W9-BJQ-970

Christian Writers'
Market Guide | 2006

THE REFERENCE TOOL FOR THE CHRISTIAN WRITER

SALLY E. STUART

WATERBROOK
PRESS

Christian Writers' Market Guide 2006
PUBLISHED BY WATERBROOK PRESS
12265 Oracle Boulevard, Suite 200
Colorado Springs, Colorado 80921
A division of Random House, Inc.

ISSN 1080-3955

ISBN 1-4000-7124-0

Copyright © 2006 by Sally E. Stuart

Printed in the United States of America
2006—First Edition

10 9 8 7 6 5 4 3 2 1

CONTENTS

III. BOOK PUBLISHERS

VII. INDEXES AND GLOSSARY

INTRODUCTION

In my mind, the 2006 edition of the *Christian Writers' Market Guide* will forever be associated with advances in the use of electronic media. Although those increases have been inching up each year, this year they seem to have become full blown. It started a few years ago when I saw the small collection of publishers with an e-mail listing grow to include almost every publishing house. Next it was Websites—going from the few who were technologically advanced to virtually every publisher having their own site. Today, some publishers have very effective sites, while others are still wondering why they have a site at all.

Next came the stage in which publishers had e-mail but most still preferred to be contacted by mail, phone, or fax. Then e-mail became preferable to phone or fax, but publishers liked snail mail the best. Now we are at the point where a good number of publishers have indicated that e-mail is their first (or only) preference. This year, some have even started asking that I not list their phone or fax numbers at all.

A few years ago we started the transition to sending manuscripts on disk rather than sending a hard copy. Similarly, publishers that used to provide printed copies of their guidelines by mail began to let writers request them by e-mail. Then many publishers added guidelines to their Websites, and now some houses provide guidelines through the Website only. Writers who do not have e-mail or Internet access are in danger of becoming obsolete—if they aren't already.

Again this year, the guide reflects a great many changes. We have seen more publishers either go out of business or drop into the ranks of those not accepting freelance writing. Surprisingly, however, there seems to be no shortage of new publishers. This edition has forty new book publishers, eighty-three new periodicals, seventeen new card/specialty markets, and thirty-four new agents. Although many of those new publishers don't pay yet, they do provide even more opportunities to get published and work at establishing your reputation in your area of expertise.

I did add a special new feature this year. Lately I've been hearing from artists who want some of the same information writers need for finding markets for their artwork. For that reason, I have started asking book publishers if they are open to freelance submissions from artists. So you will find that information in the section with photos. I also added a few new topics for both book publishers and periodicals. Those will be marked with an asterisk in the table of contents.

In addition to the new topics, you will find over 300 new entries to the "Resources for Writers" section. My special thanks to Pat Mohney, my new assistant, for the wonderful job she did updating the listings in that section, plus adding all those new ones. I encourage you to spend some time in that section identifying those listings that will help you do your job better and more easily. We also added new sections on blogging and grants.

This year I want to remind you again not to rely entirely on the topical listings for potential markets. There are many good markets that have never filled out their list of topics, so they won't be found that way. As time permits, start checking out those markets that indicate they are not listed in the topical listings. You may find some real jewels that perfectly fit your skills.

I'm still tracking e-book publishers to see if their number may be rising, but actually this year it dropped to twenty-six from thirty last year. Print-on-demand publishers gained one, going from twenty-nine to thirty. We are seeing more periodicals moving to online versions exclusively, as circulation numbers for most print magazines continue to fall (although we did see more than usual increase this year). For that reason, I encourage you to learn how to write for those online publications. Their needs often vary from their print counterparts.

Check the publishers' individual listings to see which publishers make their guidelines available by e-mail or Website. Changes in technology are improving our market research, making it much easier and less time-consuming to learn a great deal more about the publishers and publications we want to write for. Keep in mind that you can access all those publishers with e-mail or links through my Website at www.stuartmarket.com.

Since a number of publishers are now making assignments only, it is even more important that you establish a reputation in your areas of interest and expertise. Once you have acquired a number of credits in a given field, write to some of those assignment-only editors, giving your credits, and ask for an assignment. In general, you will be better off striving to get some of those assignments rather than hoping to fill one of the few slots left for unsolicited material.

We did lose a few agents from the list this year, but I was able to add about thirty-four, as more publishers are preferring to be contacted by agents. (Your help is always appreciated if you have an agent or know of an agent who isn't listed already.) It is crucial that you carefully check out agents before signing a contract or committing to work with them. See the introduction to the agent section for some tips on how to do that. (Do not assume that because they are listed I can personally vouch for them. I am not able to check out each one as thoroughly as you need to.) This year I have tried to drop the few remaining agents on the list who charge fees (the prevailing consensus is that agents should not charge fees other than actual office expenses—such as long-distance phone calls and photocopying). Because contacting agents has become more important, I indicate which conferences have agents, as well as editors, on staff.

As with any new reference book, I suggest you spend some time becoming familiar with its contents and structure. Even if you get the book each year, you need to keep up with any additions or changes that will affect the way you use it. It is a good idea each year to study the market analysis sections of this book for more insight into what is happening in the industry. Discover the supplementary lists available throughout the book. Read through the glossary and spend a few minutes learning terms you are not familiar with. Review the lists of writers' groups and conferences and mark those you might be interested in pursuing during the coming months. The denominational listing and corporate-family listing will help you start making the important connection between periodicals and book publishers associated with different denominations or publishing groups. With so many publishers being bought out or merging, this will help keep you up to date with the new members of these growing families.

Also be sure to carefully study the "How to Use This Book" section. It will save you a lot of time and frustration in trying to understand the meaning of all the notations in the primary listings, and it's full of helpful hints. Remember to send for sample copies (or a catalog) and guidelines for any of the publishers or periodicals you are not familiar with. Then study those carefully before submitting anything to that publisher. I've noticed that publishers who make their guidelines available on their Website often include a great deal more information than you get in the usual guidelines sheet.

Editors tell me repeatedly that they are looking for writers who understand them, their periodical or publishing house, and, most of all, their unique approach to the marketplace. One of the biggest complaints I've gotten from publishers over the years is that the material they receive is often not appropriate for their needs. Those complaints are coming less often these days, so I hope that is an indication that writers are doing a better job of market research. With a little time and effort, you can meet an editor's expectations, distinguish yourself as a professional, and sell what you write.

As always, I wish you well as you embark on this exciting road to publication, whether for the first time or as a longtime veteran. And as I remind you every year, each of you has been given a specific mission in the field of writing. You and I often feel inadequate to the task, but I learned a long time ago that the writing assignments God has given me cannot be written quite as well by anyone else.

> Sally E. Stuart
> 1647 S.W. Pheasant Dr.
> Aloha, OR 97006
> (503)642-9844 (Please call after 9 a.m. Pacific time.)
> Fax (503)848-3658
> E-mail: stuartcwmg@aol.com
> Website: www.stuartmarket.com

For information on how to receive the market guide automatically every year and freeze the price at $24.99, plus postage, for future editions, or for information on getting the guide at a discounted group rate or getting books on consignment for your next seminar or conference, contact me at the address, e-mail, or numbers above.

HOW TO USE THIS BOOK

The purpose of this market guide is to make your marketing job easier and more targeted. However, it will serve you well only if you put some time and effort into studying its contents and using it as a springboard for discovering and becoming an expert on those publishers best suited to your writing topics and style.

Below you will find information on its general setup and instructions for its use. In order to help you become more of an expert on marketing, I am including an explanation of each entry in the alphabetical listings for both the book section and the periodical section. Be sure to study these before trying to use this book.

1. Spend some time initially getting acquainted with the contents and setup of this resource book. You cannot make the best use of it until you know exactly what it has to offer.

2. Study the contents pages, where you will find listings of all the periodical and book topics. When selecting a topic, be sure to check related topics as well. Some cross-referencing will often be helpful. For example, if you have a novel that deals with doctor-assisted suicide, you might find the list for adult novels and the list for controversial issues and see which publishers are on both lists. Those would be good potential markets. In the topical sections you will find a letter *R* following publishers who accept reprints (pieces that have been printed in other publications but for which you retain the rights). You will find a dollar sign ($) in front of the paying markets. That will help you pick those out quickly when getting paid is your necessary goal for a particular piece.

3. The primary/alphabetical listings for book and periodical publishers contain those publishers who answered the questionnaire and those who did not. The listings preceded by an asterisk (*) are those publishers who didn't respond and whose information I was unable to update from other sources. Those with a number symbol (#) were updated from their printed guidelines or other current sources. Since the information in those two groups was not verified by the publisher, you are encouraged to send for sample copies or catalogs and writer's guidelines before submitting to them or get that information by e-mail or on their Websites. A plus sign (+) indicates a new listing.

4. In each **book publisher listing** you will find the following information (as available) in this format:

 a) Name of publisher

 b) Address, phone and fax numbers, e-mail address, Website

 c) Denomination or affiliation

 d) Name of editor—This may include the senior editor's name, followed by the name of another editor to whom submissions should be sent. In a few cases, several editors are named with the type of books each is responsible for. Address to appropriate editor.

 e) Sometimes a statement of purpose

 f) Sometimes a list of imprint names

 g) Number of inspirational/religious titles published per year

 h) Number of submissions received annually

 i) Percentage of books from first-time authors

 j) In the past, it has indicated only those publishers who do not accept manuscripts through agents. If it said nothing about agents, you could assume they did accept manuscripts through agents. Some listings will indicate whether they accept, prefer, require, or don't accept manuscripts through agents.

 k) The percentage of books from freelance authors they subsidy publish (if any). This does not refer to percentage paid by author. If percentage of subsidy is over 50%, the publisher will be listed in a separate section under Subsidy Publishers.

 l) Whether they reprint out-of-print books from other publishers

m) Preferred manuscript length in words or pages; if pages, it refers to double-spaced manuscript pages.

n) Average amount of royalty, if provided. If royalty is a percentage of wholesale or net, it is based on price paid by bookstores or distributors. If it is on retail price, it is based on cover price of the book.

o) Average amount paid for advances. Whether a publisher pays an advance or not is noted in the listing; if they did not answer the question, there is no mention of it.

p) Whether they make any outright purchases and amount paid. In this kind of sale, an author is paid a flat fee and receives no royalties.

q) Average first printing (number of books usually printed for a first-time author)

r) Average length of time between acceptance of a manuscript and publication of the work

s) Whether they consider simultaneous submissions. This means you can send a query or complete manuscript simultaneously to more than one publisher, as long as you advise everyone involved that you are doing so.

t) Length of time it should take them to respond to a query/proposal or to a complete manuscript (when two lengths of time are given, the first generally refers to a query and the latter to a complete manuscript). Give them a one-month grace period beyond that and then send a polite follow-up letter if you haven't heard from them.

u) Whether a publisher "accepts," "prefers," or "requires" the submission of an accepted manuscript on disk (do not send your unsolicited manuscripts/submissions on disk). Most publishers now do accept or require that books be sent on a computer disk (usually along with a hard copy) or by e-mail, but since each publisher's needs are different, that information will be supplied to you by the individual publisher when the time comes. This section also indicates if they accept submissions by e-mail and whether they want it sent as an attachment or copied into the message.

v) If they have a preference, it will indicate what Bible version they prefer.

w) It will also indicate if they do print-on-demand publishing.

x) Availability and cost for writer's guidelines and book catalogs—If the listing says "guidelines," it means they are available for a #10 (business size) SASE with a first-class stamp. The cost of the catalog (if any), the size of envelope, and amount of postage are given, if specified (affix stamps to envelope; don't send loose). Tip: If postage required is more than $1.42, I suggest you put $1.42 in postage on the envelope and clearly mark it "Media Mail." (That is enough for up to 1 pound.) (Please note that if the postage rates increase this year, this amount may change. Check with your local post office.) If the listing says "free catalog," it means you need only request it; they do not ask for payment or SASE. Note: If sending for both guidelines and catalog, it is not necessary to send two envelopes; guidelines will be sent with catalog. If guidelines are available by e-mail or Website, that will be indicated.

y) Nonfiction Section—Preference for query letter, book proposal, or complete manuscript, and if they accept phone, fax, or e-queries (if it does not say they accept them, assume they do not; this reference applies to fiction as well as nonfiction). If they want a query letter, send just a letter describing your project. If they want a query letter/proposal, you can add a chapter-by-chapter synopsis and the number of sample chapters indicated. If not specified, send one to three chapters. This data is often followed by a quote from them about their needs or what they don't want to see.

z) Fiction Section—Same information as nonfiction section

aa) Special Needs—If they have specific topics needs, especially those that are not included in the subject listings, they are indicated here.

bb) Ethnic Books—Usually specifies which ethnic groups they target or any particular needs

cc) Also Does—Indicates which publishers also publish booklets, pamphlets, tracts, or e-books

dd) Photos/Artwork—Indicates if they accept freelance photos for book covers. If interested, contact them for details or photography guidelines. This year I have also added a reference to artwork, indicating if they will accept queries about artwork from freelancers.

  ee) Tips—Specific tips provided by the editor/publisher.

  Note: At the end of some listings you will find an indication that the publisher receives mailings of book proposals from The Writer's Edge (see Editorial Services/Illinois for an explanation of that service) and/or First Edition (see index).

  5. In each **periodical listing** you will find the following information (as available) in this format:

   a) Name of periodical

   b) Address, phone, fax, e-mail address, Website

   c) Denomination or affiliation

   d) Name of editor and editor to submit to (if different)

   e) Theme of publication—This will help you understand their particular slant.

   f) Format of publication, frequency of publication, number of pages and size of circulation—Tells whether magazine, newsletter, journal, tabloid, newspaper, or take-home paper. Frequency of publication indicates quantity of material needed. Number of pages usually indicates how much material they can use. Circulation indicates the amount of exposure your material will receive and often indicates how well they might pay or the probability that they will stay in business.

   g) Subscription rate—Amount given is for a one-year subscription in the country of origin. I suggest you subscribe to at least one of your primary markets every year to become better acquainted with its specific focus.

   h) Date established—Included only if 2003 or later

   i) Openness to freelance; percentage freelance written. Again this year this information has been expanded to indicate the percentage of unsolicited freelance and the percentage of assigned. Since not all publishers have responded to this question, some will still give the two percentages combined or indicate only the unsolicited number. If they buy only a small percentage, it often means they are open but receive little that is appropriate. The percentage of freelance written indicates how great your chances are of selling to them. When you have a choice, choose those with the higher percentage, but only if you have done your homework and know they are an appropriate market for your material.

   j) Preference for query or complete manuscript also tells if they want a cover letter with complete manuscripts and whether they will accept phone, fax, or e-mail queries. (If it does not mention cover letters or phone, fax, or e-mail queries, assume they do not accept them.)

   k) Payment schedule, payment on acceptance (they pay when the piece is accepted) or publication (they pay when it is published), and rights purchased. (See glossary for definitions of different rights.)

   l) If a publication does not pay, or pays in copies or subscription, that is indicated in bold capital letters.

   m) If a publication is not copyrighted, that is indicated. That means you should ask for your copyright notice to appear on your piece when they publish it so your rights will be protected.

   n) Preferred word lengths and average number of manuscripts purchased per year (in parentheses)

   o) Response time—The time they usually take to respond to your query or manuscript submission (add at least two weeks for delays for mailing).

   p) Seasonal material (also refers to holiday)—Holiday or seasonal material should reach them at least the specified length of time in advance.

   q) Acceptance of simultaneous submissions and reprints—If they accept simultaneous submissions, it means they will look at submissions (usually timely topic or holiday material) sent simultaneously to several publishers. Best to send to nonoverlapping markets (such as denominational), and be sure to always indicate that it is a simultaneous submission. Reprints are pieces you have sold previously, but to which you hold the rights (which means you sold only first or one-time rights to the original publisher and the rights reverted to you as soon as they were published).

r) If they accept, prefer, or require submissions on disk or by e-mail. Many now prefer an e-mail submission, rather than on disk. Most will want a query or hard copy first. If it does not say they prefer or require disks, you should wait and see if they ask for them. If they accept an e-mail submission, it will indicate whether they want it as an attached file or copied into the message. If it says they accept e-mail submissions, but doesn't indicate a preference, it usually means they will take it either way.

s) Average amount of kill fee, if they pay one (see glossary for definition)

t) Whether or not they use sidebars (see glossary for definition), and whether they use them regularly or sometimes

u) Their preferred Bible version is indicated. The most popular version is the NIV (New International Version). If no version is indicated, they usually have no preference. See glossary for Bible Versions list.

v) It will indicate if they accept submissions from children or teens. These young writers will find a list of the publishers open to submissions from them in the topical listings under "Young Writer Markets."

w) Availability and cost for writer's guidelines, theme list, and sample copies—If the listing says "Guidelines," it means they are available for a #10 SASE (business size) with a first-class stamp. Many more now have guidelines available by e-mail or Website, and the listing will indicate that. The cost for a sample copy, the size of envelope, and number of stamps required are given, if specified (affix stamps to envelope; don't send loose). Tip: If postage required is more than $1.42, I suggest you put $1.42 in postage on the envelope and clearly mark it "Media Mail." (That is enough for up to one pound.) If the listing says "free sample copy," it means you need only to request them; they do not ask for payment or SASE. Note: If sending for both guidelines and sample copy, it is not necessary to send two envelopes; guidelines will be sent with sample copy. If a listing doesn't mention guidelines or sample copy, they probably don't have them.

x) "Not in topical listings" means the publisher has not supplied a list of topics they are interested in. Send for their guidelines or study sample copies to determine topics used.

y) Poetry—Name of poetry editor (if different). Average number of poems bought each year. Types of poetry; number of lines. Payment rate. Maximum number of poems you may submit at one time.

z) Fillers—Name of fillers editor (if different). Types of fillers accepted; word length. Payment rate.

aa) Columns/Departments—Name of column editor. Names of columns in the periodical (information in parentheses gives focus of column); word length requirements. Payment rate. Be sure to see sample before sending ms or query. Most columns require a query.

bb) Special Issues or Needs—Indicates topics of special issues they have planned for the year or unique topics not included in regular subject listings

cc) Ethnic—Any involvement they have in the ethnic market

dd) Contest—Information on contests they sponsor or how to obtain that information. See Contest section at back of book for full list of contests. They are listed by genre—poetry, fiction, nonfiction, etc.

ee) Tips—Tips from the editor on how to break into this market or how to be successful as an author.

ff) At the end of some listings you will find a notation as to where that particular periodical placed in the Top 50+ Christian Periodical list in 2004, and/or their place in previous years. This list is compiled annually to indicate the most writer-friendly publications. To receive a complete listing, plus a prepared analysis sheet and writer's guidelines for the top 50 of those markets, send $25 (includes postage) to: Sally Stuart, 1647 S.W. Pheasant Dr., Aloha, OR 97006, or order from this Website: www.stuartmarket.com.

gg) Some listings also include EPA winners. These awards are made annually by the Evangelical Press Association (a trade organization for Christian periodicals). We have also indicated the top 10 best-selling magazines in Christian retail stores.

6. It is important that you adhere closely to the guidelines set out in these listings. If a publisher asks for a query only, do not send a complete manuscript. Following these guidelines will mark you as a professional.

7. If your manuscript is completed, select the proper topical listing and target audience, and make up a list of possible publishers. Check first to see which ones will accept a complete manuscript (if you want to send it to those that require a query, you will have to write a query letter or book proposal to send first). Please do not assume that your manuscript will be appropriate for all those on the list. Read the primary listing for each, and if you are not familiar with a publisher, read their writer's guidelines and study one or more sample copies or book catalog. (The primary listings tell how to get these.) Be sure the slant of your manuscript fits the slant of the publisher.

8. If you have an idea for an article, short story, or book but you have not written it yet, a reading of the appropriate topical listing will help you decide on a possible slant or approach. Select some publishers to whom you might send a query about your idea. If your idea is for an article, do not overlook the possibility of writing on the same topic for a number of different periodicals listed under that topic, either with the same target audience or another from the list that indicates an interest. For example, you could write on money management for a general adult magazine, a teen magazine, a women's publication, or a magazine for pastors. Each would require a different slant, but you would get a lot more mileage from that idea.

9. If you do not have an idea, simply start reading through the topical listings or the primary listings. They are sure to trigger any number of book or magazine article ideas you could go to work on.

10. If you run into words or terms you are not familiar with, check the glossary at the back of the book for definitions.

11. If you need someone to look at your material to evaluate it or to give it a thorough editing, look up the section on Editorial Services and find someone to send it to for such help. That often will make the difference between success or failure in publishing.

12. If you are a published author with other books to your credit, you may be interested in finding an agent. Unpublished authors generally don't need or won't be able to interest an agent. However, some agents will consider unpublished authors (their listing will indicate that), but you must have a completed manuscript before you approach an agent (see agent list). Christian agents are at a premium, so realize it will be hard to find an agent unless you have had some success in book writing. The agent list also includes secular agents who handle religious/inspirational material.

13. Check the Group list to find a group to join in your area. Go to the Conference list to find a conference you might attend this year. Attending a conference every year or two is almost essential to your success as a writer, especially when you get into book writing.

14. **ALWAYS SEND AN SASE WITH EVERY QUERY OR MANUSCRIPT,** unless your cover letter indicates that you do not want it returned. If that is the case, send a #10 SASE for their acceptance or rejection, and indicate that's what you are doing in your cover letter.

15. **DO NOT RELY SOLELY ON THE INFORMATION PROVIDED IN THIS MARKET GUIDE.** It is just that—a guide—and is not intended to be complete by itself. It is important to your success as a freelance writer that you learn how to use writer's guidelines and study book catalogs or sample copies before submitting to any publisher. Be a professional!

ADDITIONAL RESOURCES TO HELP WITH YOUR WRITING AND MARKETING

Note: Here are additional resources to help with your every writing need. They are divided into interest areas to help you make the best selections. See instructions for ordering at the end of the list.

GENERAL HELPS

1. **Sally Stuart's Guide to Getting Published**—The author of the *Christian Writers' Market Guide* has compiled all the information you need to understand and function in the world of Christian publishing. Takes you through all the steps needed to be successful as a freelance writer. Serves as both a text and a reference book. One of the most important and useful resources you'll ever find for your writing library. $17, postpaid. Special price.

2. **New! The Little Style Guide to Great Christian Writing and Publishing**—At last an up-to-date style guide that deals with style concerns unique to Christian writing and editing. $16 postpaid.

3. **Just Write! An Essential Guide for Launching Your Writing Career**—Information on how to do research, common grammatical pitfalls, writing for children, interviewing, and short stories—plus much more. $15 postpaid.

4. **The Complete Guide to Christian Writing and Speaking**—A how-to handbook for beginning and advanced writers and speakers written by the 19 members of the editorial staff of *The Christian Communicator.* $18 postpaid.

5. **The Complete Guide to Writing for Publication**—Written by top experts in the field. Contains chapters on various genres of fiction, marketing tips, and writing for children, plus everything you wanted to know about writing for publication. $18 postpaid.

6. **Small, Easy Ways to Break into Print**—Becoming a columnist, writing and selling microfiction, holiday articles, using an almanac, and publication release forms. $5 postpaid.

7. **The Real American Dream: Creating Independence & Running a One-Person Business**—Let this workbook coach you, step by step, through creating a one-person business to freedom and control of your life as a professional writer. $26 postpaid.

FICTION RESOURCES

8. **Getting into Character: Seven Secrets a Novelist Can Learn from Actors**—A valuable resource for the novelist wanting to create multidimensional characters. $19 postpaid.

9. **How to Write and Sell a Christian Novel**—Leads you step by step through the process of writing a novel. $15 postpaid.

10. **The Professional Way to Write Dialogue**—$5 postpaid.

11. **The Professional Way to Create Characters**—$5 postpaid.

INTERNET RESOURCES

12. **WriterSpeaker.Com**—A friendly guide to Internet research and marketing. Plus how to set up and promote your own Website. $18 postpaid.

13. **2006 Internet Directory of Christian Publishers**—A handy listing of nearly 900 Christian publishers who have Websites or e-mail addresses. This resource now comes spiral bound for easier reference. $10 postpaid.

LEGAL CONCERNS

14. **Permissions Packet**—A compilation of over 16 pages of information directly from publishers on how and when to ask permission to quote from other people's material or from Bible paraphrases. Information not available elsewhere in printed form. $6 postpaid.

15. **Copyright Law: What You Don't Know Can Cost You**—Answers all the questions about rights and copyright law that affect you as a writer. Simple Q&A format followed by the actual wording of the law. Includes reproducible copyright forms and instructions. $18 postpaid.

16. **Updated! Totally Honest Tax Tips for Writers**—Answers all those tax questions specifically applicable to the Christian writer. $10 postpaid.

MARKETING RESOURCES

17. **2006 Christian Writers' Market Guide on Computer Disk**—in ASCII Text on 3.5" HD disk or CD, for quick marketing reference. This is currently in text form as it appears in the book, not in a database. $30 postpaid.

18. **2006 Top 50+ Christian Periodical Publishers Packet**—Includes a list of the Top 50+ "writer-friendly" periodicals, pre-prepared analysis sheets, and publisher's guidelines for each of the top 50, plus a master form for analyzing your own favorite markets. Saves more than $40 in postage and 25-30 hours of work. $25, postpaid. New packet every year.

19. **A Market Plan for More Sales**—A step-by-step plan to help you be successful in marketing. Includes 5 reproducible forms. $5 postpaid.

20. **Keeping Track of Your Periodical Manuscripts**—These pages can be duplicated to keep track of every step involved in sending out your periodical manuscripts to publishers. $5 postpaid.

21. **Keeping Track of Your Book Manuscripts**—A similar booklet summarizing the steps in tracking a book manuscript from idea to publication. $5 postpaid.

22. **How to Submit a Book Proposal to a Publisher**—Contains all you need to know to present a professional-looking book proposal to a publishing house. $5 postpaid.

23. **New! Book Proposals That Sell**—An inside look at the process from a successful writer and acquisitions editor. $17 postpaid.

24. **New! A Sample Book Proposal**—Includes a sample of the chapter-by-chapter synopsis. $5 postpaid.

25. **How to Submit an Article or Story to a Publisher**—Shows how to write a query, prepare a professional-looking manuscript, and more. $5 postpaid.

26. **Marketing Manuscripts**—Locating the markets, analyzing magazines, page set-up, book proposals, query letters, and literary agents. $5 postpaid.

NONFICTION RESOURCES

27. **New! The Train-of-Thought Writing Method**—Practical, user-friendly help for beginning writers. $18 postpaid.

28. **Write on Target: A Five-Phase Program for Nonfiction Writers,** by Dennis Hensley and Holly Miller—The craft of writing, the nuts and bolts, finding your niche, selling your manuscript, and mapping your future success as a writer. $16 postpaid.

29. **How to Write That Sure-Sell Magazine Article**—Contains a 3-step writing plan for articles, a list of article types, 12 evaluation questions, a sample manuscript page, and more. $5 postpaid.

30. **How to Write Personal Experience Articles**—Includes how to write a query letter/sample, components of the personal experience article, interviewing tips, and more. $5 postpaid.

31. **How to Write and Sell Interviews and Personality Profiles**—Effective listening skills, open-ended questions, sample interview, photo release form, and basics of interviewing. $5 postpaid.

32. **The Art of Researching the Professional Way**—$5 postpaid.

33. **Interviewing the Professional Way**—$5 postpaid.

SELF PROMOTION

34. **You Can Market Your Book: All the Tools You Need to Sell Your Published Book**—All the best resources and ideas for promoting and selling your book—from someone who has done it successfully. $18 postpaid.

35. **A Savvy Approach to Book Sales: Marketing Advice to Get the Buzz Going**—by Elaine Wright Colvin. A wealth of information on how to promote your self-published book, as well as many ideas for the author wanting to boost the sales of a book from a royalty publisher. $16 postpaid.

SPECIALTY AREAS

36. **Screenwriting: A Manual for Christian Writers**—Written by the director of *Act One: Writing for Hollywood.* $20 postpaid.

37. **New! Poetry: Taking Its Course**—The successful poetry writing course, now available in book form. $23 postpaid.

38. **You Can Do It: A Guide to Christian Self-Publishing**—Takes you step-by-step through the process of self-publishing, including the preparation, cost, and promotion of the book. $13 postpaid.

39. **Preparing for a Writing Conference**—A spiral-bound pamphlet that helps you prepare effectively for your first—or next—writer's conference. $7 postpaid

40. **How to Write a Picture Book**—An inside look at how to write, format, and lay out a children's picture book, with tips for those all-important finishing touches. $5 postpaid.

41. **How to Write Daily Devotionals That Inspire**—Includes the basic format and patterns for daily devotionals, marketing tips, 12 evaluation questions, and polishing. $5 postpaid.

42. **Agents: What You Need to Know**—Includes why an agent would want you for a client, do you need an agent, and signing with an agent. $5 postpaid.

43. **Writing and Selling Comedy and Humor**—Includes forms of comedy, markets for humor, how to be funny, and how to stimulate humorous thinking. $5 postpaid.

44. **Ghostwriting, Co-Authoring and Collaborations**—Ghostwriting basics, expense sheets, payment guidelines, multiauthor contracts, breaking in, working with book editors, and using a pen name. $5 postpaid.

45. **Writing Junior Books the Professional Way** (writing for ages 8-12)—$5 postpaid.

46. **Writing for Young Adults the Professional Way**—$5 postpaid.

47. **How to Develop a Professional Writers' Group**—$5 postpaid.

SPIRITUAL/PERSONAL HELPS

48. **New! For the Write Reason**—Drawing on the wisdom of experienced writers, agents, and editors, this in-depth Bible study (for writers) offers writers of all levels a valuable source of encouragement and wisdom. $21 postpaid.

49. **How to Keep a Spiritual Journal**—Learning to set up and maintain a regular spiritual journal can be one of the best tools for a successful Christian writer. $17 postpaid.

50. **100 Plus Motivational Moments for Writers and Speakers**—A devotional book specifically for writers and speakers written by successful writers and speakers. $13 postpaid.

51. **Write His Answer: A Bible Study for Christian Writers**—A Bible-study guide that deals specifically with the struggles of the Christian writer. $15 postpaid.

52. **Managing Stress as a Freelance Writer**—Stress response, self-assessment exercise, coping, handling anger and stress from editors. $5 postpaid.

53. **Time Management for Writers**—How to make time for writing, time-management contract, life map, etc. $5 postpaid.

Note: Any of the above $5 booklets may be purchased at 2 for $9, 4 for $17, 6 for $25, 8 for $33, 10 for $40, or 12 for $47.

To order any of the above resources, send a list of what you want with your check or money order to: Sally E. Stuart, 1647 S.W. Pheasant Dr., Aloha OR 97006, (503)642-9844. Fax (503)848-3658; stuartcwmg@aol.com. Or order by credit card through PayPal on Website: www.stuartmarket.com.

RESOURCES FOR WRITERS

Below you will find a variety of resources that will help you as you carry out your training or work as a freelance writer. In addition to the resources here, also check out the separate listings for groups, conferences, editorial services, and contests. You are encouraged to spend some time checking out these resources, as they represent a wealth of knowledge and contacts that will help you be more successful in this business of writing and publishing. Note that we have added two new sections this year: Blogging and Grants, as well as over 300 new resources throughout.

(*) New category this year
(+) New listing this year

BLOGGING*

Blog is a word made from *Web* plus *log*. A Web log, or blog, is a chronicle of the writings and thoughts of one individual. For a writer, it is a place to muse, usually about a particular theme, which is the best way to gather devoted readers and to develop a niche.

+BLOG FOR FUN AND PROFIT. This site contains a wealth of information about blogging sites, newest developments, and how to use blogs for profit. Website: http://blogforfunand profit.blogware.com.

+BLOGGING ABOUT BLOGS. (1) Ken Leebow reports on incredible blogs. Website: http:// bloggingaboutblogs.blogspot.com. (2) Another Website: http://tourbus.com/blognews.html.

BLOG SITES FOR WRITERS. Contact: Karen Whiting, 10936 S.W. 156th Pl. Miami FL 33196. (954)463-0982. Website: www.karenhwhiting.com.

BOOK BLOG. Website: www.bookblog.net.

+CREATE YOUR OWN BLOG. This site shows you how to create your own blog in three easy steps. Website: www.blogger.com/start.

FREE COUNTER. Website: (1) www.sitemeter.com. Offers option of receiving a daily e-mail with the previous day's stats. Other fee-based counters are at (2) www.mycomputer.com and (3) www.thecounter.com.

+THE MASTER'S ARTIST. A blogging site with musings, insights, and opinions about being a Christian writer. Website: http://themastersartist.blogspot.com.

+WEB BLOGGING SERVER. Website: www.typepad.com.

+WRITERS HOOD.COM. Though Writers Hood.com is offline, Blog the Hood is up and running, with a place to post your stories and poems. Website: http://writershood.com/blog.

CONNECTING WITH OTHER WRITERS

AUTHOR'S DEN. Website: www.authorsden.com. Where authors and readers come together. Discover and meet thousands of authors and readers from around the world.

+BACKSPACE. Offers critique forums, tips, and writing resources, plus agents, authors, and editors as guest speakers in discussion forums. The critique forums have a $30 annual membership fee and offer a free five-day trial. Website: www.bksp.org.

+CHRISTIAN MARKET LISTSERV. Designed for networking and for discussing issues around publication and marketing to the Christian marketplace. To join this group, send a message to christianpublishers-subscribe@yahoogroups.com or visit Christian Small Publishers group at Yahoo Groups.

CHRISTIAN WRITERS' GROUP (CWG). Website: http://christianwritersgroup.org. A discussion group and organization for published or aspiring, born-again writers. Purposes: To share ideas, tips, conference/seminar information, encouragement, support, and prayer requests. Editors/publishers also welcome. Offers scholarships for writers' conferences. To join, send a blank e-mail to: CWG-subscribe@yahoogroups.com or sign up on Website. Director and list owner: Lisa Wiener. Membership (300+) open.

DEDICATED AUTHOR. Website: http://groups.yahoo.com/group/eDedicatedAuthor. Free list of opportunities, jobs, and contests for writers. This list does not chat or discuss. Editor, Sheila Seifert. Over 550 members.

DISCUSSION FORUMS. Freelance Writing. Website for Today's Working Writers: www.free lancewriting.com. Numerous forums to meet and network with other writers.

FCW's FREE LIST SERVE. (Fellowship of Christian Writers), http://groups.yahoo.com/group/fcw, or send an e-mail to FCW-subscribe@yahoo.com. Must apply online at Yahoo groups and fill out questionnaire. 500+ members. Has weekly topics, daily interaction, markets, encouragement, tips, definitions, prayer, contests, and more. Online moderated critique groups for fiction, nonfiction, and poetry for list members which must be joined after you join the main list. Members may also be paired with an accountability partner, if you wish.

+FORWARD MOTION. Free site that offer 50 forums covering different genres, workshops, contests, and more. Website: www.fmwriters.com.

INTERNATIONAL@WRITERS CLUB. Website: http://members.tripod.com/awriters/iwc.htm. Provides writers worldwide with a host of services and opportunities including a base for networking, job opportunities, and invaluable writing resources.

KINGDOM WRITERS. Leaders: Marilyn Phemister (marilyp@larned.com) and Sue Hoover (Szanne@sprynet.com). An e-mail critique group and fellowship for Christian writers. You may submit work for critique and critique the works of others in return. To subscribe, send a blank e-mail message to: KingdomWriters-subscribe@egroups.com. Website: www.angel fire.com/ks/kingwrit/index.html. Membership open.

+THE MUSE IT UP CLUB. A club for anyone who enjoys writing anything from flash fiction to novels. The main goal is to match up critique partners for authors who are willing to revise a fellow writer's work. Website: http://museitupclub.tripod.com.

SMALL PUBLISHERS, ARTISTS, AND WRITERS NETWORK (SPAWN). Website: www.spawn .org. Newsletter and local networking chapters. To start a new chapter, refer to 10 Steps to Starting a SPAWN Chapter.

WORDSMITH SHOPPE. Website: http://wordsmithshoppe.com. This is a Christian writers group that offers a free twice monthly e-mail newsletter, Wordsmith Shoppe News, with over 500 subscribers. The newsletter contains information of general interest to writers including conference listings, contests, and other writing opportunities. A weekly chat meets Tuesdays at 9:00 p.m. ET with special guest workshops on the first and third Tuesday of the month.

THE WRITERS VIEW. Website: http://groups.yahoo.com/group/TheWritersView. Over 500 members. A great network of authors, editors, agents, freelance writers, journalists, publicists, and publishers. Offers focused panel discussions with 15 CBA professionals on advanced writing topics and issues.

WRITING.COM. Website: www.writing.com. The online community for readers and writers of all ages and interests. Over 300,000 active members.

WRITING GROUPS. Website: www.6ftferrets.com. Tips for starting and maintaining a group.

YAHOO CHRISTIAN WRITERS CLUB. Website: http://clubs.yahoo.com/clubs/christianwritersclub. A place to learn and share about Christian writing and publishing. Over 400 members.

DENOMINATIONS

CHRISTIANITY, CULTS & RELIGIONS. Rose Publishing, 4455 Torrance Blvd., #259, Torrance CA 90503. (310)370-7152. Fax (310)370-7492. Toll-free (800)532-4278. E-mail:

info@Rose-publishing.com. Website: www.rose-publishing.com. A wall chart or pamphlet compares 18 world religions and cults at a glance.

COMPARISON CHART OF CHRISTIAN BELIEFS. Website: www.saintaquinas.com/christian_comparison.html.

DENOMINATIONAL DIFFERENCES FOR SPEAKERS by Marita Littauer. A ten-page booklet explaining the major differences between denominations. To order, call (800)433-6633 or e-mail erin@classervices.com. $5.

HANDBOOK OF DENOMINATIONS IN THE U.S. by Frank Spencer Mead and Samuel S. Hill, Abingdon Press (2001), ISBN 0687069831, $20.

THE UNAUTHORIZED GUIDE TO CHOOSING A CHURCH by Carmen Renee Berry, Brazos Press (2003), ISBN 1587430363, $19. A conversational guide that discusses the nuances between denominations.

WORLD RELIGIONS. Virtual Religion Index. Website: http://virtualreligion.net/vri. Analyzes and highlights content of religion-related Websites to speed research. Refer to heading "Confessional Agencies."

ELEMENTS OF STYLE

THE ASSOCIATED PRESS STYLEBOOK AND BRIEFING ON MEDIA LAW. Edited by Norm Goldstein. Basic Books (2004), ISBN 0465004881, $17.95.

THE CHICAGO MANUAL OF STYLE. Website: www.press.uchicago.edu/Misc/Chicago/cmosfaq/cmosfaq.html. The definitive guide (15th edition) online.

A CHRISTIAN WRITER'S MANUAL OF STYLE by Hudson & Townsend. Zondervan (2004), ISBN 0310487714, $19.99. Focuses on unique spellings, capitalization, etc., of religious terms.

CITATION SITES. (1) Citation Styles Online. Website: www.bedfordstmartins.com/online/citex.html. Lists all the correct versions of citation style and related links; (2) www.upa.pdx.edu/BB/citation.htm.

CLEAR ENGLISH. Website: www.clearenglish.net/grammar.htm. Online references and resources to help with grammar and usage.

COLUMBIA GUIDE TO ONLINE STYLE by Janice R. Walker and Todd Taylor, Columbia University Press, New York (1998). $40.50 hardback, $19.50 paperback. Available at local bookstores. Website: www.columbia.edu/cu/cup/cgos/idx_basic.html.

ELEMENTS OF STYLE. William Strunk Jr.'s classic online. Websites: (1) www.diku.dk/hjemmesider/studerende/myth/EOS; (2) www.crockford.com/wrrrld/style.html; (3) www.bartleby.com/141.

ONLINE ENGLISH COURSES. Website: http://owl.english.purdue.edu/sitemap.html. Purdue University's Online Writing Lab (OWL).

STYLE AND PROOFREADING HELPS. Websites: (1) www.proofread.com; (2) www.theslot.com; (3) www.webgrammar.com; (4) www.editavenue.com/writingtip.asp?cid=1600; (5) www.mla.org, for more scholarly works; (6) www.rbs0.com, for technical writers; (7) http://uwadmnweb.uwyo.edu/Pubrel/publications/StyleManual.htm.

+TYPEFACE FOR MANUSCRIPTS. Website: www.right-writing.com/insight-typeface.html.

+WHAT'S THE RULE? Quick, easy, and practical reference guide to business English. Free trial version. Website: www.whatstherule.com.

FIND: BOOKS

ABEBOOKS.COM. Website: www.abebooks.com. If you tell them what book you want, they can tell you which stores carry it. You then work directly with the appropriate store to order the book.

+ABSTRACTS. Get 3000 word abstract book summaries. Website: www.getabstract.com.

ALIBRIS BOOKS. Website: www.alibris.com. Over 40 million new, used, out-of-print, and hard-to-find books.

ALLBOOKS4LESS.COM. Website: www.AllBooks4Less.com. Provides inexpensively priced books.

BIBLIOFIND. Website: www.bibliofind.com. Partnering with Amazon.com. Searches over 10 million used, rare and out-of-print books offered for sale by thousands of booksellers worldwide.

+BOOK FINDER. Find over 60 million new, used, rare, and out-of-print books. Website: www.bookfinder.com.

BOOKSINPRINT.COM. The world's most inclusive, most accurate, most up-to-date database of book, audiobook, and video titles. For subscription information, visit: (1) www.bowker.com; (2) www.booksinprint.com or call toll-free (800)526-9537. Links to U.S. ISBN agency.

+BOOKSTORE LOCATOR. To find a Christian bookstore anywhere, go to Website: http://cba.know-where.com/cba.

BOOK WIRE. Website: www.bookwire.com. Comprehensive online portal into the book industry.

CHRISTIAN BOOK DISTRIBUTORS (CBD). Website: www.christianbook.com. Check out what's selling in the marketplace. Books can be found by publisher, author, or subject.

+DISCOUNT BOOKS. Offers new and used book price comparison from 106 online book-stores worldwide. Website: www.alldiscountbooks.net.

FETCHBOOK. Website: www.fetchbook.info. A quick way to compare prices of new and used books.

+FREE ONLINE BOOKS. Site offers thousands of free online books for students, teachers, and the classic enthusiast. Website: www.readprint.com.

+FROOGLE BOOK SEARCH. Go to www.froogle.com and type in the title of a book. Lists stores carrying the book and compares prices.

HALF.COM. An inexpensive source for both Christian and secular books. Also a place to sell books you no longer need. Not an auction; sellers list books they have and their asking price, and you pick the ones you want. Refer to Help Desk for details. Website: www.Half.com.

KREGEL BOOKS. Website: www.gospelcom.net/kregel. Offers new, used, and hard-to-find Christian books, publications, and resources.

OUT OF PRINT BOOKS. Website: http://marylaine.com/bookbyte/getbooks.html. Excellent guide on how to find out-of-print books by Marylaine Block.

+POWELL'S BOOKS. Website: www.powells.com.

+TEXTBOOKS AND MEDICAL BOOKS. For discounted new and used textbooks, medical and professional books, go to Website: www.discounttextbooks.net. Offers book price comparison from 112 online bookstores worldwide.

THE WRITE RESOURCE. Websites: (1) www.writerswrite.com; (2) www.readersread.com. Contains hundreds of categorized links to best book-related sites on the Web.

FIND: INFORMATION

+ABOUT.COM. When you don't know anything about a topic, search Website: www.about.com for hundreds of information links.

ASK-AN-EXPERT SITES. (1) Website: www.K12Science.org/askanexpert.html. Also see: (2) www.askanexpert.com; (3) www.askjeeves.com. (4) The Yearbook of Experts, Authorities, and Spokespersons is another Website that lists hundreds of links to experts in dozens of categories: www.yearbook.com.

BIOGRAPHICAL INFORMATION. Website: www.biography.com. Short biographies on over 25,000 personalities.

COUNTRIES. These sites give information on various countries of the world: (1) CIA's World Factbook. Website: www.cia.gov/cia/publications/factbook; (2) Library of Congress's Portals to the World, www.loc.gov/rr/international/portals.html; (3) Country Reports, www.countryreports.org; (4) www.worldinformation.com; (5) www.economist.com/countries.

EXPERTS. (1) Website: www.experts.com. A diverse source of experts, academic and otherwise. A directory that lists expertise of more than 1,000 University of Southern California scientists, scholars, administrators, and physicians as a service to editors, reporters, and producers can be found at www.usc.edu/uscnews/experts. (2) Also, check out www.profnet.com.

+FACT PORTAL. Colin Powell's favorite site links to sources of information on a multitude of topics. Website: www.refdesk.com.

FEDERAL CITIZEN INFORMATION CENTER SITES. (1) Website: www.helenginger.com/links_govt_crime_pg.htm. Brochures on just about any subject. News, links, topics, resources, fun stuff, and more. (2) Website: www.pueblo.gsa.gov. Information about anything and everything one could need. Free and low-cost booklets.

HOLIDAYS/FESTIVALS. To find information on holidays and festivals worldwide, visit www.holidayfestival.com. Hosted by www.joeant.com.

HOW STUFF WORKS. (1) Website: www.howstuffworks.com. Explains how things work from vacuum cleaners to earthquakes, using text, pictures, and animations. (2) See also www.ehow.com.

INFORMATION PLEASE. Website: www.InfoPlease.com. This 50-year-old print resource is now available on the Internet.

MAG PORTAL. Website: www.MagPortal.com. This site lets you search for articles online simultaneously, without having to visit each magazine's Website individually.

PHONE BOOK SEARCH USA. Websites: (1) www.switchboard.com; (2) www.infobel.com/teldir.

+PUBLIC RECORDS. To find public records online, go to Website: www.oatis.com.

+REFERENCE SITES. A list of free reference sites useful to writers and anyone looking for free information. Website: www.writers-free-reference.com.

WRITERS' KNOWLEDGE SWAP. Website: http://groups.yahoo.com/group/writerswap. An information-exchange mailing list for writers doing research. Membership 220+.

FIND: QUOTES

BARTLETT'S FAMILIAR QUOTATIONS. Website: www.bartleby.com/100. Enter the word or words and it gives you the quotations.

JOURNALISM QUOTES. Website: www.schindler.org/quote.shtml.

THE QUOTABLE WRITER by William A. Gordon. McGraw Hill. ISBN 0071355766, $14.95. Quotes by writers on writing. Available at your local bookstore. To read excerpts from this book, go to: http://members.aol.com/williamagordon/writers_quotations.html.

QUOTESPLACE. Searchable categories include people, occupations, literary works, proverbs, films, TV shows, themes, and more. Website: www.quotesplace.com.

WEBSITES FOR QUOTATIONS. (1) Website: www.itools.com. Go to "Research Tools" section, enter word in Quotations box. Search by topic, author, etc., including Bible quotations. Also: (2) www.quotationspage.com; (3) www.quoteland.com; (4) www.aphids.com/quotes/index.shtml; (5) www.brainyquote.com; (6) www.startingpage.com/html/quotations.html; (7) www.cybernation.com/victory/quotations/directory.html; (8) www.geocities.com/Athens/7186; (9) www.quotecha.com; (10) http://members.aol.com/Jainster/Quotes/quotes.html; (11) www.quotablequotes.net; (12) www.motivationalquotes.com;

(13) www.thinkexist.com/English; (14) www.madwed.com. Click on the quotations section. The quotations are numbered; authors are in alphabetical order under each topic.

WORD CRAFTERS. Bob Kelly, 10225 E. Stoney Vista Dr., Sun Lakes AZ 85248. (480)895-7617. Fax (480)895-7618. E-mail: quotes@robsoncom.net. Website: www.wordcrafters.info. Free Quotation Search Service and newsletters.

FIND: STATISTICS

BARNA RESEARCH GROUP. Website: www.barna.org/FlexPage.aspx?Page=Home. Click on "Ministry Resources" for information about the intersection of faith and culture in the U.S. Some subjects include: church health, discipleship, stewardship, youth, evangelism, leaders, and trends.

BOOK INDUSTRY STATISTICS. (1) To find out statistics about the book industry (i.e. how many books sold last year), check out: www.publishers.org/industry/index.cfm. (2) Also visit Dan Poynter's Website: http://parapub.com/statistics.

BUREAU OF JUSTICE STATISTICS. Website: www.ojp.usdoj.gov/bjs.

+FEDERAL STATISTICS. Statistics from over 100 U.S. federal agencies. Website: www.fedstats.gov.

INTERNET STATISTICS. Website: www.nua.ie/surveys. "The world's leading resource for Internet trends and statistics."

THE PEW FORUM ON RELIGION & PUBLIC LIFE. Research and discussion of issues about the intersection of religion and public affairs. Website: www.pewforum.org.

STATISTICS SOURCE. Website: www.nilesonline.com/data. How to find data on the Internet and access stats of all kinds.

+TRACK BOOK SALES BY PHONE. The Ingram Book Group distributes more than a million titles to more than 30,000 stores. You can track the sales of a title by calling (800)937-8000. Press 4, then enter extension 36803. You will be asked for the book's ISBN or UPC number. When prompted, enter it and you'll be given recent and year-to-date sales.

UNIVERSITY OF MICHIGAN'S DOCUMENTS CENTER STATISTICAL RESOURCES ON THE WEB. Website: www.lib.umich.edu/govdocs/stats.html.

FREELANCE JOBS

+THE CHRISTIAN PEN: PROOFREADERS AND EDITORS NETWORK. Website: www.TheChristianPEN.com. Contact: Kathy Ide, Kathy@kathyide.com. Provides proofreaders and editors with a venue for "cooperative competition" through mutual support and exchange of information, leads, and resources. Has a free online group where members can exchange ideas, tips, news, findings, questions/answers, resources, and suggestions, as well as pass on job leads. Also offers online courses of interest to editorial freelancers. For $25/year, contributing members can post their bios and résumés on the Christian PEN Website, receive a quarterly e-newsletter, get discounts on online courses, and more. Open to anyone who is a full-time or part-time proofreader or editor (at any level), is seriously planning to become an editorial freelancer, or is simply investigating the possibility. (If you're a writer looking for an editor or proofreader, check the Members page of our Website or contact Kathy Ide by e-mail for a referral.)

CREATIVE FREELANCERS. Website: www.freelancers.com. Connecting freelancers and clients for over twenty years.

+ECPA CAREER CENTER. The Evangelical Christian Publishers Assoc. (ECPA) offers new free online resource to connect publishers and other industry employers with the largest, most qualified audience of publishing industry professionals. Employment opportunities include editorial, marketing, executive, operations, production, rights, sales, and administrative positions. Receive automatic notification of new jobs matching your criteria. Post your résumé, confidentially if preferred, so employers can actively search for you. Website: www .ecpa.org/careers.

FREELANCE SUCCESS. Website: www.freelancesuccess.com.

FREELANCE WRITING: Website for Today's Working Writer. (1) Job Bank at: www.free lancewriting.com/fjb.html. (2) Get a free e-book with 400+ paying freelance writing markets at www.writerscrossing.com.

JOB SITES. Websites: (1) www.writerfind.com/freelance_jobs; (2) www.writejobs.com/jobs; (3) www.writersdigest.com; (4) www.epassoc.org/jobs.html; (5) www.prostogo.com; (6) http://allfreelance.com; (7) www.freelanceworkexchange.com; (8) www.nytimes.com/ pages/jobs/index.html; (9) www.mediabistro.com; (10) www.writersweekly.com/markets _and_jobs.php.

JOURNALISM JOBS & SIMILAR SITES. Websites: (1) www.journalismjobs.com; (2) www .newsjobs.net; (3) www.sunoasis.com/intern.html; (4) www.writejobs.com; (5) www.news link.org/joblink.html; (6) www.iwantmedia.com/jobs/index.html.; (7) jobs and communities for journalists of color: www.journalismnext.com.

+SNAPDRAGON GROUP EDITORIAL SERVICES. PO Box 3024, Tulsa OK 74101-3024. (918)245-0559. E-mail info@snapdragongroup.com. This group aims to provide the best professional freelancers for publishers' outsourced projects. For details about their story needs, visit Website: www.snapdragongroup.com.

+WASHINGTON D.C. AREA OPPORTUNITY. Check out the DC WritersCorps at http://dcwriters corps.org. They send writers to teach middle-school students throughout the DC area.

WORLDWIDE FREELANCE. Website: www.worldwidefreelance.com. Extensive lists of travel writing markets, Christian markets, technology markets, and more. Subscribe to free newsletter online.

+WRITERS AND EDITORS FOR HIRE. Elizabeth Lyon of M. Evans & Company is putting together a national directory of editors and writers for hire. There is no charge for the listing. E-mail: elyon@ordata.com.

WRITING EMPLOYMENT CENTER. Website: www.poewar.com/jobs.htm.

FULL-TIME FREELANCING

ABOUT FREELANCING. Website: www.freelancewrite.about.com. Provides the essentials for freelance writers.

THE E-MYTH REVISITED by Michael E. Gerber. ISBN 0887307280. This book looks at and dispels myths involved with starting and maintaining your own business. Available at www.amazon.com.

FREELANCE BIDDING SERVICES. Websites: (1) www.elance.com. Writers, editors, and other professionals in a broad range of fields bid for projects posted by companies looking for freelance workers; (2) www.guru.com. An online marketplace for freelance talent.

FREELANCE WRITING ORG. INT'L. Website: www.fwointl.com. Site offers more than 3,000 links to writing resources in over 60 categories.

FUNDS FOR WRITERS. Website: www.fundsforwriters.com. Helping writers earn a living doing what they love.

HEALTH INSURANCE CONCERNS. Websites: (1) www.christianet.com/blessed; (2) www.biblical healthcare.com. These sites are not insurance sites, rather they are biblically based Medi-Share alternatives.

HEALTH SAVINGS ACCOUNTS. Golden Rule Insurance, 712 Eleventh St., Lawrenceville IL 62439-2395. Website: www.goldenrule.com. Provides a health insurance alternative to the self-employed.

WRITING FOR DOLLARS NEWSLETTER. Website: www.writingfordollars.com. Information for the business side of freelance writing.

GRANTS*

CANADIAN SUBSIDY DIRECTORY. A guide containing more than 3,100 direct and indirect financial subsidies, grants, and loans offered by government departments and agencies, foundations, associations, and organizations. Cost is $49.95. Order from one of the following distributors: Canadian Business Resource Center: (250)381-4822 or Fureteur Bookstore: (450)465-5597 or fax (450)465-8144.

FUNDS FOR WRITERS. Website: www.fundsforwriters.com. Helping writers earn a living doing what they love.

+GRANT WRITING. Check out WriteThisInstant.com. Website: www.writethisinstant.com. Click on "writing." Then click on "grant writing" in the right side bar. Lots of sights on grants and grant writing.

+JOURNALISM GRANTS & FELLOWSHIPS. Visit Website: www.newswise.com/grants.htm.

PEN AMERICAN CENTER, 588 Broadway, Ste. 303, New York NY 10012. (212)334-1660. Fax (212)334-2181. E-mail: pen@pen.org. Website: www.pen.org. Membership open to playwrights, editors, essayists, and novelists. For information on finding grants for writers, request a copy of the book *Pen Grants and Awards Available to American Writers* ($19.50).

GROUPS/ORGANIZATIONS OF INTEREST

+AMERICAN ACADEMY OF RELIGION. Find an expert on virtually any aspect of religion at www.religionsource.org.

AMERICAN BOOKSELLERS ASSN. Website: www.bookweb.org. A not-for-profit trade organization devoted to meeting the needs of its core members of independently owned bookstores with retail store-front locations through advocacy, education, research, and information dissemination.

AMERICAN CHRISTIAN WRITERS, PO Box 110390, Nashville TN 37222. Toll-free (800)21-WRITE. Website: www.ACWriters.com. Reg Forder, dir. Ministry with a goal to provide full service to Christian writers and speakers. Publishes two writers' periodicals, operates two correspondence schools, hosts three dozen conferences each year, offers a critique service and book publishing division, and has a mail-order learning center that offers thousands of books, cassette tapes, and software programs for writers.

AMERICAN SELF-PUBLISHING ASSN., PO Box 232233, Sacramento CA 95823. (916)422-8435. Toll-free (800)929-7889. Website: http://bchrist.rwh.net/AmericanSelfPublisher. Offers nationwide seminars, a monthly newsletter, and a 58-page booklet *Writing, Publishing, & Marketing Your 1st Book (or 7th) on a Shoe-String Budget*. Dues are $195/year. For free sample, e-mail: BooksAmerica@aol.com.

AMERICAN SOCIETY OF JOURNALISTS AND AUTHORS, 1501 Broadway, Ste. 302, New York NY 10036. (212)997-0947. Fax (212)768-7414. Website: www.asja.org. Dues are $195/year.

THE AMY FOUNDATION sponsors the Amy Writing Awards, which is a call to present spiritual truth reinforced with biblical references in secular, nonreligious publications. First prize is $10,000 with a total of $34,000 given annually. The Amy Writing Awards are designed to recognize creative, skillful writing that presents in a sensitive, thought-provoking manner a biblical position on issues affecting the world today. To be eligible, submitted articles must be published in a secular, nonreligious publication and must be reinforced with at least one passage of Scripture. To request guidelines and a copy of last year's winning entries, go to the order information page or write: The Amy Foundation, PO Box 16091, Lansing MI 48901-6091. (517)323-6233. Website: www.amyfound.org.

ASSOCIATED CHURCH PRESS, 1410 Vernon St., Stoughton WI 53589. (608)877-0011. Fax (608)877-0062. Mary Lynn Hendrickson, exec. dir. E-mail: acpoffice@earthlink.net. Website: www.theacp.org. Individual membership in ACP is open to freelance writers, journalists, designers, Web designers, and marketers as well as former ACP editors. Cost: $40/yr.

ASSOCIATED PRESS. Website: www.ap.org.

ASSN. OF AMERICAN PUBLISHERS. Website: www.publishers.org. The principal trade association of the book publishing industry.

THE ASSN. OF AUTHOR'S REPRESENTATIVES, Website: www.aar-online.org. Assists agents in representing their client's interests.

+ASSN. OF HEALTH CARE JOURNALISTS (AHCJ). Website: www.ahcj.umn.edu/jour _basics.htm.

AUTHOR'S GUILD, 31 E. 28th St., 10th Fl., New York NY 10016. (212)563-5904. Fax (212)564-5363. E-mail: staff@authorsguild.org. Website: www.authorsguild.org. The nation's largest society of published authors. Provides contract reviews, legal assistance, and access to group health insurance.

+BOOK GROUPS. Find a book group in your area and tips for starting and leading book clubs. Website: www.generousbooks.com.

R. R. BOWKER, 630 Central Ave., New Providence NJ 07974. Toll-free (800)526-9537. E-mail: customerservice@bowker.com. Website: www.bowker.com. This company issues International Standard Book Numbers (ISBN), Standard Account Numbers (SAN), and Advanced Book Information forms. Forms can be printed off their Website.

CANADIAN AUTHORS ASSN., Box 419, Campbellford ON K0L 1L0, Canada. Toll-free (866)216-6222. (705)653-0323. Fax (705)653-0593. E-mail: admin@canauthors.org. Website: www.canauthors.org. Addresses the needs of writers at all stages of development through meetings, workshops, and an annual conference. Publishes *The Canadian Writer's Guide.*

CANADIAN CHURCH PRESS, 2450 Milltower Court, Mississauga ON L5N 5Z6 Canada. Contact: Sue Newbery. (905)521-2240. E-mail: cdnchurchpress@hotmail.com. Website: www .Canadianchurchpress.com.

CANSCAIP. Canadian Society of Children's Authors, Illustrators, and Performers. Website: www .canscaip.org.

CATHOLIC PRESS ASSN., 3555 Veterans Memorial Hwy., Unit O, Ronkonkoma NY 11779. (631)471-4730. Fax (631)471-4804. Owen McGovern, exec. dir. E-mail: rosep@catholic press.org. Website: www.catholicpress.org.

CHRISTIANBOOK.COM. Website: www.Christianbook.com. The largest e-commerce business site for Christian books and merchandise. Customer service: Toll-free (800)247-4784.

CHRISTIAN NEWSPAPER ASSN. Website: www.christiannewsassoc.com. Call toll-free (866)586-5200 or e-mail Mary Ann Marchbanks at publisher@christianbanner.com.

+CHRISTIAN SMALL PUBLISHERS ASSOCIATION/CSPA, PO Box 5820, Lynnwood WA 98046. (206)265-9741. E-mail: cspa@christianpublishers.net. Website: www.christian publishers.net.

CHRISTIANWRITERS.COM. Website: http://christianwriters.com. A free online writers' resource community. Their mission is to provide a supportive, family atmosphere where writers may easily access the tools and resources to create, market, and publish their work.

CHRISTIAN WRITERS FELLOWSHIP INTL. Sandy Brooks, 1624 Jefferson Davis Rd., Clinton SC 29325-6401. (864)697-6035. E-mail: cwfi@cwfi-online.org. To contact Sandy Brooks personally: sandybrooks@cwfi-online.org. Website: www.cwfi-online.org. Offers market consultations, critique service, writers' instructional materials, and conference workshop tapes. Connects writers living in the same area and helps start writers' groups. *Cross & Quill* is the organizational newsletter.

COUNCIL FOR INTERNATIONAL EXCHANGE OF SCHOLARS. The Fulbright Scholar Program for faculty and professionals is offering more than 70 awards in communications and journalism for lecturing and/or doing research abroad during the coming academic year. For details, go to: www.iie.org/cies.

+COUNCIL OF LITERARY MAGAZINES AND PUBLISHERS (CLMP). A guide for new literary publishers. Website: www.clmp.org/resources/guide.html.

EDITORIAL FREELANCERS ASSN. Website: www.the-efa.org. A national, nonprofit, professional organization of self-employed workers in the publishing and communications industry.

EVANGELICAL CHRISTIAN PUBLISHERS ASSN. (ECPA), 4816 S. Ash, Ste. 101, Tempe AZ 85282. (480)966-3998. Fax (480)966-1944. Mark Kuyper, pres./CEO. E-mail: info@ ecpa.org. Website: www.ecpa.org. Proclaiming the gospel through books, Bibles, gifts, curriculum, video, and audio products. Also offers a submission service on the Internet where Christian publishers who are members of this association can review your book proposal. Cost is $79. Visit their Website and click on 1st Edition for more information.

EVANGELICAL PRESS ASSN., PO Box 28129, Crystal MN 55428. (763)535-4793. Fax (763)535-4794. E-mail: director@epassoc.org. Website: www.epassoc.org. Doug Trouten, exec. dir. The professional association for the evangelical periodical publishing industry. EPA offers memberships to writers and tools to help freelancers connect with editors.

FREEDOM FORUM ONLINE. Website: www.freedomforum.org. News about free press.

INTERNATIONAL CHRISTIAN RETAIL (formerly CBA). The international trade association of Christian retailers and product suppliers. PO Box 62000, Colorado Springs CO 80962-2000. Toll-free (800)252-1950. Bill Anderson, president. E-mail: info@cbaonline.org. Website: www.cbaonline.org.

INTERNATIONAL CHRISTIAN WRITERS, Stanley C. Baldwin, dir., 12900 S.E. Nixon, Milwaukie OR 97222 (include SASE for reply). E-mail: SCBaldwin@juno.com. A point of contact for writers around the world. Prayer Fellowship: Joyce Tomanek. E-mail: neh_8 _10@alltel.net.

INTERNATIONAL JOURNALISTS' NETWORK. Website: www.ijnet.org. Online source for media assistance, news, and journalism training opportunities.

INTERNATIONAL WOMEN'S WRITING GUILD, PO Box 810, Gracie Station, New York NY 10028-0082. (212)737-7536. Fax (212)737-9469. Hannelore Hahn, exec. dir. E-mail: dirhahn@aol.com. Website: www.iwwg.com. A network for the personal and professional empowerment of women through writing. Annual membership is $45.

JERRY B. JENKINS CHRISTIAN WRITERS GUILD. Dir. Rick Anderson, PO Box 88196, Black Forest, CO 80908. Toll-free (866)495-5177. E-mail: ContactUs@ChristianWriters Guild.com. Website: www.ChristianWritersGuild.com. This International organization owned by Jerry B. Jenkins, author of more than 150 books including the best-selling Left Behind series, has more than 1,500 members worldwide. The Guild offers annual memberships, mentor-guided correspondence courses for adults (two-year *Apprentice* and advanced one-year *Journeyman*) and youth (*Pages*: ages 9-12 and *Squires*: 13 and up), writing contests (winners receive large cash advance and book contract with a major CBA publisher), Writing for the Soul conferences, critique service, writers resource books, monthly newsletter, and more. Call for a Free Starter Kit.

NATIONAL ASSN. OF SCIENCE WRITERS, PO Box 890, Hedgesville WV 25427. (304)754-5077. E-mail: info@nasw.org. Website: www.nasw.org.

NATIONAL ASSN. OF WOMEN WRITERS, PO Box 700696, San Antonio TX 78270-0696. Website: www.naww.org. Offers an e-book library, online critique and discussion groups, and industry-related legal advice. Also has a free weekly e-zine. Send a blank e-mail to: naww@onebox.com with "Subscribe" in the subject line or visit the Website.

+NATIONAL BOOK FOUNDATION. To find out about National Book Awards, visit Website: www.nationalbook.org.

NATIONAL RELIGIOUS BROADCASTERS, 9510 Technology Dr., Manassas VA 20110. (703)330-7000. Fax (703)330-7100. E-mail: info@nrb.org. Website: www.nrb.org. Request information on the Directory of Religious Media.

NATIONAL SPEAKERS ASSN., 1500 S. Priest Dr., Tempe AZ 85281. (480)968-2552. Fax (480)968-0911. Website: www.nsaspeaker.org. Conventions and training for professional speakers. Puts out *Professional Speaker Magazine.*

NATIONAL WRITERS UNION, 113 University Pl., 6th Fl., New York NY 10003. (212)254-0279. Fax (212)254-0673. E-mail: nwu@nwu.org. Website: www.nwu.org. The National Writers Union is the only U.S. trade union for freelance and contract writers. Offers contract advice, grievance resolution, health and dental plans, member education, Job Hotline, and networking. Employers list contract and freelance jobs for free and deal directly with writers. See Website for list of local groups.

NEWSPAPER ASSN. OF AMERICA. Website: www.naa.org. Focuses on strategic issues such as marketing, public policy, diversity, industry development, and newspaper operations.

PEN AMERICAN CENTER, 588 Broadway, Ste. 303, New York NY 10012. (212)334-1660. Fax (212)334-2181. E-mail: pen@pen.org. Website: www.pen.org. Membership open to playwrights, editors, essayists, and novelists. For information on finding grants for writers, request a copy of the book *Pen Grants and Awards Available to American Writers* ($19.50).

PEN CENTER USA WEST, 672 S. Lafayette Park Pl., #42, Los Angeles CA 90057. (213)365-8500. Fax (213)365-9616. E-mail: pen@penusa.org. Website: www.pen-usa-west.org.

PUBLISHERS WEEKLY is the international news magazine and trade journal for the secular book publishing and bookselling industry. Website: www.publishersweekly.com.

RELIGION NEWS SERVICE, 1101 Connecticut Ave. N.W., Ste. 350, Washington DC 20036. (202)463-8777. Toll-free (800)767-6781. Fax (202)463-0033. E-mail: info@religion news.com. Website: www.religionnews.com. A secular news service devoted to unbiased coverage of religion and ethics.

+RELIGION NEWSWRITERS ASSN. Website: www.rna.org.

+RELIGION NEWSWRITERS FOUNDATION (RNF). Website: www.religionwriters.com/ religionjournalism.php.

SMALL PUBLISHERS ASSN. OF NORTH AMERICA (SPAN), PO Box 1306, Buena Vista CO 81211. (719)395-4790. Fax (719)395-8374. E-mail: Span@SPANnet.org. Website: www .SPANnet.org. A nonprofit professional trade association for independent presses, self-publishers, and authors.

+SOCIETY OF AMERICAN TRAVEL WRITERS. Provides support and development for its 1,200 members. Annual membership: $130-$250. Website: www.satw.org.

+SOCIETY OF PROFESSIONAL JOURNALISTS. Offers its members career training and support. Annual membership: $36-90. Website: www.spj.org.

WRITERS GUILD OF AMERICA EAST, 555 W. 57th St., Ste. 1230, New York NY 10019. (212)767-7800. Fax (212)582-1909. Website: www.wgaeast.org.

WRITERS GUILD OF AMERICA WEST, 7000 W. 3rd St., Los Angeles CA 90048. (323)951-4000. Toll-free (800)548-4532. Fax (323)782-4800. Website: www.wga.org.

WRITERS INFORMATION NETWORK, PO Box 11337, Bainbridge Island WA 98110. (206)842-9103. Contact: Elaine Wright Colvin. E-mail: writersinfonetwork@juno.com. Website: www.Christianwritersinfo.net. A professional association for Christian writers that links writers, speakers, agents, editors, publishers, and publicists. Newsletter, seminars, editorial services. Annual membership fee is $49.95 per year and includes the bimonthly in-depth magazine *WIN-Informer.*

WRITERS' UNION OF CANADA, 90 Richmond St. E., Ste. 200, Toronto ON M5C 1P1 Canada. (416)703-8982. Fax (416)504-9090. E-mail: info@writersunion.ca. Website: www.writers union.ca.

ILLUSTRATION SOURCES

+BOOK COVERS AND MORE. For made-to-order, original illustration, layout and design of book covers, contact Mike Bennett Graphics at (860)627-9772. Visit Mike's Website to see many examples of his cover designs and additional graphic arts including logo designs, Website designs, and more: www.mikebennettgraphics.com.

+BUREAU OF LAND MANAGEMENT PHOTOS. For historical pictures of the Western United States from the 1890s to 1970, go to Website: www.photos.blm.gov/hist_index.html. This site is currently offline. Check back from time to time. It is worth the wait.

CARTOONS. (1) Contact: Ron Wheeler. E-mail: ron@cartoonworks.com. Website: www.cartoon works.com. Provides cartoon illustrations for articles. (2) See latest portfolio additions at: www.ronwheeler.com. (3) For Christian cartoons, visit Dan Rosandich's site: www.dans cartoons.com. He offers existing images to license for usage in newsletters, presentations, magazines, Websites, books, calendars, etc.

+CELEBRITY PHOTOS. If you need pictures of famous folks, try these two Websites: (1) www .mptv.net or (2) www.celebritypictures.co.uk.

CORBIS. Website: www.corbis.com. Stock photography and digital pictures.

+GOVERNMENT PHOTOS. (1) In the U.S., weather-related photographs are available at the National Oceanic and Atmospheric Administration Website: www.photolib.noaa.gov. (2) The United States Library of Congress site includes historical photographs and American celebrities. Website: www.loc.gov.

+GRAPHIC ARTIST. Contact Barbara McDonald at logolady1@aol.com. For an example of her work, go to Amazon.com and search for a book entitled *Gourmet Meetings on a Microwave Schedule.* She did the cover for the book.

INTERNATIONAL MUSEUM OF CARTOON ART. Website: http://cartoon.org /home.htm. Click on Advice for information on getting started.

+INTERNET PHOTO SOURCES. (1) AP Wide World Photos offers an online collection of 700,000 photos of people and events around the world. Price varies. Website: www.apwide world.com; (2) Fotosearch combines several major online stock photo supplies into one site. Website: www.fotosearch.com; (3) Getty Image. Around the world current photos. Website: www.gettyimages.com; (4) MGN Online has fewer images but lower prices than Getty. Website: www.mgnonline.com; (5) Newscom brings together images from many news agencies. Website: www.newscom.com; (6) Photos to Go has a library of a half-million digital images available for licensing. This company also offers collections of royalty-free images on CD. Website: www.photostogo.com. Other stock photo sites include: (7) www .blackstar.com; (8) www.comstock.com; (9) www.coopstock.com; (10) www.eyewire .com; (11) www.images.com; (12) www.indexstock.com; (13) www.mira.com; (14) www .photodisc.com; (15) www.picturequest.com; (16) www.stockbyte.com; (17) www.stock photo.com; (18) www.zephyrimages.com; (19) http://images.google.com.

LIDIA SIMEONOVA, 53166 Gaskill Court E., Shelby Twp. MI 48316. (248)650-6086. E-mail: simeonov1@comcast.net. Available for designing book covers for writers/publishers.

MAZZOCCHI GROUP GRAPHIC DESIGN, PO Box 68, Three Rivers MI 49093. (269)273-7070. E-mail: omega777@net-link.net. Website: www.whimsicalwings.com/contact.html.

Specializes in custom, full-color designs for the book cover of your self-published book. Designed by a Christian artist with over 20 years' experience.

+MINISTRY PHOTOS. Worldwide Challenge Photo Gallery offers real life "ministry in action" photos. Website: www.wwcmagazine.org/photos.

+PHOTOGRAPHERS. (1) If you are looking for a photographer rather than a photograph, go to Website: www.christiansinphotojournalism.org. (2) Also visit secular Website: www.photographers.com.

PHOTOSOURCEBANK. PhotoSource Intl., Rohn Engh, dir. Toll-free (800)624-0266, ext. 21. Fax (800)photofax. E-mail: info@photosource.com. Website: www.photosource.com. Good source of stock photos, and an opportunity for you to post a description of the photos you have for sale on this Website.

+RELIGIOUS STOCK PHOTOGRAPHY. Ponkawonka Inc. specializes in Christianity and other world religions. Contributions from 90 photographers of professional quality. Website: www.ponkawonka.com.

+RON ANDERSON PHOTO. For book covers, book content, inspirational calendars, or daily journals, visit Website: www.ronandersonphoto.com.

ROYALTY STOCK, INC. PO Box 551337, Jacksonville FL 32255. E-mail: info@royaltystock.com. Website: www.royaltystock.com. Previously known as Eye Abide, Inc. A stock photography agency providing collections of inspirational images. Also looking for photographers and submissions.

SKJOLD PHOTOGRAPHS. Steve and Mary Skjold. Toll-free (800)484-9655, Security Code 9750. E-mail: skjfoto@skjoldphotographs.com. Website: www.skjoldphotographs.com. Interactive site with large clear pictures available for downloading and placement. Features stock photos of children, teens, classrooms, homeless, religious, and holidays.

+SPORTS PHOTOS. Sports photos are available at Websites: (1) www.empics.com; (2) www.allsportusa.com.

+TIPS ON FINDING & USING PHOTOS. Visit Sree's Tips on finding and using photos at Website: www.sree.net/tips/graphics.html; useful information.

LANGUAGE/VOCABULARY

ACRONYM AND ABBREVIATION LIST. Website: www.AcronymFinder.com. Allows you to search for over 403,000 acronyms, abbreviations, and definitions about all subjects, including information technology, business, telecommunications, military, government, and much more.

APHORISMS. Website: www.aphorismsgalore.com.

AUSTRALIAN SLANG DICTIONARY. Website: www.koalanet.com.au/australian-slang.html.

CLICHÉ FINDER. (1) Website: www.westegg.com/cliche. (2) Also see: www.plainenglish.co.uk for the Plain English Campaign against clichés.

COMMON ERRORS IN ENGLISH. Website: www.wsu.edu/~brians/errors/errors.html.

+CONJUGATE VERBS. Check out this site for languages, modern and ancient. Website: www.verbix.com/webverbix.

DE-MYSTIFYING BUZZWORDS. Website: www.buzzwhack.com. Sign up for the buzzword of the day.

THE DIALECTIZER. Website: www.rinkworks.com/dialect. Converts English to Redneck, Jive, Cockney, Elmer Fudd, Swedish Chef, or Pig Latin.

DICTIONARY.COM. Website: www.dictionary.com. Type in the word you are looking for, and if there is no match, it makes suggestions that are hyperlinked so you can check the meaning to make sure it is the word you are actually seeking.

ENGLISH LESSONS. Website: www.englishpage.com. Free online English lessons.

ENGLISH WORDS AND PHRASES. Website: www.worldwidewords.org. What words mean, where they came from, how they have evolved, and the ways people misuse them.

FUN WITH WORDS. Website: www.fun-with-words.com. "The Wordplay Website."

+THE GLOSSARIST. A searchable directory of glossaries and topical dictionaries. Website: www.glossarist.com.

GOOGLE TOOLS. (1) Language Tools allows you to search by specific languages or countries and translates texts. Website: www.google.com/language_tools?hl=en. (2) Another Google feature when you need a quick word definition: Type "define:word" (no spaces), and Google will define the word.

GRAMMAR. Websites: (1) www.grammarcheck.com. Free weekly e-mail newsletter that helps improve your grammar, punctuation, and writing skills; (2) http://ccc.commnet.edu/grammar. Offers an exhaustive index of grammar and composition references; (3) www.edufind .com/english/grammar; (4) www.grammarlady.com; (5) www.ruthvilmi.net/hut/help/ grammar_help; (6) www.writingenglish.com; (7) http://finance.groups.yahoo.com/group/ writing-tips; (8) www.webgrammar.com.

IDIOMS. Website: www.idiomsite.com. Learn the origin of phrases that have found their way into our everyday language.

LANGUAGE CONSTRUCTION KIT. Website: www.zompist.com/kit.html. Create your own language.

LEXICAL SITE. Website: www.lexfn.com. Goes beyond giving synonyms; it also links words so that synonyms, antonyms, or words related by any of 16 different criteria may be found.

LINGUISTICS. Website: www.sfwa.org/members/elgin/Linguistics/RWL05.html. A lesson, *Real World Linguistics 101* by Suzette Haden Elgin.

+MISSPELLED WORDS. For a list of 100 most commonly misspelled words, visit Website: http://yourdictionary.com/library/misspelled.html.

OXYMORON: CONTRADICTORY WORDS. Website: www.oxymoronlist.com. Here's a self-proclaimed "Largest List of Oxymorons Ever Collected Online!"

PRONUNCIATION GUIDE. The Voice of America Pronunciation Guide. Website: http://ibb7 .ibb.gov/pronunciations.

SLANG. Website: www.slangsite.com. Here's a site where you can find the latest hip lingo. For UK slang visit: www.peevish.co.uk/slang/index.htm.

TEEN LINGO. Website: www.thesourcefym.com/teenlingo.

+TEXT ANALYSER. This site will analyze your text for word count, readability, sentence count, average sentence length, and most frequently used words. Website: http://textalyser.net.

TRANSLATIONS. Websites: (1) http://babelfish.altavista.com/translate.dyn. Babelfish Translations. Type anything in English and it will translate it into either Spanish, French, Portuguese, Italian, German—or the other way around; (2) http://translate.google.com/ translate_t. Instantly translates from English to German, Spanish, French, Italian, and Portuguese, and from each of these into the others. Will even translate Website addresses; (3) http://translation2.paralink.com. English, French, German, Russian, and Spanish; (4) Logos translates 188 languages: www.logos.it.

+THE VERB E-ZINE. Offers an active guide to better writing. Website: www.readingwriters.com.

THE VOCABULA REVIEW. Website: www.vocabula.com. An online journal about the state of the English language, with tips on grammar, articles, and more.

+WEBSTER'S ONLINE DICTIONARY. Search over 3 million words and expressions and find background origins, definitions, crosswords, rhyming words, quotations, and more. Website: www.websters-online-dictionary.org.

A WORD A DAY. (1) Website: www.wordsmith.org/awad/index.html. Sign up to get a new word and its definition sent each day. (2) The Merriam-Webster Website also offers a word-a-day at: www.m-w.com. (3) To subscribe to Hebrew word-a-day, go to: http://Hebrew Resources.com. (4) Another site is www.vocabvitamins.com. It features a word-a-day with definitions, word origins, and an example of the word in text. Check out the "Additional Services" page for more links to interesting sites. Also see: (5) www.nationalreview.com/word/word.asp; (6) http://dictionary.reference.com/wordoftheday.

WORD COUNTER. (1) Website: www.wordcounter.com. Ranks the most frequently used words in any body of text. (2) Another interesting site ranks words in order from the most to least frequently used. Website: www.wordcount.org/main.php.

WORD POLICE. Website: www.theatlantic.com/unbound/wordpolice/six.

WORDS. Websites: (1) www.wordspy.com; (2) www.verbatimmag.com. Two sources of popular new words or new uses.

WORTHLESS WORD OF THE DAY. Website: http://home.mn.rr.com/wwftd.

LEGAL CONCERNS

ASJA CONTRACTS WATCH. Offers free e-newsletter from the American Society of Journalists and Authors that keeps writers up to date on latest contract developments. See Website to subscribe: www.asja.org.

BETTER BUSINESS BUREAU. If you are the victim of fraud or have questions/concerns about an agent or publisher, contact the Better Business Bureau in their town, as well as their local attorney general or their state attorney general's office of consumer protection. You can also contact the Better Business Bureau online to see if a certain company has any complaints on file. Website: www.bbb.org.

BOOKS FOR LEGAL CONCERNS. (1) *The Copyright Permission and Libel Handbook: A Step-by-Step Guide for Writers, Editors, and Publishers* by Lloyd J. Jassin and Steve C. Schecter. (2) *The Practical Guide to Libel Law* by Neil J. Rosini. (3) *The Writer's Legal Companion* by Brad Bunnin and Peter Beren. Covers contracts, agents, copyright, taxes, libel, permissions, and more. Books available through local retailer.

COPYRIGHT AND COPY WRONGS. Website: www.education-world.com/a_curr/curr280a.shtml. Multipart article for teachers and writers.

COPYRIGHT AND PUBLISHING LAW ATTORNEY. Law Office of Sallie G. Randolph, 520 Franklin St., Buffalo NY 14202. (716)885-1847. E-mail: info@authorlaw.com. Website: www.authorlaw.com. Available to consult with writers or their attorneys about publishing law issues. Available for speaking and teaching. Coauthor of a new book called *Author Law A to Z*. See Website.

COPYRIGHT INFORMATION. Websites: (1) www.templetons.com/brad/copymyths.htm. Brad Templeton's article gives important information on copyrights; (2) www.writing-world.com/rights/topten.shtml. Answers the top ten questions about copyright permissions.

COPYRIGHT LAW—LIBRARY OF CONGRESS COPYRIGHT OFFICE, 101 Independence Ave. S.E., Washington DC 20559-6000. (202)707-3000. (1) Website: www.copyright.gov. Available in Spanish: www.copyright.gov/espanol. You may call or write for forms, or get them from the Website. To view the most current copyright rates, go to: www.copyright.gov/docs/fees.html. (2) Also check out these copyright information sites: www.benedict.com and (3) www.whatiscopyright.org.

COPYRIGHT PIRACY. Website: www.sharpwriter.com/content/piracy.htm. Offers one writer's experience with pirates.

FAIR BUSINESS PRACTICES BRANCH, COMPETITION BUREAU, INDUSTRY CANADA. (1) Website: http://competition.ic.gc.ca. Contact about illegal or unethical behavior by an agent or publisher in Canada. (2) You also might notify or contact The Canadian Author's Assn. at: Box 419, Campbellford ON K0L 1L0, Canada. (705)653-0323. Toll-free (866)216-6222. Fax (705)653-0593. E-mail: admin@canauthors.org. Website: www.canauthors.org.

THE FEDERAL TRADE COMMISSION, BUREAU OF CONSUMER PROTECTION, Consumer

Response Center (CRC). (202)326-2222. Website: www.ftc.gov. Contact about illegal or unethical behavior by an agent or publisher in the U.S. Click "File a Complaint" in the menu bar to access FTC's Public Complaint Form.

FREEDOM OF INFORMATION ACT BY THE SOCIETY OF PROFESSIONAL JOURNALISTS. Website: http://spj.org/foia.asp.

INTELLECTUAL PROPERTY LAW. Website: www.intelproplaw.com. Look up copyrights or connect to legal reference sites.

INTERNATIONAL TRADEMARK ASSN. (1) Website: www.inta.org. Offers free information about trademarks. (2) Visit www.inta.org/hotline to reach the Trademark Hotline for free and immediate answers on proper usage.

+ISBN CHANGES. Beginning January 1, 2007, ISBN agencies all over the world will assign new ISBN numbers that are 13 digits long, replacing the 10 digit numbers currently provided. The bar codes will not change. For more information, go to Website: www.isbn-13.info.

LEGAL SITE FOR WRITERS. Daniel N. Steven, publishing attorney and consultant. Website: www.publishlawyer.com. The legal resource for publishing professionals.

NOLO: Law for All. Website: www.nolo.com/encyclopedia/tc_ency.html. Includes comprehensive legal explanations about trademarks and copyrights.

PATENT CAFÉ. Website: www.patentcafe.com. "Intellectual Property Management."

PERMISSIONS CONTACTS. Websites: (1) www.publist.com. Lists over 150,000 publications with basic information, including who to contact for permissions; (2) www.ucpress.edu/press/authors/perms.html.

PLAGIARISM. (1) For articles dealing with plagiarism, go to: www.writersweekly.com/search.html and enter the search word Plagiarism. (2) Another Website: www.web-miner.com/plagiarism.

+PROTECTING YOUR SCRIPT/COPYRIGHT. Registration facts and fiction: www.writers store.com/article.php?articles_id=532&discount=ezine@source=ezine.

THE PUBLISHING LAW CENTER, Lloyd L. Rich, Property Rights Attorney, 1163 Vine St., Denver CO 80206. (303)388-5215. E-mail: info@publaw.com. Website: www.publaw.com. Offers a free newsletter.

SMALL BUSINESSES. Website: www.businesslaw.gov. Launched by the Small Business Administration to provide indexes in one central location and links to credible sources of information such as licenses, permits, e-commerce, and exporting. The site also includes information specific to each state and territory.

+STANDARD JOURNALISM CONTRACTS. National Writers Union has free templates to download: www.nwu.org/journ/jsjc.htm.

TRADE BOOK PUBLISHING AGREEMENT CHECKLIST. Website: www.copylaw.com/forms/pub chk.html. Gives a good overview of items commonly found in a book publishing agreement.

U.S. PATENT AND TRADEMARK OFFICE. Website: www.uspto.gov. Trademark process information in easy terms.

VOLUNTEER LAWYERS FOR THE ARTS, 1 East 53rd St., 6th Fl., New York NY 10022. (212)319-2787, ext. 1. Fax (212)752-6575. E-mail: askvla@vlany.org. Website: www.vlany.org.

WARNINGS. (1) A Website to check out when you are having trouble getting payment or wondering about the legitimacy of a publisher is www.writersweekly.com/search.html and enter the search words "Whispers and Warnings." (2) Also see: www.nwu.org/alerts/alrthome.htm.

WRITER'S POCKET TAX GUIDE. Website: www.foolscap-quill.com. An annual tax guide book.

MARKET SOURCES

ANTHOLOGIES ONLINE. Website: www.anthologiesonline.com. A listing of anthologies looking for contributors. Writers should subscribe and send in brief bio and best writing sample (up to 1,200 words total) to apply to become a feature writer.

+AREOPAGUS GUIDE TO UK CHRISTIAN PUBLICATIONS. Published biannually. U.S. price $6. Order off Website: www.areopagus.org.uk/index.html.

BOOK MARKETING/PROMOTION CHECKLIST: 22 Ways to Promote and Sell Books by John B. McHugh. Free. Website: www.johnbmchugh.com. Click on Free McHugh Publications.

+BOOK PROPOSALS. (1) To purchase a copy of *Book Proposals that Sell: 21 Secrets to Speed Your Success* by W. Terry Whalin, go to Website: www.bookproposals.ws. (2) To download e-book *Writing a Winning Book Proposal* from Thomas Nelson Publishers, go to Website: www.thomasnelson.com/consumer/downloads/writingabookproposal.pdf.

CANADIAN MAGAZINE PUBLISHERS ASSN., 425 Adelaide St., Ste. 700, Toronto ON M5V 3C1 Canada. (416)504-0274. Fax (416)504-0437. E-mail: cmpainfo@cmpa.ca. Website: www.cmpa.ca.

CANADIAN MARKETS. (1) *Canadian Markets* (and other publications) at Website: www.pwac.ca/resources/publications.htm; (2) Directory of members at www.writers.ca, which is a free searchable database; (3) *Roughing It in the Market: A Survival Toolkit for the Savvy Writer,* 215 Spadina Ave., Ste. 123, Toronto ON M5T 2C7, Canada; (4) www.booklocker.com/books/1188.html for the e-book *A Writer's Guide to Canadian Markets and On-line Resources* by Diana M. VandeHoef.

CHRISTIAN WRITERS' MARKET GUIDE WEBSITE. Website: www.stuartmarket.com. Sally Stuart's Website with information on the latest guide, links to the Websites or e-mail of all the Christian publishers or publications that have them, and a listing of conferences for the year. Lots more in the works.

+DIRECTORY OF PUBLISHERS AND VENDORS. Search for publishers' Websites using this handy subject directory. Website: http://acqweb.library.vanderbilt.edu/pubr.html#subj.

FIRST EDITION MANUSCRIPT SERVICE. Website: www.ecpa.org. Click on 1st Edition. This is an online submission service provided by ECPA publishing houses. Fee is $79.

+GUIDELINES DATABASE. Writer's Digest has the Web's largest database of guidelines provided by book and magazine editors. Searchable by keyword, specific words, or phrases. Website: www.writersdigest.com/guidelines.asp.

IDEAMARKETERS.COM. Contact: Marnie L. Pehrson, dir., 514 Old Hickory Ln., Ringgold GA 30736. (706)866-2295. E-mail: webmaster@ideamarketers.com. Website: www.ideamarketers.com. A media-matching service that unites writers and publishers. Writers post their articles for free, and they are stored in a searchable database. Publishers, Web masters, and e-zine editors can then come and find content. There is a link at the top of each article they can click on to ask author's permission to use the article.

LINKS TO FOREIGN MAGAZINES & NEWSPAPERS. Websites: (1) http://dir.yahoo.com/News_and_Media/By_Region/countries; (2) www.cmpa.ca (Canadian); (3) www.vicnet.net.au/~ozlit (Australian); (4) www.newsdirectory.com.

LITERARY JOURNALS. Website: www.jefferybahr.com/Publications/default.htm. Links to literary journals, journal response times, statistics, ranking, and more.

LITERARY MARKETPLACE. Website: www.literarymarketplace.com. General market guide put out by Information Today, Inc., 143 Old Marlton Pike, Medford NJ 08055. Toll-free (800)300-9868. E-mail: custserv@infotoday.com. Cost $399 annually or $19.95 for weekly subscription.

+NICHE PUBLISHING. Find the best ways to publish to niche markets. Go to Gordon Burgett's site and click on his book titled *Niche Markets for Writers and Speakers.* Website: www.gordonburgett.com.

ONLINE MARKETS FOR WRITERS. Website: www.marketsforwriters.com. This book is the guide for online markets.

PUBLISHER'S CATALOGS. Website: www.lights.com/publisher. Includes over 7,700 publishers. Search by publisher's name or city; takes you to the publisher's Website.

PUBLISHERS MARKETING ASSOCIATION ONLINE. Website: http://pma-online.org. Lists basic contact information on hundreds of publishers.

PUBLISHERS OF CHRISTIAN MATERIALS. Website: www.idisciple.net/christianpublishers .shtml. Lists Websites of Christian publishers.

PUBLIST. Website: www.publist.com. List over 150,000 publications with basic contact information.

ROSEDOG.COM. Website: www.rosedog.com. Connects writers, agents, and publishers. Service is $9.95 for writers; free to agents and publishers.

SHELOVESGOD.COM. Contact: Marnie L. Pehrson, dir., 514 Old Hickory Ln., Ringgold GA 30736. (706)866-2295. E-mail: webmaster@SheLovesGod.com. Website: www.SheLoves God.com. A community for Christian women. Read and/or submit faith-promoting articles, stories, testimonies, and poems. Writers post their submissions for free, and they are stored in a searchable database. Churches, editors, women's groups, and others can access content. There is a link at the top of each item that they can click to ask author's permission to reprint.

WEB-ZINE ARTICLE DISTRIBUTION SITES. Websites: (1) www.ideamarketers.com and (2) www.EzineArticles.com. Free content for your e-zine or Website.

WOODEN HORSE PUBLISHERS. Market database for nonfiction writers at: www.wooden horsepub.com. Also contains an extensive glossary for writers.

+WORLDWIDE FREELANCE. Dozens of market links. Website: www.worldwidefreelance .com/markets.htm.

WRITER'S DIGEST WEBSITE. (1) Website: www.writersdigest.com. Lots of writer's helps, including copies of writer's guidelines you can print right off the site. Website for guidelines: (2) www.writersdigest.com/guidelines.asp.

WRITER'S EDGE. Website: www.WritersEdgeService.com. Their list includes 75 participating publishers.

WRITER'S GUIDELINES DATABASE. Website: www.freelancewriting.com/guidelines/pages/ index.html. Lists over 670 writer's guidelines to paying markets.

WRITERS MARKET. Website: www.writersmarket.com. A searchable database of over 5,600 writing markets. Listings are updated daily. Site also includes Submission Tracker, Expert Advice articles, Market Watch, Agent Q&A, and much more.

WRITER'S RELIEF, INC., 245 Teaneck Rd., #3, Ridgefield Park NJ 07660. (201)641-3003. Fax (201)641-1253. E-mail: Ronnie@wrelief.com. Website: www.wrelief.com. An author's submission service, handling your manuscript submissions for an hourly rate of $45-60 plus postage and copying (after initial free reading), or a flat fee after completing review. Prepares manuscripts, proofreads, writes query and cover letters, tracks submissions, keeps records, etc.

YAHOO'S LIST OF CHRISTIAN PUBLICATIONS ON THE WEB. Go to Yahoo's search engine (www.yahoo.com). Click on Society and Culture: Religion and Spirituality: Faith and Practices: Christianity.

PROMOTION

+AMAZON RATINGS. To see how your book is doing on Amazon.com and to understand sales rankings, visit these sites: (1) www.junglescan.com; (2) www.greententacles.com/articles/ 2/18; (3) www.murdermustadvertise.com/FAQ/amazon.html.

ARTICLES AND BOOKS OF INTEREST. (1) *The Art of Creating an Unfair Advantage: 200+ Ideas to Market Yourself and Your Books* edited by Ted Decorte. To read article, go to www.geocities.com/MadisonAvenue/Boardroom/4278/aaideas.html; (2) *35 Ways to Make Your Next Book Signing an Event* by Larry James. Website: www.writerswrite.com/journal/

jan00/james.htm; (3) other book-signing articles: www.writing-world.com/promotion/ james.shtml; (4) Book: *You CAN Market Your Book!* by Carmen Leal (ACW 2003). Website: http://carmenleal.com/WS/books.html; (5) Book: *Sell Yourself Without Selling Your Soul* by Susan Harrow (HarperCollins 2002). Website: www.prsecrets.com.

AUTHORLINK. (1) Website: www.authorlink.com. Includes a place to advertise and sell self-published books. Other resources for self-publishers and print-on-demand authors: (2) contact Julie Bonn Heath, e-mail: jheath500@aol.com or (3) Rita Gerlach, e-mail: rpkg@erols.com.

+AUTHORS@YOUR LIBRARY. Authors@Your Library is a free, online database connecting librarians with authors and book publicists looking to promote their books. Website: www.ala.org/ala/ppo/progresources/authors/authorsyour.htm.

BANNERS/POSTERS. Websites: (1) www.poster.com; (2) www.brittenmedia.com. Visual Display Solutions also offers merchandising and display products. Call toll-free (800)688-5104 for information.

BOOK MARKETING UPDATE. Edited by John Kremer. A 12-page newsletter for book writers to help gain national publicity and more book sales. Cost is $297/year (24 issues/year). Contact: Open Horizons, PO Box 205, Fairfield IA 52556. Toll-free (800)796-6130. (641)472-6130. Fax (641)472-1560. E-mail: info@bookmarket.com. Website: www .bookmarket.com.

+BOOK PROMOTION NEWSLETTERS. (1) A biweekly interactive e-zine for authors, publicists, editors, book reviewers, and book coaches. 1350 members. Offers tips, encouragement and networking opportunities. Website: www.bookpromotionnewsletter.com. (2) Another site: www.earthlycharms.com/ecpromo.htm. (3) For a list of articles on online and offline promotion by Judy Cullins, send a request to category-online-promotion@ bookcoaching.com.

BOOKWIRE. Website: www.bookwire.com. Lets general public and industry professionals know about authors touring in their area. Click on Calendar of Events.

BROCHURES/BUSINESS CARDS. (1) Contact: Bill Spilman, Innovative Media Solutions, 1134 N. Henderson St., Galesburg IL 61401. (309)342-3211. Fax (309)342-3212. E-mail: bill@innovativemediasolutions.com. (2) Another recommended site: www.vistaprint.com.

+CD OR DVD DUPLICATION. (1) Visit Website: www.tapeanddisc.com/site.html. (2) Also contact Toby Russell, Velocity AVS in San Diego. E-mail: toby@velocityavs.com.

+CHRISTIAN AUTHORS NETWORK. This newly formed cooperative of CBA authors dedicated to promoting Christian fiction and nonfiction will promote affiliate authors through retailer events and promotions, media campaigns, distribution of a monthly e-zine, and speaker's bureau. For more information, e-mail Cindy Salzmann at cyndysalzmann@earthlink.net.

+CHRISTIAN AUTHORS PROMOTIONAL ALLIANCE (CAPA). Helps small press authors connect with retail outlets. Also has CD catalog. Website: www.capalliance.org. Membership is $30.

CHRISTIAN E-AUTHORS. Website: http://christianeauthor.com. Purpose of site is to promote the electronic works of inspirational authors from around the world. Site offers a variety of e-books in different genres. Author links take you directly to member Websites for more information on each author. A links page offers a glimpse into the world of e-books and e-publishing. A banner, link exchanges, and a Yahoo list group are also available.

+DEARREADER.COM. Reaches Websites, corporations, booksellers, and over 3,000 libraries. Subscribers receive 5-minute read from a chapter of a featured book. For information on getting your book listed, e-mail Suzanne Beecher at Suzanne@dearreader.com. Website: http://dearreader.com.

FRUGAL MARKETING. Website: www.frugalmarketing.com. Shel Horowitz offers tips and information and his book, *Grassroots Marketing: Getting Noticed in a Noisy World.*

GUERRILLA MARKETING FOR WRITERS by Jay Conrad Levinson, Rick Frishman, and Michael Larsen. Ideas on how to promote your book on the Internet, including using your own Website to increase sales. Available at local bookstores, Writer's Digest Book Club, or find information at: www.writersdigest.com/store/booksearch.asp.

GUIDE TO FREELANCERS. Website: www.epassoc.org. Click on "Freelance Guide" or call (763)535-4793. A joint project of the Evangelical Press Association, Associated Church Press, and Fellowship of Christian Newspapers. This annual guide is distributed free of charge to hundreds of Christian periodical editors and is designed to help them find free-lance writers, photographers, and artists. Indexed by specialty and location. Listings available to professional freelancers for a small fee.

INTERNET FOR CHRISTIANS NEWSLETTER. Weekly newsletter from gospelcom.net that highlights and reviews Websites of interest to Christians. Website: www.gospelcom.net/ifc/newsletter.shtml. To recommend a Website, e-mail ifc@internetforchristians.org.

INTERVIEWS. (1) Website: www.willwrite4food.com. Will do author interviews. Websites: (2) www.robinfriedman.com; (3) www.olswanger.com. Both of these author sites have wonderful interviews with editors and agents.

MAILING LISTS. ParaLists, Dan Poynter, PO Box 8206-240, Santa Barbara CA 93118-8206. (805)968-7277. Toll-free (800)727-2782. Fax (805)968-1379. Website: www.parapub.com. ParaLists offers many categories of book promotion and how to obtain mailing lists. E-mail: info@ParaPublishing.com

MARKETING HELP. (1) Website: http://cba.know-where.com/cba. Search for Christian book-stores in your area, or any area you might want to target. (2) Website: www.stretcher.com/stories/01/010409j.cfm. Tips on marketing yourself without money.

MARKETING TIP OF THE WEEK NEWSLETTER. Website: http://bookmarket.com. Plus other helps for promoting your book.

MEDIA KIT. "How to Prepare a Media Kit." Website: www.publicityhound.com/mediakitspeak.

MEDIA LISTS. Publicity Tools is a source for unlimited-use media lists, including Book Industry, Christian, Library, Radio, Newspapers, and National Media Lists. Call toll-free (888)330-4919. E-mail: sendlistinfo@netscape.net.

MINI-CD BUSINESS CARDS. Website: www.cardiscs.com.

NRB DIRECTORY OF RELIGIOUS MEDIA. Produced by National Religious Broadcasters and available for purchase online (download version). It offers searchable databases for media listings, a Buyers' Guide, NRB membership, and unique advertising opportunities. NRB Store Website: www.nrb.org. Contact: Valerie Fraedrich, 9510 Technology Dr., Manassas VA 20110. (703)330-7000, ext. 513. E-mail: vfraedrich@nrb.org.

ONLINE PRESS RELEASE DISTRIBUTION SERVICE. Website: www.prweb.com. Also offers press release tips and templates.

PREMIUM POST CARDS. The U.S. Post Office will print and mail customized postcards. Website: www.usps.com/netpost/premiumpostcard.htm.

PRESS KITS. Website: www.murdermustadvertise.com/FAQ/PressKit.html. Advice on what a press kit should contain and how to make yours stand out.

PRESS RELEASES. Websites: (1) www.prsa.org. Offers information about chapters and other resources; (2) www.prweek.com. A weekly magazine, offering news of interest to PR writers; (3) www.Imediafax.com. A "Trash Proof News Release Tutorial" can be downloaded for free; (4) www.stetson.edu/~rhansen/prhowto.html; (5) www.press-release-writing.com/10_essential_tips.htm; (6) www.thewritemarket.com/articles/pond.htm; (7) www.thewritemarket.com/articles/moore.htm; (8) www.thewritemarket.com/articles/ventura5.htm; (9) www.thewritemarket.com/articles/lock.htm; (10) Book: *Handbook of Strategic Public Relations and Integrated Communications* edited by Clarke L. Caywood (McGraw-Hill).

PRINTING. Websites: (1) www.megacolor.com; (2) www.qualityprintingcheap.com; www.cfre.com.

+PROMOTIONAL PRODUCTS. (1) A source for creative paper products and special printing for promotion pieces. Website: www.flourishgreetings.com. (2) For bookmarks, go to: www.qualityprintingcheap.com. (3) To create a book cover or to put your picture on a stamp, visit Website: http://photo.stamps.com/photostamps.

+PROMOTIONAL SITE. List your book here and see what happens. Website: www.ordinary woman.com/bookshelves-splash.html.

PUBLICITY HOUND. Joan Stewart, 3434 County KK, Port Washington WI 53074. (263)284-7451. Fax (262)284-1737. E-mail: jstewart@publicityhound.com. Website: www.publicity hound.com. Excellent site for publicity solutions.

RADIO-TV INTERVIEW REPORT, Bradley Communications, PO Box 1206, Lansdowne PA 19050-8206. (610)259-0707. Fax (610)284-3704. E-mail: contactus@rtir.com. Website: www.rtir.com. Authors pay to have their profile included in this publication that goes to over 4,000 radio and TV producers who are looking for talk-show guests.

A SAVVY APPROACH TO BOOK SALES: Marketing Advice to Get the Buzz Going by Elaine Wright Colvin. $16 postpaid from Christian Writers Marketplace, 1647 S.W. Pheasant Dr., Aloha OR 97006. Website: www.stuartmarket.com.

STICKERS. Websites: (1) www.maysmall.com/order.htm (10 for $3.00); (2) www.spannet.org/stickers.htm (200 for $10); (3) www.abflink.com/abflink/product_page.asp; (4) www.bookweb.org/graphics/pdfs/orderform.pdf (500 for $5).

TALK RADIO STATIONS. Websites: (1) http://newslink.org/rneradi.html; (2) www.radio-locator.com. Search for stations on either site.

PROMOTION: BOOK REVIEWERS

BOOK CROSSING. Website: www.bookcrossing.com. Book Crossing encourages people to "release books into the wild," to leave books in public places for anyone to pick up and read for free. Register your book online, then "release" it. When someone picks up your book and reads it, he/she is then encouraged to go to the site and leave feedback about it. Over a million books are registered.

+BOOK PROMOTION MAILING LISTS. Lists magazines, newsletters, and newspapers with book review columns. Use these lists to send review copies of books and news releases. List questions? Call 800-PARAPUB. Website: http://parapub.com/maillist.cfm.

BOOKS AND AUTHORS. Website: www.booksandauthors.net. Seeking book reviews and reviewers. E-mail: editor@booksandauthors.net.

+BOOK TALK RADIO. This program is currently looking for authors to interview. Send your book synopsis, author bio, and contact information to RadioTalkers@aol.com.

CHRISTIAN BOOK PREVIEWS.COM. Website: www.christianbookpreviews.com. Features book excerpts, reviews, author bios, and interviews. Also offers a price comparison tool for buyers who want to find the best prices online before purchasing.

+CHRISTIAN FICTION REVIEWER. If you have a newly released novel or one coming out this year and would like Sara Mills to review it, contact her at sara@christianfiction reviewer.com. Website: www.christianfictionreviewer.com.

CO-OP REVIEWERS DATABASE. A free co-op review site listing reviews by genre (including Christian, Spiritual, Religion, and Inspirational). Website: www.bookzonepro.com/reviewers.

EXTREME CHRISTIANITY. Website: www.eczine.com/features/reviews. Brian Groce, publisher. See submission guidelines on site or e-mail: submissions@extremechristianity.com.

+FAITHFULREADER.COM. Edited for Christian readers, this site includes book reviews, author interviews, book excerpts, and a daily devotional. Website: www.faithfulreader.com.

GLORY GIRLS, 33290 W. 14 Mile Rd., #482, West Bloomfield MI 48322. Website: www.glory girlsread.net. Reading groups for African American Christian women who love God and like to read. If you would like the group to consider your book, send 3 copies of each work, press kit, and contact information to the address above.

THE MIDWEST BOOK REVIEW, 278 Orchard Dr., Oregon WI 53575. (608)835-7937. E-mail: mbr@execpc.com. Website: www.midwestbookreview.com. James Cox, ed-in-chief. Send copy of your book to be reviewed for library resource newsletters, etc.

WEBSITES FOR BOOK REVIEWS. Websites: (1) www.barnesandnoble.com; (2) www.christian books.com; (3) www.amazon.com; (4) www.churchfolk.com. Click on Book Club section; (5) www.byauthor.com. Will link to authors' Websites. Other Websites: (6) www.christianity today.com/books, includes a free newsletter; (7) www.bookreviewcafe.com; (8) www .cbaonline.org. Click on CBA Marketplace; (9) www.romantictimes.com; (10) www.library journal.com; (11) www.christianity.net. (12) The Author's Choice Book Review site reviews several books every month. Maintained by Carolyn R. Scheidies. Refer to author's Choice Book Review Website Guidelines. E-mail: crscheidies@mail2faith.com. Website: http://come.to/bookreviews.

PROMOTION: PUBLICISTS

B & B MEDIA GROUP. Client Development: Tina Jacobson. Toll-free (800)927-0517. E-mail: tbbmedia@tbbmedia.com. Website: www.tbbmedia.com. A full service publicity and public relations media communications firm that works with publishers, speakers, writers, and organizations.

BOOKMAN MARKETING. This firm represents your self-published or print-on-demand book in bookstores. Website: www.bookmanmarketing.com. Toll-free (800)342-6068. E-mail: information@bookmanmarketing.com to request author's information packet.

CLASS PROMOTIONAL SERVICES, INC., PO Box 66810, Albuquerque NM 87193. (505)899-4283. Fax (505)899-9282. Toll-free (800)433-6633. Contact: Kim Garrison. E-mail: info@ classervices.com. Christian leaders, authors, and speaker services. Website: www.classervices .com. Click on "Promotional Services." Specializing in radio and TV interview campaigns for Christian authors, speakers, and ministries. E-mail: interviews@classervices.com.

CREATIVE RESOURCES. Contact: Susan Otis, PO Box 1665, Sandpoint ID 83864. (208)263-8055. Fax (208)263-9055. E-mail: CMResource@aol.com. A Christian consulting and publicity firm that schedules 2,000 broadcast interviews annually and arranges numerous reviews, articles, and interviews in major publications. Provides services for communications and media relations to parachurch groups, publishers, broadcast ministries, and others. Publishes *Media Connections,* which links individuals, organizations, and media.

DECHANT HUGHES ASSOCIATES INC. Public Relations/Media Tours. Contacts: Kelly Hughes, president; 1440 N. Kingsbury, Chicago IL 60622. (312)280-8126. Fax (312)280-8362. E-mail: dha@dechanthughes.com. Website: www.dechanthughes.com.

GUEST FINDER. (1) NewsBuzz, Inc. PO Box 40304, Raleigh NC 27629. A place to get noticed for possible interviews, plus tips on being a better guest. Website: www.guestfinder.com. E-mail: info@newsbuzz.com. (2) Also see www.newsbuzz.com for their GreatGuests newsletter.

+THE IDEA NETWORK (Erin Saxton & Jennifer Urezzio). Visit Website: theidea network.net.

INTEGRATED BOOK MARKETING. Sharon H. Castlen, PO Box 321, Kings Park NY 11754. (631)979-5990. E-mail: ibmarket@optonline.net. Integrates publicity with distribution to generate the greatest sales. Refer to Website: www.bookmarketing.com/101bkmart.html.

ANNIE JENNINGS; PUBLICIST. Offers TV, radio, and print publicity opportunities, tele-seminars, and extensive book promotion. (908)281-6201. Fax (908)281-5221. E-mail: annie@anniejenningspr.com. Website: www.anniejenningspr.com.

M&M PUBLIC RELATIONS (formerly McClure/Muntsinger Public Relations). Contact: Jana Muntsinger, (804)754-2118. Fax (804)754-2117. E-mail: jana@mmpublicrelations.com. Or contact Pam McClure (615)595-8321. Fax (615)595-8322. E-mail: pamela@mmpublic relations.com. Website: www.mmpublicrelations.com.

+MCALLISTER COMMUNICATIONS (Margaret McAllister). Visit Website: www.mcallcom.com.

+MICHELE BUC. Specializes in the Christian market and worked with the publisher of *Chicken Soup for the Christian Woman's Soul*. (615)297-2379. E-mail: michelerbuc@aol.com.

MINISTRY MARKETING SOLUTIONS. Marc and Pamela Perry, Publicists. (248)426-2300. Fax (248)471-2422. E-mail: pamperry@ministrymarketingsolutions.com. Website: www.ministrymarketingsolutions.com. A consulting firm that provides a blend of services in marketing and public relations, targeting African American Christian Market (AACM).

PHENIX & PHENIX, 2100 Kramer Ln., Ste. 300, Austin TX 78758. (512)478-2028. Fax (512)478-2117. Website: www.bookpros.com. A literary publicity firm specializing in find-ing readers for your books through extensive media contacts.

PR-LINK PUBLIC RELATIONS. 8190 Beechmont Ave., #361, Cincinnati OH 45255. (513)233-9090. E-mail: pgiechrist@pr-link.com. Website: www.pr-link.com.

PROMOTE YOURSELF PUBLIC RELATIONS AND SEMINARS. Raleigh Pinskey, PO Box 701, Carefree AZ 85377. (480)488-4840. E-mail: raleigh@promoteyourself.com. Website: www.promoteyourself.com. Offers free monthly newsletter, articles, and tips.

+PR/PR PUBLIC RELATIONS. Publicist Pam Lontos of PR/PR worked with the publisher of *Chicken Soup for the Caregiver's Soul*. (407)299-6128. E-mail: pam@prpr.net. Website: www.prpr.net.

+PS MEDIA RELATIONS. Contact Paige Harvey: (615)579-4515, paige@psmedia relations.com or Shannon Underwood (615)498-2189, Shannon@psmediarelations.com. Fax (615)523-1368. Website: www.psmediarelations.com.

PUBLICITY HOUSE. Tim Shook, 722-A Johanne Pl., Colorado Springs CO 80906. (719)579-6472. E-mail: Tim@publicityhouse.com. Website: www.publicityhouse.com.

BEVERLY RYKERD PUBLIC RELATIONS. Beverly Rykerd, PO Box 88180, Colorado Springs CO 80908. (719)495-3920. E-mail: brykerd@ix.netcom.com.

+VERITAS COMMUNICATIONS. Don Otis, PO Box 761, Sandpoint ID 83864. (208)263-0342. E-mail: Veritas_com@yahoo.com. Provides communications services that help provide corporate, nonprofit, or author exposure in the marketplace. Services include writing and conceptualization, media consulting, and corporate and nonprofit consulting.

WYNN-WYNN MEDIA. Jeane Wynn, 410 N. Chickasaw Ave., Claremore OK 74017. (918)283-1834. E-mail: Jeane@WynnWynnMedia.com.

REFERENCE TOOLS

ALMANACS. Website: www.infoplease.com/almanacs.html. Search dozens of almanacs at once. Topics include history, government, biography, sports, arts, entertainment, business, finance, health, science, and weather. There is even a "Fact Monster" for kids.

AMERICAN DIALECT SOCIETY. Website: www.americandialect.org. Offers e-mail discussion list, Words of the Year, and reference links.

BARTLEBY'S REFERENCE LIBRARIES. Website: www.bartleby.com. (1) *American Heritage Dictionary:* www.bartleby.com/61. Over 90,000 entries, 900 full-page color illustrations,

and 70,000 audio word pronunciations. (2) *The Columbia Encyclopedia:* www
.bartleby.com/65. Over 51,000 entries. (3) *Strunk's Elements of Style:* www
.bartleby.com/141; (4) *The Encyclopedia of World History:* www.bartleby.com/67; (5)
Roget's II: The New Thesaurus: www.bartleby.com/62; (6) Quotations: www.bartleby.com/
quotations; (7) *Gray's Anatomy:* www.bartleby.com/107.

COMPUTER-USER HIGH-TECH DICTIONARY. Website: www.computeruser.com/
resources/dictionary. Includes emoticons, file types, chat stuff, domains, HTML tags, and
much more.

DEPT. OF DEFENSE DICTIONARY OF MILITARY TERMS. Website: www.dtic.mil/doctrine/
jel/doddict.

DICTIONARY.COM. Website: www.dictionary.com. Type in the word you are looking for, and if
there is no match, it makes suggestions that are hyperlinked so you can check the meaning to make sure it is the word you are actually seeking.

+DICTIONARY DATABASE. A dictionary for everything. Website: www.onelook.com/
browse.shtml#all_gen.

ENCYCLOPEDIA BRITANNICA. Website: www.britannica.com.

FREE INTERNET ENCYCLOPEDIA. Website: www.cam-info.net/enc.html

LAW DICTIONARY. Website: www.duhaime.org/diction.htm. Also offers references to many
other law topics. Check on site map to find the Law Fun page for jokes and great dumb
stuff.

MERRIAM-WEBSTER ONLINE DICTIONARY/THESAURUS. Website: http://m-w.com.

ONELOOK DICTIONARIES. Website: www.onelook.com. Definitions from over 900 dictionaries.

OXFORD ENGLISH DICTIONARY. Website: www.oed.com.

REFERENCE BOOKS ONLINE. Website: www.xrefer.com. World's largest online reference
service, offering access to 167 reference books from 36 of the world's leading publishers.

RESEARCH & RESOURCES FOR WRITERS. Website: www.fontayne.com/ink. Links to lots of
short articles and links to writers' resources.

RHYMING DICTIONARY. Website: www.rhymezone.com.

**ROGET'S DESCRIPTIVE WORD FINDER: A Dictionary/Thesaurus of Adjectives and
Adverbs** by Barbara Ann Kipfer (Writer's Digest Books, 2003). $24.99. ISBN
1582971706.

ROGET'S ONLINE THESAURUS. Website: www.thesaurus.com.

**SUPER SEARCHER, AUTHOR, SCRIBE: Successful Writers Share Their Internet
Research Secrets** by Loraine Page. A book that features in-depth interviews with 14 writers who regularly use the Internet as a research tool. Website links to nearly 300 Internet
resources including Websites, search engines, mailing lists, online databases, and software. Available at your local bookstore for $24.95 (ISBN 0-910965-58-7) or call
(800)300-9868. Website: www.supersearchers.com.

VISUAL THESAURUS. Website: www.visualthesaurus.com. A visual representation of the English language. Be sure to take the Guided Tour.

A WEB OF ON-LINE DICTIONARIES. Website: www.yourdictionary.com. Linked to more than
2500 dictionaries in over 300 different languages.

WEBOPEDIA. Website: www.webopedia.com. Online dictionary and search engine for computer and Internet technology definitions.

WORD WEB. Website: www.wordweb.info. A free trial version and download of a dictionary.

WORLD BOOK ONLINE. Website: www.worldbook.com.

WORLD FACTBOOK. Website: www.odci.gov/cia/publications/factbook. Published by the U.S.
Central Intelligence Agency, the *World Factbook* offers data on every country in the world,
including maps, background, geography, people, government, economy, and military.

WRITER'S FREE REFERENCE. Website: www.writers-free-reference.com. Contains maps, encyclopedias, copyright information, zip codes, telephone directories, currency conversions, distance calculations, and more.

RESEARCH: BIBLE

ARCHAEOLOGY. Website: www.bib-arch.org. Lists links related to archaeology and Bible scholarship.

BIBLE ANSWER MACHINE. Website: http://BibleAnswerMachine.ww7.com.

BIBLE GATEWAY. Website: http://bible.gospelcom.net. Searches different Bible versions in over 30 languages.

BIBLEPROBE. Website: www.bibleprobe.com. A nondenominational reference site for Christians and Jews.

BIBLE PROPHECY. Website: www.armageddonbooks.com. Links to over 275 Bible prophecy sites on the Web.

THE BIBLE STUDIES FOUNDATION. Website: www.bible.org. Home of the Net Bible.

BIBLE STUDY TOOLS. Websites: (1) www.biblestudytools.com; (2) www.biblestudytools.net; (3) www.e-sword.net. A free Bible Study software with many free add-ons.

BIBLE TIMES & CUSTOMS. Website: www.middletownbiblechurch.org/biblecus/biblec.htm. Includes topics such as: Customs and Manners, Bible Measurements, Eating and Dressing, Transportation and Communication, Farming, Animals, Occupations, and Holidays.

CHRISTIAN INFORMATION MINISTRIES/RESEARCH SERVICE. 2050 N. Collins Blvd., Ste. 100, Richardson, TX 75080. (972)690-1975. E-mail: info@christianinformation.org. Provides research links including topics related to the Bible, theology, and Christian living. Website: www.christianinformation.org/links.asp.

CHURCHLINK. Website: www.churchlink.com.au. Christian Resource Networking.

CONCORDANCE. *Where to Find It in the Bible: The Ultimate A-Z Resource* by Ken Anderson (Nelson Reference Publishers). A topical concordance listing contemporary topics and issues. Available at local bookstores.

CROSS DAILY. Website: www.crossdaily.com. Click on "Bible Search."

ONEPLACE.COM. Website: www.oneplace.com. Provides Bible study tools, such as words in Greek and Hebrew, and Strong's Concordance.

ONLINE BIBLE. Website: www.onlinebible.net.

STUDY LIGHT. Website: www.studylight.org. Study resources, forums, and weekly columns, plus an outstanding collection of historical Bible maps.

UNBOUND BIBLE. Website: http://unbound.biola.edu. A collection of searchable Bibles, consisting of ten English versions, Greek and Hebrew versions, four ancient versions, and 42 other languages.

VINE'S EXPOSITORY DICTIONARY OF NEW TESTAMENT WORDS. Website: www.menfak.no/bibel/vines.html.

VIRTUAL CHRISTIANITY: Bibles. Website: www.internetdynamics.com/pub/vc/bibles.html. A comprehensive list of online Bibles in English and other languages.

RESEARCH: LIBRARIES

THE DIGITAL LIBRARY. Website: www.hti.umich.edu/cgi/b/bib/bib-idx?c-dlfcoll. Indexes hundreds of collections from libraries and museums with raw material of social history: diaries, manuscripts, pictures, sheet music, campaign buttons, oral histories, films, recordings, etc.

E-LIBRARY. Website: www.highbeam.com. Search magazines, books, newspapers, maps, TV and radio transcripts.

THE LIBRARY OF CONGRESS. Website: www.loc.gov.

LIBRARYSPOT. Website: www.libraryspot.com. A free gateway to more than 5,000 libraries worldwide.

PROJECT BARTLEBY. Website: www.bartleby.com. The most comprehensive public reference library ever published on the Web.

REFDESK. Website: www.refdesk.com. Well-organized and useful information.

RESEARCH LIBRARY. Website: www.researchlibrary.net.

RESEARCH: NEWS

ABYZ NEWS LINKS. Website: www.abyznewslinks.com. Portal to online news sources from around the world.

+AMERICAN SOCIETY OF NEWSPAPER EDITORS (ASNE). For careers in newspapers, visit Website: asne.org/index.cfm?id=2.

ARCHIVED NEWSPAPERS. (1) To find something in an archived newspaper, check out Newspaper Links at: www.newspaperlinks.com; (2) U.S. News Archives on the Web at: www.ibiblio.org/slanews/internet/archivesindex.html; (3) http://newslibrary.com.

ASSIST NEWS SERVICE. Founded by journalist and author Dan Wooding. Website: www.assist news.net. Provides a wide variety of national and international stories that go to 2,400 media around the world.

BBC NEWSLINE. Website: www.bbc.co.uk/newsline. Desktop news center delivering updates automatically throughout the day.

CHRISTIAN NEWSPAPERS. Website: www.christiannewsassoc.com.

CHRISTIAN SCIENCE MONITOR NEWS SITE. Website: www.csmonitor.com.

DAILY ROTATION. Website: www.dailyrotation.com. Collects and displays links to the latest tech news stories from over 300 different sites.

DEMOSSNEWSPOND.COM. Website: www.DeMossNewsPond.com. Offers primary news about some of the major faith-based organizations, leaders, and enterprises in the world. Designed specifically for the media (reporters, editors, producers), the site is filled with timely and reliable story leads and interactive resources.

EDITOR & PUBLISHER. Website: www.editorandpublisher.com. The trade magazine for the newspaper industry publishes an annual yearbook. Order yearbook on Website.

EP NEWS SERVICE. c/o Bryan Malley, *Minnesota Christian Chronicle*, 7317 Cahill Rd., Ste. 201, Minneapolis MN 55439. (952) 562-1234. E-mail: editor@mcchronicle.com. Website: www.epnews.com/epnews/services.html.

FIND ARTICLES. 5,000,000 articles not found on any other search engine. Website: www.find articles.com.

JOURNALISM NET (UK). Website: www.journalismnet.com/uk/index.htm. Portal of online tools and worldwide news.

NEWSPAPER DIRECTORY. Website: www.newsd.com.

NEWSPAPERS.COM. Website: www.newspapers.com. Exceptional tool for referencing the world's newspapers.

THE NEWSROOM HOMEPAGE. Website: http://assignmenteditor.com. Connect to virtually any newspaper in the world, check news wires, access, and people finders, etc.

NEWS STORY RESEARCH. (1) Website: www.newstream.com. Click on "Business Wire." Offers keyword searches on news stories. (2) Search for specific news items at: www.news trawler.com.

NEWS STORY SOURCES. Websites: (1) www.ap.org; (2) http://dailynews.yahoo.com; (3) www.slate.com/code/todayspapers/todayspapers.asp; (4) www.newshub.com; (5) http://total news.com; (6) www.newsindex.com; (7) http://fullcoverage.yahoo.com; (8) www.all-links.com/newscentral; (9) http://news.google.com; (10) www.newseum.org/todaysfrontpages. Lets you view the current front pages of 377 newspapers from 44 different countries; (11) http://newslink.org. You can pull up all media (newspaper, TV, radio) by city.

+PUBLISHING INDUSTRY. For current news and information about the publishing industry, visit Website: www.writenews.com.

+REGIONAL REPORTERS ASSOCIATION (RRA). To-do list for new reporters in Washington, D.C. Website: www.rra.org/dc_guide.html.

+RELIGIONLINK.ORG. Linking journalists to ideas and sources for reporting today's news. Website: religionlink.org.

USA WEEKEND. Website: www.usaweekend.com. Click on Newspaper sites. Links to over 600 newspapers, listed by state.

+VANDERBUILT TELEVISION NEWS ARCHIVE. Http://tvnews.vanderbuilt.edu.

+THE WHY FILES. This site uses news and current events as springboards to explore science, health, environment, and technology. Website: http://whyfiles.org.

RESOURCES: CHILDREN'S WRITING

+AWARDS. The Paul A. Witty Short Story Award is given to the author of an original short story published for the first time during 2005 in a periodical for children. The award carries a $1,000 stipend. The short story should serve as a literary standard that encourages young readers to read periodicals. Website: www.reading.org/association/awards/childrens_witty.html.

+BECOME A CHILDREN'S BOOK AUTHOR. Visit FabJob.com to order *Become a Children's Book Author* by Jeannie Harmon (previous Editor at Cook Communications—Kid's book division for 15 years) and Sheila Seifert. Book topics include how to come up with a book idea that will attract an editor's attention; step-by-step advice on how to write picture books, nonfiction books and juvenile fiction; what you need to know about format, plotting, illustrations, research, characterization, and more. Website: www.fabjob.com/child author.asp?affiliate=262.

BLUE PHANTOM CRITIQUE GROUP FOR CHILDREN'S WRITERS. Website: www.blue phantomwriters.com. Free critique group and newsletter.

BOOKS OF INTEREST. (1) *Children's Writer Guide to 2006;* (2) *Children's Newsletter;* (3) *2006 Book Market for Children's Writers;* (4) *2006 Magazine Market for Children's Writers.* Order at www.writersbookstore.com. Also check out (5) *Books to Grow With: A Guide to Using the Best Children's Fiction for Everyday Issues and Tough Challenges.* The book includes more than 500 recommended books, tips on how to use fiction to help children, helpful indexes by author and title and multicultural books. Published children's writers can contact Lutra Press and request that they include their book in Lutra's online newsletter which lists updates and new books not included in *Books to Grow With.* Website: www.lutrapress.com.

THE CHILDREN'S BOOK COUNCIL, 12 W. 37th St., 2nd Fl., New York NY 10018-7480. (212)966-1990. Fax (212)966-2073. E-mail: Use contact order form. Website: www.cbc books.org. Go to Getting Your Book Published/FAQs page for marketing information and beginner instruction for writers and illustrators of children's books, plus lots of good links.

CHILDREN'S BOOK PUBLISHERS. (1) Website: www.scils.rutgers.edu/%7Ekvander/Children Lit/publish.html. Lists links to various children's book publishers. (2) Also visit the Colossal Directory of Children's Publishers. Website: http://childrenswriters.signaleader.com.

THE CHILDREN'S LITERATURE WEB GUIDE. Website: www.acs.ucalgary.ca/~dkbrown. Internet resources related to books for children and young adults.

CHILDREN'S WRITER NEWSLETTER. Website: www.childrenswriter.com. A monthly newsletter featuring reports on the marketplace for children's writing, and current news, trends, and tips in the publishing industry. Susan Tierney, ed.

CHILDREN'S WRITING SUPERSITE. Children's Book Insider LLC, 901 Columbia Rd., Fort Collins CO 80525. (970)495-0056. Toll-free (800)807-1916 (orders only). E-mail: mail@write4kids.com. Website: www.write4kids.com. To subscribe to the free e-zine *Children's Book Insider,* and for more free offers, go to the Website. Also includes market news, tutorials, FAQ, files to download, surveys, and links to other resources for children's writers.

CONTESTS. Check the Contests section in this guide for "Writing for Children/Young Adult Contests."

GLORY PRESS/PROF. DICK BOHRER, MS, MA (teacher, 39 years; editor, 11 years including editor of two newspapers and managing editor of *Moody Monthly;* author of 16 books), PO Box 624, West Linn OR 97068. (503)638-7711. E-mail: dickbohrer@comcast.net. Offers 3 writing courses: (1) "4+20 Ways to Write Stories for Christian Kids," (2) "4+20 Ways, Christian, to Write Features Like a Pro," and (3) "4+20 Ways, Christian, to Write What You Think." Charges $35 for each manual plus $1 per double-spaced typed page plus SASE for editing and critiquing assignments of poems, stories, and books. Asks for written testimony regarding applicant's salvation testimony of how he/she came to faith in Christ. References: gude@juno.com; k&kyoung@stic.net; asrduff@aol.com.

INSTITUTE OF CHILDREN'S LITERATURE, 93 Long Ridge Rd., West Redding CT 06896. (203)792-8600. Toll-free (800)243-9645. Fax (203)792-8406. E-mail: information services@InstituteChildrensLit.com. Website: www.InstituteChildrensLit.com. Writing programs and aptitude tests, plus a chat room and other resources for writers.

+KIDBIBS.COM. Bringing kids and books together, this site features award winning books and reading lists. It also has dozens of sites reporting on statistics and topics related to education. Website: http://kidbibs.com.

PICTURE-BOOK.COM. Website: www.picture-book.com. "The online resource for children's illustrators, publishers, and book lovers." Dozens of links for writers.

THE SOCIETY OF CHILDREN'S BOOK WRITERS AND ILLUSTRATORS, 8271 Beverly Blvd., Los Angeles CA 90048. (323)782-1010. Fax (323)782-1892. E-mail: membership@scbwi.org. Website: www.scbwi.org. Founded in 1971, this is the professional organization for children's book writers and illustrators. Over 19,000 members. Site includes a newsletter, critique groups, workshops, market resources, and other general information.

TRENDS IN CHILDREN'S PUBLISHING. Website: www.underdown.org/trends.htm.

VERLA KAY'S WEBSITE FOR CHILDREN'S WRITERS. Website: www.verlakay.com.

WRITING FOR CHILDREN WORKSHOP. Website: www.bethanyroberts.com. Offers writer quotes, tips, FAQs, resources, book recommendations, and a directory of children's authors and illustrators.

RESOURCES: ETHNIC WRITERS

AFRICAN-AMERICAN GUIDE TO WRITING AND PUBLISHING NONFICTION by Jewell Parker Rhodes (Broadway Books). ISBN 0767905784.

ASIAN AMERICAN JOURNALISTS ASSN. (AAJA), 1182 Market St., Ste. 320, San Francisco CA 94102. (415)346-2051. Fax (415)346-6343. E-mail: National@aaja.org. Website: www.aaja.org. A nonprofit organization whose mission is to encourage Asian Pacific Americans to enter ranks of journalism, to work for fair and accurate coverage of Asian Pacific

Americans, and to increase the number of Asian Pacific American journalists and news managers in the industry. 2,300 members.

BLACK WRITERS UNITED. The offshoot of Black Writers Alliance, Black Writers United exists to promote fellowship and the sharing of resources and information among writers. Join at: http://groups.yahoo.com/group/bwunited.

CENTER FOR RESEARCH LIBRARIES. Website: wwwcrl.uchicago.edu. Offers 7,000 periodical titles rarely held in North American libraries. Emphasis on materials produced outside USA including developing nations.

COPYRIGHT INFORMATION IN SPANISH. Website: www.copyright.gov/espanol.

MANY VOICES, ONE CITY: The Independent Press Assn. 115 West 29th St., #606, New York NY 10001. Contact: Abby Scher, dir., IPA, New York, at (212)279-1442. Fax (212)239-8571. E-mail: refer to contact form. Assisting New York's ethnic and community press committed to social justice. Website: www.indypress.org.

MAYNARD INSTITUTE, Robert C. Maynard Institute for Journalism Education. 1211 Preservation Pkwy., Oakland CA 94612. (510)891-9202. Fax (510)891-9565. E-mail: mije@maynardije.org. Website: www.maynardije.org. Provides advanced training and services nationally to help news organizations better reflect their diverse communities, improve communication with the public, and uncover new business opportunities.

MULTICULTURAL MARKETING RESOURCES. Website: www.multicultural.com. Lists annual seminars and conferences of interest to marketing professionals targeting all ethnic backgrounds.

NATIONAL ASSN. OF BLACK JOURNALISTS (NABJ), 8701 Adelphi Rd., Adelphi MD 20783. (301)445-7100. Fax (301)445-7101. E-mail: refer to online form. Website: www.nabj.org. Goal is to strengthen ties among African American journalists, providing professional development and training. 3,300 members.

NATIONAL ASSN. OF HISPANIC JOURNALISTS (NAHJ), 1000 National Press Building, 529 14th St. N.W., Washington DC 20045-2100. Toll-free (888)346-6245. (202)662-7145. Fax (202)662-7144. E-mail: nahj@nahj.org. Website: www.nahj.org. Dedicated to the recognition and professional advancement of Hispanics in the news industry. Approx. 2,300 members.

+NATIVE AMERICAN ISSUES IN CHRISTIANITY. Visit Rebekah Fawn Cochran's site and click on "Links-Word Bytes and Sites" to access links related to Native American culture and Christianity. Website: http://theriskywriter.com.

NATIVE AMERICAN JOURNALISTS ASSN. (NAJA), 555 N. Dakota St., Vermillion SD 57069. (605)677-5282. Fax (866)694-4264. E-mail: info@naja.com. Website: www.naja.com. Serves and empowers Native journalists through programs and actions designed to enrich journalism and to promote Native cultures. Includes news articles, media resources, and links.

ORGANIZATION OF BLACK SCREENWRITERS. E-mail: refer to online form. Website: www.obswriter.com. Represents African American writers in the entertainment industry.

UNITY: JOURNALISTS OF COLOR, 1601 N. Kent St., Ste. 1003, Arlington VA 22209. (703)469-2100. Fax (703)469-2108. E-mail: info@unityjournalists.org. Website: www.unityjournalists.org. Four national minority journalism associations (AAJA, NABJ, NAHJ, NAJA) seeking to promote diversity within the nation's media.

RESOURCES: FICTION WRITING

+ADVANCED FICTION WRITING. According to Randy Ingermanson, you need only three things to get your novel published: content, craft, and connections. For his free e-zine, go to www.advancedfictionwriting.com.

AMERICAN CHRISTIAN FICTION WRITERS. Formerly American Christian Romance Writers (ACRW). Website: www.americanchristianfictionwriters.com/index.html. "To encourage writers of Christian fiction, develop their skills, educate them in the market, and be a fellowship for writers of like interests." E-mail: sectry@americanchristianfictionwriters.com. E-mail loop, online courses, and newsletter. Sponsors an annual conference and writing contest.

AMERICAN CRIME WRITERS LEAGUE, 18645 S.W. Farmington Rd., #255, Aloha OR 97007. Website: www.acwl.org. Dues $25/year. E-mail: acwl@pacbell.net.

+AMERICAN WRITERS & ARTISTS INSTITUTE. Learn the insider secrets and techniques of being a published romance writer. Toll free (866)879-2924 or visit Website: www.the romancewriterslife.com/readers.

AT-HOME WRITING WORKSHOPS. Director: Marlene Bagnull, LittD, Write His Answer Ministries, 316 Blanchard Rd., Drexel Hill PA 19026. E-mail: mbagnull@aol.com. Website: www.writehisanswer.com. Fiction, 10 units, $255. Units may also be purchased individually for $30.

BOOKS OF INTEREST. (1) *Self-Editing for Fiction Writers: How to Edit Yourself into Print* by Renni Browne and Dave King, HarperResource (2004). $13.95. ISBN 0060545690; (2) *The First Five Pages: A Writer's Guide to Staying Out of the Rejection Pile* by Noah Lukeman, Fireside (2000). ISBN 068485743X; (3) *Behind the Stories* by Diane Eble, Bethany House (2002). ISBN 0764224638. Book is based on interviews with Christian novelists. Provides readers with a glimpse into personal lives of many best-selling fiction writers; (4) *Sometimes the Magic Works: Lessons from a Writing Life* by Terry Brooks, Del Rey (2004). ISBN 0345465512.

CHARACTER BIOGRAPHY. Use these Websites to help develop a character biography or personality profile for your fiction characters: (1) www.queendom.com/tests/personality/index.html; (2) www.2h.com/personality-tests.shtml; (3) www.susettewilliams.com/Work shops/CharacterSheet.htm.

+CHARACTER DEVELOPMENT. (1) Do you need an occupation for your character or does your character need to do something in an emergency? Here is a site that will tell you all about anything and everything your character might need to know. Website: www.ehow.com. (2) Writing a mystery and your character has a side effect or deadly reaction to a substance? On this Website you can read about side effects, interactions, and warnings about certain herbs and supplements: www.personalhealthzone.com/herb safety.html. (3) For background, visit: www.greatmuseums.org/museumworld.html.

CHARACTER NAME SOURCES. (1) Link to the U.S. Census Bureau to find lists of male and female first and last names. Website: www.craigcentral.com/names.asp. Other Websites: (2) www.babynames.com; (3) www.census.gov/genealogy/names; (4) www.ssa.gov. Site gives most popular baby names; (5) http://parenting.ivillage.com/namefinder; (6) www .babycenter.com/babyname/index.html; (7) www.babynamenetwork.com; (8) www.behind thename.com; (9) www.thinkbabynames.com; (10)www.geocities.com/edgarbook/names/welcome.html; (11) medieval names: www.s-gabriel.org/names/english.shtml; (12) www.parenthoodweb.com/babynames.html; (13) www.kleimo.com/random/; (14) www .rinkworks.com/namegen.name.cfm. Randomly generates names from the U.S. Census; (15) http://babynamewizard.com.

CHARACTER NAME SOURCES OF DIFFERENT NATIONALITIES. Websites: (1) African names: www.namesite.com/namesite/mainpage.html; (2) Afrocentric names: www.swagga .com/name.htm; (3) Arabic names, masculine: www.ummah.org.uk/family/masc.html; (4) Arabic names, feminine: www.ummah.org.uk/family/fem.html; (5) Chinese names: www .mandarintools.com/chinesename.html.

+CHRISTIAN CHICK LIT. *USA Today* ran an article on one of the newest genres in Christian publishing—Chick Lit. The article explains the terms and mentions some specific Christian books that fall into this genre. Read the article at www.usatoday.com/life/books/news/2003-10-29-church-lit_x.htm.

CONTESTS. Check the Contest section in this guide for "Fiction Contests."

CRIME MYSTERY WRITING/FORENSIC SITES. Websites: (1) www.visualexpert.com; (2) www.tritechusa.com; (3) www.crime-scene-investigator.net; (4) www.pimall.com/nais/home.html. This is the site for the National Assn. of Investigative Specialists; (5) http://dir.yahoo.com/Society_and_Culture/Crime. Yahoo's Crime Directory; www.officer.com. Offers links to agencies, criminal justice, investigations, special ops, most-wanted worldwide, and other law enforcement sites; (6) http://foia.fbi.gov. This Freedom of Information Act site offers an electronic reading room with categories such as espionage, famous persons, gangster era, historical interests, unusual phenomena, and violent crimes. (7) Also visit S. G. R. MacMillan, Barrister for links to resources about organized crime and money laundering: www.sgrm.com.

ECLECTIC FICTION. (1) Website: www.eclectics.com. Site offers a newsletter, links, articles, and contests. (2) Go to www.eclectics.com/articles/character.html. Find a form to use in laying out the characteristics of characters in your stories.

FAITH, HOPE & LOVE (1) The inspirational chapter of Romance Writers of America. Dues for the chapter are $24/yr., but you must also be a member of RWA to join (dues $75/yr.). Chapter offers these services: online list service for members, bimonthly newsletter, annual contest, connects critique partners by mail or e-mail, and latest romance market information. To join, contact RWA National Office, 16000 Stuebner Airline Rd., Ste. 140, Spring TX 77379. (832)717-5200. Fax (832)717-5201. Website: www.rwanational.com. (2) Or go to FHL Website: www.faithhopelove-rwa.org. E-mail: info@rwanational.com. Over 180 members in FHL, over 9,000 in RWA.

FEDERAL CITIZEN INFORMATION CENTER. Website: www.pueblo.gsa.gov. Need information about your character's livelihood? The Center offers free and low-cost booklets about nearly everything.

+FEELINGS & EMOTIONS. Looking for exactly the right word to show feelings and emotions? Go to Website: http://eqi.org/elit.htm.

FICTION & SCI-FI/FANTASY E-GROUPS. (1) Website: http://groups.yahoo.com. Type into box: Christian_fic2 (for genre fiction), or ChristSF (for science fiction and Christianity). (2) A Christian fantasy site: www.christianfantasy.com. (3) A Christian sci-fi site: www.christian-fandom.org. (4) Another site: www.critters.org.

FICTIONETTE/SHORT STORIES. Website: www.fictionette.com. With a free membership comes the ability to submit and critique short fiction works.

FICTION FACTOR. Website: www.fictionfactor.com. Free monthly newsletter, plus tips and articles on writing better fiction, promoting and marketing your work, and more.

FICTION FIX NEWSLETTER: The Nuts and Bolts of Crafting Fiction. Website: www.coffeehouseforwriters.com/news.html.

FICTION HOW-TO ESSAYS. Website: www.storyispromise.com. Essays on the craft of writing by Bill Johnson.

FICTION SOFTWARE. Website: http://story.exis.net/masterlink. Story development software.

FICTION WRITER'S CONNECTION. Website: www.fictionwriters.com. Provides help with novel writing and information on finding agents/editors and getting published. Website includes newsletters (online and hard copy), critiquing, editor/agent information, free tip sheets and consultations, and scam warnings. Toll-free (800)248-2758. E-mail: Bcamenson@aol.com.

FICTION WRITING CLASSES (F2K). Website: http://fiction.4-writers.com/creative-writing-classes.shtml.

FREE CHRISTIAN FICTION. Website: www.edelayne.com. Fiction writer Elizabeth Delayne's site offers free fiction as well as links to other Christian fiction sites.

+HISTORY DATABASE. What happened in 1014 AD? Here's an interactive timeline database extending from 1000 AD to the present. Website: www.sbrowning.com/whowhatwhen/index.php.

THE HISTORICAL NOVEL SOCIETY. Website: www.historicalnovelsociety.org. Founded in 1997, this group aims to promote all aspects of historical fiction. Offers an annual conference, discussion list, book reviews, and more. E-mail: histnovel@aol.com.

LEGAL INFORMATION INSTITUTE. (1) Website: www4.law.cornell.edu/uscode. Is your character in trouble with the law? Learn about court processes and other legalities. (2) See also: FindLaw at www.findlaw.com for useful legal links.

+LEGENDS & RUMORS. Visit Snopes.com at www.snopes.com for 25 hottest urban legends and more.

MYSTERYNET NETWORK, 3616 Far West Blvd., #117-298, Austin TX 78731. (512)342-8377. E-mail: comment@MysteryNet.com. Website: www.mysterynet.com.

MYSTERY WRITERS OF AMERICA, 17 E. 47th St., 6th Fl., New York NY 10017. (212)888-8171. Fax (212)888-8107. E-mail: mwa@mysterywriters.org. Website: www.mystery writers.org.

MYSTERY WRITERS SITES OF INTEREST. Websites: (1) www.cluelass.com; (2) www .crime.org; (3) http://crime.about.com; (4) www.MurderMustAdvertise.com. Offers an e-mail discussion list for authors wanting to promote new mystery books: www.deadly pleasures.com.

+NICHOLAS SPARKS' ADVICE. This site is a collection of advice for writers from Nicholas Sparks (*A Walk to Remember, The Notebook*). Website: www.nicholassparks.com/writers corner/index.html.

NOVEL ADVICE. Website: www.noveladvice.com. Online courses, chat sessions, and writing links.

NOVEL PRO. Website: http://novelcode.com. Software that helps organize ideas, work on pieces of the story without getting lost, brainstorm creation of characters and scenes, etc. Cost is $29.95.

ONLINE NEWSLETTER. Website: www.fictionaddiction.net.

ROBIN'S NEST. Website: www.robinsnest.com. Offers links, articles, online courses, and workshops for all genres of fiction writers.

ROMANCE WRITERS. Websites: (1) www.eHarlequin.com; (2) www.rchzine.com; (3) www .romanceink.com.

ROMANCE WRITERS OF AMERICA, (832)717-5200. Fax (832)717-5201. E-mail: info@ rwanational.org. Website: www.rwanational.org.

SCIENCE FICTION AND FANTASY WRITERS OF AMERICA, Jane Jewell, exec. dir., PO Box 877, Chestertown MD 21620. (207)861-8078. E-mail: execdir@sfwa.org. Website: www.sfwa.org.

SCIENCE FICTION LANGUAGE. Website: www.langmaker.com.

SCIENCE FICTION SITES. (1) Ralan Conley's SpecFic & Humor Webstravaganza. Website: www.ralan.com; science fiction romance, (2) www.sfronline.com.

+SHAKESPEARE'S COMPLETE WORKS. Find a sonnet or a play for inspiration at Website: http://education.yahoo.com/reference/shakespeare.

SHORT MYSTERY FICTION SOCIETY. Website: www.thewindjammer.com/smfs.

SISTERS IN CRIME, PO Box 442124, Lawrence KS 66044-8933. (785)842-1325. Website: www.sistersincrime.org.

SPECULATIVE (sci-fi & fantasy) FICTION LINKS. Spicy Green Iguana, Inc. Website: www.spicygreeniguana.com.

+STORYBOARDING. Fiction writers may be interested in this software called StoryBoarding. To order, go to Website: www.writerssupercenter.com/boardmaster.

STORYCRAFT STORY DEVELOPMENT SOFTWARE. Website: www.writerspage.com. Guides writers through the entire process of writing novels, screenplays, teleplays, plays, and short stories.

+STORYTELLING TECHNIQUES. To get a better grasp of storytelling techniques, visit these Websites: (1) For a cross-cultural history of fairy tales, www.surlalunefairytales.com; (2) www.storyteller.net; (3) www.storynet.org. Books include: (4) *Telling Your Own Stories* by Donald Davis; (5) *Telling Time* by Nancy Willard; (6) *Steering the Craft* by Ursula K. Le Guin; (7) *Zen in the Art of Writing* by Ray Bradbury; (8) *Take Joy* by Jane Yolen; (9) *On Writing* by Eudora Welty.

SYNOPSES. "Conquering the Dreaded Synopsis" by Lisa Gardner. Website: www.rosecity romancewriters.com.

TIME TICKER. Website: www.timeticker.com. Keep track of characters in other time zones.

TOP 100 FICTIONAL CHARACTERS. (1) Website: www.fictional100.com. Features the most influential characters in world literature and legend. Compiled by Lucy Pollard-Gott. (2) Also check: www.npr.org/programs/totn/features/2002/mar/020319.characters.html for *Book* magazine's list of the top 100 fictional characters since 1900.

TRADEMARK SEARCHES. (1) If you are concerned that you may have chosen a name for a fictitious business or brand in your story that exists in real life, go to: www.uspto .gov/main/trademarks.htm and click Search. (2) In Canada, go to: http://strategis.ic.gc.ca/ sc_mrksv/cipo/tm/tm_main-e.html.

VICTORIAN SETTING. Websites: (1) www.victorianweb.org. Provides history and cultural information for fiction set in the Victorian age; (2) www.thelondonhouse.co.uk; (3) www .victorianlondon.org.

WESTERN WRITERS OF AMERICA. Website: www.westernwriters.org. For membership information, contact: Larry K. Brown, 209 E. Iowa, Cheyenne WY 82009. E-mail: mailto.hogranch@email.msn.comg. Current membership over 500 published writers.

WRITER'S BLOCKS 3.0. Website: www.writersblocks.com. Organize story elements for your fiction.

WRITER'S DIGEST. 4700 E. Galbraith Rd., Cincinnati OH 45236. Toll-free (800)759-0963. Fax (513)531-0798. E-mail: writersdig@fwpubs.com. Website: www.writersonlinework shops.com. Novel Writing Workshop, Writing & Selling Short Stories, and others. This is a secular course, but you may request a Christian instructor. Note that Writer's Digest School is shifting its focus to Web-based workshops.

XIANWORLDVIEW.COM. Website: www.xianworldview.com. From a Christian world-view, this site provides book reviews, articles, interviews, forums, and other science fiction and fantasy resources.

RESOURCES: POETRY WRITING

ACADEMY OF AMERICAN POETS, 584 Broadway, Ste. 604, New York NY 10012-5243. (212)274-0343. Fax (212)274-9427. Website: www.poets.org. Site offers 500 poet biographies, 1,700 poems, RealAudio poet clips, poetry exhibits, essays, and a National Poetry Map.

ALBANY POETRY WORKSHOP. Website: www.sonic.net/poetry/albany.

CONTESTS. Check the Contest section in this guide for "Poetry Contests."

CREATIVE-POEMS.COM. Website: www.creative-poems.com. "Join the world's friendliest free poetry site. Add poems to be rated and commented on. Then rate and comment on other's poetry as well." Over 6,000 members.

CROSSHOME.COM. A site where Christian poetry is featured. To have your work considered, go to: www.crosshome.com/poetry.shtml. E-mail: webmaster@crosshome.com.

DIRECTORY OF POETRY PUBLISHERS. Website: http://acqweb.library.vanderbilt.edu/pubr/poem.htm.

FELLOWSHIP OF CHRISTIAN POETS, John and Marilyn Marinelli, cofounders. PO Box 831413, Ocala FL 34483. Offers books, a newsletter, contests, critiques, and members are guaranteed publication of 52 poems per year, one per week, in the Library of Poetic Expression. One time fee $50. Website: www.christianpoets.com.

HAIKU. Websites devoted to haiku: (1) www.gardendigest.com/poetry/index.htm; (2) www.execpc.com/~ohaus/haiku.html; (3) www.everypoet.com/absurdities/index.htm. The following organizations also provide additional resources for haiku writers: (4) British Haiku Society, 38 Wayside Ave., Hornchurch, Essex RM 12 4LL, England. Website: www.britishhaiku society.org; (5) Haiku Oz, Katherine Samuelowicz, contact officer. E-mail: ksamuelowicz@ mail.optusnet.com.au. Website: www.haikuoz.org; (6) Haiku Society of America, Membership Secretary, C2 Jamestown House, Meadville PA 16335-1027; Website: www.hsa-haiku.org; (7) World Haiku Club, Susumu Takiguchi, chairman. E-mail: susumu.takiguchi@tbinternet.com. Website: www.worldhaikuclub.org. (8) Also check out *The Haiku Box* by Lonnie Hull DuPont, Journey Editions (2001). ISBN 1582900302.

+ONLINE COMMUNITIES FOR POETS. (1) Utmost Christian Writers exists solely to encourage Christian poets. Check out writer's guidelines. Payment for each poem accepted is $10; (2) The Belvedere Room is a place where you can enjoy and discuss poetry with other poets. Website: www.belvederepoets.com. Note: The Belvedere Room is a discussion site, not a paying site.

ONLINE POETRY CLASSROOM. Website: www.onlinepoetryclassroom.org. Online classes geared toward high school poetry teachers, but helpful for all poets.

POETIC VOICES. Website: www.poeticvoices.com. A ton of information for poets, including market listings, contests, conferences, articles, columns, and more.

POETRY AND WRITERS PORTAL. Website: www.voicesnet.com/poetrylinks.htm. Offers an international contest, forums, an e-zine, self-publishing options, and more.

+POETRY ARCHIVES. An educational resource to aid students, educators, and writers seeking a poem. A searchable database by first line, author, and poem title. Website: www .emule.com/poetry.

+POETRY CONTEST SCAMS AND RIP-OFFS. (1) This site warns about poetry scams and is provided as a public service. Poets seeking recognition for their work might consider submitting to literary magazines rather then poetry contests. Website: www.windpub.com/literary.scams/ripoffs.htm. See also (2) www.winningwriters.com/warningsigns.htm; (3) www.sfwa.org/beware/contests.html.

THE POETRY LIST. Website: www.thepoetrylist.com. A free up-to-date listing of domestic, foreign, and online literary journals that regularly publish poetry.

POETRY SOCIETY OF AMERICA, 15 Gramercy Park, New York NY 10003. (212)254-9628. Website: www.poetrysociety.org.

+POETRY: TAKING ITS COURSE. Written by poetry editor and instructor Mary Harwell Sayler, this book covers techniques of free verse, syllabic, and traditional metered poetry. Order from Website: www.stuartmarket.com.

POETS & WRITERS. Website: www.pw.org. Publishing advice, conference list, grants and awards, literary links, news from the writing world, and resources.

RHYMING DICTIONARY. Website: www.rhymer.com.

THE SCROLL. Website: www.Christian-poetry.com/thescroll.html. E-mail: thescroll@ christian-poetry.com. Online Christian magazine designed to share Christian poetry, creative writing, and articles.

UNIVERSITY OF NEW YORK AT BUFFALO POETRY LINKS. Website: http://wings.buffalo .edu/epc/connects/poetrywebs.html.

WRITING POETRY by Shelly Tucker, GoodYear Books. ISBN 0673360393. A very "reader-friendly" book with clear examples of imagery, figures of speech, and guidelines for free and rhymed verse. Find a copy at www.alibris.com.

RESOURCES: SCREENWRITING/SCRIPTWRITING

ACADEMY OF MOTION PICTURE ARTS AND SCIENCES, 8949 Wilshire Blvd., Beverly Hills CA 90211-1972. (310)247-3000. Fax (310)271-3395 or (310)859-9619. E-mail: ampas@oscars.org. Website: www.oscars.org. Script library, Academy Players Directory, and listings for industry events.

ACADEMY WRITERS CLINIC, 2118 Wilshire Blvd., Ste. 160A, Santa Monica CA 90403. E-mail: info@academywriters.com. Website: www.academywriters.com. For screenwriters who wish to improve their art, sell their material, and be discovered.

ACT ONE: Writing for Hollywood. 2690 Beachwood Dr., Lower Fl., Hollywood CA 90028. (323)464-0815. E-mail: info@ActOneprogram.com. Website: www.ActOneprogram.com. Offering two summer programs: Writing for Hollywood for aspiring film and TV writers; Executive Program for aspiring entertainment executives. See Website for dates and for information about weekend seminars.

AMERICAN SCREENWRITERS ASSOCIATION, 269 S. Beverly Dr., Ste. 2600, Beverly Hills CA 90212-3807. Toll-free phone/fax (866)265-9091. E-mail: asa@goasa.com. Website: www.asascreenwriters.com. Nonprofit group that encourages the public's participation in and knowledge of screenwriting.

ANGELIC ENTERTAINMENT, 555 W. Beech St., Ste. 225, San Diego CA 92101-2957. (619)238-8234. E-mail: refer to online contact form. Website: www.AngelicEntertainment .com. An entertainment group in search of properties in manuscript and/or screenplay form. Their mission is to produce "content-responsible" entertainment. Go to the Website to view their credits and experience.

ART WITHIN. Contact: Bryan Coley, artistic director, 1940 Minnewil Ln., Marietta GA 30068, (770)558-8179. E-mail: artwithin@artwithin.org. Website: www.artwithin.org. A professional theater company whose emphasis is new works that uniquely blend hope and truth from a Christian perspective and that are relevant to a contemporary (secular) audience.

BOOKS OF INTEREST. (1) *The Writers Journey: Mythic Structure for Writers* by Christopher Vogler (Michael Weise Productions). ISBN 0941188701; (2) *Screen Play: The Foundations of Screenwriting* by Syd Field (Dell Books); (3) *The Writer's Guide to Writing Your Screenplay* and *The Writer's Guide to Selling Your Screenplay* by Cynthia Whitcomb (Kalmbach Publishing). Find both books at www.thewriterbooks.com; (4) *How to Build a Great Screenplay: A Master Class in Storytelling for Film* by David Howard (St. Martin's Press); (5) *Screenwriting Is Storytelling: Creating an A-List Screenplay That Sells!* By Kate Wright (Perigee); (6) *Pitching Hollywood: How to Sell Your TV and Movie Ideas* by Jonathan Koch and Robert Kosberg (Quill Driver Books).

+BOOKS TO FILM. Some of the best movies have been based on books. To get your full-page color ad in a catalog containing book summary, book review, book photo, book ordering information, author bio, and author contact information, e-mail info@bookstofilm.com. Website: www.bookstofilm.com.

CHRISTIAN DRAMA NORTHWEST. An e-mail group for those interested in drama. Website: http://groups.yahoo.com/groups/CDNW.

CHRISTIANS IN HOLLYWOOD. (1) Contact: Victorya Rogers Communications, PO Box 30202, Edmond OK 73003. (405)341-7621. Fax (405)348-3343. E-mail: victorya@victorya.com.

Websites: www.victorya.com and (2) www.thrillinglife.com. A publication for Christians interested in breaking into Hollywood.

CHRISTIANS IN THEATER ARTS, PO Box 26471, Greenville SC 29616. (864)679-1898. E-mail: information@cita.org. Website: www.cita.org. Holds an annual conference.

COLLABORATOR SOFTWARE/SERVICES FOR SCREEN WRITERS AND NOVELISTS. Website: www.collaborator.com.

THE COMPLETE BOOK OF SCRIPTWRITING by J. Michael Straczynski, Writer's Digest Books. ISBN 1582971587. Order at: www.writersdigest.com or through local bookstore.

CREATIVE SCREENWRITING, 6404 Hollywood Blvd., Ste. 415, Los Angeles CA 90028. Toll-free (800)727-6978. (323)957-1405. Fax (323)957-1406. E-mail: info@creativescreenwriting .com. Website: www.creativescreenwriting.com. A magazine for professional screenwriters.

DONE DEAL. Website: www.scriptsales.com. A wealth of resources for screenwriters.

DRAMASHARE CHRISTIAN DRAMA THEATRE RESOURCES, 82 St. Lawrence Crescent, Saskatoon SK S7K 1G5 Canada. Toll-free (877)363-7262. Fax (306)653-0653. E-mail: contactus@dramashare.org. Website: www.dramashare.org. Supports those involved in Christian drama ministry worldwide, with how-to manuals, scripts, seminars, and newsletters.

THE DRAMATISTS GUILD OF AMERICA, 1501 Broadway, Ste. 701, New York NY 10036. (212)398-9366. Fax (212)944-0420. E-mail: membership@Dramatistguild.com. Website: www.dramaguild.com. Professional association of playwrights, composers, and lyricists with over 6,000 members.

DRAMA WORKSHOP. Website: http://Chdramaworkshop.homestead.com/Home.html. "Nuts & Bolts of Dramatic Writing." Includes: dramatic structures, script formats, screenwriting, reading list, and exercises.

ESSAYS. An index of essays on the craft of dramatic writing can be found at www.storyis promise.com.

FADE IN ONLINE. Website: www.fadeinonline.com. Annual screenplay and fiction competition.

GETTING YOUR ACTS TOGETHER by Frank V. Priore. A complete step-by-step guide on how to write and sell a full-length play for the school market. ISBN 0963749846. This and other books available at: www.writersbookcase.com.

GRIZZLY ADAMS PRODUCTIONS, PO Box 298, Baker City OR 97814. (541)523-4697. Fax (541)523-1803. E-mail: orders@grizzlyadams.tv. Website: www.grizzlyadams.tv. Producers of network television "Encounters with the Unexplained" (PAX-TV Network) and home videos, including Christian films. Producer for a variety of networks. Occasionally on the lookout for beginning screenwriters.

HOLLYWOOD CREATIVE DIRECTORY, 5055 Wilshire Blvd., Hollywood CA 90036-4396. (323)525-2348 (research). Toll-free (800)815-0503. Fax (323)525-2393. Website: www.hcdonline.com. Updated 3 times a year. Lists production companies and staff (the ones who option or buy screenplays for production). Commonly referred to as the "Phone-books to Hollywood." They also publish the Hollywood Representation Directory—managers, agents, attorneys, publicity.

HOLLYWOOD JESUS. Website: www.hollywoodjesus.com. Movie reviews and pop culture from a spiritual point of view.

HOLLYWOOD LIT SALES. Website: www.hollywoodlitsales.com. A place to submit screenplays and to learn how to write them.

HOLLYWOOD SCRIPTWRITING. Website: www.HowToWriteScripts.com. Teaches how to go from idea, to screenplay, to sale. Also includes free newsletter and links.

ILLINOIS/CHICAGO SCREENWRITING COMPETITION. Website: www.illinoisbiz.biz/ film/index.html. This is a biennial event sponsored by the Chicago and Illinois Film Offices to support and promote local screenwriters. It is offered exclusively to Illinois resident writers who have completed a feature-length script. Winners receive a cash prize and their scripts are sent to a select group of production companies and Hollywood producers and studios. Call (312)814-8711 for general information. Application, rules, and regulations download available on site.

INKTIP.COM. Website: www.InkTip.com. The fastest and easiest way to give your screenplays more exposure.

INTER-MISSION. Website: www.inter-mission.net. A community of Christians involved in the entertainment industry.

INTERNATIONAL SCREENPLAY COMPETITION. Website: http://writersdigest.com /contests/ internat_screenplay.asp. Sponsored by the American Screenwriters Association and Writer's Digest.

MOVIEBYTES.COM. Website: www.moviebytes.com. Screenwriting contests and markets online. Lists rules and advance information on contests held monthly, yearly, internationally, and those which charge no fees to enter.

+NASHVILLE SCREENWRITING CONFERENCE. Find information about this annual conference at Website: www.scriptjournal.com/newsletter.htm.

ONLINE SCREENWRITING AND WRITING COURSES. (1) Website: www.absolutewrite.com/ classes. John Jarvis and Christina Hamlett teach beginning screenwriters and novelists how to go from idea to completed manuscript in online classes; (2) UCLA offers a one-year graduate level certificate screenwriting program online. Website: www.filmprograms .ucla.edu; (3) www.screenplay.com.

ORGANIZATION OF BLACK SCREENWRITERS, 1968 W. Adams Blvd., Los Angeles CA 90018. (323)735-2050. Fax (323)735-2051. E-mail: refer to online form. Website: www.obswriter .com. Helps African American writers get their work presented to Hollywood.

THE PLAYWRIGHTS GUILD OF CANADA (formerly The Playwrights Union of Canada). (416)703-0201. Fax (416)703-0059. E-mail: info@playwrightsguild.ca. Website: www.playwrightsguild.com/pgc. A national association of professional playwrights. Approx. 440 members. Site is under construction.

PLAYWRITING SEMINARS. Website: www.vcu.edu/artweb/playwriting. "An opinionated Web companion on the Art & Craft of Playwriting."

SCREENPLAY FESTIVAL. Website: www.screenplayfestival.com. Annual festival to submit your screenplay.

SCREENPLAY MASTERY. Website: www.screenplaymastery.com. Michael Hauge offers coaching and consultation services dedicated to the art, craft, and business of screenwriting. His site offers articles, services, newsletters, and events for entertainment professionals. Call (818)995-4209.

SCREENWRITERS MAGAZINE. Website: www.screenwritersutopia.com.

+THE SCRIPT JOURNAL. This free online publication gives an inside look at the film-making community. Website: www.scriptjournal.com/newsletter.htm.

SCR(i)PT MAGAZINE. Website: www.scriptmag.com. The magazine for the craft and business of screenwriting. Subscribe online and also check out screenwriting advice and contests.

SCRIPTSHARK, 520 Broadway St., Ste. 230, Santa Monica CA 90401. (310)260-5645. E-mail: scriptshark@filmtracker.com. Website: www.scriptshark.com. Helps screenwriters connect to studios, agents, managers, and production companies. Newsletter provides Film Tracker Insider Report, Reader Portfolios, and specials. Also provides professional analysis of your script.

SCRIPT VIKING. Website: www.scriptviking.com. Evaluates, develops, and sells scripts.

SCRIPTWRITERS NETWORK. (1) Website: http://scriptwritersnetwork.com. Also see: (2) www.screenwriters.com; (3) www.screenwriter.com; (4) www.hollywoodawards.com.

SCRIPTWRITING CONFERENCES. Website: www.writersdigest.com/conferences. Type in "Scriptwriting" in the Search box.

SCRIPTWRITING RECOMMENDED BOOKS. Also see Books of Interest on page 46. (1) *Making a Good Script Great* by Linda Seger; (2) *Writing Screenplays That Sell* by Michael Hauge; (3) *Story* by Robert McKee; (4) *The Writer's Journey* by Chris Vogler; (5) *Writing Treatments That Sell* by Ken Atchity.

SELLING TO HOLLYWOOD. Website: www.sellingtohollywood.com. American Screenwriters Assn. International Screenwriters Conference.

SOFTWARE FOR SCREEN/SCRIPT WRITERS. Add-ons: (1) ScreenStyle at www.screen style.com; (2) Script Werx at www.originalvision.com; (3) Script Wizard at www.warren assoc.com; (4) HollyWord at www.hollyword.com. Programs: (5) Final Draft at www.final draft.com; (6) Movie Magic Screenwriter 2000 at www.screenplay.com; (7) Scriptware at www.scriptware.com; (8) Page 2 Stage at www.page2stage.com. Download and try the free demos before buying. (9) More software at www.writersstore.com/products.php?cPath=22; http://indelibleink.com.

STORIE ARTS, INC., 407 S. Vail Ave., Arlington Heights IL 60005. (847)843-2047. E-mail: info@storie.com. Website: www.storie.com. A Christian film/video company looking for original scripts to be produced as film shorts, half-hour shows for broadcast/video, or feature-length films. Producing for various markets including youth, comedy, and drama.

STUDIO NOTES. Website: www.studionotes.com. E-mail: info@writerssupercenter.com. A place where writers can receive a level of professional feedback and access denied those outside the Hollywood system.

WRITE BROTHERS, INC. (formerly Screenplay Systems, Inc.), 138 N. Brand Blvd., Ste. 201, Glendale CA 91203. (818)843-6557. Fax (818)843-8364. Websites: (1) www.screen play.com; (2) www.write-bros.com. Excellent software for writing screenplays and stories.

WRITER'S FILM PROJECT (WFP). Website: www.chesterfield-co.com. Offers fiction, theater, and film writers the opportunity to begin a career in screenwriting. Selected writers form a yearlong screenwriting workshop, using their storytelling skills to begin a career in film. The Chesterfield Film Company—Writer's Film Project is currently on hiatus. For notification of the next application deadline, e-mail: info@chesterfield-co.com.

THE WRITERS STORE. Website: www.writersstore.com. Essentials for writers and filmmakers.

ZOETROPE. Website: www.zoetrope.com. "The Virtual Studio is a submission destination and collaboration tool for filmmakers—a community where artists can submit and workshop original work and where producers can make movies using build-in production tools." Membership is free.

RESOURCES: SONGWRITING

Note: Also see "Music Markets" in Periodical section.

ADORATION PUBLISHING, CO. Website: www.adorationpublishing.com. E-mail: larry@ adorationpublishing.com. Publishes choral and instrumental music for Christian worship. Click on "Submit Your Music."

THE ART OF WRITING LOVE SONGS by Pamela Phillips Oland, Allworth Press, ISBN 158115271, $19.95. Order this book and many others at www.allworth.com.

CHORDANT MUSIC GROUP. EMI Music/Chordant Music Group Distribution. Website: www.chordant.com. Click on "Products," then "Labels" for Chordant labels.

CHRISTIAN MUSIC DIRECTORIES/CHRISTIAN MUSIC FINDER. Resource Publications, Inc., 160 E. Virginia St., #290, San Jose CA 95112-5876. Toll-free (888)273-7782. Fax (408)287-8748. E-mail: info@rpinet.com. Website: www.rpinet.com/products/cmf.html. A comprehensive information source for Christian music. Christian Music Finder is available on CD-ROM.

CHRISTIAN MUSIC ONLINE. Website: www.cmo.com.

CHRISTIAN SONGWRITING ORGANIZATION. Website: www.christiansongwriting.org. A group for songwriters to share ideas/experiences and to critique each other's work.

+CONTEST FOR SONGWRITERS. Contact The American Dream Group. Website: http://achieve-the-dream.net. Click on "Contests."

THE DRAMATISTS GUILD OF AMERICA, 1501 Broadway, Ste. 701, New York NY 10036. (212)398-9366. Fax (212)944-0420. E-mail: membership@dramatistguild.com. Website: www.dramaguild.com. Professional association of playwrights, composers, and lyricists.

FINDING A COLLABORATOR. Helpful article at: www.writersdigest.com/articles/excerpts/99songmarket_find_collaborator.asp.

GETTING STARTED IN CHRISTIAN MUSIC. Reed Arvin, editor. Harvest House Publishers. ISBN 0736902678. Find a balance between music, ministry, and fame; how to record with a major label or on your own; learn basic poetic techniques for lyric writers.

GOSPEL MUSIC ASSN., 1205 Division St., Nashville TN 37203. (615)242-0303. Fax (615)254-9755. Website: www.gospelmusic.org. Annual GMA conference, critique service, and resources.

INDIEHEAVEN. Website: www.indieheaven.com. Information and resources for independent Christian artists, radio stations, venues. Offers the *50 Point Tune-up* song evaluation.

+LYRICS FINDER. Can't remember lyrics to a song? Does your character need a song to sing? Go to Website: www.findmeatune.com for searchable source.

THE NASHVILLE SONGWRITERS ASSOCIATION INTERNATIONAL, 1701 West End Ave., 3rd Fl., Nashville TN 37203. Toll-free (800)321-6008. (615)256-3354. Fax (615)256-0034. E-mail: nsai@NashvilleSongwriters.com. Website: www.nashvillesongwriters.com. Over 100 workshops around the country.

PERFORMING RIGHTS SOCIETIES. These three groups collect royalties due their members from radio, TV, and concert performances. The three societies are (1) ASCAP (American Society of Composers, Authors and Publishers), 1 Lincoln Plaza, New York NY 10023. (212)621-6000. E-mail: info@ascap.com. Website: www.ascap.com. (2) BMI (Broadcast Music Inc.), 320 W. 57th St., New York NY 10019-3790. (212)586-2000. Website: http://bmi.com. (3) SESAC (not an acronym), 55 Music Square E., Nashville TN 37203. (615)320-0055. Fax (615)329-9627. Website: www.sesac.com.

PROVIDENT MUSIC GROUP, 741 Cool Springs Blvd. E., Franklin TN 37067. Website: www.providentmusic.com. Site provides links to retailers, Provident labels, artists, concerts, jobs, FAQs, features, and more.

THE RECORDING ACADEMY, 3402 Pico Blvd., Santa Monica CA 90405. (310)392-3777. Fax (310)399-3090. E-mail: refer to online contact form. Website: www.grammy.com/academy. Presents the Grammy Awards. Also engages in professional educational activities, such as seminars; provides scholarships; offers associate memberships.

RESOURCES. Website: www.musesmuse.com. Order Songwriter's Toolkit.

RHYMING DICTIONARY. Website: www.rhymer.com.

THE SONGWRITERS GUILD, 209—10th Ave. S., Ste. 534, Nashville TN 37203. (615)742-9945. Fax (615)742-9948. E-mail: nash@songwritersguild.com. Website: www.songwriters.org. Protects the rights of songwriters.

THE SONGWRITER'S MARKET GUIDE. Website: www.writersdigest.com. Order the *Songwriter's Market* from the Writer's Digest Bookstore.

SONGWRITING COMPETITION. International Songwriting Competition, Zero Governors Ave., #6, Medford MA 02155. (781)306-0441. Website: www.songwritingcompetition.com.

SONGWRITING LINKS. Website: www.lyricist.com.

YOU CAN WRITE SONG LYRICS by Terry Cox. ISBN 0898799899. $14.99. Order at www.writers digest.com.

RESOURCES: YOUNG WRITERS

+AWARDS & CONTESTS. (1) Chattanooga Writers Guild sponsors an annual contest with adult and student (grades 6-12) divisions. Children's categories include poetry, fiction, and personal essay. Contact Jennifer Hoff, President, to get information on current contest. E-mail: cwguild@aol.com. Website: www.chattanoogawritersguild.org; (2) The Kenyon Review sponsors the Patricia Grodd Poetry Prize for Young Writers. The award recognizes outstanding young poets and is open to high school sophomores and juniors throughout the world. The winner receives a full scholarship to the Kenyon Review Young Writers Workshop. In addition, the winning poem will be published in *The Kenyon Review*. Check Website for submission guidelines and application: www.kenyonreview.org/programs/ywpp.php.

+BOOK PUBLISHERS. (1) Dawn of Day publishes books written by kids 18 and under. Also hires young artists. Website: www.dawnofday.com; (2) SynergEbooks publishes all genres of e-books. Website: www.synergebooks.com.

CONFERENCES. Check "Christian Writers' Conferences and Workshops" section in this guide for those that provide a separate track or sessions for young writers.

CREATIVE WRITING FOR TEENS. Website: http://teenwriting.about.com/teens/teenwriting. Devoted to helping young authors develop their writing skills and creativity. Covers over 30 subjects. Lots of links listed.

+GUIDEPOSTS FOR TEENS. Accepts true stories about teens by teens—ages 12 to 18. Website: www.gp4teens.com.

JO: JOURNALISM ONLINE, 6118 Bend of River, Dunn NC 28334. Phone/fax (910)980-1126. E-mail: publisher@teenlight.org. Website: www.writershelper.org/workshop. Annette Dammer, founder. Offers a free online workshop to Christian teens and home schooling families.

JUST4TEENS. Website: www.lovepoetscafe.net/teens. Site where teens can post stories and poems.

LISSA EXPLAINS IT ALL. Website: www.lissaexplains.com. An excellent site for learning HTML (the language in which Web pages are written), especially for kids, but equally helpful for any HTML novice.

MYSTERY WRITING. Mystery writing lesson plans for kids is offered at: http://kids.mystery net.com.

PERIODICAL MARKETS. Check "Periodical Topics" in this guide for "Young Writer Markets."

+SCI-FI & FANTASY WRITING FOR TEENS. A great list of resources including contests, workshops, and markets. Website: http://snipurl.com/9wda.

SECULAR PERIODICAL MARKETS. (1) *Stone Soup* publishes stories, poems, and art by kids 13 and under. Website: www.stonesoup.com; (2) *Insight Magazine* publishes stories and poems by teens ages 13 to 19. Website: www.insightmagazine.org. (3) *Creative Kids:* www.prufrock.com. Click "Journals & Magazines"; (4) *Potluck Children's Literary Magazine:* http://members.aol.com/_ht_a/potluckmagazine/index.html; (5) *Merlyn's Pen:* www.merlynspen.com; (6) *Skipping Stones:* www.efn.org/~skipping/submissions.htm; (7) *Teen Ink Magazine:* http://teenink.com; (8) *The Writers' Slate:* www.writingconference .com; (9) *I Love Cats:* www.iluvcats.com; (10) *Kids Online Magazine:* www.kidson linemagazine.com. (11) Also, check out: www.jhu.edu/~gifted/ts/writing_resources.htm.

STORYBOOK WEAVER DELUXE. A computer CD for children ages 8-12 that encourages writing. Students author and illustrate stories with easy-to-use word processor and graphic features. For more information, go to www.riverdeep.net/support/product_support/s/strybkwv11569.jhtml.

UPPER ROOM MINISTRIES. Website: www.MethodX.org. At this site young adults can reflect on their faith through music, personal journal space, reviews, and more.

THE WRITE STUFF. Website: www.geocities.com/writestuffclub. A club for young adult writers ages 13 to 23.

WRITING WITH WRITERS. Website: http://teacher.scholastic.com/activities. Students work with authors, editors, and illustrators in exclusive workshops designed to guide them in developing their writing skills.

YAHOOLIGANS. Website: www.yahooligans.com. Search engine for kids. Geared toward elementary age children or adults seeking information in a simple format.

YOUNG AUTHOR EDITION OF WRITING SMARTER NOT HARDER (1) by Colleen Reece. A how-to book for elementary-school-age children. Great for children's writing classes or home schoolers. To order a copy, send $7.95, plus $1.50 shipping to: Kaleidoscope Press, 2507—94th Ave. E., Edgewood WA 98371, or call (253)848-1116. (2) *Writing Smarter Not Harder* (for jr. high through adults) is also available for $13.95 plus $1.50 shipping.

YOUNG WRITERS CLUBS. (1) Real Kids, Real Adventures, PO Box 461572, Garland TX 75046-1572. Website: www.realkids.com. From author Deborah Morris: tips on how to get started writing, a writing contest, an e-mail list, and a critique group for kids; (2) The Young Writers Club, www.cs.bilkent.edu.tr/~david/derya/ywc.html.

YOUNG WRITERS SERIES. *Young Writers Contest Manual, Young Writers Market Manual,* and *Young Writers Manuscript Manual* by Penny Lent. For kindergarten to college-age students interested in selling nonfiction, poetry, photos, and art. To order, send $7.95, plus $1.50 shipping, for each book to: Kaleidoscope Press, 2507—94th Ave. E., Edgewood WA 98371, or call (253)848-1116.

SEARCH ENGINES

ALTAVISTA. Website: www.altavista.com.

A9. Website: http://a9.com. Amazon.com's search engine. "In addition to Web search results, we present book results from Amazon.com that include 'Search Inside the Book.'"

BRITANNICA. Website: www.britannica.com. The *Encyclopedia Britannica*'s Website. Includes the Britannica Internet Guide, all of the articles in the *Encyclopedia Britannica,* and much more.

CHRISTIAN SEARCH ENGINES. Websites: (1) www.christianlink.com; (2) www.crosssearch.com; (3) www.crosswalk.com; (4) www.everythingchristian.org; (5) www.his-net.com; (6) www.ibelieve.com; (7) www.injesus.com; (8) www.praize.com; (9) www.religiousresources.org; (10) www.chritech.com; (11) www.worthylinks.com.

+CLUSTY.COM. Similar to Google but offers alternate categories. Website: www.clusty.com.

CNET. Website: http://cnet.com. A conglomeration of dozens of tech sites and tools.

COPERNIC. Website: www.copernic.com. A meta-search engine.

DIRECT SEARCH. Website: www.freepint.com/gary/direct.htm. A growing compilation of links to the search interfaces of resources not easily searchable from general search tools.

DITTO. Website: www.ditto.com. A family-friendly-image search engine; will not link to any offensive images.

DOGPILE. Website: www.dogpile.com. Uses over a dozen search engines to find your search topic.

EXPERT CLICK. Website: www.expertclick.com. Search for experts by topic, geography, or organization.

FREEALITY INTERNET SEARCH ENGINES. Website: www.freeality.com. Links to search engines.

GOOGLE. Website: www.google.com. Sorts hits based on how "popular" they are—in other words, by how many other sites point to that particular hit.

GOOGLE PRINT. Website: http://print.google.com/print/faq.html.

+GOOGLE TIPS. Check out an article entitled *Better Googling: Things You Didn't Know Google Does* on Website: www.sreetips.com/google.html.

GOOGLE WEBQUOTES. Website: http://labs.google.com/cgi-bin/webquotes. Annotates the results of your Google search with comments from other Websites. This offers a convenient way to get a third party's opinion about each of the returns for your search, providing you with more information about that site's credibility and reputation.

HOTBOT. Website: www.hotbot.com.

INFO. Website: www.info.com. Displays results from 12 search engines.

KARNAK. Website: www.karnak.com. Specifically designed for structured and productive research. You can construct a personal library of past research topics for easy referral.

LISTFISH. Website: www.listfish.com. Specifically designed to help you find e-mail publications, and is updated regularly. Topics include science, computers, sports, fashion, government, culture, and even a category for Internet users who are under 21.

LOOKSMART. Website: www.looksmart.com. Find resources for improving your writing and getting published.

LYCOS. Website: www.lycos.com.

METOR SEARCH ENGINE. Website: www.metor.com. A more comprehensive search engine with both general and specific collections of sites.

MSN SEARCH. Website: www.search.msn.com.

QUICKBROWSE. Website: www.quickbrowse.com. Service that combines your favorite sites into a single page for faster viewing.

+SEARCH ENGINE OPTIMIZATION. Website: http://thedabblingmum.com/business/seo/index.htm.

SEARCH ENGINE WATCH. Website: www.searchenginewatch.com. Good site to learn information about search engines. Click on "Web Searching Tips" to learn how to search the Web.

711.NET. Website: www.711.net. A Christian-oriented search engine that includes categories such as apologetics, Bible, faith, church, and theology.

TURBO10 METASEARCH ENGINE. Website: http://turbo10.com. Topics are generated for each search and are listed in a pull-down menu at the top of the search results to help refine it to the most specific search.

VIVISIMO. Website: http://vivisimo.com/. New clustering search engine.

YAHOO! Website: www.yahoo.com; http://search.yahoo.com.

SERVICES FOR WRITERS

Note: Check out these services before hiring any of them. Their listing here in no way indicates an endorsement.

+ABC'S OF POD. Order *The ABC's of POD: A Beginner's Guide to Fee-Based Print-on-Demand Publishing* from author Dehanna Bailee's Website: www.dehanna.com. The site also features a POD database.

+AGENT ADDRESSES. See http://tinyurl.com/6vcq5 for a free list of agent e-mail addresses.

+AGENT QUERY. (1) The Internet's largest and most current database of literary agents. Website: www.agentquery.com. (2) See also Nebraska Center for Writers. Website: http://mocking bird.creighton.edu/NCW/litag.htm.

AGENT RESEARCH & EVALUATION, INC., 25 Barrow St., New York, NY 10014. (212)924-9942. Fax (212)924-1864. E-mail: info@agentresearch.com. Website: www.agent research.com. Tracks public record of literary agents and agents for the sale of dramatic and other subsidiary rights involving books and manuscripts. Database contains over 2,000 agents and more than 20,000 of their clients. Offers two consulting services—The Fingerprint and Dead Reckoning—and a new agent list and publishes a newsletter, *Talking Agents.*

ALL ABOUT QUOTES. Website: www.allaboutquotes.com/Daily.asp. Do you use quotations in your writing and speaking? Subscribe to the free daily e-mail quote service.

ALL WRITING SERVICES (formerly AuthorShowcase). Website: www.allwritingservices.com. Offers a variety of services for writers.

BUSINESS CARDS. Website: www.VistaPrint.com. They offer 250 free business cards.

CHRISTIAN INFORMATION MINISTRIES/RESEARCH SERVICE. 2050 N. Collins Blvd., Ste. 100, Richardson, TX 75080. (972)690-1975. E-mail: info@christianinformation.org. Provides research links including topics related to the Bible, theology, and Christian living. Website: www.christianinformation.org/links.asp.

CLASS PERSONAL MENTOR. Florence Littauer, who founded CLASS (Christian Leaders and Speakers Seminars) is offering to be a personal mentor to a limited number of CLASS graduates. This will be done in small classes in various locations. For more information, contact: CLASS, 3311 Candelaria N.E., Ste. I, Albuquerque, NM 87107-1952. (800)433-6633. Fax (505)899-9282. Website: www.classervices.com.

CORRESPONDENCE COURSE FOR MANUSCRIPT EDITING. The University of Wisconsin offers a correspondence course in manuscript editing for those wanting to do editing on a professional level or for writers wanting to improve their personal editing skills. Contact: University of Wisconsin Research Park, 505 S. Rosa Rd., Madison WI 53719-1257. Toll-free (877)895-3276. (608)265-9379. Fax (608)265-9396. E-mail: info@learn.uwsa.edu. Ask about Manuscript Editing C350-A52 or go to Fundamentals of Manuscript Editing under Independent Learning section. Website: http://learn.wisconsin.edu/il.

+CRITIQUE & PUBLICATION WEBSITE. 57 Story Lane offers automatic publication for all genres of writing including Christian writing. Writers receive critiques and advice from other writers and readers. Website: www.57storylane.com.

EDITORIAL SERVICES. Lynda Lotman offers various services to writers and editors. Find the specific service you need in one of these Websites she coordinates: (1) www.English Edit.com; (2) www.ManuscriptEditing.com; (3) www.QueryLetters.com; (4) www.SciFi Editor.com; (5) www.StatisticsTutors.com; (6) www.DissertationWriting.com; (7) www .DissertationAdvisors.com; (8) www.Book-Editing.com; (9) www.WritingNetwork.com.

E-MAIL LISTS. Sources for free mailing list companies. Websites: (1) www.christianemailservice .com; (2) www.topica.com; (3) http://groups.yahoo.com; (4) http://groups.google.com.

FAX SERVICES WHEN YOU DON'T HAVE A FAX. You can now receive faxes through an existing e-mail address. Check out these sites: (1) www.efax.com and (2) www.faxaway.com. Both offer free trials.

FIRST EDITION MANUSCRIPT SERVICE. Now your book can be submitted to over 70 Christian publishers in one simple step by logging on to www.ecpa.org. First edition is an online manuscript service of the Evangelical Christian Publishers Assn. Fee is $79.

FREE E-MAIL SERVICES. (1) Website: www.juno.com. Provides a free service to those who want the ability to correspond with others by e-mail, but don't need additional access to the Internet. Sign up online or call toll-free (800)879-5866 to order a Juno CD for $9.95. (2) For another option to set up a free e-mail address, check out www.mail.com. (3) For a guide to free Internet Providers, go to www.fepg.net.

LOGOS RESEARCH SYSTEMS, 1313 Commercial St., Bellingham WA 98225-4372. (360)527-1700. Toll-free (800)875-6467. Fax (360)527-1700. E-mail: customerservice@ logos.com. Website: www.logos.com. Publishes the all-new Logos Bible Software Series X-Scholar's Library, Pastor's Library, and the Bible Study Library. Over 3,000 titles from more than 100 publishers are now compatible with the system.

MANUSCRIPT BOXES. To obtain rugged boxes for mailing manuscripts, contact: Papyrus Place, 2210 Goldsmith Ln., Louisville KY 40218. (502)451-9748. Fax (502)451-5487. E-mail: info@papyrusplace.com. Website: www.papyrusplace.com.

MANUSCRIPT TRACKING PROGRAM. Website: www.sandbaggers.8m.com. Free download.

MARKETING LISTS. Toll-free (888)330-4919. E-mail: sendlistinfo@netscape.net. If they don't have the list you need, they will compile a custom list according to your specifications. Lists include: Libraries, Bookstores, Media, and more.

+THE NATIONAL DIRECTORY OF EDITORS AND WRITERS FOR HIRE. This book by Elizabeth Lyon contains 600 freelance business, proofreading, copy, technical, and literary editors, plus book doctors, ghostwriters, consultants, and writing coaches. Publisher: M. Evans & Company, Inc. (March, 2005); ISBN 1590770692.

POSTAGE CHART. Writer's Postage Chart. Website: www.mirror.org/terry.hickman/ Postage.htm. Gregory Koster and Terry Hickman's postage rates for mailing manuscripts to and from most English-speaking countries.

+QUOTATION SEARCH SERVICE. Bob Kelly has collected 400 volumes of quotes, numbering 1.5 million entries. Visit Website: www.wordcrafters.info to find out more about his services.

+RESIDENCIES. (1) Soapstone serves the needs of women writers working on fiction, poetry, drama, screenwriting, and other literary writing. Residencies are offered at no charge. For further information and applications, go to Website: www.soapstone.org. (2) A Studio in the Woods provides residencies of two to four weeks during which time the artist lives on site, is provided with a private studio, meals and uninterrupted work time for a small fee to cover food costs. Shorter residencies of one day to a week are possible and happen throughout the year on an informal basis. Visit Website: www.astudiointhewoods.org.

P. L. SCHLACHTER CONSULTING, INC., PO Box 22443, Denver CO 80222. (303)588-2351. E-mail: software@livebytheword.com. Website: www.livebytheword.com. Will work with you directly to develop custom software designed to meet your needs, regardless of your industry. Developed database for the *Christian Writers' Market Guide.*

SCORE (Service Corps of Retired Executives). Website: www.score.org. Offers free advice to small businesses by e-mail.

STAMPS.COM. Website: www.stamps.com. Free software for printing postage on your computer.

+SUBMISSION SERVICE. A site to connect writers with publishers, editors, and agents. Website: www.publishersandagents.net.

TELEPHONE HANDSET RECORDING CONTROL. To record phone calls for interviewing purposes. Available at Radio Shack. Website: www.radioshack.com. Enter Product #43-1237. $15-20.

+TO PRESS AND BEYOND. As "book shepherds," this publisher takes your book project through the writing, editing, design, layout, distribution, sales, and promotion stages. Website: www.topressandbeyond.com.

TRANSLATORS. (1) Slavic Christian Publishing (SCP). Group specializes in English-Russian translation of Christian materials. Contact: Bogdan Michka, exec. dir., SCP Group, PO Box 13111, Salem OR 97309. (503)589-9906. Fax (503)589-9908. E-mail: scpg@cityofgod .org. Website: www.cityofgod.org/scpgroup/scp.htm. Other translators: (2) Julia Borovik. E-mail: boroviki@mail.ru. Charges $4/page or $3.50/page for more than 100 pages. She provides services over the Internet as she is a Ukrainian resident; (3) Lean Terentyeva.

E-mail: terentyeva@ukr.net. A professional Christian translator, with 8 years of experience. Russian/English; (4) Francisco Chavarria. E-mail: inspanish@juno.com. Translator and registered court interpreter. Spanish/English; (5) Cristina Mershon, Spanish/English translator and graphic designer. Contact information: Christina Mershon, Art Director, Mpower Media, 424 Second Ave. W., Seattle WA 98119, (206)274-2500.

ULINE. Website: www.uline.com. Sells a variety of mailing supplies. Order by phone, online, or catalog.

+WRITER-REMINDERS. E-zine to organize your writing with free daily, weekly, and monthly checklists, tips, and resources. Website: http://groups.yahoo.com/group/writer-reminders. To subscribe: writer-reminders-subscribe@yahoogroups.com.

WRITERS' EDGE. Website: www.WritersEdgeService.com. Submission and critique service. Their list includes 75 participating publishers. Charge is $79.

WRITER'S HAVEN. Contact: Beverly Caruso. (951)245-4082. E-mail: Rancho@across2u.com. Website: www.across2u.com/haven.html. A haven near Lake Elsinore where Christian writers who need time and solitude to write will not be interrupted. Room and board included. Write for available dates, and for information about upcoming writer's seminars.

+WRITERS RESOURCE EXCHANGE. Buy, sell, or trade your books and other writing resources, but it is not to promote your own book. To subscribe, send a blank e-mail to: writers_resource-subscribe@yahoogroups.com.

SPEAKING

AMERICAN SPEAKERS BUREAU, 10151 University Blvd., #197, Orlando FL 32817. (407)826-4248. Fax (407)629-7752. E-mail: info@speakersbureau.com. Website: www.speakers bureau.com.

CLASS PERSONAL MENTOR. Florence Littauer, who founded CLASS (Christian Leaders and Speakers Seminars) is offering to be a personal mentor to a limited number of CLASS graduates. This will be done in small classes in various locations. For more information, contact: CLASS, 3311 Candelaria N.E., Ste. I, Albuquerque, NM 87107-1952. (800)433-6633. Fax (505)899-9282. Website: www.classervices.com.

CLASS SERVICES, INC. (Christian Leaders, Authors & Speakers Services), PO Box 66810, Albuquerque, NM 87193-6810. (505)899-4283. Fax (505)899-9282. E-mail: info@ classervices.com. Website: www.classervices.com. Specializing in radio and TV interview campaigns for Christian authors, speakers, and ministries, providing resources, training, and promotion for Christian authors and speakers.

DAYBOOK NEWS. Website: www.daybooknews.com. Information and updates on press releases, conferences, speaking engagements, conventions, and book release dates.

NATIONAL SPEAKERS ASSN., 1500 S. Priest Dr., Tempe AZ 85281. (480)968-2552. Fax (480)968-0911. Website: www.nsaspeaker.org. Convention and training for professional speakers. Puts out *Professional Speaker Magazine.*

ONE-SHEET PRINTING. Website: www.cfre.com. Click on "Personal Brochures."

ONLINE SPEAKERS BUREAU. Website: www.espeakersbureau.com. Allows speakers to register their background information online so meeting planners have greater access to available talent and can contact speakers directly. For more information, contact pjdoland@espeakers bureau.com.

SERMON AND SPEECH ILLUSTRATIONS. Website: www.bible.org/illus/illustoc.htm. Over 10,000 illustrations in their database.

SPEAKER SPOTLIGHT, 7247 W. Colt, #300, Boise ID 83709. (208)362-6611. Website: www.speakerspotlight.com. Add your link to their directory.

SPEAKING.COM. Website: www.speaking.com. Speakers platform. (415)861-1700. E-mail: speakers@speaking.com.

+SPEECH & TRANSCRIPT CENTER. (1) For current and historical transcripts, go to Website: www.freepint.com/gary/speech.htm; (2) also visit www.historychannel.com/speeches.

SPEECH COACHING. Websites: (1) http://fripp.com/forspeaker.html; (2) www.professional speaker.com/catalog.htm.

TOASTMASTERS. Website: www.toastmasters.org. Worldwide speaking organization offering tips for professionals and nonprofessionals alike.

VOICE COACHING. Roy Hanschke, voice coach. Toll-free (800)604-8843. Website: www.voicepersonality.com. Ron Hanschke does voice coaching via audiotape. He listens to your tape, critiques it, and records instructions to you, which are cut into your tape where the correction is needed.

WOMEN'S MINISTRY. Website: www.womensministry.net. Ideas, resources, and information exchange among Christian women and worldwide ministry organizations.

WRITERSPEAKER.COM. Website: www.writerspeaker.com. Offers all kinds of help for the writer or speaker, including a free newsletter. Editor Carmen Leal is seeking subscribers (it's free) and also submissions of articles. Although there is no payment, she will include a generous bio at the end of your piece with e-mail and Website contact information.

WEB PAGE DEVELOPMENT/RESOURCES

+ADDING LINKS. (1) To draw traffic to your book's Website, add your link to Literary Leaps, one of the most comprehensive collections of book-related sites. For free site submission, go to Website: www.literaryleaps.com. (2) To add Google search to your site, go to www.google.com/services/websearch.html to learn more. (3) To add Gospelcom to your site, go to www.biblegateway.com/usage/.

CHRISTIAN WEB DESIGN AND HOSTING. Website: www.webtechdg.com. WebTech Design Group: a full service Christian company offering site design, hosting, domain registration, and more.

CREATE-IT 101: Basic HTML. Website: www.geocities.com/Karenw/index.html. Great tutorial on making Web pages.

+CROSSWAY CHRISTIAN ISP. A family-friendly and Christian filtered Internet service. Website: http://crosswayisp.com.

DOMAIN NAMES. To see if the domain name you want to use is already in use, go to: (1) www.networksolutions.com/cgi-bin/whois/whois. To register your domain name, go to: (2) www.networksolutions.com; (3) www.rcomexpress.com; or (4) www.namezero.com. For domain name system management and a list of accredited registrars, go to: (5) www.icann.org/registrars/accredited-list.html. Other sites for domain names include: (6) www.names4ever.com; (7) www.godaddy.com; (8) www.homewithgod.com; (9) www.westhost.com.

FREE COUNTERS. Websites: (1) www.sitemeter.com. Other fee-based counters are at (2) www.mycomputer.com and (3) www.thecounter.com.

FREE GREETING CARDS. Website: http://associates.123greetings.com.

FREE ONLINE CUSTOMER SERVICE. Website: http://humanclick.com.

FREE POLLS. Website: www.freepolls.com.

FREE WEB-BASED E-MAIL SERVICE. Website: www.zzn.com.

FREE WEB TOOLS. (1) Website: www.bravenet.com. Some tools include guest books, message forums, counters, polls, site searches, audio clips, and more. (2) Another Website: www.wordpress.org.

HELPFUL WEBSITES. Websites: (1) www.BigNoseBird.com; (2) www.hotwired.com/webmonkey. Free Websites that offer downloads of the language and free CGI scripts.

HOMESTEAD WEB SERVER. Website: www.homestead.com.

HOW TO PROMOTE YOUR WEBSITE. Website: www.wilsonweb.com.

LISSA EXPLAINS IT ALL. Website: www.lissaexplains.com. An excellent site for learning HTML (the language in which Web pages are written), especially for kids, but equally helpful for any HTML novice.

MAINTAINING YOUR WEBSITE. Website: www.workz.com.

MEDIA BUILDER. Website: www.mediabuilder.com. Offers free fonts and Web graphics to use on your Web page.

OURCHURCH.COM. Website: www.OurChurch.com. Free Christian Web server; easy to use.

SCRIPT ARCHIVE. Website: www.scriptarchive.com. Interactive Website gadgets. Site includes working CGI scripts that you can install on your server. Some programming skills required, as well as permission from your ISP or Web-hosting service to install and run your own CGI programs.

SEARCH ENGINE OPTIMIZATION & SUBMISSION. Website: www.webtechdg.com. Click on "Free Resource Page." Before you submit your site to search engines, let them evaluate your site for search-engine readiness free. After they let you know what is needed to make your site rank higher in major search engines, you can submit your site to over 200 search engines from their site for free.

+SITE BUILDING. (1) For Site Build It software, go to Website: www.sitesell.com. (2) Also see Website: www.2-tiersoftware.com. They offer Website hosting and 25 pages of template-based design tools specifically for writers and more.

WEB HOSTS. Websites: (1) www.wyenet.com; (2) www.arkwebs.com; (3) www.halfpricehosting .com; (4) www.catalog.com; (5) www.freepagehosting.com; (6) www.westhost.com; (7) www.ilovejesus.com; (8) www.truepath.com; (9) http://smallbusiness.yahoo.com/ webhosting. (10) For a list of the "100 Best Web Site & Domain Hosting Services," go to: http://100best-web-hosting.com.

WEB PAGE DESIGN. Websites: (1) www.webaim.org/standards/508/checklist; (2) www.fresno state.edu/webaccess/; (3) www.webposition.com; (4) www.webstyleguide.com/index.html?/ contents.html.

WEBSITE OPTIMIZATION. Website: http://websiteoptimization.com/speed/toc. Website Optimization (WSO) is a series of techniques that minimize Web page file sizes and maximize page display speeds.

WEBSITE WORKSTATION. Website: www.davesite.com/webstation. All kinds of advice on Website design, etc.

WEB-ZINE ARTICLE DISTRIBUTION SITES. Websites: (1) www.ideamarketers.com; (2) www.EzineArticles.com. Free articles to put on your Web page.

WRITERSPEAKER WEB DESIGN AND DEVELOPMENT. Gary Scott, PO Box 9426, Naples FL 34101-9426. E-mail: Gary@writerspeaker.com. Website: www.writerspeaker.com. A Christian company whose focus is helping writers and speakers set up effective Websites.

WEBSITES OF INTEREST TO WRITERS: GENERAL

ABSOLUTE WRITE. Website: www.absolutewrite.com. Good links, market info, and Q&As.

ACW PRESS: RESOURCES FOR THE CHRISTIAN WRITER. Website: www.acwpress.com/ links.htm. Links to lots of great resources.

AMERICAN CHRISTIAN WRITERS. Website: www.ACWriters.com.

AMERICAN JOURNALISM REVIEW'S NEWS LINK. Website: www.newslink.org. Links more than 60 Websites including The Freedom Forum, Pulitzer Prizes, American Society of Magazine Editors, American Society of Newspaper Editors, Newsletter Publishers Assn., and the Committee to Protect Journalists.

+ANGEL IN YOUR INKWELL. Site features workshops, coaching, other services, and fun stuff for writers by Carol Newman. Website: www.angelinyourinkwell.com.

+AUTHOR WEBSITES. If you are planning an author Website, you may want to check out these sites for ideas: (1) www.traciepeterson.com; (2) http://BrandilynCollins.com; (3) http://KathyIde.com; and (4) www.charlottedillon.com (for romance writers).

+BEST OF THE BEST. Find the "best of" books, movies, and music. Website: http://listsof bests.com.

+BEST SELLERS LIST. *USA Today* offers a searchable-only database of its weekly top 150 best seller lists since October 1993. Website: http://asp.usatoday.com/life/books/books database/default.aspx.

BIOGRAPHIES. Website: www.amillionlives.com. A large guide to posthumous biographies.

+BOOKPROPOSALS.WS. Website: www.bookproposals.ws. Learn more on this site about the secrets of getting published from author/editor W. Terry Whalin. The site includes two excerpts from *Book Proposals That Sell* along with information about what editors, literary agents, and best-selling authors are saying about it.

BOOKZONE. Website: www.bookzonepro.com. Current information for writers and publishers, plus a newsletter, service directory, events calendar, and reviewers' database.

BURRYMAN WRITERS CENTER. Website: www.burryman.com. Lists freelance jobs, resources for fiction and nonfiction writers, working professionals and beginners.

CHRISTIAN E-AUTHORS. Website: www.christianeauthor.com. Offers support to Christian authors with a specific call to write for the Internet. Welcomes e-book/e-zine authors, poets, playwrights, publishers, online ministries, and those interested in learning more about writing for the Internet. Discussion list, Website, workshops.

CHRISTIAN MINISTRY LINKS. Website: www.CrossSearch.com. Links to over 40 Christian ministries.

CHRISTIAN PARADISE. Website: www.christianparadise.com. A great site for just about everything Christian, from music and entertainment to articles by some great writers.

CHRISTIAN RETAILING. Website: www.christianretailing.com. Monitors the heartbeat of the Christian retail industry. Offers free newsletter.

CHRISTIANWRITERS.COM. Website: http://christianwriters.com. A free online writers' resource community. Their mission is to provide a supportive, family atmosphere where writers may easily access the tools and resources to create, market, and publish their work.

COFFEEHOUSE FOR WRITERS. Website: www.coffeehouseforwriters.com. Online writing workshops, critique groups, discussion lists, contests, and newsletter.

COURSE MATERIALS. Website: http://ocw.mit.edu. MIT's OpenCourseWare site. Course materials from MIT classes, at no charge.

CREATIVITY SITES. (1) Eric Maisel's *Creativity Newsletter.* Website: www.ericmaisel.com. (2) Also take a look at Stickyideas for sources of inspiration and a weekly column about creativity. Website: www.stickyideas.com.

CRITIQUE AND DISCUSSION FORUMS. Website: www.writersbbs.com.

CROSSHOME. Website: www.crosshome.com. Your Christian home on the Internet.

ECONOMY INFORMATION. Website: www.dismal.com. Economic data you can use in your writing.

EPISTLEWORKS CREATIONS, JoAnn Reno Wray, 812 W. Glenwood St., Broken Arrow OK 74011-6419. (918)451-4017. Website: http://epistleworks.com. E-mail: refer to online contact form. Experienced speaker on writing topics; taught at national, local, and regional conferences and groups. Sells illustrated bookmarks and framed poems. Hundreds of links on her site to guidelines, research sites, resources for writers, news services, greeting card markets, and more.

THE EUROPEAN CHRISTIAN WRITERS' RESOURCES. Website: www.christian writer.co.uk. Features author Ms. Abidemi Sanusi, ed.

E-ZINES. Websites: (1) www.zinebook.com; (2) www.e-zinez.com.

FAITHFUL READER. Website: www.faithfulreader.com. Helps a writer keep track of current market trends by providing book reviews, author interviews, excerpts, a devotional, and more.

FAITH WRITERS. Website: www.faithwriters.com. Offers free services and information for writers, readers, and publishers.

+FAMILY LINKS. Find dozens of links to topics related to families. Website: www.thewriting family.com/index.shtml.

FEDWORLD INFORMATION NETWORK. Website: www.fedworld.gov. Source of federal reports for your research.

+FIRST LINES. There are lots of sites that feature first lines of books and poems. Check these sites: (1) http://people.cornell.edu/pages/jad22; (2) http://bridge.lexingtonma.org/library/lines.html; (3) www.bookreporter.com/community/trivia/1996-triv.asp.

+FOG INDEX FOR READABILITY. Website: www.tech-head.com/fog.htm.

THE GENDER GENIE. Website: www.bookblog.net/gender/genie.html. Find out if your writing voice is male or female for developing your fiction characters.

+GUIDELINES FOR WRITERS. For a free e-zine called Writer's Guidelines Magazine, visit Website: www.powerpenmarketsearch.com. Click on Writer's Guidelines Magazine.

GUIDE TO LITERARY AGENTS. Website: http://literaryagents.org.

+THE HOLLYWOOD PRAYER NETWORK. Website: www.hollywoodprayernetwork.org. Request free video/DVD *The Hollywood Crisis.*

IBELIEVE.COM. Website: www.ibelieve.com. One of the most active Christian Websites.

INDEPENDENT CHRISTIAN MEDIA NETWORK. Website: www.christianindy.com. A site for writers, photographers, recording artists, painters, and any independent Christian artist to showcase his/her talents to the world. Also designs and hosts Websites.

INTERNET FOR CHRISTIANS. Website: www.gospelcom.net/ifc (includes hyperlinks to all listed sites).

INTERNET-RESOURCES.COM. Website: www.internet-resources.com/writers. A wealth of valuable resource links.

IUNIVERSE.COM/SELF-PUBLISHING GUIDE. Website: www.iuniverse.com.

+JOURNALISM GUIDES & TIPS. (1) Check out Pulitzer-winner Bill Dedman's suggestions at www.powerreporting.com. Thousands of free research tools for journalists; (2) Journalist-ToolBox offers 12,000 links from Mike Reilly. Website: www.journaliststoolbox.com; (3) The Journalist Guide provides links to 16 categories of information and resources. Website: http://reporter.umd.edu; (4) For an investigative guide to Internet research, go to www.journalism.org; (5) IRE Tip Sheets offer 20,000 investigative stories at www.ire.org/resourcecenter.

KAZOODLES. Website: http://groups.yahoo.com/group/kazoodles. Bimonthly newsletter featuring e-zines, lists, books, and sites on writers and writing.

MAGAZINE ARTICLE. Website: www.pcmag.com/article2/0,4149,1043161,00.asp. Article from PC Magazine about print-on-demand (POD). PC Magazine has rated six POD firms and lists the results.

MAGAZINES FOR WRITERS. (1) *The Writer.* Website: www.writermag.com. (2) *Writer's Digest.* Website: www.writersdigest.com.

MAGAZINE SUBSCRIPTIONS. Website: www.magazinevalues.com. A great source for really cheap magazines, including 24 religious magazines.

MOM WRITERS. Support, encouragement, and tips for mothers who write. Discussion group at http://groups.yahoo.com/group/momwriters.

MR. MAGAZINE. Website: www.mrmagazine.com. Provides the latest information on consumer magazines, including the 30 Most Notable Launches of the previous year.

MY HIDDEN TALENT. Website: www.myhiddentalent.com. A place to read other writers' work and get your work reviewed.

MY WRITER BUDDY. Website: www.writerbuddy.com. "A community and reference center for writers of all ages, writing interests, and experience. Provides mutual support, assistance, and friendship."

+NICHOLAS SPARKS (A Walk to Remember) AND AGENTS. Sparks tells how he found an agent and publisher and shares his experiences with learning the craft and the business of writing. See Website: http://Tinyurl.com/68ur9.

+101 BEST WEBSITES FOR WRITERS. For the Writer's Digest annual list of best Websites for writers, go to Website: www.writersdigest.com/101/sites/2005_index.asp. Search by one of these categories or by the A-Z list: articles; tips and discussion boards; creativity; general resources; genres; jobs; just for fun; media resources; niches; online writing and critique groups; online writing groups offering classes; organizations; and publishing resources.

101 WRITING ANSWERS. Website: www.101writinganswers.com. A directory of writing and related sources. Lists associations, forums, and groups, writing by genre, markets, and showcasing, and much more. Has a link to publishing and media resources.

ON THIS DAY IN HISTORY. (1) Website: www.dmarie.com/timecap. Details about any period in history. (2) For a search engine to look up any date, any month, any year in history or a birth date, visit Website: www.scopesys.com/today.

+OPENING HOOKS. A collection of literary beginnings. Website: www.openingbooks.us.

+OVERCOMING WRITER'S BLOCK. (1) This site features a ton of generators for ideas, characters, and names. Website: www.seventhsanctum.com/index-writ.php. (2) For more inspiration go to www.profitable-pen.com.

PAGE ONE LITERARY NEWSLETTER. Website: www.pageonelit.com.

PAGE WISE. Website: www.essortment.com/in/hobbies.writing. Site contains a large assortment of helpful articles to answer any question about writing.

PICTURES OF PUBLISHING. Website: www.geocities.com/visualsofpublish. A very informative slide show of 50 photos related to the New York publishing community.

POSTAGE RATES WORLDWIDE. Website: www.geocities.com/wallstreet/exchange/1161/index.htm. International postage rates. Writers living in foreign countries seeking U.S. postage can order online at: www.usps.gov.

PRAYER WALKING. Websites: (1) www.dailyprayerwalking.com; (2) www.janetmchenry.com. Janet Holm McHenry, speaker and author of *Prayer Changes Teens, Prayerwalk,* and *Daily Prayerwalk.*

PUBLIC OPINION POLLS. Website: www.pollingreport.com. Add substance to your articles with the latest opinion poll results.

RADIO STATIONS. Website: www.radio-locator.com/cgi-bin/home. The MIT List of Radio Stations on the Internet, or "radio-locator." Over 10,000 radio stations from all around the world.

REJECTIONS. Review "Read 'em and Weep" at www.rejectioncollection.com. A place to post your rejections and vent your frustrations. Contact: PO Box 443, Shrub Oak NY 10588-0443.

RIGHT WRITING. Website: www.right-writing.com. W. Terry Whalin, best-selling author and longtime editor, wants to help anyone with his/her written communication, from novels to thank-you letters. Offers the e-zine *Right Writing News.*

SELF-PUBLISHING. (1) Website: www.parapublishing.com. (2) And check out Dan Poynter's book *The Self-Publishing Manual.* Also check out (3) www.instantpublisher.com; (4) www.selfpublishersdigest.com.

SHARP WRITER. Website: www.sharpwriter.com. A site with quick references and lots of useful writer's links.

TIME WARNER CHRISTIAN BOOKS NEWSLETTER. Free monthly newsletter. Sign up at their Website: www.twbookmark.com. Click on "Excerpts" to read an excerpt from the books listed for free.

TIME ZONE SITES. Website: (1) www.timezoneconverter.com; (2) www.disastercenter.com/time.htm.

TOASTED CHEESE. Website: www.toasted-cheese.com. Excellent site providing forums, chats, news, musings, book reviews, and the *Toasted Cheese Literary Journal*.

TOURBUS. Website: www.TOURBUS.com. An informative e-newsletter about what's happening on the Internet, including information on current Internet viruses and hoaxes.

+USA COMMUNITIES. To get information on any community in the USA, go to the Power of Place. Search out demographics, crime, economy, special events, and more. Website: www.epodunk.com.

WILLWRITE4FOOD.COM. Website: www.willwrite4food.com. Geared toward creating community between writers. Forums, updates on the markets, a list of writers conferences, articles on writing, and more.

+WORKING WITH AN EDITOR. View this 9-page resource at www.laurelcook.com. Click on the left column.

WRITE DIRECTIONS. Website: www.writedirections.com. Articles, resources, bookstore, and consulting by Beth Mende Conny. E-mail: admin@writedirections.com.

WRITE FROM HOME. Website: www.writefromhome.com. Here you will find a collection of articles to help you juggle your home life with your writing career.

WRITERS' BREAK. Website: www.writersbreak.com. Articles, interview, and links.

WRITERSPEAKER.COM. Website: www.writerspeaker.com. Offers all kinds of help for the writer or speaker, including a free newsletter. Editor Carmen Leal is seeking subscribers (it's free) and also submissions of articles. Although there is no payment, she will include a generous bio at the end of your piece with e-mail and Website contact information.

A WRITER'S PRAYER. Website: www.booksandauthors.net/Fromtheauthor/LBlock.html. A prayer that offers some food for thought to which all writers can relate.

+WRITERS SUITE. An online publishing community of writers, readers, and educators featuring 22 communities, 530 feature writers and 87,000 articles. Website: www.suite101.com.

WRITERS' WORDS GLOSSARY. Website: www.everywriter.com/newwriters.htm.

WRITE TO INSPIRE.COM. Website: www.writetoinspire.com. A site for inspirational and Christian writers.

WRITING CORNER. Website: www.writingcorner.com. Links to agents, markets, newsletters, writing schools, recommended books, and grammar tips.

+WRITING FOR DOLLARS. www.writingfordollars.com.

+WRITING-PORTAL.COM DIRECTORY. Lists links for fiction, freelancing, screenwriting, nonfiction, and hundreds of other sites for writers. Website: www.writing-portal.com.

WRITING RESOURCES. For lists of publishers, writing links, resources, and research sites, go to Websites: (1) www.seliterary.homestead.com/links.html; (2) www.write-resource.com; (3) www.writershome.com/index.htm; (4) www.writecraftweb.com/wcarticles.html; (5) http://thinkers.net; (6) www.forwriters.com; (7) http://writesuccess.com.

YOU CAN WRITE. Website: www.youcanwrite.com/. Good site for nonfiction writers but with a boatload of good information for others, too.

WEBSITES OF INTEREST TO WRITERS: SPECIALTY TOPICS

+ADOPTION RESOURCES. (1) Adoption Network: www.adopt-usa.org; (2) All God's Children Intl: www.allgodschildren.org; (3) America World Adoption Assoc.: www.awaa.org; (4) Bethany Christian Services: www.bethany.org; (5) Christian World Adoption: www.cwa.org;

(6) North American Council on Adoptable Children: www.nacac.org; (7) Shaohannah's Hope: www.shaohannahshope.org; (8) free adoption posters, videos, radio spots: www.davethomasfoundation.com.

ASSOCIATED PRESS PHOTO ARCHIVE. Website: http://photoarchive.ap.org.

ASSN. OF PERSONAL HISTORIANS. Website: www.personalhistorians.org. Information for memoir writing.

+BABY BOOMER'S ONLINE COMMUNITY. See how wise, warm, and witty baby boomer women are connecting, encouraging, and supporting one another. Website: www.boomerwomenspeak.com.

+BIBLICAL VERSUS EASTERN RELIGIOUS VIEWS. Free chart comparing biblical and eastern religious views and a book review of *The Dark Side of Karate* by Linda Nathan can be found on Website: www.logosword.com/karate.htm.

BRITISH ROYALTY. Website: www.royal.gov.uk.

CHRISTIAN HISTORY. Websites: (1) www.christianhistory.net; (2) www.gospelcom.net/chi/index.html.

CLOTHING OF PAST ERAS. Website: www.costumepage.org/tcpinfo2.html. Covers everything from ancient Greece to the Middle Ages to the 1950s.

COMIX35 CHRISTIAN COMICS TRAINING. Nathan Butler, PO Box 27470, Albuquerque NM 87125-7470. (505)232-3500. Fax (775)307-8202. E-mail: comix35@comix35.org. Website: www.comix35.org. Sponsors The Christian Comics Competition, a biannual event.

+DEMOLITION SCENES. If you have a demolition in your novel and you need to describe what happens when the detonation is triggered, you can study pictures of all kinds of implosions on this site to see how they fall. Website: www.implosionworld.com/gallery.htm.

DOMESTIC ABUSE. Website: www.womeninneed.org. An outreach recovery program for domestic and intimate partner abuse.

EDUCATORS. Websites: (1) www.teacherfocus.com. More than 2,000 unique lesson plans submitted by teachers; (2) www.merlot.org. MERLOT, the Multimedia Educational Resource for Learning and Online Teaching, is a free, peer-reviewed collection of over 8,000 different online learning tools and simulations developed mostly by college professors around the world.

GLASS BLOWING. Website: www.lamberts.de/elambhom.htm. Check here for answers to your questions about mouth-blown glass and lots of other kinds of glass (i.e. restoration, flashed, crackled, cathedral) and glass around the world.

+HISTORY ONLINE. (1) Site lists all kinds of information by type, geographical area, or time period. Website: www.history.ac.uk/hr/resources/historical/index.html. Other Websites: (2) www.historynet.com; (3) www.historychannel.com. Historical research by topic, time, event, etc. (4) Life in the Middle Ages: www.mnsu.edu/emuseum/history/middleages/contents.html.

HOMESCHOOLING. Websites: (1) www.homeschoolheadquarters.com; (2) www.hsrc.com; (3) www.crosswalk.com/family/home_school. For writers in homeschool market.

INDEPENDENT CHRISTIAN MEDIA NETWORK. Website: www.christianindy.com. A Website for writers, photographers, recording artists, painters, and any independent Christian artists.

INTERNET IMAGES. Make sure your book's cover is on the Internet. Search at: http://images.google.com. Type in your book's ISBN number without hyphens.

JOIN HANDS. If writing for pastors, Christian education leaders, or music directors, you may find some helpful resources at (1) www.woodlakebooks.com or (2) www.logosproductions.com.

+MAPS. (1) For Ancient World maps, check out this site of cartography and geographic study. Website: www.unc.edu/awmc/. (2) For Civil War maps, go to Website: www.msnbc.msn.com/id/6807551. (3) For "online maps to everywhere," go to Website: www.multimap.com.

+MEDICAL & FORENSICS LAB. Archives of crime scenes where you can ask questions about related topics. Website: www.dplylemd.com.

+MEDICAL SITES. (1) For information to construct your character's medical condition, visit www.webmd.com. Click "Condition Centers A-Z." (2) Or go to www.mayoclinic.com.

MEDLINE PLUS. Website: www.nlm.nih.gov/medlineplus/. Dedicated to medical professionals and experts of all kinds. From a medical encyclopedia to all kinds of drug information.

MEMOIRS. Website: www.turningmemories.com. A resource for memoirs. Has articles that are extremely helpful in getting started.

MOVIES. (1) Internet Movie Database. Website: www.imdb.com. Free, searchable database of over 260,000 film and television productions made since 1910; (2) www.metacritic.com. Movie Reviews. A place where movie fans easily find the most important reviews for each new movie.

+MUSIC LOVERS. If you are a music lover or have a character who is a music lover, check out this site from the Rock and Roll Hall of Fame and Museum. Website: www.rock hall.com/timeline.

NEWSPAPERS AND MAGAZINES. Website: www.prLeads.com. Learn about articles before they are written. Dan Janal will supply you with target leads on the subjects you select. Then you contact the editor or freelancer to help him or her with the article. E-mail: Dan@ prLeads.com.

PARENT SOUP. Website: http://parenting.ivillage.com. For writers of parenting articles.

PROPHETIC NEWS SITES. (1) Website: www.prophezine.com. News about Israel from a Zionist perspective. (2) Discussion group at: http://groups.yahoo.com/group/zincisrael.

REGENCY ERA. Website: www.regencylibrary.com.

REVIEW COPY HELPER. Website: www.twowriters.net/reviewcopies.html. A site for book reviewers to get publisher contact information.

+SLOGANS. Check this site out see when some of our more popular slogans and jingles came into being. For example, "The pause that refreshes" (Coca Cola, 1929).

TRAVELWRITERS.COM. Website: www.travelwriters.com. E-source for travel writers. Contact info on over 500 travel publications. Free market news and press trip announcements.

TRAVEL WRITING TIPS. (1) Website: www.travelwritingtips.com; (2) for useful tips and sites for the travel writer, go to www.sree.net/tips/travel.html.

UPPER ROOM MINISTRIES. Website: www.MethodX.org. Young adults can reflect on their faith through music, personal journal space, reviews, and more. Good resource for those whose target audience is teens/young adults.

U.S. MILITARY INFORMATION. Websites: (1) www.usmilitary.com; (2) www.defenselink.mil; (3) www.dtic.mil/doctrine/jel/doddict. Army Websites: (4) www.army.mil; (5) www.goarmy .com; (6) www.army.mil/usar; (7) www.qmfound.com/army_heraldry.htm. Navy Websites: (8) www.navy.mil; (9) www.navy.com; (10) www.navyseals.com. Air force Websites: (11) www.af.mil; (12) www.airforce.com. Marine Websites: (13) www.usmc.mil; (14) www .marines.com; (15) www.marinecorps.com; (16) www.usmc.mil/marinelink/ind.nsf/ranks. Coast Guard Websites: (17) www.uscg.mil; (18) www.gocoastguard.com; (19) www.cgaux .org. (20) Special Ops Website: www.specialoperations.com.

VICTORIAN ERA. Websites: (1) www.victorianlondon.org; (2) www.victorianweb.org; (3) www.thelondonhouse.co.uk; (4) http://dept.kent.edu/museum/costume.

WOMEN'S WRITING RESOURCES. Website: www.womensministry.net.

WORD COUNT. *Word Counts: What Is a Word?* by Chuck Rothman. Website: www.sfwa.org/ writing/wordcount.htm.

WORLD WAR II INFO. Websites: www.ibiblio.org/pha; www.worldwar2history.info.

WRITERS' SOFTWARE

DRAMATICA PRO. Website: http://storymind.com.

+MANUSCRIPT TRACKING. Website: www.sandbaggers.8m.com/samm.htm.

+MY BOOK PROPOSAL SOFTWARE. Easy-to-use software templates for composing book proposals and query letters developed by Mark Shaw. To order call (970)544-3398 or visit Website: www.booksforlifefoundation.com/. Cost: $129.95.

+NEWNOVELIST. Software tools draw out your ideas, giving body to your characters and strength to your story lines, and keeping notes alongside each element of your work. To learn more, visit Website: www.newnovelist.com/?source=aw10.

OUTLOOK EXPRESS ADD-INS. Website: www.SperrySoftware.com.

QUICKPLOT. Website: www.typingchimp.com/index.html. Freeware program to help organize your thoughts in the planning stages.

S.A.M.M. Website: www.sandbaggers.8m.com/samm.htm. A manuscript tracking freeware program.

SCREEN/SCRIPT WRITING SOFTWARE. See Resources section: "Screenwriting/Scriptwriting."

+SOFTWARE WEBSITES: (1) Character Pro, www.characterpro.com; (2) Dramatic Pro and Movie Magic Screenwriter, Writer's DreamKit, www.write-bros.com; (3) Final Draft, www.finaldraft.com; (4) LifeJournal, www.lifejournal.com; (5) Personal Knowbase, www.bitsmithsoft.com; (6) Power Structure, Power Tracker, and Power Writer, www.write-brain.com; (7) TextAloud MP3, www.textaloud.com; (8) Truby's Blockbuster, www.truby.com; (9) Word Menu, www.wordmenu.com; (10) Writer's Blocks, www.writersblocks.com; (11) WriteItNow, www.ravensheadservices.com.

STORYBASE. Website: www.storybase.net. Toll-free (800)833-7568.

STORYCRAFT STORY DEVELOPMENT SOFTWARE. Website: www.storycraft.org. Guides writers through the entire process of writing novels, screenplays, teleplays, plays, and short stories.

STORYVIEW 2.0. Website: www.storyview.com. A writing tool that lets you create the elements of your story and arrange them on a timeline. You add the building blocks of your story in any order and immediately see any gaps.

STORYWEAVER. Website: http://storymind.com.

WORD MENU. Website: www.wordmenu.com. Word Menu (by Write Brothers, Inc.) organizes words by the way we actually use them: by subject matter. Cost: $34.95.

WRITE-BRAIN. Website: www.write-brain.com. Software to help you plot and write your stories.

WRITE PRO. Website: www.writepro.com. Also, FictionMaster by Sol Stein and WritePro.

WRITER'S BLOCKS 3.0. Website: www.writersblocks.com. Organize story elements for your fiction.

WRITER'S SUPERCENTER. Website: www.writerssupercenter.com. Offers a wide variety of software to help writers of all genres and forms.

WRITING MANAGEMENT SOFTWARE. Website: www.write-again.com. Can download on trial basis. Costs $49.95.

WRITING INSTRUCTION: CDs/CASSETTE TAPES

THE CHRISTIAN COMMUNICATOR MANUSCRIPT CRITIQUE SERVICE CASSETTE HANDS-ON COURSE. For information contact: Susan Titus Osborn, 3133 Puente St., Fullerton CA 92835-1952. (714)990-1532. Toll-free (877)428-7992. E-mail: Susanosb@aol.com. Website: www.christiancommunicator.com. Offers basic writing course available by cassette. Includes 6 lessons on 12 cassettes, handouts, and critiqued assignments. Cost for entire course: $180; by the lesson: $35.

CHRISTIAN WRITERS LEARNING CENTER. Website: www.ACWriters.com. Over 1,000 cassette tapes to choose from. Cost is $5-6 each, depending on quantity. Request the complete catalog by contacting American Christian Writers, PO Box 110390, Nashville TN 37222. (800)21-WRITE. Call for free catalog.

CREATIVE CHRISTIAN MINISTRIES, PO Box 12624, Roanoke VA 24027. E-mail: ccmbbr@ juno.com. Website: www.CreativeChristianMinistries.com. Tapes on a variety of topics for Christian writers (recorded at past writers' conferences by top writer/speakers).

NO FEAR STRATEGIES FOR PUBLISHING YOUR FIRST ARTICLES AND BOOK. David Sanford's 45-minute audio seminar. For a copy of the seminar, send a check for $15 to: Sanford Communications, Inc., 6406 N.E. Pacific St., Portland OR 97213.

WRITE HIS ANSWER MINISTRIES. Director: Marlene Bagnull, LittD, 316 Blanchard Rd., Drexel Hill PA 19026. E-mail: mbagnull@aol.com. Website: www.writehisanswer.com. Tapes on 20+ topics, $5 ea. Topics include: Taking the Pain Out of Marketing; Writing Manuscripts That Sell and Touch Lives; Turning Personal Experience into Print; and Self-Publishing. Tapes of Marlene's 8.5-hour Write His Answer Seminar are $27.95 and include handouts.

WRITE-TO-PUBLISH CONFERENCE. Director: Lin Johnson, 9731 N. Fox Glen Dr., #6F, Niles IL 60714-4222. E-mail: lin@writetopublish.com. Website: www.writetopublish.com. Bring speakers from the Write-to-Publish Conference into your home and car via these cassettes. Tapes from past conferences on all aspects of writing and publishing, as well as editors' panels telling what they are looking for now. $5 each, $4 for 21 or more. Lists are available on the Website, or send SASE to above address.

WRITING INSTRUCTION: CORRESPONDENCE COURSES

AMERICAN SCHOOL OF CHRISTIAN WRITING. Website: www.ACWriters.com. This division of American Christian Writers offers a 3-year, 36-lesson correspondence course that covers the entire field of Christian writing. Students may purchase full course or selected portions. Several payment plans available. For school brochure contact: American Christian Writers, PO Box 110390, Nashville TN 37222. (800)21-WRITE.

ASSOCIATED WRITING PROGRAMS, George Mason University, MS 1E3, Fairfax VA 22030. (703)993-4301. Fax (703)993-4302. E-mail: awp@awpwriter.org. Website: www.awp writer.org.

AT-HOME WRITING WORKSHOPS. Director: Marlene Bagnull, LittD, Write His Answer Ministries, 316 Blanchard Rd., Drexel Hill PA 19026. E-mail: mbagnull@aol.com. Website: www.writehisanswer.com. Offers 3 courses of study with 5-10 study units in each. (1) Putting Your Best Foot Forward (lays foundation for your writing ministry), 5 units, $145; (2) Nonfiction (articles, tracts, curriculum, devotionals, how-tos, etc., plus planning a nonfiction book and book proposal), 10 units, $272; (3) Fiction, 10 units, $255. Units may also be purchased individually for $30-34.

CHRISTIAN WRITERS INSTITUTE CORRESPONDENCE COURSES. Website: www.ACWriters .com. This 60-year-old institution, founded by veteran publisher Robert Walker, is a division of American Christian Writers. Offers six, 1-year courses with an assigned instructor/mentor. Writing assignments are given with a goal of having a publishable manuscript by the end of each course. Two payment plans available. Contact: Christian Writers Institute, PO Box 110390, Nashville TN 37222. (800)21-WRITE.

CORRESPONDENCE COURSE FOR MANUSCRIPT EDITING. Website: http://learn.wisconsin .edu/il. The University of Wisconsin offers a correspondence course in manuscript editing for those wanting to do editing on a professional level or for writers wanting to improve their personal editing skills. Reasonable cost. Contact: University of Wisconsin Research Park, 505 S. Rosa Rd., Madison WI 53719-1257. Toll-free (877)895-3276. (608)265-9379. Fax (608)265-9396. E-mail: info@learn.uwsa.edu. Ask about Manuscript Editing C350-A52.

GLORY PRESS/PROF. DICK BOHRER, MS, MA (teacher, 39 years; editor, 11 years including editor of two newspapers and managing editor of *Moody Monthly;* author of 16 books), PO Box 624, West Linn OR 97068. (503)638-7711. E-mail: dickbohrer@comcast.net. Offers 3 writing courses called "4+20 Ways to Write Stories for Christian Kids," "4+20 Ways, Christian, to Write Features Like a Pro," and "4+20 Ways, Christian, to Write What You Think." Charges $35 for each manual plus $1 per double-spaced typed page plus SASE for editing and critiquing assignments of poems, stories, and books. Asks for written testimony regarding applicant's salvation testimony of how he/she came to faith in Christ. References: gude@juno.com; k&kyoung@stic.net; asrduff@aol.com.

THE INSTITUTE OF CHILDREN'S LITERATURE, 93 Long Ridge Rd., West Redding CT 06896. Toll-free (800)243-9645. (203)792-8600. Fax (203)792-8406. E-mail: information services@InstituteChildrensLit.com. Website: www.InstituteChildrensLit.com. Several writing programs and a writing aptitude test; also a chat room and other resources for writers.

JERRY B. JENKINS CHRISTIAN WRITERS GUILD. Contact: Wayne Atcheson, Admissions Mgr., PO Box 88196, Black Forest, CO 80908. Toll-free (866)495-5177. E-mail: Contact Us@ChristianWritersGuild.com. Website: www.ChristianWritersGuild.com. This International organization of more than 1,500 members offers mentor-guided correspondence courses for adults (two-year *Apprentice* and advanced one-year *Journeyman*) and youth (*Pages*: ages 9-12 and *Squires*: 13 and up) with two payment plans available. The Guild also offers annual memberships, writing contests (winners receive large cash advance and book contract with a major CBA publisher), Writing for the Soul conferences, critique service, writers resource books, monthly newsletter, and more. Call for a Free Starter Kit.

LONG RIDGE WRITERS GROUP, 95 Long Ridge Rd., West Redding CT 06896. Toll-free (800)624-1476. Fax (203)792-8406. E-mail: studentservices@longridgewriters group.com. Website: www.longridgewritersgroup.com. Secular correspondence course, but you may request a Christian instructor.

RIGHTEOUS WRITING. Dr. Kenneth Gentry, E-mail: kennethgentry@cs.com. Website: www.kennethgentry.com. Intensive writing course covering research, library strategy, note taking, cultivating a topic, outlining, polishing, avoiding pitfalls, approaching editors, copyrighting, marketing, and more.

WRITER'S DIGEST SCHOOL, 4700 E. Galbraith Rd., Cincinnati OH 45236. Toll-free (800)759-0963. Fax (513)531-0798. E-mail: writersdig@fwpubs.com. Website: www.writers digest.com/wds. Novel Writing Workshop, Writing & Selling Short Stories, Writing & Selling Nonfiction Articles, and others. This is a secular correspondence course, but you may request a Christian instructor.

THE WRITING ACADEMY SEMINAR. Inez Schneider, New Member Coordinator, 4010 Singleton Rd., Rockford IL 61114. (815)877-9675. E-mail: pattyk@wams.org. Website: www.wams.org. Sponsors year-round Christian correspondence writing program and annual seminar in various locations.

WRITING SERVICES INSTITUTE (WSI), Marsha L. Drake, #109—4351 Rumble St., Burnaby B.C. V5J 2A2, Canada. Phone/fax (604)321-3555. E-mail: writeone@shaw.ca. Offers several correspondence and online courses: Write for Fun and Profit; Write for Success; Write Fiction from Plot to Print; Write with Power; Write for You: Magazine Article Writing; Write Yes!; Write Now: Young Author's Tutorial; Write Right—With Computers; and Write On! Write or e-mail for details and information on correspondence courses. Also writes company histories, biographies, résumés, and offers online tutorials. Charges negotiable fees for consultation, editing, and critique. See: www.vsb-adult-ed.com for more information on courses and author biography.

WRITING INSTRUCTION: E-MAIL/INTERNET COURSES

ABSOLUTE WRITE UNIVERSITY. Website: www.absoluteclasses.com. Online courses in photo-journalism, romance writing, writing children's picture books, creativity, spiritual writing, and more.

BARNES & NOBLE ONLINE WRITING COURSES. Website: www.bn.com. Click on "B&N University."

THE CHRISTIAN COMMUNICATOR MANUSCRIPT CRITIQUE SERVICE E-MAIL HANDS-ON COURSE. For information contact: Susan Titus Osborn, 3133 Puente St., Fullerton CA 92835-1952. (714)990-1532. Toll-free (877)428-7992. E-mail: Susanosb@aol.com. Website: www.christiancommunicator.com. Offers basic writing course available by e-mail. Includes 6 lessons online, handouts, and critiqued assignments. Cost for entire course: $150, by the lesson: $30.

COFFEEHOUSE FOR WRITERS. Website: http://members.tripod.com/coffeehouse4writers. Offers a variety of 4-week writing workshops for $80.

E-MAIL NEWSLETTERS FOR WRITERS. Websites: (1) www.publishersweekly.com; (2) www.parapub.com; (3) www.writing-world.com.

EZ WRITER ONLINE. Website: www.ezwriteronline.com. E-mail: information@ezwriteronline.com. Beginning and intermediate fiction writing classes. Multipublished, award-winning Lauraine Snelling with fiction coach Kathleen Wright. Developing characters, pacing, etc. Download lessons, get feedback on your work. Some feedback courses, some lecture. Free motivational sound file to download when you visit. Single classes offered for that one spot where you need most help. Intermediate classes offered intermittently: Fiction Fundementals ongoing. Costs vary. Check Website.

HOW TO LAND HIGH-PAYING ASSIGNMENTS. E-book encourages writers to "seek the assignment, NOT the sale." Shows aspiring writers how to get an editor's attention without spending hours, days, and weeks on a manuscript. Website: www.dougschmidt.com.

LIFE WRITE. Website: http://LifeWrite.com. Free 9-lesson writing course.

NOVEL ADVICE. Offers online courses and resources for writers. Website: www.noveladvice.com.

ONLINE WORKSHOPS BY MARY EMMA ALLEN, 55 Binks Hill Rd., Plymouth NH 03264. Fax (603)536-4851. E-mail: me.allen@juno.com. Website: http://homepage.fcgnetworks.net/jetent/mea. Topics include: Column Writing 101, Introduction to Self-Publishing, Writing for Children, Writing Your Family History, Writing for Regional Markets, Writing for the Weekly Newspaper, Travel Writing, Marketing Your Manuscripts, Poetry Writing, Writing & Publishing on the Internet, Writing Life Essays, and Scrapbooking Your Family History. Mary Emma offers these workshops at conferences, in schools and libraries, as well as online. She also develops writing workshops for children.

ONLINE WRITING COURSES. Website: www.ed2go.com/courses.html. Click on "Writing Courses" for a list of 20 online writing classes.

PARADIGM ONLINE WRITING ASSISTANT. Website: www.powa.org. An interactive, menu-driven, online writer's guide. Useful for all writers, from inexperienced to advanced.

+PERELANDRA COLLEGE. Offers online degrees in Creative Writing (some short in-residence may be required) to fill the need for skilled, imaginative, thoughtful Christian writers to offer alternatives to the primarily formulaic offerings of Christian publishers and books of secular presses.

+SENTENCE SENSE. A free online writing composition class. Website: Webster.commnet.edu/sensen.

+TRINITY COLLEGE WRITING CENTER ONLINE. Some good tips and lots of help. Website: www.trincoll.edu/depts/writcent/.

VIRTUAL UNIVERSITY. Website: http://vu.org/calendar.html. Offers online courses for writers.

WRITERS' HELPER. Phone/fax (910)980-1126. E-mail: publisher@teenlight.org. Website: www.writershelper.org/workshop.htm. Annette Dammer, administrator. Dedicated to Christian writers and their dreams. Interactive, easy-to-use, online workshops taught by Christian published authors. Many free resources, workshops, e-zine, and support group. Home of the free, award-winning "Write From the Bible" workshop.

WRITERS' ONLINE WORKSHOPS, 4700 E. Galbraith Rd., Cincinnati OH 45236. (513)531-0798. Toll-free (800)759-0963. Website: www.WritersOnlineWorkshops.com. Beginning to advanced workshops in fiction, nonfiction, proposal writing, and more. This is a secular Internet-based course, but you may request a Christian instructor. Sponsored by Writer's Digest. New courses to improve your writing and advance your career: Essentials of Mystery Writing; Essentials of Business Writing; Essentials of Romance Writing; Writing Effective Dialogue; Point of View Workshop; Writing the Query Letter Workshop; Focus on Writing for Children; Advanced Memoir and Nonfiction Book Writer's Workshop. If you want to work on your writing but feel you don't have the time, extended workshops give you the same instruction and information but with seven months instead of the usual two or three months: Extended Getting Started in Writing Workshop; Extended Novel Writing Workshop.

WRITERS ON THE NET. Website: www.writers.com. Online classes and a Writing Tips section.

WRITERS WEEKLY UNIVERSITY. Website: http://writersweekly.com/wwu/courses. Offers online courses for writers. Topics include: plot, characters, life stories, marketing, newsletter writing, and novels.

WRITING BASICS. Website: www.write4christ.com. E-books that integrate faith and writing.

WRITING CLASSES. Website: www.writingclasses.com.

THE WRITING SCHOOL HOME PAGE. Website: www.mythbreakers.com/writingschool.

WRITING INSTRUCTION: MISCELLANEOUS HELPS

+A TO Z WRITING. Writing tips for every writing need. Website: www.atozwriting.com.

BOOKS ON WRITING. (1) *Art and Soul: 156 Ways to Free Your Creative Spirit* by Pam Grout (2000), Andrews McNeel Pub., ISBN 0740704826. (2) *On Writing: A Memoir of the Craft* by Stephen King (2000), Scribner, ISBN 0684853523. (3) *Forest for the Trees: An Editor's Advice to Writers* by Betsy Lerner (2000), Riverhead Books, ISBN 1573228575. (4) *Feature & Magazine Writing: Action, Angle and Anecdotes* by David E Sumner and Holly G. Miller (2005), Blackwell Publishing, ISBN 0813805198.

CARTOONING. Website: www.cartoon.org/home.htm. Website for the International Museum of Cartoon Art. Includes information on how to become a cartoonist. Click on "Advice."

COMIC BOOKS. Website: www.jazmaonline.com. Offers information for aspiring comic book writers with interviews, reviews, message board, and classifieds.

+THE EASY WAY TO WRITE. Excellent resources for writers of any genre and level writing skill. Offers free writing lessons and a newsletter. Website: www.easywaytowrite.com?hop=bizwings.

E-BOOK PUBLISHING. *How to Get Your E-Book Published: An Insider's Guide to the World of Electronic Publishing* by Richard Curtis and William Thomas Quick. ISBN 1582970955.

THE ECLECTIC WRITER. How-to articles for writers. Website: www.eclectics.com/writing/writing.html.

EDITING. Website: www.queryletters.com. Provides in-depth editing of fiction and nonfiction manuscripts. See also the "Editorial Services" section in the back of this Market Guide.

FIFTEEN WRITING EXERCISES. Website: www.poewar.com/articles/15_exercises.htm.

+FONT IDENTIFYER. Need to find the name of a typeface? See What the Font? Website: www.myfonts.com/WhatTheFont/.

FREELANCE WRITING. Website: www.suite101.com/topics/page.cfm/1639. Practical helps for freelancers, such as how to write a query letter.

GETTING ORGANIZED. Websites: (1) www.onlineorganizing.com; (2) www.succeedingin business.com/catalog. Offers many e-books, including *Winning the Fight Between You and Your Desk* by Jeffrey Mayer.

MANUSCRIPT FORMAT. For a sample and instructions on format for an article or a book, go to: (1) www.shunn.net/format.html, or (2) www.sfwa.org/writing/format_betancourt.htm.

+ME WRITE A SYNOPSIS? This site might help to handle that dreaded sales tool. Website: www.vivianbeck.com/writing/tips/mewrite.htm.

+NEWSTHINKING. Thoughts on writing by Bob Baker, LA Times editor. Website: www.news thinking.com.

NONFICTION BOOK PROPOSAL. Website: http://co.essortment.com/bookproposal_rjwi.htm.

+PEN NAME. Here's a fun site to find your own pen name by supplying personal info. Website: www.testcafe.com/pen/.

PERSONAL WRITING COACH. Expert help for those seeking a life coach to guide them in their writing career. E-mail: maryanne@LifeCoachingConsultants.us. Website: www.LifeCoaching Consultants.us.

PRINT ON DEMAND. Website: www.booksandtales.com/pod. *An Incomplete Guide to Print on Demand Publishers* by Clea Saal compares different POD publishers and their services.

PROFESSIONAL WRITING DEGREE. Website: http://fw.taylor.edu/academics/departments/cas/programs/pwr. Taylor University Fort Wayne has initiated the country's first Professional Writing major at an accredited Christian university. The four-year bachelor of arts program includes freelance writing, fiction, business and technical writing, journalism, scriptwriting, public relations, editorial and opinion writing, TV and radio news broadcasting, speech writing, and academic research writing. Write to Office of Admissions, TUFW, 1025 W. Rudisill Blvd., Fort Wayne IN 46807. (260)744-8600. Toll-free (800)233-3922. E-mail: refer to online contact form.

+PROVIDENCE JOURNAL TIPS. Writing tips from the Providence Journal include weekly lessons on the craft of newspaper writing. Website: www.projo.com/words.

Q&A COLUMN. The University of Chicago Press (publisher of the *Chicago Manual of Style*, 15th edition) has a Q&A column written by their Manuscript Editing Department on their Website: www.press.uchicago.edu/Misc/Chicago/cmosfaq.cmosfaq.html.

QUERY LETTERS. Websites: (1) http://personal.rockbridge.net/gavaler/TheArtoftheQuery .html. The Art of the Query; (2) www.writing-world.com/basics/query.shtml. How to Write a Successful Query Letter; (3) www.writing-world.com/basics/email.shtml. Preparing E-mail Queries; (4) www.powernet.net/~scrnplay/Queryletterbk.html. Query letter sample; (5) www.eclectics.com/articles/query.html; (6) www.poewar.com/articles/query_letter .htm; (7) www.jkelman.com/misc/queryletter.html; (8) www.geocities.com/charlottedillon 2000/query.html.

RENSSELEAR WRITING CENTER ONLINE HANDOUTS. Website: www.rpi.edu/web/writing center/handouts.html. Includes 18 handouts on Basic Punctuation and Mechanics under Revising Prose heading.

SALLY STUART'S GUIDE TO GETTING PUBLISHED. This book tells you everything you need to know about how to write for publication and get published. Special $10 postpaid from Christian Writers Marketplace, 1647 S.W. Pheasant Dr., Aloha OR 97006. Website: www .stuartmarket.com.

+SPARE TIME NOVELIST. Website: http://sparetimenovelist.netfirms.com/stntitanic.html.

SPIRITUAL JOURNAL. Ron Klug has revised his book *How to Keep a Spiritual Journal: A Guide to Journal Keeping for Inner Growth and Personal Discovery* (Augsburg Books, 2002). For the writer, a journal is a safe place to practice writing, to capture ideas and material, and to explore the writing process. This substantial revision of a widely read book on journaling from a Christian perspective offers dozens of writing exercises, a new chapter on writing for healing, and ideas on how to harvest the journal. Included is a guide for forming a journaling group and an extensive bibliography of books, tapes, and Websites. You may order the guide ($17 postpaid) from Christian Writers Marketplace, 1647 S.W. Pheasant Dr., Aloha OR 97006. Website: www.stuartmarket.com.

SUBMISSIONS. Website: www.yudkin.com/publish.htm. Article about freelance writing and submission procedures.

TEACHING RESOURCES. (1) *You Can Improve Your Students' Writing Skills Immediately* by David Melton, ISBN 0933849672; (2) *Writing Toward Home* by Georgia Heard, ISBN 0435081241; and (3) *Where I'm From* by George Ella Lyon, ISBN 1888842121.

TESTIMONIES. Website: www.gospelcom.net/guide/resources/angie/php. Article showing how to make a testimony target non-Christian readers. Also in English; click on Leia em Ingles.

+WRITENOW! Lynn Colwell is launching a program to help aspiring writers kick start their writing careers. You can help with the design per your needs. Input welcome. Website: www.bloomngrow.net/page/page/1277566.htm.

WRITER'S APPRENTICE. Website: www.writersapprentice.com. Tina Miller, publisher. Free print magazine for new and intermediate writers.

WRITERS CONFERENCE GUIDELINES. Website: www.WritersConferenceGuidelines.com. A Website dedicated to helping writers master the conference submissions process. Learn what goes into writing your submission package, and how to do it right. Information on cover letters, queries, book proposals, article and manuscript formats, genre tips, meeting with faculty, making the most of your conference, and much more. Contributions from editors, publishers, agents, and experienced writers.

WRITER'S ULTIMATE RESOURCE GUIDE. Website: www.writersdigest.com. This book contains 1600 conferences, writing books that belong on your shelf, specific contact information and Website links, and much more.

WRITERS WEEKLY. Website: www.writersweekly.com/index-starterkit.htm. Free Internet newsletter for writers. Subscribe and receive the free e-book *How to Be a Freelance Writer* (with 103 paying markets).

WRITING ARTICLES. Website: www.writing.org. Durant Imboden's articles for writers.

WRITING UPDATE FROM WRITER'S DIGEST. This is a periodic, free e-mail newsletter from the editors at Writer's Digest that includes up-to-date writing-related news and tips. Subscribe at their Website: www.writersdigest.com. Click on "Tip of the Week."

WRITING WORLD. Website: www.writing-world.com. Good site for writers including a step-by-step guide to launching a writing career and other important tips.

YOU CAN BE A COLUMNIST by Charlotte Digregorio (1993), Baker & Taylor, ISBN 0962331813. Available at www.alibris.com.

TOPICAL/SUBJECT LISTINGS OF BOOK PUBLISHERS

One of the most difficult aspects of marketing is trying to determine which publishers might be interested in the book you want to write. This topical listing was designed to help you do just that.

First, look up your topic of interest in the following lists. If you don't find the specific topic, check the list of topics in the table of contents, find any related topics, and pursue those. Once you have discovered which publishers are interested in a particular topic, the next step is to secure writer's guidelines and book catalogs from those publishers. Just because a particular publisher is listed under your topic, don't assume that it would automatically be interested in your book. It is your job to determine whether your approach to the subject will fit within the unique scope of that publisher's catalog. It is also helpful to visit a Christian bookstore to actually see some of the books produced by each publisher you are interested in pursuing.

Note, too, that the primary listings for each publisher indicate what the publisher prefers to see in the initial contact—a query, book proposal, or complete manuscript.

R—Indicates which publishers reprint out-of-print books from other publishers.

An asterisk (*) following a topic indicates it is a new topic this year.

An (s) before a listing indicates it is a publisher listed in the Subsidy Publishers' section and does at least 50% subsidy publishing or print-on-demand. Please note that some of these publishers do some royalty publishing as well (check their listings), so if you aren't interested in a subsidy deal, you can contact them indicating you are interested only in a royalty contract.

APOLOGETICS

Aadeon Publishing
Alba House—R
AMG Publishers—R
Canticle Books—R
Christian Focus—R
(s)-Creation House—R
Crossway Books
CSS Publishing
Earthen Vessel—R
Emmaus Road—R
Fair Havens—R
(s)-Fairway Press—R
Forward Movement
Green Key Books
Harvest House
Holy Fire Publishing—R
Hope Publishing—R
InterVarsity Press—R
Lighthouse eBooks—R
Lutheran Univ. Press
Lutterworth Press—R
Magnus Press—R
(s)-One World—R
Our Sunday Visitor—R
(s)-Pleasant Word—R
(s)-Providence—R
Randall House—R

Rose Publishing
Tate Publishing
Tyndale/SaltRiver
WindRiver—R
(s)-WinePress—R
(s)-Word Alive
World Publishing—R

ARCHAEOLOGY

(s)-American Binding—R
Baker Books
Baker Trittin
Baker's Plays—R
Basic Books—R
Baylor Univ. Press—R
(s)-Black Forest—R
(s)-Brentwood—R
Christian Focus—R
Christian Writer's Ebook—R
Conciliar Press—R
Continuum Intl.—R
(s)-Creation House—R
Doubleday
Dover Publications—R
Eerdmans Publishing—R
(s)-Elderberry Press
(s)-Essence—R
Facts on File
Fair Havens—R

(s)-Fairway Press—R
FaithWalk
Four Courts Press—R
Green Key Books
(s)-Guardian Books—R
HarperSanFrancisco
Hendrickson—R
Hill Street Press—R
Holy Fire Publishing—R
InterVarsity Press—R
Johns Hopkins—R
Kirk House
Kregel—R
Lighthouse eBooks—R
(s)-Longwood—R
Lutterworth Press—R
Monarch Books—R
Mt. Olive College Press
New Seeds Books—R
New York Univ. Press
(s)-One World—R
Pacific Press
(s)-Pleasant Word—R
Randall House—R
Read 'N Run—R
Rose Publishing
T & T Clark—R
Tate Publishing
Third World Press—R

Univ. Press of America—R
WindRiver—R
(s)-WinePress—R
(s)-Word Alive
World Publishing—R
Yale Univ. Press—R

AUTOBIOGRAPHY

Ambassador-Emerald—R
(s)-American Binding—R
Baker Books
Baylor Univ. Press—R
Bethany House
Blue Dolphin
(s)-Book Publishers
(s)-Brentwood—R
Carey Library, Wm.—R
Charisma House—R
Christian Focus—R
Christian Writer's Ebook—R
Continuum Intl.—R
Created in Christ
(s)-Creation House—R
Cross Cultural—R
(s)-Dean Press, Robbie—R
Doubleday
(s)-Elderberry Press
(s)-Essence—R
Evergreen Press
(s)-Fairway Press—R
Friends United Press
Genesis Press
Georgetown Univ. Press
Greenwood/Praeger
(s)-Guardian Books—R
Guernica Editions—R
HarperSanFrancisco
Hill Street Press—R
Holy Fire Publishing—R
Kirk House
Lighthouse eBooks—R
Lighthouse Trails—R
(s)-Lightning Star Press—R
Living Books for All
(s)-Longwood—R
Lutterworth Press—R
(s)-McDougal Publishing—R
Monarch Books—R
New Seeds Books—R
(s)-One World—R
Pacific Press
(s)-Pleasant Word—R
(s)-Providence—R
Randall House—R
Read 'N Run—R
Regnery—R
Selah Publishing—R
(s)-So. Baptist Press—R

Still Waters Revival—R
Tate Publishing
(s)-TEACH Services—R
Univ. Press of America—R
VMI Publishers
WaterBrook Press
Whitaker House—R
WindRiver—R
(s)-WinePress—R
(s)-Word Alive

BIBLE/BIBLICAL STUDIES

Abingdon Press
ACU Press
Ambassador-Emerald—R
(s)-American Binding—R
AMG Publishers—R
Baker Books
Baker Trittin
Baylor Univ. Press—R
Bethany House
(s)-Brentwood—R
Bridge Resources
Broadman & Holman
Canon Press—R
Canticle Books—R
Carey Library, Wm.—R
Caribe-Betania Editores
Carson-Dellosa—R
Catholic Answers—R
Chalice Press
Charisma House—R
Christian Ed. Pub.
Christian Focus—R
Christian Writer's Ebook—R
College Press—R
Conciliar Press—R
Contemporary Drama
Continuum Intl.—R
Created in Christ
(s)-Creation House—R
Cross Cultural—R
CSS Publishing
(s)-DCTS Publishing—R
(s)-Dean Press, Robbie—R
Doubleday
Editorial Portavoz—R
Educational Ministries
Emmaus Road—R
(s)-Essence—R
Evergreen Press
(s)-Fairway Press—R
FaithWalk
5th Estate
Fortress Press
Forward Movement
Geneva Press
Good Book—R

Greenwood/Praeger
Group Publishing
(s)-Guardian Books—R
Harcourt Religion
Harrison House
Harvest House
Hensley Publishing
Holy Fire Publishing—R
Inkling Books—R
InterVarsity Press—R
Jubilant Press—R
Judson Press
Latimer Press—R
Libros Liguori
Lighthouse eBooks—R
(s)-Longwood—R
Lutheran Univ. Press
Lutterworth Press—R
Magnus Press—R
(s)-McDougal Publishing—R
MegaGrace Books
Mercer Univ. Press—R
Messianic Jewish—R
Monarch Books—R
New Hope—R
New Leaf Press—R
(s)-One World—R
Our Sunday Visitor—R
P & R Publishing—R
Pacific Press
Paradise Research—R
Pathway Press
Paulist Press
Pilgrim Press—R
(s)-Pleasant Word—R
(s)-Providence—R
Randall House—R
Read 'N Run—R
Rose Publishing
Sheed & Ward—R
Smyth & Helwys
(s)-So. Baptist Press—R
St. Anthony Messenger
T & T Clark—R
Tate Publishing
UMI Publishing—R
Univ. Press of America—R
VMI Publishers
Walk Worthy—R
WaterBrook Press
Wesleyan Publishing
Westminster John Knox
WindRiver—R
(s)-WinePress—R
Woodland Gospel
(s)-Word Alive
World Publishing—R
Yale Univ. Press—R

Youth Specialties
Zondervan

BIBLE COMMENTARY

Alba House—R
Ambassador-Emerald—R
(s)-American Binding—R
AMG Publishers—R
Baker Books
Baylor Univ. Press—R
(s)-Black Forest—R
Canon Press—R
Carey Library, Wm.—R
Caribe-Betania Editores
Catholic Answers—R
Chalice Press
Chapter Two—R
Christian Focus—R
Christian Writer's Ebook—R
College Press—R
Conciliar Press—R
Continuum Intl.—R
Cook Communications
(s)-Creation House—R
CSS Publishing
Discovery House—R
Doubleday
Editorial Portavoz—R
Eerdmans Publishing—R
(s)-Elderberry Press
(s)-Fairway Press—R
5th Estate
Forward Movement
Four Courts Press—R
Greenwood/Praeger
(s)-Guardian Books—R
Harrison House
Hendrickson—R
Holy Fire Publishing—R
Inkling Books—R
InterVarsity Press—R
Kregel—R
Libros Liguori
Lighthouse eBooks—R
Lutterworth Press—R
Messianic Jewish—R
Monarch Books—R
New Canaan
New Leaf Press—R
(s)-One World—R
Our Sunday Visitor—R
P & R Publishing—R
Pauline Books—R
Paulist Press
(s)-Pleasant Word—R
(s)-Providence—R

Randall House—R
Read 'N Run—R
Rose Publishing
Sheed & Ward—R
St. Anthony Messenger
Tate Publishing
Twenty-Third Public.
Tyndale House—R
UMI Publishing—R
Verbinum
Victor Books
Westminster John Knox
WindRiver—R
(s)-WinePress—R
(s)-Word Alive
World Publishing—R
Zondervan

BIOGRAPHY

Ambassador-Emerald—R
(s)-American Binding—R
American Book Publishing
Baker Books
Baker Trittin
Baker's Plays—R
Ballantine Books
Barbour Publishing
Basic Books—R
Baylor Univ. Press—R
Bethany House
BJU/Journey Forth—R
(s)-Black Forest—R
Blue Dolphin
(s)-Book Publishers
Boyds Mills Press—R
Branden Publishing
(s)-Brentwood—R
Canon Press—R
Canticle Books—R
Carey Library, Wm.—R
Carson-Dellosa—R
Catholic Answers—R
Chapter Two—R
Charisma House—R
CharismaKids
Christian Focus—R
Christian Writer's Ebook—R
Conciliar Press—R
Continuum Intl.—R
Created in Christ
(s)-Creation House—R
Cross Cultural—R
Crossroad Publishing—R
Cumberland House
(s)-Dean Press, Robbie—R
Dimension Books—R

Doubleday
Earthen Vessel—R
Eerdmans Publishing—R
Eerdmans/Young Readers
(s)-Elderberry Press
(s)-Essence—R
Facts on File
Fair Havens—R
(s)-Fairway Press—R
FaithWalk
Forward Movement
Four Courts Press—R
Genesis Press
Georgetown Univ. Press
Greenwood/Praeger
(s)-Guardian Books—R
HarperSanFrancisco
Hiddenspring Books
Hill Street Press—R
Holy Fire Publishing—R
Hope Publishing—R
ICS Publications—R
Inkling Books—R
Jossey-Bass
Kaleidoscope Press—R
Lighthouse eBooks—R
Lighthouse Trails—R
Living Books for All
(s)-Longwood—R
Lutterworth Press—R
Magnus Press—R
(s)-McDougal Publishing—R
Mercer Univ. Press—R
Meredith Books
Monarch Books—R
Mt. Olive College Press
New Hope—R
New Seeds Books—R
(s)-One World—R
P & R Publishing—R
Pacific Press
Pauline Books—R
(s)-Pleasant Word—R
PREP Publishing—R
(s)-Providence—R
Quintessential Books—R
Randall House—R
Ravenhawk Books—R
Read 'N Run—R
Regnery—R
Rose Publishing
Scarecrow Press—R
Scepter Publishers—R
Selah Publishing—R
Sheed & Ward—R
(s)-So. Baptist Press—R

Still Waters Revival—R
Summit Pub. Group—R
Tate Publishing
(s)-TEACH Services—R
Univ. of AR Press—R
Univ. Press of America—R
VMI Publishers
W Publishing
WaterBrook Press
Whitaker House—R
WindRiver—R
(s)-WinePress—R
Woodland Gospel
(s)-Word Alive
Yale Univ. Press—R

BOOKLETS

(s)-American Binding—R
Canon Press—R
Carson-Dellosa—R
Catholic Answers—R
Chapter Two—R
Charisma House—R
Christian Writer's Ebook—R
Created in Christ
(s)-Creation House—R
(s)-Dean Press, Robbie—R
(s)-Essence—R
Evergreen Press
Forward Movement
(s)-Fruit-Bearer Pub.
Good Book—R
(s)-Guardian Books—R
Holy Fire Publishing—R
(s)-Insight Publishing—R
InterVarsity Press—R
Intl. Awakening—R
Latimer Press—R
Libros Liguori
(s)-Lightning Star Press—R
Liguori
(s)-Longwood—R
Lutterworth Press—R
MegaGrace Books
(s)-One World—R
Our Sunday Visitor—R
P & R Publishing—R
Pacific Press
Paradise Research—R
Paulist Press
Read 'N Run—R
Rose Publishing
Tate Publishing
Trinity Foundation—R
Twenty-Third Public.
(s)-WinePress—R

(s)-Word Alive
(s)-Xulon Press—R

CANADIAN/FOREIGN

Canadian Inst. for Law—R
Christian Focus—R
Continuum Intl.—R
(s)-Essence—R
(s)-Guardian Books—R
Guernica Editions—R
Hidden Brook Press
Kindred Productions
Lighthouse eBooks—R
Lutterworth Press—R
Monarch Books—R
Northstone—R
(s)-One World—R
Skysong Press
Still Waters Revival—R
Tate Publishing
Univ./Ottawa Press
Wood Lake Books—R
(s)-Word Alive
Writers Exchange

CELEBRITY PROFILES

Baker Books
(s)-Black Forest—R
Blue Dolphin
Branden Publishing
Christian Writer's Ebook—R
Continuum Intl.—R
(s)-Creation House—R
(s)-Essence—R
(s)-Fairway Press—R
FaithWalk
Genesis Press
Good News Publishers
Greenwood/Praeger
(s)-Guardian Books—R
Hay House
Hill Street Press—R
Judson Press
Kirk House
Lighthouse eBooks—R
Lutterworth Press—R
Meredith Books
(s)-One World—R
(s)-Pleasant Word—R
Ravenhawk Books—R
Read 'N Run—R
Selah Publishing—R
Tate Publishing
TowleHouse—R
VMI Publishers
Warner Faith

Whitaker House—R
WindRiver—R
(s)-WinePress—R
Woodland Gospel
(s)-Word Alive

CHARISMATIC*

Alba House—R
(s)-American Binding—R
Canticle Books—R
Carson-Dellosa—R
(s)-Creation House—R
CSS Publishing
(s)-Fairway Press—R
Good Book—R
Holy Fire Publishing—R
Latimer Press—R
Lighthouse eBooks—R
Lutheran Univ. Press
Magnus Press—R
Nelson Ignite
(s)-One World—R
(s)-Pleasant Word—R
(s)-Providence—R
Rose Publishing
Tate Publishing
Warner Faith
WindRiver—R
(s)-WinePress—R
(s)-Word Alive
World Publishing—R
Zondervan

CHILDREN'S BOARD BOOKS

Big Idea
Candy Cane Press
Canon Press—R
Carson-Dellosa—R
Eerdmans/Young Readers
Kregel—R
Kregel Kidzone—R
Legacy Press—R
(s)-One World—R
(s)-Providence—R
Tate Publishing
WindRiver—R
(s)-Word Alive
Zondervan

CHILDREN'S EASY READERS

Ambassador Books
Baker Books
Big Idea
Branden Publishing

Canon Press—R
Carson-Dellosa—R
CharismaKids
Christian Focus—R
Conciliar Press—R
Cook Communications
(s)-Creation House—R
Creative Teaching
(s)-Dean Press, Robbie—R
E-Digital Books
Eerdmans/Young Readers
(s)-Essence—R
Evergreen Press
(s)-Fairway Press—R
Faith Kidz
5th Estate
Green Pastures—R
(s)-Guardian Books—R
Holy Fire Publishing—R
Honor Kidz
Inkling Books—R
Latimer Press—R
Legacy Press—R
Lighthouse eBooks—R
(s)-Lightning Star Press—R
McRuffy Press
(s)-One World—R
OnStage Publishing
Our Sunday Visitor—R
Pacific Press
Pauline Books—R
Pelican Publishing—R
(s)-Poetry of Today
(s)-Providence—R
Randall House—R
Ravenhawk Books—R
Read 'N Run—R
Standard Publishing
Tate Publishing
Tyndale House—R
Verbinum
VMI Publishers
WindRiver—R
(s)-Word Alive
Zondervan

CHILDREN'S PICTURE BOOKS

Ambassador Books
Baker Books
Big Idea
(s)-Black Forest—R
(s)-Book Publishers
Boyds Mills Press—R
Candy Cane Press
Canon Press—R
Carson-Dellosa—R

CharismaKids
Christian Focus—R
Conciliar Press—R
Cook Communications
Devoted to You
E-Digital Books
Editorial Portavoz—R
Eerdmans/Young Readers
(s)-Elderberry Press
(s)-Essence—R
Evergreen Press
Extreme Diva
Faith Communications
Faith Kidz
5th Estate
(s)-Guardian Books—R
Illumination Arts
Kaleidoscope Press—R
Kregel—R
Kregel Kidzone—R
Lamplighter—R
(s)-Lightning Star Press—R
Living Books for All
(s)-One World—R
OnStage Publishing
Pauline Books—R
Pelican Publishing—R
(s)-Poetry of Today
(s)-Providence—R
Randall House—R
Read 'N Run—R
Selah Publishing—R
Storytime Press
Tate Publishing
Third World Press—R
Tyndale House—R
Warner Press
WaterBrook Press
WindRiver—R
Zondervan

CHRIST

(s)-American Binding—R
Baker Trittin
Baker's Plays—R
(s)-Black Forest—R
Canticle Books—R
Catholic Answers—R
Charisma House—R
CharismaKids
Christian Focus—R
Christian Writer's Ebook—R
Cook Communications
(s)-Creation House—R
CSS Publishing
Doubleday
(s)-Fairway Press—R

5th Estate
Forward Movement
Holy Fire Publishing—R
InterVarsity Press—R
Kregel—R
Latimer Press—R
Lighthouse eBooks—R
(s)-Longwood—R
Magnus Press—R
Meredith Books
(s)-One World—R
Our Sunday Visitor—R
Pilgrim Press—R
(s)-Pleasant Word—R
(s)-Poetry of Today
(s)-Providence—R
Randall House—R
Rose Publishing
St. Anthony Messenger
Tate Publishing
VMI Publishers
Warner Faith
Wesleyan Publishing
Whitaker House—R
WindRiver—R
(s)-WinePress—R
(s)-Word Alive
World Publishing—R

CHRISTIAN BUSINESS

(s)-American Binding—R
American Book Publishing
(s)-Black Forest—R
Brown Books
Charisma House—R
Christian Focus—R
Christian Writer's Ebook—R
Cook Communications
(s)-Creation House—R
CSS Publishing
Doubleday
Evergreen Press
Fair Havens—R
(s)-Fairway Press—R
5th Estate
Green Key Books
Holy Fire Publishing—R
InterVarsity Press—R
Jossey-Bass
Jubilant Press—R
Kirk House
Lighthouse eBooks—R
Living Books for All
(s)-Longwood—R
Lutheran Univ. Press
Meredith Books
Millennium III—R

Nelson Books
(s)-One World—R
(s)-Pleasant Word—R
(s)-Poetry of Today
(s)-Providence—R
Quintessential Books—R
Randall House—R
Ravenhawk Books—R
Rose Publishing
St. Anthony Messenger
Tate Publishing
VMI Publishers
Warner Faith
WaterBrook Press
Westminster John Knox
Whitaker House—R
WindRiver—R
(s)-WinePress—R
(s)-Word Alive
World Publishing—R

CHRISTIAN EDUCATION

ACU Press
Ambassador-Emerald—R
(s)-American Binding—R
Andros Book Publishing
Baker Books
Baker Trittin
Baylor Univ. Press—R
Big Idea
(s)-Black Forest—R
Bogard Press
(s)-Brentwood—R
Bridge Resources
Broadman & Holman
Canon Press—R
Carson-Dellosa—R
Chalice Press
Christian Ed. Pub.
Christian Writer's Ebook—R
College Press—R
Contemporary Drama
Cook Communications
Created in Christ
(s)-Creation House—R
Cross Cultural—R
CSS Publishing
(s)-DCTS Publishing—R
(s)-Dean Press, Robbie—R
Doubleday
Educational Ministries
(s)-Essence—R
ETC Publications
(s)-Fairway Press—R
Faith Alive
5th Estate
Forward Movement

Gospel Publishing
Group Publishing
(s)-Guardian Books—R
Harcourt Religion
Hensley Publishing
Hill Street Press—R
Holy Fire Publishing—R
InterVarsity Press—R
Kregel—R
Lighthouse eBooks—R
Liturgical Press
Lutheran Univ. Press
Lutterworth Press—R
Master Books
Meriwether—R
Millennium III—R
Monarch Books—R
New Canaan
New Hope—R
New Leaf Press—R
Northwestern
(s)-One World—R
Our Sunday Visitor—R
P & R Publishing—R
Pacific Press
Pathway Press
Pauline Books—R
Pflaum Publishing
Pilgrim Press—R
(s)-Pleasant Word—R
(s)-Poetry of Today
(s)-Providence—R
Quintessential Books—R
Randall House—R
Reference Service
Religious Education
Rose Publishing
Scarecrow Press—R
Smyth & Helwys
(s)-So. Baptist Press—R
St. Anthony Messenger
Standard Publishing
Still Waters Revival—R
Tate Publishing
Trinity Foundation—R
UMI Publishing—R
Univ. Press of America—R
Verbinum
WindRiver—R
(s)-WinePress—R
Wood Lake Books—R
(s)-Word Alive

CHRISTIAN HOMESCHOOLING

Ambassador-Emerald—R
Andros Book Publishing

Baker Books
Big Idea
(s)-Brentwood—R
Broadman & Holman
Canon Press—R
Carson-Dellosa—R
Christian Focus—R
Christian Publications
Christian Writer's Ebook—R
Created in Christ
(s)-Creation House—R
CSS Publishing
(s)-Dean Press, Robbie—R
Emmaus Road—R
(s)-Essence—R
ETC Publications
Fair Havens—R
(s)-Fairway Press—R
5th Estate
(s)-Guardian Books—R
Harcourt Religion
Harvest House
Hensley Publishing
Hill Street Press—R
Holy Fire Publishing—R
Inkling Books—R
Jubilant Press—R
Kaleidoscope Press—R
Lighthouse eBooks—R
(s)-Longwood—R
New Leaf Press—R
(s)-One World—R
P & R Publishing—R
Pacific Press
(s)-Pleasant Word—R
(s)-Providence—R
Rainbow Publishers—R
Ravenhawk Books—R
Rose Publishing
Scarecrow Press—R
Standard Publishing
Still Waters Revival—R
Tate Publishing
Virginia Pines Press
WindRiver—R
(s)-WinePress—R
(s)-Word Alive

CHRISTIAN LIVING

Abingdon Press
Ambassador Books
Ambassador-Emerald—R
(s)-American Binding—R
AMG Publishers—R
Baker Books
Baker Trittin
Barbour Publishing

Baylor Univ. Press—R
Beacon Hill Press—R
Bethany House
(s)-Black Forest—R
(s)-Brentwood—R
Broadman & Holman
Canon Press—R
Carson-Dellosa—R
Chalice Press
Charisma House—R
Christian Focus—R
Christian Publications
Christian Writer's Ebook—R
Cladach Publishing—R
Continuum Intl.—R
Cook Communications
Created in Christ
(s)-Creation House—R
Cross Cultural—R
CSS Publishing
(s)-DCTS Publishing—R
Dimensions for Living
Discovery House—R
Doubleday
Editorial Portavoz—R
Eerdmans Publishing—R
Elijah Press
(s)-Essence—R
Evergreen Press
Fair Havens—R
(s)-Fairway Press—R
FaithWalk
5th Estate
Forward Movement
Friends United Press
(s)-Fruit-Bearer Pub.
Good News Publishers
Green Key Books
Green Pastures—R
Greenwood/Praeger
(s)-Guardian Books—R
(s)-Hannibal Books—R
HarperSanFrancisco
Harrison House
Harvest House
Haworth Pastoral—R
Hensley Publishing
Hill Street Press—R
Holy Fire Publishing—R
Hope Publishing—R
Howard Publishing
(s)-Impact Christian—R
InterVarsity Press—R
Jireh Publishing
Jossey-Bass
Judson Press

Kindred Productions
Kirk House
Kregel—R
Lamplighter—R
Latimer Press—R
Life Cycle Books—R
Lighthouse eBooks—R
Lighthouse Trails—R
Liturgical Press
Living Books for All
(s)-Longwood—R
Lutterworth Press—R
Magnus Press—R
(s)-McDougal Publishing—R
MegaGrace Books
Meredith Books
Monarch Books—R
Moody Publishers
Morehouse
Nelson Books
Nelson Ignite
New Leaf Press—R
(s)-One World—R
Our Sunday Visitor—R
P & R Publishing—R
Paradise Research—R
Pathway Press
Pilgrim Press—R
(s)-Pleasant Word—R
(s)-Poetry of Today
PREP Publishing—R
(s)-Providence—R
Quintessential Books—R
Ragged Edge—R
Randall House—R
Read 'N Run—R
RiverOak—R
Rose Publishing
Selah Publishing—R
Smyth & Helwys
St. Anthony Messenger
Standard Publishing
Still Waters Revival—R
Tate Publishing
Tau-Publishing—R
(s)-TEACH Services—R
Tyndale House—R
Tyndale/SaltRiver
UMI Publishing—R
Univ. Press of America—R
Verbinum
VMI Publishers
W Publishing
Warner Faith
WaterBrook Press
Wesleyan Publishing

Westminster John Knox
Whitaker House—R
WindRiver—R
(s)-WinePress—R
(s)-Winer Foundation—R
Woodland Gospel
(s)-Word Alive
World Publishing—R
Zondervan

CHRISTIAN SCHOOL BOOKS

Andros Book Publishing
Baker Books
Baker Trittin
Baylor Univ. Press—R
Big Idea
Broadman & Holman
Carson-Dellosa—R
Christian Liberty Press
Christian Writer's Ebook—R
Created in Christ
CSS Publishing
(s)-Dean Press, Robbie—R
ETC Publications
(s)-Fairway Press—R
5th Estate
(s)-Guardian Books—R
Holy Fire Publishing—R
Inkling Books—R
Kaleidoscope Press—R
Lighthouse eBooks—R
Lutterworth Press—R
New Canaan
(s)-One World—R
Our Sunday Visitor—R
Pacific Press
(s)-Pleasant Word—R
(s)-Providence—R
Rose Publishing
(s)-So. Baptist Press—R
Tate Publishing
Trinity Foundation—R
WindRiver—R
(s)-WinePress—R
Wood Lake Books—R
(s)-Word Alive
Wordsmiths

CHURCH HISTORY

Abingdon Press
Ambassador-Emerald—R
(s)-American Binding—R
American Cath. Press—R
Baker Books
Baker Trittin

Baker's Plays—R
Baylor Univ. Press—R
(s)-Black Forest—R
Boyds Mills Press—R
Broadman & Holman
Canon Press—R
Canticle Books—R
Carey Library, Wm.—R
Catholic Answers—R
Chalice Press
Chapter Two—R
Christian Focus—R
Christian Publications
Christian Writer's Ebook—R
College Press—R
Continuum Intl.—R
Created in Christ
(s)-Creation House—R
Cross Cultural—R
Crossroad Publishing—R
CSS Publishing
Discovery House—R
Doubleday
Editorial Portavoz—R
Eerdmans Publishing—R
Elijah Press
(s)-Fairway Press—R
FaithWalk
Fortress Press
Forward Movement
Founders Press
Four Courts Press—R
Geneva Press
Green Pastures—R
Greenwood/Praeger
HarperSanFrancisco
Hiddenspring Books
Holy Fire Publishing—R
InterVarsity Press—R
Intl. Awakening—R
Johns Hopkins—R
Jossey-Bass
Kregel—R
Libros Liguori
Lighthouse eBooks—R
(s)-Longwood—R
Loyola Press
Lutheran Univ. Press
Lutterworth Press—R
Millennium III—R
Monarch Books—R
New Canaan
(s)-One World—R
Our Sunday Visitor—R
P & R Publishing—R
Pacific Press

Paulist Press
(s)-Pleasant Word—R
(s)-Providence—R
Quintessential Books—R
Randall House—R
Resource Public.
Rose Publishing
Scepter Publishers—R
Selah Publishing—R
Sheed & Ward—R
Smyth & Helwys
Summit Pub. Group—R
Tate Publishing
Trinity Foundation—R
Twenty-Third Public.
Univ. of AR Press—R
Univ. Press of America—R
Univ./Ottawa Press
Verbinum
Victor Books
Westminster John Knox
Whitaker House—R
WindRiver—R
(s)-WinePress—R
Wood Lake Books—R
(s)-Word Alive
World Publishing—R
Zondervan

CHURCH LIFE

Abingdon Press
ACU Press
Ambassador-Emerald—R
(s)-American Binding—R
Baker Books
Baker's Plays—R
Baylor Univ. Press—R
Bethany House
(s)-Black Forest—R
(s)-Brentwood—R
Broadman & Holman
Canon Press—R
Canticle Books—R
Chalice Press
Charisma House—R
CharismaKids
Christian Focus—R
Christian Writer's Ebook—R
Continuum Intl.—R
(s)-Creation House—R
Cross Cultural—R
CSS Publishing
(s)-DCTS Publishing—R
Destiny Image—R
Doubleday
Educational Ministries

Eerdmans Publishing—R
(s)-Essence—R
Fair Havens—R
(s)-Fairway Press—R
FaithWalk
Forward Movement
Four Courts Press—R
Friends United Press
Gospel Publishing
Greenwood/Praeger
Group Publishing
(s)-Guardian Books—R
HarperSanFrancisco
Harrison House
Hill Street Press—R
Holy Fire Publishing—R
Hope Publishing—R
(s)-Impact Christian—R
InterVarsity Press—R
Jossey-Bass
Jubilant Press—R
Judson Press
Kregel—R
Libros Liguori
Lighthouse eBooks—R
Lighthouse Trails—R
Lutterworth Press—R
Monarch Books—R
(s)-One World—R
P & R Publishing—R
Pacific Press
Pathway Press
Pilgrim Press—R
(s)-Pleasant Word—R
(s)-Poetry of Today
(s)-Providence—R
Quintessential Books—R
Randall House—R
Read 'N Run—R
RiverOak—R
Rose Publishing
Selah Publishing—R
Smyth & Helwys
Tate Publishing
Twenty-Third Public.
Verbinum
VMI Publishers
W Publishing
Warner Faith
Wesleyan Publishing
Westminster John Knox
Whitaker House—R
WindRiver—R
(s)-WinePress—R
(s)-Winer Foundation—R
Wood Lake Books—R

Woodland Gospel
(s)-Word Alive
Youth Specialties
Zondervan

CHURCH MANAGEMENT*

(s)-American Binding—R
Chalice Press
CSS Publishing
Doubleday
(s)-Fairway Press—R
5th Estate
Forward Movement
Holy Fire Publishing—R
Hope Publishing—R
InterVarsity Press—R
Lighthouse eBooks—R
Lutterworth Press—R
(s)-One World—R
Our Sunday Visitor—R
(s)-Pleasant Word—R
(s)-Providence—R
Resource Public.
Tate Publishing
Warner Faith
WindRiver—R
(s)-WinePress—R
(s)-Word Alive

CHURCH RENEWAL

Abingdon Press
Ambassador-Emerald—R
(s)-American Binding—R
AMG Publishers—R
Baker Books
Baylor Univ. Press—R
Bethany House
(s)-Black Forest—R
(s)-Brentwood—R
Broadman & Holman
Canon Press—R
Canticle Books—R
Carey Library, Wm.—R
Chalice Press
Charisma House—R
CharismaKids
Christian Focus—R
Christian Writer's Ebook—R
Continuum Intl.—R
Created in Christ
(s)-Creation House—R
Cross Cultural—R
Crossroad Publishing—R
CSS Publishing
Destiny Image—R

Dimension Books—R
Doubleday
Eerdmans Publishing—R
(s)-Essence—R
Fair Havens—R
(s)-Fairway Press—R
FaithWalk
Forward Movement
Geneva Press
Greenwood/Praeger
Group Publishing
(s)-Guardian Books—R
HarperSanFrancisco
Hill Street Press—R
Holy Fire Publishing—R
Hope Publishing—R
(s)-Impact Christian—R
InterVarsity Press—R
Intl. Awakening—R
Jossey-Bass
Judson Press
Kregel—R
Latimer Press—R
Libros Liguori
Lighthouse eBooks—R
(s)-Longwood—R
Lutheran Univ. Press
Lutterworth Press—R
Magnus Press—R
(s)-McDougal Publishing—R
MegaGrace Books
Monarch Books—R
Nelson Books
(s)-One World—R
P & R Publishing—R
Pacific Press
Pilgrim Press—R
(s)-Pleasant Word—R
(s)-Providence—R
Quintessential Books—R
Randall House—R
Read 'N Run—R
Resource Public.
Rose Publishing
Selah Publishing—R
(s)-Sermon Select Press
Smyth & Helwys
(s)-So. Baptist Press—R
Tate Publishing
Twenty-Third Public.
VMI Publishers
Warner Faith
Westminster John Knox
Whitaker House—R
WindRiver—R
(s)-WinePress—R

(s)-Word Alive
Zondervan

CHURCH TRADITIONS

(s)-American Binding—R
Baker Books
Baker's Plays—R
Baylor Univ. Press—R
(s)-Black Forest—R
Boyds Mills Press—R
Broadman & Holman
Carey Library, Wm.—R
Catholic Answers—R
Chalice Press
Charisma House—R
Christian Writer's Ebook—R
Conciliar Press—R
Continuum Intl.—R
Created in Christ
(s)-Creation House—R
Cross Cultural—R
Crossroad Publishing—R
CSS Publishing
Doubleday
Eerdmans Publishing—R
(s)-Essence—R
(s)-Fairway Press—R
FaithWalk
Forward Movement
Founders Press
Greenwood/Praeger
(s)-Guardian Books—R
Hill Street Press—R
Holy Fire Publishing—R
Inkling Books—R
InterVarsity Press—R
Latimer Press—R
Libros Liguori
Lighthouse eBooks—R
Lutheran Univ. Press
Lutterworth Press—R
(s)-One World—R
Our Sunday Visitor—R
Pacific Press
Pauline Books—R
(s)-Pleasant Word—R
(s)-Poetry of Today
(s)-Providence—R
Read 'N Run—R
Resource Public.
Rose Publishing
Tate Publishing
Twenty-Third Public.
VMI Publishers

Warner Faith
Whitaker House—R
WindRiver—R
(s)-WinePress—R
Wood Lake Books—R
(s)-Word Alive
Zondervan

COMPILATIONS

(s)-American Binding—R
Baker's Plays—R
Baylor Univ. Press—R
(s)-Brentwood—R
Christian Focus—R
Christian Writer's Ebook—R
Continuum Intl.—R
(s)-Creation House—R
Doubleday
(s)-Fairway Press—R
Group Publishing
Lighthouse eBooks—R
Lighthouse Trails—R
(s)-Longwood—R
Lutterworth Press—R
Meredith Books
Obadiah Press
(s)-One World—R
(s)-Pleasant Word—R
(s)-Providence—R
RiverOak—R
Tate Publishing
Univ. Press of America—R
VMI Publishers
WaterBrook Press
Whitaker House—R
WindRiver—R
(s)-WinePress—R
Woodland Gospel
(s)-Word Alive

CONTROVERSIAL ISSUES

Aadeon Publishing
Ambassador-Emerald—R
(s)-American Binding—R
AMG Publishers—R
Baker Books
Baker's Plays—R
(s)-Black Forest—R
Blue Dolphin
Branden Publishing
(s)-Brentwood—R
Broadman & Holman
Canadian Inst. for Law—R
Canon Press—R
Canticle Books—R

Catholic Answers—R
Charisma House—R
Christian Focus—R
Christian Writer's Ebook—R
Conciliar Press—R
Continuum Intl.—R
(s)-Creation House—R
Cross Cultural—R
(s)-Dean Press, Robbie—R
Destiny Image—R
Doubleday
(s)-Essence—R
(s)-Fairway Press—R
FaithWalk
5th Estate
Genesis Press
Green Key Books
Greenwood/Praeger
(s)-Guardian Books—R
HarperSanFrancisco
Haworth Pastoral—R
Hay House
Hill Street Press—R
Holy Fire Publishing—R
Hope Publishing—R
Inkling Books—R
InterVarsity Press—R
Jireh Publishing
Kirk House
Kregel—R
Life Journey Books—R
Lighthouse eBooks—R
Lighthouse Trails—R
Lutterworth Press—R
Magnus Press—R
Millennium III—R
Monarch Books—R
New Leaf Press—R
New Seeds Books—R
(s)-One World—R
Pilgrim Press—R
(s)-Pleasant Word—R
Quintessential Books—R
Ravenhawk Books—R
Read 'N Run—R
Regnery—R
Rising Star Press
RiverOak—R
Rose Publishing
Selah Publishing—R
Still Waters Revival—R
Tate Publishing
Virginia Pines Press
VMI Publishers
Warner Faith
Whitaker House—R

WindRiver—R
(s)-WinePress—R
(s)-Word Alive

COOKBOOKS

(s)-American Binding—R
Ballantine Books
(s)-Black Forest—R
(s)-Book Publishers
(s)-Brentwood—R
Christian Writer's Ebook—R
Countryman, J.
(s)-Creation House—R
Cumberland House
Dover Publications—R
(s)-Elderberry Press
Evergreen Press
Extreme Diva
(s)-Fairway Press—R
(s)-Guardian Books—R
Hill Street Press—R
(s)-Longwood—R
(s)-One World—R
Pacific Press
Pelican Publishing—R
(s)-Pleasant Word—R
(s)-Providence—R
Read 'N Run—R
Siloam
(s)-So. Baptist Press—R
Summit Pub. Group—R
Tate Publishing
(s)-TEACH Services—R
WindRiver—R
(s)-WinePress—R
(s)-Word Alive

COUNSELING AIDS

Ambassador-Emerald—R
(s)-American Binding—R
Baker Books
Bethany House
(s)-Black Forest—R
(s)-Brentwood—R
Broadman & Holman
Chalice Press
Charisma House—R
Christian Focus—R
Christian Writer's Ebook—R
Continuum Intl.—R
Created in Christ
(s)-Creation House—R
CSS Publishing
(s)-Dean Press, Robbie—R
Dimension Books—R
Editorial Portavoz—R

(s)-Elderberry Press
(s)-Essence—R
Evergreen Press
Fair Havens—R
(s)-Fairway Press—R
FaithWalk
5th Estate
(s)-Guardian Books—R
Harcourt Religion
Harrison House
Haworth Pastoral—R
Hill Street Press—R
Holy Fire Publishing—R
InterVarsity Press—R
Judson Press
Kaleidoscope Press—R
Kregel—R
Langmarc
Life Cycle Books—R
Life Journey Books—R
Lighthouse eBooks—R
(s)-Longwood—R
(s)-McDougal Publishing—R
MegaGrace Books
Monarch Books—R
(s)-One World—R
Pilgrim Press—R
(s)-Pleasant Word—R
Quintessential Books—R
Read 'N Run—R
RiverOak—R
Rose Publishing
(s)-Sermon Select Press
Silas Publishing (books)—R
(s)-So. Baptist Press—R
Tate Publishing
VMI Publishers
WindRiver—R
(s)-WinePress—R
(s)-Word Alive
Youth Specialties

CREATION SCIENCE

Allegiance Books—R
Ambassador-Emerald—R
(s)-American Binding—R
AMG Publishers—R
(s)-Black Forest—R
Canon Press—R
Christian Focus—R
Christian Writer's Ebook—R
(s)-Creation House—R
Editorial Portavoz—R
(s)-Elderberry Press
(s)-Essence—R

Fair Havens—R
(s)-Fairway Press—R
5th Estate
Green Pastures—R
(s)-Guardian Books—R
Hill Street Press—R
Holy Fire Publishing—R
Hope Publishing—R
Inkling Books—R
Kaleidoscope Press—R
Lighthouse eBooks—R
(s)-Longwood—R
Millennium III—R
New Leaf Press—R
(s)-One World—R
Pacific Press
(s)-Pleasant Word—R
Rose Publishing
Tate Publishing
Whitaker House—R
WindRiver—R
(s)-WinePress—R
(s)-Word Alive

CULTS/OCCULT

Ambassador-Emerald—R
AMG Publishers—R
Baker Books
Baker Trittin
Baker's Plays—R
Bethany House
(s)-Black Forest—R
Broadman & Holman
Catholic Answers—R
Christian Focus—R
Christian Writer's Ebook—R
Conciliar Press—R
Continuum Intl.—R
Created in Christ
(s)-Creation House—R
Editorial Portavoz—R
(s)-Essence—R
(s)-Fairway Press—R
5th Estate
Greenwood/Praeger
(s)-Guardian Books—R
HarperSanFrancisco
Harrison House
Harvest House
Hill Street Press—R
Holy Fire Publishing—R
(s)-Impact Christian—R
Lighthouse eBooks—R
Lighthouse Trails—R
Living Books for All
Lutterworth Press—R

(s)-One World—R
Open Court—R
P & R Publishing—R
(s)-Pleasant Word—R
Randall House—R
Ravenhawk Books—R
Read 'N Run—R
RiverOak—R
Rose Publishing
Scarecrow Press—R
Selah Publishing—R
Tate Publishing
Warner Faith
Whitaker House—R
WindRiver—R
(s)-WinePress—R
(s)-Word Alive
Zondervan

CURRENT/SOCIAL ISSUES

Aadeon Publishing
Allegiance Books—R
Ambassador-Emerald—R
(s)-American Binding—R
Baker Books
Baker Trittin
Baker's Plays—R
Beacon Hill Press—R
Bethany House
(s)-Black Forest—R
Blue Dolphin
Branden Publishing
(s)-Brentwood—R
Broadman & Holman
Canadian Inst. for Law—R
Catholic Answers—R
Charisma House—R
Christian Focus—R
Christian Publications
Christian Writer's Ebook—R
Continuum Intl.—R
Created in Christ
(s)-Creation House—R
Cross Cultural—R
Cumberland House
(s)-DCTS Publishing—R
Destiny Image—R
Discovery House—R
Doubleday
Editorial Portavoz—R
Eerdmans Publishing—R
(s)-Elderberry Press
(s)-Essence—R
(s)-Fairway Press—R
FaithWalk

5th Estate
Four Courts Press—R
Georgetown Univ. Press
Greenwood/Praeger
(s)-Guardian Books—R
(s)-Hannibal Books—R
HarperSanFrancisco
Harrison House
Haworth Pastoral—R
Hill Street Press—R
Holy Fire Publishing—R
Howard Publishing
Inkling Books—R
InterVarsity Press—R
Judson Press
Kregel—R
Lamplighter—R
Life Cycle Books—R
Life Journey Books—R
Lighthouse eBooks—R
Lighthouse Trails—R
(s)-Longwood—R
Loyola Press
Lutterworth Press—R
Millennium III—R
Monarch Books—R
Nelson Books
New Hope—R
New Leaf Press—R
(s)-One World—R
Pilgrim Press—R
(s)-Pleasant Word—R
Quintessential Books—R
Ravenhawk Books—R
Read 'N Run—R
Regnery—R
Rising Star Press
RiverOak—R
Rose Publishing
Scarecrow Press—R
Selah Publishing—R
Sheed & Ward—R
Smyth & Helwys
St. Anthony Messenger
Still Waters Revival—R
Tate Publishing
Univ./Ottawa Press
VMI Publishers
W Publishing
Warner Faith
Whitaker House—R
WindRiver—R
(s)-WinePress—R
Wood Lake Books—R
(s)-Word Alive

CURRICULUM

Andros Book Publishing
Baker Trittin
Big Idea
Bogard Press
Canon Press—R
Christian Ed. Pub.
Christian Focus—R
Christian Liberty Press
Cook Communications
Created in Christ
Curriculum Associates
Easum, Bandy
(s)-Elderberry Press
(s)-Fairway Press—R
Gospel Publishing
Group Publishing
Harcourt Religion
Hill Street Press—R
Invert Books
Kremer
Lighthouse eBooks—R
Master Books
Monarch Books—R
Northwestern
(s)-One World—R
Rainbow Publishers—R
Randall House—R
Scarecrow Press—R
Smyth & Helwys
Standard Publishing
Tate Publishing
UMI Publishing—R
Univ. Press of America—R
W Publishing
(s)-WinePress—R
(s)-Word Alive
Youth Specialties

DATING/SEX

AMG Publishers—R
Baker's Plays—R
Ballantine Books
Canon Press—R
Catholic Answers—R
Charisma House—R
Christian Focus—R
Christian Writer's Ebook—R
Cook Communications
Created in Christ
(s)-Creation House—R
Discovery House—R
Doubleday
Evergreen Press
(s)-Fairway Press—R

FaithWalk
FamilyLife—R
Frederick Fell—R
5th Estate
Genesis Press
Greenwood/Praeger
HarperSanFrancisco
Harrison House
Harvest House
Holy Fire Publishing—R
InterVarsity Press—R
Invert Books
Kirk House
Kregel—R
Life Journey Books—R
Lighthouse eBooks—R
(s)-Longwood—R
(s)-One World—R
Peter Pauper Press
(s)-Pleasant Word—R
Quintessential Books—R
Randall House—R
Rose Publishing
Silas Publishing (books)—R
Siloam
Tate Publishing
VMI Publishers
Walk Worthy—R
Warner Faith
WaterBrook Press
Whitaker House—R
WindRiver—R
(s)-WinePress—R
(s)-Word Alive
Youth Specialties
Zondervan

DEATH/DYING

(s)-American Binding—R
Baker Books
Baker's Plays—R
Barbour Publishing
(s)-Black Forest—R
Blue Dolphin
(s)-Book Publishers
Chalice Press
Charisma House—R
Christian Focus—R
Christian Writer's Ebook—R
Continuum Intl.—R
Cook Communications
Created in Christ
(s)-Creation House—R
CSS Publishing
Discovery House—R
Doubleday

Editorial Portavoz—R
Eerdmans Publishing—R
(s)-Essence—R
Evergreen Press
Fair Havens—R
(s)-Fairway Press—R
FaithWalk
5th Estate
Forward Movement
Greenwood/Praeger
(s)-Guardian Books—R
HarperSanFrancisco
Harrison House
Harvest House
Haworth Pastoral—R
Hill Street Press—R
Holy Fire Publishing—R
Hope Publishing—R
InterVarsity Press—R
Kirk House
Life Cycle Books—R
Life Journey Books—R
Lighthouse eBooks—R
Liturgy Training
(s)-Longwood—R
Lutterworth Press—R
Monarch Books—R
Nelson Books
New Seeds Books—R
(s)-One World—R
Pacific Press
Paulist Press
Pilgrim Press—R
(s)-Pleasant Word—R
PREP Publishing—R
(s)-Providence—R
Quintessential Books—R
Randall House—R
Read 'N Run—R
Resource Public.
RiverOak—R
Rose Publishing
Sheed & Ward—R
Siloam
Smyth & Helwys
St. Anthony Messenger
Tate Publishing
Twenty-Third Public.
Verbinum
VMI Publishers
Warner Faith
WaterBrook Press
Whitaker House—R
WindRiver—R
(s)-WinePress—R
(s)-Word Alive
Zondervan

DEVOTIONAL BOOKS

Abingdon Press
ACU Press
Ambassador Books
Ambassador-Emerald—R
(s)-American Binding—R
AMG Publishers—R
Baker Books
Baker Trittin
Barbour Publishing
(s)-Black Forest—R
(s)-Brentwood—R
Broadman & Holman
Canticle Books—R
Carson-Dellosa—R
Chalice Press
Charisma House—R
Christian Focus—R
Christian Publications
Christian Writer's Ebook—R
Contemporary Drama
Continuum Intl.—R
Cook Communications
Countryman, J.
Created in Christ
(s)-Creation House—R
Cross Cultural—R
CSS Publishing
Devoted to You
Dimensions for Living
Discovery House—R
Doubleday
Easum, Bandy
Editorial Portavoz—R
(s)-Essence—R
Evergreen Press
Extreme Diva
Fair Havens—R
(s)-Fairway Press—R
FaithWalk
5th Estate
Forward Movement
Founders Press
Friends United Press
(s)-Fruit-Bearer Pub.
Glory Bound Books
Good Book—R
Green Key Books
Green Pastures—R
Greenwood/Praeger
Group Publishing
(s)-Guardian Books—R
HarperSanFrancisco
Harrison House
Harvest House
Hensley Publishing

Holy Fire Publishing—R
Honor Books
Honor Kidz
(s)-Impact Christian—R
Inkling Books—R
Inspirio Gifts
InterVarsity Press—R
Jireh Publishing
Judson Press
Kirk House
Kregel—R
Lamplighter—R
Latimer Press—R
Legacy Press—R
Libros Liguori
Lighthouse eBooks—R
(s)-Lightning Star Press—R
Living Books for All
Lutterworth Press—R
Magnus Press—R
(s)-McDougal Publishing—R
MegaGrace Books
Monarch Books—R
Nelson Books
New Seeds Books—R
(s)-One World—R
Opine Publishing—R
P & R Publishing—R
Pauline Books—R
Pilgrim Press—R
(s)-Pleasant Word—R
(s)-Poetry of Today
(s)-Providence—R
Ragged Edge—R
Randall House—R
Read 'N Run—R
RiverOak—R
Rose Publishing
Selah Publishing—R
Smyth & Helwys
St. Anthony Messenger
Standard Publishing
Tate Publishing
(s)-TEACH Services—R
Tyndale House—R
VMI Publishers
W Publishing
Warner Faith
WaterBrook Press
Whitaker House—R
WindRiver—R
(s)-WinePress—R
(s)-Winer Foundation—R
(s)-Word Alive
World Publishing—R
Youth Specialties
Zondervan

DISCIPLESHIP

ACU Press
Ambassador-Emerald—R
(s)-American Binding—R
AMG Publishers—R
Baker Books
Baker Trittin
Baker's Plays—R
Barbour Publishing
Baylor Univ. Press—R
Beacon Hill Press—R
Bethany House
(s)-Black Forest—R
(s)-Brentwood—R
Broadman & Holman
Canticle Books—R
Carey Library, Wm.—R
Carson-Dellosa—R
Chalice Press
Charisma House—R
CharismaKids
Christian Focus—R
Christian Writer's Ebook—R
College Press—R
Continuum Intl.—R
Cook Communications
Created in Christ
(s)-Creation House—R
Cross Cultural—R
Crossway Books
CSS Publishing
(s)-DCTS Publishing—R
Discovery House—R
Doubleday
Editorial Portavoz—R
Educational Ministries
(s)-Essence—R
Evergreen Press
Fair Havens—R
(s)-Fairway Press—R
FaithWalk
5th Estate
Forward Movement
Founders Press
Good News Publishers
Gospel Publishing
Green Key Books
Group Publishing
(s)-Guardian Books—R
(s)-Hannibal Books—R
HarperSanFrancisco
Harrison House
Hensley Publishing
Hill Street Press—R
Holy Fire Publishing—R
Inkling Books—R

InterVarsity Press—R
Jossey-Bass
Judson Press
Kirk House
Kregel—R
Lamplighter—R
Lighthouse eBooks—R
Living Books for All
(s)-Longwood—R
Lutheran Univ. Press
Lutterworth Press—R
(s)-McDougal Publishing—R
MegaGrace Books
Monarch Books—R
Moody Publishers
Nelson Books
New Hope—R
(s)-One World—R
P & R Publishing—R
Pacific Press
Pathway Press
Pilgrim Press—R
(s)-Pleasant Word—R
(s)-Poetry of Today
(s)-Providence—R
Quintessential Books—R
Randall House—R
Read 'N Run—R
RiverOak—R
Rose Publishing
Smyth & Helwys
(s)-So. Baptist Press—R
Standard Publishing
Tate Publishing
VMI Publishers
W Publishing
Warner Faith
WaterBrook Press
Wesleyan Publishing
Whitaker House—R
WindRiver—R
(s)-WinePress—R
(s)-Winer Foundation—R
(s)-Word Alive
World Publishing—R
Youth Specialties
Zondervan

DIVORCE

(s)-American Binding—R
AMG Publishers—R
Baker Books
Baker's Plays—R
Bethany House
(s)-Black Forest—R
(s)-Brentwood—R
Charisma House—R

Christian Focus—R
Christian Writer's Ebook—R
Continuum Intl.—R
Cook Communications
Created in Christ
(s)-Creation House—R
CSS Publishing
(s)-Dean Press, Robbie—R
Editorial Portavoz—R
(s)-Essence—R
Fair Havens—R
(s)-Fairway Press—R
Faith One
FaithWalk
5th Estate
Greenwood/Praeger
(s)-Guardian Books—R
Harvest House
Haworth Pastoral—R
Hill Street Press—R
Holy Fire Publishing—R
InterVarsity Press—R
Life Journey Books—R
Lighthouse eBooks—R
Lutterworth Press—R
Monarch Books—R
Nelson Books
(s)-One World—R
Pacific Press
(s)-Pleasant Word—R
Quintessential Books—R
Randall House—R
Read 'N Run—R
Regnery—R
RiverOak—R
Rose Publishing
Silas Publishing (books)—R
(s)-So. Baptist Press—R
Tate Publishing
VMI Publishers
WaterBrook Press
Whitaker House—R
WindRiver—R
(s)-WinePress—R
(s)-Word Alive
Zondervan

DOCTRINAL

ACU Press
Ambassador-Emerald—R
(s)-American Binding—R
AMG Publishers—R
Baker Books
Baker's Plays—R
Baylor Univ. Press—R
Beacon Hill Press—R
Bethany House

(s)-Black Forest—R
(s)-Brentwood—R
Broadman & Holman
Canon Press—R
Canticle Books—R
Catholic Answers—R
Chapter Two—R
Charisma House—R
Christian Focus—R
Christian Publications
Christian Writer's Ebook—R
College Press—R
Continuum Intl.—R
Created in Christ
(s)-Creation House—R
Cross Cultural—R
Crossway Books
(s)-DCTS Publishing—R
Discovery House—R
Doubleday
Editorial Portavoz—R
(s)-Essence—R
(s)-Fairway Press—R
5th Estate
Friends United Press
(s)-Guardian Books—R
Harrison House
Hill Street Press—R
Holy Fire Publishing—R
(s)-Impact Christian—R
InterVarsity Press—R
Intl. Awakening—R
Kregel—R
Latimer Press—R
Libros Liguori
Lighthouse eBooks—R
Lighthouse Trails—R
Liturgical Press
Lutheran Univ. Press
Lutterworth Press—R
Magnus Press—R
MegaGrace Books
Millennium III—R
Monarch Books—R
(s)-One World—R
P & R Publishing—R
Pacific Press
Pauline Books—R
(s)-Pleasant Word—R
Read 'N Run—R
RiverOak—R
Rose Publishing
Scepter Publishers—R
(s)-So. Baptist Press—R
Still Waters Revival—R
Tate Publishing

Trinity Foundation—R
UMI Publishing—R
Whitaker House—R
WindRiver—R
(s)-WinePress—R
(s)-Word Alive
Zondervan

DRAMA

(s)-American Binding—R
Baker Trittin
Baker's Plays—R
Big Idea
(s)-Black Forest—R
(s)-Brentwood—R
Contemporary Drama
Created in Christ
(s)-Creation House—R
Easum, Bandy
(s)-Elderberry Press
Eldridge Plays
(s)-Fairway Press—R
Genesis Press
Group Publishing
(s)-Guardian Books—R
InterVarsity Press—R
Invert Books
Lighthouse eBooks—R
Lutterworth Press—R
Meriwether—R
Monarch Books—R
New Hope—R
(s)-One World—R
OnStage Publishing
Players Press—R
(s)-Pleasant Word—R
(s)-Poetry of Today
Ravenhawk Books—R
Read 'N Run—R
(s)-So. Baptist Press—R
Tate Publishing
WindRiver—R
(s)-WinePress—R
(s)-Word Alive
Youth Specialties

E-BOOKS

Booklocker Jr.
Broadman & Holman
Canon Press—R
Christian Writer's Ebook—R
College Press—R
Created in Christ
Cross Cultural—R
(s)-Dean Press, Robbie—R
Descant Publishing

Easum, Bandy
(s)-Ekklesia Press
Jireh Publishing
Jubilant Press—R
Lighthouse eBooks—R
(s)-Lightning Star Press—R
(s)-One World—R
Paradise Research—R
(s)-Poetry of Today
Read 'N Run—R
Resource Public.
Selah Publishing—R
Smyth & Helwys
Tyndale House—R
Whitaker House—R
(s)-Word Alive
Writers Exchange
(s)-Xulon Press—R

ECONOMICS

Allegiance Books—R
(s)-American Binding—R
Baker Books
Basic Books—R
(s)-Brentwood—R
Canadian Inst. for Law—R
Christian Focus—R
Christian Writer's Ebook—R
Cross Cultural—R
Dimension Books—R
(s)-Essence—R
(s)-Fairway Press—R
FaithWalk
Frederick Fell—R
5th Estate
(s)-Guardian Books—R
Harvest House
Haworth Pastoral—R
Hill Street Press—R
Holy Fire Publishing—R
InterVarsity Press—R
Lighthouse eBooks—R
Lutterworth Press—R
Monarch Books—R
New York Univ. Press
(s)-One World—R
(s)-Pleasant Word—R
(s)-Providence—R
Quintessential Books—R
Read 'N Run—R
Regnery—R
RiverOak—R
Sheed & Ward—R
Summit Pub. Group—R
Tate Publishing
Trinity Foundation—R

Univ. Press of America—R
VMI Publishers
Whitaker House—R
WindRiver—R
(s)-WinePress—R
(s)-Word Alive

ENCOURAGEMENT*

(s)-American Binding—R
Baker's Plays—R
(s)-Creation House—R
CSS Publishing
Diamond Eyes—R
Doubleday
Fair Havens—R
(s)-Fairway Press—R
5th Estate
Holy Fire Publishing—R
Howard Publishing
InterVarsity Press—R
Lighthouse eBooks—R
Lutterworth Press—R
(s)-One World—R
Peter Pauper Press
(s)-Pleasant Word—R
(s)-Poetry of Today
(s)-Providence—R
Randall House—R
Rose Publishing
Tate Publishing
Warner Faith
WaterBrook Press
WindRiver—R
(s)-WinePress—R
(s)-Word Alive
Zondervan

ENVIRONMENTAL ISSUES

Allegiance Books—R
(s)-American Binding—R
Baker Books
Baker's Plays—R
Basic Books—R
Baylor Univ. Press—R
(s)-Black Forest—R
Blue Dolphin
Christian Focus—R
Christian Writer's Ebook—R
Doubleday
Eerdmans/Young Readers
(s)-Elderberry Press
(s)-Essence—R
Facts on File
(s)-Fairway Press—R
FaithWalk
5th Estate

Georgetown Univ. Press
(s)-Guardian Books—R
Haworth Pastoral—R
Hill Street Press—R
Holy Fire Publishing—R
InterVarsity Press—R
Johns Hopkins—R
Judson Press
Lighthouse eBooks—R
Liturgy Training
Lutterworth Press—R
Monarch Books—R
(s)-One World—R
Paragon House
(s)-Pleasant Word—R
Quintessential Books—R
Ravenhawk Books—R
Read 'N Run—R
RiverOak—R
Sheed & Ward—R
(s)-So. Baptist Press—R
St. Anthony Messenger
Tarcher, Jeremy P.
Tate Publishing
Univ. Press of America—R
VMI Publishers
WindRiver—R
(s)-WinePress—R
(s)-Word Alive

ESCHATOLOGY

Ambassador-Emerald—R
Baker Books
(s)-Black Forest—R
Broadman & Holman
Canon Press—R
Caribe-Betania Editores
Chapter Two—R
Charisma House—R
Christian Focus—R
Christian Writer's Ebook—R
College Press—R
Continuum Intl.—R
(s)-Creation House—R
CSS Publishing
(s)-DCTS Publishing—R
Fair Havens—R
(s)-Fairway Press—R
5th Estate
Four Courts Press—R
(s)-Guardian Books—R
Hill Street Press—R
Holy Fire Publishing—R
InterVarsity Press—R
Kregel—R
Lighthouse eBooks—R

Lighthouse Trails—R
(s)-Longwood—R
Lutheran Univ. Press
Lutterworth Press—R
Millennium III—R
Monarch Books—R
(s)-One World—R
P & R Publishing—R
Pacific Press
(s)-Pleasant Word—R
Rose Publishing
Selah Publishing—R
Tate Publishing
Verbinum
Victor Books
Whitaker House—R
WindRiver—R
(s)-WinePress—R
(s)-Word Alive
World Publishing—R
Zondervan

ETHICS

Aadeon Publishing
ACU Press
Alba House—R
(s)-American Binding—R
Andros Book Publishing
Baker Books
Baker's Plays—R
Baylor Univ. Press—R
Bethany House
(s)-Black Forest—R
(s)-Book Publishers
(s)-Brentwood—R
Broadman & Holman
Catholic Answers—R
Chalice Press
Charisma House—R
Christian Focus—R
Christian Writer's Ebook—R
Conciliar Press—R
Continuum Intl.—R
(s)-Creation House—R
Cross Cultural—R
Discovery House—R
Dover Publications—R
Eerdmans Publishing—R
Eerdmans/Young Readers
(s)-Elderberry Press
(s)-Essence—R
(s)-Fairway Press—R
FaithWalk
5th Estate
Fortress Press
Forward Movement

Geneva Press
Georgetown Univ. Press
Greenwood/Praeger
(s)-Guardian Books—R
Haworth Pastoral—R
Hill Street Press—R
Holy Fire Publishing—R
Howard Publishing
Inkling Books—R
InterVarsity Press—R
Jossey-Bass
Judson Press
Libros Liguori
Life Cycle Books—R
Lighthouse eBooks—R
(s)-Longwood—R
Lutheran Univ. Press
Lutterworth Press—R
Monarch Books—R
New Seeds Books—R
(s)-One World—R
Open Court—R
Opine Publishing—R
Our Sunday Visitor—R
P & R Publishing—R
Pacific Press
Paulist Press
Pilgrim Press—R
(s)-Pleasant Word—R
(s)-Providence—R
Quintessential Books—R
Randall House—R
Read 'N Run—R
Regnery—R
Rising Star Press
RiverOak—R
Sheed & Ward—R
Smyth & Helwys
St. Augustine's Press—R
Still Waters Revival—R
Tate Publishing
Trinity Foundation—R
Twenty-Third Public.
Univ. Press of America—R
Univ./Ottawa Press
Verbinum
Victor Books
VMI Publishers
Walk Worthy—R
Westminster John Knox
WindRiver—R
(s)-WinePress—R
Wood Lake Books—R
(s)-Word Alive
World Publishing—R
Yale Univ. Press—R

ETHNIC/CULTURAL

ACU Press
(s)-Ali Literary, Alfred—R
(s)-American Binding—R
Baker Books
Baker Trittin
Baker's Plays—R
Basic Books—R
Baylor Univ. Press—R
(s)-Black Forest—R
Boyds Mills Press—R
Branden Publishing
Broadman & Holman
Carey Library, Wm.—R
Caribe-Betania Editores
Christian Focus—R
Christian Writer's Ebook—R
College Press—R
Continuum Intl.—R
(s)-Creation House—R
Cross Cultural—R
(s)-Dean Press, Robbie—R
E-Digital Books
Facts on File
(s)-Fairway Press—R
FaithWalk
5th Estate
Fortress Press
Frederick Fell—R
Friends United Press
Genesis Press
Georgetown Univ. Press
(s)-Guardian Books—R
Guernica Editions—R
HarperSanFrancisco
Haworth Pastoral—R
Hensley Publishing
Hill Street Press—R
Holy Fire Publishing—R
InterVarsity Press—R
Judson Press
Kaleidoscope Press—R
Libros Liguori
Lighthouse eBooks—R
Lutterworth Press—R
Moody Publishers
New York Univ. Press
(s)-One World—R
Oregon Catholic Press
Pacific Press
Paulist Press
Pilgrim Press—R
(s)-Pleasant Word—R
(s)-Providence—R
Read 'N Run—R

Standard Publishing
Tate Publishing
Third World Press—R
UMI Publishing—R
Univ. of AR Press—R
Univ. Press of America—R
Verbinum
VMI Publishers
Walk Worthy—R
WindRiver—R
(s)-WinePress—R
(s)-Word Alive

EVANGELISM/WITNESSING

Abagail Press
ACU Press
Ambassador-Emerald—R
(s)-American Binding—R
Baker Books
Baker Trittin
Barbour Publishing
Baylor Univ. Press—R
Bethany House
(s)-Black Forest—R
(s)-Brentwood—R
Broadman & Holman
Carey Library, Wm.—R
Charisma House—R
Christian Focus—R
Christian Writer's Ebook—R
Church Growth Inst.
Continuum Intl.—R
Cook Communications
Created in Christ
(s)-Creation House—R
CSS Publishing
(s)-DCTS Publishing—R
Discovery House—R
Earthen Vessel—R
Editorial Portavoz—R
(s)-Ekklesia Press
(s)-Essence—R
Evergreen Press
Fair Havens—R
(s)-Fairway Press—R
Faith Alive
Faith One
FaithWalk
5th Estate
Forward Movement
Founders Press
Friends United Press
Gospel Publishing
Group Publishing
(s)-Guardian Books—R
(s)-Hannibal Books—R

Harrison House
Harvest House
Holy Fire Publishing—R
(s)-Impact Christian—R
InterVarsity Press—R
Judson Press
Kregel—R
Lamplighter—R
Lighthouse eBooks—R
(s)-Lightning Star Press—R
Living Books for All
(s)-Longwood—R
Lutheran Univ. Press
Lutterworth Press—R
(s)-McDougal Publishing—R
MegaGrace Books
Millennium III—R
Monarch Books—R
Moody Publishers
Nelson Books
Nelson Ignite
New Hope—R
New Leaf Press—R
(s)-One World—R
P & R Publishing—R
Pacific Press
Pilgrim Press—R
(s)-Pleasant Word—R
(s)-Poetry of Today
(s)-Providence—R
Randall House—R
Read 'N Run—R
RiverOak—R
Rose Publishing
Selah Publishing—R
(s)-So. Baptist Press—R
Still Waters Revival—R
Tate Publishing
Tyndale House—R
VMI Publishers
W Publishing
Warner Faith
Wesleyan Publishing
Whitaker House—R
WindRiver—R
(s)-WinePress—R
Woodland Gospel
(s)-Word Alive
World Publishing—R
Zondervan

EXEGESIS

Baker Books
Baylor Univ. Press—R
(s)-Black Forest—R

Canon Press—R
Catholic Answers—R
Christian Focus—R
Christian Writer's Ebook—R
Cistercian—R
College Press—R
Continuum Intl.—R
(s)-Creation House—R
CSS Publishing
Discovery House—R
Doubleday
Eerdmans Publishing—R
(s)-Essence—R
(s)-Fairway Press—R
5th Estate
Geneva Press
Greenwood/Praeger
(s)-Guardian Books—R
Holy Fire Publishing—R
InterVarsity Press—R
Johns Hopkins—R
Lighthouse eBooks—R
Lutheran Univ. Press
Lutterworth Press—R
(s)-McDougal Publishing—R
Monarch Books—R
(s)-One World—R
Open Court—R
P & R Publishing—R
Paulist Press
(s)-Pleasant Word—R
(s)-Providence—R
Randall House—R
Read 'N Run—R
Rose Publishing
Tate Publishing
Twenty-Third Public.
VMI Publishers
Westminster John Knox
Whitaker House—R
WindRiver—R
(s)-WinePress—R
(s)-Word Alive
World Publishing—R
Zondervan

EXPOSÉS

(s)-American Binding—R
Baker Books
(s)-Black Forest—R
(s)-Brentwood—R
Christian Writer's Ebook—R
(s)-Fairway Press—R
5th Estate
Greenwood/Praeger
(s)-Guardian Books—R

Holy Fire Publishing—R
Lighthouse eBooks—R
Lighthouse Trails—R
Lutterworth Press—R
(s)-One World—R
Read 'N Run—R
(s)-So. Baptist Press—R
WindRiver—R
(s)-WinePress—R
(s)-Word Alive

FAITH

Abingdon Press
Alba House—R
Ambassador-Emerald—R
(s)-American Binding—R
Baker Books
Baker Trittin
Baker's Plays—R
Baylor Univ. Press—R
(s)-Black Forest—R
Canticle Books—R
Caribe-Betania Editores
Carson-Dellosa—R
Chalice Press
Charisma House—R
Christian Focus—R
Christian Writer's Ebook—R
Continuum Intl.—R
Created in Christ
(s)-Creation House—R
Cross Cultural—R
(s)-DCTS Publishing—R
Destiny Image—R
Discovery House—R
Doubleday
Educational Ministries
Eerdmans Publishing—R
Eerdmans/Young Readers
(s)-Elderberry Press
(s)-Essence—R
Evergreen Press
Fair Havens—R
(s)-Fairway Press—R
Faith Communications
Faith One
FaithWalk
5th Estate
Forward Movement
(s)-Fruit-Bearer Pub.
Genesis Press
Good News Publishers
Gospel Publishing
Green Key Books
Greenwood/Praeger
Group Publishing

(s)-Guardian Books—R
HarperSanFrancisco
Harrison House
Harvest House
Hensley Publishing
Hill Street Press—R
Holy Fire Publishing—R
Howard Publishing
InterVarsity Press—R
Jireh Publishing
Jossey-Bass
Kirk House
Legacy Publishers
Lighthouse eBooks—R
Living Books for All
Loyola Press
Lutterworth Press—R
Magnus Press—R
(s)-McDougal Publishing—R
MegaGrace Books
Meredith Books
Monarch Books—R
Nelson Books
(s)-One World—R
Opine Publishing—R
P & R Publishing—R
Pacific Press
Paradise Research—R
Peter Pauper Press
Pilgrim Press—R
(s)-Pleasant Word—R
(s)-Poetry of Today
PREP Publishing—R
(s)-Providence—R
Quintessential Books—R
Randall House—R
Read 'N Run—R
Rising Star Press
RiverOak—R
Rose Publishing
Scepter Publishers—R
Selah Publishing—R
St. Anthony Messenger
Tate Publishing
(s)-TEACH Services—R
Twenty-Third Public.
Tyndale House—R
Tyndale/SaltRiver
UMI Publishing—R
Verbinum
Virginia Pines Press
VMI Publishers
W Publishing
Warner Faith
WaterBrook Press
Wesleyan Publishing
Whitaker House—R

WindRiver—R
(s)-WinePress—R
(s)-Word Alive
World Publishing—R
Youth Specialties

FAMILY LIFE

ACU Press
Ambassador-Emerald—R
(s)-American Binding—R
AMG Publishers—R
Andros Book Publishing
Baker Books
Baker Trittin
Baker's Plays—R
Barbour Publishing
Beacon Hill Press—R
BelleBooks—R
Bethany House
Big Idea
(s)-Black Forest—R
Blue Dolphin
(s)-Book Publishers
Boyds Mills Press—R
(s)-Brentwood—R
Broadman & Holman
Canon Press—R
Carson-Dellosa—R
Chalice Press
Charisma House—R
Christian Family
Christian Focus—R
Christian Publications
Christian Writer's Ebook—R
Cladach Publishing—R
College Press—R
Continuum Intl.—R
Cook Communications
Created in Christ
(s)-Creation House—R
Crossway Books
(s)-DCTS Publishing—R
Destiny Image—R
Devoted to You
Dimensions for Living
Discovery House—R
Editorial Portavoz—R
Eerdmans/Young Readers
(s)-Elderberry Press
(s)-Essence—R
Evergreen Press
Extreme Diva
Fair Havens—R
(s)-Fairway Press—R
Faith Communications
FaithWalk
FamilyLife (books)—R

5th Estate
Focus on the Family—R
(s)-Fruit-Bearer Pub.
Glory Bound Books
Green Pastures—R
Greenwood/Praeger
(s)-Guardian Books—R
HarperSanFrancisco
Harrison House
Harvest House
Haworth Pastoral—R
Hensley Publishing
Hill Street Press—R
Holy Fire Publishing—R
Hope Publishing—R
Ideals Books
InterVarsity Press—R
Jireh Publishing
Judson Press
Kirk House
Lamplighter—R
Langmarc
Life Cycle Books—R
Life Journey Books—R
Lighthouse eBooks—R
Liguori
(s)-Longwood—R
Loyola Press
Lutterworth Press—R
(s)-McDougal Publishing—R
Meredith Books
Monarch Books—R
Nelson Books
Nelson Ignite
New Hope—R
New Leaf Press—R
(s)-One World—R
Our Sunday Visitor—R
P & R Publishing—R
Pacific Press
Pauline Books—R
Peter Pauper Press
Pflaum Publishing
Pilgrim Press—R
(s)-Pleasant Word—R
PREP Publishing—R
(s)-Providence—R
(s)-Quiet Waters
Quintessential Books—R
Randall House—R
Read 'N Run—R
(s)-Recovery Commun.
RiverOak—R
Rose Publishing
Selah Publishing—R
Silas Publishing (books)—R
(s)-So. Baptist Press—R

Sower's Press
St. Anthony Messenger
Still Waters Revival—R
Tate Publishing
Twenty-Third Public.
Tyndale House—R
Verbinum
VMI Publishers
W Publishing
Warner Faith
WaterBrook Press
Whitaker House—R
WindRiver—R
(s)-WinePress—R
Wood Lake Books—R
Woodland Gospel
(s)-Word Alive
World Publishing—R
Zondervan

FICTION: ADULT/ RELIGIOUS

Ambassador Books
Ambassador-Emerald—R
(s)-American Binding—R
Baker Books
Baker's Plays—R
Barbour Publishing
BelleBooks—R
Bethany House
(s)-Black Forest—R
Blue Dolphin
(s)-Book Publishers
Branden Publishing
Bridge Resources
Broadman & Holman
Canon Press—R
Charisma House—R
Christian Focus—R
Christian Writer's Ebook—R
Cladach Publishing—R
(s)-Creation House—R
Cross Cultural—R
Crossroad Publishing—R
Crossway Books
(s)-DCTS Publishing—R
Descant Publishing
Destiny Image—R
Diamond Eyes—R
DiskUs Publishing
E-Digital Books
Eerdmans Publishing—R
(s)-Elderberry Press
Elijah Press
(s)-Essence—R
Evergreen Press
Fair Havens—R

(s)-Fairway Press—R
FaithWalk
5th Estate
Focus on the Family—R
Frederick Fell—R
Genesis Press
Green Pastures—R
(s)-Guardian Books—R
Guernica Editions—R
Harvest House
Hay House
Heart Quest
Heartsong Presents
Holy Fire Publishing—R
Howard Publishing
(s)-Insight Publishing—R
Jireh Publishing
Kregel—R
Lighthouse eBooks—R
Lighthouse Trails—R
(s)-Lightning Star Press—R
(s)-Longwood—R
(s)-McDougal Publishing—R
Meredith Books
Messianic Jewish—R
Millennium III—R
Moms in Print
Moody Publishers
MountainView
Mt. Olive College Press
New Spirit
(s)-One World—R
Opine Publishing—R
Pacific Press
(s)-Pleasant Word—R
(s)-Poetry of Today
(s)-Providence—R
Quintessential Books—R
Randall House—R
Ravenhawk Books—R
Read 'N Run—R
RiverOak—R
Scepter Publishers—R
Selah Publishing—R
(s)-Self Publish Press—R
Silas Publishing (books)—R
Steeple Hill
(s)-Strong Tower
Tate Publishing
Vintage Romance
Virginia Pines Press
VMI Publishers
Walk Worthy—R
Warner Faith
WaterBrook Press
Westbow Press
Whitaker House—R

WindRiver—R
(s)-WinePress—R
Wood Lake Books—R
(s)-Xulon Press—R
Zondervan

FICTION: ADVENTURE

Ambassador Books
Ambassador-Emerald—R
(s)-American Binding—R
Baker Books
Baker Trittin
Baker's Plays—R
Bethany House
BJU/Journey Forth—R
(s)-Black Forest—R
(s)-Book Publishers
(s)-Brentwood—R
Broadman & Holman
Canon Press—R
Carson-Dellosa—R
Christian Ed. Pub.
Christian Focus—R
Christian Writer's Ebook—R
Cook Communications
(s)-Creation House—R
Crossway Books
DiskUs Publishing
E-Digital Books
(s)-Elderberry Press
(s)-Essence—R
Evergreen Press
Fair Havens—R
(s)-Fairway Press—R
FaithWalk
5th Estate
Forward Movement
Glory Bound Books
Group Publishing
(s)-Guardian Books—R
Harvest House
Holy Fire Publishing—R
Howard Publishing
(s)-Insight Publishing—R
Kaleidoscope Press—R
Kregel—R
Legacy Press—R
Lighthouse eBooks—R
Lighthouse Trails—R
(s)-Lightning Star Press—R
(s)-Longwood—R
MountainView
(s)-One World—R
OnStage Publishing
Opine Publishing—R
(s)-Pleasant Word—R
PREP Publishing—R

(s)-Providence—R
Quintessential Books—R
Randall House—R
Ravenhawk Books—R
Read 'N Run—R
Selah Publishing—R
(s)-Self Publish Press—R
(s)-So. Baptist Press—R
Steeple Hill
Tate Publishing
Tweener Press
Virginia Pines Press
VMI Publishers
Warner Faith
WaterBrook Press
Whitaker House—R
WindRiver—R
(s)-WinePress—R
Zondervan

FICTION: ALLEGORY

(s)-American Binding—R
Baker Books
Baker Trittin
Baker's Plays—R
(s)-Black Forest—R
Canon Press—R
Charisma House—R
Christian Focus—R
Christian Writer's Ebook—R
(s)-Creation House—R
CSS Publishing
(s)-Elderberry Press
(s)-Essence—R
Evergreen Press
(s)-Fairway Press—R
5th Estate
Group Publishing
(s)-Guardian Books—R
Holy Fire Publishing—R
Howard Publishing
(s)-Insight Publishing—R
Lighthouse eBooks—R
MountainView
(s)-One World—R
Opine Publishing—R
(s)-Pleasant Word—R
(s)-Providence—R
Read 'N Run—R
Realms
Selah Publishing—R
Tate Publishing
VMI Publishers
Whitaker House—R
WindRiver—R
(s)-WinePress—R

FICTION: BIBLICAL

(s)-American Binding—R
Baker Books
Baker Trittin
Baker's Plays—R
BJU/Journey Forth—R
(s)-Black Forest—R
(s)-Brentwood—R
Canon Press—R
Carson-Dellosa—R
Charisma House—R
CharismaKids
Christian Focus—R
Christian Writer's Ebook—R
Cladach Publishing—R
College Press—R
(s)-Creation House—R
Creative Teaching
(s)-DCTS Publishing—R
Destiny Image—R
Eerdmans Publishing—R
(s)-Elderberry Press
Evergreen Press
Fair Havens—R
(s)-Fairway Press—R
5th Estate
Forward Movement
Group Publishing
(s)-Guardian Books—R
Holy Fire Publishing—R
Howard Publishing
(s)-Insight Publishing—R
Lighthouse eBooks—R
(s)-Longwood—R
Messianic Jewish—R
Moody Publishers
MountainView
Mt. Olive College Press
(s)-One World—R
Opine Publishing—R
Pacific Press
(s)-Pleasant Word—R
(s)-Poetry of Today
PREP Publishing—R
(s)-Providence—R
Read 'N Run—R
Realms
(s)-Self Publish Press—R
(s)-So. Baptist Press—R
Steeple Hill
(s)-Strong Tower
Tate Publishing
VMI Publishers
Walk Worthy—R
WaterBrook Press
Whitaker House—R

WindRiver—R
(s)-WinePress—R

FICTION: CHICK LIT

Baker's Plays—R
BelleBooks—R
Christian Writer's Ebook—R
(s)-Elderberry Press
Heart Quest
Holy Fire Publishing—R
Howard Publishing
(s)-Insight Publishing—R
Kregel—R
Lighthouse eBooks—R
Meredith Books
(s)-One World—R
Opine Publishing—R
(s)-Pleasant Word—R
RiverOak—R
Steeple Hill
Tate Publishing
Warner Faith
WaterBrook Press
Westbow Press
WindRiver—R
(s)-WinePress—R

FICTION: CONTEMPORARY

Ambassador Books
(s)-American Binding—R
Baker Books
Baker Trittin
Baker's Plays—R
BelleBooks—R
Bethany House
(s)-Black Forest—R
Branden Publishing
(s)-Brentwood—R
Broadman & Holman
Canon Press—R
CharismaKids
Christian Ed. Pub.
Christian Focus—R
Christian Writer's Ebook—R
Cladach Publishing—R
Cook Communications
(s)-Creation House—R
Creative Teaching
Crossway Books
Descant Publishing
Destiny Image—R
Diamond Eyes—R
DiskUs Publishing
E-Digital Books
(s)-Elderberry Press
(s)-Essence—R

(s)-Fairway Press—R
FaithWalk
Focus on the Family—R
Genesis Press
Glory Bound Books
(s)-Guardian Books—R
Harvest House
Heart Quest
Heartsong Presents
Hill Street Press—R
Holy Fire Publishing—R
Howard Publishing
(s)-Insight Publishing—R
Jireh Publishing
Kindred Productions
Kregel—R
Lighthouse eBooks—R
Lighthouse Trails—R
(s)-Longwood—R
(s)-McDougal Publishing—R
Meredith Books
Meriwether—R
Moody Publishers
MountainView
Mt. Olive College Press
New Spirit
(s)-One World—R
OnStage Publishing
Opine Publishing—R
(s)-Pleasant Word—R
(s)-Poetry of Today
(s)-Providence—R
Putnam's Sons, G. P.
Quintessential Books—R
Randall House—R
Ravenhawk Books—R
Read 'N Run—R
RiverOak—R
(s)-Self Publish Press—R
(s)-So. Baptist Press—R
Steeple Hill
Tate Publishing
Third World Press—R
Tweener Press
VMI Publishers
Walk Worthy—R
Warner Faith
WaterBrook Press
Westbow Press
Whitaker House—R
WindRiver—R
(s)-WinePress—R
Zondervan

FICTION: ETHNIC

(s)-American Binding—R
Baker Books

Baker Trittin
Baker's Plays—R
(s)-Black Forest—R
Blue Dolphin
Boyds Mills Press—R
Branden Publishing
Canon Press—R
Christian Focus—R
Christian Writer's Ebook—R
(s)-Creation House—R
(s)-DCTS Publishing—R
Destiny Image—R
DiskUs Publishing
E-Digital Books
(s)-Elderberry Press
(s)-Essence—R
Evergreen Press
(s)-Fairway Press—R
Focus on the Family—R
Genesis Press
(s)-Guardian Books—R
Guernica Editions—R
Holy Fire Publishing—R
(s)-Insight Publishing—R
Kaleidoscope Press—R
Lighthouse eBooks—R
Living Books for All
Messianic Jewish—R
MountainView
(s)-One World—R
Opine Publishing—R
(s)-Pleasant Word—R
(s)-Providence—R
Putnam's Sons, G. P.
Tate Publishing
Third World Press—R
Walk Worthy—R
WindRiver—R
(s)-WinePress—R

FICTION: FABLES/ PARABLES*

Baker's Plays—R
Holy Fire Publishing—R
Lighthouse eBooks—R
MountainView
(s)-One World—R
(s)-Pleasant Word—R
(s)-Providence—R
Tate Publishing
WindRiver—R
(s)-WinePress—R

FICTION: FANTASY

(s)-American Binding—R
American Book Publishing
AMG Publishers—R

Baker Trittin
Baker's Plays—R
BelleBooks—R
Big Idea
(s)-Black Forest—R
(s)-Book Publishers
Canon Press—R
Charisma House—R
Christian Focus—R
Christian Writer's Ebook—R
Cook Communications
(s)-Creation House—R
Descant Publishing
Destiny Image—R
DiskUs Publishing
Dover Publications—R
E-Digital Books
(s)-Elderberry Press
Evergreen Press
(s)-Fairway Press—R
Forward Movement
Genesis Press
(s)-Guardian Books—R
Holy Fire Publishing—R
(s)-Insight Publishing—R
Lighthouse eBooks—R
MountainView
(s)-One World—R
OnStage Publishing
(s)-Pleasant Word—R
Putnam's Sons, G. P.
Ravenhawk Books—R
Read 'N Run—R
Realms
Tate Publishing
VMI Publishers
WaterBrook Press
Whitaker House—R
WindRiver—R
(s)-WinePress—R

FICTION: FRONTIER

Ambassador-Emerald—R
(s)-American Binding—R
Baker Books
Baker Trittin
Baker's Plays—R
Bethany House
BJU/Journey Forth—R
(s)-Black Forest—R
(s)-Brentwood—R
Canon Press—R
Christian Focus—R
Christian Writer's Ebook—R
Cladach Publishing—R
(s)-Elderberry Press
(s)-Fairway Press—R

Glory Bound Books
(s)-Guardian Books—R
Holy Fire Publishing—R
Howard Publishing
(s)-Insight Publishing—R
Kaleidoscope Press—R
Lighthouse eBooks—R
(s)-Longwood—R
MountainView
(s)-One World—R
Opine Publishing—R
(s)-Pleasant Word—R
(s)-Providence—R
Randall House—R
Ravenhawk Books—R
Read 'N Run—R
RiverOak—R
(s)-Self Publish Press—R
(s)-So. Baptist Press—R
Tate Publishing
VMI Publishers
Whitaker House—R
WindRiver—R
(s)-WinePress—R

FICTION: FRONTIER/ ROMANCE

Ambassador-Emerald—R
(s)-American Binding—R
Baker Books
Baker's Plays—R
Barbour Publishing
Bethany House
(s)-Black Forest—R
(s)-Brentwood—R
Christian Writer's Ebook—R
(s)-Elderberry Press
(s)-Fairway Press—R
(s)-Guardian Books—R
Heartsong Presents
Holy Fire Publishing—R
Howard Publishing
(s)-Insight Publishing—R
Lighthouse eBooks—R
(s)-Lightning Star Press—R
(s)-Longwood—R
MountainView
(s)-One World—R
Opine Publishing—R
(s)-Pleasant Word—R
PREP Publishing—R
Ravenhawk Books—R
Read 'N Run—R
RiverOak—R
(s)-Self Publish Press—R
(s)-So. Baptist Press—R
Tate Publishing

Vintage Romance
VMI Publishers
Whitaker House—R
WindRiver—R
(s)-WinePress—R

FICTION: HISTORICAL

Ambassador Books
Ambassador-Emerald—R
(s)-American Binding—R
Baker Books
Baker Trittin
Baker's Plays—R
Bethany House
BJU/Journey Forth—R
(s)-Black Forest—R
Boyds Mills Press—R
Branden Publishing
(s)-Brentwood—R
Broadman & Holman
Canon Press—R
Charisma House—R
CharismaKids
Christian Focus—R
Christian Writer's Ebook—R
Cook Communications
(s)-Creation House—R
Crossroad Publishing—R
Crossway Books
Cumberland House
DiskUs Publishing
E-Digital Books
Eerdmans Publishing—R
Eerdmans/Young Readers
(s)-Elderberry Press
(s)-Essence—R
Fair Havens—R
(s)-Fairway Press—R
Faith Kidz
Green Pastures—R
(s)-Guardian Books—R
Heart Quest
Holy Fire Publishing—R
Howard Publishing
(s)-Insight Publishing—R
Lighthouse eBooks—R
(s)-Longwood—R
Millennium III—R
Mission City Press
Moody Publishers
MountainView
(s)-One World—R
OnStage Publishing
Opine Publishing—R
P & R Publishing—R
(s)-Pleasant Word—R
(s)-Providence—R

Putnam's Sons, G. P.
Quintessential Books—R
Randall House—R
Read 'N Run—R
Realms
RiverOak—R
(s)-Self Publish Press—R
(s)-So. Baptist Press—R
Steeple Hill
Tate Publishing
Third World Press—R
VMI Publishers
Warner Faith
WaterBrook Press
Whitaker House—R
WindRiver—R
(s)-WinePress—R
Zondervan

FICTION: HISTORICAL/ ROMANCE

Ambassador-Emerald—R
(s)-American Binding—R
Baker Books
Baker's Plays—R
Barbour Publishing
Bethany House
(s)-Black Forest—R
(s)-Book Publishers
(s)-Brentwood—R
Broadman & Holman
Christian Writer's Ebook—R
(s)-Elderberry Press
(s)-Fairway Press—R
(s)-Guardian Books—R
Heartsong Presents
Holy Fire Publishing—R
Howard Publishing
(s)-Insight Publishing—R
Lighthouse eBooks—R
(s)-Longwood—R
MountainView
(s)-One World—R
Opine Publishing—R
(s)-Pleasant Word—R
Putnam's Sons, G. P.
Read 'N Run—R
RiverOak—R
(s)-Self Publish Press—R
(s)-So. Baptist Press—R
Steeple Hill
Tate Publishing
Vintage Romance
VMI Publishers
Warner Faith
WaterBrook Press
Whitaker House—R

WindRiver—R
(s)-WinePress—R
Zondervan

FICTION: HUMOR

Ambassador Books
Ambassador-Emerald—R
(s)-American Binding—R
American Book Publishing
Baker Books
Baker Trittin
Baker's Plays—R
BelleBooks—R
Big Idea
BJU/Journey Forth—R
(s)-Black Forest—R
Canon Press—R
Carson-Dellosa—R
Christian Focus—R
Christian Writer's Ebook—R
DiskUs Publishing
E-Digital Books
(s)-Elderberry Press
(s)-Essence—R
Evergreen Press
(s)-Fairway Press—R
Glory Bound Books
(s)-Guardian Books—R
Holy Fire Publishing—R
Howard Publishing
(s)-Insight Publishing—R
Kaleidoscope Press—R
Lighthouse eBooks—R
(s)-Longwood—R
Meredith Books
Meriwether—R
MountainView
(s)-One World—R
OnStage Publishing
Opine Publishing—R
(s)-Pleasant Word—R
(s)-Poetry of Today
Putnam's Sons, G. P.
Read 'N Run—R
RiverOak—R
Selah Publishing—R
Tate Publishing
Vintage Romance
VMI Publishers
Warner Faith
WindRiver—R
(s)-WinePress—R

FICTION: JUVENILE (Ages 8-12)

Ambassador Books
Ambassador-Emerald—R

(s)-American Binding—R
Baker Books
Baker Trittin
BelleBooks—R
Bethany House
Big Idea
BJU/Journey Forth—R
(s)-Black Forest—R
Boyds Mills Press—R
Branden Publishing
Canon Press—R
Carson-Dellosa—R
Christian Focus—R
Cook Communications
(s)-Creation House—R
(s)-DCTS Publishing—R
(s)-Dean Press, Robbie—R
DiskUs Publishing
Dover Publications—R
E-Digital Books
Eerdmans/Young Readers
(s)-Elderberry Press
(s)-Essence—R
Evergreen Press
Fair Havens—R
(s)-Fairway Press—R
Faith Kidz
5th Estate
Forward Movement
Glory Bound Books
Green Pastures—R
Group Publishing
(s)-Guardian Books—R
Holy Fire Publishing—R
(s)-Insight Publishing—R
Kaleidoscope Press—R
Kindred Productions
Kregel—R
Lamplighter—R
Legacy Press—R
Lighthouse eBooks—R
(s)-Lightning Star Press—R
(s)-Longwood—R
Mission City Press
Moody Publishers
(s)-One World—R
OnStage Publishing
Opine Publishing—R
P & R Publishing—R
Pacific Press
Pauline Books—R
Pelican Publishing—R
(s)-Pleasant Word—R
(s)-Poetry of Today
(s)-Providence—R
Putnam's Sons, G. P.
Randall House—R

Ravenhawk Books—R
Read 'N Run—R
Selah Publishing—R
(s)-Self Publish Press—R
Tate Publishing
Third World Press—R
Tweener Press
VMI Publishers
Walk Worthy—R
WindRiver—R
(s)-WinePress—R
Zondervan

FICTION: LITERARY

Ambassador Books
Ambassador-Emerald—R
(s)-American Binding—R
Baker Books
Baker's Plays—R
BJU/Journey Forth—R
(s)-Black Forest—R
Branden Publishing
Broadman & Holman
Canon Press—R
Christian Focus—R
Christian Writer's Ebook—R
Cladach Publishing—R
Crossway Books
DiskUs Publishing
Dover Publications—R
E-Digital Books
Eerdmans Publishing—R
Eerdmans/Young Readers
(s)-Elderberry Press
(s)-Fairway Press—R
FaithWalk
Focus on the Family—R
(s)-Guardian Books—R
Guernica Editions—R
Hill Street Press—R
Holy Fire Publishing—R
Howard Publishing
(s)-Insight Publishing—R
Lighthouse eBooks—R
Millennium III—R
Moody Publishers
Mt. Olive College Press
(s)-One World—R
OnStage Publishing
Opine Publishing—R
(s)-Pleasant Word—R
(s)-Poetry of Today
PREP Publishing—R
(s)-Providence—R
Putnam's Sons, G. P.
Quintessential Books—R
Ravenhawk Books—R

Read 'N Run—R
RiverOak—R
(s)-Self Publish Press—R
Skysong Press
Steeple Hill
Tate Publishing
Third World Press—R
Virginia Pines Press
VMI Publishers
Walk Worthy—R
Warner Faith
WaterBrook Press
WindRiver—R
(s)-WinePress—R

FICTION: MYSTERY/ ROMANCE

(s)-American Binding—R
Baker Books
Baker's Plays—R
Bethany House
(s)-Black Forest—R
(s)-Book Publishers
(s)-Brentwood—R
Christian Writer's Ebook—R
Cook Communications
Destiny Image—R
(s)-Elderberry Press
(s)-Fairway Press—R
Genesis Press
(s)-Guardian Books—R
Harvest House
Heartsong Presents
Holy Fire Publishing—R
Howard Publishing
(s)-Insight Publishing—R
Kregel—R
Lighthouse eBooks—R
(s)-Lightning Star Press—R
(s)-Longwood—R
Love Inspired
Meredith Books
MountainView
(s)-One World—R
OnStage Publishing
Opine Publishing—R
(s)-Pleasant Word—R
PREP Publishing—R
Ravenhawk Books—R
Read 'N Run—R
RiverOak—R
Selah Publishing—R
(s)-Self Publish Press—R
(s)-So. Baptist Press—R
Steeple Hill
Tate Publishing

Vintage Romance
VMI Publishers
Warner Faith
Whitaker House—R
WindRiver—R
(s)-WinePress—R
Zondervan

FICTION: MYSTERY/ SUSPENSE

Ambassador-Emerald—R
(s)-American Binding—R
American Book Publishing
Baker Books
Baker's Plays—R
Bethany House
BJU/Journey Forth—R
(s)-Black Forest—R
Christian Ed. Pub.
Christian Focus—R
Christian Writer's Ebook—R
Cumberland House
Descant Publishing
DiskUs Publishing
E-Digital Books
(s)-Elderberry Press
(s)-Essence—R
Fair Havens—R
(s)-Fairway Press—R
Focus on the Family—R
Glory Bound Books
(s)-Guardian Books—R
Heart Quest
Holy Fire Publishing—R
Howard Publishing
(s)-Insight Publishing—R
Jireh Publishing
Kregel—R
Lighthouse eBooks—R
(s)-Longwood—R
Meredith Books
Moody Publishers
MountainView
Mt. Olive College Press
(s)-One World—R
OnStage Publishing
Opine Publishing—R
(s)-Pleasant Word—R
(s)-Providence—R
Putnam's Sons, G. P.
Quintessential Books—R
Randall House—R
Ravenhawk Books—R
Read 'N Run—R
Selah Publishing—R
(s)-Self Publish Press—R

Tate Publishing
VMI Publishers
Warner Faith
WindRiver—R
(s)-WinePress—R
Zondervan

FICTION: NOVELLAS

(s)-American Binding—R
Baker Books
Canon Press—R
Christian Writer's Ebook—R
Cook Communications
(s)-Elderberry Press
(s)-Fairway Press—R
(s)-Guardian Books—R
Holy Fire Publishing—R
Howard Publishing
(s)-Insight Publishing—R
Lighthouse eBooks—R
MountainView
(s)-One World—R
Opine Publishing—R
(s)-Pleasant Word—R
Quintessential Books—R
Read 'N Run—R
Tate Publishing
Vintage Romance
WindRiver—R

FICTION: PLAYS

A.D. Players Theater
(s)-American Binding—R
Baker's Plays—R
(s)-Brentwood—R
Bridge Resources
Canon Press—R
Diamond Eyes—R
Dover Publications—R
Eldridge Plays
(s)-Essence—R
(s)-Fairway Press—R
Group Publishing
(s)-Guardian Books—R
L.A. Designers' Theatre
Lillenas
Meriwether—R
Mt. Olive College Press
(s)-One World—R
Players Press—R
(s)-Pleasant Word—R
Read 'N Run—R
Resource Public.
(s)-So. Baptist Press—R
Third World Press—R

FICTION: ROMANCE

Ambassador Books
(s)-American Binding—R
American Book Publishing
Baker Books
Baker's Plays—R
Barbour Publishing
Bethany House
(s)-Black Forest—R
Christian Writer's Ebook—R
DiskUs Publishing
(s)-Elderberry Press
(s)-Fairway Press—R
Genesis Press
(s)-Guardian Books—R
(s)-Hannibal Books—R
Harvest House
Heartsong Presents
Holy Fire Publishing—R
Howard Publishing
(s)-Insight Publishing—R
Jireh Publishing
Lighthouse eBooks—R
(s)-Lightning Star Press—R
(s)-Longwood—R
Love Inspired
Meredith Books
MountainView
(s)-One World—R
OnStage Publishing
Opine Publishing—R
(s)-Pleasant Word—R
PREP Publishing—R
Read 'N Run—R
RiverOak—R
Selah Publishing—R
Steeple Hill
Tate Publishing
Vintage Romance
VMI Publishers
Warner Faith
WaterBrook Press
Whitaker House—R
WindRiver—R
(s)-WinePress—R
Zondervan

FICTION: SCIENCE FICTION

(s)-American Binding—R
American Book Publishing
Baker's Plays—R
(s)-Black Forest—R
Canon Press—R
Charisma House—R
Christian Focus—R

Christian Writer's Ebook—R
Descant Publishing
Destiny Image—R
DiskUs Publishing
Dover Publications—R
(s)-Elderberry Press
Evergreen Press
Fair Havens—R
(s)-Fairway Press—R
Forward Movement
Group Publishing
(s)-Guardian Books—R
Holy Fire Publishing—R
Howard Publishing
(s)-Insight Publishing—R
Lighthouse eBooks—R
(s)-Lightning Star Press—R
Meredith Books
MountainView
(s)-One World—R
OnStage Publishing
(s)-Pleasant Word—R
Putnam's Sons, G. P.
Ravenhawk Books—R
Read 'N Run—R
Realms
RiverOak—R
Skysong Press
Tate Publishing
VMI Publishers
WaterBrook Press
Whitaker House—R
WindRiver—R
(s)-WinePress—R

FICTION: SHORT STORY COLLECTION

(s)-American Binding—R
Baker Books
Baker Trittin
BelleBooks—R
(s)-Black Forest—R
Branden Publishing
Canon Press—R
Christian Writer's Ebook—R
(s)-DCTS Publishing—R
DiskUs Publishing
E-Digital Books
Eerdmans Publishing—R
(s)-Elderberry Press
(s)-Essence—R
(s)-Fairway Press—R
Glory Bound Books
Green Pastures—R
Group Publishing
(s)-Guardian Books—R

Holy Fire Publishing—R
(s)-Insight Publishing—R
Kaleidoscope Press—R
Lighthouse eBooks—R
(s)-Lightning Star Press—R
(s)-Longwood—R
MountainView
Mt. Olive College Press
(s)-One World—R
Opine Publishing—R
(s)-Pleasant Word—R
(s)-Providence—R
Read 'N Run—R
RiverOak—R
Tate Publishing
Third World Press—R
VMI Publishers
Walk Worthy—R
Whitaker House—R
WindRiver—R
(s)-WinePress—R

FICTION: SPECULATIVE

(s)-American Binding—R
Baker Books
Baker's Plays—R
Canon Press—R
Charisma House—R
Christian Focus—R
Christian Writer's Ebook—R
(s)-Elderberry Press
Holy Fire Publishing—R
Howard Publishing
(s)-Insight Publishing—R
Lighthouse eBooks—R
MountainView
(s)-One World—R
(s)-Pleasant Word—R
(s)-Poetry of Today
Ravenhawk Books—R
Realms
RiverOak—R
Tate Publishing
VMI Publishers
Whitaker House—R
WindRiver—R
(s)-WinePress—R

FICTION: TEEN/YOUNG ADULT

Ambassador Books
(s)-American Binding—R
American Book Publishing
AMG Publishers—R
Baker Books
Baker Trittin

BelleBooks—R
Bethany House
Big Idea
BJU/Journey Forth—R
(s)-Book Publishers
Boyds Mills Press—R
Canon Press—R
Christian Focus—R
Christian Writer's Ebook—R
(s)-Creation House—R
Diamond Eyes—R
DiskUs Publishing
E-Digital Books
Eerdmans/Young Readers
(s)-Elderberry Press
(s)-Essence—R
Evergreen Press
Fair Havens—R
(s)-Fairway Press—R
Faith Communications
5th Estate
Forward Movement
Glory Bound Books
Green Pastures—R
Group Publishing
(s)-Guardian Books—R
Holy Fire Publishing—R
(s)-Insight Publishing—R
Invert Books
Kregel—R
Lighthouse eBooks—R
(s)-Lightning Star Press—R
(s)-Longwood—R
Moody Publishers
MountainView
New Canaan
(s)-One World—R
Opine Publishing—R
P & R Publishing—R
(s)-Pleasant Word—R
(s)-Poetry of Today
(s)-Providence—R
Putnam's Sons, G. P.
Quintessential Books—R
Randall House—R
Ravenhawk Books—R
Read 'N Run—R
Selah Publishing—R
Tate Publishing
Third World Press—R
Virginia Pines Press
Walk Worthy—R
WaterBrook Press
WindRiver—R
(s)-WinePress—R
Youth Specialties
Zondervan

FICTION: WESTERNS

(s)-American Binding—R
Baker Books
Baker Trittin
Baker's Plays—R
BJU/Journey Forth—R
(s)-Black Forest—R
Canon Press—R
Christian Focus—R
Christian Writer's Ebook—R
DiskUs Publishing
E-Digital Books
(s)-Elderberry Press
(s)-Fairway Press—R
Glory Bound Books
Holy Fire Publishing—R
Howard Publishing
(s)-Insight Publishing—R
Lighthouse eBooks—R
(s)-Longwood—R
Meredith Books
MountainView
(s)-One World—R
Opine Publishing—R
(s)-Pleasant Word—R
(s)-Providence—R
Ravenhawk Books—R
RiverOak—R
Tate Publishing
VMI Publishers
Whitaker House—R
WindRiver—R
(s)-WinePress—R

FORGIVENESS

(s)-American Binding—R
Baker Trittin
Baker's Plays—R
(s)-Black Forest—R
Charisma House—R
Christian Focus—R
Christian Writer's Ebook—R
Continuum Intl.—R
Created in Christ
(s)-Creation House—R
CSS Publishing
(s)-DCTS Publishing—R
Doubleday
Editorial Portavoz—R
Eerdmans Publishing—R
Eerdmans/Young Readers
(s)-Elderberry Press
Evergreen Press
Fair Havens—R
(s)-Fairway Press—R
FaithWalk

5th Estate
Forward Movement
Good News Publishers
Gospel Publishing
Green Key Books
Greenwood/Praeger
HarperSanFrancisco
Harrison House
Harvest House
Holy Fire Publishing—R
Howard Publishing
InterVarsity Press—R
Jossey-Bass
Life Journey Books—R
Lighthouse eBooks—R
Living Books for All
Lutterworth Press—R
MegaGrace Books
Meredith Books
Nelson Books
(s)-One World—R
Opine Publishing—R
Pacific Press
Pilgrim Press—R
(s)-Pleasant Word—R
(s)-Poetry of Today
(s)-Providence—R
Randall House—R
Rose Publishing
Silas Publishing (books)—R
St. Anthony Messenger
Tate Publishing
Twenty-Third Public.
Verbinum
VMI Publishers
Warner Faith
Whitaker House—R
WindRiver—R
(s)-WinePress—R
(s)-Word Alive
World Publishing—R
Zondervan

GAMES/CRAFTS

Ambassador-Emerald—R
Baker Books
Barbour Publishing
Big Idea
Carson-Dellosa—R
Contemporary Drama
Creative Teaching
Devoted to You
(s)-Essence—R
(s)-Fairway Press—R
Frederick Fell—R
(s)-Guardian Books—R
Harcourt Religion

Holy Fire Publishing—R
Jubilant Press—R
Judson Press
Kaleidoscope Press—R
Legacy Press—R
Lighthouse eBooks—R
Lutterworth Press—R
Meriwether—R
Monarch Books—R
(s)-One World—R
Pflaum Publishing
Players Press—R
Rainbow Publishers—R
Randall House—R
Standard Publishing
Tate Publishing
WindRiver—R
Wood Lake Books—R

GIFT BOOKS

Ambassador-Emerald—R
(s)-American Binding—R
Baker Books
Ballantine Books
Barbour Publishing
Big Idea
(s)-Black Forest—R
Blue Mountain Arts
(s)-Book Publishers
Broadman & Holman
Chalice Press
Christian Focus—R
Christian Writer's Ebook—R
Contemporary Drama
Cook Communications
Countryman, J.
(s)-Creation House—R
Cumberland House
(s)-DCTS Publishing—R
(s)-Dean Press, Robbie—R
Devoted to You
Dimensions for Living
Editorial Portavoz—R
Eerdmans Publishing—R
(s)-Elderberry Press
(s)-Essence—R
Evergreen Press
(s)-Fairway Press—R
Faith Communications
5th Estate
Green Key Books
Green Pastures—R
(s)-Guardian Books—R
HarperSanFrancisco
Harvest House
Hensley Publishing
Hill Street Press—R

Holy Fire Publishing—R
Howard Publishing
Judson Press
Kaleidoscope Press—R
Kirk House
Lighthouse eBooks—R
(s)-Longwood—R
Lutterworth Press—R
Mt. Olive College Press
New Leaf Press—R
(s)-One World—R
Opine Publishing—R
Our Sunday Visitor—R
Peter Pauper Press
(s)-Pleasant Word—R
(s)-Providence—R
Randall House—R
Ravenhawk Books—R
Rose Publishing
Tate Publishing
VMI Publishers
Whitaker House—R
WindRiver—R
(s)-WinePress—R
Woodland Gospel
(s)-Word Alive

GROUP STUDY BOOKS

(s)-American Binding—R
Baker Books
Baker Trittin
(s)-Brentwood—R
Bridge Resources
Carey Library, Wm.—R
Chalice Press
Charisma House—R
Christian Focus—R
Christian Writer's Ebook—R
Continuum Intl.—R
Created in Christ
(s)-Creation House—R
CSS Publishing
Easum, Bandy
Educational Ministries
Emmaus Road—R
(s)-Essence—R
Evergreen Press
Fair Havens—R
(s)-Fairway Press—R
Forward Movement
Founders Press
Gospel Publishing
(s)-Guardian Books—R
Hensley Publishing
Hill Street Press—R
InterVarsity Press—R
Invert Books

Jubilant Press—R
Judson Press
Latimer Press—R
Lighthouse eBooks—R
Living Books for All
(s)-Longwood—R
Lutterworth Press—R
Monarch Books—R
New Hope—R
(s)-One World—R
P & R Publishing—R
Pacific Press
Pilgrim Press—R
(s)-Pleasant Word—R
(s)-Providence—R
Randall House—R
Rose Publishing
Smyth & Helwys
(s)-So. Baptist Press—R
Tate Publishing
UMI Publishing—R
VMI Publishers
WindRiver—R
(s)-WinePress—R
(s)-Word Alive
Zondervan

HEALING

Abagail Press
(s)-American Binding—R
Baker Books
Baker's Plays—R
Bethany House
(s)-Black Forest—R
Blue Dolphin
(s)-Book Publishers
(s)-Brentwood—R
Canticle Books—R
Carson-Dellosa—R
Charisma House—R
Christian Focus—R
Christian Writer's Ebook—R
Continuum Intl.—R
Cook Communications
Created in Christ
(s)-Creation House—R
CSS Publishing
Destiny Image—R
(s)-Essence—R
(s)-Fairway Press—R
Faith One
FaithWalk
5th Estate
Greenwood/Praeger
(s)-Guardian Books—R
Harrison House
Harvest House

Haworth Pastoral—R
Hay House
Hensley Publishing
Hill Street Press—R
Holy Fire Publishing—R
Hope Publishing—R
(s)-Impact Christian—R
InterVarsity Press—R
Jireh Publishing
Jossey-Bass
Latimer Press—R
Life Journey Books—R
Lighthouse eBooks—R
(s)-Lightning Star Press—R
Living Books for All
Loyola Press
Lutterworth Press—R
Magnus Press—R
(s)-McDougal Publishing—R
Monarch Books—R
Northstone—R
(s)-One World—R
Pacific Press
Paradise Research—R
Pilgrim Press—R
(s)-Pleasant Word—R
(s)-Poetry of Today
PREP Publishing—R
(s)-Providence—R
Read 'N Run—R
(s)-Recovery Commun.
RiverOak—R
Selah Publishing—R
Silas Publishing (books)—R
Siloam
(s)-So. Baptist Press—R
Tate Publishing
Verbinum
VMI Publishers
Warner Faith
Whitaker House—R
WindRiver—R
(s)-WinePress—R
Wood Lake Books—R
(s)-Word Alive
World Publishing—R

HEALTH

(s)-American Binding—R
Baker Books
Baker's Plays—R
Ballantine Books
Basic Books—R
Bethany House
(s)-Black Forest—R
Blue Dolphin
(s)-Book Publishers

Branden Publishing
(s)-Brentwood—R
Charisma House—R
Christian Focus—R
Christian Writer's Ebook—R
Cladach Publishing—R
Continuum Intl.—R
Created in Christ
(s)-Creation House—R
(s)-Elderberry Press
(s)-Essence—R
Evergreen Press
Facts on File
(s)-Fairway Press—R
Faith One
Frederick Fell—R
5th Estate
Greenwood/Praeger
(s)-Guardian Books—R
Harrison House
Harvest House
Haworth Pastoral—R
Hay House
Hill Street Press—R
Holy Fire Publishing—R
Hope Publishing—R
InterVarsity Press—R
Kaleidoscope Press—R
Langmarc
Legacy Publishers
Life Cycle Books—R
Lighthouse eBooks—R
Lighthouse Trails—R
(s)-Longwood—R
Loyola Press
Lutterworth Press—R
Meredith Books
Monarch Books—R
Nelson Books
(s)-One World—R
Pacific Press
(s)-Pleasant Word—R
(s)-Providence—R
Quintessential Books—R
Read 'N Run—R
(s)-Recovery Commun.
Regnery—R
RiverOak—R
Silas Publishing (books)—R
Siloam
(s)-So. Baptist Press—R
Square One—R
Summit Pub. Group—R
Tarcher, Jeremy P.
Tate Publishing
(s)-TEACH Services—R
Third World Press—R

Tyndale/SaltRiver
VMI Publishers
Warner Faith
Whitaker House—R
WindRiver—R
(s)-WinePress—R
Wood Lake Books—R
(s)-Word Alive

HISTORICAL

Aadeon Publishing
Allegiance Books—R
Ambassador-Emerald—R
(s)-American Binding—R
American Book Publishing
Baker Books
Baker's Plays—R
Basic Books—R
Baylor Univ. Press—R
Bethany House
(s)-Black Forest—R
(s)-Book Publishers
Boyds Mills Press—R
Branden Publishing
(s)-Brentwood—R
Canon Press—R
Canticle Books—R
Carey Library, Wm.—R
Catholic Answers—R
Chapter Two—R
Christian Focus—R
Christian Writer's Ebook—R
Conciliar Press—R
Continuum Intl.—R
(s)-Creation House—R
Cross Cultural—R
Cumberland House
Custom Communications
Dimension Books—R
Doubleday
E-Digital Books
Eerdmans Publishing—R
Eerdmans/Young Readers
(s)-Elderberry Press
(s)-Essence—R
ETC Publications
Facts on File
(s)-Fairway Press—R
FaithWalk
5th Estate
Founders Press
Four Courts Press—R
Friends United Press
Greenwood/Praeger
(s)-Guardian Books—R
HarperSanFrancisco
Hill Street Press—R

Holy Fire Publishing—R
(s)-Impact Christian—R
Inkling Books—R
InterVarsity Press—R
Johns Hopkins—R
Judson Press
Lighthouse eBooks—R
(s)-Longwood—R
Lutheran Univ. Press
Lutterworth Press—R
Mercer Univ. Press—R
Monarch Books—R
Mt. Olive College Press
New York Univ. Press
Northstone—R
(s)-One World—R
OnStage Publishing
Open Court—R
(s)-Pleasant Word—R
(s)-Providence—R
Quintessential Books—R
Ragged Edge—R
Read 'N Run—R
Regnery—R
RiverOak—R
Scepter Publishers—R
(s)-So. Baptist Press—R
St. Augustine's Press—R
Still Waters Revival—R
Tate Publishing
Third World Press—R
Trinity Foundation—R
Univ. of AR Press—R
Univ. Press of America—R
Univ./Ottawa Press
Virginia Pines Press
Whitaker House—R
WindRiver—R
(s)-WinePress—R
(s)-Winer Foundation—R
Wood Lake Books—R
(s)-Word Alive

HOLIDAY/SEASONAL

(s)-American Binding—R
AMG Publishers—R
Baker Trittin
Baker's Plays—R
Chalice Press
Charisma House—R
Christian Writer's Ebook—R
Continuum Intl.—R
Cook Communications
(s)-Creation House—R
CSS Publishing
Cumberland House
Educational Ministries

Eerdmans/Young Readers
Evergreen Press
(s)-Fairway Press—R
5th Estate
Glory Bound Books
Gospel Publishing
Greenwood/Praeger
(s)-Hannibal Books—R
HarperSanFrancisco
Holy Fire Publishing—R
Howard Publishing
InterVarsity Press—R
Latimer Press—R
Lighthouse eBooks—R
(s)-Longwood—R
Lutterworth Press—R
Meriwether—R
(s)-One World—R
P & R Publishing—R
Pelican Publishing—R
Peter Pauper Press
(s)-Pleasant Word—R
(s)-Poetry of Today
(s)-Providence—R
Rainbow Publishers—R
Randall House—R
Tate Publishing
VMI Publishers
Warner Faith
Whitaker House—R
WindRiver—R
(s)-WinePress—R
(s)-Word Alive

HOLY SPIRIT

(s)-American Binding—R
Baker Trittin
Baker's Plays—R
Baylor Univ. Press—R
(s)-Black Forest—R
Canticle Books—R
Carson-Dellosa—R
Chapter Two—R
Charisma House—R
Christian Focus—R
Christian Writer's Ebook—R
Continuum Intl.—R
Created in Christ
(s)-Creation House—R
CSS Publishing
Destiny Image—R
(s)-Fairway Press—R
5th Estate
(s)-Fruit-Bearer Pub.
Gospel Publishing
Greenwood/Praeger
Harrison House

Holy Fire Publishing—R
InterVarsity Press—R
Kregel—R
Lighthouse eBooks—R
Living Books for All
Lutheran Univ. Press
Lutterworth Press—R
Magnus Press—R
(s)-One World—R
P & R Publishing—R
Pacific Press
Pathway Press
Pilgrim Press—R
(s)-Pleasant Word—R
(s)-Poetry of Today
(s)-Providence—R
Rose Publishing
Tate Publishing
Verbinum
VMI Publishers
Warner Faith
Wesleyan Publishing
Westminster John Knox
Whitaker House—R
WindRiver—R
(s)-WinePress—R
(s)-Word Alive

HOMESCHOOLING RESOURCES

Andros Book Publishing
Baker Books
Big Idea
(s)-Book Publishers
(s)-Brentwood—R
Broadman & Holman
Canon Press—R
Carson-Dellosa—R
Christian Focus—R
Christian Publications
Christian Writer's Ebook—R
Created in Christ
(s)-Creation House—R
Curriculum Associates
Fair Havens—R
(s)-Fairway Press—R
5th Estate
Harvest House
Heart of Wisdom
Holy Fire Publishing—R
Lighthouse eBooks—R
Lutterworth Press—R
McRuffy Press
New Canaan
(s)-One World—R
P & R Publishing—R
(s)-Providence—R

Rainbow Publishers—R
Rose Publishing
Scarecrow Press—R
Tate Publishing
Virginia Pines Press
(s)-WinePress—R
(s)-Word Alive

HOMILETICS

Abingdon Press
Alba House—R
Baker Books
(s)-Black Forest—R
Broadman & Holman
Christian Focus—R
Christian Writer's Ebook—R
Continuum Intl.—R
(s)-Creation House—R
CSS Publishing
(s)-DCTS Publishing—R
Earthen Vessel—R
Eerdmans Publishing—R
(s)-Fairway Press—R
5th Estate
Group Publishing
(s)-Guardian Books—R
Holy Fire Publishing—R
InterVarsity Press—R
Judson Press
Kregel—R
Lighthouse eBooks—R
Lutterworth Press—R
Monarch Books—R
(s)-One World—R
(s)-Pleasant Word—R
(s)-Providence—R
Randall House—R
Resource Public.
Tate Publishing
Twenty-Third Public.
Verbinum
Victor Books
VMI Publishers
Westminster John Knox
Whitaker House—R
WindRiver—R
(s)-WinePress—R
Wood Lake Books—R
(s)-Word Alive

HOW-TO

(s)-American Binding—R
American Book Publishing
Baker Books
Ballantine Books
Bethany House
(s)-Black Forest—R

Blue Dolphin
(s)-Book Publishers
(s)-Brentwood—R
Broadman & Holman
Carson-Dellosa—R
Christian Writer's Ebook—R
Church Growth Inst.
(s)-Creation House—R
Cumberland House
Descant Publishing
Destiny Image—R
Diamond Eyes—R
Discovery House—R
Educational Ministries
(s)-Elderberry Press
(s)-Essence—R
Evergreen Press
(s)-Fairway Press—R
FaithWalk
Frederick Fell—R
5th Estate
Greenwood/Praeger
(s)-Guardian Books—R
(s)-Hannibal Books—R
Harcourt Religion
Hill Street Press—R
Holy Fire Publishing—R
Inkling Books—R
InterVarsity Press—R
Judson Press
Kaleidoscope Press—R
Lighthouse eBooks—R
(s)-Lightning Star Press—R
(s)-Longwood—R
Lutterworth Press—R
MegaGrace Books
Meredith Books
Meriwether—R
Monarch Books—R
Mt. Olive College Press
(s)-One World—R
Our Sunday Visitor—R
Pacific Press
Perigee Books
Players Press—R
(s)-Pleasant Word—R
(s)-Poetry of Today
(s)-Providence—R
Quintessential Books—R
Randall House—R
Ravenhawk Books—R
Read 'N Run—R
(s)-Recovery Commun.
RiverOak—R
Rose Publishing
(s)-So. Baptist Press—R
Standard Publishing

Still Waters Revival—R
Tarcher, Jeremy P.
Tate Publishing
VMI Publishers
Walk Worthy—R
Warner Faith
Wilshire Book—R
WindRiver—R
(s)-WinePress—R
(s)-Winer Foundation—R
(s)-Word Alive

HUMOR

(s)-American Binding—R
American Book Publishing
Baker Books
Baker's Plays—R
Ballantine Books
BelleBooks—R
(s)-Black Forest—R
Blue Dolphin
(s)-Brentwood—R
Broadman & Holman
Canon Press—R
Carson-Dellosa—R
Christian Writer's Ebook—R
Cook Communications
Countryman, J.
(s)-Creation House—R
Cumberland House
Dimension Books—R
(s)-Elderberry Press
(s)-Essence—R
Evergreen Press
(s)-Fairway Press—R
5th Estate
Friends United Press
Glory Bound Books
(s)-Guardian Books—R
Harvest House
Hill Street Press—R
Holy Fire Publishing—R
Howard Publishing
Ideals Books
InterVarsity Press—R
Judson Press
Kaleidoscope Press—R
Lighthouse eBooks—R
Living Books for All
(s)-Longwood—R
Loyola Press
Lutterworth Press—R
Meredith Books
Meriwether—R
Monarch Books—R
(s)-One World—R
OnStage Publishing

Pacific Press
(s)-Pleasant Word—R
PREP Publishing—R
Randall House—R
Read 'N Run—R
Regnery—R
RiverOak—R
Rose Publishing
Selah Publishing—R
(s)-So. Baptist Press—R
Tate Publishing
Verbinum
VMI Publishers
Walk Worthy—R
Warner Faith
WindRiver—R
(s)-WinePress—R
(s)-Word Alive

INSPIRATIONAL

ACU Press
(s)-Ali Literary, Alfred—R
Ambassador Books
Ambassador-Emerald—R
(s)-American Binding—R
AMG Publishers—R
Baker Books
Baker Trittin
Baker's Plays—R
Barbour Publishing
Baylor Univ. Press—R
Beacon Hill Press—R
Bethany House
(s)-Black Forest—R
Blue Dolphin
(s)-Book Publishers
(s)-Brentwood—R
Broadman & Holman
Brown Books
Canticle Books—R
Catholic Book
Chapter Two—R
Charisma House—R
CharismaKids
Christian Focus—R
Christian Publications
Christian Writer's Ebook—R
Cladach Publishing—R
Continuum Intl.—R
Countryman, J.
Created in Christ
(s)-Creation House—R
Cross Cultural—R
CSS Publishing
(s)-DCTS Publishing—R
Destiny Image—R
Dimensions for Living

Discovery House—R
Doubleday
Eerdmans/Young Readers
(s)-Elderberry Press
(s)-Essence—R
Evergreen Press
Fair Havens—R
(s)-Fairway Press—R
Faith Communications
FaithWalk
Frederick Fell—R
5th Estate
Friends United Press
Genesis Press
Glory Bound Books
Good Book—R
Green Key Books
(s)-Guardian Books—R
Harrison House
Harvest House
Hay House
Hensley Publishing
Hill Street Press—R
Holy Fire Publishing—R
Honor Books
Honor Kidz
Hope Publishing—R
Howard Publishing
ICS Publications—R
Ideals Books
(s)-Impact Christian—R
InterVarsity Press—R
Judson Press
Kaleidoscope Press—R
Kindred Productions
Kregel—R
Lamplighter—R
Langmarc
Lighthouse eBooks—R
Lighthouse Trails—R
(s)-Lightning Star Press—R
Living Books for All
(s)-Longwood—R
Lutheran Univ. Press
Lutterworth Press—R
Magnus Press—R
(s)-McDougal Publishing—R
MegaGrace Books
Meredith Books
Messianic Jewish—R
Monarch Books—R
MountainView
Nelson Books
New Leaf Press—R
(s)-One World—R
Opine Publishing—R
P & R Publishing—R

Pacific Press
Paulist Press
Pelican Publishing—R
Perigee Books
Peter Pauper Press
Pilgrim Press—R
(s)-Pleasant Word—R
(s)-Poetry of Today
PREP Publishing—R
(s)-Providence—R
Ragged Edge—R
Randall House—R
Read 'N Run—R
RiverOak—R
Selah Publishing—R
Smyth & Helwys
(s)-So. Baptist Press—R
St. Anthony Messenger
Tate Publishing
Tau-Publishing—R
(s)-TEACH Services—R
TowleHouse—R
Tyndale House—R
VMI Publishers
W Publishing
Warner Faith
WaterBrook Press
Wesleyan Publishing
Whitaker House—R
WindRiver—R
(s)-WinePress—R
(s)-Winer Foundation—R
Wood Lake Books—R
Woodland Gospel
(s)-Word Alive
World Publishing—R
Zondervan

LEADERSHIP

ACU Press
(s)-American Binding—R
AMG Publishers—R
Baker Books
Baker's Plays—R
Baylor Univ. Press—R
Beacon Hill Press—R
(s)-Black Forest—R
(s)-Book Publishers
Bridge Resources
Broadman & Holman
Chalice Press
Charisma House—R
Christian Focus—R
Christian Publications
Christian Writer's Ebook—R
Church Growth Inst.
College Press—R

Continuum Intl.—R
Cook Communications
Created in Christ
(s)-Creation House—R
CSS Publishing
(s)-DCTS Publishing—R
Destiny Image—R
Discovery House—R
Editorial Portavoz—R
(s)-Elderberry Press
(s)-Essence—R
Evergreen Press
Fair Havens—R
(s)-Fairway Press—R
FaithWalk
Frederick Fell—R
5th Estate
Gospel Publishing
Greenwood/Praeger
Group Publishing
(s)-Guardian Books—R
Harrison House
Harvest House
Hill Street Press—R
Holy Fire Publishing—R
Howard Publishing
InterVarsity Press—R
Jubilant Press—R
Judson Press
Kirk House
Lamplighter—R
Lighthouse eBooks—R
Living Books for All
(s)-Longwood—R
Lutterworth Press—R
(s)-McDougal Publishing—R
MegaGrace Books
Monarch Books—R
Neibauer Press—R
Nelson Books
(s)-One World—R
Pilgrim Press—R
(s)-Pleasant Word—R
(s)-Providence—R
Quintessential Books—R
Randall House—R
Read 'N Run—R
Resource Public.
Rose Publishing
Selah Publishing—R
Standard Publishing
Tate Publishing
Tyndale/SaltRiver
UMI Publishing
Univ. Press of America—R
VMI Publishers
Warner Faith

WaterBrook Press
Wesleyan Publishing
Whitaker House—R
WindRiver—R
(s)-WinePress—R
(s)-Winer Foundation—R
Wood Lake Books—R
(s)-Word Alive

LITURGICAL STUDIES

American Cath. Press—R
Baker Books
Baker's Plays—R
Baylor Univ. Press—R
Blue Dolphin
(s)-Brentwood—R
Canon Press—R
Catholic Answers—R
Catholic Book
Christian Writer's Ebook—R
Cistercian—R
Conciliar Press—R
Continuum Intl.—R
Cross Cultural—R
CSS Publishing
Doubleday
Eerdmans Publishing—R
(s)-Fairway Press—R
5th Estate
Forward Movement
Greenwood/Praeger
(s)-Guardian Books—R
Holy Fire Publishing—R
InterVarsity Press—R
Johns Hopkins—R
Judson Press
Lighthouse eBooks—R
Liturgy Training
Lutheran Univ. Press
Lutterworth Press—R
Morehouse
New Seeds Books—R
(s)-One World—R
Oregon Catholic Press
Pilgrim Press—R
(s)-Pleasant Word—R
(s)-Providence—R
Read 'N Run—R
Resource Public.
(s)-So. Baptist Press—R
Tate Publishing
Twenty-Third Public.
Univ. Press of America—R
WindRiver—R
(s)-WinePress—R
(s)-Word Alive

MARRIAGE

Ambassador Books
Baker Books
Baker's Plays—R
Barbour Publishing
Beacon Hill Press—R
BelleBooks—R
Bethany House
(s)-Black Forest—R
(s)-Brentwood—R
Broadman & Holman
Canon Press—R
Catholic Answers—R
Charisma House—R
Christian Focus—R
Christian Publications
Christian Writer's Ebook—R
College Press—R
Continuum Intl.—R
Cook Communications
Created in Christ
(s)-Creation House—R
Crossway Books
CSS Publishing
(s)-Dean Press, Robbie—R
Destiny Image—R
Dimensions for Living
Discovery House—R
Doubleday
Editorial Portavoz—R
Eerdmans Publishing—R
(s)-Elderberry Press
Emmaus Road—R
(s)-Essence—R
Evergreen Press
Fair Havens—R
(s)-Fairway Press—R
FaithWalk
FamilyLife (books)—R
5th Estate
Focus on the Family—R
Greenwood/Praeger
Group Publishing
(s)-Guardian Books—R
HarperSanFrancisco
Harrison House
Harvest House
Haworth Pastoral—R
Hensley Publishing
Hill Street Press—R
Holy Fire Publishing—R
Hope Publishing—R
InterVarsity Press—R
Judson Press
Kirk House
Latimer Press—R
Legacy Publishers

Life Journey Books—R
Lighthouse eBooks—R
Living Books for All
(s)-Longwood—R
Loyola Press
Lutterworth Press—R
(s)-McDougal Publishing—R
Meredith Books
Millennium III—R
Moms in Print
Monarch Books—R
Nelson Books
Nelson Ignite
(s)-One World—R
P & R Publishing—R
Pacific Press
Paulist Press
Pilgrim Press—R
(s)-Pleasant Word—R
(s)-Providence—R
(s)-Quiet Waters
Quintessential Books—R
Randall House—R
Read 'N Run—R
Resource Public.
RiverOak—R
Rose Publishing
Scepter Publishers—R
Selah Publishing—R
Silas Publishing (books)—R
(s)-So. Baptist Press—R
Sower's Press
St. Anthony Messenger
Standard Publishing
Still Waters Revival—R
Tate Publishing
(s)-TEACH Services—R
Twenty-Third Public.
Tyndale House—R
Verbinum
VMI Publishers
W Publishing
Warner Faith
WaterBrook Press
Whitaker House—R
WindRiver—R
(s)-WinePress—R
(s)-Word Alive
World Publishing—R
Zondervan

MEMOIRS

(s)-American Binding—R
Baker Books
Baker's Plays—R
Ballantine Books
Basic Books—R

BelleBooks—R
(s)-Book Publishers
Christian Focus—R
Christian Writer's Ebook—R
Cladach Publishing—R
Continuum Intl.—R
(s)-Creation House—R
Crossroad Publishing—R
Cumberland House
Descant Publishing
Doubleday
(s)-Elderberry Press
(s)-Fairway Press—R
FaithWalk
5th Estate
(s)-Fruit-Bearer Pub.
Glory Bound Books
Greenwood/Praeger
HarperSanFrancisco
Hill Street Press—R
Holy Fire Publishing—R
Ideals Books
Jossey-Bass
Lighthouse eBooks—R
Lighthouse Trails—R
Lutterworth Press—R
Meredith Books
(s)-One World—R
Pacific Press
(s)-Pleasant Word—R
(s)-Providence—R
Tate Publishing
TowleHouse—R
Tyndale/SaltRiver
Univ. Press of America—R
VMI Publishers
Whitaker House—R
WindRiver—R
(s)-WinePress—R
(s)-Word Alive

MEN'S BOOKS

Ambassador-Emerald—R
AMG Publishers—R
Baker Books
Beacon Hill Press—R
Bethany House
(s)-Black Forest—R
Blue Dolphin
Broadman & Holman
Canon Press—R
Christian Focus—R
Christian Writer's Ebook—R
College Press—R
Continuum Intl.—R
Created in Christ
(s)-Creation House—R

Crossway Books
Dimensions for Living
Discovery House—R
Doubleday
Editorial Portavoz—R
(s)-Elderberry Press
Emmaus Road—R
(s)-Essence—R
Evergreen Press
Fair Havens—R
(s)-Fairway Press—R
Faith Communications
FaithWalk
5th Estate
Green Key Books
(s)-Guardian Books—R
Harvest House
Hensley Publishing
Hill Street Press—R
Holy Fire Publishing—R
Inkling Books—R
InterVarsity Press—R
Judson Press
Latimer Press—R
Life Journey Books—R
Lighthouse eBooks—R
(s)-Longwood—R
Loyola Press
Lutterworth Press—R
(s)-McDougal Publishing—R
Monarch Books—R
Nelson Books
(s)-One World—R
Pacific Press
Pilgrim Press—R
(s)-Pleasant Word—R
(s)-Poetry of Today
(s)-Providence—R
Quintessential Books—R
Randall House—R
Read 'N Run—R
RiverOak—R
Rose Publishing
Selah Publishing—R
St. Anthony Messenger
Tate Publishing
VMI Publishers
W Publishing
Warner Faith
WaterBrook Press
Whitaker House—R
WindRiver—R
(s)-WinePress—R
(s)-Word Alive

MINIBOOKS*

(s)-American Binding—R

Carson-Dellosa—R
InterVarsity Press—R
Legacy Press—R
Lighthouse eBooks—R
(s)-One World—R
Peter Pauper Press
Tate Publishing

MIRACLES

Ambassador-Emerald—R
(s)-American Binding—R
Baker Books
Baker's Plays—R
(s)-Black Forest—R
(s)-Brentwood—R
Canticle Books—R
Carson-Dellosa—R
Charisma House—R
Christian Writer's Ebook—R
Continuum Intl.—R
(s)-Creation House—R
Cross Cultural—R
CSS Publishing
(s)-Elderberry Press
(s)-Essence—R
Evergreen Press
(s)-Fairway Press—R
5th Estate
Friends United Press
Greenwood/Praeger
HarperSanFrancisco
Harrison House
Harvest House
Holy Fire Publishing—R
(s)-Impact Christian—R
InterVarsity Press—R
Lighthouse eBooks—R
Loyola Press
(s)-McDougal Publishing—R
Monarch Books—R
(s)-One World—R
Pacific Press
(s)-Pleasant Word—R
(s)-Providence—R
Read 'N Run—R
Rose Publishing
Selah Publishing—R
(s)-So. Baptist Press—R
Tate Publishing
Verbinum
VMI Publishers
Whitaker House—R
WindRiver—R
(s)-WinePress—R
(s)-Word Alive
World Publishing—R

MISSIONARY

ACU Press
Ambassador-Emerald—R
(s)-American Binding—R
Baker Books
Baker's Plays—R
Baylor Univ. Press—R
(s)-Black Forest—R
(s)-Brentwood—R
Carey Library, Wm.—R
Carson-Dellosa—R
Charisma House—R
Christian Focus—R
Christian Writer's Ebook—R
Continuum Intl.—R
Created in Christ
(s)-Creation House—R
Cross Cultural—R
CSS Publishing
Discovery House—R
(s)-Essence—R
Evergreen Press
(s)-Fairway Press—R
FaithWalk
5th Estate
Friends United Press
Glory Bound Books
Greenwood/Praeger
(s)-Guardian Books—R
Harrison House
Holy Fire Publishing—R
Hope Publishing—R
InterVarsity Press—R
Judson Press
Lamplighter—R
Lighthouse eBooks—R
Lighthouse Trails—R
Living Books for All
(s)-Longwood—R
Lutheran Univ. Press
Lutterworth Press—R
(s)-McDougal Publishing—R
Messianic Jewish—R
Monarch Books—R
New Hope—R
(s)-One World—R
Pacific Press
(s)-Pleasant Word—R
(s)-Poetry of Today
(s)-Providence—R
(s)-Quiet Waters
Randall House—R
Read 'N Run—R
Rose Publishing
(s)-So. Baptist Press—R
Tate Publishing
Verbinum

VMI Publishers
WindRiver—R
(s)-WinePress—R
(s)-Word Alive

MONEY MANAGEMENT

(s)-American Binding—R
Baker Books
Barbour Publishing
Basic Books—R
Bethany House
Blue Dolphin
(s)-Book Publishers
(s)-Brentwood—R
Christian Writer's Ebook—R
Cook Communications
Created in Christ
(s)-Creation House—R
Diamond Eyes—R
Editorial Portavoz—R
(s)-Elderberry Press
(s)-Essence—R
Evergreen Press
(s)-Fairway Press—R
FaithWalk
Frederick Fell—R
5th Estate
Greenwood/Praeger
(s)-Guardian Books—R
Harrison House
Harvest House
Hensley Publishing
Holy Fire Publishing—R
InterVarsity Press—R
Legacy Publishers
Life Journey Books—R
Lighthouse eBooks—R
Living Books for All
Moms in Print
Moody Publishers
Nelson Books
(s)-One World—R
Pacific Press
(s)-Pleasant Word—R
(s)-Providence—R
Quintessential Books—R
Randall House—R
Read 'N Run—R
Regnery—R
RiverOak—R
Rose Publishing
Silas Publishing (books)—R
(s)-So. Baptist Press—R
Summit Pub. Group—R
Tate Publishing
VMI Publishers
Walk Worthy—R

Warner Faith
WaterBrook Press
Wesleyan Publishing
Whitaker House—R
WindRiver—R
(s)-WinePress—R
(s)-Winer Foundation—R
(s)-Word Alive

MUSIC-RELATED BOOKS

ACU Press
Ambassador-Emerald—R
American Cath. Press—R
Baker Books
Christian Writer's Ebook—R
Contemporary Drama
Countryman, J.
Dimension Books—R
(s)-Essence—R
(s)-Fairway Press—R
FaithWalk
(s)-Guardian Books—R
Hill Street Press—R
Holy Fire Publishing—R
Judson Press
Lighthouse eBooks—R
Liturgy Training
Lutterworth Press—R
MegaGrace Books
(s)-One World—R
Read 'N Run—R
Scarecrow Press—R
Standard Publishing
T & T Clark—R
Tate Publishing
VMI Publishers
Warner Faith
Whitaker House—R
(s)-WinePress—R
(s)-Word Alive

NOVELTY BOOKS FOR KIDS

Baker Books
Baker Trittin
Big Idea
Creative Teaching
(s)-Fairway Press—R
Kregel Kidzone—R
Legacy Press—R
(s)-One World—R
(s)-Poetry of Today
Ravenhawk Books—R
Standard Publishing
Tate Publishing
(s)-Word Alive

PAMPHLETS

Chalice Press
Chapter Two—R
Christian Writer's Ebook—R
(s)-Essence—R
Forward Movement
Founders Press
(s)-Fruit-Bearer Pub.
Good Book—R
Good News Publishers
(s)-Guardian Books—R
InterVarsity Press—R
Intl. Awakening—R
Libros Liguori
Liguori
(s)-Longwood—R
Neibauer Press—R
(s)-One World—R
Our Sunday Visitor—R
Paradise Research—R
Paulist Press
Read 'N Run—R
Rose Publishing
Trinity Foundation—R

PARENTING

ACU Press
Ambassador Books
(s)-American Binding—R
AMG Publishers—R
Andros Book Publishing
Baker Books
Baker Trittin
Baker's Plays—R
Ballantine Books
Barbour Publishing
Basic Books—R
Beacon Hill Press—R
Bethany House
(s)-Black Forest—R
(s)-Book Publishers
(s)-Brentwood—R
Broadman & Holman
Carson-Dellosa—R
Charisma House—R
Christian Family
Christian Focus—R
Christian Publications
Christian Writer's Ebook—R
Cladach Publishing—R
College Press—R
Conciliar Press—R
Continuum Intl.—R
Cook Communications
Created in Christ
(s)-Creation House—R

Crossway Books
(s)-Dean Press, Robbie—R
Devoted to You
Dimensions for Living
Discovery House—R
Editorial Portavoz—R
(s)-Essence—R
Evergreen Press
Fair Havens—R
(s)-Fairway Press—R
FamilyLife (books)—R
Focus on the Family—R
Frederick Fell—R
5th Estate
(s)-Fruit-Bearer Pub.
Greenwood/Praeger
Group Publishing
(s)-Guardian Books—R
(s)-Hannibal Books—R
Harrison House
Harvest House
Hensley Publishing
Hill Street Press—R
Holy Fire Publishing—R
InterVarsity Press—R
Judson Press
Kaleidoscope Press—R
Kirk House
Kregel—R
Langmarc
Life Journey Books—R
Lighthouse eBooks—R
Liguori
Living Books for All
(s)-Longwood—R
Lutterworth Press—R
(s)-McDougal Publishing—R
Meredith Books
Moms in Print
Monarch Books—R
Nelson Books
(s)-One World—R
Our Sunday Visitor—R
P & R Publishing—R
Pacific Press
Pauline Books—R
Pflaum Publishing
(s)-Pleasant Word—R
(s)-Providence—R
Quintessential Books—R
Randall House—R
Read 'N Run—R
RiverOak—R
Rose Publishing
Scepter Publishers—R
Selah Publishing—R
Silas Publishing (books)—R

Square One—R
Standard Publishing
Still Waters Revival—R
Tarcher, Jeremy P.
Tate Publishing
Twenty-Third Public.
Tyndale House—R
VMI Publishers
W Publishing
Walk Worthy—R
Warner Faith
WaterBrook Press
Whitaker House—R
WindRiver—R
(s)-WinePress—R
Wood Lake Books—R
(s)-Word Alive
World Publishing—R
Zondervan

PASTORS' HELPS

Abingdon Press
Ambassador-Emerald—R
(s)-American Binding—R
AMG Publishers—R
Baker Books
Beacon Hill Press—R
Bethany House
(s)-Brentwood—R
Broadman & Holman
Christian Focus—R
Christian Publications
Christian Writer's Ebook—R
Church Growth Inst.
Continuum Intl.—R
Created in Christ
(s)-Creation House—R
Cross Cultural—R
CSS Publishing
(s)-DCTS Publishing—R
Earthen Vessel—R
Editorial Portavoz—R
(s)-Essence—R
Fair Havens—R
(s)-Fairway Press—R
5th Estate
Fortress Press
Gospel Publishing
Greenwood/Praeger
Group Publishing
(s)-Guardian Books—R
Harcourt Religion
Harrison House
Harvest House
Haworth Pastoral—R
Hendrickson—R
Holy Fire Publishing—R

InterVarsity Press—R
Judson Press
Kregel—R
Lighthouse eBooks—R
Monarch Books—R
Neibauer Press—R
(s)-One World—R
P & R Publishing—R
Pathway Press
Pilgrim Press—R
(s)-Pleasant Word—R
(s)-Providence—R
Randall House—R
Read 'N Run—R
Rose Publishing
(s)-Sermon Select Press
(s)-So. Baptist Press—R
Standard Publishing
Tate Publishing
Twenty-Third Public.
Verbinum
Victor Books
VMI Publishers
WindRiver—R
(s)-WinePress—R
(s)-Winer Foundation—R
(s)-Word Alive
Zondervan

PERSONAL EXPERIENCE

Abagail Press
Ambassador-Emerald—R
(s)-American Binding—R
Baker Books
Baker's Plays—R
(s)-Black Forest—R
(s)-Brentwood—R
Canon Press—R
Canticle Books—R
Charisma House—R
Christian Focus—R
Christian Writer's Ebook—R
Continuum Intl.—R
Created in Christ
(s)-Creation House—R
(s)-DCTS Publishing—R
Destiny Image—R
(s)-Essence—R
Fair Havens—R
(s)-Fairway Press—R
FaithWalk
5th Estate
Friends United Press
(s)-Fruit-Bearer Pub.
Green Pastures—R
Greenwood/Praeger

(s)-Guardian Books—R
(s)-Hannibal Books—R
HarperSanFrancisco
Harvest House
Hensley Publishing
Holy Fire Publishing—R
InterVarsity Press—R
Lamplighter—R
Lighthouse eBooks—R
Lighthouse Trails—R
Living Books for All
(s)-Longwood—R
Lutterworth Press—R
(s)-McDougal Publishing—R
Monarch Books—R
(s)-One World—R
Pacific Press
(s)-Pleasant Word—R
(s)-Poetry of Today
(s)-Providence—R
Read 'N Run—R
RiverOak—R
(s)-So. Baptist Press—R
Tate Publishing
Twenty-Third Public.
VMI Publishers
W Publishing
Whitaker House—R
WindRiver—R
(s)-WinePress—R
(s)-Winer Foundation—R
(s)-Word Alive

PERSONAL GROWTH

Abagail Press
(s)-Ali Literary, Alfred—R
Ambassador Books
Ambassador-Emerald—R
(s)-American Binding—R
AMG Publishers—R
Baker Books
Baker's Plays—R
Barbour Publishing
Bethany House
(s)-Black Forest—R
(s)-Book Publishers
Broadman & Holman
Canon Press—R
Canticle Books—R
Charisma House—R
CharismaKids
Christian Focus—R
Christian Writer's Ebook—R
Continuum Intl.—R
Created in Christ
(s)-Creation House—R
(s)-DCTS Publishing—R

Destiny Image—R
Discovery House—R
(s)-Essence—R
Evergreen Press
Fair Havens—R
(s)-Fairway Press—R
FaithWalk
Forward Movement
Frederick Fell—R
5th Estate
(s)-Fruit-Bearer Pub.
Green Pastures—R
Greenwood/Praeger
(s)-Guardian Books—R
(s)-Hannibal Books—R
HarperSanFrancisco
Hay House
Hensley Publishing
Hill Street Press—R
Holy Fire Publishing—R
Howard Publishing
InterVarsity Press—R
Jossey-Bass
Judson Press
Life Journey Books—R
Lighthouse eBooks—R
Living Books for All
(s)-McDougal Publishing—R
MegaGrace Books
Meredith Books
Monarch Books—R
Nelson Books
(s)-One World—R
Pacific Press
Pathway Press
Peter Pauper Press
Pilgrim Press—R
(s)-Pleasant Word—R
(s)-Poetry of Today
(s)-Providence—R
Randall House—R
Read 'N Run—R
Rising Star Press
RiverOak—R
Silas Publishing (books)—R
Tate Publishing
(s)-TEACH Services—R
Twenty-Third Public.
Tyndale House—R
Verbinum
VMI Publishers
W Publishing
Warner Faith
WaterBrook Press
Wesleyan Publishing
Whitaker House—R
WindRiver—R

(s)-WinePress—R
(s)-Winer Foundation—R
(s)-Word Alive
World Publishing—R

PERSONAL RENEWAL

Abagail Press
(s)-Ali Literary, Alfred—R
Ambassador-Emerald—R
AMG Publishers—R
Baker Books
Baker's Plays—R
Bethany House
(s)-Black Forest—R
Blue Dolphin
Broadman & Holman
Canon Press—R
Charisma House—R
CharismaKids
Christian Focus—R
Christian Writer's Ebook—R
Cladach Publishing—R
Continuum Intl.—R
Created in Christ
(s)-Creation House—R
(s)-DCTS Publishing—R
Destiny Image—R
Discovery House—R
(s)-Essence—R
Evergreen Press
Fair Havens—R
(s)-Fairway Press—R
FaithWalk
5th Estate
Forward Movement
Friends United Press
(s)-Fruit-Bearer Pub.
Green Pastures—R
Greenwood/Praeger
(s)-Guardian Books—R
(s)-Hannibal Books—R
HarperSanFrancisco
Haworth Pastoral—R
Hensley Publishing
Hill Street Press—R
Holy Fire Publishing—R
(s)-Impact Christian—R
InterVarsity Press—R
Intl. Awakening—R
Judson Press
Latimer Press—R
Life Journey Books—R
Lighthouse eBooks—R
Living Books for All
(s)-Longwood—R
(s)-McDougal Publishing—R

MegaGrace Books
Meredith Books
Monarch Books—R
(s)-One World—R
P & R Publishing—R
Pacific Press
Pilgrim Press—R
(s)-Pleasant Word—R
(s)-Poetry of Today
(s)-Providence—R
Quintessential Books—R
Randall House—R
Read 'N Run—R
RiverOak—R
Rose Publishing
Silas Publishing (books)—R
Tate Publishing
Tyndale House—R
VMI Publishers
Warner Faith
Wesleyan Publishing
Whitaker House—R
WindRiver—R
(s)-WinePress—R
(s)-Winer Foundation—R
(s)-Word Alive
World Publishing—R

PHILOSOPHY

ACU Press
Baker Books
Baker's Plays—R
Basic Books—R
Baylor Univ. Press—R
(s)-Black Forest—R
(s)-Brentwood—R
Cambridge Univ. Press
Christian Focus—R
Christian Writer's Ebook—R
Continuum Intl.—R
(s)-Creation House—R
Cross Cultural—R
Doubleday
Dover Publications—R
Eerdmans Publishing—R
(s)-Elderberry Press
(s)-Essence—R
(s)-Fairway Press—R
FaithWalk
5th Estate
Friends United Press
Greenwood/Praeger
(s)-Guardian Books—R
HarperSanFrancisco
Hill Street Press—R
Holy Fire Publishing—R
Inkling Books—R

InterVarsity Press—R
Larson Publications
Lighthouse eBooks—R
Lutterworth Press—R
Mercer Univ. Press—R
Monarch Books—R
(s)-One World—R
Open Court—R
Paragon House
Pelican Publishing—R
(s)-Pleasant Word—R
Quintessential Books—R
Ravenhawk Books—R
Read 'N Run—R
Regnery—R
Rose Publishing
Scarecrow Press—R
St. Augustine's Press—R
Still Waters Revival—R
Tarcher, Jeremy P.
Tate Publishing
Third World Press—R
Trinity Foundation—R
Univ. Press of America—R
VMI Publishers
Whitaker House—R
WindRiver—R
(s)-WinePress—R
(s)-Winer Foundation—R
(s)-Word Alive
Yale Univ. Press—R

PHOTOGRAPHS
(For Covers)

Abingdon Press
(s)-Ali Literary, Alfred
(s)-Black Forest
Canadian Inst. for Law
Canon Press
Carey Library, Wm.
Catholic Answers
Christian Focus
Church Growth Inst.
Conciliar Press
Continuum Intl.
Created in Christ
(s)-Creation House
Cross Cultural
(s)-Dean Press, Robbie
Devoted to You
ETC Publications
Fair Havens
FaithWalk
5th Estate
Glory Bound Books
(s)-Guardian Books
Guernica Editions

Harcourt Religion
Intl. Awakening
Jireh Publishing
Jubilant Press
Lighthouse eBooks
(s)-Lightning Star Press
Lutheran Univ. Press
Millennium III
Neibauer Press
New Canaan
New Hope
(s)-One World
Oregon Catholic Press
Our Sunday Visitor
Paulist Press
Players Press
(s)-Poetry of Today
Quintessential Books
Read 'N Run
Rising Star Press
Selah Publishing
Sheed & Ward
St. Anthony Messenger
Tate Publishing
(s)-TEACH Services
Touch Publications
Trinity Foundation
Twenty-Third Public.
United Methodist
Univ. of AR Press
Virginia Pines Press
Wilshire Book

POETRY

(s)-American Binding—R
Baker's Plays—R
(s)-Black Forest—R
(s)-Book Publishers
Boyds Mills Press—R
(s)-Brentwood—R
Canon Press—R
Christian Writer's Ebook—R
Cladach Publishing—R
Continuum Intl.—R
Created in Christ
(s)-Creation House—R
(s)-Dean Press, Robbie—R
Destiny Image (books)—R
Eerdmans/Young Readers
(s)-Elderberry Press
(s)-Essence—R
(s)-Fairway Press—R
5th Estate
(s)-Fruit-Bearer Pub.
Glory Bound Books
(s)-Guardian Books—R
Guernica Editions—R

Hidden Brook Press
Holy Fire Publishing—R
Lamplighter—R
Lighthouse eBooks—R
(s)-Lightning Star Press—R
Lutterworth Press—R
Moms in Print
Mt. Olive College Press
(s)-One World—R
(s)-Pleasant Word—R
(s)-Poems By Me—R
(s)-Poetry of Today
(s)-Poets Cove Press
Read 'N Run—R
Selah Publishing—R
(s)-So. Baptist Press—R
Tate Publishing
Verbinum
Vintage Romance
WindRiver—R
(s)-WinePress—R
(s)-Word Alive

POLITICAL

Allegiance Books—R
Baker Books
Baker's Plays—R
Basic Books—R
Baylor Univ. Press—R
(s)-Black Forest—R
Branden Publishing
(s)-Brentwood—R
Canadian Inst. for Law—R
Christian Focus—R
Christian Writer's Ebook—R
Continuum Intl.—R
(s)-Creation House—R
Cross Cultural—R
Cumberland House
Doubleday
(s)-Elderberry Press
(s)-Essence—R
(s)-Fairway Press—R
5th Estate
Four Courts Press—R
Georgetown Univ. Press
Greenwood/Praeger
(s)-Guardian Books—R
HarperSanFrancisco
Hill Street Press—R
Holy Fire Publishing—R
Inkling Books—R
InterVarsity Press—R
Judson Press
Lighthouse eBooks—R
Lutterworth Press—R
Mercer Univ. Press—R

Millennium III—R
Monarch Books—R
New York Univ. Press
(s)-One World—R
Open Court—R
(s)-Pleasant Word—R
Quintessential Books—R
Ravenhawk Books—R
Read 'N Run—R
Regnery—R
Scarecrow Press—R
Still Waters Revival—R
Tate Publishing
Third World Press—R
Univ. Press of America—R
VMI Publishers
WindRiver—R
(s)-WinePress—R
(s)-Word Alive

PRAYER

Abingdon Press
ACU Press
Alba House—R
Ambassador-Emerald—R
(s)-American Binding—R
American Cath. Press—R
AMG Publishers—R
Baker Books
Baker Trittin
Baker's Plays—R
Barbour Publishing
Baylor Univ. Press—R
Beacon Hill Press—R
Bethany House
(s)-Black Forest—R
(s)-Brentwood—R
Broadman & Holman
Carson-Dellosa—R
Catholic Book
Chalice Press
Chapter Two—R
Charisma House—R
CharismaKids
Christian Focus—R
Christian Publications
Christian Writer's Ebook—R
College Press—R
Continuum Intl.—R
Cook Communications
Created in Christ
(s)-Creation House—R
Cross Cultural—R
CSS Publishing
(s)-DCTS Publishing—R
Destiny Image—R
Diamond Eyes—R

Discovery House—R
Doubleday
Eerdmans Publishing—R
Eerdmans/Young Readers
(s)-Elderberry Press
(s)-Essence—R
Evergreen Press
(s)-Fairway Press—R
Faith One
FaithWalk
5th Estate
Forward Movement
Friends United Press
(s)-Fruit-Bearer Pub.
Good News Publishers
Gospel Publishing
Green Pastures—R
Greenwood/Praeger
(s)-Guardian Books—R
(s)-Hannibal Books—R
Harcourt Religion
HarperSanFrancisco
Harrison House
Harvest House
Hensley Publishing
Hill Street Press—R
Holy Fire Publishing—R
Hope Publishing—R
ICS Publications—R
(s)-Impact Christian—R
InterVarsity Press—R
Intl. Awakening—R
Jireh Publishing
Judson Press
Kirk House
Kregel—R
Latimer Press—R
Libros Liguori
Lighthouse eBooks—R
(s)-Lightning Star Press—R
Liguori
Liturgy Training
Living Books for All
(s)-Longwood—R
Lutterworth Press—R
(s)-McDougal Publishing—R
Meredith Books
Monarch Books—R
Moody Publishers
New Hope—R
New Leaf Press—R
New Seeds Books—R
(s)-One World—R
Our Sunday Visitor—R
P & R Publishing—R
Pacific Press
Pauline Books—R

Paulist Press
Peter Pauper Press
Pflaum Publishing
Pilgrim Press—R
(s)-Pleasant Word—R
(s)-Poetry of Today
(s)-Providence—R
Randall House—R
Read 'N Run—R
RiverOak—R
Rose Publishing
Scepter Publishers—R
Selah Publishing—R
Smyth & Helwys
(s)-So. Baptist Press—R
Standard Publishing
Still Waters Revival—R
Tate Publishing
(s)-TEACH Services—R
Twenty-Third Public.
Tyndale House—R
Verbinum
VMI Publishers
W Publishing
Walk Worthy—R
Warner Faith
WaterBrook Press
Wesleyan Publishing
Westminster John Knox
Whitaker House—R
WindRiver—R
(s)-WinePress—R
(s)-Winer Foundation—R
Wood Lake Books—R
Woodland Gospel
(s)-Word Alive
World Publishing—R
Zondervan

PRINT-ON-DEMAND

Aadeon Publishing
(s)-American Binding—R
(s)-Black Forest—R
Blue Dolphin
Booklocker Jr.
(s)-Brentwood—R
Christian Writer's Ebook—R
Continuum Intl.—R
Created in Christ
Crossroad Publishing—R
(s)-Dean Press, Robbie—R
(s)-Ekklesia Press
(s)-Elderberry Press
Evergreen Press
5th Estate
Georgetown Univ. Press
Holy Fire Publishing—R

Inkling Books—R
(s)-Insight Publishing—R
(s)-Lightning Star Press—R
(s)-One World—R
(s)-Pleasant Word—R
(s)-Poems By Me—R
(s)-Poetry of Today
Ravenhawk Books—R
(s)-Self Publish Press—R
(s)-Strong Tower
Univ. Press of America—R
(s)-Word Alive
(s)-Xulon Press—R

PROPHECY

Ambassador-Emerald—R
(s)-American Binding—R
Baker Books
Baker's Plays—R
Baylor Univ. Press—R
(s)-Black Forest—R
Blue Dolphin
(s)-Brentwood—R
Broadman & Holman
Chapter Two—R
Charisma House—R
CharismaKids
Christian Focus—R
Christian Writer's Ebook—R
Continuum Intl.—R
Created in Christ
(s)-Creation House—R
CSS Publishing
(s)-Elderberry Press
(s)-Essence—R
Fair Havens—R
(s)-Fairway Press—R
FaithWalk
5th Estate
(s)-Fruit-Bearer Pub.
Greenwood/Praeger
(s)-Guardian Books—R
Harrison House
Harvest House
Holy Fire Publishing—R
Kregel—R
Lighthouse eBooks—R
Living Books for All
(s)-Longwood—R
Lutheran Univ. Press
Lutterworth Press—R
(s)-McDougal Publishing—R
Millennium III—R
Monarch Books—R
(s)-One World—R
P & R Publishing—R
Pacific Press

(s)-Pleasant Word—R
(s)-Providence—R
Read 'N Run—R
RiverOak—R
Rose Publishing
Selah Publishing—R
(s)-So. Baptist Press—R
Still Waters Revival—R
Tate Publishing
Victor Books
VMI Publishers
W Publishing
Warner Faith
Whitaker House—R
WindRiver—R
(s)-WinePress—R
(s)-Word Alive
Zondervan

PSYCHOLOGY

Baker's Plays—R
Basic Books—R
Baylor Univ. Press—R
Bethany House
(s)-Black Forest—R
Blue Dolphin
(s)-Brentwood—R
Christian Focus—R
Christian Writer's Ebook—R
Continuum Intl.—R
Created in Christ
(s)-Creation House—R
Dimension Books—R
(s)-Elderberry Press
(s)-Essence—R
Evergreen Press
(s)-Fairway Press—R
FaithWalk
5th Estate
Greenwood/Praeger
(s)-Guardian Books—R
Harvest House
Haworth Pastoral—R
Hill Street Press—R
Holy Fire Publishing—R
Hope Publishing—R
InterVarsity Press—R
Jossey-Bass
Judson Press
Larson Publications
Life Journey Books—R
Lighthouse eBooks—R
Lutterworth Press—R
Monarch Books—R
New Seeds Books—R
New York Univ. Press
(s)-One World—R

Open Court—R
P & R Publishing—R
Paragon House
(s)-Pleasant Word—R
(s)-Providence—R
Quintessential Books—R
Read 'N Run—R
(s)-Recovery Commun.
Religious Education
Rose Publishing
Silas Publishing (books)—R
Siloam
(s)-So. Baptist Press—R
Tarcher, Jeremy P.
Tate Publishing
Third World Press—R
Tyndale House—R
Univ. Press of America—R
VMI Publishers
Warner Faith
Wilshire Book—R
WindRiver—R
(s)-WinePress—R
(s)-Winer Foundation—R
(s)-Word Alive
Yale Univ. Press—R
Zondervan

RACISM

(s)-Ali Literary, Alfred—R
American Cath. Press—R
Baker Books
Baker's Plays—R
(s)-Black Forest—R
Christian Writer's Ebook—R
Continuum Intl.—R
(s)-Creation House—R
Cross Cultural—R
(s)-DCTS Publishing—R
Destiny Image—R
Eerdmans/Young Readers
(s)-Fairway Press—R
FaithWalk
5th Estate
Greenwood/Praeger
Hill Street Press—R
Holy Fire Publishing—R
InterVarsity Press—R
Kirk House
Lighthouse eBooks—R
Lutterworth Press—R
Monarch Books—R
(s)-One World—R
Open Court—R
Pilgrim Press—R
(s)-Pleasant Word—R
Summit Pub. Group—R

Tate Publishing
Univ. Press of America—R
VMI Publishers
WindRiver—R
(s)-WinePress—R
(s)-Word Alive

RECOVERY BOOKS

Ambassador Books
Baker Books
(s)-Black Forest—R
Broadman & Holman
Charisma House—R
Christian Focus—R
Christian Writer's Ebook—R
Continuum Intl.—R
(s)-Creation House—R
CSS Publishing
(s)-Essence—R
Evergreen Press
Fair Havens—R
(s)-Fairway Press—R
Faith Communications
FaithWalk
5th Estate
Forward Movement
Good Book—R
Greenwood/Praeger
(s)-Guardian Books—R
(s)-Hannibal Books—R
HarperSanFrancisco
Haworth Pastoral—R
Hill Street Press—R
Holy Fire Publishing—R
Hope Publishing—R
InterVarsity Press—R
Judson Press
Langmarc
Life Journey Books—R
Lighthouse eBooks—R
Lutterworth Press—R
(s)-McDougal Publishing—R
Meredith Books
Monarch Books—R
(s)-One World—R
Paradise Research—R
(s)-Pleasant Word—R
(s)-Providence—R
Quintessential Books—R
Randall House—R
Read 'N Run—R
(s)-Recovery Commun.
RiverOak—R
Rose Publishing
Silas Publishing (books)—R
Siloam
Tate Publishing

Tyndale House—R
VMI Publishers
WaterBrook Press
Whitaker House—R
Wilshire Book—R
WindRiver—R
(s)-WinePress—R
(s)-Word Alive

REFERENCE BOOKS

Ambassador-Emerald—R
AMG Publishers—R
Baker Books
Baylor Univ. Press—R
Bethany House
(s)-Black Forest—R
Branden Publishing
(s)-Brentwood—R
Christian Focus—R
Christian Writer's Ebook—R
Continuum Intl.—R
Cook Communications
(s)-Creation House—R
Cumberland House
Doubleday
Dover Publications—R
Editorial Portavoz—R
Eerdmans Publishing—R
(s)-Elderberry Press
Facts on File
(s)-Fairway Press—R
FaithWalk
5th Estate
(s)-Guardian Books—R
HarperSanFrancisco
Hendrickson—R
Hill Street Press—R
Holy Fire Publishing—R
(s)-Impact Christian—R
InterVarsity Press—R
Intl. Awakening—R
Johns Hopkins—R
Judson Press
Kaleidoscope Press—R
Kregel—R
Lighthouse eBooks—R
Lutterworth Press—R
MegaGrace Books
Messianic Jewish—R
Millennium III—R
Monarch Books—R
New Leaf Press—R
(s)-One World—R
Our Sunday Visitor—R
(s)-Providence—R
Randall House—R
Read 'N Run—R

Religious Education
Rose Publishing
Scarecrow Press—R
Sheed & Ward—R
(s)-So. Baptist Press—R
Square One—R
Still Waters Revival—R
Tate Publishing
Third World Press—R
Tyndale House—R
Univ. Press of America—R
Victor Books
Whitaker House—R
WindRiver—R
(s)-WinePress—R
(s)-Word Alive
World Publishing—R
Zondervan

RELIGION

Abingdon Press
ACTA Publications
ACU Press
Alba House—R
(s)-Ali Literary, Alfred—R
Ambassador-Emerald—R
(s)-American Binding—R
Baker Books
Baker Trittin
Baker's Plays—R
Ballantine Books
Basic Books—R
Baylor Univ. Press—R
Bethany House
(s)-Black Forest—R
Blue Dolphin
Boyds Mills Press—R
(s)-Brentwood—R
Broadman & Holman
Brown Books
Cambridge Univ. Press
Catholic Answers—R
Chalice Press
Charisma House—R
Christian Focus—R
Christian Writer's Ebook—R
Continuum Intl.—R
Created in Christ
(s)-Creation House—R
Cross Cultural—R
CSS Publishing
Descant Publishing
Diamond Eyes—R
Dimension Books—R
Doubleday
E-Digital Books
Educational Ministries

Eerdmans Publishing—R
Eerdmans/Young Readers
(s)-Elderberry Press
(s)-Essence—R
Facts on File
(s)-Fairway Press—R
FaithWalk
5th Estate
Fortress Press
Four Courts Press—R
Friends United Press
Georgetown Univ. Press
Greenwood/Praeger
(s)-Guardian Books—R
HarperSanFrancisco
Hiddenspring Books
Hill Street Press—R
Holy Fire Publishing—R
(s)-Impact Christian—R
InterVarsity Press—R
Johns Hopkins—R
Judson Press
Kregel—R
Larson Publications
Libros Liguori
Lighthouse eBooks—R
Liturgy Training
Lutterworth Press—R
(s)-McDougal Publishing—R
Mercer Univ. Press—R
Messianic Jewish—R
Millennium III—R
Monarch Books—R
Morehouse
Mt. Olive College Press
Nelson Books
New Hope—R
New Seeds Books—R
New York Univ. Press
Northstone—R
(s)-One World—R
Open Court—R
Oregon Catholic Press
Our Sunday Visitor—R
P & R Publishing—R
Pacific Press
Paragon House
Paulist Press
Pflaum Publishing
Pilgrim Press—R
(s)-Pleasant Word—R
(s)-Poetry of Today
PREP Publishing—R
(s)-Providence—R
Ragged Edge—R
Read 'N Run—R
Regnery—R

Religious Education
Rising Star Press
RiverOak—R
Rose Publishing
Sheed & Ward—R
Smyth & Helwys
(s)-So. Baptist Press—R
Square One—R
Still Waters Revival—R
T & T Clark—R
Tarcher, Jeremy P.
Tate Publishing
Tau-Publishing—R
Third World Press—R
Twenty-Third Public.
Univ. of AR Press—R
Univ. Press of America—R
Univ./Ottawa Press
Verbinum
VMI Publishers
W Publishing
Warner Faith
WaterBrook Press
Westminster John Knox
Whitaker House—R
WindRiver—R
(s)-WinePress—R
Wood Lake Books—R
(s)-Word Alive
World Publishing—R
Yale Univ. Press—R

RELIGIOUS TOLERANCE

(s)-American Binding—R
American Cath. Press—R
Baker Books
Baker's Plays—R
Baylor Univ. Press—R
(s)-Black Forest—R
Canticle Books—R
Charisma House—R
Christian Writer's Ebook—R
Continuum Intl.—R
Created in Christ
Cross Cultural—R
Eerdmans/Young Readers
(s)-Elderberry Press
(s)-Fairway Press—R
FaithWalk
5th Estate
Forward Movement
Greenwood/Praeger
Hill Street Press—R
Holy Fire Publishing—R
InterVarsity Press—R
Johns Hopkins—R
Jossey-Bass

Lighthouse eBooks—R
Lutterworth Press—R
Magnus Press—R
Meredith Books
New Canaan
(s)-One World—R
Open Court—R
Paragon House
(s)-Pleasant Word—R
(s)-Poetry of Today
(s)-Providence—R
Rising Star Press
Rose Publishing
Tate Publishing
Verbinum
VMI Publishers
Westminster John Knox
WindRiver—R
(s)-WinePress—R
(s)-Word Alive

RETIREMENT

(s)-American Binding—R
Baker Books
Baker's Plays—R
Barbour Publishing
Bethany House
(s)-Book Publishers
Broadman & Holman
Christian Focus—R
Christian Publications
Christian Writer's Ebook—R
Cladach Publishing—R
College Press—R
Continuum Intl.—R
(s)-Creation House—R
Discovery House—R
(s)-Elderberry Press
(s)-Essence—R
Fair Havens—R
(s)-Fairway Press—R
5th Estate
Greenwood/Praeger
(s)-Guardian Books—R
Harvest House
Hill Street Press—R
Holy Fire Publishing—R
InterVarsity Press—R
Judson Press
Kirk House
Life Journey Books—R
Lighthouse eBooks—R
(s)-Longwood—R
Lutterworth Press—R
(s)-One World—R
(s)-Pleasant Word—R
(s)-Providence—R

Read 'N Run—R
Regnery—R
Rose Publishing
(s)-So. Baptist Press—R
Square One—R
Tate Publishing
WindRiver—R
(s)-WinePress—R
(s)-Word Alive

SCHOLARLY

Amcrican Book Publishing
Baker Books
Baker's Plays—R
Baylor Univ. Press—R
(s)-Black Forest—R
Canon Press—R
Chalice Press
Christian Focus—R
Christian Writer's Ebook—R
Cistercian—R
Continuum Intl.—R
Cook Communications
(s)-Creation House—R
Cross Cultural—R
Crossway Books
Doubleday
Eerdmans Publishing—R
(s)-Elderberry Press
(s)-Essence—R
Fair Havens—R
(s)-Fairway Press—R
5th Estate
Fortress Press
Georgetown Univ. Press
Gospel Publishing
Greenwood/Praeger
(s)-Guardian Books—R
Haworth Pastoral—R
Hendrickson—R
Hill Street Press—R
Holy Fire Publishing—R
(s)-Impact Christian—R
Inkling Books—R
InterVarsity Press—R
Intl. Awakening—R
Kregel—R
Lighthouse eBooks—R
Lutheran Univ. Press
Lutterworth Press—R
Mercer Univ. Press—R
Millennium III—R
Monarch Books—R
Mt. Olive College Press
New Leaf Press—R
New Seeds Books—R
New York Univ. Press

(s)-One World—R
Open Court—R
P & R Publishing—R
Paragon House
Pilgrim Press—R
(s)-Pleasant Word—R
(s)-Providence—R
(s)-Quiet Waters
Read 'N Run—R
Religious Education
Scarecrow Press—R
Smyth & Helwys
T & T Clark—R
Tate Publishing
Trinity Foundation—R
Univ. of AR Press—R
Univ. Press of America—R
Univ./Ottawa Press
Victor Books
VMI Publishers
Westminster John Knox
Whitaker House—R
WindRiver—R
(s)-WinePress—R
(s)-Word Alive
Youth Specialties

SCIENCE

Allegiance Books—R
(s)-American Binding—R
Baker Books
Baker's Plays—R
(s)-Black Forest—R
Boyds Mills Press—R
Broadman & Holman
Carson-Dellosa—R
Christian Focus—R
Christian Writer's Ebook—R
Continuum Intl.—R
Cross Cultural—R
Doubleday
(s)-Elderberry Press
Facts on File
(s)-Fairway Press—R
5th Estate
Glory Bound Books
Greenwood/Praeger
(s)-Guardian Books—R
Hill Street Press—R
Holy Fire Publishing—R
Inkling Books—R
InterVarsity Press—R
Kaleidoscope Press—R
Lighthouse eBooks—R
Lutterworth Press—R
Master Books
Millennium III—R

Monarch Books—R
New Leaf Press—R
(s)-One World—R
OnStage Publishing
(s)-Pleasant Word—R
Ravenhawk Books—R
Read 'N Run—R
Regnery—R
Summit Pub. Group—R
Tate Publishing
Tyndale/SaltRiver
Whitaker House—R
WindRiver—R
(s)-WinePress—R
(s)-Word Alive

SELF-HELP

(s)-Ali Literary, Alfred—R
Ambassador Books
(s)-American Binding—R
Baker Books
Ballantine Books
(s)-Black Forest—R
Blue Dolphin
(s)-Book Publishers
Broadman & Holman
Brown Books
Charisma House—R
Christian Focus—R
Christian Writer's Ebook—R
Continuum Intl.—R
(s)-Creation House—R
(s)-DCTS Publishing—R
(s)-Dean Press, Robbie—R
Descant Publishing
Destiny Image—R
Diamond Eyes—R
Dimensions for Living
(s)-Essence—R
Evergreen Press
Extreme Diva
Fair Havens—R
(s)-Fairway Press—R
FaithWalk
Frederick Fell—R
5th Estate
(s)-Fruit-Bearer Pub.
Genesis Press
Glory Bound Books
Good Book—R
(s)-Guardian Books—R
HarperSanFrancisco
Harvest House
Hay House
Hill Street Press—R
Holy Fire Publishing—R
InterVarsity Press—R

Judson Press
Langmarc
Life Journey Books—R
Lighthouse eBooks—R
(s)-Lightning Star Press—R
(s)-Longwood—R
Lutterworth Press—R
MegaGrace Books
Meredith Books
Monarch Books—R
Mt. Olive College Press
Nelson Books
New Seeds Books—R
Northstone—R
(s)-One World—R
P & R Publishing—R
Paradise Research—R
Perigee Books
Peter Pauper Press
Pilgrim Press—R
(s)-Pleasant Word—R
(s)-Poetry of Today
(s)-Providence—R
Quintessential Books—R
Ragged Edge—R
Randall House—R
Read 'N Run—R
RiverOak—R
Selah Publishing—R
Silas Publishing (books)—R
Square One—R
Summit Pub. Group—R
Tarcher, Jeremy P.
Tate Publishing
(s)-TEACH Services—R
Third World Press—R
VMI Publishers
Walk Worthy—R
Warner Faith
WaterBrook Press
Whitaker House—R
Wilshire Book—R
WindRiver—R
(s)-WinePress—R
(s)-Winer Foundation—R
(s)-Word Alive
Zondervan

SENIOR ADULT CONCERNS

(s)-American Binding—R
AMG Publishers—R
Baker Books
Baker's Plays—R
Bethany House
(s)-Black Forest—R
Charisma House—R
Christian Focus—R

Christian Publications
Christian Writer's Ebook—R
Cladach Publishing—R
Continuum Intl.—R
Cook Communications
Created in Christ
(s)-Creation House—R
Discovery House—R
Educational Ministries
(s)-Essence—R
Evergreen Press
Fair Havens—R
(s)-Fairway Press—R
5th Estate
Focus on the Family—R
Gospel Publishing
(s)-Guardian Books—R
(s)-Hannibal Books—R
Haworth Pastoral—R
Hensley Publishing
Hill Street Press—R
Holy Fire Publishing—R
InterVarsity Press—R
Judson Press
Langmarc
Life Journey Books—R
Lighthouse eBooks—R
(s)-Longwood—R
Lutterworth Press—R
Monarch Books—R
(s)-One World—R
(s)-Pleasant Word—R
(s)-Providence—R
Quintessential Books—R
Randall House—R
Read 'N Run—R
Rose Publishing
(s)-So. Baptist Press—R
St. Anthony Messenger
Tate Publishing
VMI Publishers
WindRiver—R
(s)-WinePress—R
(s)-Word Alive

SERMONS

Alba House—R
Ambassador-Emerald—R
(s)-American Binding—R
Baker Books
(s)-Brentwood—R
Carson-Dellosa—R
Chalice Press
Christian Focus—R
Christian Writer's Ebook—R
Church Growth Inst.
Continuum Intl.—R

Created in Christ
(s)-Creation House—R
CSS Publishing
(s)-DCTS Publishing—R
Editorial Portavoz—R
Educational Ministries
(s)-Elderberry Press
(s)-Fairway Press—R
5th Estate
Group Publishing
(s)-Guardian Books—R
(s)-Hannibal Books—R
Holy Fire Publishing—R
Judson Press
Kirk House
Lighthouse eBooks—R
Liturgical Press
Lutterworth Press—R
(s)-McDougal Publishing—R
Monarch Books—R
(s)-One World—R
Pacific Press
(s)-Pleasant Word—R
(s)-Providence—R
Read 'N Run—R
(s)-Sermon Select Press
(s)-So. Baptist Press—R
Still Waters Revival—R
Tate Publishing
Verbinum
VMI Publishers
WindRiver—R
(s)-WinePress—R
(s)-Word Alive

SINGLES ISSUES

Ambassador Books
AMG Publishers—R
Baker Books
Baker's Plays—R
Barbour Publishing
Bethany House
(s)-Brentwood—R
Broadman & Holman
Charisma House—R
Christian Focus—R
Christian Writer's Ebook—R
Continuum Intl.—R
Cook Communications
(s)-Creation House—R
(s)-Dean Press, Robbie—R
Destiny Image—R
Discovery House—R
(s)-Elderberry Press
(s)-Essence—R
Evergreen Press
(s)-Fairway Press—R

FaithWalk
5th Estate
Green Key Books
Greenwood/Praeger
(s)-Guardian Books—R
Harrison House
Harvest House
Hensley Publishing
Hill Street Press—R
Holy Fire Publishing—R
InterVarsity Press—R
Judson Press
Kregel—R
Life Journey Books—R
Lighthouse eBooks—R
Lutterworth Press—R
(s)-McDougal Publishing—R
Monarch Books—R
(s)-One World—R
P & R Publishing—R
Pacific Press
Perigee Books
(s)-Pleasant Word—R
(s)-Providence—R
Quintessential Books—R
Randall House—R
Ravenhawk Books—R
Read 'N Run—R
Rose Publishing
Tate Publishing
VMI Publishers
Walk Worthy—R
Warner Faith
Whitaker House—R
WindRiver—R
(s)-WinePress—R
(s)-Word Alive

SOCIAL JUSTICE ISSUES

Aadeon Publishing
Allegiance Books—R
Baker Books
Baker's Plays—R
Baylor Univ. Press—R
Bethany House
(s)-Black Forest—R
(s)-Brentwood—R
Broadman & Holman
Canadian Inst. for Law—R
Christian Focus—R
Christian Writer's Ebook—R
Continuum Intl.—R
(s)-Creation House—R
Cross Cultural—R
Crossroad Publishing—R
(s)-DCTS Publishing—R
Destiny Image—R

Eerdmans Publishing—R
Eerdmans/Young Readers
(s)-Essence—R
(s)-Fairway Press—R
5th Estate
Georgetown Univ. Press
Greenwood/Praeger
(s)-Guardian Books—R
HarperSanFrancisco
Haworth Pastoral—R
Hill Street Press—R
Holy Fire Publishing—R
Hope Publishing—R
Inkling Books—R
InterVarsity Press—R
Jossey-Bass
Judson Press
Libros Liguori
Life Cycle Books—R
Lighthouse eBooks—R
Liturgy Training
Lutterworth Press—R
Monarch Books—R
(s)-One World—R
Our Sunday Visitor—R
Paulist Press
Pilgrim Press—R
(s)-Pleasant Word—R
(s)-Providence—R
Read 'N Run—R
Regnery—R
Rose Publishing
Sheed & Ward—R
St. Anthony Messenger
Still Waters Revival—R
Tate Publishing
Univ./Ottawa Press
Verbinum
VMI Publishers
Whitaker House—R
WindRiver—R
(s)-WinePress—R
(s)-Word Alive
Youth Specialties

SOCIOLOGY

Allegiance Books—R
(s)-American Binding—R
Baker Books
Baker's Plays—R
Basic Books—R
Baylor Univ. Press—R
Bethany House
(s)-Black Forest—R
Branden Publishing
(s)-Brentwood—R
Carey Library, Wm.—R

Christian Writer's Ebook—R
Continuum Intl.—R
(s)-Elderberry Press
(s)-Essence—R
(s)-Fairway Press—R
FaithWalk
5th Estate
Greenwood/Praeger
(s)-Guardian Books—R
Haworth Pastoral—R
Hill Street Press—R
Holy Fire Publishing—R
InterVarsity Press—R
Judson Press
Lighthouse eBooks—R
Lutterworth Press—R
(s)-McDougal Publishing—R
Monarch Books—R
New York Univ. Press
(s)-One World—R
(s)-Pleasant Word—R
Read 'N Run—R
RiverOak—R
Still Waters Revival—R
Tate Publishing
Third World Press—R
Univ. Press of America—R
VMI Publishers
WindRiver—R
(s)-WinePress—R
(s)-Word Alive

SPIRITUAL GIFTS

Ambassador Books
(s)-American Binding—R
Baker Books
Baker's Plays—R
(s)-Black Forest—R
Broadman & Holman
Canticle Books—R
Caribe-Betania Editores
Carson-Dellosa—R
Charisma House—R
Christian Focus—R
Christian Writer's Ebook—R
Continuum Intl.—R
Created in Christ
(s)-Creation House—R
Crossroad Publishing—R
CSS Publishing
(s)-Dean Press, Robbie—R
Destiny Image—R
(s)-Essence—R
(s)-Fairway Press—R
Faith One
FaithWalk
5th Estate

Forward Movement
Gospel Publishing
Greenwood/Praeger
Group Publishing
(s)-Guardian Books—R
Harrison House
Harvest House
Hensley Publishing
Hill Street Press—R
Holy Fire Publishing—R
InterVarsity Press—R
Kirk House
Lighthouse eBooks—R
Living Books for All
Lutheran Univ. Press
Lutterworth Press—R
Magnus Press—R
Monarch Books—R
Nelson Books
(s)-One World—R
P & R Publishing—R
Pacific Press
(s)-Pleasant Word—R
(s)-Providence—R
Read 'N Run—R
RiverOak—R
Rose Publishing
Selah Publishing—R
Silas Publishing (books)—R
Tate Publishing
Tau-Publishing—R
VMI Publishers
W Publishing
Warner Faith
Wesleyan Publishing
Whitaker House—R
WindRiver—R
(s)-WinePress—R
(s)-Word Alive
Zondervan

SPIRITUALITY

Abingdon Press
ACTA Publications
ACU Press
Alba House—R
(s)-Ali Literary, Alfred—R
Ambassador Books
(s)-American Binding—R
American Book Publishing
AMG Publishers—R
Baker Books
Baker's Plays—R
Ballantine Books
Basic Books—R
Baylor Univ. Press—R
Bethany House

(s)-Black Forest—R
Blue Dolphin
(s)-Book Publishers
(s)-Brentwood—R
Broadman & Holman
Brown Books
Canticle Books—R
Carson-Dellosa—R
Chalice Press
Charisma House—R
Christian Focus—R
Christian Writer's Ebook—R
Cistercian—R
Continuum Intl.—R
Created in Christ
(s)-Creation House—R
Cross Cultural—R
CSS Publishing
Descant Publishing
Destiny Image—R
Dimension Books—R
Doubleday
E-Digital Books
Educational Ministries
Eerdmans Publishing—R
Eerdmans/Young Readers
Elijah Press
Emmaus Road—R
(s)-Essence—R
Evergreen Press
(s)-Fairway Press—R
Faith Communications
FaithWalk
Forward Movement
Frederick Fell—R
5th Estate
Friends United Press
Good News Publishers
Greenwood/Praeger
(s)-Guardian Books—R
(s)-Hannibal Books—R
HarperSanFrancisco
Hay House
Hiddenspring Books
Hill Street Press—R
Holy Fire Publishing—R
(s)-Impact Christian—R
InterVarsity Press—R
Johns Hopkins—R
Jossey-Bass
Judson Press
Kirk House
Kregel—R
Larson Publications
Libros Liguori
Lighthouse eBooks—R
Liguori

Living Books for All
Loyola Press
Lutheran Univ. Press
Lutterworth Press—R
Magnus Press—R
Meredith Books
Monarch Books—R
Morehouse
Mt. Olive College Press
Nelson Books
New Seeds Books—R
Northstone—R
(s)-One World—R
P & R Publishing—R
Pacific Press
Paragon House
Pauline Books—R
Paulist Press
Perigee Books
Peter Pauper Press
Pflaum Publishing
Pilgrim Press—R
(s)-Pleasant Word—R
(s)-Poetry of Today
PREP Publishing—R
(s)-Providence—R
Quintessential Books—R
Ragged Edge—R
Randall House—R
Read 'N Run—R
Regnery—R
Resource Public.
Rising Star Press
RiverOak—R
Rose Publishing
Selah Publishing—R
Sheed & Ward—R
Smyth & Helwys
(s)-So. Baptist Press—R
St. Anthony Messenger
Tate Publishing
Tau-Publishing—R
Twenty-Third Public.
Tyndale House—R
Verbinum
Victor Books
VMI Publishers
W Publishing
Warner Faith
WaterBrook Press
Wesleyan Publishing
Whitaker House—R
WindRiver—R
(s)-WinePress—R
(s)-Winer Foundation—R
Wood Lake Books—R
(s)-Word Alive

SPIRITUAL LIFE

ACTA Publications
Alba House—R
(s)-American Binding—R
Baker Trittin
Baker's Plays—R
(s)-Black Forest—R
Carson-Dellosa—R
Chapter Two—R
Charisma House—R
Christian Focus—R
Christian Publications
Christian Writer's Ebook—R
Created in Christ
(s)-Creation House—R
Crossway Books
CSS Publishing
Evergreen Press
Fair Havens—R
(s)-Fairway Press—R
FaithWalk
5th Estate
Focus on the Family—R
Forward Movement
Gospel Publishing
(s)-Hannibal Books—R
HarperSanFrancisco
Harrison House
Harvest House
Holy Fire Publishing—R
Howard Publishing
InterVarsity Press—R
Jossey-Bass
Kirk House
Kregel—R
Latimer Press—R
Legacy Publishers
Lighthouse eBooks—R
Living Books for All
(s)-Longwood—R
Lutheran Univ. Press
Lutterworth Press—R
MegaGrace Books
Meredith Books
New Seeds Books—R
(s)-One World—R
Paradise Research—R
Pathway Press
Paulist Press
Pilgrim Press—R
(s)-Pleasant Word—R
(s)-Providence—R
Quintessential Books—R
Rose Publishing
Tate Publishing
(s)-TEACH Services—R

Tyndale/SaltRiver
Verbinum
Victor Books
VMI Publishers
Warner Faith
WaterBrook Press
Wesleyan Publishing
Whitaker House—R
WindRiver—R
(s)-WinePress—R
(s)-Word Alive
World Publishing—R
Zondervan

SPIRITUAL WARFARE

(s)-American Binding—R
Baker Books
Baker's Plays—R
Baylor Univ. Press—R
(s)-Black Forest—R
Broadman & Holman
Carey Library, Wm.—R
Caribe-Betania Editores
Carson-Dellosa—R
Charisma House—R
Christian Focus—R
Christian Writer's Ebook—R
Continuum Intl.—R
Created in Christ
(s)-Creation House—R
Destiny Image—R
Editorial Portavoz—R
(s)-Essence—R
Evergreen Press
(s)-Fairway Press—R
FaithWalk
5th Estate
Greenwood/Praeger
(s)-Guardian Books—R
Harrison House
Harvest House
Holy Fire Publishing—R
(s)-Impact Christian—R
InterVarsity Press—R
Jireh Publishing
Lamplighter—R
Latimer Press—R
Legacy Publishers
Lighthouse eBooks—R
(s)-Lightning Star Press—R
Living Books for All
(s)-Longwood—R
Lutterworth Press—R
(s)-McDougal Publishing—R
Monarch Books—R
(s)-One World—R
Paradise Research—R

(s)-Pleasant Word—R
(s)-Providence—R
Read 'N Run—R
Rose Publishing
Selah Publishing—R
Tate Publishing
Virginia Pines Press
W Publishing
Warner Faith
Whitaker House—R
WindRiver—R
(s)-WinePress—R
(s)-Winer Foundation—R
(s)-Word Alive
World Publishing—R

SPORTS/RECREATION

ACTA Publications
Ambassador Books
(s)-American Binding—R
Baker Books
Baker's Plays—R
Ballantine Books
Canon Press—R
Christian Focus—R
Christian Writer's Ebook—R
Continuum Intl.—R
Cumberland House
(s)-Essence—R
Evergreen Press
Facts on File
(s)-Fairway Press—R
5th Estate
Good News Publishers
Greenwood/Praeger
(s)-Guardian Books—R
Hill Street Press—R
Holy Fire Publishing—R
Lighthouse eBooks—R
Lutterworth Press—R
New York Univ. Press
(s)-One World—R
(s)-Pleasant Word—R
Randall House—R
Read 'N Run—R
Tate Publishing
TowleHouse—R
VMI Publishers
WindRiver—R
(s)-WinePress—R
(s)-Word Alive

STEWARDSHIP

Ambassador-Emerald—R
(s)-American Binding—R
Baker Books
(s)-Black Forest—R

Charisma House—R
Christian Focus—R
Christian Writer's Ebook—R
College Press—R
Continuum Intl.—R
Created in Christ
(s)-Creation House—R
CSS Publishing
Discovery House—R
Educational Ministries
(s)-Essence—R
Evergreen Press
(s)-Fairway Press—R
FaithWalk
5th Estate
Forward Movement
Geneva Press
(s)-Guardian Books—R
Harrison House
Hensley Publishing
Hill Street Press—R
Holy Fire Publishing—R
Hope Publishing—R
InterVarsity Press—R
Judson Press
Kirk House
Lighthouse eBooks—R
(s)-McDougal Publishing—R
Neibauer Press—R
(s)-One World—R
Our Sunday Visitor—R
Pacific Press
Pilgrim Press—R
(s)-Pleasant Word—R
(s)-Providence—R
Randall House—R
Read 'N Run—R
RiverOak—R
Rose Publishing
Tate Publishing
VMI Publishers
Wesleyan Publishing
Westminster John Knox
Whitaker House—R
WindRiver—R
(s)-WinePress—R
(s)-Winer Foundation—R
(s)-Word Alive
World Publishing—R
Zondervan

THEOLOGY

ACU Press
Alba House—R
Ambassador-Emerald—R
(s)-American Binding—R

American Cath. Press—R
Baker Books
Baker's Plays—R
Baylor Univ. Press—R
Bethany House
(s)-Black Forest—R
Blue Dolphin
(s)-Brentwood—R
Bridge Resources
Broadman & Holman
Canon Press—R
Canticle Books—R
Catholic Answers—R
Chalice Press
Christian Focus—R
Christian Writer's Ebook—R
Cistercian—R
College Press—R
Conciliar Press—R
Continuum Intl.—R
Cook Communications
Created in Christ
(s)-Creation House—R
Cross Cultural—R
Crossroad Publishing—R
Crossway Books
CSS Publishing
Dimension Books—R
Discovery House—R
Doubleday
Earthen Vessel—R
Eerdmans Publishing—R
(s)-Essence—R
(s)-Fairway Press—R
FaithWalk
5th Estate
Fortress Press
Forward Movement
Founders Press
Four Courts Press—R
Friends United Press
Geneva Press
Georgetown Univ. Press
(s)-Guardian Books—R
HarperSanFrancisco
Hendrickson—R
Hill Street Press—R
Holy Fire Publishing—R
(s)-Impact Christian—R
Inkling Books—R
InterVarsity Press—R
Intl. Awakening—R
Judson Press
Kregel—R
Lighthouse eBooks—R
Lighthouse Trails—R

Liturgical Press
Liturgy Training
Lutheran Univ. Press
Lutterworth Press—R
Magnus Press—R
Mercer Univ. Press—R
Millennium III—R
Monarch Books—R
New Seeds Books—R
(s)-One World—R
P & R Publishing—R
Pacific Press
Paulist Press
Pilgrim Press—R
(s)-Pleasant Word—R
(s)-Poetry of Today
(s)-Providence—R
Quintessential Books—R
Randall House—R
Read 'N Run—R
Religious Education
Resource Public.
RiverOak—R
Rose Publishing
Sheed & Ward—R
Smyth & Helwys
(s)-So. Baptist Press—R
St. Augustine's Press—R
Still Waters Revival—R
T & T Clark—R
Tate Publishing
Trinity Foundation—R
Twenty-Third Public.
Tyndale House—R
UMI Publishing—R
Univ. Press of America—R
Univ./Ottawa Press
Verbinum
Victor Books
VMI Publishers
Westminster John Knox
Whitaker House—R
WindRiver—R
(s)-WinePress—R
(s)-Word Alive
World Publishing—R
Zondervan

TIME MANAGEMENT

(s)-American Binding—R
Baker Books
Barbour Publishing
(s)-Black Forest—R
Broadman & Holman
Christian Writer's Ebook—R
Continuum Intl.—R

Cook Communications
(s)-Creation House—R
(s)-DCTS Publishing—R
(s)-Elderberry Press
(s)-Essence—R
Evergreen Press
(s)-Fairway Press—R
5th Estate
(s)-Guardian Books—R
Harvest House
Hensley Publishing
Hill Street Press—R
Holy Fire Publishing—R
InterVarsity Press—R
Kirk House
Life Journey Books—R
Lighthouse eBooks—R
Lutterworth Press—R
Moms in Print
Monarch Books—R
Nelson Books
(s)-One World—R
(s)-Pleasant Word—R
(s)-Providence—R
Randall House—R
Ravenhawk Books—R
Read 'N Run—R
RiverOak—R
Rose Publishing
Summit Pub. Group—R
Tate Publishing
VMI Publishers
Walk Worthy—R
Warner Faith
Whitaker House—R
WindRiver—R
(s)-WinePress—R
(s)-Winer Foundation—R
(s)-Word Alive

TRACTS

Bible Advocate Press
Chapter Two—R
Christian Writer's Ebook—R
(s)-Essence—R
5th Estate
Forward Movement
(s)-Fruit-Bearer Pub.
Good News Publishers
Gospel Tract Society
(s)-Guardian Books—R
Intl. Awakening—R
Lamplighter—R
Libros Liguori
Living Books for All
(s)-Longwood—R

Lutterworth Press—R
Neibauer Press—R
(s)-One World—R
Read 'N Run—R
Rose Publishing
Tract League
Trinity Foundation—R
(s)-Word Alive

TRAVEL

(s)-American Binding—R
Baker Books
Baker's Plays—R
Ballantine Books
(s)-Black Forest—R
(s)-Brentwood—R
Christian Focus—R
Christian Writer's Ebook—R
Cumberland House
Destiny Image (books)—R
E-Digital Books
(s)-Elderberry Press
(s)-Essence—R
(s)-Fairway Press—R
FaithWalk
5th Estate
Greenwood/Praeger
(s)-Guardian Books—R
Hill Street Press—R
Holy Fire Publishing—R
Hope Publishing—R
Ideals Books
Lighthouse eBooks—R
Liguori
Lutterworth Press—R
(s)-One World—R
Peter Pauper Press
(s)-Pleasant Word—R
Read 'N Run—R
Tate Publishing
Whitaker House—R
WindRiver—R
(s)-WinePress—R
(s)-Word Alive

WOMEN'S ISSUES

Ambassador Books
Ambassador-Emerald—R
AMG Publishers—R
Baker Books
Baker's Plays—R
Ballantine Books
Barbour Publishing
Basic Books—R
Beacon Hill Press—R
BelleBooks—R

Bethany House
(s)-Black Forest—R
Blue Dolphin
(s)-Book Publishers
Broadman & Holman
Brown Books
Charisma House—R
Christian Focus—R
Christian Writer's Ebook—R
College Press—R
Continuum Intl.—R
Cook Communications
Created in Christ
(s)-Creation House—R
Crossway Books
(s)-Dean Press, Robbie—R
Destiny Image—R
Discovery House—R
Doubleday
Emmaus Road—R
(s)-Essence—R
Evergreen Press
(s)-Fairway Press—R
Faith Communications
FaithWalk
FamilyLife (books)—R
5th Estate
Focus on the Family—R
Fortress Press
Genesis Press
Gospel Publishing
Green Key Books
Greenwood/Praeger
(s)-Guardian Books—R
Guernica Editions—R
HarperSanFrancisco
Harrison House
Harvest House
Haworth Pastoral—R
Hensley Publishing
Hill Street Press—R
Holy Fire Publishing—R
Hope Publishing—R
Inkling Books—R
InterVarsity Press—R
Johns Hopkins—R
Jubilant Press—R
Judson Press
Kirk House
Kregel—R
Langmarc
Legacy Publishers
Life Cycle Books—R
Life Journey Books—R
Lighthouse eBooks—R
Lighthouse Trails—R

(s)-Lightning Star Press—R
(s)-Longwood—R
Loyola Press
Lutterworth Press—R
(s)-McDougal Publishing—R
Meredith Books
Monarch Books—R
Moody Publishers
Morehouse
Nelson Books
New Hope—R
New Leaf Press—R
New York Univ. Press
(s)-One World—R
P & R Publishing—R
Perigee Books
Pilgrim Press—R
(s)-Pleasant Word—R
(s)-Poetry of Today
(s)-Providence—R
Quintessential Books—R
Randall House—R
Ravenhawk Books—R
Read 'N Run—R
RiverOak—R
Rose Publishing
Scarecrow Press—R
Selah Publishing—R
Sheed & Ward—R
(s)-So. Baptist Press—R
Still Waters Revival—R
Summit Pub. Group—R
Tarcher, Jeremy P.
Tate Publishing
Third World Press—R
Twenty-Third Public.
Univ. of AR Press—R
VMI Publishers
W Publishing
Warner Faith
Whitaker House—R
WindRiver—R
(s)-WinePress—R
(s)-Word Alive

WORLD ISSUES

Allegiance Books—R
AMG Publishers—R
Baker Books
Baker's Plays—R
Bethany House
(s)-Black Forest—R
Blue Dolphin
Carey Library, Wm.—R
Charisma House—R
Christian Focus—R
Christian Writer's Ebook—R

Continuum Intl.—R
(s)-Creation House—R
Cross Cultural—R
Doubleday
(s)-Essence—R
(s)-Fairway Press—R
FaithWalk
5th Estate
Georgetown Univ. Press
Greenwood/Praeger
(s)-Guardian Books—R
Guernica Editions—R
HarperSanFrancisco
Harrison House
Hill Street Press—R
Holy Fire Publishing—R
InterVarsity Press—R
Kirk House
Lighthouse eBooks—R
(s)-Longwood—R
Lutterworth Press—R
Monarch Books—R
New Leaf Press—R
New Seeds Books—R
(s)-One World—R
Pilgrim Press—R
(s)-Pleasant Word—R
(s)-Providence—R
Quintessential Books—R
Ravenhawk Books—R
Read 'N Run—R
Regnery—R
RiverOak—R
Rose Publishing
Selah Publishing—R
Still Waters Revival—R
Tate Publishing
Tyndale House—R
Tyndale/SaltRiver
VMI Publishers
Warner Faith
Whitaker House—R
WindRiver—R
(s)-WinePress—R
(s)-Word Alive
Zondervan

WORSHIP

Abingdon Press
Ambassador-Emerald—R
(s)-American Binding—R
Baker's Plays—R
Baylor Univ. Press—R
(s)-Black Forest—R
Broadman & Holman
Canon Press—R
Chalice Press

Chapter Two—R
Charisma House—R
CharismaKids
Christian Focus—R
Christian Writer's Ebook—R
College Press—R
Continuum Intl.—R
Cook Communications
Created in Christ
(s)-Creation House—R
CSS Publishing
Destiny Image—R
Educational Ministries
(s)-Fairway Press—R
Faith Alive
FaithWalk
5th Estate
Founders Press
Greenwood/Praeger
Harrison House
Harvest House
Hill Street Press—R
Holy Fire Publishing—R
InterVarsity Press—R
Kirk House
Kregel—R
Life Journey Books—R
Lighthouse eBooks—R
Living Books for All
(s)-One World—R
Oregon Catholic Press
P & R Publishing—R
Pacific Press
Pilgrim Press—R
(s)-Pleasant Word—R
(s)-Poetry of Today
(s)-Providence—R
Randall House—R
Resource Public.
Rose Publishing
Selah Publishing—R
Tate Publishing
Verbinum
Victor Books
VMI Publishers
W Publishing
Wesleyan Publishing
Westminster John Knox
Whitaker House—R
WindRiver—R
(s)-WinePress—R
(s)-Word Alive

WORSHIP RESOURCES

Abingdon Press
American Cath. Press—R
Baker Books

Baylor Univ. Press—R
Bethany House
Catholic Book
Chalice Press
Charisma House—R
Christian Writer's Ebook—R
Continuum Intl.—R
Created in Christ
CSS Publishing
(s)-DCTS Publishing—R
(s)-Elderberry Press
(s) Essence—R
(s)-Fairway Press—R
Faith Alive
FaithWalk
5th Estate
Forward Movement
Founders Press
Geneva Press
Greenwood/Praeger
Group Publishing
(s)-Guardian Books—R
Hill Street Press—R
Holy Fire Publishing—R
InterVarsity Press—R
Judson Press
Lighthouse eBooks—R
Liturgical Press
Liturgy Training
(s)-One World—R
Our Sunday Visitor—R
Pilgrim Press—R
(s)-Pleasant Word—R
(s)-Providence—R
Randall House—R
Read 'N Run—R
Resource Public.
Rose Publishing
Smyth & Helwys
Standard Publishing
Tate Publishing
Twenty-Third Public.
VMI Publishers
Wesleyan Publishing
Westminster John Knox
WindRiver—R
(s)-WinePress—R
Wood Lake Books—R
(s)-Word Alive

WRITING HOW-TO

(s)-American Binding—R
(s)-Black Forest—R
Christian Writer's Ebook—R
Diamond Eyes—R
(s)-Essence—R
Evergreen Press

(s)-Fairway Press—R
FaithWalk
Filbert Publishing
Green Pastures—R
(s)-Guardian Books—R
Holy Fire Publishing—R
Jubilant Press—R
Lighthouse eBooks—R
(s)-One World—R
(s)-Pleasant Word—R
Selah Publishing—R
Square One—R
Tate Publishing
VMI Publishers
(s)-WinePress—R
(s)-Word Alive
Write Now—R

YOUTH BOOKS (Nonfiction)

Note: Listing denotes books for 8- to 12-year-olds, junior highs, or senior highs. If all three, it will say "all." If no age group is listed, they did not specify.

Ambassador Books (All)
Ambassador-Emerald—R
(s)-American Binding—R (Jr./Sr. High)
Baker Books
Baker Trittin (All)
Barbour Publishing
Bethany House
Big Idea (8-12/Jr. High)
BJU/Journey Forth—R (8-12)
(s)-Black Forest—R (All)
Boyds Mills Press—R (8-12/Jr. High)
Broadman & Holman
Canon Press—R
Carson-Dellosa—R (8-12)
CharismaKids (8-12/Jr. High)
Christian Ed. Pub.
Christian Focus—R (All)
Christian Writer's Ebook—R (All)
Cladach Publishing—R (8-12)
Contemporary Drama
(s)-Creation House—R (All)
Educational Ministries
Eerdmans/Young Readers
(s)-Essence—R
Evergreen Press
Facts on File
Fair Havens—R (8-12/Jr. High)
(s)-Fairway Press—R
5th Estate (8-12)
Focus on the Family—R (Sr. High)
Friends United Press

Genesis Press
Glory Bound Books (All)
Green Pastures—R (8-12)
(s)-Guardian Books—R
Harcourt Religion (Sr. High)
Harrison House (All)
Health Commun.
Hensley Publishing
Holy Fire Publishing—R (All)
Honor Kidz (8-12)
Invert Books (Jr./Sr. High)
Judson Press
Kaleidoscope Press—R
Kregel—R (All)
Lamplighter—R
Latimer Press—R (Jr./Sr. High)
Legacy Press—R (8-12)
Lighthouse eBooks—R (All)
McRuffy Press (8-12)
Moody Publishers
New Canaan
New Hope—R
(s)-One World—R (All)
OnStage Publishing
P & R Publishing—R (Jr. High)
Pacific Press
Pauline Books—R
Pelican Publishing—R (8-12)
Peter Pauper Press (8-12)
Pflaum Publishing (8-12/Jr. High)
(s)-Pleasant Word—R (All)
Quintessential Books—R (Jr./Sr. High)
Randall House—R (All)
Ravenhawk Books—R (All)
Read 'N Run—R
(s)-So. Baptist Press—R
Still Waters Revival—R
Tate Publishing (All)
Verbinum (All)
VMI Publishers (All)
WaterBrook Press (All)
WindRiver—R (All)
(s)-WinePress—R (All)
Wood Lake Books—R
(s)-Word Alive (All)
Youth Specialties (Jr./Sr. High)
Zondervan (All)

YOUTH PROGRAMS

(s)-American Binding—R
Baker Books
Carson-Dellosa—R
Christian Writer's Ebook—R
Church Growth Inst.
Contemporary Drama
Educational Ministries

(s)-Fairway Press—R
Gospel Publishing
Group Publishing
(s)-Guardian Books—R
Harcourt Religion
Hensley Publishing

Holy Fire Publishing—R
Invert Books
Judson Press
Latimer Press—R
(s)-One World—R
Pflaum Publishing

Pilgrim Press—R
Randall House—R
Read 'N Run—R
Rose Publishing
Standard Publishing
Tate Publishing

ALPHABETICAL LISTINGS OF BOOK PUBLISHERS

(*) An asterisk before a listing indicates unconfirmed or no information update.
(#) A number symbol before a listing indicates it was updated from their guidelines or other current sources.
(+) A plus sign before a listing indicates it is a new listing this year and was not included last year.

If you do not find the publisher you are looking for, check the General Index. See the introduction to that index for the codes used to identify the current status of each unlisted publisher. If you do not understand all the terms or abbreviations used in these listings, read the "How to Use This Book" section, or check the glossary.

+AADEON PUBLISHING COMPANY, PO Box 223, Hartford CT 06141. Fax 206-666-5132. E-mail: submissions@aadeon.com. Website: www.aadeon.com. George Burgess, pub; submit to The Editor. Addresses social, cultural, and political issues related to the United States of America; must be insightful, historically and biblically accurate, and focused toward a Christian readership. Publishes 1 title/yr. Accepts mss through agents. Does print-on-demand. Reprints books. Prefers 160 pgs. Royalty 8% on net; no advance. Average first printing 100-5,000. Publication within 1 yr. Considers simultaneous submissions. Requires accepted ms on disk in Microsoft Word. Responds in 1-4 mos. Requires NKJV. Guidelines on Website; no catalog.

> **Nonfiction:** Proposal/3 chapters or complete ms; no phone/fax/e-query.
>
> **Photos/Artwork:** Open to queries from freelance artists.
>
> **Tips:** "We are particularly interested in manuscripts that challenge average people to confront and overcome the negative influences of an increasingly secular and godless society. Manuscripts must be well organized, professionally edited, easy to understand, biblically based, and scripturally supported (frequent quotations from the Bible—chapter and verse—to support writings). Manuscripts must clearly speak to both a Christian and non-Christian audience."

ABAGAIL PRESS, PO Box 1477, Cordova TN 38088-1477. (901)465-7224. Websites: www.abagailpress.com, or www.alexandraclair.com. Nondenominational. Alexandra F. Clair, ed.; John A. Bailey, acq. ed. Every believer has a testimony and story, and we want to give voice to some of those stories. 90% of books from first-time authors. Print-on-demand publisher (no charge to author). No reprints. Prefers 100-150 pgs. Royalty 8-12% of net; no advance. Publication within 6 mos. Considers simultaneous submissions. Responds in 4-6 wks. Guidelines (also on Website); no catalog.

> **Nonfiction:** Proposal/first 3 chapters; prefers mail query; phone/e-query OK. "Only true stories of salvation, deliverance, and healing."
>
> **Tips:** "Looking for personal stories about or by those who overcome challenges in Christian faith. We want well-written material, conversational, honest." Offers advice and helps with promotion.

#ABINGDON PRESS, 201—8th Ave. S., PO Box 801, Nashville TN 37202. (615)749-6301. Fax (615)749-6512. E-mail: (first initial and last name) @umpublishing.org. Website: www.abingdonpress.com. United Methodist Publishing House. Editors: Harriett Jane Olson, ed. dir.; Ron Kidd, gen. interest bks.; Robert Ratcliff, professional and academic bks.; Paul Franklyn, reference bks.; Joseph A. Crowe, gen. interest bks.; Peg Augustine, children's bks.; Crys Zinkiewicz, youth bks. Books and church supplies directed primarily to a mainline religious market. Imprint: Dimensions for Living (see separate listing). Publishes 120 titles/yr. Receives 3,000 submissions annually. Less than 5% of books from first-time authors. Accepts mss through agents. No reprints. Prefers 144 pgs. Royalty 5-10% on retail; advance. Average first printing 3,500-4,000. Publication within 18 mos. Prefers no simultaneous submissions. Requires requested ms on disk. Responds in 8-12 wks. Prefers NRSV or a variety of which NRSV is one. Guidelines (also by e-mail); free catalog.

Nonfiction: Proposal/2 chapters; no phone/fax/e-query.

Ethnic Books: African American, Hispanic, Native American, Korean.

Photos/Artwork: Accepts freelance photos for book covers.

Tips: "We develop and produce materials to help more people in more places come to know and love God through Jesus Christ and to choose to serve God and neighbor."

ACTA PUBLICATIONS, 5559 W. Howard St., Skokie IL 60077-2621. Toll-free (800)397-2282. Fax (800)397-0079. E-mail: actapublications@aol.com. Website: www.actapublications.com. Catholic. Gregory F. Augustine Pierce, pres. & co-publisher. Resources for the "end user" of the Christian faith. Publishes 10 titles/yr. Receives 100 submissions annually. 50% of books from first-time authors. Prefers 150-200 pgs. Royalty 10-12% of net; no advance. Average first printing 3,000. Publication within 1 yr. Responds in 2 mos. Prefers NRSV. Guidelines; catalog for 9x12 SAE/2 stamps.

Nonfiction: Query or proposal/1 chapter; no phone/fax/e-query.

Tips: "Most open to books that are useful to a large number of average Christians. Read our catalog and one of our books first."

ACU PRESS, 1648 Campus Ct., Abilene TX 79601, or ACU Station Box 29138, Abilene TX 79699. (325)674-2720. Fax (325)674-6471. E-mail: LEMMONST@acu.edu. Website: www.acu.edu/acupress, or www.hillcrestpublishing.com. Church of Christ/Abilene Christian University. Thom Lemmons, ed.; Karen Cukrowski, asst. ed. Guidance in the religious life for members and leaders of the denomination, general Christian readership. Publishes 5 titles/yr. Receives 100 submissions annually. 10% of books from first-time authors. Royalty 10%. Average first printing 1,000. Publication within 18 mos. Considers simultaneous submissions. Responds in 2 mos. Catalog.

Nonfiction: Proposal/3 chapters.

A.D. PLAYERS THEATER, 2710 W. Alabama, Houston TX 77098. (713)526-2721. E-mail: lee@adplayers.org. Website: www.adplayers.org. Lee Walker, literary mngr. Produces full-length plays and musicals with Judeo-Christian world-view; interested only in scripts suitable for production. Payment negotiable. Guidelines available by e-mail or Website.

Fiction: Play scripts only/query first; phone/fax/e-query OK. "Send synopsis and/or brief scene or demo tape/CD. Include cast list."

Tips: "Our only consideration is whether the scripts are suitable for production in our theater—we don't publish them." They do not publish books, scripts, etc.

ALBA HOUSE, 2187 Victory Blvd., Staten Island NY 10314-6603. (718)761-0047. Fax (718)761-0057. E-mail: Edmund_Lane@juno.com. Website: www.alba-house.com. Catholic/Society of St. Paul. Edmund C. Lane SSP, ed-in-chief; Frank Sadowski, SSP, ed.; Father Victor Viberti, SSP, acq. ed. Imprint: St. Pauls. Publishes 24 titles/yr. Receives 450 submissions annually. 20% of books from first-time authors. No mss through agents. Reprints books. Prefers 124 pgs. Royalty 7-10% on retail; no advance. Average first printing 3,500. Publication within 9 mos. Prefers requested ms on disk. Responds in 1-2 mos. Free guidelines/catalog.

Nonfiction: Query.

Special Needs: Spirituality in the Roman Catholic tradition; lives of the saints.

#ALLEGIANCE BOOKS, 380 Crown Oak Centre Dr., Longwood FL 32750. Toll-free (866)381-2665, ext. 103. E-mail: tfreiling@allegiancepress.com. Website: www.allegiancepress.com. Xulon

Press. Tom Freiling, pub. Gives readers the truth about today's most relevant cultural and public policy issues from a Christian world-view. Publishes 12 titles/yr. 20% of books from first-time authors. Prefers mss through agents. Reprints books. Prefers 200-400 pgs. Royalty 15-20% of net. Average first printing 10,000. Publication within 9-18 mos. Considers simultaneous submissions. Prefers requested mss by e-mail. Guidelines on Website; no catalog.

> **Nonfiction:** Proposal/2 chapters; e-query OK.

> **Tips:** Most open to history, political, or current events.

AMBASSADOR BOOKS, INC., 91 Prescott St., Worcester MA 01605-1702. (508)756-2893. Fax (508)757-7055. E-mail: info@ambassadorbooks.com. Website: www.ambassador books.com. Catholic. Chris Driscoll, acq. ed. Books of intellectual and spiritual excellence. Publishes 7 titles/yr. Receives 2,000 submissions annually. 50% of books from first-time authors. Accepts mss through agents. No reprints. Royalty 8-12% of retail; no advance. Publication within 1 yr. Considers simultaneous submissions. Responds in 3-4 mos. Prefers NAB. Guidelines (also by e-mail/Website); free catalog (or on Website).

> **Nonfiction:** Query; no phone/fax/e-query.

> **Fiction:** Query. Juvenile, young adult, and adult; picture books.

> **Photos/Artwork:** Accepts freelance photos for book covers.

> **Tips:** "Most open to books that will have a positive impact on readers' lives. Must be well written and fit with our mission."

AMBASSADOR-EMERALD, INTL., 427 Wade Hampton Blvd., Greenville SC 29609. (864)235-2434. Fax (864)235-2491. E-mail: publisher@emeraldhouse.com. Website: www.emerald house.com. European office: Ambassador Productions, Providence House, Ardenlee, Belfast BT6 8QJ, N. Ireland. Phone 028 90450010. Fax 028 90739659. E-mail: info@ambassador-productions.com. Emerald House Group, Inc. Tim Lowry, ed. Dedicated to spreading the gospel of Christ and empowering Christians through the written word. Publishes 55 titles/yr. Receives 400 submissions annually. 15% of books from first-time authors. Accepts mss through agents. **SUBSIDY PUBLISHES 1%.** Reprints books. Prefers 150-200 pgs. Royalty 5-15% of net; advance $1,000. Average first printing 5,000. Publication within 1 yr. Considers simultaneous submissions. Prefers requested ms on disk or by e-mail. Responds in 3 mos. Prefers KJV. Guidelines (also by e-mail); free catalog.

> **Nonfiction:** Query only; fax/e-query OK.

> **Fiction:** Query only; fax/e-query OK. All ages.

> **Tips:** "We're most open to nonfiction writing for women."

+AMERICAN BOOK PUBLISHING. E-mail: acqeditor@american-book.com (submissions), or info@american-book.com (guidelines). Website: www.american-book.com. Open to spiritual books. Guidelines by e-mail/Website. Incomplete topical listings. No questionnaire returned.

> **Nonfiction:** E-query required; submission instructions on Website.

> **Fiction:** E-query required; submission instructions on Website.

> **Tips:** "We offer a variety of publishing options, which may include a contract with an advance for well-established authors; a contract without an advance or deposit for professional writers; or a contract with a $780 deposit for the promising author. The deposit is returned to the author the first quarter after the book is released when minimum sales have been met."

AMERICAN CATHOLIC PRESS, 16565 State St., South Holland IL 60473-2025. (708)331-5485. Fax (708)331-5484. E-mail: acp@acpress.org. Website: www.acpress.org, or www.leafletmissal.com. Catholic worship resources. Father Michael Gilligan, ed. dir. Publishes 4 titles/yr. Receives 10 submissions annually. Reprints books. Pays $25-100 for outright purchases only. Average first printing 3,000. Publication within 1 yr. No simultaneous submissions. Responds in 2 mos. Prefers NAS. No guidelines; catalog for SASE.

Nonfiction: Query first; no phone/fax/e-query.

Tips: "We publish only materials on the Roman Catholic liturgy. Especially interested in new music for church services."

AMG PUBLISHERS, 6815 Shallowford Rd. (37421), PO Box 22000, Chattanooga TN 37422. Toll-free (800)266-4977. (423)894-6060. Fax (800)265-6690 or (423)894-9511. E-mail: danp@amginternational.org. Website: www.amgpublishers.com. AMG International. Dan Penwell, dir. of product development/acquisitions; Dr. Warren Baker, sr. ed.; Richard Steele, assoc. ed. To provide biblically oriented books for reference, learning, and personal growth. Imprint: Living Ink Books. Publishes 35 titles/yr. Receives 1,500 submissions annually. 20% of books from first-time authors. Accepts mss through agents. Reprints books. Prefers 50,000 wds. or 175 pgs. Royalty 10-16% of net; advance $1,500 and up. Average first printing 3,000. Publication within 18 mos. Accepts simultaneous submissions. Prefers accepted ms by mail. Responds in 1-4 mos. Prefers KJV, NASB, NIV, NKJV, NLT. Guidelines (also by e-mail/Website); catalog for 9x12 SAE/5 stamps.

Nonfiction: Query letter first; e-query preferred. "Looking for well-written nonfiction. We have a broad interest in biblically oriented books."

Fiction: Teen fantasy.

Special Needs: Women's issues and men's issues.

Also Does: Bible software, Bible audio cassettes, CD-ROMs.

Tips: "Most open to a book that is well thought out, clearly written, and finely edited. A professional proposal, following our specific guidelines, has the best chance of acceptance."

**Note: This publisher serviced by The Writer's Edge.

#ANDROS BOOKS PUBLISHING, 3038 E. Irwin Ave., Mesa AZ 85204-7270. (928)778-4491. Fax (928)778-4620. E-mail: androsbks@aol.com. Website: www.hometown.aol.com/androsbks. Small publisher. Susanne Bain, pub. Specializes in homeschooling and parental involvement in education. Prefers 200 pgs. Considers simultaneous submissions. Responds within 6 wks. No e-mail submissions (mail only). Guidelines (also by e-mail); no catalog.

Nonfiction: Query only first; no phone/fax query, e-query OK.

Tips: "We are currently seeking uplifting works about homeschool and positive parental involvement in children's education or continuing education. We prefer 'how to do it' or 'how we did it' from homeschooling parents only. We want personal experience."

BAKER BOOKS, Box 6287, Grand Rapids MI 49516-6287. (616)676-9185. Fax (616)676-9573. Website: www.bakerbooks.com, or www.thenarrowroad.net. Baker Publishing Group. Ministry titles for the church. No freelance submissions. Submit only through an agent, Writer's Edge, or ECPA First Edition.

BAKER'S PLAYS, INC., PO Box 699222, Quincy MA 02269-9222. (617)745-0805. Fax (617)745-9891. Website: www.bakersplays.com. Deirdre Shaw, mng. dir. Publishes 2-8 titles/yr. Receives 800 submissions annually. 60% of plays from first-time authors. Accepts mss through agents. Reprints plays. Book royalty 10% on retail; performance royalty 50%; no advance. Average first printing 1,000. Publication within 6 mos. Considers simultaneous submissions. Accepts requested ms on disk. Responds in 6-8 mos. Free guidelines; separate section in their general catalog, $4.

Plays: Complete ms. "Most open to plays that involve biblical stories or skits on modern Christian life."

Contest: High School Play Writing Contest. Deadline: January 31. No entry fee. Prizes: $500 (with publication), $250, $100. Plays about the high-school experience or appropriate for high school productions. Requires a signature from a sponsoring drama or English teacher.

Tips: "We currently publish full-length plays, one-act plays for young audiences, theater texts and musicals, plays written by high schoolers, with a separate division which publishes religious plays. We consider plays year round." If your play has been produced, send copies of press clippings.

BAKER TRITTIN PRESS, PO Box 277, Winona Lake IN 46590. (574)269-6100. Fax (574)269-6130. E-mail: info@btconcepts.com. Website: www.bakertrittinpress.com. Marvin G. Baker, ed-in-chief. Imprints: Tweener Press; Innovative Christian Publications. Books for 8- to 12-year-olds. Publishes 4-5 religious titles/yr. New publisher. 50% of books from first-time authors. Accepts mss through agents. No reprints. Prefers 20,000-40,000 wds. Royalty 7-10% on retail; no advance. Average first printing 2,500. Publication within 1 yr. No simultaneous submissions. Responds in 1 mo. Accepts mss on disk or by e-mail. Prefers NIV. No guidelines; catalog available soon.

    Nonfiction: Proposal/3 chapters; no phone query; fax/e-query OK.

    Fiction: Proposal/3 chapters; no phone query; fax/e-query OK.

BALLANTINE BOOKS, 1745 Broadway, 18th Fl., New York NY 10019. (212)782-9000. Website: www.randomhouse.com/BB. A Division of Random House. Dan Smetanka, religion ed. General publisher that does a few religious books. Mss from agents only. No e-query. Royalty 8-15%; variable advances. Guidelines on Website; no catalog.

BANTAM BOOKS—See Doubleday.

BARBOUR PUBLISHING, INC., 1810 Barbour Dr., PO Box 719, Uhrichsville OH 44683. (740)922-6045. Fax (740)922-5948. E-mail: info@barbourbooks.com. Website: www.barbourbooks.com. Paul Muckley, sr. ed./nonfiction (pmuckley@barbourbooks .com); Rebecca Germany (rgermany@barbourbooks.com), sr. ed./romance and women's fiction (novels & novellas); Kelly Williams (kwilliams@barbourbooks.com), mng. ed. and youth/children/gift acquisitions. Distributes Christian books at value prices. Imprints: Barbour Books (fiction and nonfiction) and Heartsong Presents (romance: see separate listing). Publishes 170 titles/yr. (80 fiction titles). Receives 2,000 submissions annually. 20% of books from first-time authors. Few mss through agents. Prefers 50,000 wds. (novels & nonfiction). Royalty 8-12% of net; outright purchases $500-5,000; advance $500-7,500. Average first printing 15,000-20,000. Publication within 2 yrs. Considers simultaneous submissions. Responds in 3-6 mos. Prefers NIV, KJV. Guidelines (also by e-mail/Website); catalog $2.

    Nonfiction: Proposal/3 chapters; no phone/fax/e-query.

    Fiction: Proposal/2 chapters to Rebecca Germany, fiction ed. Novellas 20,000 wds. "We are interested in a mystery/romance series." See separate listing for Heartsong Presents.

    Tips: "We seek solid, evangelical books with the greatest mass appeal. A good title on practical Christian living will go much farther with Barbour than will a commentary on Jude. Do your homework before sending us a manuscript; send material that will work well within our publishing philosophy."

    **Note: This publisher serviced by The Writer's Edge.

#BARCLAY PRESS, 211 N. Meridian St., Newberg OR 97132. (503)538-9775. Fax (503)554-8597. E-mail: info@barclaypress.com. Website: www.barclaypress.com. Friends/Quaker. Dan McCracken, gen. mngr. No unsolicited manuscripts.

    **Note: This publisher serviced by The Writer's Edge.

BASIC BOOKS, 387 Park Ave. S., 12th Fl., New York NY 10016-8810. (212)340-8100. Fax (212)340-8115. Website: www.basicbooks.com. Elizabeth Maguire, VP, assoc. ed. Perseus Books Group. Secular publisher that does books on religion and spirituality. Publishes 100 titles/yr. Receives 800 submissions annually. 5% of books from first-time authors. Accepts mss through agents. Reprints books. Royalty 10-15% on retail; advance to $10,000. Publication within 1 yr. Considers simultaneous submissions. Responds in 3-6 mos. No submissions on disk or by e-mail. Prefers NIV. Guidelines on Website; free catalog.

Nonfiction: Query by mail, or send proposal/3 chapters. No complete mss. "We do not do poetry, romance, children's books, or conventional thrillers."

BAYLOR UNIVERSITY PRESS, One Bear Pl., #97363, Waco TX 76798-7308. (254)710-3164. Fax (254)710-3440. E-mail: Carey_Newman@baylor.edu. Website: www.baylorpress.com. Baptist. Carey C. Newman, dir. Imprint: Markham Press Fund. Academic press producing scholarly books on religion and social sciences; church-state studies. Publishes 5 titles/yr. Receives 120 submissions annually. 10% of books from first-time authors. Accepts mss through agents. Reprints books. Prefers 250 pgs. Royalty 10% of net; no advance. Average first printing 1,000. Publication within 6 mos. No simultaneous submissions. Responds in 2 mos. Guidelines on Website; free catalog.

> **Nonfiction:** Query/outline & 1-3 chapters; no phone query, e-query OK. Looking for academic books.

BEACON HILL PRESS OF KANSAS CITY, PO Box 419527, Kansas City MO 64141. (816)931-1900. Fax (816)753-4071. E-mail: jap@bhill.com. Website: www.bhillkc.com. Nazarene Publishing House/Church of the Nazarene. Bonnie Perry, pub. dir.; Richard Buckner, ministry line ed.; Judi Perry, consumer ed. A Christ-centered publisher that provides authentically Christian resources that are faithful to God's Word and relevant to life. Imprint: Beacon Hill Books. Publishes 30 titles/yr. Accepts mss through agents. Reprints books. Prefers 30,000-60,000 wds. or 250 pgs. Royalty 12-14% of net; advance; some outright purchases. Average first printing 5,000. Publication within 1 yr. Considers simultaneous submissions. Responds in 3 mos. or longer. Free guidelines/catalog.

> **Nonfiction:** Proposal/2 chapters; no phone/fax query. "Looking for practical Christian living, felt needs, Christian care, spiritual growth, and ministry resources."

> **Tips:** "Nearly all our titles come through acquisitions, and the number of freelance submissions has declined dramatically. If you wish to submit, follow guidelines above. You are always welcome to submit after sending for guidelines."

> ****Note:** This publisher serviced by The Writer's Edge.

+BELLEBOOKS, PO Box 67, Smyrna GA 30081. Phone/fax (770)432-4860. E-mail: belle books@bellebooks.com. Website: www.bellebooks.com. Deborah Smith, ed. Publishes southern, wholesome, feel-good fiction and nonfiction. Publishes 1 title/yr. Receives 25-40 submissions annually. 0% of books from first-time authors. Accepts mss through agents. Reprints books. Prefers 75,000 wds. or 300 pgs. Royalty; advance. Average first printing 3,000. Publication within 12 mos. Considers simultaneous submissions. Responds in 3 mos. No guidelines or catalog.

> **Nonfiction:** Query by e-mail only. "Looking for nondenominational books with an emphasis on general spirituality."

> **Fiction:** Query by e-mail only "We only publish books with Southern (S.E. USA) settings."

> **Photos/Artwork:** Open to queries from freelance artists.

> **Tips:** "We publish humorous, nondenominational, general inspiration suitable for mainstream as well as Christian readers."

BETHANY HOUSE PUBLISHERS, 11400 Hampshire Ave. S., Bloomington MN 55438. (952)829-2500. Fax (952)996-1304 or (952)829-2768. Website: www.bethanyhouse .com. Baker Publishing Group. Submit to nonfiction, fiction, or juvenile ed. To publish books communicating biblical truth that will inspire and challenge people in both spiritual and practical areas of life. Publishes 90-100 titles/yr. 2% of books from first-time authors. Accepts mss through agents. No reprints. Negotiable royalty on net; negotiable advance. Publication within 1 yr. Considers simultaneous submissions. Responds in 13 wks. Guidelines for fiction/nonfiction/juvenile on Website; catalog for 9x12 SAE/5 stamps.

> **Nonfiction:** One-page fax query only; all unsolicited submissions returned unopened. "Seeking well-planned and developed books in the following categories: personal growth,

deeper-life spirituality, contemporary issues, women's issues, reference, applied theology, and inspirational."

Fiction: One-page fax query only; all unsolicited submissions returned unopened. "We publish adult fiction in several genres, teen/young adult fiction, and children's fiction series (6-12 yrs.)."

Tips: "We do not accept unsolicited queries or proposals via telephone, regular mail, or e-mail, but will consider one-page queries sent by facsimile (fax) and directed to Adult Nonfiction, Adult Fiction, or Young Adult/Children."

**Note: This publisher serviced by The Writer's Edge.

+BIBLE ADVOCATE PRESS, PO Box 33677, Denver CO 80233. (303)452-7973. Fax (303)452-0657. E-mail: bibleadvocate@cog7.org. Website: www.cog7.org (see Publications). Sherri Langton, assoc. ed. Publishes new line of outreach tracts *Light for Life,* geared for the seeker, with topics that address current concerns in society (*The Da Vinci Code,* tragedy, homosexuality, etc.). Byline given. Pays $60-65. Word count: 1,200 wds. The tract would probably appear in the *Bible Advocate* magazine and be featured online. Responds in 4-8 wks. Complete ms. Most open to e-mail submissions (no attachments). Contributor's copies upon publication. Samples for #10 SAE/2 stamps.

BIG IDEA, INC., 230 Franklin Rd., Franklin TN 37064. (615)224-2200. E-mail: cindy.kenney@ bigidea.com. Website: www.bigidea.com. Classic Media. Cindy Kenney, sr. mng. ed. To creatively impact the lives of children, ages 2 through 12, with stories that teach biblical values. Publishes 15-20 titles/yr. Receives 1,000 submissions annually. 25% of books from first-time authors. Accepts mss through agents. No reprints. Prefers 1,500-2,000 wds. Negotiable outright purchase (no royalties); no advance. Average first printing 10,000-20,000. Publication within 18 mos. Considers simultaneous submissions. Responds in 4-6 mos. Prefers NIRV or NIV. No catalog (see online).

Nonfiction: Query first; complete ms for picture or board books; no phone/fax query; e-query OK.

Fiction: Query first; complete ms for picture books; no phone/fax query; e-query OK.

Special Needs: Looking for picture books and tween books.

Tips: "Come up with stories/materials that are highly innovative, clever, witty, and teach a biblical value. Looking for children's curriculum writers."

BJU PRESS/JOURNEY FORTH, 1700 Wade Hampton Blvd., Greenville SC 29614. (864)370-1800, ext. 4350. Fax (864)298-0268, ext. 4324. E-mail: jb@bju.edu. Website: www.bjup.com. Bob Jones University Press. Nancy Lohr, youth ed. Our goal is to publish excellent, trustworthy books for children. Publishes 10 titles/yr. Receives 500 submissions annually. 30% of books from first-time authors. Accepts mss through agents. Reprints books. Royalty on net; outright purchases (for first-time authors). Average first printing 5,000. Publication within 12-18 mos. Considers simultaneous submissions. No submissions by disk or e-mail. Responds in 8-12 wks. Requires KJV. Guidelines (also by e-mail/Website); catalog for 9x12 SAE/3 stamps.

Nonfiction: Query only first; fax query OK.

Fiction: Proposal/5 chapters or complete ms. For children & teens. "We prefer overtly Christian or Christian world-view."

Photos/Artwork: Open to queries from freelance artists.

Tips: "Any of the topics marked have a good chance, provided the writing is clear and compelling. Mediocre writing is not going to get past the first reader. Take time to learn about and hone your craft. The precollege, homeschool market welcomes print-rich, well-written books, and we welcome youth manuscripts that fit that bill. No picture books, please, but compelling novels for early readers are always good for us. Biographies on the lives of Christian heroes and statesmen are also a good fit."

**Note: This publisher serviced by The Writer's Edge.

BLUE DOLPHIN PUBLISHING, INC., PO Box 8, Nevada City CA 95959. (530)265-6925. Fax (530)265-0787. E-mail: Bdolphin@netshel.net. Website: www.bluedolphinpublishing .com. Paul M. Clemens, pub. Imprint: Pelican Pond (fiction & poetry), Papillon Publishing (juvenile), and Symposium Publishing (nonfiction). Books that help people grow in their social and spiritual awareness. Publishes 20-24 titles/yr. (includes 10-12 print-on-demand). Receives 4,800 submissions annually. 90% of books from first-time authors. Prefers about 60,000 wds. or 200-300 pgs. Royalty 10-15% of net; no advance. Average first printing 300, then on demand. Publication within 10 mos. Considers simultaneous submissions. Requires requested ms on disk. Responds in 3-6 mos. Guidelines (also on Website); catalog for 6x9 SAE/2 stamps.

> **Nonfiction:** Query or proposal/1 chapter; no phone/e-query. "Looking for books that will increase people's spiritual and social awareness. We will consider all topics."
>
> **Fiction:** Query/2-pg. synopsis. Pelican Pond Imprint. Will consider all genres for all ages, except children's board books or picture books.
>
> **Tips:** "We look for topics that would appeal to the general market, are interesting, different, and will aid in the growth and development of humanity. See Website before submitting."
>
> **Note:** This publisher also publishes books on a range of topics, including cross-cultural spirituality. They also offer a co-publishing arrangement, not necessarily a royalty deal.

+BOGARD PRESS, 4605 N. State Line Ave., Texarkana TX 75503. (903)792-2783. Fax (903)792-8128. E-mail: larryclements@abaptist.org. Website: www.abaptist.org. American Baptist. Larry Clements, ed-in-chief; Libby Gill, children's ed. (children@abaptist.org); Jim Jones, ad. curriculum ed. (jimjones@abaptist.org); Kyle Elkins, high school, electives, and Spanish ed, (kelkins@abaptist.org). Curriculum publisher. Incomplete topical listings. No questionnaire returned.

BOOKLOCKER.COM, INC., PO Box 2399, Bangor ME 04402-2399. Fax (207)262-5544. E-mail from Website. Website: www.booklocker.com. E-books or print-on-demand. Royalty varies according to product/price. Prices and terms on Website; also contract. No questionnaire returned.

BOOKLOCKER JR, PO Box 2399, Bangor ME 04402-2399. Fax (207)262-5544. E-mail from Website. Website: www.booklocker.com/getpublished/published.html. E-books or print-on-demand. Seeking submissions from young authors, under 18 years. Royalty varies according to product/price. Prices and terms on Website; also contract. Not included in topical listings. No questionnaire returned.

*BORDEN BOOKS, 6532 E. 71st St., Ste. 105, Tulsa OK 74133. Dave Borden, ed. Not included in topical listings. No questionnaire returned.

BOYDS MILLS PRESS, 815 Church St., Honesdale PA 18431-1895. (570)253-1164. Fax (570)253-0179. E-mail: admin@boydsmillspress.com. Website: www.boydsmillspress .com. Highlights for Children. Larry Rosler, ed. dir. Publishes a wide range of literary children's titles, for preschool through young adult; very few religious. Publishes 50 titles/yr. Receives 10,000 submissions annually. 40% of books from first-time authors. Reprints books. Royalty 4-12% on retail; advances vary. Considers simultaneous submissions. Responds in 1 mo. Guidelines and catalog on Website.

> **Nonfiction:** Query/proposal package, outline, 3 sample chapters; no fax or e-query.
>
> **Fiction:** Outline/synopsis/first 3 chapters for novels; complete ms for picture books. "We are always interested in multicultural settings."
>
> **Tips:** "Looking for picture books for pre-readers that contain simple, focused, and fun concepts for children ages 3-5, and concept books. We are primarily a general trade book publisher. For us, if stories include religious themes, the stories should still have a wide enough appeal for a general audience."

BRANDEN PUBLISHING CO., PO Box 812094, Wellesley MA 02482. (781)235-3634. Fax (781)790-1056. E-mail: Branden@branden.com. Website: www.branden.com. Adolph Caso, ed. Books by or about women, children, military, Italian American or African American themes; religious fiction. Publishes 15 titles/yr. Receives 1,000 submissions annually. Accepts mss through agents. Reprints books. Royalty 5-10% of net; advance $1,000 max. Publication within 10 mos. Responds in 1 mo.

>**Nonfiction:** Paragraph query only with author's vita & SASE; no phone/fax/e-query.

>**Fiction:** Paragraph query only with author's vita & SASE. Ethnic, religious fiction.

BRAZOS PRESS, PO Box 6287, Grand Rapids MI 49516-6287. Website: www.BrazosPress.com. Division of Baker Publishing Group. Publishes books by evangelical, Roman Catholic, Protestant mainline, and Eastern Orthodox writers. No freelance submissions. Submit through Writer's Edge or ECPA First Edition.

BRIDGE-LOGOS, PO Box 141630, Gainesville FL 32614-1640. (352)472-7900. Fax (352)472-7908. E-mail: editorial@bridgelogos.com. Website: www.bridgelogos.com. Beverly G. Browning, mng. ed. Purpose is to clearly define God's changeless Word to a changing world. Imprints: Logos, Bridge, Selah, and Synergy. Publishes 25 titles/yr. Receives 2,000 submissions annually. **SUBSIDY PUBLISHES 12%.** Royalty 6-25% of net; some advances, $1,000-10,000. Average first printing 5,000. Publication within 6 mos. Considers simultaneous submissions. Responds in 15 wks. No disk. Guidelines (also by e-mail/Website); no catalog.

>**Nonfiction:** Query only. "Most open to evangelism, spiritual growth, self-help, and education."

>**Special Needs:** Reference, biography, current issues, controversial issues, church renewal, women's issues, and Bible commentary.

>**Photos/Artwork:** Accepts freelance photos for book covers.

>**Tips:** "Have a great message, a well-written manuscript, and a specific plan and willingness to market your book. Looking for previously published authors with an active ministry who are experts on their subject."

BRIDGE RESOURCES/WITHERSPOON PRESS, 100 Witherspoon St., Louisville KY 40202-1396. Toll-free (888)728-7228, ext. 5124. (502)569-5124. Fax (502)569-8329. E-mail: mgilliss@ctr.pcusa.org. Website: www.pcusa.org/cmd/cmp. Congregational Ministries Publishing/Presbyterian Church (U.S.A.). Sandra Albritton Moak, pub. Prefers NRSV. Publishes nonfiction works that help congregations fulfill their ministries and individuals more thoroughly understand the Presbyterian Church (U.S.A.); Bible studies, resources for children, youth and adults; bringing those with special needs into fuller participation; lay leadership. Reformed theology only. Guidelines on Website. Incomplete topical listings.

>**Nonfiction:** Proposal/sample chapters. "Treatment/sample chapters required for consideration."

BROADMAN & HOLMAN, 127—9th Ave. N., Nashville TN 37234-0115. (615)251-2392. Fax (615)251-3752. E-mail: courtney.brooks@lifeway.com. Website: www.broadmanholman.com. Book and Bible division of LifeWay Christian Resources. Leonard Goss, ed. dir.; David Shepherd, Sr. VP-publisher. Publishes books in the conservative, evangelical tradition by and for the larger Christian world. Publishes 90-100 titles/yr. Receives 3,000 submissions annually. 10% of books from first-time authors. Prefers 60,000-80,000 wds. Variable royalty on net; advance. Average first printing 5,000. Publication within 12-18 mos. Considers simultaneous submissions. Responds in 2-3 mos. Requires requested ms on disk. Prefers HCSB, NIV, NASB. Guidelines; no catalog.

>**Nonfiction:** Query first; no phone/fax query.

>**Fiction:** Query first. Prefers adult contemporary.

>**Ethnic:** Spanish translations.

>**Also Does:** Rocket e-books.

Tips: "Follow guidelines when submitting. Be informed about the market in general and specifically related to the book you want to write." Expanding into fiction, gift books, and children's books.

**Note: This publisher serviced by The Writer's Edge.

CAMBRIDGE UNIVERSITY PRESS, 40 W. 20th St., New York NY 10011-4211. Toll-free (800)872-7423. (212)924-3900 or (212)337-5941. Fax (212)691-3239. E-mail: information@cup.org. Specific e-mails on Website. Website: www.cup.org. University of Cambridge. Andrew Beck, religion ed. (abeck@cambridge.org).

Nonfiction: Proposal; no complete mss. Scholarly nonfiction.

CANADIAN INSTITUTE FOR LAW, THEOLOGY & PUBLIC POLICY, INC., 7203—90th Ave., Edmonton AB T6B 0P5, Canada. (780)465-4581. Fax (780)465-4581. E-mail: ciltpp@cs.com. Website: www.ciltpp.com. Will Moore, pres. Integrating Christianity with the study of law and political science. Publishes 2-4 titles/yr. Receives 4-5 submissions annually. 1% of books from first-time authors. Accepts mss through agents. Reprints books. Royalty 7% of retail; no advance. Average first printing 1,000. Publication within 12-24 mos. No simultaneous submissions. Responds in 6-12 mos. Prefers NIV. Free guidelines (also by e-mail) /catalog.

Nonfiction: Proposal/1 chapter. "Looking for books integrating Christianity with law and political science."

Photos/Artwork: Accepts freelance photos for book covers.

CANDY CANE PRESS, 535 Metroplex Dr., Ste. 250, Nashville TN 37211. Toll-free (800)586-2572. (615)333-0478. Fax (888)815-2759. Website: www.idealspublications.com. Ideals Publications/Guideposts. Patricia Pingry, ed.; submit to Peggy Schaefer, mng. ed. Board books for 3- to 5-year-olds (holiday oriented, religious, or Americana). Publishes 5-10 titles/yr. Maximum 1,000 wds. Royalty; variable advance. Responds in 2 mos. Send for guidelines/catalog.

Fiction: Complete mss for board books.

Tips: "We are looking in particular for subjects pertaining to holidays (Christmas, Valentine, Easter, etc.), either secular or religious."

CANON PRESS, PO Box 9025, Moscow ID 83843. (208)892-8074. Fax (208)892-8143. E-mail: canonads@moscow.com. Website: www.canonpress.org. Christ Church (Reformed; Presbyterian). Jeffrey C. Evans, ed. Aims to expand "medieval Protestantism" in terms of truth, beauty, and goodness. Publishes 10 titles/yr. Receives 500 submissions annually. 10% of books from first-time authors. Accepts mss through agents. Reprints books. Prefers 100-300 pgs. Royalty 10-15% on net or retail; no advance. Average first printing 3,000. Publication within 18 mos. Considers simultaneous submissions. Prefers accepted ms by e-mail. Responds in 1 mo. Prefers NKJV. Guidelines/catalog on Website.

Nonfiction: Proposal/3 chapters; no phone/fax query; e-query OK.

Fiction: Proposal/3 chapters. "We want literary fiction, but not genre."

Also Does: Booklets, e-books (soon).

Tips: "Most open to books from a Trinitarian world-view. Avoid the typical, modern, sentimental evangelical thinking, as well as intellectualistic Presbyterianism. We delight in beauty and humor, creation, and the reformed tradition. Please consult guidelines on Website before submitting."

CANTICLE BOOKS, PO Box 2666, Carlsbad CA 92018. (760)806-3743. Fax (760)806-3689. E-mail: magnuspres@aol.com. Website: www.magnuspress.com. Imprint of Magnus Press. Warren Angel, ed. dir. To publish biblical studies by Catholic authors which are written for the average person and which minister life to Christ's Church. Publishes 2 titles/yr. Receives 60 submissions annually. 50% of books from first-time authors. Accepts mss through agents. Reprints books. Prefers 105-300 pgs. Royalty 6-12% on retail; no advance.

Average first printing 2,500. Publication within 1 yr. Considers simultaneous submissions. Accepts requested ms on disk. Responds in 1 mo. Guidelines (also by e-mail); free catalog.

Nonfiction: Query or proposal/2-3 chapters; fax query OK. " Looking for spirituality, thematic biblical studies, unique inspirational/devotional books."

Tips: "Our writers need solid knowledge of the Bible and a mature spirituality that reflects a profound relationship with Jesus Christ. Most open to well-researched, popularly written biblical studies geared to Catholics, or personal experience books which share/emphasize a person's relationship with Christ."

WILLIAM CAREY LIBRARY, 1605 E. Elizabeth St., Pasadena CA 91104. (626)720-8210. Fax (626)794-0477. E-mail: publishing@WCLBooks.com, or info@WCLBooks.com. Website: www.wclbooks.com. Greg Parsons, mngr. Purpose is to publish the best in Evangelical Christian Mission literature. Imprint: Mandate Press. Publishes 10-15 titles/yr. Reprints books. Variable lengths. Royalty 10% on net; no advance. Publication time varies. Guidelines on Website; free catalog.

Nonfiction: Query only; e-query OK. Charges a processing fee. "As a specialized publisher, we do only books and studies of church growth, missions, world issues, and ethnic/cultural issues."

Special Needs: Anthropology and cross-cultural.

Photos/Artwork: Accepts freelance photos for book covers.

Tips: "We mostly publish books on missions, evangelization, and unreached people groups. We welcome books that missionaries and mission-minded people would find useful and encouraging. Please see the Manuscript Submissions Guidelines on our Website for more information."

#CARIBE-BETANIA EDITORES, PO Box 141000, Nashville TN 37214. Toll-free (800)322-7423. (615)902-2372/2375. Fax (615)883-9376. E-mail: info@editorialcaribe.com. Website: www.caribebetania.com. Subsidiary of Thomas Nelson. Tod Shuttleworth, VP/Publisher; Juan Rojas, ed. Targets the needs and wants of the Hispanic community. Imprints: Betania and Caribe. Publishes 45 titles/yr. Receives 50 submissions annually. 90% of books from first-time authors. No mss through agents. Prefers 192 pgs. Royalty on net; advance $500. Average first printing 4,000. Publication within 15 mos. Accepts e-mail submissions. No guidelines; free catalog.

Nonfiction: Query letter only; no phone/fax/e-query. "We currently have a backlog of 18 months."

Ethnic Books: Hispanic imprint.

Also Does: Computer games.

Tips: "Most open to Christian books based on the Bible."

+CARSON-DELLOSA CHRISTIAN, 7027 Albert Pick Rd., PO Box 35665, Greensboro NC 27425. (336)632-0084. Fax (336)808-3249. E-mail: clayton@carsondellosa.com Website: www.carsondellosa.com. Carson-Dellosa Publishing, Inc. Carol Layton, ed. dir. Creates high quality children's products that teach the Word of God, share His love and goodness, assist in faith development, and glorify His Son, Jesus Christ. Publishes 20 titles/yr. Receives 50 submissions annually. 25% of books from first-time authors. Prefers mss through agents. Reprints books rarely. Prefers 64 pgs. Royalty & advance confidential. Publication within 12 mos. Considers simultaneous submissions. Responds in 6 wks. Prefers NIV. Guidelines by e-mail; free catalog.

Nonfiction: Proposal/2 chapters; hard copy only. "Looking for books that teach the Word of God to children in an engaging and fun way—particularly in a classroom setting."

Fiction: Proposal/2 chapters. "Fiction must be suited for classroom use."

Photos/Artwork: Accepts queries from freelance artists.

Also Does: Board games, beach balls, Pocket Cubes.

**Note: This publisher serviced by ECPA First Edition.

CASCADIA PUBLISHING HOUSE, 126 Klingerman Rd., Telford PA 18969. (215)723-9125. E-mail: editor@cascadiapublishinghouse.com. Website: www.cascadiapublishinghouse.com. Mennonite. Michael A. King, ed. Imprint: DreamSeeker Books. Open to freelance; uses little unsolicited. Some books are subsidized by interested institutions. Guidelines/catalog on Website. Not included in topical listings. No questionnaire returned.

Nonfiction: Query only/vita; e-query OK.

CATHOLIC ANSWERS, 2020 Gillespie Way, El Cajon CA 92020. (619)387-7200. Fax (619)387-0042. E-mail: jakin@catholic.com. Website: www.catholic.com. Trask Tapperson, dir. of publications. Publishes 10-20 titles/yr. Accepts mss through agents. Reprints books. Prefers 30,000-60,000 wds. Royalty on retail; advance $500 (if manuscript is on time). Average first printing 5,000. Publication within 6-12 mos. No simultaneous submissions. Prefers RSV-CE. Guidelines; free catalog.

Nonfiction: Query first; no phone/fax/e-query.

Photos/Artwork: Accepts freelance photos for book covers.

Tips: "Most open to Catholic apologetics and evangelization."

CATHOLIC BOOK PUBLISHING CO., 77 West End Rd., Totowa NJ 07512. (973)890-2400. Fax (973)890-2410. E-mail: info@catholicbookpublishing.com. Website: http://catholic bookpublishing.com. Catholic. Anthony Buono, mng. ed. Inspirational books for Catholic Christians. Acquired Resurrection Press and World Catholic Press. Publishes 15-20 titles/yr. Receives 75 submissions annually. 30% of books from first-time authors. No mss through agents. Variable royalty or outright purchases; no advance. Average first printing 3,000. Publication within 12-15 mos. No simultaneous submissions. Responds in 2-3 mos. Catalog for 9x12 SAE/5 stamps.

Nonfiction: Query letter only; no phone/fax query.

Tips: "We publish mainly liturgical books, Bibles, Missals, and prayer books. Most of the books are composed in-house or by direct commission with particular guidelines. We strongly prefer query letters in place of full manuscripts."

+CENTER STREET/TIME WARNER BOOK GROUP, 1271 Avenue of the Americas, New York NY 10020. Rolf Zettersten, pub. Focuses on traditional-values titles. Not included in topical listings. No questionnaire returned.

*CERDIC-PUBLICATIONS, PJR-RIC, 11, Rue Jean Sturm, 67520 Nordheim, France. Phone (03)88.87.71.07. Fax (03)88.87.71.25. Marie Zimmerman, dir. Publishes 3-5 titles/yr. 50+% of books from first-time authors. Prefers 230 pgs. The first print run in the field of law in religion does not make money; no payment. Average first printing 2,200. Publication within 3 mos.(varies). Considers simultaneous submissions. Responds in 4 wks. No guidelines; free catalog.

Nonfiction: Complete ms; phone/fax query OK. "Looking for books on law and religion. All topics checked in topical listings must relate to the law."

Tips: "We publish original studies in law of religion (any) with preference for young, beginning authors; in French only."

CHALICE PRESS, Box 179, St. Louis MO 63166-0179. (314)231-8500. Fax (314)231-8524. E-mail: chalice@cbp21.com. Website: www.chalicepress.com. Christian Church (Disciples of Christ). Dr. Trent Butler, ed. dir. Books for a thinking, caring church; in Bible, theology, ethics, homiletics, pastoral care, Christian education, Christian living, and spiritual growth. Publishes 50 titles/yr. Receives 500 submissions annually. 15% of books from first-time authors. No mss through agents. Prefers 144-160 pgs. for general books, 160-300 pgs. for academic books. Royalty 14-18% of net. Average first printing 2,500-3,000. Publication within 1 yr. Accepts simultaneous submissions. Requires requested proposal and ms by e-mail. Responds in 1-3 mos. Guidelines on Website; catalog for 9x12 SAE/2 stamps.

Nonfiction: Proposal/1 chapter; e-proposal preferred. "Looking for books in evangelism, leadership, and spiritual growth."

Also Does: Pamphlets.

+CHAPTER TWO, Fountain House, Conduit Mews, London SE18 7AP, United Kingdom. Phone ++44 (0) 20 8316 5389. Fax ++44 (0) 20 8854 5963. E-mail: chapter2uk@aol.com. Website: www.chaptertwobooks.org.uk. Plymouth Brethren. Mr. E. Cross, ed. Promotes the Christian faith in its primitive state, i.e. New Testament Christianity. Publishes 20-30 titles/yr. No mss through agents. Reprints books. Royalty 0-10% on retail (most of their authors donate their work). Average first printing 3.000. Publication within 12 mos. No simultaneous submissions. Prefers KJV, NKJV. No guidelines; free catalog.

Nonfiction: Query first; phone/e-query OK.

Special Needs: Plymouth Brethren commentaries.

CHARIOT BOOKS—See Cook Communications Ministries.

CHARIOT VICTOR PUBLISHING—See Cook Communications Ministries.

CHARISMA HOUSE, 600 Rinehart Rd., Lake Mary FL 32746. (407)333-0600. Fax (407)333-7100. E-mail: charismahouse@strang.com. Website: www.charismahouse.com. Strang Communications. Atalie Anderson, acquisitions asst. To inspire and equip people to live a Spirit-led life and walk in the divine purpose for which they were called. Imprints: Creation House Press (co-publishing), Siloam (health), CharismaKids. Publishes 40-50 titles/yr. Receives 600+ submissions annually. 2% of books from first-time authors. Accepts mss through agents. Reprints books. Prefers 50,000+ wds. Royalty 4-18% on retail; $1,500-5,000 advance. Average first printing 7,500. Publication within 9 mos. Considers simultaneous submissions. Accepts requested ms on disk or by e-mail. Responds in 6-12 mos. Guidelines on Website; free catalog.

Nonfiction: Proposal/1-2 chapters; no phone/fax query; e-query OK.

Fiction: Query first. For adults. Also open to supernatural thrillers or spiritual-warfare novels. "Looking for speculative fiction and sophisticated historical fiction in eras and events when Christ and Christianity were part of the culture (medieval, biblical, crusades, Awakenings, etc.)."

CHARISMAKIDS, 600 Rinehart Rd., Lake Mary FL 32746. (407)333-0600. Fax (407)333-7100. E-mail: matuszak@strang.com. Website: www.charismakids.com. Strang Communications. Submit to The Editor. Books to help children experience God's presence, find His purpose for their lives, and receive the power of the Holy Spirit. Publishes 12 titles/yr. Receives 100s of submissions annually. 10% of books from first-time authors. Prefers mss through agents. No reprints. Prefers 2,400 wds. or 32 pgs. Royalty on net; advance. Average first printing 10,000. Publication within 1 yr. Considers simultaneous submissions. Responds in 6 mos. Guidelines & catalog on Website.

Nonfiction: Proposal/1 chapter; fax/e-query OK.

Fiction: Proposal/1 chapter. Charismatic children's books; for children 4-8 years.

Ethnic Books: Black, Charismatic.

Tips: "Most open to books with a Charismatic world-view for children."

CHICKEN SOUP BOOKS—See listing in Periodical section.

CHOSEN BOOKS, Division of Baker Publishing Group, 3985 Bradwater St., Fairfax VA 22031-3702. (703)764-8250. Fax (703)764-3995. E-mail: JECampbell@aol.com. Website: www.bakerpublishinggroup.com. Charismatic; Spirit-filled life titles. Jane Campbell, ed. dir. No freelance. Submit through Writer's Edge or ECPA First Edition.

CHRISTIAN ED. PUBLISHERS, Box 26639, San Diego CA 92196. (858)578-4700. Fax (858)578-2431 (for queries only). E-mail: Editor@cepub.com or Jackelson@cepub.com.

Website: www.ChristianEdWarehouse.com. Janet Ackelson, asst. ed. An evangelical publisher of Bible Club materials for ages two through high school, church special-event programs, and Bible-teaching craft kits. Publishes 80 titles/yr. Receives 150 submissions annually. 10% of books from first-time authors. No mss through agents. Outright purchases for .03/wd.; no advance. Publication within 1 yr. No simultaneous submissions. Accepts requested ms on disk or by e-mail. Responds in 3-5 mos. Prefers NIV, KJV. Guidelines (also by e-mail); catalog for 9x12 SAE/4 stamps.

Nonfiction: Query only; phone/fax/e-query OK. Bible studies, curriculum, and take-home papers.

Fiction: Query only. Juvenile fiction for take-home papers. "Each story is about 900 wds. Write for an application; assignments only."

Photos/Artwork: Open to freelance illustrators. Send files in Adobe Illustrator.

Tips: "All writing done on assignment. Request our guidelines, then complete a writer application before submitting. Need Bible-teaching ideas for preschool through sixth grade. Also publishes Bible stories for preschool and primary take-home papers, 200 words."

CHRISTIAN FAMILY PUBLICATIONS, 58 S. Bay Ave., Islip NY 11751. E-mail: Gfedele@ cmp.com. Website: www.christianfamilybooks.com. Gene Fedele, ed. Incomplete topical listings. No questionnaire returned.

CHRISTIAN FOCUS PUBLICATIONS, LTD., Geanies House, Fearn, Tain, Ross-shire IV20 1TW Scotland UK. Phone +44 (0) 1862 871011. Fax +44 (0) 1862 871699. E-mail: info@ christianfocus.com. Website: www.christianfocus.com. Willie Mackenzie, adult editorial mngr.; Catherine McKenzie, children's ed. Focuses on having strong biblical content. Imprints: Mentor, Christian Heritage, Christian Focus, Christian Focus 4 Kids. Publishes 90 titles/yr. Receives 300+ submissions annually. 10% of books from first-time authors. Accepts mss through agents. Reprints books. Royalty on net or outright purchase. Publication within 24 mos. Considers simultaneous submissions. Accepts requested ms on disk. Responds typically in 4 mos. Guidelines on Website; free catalog.

Nonfiction: Proposal/2 chapters; fax/e-query OK.

Fiction: Complete ms. For children and teens only. See guidelines for descriptions of children's fiction lines.

Photos/Artwork: Accepts freelance photos for book covers.

Tips: "We are 'reformed,' though we don't insist all our authors would consider themselves reformed." A prize-winning British publisher with good worldwide coverage.

CHRISTIAN LIBERTY PRESS, 502 W. Euclid Ave., Arlington Heights IL 60064. (847)259-4444. Fax (847)259-2941. Website: www.christianlibertypress.com. Publishing arm of Christian Liberty Academy. Curriculum. Incomplete topical listings. No questionnaire returned.

CHRISTIAN PUBLICATIONS, 3825 Hartzdale Dr., Camp Hill PA 17011. (717)761-7044. Fax (717)761-7273. E-mail: editorial@christianpublications.com. Website: www.christian publications.com. Christian and Missionary Alliance. Pamela Brossman, ed. Publishes books which emphasize the deeper Christian life. Publishes 10 titles/yr. Receives 250 submissions annually. 30% of books from first-time authors. Prefers 50,000 wds. or 150-300 pgs. Royalty 5-10% of net; variable advance. Average first printing 3,000-5,000. Publication within 18 mos. Considers simultaneous submissions on full proposals. Requires requested ms on disk. Responds in 6-8 wks. Guidelines (also by e-mail/Website); no catalog.

Nonfiction: One-page query letter describing book; fax query OK. "Looking for books on spiritual growth and women's concerns (Bible based)."

Tips: "Most open to Christian living with depth, homeschooling resources, and church/Christian history. The books we publish are selected for their potential to promote real spiritual growth in the lives of our readers."

**Note: This publisher serviced by The Writer's Edge.

CHRISTIAN WRITER'S EBOOK NET, PO Box 446, Ft. Duchesne UT 84026. (435)772-3429. E-mail: editor@writersebook.com. Website: www.writersebook.com. Nondenominational/ Evangelical Christian. Linda Kay Stewart Whitsitt, ed-in-chief; Terry Gordon Whitsitt, asst. ed. Gives first-time authors the opportunity to bring their God-given writing talent to the Christian market. Publishes 30 titles/yr. Receives 200 submissions annually. 95% of books from first-time authors. Accepts mss through agents. **SUBSIDY PUBLISHES 25%.** Reprints books. Prefers 60+ pgs. Royalty 35-50%; no advance. E-Books only. Publication within 6 mos. Considers simultaneous submissions. Electronic queries and submissions only; mss need to be in electronic form (MS Word, WordPerfect, ASCII, etc.) to be published; send by e-mail (preferred). Responds in 1-2 mos. Guidelines on Website.

> **Nonfiction:** E-query only. Any topic.
>
> **Fiction:** E-query only. Any genre.
>
> **Also Does:** Booklets, pamphlets, tracts.
>
> **Tips:** "Make sure your work is polished and ready for print. The books we publish are sold in our online store. If you are not sure what an e-book is, check out our Website's FAQ page."

CHURCH & SYNAGOGUE LIBRARY ASSN. INC., PO Box 19357, Portland OR 97280-0357. (503)244-6919. Fax (503)977-3734. E-mail: csla@worldaccessnet.com. Website: www.csla.info. Karen Bota, ed. An interfaith group set up to help librarians set up and organize/reorganize their religious libraries. Publishes 6 titles/yr. No mss through agents. No royalty. Average first printing 750. Catalog.

CHURCH GROWTH INSTITUTE, PO Box 7, Elkton MD 21922-0007. E-mail: cgimail@church growth.org. Website: www.churchgrowth.org. Ephesians Four Ministries. Cindy G. Spear, resource development dir. Providing practical tools for leadership, evangelism, and church growth. Publishes 4 titles/yr. Receives 40 submissions annually. 7% of books from first-time authors. No mss through agents. Prefers 64-160 pgs. Royalty 6% on retail or outright purchase; no advance. Average first printing 100. Publication within 1 yr. Considers simultaneous submissions. Responds in 3 mos. Requires requested ms on disk. Guidelines; catalog for 9x12 SAE/3 stamps, or on Website.

> **Nonfiction:** Proposal/1 chapter; no phone/fax; e-query OK. "We prefer our writers to be experienced in what they write about, to be experts in the field."
>
> **Special Needs:** Topics that help churches grow spiritually and numerically; leadership training; attendance and stewardship programs; new or unique ministries (how-to). Self-discovery and evaluation tools, such as our Spiritual Gifts Inventory and Spiritual Growth Survey.
>
> **Photos/Artwork:** Accepts freelance photos for book covers.
>
> **Tips:** "Most open to a practical manual or audio album (CDs/audiotapes and workbooks) for the pastor or other church leaders—something unique with a special niche. Must be practical and different from anything else on the same subject—or must be a topic/slant few others have published. Also very interested in evaluation tools as mentioned above. Please no devotionals, life testimonies, commentaries, or studies on books of the Bible."

CISTERCIAN PUBLICATIONS, INC., WMU Station, 1903 W. Michigan Ave., Kalamazoo MI 49008-5415. (269)387-8920. Fax (269)387-8390. E-mail: cistpub@wmich.edu. Website: www .spencerabbey.org/cistpub. Catholic/Order of Cistercians of the Strict Observance. Dr. E. Rozanne Elder, ed. dir. Works of monastic tradition and studies that foster renewal, spirituality, and ongoing formation of monastics. Publishes 8-14 titles/yr. Receives 30 submissions annually. 50% of books from first-time authors. No mss through agents. Reprints books. Prefers 204-286 pgs. Royalty on net; no advance. Average first printing 1,500. Publication within 2-10 yrs. Requires requested ms on disk. No guidelines; free style sheet/catalog.

> **Nonfiction:** Query only; no phone query; fax query OK. History, spirituality, and theology.

Photos/Artwork: Accepts freelance photos for book covers.

Tips: "We publish only on the Christian Monastic Tradition. Most open to a translation of a monastic text, or study of a monastic movement, author, or subject."

CLADACH PUBLISHING, PO Box 336144, Greeley CO 80633. (970)371-9530. E-mail: staff@cladach.com. Website: www.cladach.com. Independent Christian publisher. Catherine Lawton, pub./ed. Seeks to influence those inside and outside the body of Christ by giving a voice to little-known but talented writers with a clear, articulate, and Christ-honoring vision. Publishes 2-3 titles/yr. Receives 100 submissions annually. 65% of books from first-time authors. Accepts mss through agents. No reprints. Prefers 128-224 pgs. Royalty 7-10% on net; no advance. Average first printing 1,000. Publication within 1 yr. Considers simultaneous submissions. Accepted mss by e-mail. Responds in 1-6 mos. Guidelines on Website; free catalog.

Nonfiction: Query letter; phone/e-query OK. "Looking for nonfiction that helps people in their relationship with God."

Fiction: Query letter; phone/e-query OK. For adults. "Prefers gripping stories depicting inner struggles and real-life issues; well crafted. Would like to see Christian world-view, literary fiction."

Tips: "Write from your heart and experience, true to the Word of God. Most open to books that inspire or meet a need and that the author can help market."

COLLEGE PRESS PUBLISHING CO., INC., 223 W. Third St. (64801), Box 1132, Joplin MO 64802. Toll-free (800)289-3300. (417)623-6280. Fax (417)623-8250. Website: www.college press.com. Christian Church/Church of Christ. Submit to Acquisitions Ed. Christian materials that will help fulfill the Great Commission and promote unity on the basis of biblical truth and intent. Imprint: HeartSpring Publishing. Publishes 15-20 titles/yr. Receives 700 submissions annually. 25% of books from first-time authors. Accepts mss through agents. Reprints books. Prefers 250-300 pgs. (paperback) or 300-600 pgs.(hardback). Royalty 5-15% of net; no advance. Average first printing 3,000. Publication within 6 mos. Considers simultaneous submissions. Requires requested ms on disk; no e-mail submissions. Responds in 3 mos. Prefers NIV, NASB, NAS. Guidelines on Website; catalog for 9x12 SAE/5 stamps.

Nonfiction: Query only, then proposal/2-3 chapters; no phone/fax query. "Looking for Bible study, reference, divorced leaders, blended families, and leadership."

Ethnic Books: Reprints their own books in Spanish.

Also Does: E-books.

Tips: "We are interested in biblical studies and resources that come from an 'Arminian' view and/or 'amillennial' slant."

CONARI PRESS, 368 Congress St., Boston MA 02210. Toll-free (800)423-7087. Fax (877)337-3309. E-mail: info@redwheelweiser.com. Website: www.conari.com or www.redwheel weiser.com. An imprint of Red Wheel/Weiser, LLC. Ms. Pat Bryce, ed. To inspire readers on their life path, on family and parenting, on love—and its loss, about women in history and now. Publishes 30 titles/yr. Guidelines and catalog on Website. Incomplete topical listings.

#CONCILIAR PRESS, PO Box 76, Ben Lomand CA 95005. Toll-free (800)967-7377. (831)336-5118. Fax (831)336-8882. Website: www.conciliarpress.com. Antiochian Orthodox Christian Archdiocese of N.A., Father Thomas Zell, ed. Publishes 5-10 titles/yr. Receives 50 submissions annually. 20% of books from first-time authors. Accepts mss through agents. **SUBSIDY PUBLISHES 10%.** Reprints books. Royalty; no advance. Average first printing 5,000. Prefers e-mail submission. Prefers NKJV. Guidelines (also by e-mail); catalog for 9x12 SAE/5 stamps.

Nonfiction: Query only; phone/fax/e-query OK.

Photos/Artwork: Accepts freelance photos for book covers.

CONCORDIA ACADEMIC PRESS, 3558 S. Jefferson Ave., St. Louis MO 63118-3968. (314)268-1098. Fax (314)268-1329. E-mail: mark.sell@cph.org. Website: www.concordia academicpress.org. Lutheran Church/Missouri Synod. Imprint of Concordia Publishing House. Mark E. Sell, ed. Scholarly and professional books in biblical studies, 16th-century studies, historical theology, and theology and culture. Publication within 2 yrs. Responds in 8-12 wks. Guidelines on Website.

> **Tips:** "Freelance submissions are welcome. Prospective authors should consult the guidelines on the Website for an author prospectus and submissions guidelines."

CONCORDIA PUBLISHING HOUSE, 3558 S. Jefferson Ave., St. Louis MO 63118-3968. (314)268-1187. Fax (314)268-1329. Website: www.cph.org. Lutheran Church/Missouri Synod. Peggy Kuethe: children's resources, children's and family devotions, teaching resources, adult nonfiction and devotionals; Mark Sell: academic books; Fred Baue: pastoral and congregational resources; Hector Hoppe: multiethnic resources; Brandy Overton: guidelines for adults, children's resources. Publishes 50 titles/yr. Receives 3,000 submissions annually. 10% of books from first-time authors. Royalty 2-12% on retail; some outright purchases; some advances $500-1,500. Average first printing 6,000-8,000. Publication within 2 yrs. Considers simultaneous submissions. Responds in 6 mos. Prefers accepted submissions on disk. Prefers NIV. Guidelines on Website; catalog for 9x12 SAE/4 stamps.

> **Nonfiction:** Proposal/2 chapters; no phone/fax query. No poetry, personal experience, or biography.
> **Ethnic Books:** Hispanic; Asian American.
> **Also Does:** Pamphlets, booklets.
> **Tips:** "Publishes Christ-centered resources for The Lutheran Church—Missouri Synod. Most open to family, devotional, and teaching resources. Any proposal should be Christ centered, Bible based, and life directed. It must be creative in its presentation of solid scriptural truths."
> ****Note:** This publisher serviced by The Writer's Edge.

#CONTEMPORARY DRAMA SERVICE, Meriwether Publishing Co., 885 Elkton Dr., Colorado Springs CO 80907. E-mail: merPCDS@aol.com. Website: www.meriwetherpublishing.com. Publishes plays and supplemental textbooks on theatrical subjects for middle school, high school, and college students. Prefers comedy, but does some serious works. Accepts full-length or one-act plays—comedy or musical. Secular and Christian. Publishes 30 plays/yr. See the Meriwether Publishing listing for additional details.

CONTINUUM INTERNATIONAL PUBLISHING, 15 E. 26th St., Ste. 1703, New York NY 10010. Toll-free (800)561-7704. (212)953-5858. Fax (212)953-5944. E-mail: info@continuum books.com. Website: www.continuumbooks.com. Robin J. Baird-Smith, pub. dir. Philip J. Laird, ed. dir. Imprints: Morehouse; T and T Clark/Sheffield Academic Press; Burns & Oates. Publishes 350-400 titles/yr. Receives 1,400 submissions annually. 10% of books from first-time authors. Accepts mss through agents. Does print-on-demand. Reprints books. Royalty to 15%; advance. Publication within 9 mos. No simultaneous submissions. Responds in 1 mo. Guidelines by e-mail; free catalog.

> **Nonfiction:** Proposal/1 chapter; phone/fax/e-query OK.
> **Photos/Artwork:** Accepts freelance photos for book covers.
> **Contest:** Trinity Prize.

COOK COMMUNICATIONS MINISTRIES, 4050 Lee Vance View, Colorado Springs CO 80918. (719)536-0100. Fax (719)536-3269. Website: www.cookministries.com. Dan Benson, ed. dir.; Lora Riley, mng. ed.; Mike Nappa, acq. ed. for nonfiction. Discipleship is foundational; everything we publish needs to move the reader one step closer to maturity in Christ. Brands: NexGen (for teachers or program leaders who want Bible-based discipleship resources); Victor (Bible and study resources for serious Bible students); Life Journey (books for Christian families seeking biblical answers to life problems); Honor Books (devotional books that inspire and motivate, packaged as gift books); RiverOak (historical, contemporary fiction); Faith Kidz (equipping kids—birth to age 12—for life; see separate listing). Publishes 125 titles/yr. 10% of books from first-time authors. Prefers mss through agents. Average first printing 5,000. Publication within 1-2 yrs. Considers simultaneous submissions. Responds in 3-6 mos. Prefers requested ms by e-mail. Prefers NIV. Guidelines (also by e-mail/Website).

Nonfiction: Proposal/2 chapters. All book proposals must be sent via Website: www.cook ministries.com/booksubmissions.

Fiction: Proposal/3 chapters or complete ms. All book proposals must be sent via Website: www.cookministries.com/booksubmissions.

Tips: "Most open to a book that combines expertise with experience—both are important here."

**Note: This publisher serviced by The Writer's Edge.

DAVID C. COOK PUBLISHING CO.—See Cook Communications Ministries.

J. COUNTRYMAN, PO Box 141000, Nashville TN 37214-1000. (615)902-3134. Fax (615)902-3200. Website: www.jcountryman.com. Thomas Nelson Inc. Troy Johnson, pub./exec. VP; Lisa Stilwell, ed-in-chief; Terri Gibbs, VP, acq. and product development. Gift-book imprint presenting strong, Bible-based messages in beautifully designed books. No longer accepting unsolicited manuscripts or proposals.

**Note: This publisher serviced by The Writer's Edge.

CREATIVE TEACHING PRESS, 15342 Graham St., Huntington Beach CA 92649. Toll-free (800)287-8879. (714)895-5047. Fax (714)895-5087. E-mail: carolea.williams@creative teaching.com. Website: www.creativeteaching.com. Rebecca Cleland, ed. Produces teacher-developed materials for school and home. Publishes 50 titles/yr. Outright purchases. Publication within 9-12 mos. Considers simultaneous submissions. Accepts disk or e-mail submissions. Guidelines on Website; free catalog.

Nonfiction: Proposal; e-query OK.

Fiction: For children. Proposal; e-query OK.

Special Needs: Sunday school activity books.

Tips: "Most open to teacher resource books for use by a Christian school teacher or Sunday school teacher; grades prekindergarten through 3rd grade." Submission form on Website.

CROSS CULTURAL PUBLICATIONS, INC., PO Box 506, Notre Dame IN 46556. Toll-free (800)561-6526. (574)273-6526. Fax (574)273-5973. E-mail: crosscult@aol.com, or info@crossculturalpub.com. Website: www.crossculturalpub.com. Catholic. Cyriac K. Pullapilly, gen. ed. Promotes intercultural and interfaith understanding. Imprint: CrossRoads Books. Publishes 30 titles/yr. Receives 5,000 submissions annually. 30% of books from first-time authors. Accepts mss through agents. Reprints books. Prefers 250 pgs. Royalty 10% on net; no advance. Publication within 6 mos. Considers simultaneous submissions. Requires requested ms on disk. Responds in 3-4 mos. No guidelines; free catalog.

Nonfiction: Prefers query letter/sample chapters; will accept a proposal; e-query OK.

Fiction: Prefers query letter/sample chapters; will accept a proposal; e-query OK. For adults only.

Ethnic Books: Seeks to serve the cross-cultural, intercultural, and multicultural aspects of religious traditions.

Also Does: Will soon be doing e-books.

Photos/Artwork: Accepts freelance photos for book covers.

Tips: "Most open to solidly researched, well-written books on serious issues: intercultural, interfaith topics. Do a thorough job of writing/editing, etc. Have something constructive, noble, and worthwhile to say."

THE CROSSROAD PUBLISHING CO., 16 Penn Plaza, Ste. 1550, New York NY 10001. (212)868-1801. Fax (212)868-2171. E-mail: rgreer@crossroadpublishing.com. Website: www.crossroadpublishing.com. Dr. John Jones, exec. mngr. Books on religion, spirituality, and personal growth that speak to the diversity of backgrounds and beliefs; books that inform, enlighten, and heal. Imprints: see below. Publishes 50 titles/yr. Receives 1,200 submissions annually. 50% of books from first-time authors. Prefers mss through agents. **SUBSIDY PUBLISHES 5%.** Does print-on-demand. Reprints books. Prefers 50,000-60,000 wds. or 160-176 pgs. Royalty 8-10-12% of net; small advance (more for established authors). Average first printing 5,000. Publication within 1 yr. Considers simultaneous submissions. Responds in 3-4 mos. Accepts requested ms on disk. Guidelines by e-mail.

> **Nonfiction:** Proposal/2 chapters; fax/e-query OK. Books that explore and celebrate the Christian life.

> **Fiction:** Query only; does little fiction. For adults. Prefers historical fiction that focuses on important figures or periods in the history of Christianity. Must have a spiritual purpose or message.

> **Herder & Herder:** 200 years of international publishing in the service of theology and church. Monographs, reference works, theological, and philosophical discourse.

CROSS TRAINING PUBLISHING, PO Box 1541, Grand Island NE 68801. Toll-free (800)430-8588. Fax (308)384-9974. E-mail: gordon@crosstrainingpublishing.com. Website: www.cross trainingpublishing.com. Gordon Thiessen, pub. Sports books for children and adults.

CROSSWAY BOOKS AND BIBLES, 1300 Crescent St., Wheaton IL 60187. (630)682-4300. Fax (630)682-4785. E-mail: editorial@gnpcb.org. Website: www.crosswaybooks.org. A publishing ministry of Good News Publishers. Marvin Padgett, VP editorial; submit to Jill Carter, editorial administrator. Publishes books that combine the Truth of God's Word with a passion to live it out, with unique and compelling Christian content. Publishes 80 titles/yr. Receives 2,500 submissions annually. 1% of books from first-time authors. Accepts mss through agents. No reprints. Prefers 25,000 wds. & up. Royalty 10-21% of net; advance varies. Average first printing 5,000-10,000. Publication within 18 mos. Considers simultaneous submissions. Responds in 6-8 wks. Prefers ESV. Guidelines (also on Website); free catalog.

> **Nonfiction:** Currently not accepting unsolicited submissions.

> **Fiction:** Currently not accepting unsolicited submissions.

> **Also Does:** Tracts. See Good News Publishers.

> ****Note:** This publisher serviced by The Writer's Edge and ECPA First Edition.

CSS PUBLISHING GROUP, INC., PO Box 4503, 517 S. Main St., Lima OH 45802-4503. (419)227-1818. Fax (419)228-9184. E-mail: rbrandt@csspub.com. Website: www .csspub.com. Rebecca Allen Brandt, ed.; Stan Purdum, acq. ed. Serves the needs of pastors, worship leaders, and parish program-planners in the broad Christian mainline of the American church. Publishes 60 titles/yr. Receives 1,200-1,500 submissions annually. 50% of books from first-time authors. **SUBSIDY PUBLISHES 40%** through Fairway Press. Prefers 100-125 pgs. Royalty 3-7% or outright purchases for $25-400. Average first printing 1,000. Publication within 6-10 mos. Considers simultaneous submissions. Requires requested mss by mail. Responds in 3 wks. to 3 mos.; final decision within 6 mos. Accepts requested ms on disk. Prefers NRSV. Free guidelines (also on Website)/catalog.

> **Nonfiction:** Query or proposal/3 chapters; fax/e-query OK (no attachments); complete ms for short works. "Looking for pastoral resources for ministry. Our material is practical in nature."

> **Fiction:** Complete ms. Easy-to-perform dramas and pageants for all age groups. "Our drama interest primarily includes Advent, Christmas, Epiphany, Lent, and Easter. We do not publish long plays."

> **Tips:** "Suggest what you can do to help promote the book."

CUMBERLAND HOUSE PUBLISHING, 431 Harding Industrial Dr., Nashville TN 37211. (615)832-1171. Fax (615)832-0633. E-mail: info@cumberlandhouse.com. Website: www.cumberlandhouse.com. Tilly Katz, acq. ed. Historical nonfiction, cooking, mystery, and Christian titles. Publishes 60 titles/yr. Receives 3,500 submissions annually. 30% of books from first-time authors. Accepts mss through agents. Royalty 10-15% on net; advance $500-5,000. Publication within 1 yr. Considers simultaneous submissions. Prefers accepted ms on disk; no e-mail submissions. Responds in 6-12 mos. Guidelines on Website; catalog for 8x10 SAE/4 stamps.

> **Nonfiction:** Query/outline; fax query OK; no phone/e-query. See guidelines for how to submit cookbooks.
>
> **Fiction:** Query only. Historical mystery/suspense.
>
> **Tips:** "Most open to history or biography. In your cover letter, briefly describe the book and the market for the book. In a statement or two indicate who you are and why you have written or plan to write the book you are proposing." Has acquired WND Books (WorldNet-Daily)

+CURRICULUM ASSOCIATES, INC., 153 Rangeway Rd., PO Box 2001, North Billerica MA 01862. Toll-free (800)225-0248. Fax (800)366-1158. E-mail: cainfo@curriculumassociates .com, or homeschool@curriculumassociates.com. Website: www.curriculumassociates .com. Produces home school curriculum and resources. Open to freelance submissions. Submit hard copy first; will request ms on disk if accepted. Royalty negotiated. Guidelines on Website.

> **Nonfiction:** Query first with a signed release form (on Website).
>
> **Special Needs:** Focus your ideas on instructional programs or series that can be used in the following classrooms: K-8, ESL, special needs, and Chapter I. Also submit ideas for testing programs, early childhood programs, and state-specific products.
>
> **Photos/Artwork:** Do not send original artwork; sketches are acceptable, especially if they are integral to the product.

#CUSTOM COMMUNICATIONS SERVICES, INC./SHEPHERD PRESS/CUSTOM BOOK, 77 Main St., Tappan NY 10983. (845)365-0414. Fax (845)365-0864. E-mail: customusa@ aol.com. Website: www.customstudios.com. Norman Shaifer, pres. Publishes 50-75 titles/yr. 50% of books from first-time authors. No mss through agents. Royalty on net; some outright purchases for specific assignments. Publication within 6 mos. Responds in 1 mo. Guidelines.

> **Nonfiction:** Query/proposal/chapters. "Histories of individual congregations, denominations, or districts."
>
> **Tips:** "Find stories of larger congregations (750 or more households) who have played a role in the historic growth and development of the community or region."

DESCANT PUBLISHING, PO Box 12973, Mill Creek WA 98082. (206)235-3357. Fax (646)365-7513. E-mail: bret@descantpub.com. Website: www.descantpub.com. Bret Sable, nonfiction ed.; Alex Royal, fiction ed. Secular publisher that does books on religion and spirituality, and religious fiction. Publishes 10-12 titles/yr. Does some e-books. Receives 1,200 submissions annually. 50% of books from first-time authors. Accepts mss through agents. Royalty 6-15%. Publication within 18 mos. Considers simultaneous submissions. Responds in 3 mos. Guidelines for SASE.

> **Nonfiction:** For adults and children. Query by mail.
>
> **Fiction:** Adult. Query by mail.

DESTINY IMAGE PUBLISHERS, PO Box 310, Shippensburg PA 17257. (717)532-3040. Fax (717)532-9291. E-mail: dlm@destinyimage.com. Website: www.destinyimage.com. Don Milam, ed. mngr. Publishes biblically sound prophetic words to strengthen the church as a whole. Imprints: Destiny Image, Revival Press, Treasure House, Fresh Bread. Publishes

36 titles/yr. Receives 1,500 submissions annually. 10% of books from first-time authors. Accepts mss through agents. **SUBSIDY PUBLISHES 1-2%.** Reprints books. Prefers 128-190 pgs. Royalty 10-15% on net; no advance. Average first printing 10,000. Publication within 9 mos. Considers simultaneous submissions. No disk or e-mail submissions. Responds in up to 6 mos. Guidelines on Website; free catalog.

Nonfiction: Query or proposal/chapters; no e-query. Charges a $25 fee for unsolicited manuscripts (enclose).

Fiction: Proposal. Adult. Biblical.

Tips: "Most open to books on the deeper life, Charismatic interest." See Website for Manuscript Submission Questionnaire.

DEVOTED TO YOU BOOKS, 515 County Rd. 18, Wrenshall MN 55797-9103. Toll-free (800)704-7250. Website: www.scrapclubministries.org. Nondenominational. Tracy Ryks, pub. Seeks to teach children that God is present in their lives today; children's picture books for ages 1-8. Publishes 2 titles/yr. No reprints. Royalty; no advance. Publication within 18 mos. Considers simultaneous submissions. Responds in 2-4 mos. Prefers NIV. Guidelines on Website; free catalog.

Nonfiction: Complete ms or mock-up dummy book; e-submission OK. Now open to picture stories.

Fiction: Complete ms (dummy of book); e-submission OK. Contemporary children's picture books. "Books that portray God working in children's lives, prayer, or those that teach children how to develop a personal relationship with Jesus."

Special Needs: "We are looking for contemporary Christian picture books that show God in children's lives. Also parenting books—could be in devotional form—that inspire parents. Not how-to tips on parenting; we prefer books that make parents better parents by reminding them of their blessings, something heartwarming and inspirational."

Photos/Artwork: Accepts freelance photos for book covers.

Contest: Sponsors a contest.

Tips: "Most open to contemporary books for today, children's picture books, and inspirational parenting. Creative, innovative books that meet the needs of a changing society without compromising or changing our core Christian beliefs."

DIAMOND EYES PUBLISHING, 2309 Mountain Spruce St., Ocoee FL 347651. Toll-free (888)769-9931. (407)654-6652. Fax (208)977-1164. E-mail: Wordsarelife@yahoo.com. Website: www.depublishing.com. Jessica Adriel, sr. ed. Imprints: Trident Books, Lauren's Box. Books that view life from God's perspective. Publishes 5 titles/yr. Receives 350 submissions annually. 80% of books from first-time authors. Accepts mss through agents. Accepts reprints. Prefers under 75,000 words or 250 pgs. Royalty 7-10% on retail; no advance. Average first printing 2,000-3,000. Publication within 1 yr. Considers simultaneous submissions. Responds in 2-4 mos. Prefers KJV. Guidelines/catalog on Website.

Nonfiction: Query only by e-mail preferred (can send by mail). No phone/fax query. "Need prophecy pertaining to writing a book; prayer pertaining to writing a book; and writers' helps."

Fiction: Query by e-mail.

Photos/Artwork: Accepts freelance photos for book covers.

Tips: "Looking for writers' helps, journals for writers, success stories for compilation book. We also accept drama and screenplay instruction."

DIMENSION BOOKS, INC., PO Box 9, Starrucca PA 18462. (570)727-2486. Fax (570)727-2813. Catholic; general nonfiction. Thomas P. Coffey, ed. Not currently open to submissions.

DIMENSIONS FOR LIVING, 201—8th Ave. S., Nashville TN 37203. Fax (615)749-6512. Website: www.abingdonpress.com. United Methodist Publishing House. Joseph A. Crowe, ed.; submit to Shirley Briese (sbriese@umpublishing.org). Books for the general Christian reader. Publishes 120 titles/yr. Receives 2,000 submissions annually. Less than 1% of books from first-time authors. No reprints. Prefers 144 pgs. Royalty 7.5% on retail; some outright purchases; no advance. Average first printing 3,000. Publication within 2 yrs. Requires requested ms on disk. Responds in 6-8 wks. Guidelines on Website; free catalog.

Nonfiction: Proposal/2 chapters; no phone query. Open to inspiration/devotion, self-help, home/family, special occasion gift books.

#DISCOVERY HOUSE PUBLISHERS, PO Box 3566, Grand Rapids MI 49501. Toll-free (800)653-8333. (616)942-9218. Fax (616)957-5741. E-mail: dph@rbc.net. Website: www.rbc.net. RBC Ministries. Carol Holquist, pub.; submit to ms. review ed. Publishes books that foster Christian growth and godliness. Publishes 12-18 titles/yr. Accepts mss through agents. Reprints books. Royalty 10-14% on net; no advance. Publication within 12-18 mos. Considers simultaneous submissions. Requires accepted mss on disk or by e-mail. Responds in 4-6 wks. Guidelines (also by e-mail/Website); free catalog.

Nonfiction: Query letter only; e-query OK.

Also Does: Bible study software.

**Note: This publisher serviced by The Writer's Edge.

+DISKUS PUBLISHING, PO Box 43, Albany IN 47320. E-mail: editor@diskuspublishing.com; submissions to: submissions@diskuspublishing.com. Website: www.diskuspublishing .com. Marilyn Nesbitt, ed-in-chief; Joyce McLaughlin, inspirational ed. E-book publisher. Publishes 50 titles/yr. Royalty 40%. Publication within 6-8 mos. Considers simultaneous submissions. Guidelines (also on Website); catalog for #10 SAE.

Fiction: Complete ms. or query. Includes religious fiction.

Tips: "Follow very specific guidelines on Website."

DOUBLEDAY RELIGION, 1745 Broadway, New York NY 10019. (212)782-9762. Fax (212)782-8338. E-mail: mrapkin@randomhouse.com, or tmurphy@randomhouse.com. Website: www.randomhouse.com. Random House, Inc. Michelle Rapkin, VP, Dir. of Religious Publishing; submit to Trace Murphy, editorial dir. Imprints: Image, Galilee, Doubleday Hardcover, Three Leaves Press, Anchor Bible Commentaries, Anchor Bible Reference Library. Publishes 45-50 titles/yr. Receives 1,500 submissions annually. 10% of books from first-time authors. Requires mss through agents. Royalty 7.5-15% on retail; advance. Average first printing varies. Publication within 8 mos. Considers simultaneous submissions. Responds in 4 mos. No disk. No guidelines; catalog for 9x12 SAE/3 stamps.

Nonfiction: Agented submissions only. Proposal/3 chapters; no phone query.

Ethnic Books: African American; Hispanic.

Tips: "Most open to a book that has a big and well-defined audience. Have a clear proposal, lucid thesis, and specified audience."

DOVER PUBLICATIONS, INC., 31 E. 2nd St., Mineola NY 11501-3852. (516)294-7000. Fax (516)873-1401 or (516)742-6953. E-mail: rights@doverpublications.com. Website: www.doverpublications.com. Mary Carolyn Waldrep, ed-in-chief. Publishes some religious titles, reprints only. Makes outright purchases. Query. Free catalog online.

Nonfiction: Query. Religion topics.

+EARTHEN VESSEL PUBLISHING, 289 Miller Ave., Mill Valley CA 94941. Phone/fax (415)381-6020. E-mail: kentphilpott@comcast.net. Website: www.earthenvessel.net. Reformed Baptist. Kent Philpott, ed. Publishes 2 titles/yr. Receives 1-3 submissions annually. 50% of books from first-time authors. No mss through agents. Reprints books. Outright purchases. Average first printing varies. Publication time varies. Considers simultaneous submissions. Responds soon. No guidelines or catalog.

Nonfiction: Accepts phone query.

Photos/Artwork: Open to queries from freelance artists.

EASUM, BANDY & ASSOCIATES, INC., PO Box 780, Port Aransas TX 78373-0780. (361)749-5364. Fax (361)749-5800. E-mail: easum@easumbandy.com, or bandy@easumbandy.com. Website: www.easumbandy.com. Bill Easum, pub. Submit to Sandra Pearson (attached file to: Sandra@easumbandy.com). E-book publisher. Company keeps 20% of proceeds from sales of book. Guidelines on Website.

> **Nonfiction:** Produces books in Adobe format to be downloaded. Author sets price.
>
> **Special Needs:** Does workbooks, study guides, PowerPoint presentations, and curriculum.
>
> **Also Does:** Audio, video.

+E-DIGITAL BOOKS, LLC., 1155 S. Havana St., #11-364, Aurora CO 80012. E-mail: submissions@edigitalbooks.com. Website: www.edigitalbooks.com. T. R. Allen, ed-in-chief. Publishes 10-12 titles/yr. Receives 10 submissions annually. 50% of books from first-time authors. No mss through agents. Royalty 30-60% on retail. Publication within 6 mos. Considers simultaneous submissions. Responds in 6 mos. Guidelines/catalog by e-mail.

> **Nonfiction:** Query by e-mail.
>
> **Fiction:** Query by e-mail.
>
> **Tips:** "Interested in Christian religious poetry with uplifting, positive, and inspirational themes. We have a family-oriented Christian audience."

EDITORIAL PORTAVOZ, PO Box 2607, Grand Rapids MI 49501-2607. Toll-free (800)733-2607. (616)451-4775. Fax (616)451-9330. E-mail: editor@portavoz.com. Website: www.portavoz.com. Spanish Division of Kregel Publishing. Andres Schwartz, ed. dir. To provide trusted, biblically based resources that challenge and encourage Spanish-speaking individuals in their Christian lives and service. Publishes 40+ titles/yr. 2-5% of books from first-time authors. Accepts mss through agents. Does print-on-demand. No reprints. Negotiable royalty on net; negotiable advance. Purchases artwork outright. Average first printing 5,000. Publication within 13 mos. Considers simultaneous submissions. Responds in 2-4 mos. Guidelines on Website.

> **Nonfiction:** Send proposal by e-mail or CD-ROM, with 2-3 chapters. "Looking for original Spanish reference works."

EDITORIAL UNILIT, 1360 N.W. 88th Ave., Miami FL 33172-3093. Toll-free (800)767-7726. (305)592-6136. Fax (305)592-0087. Website: www.editorialunilit.com. Spanish House. Submit to The Editor. To glorify God by providing the church and Spanish-speaking people with the tools to communicate clearly the gospel of Jesus Christ and help them grow in their relationship with Him and His church.

> ****Note:** This publisher selected as Publisher of the Year (1999) by the Spanish Evangelical Publishers Assn.

EDUCATIONAL MINISTRIES, 165 Plaza Dr., Prescott AZ 86303. (928)771-8601. Fax (928)771-8621. E-mail: edmin2@aol.com. Website: www.educationalministries.com. Linda Davidson, ed. Our liberal theology sets us apart—our books do not give pat answers. Periodicals: *Church Educator* and *Church Worship.* Publishes 2-3 titles/yr. Receives 30 submissions annually. 15% of books from first-time authors. No mss through agents. No reprints. Outright purchases; no advance. Average first printing 500. Publication within 6 mos. Considers simultaneous submissions. Prefers accepted ms on disk. Responds in 2-3 mos. Guidelines; catalog for 9x12 SAE/3 stamps.

> **Nonfiction:** Complete ms; phone query OK.

EERDMANS BOOKS FOR YOUNG READERS, 255 Jefferson S.E., Grand Rapids MI 49503. Toll-free (800)253-7521. (616)459-4591. Fax (616)459-6540. E-mail: jzylstra@eerdmans.com; or youngreaders@eerdmans.com. Website: www.eerdmans.com/youngreaders. Wm. B. Eerdmans Publishing. Judy Zylstra, ed-in-chief. Produces books for general trade, school, and library markets. Publishes 12-15 titles/yr. Receives 6,000 submissions annually.

5% of books from first-time authors. Age-appropriate length. Royalty 5-7% of retail; advance to previously published authors. Average first printing 10,000 (picture books) and 5,000-6,000 (chapter books/novels). Publication within 1-3 yrs. Considers simultaneous submissions if marked on envelope. Responds in 3-6 mos. Guidelines (also by e-mail/Website); catalog for 9x12 SAE/4 stamps.

Nonfiction: Proposal/3-4 chapters for book length; complete ms for picture books; no phone/fax/e-query. For children and teens.

Fiction: Proposal/3 chapters for book length; complete ms for picture books. For children and teens.

Tips: "Many of our books do not have overtly religious content, but all submissions must have some depth to them."

Photos/Artwork: Please do not send illustrations with picture book manuscripts unless you are a professional illustrator. When submitting artwork, send color copies, not originals.

**Note: This publisher serviced by The Writer's Edge.

WM. B. EERDMANS PUBLISHING CO., 255 Jefferson Ave. S.E., Grand Rapids MI 49503. Toll-free (800)253-7521. (616)459-4591. Fax (616)459-6540. E-mail: info@eerdmans.com. Website: www.eerdmans.com. Protestant/Academic/Theological. Jon Pott, ed-in-chief. Imprint: Eerdmans Books for Young Readers (Judy Zylstra, ed-in-chief). Publishes 120-130 titles/yr. Receives 3,000-4,000 submissions annually. 10% of books from first-time authors. Accepts mss through agents. Reprints books. Royalty; occasional advance. Average first printing 4,000. Publication within 1 yr. Considers simultaneous submissions. Responds in 6 wks. to query; longer for mss. Guidelines on Website; free catalog.

Nonfiction: Proposal/2-3 chapters; no fax/e-query. "Looking for religious approaches to contemporary issues, spiritual growth, scholarly works."

Fiction: Proposal/chapter; no fax/e-query. "We are looking for adult novels with high literary merit."

Tips: "Most open to material with general appeal, but well-researched, cutting-edge material that bridges the gap between evangelical and mainline worlds."

**Note: This publisher serviced by The Writer's Edge.

ELDRIDGE CHRISTIAN PLAYS & MUSICALS, PO Box 14367, Tallahassee FL 32317. Toll-free (800)95-CHURCH. Fax (800)453-5179. E-mail: info@95church.com. Website: www.95 church.com. Independent Christian drama publisher. Susan Shore, religious ed. To provide superior religious drama to enhance preaching and teaching, whatever your Christian denomination. Publishes 12 plays and 1-2 musicals/yr. Receives 350-400 plays annually. 75% of plays from first-time authors. One-act to full-length plays. Outright purchases of $100-1,000 on publication; no advance. Publication within 1 yr. Considers simultaneous submissions. Responds in 1-3 mos. Requires requested ms on disk or by e-mail. Free guidelines (also by e-mail or Website)/catalog.

Plays: Complete ms; e-query OK. For children, teens, and adults.

Special Needs: Always looking for high quality Christmas and Easter plays but open to other holiday and "anytime" Christian plays too. Can be biblical or current day, for performance by all ages, children through adult.

Tips: "Have play produced at your church and others prior to submission, to get out the bugs. At least try a stage reading."

#ELIJAH PRESS, Meadow House Communications, Inc., PO Box 317628, Cincinnati OH 45231-7628. (513)521-7362. Fax (513)521-7364. Website: www.elijahpress.com. Publishes quality religious/spiritual fiction and nonfiction books and tapes on and related to Christian living, church history, and spiritual reflection. S. R. Davis, ed. Publishes 3-5 titles/yr. Prefers 50,000-100,000 wds. Responds in 1 mo. Guidelines on Website. Incomplete topical listings.

Nonfiction: One-page query; must have completed ms; no phone/e-query.

Fiction: Accepts fiction.

EMMAUS ROAD PUBLISHING, 827 N. Fourth St., Steubenville OH 43952. Toll-free (800)398-5470. (740)281-2404. Fax (740)283-4011. E-mail: shughes@emmausroad.org. Website: www.emmausroad.org. Catholics United for the Faith. Regis J. Flaherty, ed-in-chief. Publishes 8-10 titles/yr. Receives 50 submissions annually. 10% of books from first-time authors. No mss through agents. Reprints books. Royalty on net; advance $500. Publication within 1 yr. Considers simultaneous submissions. Guidelines on Website; free catalog.

Nonfiction: Query only; e-query OK.

ETC PUBLICATIONS, 700 E. Vereda del Sur, Palm Springs CA 92262. (760)325-5352. Fax (760)325-8841. E-mail: etcbooks@earthlink.net. LeeOna S. Hostrop, sr. ed. Publishes textbooks for the Christian and secular markets at all levels of education. Publishes 3 textbook/yr. Receives 50 submissions annually. 90% of books from first-time authors. Accepts mss through agents. No reprints. Prefers 128-256 pgs. Royalty 5-15% of net; no advance. Average first printing 1,500-2,500. Publication within 6 mos. No simultaneous submissions. Responds in 10 days. No guidelines (use *Chicago Manual of Style*); catalog for #10 SAE/1 stamp.

Nonfiction: Query only; e-query OK. "We are interested only in Christian-oriented state history textbooks to be used in Christian schools and by homeschoolers."

Photos/Artwork: Accepts freelance photos for book covers.

Tips: "Open only to state histories that are required at a specific grade level and are Christian oriented, with illustrations."

EVERGREEN PRESS, 5821 Rangeline Rd., Bldg. 102, Theodore AL 36582. Toll-free (800)367-8203. Fax (251)408-0857. E-mail: kathy@evergreen777.com. Website: www.evergreen pressbooks.com. Genesis Communications. Kathy Banashak, ed-in-chief. Publishes books that empower people for breakthrough living by being practical, biblical, and engaging. Imprints: Evergreen Press, Gazelle Press. Publishes 30 titles/yr. Receives 250 submissions annually. 40% of books from first-time authors. Accepts mss through agents. **SUBSIDY PUBLISHES 35%.** Does print-on-demand. No reprints. Prefers 96-160 pgs. Royalty on net; no advance. Average first printing 4,000. Publication within 6 mos. Considers simultaneous submissions. Requires requested ms on disk or by e-mail. Responds in 4-6 wks. Guidelines (also by e-mail); free catalog.

Nonfiction: Complete ms; phone/fax/e-query OK.

Fiction: For all ages. Complete ms; phone/fax/e-query OK.

Special Needs: Business, finance, personal growth, women's issues, family/parenting, relationships, prayer, humor, and angels.

Also Does: Booklets.

Tips: "Most open to books with a specific market (targeted, not general) that the author is qualified to write for and that is relevant to today's believers and seekers. Author must also be open to editorial direction."

+THE EXTREME DIVA PUBLISHING. E-mail: queries@theextremediva.com. Website: www.the extremediva.com. Publishes books in 4 areas: reducing stress, increasing joy, simplifying life, and enhancing relationships. Guidelines on Website.

Nonfiction: Query by e-query. Full manuscripts will be discarded unless requested.

Fiction: Currently not accepting fiction, except children's picture books.

Special Needs: Devotions to Go (30-day devotionals); Self Improvement; Cookbooks/ Entertainment Guides; Mommy/Daddy and Me (children's daily activities); Children's Picture Books.

Tips: "Joy is a factor in everything we do."

FACTS ON FILE, INC., 132 W. 31st St., 17th Fl., New York NY 10011. Toll-free (800)322-8755. (212)967-8800. Fax (212)967-9196. E-mail: llikoff@factsonfile.com, or editorial@factson file.com. Website: www.factsonfile.com. Laurie Likoff, ed. dir. School and library reference and trade books (for middle- to high-school students) tied to curriculum and areas of cross-cultural studies, including religion. Imprints: Facts On File, Checkmark Books. Publishes 3-5 religious titles/yr. Receives 10-20 submissions annually. 2% of books from first-time authors. Accepts mss through agents. No reprints. Prefers 224-480 pgs. Royalty 10% on retail; outright purchases of $2,000-10,000; advance $5,000-10,000. Some work-for-hire. Average first printing 3,000. Publication within 9-12 mos. Considers simultaneous submissions. Responds in 2 mos. Requires requested ms on disk. Guidelines (also by e-mail/Website)/free catalog.

Nonfiction: Query or proposal/1 chapter; fax/e-query OK.

Tips: "Most open to reference books tied to curriculum subjects or disciplines."

FAIR HAVENS PUBLICATIONS, PO Box 1238, Gainesville TX 76241-1238. Toll-free (800)771-4861. (940)668-6044. Fax (940)668-6984. E-mail: fairhavens@fairhavenspub.com. Website: www.fairhavenspub.com. J. Ray Smith, chief ed.; D. Joan Smith, children's ed. Produces quality books, teaching and evangelistic literature, audiotapes and videotapes, CD-ROMs, dramas, and artworks that inspire faith and courage. Publishes 4-5 titles/yr. Receives 200 submissions annually. No first-time authors considered for 2006. Accepts mss through agents. **SUBSIDY PUBLISHES 5%.** Reprints books. Prefers 250-300 pgs. Royalty 10-20% on sale price; no advance for first-time authors; negotiable for published authors. Average first printing 4,000 (runs 3,000-12,000). Publication within 8 mos. Considers simultaneous submissions. Requires requested on disk. Responds in 8 wks. Prefers NIV. Guidelines on Website; no catalog.

Nonfiction: Proposal/3 chapters; no phone/fax/e-query.

Fiction: Proposal/2 chapters; for all ages.

Special Needs: Biography, Bible prophecy, personal experience, animal stories, inspirational, how-to, trend analysis, self-help, and ministry aids.

Also Does: Booklets, audio & videotapes, CD-ROMs, dramas, artwork.

Photos/Artwork: Accepts freelance photos for book covers.

Tips: "We are particularly interested in books based on original research: case histories, surveys, unpublished documents, etc. We prefer books that follow traditional standards of grammar and style."

FAITH ALIVE CHRISTIAN RESOURCES, 2850 Kalamazoo Ave. S.E., Grand Rapids MI 49560. Toll-free (800)333-8300. (616)224-0819. E-mail: editors@faithaliveresources.org. Website: www.faithaliveresources.org. CRC Publications/Christian Reformed Church. Incomplete topical listings. No questionnaire returned.

FAITH COMMUNICATIONS, 3201 S.W. 15th St., Deerfield Beach FL 33442. (954)360-0909. Fax (954)360-0034. E-mail: susant@hcibooks.com. Website: www.hcibooks.com. Christian imprint of Health Communications, Inc. Susan Tobias, ed.; submit to Editorial Committee. No phone/e-queries. Guidelines on Website. Incomplete topical listings. No questionnaire returned.

Tips: "Books should have a very clear Christian focus—fiction or nonfiction."

+FAITHGIRLZ!/ZONDERKIDZ, 5300 Patterson S.E., Grand Rapids MI 49530-0002. (616)698-3400. Fax (616)698-3326. E-mail: zpub@zondervan.com. Website: www.zonder kidz.com. Zondervan/HarperCollins. Bruce Nuffer, children's pub. Girl's book line of Zonderkidz; fiction and nonfiction for tween girls, ages 8-12; about inner beauty and outward faith. Not accepting unsolicited manuscripts or proposals by air or surface mail.

Nonfiction: Fax proposal to Book Proposal Review Editor, (616)698-3454. No e-mail submissions.

Fiction: Fax proposal to Book Proposal Review Editor, (616)698-3454. No e-mail submissions.

**Note: This publisher serviced by ECPA First Edition.

FAITH KIDZ BOOKS, 4050 Lee Vance View, Colorado Springs CO 80918. (719)536-3271. Fax (719)536-3265. Website: www.cookministries.com. Cook Communications. Heather Gemmen, sr. ed. Publishes inspirational books for children, ages 1-12, with a strong spiritual emphasis. Publishes 40-50 titles/yr. Receives 1,000-1,500 submissions annually. Accepts mss through agents. Variable royalty on retail, usually an outright purchase $2,000-10,000; rarely offers advance. Publication within 18 mos. Considers simultaneous submissions. Responds in 6 mos. Guidelines on Website; free catalog.

> **Nonfiction:** Proposal via their Website: www.cookministries.com/proposals. For picture books send complete manuscript.

> **Fiction:** Prefers proposals from previously published authors or agents.

FAITH ONE PUBLISHING, PO Box 90000, Los Angeles CA 90009. (323)758-3777. E-mail: nicolla@inspiredlivingmag.com. Website: www.faithdome.org. Ever Increasing Faith Ministries. Nicolla Moore, ed. Primary focus is to publish works by the pastors and ministers of the Crenshaw Christian Center. Publishes 5-8 titles/yr. Receives 10-25 submissions annually. 15% of books from first-time authors. No mss through agents. No guidelines or catalog.

> **Nonfiction:** Query only.

> **Tips:** "We have not yet begun to pay for manuscripts." Changes in the works for this publisher; check Website.

FAITHWALK PUBLISHING, 333 Jackson St., Grand Haven MI 49417. Toll-free (800)335-7177. (616)846-9360. Fax (616)846-0072. E-mail: submissions@faithwalkpub.com. Website: www.faithwalkpub.com Dirk Wierenga, ed. Called to publish books which appeal to seekers and believers who might otherwise never purchase a religious book. Publishes 10 titles/yr. Receives 300 submissions annually. 25% of books from first-time authors. Accepts mss through agents. No reprints. Prefers 160-356 pgs. Royalty 7-10% of retail; advance. Average first printing 5,000. Publication within 9-12 mos. Considers simultaneous submissions (if indicated). Responds in 2-3 mos. Prefers NIV, NRSV. Guidelines (also by e-mail); catalog.

> **Nonfiction:** Proposal/1-2 chapters; e-query OK. No children's or gift books.

> **Fiction:** Proposal/1-2 chapters; e-query OK. Adult; adventure, contemporary, and literary.

> **Photos/Artwork:** Accepts freelance photos for book covers.

FAMILYLIFE PUBLISHING, 5800 Ranch Dr., Little Rock AR 72223. Toll-free (800)404-5052. E-mail: acquisitions_editor@familylife.com. Website: www.familylife.com. Campus Crusade for Christ. Margie Clark, product development mngr. Our uniqueness is creating/publishing connecting resources: marrying together truth, relationship, and experience. Publishes 10 titles/yr. Receives 100 submissions annually. 10% of books from first-time authors. Accepts mss through agents. Reprints books. Royalty 2-18% of net or outright purchase; advance. Average first printing 10,000. Publication within 12 mos. Considers simultaneous submissions. Requires submissions on disk or by e-mail. Responds in 6 mos. Prefers NASB, ESV, NIV. Guidelines (also by e-mail/Website); catalog on Website or for 9x12 SAE/4 stamps.

> **Nonfiction:** Proposal/2 chapters; e-query OK. "Looking for books on marriage: intimacy, communication."

> **Also Does:** Booklets; multipiece activity packs.

> **Photos/Artwork:** Accepts freelance photos for book covers; open to queries from freelance artists.

> **Tips:** "Most open to multipiece, interactive products. The query and proposal should be professional. Before you submit to us, be sure to read our writer's guidelines and The Family Manifesto (both on Website). If you don't know who we are or what we do, please send your material elsewhere."

> ****Note:** This publisher serviced by ECPA First Edition.

FREDERICK FELL PUBLISHERS, INC., 2131 Hollywood Blvd., Ste. 305, Hollywood FL 33020-6750. (954)925-5242. Fax (954)925-5244. E-mail: info@fellpub.com. Website: www.fellpub.com. Barbara Newman, sr. ed. General publisher that publishes 2-4 religious titles/yr. Receives 4,000 submissions annually. 95% of books from first-time authors. Reprints books. Prefers 60,000 wds. or 200-300 pgs. Royalty 6-15% on retail; advance of $500-10,000. Average first printing 7,500. Publication within 1 yr. Considers simultaneous submissions. Responds in 5-13 wks. Requires submissions by e-mail. Guidelines on Website.

> **Nonfiction:** Proposal/3 chapters; no phone/fax/e-query. Looking for self-help and how-to books. Include a clear marketing and promotional strategy.
>
> **Fiction:** Complete ms; no phone/fax/e-query. For adults; adventure and historical. "Looking for great story lines, with potential movie prospects."
>
> **Tips:** "Spirituality, optimism, and a positive attitude have international appeal. Steer clear of doom and gloom; less sadness and more gladness benefits all." Also publishes New Age books. SASE required.

+5TH ESTATE, PO Box 116, Blountsville AL 35031. (205)625-5733. E-mail: admin@fifth-estate.net. Website: www.fifth-estate.net. Joyce Dujardin, exec. ed. Publishes 20 titles/yr. Receives 100 submissions annually. 85% of books from first-time authors. Prefers mss through agents. Does print-on-demand. Prefers 120+ pgs. Royalty; no advance. Considers simultaneous submissions. Responds in 1 mo. Requires accepted ms on disk or by e-mail. Guidelines (also by e-mail or Website); free catalog for SASE.

> **Nonfiction:** Query only first; e-query OK. "Looking for spiritual and children's books."
>
> **Fiction:** Query only first; e-query OK. For all ages.
>
> **Photos/Artwork:** Accepts freelance photos for book covers; queries from freelance artists.

+FILBERT PUBLISHING, Box 326, Kandiyohi MN 56251.(320)382-6662. E-mail: filbertpublishing@filbertpublishing.com. Website: http://filbertpublishing.com.www. Maurice Erickson, dir. of acquisitions. Publishes 6 titles/yr. 70% of books from first-time authors. No mss through agents. Royalty 10-15% on retail. Considers simultaneous submissions. Catalog for 6x9 SAE/4 stamps. Publishes how-to books for writers and small-business titles.

FIRST FRUITS OF ZION, PO Box 620099, Littleton CO 80162-0099. Fax (303)933-0997. Website: www.FFOZ.org. Hope Egan, ed. A nonprofit ministry devoted to strengthening the love and appreciation of the Body of Messiah for the land, people, and Scripture of Israel. Publishes 2-6 titles/yr. No mss through agents. Royalty; no advance. Publication within 6 mos. Considers simultaneous submissions. Responds in 1 mo. Prefers NASB.

> **Nonfiction:** Query first; no phone/fax/e-query.
>
> **Special Needs:** Books on Hebrew roots only.
>
> **Tips:** "Be very familiar with our material before submitting to us."

FOCUS ON THE FAMILY BOOK PUBLISHING AND RESOURCE DEVELOPMENT, 8605 Explorer Dr., Colorado Springs CO 80920-1051. (719)531-3400. Fax (719)531-3448. Website: www.family.org. Submit to Acquisitions Assistant. Exists to support the family; all our products are about topics pertaining to families. Publishes 30-40 titles/yr. 12% of books from first-time authors. Rarely reprints books. Length depends on genre. Royalty or work for hire; advance varies. Average first printing varies. Publication within 12 mos. No longer considers unsolicited submissions. Responds in 1-3 mos. Prefers NIV (but accepts 7 others). Guidelines by e-mail; no catalog.

> **Nonfiction:** Query Letter only through an agent or writer's conference contact with a Focus editor. "Most open to family advice topics. We look for excellent writing and topics that haven't been done to death—or that have a unique angle."
>
> **Fiction:** Query Letter only through an agent or writer's conference contact with a Focus editor. Stories must incorporate traditional family values. Also does MomLit.

Photos/Artwork: Open to queries from freelance artists (but not for specific projects).

**Note: This publisher serviced by The Writer's Edge and ECPA First Edition.

FORTRESS PRESS, Box 1209, Minneapolis MN 55440-1209. (612)330-3300. Fax (612)330-3215. Website: www.fortresspress.com. J. Michael West, ed-in-chief; submit to Dr. K. C. Hanson, acq. ed. Publishes religious academic books. Publishes 60 titles/yr. Receives 1,000 submissions annually. 5-10% of books from first-time authors. Accepts mss through agents. Royalty on retail. Publication within 1 yr. Considers simultaneous submissions. Responds in 3 mos. Guidelines on Website; free catalog (call 1-800-328-4648).

> **Nonfiction:** Query. "Please study guidelines before submitting."
>
> **Ethnic Books:** African American studies.

FORWARD MOVEMENT, 300 W. 4th St., Cincinnati OH 45202-2665. Toll-free (800)543-1813. (513)721-6659. Fax (513)721-0729. E-mail: orders@forwarddaybyday.com. Website: www.forwardmovement.org. Episcopal. Submit to The Editor. Provides resources to support persons in their lives of prayer and faith. Publishes 12 titles/yr. Receives 1,000 submissions annually. 50% of books from first-time authors. No mss through agents. Rarely reprints books. Prefers 150 pgs. One-time honorarium; no advance. Average first printing 5,000. Publication within 9 mos. Considers simultaneous submissions. Prefers requested ms on disk as an .RTF file. Responds in 1-2 mos. Prefers NRSV. Guidelines; free catalog.

> **Nonfiction:** Query for book, complete ms if short; no phone/fax/e-query. "Looking for books on prayer and spirituality, devotionals, Christian living, and spiritual life."
>
> **Fiction:** Query. For teens. Biblical. Send for guidelines.
>
> **Ethnic Books:** Hispanic pamphlets.
>
> **Also Does:** Booklets, 4-32 pgs.; pamphlets 4-8 pgs.; tracts.
>
> **Tips:** "We sell primarily to a mainline Protestant audience. Most open to books that deal with the central doctrines of the Christian faith."

+FOUNDERS PRESS, PO Box 150931, Cape Coral FL 33915. (239)772-1400. Fax (239)772-1140. Website: www.founders.org. Founders Ministries/Southern Baptist. Kenneth Puls, ed. Committed to producing and distributing books, pamphlets, and other materials that are consistent with the doctrines of grace and that speak from a historic Southern Baptist perspective. Responds in 4 mos. (or contact them). Guidelines on Website. Incomplete topical listings. No questionnaire returned.

> **Nonfiction:** Proposal, plus completed author information sheet (available on the Website).
>
> **Also Does:** Pamphlets.

FOUR COURTS PRESS, 7 Malpas St., Dublin 8, Ireland. International phone +3531 4534668. Fax +3531 4534672. Martin Fanning, ed. Imprint: Open Air. Publishes 5 titles/yr. Receives 40 submissions annually. 10% of books from first-time authors. Accepts mss through agents. Reprints books. Prefers 70,000 wds. Royalty 10% of net; sometimes no royalty is paid; no advance. Average first printing 500-700. Publication within 6-10 mos. Considers simultaneous submissions. Responds in 2-10 wks. Prefers RSV. Guidelines being revised; free catalog.

> **Nonfiction:** Unsolicited mss will not be returned. Phone/fax/e-query OK. "We're looking for scholarly/academic books."

FRIENDS UNITED PRESS, 101 Quaker Hill Dr., Richmond IN 47374. (765)962-7573. Fax (765)966-1293. E-mail: friendspress@fum.org. Website: www.fum.org. Friends United Meeting (Quaker). Barbara Bennett Mays, ed. To gather persons into a fellowship where Jesus Christ is known as Lord and Teacher. Publishes 2 titles/yr. Receives 50 submissions annually. 50% of books from first-time authors. No mss through agents. Prefers 150-200 pgs. Royalty 7.5% of net; no advance. Average first printing 1,000-1,500. Publication within 1 yr. Considers simultaneous submissions; e-mail submissions preferred. Responds in 3 mos. Prefers requested ms on disk or by e-mail. Guidelines (also on Website); free catalog.

Nonfiction: Proposal/2 chapters; e-query preferred.

Ethnic Books: Howard Thurman Books (African American).

Tips: "Primarily open to Quaker authors. Looking for Quaker-related spirituality, or current faith issues/practice addressed from a Quaker experience or practice."

GENESIS PRESS, INC., PO Box 101, Columbus MS 39703-0101. (662)329-9927. Fax (662)329-9399. E-mail: ncolom@genesis-press.com. Website: www.genesis-press.com. Angelique Justin, acq. ed. Wants to approach romance with a classy, realistic, and fun, yet inspirational, Christian outlook. Imprints: Indigo Christian Romance; Indigo Glitz, and Indigo Vibe (all fiction); and Mount Blue (Christian living). Publishes 2 titles/yr. Receives 300+ submissions annually. 75% of books from first-time authors. **SOME SUBSIDY.** No reprints. Prefers 85,000 wds. Royalty 6-8% of net; advance $750. Average first printing 15,000. Publication within 6 mos. Considers simultaneous submissions. Responds in 3 mos. Guidelines by e-mail/Website; free catalog.

Nonfiction: Query first; proposal/150 pgs.; no phone/fax/e-query. Hard copy only.

Fiction: Query first; proposal/150 pgs.; no phone/fax/e-query. Hard copy only. Christian/inspirational romance. Prefers African American or cross-cultural fiction. Also does teen fiction for 12- to 18-year-olds, and fiction for 21- to 30-year-olds (under Indigo Vibe Imprint).

Ethnic Books: African American and multicultural romances.

GENEVA PRESS, 100 Witherspoon St., Louisville KY 40202-1396. Fax (502)569-5113. E-mail: ldowell@presbypub.com. Website: www.genevapress.com. Presbyterian Church (USA). Submit to Lori Dowell, ed. asst. Imprint of Presbyterian Publishing Corp. Publishes in three categories: (1) heritage, history, doctrine, policy, and institutions of the denomination; (2) theological, social, and ethical issues confronting the church; and (3) congregational mission (books for Christian educators, pastors, lay leaders, and laity); for a Presbyterian-specific audience. Publishes 10 titles/yr. Receives 1,500 submissions annually. 10% of books from first-time authors. No mss through agents. No reprints. Average length 120-250 pgs. Royalty on retail; no advance for first-time authors. Average first printing 2,000. Considers simultaneous submissions. Accepts hard copy by mail. Responds within 8 wks. Prefers NRSV. Guidelines by e-mail/Website; free catalog.

Nonfiction: Proposal/1 chapter; fax/e-query OK.

Tips: "We do not publish fiction, poetry, or children's books."

GEORGETOWN UNIVERSITY PRESS, 3240 Prospect St. N.W., Washington DC 20007. (202)687-5889. Fax (202)687-6340. E-mail: reb7@georgetown.edu, or gupress@georgetown.edu. Website: www.press.georgetown.edu. Georgetown University. Richard Brown, dir. Scholarly books in religion, theology, ethics, and other fields, with an emphasis on cross-disciplinary and cross-cultural studies. Publishes 10 titles/yr. Receives 100 submissions annually. 10% of books from first-time authors. Accepts mss through agents. No reprints. Prefers 80,000 wds. Royalty 8-12% on net; negotiable advance. Average first printing 2,000-3,000. Publication within 9-10 mos. Considers simultaneous submissions. Requires requested ms on disk. Responds in 6-8 wks. Prefers NRSV. Does print-on-demand. Guidelines on Website; free catalog.

Nonfiction: Proposal/1 chapter; fax/e-query OK. "Should be thoroughly researched and original."

Special Needs: Work relations, theology, ethics—with scholarly bent.

Ethnic Books: Hispanic.

Also Does: CD-ROMs.

Photos/Artwork: Accepts freelance photos for book covers.

GILGAL PUBLICATIONS, Box 3399, Sunriver OR 97707. Phone/fax (541)593-8418. E-mail: judyo@gilgal.com. Website: www.gilgal.com. Judy Osgood, exec. ed. Focuses on collections of meditations on specific themes. Publishes 1 title/yr. Receives 100+ submissions annually. 25-30% of submissions from first-time authors. No mss through agents. Pays $25/meditation on acceptance, plus 2 copies of the book. Average first printing 3,000. Publication time varies. Responds in 1-2 mos. No disk. Guidelines on Website.

Nonfiction: Complete ms (after reading guidelines); fax query OK. "Our books are all anthologies on coping with stress and resolving grief. Not interested in other book mss. Currently interested in meditations on bereavement of various kinds."

Tips: "For the foreseeable future, we will only be continuing our Gilgal Meditation Series and will not be buying book manuscripts."

GLORY BOUND BOOKS, PO Box 278, Cass City MI 48726. Phone (989)635-7520. E-mail: glory bound@centurytel.net. Website: www.thcgloryboundbookcompany.com. Leah Berry, pub. Sharing with children and families around the world that there is a home in heaven that can never be taken from them and that the family of God waits to welcome them in. Publishes 10+ titles/yr. (growing). New publisher. 100% of books from first-time authors. No mss through agents. No reprints. Prefers 5,000 wds. Royalty 25% of net; no advance. Average first printing 500. Publication within 12-24 mos. Considers simultaneous submissions. Responds in 3 mos. Prefers KJV (but not limited to). Guidelines on Website; catalog $1/#10 SAE/2 stamps.

Nonfiction: Complete ms; no phone/fax/e-query. "We are specifically looking for missionary adventure stories, and real-life family ministry memoirs. Submissions in all categories are welcome."

Fiction: Complete ms by mail only; no phone/fax/e-query. "Humorous family fiction. Life is funny—give us a giggle and make us smile! 1 Peter 1:18."

Special Needs: "We specialize in fables, poetry books, and juvenile fiction." Looking for humorous books and mystery novels.

Ethnic Books: Actively seeking foreign language submissions with English translation.

Photos/Artwork: Accepts freelance photos for book covers.

Contest: Sponsors a fiction contest; see contest listings.

Tips: "We cherish the humor of family life and the nostalgic moments that weave us together. Our books are rich in feeling and descriptive detail, literally transporting the reader to another time and place. Take us on a journey through the eyes of a child or let us peek through the window of a family's home. Allow us to become a part of the experience where children and families have allowed Jesus to become their friend."

Note: Watch Website for details about current contact information, as this publisher will be relocating.

GOOD BOOK PUBLISHING COMPANY, PO Box 837, Kihei HI 96753-0837. Phone/fax (808)874-4876. E-mail: dickb@dickb.com. Website: www.dickb.com/index.shtml.Christian/ Protestant/Bible Fellowship. Ken Burns, pres. Researches and publishes books on the biblical/Christian roots of Alcoholics Anonymous. Publishes 1 title/yr. Receives 8 submissions annually. 80% of books from first-time authors. No mss through agents. Reprints books. Prefers 250 pgs. Royalty 10%; no advance. Average first printing 3,000. Publication within 2 mos. Considers simultaneous submissions. Responds in 1 wk. No disk. Prefers KJV. No guidelines; free catalog.

Nonfiction: Proposal; no phone/fax/e-query. Books on the spiritual history and success of AA; 12-step spiritual roots.

Also Does: Pamphlets, booklets.

GOOD NEWS PUBLISHERS, 1300 Crescent St., Wheaton IL 60187. (630)682-4300, ext. 308. Fax (630)682-4785. E-mail: jwest@gnpcb.org. Website: www.goodnewspublishers.org. Jutti West, ed. Tracts only; publishing the gospel message in an attractive and relevant format. Publishes 30 tracts/yr. Receives 500 submissions annually. 2% of tracts from first-time authors. Prefers 650-800 wds. Pays about $150 or a quantity of tracts. Average first printing 250,000. Publication within 16 mos. Considers simultaneous submissions. Responds in 6 wks. Prefers ESV. Guidelines; free tract catalog.

Tracts: Complete ms.

Also Does: Pamphlets.

GOSPEL PUBLISHING HOUSE, 1445 N. Boonville Ave., Springfield MO 65802. Toll-free (800)641-4310. (417)831-8000. E-mail: newproducts@gph.org. Website: www.gospel publishing.com. Assemblies of God. Julie Horner, ed. The majority of titles specifically address Pentecostal audiences in a variety of ministries in the local church. Publishes 10-15 titles/yr. Receives 250 submissions annually. 25% of books from first-time authors. Accepts mss through agents. No reprints. Royalty 5-10% of retail; no advance. Average first printing 5,000. Publication within 1 yr. Considers simultaneous submissions. Responds in 4 mos. Requires accepted mss on disk or by e-mail. Guidelines on Website; free catalog.

Nonfiction: Proposal/1 chapter; no phone query, e-query OK. "Looking for Holy Spirit; Pentecostal focus for pastors, local church lay leaders, and individuals; children's ministry programs and resources."

Tips: "Most open to a new program or resource for children's ministry, compassion ministry, or evangelistic outreach."

GOSPEL TRACT SOCIETY, INC., PO Box 1118, Independence MO 64051. (816)461-6086. Fax (816)461-4305. Gospel Tract Society, Inc. David Buttram, ed. All tracts must be camera-ready (artwork, typeset, etc.). "We always need good, Bible-based articles that will fit a tract format. We also use poems in tract form."

GREEN KEY BOOKS, 2514 Aloha Pl., Holiday FL 34691. Toll-free (888)900-0197. (727)934-0927. Fax (727)934-4241. E-mail: acquisitions@greenkeybooks.com. Website: www .greenkeybooks.com. Christian publisher. Krissi Castor, mng. ed./acquisitions. Publishes 10-12 titles/yr. Receives 300 submissions annually. 95% of books from first-time authors. Accepts mss through agents. No reprints. Royalty; no advance. Average first printing 5,000. Publication within 9-12 mos. No simultaneous submissions. Accepts mss by e-mail. Responds in 8-12 wks. Guidelines on Website; free catalog.

Nonfiction: Query first; e-query OK. Query can include a synopsis or brief project outline. "Looking for men's books, niche topics, books for military families."

Fiction: Not currently considering fiction.

Tips: "Most open to a book that is editorially tight (specifically grammar and punctuation)—in adherence to the *Chicago Manual of Style*."

**Note: Serviced by ECPA First Edition.

GREEN PASTURES PRESS, HC 67 Box 91-A, Mifflin PA 17058. (717)436-9115. E-mail: green pastures@emypeople.net. Mennonite. Don L. Martin, ed. High-quality, inspirational, character-building literature for children & young people. Publishes 1-4 titles/yr. Reprints books. Prefers 100-200 pgs. Royalty on net. Prefers KJV. No guidelines; free catalog.

Nonfiction: Query first; phone query OK. "Looking for children's devotionals."

Fiction: For all ages. Query first; phone query OK. "Looking for short-story collections and inspirational children's fiction. We prefer historical fiction; we are very conservative and avoid romance, violence, women preachers, and evangelism of children who are too young to understand."

Tips: "We are most open to well-researched historical Christian fiction for middle grades to teens; short stories with moral and inspirational value; and children's or family devotionals."

GREENWOOD PUBLISHING GROUP/PRAEGER PUBLISHERS, 88 Post Road W., Westport CT 06881. (203)226-3571. Fax (203)226-6009. E-mail: sstaszak@greenwood.com. Website: www.Greenwood.com. Reed Elsevier Co. Suzanne Staszak-Silva, sr. ed. Imprints: Greenwood and Praeger. Publishes 5-30 titles/yr. Receives 40-60 submissions annually. No reprints. Prefers up to 100,000 wds. Royalty on net; some advances. Average first printing 1,500. Publication within 8-10 mos. Considers simultaneous submissions. Requires accepted ms on disk. Responds in 1-3 mos. Guidelines (by e-mail or Website); free catalog.

Nonfiction: Book proposal/1-2 chapters or all chapters available; e-query OK.

Special Needs: Religious studies (general interest); criminology (general interest); literary studies.

Ethnic Books: Black studies (general interest); Islamic studies; Jewish studies.

Tips: "Most open to general interest books."

GROUP PUBLISHING, INC., 1515 Cascade Ave., Loveland CO 80539-0481. Toll-free (800)447-1070. (970)292-4243. Fax (970)622-4370. E-mail: kloesche@group publishing.com. Website: www.group.com. Nondenominational. Kerri Loesche, ed. asst./ copyright coordinator. Imprints: Group Books. To encourage Christian growth in children, youth, and adults with resources that are R.E.A.L. (relational, experiential, applicable, learner based). Publishes 40 titles/yr. Receives 1,000+ submissions annually. 5% of books from first-time authors. Prefers mss through agents. Some subsidy. No reprints. Prefers 128-250 pgs. Outright purchases of $25-3,000 or royalty of 6-10% of net; advance $1,500. Average first printing 5,000. Publication within 12-18 mos. Considers simultaneous submissions. Responds in 3 mos. Requires requested ms on disk. Prefers NIV. Guidelines on Website; no catalog.

Nonfiction: Query or proposal/2 chapters/intro/cover letter/SASE; no phone/fax/e-query. "Looking for practical ministry tools for pastors, youth workers, C. E. directors, and teachers with an emphasis on active learning. Read *Why Nobody Learns Much of Anything at Church: And How to Fix It* and *The Dirt on Learning* and *The 1 Thing* by Thom and Joani Schultz."

Tips: "Most open to a practical resource that will help church leaders change lives."

**Note: This publisher serviced by The Writer's Edge.

GUERNICA EDITIONS, PO Box 117, Sta. P, Toronto ON M5S 2S6, Canada. (416)658-9888. Fax (416)657-8885. E-mail: guernicaeditions@cs.com. Website: www.guernicaeditions.com. Antonio D'Alfonso, ed. Interested in the next generation of writers. Publishes 1 religious title/yr. Receives 100 submissions annually. 5% of books from first-time authors. No mss through agents. Reprints books. Prefers 100 pgs. Royalty 8-10% of retail; some outright purchases of $200-5,000; $200-2,000 advance. Average first printing 1,500. Publication within 10 mos. Responds in 1-6 mos. Requires requested ms on disk; no e-mail. No guidelines (read one of our books to see what we like); catalog online.

Nonfiction: Query first; no phone/fax/e-query. "Looking for books on world issues."

Fiction: Query first. "Looking for short and profound literary works."

Ethnic Books: Concentration on other cultures. "We are involved in translations and ethnic issues."

Photos/Artwork: Accepts freelance photos for book covers.

Tips: "Know what we publish. We're interested in books that bridge time and space; works that fit our editorial literary policies."

HARCOURT RELIGION PUBLISHERS, 6277 Sea Harbor Dr., Orlando FL 32887. Toll-free (800)922-7696. (407)345-3800. Fax (407)345-3798 (to Sebrina Kersanac for submissions). Website: www.harcourtreligion.com. Catholic. Craig O'Neil, sr. ed. Catholic educational market; high school curriculum. Publishes 50-100 titles/yr. Receives 100-300 submissions annually. Variable royalty or outright purchase; rarely pays advance. Average first printing 1,000-3,000. Publication within 1 yr. Considers simultaneous submissions. Responds in 6 mos. Free catalog.

Nonfiction: Complete ms. "Looking primarily for school and parish textbooks."

Photos/Artwork: Accepts freelance photos for book covers. Submit to Lynn Molony, production mngr.

HARPERSANFRANCISCO, 353 Sacramento St., #500, San Francisco CA 94111-3653. (415)477-4400. Fax (415)477-4444. E-mail: hcsanfrancisco@harpercollins.com. Website: www.harpercollins.com. Religious division of HarperCollins. Michael G. Maudlin, ed. dir. Strives to be the preeminent publisher of the most important books across the full spectrum of religion and spiritual literature, adding to the wealth of the world's wisdom by respecting all traditions and favoring none; emphasis on quality Christian spirituality and literary fiction. Publishes 75 titles/yr. Receives 10,000 submissions annually. 5% of books from first-time authors. Prefers mss through agents. No reprints. Prefers 160-256 ms pgs. Royalty 7.5-15% on retail; advance $20,000-100,000. Average first printing 10,000. Publication within 12 mos. Considers simultaneous submissions. Responds in 3 mos. Requires requested ms on disk. No guidelines/catalog.

> **Nonfiction:** Proposal/1 chapter; fax query OK.
>
> **Fiction:** Complete ms; contemporary adult fiction.
>
> **Tips:** "Agented proposals only."

HARRISON HOUSE PUBLISHERS, Box 35035, Tulsa OK 74153. Toll-free (800)888-4126. (918)523-5400. E-mail: customerservice@harrisonhouse.com. Website: www.harrison house.com. Evangelical/charismatic. Julie Lechlider, mng. ed. To challenge Christians to live victoriously, grow spiritually, and know God intimately. Publishes 20 titles/yr. 5% of books from first-time authors. No mss through agents. No reprints. Royalty on net or retail; no advance. Average first printing 5,000. Publication within 12-24 mos. Responds in 6 mos. No guidelines or catalog. Not currently accepting proposals or manuscripts.

> **Nonfiction:** Query first; then proposal/table of contents/1 chapter; no phone/fax query; e-query OK.

HARVEST HOUSE PUBLISHERS, 990 Owen Loop N., Eugene OR 97402. (541)343-0123. E-mail: admin@harvesthousepublishers.com. Evangelical. Books and products that affirm biblical values and help people grow spiritually strong. Publishes 190 titles/yr. No longer accepting unsolicited submissions, proposals, queries, etc.

> **Nonfiction:** Self-help; Christian living.
>
> **Fiction:** Interesting women's fiction.
>
> ****Note:** This publisher serviced by The Writer's Edge and ECPA First Edition.

THE HAWORTH PASTORAL PRESS, an imprint of The Haworth Press, 10 Alice St., Binghamton NY 13904-1580. Toll-free (800)429-6784. (607)722-5857. Fax (607)771-0012. E-mail: getinfo@haworthpress.com. Website: www.haworthpress.com. Bill Palmer, VP of Publications. Publishes 10 titles/yr. Receives 100 submissions annually. 60% of books from first-time authors. Reprints books. Prefers up to 250 pgs. Royalty 7-15% of net; advance $500-1,000. Average first printing 1,500. Publication within 1 yr. Requires requested ms on disk. Responds in 2 mos. Guidelines; free catalog.

> **Nonfiction:** Proposal/3 chapters; no phone/fax query. "Looking for books on psychology/social work, etc., with a pastoral perspective."

HAY HOUSE, INC., PO Box 5100, Carlsbad CA 92018-5100. (760)431-7695. Fax (760)431-6948. E-mail: slittrell@hayhouse.com. Website: www.hayhouse.com. Jill Kramer, ed. dir.; Shannon Littrell, submissions ed. (slittrell@hayhouse.com). Books to help heal the planet. Publishes 1 religious title/yr. Receives 200 religious submissions annually. 5% of books from first-time authors. Agented submissions only. Prefers 70,000 wds. or 250 pgs. Royalty. Average first printing 5,000. Publication within 12-15 mos. Considers simultaneous submissions. Responds in 1-2 mos. Guidelines (also by e-mail); free catalog for SASE.

> **Nonfiction:** Proposal/3 chapters; hard copy only. "Looking for self-help/spiritual with a unique ecumenical angle."

Also Does: Some gift books.

Tips: "We are looking for books with a unique slant, ecumenical, but not overly religious. We want an open-minded approach." Includes a broad range of religious titles, including New Age.

HEALTH COMMUNICATIONS, INC., 3201 S.W. 15th St., Deerfield Beach FL 33442. (954)360-0909 (no phone calls). Fax (954)360-0034. E-mail: editorial@hcibooks.com. Website: www.hci-online.com, or www.hcibooks.com. Submit to Editorial Committee. Nonfiction that emphasizes self-improvement, personal motivation, psychological health, and overall wellness; recovery/addiction, self-help/psychology, health/wellness, soul/spirituality, inspiration, women's issues, relationships, and family. Imprint: HCI Teens. Publishes 40 titles/yr. 20% of books from first-time authors. Accepts mss through agents. Prefers 250 pgs. Royalty 15% of net. Publication within 9 mos. Considers simultaneous submissions. Responds in 1-3 mos. Must get and follow guidelines for submission. Guidelines (also on Website); catalog for 9x12 SASE. Not in topical listings.

Nonfiction: Query/outline and 2 chapters; no phone/fax/e-query. Needs books for Christian teens.

HEART OF WISDOM PUBLISHERS, 146 Chriswood Ln., Stafford VA 22556-6601. (540)752-2593. E-mail: info@heartofwisdom.com. Website: www.heartofwisdom.com. Publishes a variety of academic materials to help Christian families bring up children with a heart's desire for and knowledge of the Lord. Robin Sampson, ed. Query only. Guidelines at: http://homeschoolunitstudies.com/guidelines.htm.

Special Needs: Currently accepting queries for high-quality history, science, and life skills unit studies for grades 4-12. Not accepting any other titles.

Tips: "We market to home educators and Christian schools."

HEARTQUEST/TYNDALE HOUSE PUBLISHERS, PO Box 80, Wheaton IL 60189-0080. (630)668-8300. Fax (630)784-5011. E-mail: through Website. Website: www.tyndale.com. Anne Goldsmith, sr. ed. To encourage and challenge readers in their faith journey and Christian walk. Accepts mss through agents or by request only. Prefers 75,000-90,000 wds. (contemporary), and 100,000+ wds. (historical). Responds in 3 mos. Royalty on net; advance. Guidelines (also by e-mail).

Fiction: One-to-two-page query/synopsis/3 chapters; no phone/fax query. "Must incorporate three plot lines—action, emotion, and faith (see guidelines for details). None set in Civil War period."

Tips: "We are actively acquiring contemporary novels, suspense novels, and women's fiction. We look for strong writing, gripping stories, and powerful Christian content. We publish historicals (set in 1600–1945), contemporaries, and 3-book series."

HEARTSONG PRESENTS, Imprint of Barbour Publishing, Inc., PO Box 721, 1810 Barbour Dr., Uhrichsville, OH 44683. (740)922-7280. Fax (740)922-5948. E-mail: fictionsubmit@barbour books.com, or info@heartsongpresents.com. Website: www.heartsongpresents.com. Jim & Tracie Peterson, mng. eds. Produces affordable, wholesome entertainment through a book club that also helps to enhance and spread the gospel. Publishes 52 titles/yr. Receives 1,000+ submissions annually. 10% of books from first-time authors. Prefers 45,000-50,000 wds. Royalty 8% of net; advance $2,200. Average first printing 15,000-20,000. Publication within 1 yr. Considers simultaneous submissions. Responds in 3-6 mos. Requires electronic submission; no proposals via regular mail. Prefers KJV for historicals; NIV for contemporary. Guidelines (also by e-mail/Website); no catalog.

Fiction: Proposal/3-4 chapters; electronic submissions only (fictionsubmit@barbour books.com). Adult. "We publish 2 contemporary and 2 historical romances every 4 weeks. We cover all topics and settings. Specific guidelines available."

Tips: "Romance only, with a strong conservative-Christian theme. Read our books and study our style before submitting."

HENDRICKSON PUBLISHERS, 140 Summit St., PO Box 3473, Peabody MA 01961. (978)532-6546. Fax (978)531-8146. E-mail: editorial@hendrickson.com. Website: www.hendrickson.com. Submit to: Acquisitions. To provide biblically oriented books for reference, learning, and personal growth, and resources for pastors. Publishes 25-35 titles/yr. Receives 500-600 submissions annually. 25% of books from first-time authors. Accepts mss through agents. Reprints books. Prefers 200-500 pgs. Royalty 10-14% of net; some advances. Average first printing 3,000. Publication within 12-18 mos. No simultaneous submissions. Responds in 3-6 mos. Prefers accepted ms by e-mail. Follow *Chicago Manual of Style.* Prefers NIV. Guidelines (also by e-mail/Website); catalog for 9x12 SAE/$1.42 postage (mark "Media Mail").

Nonfiction: Proposal/1-2 chapters; e-query OK. "Looking for popular reference material." Also publishes academic books through their Academic Book Division.

Special Needs: Books that help the reader's confrontation and interaction with Scripture, leading to a positive change in thought and action; books that give a hunger to studying, understanding, and applying Scripture; books that encourage and facilitate personal growth in such areas as personal devotions and a skillful use of the Bible.

Tips: "Most open to books about current 'hot' topics in churches; books that help readers understand and explore Scripture and early church history; and books that encourage Bible study and application of theology in practical life."

**Note: This publisher serviced by The Writer's Edge.

HENSLEY PUBLISHING, 6116 E. 32nd St., Tulsa OK 74135. (918)664-8520. Fax (918)664-8562. E-mail: editorial@hensleypublishing.com. Website: www.hensleypublishing.com. Terri Kalfas, dir. of publishing. Goal is to get people studying the Bible instead of just reading books about the Bible; Bible study only. Publishes 5-10 titles/yr. Receives 800 submissions annually. 50% of books from first-time authors. No mss through agents. No reprints. Prefers up to 200 pgs. Royalty on net; some outright purchases; no advance. Average first printing 2,500. Publication within 12-18 mos. Considers simultaneous submissions. Requires requested ms on disk, in MAC format or e-mail submissions. Responds in 2 mos. Guidelines & catalog on Website.

Nonfiction: Query first, then proposal/first 3 chapters; no phone/fax query. "Looking for Bible studies of varying length for use by small or large groups or individuals."

Special Needs: Bible study workbooks for small or large groups or individuals.

**Note: This publisher serviced by The Writer's Edge.

HIDDEN BROOK PRESS, 109 Bayshore Rd., RR#4, Brighton ON K0K 1H0, Canada. (613)475-2368. Fax (801)751-1837. E-mail: writers@hiddenbrookpress.com. Website: www.hiddenbrookpress.com. Richard M. Grove, ed. Poetry books.

HIDDENSPRING BOOKS, 997 Macarthur Blvd., Mahwah NJ 07430. (201)825-7300. Fax (201)825-8345. E-mail: Info@hiddenspringbooks.com. Website: www.hiddenspringbooks.com, or www.paulistpress.com. Paulist Press. Paul McMahon, mng. ed. A mainstream Catholic publishing house that specializes in parish and theology resources. Publishes 95 titles/yr. Receives 700 submissions annually. 30-40% of books from first-time authors. Accepts mss through agents. No reprints. Prefers 160 pgs. Royalty 8% on net; advance $1,000. Average first printing 5,000. Publication within 18 mos. Considers simultaneous submissions. Accepts ms on disk. Responds in 2 mos. Prefers NRSV. Guidelines on Website; free catalog.

Nonfiction: Query only first, proposal/3 chapters, or complete ms.; phone query OK.

Tips: "Most open to books on classic spirituality, mysticism, and prayer." This publisher is currently overstocked and is accepting no freelance submissions until April 2006.

HILLCREST PUBLISHING, 1648 Campus Ct., Abilene TX 79601. Toll-free (877)816-4455. (325)674-6950. Fax (325)674-6471. E-mail: Lemmonst@acuprs.acu.edu, or contact@ hillcrestpublishing.com. Website: www.hillcrestpublishing.com. To provide books, software, and other media of the highest quality and value, that will honor the God who is revealed in the Holy Bible, encourage the spiritual quest and personal devotion, and promote service to others. Not included in topical listings. No questionnaire returned.

HILL STREET PRESS, 191 E. Broad St., Ste. 209, Athens GA 30601-2848. (706)613-7200. Fax (706)613-7204. E-mail: editorial@hillstreetpress.com. Website: www.hillstreetpress.com. Judy Long (long@hillstreetpress.com), ed. Liberal, ecumenical, progressive. Imprint: Hill Street Classics. Publishes 1-2 titles/yr. Receives 75-100 submissions annually. 40% of books from first-time authors. Prefers mss through agents. Reprints books. Prefers 50,000-85,000 wds. Royalty; sometimes gives advance. First printing varies. Publication within 12-15 mos. Considers simultaneous submissions. Responds in 6-8 mos. Guidelines on Website; catalog online only.

> **Nonfiction:** Proposal/3 chapters/query letter/résumé; no phone/fax/e-query. "All electronic submissions are returned unread."
>
> **Fiction:** Proposal/3 chapters/query letter/résumé; no phone/fax/e-query. Contemporary and literary. Not encouraging fiction submissions at this time, except by previously published authors.
>
> **Ethnic Books:** Jewish, Black.
>
> **Tips:** "Most open to a book that is short, ecumenical, and liberal."

+HOLY FIRE PUBLISHING, 531 Constitution Blvd., Martinsburg WV 25401. (304)579-4269. E-mail: publisher@christianpublish.com. Website: www.christianpublish.com. Venessa Hensel, VP. A ministry helping the Christian author reach the world through the printed word. Publishes 50+ titles/yr. Receives 2,000+ submissions annually. 50% of books from first-time authors. Accepts mss through agents. Does print-on-demand. Reprints books. Prefers 48-750 pgs. Royalty 20-30% on net; no advance. Publication within 2 mos. Prefers submissions on disk or by e-mail. Guidelines on Website; no catalog.

> **Nonfiction:** Proposal/1 chapter; phone/fax/e-query OK. "Looking for Christian Living."
>
> **Fiction:** Proposal/1 chapter; phone/fax/e-query OK. For all ages.
>
> **Photos/Artwork:** Open to queries from freelance artists.

HONOR BOOKS, Devotional books that inspire and motivate, packaged as gift books. Submit to The Editor. See Cook Communications Ministries for details.

HONOR KIDZ, 4050 Lee Vance View, Colorado Springs CO 80918. Toll-free (800)708-5550. (719)536-0100. E-mail through Website. Website: www.cookministries.com/books/ honor. Inspirational/devotional books for children. Children's imprint of Honor Books. No freelance submissions. Accepting submissions only through The Writer's Edge or First Edition.

+HOPE PUBLISHING HOUSE, PO Box 60008, Pasadena CA 91106. (626)792-6123. Fax (626)792-2121. E-mail: hopepub@sbcglobal.net. Website: www.hope-pub.com. Southern California Ecumenical Council. Faith A. Sand, pub. Produces thinking books that challenge the faith community to be serious about their pilgrimage of faith. Imprint: New Paradigm Books. Publishes 6 titles/yr. Receives 40 submissions annually. 30% of books from first-time authors. No mss through agents. Reprints books. Prefers 200 pgs. Royalty 10% on net; no advance. Average first printing 3,000. Publication within 6 mos. No simultaneous submissions. Accepts mss by disk or e-mail. Responds in 3 mos. Prefers NRSV. No guidelines; catalog for 7x10 SAE/4 stamps.

> **Nonfiction:** Query only first; no phone/fax query; e-query OK.
>
> **Tips:** "Most open to a well-written manuscript with correct grammar that is provocative, original, challenging, and informative."

HOURGLASS BOOKS, 387 Northgate Rd., Lindenhurst IL 60046. E-mail: editor@hourglass books.org. Website: www.hourglassbooks.org/submissions.html. Gina Frangello and Molly McQuade, eds. Publishes anthologies of short stories assembled around a common theme. Accepts simultaneous submissions & reprints. Shared royalties for contributors to the anthologies. Guidelines on Website.

> **Fiction:** Submit by e-mail (copied into message). Literary fiction only. Currently working on "Leaving Home," a collection of stories about the experience of departure and change. No word limits, or fixed closing dates.

HOWARD PUBLISHING CO., INC., 3117 N. 7th St., West Monroe LA 71291. (318)396-3122. Fax (318)397-1882. E-mail: dennyb@howardpublishing.com. Website: www.howard publishing.com. John Howard, pres.; Denny Boultinghouse, exec. ed.; submit to Manuscript Review Committee. Christian publisher. Imprint: Howard Fiction. Publishes 46 titles/yr. Receives 600 submissions annually. 10% of books from first-time authors. Prefers 200-250 pgs. Negotiable royalty & advance. Average first printing 10,000. Publication within 16 mos. Considers simultaneous submissions. Accepted ms by e-mail. Responds in 6-8 mos. No disk. Prefers NIV. Free guidelines (also on Website); no catalog.

> **Nonfiction:** Accepting queries only, by e-mail.
>
> **Fiction:** Accepting queries only, by e-mail (Twhalin@howardpublishing.com). Adult.
>
> **Tips:** "Our authors must first be Christ-centered in their lives and writing, then qualified to write on the subject of choice. Public name recognition is a plus. Authors who are also public speakers usually have a ready-made audience."
>
> ****Note:** This publisher serviced by The Writer's Edge.

ICS PUBLICATIONS, 2131 Lincoln Rd. N.E., Washington DC 20002-1199. Toll-free (800)832-8389. (202)832-8489. Fax (202)832-8967. E-mail: editorial@icspublications.org. Website: www.icspublications.org. Catholic/Institute of Carmelite Studies. John Sullivan, pub. For those interested in the Carmelite tradition with focus on prayer and spirituality. Publishes 6 titles/yr. Receives 10 submissions annually. 10% of books from first-time authors. Reprints books. Prefers 200 pgs. Royalty 2-6% on retail; some outright purchases; advance $500. Average first printing 3,000-7,000. Publication within 4 yrs. Considers simultaneous submissions. Accepts requested ms on disk. Responds in 6 mos. No guidelines; catalog for 7x10 SAE/2 stamps.

> **Nonfiction:** Query or outline/1 chapter; phone/fax/e-query OK.
>
> **Tips:** "Most open to translation of Carmelite classics; popular introductions to Carmelite themes which show a solid grasp of the tradition."

IDEALS CHILDREN'S BOOKS, 535 Metroplex Dr., Ste. 250, Nashville TN 37211. Toll-free (800)586-2572 (615)333-0478. Website: www.idealspublications.com. Ideal Publications/Guideposts. Patricia Pingry, pub. Hard- and soft-cover books for 3- to 10-year-olds. Publishes 5-10 titles/yr. Maximum 1,000 wds. Royalty; variable advance. Responds in 8-12 wks. Send for guidelines/catalog.

> **Fiction:** Complete mss for picture books; sample chapters for children's chapter books; no fax/e-mail. No original artwork.
>
> **Tips:** "We are looking in particular for subjects pertaining to holidays (Christmas, Valentine, Easter, etc.), either secular or religious." Address submissions to: Submissions, Ideals Children's Books (at above address).

IDEALS PRESS, 535 Metroplex Dr., Ste. 250, Nashville TN 37211. Toll-free (800)932-2145. (615)333-0478. Website: www.idealspublications.com. Guideposts. Patricia Pingry, pub.; submit to Peggy Schaefer, mng. ed. Imprint: Candy Cane Press. Publishes 8-10 adult and 25-30 children's titles/yr. Variable advance. Publication within 18 mos. Considers simultaneous submissions. Responds in 2 mos. Guidelines.

Nonfiction: Accepting manuscripts. Subjects include memoirs, humorous family stories, inspiration, reflections on nature, patriotism, or travel.

ILLUMINATION ARTS PUBLISHING CO., INC., PO Box 1865, Bellevue WA 98009. (425)644-7185. Fax (425)644-9274. E-mail: LiteInfo@Illumin.com. Website: www.Illumin.com. Ruth Thompson, ed. dir. Publishes high quality, enlightening children's picture books with enduring, inspirational, and spiritual values (inspirational, not religious). Publishes 4-5 titles/yr. Prefers 500-1,500 wds. Royalty on net; advance for artists. Responds in 1 mo. Guidelines/catalog on Website.

Nonfiction: Complete ms/cover letter.

Fiction: Complete ms/cover letter. Picture books under 1,000 wds. (preferred); 1,500 wds. max.

Special Needs: Picture books only.

Tips: "Include a description of what makes your book special or different from others currently on the market."

INKLING BOOKS, 6528 Phinney Ave. N., Seattle WA 98103. (206)365-1624. E-mail: editor@inklingbooks.com. Website: www.InklingBooks.com. Michael W. Perry, pub. Publishes 6 titles/yr. No mss through agents. Reprints books. Prefers 150-400 pgs. No advance. Print-on-demand. Publication within 2 mos. No guidelines or catalog. Not currently accepting submissions.

INTERNATIONAL AWAKENING PRESS, 139 N. Washington, PO Box 232, Wheaton IL 60189. Phone/fax (630)653-8616. E-mail: internationalawakening@juno.com. Website: www.intl-awaken.com. Intl. Awakening Ministries, Inc. Richard Owen Roberts, pres. Scholarly books on religious awakenings or revivals. Publishes 4 titles/yr. Receives 12 submissions annually. Reprints books. Royalty negotiated; no advance. Average first printing 3,000. Publication within 6 mos. Responds in 3 mos. Prefers requested ms on disk. Any translation; no paraphrases. No guidelines; free catalog.

Nonfiction: Query only; no phone/fax/e-query. "Looking for scholarly theology, especially Bible commentaries, church history, and revival-related material."

Also Does: Booklets, pamphlets, tracts.

Photos/Artwork: Accepts freelance photos for book covers.

INTERVARSITY PRESS, Box 1400, Downers Grove IL 60515-1426. Receptionist: (630)734-4000. Fax (630)734-4200. E-mail: submissions@ivpress.com. Website: www.ivpress.com. InterVarsity Christian Fellowship. Andrew T. LePeau, ed. dir.; submit to Elaina Whittenhall, ms reviewer. IVP books are characterized by a thoughtful, biblical approach to the Christian life that transforms the hearts, souls, and minds of readers in the university, church, and the world, on topics ranging from spiritual disciplines to apologetics, to current issues, to theology. Imprint: LifeGuide Bible Studies. Publishes 90 titles/yr. Receives 2,500 submissions annually. 15% of books from first-time authors. Accepts mss through agents. Reprints books. Prefers 50,000 wds. or 200 pgs. Negotiable royalty on retail or outright purchase; negotiable advance. Average first printing 5,000. Publication within 18 mos. Considers simultaneous submissions. Responds in 1-12 wks. Prefers NIV, NRSV. Accepts e-mail submissions after acceptance. Guidelines (also by e-mail/Website); catalog for 9x12 SAE/$1.42 postage (mark "Media Mail").

Nonfiction: Query only first, with detailed letter according to submissions guidelines, then proposal with 2 chapters; e-query OK.

Ethnic Books: Especially looking for ethnic writers (Black, Hispanic, Asian American).

Also Does: Booklets, 5,000 wds.; pamphlets; e-books.

Tips: "We look for a thoughtful, fresh approach. We shy away from simple answers. Writers who are nuanced, subtle, discerning, and perceptive will get farther at IVP. Writers who know and read IVP books regularly will have the best sense of what kind of books work for us. We are especially interested in apologetics, spiritual disciplines, Christianity and society issues, and theology and doctrine."

Note: This publisher serviced by The Writer's Edge.

+**INVERT BOOKS,** 5300 Patterson S.E., Grand Rapids MI 49530. (619)440-2333. Website: www.youthspecialties.com. Jay Howver, pub. Books for teenagers. Imprints: invert, Youth Specialties, emergentYS. Publishes 30 titles/yr. Accepts mss through agents. No reprints. Prefers 35,000 wds. Royalty on net, or outright purchase of $3,000-8,000; advance. Average first printing 3,000. Publication within 1 yr. Considers simultaneous submissions. Responds in 4-6 wks. Prefers NIV. Guidelines by e-mail/Website; free catalog.

Nonfiction: Proposal/2 chapters.

Fiction: Proposal/2 chapters. Teen/YA fiction only.

Tips: "We prefer books from youth workers who are in the trenches working with students."

JIREH PUBLISHING CO., 1920 Oliveglen Ct., Fairfield CA 94534-6427. E-mail: jaholman@ jirehpublishing.com. Website: www.jirehpublishing.com. Janice Holman, ed. To spread the gospel and teach the Word of God throughout the world. Publishes 2-5 titles/yr. Receives 275 submissions annually. 95% of books from first-time authors. Accepts mss through agents. No reprints. Prefers 96+ pgs. Royalty 10-12% on net; no advance. Average first printing 500-1,000. Publication within 9-12 mos. Considers simultaneous submissions. Responds in 5-13 wks. Guidelines/catalog on Website.

Nonfiction: Proposal/3 chapters; fax/e-query OK. "Looking for manuscript which helps teach believers how to walk by faith and receive all the blessings that God has for them." Likes to see first and last chapter.

Fiction: Proposal/3 chapters. Adult only. Contemporary, mystery/romance, and mystery/suspense.

Also Does: E-books.

Photos/Artwork: Accepts freelance photos for book covers.

Tips: "We are looking for authors who would like to work with us to create e-books (initially fiction titles)." Responds only to accepted manuscripts.

JOHNS HOPKINS UNIVERSITY PRESS, 2715 N. Charles St., Baltimore MD 21218-4363. (410)516-6900. Fax (410)516-6968. E-mail: tcl@mail.press.jhu.edu. Website: www.press .jhu.edu. Nondenominational. Henry Tom, exec. ed. Publishes 4-6 religious titles/yr. Receives 50-75 submissions annually. 10-25% of books from first-time authors. Accepts mss through agents. Reprints books. Prefers 100,000 wds. Publication within 10-12 mos. Considers simultaneous submissions only on proposals. Guidelines/catalog on Website.

Nonfiction: Query only; no phone/fax/e-query.

JOSSEY-BASS, a John Wiley & Sons Imprint, 989 Market St., 5th Fl., San Francisco CA 94103-1741. (415)782-3145. Fax (415)433-0499. E-mail: Sfullert@jbp.com. Website: www .jossey-bass.com. John Wiley & Sons, Inc. Sheryl Fullerton, exec. ed.; Julianna Gustafson, ed. Because of a nondenominational focus on Christian spirituality and secular corporate ownership, they are able to reach the broadest range of markets and readership. Imprint: Religion in Practice. Publishes 40 titles/yr. Receives hundreds of submissions annually. Up to 20% of books from first-time authors. Accepts mss through agents. No reprints. Prefers 60,000 wds. or 250 pgs. Royalty negotiable on net; advance. Average first printing 10,000. Publication within 1 yr. Considers simultaneous submissions. Responds in 1 mo. Prefers NRSV, NIV. Guidelines (also by e-mail); free catalog.

Nonfiction: Proposal/2 chapters; e-query OK. "Looking for fresh, vital resources to deepen faith and Christian identity."

Also Does: E-books.

Tips: "Our mission is to provide innovative, thoughtful, and useful resources for people on their faith journeys. We're looking for writers who have fresh ideas clearly positioned among existing books in the market and who have a platform (and/or track record) from which to promote and market themselves, as well as clearly relevant credentials and expertise. We are not interested in books that would be considered 'more of the same,' nor in books that are narrow or marginal in their perspective. We are particularly interested in books for the emerging church and those that encourage a generous orthodoxy."

JUBILANT PRESS: An Electronic Publisher, PO Box 6421, Longmont CO 80501. E-mail: jubilantpress@aol.com. Website: www.JubilantPress.com. Supports Right to the Heart Ministries. Linda Shepherd, pub. Publishes downloadable e-books with instant information to change your life. Publishes 20 titles/yr. Acquires by invitation only. 0% of books from first-time authors. Accepts mss through agents. Reprints books. Prefers 20-100 pgs. Pays for the right to publish, plus a percentage of author's online sales (author must have an active Web page); variable advance. Publication within 6 mos. Prefers NIV. Guidelines on Website.

Nonfiction: Brief e-mail query only; no phone/fax query.

Special Needs: Women's ministry helps, wedding helps, funeral helps, birthday party helps, kid games, weight-loss helps, speaking and writing helps.

Photos/Artwork: Accepts freelance photos for book covers.

Tips: "Submissions accepted by invitation only. Best to send a brief e-mail with description of your idea. Please see our Web page to best understand our publishing program. Most open to a how-to, informational book with a need-to-know marketability."

JUDSON PRESS, Box 851, Valley Forge PA 19482-0851. (610)768-2109. Fax (610)768-2441. E-mail: randy.frame@abc-usa.org. Website: www.judsonpress.com. American Baptist Churches USA. Randy Frame, acq. ed.; Laura Alden, pub. Publishes 30 titles/yr. Receives 700 submissions annually. 20% of books from first-time authors. Accepts mss through agents. No reprints. Prefers 140-180 pgs., or 30,000-40,000 wds. Royalty 10-15% on net; some work-for-hire agreements; advance $500. Average first printing 4,500. Publication within 8 mos. Considers simultaneous submissions. Responds in 3 mos. Free guidelines (also on Website; click on Free Downloads)/catalog.

Nonfiction: Proposal/2 chapters.

Ethnic Books: African American.

Tips: "Authors should avoid books based primarily on their own experiences and personal reflections. Writing style must be engaging, and the writer should be well qualified to address the topic. We want books that are unusually well written."

**Note: This publisher serviced by The Writer's Edge.

JUST FOLKS PUBLISHING CO., PO Box 2012, Columbus IN 47202. (812)372-1663. E-mail: eb@hsonline.net. Website: www.prayerofhannah.com. Kenn Gividen, ed. Query; phone/fax query OK. New publisher. Not included in topical listings.

KINDRED PRODUCTIONS, 1310 Taylor Ave., Winnipeg MB R3M 3Z6, Canada. (204)669-6575. Fax (204)654-1865. E-mail: kindred@mbconf.ca. Website: www.kindredproductions .com. Mennonite Brethren. Marilyn Hudson, mngr. To resource the churches within the denomination (Anabaptist perspective) for Christlike living and ministry. Publishes 2-3 titles/yr. Receives 30 submissions annually. 90% of books from first-time authors. No mss through agents. **SUBSIDY PUBLISHES 5%.** No reprints. Prefers 60,000 wds. or 213 pgs. Royalty 10-15% on net; no advance. Average first printing 1,000-2,000. Publication within 9-12 mos. Considers simultaneous submissions. Responds within 4-5 mos. Requires requested ms on disk or by e-mail. Prefers NIV. Free guidelines (also by e-mail)/catalog.

Nonfiction: Proposal/2-3 chapters; no phone query, fax/e-query OK. "Looking for books that help people meet God in a nonthreatening way. Only accepting unsolicited manuscripts for inspirational reading books. A crossover potential preferred, but not mandatory."

Tips: "Most open to inspirational books that help people in everyday life encounter a relevant God. No deep theology. Material with a human interest element is best."

+KIRK HOUSE PUBLISHERS, PO Box 390759, Minneapolis MN 55439. (952)835-1828. Fax (952)835-2613. E-mail: publisher@kirkhouse.com. Website: www.kirkhouse.com. Leonard Flachman, pub. Publishes 6-8 titles/yr. Receives hundreds of submissions annually. 95% of books from first-time authors. No mss through agents. No reprints. Royalty 10-15% on net; no advance. Average first printing 500-3,000. Publication within 6 mos. No simultaneous submissions. Requires disk or e-mail submission. Responds in 2-3 wks. No guidelines; free catalog.

Nonfiction: Proposal/1-2 chapters.

KREGEL KIDZONE, PO Box 2607, Grand Rapids MI 49501-2607. (616)451-4775. Fax (616)451-9330. No e-mail. Website: www.kregelpublications.com. Publishes books and collateral materials that target both the spiritual and educational development of children. Royalty; some outright purchases. Publication within 16 mos. Responds in 4 mos. Guidelines (also by e-mail/Website); catalog for 9x12 SAE/3 stamps. No longer reviewing unsolicited queries, proposals, or manuscripts, except through agents, Writer's Edge or ECPA First Edition.

Fiction: Query, or complete ms (if 32 pages or less); no phone/fax/e-query.

**Note: This publisher serviced by The Writer's Edge and ECPA First Edition.

KREGEL PUBLICATIONS, PO Box 2607, Grand Rapids MI 49501-2607. (616)451-4775. Fax (616)451-9330. Website: www.kregelpublications.com. Evangelical/Conservative. Dennis R. Hillman, pub.; Jim Weaver, academic & professional books ed.; submit to Acquisitions Editor. To provide tools for ministry and Christian growth from a conservative, evangelical perspective. Imprints: Kregel Kidzone, Kregel Academic and Professional, and Kregel Classics. Publishes 90 titles/yr. 20% of books from first-time authors. Reprints books. Royalty 12-16% of net; some outright purchases. Average first printing 5,000. Publication within 16 mos. Responds in 3 mos. Guidelines (also by e-mail/Website); catalog for 9x12 SAE/3 stamps. No longer reviewing unsolicited queries, proposals, or manuscripts, except through agents, Writer's Edge, or ECPA First Edition.

Nonfiction: Query only; no phone/fax/e-query.

Fiction: For all ages. Query only; no phone/fax/e-query. "Looking for high-quality contemporary fiction with strong Christian themes and characters."

Tips: "We are expanding our line of children's products. Engaging stories and great art are a must. Also we are adding more fiction, but again, we are very selective. Strong story lines with an evident spiritual emphasis are required."

**Note: This publisher serviced by The Writer's Edge.

**Named a 2002 Publishers Weekly "Small Publisher Standout."

+KREMER PUBLICATIONS, INC., 12621 W. Custer Ave., Butler WI 53007. (800)669-0887. Nondenominational. Curriculum publisher.

LAMPLIGHTER PUBLISHERS, Box 2315, Brandon FL 33509-2315. (813)685-7387. Fax (813)655-3066. E-mail: lamplighterpub@verizon.net. Nondenominational. R. A. Ellinger, ed. To enlighten, educate, and entertain. No mss through agents. Makes outright purchase on acceptance. Average first printing 500-1,000. Publication within 1 yr. Considers simultaneous submissions. Accepts e-queries. Responds in 6-8 wks. Prefers KJV. Guidelines by e-mail; no catalog.

Nonfiction: Query first; e-query OK.

Fiction: For children, including picture books. Query first. "Fiction is confined to children's publications and should follow guidelines."

Special Needs: "We are looking for writers who specialize in short, moral subjects for children's tracts, no more than 500 words per tract. Topics need to be Bible based with strong moral applications. Send SASE for a sample."

Tips: "Writers should incorporate biblically sound principles with Bible reference (KJV) only. We want a clear, concise reading with no sympathy for sin or immorality. We expect submissions to be readable and double spaced on good quality paper; easy to read and understand."

LANGMARC PUBLISHING, PO Box 90488, Austin TX 78709-0488. (512)394-0989. Fax (512)394-0829. E-mail: langmarc@booksails.com. Website: www.langmarc.com. Lutheran. Lois Qualben, pub. Focuses on spiritual growth of readers. Publishes 6 titles/yr. Receives 200 submissions annually. 50% of books from first-time authors. No mss through agents. No reprints. Prefers 150-300 pgs. Royalty 10-13% on net; no advance. Average first printing varies. Publication usually within 1 yr. Considers simultaneous submissions. Responds in 2-4 mos. Requires requested ms on disk. Prefers NIV. Guidelines (also by e-mail/Website); catalog for #10 SAE/1 stamp.

Nonfiction: Proposal/3 chapters; no phone query. "Most open to inspirational books."

LARSON PUBLICATIONS/PBPF, 4936 NYS Rte. 414, Burdett NY 14818-9729. (607)546-9342. Fax (607)546-9344. E-mail: larson@lightlink.com. Website: www.larsonpublications.org. Paul Cash, dir. Books cover philosophy, psychology, religion, and spirituality. Publishes 4-5 titles/yr. Receives 1,000 submissions annually. 5% of books from first-time authors. Variable royalty; rarely gives an advance. Publication within 1 yr. Considers simultaneous submissions. Responds in 4 mos. Prefers NIV. Catalog on Website.

Nonfiction: Query by mail/outline.

+LATIMER PRESS, PO Box 763217, Dallas TX 75376. (972)293-7443. Fax (972-293-7559. E-mail: anglicansunited@sbcglobal.net. Website: www.latimerpress.com. Anglican (Orthodox Episcopalian). Cheryl M. Wetzel, ed. Provides materials for Orthodox Episcopalians. Publishes 2-3 titles/yr. Receives 20 submissions annually. 80% of books from first-time authors. Accepts mss through agents. **SOME SUBSIDY.** Reprints books. Prefers up to 125 pgs. Outright purchase for $100-500. Average first printing 2,000. Publication within 6 mos. Considers simultaneous submissions. Prefers ms by disk or e-mail. Responds in 2 mos. Prefers NIV. Guidelines (also by e-mail/Website); catalog for #10 SAE/1 stamp.

Nonfiction: Query first, plus phone conversation; e-query OK. "Looking for Anglican history and practice; adult ed."

Also Does: Booklets; Videos/DVDs.

Tips: "Most open to biblically orthodox and evangelical materials."

LEGACY PRESS, PO Box 261129, San Diego CA 92196. (858)668-3260. Fax (858)668-3328. E-mail: rainbowed@earthlink.net. Website: www.rainbowpublishers.com. Rainbow Publishers. Christy Scannell, ed. dir. Publishes nondenominational nonfiction and fiction for children in the evangelical Christian market. Publishes 15 titles/yr. Receives 250 submissions annually. 50% of books from first-time authors. Reprints books. Prefers 150 pgs. & up. Royalty 8% & up on net; advance $500+. Average first printing 5,000. Publication within 2 yrs. Considers simultaneous submissions. Prefers requested ms on disk. Responds in 3 mos. Prefers NIV. Guidelines (also on Website); catalog for 9x12 SAE/2 stamps.

Nonfiction: Proposal/3-5 chapters; no e-queries. "Looking for nonfiction for girls and boys ages 2-12."

Fiction: Proposal/3 chapters. For ages 2-12 only. Must include an additional component beyond fiction (e.g., devotional, Bible activities, etc.)

Special Needs: Nonfiction for ages 10-12, particularly Christian twists on current favorites, such as cooking, jewelry making, games, etc.

Tips: "All books must offer solid Bible teaching in a fun, meaningful way that appeals to kids. Research popular nonfiction for kids in the general market, then figure out how to present those fun ideas in ways that teach the Bible. As a smaller publisher, we seek to publish unique niche books that stand out in the market."

LEGACY PUBLISHERS INTERNATIONAL, 1301 S. Clinton St., Denver CO 80247. (303)283-7480. Fax (303)283-7536. E-mail: dmiller@hccweb.org. Website: www.legacypublishers international.com. Pool of editors; submit to Dawn Miller. Accepts some freelance. Catalog. Incomplete topical listings. No questionnaire returned.

LIBROS LIGUORI, 1 Liguori Dr., Liguori MO 63057-9999. (636)464-2500. Fax (636)464-8449. E-mail: mkessler@liguori.org. Website: www.liguori.org. Spanish division of Liguori Publications. Mathew Kessler (636)223-1471, ed. To spread the gospel in the Hispanic community by means of low-cost publications. Publishes 5 titles/yr. Receives 6-8 submissions annually. 5% of books from first-time authors. Prefers up to 30,000 wds. Royalty 8-10% of net or outright purchases of $450 (book and booklet authors get royalties; pamphlet authors get $400 on acceptance); advance. Average first printing 3,500-5,000. Publication within 18 mos. No simultaneous submissions. Requires accepted mss on electronic file. Responds in 4-8 wks. Free guidelines/catalog.

> **Nonfiction:** Proposal/2 chapters; fax/e-query OK. "Looking for issues families face today—substance abuse, unwanted pregnancies, etc.; family relations; religion's role in immigrants' experiences, pastoral Catholic faith."
>
> **Ethnic Books:** Focuses on Spanish-language products.
>
> **Also Does:** Pamphlets, booklets, tracts, PC software, clip art.
>
> **Tips:** "Contact us before writing. It's much easier to work together from the beginning of a project. We need books on the Hispanic experience in the U.S. Keep it concise, avoid academic/theological jargon, and stick to the tenets of the Catholic faith. Avoid abstract arguments."

LIFE CHANGING MEDIA, 10777 W. Sample Rd., Unit 302, Coral Springs FL 33065-3768. (954)554-1921. E-mail: Paul@lifechangingmedia.net. Website: www.lifechangingmedia.net. Life Changing Publications. Paul Gundotra, pres.; submit to Sindhu Roy (submissions@lifechangingmedia.net). Considers simultaneous submissions (if indicated). Guidelines on Website. Not included in topical listings. No questionnaire returned.

> **Nonfiction:** Query first; e-query OK. "Please include a description of the book project, brief bio including publishing history. Let us know if you have the ability for public speaking."

LIFE CYCLE BOOKS, LPO Box 1008, Niagara Falls NY 14304-1008. Toll-free (800)214-5849. (970)493-2257. Fax (888)690-8532. E-mail: paulb@lifecyclebooks.com. Website: www.lifecyclebooks.com. Paul Broughton, gen. mngr.; submit to The Editor. Specializes in pro-life material. Publishes 1-3 titles/yr. Receives 50 submissions annually. 50% of books from first-time authors. Reprints books. Royalty 8% of net; outright purchase of brochure material, $250+; advance $100-300. **SUBSIDY PUBLISHES 10%.** Publication within 10 mos. Responds in 6 wks. Free catalog.

> **Nonfiction:** Query or complete ms. "Our emphasis is on pro-life and pro-family titles."
>
> **Tips:** "We are most involved in publishing leaflets of about 1,500 words, and we welcome submissions of manuscripts of this length."

LIFE JOURNEY BOOKS, 4050 Lee Vance View, Colorado Springs CO 80918. (719)536-0100. Fax (719)536-3269. Website: www.cookministries.com. Mary McNeil, acq. ed. Guides for Christian families seeking biblical answers to life problems. Prefers mss through agents. Reprints books. Royalty 8-14% on net; advance $5,000. Average first printing 5,000. Publication within 9-12 mos. Considers simultaneous submissions. Responds in 3-9 mos. Prefers NIV. Guidelines on Website; no catalog.

> **Nonfiction:** Proposal via their Website.
>
> **Special Needs:** Family life and senior adult concerns.
>
> ****Note:** This publisher serviced by The Writer's Edge.

LIFESONG PUBLISHERS, PO Box 183, Somis CA 93066. (805)655-5644. E-mail: mailbox@lifesongpublishers.com. Website: www.lifesongpublishers.com. Laurie Donahue, pub. Provides Christian families with tools that will aid in spiritual and relational development of family members. Publishes 4 titles/yr. No mss through agents. No reprints. **SOME SUBSIDY.** Royalty 5-10% of net; small advance. Publication within 6 mos. Considers simultaneous submissions. Responds in 2-4 wks. No guidelines; catalog for 9x12 SAE/2 stamps. Not included in topical listings.

> **Nonfiction:** Proposal/3 chapters; e-query OK. "Looking for an author with an existing ministry."

LIFT EVERY VOICE, 820 N. LaSalle Blvd., Chicago IL 60610. (312)329-2101. Fax (312)329-2144. E-mail: acquisitions@moody.edu. Website: www.moodypublishers.org. African American imprint of Moody Publishers. Moody Bible Institute and Institute for Black Family Development. Submit to Acquisitions Coordinator. To advance the cause of Christ through publishing African American Christians who educate, edify, and disciple Christians. Not included in topical listings.

+LIGHTHOUSE EBOOKS, 5531 Dufferin Dr., Savage MN 55378. (952)447-8604. E-mail: Andrew_Overett@yahoo.com. Website: www.lighthouseebooks.com. Crystal Lake Communications. Andy Overett, ed.; submit to Sylvia Charvet. To distribute a wide variety of Christian media to vast parts of the globe, so people can hear about the gospel for free or very inexpensively. Imprints: LighthousePress, Lighthouse Music Publishing. Publishes 20-30 titles/yr. Receives 50-60 submissions annually. 60% of books from first-time authors. Accepts mss through agents. Plans to do print-on-demand in the future. Reprints books. All size files are accepted, but prefers 6MB disk for Website. Royalty 10-90%; no advance. Writers also generate commissions from the sale of merchandise on the Website (T-shirts, hats, pens, etc.). Publication within 1-2 mos. Considers simultaneous submissions. Prefers submissions by e-mail. Responds in 3-4 wks. Prefers NAS. Guidelines on Website; catalog $10.

> **Nonfiction:** Complete ms; e-query OK. Any topic. "Looking for children's stories and comics; self-help and science books with a Christian perspective."
>
> **Fiction:** Complete ms. Any genre, for all ages.
>
> **Also Does:** Comics, animation on CD, music CDs, plans to do Christian computer games in the future.
>
> **Photos/Artwork:** Accepts freelance photos for book covers; open to queries from freelance artists.
>
> **Contest:** Plans for a contest in the future.
>
> **Tips:** "Most open to anything with a message that will impact lives positively for Christ."

LIGHTHOUSE TRAILS PUBLISHING, PO Box 958, Silverton OR 97381. (503)873-9092. Fax (503)873-7380. E-mail: editor@lighthousetrails.com. Website: www.lighthousetrails.com. David Dombrowski, acq. ed. Books that align with the Word of God, rather than with what is popular or trendy. Publishes 2-4 titles/yr. Receives 50-100 submissions annually. 50% of books from first-time authors. Accepts mss through agents. Reprints books. Prefers 144-300 pgs. Royalty 12-17% of net, or 20% of retail; no advance. Average first printing 2,500. Publication within 6-9 mos. Considers simultaneous submissions. Requires accepted ms on disk. Responds in 4-6 wks. Prefers KJV, NAS, NKJV. Guidelines and catalog on Website.

> **Nonfiction:** Proposal/2-3 chapters; no phone/fax query; e-query OK.
>
> **Fiction:** Proposal/2-3 chapters.
>
> **Special Needs:** Clearly written exposés on New Age infiltrating the church. Will also look at autobiographies or biographies about people who have courageously endured through overwhelming circumstances (Holocaust survivors, child-abuse survivors, etc.) with a definite emphasis on the role the Lord played in these stories.
>
> **Tips:** "Any book we consider will not only challenge the educated, professional reader, but also be able to reach college-age adults who may have less experience and comprehension. Our books will include human interest and personal experience scenarios as a means of

getting the point across. Read a couple of our books to better understand the style of writing we are looking for. Also check our research Website for an in-depth look at who we are (www.lighthousetrailsresearch.com)."

LIGUORI PUBLICATIONS, 1 Liguori Dr., Liguori MO 63057-9999. Toll-free (800)325-9521. (636)464-2500. Fax (636)464-8449. Website: www.liguori.org. Catholic/Redemptorists. Submit to The Editor. Spreading the gospel of Jesus Christ, primarily through the print and electronic media. Imprints: Libros Liguori, Liguori Books, and Liguori/Triumph. Publishes 25 titles/yr. Prefers 100-300 pgs. for books; 40-100 pgs. for booklets; pamphlets 16-18 pgs. Royalty 8-12% (on trade books); outright purchase of pamphlets for $450; advance varies. Average first printing 4,000 on books & booklets, 10,000 on pamphlets. Publication within 2 yrs. No simultaneous submissions. Accepts requested ms on disk. Responds in 9-13 wks. Prefers NRSV. Guidelines (also on Website); catalog for 9x12 SASE.

Nonfiction: Query only first. "Looking for spirituality, classics, saints, prayer, travel, parenting, and family life."

Ethnic Books: Publishes books in Spanish. See separate listing for Libros Liguori.

Also Does: Booklets, pamphlets.

Tips: "Manuscripts accepted by us must have strong, middle-of-the-road, practical spirituality."

LILLENAS PUBLISHING CO., Program Builder Series and Other Drama Resources, Box 419527, Kansas City MO 64141-6527. (816)931-1900. Fax (816)412-8390. E-mail: drama@lillenas.com. Website: www.lillenasdrama.com. Kimberly R. Messer, product line mngr. Imprint: Lillenas Drama Resources. Publishes 10-12 titles/yr. Accepts mss through agents. Royalty 10% for drama resources; outright purchase of program builder material; no advance. No simultaneous submissions. Responds in 4 mos. Guidelines (also by e-mail/Website); catalog.

Drama Resources: Query or complete ms; phone/fax/e-query OK. Accepts readings, one-act and full-length plays, program and service features, monologues, and sketch collections.

Special Needs: Sketch collections and plays; full-length and one-act plays for adults. Seasonal; children's or youth 5-minute sketches.

Tips: "Most open to biblically based sketches and plays that have small- to medium-sized casts and are easy to stage; short sketches—4 to 8 minutes."

LION PUBLISHING, 4050 Lee Vance View, Colorado Springs CO 80918-7102. (719)536-3271. Cook Communications. Accepts no freelance submissions.

+LITTLE SIMON INSPIRATIONS, 1230 Avenue of the Americas, New York NY 10020. (212)698-1295. Fax (212)698-2794. Website: www.simonsayskids.com. Faith-based imprint of Simon & Schuster Children's Publishing Division. Not included in topical listings. No questionnaire returned.

THE LITURGICAL PRESS, PO Box 7500, St. John's Abbey, Collegeville MN 56321-7500. Toll-free (800)858-5450. (320)363-2213. Fax (800)445-5899 or (320)363-3299. E-mail: mtwomey@osb.org. Website: www.litpress.org. St. John's Abbey (a Benedictine group). Imprints: Liturgical Press Books, Michael Glazier Books, and Pueblo Books. Mark Twomey, ed. dir. Academic manuscripts to Linda Maloney (lmmaloney@csbsju.edu). Publishes 70 titles/yr. Prefers 100-300 pgs. Royalty 10% of net; some outright purchases; no advance. No simultaneous submissions. Responds in 3 mos. Guidelines (also on Website); free catalog.

Nonfiction: Query/proposal. Adult only.

Tips: "We publish liturgical, scriptural, and pastoral resources."

LITURGY TRAINING PUBLICATIONS, Archdiocese of Chicago, 1800 N. Hermitage Ave., Chicago IL 60622-1101. Toll-free (800)933-1800. (773)486-8970, ext. 264. Fax (773)486-7094. E-mail: editorialmanager@ltp.org. Website: www.LTP.org. Catholic/Archdiocese of Chicago. Submit to Editorial Mngr. Resources for liturgy in Christian life. Publishes 25 titles/yr. Receives 150 submissions annually. 50% of books from first-time authors. Variable royalty. Average first printing 2,000-5,000. Publication within 1 yr. Considers simultaneous submissions. Responds in 2-10 wks. Requires requested ms on disk. Catalog.

Nonfiction: Proposal/1 chapter; phone/fax/e-query OK.

LIVING BOOKS FOR ALL, PO Box 98425 (TST), Kowloon, Hong Kong. Phone 852 2723 1525. Fax 852 2366 6519. E-mail: clchk@hkstar.com. Website: www.hkstar.com/~clchk. CLC Ministries International, Hong Kong. Mrs. Mare Allison, ed. Prefers books of interest to Asians or Western readers interested in Asia. Imprint: Bellman House (Chinese); Living Books for All (LBA) English. Publishes 1-5 titles/yr. Receives 20 submissions annually. Considers Chinese translations of English books and English translations of Chinese books. No mss through agents. Prefers up to 200 pgs. Royalty 5% on retail or payment in copies of book; no advance. Average first printing 3,000. Publication within 1 yr. Considers simultaneous submissions. Responds in 2 mos. Prefers requested ms on disk or by e-mail in Rich Text Format (.RTF). Responds in 1-3 mos. Guidelines (by e-mail or Website, www.hkstar.com/~clchk/lbaguide.html.); free Chinese book catalog.

Nonfiction: Proposal with 3 chapters (up to 30 pages), or complete ms; e-query preferred. "Most open to practical, Christian living books relevant to English readers in Asia."

Fiction: "Fiction for adults in an Asian context. Must have a spiritual impact."

Special Needs: Biblically based material for teaching adults English and books to help Christian workers in China.

Ethnic Books: For Asian market.

Also Does: Pamphlets, booklets.

Photos/Artwork: Would consider freelance photos for book covers.

Tips: "Write in direct, personal, inclusive style; then simplify. No dissertations. We are looking for Chinese manuscripts." Prefers American spelling to English spelling. Accepts manuscripts in English or Chinese.

LIVING THE GOOD NEWS, 600 Grant St., Ste. 400, Denver CO 80203. Fax (303)832-4971. Division of the Morehouse Group. Not currently accepting submissions.

LONGWOOD COMMUNICATIONS, 3037 Clubview Dr., Orlando FL 32822. (407)737-0406. Fax (407)737-7378. E-mail: longcomm@bellsouth.net. Murray Fisher, VP. A service for authors who cannot get their books accepted by a traditional house. Publishes 8 titles/yr. Receives 70-80 submissions annually. 95% of books from first-time authors. No mss through agents. **30% SUBSIDY.** Reprints books. Any length. Outright purchases. Average first printing 5,000. Publication within 10-14 wks. Considers simultaneous submissions. Prefers accepted ms on disk. Responds in 2 wks. Any Bible version. No guidelines or catalog.

Nonfiction: Complete ms; phone/fax/e-query OK. Almost any topic as long as it's Christian and builds up the body of Christ. Looking for books to strengthen individuals and the church.

Fiction: Complete ms. For all ages.

Also Does: Booklets, pamphlets, tracts.

Photos/Artwork: Accepts freelance photos for book covers.

Tips: "Looking for well-written, basic Christian books: building up the church, Christian growth, and stories about real people."

LOS ANGELES DESIGNERS' THEATRE, PO Box 1883, Studio City CA 91614-0883. (323)650-9600. E-mail: ladesigners@juno.com. Full-length comedy, drama, musicals, adaptations; can incorporate unpopular religious, social, or political themes. No cast or set restrictions. 6-8 plays/season. Receives 1,200 submissions annually. 100% freelance. Royalty. Responds in 4-5 mos.

Plays: Query first; e-query OK.

LOVE INSPIRED/LOVE INSPIRED SUSPENSE, 233 Broadway, Ste. 1001, New York NY 10279-0001. (212)553-4200. Fax (212)277-8969. E-mail: Emily_Rodmell@harlequin.ca. Website: www.SteepleHill.com. Harlequin Enterprises. Submit to any of the following: Joan Marlow Golan, exec. ed.; Krista Stroever, assoc. sr. ed.; Diane Dietz, asst. ed.; Emily Rodmell, ed. asst. Mass-market Christian romance novels. Imprints: Steeple Hill (single-title trade paperback women's fiction), see separate listing. Publishes 72 titles/yr. Receives 500-1,000 submissions annually. 15% of books from first-time authors. Accepts mss through agents. No reprints. Prefers 70,000-75,000 wds. or 300-320 pgs. Royalty on retail; competitive advance. Publication within 12-24 mos. Requires accepts ms on disk/hard copy. Responds in 3 mos. Prefers KJV. Guidelines by e-mail/Website: no catalog.

> **Fiction:** Query letter or 3 chapters and up to 5-page synopsis; no phone/fax/e-query.
>
> **Special Needs:** These contemporary "sweet" romances feature Christian characters facing the many challenges of life and love in today's world. Drama, humor, and even a touch of mystery or suspense can take place in the series. Any subplots should come directly from the main story. Secondary characters (children, family, friends, neighbors, fellow church members, etc.) can also help contribute to a substantial and gratifying story. An element of faith should be well integrated into the plot. And the conflict between the main characters should be an emotional one.
>
> **Tips:** "We want character-driven fiction with an author voice that inspires, whether in a contemporary romance or contemporary romantic suspense."

LOYOLA PRESS, 3441 N. Ashland Ave., Chicago IL 60657. Toll-free (800)621-1008. (773)281-1818. Fax (773)281-0152. E-mail: durepos@loyolapress.com. Website: www .loyolapress.org. Catholic. Joseph Durepos, acq. ed. Serving faith formation in the Jesuit tradition. Publishes 40 titles/yr. Open to first-time authors. Accepts mss through agents. Prefers 40,000-80,000 wds. or 200-400 pgs. Variable royalty on net; advances $5,000-25,000. Average first printing 7,500-15,000. Considers simultaneous submissions. Responds in 8-10 wks. Prefers NRSV (Catholic Edition). Guidelines on Website.

> **Nonfiction:** Proposal/sample chapters; no phone query; e-query OK.
>
> **Tips:** "Looking for family, faith, and social/spiritual issues."
>
> ****Note:** This publisher serviced by The Writer's Edge.

+LUTHERAN UNIVERSITY PRESS, PO Box 390759, Minneapolis MN 55439. (952)835-1828. Fax (972)835-2613. E-mail: publisher@lutheranupress.org. Website: www.lutheranu press.org. Karen Walhof, ed. Publishes 8-10 titles/yr. Receives dozens of submissions annually. **SUBSIDY PUBLISHES 25%.** No print-on-demand. No reprints. Royalty 10-15% on net; no advance. Average first printing 500-2,000. Publication within 6 mos. No simultaneous submissions. Responds in 3 wks. No guidelines; free catalog.

> **Nonfiction:** Proposal/sample chapters in electronic format.
>
> **Photos/Artwork:** Accepts freelance photos for book covers.
>
> **Tips:** "We accept manuscripts only from faculty of Lutheran colleges, universities, seminaries, and Lutheran faculty from other institutions."

THE LUTTERWORTH PRESS/JAMES CLARKE & CO. LTD., PO Box 60, Cambridge CB1 2NT, England. Phone +44 (0)1223 350865. Fax +44 (0)1223 366951. E-mail: publishing @lutterworth.com. Website: www.lutterworth.com, or www.jamesclarke.co.uk. Adrian Brink, ed. Imprints: The Lutterworth Press (general); James Clarke & Co. (academic/reference). Publishes 25 titles/yr. (15 reprints, 10 new). Receives 100 submissions annually. 90% of books from first-time authors. Accepts mss through agents. Reprints books. **SUBSIDY PUBLISHES 2%.** No print-on-demand. Royalty on retail; some advances. Publication within 18 mos. No simultaneous submissions. Responds in 3 mos. Requested ms by mail. No guidelines; free catalog.

> **Nonfiction:** Proposal/2 chapters. Most open to nonfiction.

MACALESTER PARK PUBLISHING, 24558—546th Ave., Austin MN 55912. (507)396-0135. Toll-free fax (800)407-9078. E-mail: macalesterpark@macalesterparkpublishing.com. Website: www.macalesterpark.com. Focuses on reprinting books. Sue Franklin, owner.

MAGNUS PRESS, PO Box 2666, Carlsbad CA 92018. (760)806-3743. Fax (760)806-3689. E-mail: magnuspres@aol.com. Website: www.magnuspress.com. Warren Angel, ed. dir. To publish biblical studies that are written for the average person and that minister life to Christ's church. Imprint: Canticle Books. Publishes 3 titles/yr. Receives 60 submissions annually. 50% of books from first-time authors. Accepts submissions through agents. Reprints books. Prefers 105-300 pgs. Graduated royalty on retail; no advance. Average first printing 2,500. Publication within 1 yr. Considers simultaneous submissions. Accepts requested ms on disk. Responds in 1 mo. Guidelines (also by e-mail); free catalog.

> **Nonfiction:** Query or proposal/2-3 chapters; fax query OK. "Looking for spirituality, thematic biblical studies, unique inspirational/devotional books, e.g. *Sports Stories and the Bible.*"
>
> **Tips:** "Our writers need solid knowledge of the Bible and a mature spirituality that reflects a profound relationship with Jesus Christ. Most open to a popularly written biblical study that addresses a real concern/issue in the church at large today."
>
> ****Note:** This publisher serviced by The Writer's Edge.

+MARSHALL TRUMANN PUBLISHING, 3710 S. Calhoun St., Fort Wayne IN 46807. (260)744-0579. E-mail: jtolbert@wincoprint.com. Submit to: submissions@marshalltrumann.com. Website: www.marshalltrumann.com. Jim Tolbert, ed. Responds to queries in 60 days; mss in 90 days. Not included in topical listings.

> **Nonfiction:** Accepts all genres in nonfiction.
>
> **Tips:** "We are a new publisher looking for submissions from promising new authors, such as spiritual leaders, as well as from seasoned authors. Our editorial staff is eager to coach authors in finding their voice and the promotion of their work."

MASTER BOOKS, PO Box 726, Green Forest AR 72638. (870)438-5288. Fax (870)438-5120. E-mail: nlp@newleafpress.net. Website: www.masterbooks.net. Imprint of New Leaf Press. Jim Fletcher, ed. Publishes 12-15 titles/yr. Receives 1,200 submissions annually. 10% of books from first-time authors. Prefers 140-240 pgs. Royalty 10% of net; no advance. Average first printing 5,000. Considers simultaneous submissions. Responds in 90 days or longer. Free catalog.

> **Nonfiction:** Query. "Looking for biblical creationism, biblical science, creation/evolution debate material." No fiction, poetry, or personal stories.
>
> **Special Needs:** Children's books and homeschool science books.

MCDOUGAL PUBLISHING, PO Box 3595, Hagerstown MD 21742. (301)797-6637. Fax (301)733-2767. E-mail: publishing@mcdougal.org. Website: www.mcdougalpublishing .com. Pentecostal/Charismatic, nondenominational. Diane McDougal, pres.; Janet Durbin, mng. ed. Publishes books for the body of Christ. Imprints: McDougal Publishing, Fairmont Books, Parable Publishing, and Serenity Books. Publishes 15-20 titles/yr. Receives 150 submissions annually. 70% of books from first-time authors. Accepts mss through agents. **SUBSIDY PUBLISHES 20%.** Reprints books. Prefers 80-192 pgs. Royalty 10-15% of net; no advance. Requires all authors to buy 3,000 copies of their book. Average first printing 3,000-5,000. Publication within 6 mos. Considers simultaneous submissions. Responds in 2 mos. Guidelines (also on Website); free catalog.

> **Nonfiction:** Proposal/1-2 chapters (preferred); phone/fax/e-query OK. "Looking for titles on all topics relevant to the Christian life."
>
> **Fiction:** Complete ms. "Now considering adult fiction from authors with an established market; no romance."
>
> **Tips:** "Know who your audience is, and write to that audience. Also, keep focused on one central theme."

MCRUFFY PRESS, PO Box 212, Raymore MO 64083. Toll-free (888)967-1200. Fax (888)967-1300. E-mail: brian@mcruffy.com. Website: www.mcruffy.com. Brian Davis, ed. Christian publisher of children's trade books, children's audio, and homeschool materials. Open to freelance. Requires e-query. Incomplete topical listings.

Tips: "Most open to seeing elementary educational materials, any subject area. Not currently accepting picture book manuscripts."

MEGAGRACE BOOKS, PO Box 80180, Las Vegas NV 89180-0180. E-mail: ds@scherf.com, or grace@megagrace.com. Websites: www.megagrace.com, or www.scherf.com/scherfbooks .htm. Dietmar Scherf, ed. Books that positively discuss and teach the pure grace message of the Bible. Imprint: Scherf Books. Publishes 2 titles/yr. Receives 500 submissions annually. 90% of books from first-time authors. No mss through agents. No reprints. Prefers 40,000-50,000 wds. (nonfiction), or 90,000-120,000 wds. (fiction). Royalty 5-10% of retail or outright purchase; no advance. Average first printing 2,000-5,000. Publication within 18 mos. Considers simultaneous submissions. No mss by disk or e-mail. Responds in 4-6 wks. Prefers KJV, NASB, or Amplified. Guidelines and catalog on Website.

Nonfiction: Query first/SASE; no phone/fax/e-query. "Looking for Christian living and spiritual life books."

Also Does: Audio CDs on the pure grace of God.

Photos/Artwork: Accepts freelance photos for book covers.

Tips: "We like books that gently help folks discover the pure grace of God."

MERCER UNIVERSITY PRESS, 1400 Coleman Ave., Macon GA 31207-0003. (478)301-2880. Fax (478)301-2264. E-mail: jolley_ma@mercer.edu. Website: www.mupress.org. Baptist. Marc Jolley, mng. ed. Publishes 15 titles/yr. Receives 200 submissions annually. 75% of books from first-time authors. Accepts mss through agents. Some reprints. Royalty on net; no advance. Average first printing 800-1,200. Publication within 15 mos. Prefers requested ms on disk; no e-mail submissions.

Nonfiction: Proposal/2 chapters; fax/e-query OK. "We are looking for books on history, philosophy, theology, and religion, including history of religion, philosophy of religion, Bible studies, and ethics." No religious fiction, only Southern literary.

+MEREDITH BOOKS/CHRISTIAN, 1716 Locust St., Des Moines IA 50309-3023. (515)284-3000. Fax (515)284-3338. E-mail: ken.sidey@meredith.com. Website: www.meredith books.com. Meredith Corp. Ken Sidey, ed. Secular publisher developing a line of nonfiction Christian books. Requires submissions though agents; no freelance submissions. Considers simultaneous submissions.

Nonfiction: Proposal from agents.

Fiction: Proposal from agents. Adult.

Tips: "We are committed to strengthening the bonds within families and promoting the power of the family through the publication of Christian books."

MERIWETHER PUBLISHING LTD./CONTEMPORARY DRAMA SERVICE, 885 Elkton Dr., Colorado Springs CO 80918. (719)594-4422. Fax (719)594-9916. E-mail: MerPCDS@ aol.com. Website: www.meriwetherpublishing.com. Arthur L. Zapel, ed.; submit to Rhonda Wray, Christian ed. Publishes 2-3 titles/yr.; 30 plays/yr. Primarily a publisher of plays for Christian and secular; must be acceptable for use in a wide variety of Christian denominations. Imprint: Contemporary Drama Service. Publishes 3 bks./25 plays/yr. Receives 800 submissions annually (mostly plays). 50% of books from first-time authors. Accepts mss through agents. Reprints books. Prefers 200 pgs. Royalty 10% of net or retail, or fee arrangement; no advance. Average first printing of books 2,500, plays 500. Publication within 1 yr. Considers simultaneous submissions. Requires accepted mss on disk; no e-mail submissions. Responds in 3-5 wks. Guidelines (also on Website); catalog $2.

Nonfiction: Query only for books; fax/e-query OK. "Looking for creative worship books, i.e., drama, using the arts in worship, how-to books with ideas for Christian education." Submit books to Meriwether.

Fiction: Plays only, for all ages. Always looking for Christmas and Easter plays (1 hour maximum). Send complete manuscript. Submit plays to Contemporary Drama.

Special Needs: Collections of church dramas. Drama, theater, how-to in relation to theater, drama ministry, and Christian education; collection of skits, scripts, or sketches.

Tips: "Our books are on drama or any creative, artistic area that can be a part of worship. Writers should familiarize themselves with our catalog before submitting to ensure that their manuscript fits with the list we've already published." Contemporary Drama Service wants easy-to-stage comedies, skits, one-act plays, large-cast musicals, and full-length comedies for schools (junior high through college), and churches (including chancel dramas for Christmas and Easter).

MESSIANIC JEWISH PUBLISHERS, PO Box 615; 6120 Day Long Ln., Clarksville MD 21029. (410)531-6644. E-mail: guidelines@messianicjewish.net. Website: www.MessianicJewish .net. Lederer/Messianic Jewish Communications. Janet Chaiet, mng. ed. Books that build up the Messianic Jewish community, witness to unbelieving Jewish people, or help Christians understand their Jewish roots. Imprints: Lederer Books, Remnant Press (subsidy only). Publishes 10-12 titles/yr. Receives 100+ submissions annually. 50% of books from first-time authors. No mss through agents. Reprints books. Prefers 50,000-88,000 wds. Royalty 7-15% of net. Average first printing 5,000. Publication within 12-24 mos. No simultaneous submissions. Responds in 3-6 mos. Requires requested ms on disk. Prefers Complete Jewish Bible. Guidelines (also by e-mail); free catalog.

Nonfiction: Write or call for submission guidelines first. Messianic Judaism, Jewish evangelism, or Jewish roots of Christian faith. "Must have Messianic Jewish theme and demonstrate familiarity with Jewish culture and thought."

Fiction: Write or call for submission guidelines first. For adults. Jewish themes only.

Ethnic Books: Jewish; Messianic Jewish.

Tips: "Must request guidelines before submitting book proposal; all submissions must meet our requirements. Looking for Messianic Jewish commentaries. Books must address one of the following: Jewish evangelism, Jewish roots of Christianity, or Messianic Judaism."

+MILESTONES INTERNATIONAL PUBLISHERS, 4410 University Dr., Ste. 113, Huntsville AL 35816. (256)536-9402, ext. 234. Website: www.milestonesinternationalpublishers.com. Jim Rill, pres. Bringing significance to life's journey.

MILLENNIUM III PUBLISHERS, 174 N. Moore Rd., Simpsonville SC 29680. (864)967-7344. E-mail: willramsey@millenniatech.info. Website: www.millenniatech.info. Willard Ramsey, sr. ed. Restoring our culture to a Christian world-view. Publishes 4-5 titles/yr. Receives 40-50 submissions annually. 50% of books from first-time authors. Accepts mss through agents. Reprints books. Prefers 250-300 pgs. Royalty 10-15% on net; some advances. Publication within 10-12 mos. Considers simultaneous submissions. Responds in 6 wks. Prefers NKJV. Guidelines; free catalog.

Nonfiction: Query; proposal/2 chapters; phone/e-query OK.

Fiction: Proposal/2 chapters; phone/e-query OK. "Looking for historical novels of the 'Great Awakening' period. How were the churches and their message different then?"

Photos/Artwork: Accepts freelance photos for book covers.

Tips: "Most open to nonfiction books applying Christian solutions to contemporary cultural problems."

+MISSION CITY PRESS, 202—2nd Ave. S., Franklin TN 37064-2650. (615)591-1007. Fax (615)591-1006. E-mail: info@missioncitypress.com, or info@alifeoffaith.com. Website:

www.missioncitypress.com. Committed to creating products that inspire today's kids to develop a life of faith. Book for girls.

MOMS IN PRINT: The Exclusive Publisher for Moms, PO Box 241, Round Hill VA 20141. (540)338-2596. Fax (703)750-0229. E-mail: editors@momsinprint.com, or submissions@momsinprint.com. Website: www.momsinprint.com. General publisher. Terry Doherty, sr. ed. Publishes select works by a wide variety of Mom authors, producing top quality books readers will cherish. Royalty. Responds in 2 mos. Guidelines on Website. Not currently accepting submissions.

MONARCH BOOKS, Mayfield House, 256 Banbury Rd., Oxford OX2 7DH, United Kingdom. Phone +44 (0) 1865 302750. Fax +44 (0) 1865 302757. E-mail: monarch@lionhudson .com. Website: www.lionhudson.com. Lion Hudson PLC. Tony Collins, ed. dir. Publishes primarily for the evangelical Christian market, providing tools and resources for Christian leaders; publishes and distributes in U.S. and Canada through an arrangement with Kregel Books. Publishes 35 titles/yr. Receives 800-1,000 submissions annually. 20% of books from first-time authors. Accepts mss through agents. Prefers 50,000 wds. or 192 pgs. Royalty 10-15% on net; advance. Average first printing 5,000. Publication within 9 mos. Considers simultaneous submissions. Requires requested ms on disk or by e-mail. Responds in 6 wks. Prefers NIV. Guidelines by e-mail; free catalog.

> **Nonfiction:** Proposal with 2 chapters; phone/fax/e-query OK. Looking for books of substance.

> **Tips:** "Looking for books that are original, well presented, and have a clear purpose and market. Think about who you are writing for. What will a reader get as a benefit from reading your book?"

MOODY PUBLISHERS, 820 N. LaSalle Blvd., Chicago IL 60610. Fax (312)329-2144. E-mail: Acquisitions@moody.edu. Website: www.moodypublishers.org. Imprint: Northfield Publishing, and Lift Every Voice (African American). Moody Bible Institute. Submit to Acquisitions Coordinator. To provide books that evangelize, edify the believer, and educate concerning the Christian life. Publishes 65-70 titles/yr. Receives 3,500 submissions annually. 1% of books from first-time authors. Accepts mss through agents. Royalty on net; advance $500-50,000. Average first printing 10,000. Publication within 1 yr. No simultaneous submissions. Requires requested ms on disk. Responds in 2-3 mos. Prefers NAS, NLT, NIV. Guidelines (also by e-mail); catalog for 9x12 SASE/$1.42 postage (mark "Media Mail").

> **Nonfiction:** Considers agented proposals only; no phone/fax/e-query. "For nonfiction, we review only those proposals that come from professional literary agents." Closed to all other unsolicited mss.

> **Fiction:** Proposal/3-5 chapters; for all ages. "We are looking for stories that glorify God both in content and style. We believe that God gives some of his children the talents to write beautiful works of fiction, and we will seek out those artists and the stories they create. We wish to direct people toward God through beauty and truth." No picture books or romance genre fiction.

> **Ethnic Books:** African American.

> **Tips:** "Most open to books where the writer is a recognized expert and already has a platform to promote the book."

> ****Note:** This publisher serviced by The Writer's Edge.

MOREHOUSE PUBLISHING CO., 4775 Linglestown Rd., Harrisburg PA 17112. (717)541-8130. Fax (717)541-8136. E-mail: morehouse@morehousegroup.com, or dfarring@morehousegroup.com. Website: www.morehousepublishing.com. Episcopalian. Debra Farrington, ed. dir.; submit to Nancy Fitzgerald, sr. ed. Publishes 30-35 titles/yr. Receives 750 submissions annually. 60% of books from first-time authors. Accepts mss through agents. No reprints. Royalty 10% of net; advance $1,000-2,000. Average first printing 3,000. Publication within 18 mos. Considers simultaneous submissions. Responds in 4-6 wks. Guidelines (also on Website); for free catalog call (800)877-0012.

Nonfiction: Proposal/1-2 chapters; no phone/fax/e-query.

Special Needs: Spirituality, Episcopal oriented.

Tips: "We primarily accept books in our stated categories that are written by Episcopalians and written from an Anglican perspective. Not currently accepting children's book manuscripts."

WILLIAM MORROW, 10 E. 53rd St., New York NY 10022. (212)207-7000. Fax (212)207-7145. Website: www.harpercollins.com. Imprint of HarperCollins Publishers. General trade imprint; religious titles published by HarperSanFrancisco. Michael Morrison, ed. dir. Agented submissions only.

MOUNTAINVIEW PUBLISHING, 1284 Overlook Dr., Sierra Vista AZ 85635-5512. (520)458-5602. Fax (520)458-5618. E-mail: leeemory@earthlink.net. Website: www.trebleheart books.com. Division of Treble Heart Books. Lee Emory, ed./pub. Online Christian publisher. Receives 300 submissions annually. 13% of books from first-time authors. Prefers 50,000-100,000 wds. Royalty 35% of retail; no advance. Books are published electronically, and in trade-sized print. Publication usually within 12-18 mos. No simultaneous submissions (a 90-day exclusive is required on all submissions). Responds in 3-4 mos. Guidelines on Website.

Nonfiction: Submissions to: submissions@trebleheartbooks.com (e-mail submissions only). Seeking excellent nonfiction, inspirational books.

Fiction: E-mail submissions only. Historical romances, 80,000-100,000 wds.; contemporary romances, 65,000-80,000 wds.; novellas 20,000-30,000 wds. preferred (considers 35,000-40,000). "Seeking high-quality manuscripts; not necessarily romances. Looking for good mainstream and traditional inspirationals in most categories; also mysteries, westerns, and historicals."

Photos/Artwork: Accepts some high quality freelance photos for book covers.

Tips: "All inspirational fiction should contain a faith element. Challenge the reader to think, to look at things through different eyes. Avoid head-hopping and clichés; avoid heavy-handed preaching. No sci-fi or fantasy or dark angel stories. Send consecutive chapters, not random."

MOUNT OLIVE COLLEGE PRESS, 634 Henderson St., Mount Olive NC 28365. (919)658-2502. Dr. Pepper Worthington, ed. Publishes 5 titles/yr. Receives 2,500 submissions annually. 75% of books from first-time authors. Prefers 220 pgs. Negotiated royalty. Average first printing 500. Publication within 1-3 yrs. No simultaneous submissions. Responds in 6-12 mos. No disk. Free guidelines/catalog.

Nonfiction: Proposal/3 chapters; no phone query. Religion. For poetry submit 6 sample poems.

Fiction: Proposal/3 chapters. Religious; literary.

Photos/Artwork: Considers photos and artwork.

MULTNOMAH PUBLISHERS, 601 N. Larch St., Sisters OR 97759. (541)549-1144. Fax (541)549-8048. E-mail: editorial@multnomahbooks.com. Websites: www.multnomah books.com; www.letstalkfiction.com. Imprint information listed below. Publishes 75 titles/yr. Multnomah is currently not accepting unsolicited manuscripts, proposals, or queries; no proposals for biographies, poetry, or children's books. Queries will be accepted through literary agents and at writers' conferences at which a Multnomah representative is present.

Big Change Moments: Books that effect "big change" in people's lives. Website: www.bigchangemoments.com. Guy Coleman, dir. E-mail: gcoleman@mpbooks.com.

Multnomah Books: Christian living and popular theology books.

Multnomah Fiction: Well-crafted fiction that uses truth to change lives.

Multnomah Gifts: Substantive topics with beautiful, lyrical writing.

Also Does: E-books.

**Note: This publisher serviced by The Writer's Edge (especially for fiction).

+**NATIONAL BLACK THEATRE, INC.,** 2033 Fifth Ave., Harlem NY 10035. Does drama, musicals, and children's plays. Scripts need to reflect an African or African American lifestyle. Especially open to historical or inspirational forms. Also holds workshops and readings.

+**NATIONAL DRAMA SERVICE,** LifeWay Christian Resources, One Lifeway Plaza, Nashville TN 37234. E-mail: terry@lifeway.com. Website: www.lifeway.com. Publishes dramatic material for use in Christian ministry: drama in worship, puppet & clown scripts, Christian comedy, mime/movement scripts, readers theater, creative worship services, monologues.

NAVPRESS, Box 35001, Colorado Springs CO 80935. Toll-free (800)955-7767. (719)531-3548. Website: www.navpress.org or www.gospelcom.net/navs/NP. Imprints: Th1nk, and Piñon. Publishes 75 titles/yr. Guidelines on Website. "We are no longer accepting any unsolicited submissions, proposals, queries, etc."

**Note: This publisher serviced by The Writer's Edge and ECPA First Edition.

NAZARENE PUBLISHING HOUSE—See Beacon Hill Press of Kansas City.

NEIBAUER PRESS, 20 Industrial Dr., Warminster PA 18974. (215)322-6200, ext. 255. Fax (215)322-2495. E-mail: Nathan@neibauer.com. Website: www.ChurchSupplier.com. Nathan Neibauer, ed. For Evangelical/Protestant clergy and church leaders. Publishes 8 titles/yr. Receives 100 submissions annually. 5% of books from first-time authors. No mss through agents. Reprints books. Prefers 200 pgs. Royalty on net; some outright purchases; no advance. Average first printing 1,500. Publication within 6 mos. Considers simultaneous submissions. Responds in 4 wks. Prefers e-mail submissions. Prefers NIV. No guidelines/catalog.

Nonfiction: Query or proposal/2 chapters; fax query OK.

Also Does: Pamphlets, tracts.

Photos/Artwork: Accepts freelance photos for book covers.

Tips: "Publishes only religious books on stewardship and church enrollment, stewardship and tithing, and church enrollment tracts."

NELSON BOOKS, (Thomas Nelson Publishers) PO Box 141000, Nashville TN 37214-1000. (615)889-9000. Fax (615)902-2747. Website: www.thomasnelson.com. A division of Thomas Nelson, Inc. Jonathan Merkh, pub.; Brian Hampton, assoc. pub. Imprints: Nelson Business. Publishes 42 titles/yr. Less than 5% of books from first-time authors. Prefers mss through agents. No reprints. Accepts no unsolicited queries, proposals, or mss. Prefers 65,000-95,000 wds. Royalty. Prefers NKJV. No guidelines or catalog.

Nonfiction: "Looking for nonfiction dealing with the relationship and/or application of biblical principles to everyday life, 65,000-95,000 words; from agents only."

**Note: This publisher serviced by The Writer's Edge and ECPA First Edition.

+**NELSON IGNITE,** PO Box 141000, Nashville TN 37214-1000. (615)889-9000. Fax (615)902-2747. Website: www.thomasnelson.com. A division of Thomas Nelson, Inc. John Mason, VP & Publisher. New charismatic-titles imprint. Will publish 20-25 titles/yr. Incomplete topical listings.

Tips: "While our authors will have a charismatic or Pentecostal theological bent, topics in Nelson Ignite may cover some of the same Christian living, marriage, and other subjects as Nelson Books or W Publishing."

THOMAS NELSON PUBLISHERS—See Nelson Books.

TOMMY NELSON, a division of Thomas Nelson, Inc., 402 BNA Dr., Bldg. 100, Ste. 600, Nashville TN 37217. (615)889-9000. Dan Lynch, Sr. VP & pub.; Amy Parker, ed. of children's books (2-14 yrs.). Children's books and products. Submissions only through agents, by referral from one of their authors, through a manuscript service, or by meeting an editor at a conference.

Note: This publisher serviced by The Writer's Edge and ECPA First Edition.

NEW CANAAN PUBLISHING CO., INC., PO Box 752, New Canaan CT 06840. Phone/fax (203)966-3408. E-mail: info@newcanaanpublishing.com, or djm@newcanaanpublishing.com. Website: www.newcanaanpublishing.com. Kathy Mittelstadt, ed. Children's books with strong educational and moral content, for grades 1-9 (ages 5-16); also aggressively building its Christian titles list. Publishes 3-4 titles/yr. Receives 120 submissions annually. 50% of books from first-time authors. Accepts mss through agents. Prefers 20,000-50,000 wds. or 120-250 pgs. Royalty 8-10% of net; occasional advance. Average first printing 500-5,000. Publication within 1 yr. Accepts simultaneous submissions. Responds in 3-4 mos. Requires requested ms on disk; no e-mail submissions. Guidelines and catalog on Website, or for #10 SASE.

Nonfiction: Proposal/2-3 chapters or complete ms; no e-query. Does not return submissions.

Fiction: Proposal/2-3 chapters or complete ms; no e-query. For children and teens, 6-14 yrs. "We want children's books with strong educational and moral content; 10,000-20,000 wds." Now accepts picture books.

Special Needs: Middle-school-level educational books.

Photos/Artwork: Accepts freelance photos for book covers.

Tips: "Looking for teen/youth fiction and religious instructional materials for teens/youth."

NEW HOPE, Box 12065, Birmingham AL 35202-2065. (205)991-8100. Fax (205)991-4015. E-mail: new_hope@wmu.org. Website: www.newhopepubl.com. Imprint of Woman's Missionary Union; Auxiliary to Southern Baptist Convention. Andrea Mullins, pub. dir.; Rebecca England, ed. Publishes Christian nonfiction for women and families, and books with a missions or ministry focus. Publishes 24-32 titles/yr. Receives 350 submissions annually. 25% of books from first-time authors. Accepts mss through agents. Reprints books. Prefers 192-288 pgs. Royalty or outright purchase. Average first printing 5,000-10,000. Publication within 2 yrs. Considers simultaneous submissions. Requires requested ms on disk or by e-mail. Guidelines (also on Website); catalog for 9x12 SAE/3 stamps.

Nonfiction: No unsolicited submissions; no phone/fax/e-query. "All that we publish must have a missions/ministry emphasis."

Photos/Artwork: Accepts freelance photos for book covers.

Note: This publisher serviced by The Writer's Edge.

NEW LEAF PRESS, PO Box 726, Green Forest AR 72638-0726. (870)438-5288. Fax (870)438-5120. E-mail: nlp@newleafpress.net. Website: www.newleafpress.net. Jim Fletcher, ed.; Roger Howerton, acq. ed. Endeavors to bring the lost to Christ and understanding to the body of Christ. Imprints: Master Books and Balfour Books. Publishes 25-30 titles/yr. Receives 1,200 submissions annually. 15% of books from first-time authors. Accepts mss through agents. Reprints books. Prefers 100-400 pgs. Variable royalty on net; rarely gives advance. Average first printing 5,000. Publication within 12 mos. Considers simultaneous submissions. Requires accepted ms on disk. Responds in 3 mos. Prefers KJV. Guidelines (also by e-mail); catalog for 9x12 SAE/5 stamps.

Nonfiction: Proposal/2 chapters; no phone/fax query. "Looking for gift books, Christian living, creation-science, and scholarly works." No fiction, poetry, or personal stories.

Tips: "Send us a gift book or something very unique that's different from anything out there."

NEW SEEDS BOOKS, 300 Massachusetts Ave., Boston MA 02115. (617)424-0030. Fax (617)236-1563. E-mail: doneal@shambhala.com. Website: www.shambhala.com. Shambhala Publications, Inc. David O'Neal, mng. ed.; Katie Keach, asst. ed. (kkeach@shambhala.com). A new imprint devoted to publishing works of the Christian contemplative traditions, cross-traditionally; also new and readable translations of classic texts. Accepts mss through agents. Reprints books. Length open. Royalty; advance. Average first printing 10,000-30,000. Publication within 1 yr. Considers simultaneous submissions. Responds in 6 wks. Prefers accepted ms on disk or by e-mail. Guidelines; free catalog.

Nonfiction: Query, proposal/2 chapters, or complete ms; e-query OK.

+NEW SPIRIT, 850 Third Ave., 16th Fl., New York NY 10022. Website: www.bet.com/books. Imprint of BET Books. Glenda Howard, sr. ed. Responds in 4 mos. Incomplete topical listings. No questionnaire returned.

Nonfiction: Proposal/3 chapters. "We want to motivate readers by offering messages advocating personal growth, empowerment, and strong personal relationships."

Fiction: Proposal/3 chapters. "Looking for well-crafted novels featuring strong characters who overcome challenges and obstacles through the power of prayer and faith."

NEW YORK UNIVERSITY PRESS, 838 Broadway, 3rd Fl., New York NY 10003-4812. (212)998-2575. Fax (212)995-3833. E-mail: information@nyupress.org. Website: www.nyupress.org. Jennifer Hammer, religion ed. Embraces ideological diversity. Publishes 100 titles/yr. Receives 800-1,000 submissions annually. 30% of books from first-time authors. Few mss through agents. Royalty on net. Publication within 10-12 mos. Considers simultaneous submissions. Initial response usually within 1 mo. (peer reviewed). Guidelines on Website.

Nonfiction: Query or proposal/1 chapter.

Tips: "As a university press, we primarily publish works with a scholarly foundation written by PhDs affiliated with a university department. Our focus within religious studies is on religion in American history, culture, and politics. We do not publish liturgical studies, pastoral care, spiritual guides, or exegesis."

NEXGEN. For teachers or program leaders who want Bible-based discipleship resources. Janet Lee, sr. product mgr. See Cook Communications Ministries for details.

NORTHFIELD PUBLISHING CO., 820 N. LaSalle Blvd., Chicago IL 60610. (312)329-8047. Fax (312)329-2019. E-mail: acquisitions@moody.edu. Website: www.moodypublishers.org. Imprint of Moody Publishers. Submit to Acquisitions Coordinator. Books for non-Christians or those exploring the faith. Publishes 3-5 titles/yr. 1% of books from first-time authors. Royalty on net; advance $500-50,000. Publication within 1 yr. No simultaneous submissions. Responds in 2-3 mos. Guidelines (also by e-mail/Website); catalog for 9x12 SAE/2 stamps. Incomplete topical listings.

Nonfiction: Proposal/2-3 chapters. "We decline all unsolicited proposals."

Fiction: For all ages.

NORTHSTONE PUBLISHING, 9025 Jim Bailey Rd., Kelowna BC V4V 1R2, Canada. Toll-free (800)299-2926. (250)766-2778. Toll-free fax (888)841-9991. Fax (250)766-2736. E-mail: acquisitions@woodlake.com. Website: www.woodlakebooks.com. Imprint of Wood Lake Books, Inc. Michael Schwartzentruber, ed. To provide high quality products promoting positive social and spiritual values. Publishes 6 titles/yr. Receives 900 submissions annually. 30% of books from first-time authors. Prefers 192-256 pgs. Royalty 7.5-10% of retail; some advances $1,000. Average first printing 4,000. Publication within 18 months. Considers simultaneous submissions. Prefers requested ms on disk, or by e-mail. Guidelines (also by e-mail/Website); catalog $2.

Nonfiction: Proposal/2 chapters; phone/fax/e-query OK.

Tips: "Most open to truth-seeking, life-affirming books that promote positive social and spiritual values. Although we publish from a Christian perspective, we seek to attract a general audience. Our target audience is interested in spirituality and values, but may not even attend church (nor do we assume that they should)."

NORTHWESTERN PUBLISHING HOUSE, 1250 N. 113th St., Milwaukee WI 53226-3284. Toll-free (800)662-6022. Fax (414)475-7684. E-mail: braunj@nph.wels.net. Website: www.nph.net. Lutheran. Rev. John A. Braun, VP of publishing services. Open to freelance. Responds in 2-3 mos. Guidelines on Website (www.nph.net/cgi-bin/site.pl?aboutUs Manuscript). Incomplete topical listings. No questionnaire returned.

Nonfiction: Complete ms./cover letter; or query letter/outline.

OBADIAH PRESS, 607 N. Cleveland St., Merrill WI 54452. Phone/fax (715)536-3167. E-mail: tina@obadiahpress.com. Website: www.obadiahpress.com. Nondenominational/Christian. Tina L. Miller, ed-in-chief. Publishes 2-5 titles/yr. 90% of books from first-time authors. Royalty 12% of net. Prefers e-query or complete ms. by mail. Not currently accepting submissions except for their anthologies. Guidelines on Website.

> **Tips:** "We publish only a few books each year and work very closely with our authors. Check the Website before submitting as we are not currently accepting proposals or submissions except stories for our anthologies."

ONE WORLD/BALLANTINE BOOKS, 1540 Broadway, New York NY 10036. (212)782-8378. Fax (212)782-8442. Website: www.randomhouse.com. Submit to Senior Editor. Imprint of Ballantine Books. Novels that are written by and focus on African Americans, but from an American perspective. Publishes 24 titles/yr. Receives 850 submissions annually. 50% of books from first-time authors. Submissions from agents only. No reprints. Prefers 80,000 wds. Royalty 7.5-15% on retail; advance $40,000-200,000. Average first printing 10,000. Publication within 18 mos. Considers simultaneous submissions. Responds in 2 mos. No disk or e-mail. No guidelines/catalog. Not accepting submissions at this time. Note: No unsolicited submissions, proposals, manuscripts, or queries at this time.

> **Fiction:** Proposal/3 chapters; no phone/fax/e-query. "Contemporary/ethnic novels only; for African American women."
>
> **Ethnic Books:** All are ethnic books.
>
> **Tips:** "You must understand African American culture and avoid time-worn stereotypes."

ONSTAGE PUBLISHING, 214 E. Moulton St. N.E., Decatur AL 35601. Toll-free (888)420-8879. (256)308-2300. Fax (256)308-9712. Website: www.onstagebooks.com. Dianne Hamilton, sr. ed. (dianne@onstagebooks.com). Children's book publisher. Open to freelance. 80% of books from first-time authors. No mss through agents. No reprints. Prefers 3,000-9,000 wds. for ages 6-8; 10,000-40,000 wds. for ages 9-12; and 40,000-60,000 wds. for ages 12 and up. Royalty on retail; advance. Average first printing varies. Considers simultaneous submissions (if indicated). Responds in 2-4 mos. Guidelines by e-mail; catalog for 3 stamps.

> **Nonfiction:** Not currently looking for nonfiction, so query first.
>
> **Fiction:** Proposal/3 chapters or complete ms; no phone/fax/e-query. "We publish books for children or teens."
>
> **Photos/Artwork:** Open to artwork. See Website for artist guidelines.
>
> **Tips:** "Study our catalog, and get a sense of the kind of books we publish, so you'll know whether your projects is right for us."

#OPEN COURT PUBLISHING CO., PO Box 300, 315 Fifth St., Peru IL 61354. Toll-free (800)815-2280. Fax (815)224-2256. E-mail: opencourt@caruspub.com. Website: www.opencourtbooks.com. Carus Publishing Co. Submit to Acquisitions Editor. Liberal, secular publisher with a focus on critical and comparative religious studies; tends to avoid evangelical or doctrinal works. Publishes 4 religious titles/yr. Receives 1,200 submissions annually. 5-10% of books from first-time authors. Accepts mss through agents. Reprints books. Prefers 250-300 pgs. Royalty 5-12% of net; advance $1,000. Average first printing 1,000 (paperback). Publication within 1-3 yrs. No simultaneous submissions. Responds in 6 mos. Guidelines on Website; free catalog.

> **Nonfiction:** Proposal/1 chapter/résumé/vita; no fax/e-query.

Tips: "We're looking for works of high intellectual quality for a scholarly or general readership on comparative religion, philosophy of religion, and religious studies. We don't consider evangelical/doctrinal/inspirational works/poetry/fiction."

OPINE PUBLISHING, 5113 W. Running Brook Rd., Columbia MD 21044. (443)745-1004. Fax (410)730-0917. E-mail: info@opinebooks.com. Website: www.opinebooks.com, or www.opinepublishing.com. Jean Purcell, pub. Christian books on faith, marriage, and single life, plus award-winning family humor and fiction for all ages. This company is currently focusing on marketing and promoting existing titles; reviewing manuscripts that arrived prior to August 1, 2005; helping new writers through their writing program; and the *Opinari* newsletter, a subscription-only newsletter for writers and avid Opine readers (available for signup on the Website: www.opinebooks.com).

OREGON CATHOLIC PRESS, PO Box 18030, Portland OR 97218-0030. Toll-free (800)548-8749. (503)281-1191. Fax (800)462-7329. E-mail: Liturgy@ocp.org. Website: www.ocp.org. John Limb, pub.; Bari Colombari, sr. ed.; Eric Schumock, mng. ed. To enhance the worship in the Catholic Church in the United States. Imprint: Pastoral Press. Publishes 8 titles/yr. Receives 80 submissions annually. 5% of books from first-time authors. No mss through agents. No reprints. Prefers 192 pgs. Royalty 5-12% of net; no advance. Average first printing 500. Publication within 12 mos. Considers simultaneous submissions. Prefers requested ms on disk; no e-mail submissions. Responds in 3 mos. Prefers NAB. Free catalog; guidelines by e-mail/Website.

> **Nonfiction:** Proposal/1 chapter; no phone/fax/e-query. "Looking for liturgical ministries."
> **Ethnic Books:** Hispanic/Spanish language.
> **Photos/Artwork:** Accepts freelance photos for book covers.
> **Tips:** "Most open to Catholic liturgical works."

*ORIGINAL WORD PUBLISHERS, PO Box 799, Roswell GA 30077. Toll-free (800)235-9673. (770)552-8879. E-mail: drgoodwin@mindspring.com. Website: www.originalword.com. Dr. Charles Goodwin, ed. A transdenominational, nonprofit teaching ministry devoted to biblical studies.

OUR SUNDAY VISITOR, INC., 200 Noll Plaza, Huntington IN 46750-4303. Toll-free (800)348-2440. (219)356-8400. Fax (219)356-8472. E-mail: booksed@osv.com. Website: www.osv.com. Catholic. Greg Erlandson, pub./pres.; Beth McNamara, ed. dir.; Jacquelyn Lindsey, ed. dev. mngr.; submit to Acquisitions Editors: Jacquelyn Lindsey, Michael Dubruiel, and Kelley Renz (religious ed.). To assist Catholics to be more aware and secure in their faith and capable of relating their faith to others. Publishes 20-30 titles/yr. Receives 500+ submissions annually. 10% of books from first-time authors. Prefers not to work through agents. Reprints books. Royalty 10-12% of net; advance varies. Average first printing 5,000. Publication within 1 yr. Considers simultaneous submissions. Responds in 3 mos. Requires requested ms on disk. Free guidelines (also by e-mail); catalog for 9x12 SASE.

> **Nonfiction:** Proposal/2 chapters; e-query OK. "Most open to devotional books (not first person), church history, heritage and saints, the parish, prayer, and family."
> **Also Does:** Pamphlets, booklets.
> **Photos/Artwork:** Occasionally accepts freelance photos for book covers.
> **Tips:** "All books published must relate to the Catholic Church; unique books aimed at our audience. Give as much background information as possible on author qualification, why the topic was chosen, and unique aspects of the project. Follow our guidelines. We are expanding our religious education product line and programs."

PACIFIC PRESS PUBLISHING ASSN., Box 5353, Nampa ID 83653-5353. (208)465-2570. Fax (208)465-2531. E-mail: booksubmissions@pacificpress.com. Website: www.pacific press.com. Seventh-day Adventist. David Jarnes, book ed.; submit to Tim Lale, acq. ed. Books of interest and importance to Seventh-day Adventists and other Christians of all ages. Publishes 30 titles/yr. Receives 500 submissions annually. 5% of books from first-time authors. Accepts mss through agents. Prefers 40,000-70,000 wds. or 128-256 pgs. Royalty 12-15% of net; advance $1,500. Average first printing 5,000. Publication within 12-24 mos. Considers simultaneous submissions. Responds in 3 mos. Requires requested ms on disk, or by e-mail. Guidelines at www.pacificpress.com/index/php?pgName=newsBookSub; free catalog.

Nonfiction: Query only; e-query OK.

Fiction: Query only; almost none accepted; adult/biblical. Children's books: "Must be on a uniquely Seventh-day Adventist topic. No talking animals."

Ethnic Books: Occasionally publishes for ethnic market.

Also Does: Booklets.

Tips: "Most open to spirituality, inspirational, Christian living, or gift books. Our Website has the most up-to-date information, including samples of recent publications. Do not send full manuscript unless we request it after reviewing your proposal."

P & R PUBLISHING CO., PO Box 817, Phillipsburg NJ 08865. (908)454-0505. Fax (908)454-0859. E-mail: susan@prpbooks.com. Website: www.prpbooks.com. Allan Fisher, publications dir.; Melissa Craig, acq. ed. Devoted to stating, defending, and furthering the gospel in the modern world. Publishes 40 titles/yr. Receives 400 submissions annually. 5% of books from first-time authors. Accepts mss through agents. Reprints books. Prefers 140-240 pgs. Royalty 10-14% of net; no advance. Average first printing 4,000. Publication within 8-10 mos. Considers simultaneous submissions. Responds in 1-4 mos. Guidelines on Website; free catalog.

Nonfiction: Query; fax/e-query OK.

Also Does: Booklets.

Tips: "Clear, engaging, and insightful applications of reformed theology to life. Offer us fully developed proposals and polished sample chapters. All books must be consistent with the Westminster Confession of Faith."

**Note: This publisher serviced by The Writer's Edge.

PARADISE RESEARCH PUBLICATIONS, INC., PO Box 837, Kihei HI 96753-0837. Phone/fax (808)874-4876. E-mail: dickb@dickb.com. Website: www.dickb.com/index.shtml. Ken Burns, VP. Imprint: Tincture of Time Press. Publishes 5 titles/yr. Receives 8 submissions annually. 80% of books from first-time authors. No mss through agents. Reprints books. Prefers 250 pgs. Royalty 10% of retail; no advance. Average first printing 5,000. Publication within 2 mos. Considers simultaneous submission. Responds in 1 wk. No disk. Prefers KJV. No guidelines; free catalog.

Nonfiction: Query only; no phone/fax/e-query. Books on the biblical/Christian history of early Alcoholics Anonymous.

Also Does: Pamphlets, booklets, e-books.

Tips: "Most open to healing of alcoholism/addiction by power of God."

PARAGON HOUSE, 1925 Oakcrest Ave., Ste. 7, St. Paul MN 55113-2619. (651)644-3087. Fax (651)644-0997. E-mail: paragon@paragonhouse.com. Website: www.paragonhouse.com. Rosemary Yokoi, acq. ed. Serious nonfiction and texts with an emphasis on religion and philosophy. Imprints: New Era Books, Athena, Omega. Publishes 12-15 titles/yr. Receives 3,000 submissions annually. 20% of books from first-time authors. Accepts mss through agents. No reprints. Prefers 250 pgs. Royalty 7-15% (usually 10%) of net; advance $1,000. Average first printing 2,000-3,000. Publication within 10-18 mos. Considers few simultaneous submissions. Prefers requested ms as hard copy; accepts disk. Responds in 3 mos. Guidelines on Website; catalog available online.

Nonfiction: Query; proposal/2-3 chapters, or complete ms; no phone/fax/e-query. "Looking for scholarly overviews of religious teachers and movements; textbooks in philosophy; new information, theories, ecumenical subjects; and reference books."

PATHWAY PRESS, 1080 Montgomery Ave., Cleveland TN 37311. (423)478-7592. Fax (423)478-7616. E-mail: bill_george@pathwaypress.org. Website: www.pathwaypress.org. Church of God (Cleveland TN). Bill George, ed. Publishes 14-16 titles/yr. Receives 120 submissions annually. 25% of books from first-time authors. Prefers 120-300 pgs. Royalty 10% of wholesale; no advance. Average first printing 2,500-5,000. Publication within 12-18 mos. Guidelines on Website (www.pathwaypress.org/Evangel).

    Nonfiction: Proposal/1-3 chapters; no phone/fax/e-query. "Manuscripts returned only when accompanied by an SASE."

    Tips: "Pathway markets to evangelical readers and publishes from a Pentecostal/Charismatic perspective. Acquisitions committee meets quarterly."

PAULINE BOOKS & MEDIA, 50 Saint Pauls Ave., Jamaica Plain MA 02130-3491. (617)522-8911. Fax (617)524-9805. E-mail: editorial@pauline.org. Website: www.pauline.org. Catholic. Sr. Madonna Ratliff, acq. ed.; Sr. Patricia Edward Jablonski, children's ed. To help clarify Catholic belief and practice for the average reader. Publishes 50-60 titles/yr. Receives 1,500 submissions annually. 25% of books from first-time authors. No ms through agents. Royalty 8-12% of net; advance $300-500. Average first printing 3,000. Publication within 1-2 yrs. No simultaneous submissions. Responds in 6-8 wks. Requires requested ms on disk. Prefers NRSV. Guidelines on Website; catalog for 9x12 SAE/4 stamps.

    Nonfiction: Query only (no unsolicited mss), fax/e-query OK. "Looking for books on Catholic faith and moral values, spiritual growth and development, and Christian formation for families."

    Fiction: Query only (no unsolicited mss). For children only.

    Tips: "Open to religion teacher's resources and adult catechetics. No biographical or autobiographical material."

PAULIST PRESS, 997 Macarthur Blvd., Mahwah NJ 07430. (201)825-7300. Fax (201)825-8345. E-mail: info@paulistpress.com. Website: www.paulistpress.com. Catholic. Lawrence Boadt, ed. dir. Catholic publisher that publishes books for a broad spiritual market with a particular focus on ecumenism, reconciliation, and dialog with people in search of faith. Imprints: Newman Press, HiddenSpring, Stimulus. Publishes 80 titles/yr. Receives 1,000 submissions annually. 15% of books from first-time authors. Accepts mss through agents. Prefers 100-400 pgs. Royalty 7-10% of net; advance $500-1,000. Average first printing 2,500. Publication within 18 mos. Considers simultaneous submissions (prefers 1st option). Requires requested ms on disk. Responds in 2 mos. Prefers NRSV. Guidelines on Website; free catalog.

    Nonfiction: Proposal/2 chapters or complete ms; e-query OK. "Looking for theology (Catholic and ecumenical Christian), popular spirituality, liturgy, and religious education texts." Children's books for 2-5, 5-8, 8-12, 9-14 years, as per guidelines; complete ms.

    Ethnic Books: A few Hispanic.

    Also Does: Booklets, pamphlets.

    Photos/Artwork: Accepts freelance photos for book covers.

    Tips: "Most open to good spirituality books that have solid input and a clear sense of tradition behind them. Demonstrate grounded convictions. Stay well read. Pay attention to contemporary social needs."

PETER PAUPER PRESS, 202 Mamaroneck Ave., Ste. 400, White Plains NY 10601-5376. Toll-free (800)833-2311. (914)681-0144. Fax (914)681-0389. E-mail: bpaulding@peter pauper.com. Website: www.peterpauper.com. Barbara Paulding, ed. dir.; Nick Beilenson, mng. ed. (nbeilenson@peterpauper.com). Does small-format, illustrated gift books. Imprint: Inspire Books (evangelical imprint). Publishes 2 religious titles/yr. Receives 30 submissions annually. 0% of books from first-time authors. Accepts mss through agents. No reprints.

Prefers 800-2,000 wds. Outright purchase only, $250-1,000. Average first printing 10,000. Publication within 1 yr. Considers simultaneous submissions. Requires requested ms on disk. Responds in 1 mo. Guidelines (request by e-mail that a copy be faxed); no catalog.

Nonfiction: Query by mail or e-mail. General inspirational themes.

Tips: "We want original aphorisms, 67-75 to a book. Title should be focused on a holiday or special occasion, family such as mother, sister, graduation, new baby, wedding, etc."

PELICAN PUBLISHING CO., INC., 1000 Burmaster St., Gretna LA 70053. (504)368-1175. Fax (504)368-1195. E-mail: editorial@pelicanpub.com. Website: www.pelicanpub.com. Nina Kooij, ed-in-chief. To publish books of quality and permanence that enrich the lives of those who read them. Imprints: Firebird Press, Jackson Square Press. Publishes 1 title/yr. Receives 250 submissions annually. No books from first-time authors. Accepts mss through agents. Reprints books. Prefers 200+ pgs. Royalty; some advances. Publication within 9-18 mos. No simultaneous submissions. Responds in 1 mo. on queries. Requires accepted ms on disk. Prefers KJV. Guidelines (also on Website); catalog for 9x12 SAE/6 stamps.

Nonfiction: Proposal/2 chapters; no phone/fax/e-query. Children's picture books to 1,100 wds.(send complete ms); middle readers about Louisiana (ages 8 & up) at least 25,000 wds.; cookbooks at least 200 recipes.

Fiction: Complete ms. For ages 5-8 only.

Photos/Artwork: Accepts freelance photos for book covers; open to queries from freelance artists.

Tips: "On inspirational titles we need a high-profile author who already has an established speaking circuit so books can be sold at these appearances."

PERIGEE BOOKS, 375 Hudson St., New York NY 10014. (212)366-2000. Fax (212)366-2365. Website: www.penguin.com. Penguin Group (USA), Inc. John Duff, pub.; Sheila Curry Oakes, exec. ed.; Michelle Howry, ed. (spirituality). Publishes 3-5 spirituality titles out of 55-60 titles/yr. Receives 300 submissions annually. 30% of books from first-time authors. Strongly prefers mss through agents (but accepts freelance). Prefers 60,000-80,000 wds. Royalty 6-7.5%; advance $5,000-150,000. Average first printing varies. Publication within 18 mos. Considers simultaneous submissions. Responds in 2 mos. Guidelines available with contract; free catalog.

Nonfiction: Query only; no phone/e-query; fax query OK. "Looking for spiritual, prescriptive, self-help, and women's issues; no memoirs or personal histories."

PFLAUM PUBLISHING GROUP, 2621 Dryden Rd., Ste. 300, Moraine OH 45439. (935)293-1415. Fax (937)293-1310. E-mail: kcannizzo@pflaum.com, or jeanlarkin@pflaum.com. Website: www.pflaum.com. Peter Li Education Group/Catholic. Karen Cannizzo, ed. dir., or Jean Larkin, ed. dir. Religious education resources for Catholic young people (preschool through high school), plus resources for catechists and teachers who work with Catholic young people. Publishes 10-20 titles/yr. Receives 25 submissions annually. 10% of books from first-time authors. Prefers mss through agents. No reprints. Royalty on net or outright purchase; advance depends on author arrangement. Average first printing 2,000. Publication within 9 mos. No simultaneous submissions. Requires accepted ms on disk or by e-mail. Responds as soon as possible. Prefers NRSV. Free guidelines/catalog.

Nonfiction: Proposal with at least 1 chapter; e-query OK. "We like user-friendly resources."

THE PILGRIM PRESS, 700 Prospect Ave. E., Cleveland OH 44115-1100. (216)736-3755. Fax (216)736-2207. E-mail: ksadler@thepilgrimpress.com. Website: www.thepilgrimpress .com. United Church of Christ. Timothy G. Staveteig, pub.; Kim Sadler, ed. dir. Church and educational resources. Publishes 54 titles/yr. Receives 500 submissions annually. 30% of books from first-time authors. Prefers mss through agents. Reprints books. Royalty 10% of net; or work-for-hire, one-time fee; negotiable advance. Average first printing 2,000.

Publication within 18 mos. No simultaneous submissions. Responds in 13 wks. Accepts submissions on disk or by e-mail. Guidelines (also by e-mail); free catalog.

Nonfiction: Query first. Proposal/2 chapters; e-query via Website.

Special Needs: Children's sermons, worship resources, youth materials, and religious materials for ethnic groups.

Ethnic Books: African American, Native American, Asian American, Pacific Islanders, and Hispanic.

Photos/Artwork: Accepts freelance photos for book covers.

Tips: "Most open to well-written manuscripts that address mainline Protestant-Christian needs and that use inclusive language and follow the *Chicago Manual of Style.*"

PLAYERS PRESS, INC., PO Box 1132, Studio City CA 91614-0132. (818)789-4980. Robert W. Gordon, ed. To create is to live life's purpose. Publishes only dramatic works. Publishes 1-5 religious titles/yr. Receives 600-1,200 submissions annually. 15-20% of books from first-time authors. Accepts mss through agents. Reprints books. Variable length. Variable royalty and advance. Average first printing 1,000-10,000. Publication within 12 mos. No simultaneous submissions. No submissions by disk or e-mail. Responds in 3 wks. on query; 3-12 mos. on ms. Guidelines; catalog for 9x12 SAE/5 stamps.

Nonfiction/Plays: Query only; no phone/fax/e-query. "Theatrical musicals; theater/film/ television how-tos; plays and theater crafts."

Special Needs: Theatre education.

Photos/Artwork: Accepts freelance photos for book covers.

Tips: "Most open to plays and books on theater, film, and television; also how-to."

#PREP PUBLISHING, 1110 1/2 Hay St., Fayetteville NC 28305. (910)483-6611. Fax (910)483-2439. E-mail: preppub@aol.com. Website: www.prep-pub.com. PREP, Inc. Anne McKinney, mng. ed. (mckinney@prep-pub.com); submit to Frances Sweeney (sweeney@prep-pub .com). Books to enrich people's lives and help them find joy in human experience. Publishes 10 titles/yr. Receives 1,500+ submissions annually. 85% of books from first-time authors. Reprints books. Prefers 250 pgs. Royalty 6-10% of retail; advance. Average first printing 3,000-5,000. Publication within 18 mos. Considers simultaneous submissions. Responds in 1 mo. Guidelines (also on Website) & catalog for #10 SAE/2 stamps.

Nonfiction: Query only; no phone query.

Fiction: Query only (cover letter and up to 3-page synopsis). If you send a complete manuscript (send to Janet Abernathy), include a check for $150 for a paid critique. All ages. "We are attempting to grow our Judeo-Christian fiction imprint."

Tips: "Rewrite, rewrite, rewrite with your reader clearly in focus."

G. P. PUTNAM'S SONS, a division of Penguin/Books for Young Readers, 345 Hudson St., 14th Fl., New York NY 10014. (212)366-2000. Fax (212)366-2664. Website: www.penguin putnam.com. Submit to Children's Manuscript Editor. Imprint: G. P. Putnam's Sons. Publishes 45 titles/yr. Accepts mss through agents. Variable royalty on retail; variable advance. Considers simultaneous submissions. No disk or e-mail submissions. Responds in 6 mos. Guidelines free.

Nonfiction: Query only. "We publish some religious/inspirational books and books for ages 2-18."

Fiction: For children or teens. Complete ms for picture books; proposal/3 chapters for novels. Primarily picture books or middle-grade novels.

QUINTESSENTIAL BOOKS, PO Box 8755, Kansas City MO 64114-0755. (816)214-4289. Fax (816)561-4109. E-mail: mjanson@quintessentialbooks.com, or ljoyce@quintessential books.com. Website: www.quintessentialbooks.com. Laura C. Joyce, ed. dir. Books that will challenge people to think deeply and live passionately in accordance with sound principles. Publishes 3-4 titles/yr. Receives 75-100 submissions annually. 10% of books from first-time authors. Prefers mss through agents. Reprints books. Prefers 60,000-70,000 wds. or 224 pgs. Royalty on net; advance. Average first printing varies. Publication within 18 mos. Considers simultaneous submissions. Responds in 3-4 mos. Requires requested ms by e-mail. Prefers NIV or NLT. Guidelines (also by e-mail/Website).

Nonfiction: Query only; no phone/fax query. "Looking for family/parenting, personal responsibility, and leadership."

Fiction: Query only. For teens & adults.

Photos/Artwork: Accepts freelance photos for book covers; open to queries from freelance artists.

Tips: "Most open to something that is crisp, fresh, provocative, cutting-edge/iconoclastic, but kind/generous at the same time."

**Note: This publisher serviced by The Writer's Edge.

RAGGED EDGE PRESS, 73 W. Burd St., PO Box 708, Shippenburg PA 17257. (717)532-2237. Fax (717)532-6110. E-mail: marketing@whitemane.com, or editorial@whitemane.com. Website: www.whitemane.com. White Mane Publishing Co., Inc. Harold E. Collier, acq. ed. Christian, social science, and self-help books to make a difference in people's lives. Publishes 10-15 titles/yr. Receives 50-75 submissions annually. 50% of books from first-time authors. **SUBSIDY PUBLISHES 20%.** Reprints books. Prefers 200 pgs. Variable royalty on net; no advance. Average first printing 3,000. Publication within 12-18 mos. Considers simultaneous submissions. Responds in 30-90 days. Free guidelines (also by e-mail)/catalog.

Nonfiction: Query only; fax/e-query OK.

Tips: "Most open to a Protestant book in the middle of the spectrum."

RAINBOW PUBLISHERS, Box 261129, San Diego CA 92196. (858)668-3260. Fax (858)668-3328. E-mail: rainbowed@earthlink.nct. Wcbsitc: www.rainbowpublishers.com. Christy Scannell, ed. dir. Publishes Bible-teaching, reproducible books for children's teachers. Publishes 20 titles/yr. Receives 250 submissions annually. 50% of books from first-time authors. Reprints books. Prefers 96 pgs. Outright purchases $640 & up. Average first printing 2,500. Publication within 2 yrs. Considers simultaneous submissions. Responds in 3 mos. No disk or e-mail submissions. Prefers NIV. Guidelines (also on Website); catalog for 9x12 SAE/2 stamps.

Nonfiction: Proposal/2-5 chapters; no phone/e-query. "Looking for fun and easy ways to teach Bible concepts to kids, ages 2-12."

Special Needs: Creative puzzles and unique games.

Tips: "Request a catalog or visit your Christian bookstore to see what we have already published. We have over 100 titles and do not like to repeat topics, so a proposal needs to be unique for us but not necessarily unique in the market. Most open to writing that appeals to teachers who work with kids and Bible activities that have been tried and tested on today's kids. No preachy, old-fashioned methods."

+RANDALL HOUSE PUBLICATIONS, 114 Bush Rd., Nashville TN 37217. Toll-free (800)877-7030. (615)361-1221. Fax (615)367-0535. E-mail: dianne@randallhouse.com. Website: www.randallhouse.com. Free Will Baptist. Dianne Sargent, assoc. ed. Publishes Sunday school and Christian education materials to make Christ known, from a conservative perspective. Publishes 5 titles/yr. 50% of books from first-time authors. Accepts mss through agents. Reprints books. Royalty 10% on retail after start-up costs; no advance. Publication within 6 mos. Considers simultaneous submissions. Accepted ms on disk. Responds in 8 wks. Prefers KJV. Guidelines; no catalog.

Nonfiction: Query first; no phone/fax query; e-query OK. Must fill out book proposal form they provide.

Fiction: For all ages. Query first; no phone/fax query; e-query OK. Must fill out book proposal form they provide.

Special Needs: Accepts queries for articles based on the topics indicated in the Periodical Topical listings section of this guide. Follow the same procedures for submitting as the book queries.

Photos/Artwork: Open to queries from freelance artists (matt@randallhouse.com).

Tips: "We are expanding our book division with a conservative perspective."

+RAVENHAWK BOOKS, 7739 E. Broadway Blvd., #95, Tucson AZ 85710. E-mail: ravenhawk6dof@yahoo.com. The 6DOF Company. Hans B. Shepherd or Carl Lasky, eds. Publishes variable number of titles/yr. Receives 20-30 submissions annually. 70% of books from first-time authors. Print-on-demand. Reprints books. Royalty 40-55% on gross profits; no advance. Average first printing 2,500. Publication in up to 18 mos.

Nonfiction: Query first. "Looking for profitable books from talented writers."

Fiction: Query first. For all ages.

Photos/Artwork: Open to queries from freelance artists.

Tips: "Most open to crisp, creative, entertaining writing that also informs and educates. Writing, as any creative art, is a gift from God. Not everyone has the innate talent to do it well. We are author-oriented. We don't play games with the numbers."

READ 'N RUN BOOKS, PO Box 294, Rhododendron OR 97049. Crumb Elbow Publishing. Michael P. Jones, pub. Books of lasting interest. Publishes 2 titles/yr. Receives 150 submissions annually. 90% of books from first-time authors. Reprints books. Royalty 30-50% of net; no advance; **SOME COOPERATIVE PUBLISHING.** Average first printing 500-1,000. Publication within 1 yr. Considers simultaneous submissions. Responds in 2-5 wks. No disk. Guidelines; catalog $3.

Nonfiction: Complete ms; no phone/fax query. "Looking for books on cults/occult, history, and prophecy."

Fiction: Complete ms. Any type; any age. Looking for historical fiction of the Northwest, Oregon, or the West.

Ethnic Books: Open to ethnic books.

Also Does: Booklets, pamphlets, tracts, e-books, postcards, note cards, posters.

Photos/Artwork: Accepts freelance photos for book covers.

Contest: Poetry contest. Send SASE for information.

Tips: "Nature and history are two areas we are seriously looking at but are also interested in poetry and short-story collections." Send copies only; no originals.

+REALMS, 600 Rinehart Rd., Lake Mary FL 32746. (407)333-6000. E-mail: jeff.gerke@strang.com. Website: www.realmsfiction.com. Strang Communications. Jeff Gerke, sr. ed. Publishes exclusively in the realm of Christian visionary fiction. Publishes 6-10 titles/yr. Receives 500 submissions annually. 50% of books from first-time authors. Prefers mss through agents. No reprints. Prefers 75,000-125,000 wds. Royalty; advance. Average first printing 10,000. Publication within 16 mos. Considers simultaneous submissions. Responds in 3-6 mos. Guidelines on Website; free catalog.

Fiction: Query first: e-query OK. Also does time travel, alternate history, supernatural thrillers, spiritual warfare, visionary fiction.

Photos/Artwork: Open to queries from freelance artists

Tips: "The ideal Realms proposal will offer a fresh and original story with a large supernatural and/or speculative component. Every Realms novel is a portal to another world or plane of existence. Ideal proposals will be written according to the principles found in *Self-Editing for Fiction Writers*."

REFERENCE SERVICE PRESS, 5000 Windplay Dr., Ste. 4, El Dorado Hills CA 95762. (916)939-9620. Fax (916)939-9626. E-mail: info@rspfunding.com. Website: www.rspfunding.com. Stuart Hauser, ed. Books related to financial aid and Christian higher education. Publishes 1 title/yr. Receives 3-5 submissions annually. Most books from first-time authors. No reprints. Royalty 10% on net; usually no advance. Publication within 5 mos. May consider simultaneous submissions. No guidelines; free catalog for 2 stamps.

Nonfiction: Proposal/several chapters.

Special Needs: Financial aid directories for Christian college students.

REGAL BOOKS, 2300 Knoll Dr., Ventura CA 93003. Does not accept unsolicited manuscripts. ****Note:** This publisher serviced by The Writer's Edge.

REGNERY PUBLISHING, One Massachusetts Ave. N.W., Washington DC 20001. Toll-free (888)219-4747. (202)216-0600. Fax (202)216-0612. E-mail: submissions@regnery .com, or editorial@regnery.com. Website: www.regnery.com. Eagle Publishing. Harry Crocker, exec. ed.; submit to Submissions Editor. Trade publisher that does scholarly Catholic books and evangelical Protestant books. Imprint: Gateway Editions. Publishes 2-4 religious titles/yr. Receives 30-50 submissions annually. Few books from first-time authors. Requires mss through agents. Reprints books. Prefers 250-500 pgs. Royalty 8-15% on retail; advances to $50,000. Average first printing 5,000. Publication within 1 yr. Considers simultaneous submissions. Responds in 3 mos. Free catalog.

Nonfiction: Accepts manuscripts through agents only. Proposal/1-3 chapters or query; no fax/e-query. Looking for history, popular biography, and popular history.

Tips: "Religious books should relate to politics, history, current affairs, biography, and public policy. Most open to a book that deals with a topical issue from a conservative point of view—something that points out a need for spiritual renewal or a how-to book on finding spiritual renewal."

RELIGIOUS EDUCATION PRESS, 5316 Meadow Brook Rd., Birmingham AL 34242. (205)991-1000. Fax (205)991-9669. E-mail: releduc@ix.netcom.com. Website: www.bham.net/ releduc. Unaffiliated. James Michael Lee, ed. Mission is specifically directed toward helping fulfill, in an interfaith and ecumenical way, the Great Commission. Publishes 5-6 titles/yr. Receives 500 submissions annually. 40% of books from first-time authors. Prefers 200-500 pgs. Royalty 5% of net; advance. Average first printing 2,000. Publication within 9 mos. Responds in 1 mo. Requires requested ms on disk. Guidelines; free catalog.

Tips: "We are not accepting manuscripts for the foreseeable future."

RESOURCE PUBLICATIONS, INC., 160 E. Virginia St., Ste. 290, San Jose CA 95112-5876. (408)286-8505. Fax (408)287-8748. E-mail: info@rpinet.com. Website: www.rpinet.com. William Burns, pub. Publishes 10 titles/yr. Receives 450 submissions annually. 30% of books from first-time authors. Prefers 50,000 wds. Royalty 8% of net; rare advance. Average first printing 3,000. Publication within 1 yr. Responds in 10 wks. Prefers requested ms on disk. Guidelines on Website; catalog on Website or for 9x12 SAE/$1.42 postage (mark "Media Mail").

Nonfiction: Proposal/1 chapter; phone/fax/e-query OK.

Fiction: Query. Adult/teen/children. Only read-aloud stories for storytellers; fables and parables. "Must be useful in ministerial, counseling, or educational settings."

Also Does: Computer programs; aids to ministry or education. E-books.

Tips: "Know our market. We cater to ministers in Catholic and mainstream Protestant settings. We are not an evangelical house or general interest publisher."

REVELL BOOKS, Box 6287, Grand Rapids MI 49516. (616)676-9185. Fax (616)676-2315. E-mail: lhdupont@bakerbooks.com. Website: www.bakerbooks.com. Baker Publishing Group. Publishes inspirational fiction and nonfiction for the broadest Christian market. No freelance. Submit through Writer's Edge or ECPA First Edition.

REVIEW AND HERALD PUBLISHING ASSN., 55 W. Oak Ridge Dr., Hagerstown MD 21740-7390. (301)393-3000. Fax (301)393-4055. E-mail: editorial@rhpa.org. Website: www.rhpa.org. Seventh-day Adventist. Richard Coffen, VP/editorial; Jeannette Johnson, acq. ed. No freelance.

#RISING STAR PRESS, 2532 N.W. Shields Dr., Bend OR 97701-6714. E-mail: editor@ risingstarpress.com, or RSPEditor@earthlink.net. Website: www.RisingStarPress.com. Donna Jacobsen, acq. ed. Overall focus is on intellect/values/spiritual agreement in life and work. Publishes 2 titles/yr. Receives 200 submissions annually. 90% of books from first-time authors. No mss through agents. Length open. Royalty 15% of net; average advance $750. Average first printing 2,000. Publication within 10 mos. Considers simultaneous submissions. Responds in 6-8 wks. Prefers accepted mss by e-mail; disk OK. Guidelines on Website; no catalog.

> **Nonfiction:** Query only; e-query OK.
>
> **Photos/Artwork:** Accepts freelance photos for book covers.
>
> **Tips:** "Books are selected based on the combination of fit with the company mission, consistency between the author's words and life, and marketability. Looking for books on 'open' and 'accepting' religion as a topic."

RIVEROAK PUBLISHING, Historical and contemporary fiction. Jeff Dunn, acq. ed. See Cook Communications Ministries for details.

ROSE PUBLISHING, 4733 Torrance Blvd., #259, Torrance CA 90503. Toll-free (800)532-4278. (310)370-8962. Fax (310)370-7492. E-mail: carolatrose@aol.com. Website: www.rose-publishing.com. Nondenominational. Carol Witte, mng. ed. Publishes primarily Bible studies; Sunday school wall charts and visual aids. Publishes 5-10 titles/yr. 5% of projects from first-time authors. No mss through agents. No reprints. Outright purchases. Publication within 18 mos. Considers simultaneous submissions. Requires accepted mss by disk or e-mail. Responds in 2-3 mos. Catalog for 9x12 SAE/4 stamps.

> **Nonfiction:** Query only. No books, mainly booklets/pamphlets, wall charts/posters, or PowerPoints.
>
> **Special Needs:** Query with sketch of proposed chart or poster (nonreturnable); fax query OK; e-query OK if less than 100 wds. (copied into message). No e-mail attachments. Open to basic wall charts that every Sunday school classroom needs; reference wall charts that make difficult Bible topics or theological topics easier; wall charts for children and youth; wall charts on Old Testament and New Testament topics; study guides and worksheets (grades 4-8) on sharing your faith with skeptics or salvation; and wall charts on modern heroes or comfort in time of trouble. Also open to pamphlets on marriage enrichment, a book of the Bible (Acts, Romans, Luke), church history, world religions, angels, end times, prayer (conversing with God), Holy Spirit, Websites and good stuff for teens, self-respect, pornography, resisting temptation, cults, men in leadership, or mentoring boys.
>
> **Also Does:** Power Point presentations for biblical subjects.
>
> **Photos/Artwork:** Open to queries from freelance artists.
>
> **Tips:** "Now accepting more freelance submissions. Material for children, youth, Bible study charts and study guides, pamphlets, maps, time lines, and Power Points." No fiction.

SCARECROW PRESS, 4501 Forbes Blvd., Ste. 200, Lanham MD 20706. (301)459-3366. Fax (301)429-5748. E-mail: mdillon@scarecrowpress.com. Website: www.scarecrow press.com. Rowman & Littlefield Publishing Group. Martin Dillon, acq. ed. Provides reference and professional materials for librarians. Publishes 150-200 titles/yr. Receives 600-700 submissions annually. 20% of books from first-time authors. Accepts mss through agents. Reprints books. Prefers 250-300 pgs. Royalty 5-15% of net; no advance. Average first printing 500. Publication within 9 mos. No simultaneous submissions. Responds in 2-4 mos. Requires requested ms on disk. Guidelines on Website; free catalog.

> **Nonfiction:** Proposal/2-3 chapters; e-query OK. "Looking for reference, religion, and scholarly books." New: educational administration.
>
> **Tips:** "Most open to reference, music, and scholarly books. Should be well researched and

address issues from a scholarly point of view. We consider submissions only from college-educated writers."

SCEPTER PUBLISHERS, INC., PO Box 211, New York NY 10018. (212)354-0670. Fax (212)354-0736. E-mail: scepter@scepterpublishers.org. Website: www.scepterpublishers.org. Catholic. Bernard Browne, ed. Books on how to struggle to live faith and virtue in one's daily life. Publishes 20 titles/yr. 0-2% of books from first-time authors. Accepts mss through agents. Reprints books. Prefers 200-250 pgs. Royalty on net; advance $2,000-10,000. Average first printing 2,000. Publication within 24 mos. No simultaneous submissions. Responds after 12 mos. No guidelines; free catalog.

   Nonfiction: Query only first; no phone/fax/e-query.

   Fiction: Query only first; no phone/fax/e-query.

   Tips: "Looking for short, practical books addressing reader needs."

SCRIPTURE PRESS—See Cook Communications Ministries.

#SELAH PUBLISHING GROUP, LLC., 16238 W. Young St., Surprise AZ 85374-5744. E-mail: garlen@selahbooks.com. Website: www.selahbooks.com. Garlen Jackson, pub. A publisher that does not water down the author's message. Publishes 45 titles/yr. Receives 20 submissions annually. 75% of books from first-time authors. Prefers mss through agents. Reprints books. Prefers 40,000 wds. or 144 pgs. Royalty 12-18% of net; no advance. Average first printing 2,500. Publication within 6 mos. No simultaneous submissions. Prefers requested ms on disk. Responds in 2 mos. Prefers ASV. Guidelines by e-mail; free catalog.

   Nonfiction: Complete ms; no phone/fax/e-query.

   Fiction: Complete ms; no phone/fax/e-query. For all ages.

   Also Does: E-books.

   Photos/Artwork: Accepts freelance photos for book covers.

   Tips: "Most open to time-sensitive, current events, and controversial books. Writers should spend more time selling who they are in regards to character and integrity."

SHAW BOOKS—WaterBrook Press no longer publishing under this imprint.

SHEED & WARD, 4501 Forbes Blvd., Ste. 200, Lanham MD 20706. (301)459-3366. Fax (312)664-5846. E-mail: jeremy.langford@rowman.com. Website: www.sheedandward.com. Rowman & Littlefield Publishers, Inc. Submit to The Editor. Publishes books of contemporary impact and enduring merit in Catholic-Christian thought and action. Publishes 25-30 titles/yr. Receives 2,000 submissions annually. 25% of books from first-time authors. Does print-on-demand. Reprints books. Prefers 35,000-65,000 wds. Royalty 6-12% on retail; $500-2,000 advance. Average first printing 3,000. Publication within 8 mos. No simultaneous submissions. Responds in 1-2 mos. Requires requested ms on disk. Prefers NAB, NRSV (Catholic editions). Guidelines/catalog on Website.

   Nonfiction: Proposal/2 chapters; phone/fax/e-query OK. "Looking for parish ministry (health care, spirituality, leadership, general trade books for mass audiences, sacraments, small group, or priestless parish facilitating books)."

   Photos/Artwork: Considers photos/artwork as part of book package.

   Tips: "Looking for general trade titles and academic titles (oriented toward the classroom) in areas of spirituality, parish ministry, leadership, sacraments, prayer, faith formation, church history, and scripture."

SILAS PUBLISHING, 1154 Westchester Dr., Lilburn GA 30047. (404)625-9217. E-mail: info@silasinteractive.com. Website: www.silasinteractive.com. Independent Christian publisher. Scott Philip Stewart, ed. Publishes Christian care books and software to help 21st century Christians and seekers and those who minister to them. Publishes 10 titles/yr. Receives 60 submissions annually. 80% of books from first-time authors. Accepts mss through agents. Reprints books. Royalty 10-12% of net; some outright purchases; some advances. Publication within 6 mos. Considers simultaneous submissions, if notified. Accepts requested manuscript on disk or by e-mail. Responds in 1 wk. Guidelines by e-mail/Website.

Nonfiction: Proposal/2-3 chapters; prefers e-mail query.

Fiction: Novella-length, "self-help" fiction (see Website for details).

Special Needs: Self-help, personal growth, counseling aids, resources for peer and professional Christian caregivers and counselors.

Also Does: Interactive multimedia; book/CD sets

Tips: "Most open to grace-full self-help/personal growth books written from a unique angle designed to help hurting believers and seekers and those who minister to them."

SILOAM, 600 Rinehart Rd., Lake Mary FL 32746. (407)333-0600. E-mail: jeff@strang.com. Website: www.siloam.com. Strang Communications. Jeff Gerke, sr. ed. Health and fitness books from a Christian perspective. Publishes 12-15 titles/yr. Prefers mss through agents. Prefers 45,000-75,000 wds. Royalty; advance. Considers simultaneous submissions. Responds in 4-6 mos. Guidelines on Website.

Nonfiction: Query first; no phone/fax query; e-query OK.

Special Needs: Fitness, health issues, nutrition, medical issues, relationships, sex and intimacy, alternative medicine (no New Age), integrative medicine, conventional medicine, and emotional health.

Tips: "Wellness is a major concern in America, and Christians want timely answers grounded in Scripture and informed by the latest science. The ideal Siloam author is professionally qualified to write on his or her topic, writes well and with passion, has an established audience or marketing platform, writes from an evangelical world-view, and writes on a health or fitness topic about which a wide Christian audience will be interested."

SKYSONG PRESS, 35 Peter St. S., Orillia ON L3V 5A8, Canada. E-mail: sky song@bconnex.net. Website: www.bconnex.net/~skysong. Steve Stanton, ed. Imprints: Dreams & Visions, Sky Song. Publishes 2+ titles/yr. Guidelines on Website.

Fiction: Publishers of Christian literary fiction under the imprints Dreams & Visions, Sky Songs, and Skysong Science Fiction. "New authors should not submit novel manuscripts. Send us something for Dreams & Visions (see periodical section) first."

SMYTH & HELWYS PUBLISHING, INC., 6316 Peake Rd., Macon GA 31210-3960. Toll-free (800)747-3016. (478)757-0564. Fax (478)757-1305. E-mail: Proposals@helwys.com, or mcelroy@helwys.com. Website: www.helwys.com. Dr. Keith Gammons, book ed. (keith@ helwys.com); Mark McElroy, sr. ed. Quality resources for the church, the academy, and individual Christians who are nurtured by faith and informed by scholarship. Publishes 25-30 titles/yr. Receives 600 submissions annually. 40% of books from first-time authors. Prefers 144 pgs. Royalty 7%. Considers simultaneous submissions. Responds in 3 mos. Free guidelines (also by e-mail/Website); free catalog.

Nonfiction: Query only; fax/e-query OK. "Manuscripts requested for topics appropriate for mainline church and seminary/university textbook market."

Also Does: E-books. Copies of print books and original books. Go to: www.nextsunday.com.

Tips: "Most open to books with a strong secondary or special market. Niche titles and short-run options available for specialty subjects."

*SOWER'S PRESS, PO Box 666306, Marietta GA 30066. Phone/fax (770)977-3784. Jamey Wood, ed. Books to further establish the ministries of speakers and teachers. Publishes 2-3 titles/yr. Responds in 1 mo.

Nonfiction: Proposal/chapters. Marriage and family books.

SQUARE ONE PUBLISHERS, 115 Herricks Rd., New Hyde Park NY 11040-5341. (516)535-2010. Fax (516)535-2014. E-mail: sq1info@aol.com. Website: www.squareonepublishers .com. Rudy Shur, ed. Strives to satisfy readers' hunger for knowledge by providing reliable information on meaningful topics, including religion. Publishes 6 religious titles/yr. Receives 100 submissions annually. 35% of books from first-time authors. Prefers mss through agents. Reprints books. Prefers 80,000 wds. Royalty 10-15% of net; advance $2,500 & up. Average first printing 6,000-8,000. Publication within 12-18 mos. Considers simultaneous submissions. Accepts requested ms on disk. Responds in 4 wks. Guidelines on Website; free catalog.

Nonfiction: Query with overview, table of contents, author information, potential audience, and SASE; no phone/fax/e-query.

Tips: "Inspirational books and books on spirituality that do not overly focus on one particular denomination would have the greatest appeal to our firm."

STANDARD PUBLISHING, 8121 Hamilton Ave., Cincinnati OH 45231. (513)931-4050. Fax (513)931-0950. E-mail: books@standardpub.com. Website: www.standardpub.com. Standex International Corp. Diane Stortz, ed. dir., Family Resources; Ruth Frederick, ed. dir., Children & Youth Church Resources; Mark Taylor, ed. dir., Adult Church Resources. An evangelical Christian publisher of books, curriculum, classroom resources. Following are the trade book departments for this company (see guidelines or Website for details): Children & Tween (ages birth-12), publishes 25 titles/yr.; 25% freelance. Teen/Young Adult (ages 13-22). Adults. Royalty & work-for-hire; advance. Average first printing 10,000 (depends on product). Publication within 18 mos. Considers simultaneous submissions. Responds in 3-6 mos. Guidelines (also on Website); catalog $2. See Website for submissions information.

Nonfiction: Query for classroom resources.

**Note: This publisher serviced by The Writer's Edge.

ST. ANTHONY MESSENGER PRESS and **FRANCISCAN COMMUNICATIONS,** 28 W. Liberty St., Cincinnati OH 45202. Toll-free (800)488-0488. (513)241-5615, ext. 123. Fax (513)241-0399. E-mail: StAnthony@AmericanCatholic.org. Website: www.American Catholic.org. Catholic. Lisa Biedenbach, ed. dir. (lisab@AmericanCatholic.org); Katie Carroll, book ed; Mary Hackett, book ed. Seeks to publish affordable resources for living a Catholic-Christian lifestyle. Imprints: Servant Books, Franciscan Communications, Fischer Productions, and Ikonographics (videos). Publishes 10-12 titles/yr. Receives 250 submissions annually. 5% of books from first-time authors. Accepts mss through agent. Reprints books (seldom). Prefers 25,000-50,000 wds. or 100-300 pgs. Royalty 10-12% on net; advance $1,000. Average first printing 5,000. Publication within 18 mos. No simultaneous submissions. Requires accepted ms on disk; e-mail OK. Responds in 5-9 wks. Prefers NRSV. Guidelines on Website; catalog for 9x12 SAE/4 stamps.

Nonfiction: Query only/500-wd. summary; fax/e-query OK. "Looking for family-based catechetical programs; living the Catholic-Christian life at home and in workplace; and Franciscan topics."

Special Needs: Catholic identity; spirituality; resources for new and inactive Catholics.

Ethnic Books: Hispanic, occasionally.

Tips: "Most open to books with sound Catholic doctrine that include personal experiences or anecdotes applicable to today's culture. Our books are decidedly Catholic."

**Note: 2001 First Place Best Website—Catholic Press Assn. of the U.S. and Canada.

ST. AUGUSTINE'S PRESS, PO Box 2285, South Bend IN 46680. (574)291-3500. Fax (574)291-3700. E-mail: bruce@staugustine.net. Website: www.staugustine.net. A conservative, nondenominational (although mostly Catholic) scholarly publisher of academic titles, mainly in academic philosophy, theology, and cultural history. Bruce Fingerhut, pres. Publishes 20-40 titles/yr. Receives 100+ submissions annually. 5% of books from first-time authors. Accepts mss through agents. Reprints books. Royalty 6-15% of net; advance $1,000. Average first printing 1,000. Publication within 1 yr. Considers simultaneous submissions. Responds in 3 mos. No guidelines; free catalog.

Nonfiction: Query or proposal/chapters. "Most of our titles are philosophy."

Tips: "Most open to books on subjects or by authors similar to what/who we already publish."

STEEPLE HILL, 233 Broadway, Ste. 1001, New York NY 10279-0001. (212)553-4200. Fax (212)277-8969. E-mail: Emily_Rodmell@harlequin.ca. Website: www.SteepleHill.com. Harlequin Enterprises. Submit to any of the following: Joan Marlow Golan, exec. ed.; Krista Stroever, assoc. sr. ed.; Diane Dietz, asst. ed.; Emily Rodmell, ed. asst. Single title, trade paperback Christian women's fiction that will help women guide themselves and their families toward purposeful, faith-driven lives. Lines: Love Inspired (mass-market category romances), see separate listing; Love Inspired Suspense; Steeple Hill Café (women's fiction). Publishes 96-108 titles/yr. Receives 500-1,000 submissions annually. 15% of books from first-time authors. Accepts mss through agents. No reprints. Prefers 80,000-125,000 wds. or 350-500 pgs. Royalty on retail; competitive advance. Publication within 12-24 mos. Considers simultaneous submissions for trade books, not for mass market. Requires accepted ms on disk/hard copy. Responds in 3 mos. Prefers KJV. Guidelines (also by e-mail/Website): no catalog.

Fiction: Query letter for single titles or complete ms for series; no phone/fax/e-query.

Tips: "We want quality inspirational novels that focus on the more complex and thoughtfully developed stories, with many characters, subplots, and so on. They are mostly character-driven, depicting sympathetic protagonists as they learn important lessons about the power of faith. Subgenres include relationship novels, contemporary and historical romances, family dramas, Christian chick lit, romantic suspense, mysteries, and thrillers."

STILL WATERS REVIVAL BOOKS, 4710—37A Ave., Edmonton AB T6L 3T5, Canada. (708)450-3730. Fax (708)468-1096. E-mail: swrb@swrb.com. Website: www.swrb.com. Covenanter Church. Reg Barrow, pres. Publishes 100 titles/yr. Receives few submissions. Very few books from first-time authors. Reprints books. Prefers 128-160 pgs. Negotiated royalty or outright purchase. Considers simultaneous submissions. Catalog for 9x12 SAE/2 stamps.

Nonfiction: Proposal/2 chapters.

Tips: "Only open to books defending the Covenanted Reformation, nothing else."

+STORYTIME PRESS, INC., 427 W. Main, Brighton MI 48116. Toll-free (866)897-2665. Fax (810)229-8906. E-mail: storytimepress@yahoo.com. Website: www.storytimepress.com. Publishes children's picture books.

THE SUMMIT PUBLISHING GROUP, 3649 Conflans Rd., #103, Irving TX 75061. (972)399-8856. Fax (972)313-9060. E-mail: jbertolet@tapestrypressinc.com. Website: www.tapestrypressinc.com. Tapestry Press, Inc. Jill Bertolet, pub. Secular publisher of contemporary nonfiction books, including some religious; custom publishing or partnership between author and publisher. Publishes 10-15 titles/yr. Receives 1,000 submissions annually. 50% of books from first-time authors. Accepts mss through agents. Reprints books. Royalty on net; small advance. Publication within 6-12 mos. Considers simultaneous submissions. Responds in 3-6 mos. Guidelines on Website; no catalog.

Nonfiction: Query only; fax/e-query OK. Looking for gardening, cooking, and business.

Tips: "Books need national distribution appeal. Author's media experience, contacts, and exposure are a strong plus."

TAN BOOKS AND PUBLISHERS, INC., 2020 Harrison Ave., PO Box 424, Rockford IL 61105. Toll-free (800)437-5876, ext. 205. (815)226-7777. Fax (815)226-7770. E-mail: taneditor@tanbooks.com. Website: www.TanBooks.com. Catholic. Thomas A. Nelson, ed. Not included in topical listings. No questionnaire returned.

T & T CLARK INTERNATIONAL, (formerly Trinity Press International) PO Box 1321, Harrisburg PA 17108. (717)541-8130. Fax (717)541-8136. E-mail: hcarriga@morehouse group.com. Website: www.tandtclarkinternational.com. The Morehouse Group. Henry L. Carrigan Jr., ed. dir. A nondenominational, academic religious publisher. Imprints: Trinity Press International, Continuum. Publishes 50-60 titles/yr. Receives 150-200 submissions annually. 3% of books from first-time authors. Accepts mss through agents. Reprints books. Royalty 10% of net; advance $500 & up. Average first printing 1,000. Publication within 9 mos. Considers simultaneous submissions. Responds in 3-6 mos. Prefers NRSV. Guidelines (also by e-mail); free catalog.

Nonfiction: Proposal/1 chapter, or complete ms; fax/e-query OK. "Looking for biblical studies, theology, religion, and music." No dissertations or essays.

Special Needs: Religion and film; American religious history; and religion and science.

Photos/Artwork: Accepts freelance photos for book covers.

Tips: "Most open to a book that is academic, to be used in undergraduate biblical studies, theology, or religious studies programs."

TAPESTRY PRESS, INC., 3649 Conflans Rd., #103, Irving TX 75061. (972)399-8856. Fax (972)313-9060. E-mail: jbertolet@tapestrypressinc.com, or info@tapestrypressinc.com. Website: www.tapestrypressinc.com. Jill Bertolet, pub. Secular publisher of contemporary nonfiction books, including some religious; custom publishing or partnership between author and publisher. Publishes 10-15 titles/yr. Receives 1,000 submissions annually. 50% of books from first-time authors. Accepts mss through agents. Reprints books. Royalty on net. Publication within 6-12 mos. Considers simultaneous submissions. Responds in 3-6 mos. Guidelines on Website; no catalog.

Nonfiction: Query only; fax/e-query OK. Looking for gardening, cooking, and business.

Tips: "Books need national distribution appeal. Author's media experience, contacts, and exposure are a strong plus."

JEREMY P. TARCHER, 375 Hudson St., New York NY 10014. (212)366-2000. Fax (212)366-2670. Website: www.penguinputnam.com. Penguin Putnam, Inc. Mitch Horowitz, Sara Carder, eds. Publishes ideas and works about human consciousness that are large enough to include matters of spirit and religion. Publishes 40-50 titles/yr. Receives 1,500 submissions annually. 10% of books from first-time authors. Accepts mss through agents. Royalty 5-8% of retail; advance. Considers simultaneous submissions. Free catalog.

Nonfiction: Query. Religion.

TATE PUBLISHING & ENTERPRISES, LLC., Tate Publishing Bldg., 127 E. Trade Center Ter., Mustang OK 73064-4421. (405)376-4900. Fax (405)376-4401. E-mail: info@tate publishing.com. Website: www.tatepublishing.com. David Dolphin, dir. of production; submit to acq. sr. ed. Publishes 120 titles/yr. Receives 11,000 submissions annually. 90% of books from first-time authors. Accepts mss through agents. **SUBSIDY PUBLISHES 2%.** Print-on-demand possible. No reprints. Any length. Royalty 15-40% of net; variable advance. First printing varies. Publication within 6-8 mos. Considers simultaneous submissions. Responds in 3-6 wks. Accepts e-mail submissions. Any Bible version. Guidelines (also by e-mail/Website); free catalog.

Nonfiction: Proposal with synopsis & any number of chapters, or complete ms; phone/fax/e-query OK. Any topic. "Looking for books that sell."

Fiction: Proposal with synopsis & any number of chapters or complete ms; phone/fax/e-query OK. For all ages.

Ethnic Books: Hispanic

Photos/Artwork: Rarely accepts freelance photos for book covers; open to queries from freelance artists.

Tips: "We invest resources in every work we accept, and only accept first-time authors."

**Note: This publisher services by The Writer's Edge and ECPA First Edition.

TAU-PUBLISHING, 1422 E. Edgemont Ave., Phoenix AZ 85006. (602)264-4828. Fax (602)248-9656. E-mail: phoenixartist@msn.com. Website: www.tau-publishing.org. Catholic. Jeffrey Campbell, pub. Imprints: Aleph-First. Publishes 3-4 titles/yr. Receives 25 submissions annually. 50% of books from first-time authors. Prefers mss through agents. **SOME SUBSIDY.** Reprints books. Prefers 25,000-50,000 wds. or 100-200 pgs. Royalty on net; no advance. Average first printing 3,000. Publication within 8 mos. Considers simultaneous submissions. Responds in 4-6 mos. Guidelines on Website; no catalog.

  Nonfiction: Query; fax/e-query OK. "Looking for Catholic inspirational material; reflections and meditations."

  Photos/Artwork: Accepts freelance photos for book covers.

THIRD WORLD PRESS, PO Box 19730, Chicago IL 60619. (773)651-0700. Fax (773)651-7286. E-mail: GwenMTWP@aol.com, or twpress3@aol.com. Website: www.ThirdWorld PressInc.com. Bennett Johnson, ed. African American publisher. Publishes 20 titles/yr. Receives 400-500 submissions annually. 20% of books from first-time authors. Few mss through agents. Reprints books. Royalty on retail; advance varies. Publication within 18 mos. Considers simultaneous submissions. Responds in 5-6 mos. Guidelines; free catalog. Note: this company is open to submissions in July only.

  Nonfiction: Query by mail, or proposal/5 chapters.

  Fiction: Query by mail, or proposal/5 chapters. African American.

  Ethnic Books: African American.

  Tips: "Submit complete manuscript for poetry; must be African American centered."

TORCH LEGACY PUBLICATIONS, 2780 Valley Ridge Dr., Atlanta GA 30032; PO Box 165046, Irving TX 75016. Phone/fax (817)556-2918. E-mail: danielwhyteiii@yahoo.com. Website: www.torchlegacy.com. Torch Ministries, Intl. Daniel Whyte III, pres. Dedicated to publishing Bible-based books of all genres by and for African Americans and others; especially for Black pastors.

TOUCH PUBLICATIONS, 10055 Regal Row Ste. 180, Houston TX 77040-3254. Toll-free (800)735-5865. (281)497-7901, or (713)896-7478. Fax (281)497-0904, or (713)896-1874. E-mail: sboren@touchusa.org. Website: www.touchusa.org. Touch Outreach Ministries. Scott Boren, dir. of publishing. To empower pastors, group leaders, and members to transform their lives, churches, and the world through basic Christian communities called cells. Publishes 8 titles/yr. Receives 25 submissions annually. 40% of books from first-time authors. Reprints books. Prefers 75-200 pgs. Royalty 10-15% of net; no advance. Average first printing 2,000. Guidelines (also by e-mail). Not in topical listings.

  Nonfiction: Query only. "Must relate to cell church life."

  Photos/Artwork: Accepts freelance photos for book covers.

  Tips: "Our market is extremely focused. We publish books, resources, and discipleship tools for churches, using a cell group strategy."

TOWLEHOUSE PUBLISHING, 394 W. Main St., Ste. B-9, Hendersonville TN 37075. Phone/fax (615)338-0283. E-mail: vermonte@aol.com. Website: www.towlehouse.com. Mike Towle, pres. A sports-oriented publisher—mostly golf, baseball, football, and basketball—interested in books with a Christian angle. Publishes 8-10 titles/yr. Receives 250 submissions annually. 50% of books from first-time authors. Accepts mss through agents. Reprints books. Prefers 25,000-30,000 wds. Royalty 8% of net; negotiable advance. Average first printing 5,000. Publication within 6 mos. Considers simultaneous submissions. Responds in 3-4 mos. Prefers requested ms on disk. No guidelines; catalog for #10 SAE/2 stamps.

  Nonfiction: Proposal/2 chapters; fax/e-query OK. "Looking for sports books, especially golf."

  Photos/Artwork: Accepts freelance photos for book covers.

THE TRACT LEAGUE, 2627 Elmridge Dr., Grand Rapids MI 49544-1390. (616)453-7695. Fax (616)453-2460. E-mail: info@tractleague.com. Website: www.tractleague.com. Publishes very few tracts from outside writers, but willing to look at ideas. Submit to General Manager.

THE TRINITY FOUNDATION, PO Box 68, Unicoi TN 37692. (423)743-0199. Fax (423)743-2005. E-mail: jrob1517@aol.com. Website: www.trinityfoundation.org. John W. Robbins, pres. To promote the logical system of truth found in the Bible. Publishes 6 titles/yr. Receives 3 submissions annually. No books from first-time authors. No mss through agents. Reprints books. Prefers 200 pgs. Outright purchases for up to $1,500; free books; no advance. Average first printing 2,000. Publication within 9 mos. No simultaneous submissions. Requires requested ms on disk. Responds in 2 mos. No guidelines; catalog for 3 stamps.

Nonfiction: Query letter only. Open to Calvinist/Clarkian books, Christian philosophy, economics, and politics.

Also Does: Pamphlets, booklets, tracts.

Photos/Artwork: Accepts freelance photos for book covers.

Tips: "Most open to doctrinal books; nonfiction, biblical, and well-reasoned books, theologically sound, clearly written, and well organized."

TROITSA BOOKS, 400 Oser Ave., Ste. 1600, Hauppauge NY 11788-3619. (631)231-7269. Fax (631)231-8175. E-mail: Novaeditorial@earthlink.net. Website: www.novapublishers.com. Religious imprint of Nova Science Publishers, Inc. Frank Columbus, ed. Publishes 5-20 titles/yr. Receives 50-100 submissions annually. No mss through agents. Various lengths. Royalty; no advance. Publication within 6-18 mos. Considers simultaneous submissions. Accepts requested ms on disk or by e-mail (prefers e-mail for all submissions and correspondence). Responds in 1 mo. Free guidelines/catalog.

Nonfiction: Proposal/2 chapters by e-mail.

Fiction: Proposal/2 chapters by e-mail. For adults.

Photos/Artwork: Accepts freelance photos for book covers.

TWEENER PRESS, PO Box 277, Winona Lake IN 46590. Toll-free (888)471-4386. Fax (574)269-6130. E-mail: mentoring@gospelstoryteller.com. Website: www.gospelstoryteller.com. Marvin G. Baker, ed.-in-chief. Focuses on tweeners (8- to 12-year-olds) and those who love them. Imprint of Baker Trittin Press. Incomplete topical listings. No questionnaire returned.

Fiction: "Fiction that captures the imagination and interest of this forgotten age group will demonstrate healthy relationships that present strong Christian values without sermonizing."

TWENTY-THIRD PUBLICATIONS, PO Box 180, Mystic CT 06355. Toll-free (800)321-0411. (860)536-2611. Fax (860)536-5674. E-mail: ttpubsedit@aol.com. Website: www.twentythirdpublications.com. Catholic/Bayard. Gwen Costello, pub.; Mary Carol Kendzia, ed. dir. Publishes 45 titles/yr. Receives 50 submissions annually. 45% of books from first-time authors. Accepts mss through agents. No reprints. Royalty on net; advance $1,000. Average first printing 3,000. Publication within 1 yr. Considers simultaneous submissions (if indicated). Requires requested ms on disk or by e-mail. Responds in 1 mo. Prefers NRSV (Catholic Edition). Guidelines (also by e-mail); free catalog.

Nonfiction: Proposal/2 chapters; phone/e-query OK.

Also Does: Booklets, CD-ROMs.

Photos/Artwork: Accepts freelance photos for book covers.

Tips: "Most open to pastoral, catechetical, or spirituality books."

TYNDALE HOUSE PUBLISHERS, 351 Executive Dr., Carol Stream IL 60188. Toll-free (800)323-9400. (630)668-8300. E-mail: manuscripts@tyndale.com. Fax (800)684-0247. Website: www.tyndale.com. Submit to Manuscript Review Committee; Anne Goldsmith, acq. ed. Imprints: HeartQuest (see separate listing). Publishes 225-250 titles/yr. 5% of books from first-time authors. Reprints books. Royalty negotiable; outright purchase of some children's books; advance negotiable. Average first printing 5,000-10,000. Publication within 9 mos. Accepts simultaneous submissions. Responds in 3-6 mos. Prefers NLT. No unsolicited mss. Guidelines/catalog on Website.

Nonfiction: Query from agents or published authors only; no phone/fax query. Also producing e-books.

Fiction: "We accept queries only from agents, Tyndale authors, authors known to us from other publishers, or other people in the publishing industry. Novellas, 25,000-30,000 wds.; novels 75,000-100,000 wds. All must have an evangelical Christian message."

Also Does: E-books.

**Note: This publisher serviced by The Writer's Edge.

TYNDALE HOUSE/SALTRIVER BOOKS, 351 Executive Dr., Carol Stream IL 60188. (630)668-8300. Website: www.tyndale.com. Janis Long Harris, sr. acq. ed. A new nonfiction crossover imprint with a goal of "publishing thought-provoking books that draw readers further along in their journey of Christian faith—or to Christian faith." Incomplete topical listings. No questionnaire returned.

Tips: "SaltRiver Books will seek to provide accessibly intelligent conversation starters in such areas as spiritual formation, spiritual memoir, leadership, apologetics, and life with God in the real world."

**Note: This publisher serviced by The Writer's Edge.

UMI PUBLISHING, 1551 Regency Court, Calumet IL 60409. Toll-free (800)860-8642. (708)868-7100. Fax (708)868-6759. E-mail: khall@urbanministries.com. Website: www.urbanministries.com. Urban Ministries, Inc. Carl Jeffrey Wright, pub.; Kathryn Hall, mng. ed. Called of God to create, produce, and distribute quality Christian education products; to provide quality Christian educational services that will empower God's people, especially in the Black community; to evangelize, disciple, and equip people for serving Christ, his Kingdom, and his church. Publishes 2-4 titles/yr. Receives 25-40 submissions annually. 85% of books from first-time authors. Accepts mss through agents. Reprints books. Prefers 256 pgs. Royalty to 40%; no advance. Average first printing 2,500-5,000. Publication within 2 yrs. Acknowledges receipt within 4 wks.; accepts or rejects in 6-12 mos. Prefers accepted ms on disk. Prefers KJV or NIV. Guidelines by e-mail; free catalog.

Nonfiction: Query only; no unsolicited mss; no phone/fax/e-query.

Special Needs: Christian living, theology, Christian education, and Christian doctrine.

Ethnic Books: African American.

Tips: "Follow guidelines for submissions (strictly); send query letter first."

**Note: This publisher serviced by The Writer's Edge.

UNITED CHURCH PRESS, 700 Prospect Ave. E., Cleveland OH 44115-1100. (216)736-3755. Fax (216)736-2207. E-mail: sadlerk@ucc.org, or stavetet@ucc.org. Website: www.pilgrim press.com. No freelance; see listing for Pilgrim Press.

UNITED METHODIST PUBLISHING HOUSE—See Abingdon Press or Dimensions for Living.

UNIVERSITY OF ARKANSAS PRESS, 201 Ozark Dr., Fayetteville AR 72701. Toll-free (800)626-0090. (479)575-3246. Fax (479)575-6044. E-mail: uapress@uark.edu. Website: www.uapress.com. Lawrence Malley, ed. Academic publisher. Publishes 30 titles/yr. Receives 1,000 submissions annually. 30% of books from first-time authors. Accepts mss through agents. Reprints books. Prefers 300 pgs. Royalty on net; no advance. Average first printing 1,000-2,000. Publication within 1 yr. Reluctantly considers simultaneous submissions. Responds in 3 mos. Requires accepted ms on disk. No guidelines; free catalog.

Nonfiction: Query. "All our books are scholarly." Looking for regional books.

Photos/Artwork: Accepts freelance photos for book covers.

UNIVERSITY OF OTTAWA PRESS, 542 King Edward Ave., Ottawa ON K1N 6N5, Canada. (613)562-5246. Fax (613)562-5247. E-mail: press@uottawa.ca. Website: www.uottawa

press.ca. Ruth Bradley-St-Cyr, ed-in-chief. Promotes scholarly, academic publications; no inspirational. Publishes 20-25 titles/yr. Receives 75 submissions annually. 10-20% of books from first-time authors. No mss through agents. No reprints. Prefers 200-400 pgs. Royalty 8% of net; no advance. Average first printing 1,000. Publication within 3 yrs. Accepts simultaneous submissions. Responds in 2 mos. Requires requested ms on disk. Free guidelines (also by e-mail)/catalog.

Nonfiction: Query only first; e-query OK. Scholarly/academic books only. Social scientific study of religion and theology. No devotionals or memoirs.

Special Needs: Post-doctoral and senior academic research in social sciences and humanities or religion. Scholarly work with supporting footnotes/references/bibliography. Primary research, usually by individual or team of individuals with PhD in Religious Studies, Ethics, Theology, History, or Philosophy (peer review required).

Tips: "Do not send SASE with U.S. stamps. UOP is the oldest French-language university press in North America and the only officially bilingual (French/English) university press in Canada."

UNIVERSITY PRESS OF AMERICA, 4501 Forbes Blvd., Ste. 200, Lanham MD 20706. (301)459-3366. Fax (301)429-5749. E-mail: submitupa@univpress.com. Website: www.univpress.com. Rowman & Littlefield Publishing Group/academic. Judith Rothman, VP & dir.; acq. eds.: David Chao and Joseph Parry. Publishes scholarly works in the social sciences and humanities; established by academics for academics. Imprint: Hamilton Books (biographies & memoirs). Publishes 75 religion titles/yr. Receives 700 submissions annually. 75% of books from first-time authors. Accepts mss through agents. **SOME SUBSIDY.** Does Digital Printing. Reprints books. Prefers 90-300 pgs. Royalty up to 12% of net; no advance. Average first printing 200-300. Publication within 4-6 mos. Considers simultaneous submissions. Accepts e-mail submissions. Responds in 2 wks. Accepts requested ms on disk or by e-mail. Guidelines (also by e-mail/Website); free catalog.

Nonfiction: Proposal/3 chapters or complete ms; phone/fax/e-query OK. "Looking for scholarly manuscripts."

Ethnic Books: African studies; Black studies.

Tips: "Most open to timely, thoroughly researched, and well-documented books. Moderately controversial topics. We publish academic and scholarly books only. Authors are typically affiliated with a college, university, or seminary."

VERBINUM, ul. Ostrobramska 98, 04-118 Warszawa, Poland. Phone (+48 22)610 78 70. Fax (+48 22)610 77 75. E-mail: wydawnictwo@verbinum.pl. Website: www.verbinum.pl. Catholic. Fr. Michot Studnik SVD, dir. Concentrates mainly on Bible apostolate, science of religion and mission, cultural anthropology, ecumenism, and children's books.

VICTOR BOOKS, Theology books. Craig Bubeck, acq, ed. See Cook Communications Ministries for details.

VINTAGE ROMANCE PUBLISHING, LLC, 107 Clearview Cir., Goose Creek SC 29445. (843)270-3742. E-mail: submissions@vrpublishing.com, or assist2editor@vrpublishing.com. Website: http://vrpublishing.com. Dawn Carrington, ed. Old-fashioned romance set in the 1900s through the 1960s. Open to first-time authors. Prefers 35,000-75,000 wds. or novellas up to 25,000 wds. No simultaneous submissions; asks for a one-month exclusive. Responds in 1 mo. Guidelines on Website.

Fiction: Query first via e-query; no attachments.

VIRGINIA PINES PRESS, 7092 Jewell-North, Kinsman OH 44428. (330)876-3504. Fax (209)882-5803. E-mail: virginiapines@nlc.net. Website: http://virginiapines.com. Helen C. Caplan, pub. Publishes fiction with a Christian viewpoint and creative nonfiction that helps document 21st century America. Publishes 3-5 titles/yr. Receives 40-50 submissions annually. 90% of books from first-time authors. Accepts mss through agents. No reprints.

Prefers 80,000-100,000 wds. Royalty 6-8% on net; some outright purchases; no advance. Average first printing 1,000. Publication within 8 mos. Considers simultaneous submissions. Prefers requested ms on disk. Responds in 1-10 mos. Prefers NKJV. Guidelines on Website; free catalog.

Nonfiction: Query, proposal, or complete ms; phone/fax/e-query OK. "We are always on the lookout for third-person, full-length, creative nonfiction works to which we give top priority."

Fiction: Query, proposal, or complete ms; phone/fax/e-query OK. "Looking for excellent, full-length spiritual warfare works that teach by example of the characters within the story how to identify spiritual warfare in daily life and how to become victorious over these types of attacks on family, finances, business, and peace of mind."

Photos/Artwork: Accepts freelance photos for book covers.

Contest: Sponsors several cover design contests each year. See Website for details of current contest.

VMI PUBLISHERS, 26306 Metolius Meadows Dr., Camp Sherman OR 97730. (541)595-2403. Fax (541)595-5822. E-mail: bill@vmipublishers.com. Website: www.vmipublishers.com. Virtue Ministries, Inc. Bill and Nancie Carmichael, pubs. Partnering with new authors. Publishes 8-12 titles/yr. Receives dozens of submissions annually. 95% of books from first-time authors. Accepts mss through agents. No reprints. Prefers 65,000+ wds., or 192-400 pgs. Royalty 12-18% of net; no advance. Average first printing 2,500+. Publication within 6-12 mos. Considers simultaneous submissions. Requires accepted mss on disk or by e-mail. Responds in 2 mos. Guidelines on Website.

Nonfiction: Query first by e-mail only.

Fiction: Query first by e-mail only. For all ages. "Anything Christian or inspirational that is well written, especially from new authors."

Also Does: "We coach new writers in our writers' breakaways (www.writersbreak away.com)."

Tips: "Most open to well-written books. Our niche is new authors with something significant to say and who have the ability to partner with us."

WALK WORTHY PRESS, 33290 W. 14 Mile Rd., #482, West Bloomfield MI 48322. (248)737-1747. Fax (248)737-1766. E-mail: editor@walkworthypress.net. Website: www.walkworthy press.net. Denise Stinson, pub. Primarily fiction for the African American Christian. Publishes 10 titles/yr. Receives 200 submissions annually. 95% of books from first-time authors. Accepts mss through agents. Reprints books. Prefers 75,000-100,000 wds., or 300 pgs. Royalty 10-15% on retail; variable advance. Average first printing varies. Publication within 9 mos. Considers simultaneous submissions (if informed). No disk or e-mail submissions. Responds in 6-8 wks. Prefers KJV, NKJV, NIV, Amplified. Guidelines on Website; free catalog.

Nonfiction: Proposal/2 chapters; no phone/fax/e-query. "We do primarily fiction. Our nonfiction is generally from authors who have a high profile."

Fiction: Complete ms; no phone/fax/e-query. Seasoned fiction author may send proposal/3 chapters. For all ages. Contemporary, ethnic, fantasy, juvenile, literary, short-story collection. Big commercial fiction.

Ethnic Books: African American.

Tips: "Present a good package. Read our books first. Do a story synopsis, not book-jacket copy. We like manuscripts that explore little-explored areas of life in Christian books."

+WARNER FAITH, 10 Cadillac Dr., Ste. 220, Brentwood TN 37027. (615)221-0996. Fax (615)221-0962. Website: www.WarnerFaith.com. Sells the majority of their books through general market venues. Chip MacGregor, assoc. pub.; Gary Terashita, sr. ed.; Leslie Peterson, ed. Publishes 50-60 titles/yr. Receives 500 submissions annually. 5% of books from first-time authors. Requires mss through agents. No reprints. Length depends on project. Royalty on retail; advance. Average first printing depends on project. Publication within 12 mos. Considers simultaneous submissions. Accepts requested mss by e-mail. Responds in 1-2 mos. Free catalog.

Nonfiction: Query; proposal/1-2 chapters, or complete ms; phone/fax query from agents only. Unsolicited mss returned unopened.

Fiction: Query only. "Looking for women's fiction."

Tips: "Most open to an author with a demonstrated platform and a commercial idea."

WARNER PRESS, PO Box 2499, 1200 E. 5th St., Anderson IN 46018-9988. (765)644-7721. Fax (765)640-8005. E-mail: krhodes@warnerpress.org. Website: www.warnerpress.com. Church of God/Anderson IN. Karen Rhodes, sr. ed. This publisher publishes only greeting cards, bulletins, activity books (predominately Bible stories and 48 pages), a limited number of children's story books. No unsolicited manuscripts for children's story books. See listing in greeting card section. Guidelines on Website.

Tips: "We prefer e-mail submissions and queries. Unless SASE is enclosed, no submissions will be returned."

WATERBROOK PRESS, 12265 Oracle Blvd., Ste. 200, Colorado Springs CO 80921. Toll-free (800)603-7051. (719)590-4999. Fax (719)590-8977. Website: www.waterbrook press.com. Random House, Inc. Submit to The Editor. Publishes 70 titles/yr. Receives 1,000 submissions annually. 15% of books from first-time authors. Prefers mss through agents. Reprints books. Royalty; advance. Publication in approximately 12 mos. Considers simultaneous submissions. Responds in 1-2 mos. No guidelines; catalog on Website.

Nonfiction: Agented submissions only.

Fiction: Agented submissions only.

**Note: This publisher serviced by ECPA First Edition.

WESLEYAN PUBLISHING HOUSE, PO Box 50434, Indianapolis IN 46250-0434. (317)774-3853. Fax (317)774-3860. E-mail: wph@wesleyan.org. Website: www.wesleyan.org/wph, or www.wesleyan.org/writer. The Wesleyan Church. Lawrence Wilson, ed. dir. Aims to ignite a passion for God in all of life. Publishes 15 titles/yr. Receives 150 submissions annually. 10-20% of books from first-time authors. Accepts mss through agents. No reprints. Prefers 25,000-40,000 wds. Royalty and advance. Average first printing 3,000. Publication within 9-12 mos. Considers simultaneous submissions. Accepts requested ms by e-mail. Responds in 2 mos. Prefers NIV. Guidelines on Website; free catalog.

Nonfiction: Proposal/2 chapters; no phone/fax query; e-query OK.

Tips: "Most open to books that help the reader take the next step in spiritual maturing or deal with an issue or problem in life. We are not looking for Bible studies, memoirs, or devotionals."

WESTBOW PRESS, PO Box 141000, Nashville TN 37215. (615)889-9000. Website: www.West BowPress.com. Thomas Nelson, Inc. Allen Arnold, pub.; Jenny Baumgartner and Ami McConnell, acq. eds. Fiction from a Christian world-view. Publishes 25 titles/yr. Prefers mss through agents; does not accept unsolicited manuscripts. Prefers 100,000 wds. Royalty. No guidelines; free catalog.

Fiction: Proposal with at least 3 chapters.

WESTMINSTER JOHN KNOX PRESS, 100 Witherspoon St., Louisville KY 40202-1396. (502)569-5613. Fax (502)569-5113. E-mail: ldowell@presbypub.com. Website: www.wjkbooks.com. Presbyterian Publishing Co./Presbyterian Church (USA). Submit to Lori Dowell. Addresses the needs of the Christian community by fostering religious and cultural dialog by contributing to the intellectual, moral, and spiritual nurture of the church and broader human family. Publishes 50 titles/yr. Receives 2,000 submissions annually. Less than 10% of books from first-time authors. No mss through agents. Prefers 140-300 pgs. Royalty on retail; no advance for first-time authors. Average first printing 2,000. Considers simultaneous submissions. Responds in 6-8 wks. Prefers NRSV. Guidelines (also by e-mail); free catalog.

Nonfiction: Proposal/1 chapter according to guidelines; fax/e-query OK. Looking mostly for Bible studies, ethics, spirituality, and theology.

Tips: "Most open to religious/theological scholarship." Does not publish fiction, poetry, memoirs, or children's books.

WHITAKER HOUSE, 1030 Hunt Valley Cir., New Kensington PA 15068. (724)334-7000. (724)334-1200. E-mail: publisher@whitakerhouse.com. Website: www.whitakerhouse .com. Whitaker Corp. Michael McCall, sr. ed. "Looking for timely, well-crafted nonfiction and fiction manuscripts that showcase the author's knowledge of current issues with a Christian perspective." Publishes 40-50 titles/yr. Receives 1,000 submissions annually. 33% of books from first-time authors. Accepts mss through agents. **SUBSIDY PUBLISHES 25%.** No print-on-demand. Reprints books. Prefers 50,000 wds. Royalty 10-22% on retail; some variable advances. Average first printing 10,000. Publication within 6 mos. Considers simultaneous submissions. Prefers accepted ms by e-mail. Responds in 6 mos. Prefers NIV. Guidelines on Website; catalog on Website.

Nonfiction: Query only first; phone/fax/e-query OK.

Fiction: Query only first.

Ethnic Books: Hispanic translations of current English titles.

Tips: "Most open to a high-quality, well-thought-out, compelling piece of work. Do the research and work required by our guidelines."

WHITE STONE BOOKS, PO Box 2835, Lakeland FL 33806. (866)253-8622. Fax (800)830-5688. E-mail: info@whitestonebooks.com. Website: www.whitestonebooks.com. Christian books. Not included in topical listings. No questionnaire returned.

WILSHIRE BOOK COMPANY, 12015 Sherman Rd., North Hollywood CA 91605-3781. (818)765-8579. Fax (818)765-2922. E-mail: mpowers@mpowers.com. Website: www.mpowers.com. A secular publisher of motivational books. Melvin Powers, pres.; Marcia Grad, ed. Books that help you become who you choose to be tomorrow. Publishes 6 titles/yr. 80% of books from first-time authors. Accepts mss through agents. Reprints books. Prefers 30,000 wds. or 128-160 pgs. Royalty 5% on retail; variable advance. Average first printing 5,000. Publication within 6 mos. Considers simultaneous submissions. No disk or e-mail submissions. Responds in 2 mos. Guidelines (also by e-mail/Website)/catalog for SAE/2 stamps.

Nonfiction: Query or proposal/3 chapters; phone/e-query OK.

Fiction: Allegory for adults that teach principles of psychological/spiritual growth.

Photos/Artwork: Accepts freelance photos for book covers.

Tips: "We are looking for adult allegories such as *Illusions,* by Richard Bach, *The Little Prince,* by Antoine de Saint Exupery, and *The Greatest Salesman in the World,* by Og Mandino. Analyze each one to discover what elements make it a winner. Duplicate those elements in your own style, using a creative, new approach and fresh material. We need 30,000-60,000 words."

+WINDRIVER PUBLISHING, INC., 72 N. WindRiver Rd., Silverton ID 83867-0446. (208)752-1836. Fax (208)752-1876. E-mail: info@windriverpublishing.com. Website: www.wind riverpublishing.com, or www.TrumpetMedia.com. Nondenominational. Gail Howick, ed-in-chief. To provide family entertainment and education that fulfills the admonition of Paul in Philippians 4:8. Imprint: Trumpet Media. Publishes 4 titles/yr. Receives 300 submissions annually. 90% of books from first-time authors. Accepts mss through agents. Reprints books. Prefers 100,000 wds. Royalty 10-15% on net; no advance. Average first printing 4,000. Publication within 14 mos. Considers simultaneous submissions. Prefers online

submissions; accepts disk or e-mail. Responds in 4-6 mos. Guidelines at www.Trumpet
Media.com; catalog online & free on request.

Nonfiction: Proposal/3 chapters; no phone/e-query; fax query OK. "Looking for Bible
studies and how-to books this year."

Fiction: Proposal/3 chapters; no phone/e-query; fax query OK. For all ages; any genre.

Photos/Artwork: Open to queries from freelance artists.

Tips: "Obtain professional editing before submitting."

WOOD LAKE BOOKS, INC., 9025 Jim Bailey Rd., Kelowna BC V4V 1R2, Canada. (250)766-
2778. Fax (250)766-2736. E-mail: acquisitions@woodlake.com. Website: www.woodlake
books.com. Ecumenical/mainline; Wood Lake Books, Inc. Michael Schwartzentruber,
series ed. Publishes quality resources that respond to the needs of the ecumenical church
and promote spiritual growth and commitment to God. Imprint: Northstone Publishing.
Publishes 3 titles/yr. Receives 300 submissions annually. 25% of books from first-time
authors. Reprints books. Prefers 200-250 pgs. Royalty on net; compiler's fee (for compilations) $1,000-3,000; some advances $1,000. Average first printing 3,000-4,000. Publication within 18-24 mos. Considers simultaneous submissions. Prefers requested ms on
disk. Responds in 6-12 wks. Guidelines; catalog $2.

Nonfiction: Query or proposal/2 chapters; fax/e-query OK. "Books with inclusive language
and mainline, Protestant interest."

Tips: "Most open to books with inclusive language, mainline/liberal theology, truth seeking, life affirming, and those that deal positively with life and faith. We publish books, curriculum, and resources for the mainline church. All queries and submissions should reflect
this in their theological approach."

WOODLAND GOSPEL PUBLISHING HOUSE, 118 Woodland Dr., Ste. 1101, Chapmanville WV
25508. (304)752-7500. Fax (304)752-9002. E-mail: info@woodlandpress.com. Website:
www.woodlandgospel.com; and www.woodlandpress.com. Woodland Press LLC. Cheryl
Davis, ed; submit to Mike Collins. Publishes 7 titles/yr. Receives 150 submissions annually.
90% of books from first-time authors. Accepts mss through agents. No reprints. Prefers
60,000 wds. or 230 pgs. Royalty on net; no advance. Average first printing 2,000. Publication within 1 yr. No simultaneous submissions. Responds in 2 mos. No mss by disk or
e-mail. No guidelines or catalog.

Nonfiction: Proposal/3 chapters; no phone/fax/e-query.

WORDSMITHS, 1355 Ferry Rd., Grants Pass OR 97526. (541)476-3080. Fax (541)474-9756.
E-mail: frode@jsgrammar.com. Website: www.jsgrammar.com. Frode Jensen, pub./ed. To
supply quality materials for homeschools and Christian schools. Receives 8-10 submissions
annually. No mss through agents. No reprints. Prefers 100-300 pgs. Royalty on net; no
advance. Average first printing 2,000-5,000. Publication time varies. Accepts simultaneous
submissions. Responds in about 2 wks. Prefers accepted ms on disk. Prefers KJV or NKJV.
No guidelines; free catalog.

Nonfiction: Proposal/outline; no phone/fax query; e-query OK. "We're most open to educational materials, textbook and workbook formats, having to do with language."

Tips: "I am open to books that are educational in nature, primarily text books. Most of my
existing market is for junior high and high school, but books for lower grades would be
acceptable."

WORLD PUBLISHING, PO Box 145001, Nashville TN 37214-5001. Website: www.World
Publishing.com. Thomas Nelson, Inc. Ted Squires, Exec. VP.; submit to Randall Elliott. No
guidelines.

Tips: "We accept manuscripts only from ministries that have a television or radio ministry."

W PUBLISHING GROUP, PO Box 141000, Nashville TN 37214. (615)889-9000. Fax (615)902-
2112. Website: www.Wpublishinggroup.com. Thomas Nelson, Inc. David Moberg, pub.;

Greg Daniel, assoc. pub. Publishes 75 titles/yr. Less than 3% of books from first-time authors. Prefers mss through agents. No reprints. Does not accept unsolicited manuscripts. Prefers 65,000-95,000 wds. Royalty. No guidelines.

Nonfiction: Query letter only first; no unsolicited ms. "Nonfiction dealing with the relationship and/or application of biblical principles to everyday life; 65,000-95,000 words." ****Note:** This publisher serviced by The Writer's Edge.

WRITE NOW PUBLICATIONS, 5501 N. 7th Ave., PMB 502, Phoenix AZ 85013. (602)336-8910. Fax (602)532-7123. E-mail: steve.laube@acwpress.com. Website: www.writenow publications.com. Steven R. Laube, exec. ed. To train and develop quality Christian writers; books on writing and speaking for writers and speakers. Royalty division of ACW Press. Publishes 1-2 titles/yr. Receives 6 submissions annually. 0% from first-time authors. Accepts mss through agents. Reprints books. Royalty 10% of net. Average first printing 2,000. Publication within 12 mos. Considers simultaneous submissions. Requires requested ms on disk. No guidelines/catalog.

Nonfiction: Writing how-to only. Query letter only; e-query OK.

WRITERS EXCHANGE E-PUBLISHING, PO Box 372, Atherton QLD 4883, Australia. E-mail: writers@writers-exchange.com. Website: www.writers-exchange.com/epublishing. E-book publisher. Sandy Cummins, CEO & ed. All contracts and agreements are available on the Website. Publishes books in different categories, including one for Christian books. Guidelines on Website. Not included in topical listings.

Nonfiction: Proposal.

Fiction: Proposal.

Tips: "Looking for children's fiction that reveals deeper Christian truths or theology, not just fluff."

YALE UNIVERSITY PRESS, 302 Temple St., New Haven CT 06520-9040. (203)432-0960. Fax (203)432-0948. E-mail: larisa.heimert@yale.edu. Website: www.yale.edu/yup. Lara Heimert, ed./religion. Publishes 10 religious titles/yr. Receives 200 submissions annually. 15% of books from first-time authors. Accepts mss through agents. Reprints books. Prefers up to 100,000 wds. or 400 pgs. Royalty from 0% to standard trade royalties; advance $0-100,000. Average first printing varies by field. Publication within 1 yr. Considers simultaneous submissions. Requires requested ms on disk; no e-mail submissions. Responds in 1-2 mos. Free guidelines (also on Website, www.yalebooks.com)/catalog for #10 SASE.

Nonfiction: Query; fax query OK. "Excellent and salable scholarly books."

Contest: Yales Series of Younger Poets competition. Open to poets under 40 who have not had a book of poetry published. Submit manuscripts of 48-64 pages in February only. Entry fee $15. Send SASE for guidelines (also on Website).

YOUTH SPECIALTIES, 300 S. Pierce St., El Cajon CA 92020. (619)440-2333. Fax (619)440-0582. E-mail: ys@youthspecialties.com, or camille@youthspecialties.com. Website: www.youthspecialties.com. Nondenominational. Roni Meek, mng. ed.; Dave Urbanski, sr. developmental ed.; submit to Nicole Davis, product asst. Christian resources for youth workers to use in their youth groups. Publishes 40 titles/yr. Receives 60 submissions annually. 25% of books from first-time authors. Prefers mss through agents. Some subsidy. Reprints books. Royalty depends on the author; advance. Average first printing 2,000-3,000. Publication within 8 mos. Considers simultaneous submissions. Responds in 1.5 mos. Accepts requested manuscripts by e-mail. Guidelines on Website; free catalog

Nonfiction: Proposal/3 chapters.

Fiction: Proposal/3 chapters. For teens/young adults.

ZERUBBABEL PRESS, PO Box 1710, Blowing Rock NC 28605. (828)295-7982. Fax (828)295-7900. E-mail: zpressnc@aol.com. Zerubbabel, Inc. Nondenominational. Sanda Cooper, ed-in-chief. Reprints out-of-print Christian books; does not solicit mss. Publishes 1 title/yr.

100% of books from first-time authors. No mss through agents. Reprints books only. No guidelines/catalog.

Tips: "Our mission is to further the great high calling of the Lord Jesus to carry His Gospel to the whole world, and one way we accomplish this is through literature."

ZONDERKIDZ, 5300 Patterson S.E., Grand Rapids MI 49530-0002. (616)698-3400. Fax (616)698-3326. E-mail: zpub@zondervan.com. Website: www.zonderkidz.com. Zondervan/HarperCollins. Bruce Nuffer, children's pub. Children's book line of Zondervan; ages 12 and under. Imprint: Faithgirlz! (see separate listing). No longer accepting unsolicited manuscripts or proposals by air or surface mail. Submit your proposal electronically to First Edition, or fax to Book Proposal Review Editor, (616)698-3454. No e-mail submissions.

Special Needs: This imprint covers five areas: devotionals, picture books, Bibles/Bible storybooks, special format books, and partnerships with groups such as Big Idea, Mothers of Preschoolers, Focus on the Family, etc.

ZONDERVAN, General Trade Books; Academic and Professional Books, 5300 Patterson S.E., Grand Rapids MI 49530-0002. Toll-free (800)226-1122. (616)698-6900. Fax (616)698-3454. E-mail: zpub@zondervan.com. Website: www.zondervan.com. HarperCollins/News Corp. Lyn Cryderman, ed.; Diane Bloem, submissions ed. Seeks to meet the needs of people with resources that glorify Jesus Christ and promote biblical principles. Publishes 120 trade titles/yr. Receives about 3,000 submissions annually. 10% of books from first-time authors. Accepts mss through agents. No reprints. Royalty 12-14% of net; variable advance. Average first printing 10,000. Publication within 12 mos. Considers simultaneous submissions. Accepts requested ms on disk or by e-mail. Responds in 9-17 wks. Prefers NIV. Guidelines on Website; catalog free for 9x12 SAE.

Nonfiction: Outline/1 chapter; fax query required; no phone/e-query. "When faxing, proposal should include the book title; a table of contents (2 or 3 sentence description of each chapter); a brief description of the proposed book, including its unique contribution and why you feel it should be published; your intended reader; and your vita, including your qualifications to write the book. The proposal should be no more than 5 pages. If we're interested, we will respond within 6 weeks. You may fax your proposal to the Manuscript Proposal Review Editor, (616)698-3454."

Fiction: Query or outline/1 chapter; fax query required; no phone/e-query. Publishes 4 each, contemporary and historical, per year.

Children's Lines: ZonderKidz and Faithgirlz (see separate listings).

Ethnic Books: Vida Publishers division: Spanish and Portuguese.

Tips: "Absolutely stellar prose that meets demonstrated needs of our market always receives a fair and sympathetic hearing. Great writing, great content always catch our attention." Accepts no mss by air or surface mail unless requested.

**Note: This publisher serviced by ECPA First Edition.

SUBSIDY PUBLISHERS

WHAT YOU NEED TO KNOW ABOUT SUBSIDY PUBLISHERS

In this section you will find any publishers who do 50 percent or more subsidy publishing. For our purposes, I am defining a subsidy publisher as any publisher that requires the author to pay for any part of the publishing costs. They may call themselves by a variety of names, such as a book packager, a cooperative publisher, a self-publisher, or simply someone who helps authors get their books published. Note that some of these also do at least some royalty publishing, so they could be approached as any other royalty publisher. You just need to realize that they are likely to offer you a subsidy deal, so indicate in your cover letter that you are only interested in a royalty arrangement, if that is the case.

As technology makes book publishing more accessible, and with the refinement of desktop publishing, more subsidy publishers have sprung up, and there has been an increase in confusion over who or what type of subsidy publishing is legitimate, and what publishers fall in with what we call "vanity publishers." As many of the legitimate publishers (and even some questionable ones) try to distance themselves from the reputation of the vanity publisher, they have come up with a variety of names to try to form definite lines of distinction. Unfortunately, it has only served to confuse the authors who might use their services. It is my hope in offering this separate listing that I can help you understand what this side of publishing entails, what to look for in a subsidy publisher, as well as what to look out for. To my knowledge the following publishers are legitimate subsidy publishers and are not vanity publishers, but I cannot guarantee that. It is important that as a writer you understand that any time you are asked to send money for any part of the production of your book, you are entering into a nontraditional relationship with a publisher. In this constantly changing field it becomes a matter of buyer beware.

Realize, too, that some of these publishers will publish any book, as long as the author can afford to pay for it. Others are as selective about what they publish as a royalty publisher would be, or they publish only certain types of books. Fortunately I'm seeing more publishers who are being selective; consequently, the professional quality of subsidy books is improving overall. Many will do only nonfiction—no novels or children's books. These distinctions will be important as you seek the right publisher for your project.

Because there is so much confusion about subsidy publishing, with many authors going into agreements with these publishers having little or no knowledge of what to expect or even what is typical in this situation, many have come away unhappy or disillusioned. For that reason I frequently get complaints from authors who feel they have been cheated or taken advantage of. (Of course, I sometimes get similar complaints about the royalty publishers listed in this book.) Each complaint brings with it an expectation that I should drop that publisher from this book. Although I am sensitive to their complaints, I also have come to the realization that I am not in a position to pass judgment on which publishers should be dropped. It has been my experience in publishing that for every complaint I get on a publisher, I can usually find several other authors who will sing the praises of the same publisher. For that reason, I feel I can serve the needs of authors better by giving them some insight into what to expect from a subsidy publisher and what kinds of terms should send up a red flag.

Because I am not an expert in this field and because of space limitations, I will keep this brief. Let me clarify first that unless you know your book has a limited audience or you have your own method of distribution (such as being a speaker who can sell your own books when you speak), I recommend that you try all the appropriate royalty publishers first. If you are unsuccessful with the royalty publishers but feel strongly about seeing your book published and have the financial resources to do so (or have your own distribution), one of the following publishers may be able to help you.

You can go to a local printer and take your book through all the necessary steps yourself, but a legitimate subsidy publisher has the contacts, know-how, and resources to make the task easier and often less expensive. It is always good to get more than one bid to determine whether the terms you are being offered are fair and competitive with other such publishers. Note that this listing is beginning to also include printers who offer the necessary services to help you complete the printing process yourself, so you will want to check out those as well.

There is not currently any kind of watchdog organization for subsidy publishers, and since I do not have direct knowledge about all of the publishers listed below, I would recommend that no matter who makes you a first offer, you get a second one from ACW Press, Essence Publishing (in Canada), Longwood Communications, or WinePress. These are ones I can personally recommend.

As with any contract, have someone review it before signing anything. I do such reviews, as do a number of others listed in the "Editorial Services" section of this book. Be sure that any terms agreed upon are *in writing*. Verbal agreements won't be binding. A legitimate subsidy publisher will be happy to provide you with a list of former clients as references. (If they aren't willing, watch out.) Don't just ask for that list; follow through and contact more than one of those references. Get a catalog of their books or a list of books they have published, and try to find them or ask them to send you a review copy of one or two books they have published. Use those to check the quality of their work, the bindings, etc. See if their books are available through Amazon.com or similar online services. Get answers to all your questions before you commit yourself to anything.

Keep in mind that the more copies of a book that are printed, the lower the cost per copy, but never let a publisher talk you into publishing more (or fewer) copies than you think is reasonable. Also, find out up front, and have included in the contract, whether and how much promotion the publisher is going to do. Some will do as much as a royalty publisher; others do none at all. If they are not doing promotion, and you don't have any means of distribution yourself, it may not be a good idea to pursue subsidy publication. You don't want to end up with a garage full of books you can't sell. Following this section I am including the names and addresses of Christian book distributors. I don't know which ones will consider distributing a subsidy-published book, so you will want to contact them to find out before you sign a contract. For more help on marketing your book, go to: www.bookmarket.com/index.html.

LISTING OF SUBSIDY PUBLISHERS

Below is a listing of any publishers that do 50% or more subsidy publishing (author pays some or all of the production costs). Before entering into dealings with any of these publishers, be sure to read the preceding section on what you need to know.

(*) An asterisk before a listing indicates no or unconfirmed information update.

(#) A number symbol before a listing indicates it was updated from their guidelines or other current sources.

(+) A plus sign before a listing indicates it is a new listing this year or was not included last year.

ACW PRESS, 1200 Hwy. 231 South, #273, Ozark AL 36360. (877)868-9673. Fax (334)774-3375. E-mail: juliewood@acwpress.com. Website: www.acwpress.com. Steven R. Laube, owner; Julie Wood, gen. mngr. A self-publishing book packager. Imprint: Write Now Publications (see separate listing). Publishes 40 titles/yr. Reprints books. **SUBSIDY PUBLISHES**

95%. Average first printing 2,500. Publication within 4-6 mos. Responds in 48-72 hrs. Request for estimate form available on Website. Not in topical listings; will consider any nonfiction or fiction topic. Guidelines by e-mail/Website.

Tips: "We offer a high quality publishing alternative to help Christian authors get their material into print. High standards, high quality. If authors have a built-in audience, they have the best chance to make self-publishing a success." Has a marketing program available to authors.

**Note: This publisher serviced by The Writer's Edge and ECPA First Edition.

ALFRED ALI LITERARY WORKS, INC., PO Box 582, Southfield MI 48076. (248)356-5111. Fax (248)356-1367. E-mail: AALiterary@aol.com. Website: www.AlfredAli.com. San Serif, ed. Spreading the word on how the Word of God can change and improve lives. Publishes 1 title/yr. Receives 5 submissions annually. 80% of books from first-time authors. Accepts mss through agents. Reprints books. **SUBSIDY PUBLISHES 70%.** Prefers 210 pgs. Royalty 25% of retail; no advance. Average first printing 1,000-5,000. Publication within 9 mos. Accepts e-mail submissions. No guidelines; catalog $3.

Nonfiction: Query only; fax query OK.

Ethnic Books: Publishes for the African American market.

Photos/Artwork: Accepts freelance photos for book covers.

Tips: "Most open to books that are based on inspiration that leads to self-awareness."

AMERICAN BINDING & PUBLISHING CO., PO Box 60049, Corpus Christi TX 78466-0049. Toll-free (800)863-3708. E-mail: magpub@pyramid3.net. Website: www.americanbinding publishing.com. Rose Magner, pub. Publishes 60/yr. Receives 200 submissions annually. 95% of books from first-time authors. No mss through agents. Reprints books. **SUBSIDY PUBLISHES 100%.** Prefers 200 pgs. Royalty 15% on retail; no advance. Print-on-demand. Publication within 2 wks. Considers simultaneous submissions. Requires requested ms on disk (Microsoft Word format). Responds in 2 wks. Any Bible version. Guidelines (also by e-mail); free catalog. Not included in topical listings.

Nonfiction: Complete ms; phone/e-query OK. Will consider any topic.

Fiction: Complete ms; phone/e-query OK. For all ages; all genres.

Ethnic Books: Black and Hispanic.

Photos/Artwork: Accepts freelance photos for book covers.

Tips: "We are print-on-demand; authors are responsible for their own marketing. We will consider any topic—nonfiction or fiction."

AMPELOS PRESS, 316 Blanchard Road, Drexel Hill PA 19026. Phone/fax (610)626-6833. E-mail: mbagnull@aol.com. Website: www.writehisanswer.com. Marlene Bagnull, LittD, pub./ed. Services (depending on what is needed) include critiquing, editing, proofreading, typesetting, and cover design. Publishes 1-3 titles/yr. **SUBSIDY PUBLISHES 100%.** Query only. Not included in topical listings (see Tips).

Tips: "Our vision statement reads: 'Strongly, unashamedly, uncompromisingly Christ-centered. Exalting the name of Jesus Christ. Seeking to teach His ways through holding up the Word of God as the Standard.' (*Ampelos* is the Greek word for 'vine' in John 15:5.)"

BLACK FOREST PRESS, Belle Arden Run, 490 Mountain View Dr., Mosheim TN 37818. Toll-free (800)451-9404. Fax (619)482-8704. E-mail: bfp1@blackforestpress.com, or admin@blackforestbooks.com. Website: www.blackforestpress.com. Mary Inbody, sr. ed.; Sue Van Gundy, acq. ed. A self-publishing company; also does print-on-demand (POD); beginning e-books. Imprints: Kinder Books (children's adventure books); Dichter Books (ethnic & poetry); Abenteuer Books; Sonnenschein Books; Segen Books (religious). Publishes 100 titles/yr. (including POD). Receives 2,000 submissions annually. 75% of books from first-time authors. Accepts mss through agents. **SUBSIDY PUBLISHES 60%** (helps people get published). Reprints books. Prefers 75-350 pgs. Royalty 100% to authors; 68%

to authors for Website purchases; promotional contracts vary; no advance. Average first printing 2,000-3,000. Publication within 4.5 months. Considers simultaneous submissions. Requires requested ms on disk. Responds in 2-3 wks. Prefers NLT or modern Bible versions. Free 90-page catalog (also on Website).

Nonfiction: Query/phone number; phone/fax/e-query OK. "Looking for true testimonials and books on angels; also contemporary Christian issues."

Fiction: Query. For all ages. "Looking for historical novels and Civil War books; 150-350 pages."

Ethnic Books: Publishes for Black and Hispanic markets.

Photos/Artwork: Accepts freelance photos for book covers.

Tips: "Looking for books on vital Christian issues; books with literary merit and significant lessons for life."

BOOK PUBLISHERS NETWORK, PO Box 2256, Bothell WA 98041. (425)483-3040. Fax (425)483-3098. E-mail: sherynhara@earthlink.net. Sheryn Hara, ed. Publishes 5-8 titles/yr. Receives 20 submissions annually. 100% of books from first-time authors. Accepts mss through agents. **100% SUBSIDY.** Reprints books. No preference on length. No royalty/advance. Publication within 3 mos. Considers simultaneous submissions. Responds in 1 mo. Guidelines (also by e-mail); no catalog.

Nonfiction: Proposal or complete ms.; phone/fax/e-query OK.

Fiction: Proposal or complete ms.; phone/fax/e-query OK.

Photos/Artwork: Accepts freelance photos for book covers.

BRENTWOOD CHRISTIAN PRESS, 4000 Beallwood Ave., Columbus GA 31904. Toll-free (800)334-2828. (706)576-5787. Fax (706)317-5808. E-mail: Brentwood@aol.com. Website: www.BrentwoodBooks.com. Mainline. U.D. Roberts, exec. ed. Publishes 267 titles/yr. Receives 2,000 submissions annually. Reprints books. **SUBSIDY PUBLISHES 95%.** Offers InstaBooks and Just in Time publishing (print-on-demand). Average first printing 500. Publication within 1 mo. Considers simultaneous submissions. Responds in 2 days. Guidelines.

Nonfiction: Complete ms. "Collection of sermons on family topics; poetry; relation of Bible to current day."

Fiction: Complete ms. "Stories that show how faith helps overcome small, day-to-day problems."

Photos/Artwork: Accepts freelance photos for book covers.

Tips: "Keep it short; support facts with reference." This publisher specializes in small print runs of 300-1,000. Can best serve the writer who has a completed manuscript.

BROWN BOOKS PUBLISHING GROUP, 16200 N. Dallas Pkwy., Ste. 170, Dallas TX 75248. (972)381-0009. Fax (972)248-4336. E-mail: publishing@brownbooks.com. Website: www.brownbooks.com. Milli A. Brown, pub. Publishes books in the areas of self-help, religion/inspirational, relationships, business, mind/body/spirit, and women's issues. **SUBSIDY PUBLISHES 100%.** Incomplete topical listings. No questionnaire returned.

CREATED IN CHRIST, PUBLISHING DIVISION, 3725 Golfe Links Dr., Snellville GA 30039. Toll-free (877)886-6260. Fax (530)618-5767. E-mail: cicpublishing@ureach.com. Website: www.cicpublishing.org. International Gospel Fellowship. Lloyd Ocampo, dir. Develops and publishes written materials based on biblical teachings that tear down walls of denomination and religion. 100% of books from first-time authors. No mss through agents. **100% print-on-demand.** No reprints. Prefers 700 pgs. Pay 10-45% royalty on net; no advance. Publication within 3 mos. Considers simultaneous submissions. Accepts manuscripts on disk or by e-mail. Guidelines by e-mail or Website.

Nonfiction: Complete ms.; no phone query, fax/e-query OK.

Photos/Artwork: Accepts freelance photos for book covers.

Tips: "Most open to church manuals, or spiritual teachings that foster relationship development with God."

CREATION HOUSE, 600 Rinehart Rd., Lake Mary FL 32746-4872. (407)333-0600. Fax (407)333-7100. E-mail: allen.quain@strang.com. Strang Communications Co. Allen Quain, mngr. To inspire and equip people to live a Spirit-led life and to walk in the divine purpose for which they were created. Imprints: Charisma House, Siloam Press, CharismaKids. Publishes 50-100 titles/yr. Receives 500 submissions annually. 80% of books from first-time authors. Accepts mss through agents. **CO-PUBLISHES 100%.** No print-on-demand. Reprints books. Prefers 25,000+ wds. or 100-200 pgs. Royalty 12-18% of net; no advance. Average first printing 6,000. Publication within 5 mos. Considers simultaneous submissions. Responds in 6-12 wks. Open to submissions on disk or by e-mail. Guidelines (also by e-mail/Website); free catalog.

Nonfiction: Proposal or complete ms.; phone/fax/e-query OK. "Open to any books that are well-written and glorify Jesus Christ."

Fiction: Proposal or complete ms.; phone/fax/e-query OK. For all ages. "Fiction must have a biblical world-view and point the reader to Christ."

Photos/Artwork: Accepts freelance photos for book covers.

Tips: "We use the term 'co-publishing' to describe a hybrid between conventional royalty publishing and self or subsidy publishing, utilizing the best of both worlds. We produce a high quality book for our own inventory, market it, distribute it, and pay the author a royalty on every copy sold. In return, the author agrees to buy, at a deep discount, a portion of the first print run."

DCTS PUBLISHING, PO Box 40276, Santa Barbara CA 93140. Toll-free (800)965-8150. Fax (805)653-6522. E-mail: dennis@dctspub.com. Website: www.dctspub.com. Dennis Hamilton, ed. Books are designed to enrich the mind, encourage the heart, and empower the spirit. Publishes 5 titles/yr. Receives 25 submissions annually. 35% of books from first-time authors. No mss through agents. **SUBSIDY PUBLISHES 70%.** Reprints books. Prefers 100-300 pgs. Royalty 17% of retail; no advance. Average first printing 3,500. Publication within 6-8 mos. No simultaneous submissions. Prefers KJV. Guidelines; catalog for #10 SAE/1 stamp.

Nonfiction: Query or proposal/2-3 chapters; e-query OK.

Fiction: Query or proposal/2-3 chapters; e-query OK. Adult, biblical, ethnic, juvenile, or short story collections.

ROBBIE DEAN PRESS, 2910 E. Eisenhower Parkway, Ann Arbor MI 48108. (734)973-9511. Fax (734)973-9475. E-mail: Fairyha@aol.com. Website: www.RobbieDeanPress.com. Interested in works that are multiculturally appealing and that approach a topic in a unique manner. Dr. Fairy C. Hayes-Scott, owner. Publishes 1 title/yr. Receives 20 submissions annually. 100% of books from first-time authors. Accepts mss through agents. **SUBSIDY PUBLISHES 75%.** Does print-on-demand. Reprints books. Length flexible. Royalty 10-20%; no advance. Average first printing 250. Publication within 6 mos. Considers simultaneous submissions. Responds in 2-6 wks. Guidelines by e-mail; free catalog.

Nonfiction: Query first. "We're open to new ideas."

Fiction: "We seldom do fiction." For children only.

Ethnic Books: Multicultural.

Also Does: Booklets; e-books; computer games.

Photos/Artwork: Accepts freelance photos for book covers.

Tips: "Most open to self-help, reference, senior adult topics, and parenting."

+DIAKONIA PUBLISHING, PO Box 397, Summerfield NC 27358. (336)643-5849. E-mail: diakonia@bookpublishing4u.com. Website: www.bookpublishing4u.com/diakonia.html. Harlan Publishing. Jeffrey H. Pate, pub.

+EKKLESIA PRESS, PO Box 5935, Lincoln NE 68505. E-mail: timprice@kingdomcitizenship .org, or tpprice123@juno.com. Website: www.kingdomcitizenship.org/publishing.htm. Timothy L. Price, ed. A ministry to help authors publish works not considered profitable by mainstream publishers, works that will impact and motivate followers to fulfill the Great Commission. Publishes 10-12 titles/yr. Prefers 150-600 pgs.; will also do 51-149 pgs. Royalty 25-35%; no advance. Print-on-demand publisher; also does e-books. Average first printing 150 min.; 25 thereafter. Publication within 6 mos.; sometimes more. Responds in 72 hrs.

> **Nonfiction:** Query or proposal; e-query OK. Nonfiction only. "Manuscript submissions must be in Microsoft Word document form, single-spaced, and justified."
>
> **Also Does:** Pamphlets up to 50 pgs.
>
> **Tips:** "We want works that bring conviction. We want works that call the church to a higher level of living and performance. We are sympathetic to the home church movement and would like to help propagate the idea of the priesthood of every believer. Book should be practical. Submissions are to be well argued (not argumentative) and must be profuse in their use of Scripture." Does custom cover designs; designs Website to help promote author's book. Book distribution handled through Ingram Book.

ELDERBERRY PRESS, INC., 1393 Old Homestead Rd., 2nd Fl., Oakland OR 97462. Phone/fax (541)459-6043. E-mail: editor@elderberrypress.com. Website: www.elderberrypress .com. David W. St. John, exec. ed. Publishes 15 titles/yr. Receives 150-250 submissions annually. 90% of books from first-time authors. No mss through agents. **SUBSIDY PUBLISHES 50%.** Does print-on-demand. Royalty 10-25%; no advance. Publication within 3 mos. Considers simultaneous submissions. Accepts disk or e-mail submissions. Responds in 1 mo. Guidelines on Website; free catalog. Will consider any nonfiction or fiction topic. Not included in topical listings.

> **Nonfiction:** Complete ms; phone/fax/e-query OK. "We consider all topics."
>
> **Fiction:** Complete ms; phone/fax/e-query OK. All genres for all ages.

ESSENCE PUBLISHING CO. INC., 20 Hanna Ct., Belleville ON K8P 5J2, Canada. (613)962-2360. Toll-free (800)238-6376. Fax (613)962-3055. E-mail: publishing@essencegroup .com, or info@essencegroup.com. Website: www.essencegroup.com. Essence Communications Group. Cathy Jol, submissions ed.; Rikki-Anne McNaught, publishing mgr.; Renee VanderWindt and Stephanie VanderMuelen, eds. Provides affordable, short-run book publishing to the Christian community. Imprints: Guardian Books (see separate listing), Epic Press (secular). Publishes 100-150+ titles/yr. Receives 250+ submissions annually. 75% of books from first-time authors. **SUBSIDY PUBLISHES 90%.** Reprints books. Any length. Average first printing 500-1,000. Publication within 3-5 mos. Considers simultaneous submissions. Responds in 3-4 wks. Prefers requested ms on disk. Guidelines (also by e-mail/Website); catalog online (www.essencebookstore.com).

> **Nonfiction:** Complete ms; phone/fax/e-query OK. Accepts all topics.
>
> **Fiction:** Complete ms. All genres for all ages. Also picture books.
>
> **Also Does:** Pamphlets, booklets, tracts.
>
> **Contest:** The Essence Treasury Writing Competition.
>
> **Photos/Artwork:** Accepts freelance photos for book covers.

FAIRWAY PRESS, subsidy division for CSS Publishing Company, 517 S. Main St., Box 4503, Lima OH 45802-4503. (419)227-1818. Fax (419)228-9184. Website: www.csspub.com. Teresa Rhoads, ed.; submit to Stan Purdum. Imprint: Express Press. Publishes 100 titles/yr. Receives 200-300 submissions annually. 80% of books from first-time authors. Reprints books. **SUBSIDY PUBLISHES 100%.** Royalty to 50%; no advance. Average first printing 500-1,000. Publication within 6-9 mos. Considers simultaneous submissions. Responds in up to 1 mo. Prefers requested ms on disk; no e-mail submissions. Prefers NRSV. Free guidelines (also on Website)/catalog for 9x12 SAE.

Nonfiction: Complete ms; phone/fax/e-query OK. All types. "Looking for manuscripts with a Christian theme, and seasonal material."

Fiction: Complete ms. For adults, teens, or children; all types. No longer producing anything in full color or with four-color illustrations.

FRUIT-BEARER PUBLISHING, PO Box 777, Georgetown DE 19947. (302)856-6649. Fax (302)856-7742. E-mail: candy.abbott@verizon.net. Website: www.fruitbearer.com. Branch of Candy's Creations. Candy Abbott, pres. Offers editing services and advice for self-publishers. Publishes 5-10 titles/yr. Receives 10-20 submissions annually. 90% of books from first-time authors. **SUBSIDY PUBLISHES 100%.** No reprints. Average first printing 30-5,000. Publication within 1-6 mos. Responds in 3 mos. Brochure for #10 SAE/1 stamp.

Nonfiction: Proposal/2 chapters; phone/fax/e-query OK.

Also Does: Pamphlets, booklets, tracts.

Photos/Artwork: Accepts freelance photos for book covers.

Tips: "Accepting limited submissions."

GESHER—See Winer Foundation.

GUARDIAN BOOKS, 20 Hanna Ct., Belleville ON K8P 5J2, Canada. Toll-free (800)238-6376. (613)962-3294. Fax (613)962-3055. E-mail: publishing@essencegroup.com. Website: www.essencegroup.com. Essence Communications Group. Renee VanderWindt, submissions ed.; Lori Mackay, ed.; Rikki-Anne McNaught, mngr.; Gus Henne, marketing. Provides affordable, short-run book publishing to the Christian community. Imprints: Guardian Books, Epic Press (secular). Publishes 40-50 titles/yr. Receives 250+ submissions annually. 75% of books from first-time authors. **SUBSIDY PUBLISHES 90%.** Reprints books. Any length. Average first printing 500-1,000. Publication within 3-5 mos. Considers simultaneous submissions. Responds in 3-4 wks. Prefers requested ms on disk. Guidelines (also by e-mail/Website); free catalog.

Nonfiction: Complete ms; phone/fax/e-query OK. Accepts all topics.

Fiction: Complete ms. All genres for all ages. Also picture books.

Also Does: Pamphlets, booklets, tracts.

Photos/Artwork: Accepts freelance photos for book covers.

HANNIBAL BOOKS, PO Box 461592, Garland TX 75046-1592. Toll-free (800)747-0738. Fax (888)252-3022. E-mail: hannibalbooks@earthlink.net. Website: www.hannibalbooks .com. KLMK Communications, Inc. Louis Moore, pub. Evangelical Christian publisher specializing in missions, marriage and family, and critical issues. Publishes 8-10 titles/yr. Receives 50 submissions annually. 80% of books from first-time authors. Accepts mss through agents. **SUBSIDY PUBLISHES 100%;** no print-on-demand. Reprints books. Prefers 50,000-60,000 wds. Royalty on net or outright purchase; no advance. Average first printing 2,000-3,000. Publication within 3 mos. Considers simultaneous submissions. Responds in 3 mos. Prefers NIV. Guidelines; free catalog.

Nonfiction: Book Proposal/1-3 chapters; no phone/fax/e-query. "Looking for missionary, marriage restoration, homeschooling, and devotionals."

Fiction: Book Proposal/1-3 chapters; no phone/fax/e-query. "We like missionary romance novels."

Tips: "We are looking for go-get-'em new authors with a passion to be published."

IMPACT CHRISTIAN BOOKS, INC., 332 Leffingwell Ave., Ste. 101, Kirkwood MO 63122. (314)822-3309. Fax (314)822-3325. E-mail: info@impactchristianbooks.com. Website: www.impactchristianbooks.com. William D. Banks, pres. Books of healing, miraculous deliverance, and spiritual warfare, drawing individuals into a deeper walk with God. Publishes 20+ titles/yr. Receives 20-50 submissions annually. 50-70% of books from first-time authors. No mss through agents. **SUBSIDY PUBLISHES 50-70%.** Reprints books. Average first printing 5,000. Publication within 2 mos. Considers simultaneous submissions. Responds by prior arrangement in 30 days. Requires requested ms on disk. Guidelines; catalog for 9x12 SAE/5 stamps. Not in topical listings.

Nonfiction: Query only; phone/fax query OK. Outstanding personal testimonies and Christ-centered books.

+INFINITY PUBLISHING, 1094 New Dehaven St., Ste. 100, West Conshohocken PA 19428-2713. Toll-free (877)BUY-BOOK. E-mail: info@buybooksontheweb.com. Website: www.infinitypublishing.com. Print-on-demand. Charges $400 up-front fee. First order of books is at 50% discount; additional orders 40% discount. Royalty 10%.

INSIGHT PUBLISHING GROUP, 8801 S. Yale, Ste. 410, Tulsa OK 74137. (918)493-1718. Fax (918)493-2219. E-mail: info@freshword.com. Website: www.freshword.com. Christian Publisher. John Mason, ed. Owned by a best-selling author who established the company to serve authors. Publishes 50 titles/yr. Receives 50 submissions annually. 50% of books from first-time authors. Accepts mss through agents. Does print-on-demand. Reprints books. Prefers 160 pgs. Royalty 15-17% on net; no advance. Average first printing 5,000. Publication within 6 mos. Considers simultaneous submissions. Requires disk or e-mail submission. Responds in 2 mos. Guidelines by e-mail/Website; no catalog. Will consider most fiction and nonfiction topics. Incomplete topical listings.

Nonfiction: Complete ms; phone/fax/e-query OK.

Fiction: Complete ms; phone/fax/e-query OK. Nondenominational Christian. For all ages.

Also Does: Booklets.

Tips: "We help people self-publish. To those authors we can offer a variety of services including distribution and small print runs. Most open to books that are unique, authentic, and relevant."

LIGHTNING STAR PRESS, PO Box 730393, San Jose CA 95173. (408)270-0572. Fax (425)645-0423. E-mail: jessie@lightningstarpress.com, or inquiries@lightningstarpress.com. Website: www.lightningstarpress.com. Submit to The Editor. Publishes 2-4 titles/yr. Receives 50 submissions annually. 99% of books from first-time authors. Accepts mss through agents. **99% SUBSIDY.** Does print-on-demand. Reprints books. Prefers 32+ pgs. No royalty or advance. Average first printing 100+. Publication within 6 mos. Considers simultaneous submissions. Responds in 1-2 wks. Accepts e-mail submissions. Guidelines on Website; no catalog.

Nonfiction: Complete ms or proposal/2 chapters; phone/fax/e-query OK

Fiction: Complete ms or proposal/3 chapters; phone/fax/e-query OK

Photos/Artwork: Accepts freelance photos for book covers.

MARKETINGNEWAUTHORS.COM, 2910 E. Eisenhower Pkwy., Ann Arbor MI 48108. Toll-free (800)431-1579. (734)975-0028. Fax (734)973-9475. E-mail: Fairyha@aol.com, or MarketingNewAuth@aol.com. Website: www.MarketingNewAuthors.com. Imprint of Robbie Dean Press. To primarily serve authors who wish to self-publish. Dr. Fairy C. Hayes-Scott, owner. 100% of books from first-time authors. Accepts mss through agents. **SUBSIDY PUBLISHES 100%.** Reprints books. Length flexible. Publication within 6 mos. Considers simultaneous submissions. Responds in 2-6 wks. Guidelines by e-mail/Website. Offers 7 different marketing plans; see Website.

+MAZE OF WORSHIP PUBLISHING, 1036 Live Oak Dr., Hinesville GA 31313. (919)977-6761. E-mail: mowpublishing@yahoo.com. Website: www.nextgenerationpublishers.com. Thresia D. Phillips, ed. Open to religious submissions. Not included in topical listings.

ONE WORLD PRESS, 1042 Willow Creek Rd., Prescott AZ 86302. Toll-free (800)250-8171. (928)445-2081. Fax (928)717-1779. E-mail: oneworldpress@mail.com. Joe Zuccarello, operations mngr. Publishes many titles/yr. Receives 25-50 submissions annually. 50% of books from first-time authors. Accepts mss through agents. **SUBSIDY PUBLISHES 100%.** Reprints books. Does print-on-demand. Average first printing up to author. Publication within 2 mos. Considers simultaneous submissions. Responds in 2-4 wks. No guidelines or catalog.

> **Nonfiction:** Complete manuscript. All ages. "We publish about anything within decency and reason."
>
> **Also Does:** Booklets, e-books, pamphlets, tracts.

PLEASANT WORD, 1730 Railroad St., PO Box 428, Enumclaw WA 98022. Toll-free (800)326-4674. (360)802-9758. Fax (360)802-9992. E-mail: info@pleasantword.com. Website: www.pleasantword.com. WinePress Publishing. Athena Dean, pub. In an industry where print-on-demand publishers will print almost anything, Pleasant Word has high standards for both design and content of POD books. **100% SUBSIDY.** Print-on-demand division. Publishes 300+ titles/yr. Receives 500+ submissions annually. 80% of books from first-time authors. Accepts mss through agents. Reprints books. Any length, 48 to 740 pgs. Color picture books in soft cover only, 28-120 pgs. Royalty; no advance. Publication within 45-90 days; longer with editing. Considers simultaneous submissions. Responds online. Guidelines & catalog on Website.

> **Nonfiction:** Complete ms submitted online through Website; e-queries OK. "We accept all topics except books that promote the prosperity doctrine, 'Toronto Blessing,' or women in leadership over men."
>
> **Fiction:** Complete ms submitted online through Website; e-queries OK. Fiction for all ages.
>
> **Tips:** "Most subsidy/POD publishers will publish anything if you are willing to pay for it. We turn down unscriptural manuscripts and others that have no chance of recouping the original investment."

POEMS BY ME, 4000 Beallwood Ave., Columbus GA 31904. Toll-free (800)334-2828. E-mail: Brentwood@aol.com. Website: www.PoemsByMe.com. Brentwood Christian Press. Joyce Warren, ed. Poetry that is spiritual, personal, emotional. Receives 80 submissions annually. 75% of books from first-time authors. Accepts mss through agents. **100% SUBSIDY.** Print-on-demand. Reprints books. Need at least 40 poems for a book. Same-week response.

POETRY OF TODAY PUBLISHING, 2073 Stanford Village Dr., Antioch TN 37013-4450. (615)337-2725. Fax (347)823-9608. E-mail: info@poetryoftoday.com. Website: www.poetryoftoday.com. Christian Business. Patrice M. Clark, pub. Publishes 12 titles/yr. Receives 40-50 submissions annually. 85% of books from first-time authors. Accepts mss through agents. **SUBSIDY PUBLISHES 75%.** Print-on-demand. No reprints. Prefers 80 pgs. min. Royalty 60-75% on retail; no advance. Average first printing 500. Publication within 2 mos. Considers simultaneous submissions. Accepts disk. Responds in 1-2 mos. Prefers KJV. Guidelines (also by e-mail/Website); no catalog.

> **Nonfiction:** Complete ms; e-query OK. "Looking for Christian poetry and theological books."
>
> **Fiction:** Complete ms; e-query OK. For all ages. "Looking for inspirational novels."
>
> **Also Does:** E-books.
>
> **Photos/Artwork:** Accepts freelance photos for book covers; open to queries from freelance artists.
>
> **Contest:** Sponsors a monthly poetry contest.
>
> **Tips:** "We're looking for Christian poetry that is well written, new, inspiring, and educational. We specialize in first-time authors."

POET'S COVE PRESS, 4000 Beallwood Ave., Columbus GA 31904. Toll-free (800)334-2828. (706)576-5787. E-mail: Brentwood@aol.com. Website: www.BrentwoodBooks.com. Subsidiary of Brentwood Publishers Group. U.D. Roberts, exec. dir. Publishes 75 titles/yr. **SUB-**

SIDY OR CUSTOM PUBLISHES 100%. Specializes in self-publishing books of religious or inspirational poetry, in small press runs of under 500 copies. Publication in 45 days. Same-day response.

Tips: "Type one poem per page; include short bio and photo with first submission."

PROVIDENCE PUBLISHING CORPORATION, 238 Seaboard Ln., Franklin TN 37067. Toll-free (800)321-5692. (615)771-2020. Fax (615)771-2002. E-mail: mvanhook@providence house.com. Website: www.providence-publishing.com. Providence Publishing Corp. Nancy Wise, mng. ed.; Michael S. VanHook, acq. ed. A private publisher that supplies a complete list of services including editorial, design, production, marketing, and inventory management. Imprints: Providence House Publishers (religious), Hillsboro Press, Meeting House Press. Publishes 12 religious titles/yr. Receives 100 submissions annually. 90% of books from first-time authors. Accepts mss through agents. **SUBSIDY PUBLISHES 100%.** No print-on-demand. Reprints books. Prefers 96-512 pgs. Author receives 100% income from sales. Average first printing 2,000-3,000. Publication within 8-9 mos. Considers simultaneous submissions. Responds in 1-4 mos. Requires accepted ms on disk. Prefers NIV, NKJV. Guidelines/catalog on Website.

Nonfiction: Complete ms; no phone/fax/e-query.

Fiction: Complete ms; no phone/fax/e-query. "We seldom do fiction; depends on manuscript."

Tips: "Most open to well-written, historic or religious themes."

QUIET WATERS PUBLICATIONS, PO Box 34, Bolivar MO 65613-0034. (417)326-5001. Fax (617)249-0256. E-mail: QWP@usa.net. Website: www.QuietWatersPub.com. Stephen Trobisch, ed. Books on marriage, family, and missions. Open to freelance submissions.

RECOVERY COMMUNICATIONS, INC. PO Box 19910, Baltimore MD 21211. (410)243-8352. Fax (410)243-8558. E-mail: tdrews3879@aol.com. Website: www.GettingThemSober.com. Toby R. Drews, ed. Publishes 4-6 titles/yr. No mss through agents. **SUBSIDY PUBLISHER.** Prefers 110 pgs. Co-op projects; no royalty or advance. Average first printing 5,000. Publication within 9 mos. Excellent nationwide distribution and marketing in bookstores. Send for their free information packet.

Nonfiction: Query only.

Tips: "Although technically we are a subsidy publisher, we are more of a hybrid publisher in that we give the author enough free books to sell in the back of the room to totally recoup all the money they have paid; plus we share 50/50 on net sales at bookstores. Over half of our authors have gotten their money back and made a great profit. We are also aggressive in our pursuit of catalog sales and foreign rights sales (we recently sold to a German publisher). We also individually coach all our authors, at no cost to them, to help them successfully obtain speaking engagements."

SELAH PUBLISHING GROUP, LLC., 16238 W. Young St., Surprise AZ 85374-5744. E-mail: garlen@selahbooks.com. Website: www.selahbooks.com. Garlen Jackson, pub. A publisher that does not water down the author's message. Publishes 45 titles/yr. Receives 20 submissions annually. 75% of books from first-time authors. Prefers mss through agents. Reprints books. Prefers 40,000 wds. or 144 pgs. Royalty 12-18% of net; no advance. Average first printing 2,500. Publication within 6 mos. No simultaneous submissions. Prefers requested ms on disk. Responds in 2 mos. Prefers ASV. Guidelines by e-mail; free catalog.

Nonfiction: Complete ms; no phone/fax/e-query.

Fiction: Complete ms; no phone/fax/e-query. For all ages.

Also Does: E-books.

Photos/Artwork: Accepts freelance photos for book covers.

Tips: "Most open to time-sensitive, current events, and controversial books. Writers should spend more time selling who they are in regard to character and integrity."

SELF PUBLISH PRESS, 4000 Beallwood Ave., Columbus GA 31904. Toll-free (800)334-2828. (706)576-5787. Fax (706)317-5808. E-mail: Brentwood@aol.com. Website: www.Publish MyBook.com. Brentwood Publishing Group. U.D. Roberts, exec. ed.; submit to Marie Warren, ed. All books must be family suitable. Receives 100 submissions annually. 98% of books from first-time authors. Accepts mss through agents. **SUBSIDY PUBLISHES 98%.** Does print-on-demand. Offers InstaBooks and Just in Time publishing (print-on-demand). Reprints books. Prefers 64-300 pgs. Publication within 1 mo. Considers simultaneous submissions. Responds in 3 days. Guidelines on Website; no catalog.

   Nonfiction: Complete ms/diskette; no phone/fax/e-query. All religious—for family or youth.

   Fiction: Complete ms/diskette; no phone/fax/e-query. For all ages.

SERMON SELECT PRESS, 4000 Beallwood Ave., Columbus GA 31904. Toll-free (800)334-2828. (706)576-5787. Fax (706)317-5808. E-mail: Brentwood@aol.com. Website: www .BrentwoodBooks.com. Subsidiary of Brentwood Publishers Group. U. D. Roberts, exec. dir. **SUBSIDY OR CUSTOM PUBLISHES 100%.** Focus is on sermon notes, outlines, illustrations, plus news that pastors would find interesting. Publishes 100 copies. Cost of about $3-4/book. Publication in 45 days. Same-day response.

SOUTHERN BAPTIST PRESS, 4000 Beallwood, Columbus GA 31904. Toll-free (800)334-2828. (706)576-5787. E-mail: Brentwood@aol.com. Website: www.SouthernBaptistPress .com. U.D. Roberts, exec. ed. Publishes 25 books/yr. Receives 600 submissions annually. Reprints books. **SUBSIDY OR CUSTOM PUBLISHES 95%.** Average first printing 500. Publication within 2 mos. Considers simultaneous submissions. Responds in 1 week. Guidelines.

   Nonfiction: Complete ms. "Collections of sermons on family topics; poetry; relation of Bible to current day."

   Fiction: Complete ms. "Stories that show how faith helps overcome small, day-to-day problems."

   Tips: "Keep it short; support facts with reference."

*STEP-BY-STEP PUBLICATIONS, PO Box 369, Cloverdale IN 46120. Toll-free (800)709-8097. E-mail: sbs@sbspub.com. Website: www.sbspub.com. Submit to The Editor. Publishes 1-2 titles/yr. **SUBSIDY PUBLISHES 100%.** Guidelines and price list on Website. Not included in topical listings (accepts almost any topic). No questionnaire returned.

#STRONG TOWER PUBLISHING, PO Box 973, Milesburg PA 16853. E-mail: strongtower pubs@aol.com. Website: www.strongtowerpublishing.com. Heidi L. Nigro, pub. Looks for books that challenge the reader to think more deeply about their faith and scriptural truths; must be biblically responsible, doctrinally defensible, and consistent with their statement of faith. Publishes 1-2 titles/yr. 50% of books from first-time authors. No mss through agents. No reprints. **PRINT-ON-DEMAND 100%.** Royalty on retail; no advance. Average first printing 200. Publication within 3-4 mos. No guidelines or catalog. Information and prices on Website.

   Nonfiction: Query.

   Fiction: Query. Adult biblical.

   Tips: "We recommend that all first-time authors have their manuscript professionally edited. We will consider putting first-time authors into print, but by invitation only. That invitation comes only after the manuscript has been thoroughly evaluated and we have discussed the pros and cons of our unique on-demand publishing model with the author."

SYNERGY PUBLISHERS, PO Box 141630, Gainesville FL 32614-1640. (352)472-7900. E-mail: submissions@bridgelogos.com. Website: www.bridgelogos.com. **CO-OP PUBLISHING** imprint of Bridge-Logos. Pays for cost of production and royalties, but author is required to buy a certain number of books up front. Not included in topical listings. No questionnaire returned.

TEACH SERVICES, INC., 254 Donovan Rd., Brushton NY 12916. (518)358-3494. Fax (518)358-3028. E-mail: publishing@TEACHservices.com. Website: www.teachservices .com. Timothy Hullquist, pres.; submit to Wayne Reid, acq. ed. To publish uplifting books for the lowest price. Publishes 40-50 titles/yr. Receives 100 submissions annually. 35% of books from first-time authors. No mss through agents. **SUBSIDY PUBLISHES 75%** (author has to pay for first printing, then publisher keeps it in print). Reprints books. Prefers 45,000 wds. or 96 pgs. Royalty 10% of retail; no advance. Average first printing 2,000. Publication within 6 mos. Requires requested ms on disk. Responds in 2 wks. Prefers KJV. Guidelines (also by e-mail/Website)/catalog for #10 SAE/2 stamps.

> **Nonfiction:** Query only; no phone/fax query. "Looking for books on nutrition."
> **Special Needs:** Personal testimonies.
> **Photos/Artwork:** Accepts freelance photos for book covers.

WINEPRESS PUBLISHING, PO Box 428, 1730 Railroad St., Enumclaw WA 98022. Toll-free (800)326-4674. (360)802-9758. Fax (360)802-9992. E-mail: info@winepresspub.com or athena@winepresspub.com. Website: www.winepresspub.com. The WinePress Group. Athena Dean, pub. Serves Christian authors with attentive service, quick responses, and honesty. Publishes 50+ titles/yr. Receives 500+ submissions annually. 70% of books from first-time authors. Accepts mss through agents. **BOOK PACKAGERS 95%.** Reprints books. Lengths range from 48-1,300 pgs. Author pays production costs, keeps all profit from sales. Average first printing 3,000 (2,500 min.). Publication in 6 mos. Considers simultaneous submissions. Responds in 48-72 hrs. Accepts requested ms on disk. Prefers NIV. Free guidelines (also on Website)/catalog. Not included in topical listings because they consider any topic or genre.

> **Nonfiction:** Complete ms; phone/fax/e-query OK. Publishes any topic as long as it's biblical or glorifies God.
> **Fiction:** Complete ms. All ages and all genres.
> **Also Does:** Booklets, gift books, Bibles, full-color children's books. Offers a print-on-demand program with competitive prices for less than 2,500 copies.
> **Photos/Artwork:** Accepts freelance photos for book covers.
> **Tips:** "As the leader in quality self-publishing, we offer professional book packaging for Christian writers. We not only offer a full line of editorial, design, layout, and printing services, but cutting-edge marketing, publicity, promotion, order fulfillment, warehousing, and distribution as well. Our in-house team of professionals is committed to serving our authors with excellent customer service and honest advice. We don't purchase rights to books and choose not to partner with messages that don't glorify God. All manuscripts that do not have a reasonably good chance of selling at least 1,000 copies are encouraged to take advantage of our print-on-demand services (see Pleasant Word listing)."

WINER FOUNDATION, PO Box 33373, Philadelphia PA 19142-3373. (215)365-3350. Fax (215)365-3325. E-mail: info@winerfoundation.org. Website: www.winerfoundation.org. Robert Winer, pres. Helping people walk in all that God intends for them. Publishes 4 titles/yr. **SUBSIDY PUBLISHES 90%.** Reprints books. Prefers 150-250 pgs. Royalty 3-10% of retail; advance $250-500. Average first printing 3,000-5,000. Publication within 6-8 mos. Considers simultaneous submissions. Requires requested ms on disk (Word, WordPerfect, or .RTF format). Responds in 1-2 mos. Prefers NKJV. Guidelines (also by e-mail); no catalog.

> **Nonfiction:** Proposal with 2-3 chapters; e-query OK. "Books on deeper spirituality to help people mature in the Lord."
> **Special Needs:** Messianic Jewish in addition to general Christianity.
> **Tips:** "Most open to books that fulfill our mission statement."

WORD ALIVE PRESS, 131 Cordite Rd., Winnipeg MB R3W 1S1, Canada. (866)967-3782, ext. 203. Fax (800)352-9272. E-mail: Cschmidt@wordalive.ca. C. Schmidt, ed. At least 6,000 wds. or 50 pgs. **100% PRINT-ON-DEMAND.** Guidelines and price list available.

WRITE HAND PUBLISHING, 105 Willow Dr., Andalusia AL 36421. (334)222-9212. E-mail: webmail@writehand.com. Website: www.writehand.com. George Payne, ed. Reprints books. Publication within 2 mos. Not a subsidy publisher; helps Christians self-publish their books. Prefers you call for information. No catalog.

> **Nonfiction:** Phone query only. Open to anything Christian.
> **Photos/Artwork:** Accepts freelance photos for book covers.

#XLIBRIS, 2 International Plz., Ste. 340, Philadelphia PA 19113-1598. Toll-Free (888)795-4274, ext. 278. E-mail: info@xlibris.com. Website: www.xlibris.com. Random House. Mercedes Bournias, publishing consultant. Can produce novels to 700 pgs. and picture books to 24 pgs. Not included in topical listings. No questionnaire returned.

#XULON PRESS, INC., 380 Crown Oak Centre Dr., Longwood FL 32750. Toll-free (866)381-2665, ext. 103. Fax (407)339-9898. E-mail: kkochenburger@xulonpress.com, or acquisitions@xulonpress.com. Website: www.xulonpress.com. Tom Freiling, pres./CEO.; Karen Kochenburger, ed. Uses digital and print-on-demand technologies to help Christian authors get published. Publishes 1,000 titles/yr. Receives 2,500 submissions annually. 80% of books from first-time authors. **SUBSIDY PUBLISHES 80%.** Reprints books. Any length. Royalty 20-25% of net; no advance. Print-on-demand. Publication within 2 mos. Considers simultaneous submissions. Responds in 1 mo. Not in topical listings; will consider all appropriate Christian topics. Guidelines on Website; free catalog.

> **Nonfiction:** Phone/fax/e-query OK.
> **Fiction:** Phone/fax/e-query OK.
> **Also Does:** Booklets, e-books.
> **Photos/Artwork:** Accepts freelance photos for book covers.
> **Tips:** "We offer publishing, distribution, and marketing services. Our books are available in bookstores and on the Internet. Our bimonthly catalog is mailed to 4,000 bookstores and media channels, and we publicize our books at trade shows, including at the annual CBA convention."
> ****Note:** This publisher (royalty division) serviced by The Writer's Edge.

LISTING OF CHRISTIAN BOOK/MUSIC/GIFT DISTRIBUTORS

ALLIANCE—MUSIC, 4250 Coral Ridge Dr., Coral Springs FL 33065-7615. (954)255-4600. Fax (954)255-4825. E-mail: custsvc@aent.com. Website: www.aent.com. Music.

AMAZON ADVANTAGE PROGRAM. Go to Amazon.com, scroll down to "Make Money" section in left-hand column, and click on "Advantage." Site to contact if you want Amazon to distribute your book.

ANCHOR DISTRIBUTORS, 1030 Hunt Valley Cir., New Kensington PA 15068. Toll-free (800)444-4484. (724)334-7000. Fax (800)765-1960 or (724)334-1200. E-mail: purchasing@anchordistributors.com, or marketing@anchordistributors.com. Website: www.anchordistributors.com. Donna Bonarati, intl. sales mngr. (800)444-4484, ext. 246.

APPALACHIAN DISTRIBUTORS, PO Box 1573, 522 Princeton Rd., Johnson City TN 37601. Toll-free (800)289-2772. Fax (800)759-2779. Website: www.appalink.com. A full-service distributor with two locations. Includes the homeschool market.

+BOOKMAN PUBLISHING & MARKETING, 35 Industrial Dr., Ste. 104, Martinsville IN 46151. Toll-free (800)342-6068. Fax (765)342-7217. E-mail: Brien@bookmanmarketing.com. Website: www.bookmanmarketing.com. Distributes self-published and print-on-demand books for authors (even from other publishers). Contact: Brien Jones.

B. BROUGHTON CO., LTD., 2105 Danforth Ave., Toronto ON M4C 1K1, Canada. Toll-free (800)268-4449. (416)690-4777. Fax (416)690-5357. E-mail: sales@bbroughton.com. Website: www.bbroughton.com. Canadian distributor.

CBA MAILING LISTS OF CHRISTIAN BOOKSTORES, PO Box 62000, Colorado Springs CO 80962-2000. Fax (719)272-3510. Available for rental. Four different lists available, including nonmember stores, 7,300 addresses ($149); member stores, 1,700 addresses ($649); chain-store headquarters (51) plus largest independent stores 1,000 addresses ($449); or a combined list of all stores, 9,000 addresses ($699). Prices subject to change. Call toll-free (800)252-1950 for full details.

CHRISTIAN BOOK DISTRIBUTORS, PO Box 7000, Peabody MA 01961-7000. Toll-free (800)247-4784. (978)977-5080. Fax (978-977-5010. E-mail: customer.service@ christianbooks.com. Website: www.christianbooks.com.

CONEXUS MULTIFAITH MEDIA, PO Box 39218, Solon OH 44139. Toll-free (877)784-7779. (440)349-0495. E-mail: info@conexuspress.com, or csv@conexuspress.com. Website: www.conexuspress.com. Distributes interreligious/interfaith and comparative religion resources, including books, music, videos, CD-ROMs, gift items, etc. James T. Cloud, owner.

CONSORTIUM BOOK SALES & DISTRIBUTION, INC., 1045 Westgate Dr., Ste. 90, St. Paul MN 55114. Toll-free (800)283-3572. (651)221-9035. Fax (651)221-0124. Website: www .cbsd.com.

COOK COMMUNICATIONS CANADA, 55 Woodslee Ave., Box 98, Paris ON N3L 3E5, Canada. Toll-free (800)263-2664. Fax (800)461-8575. E-mail: custserv@cook.ca. Website: www .cook.ca. Can distribute only in Canada.

DICKSONS, PO Box 368, Seymour IN 47274. (812)522-1308. Fax (812)522-1319. E-mail: marketing@dicksonsgifts.com. Website: www.dicksonsgifts.com. Distributes gift products only. Website includes a list of additional distributors.

EFULFILLMENT SERVICE, INC., 6893 Sullivan Rd., Grawn MI 49637. (231)276-5057, ext. 100. Fax (231)276-5074. E-mail: alc@efulfillmentservice.com, or info@efulfillment service.com. Website: www.efulfillmentservice.com. John Lindberg, pres. Services include storage and order fulfillment.

FAITHWORKS, 9247 Hunterboro Dr., Brentwood TN 37027. Toll-free (877)323-4550. Phone/fax (615)221-6442. E-mail: lcarpenter@faithworksonline.com. Website: www.faith worksonline.com. Contact: Larry Carpenter. Christian products, including books, music, videos, audiotapes, and software.

FOUNDATION DISTRIBUTING INC., 9 Cobbledick St., PO Box 98, Orono ON L0B 1M0, Canada. (905)983-1188. Fax (905)983-1190. E-mail: info@fdi.ca. Website: www.fdi.ca. Canadian distributor.

GENESIS MARKETING, 16 Wellington Ave., Greenville SC 29609. Toll-free (800)627-2651. Website: www.genesislink.com.

GL SERVICES, 1957 Eastman Ave., Ventura CA 93003. (805)677-6815. Fax (805)644-4729. E-mail: JeffMesinoff@GLServices.com. Website: www.GLServices.com. Contact: Jeff Mesinoff. A division of Gospel Light. Does not distribute books for individual authors.

#GODSPEED COMPUTING'S DIGITAL DISTRIBUTION SYSTEM, #211, 908—17 Ave. S.W., Calgary AB T2T 0A3, Canada. Toll-free (866)463-7733. (403)274-6510. Fax (403)282-1238. E-mail: sales@godspeedcomputing.com, or info@godspeedcomputing.com. Website: http://godspeedcomputing.com. E-book distributor.

INGRAM BOOK GROUP/DISTRIBUTION, One Ingram Blvd., La Vergne TN 37086-1986. Toll-free (800)937-8000. (615)793-5000. Website: www.ingrambookgroup.com. The best way to have your book/product distributed by this company is to go through one of their trading partners. For a list of distributing partners and more information, visit their Website.

KEY MARKETING GROUP, PO Box 162, Jenks OK 74037. Toll-free (877)727-0697. (918)298-0232. Fax (413)723-4384. E-mail: info@keymarketinggroup.net. Website: www .keymarketinggroup.net. Bryan Norris, owner.

LIGHTNING SOURCE, INC., 1246 Heil Quaker Blvd., La Vergne TN 37086. (615)213-5815. Fax (615)213-4426. E-mail: inquiry@lightningsource.com. Website: www.lightning source.com.

MALACO CHRISTIAN DISTRIBUTION, 3023 W. Northside Dr., Jackson MS 39213. (877)462-3623, Fax (877)270-4508. E-mail: tgoodwin@malaco.com, or malaco@malaco.com. Website: www.malaco.com. Tony Goodwin, mng. dir. of sales. Music distributor.

MCBETH CORPORATION, Fulfillment and Distribution Headquarters, PO Box 400, Chambersburg PA 17201. Toll-free (800)876-5112. (717)263-5600. Fax (800)876-5110 or (717)263-5600. E-mail: mcbeth@mcbethcorp.com. Website: www.mcbethcorp.com. Distributes Christian gift products.

R. G. MITCHELL FAMILY BOOKS, INC., 565 Gordon Baker Rd., Willowdale ON M2H 2W2, Canada. (416)499-4615. Fax (416)499-6340. E-mail: info@rgm.ca. Website: www.rgm.ca. David Freeland, pres.

#MUSIC/CD/TAPE DISTRIBUTOR, 1705 Woodmead St. S.W., Decatur AL 35601-4631. Contact: Brian Baer.

NEW DAY CHRISTIAN DISTRIBUTORS, 126 Shivel Dr., Hendersonville TN 37075. Toll-free (800)251-3633. (615)822-3633. Fax (800)361-2533. E-mail: info@newdaychristian .com. Website: www.newdaychristian.com. Music (primarily), books, Bibles, gift items.

NEW LIFE RESOURCES, (formerly New Life Publications) 375 Hwy. 74 S., Ste. A, Peachtree City GA 30269. Toll-free (800)235-7255, or (800)827-2788. Fax (800)514-7072, or (770)631-9916. E-mail: pat.pearce@campuscrusade.org. Website: www.campuscrusade .org. Contact: Pat Pearce.

NOAH'S ARK DISTRIBUTION, 28545 Felix Valdez Ave., Ste. B4, Temecula CA 92590-1859. Toll-free (800)562-8093. (760)723-3101. Fax (760)723-1443. E-mail: Noahtwo@juno .com. Website: www.noahsarkdistribution.com. Contact: Scott Vanyo, manager.

THE PARABLE GROUP, 3563 Empleo St., San Luis Obispo CA 93401. Toll-free (800)366-6031, ext. 525. Fax (800)543-2136. E-mail: info@parable.com. Website: www.parable.com. A marketing program for Christian bookstores.

PUBLISHERS GROUP WEST, National Headquarters: 1700 Fourth St., Berkeley CA 94710. (510)528-1444. Fax (510)528-3444. E-mail: info@pgw.com. Website: www.pgw.com. Send all inquiries to National Headquarters. Distribution Center: 7326 Winton Dr., Indianapolis IN 46268.

PUBLISHERS MARKETING ASSN., 627 Aviation Way, Manhattan Beach CA 90266-7107. (310)372-2732. Fax (310)374-3342. E-mail: info@pma-online.org. Website: www.pma-online.org. Trade association of independent publishers. Provides cooperative marketing programs for books, e-books, and audiobooks. Jan Nathan, exec. dir.

QUALITY BOOKS, 1003 W. Pines Rd., Oregon IL 61061. Toll-free (800)323-4241. (815)732-4450. Fax (815)732-4499. E-mail: tiffani.griffin@quality-books.com. Website: www .quality-books.com. Owner: Dawson Holdings PLC. Tiffani Griffin, mngr. of customer service & sales. Distributes small press books, videos, audios, DVDs, and CD-ROMs to secular libraries. Asks for 1 copy of your book, plus 30 covers.

SPRING ARBOR DISTRIBUTORS, PO Box 3006, One Ingram Blvd., Mailstop 671, La Vergne TN 37086. Toll-free (800)395-4340. Fax (615)213-5192 or (800)876-0186. E-mail: custserv@springarbor.com. Website: www.springarbor.com. Contact: Karen K. Bishop, Director, National Sales. Books, music, Bibles; no gift items or church supplies.

WHITAKER HOUSE PUBLISHERS, 1030 Hunt Valley Cir., New Kensington PA 15068. Toll-free

(877)793-9800. (724)334-2920. Fax (866)773-7001 or (724)334-2932. E-mail: sales@whitakerhouse.com. Donna Bonarati, intl. sales mngr. (800)444-4484, ext. 246.

WINDFLOWER COMMUNICATIONS, 67 Flett Ave., Winnipeg MB R2K 3N3, Canada. Toll-free (800)465-6564. (204)668-7475. Fax (204)668-7475. E-mail: windflower@brandt family.com. Website: www.brandtfamily.com. Brandt Family Enterprises. Gilbert Brandt, pres. Book distributor.

WORD ALIVE, INC., 131 Cordite Rd., Winnipeg MB R3W 1S1 Canada. Toll-free (800)665-1468. Fax (800)352-9272. E-mail: orderdesk@wordalive.ca. Website: www.wordalive.ca. Distributes Christian books and giftware, CD-ROMs, audiotapes & videotapes; all kinds of Christian products.

MARKET ANALYSIS

ALL PUBLISHERS IN ORDER OF MOST BOOKS PUBLISHED PER YEAR

Continuum Intl. 350-400
Tyndale House 225-250
Harvest House 190
United Methodist 175
Barbour Publishing 170
Scarecrow Press 150-200
Cook Communications 125
Eerdmans 120-130
Abingdon Press 120
Zondervan 120
Basic Books 100
Hazelden Publishing 100
New York Univ. Press 100
Steeple Hill 96-108
Bethany House 90-100
Broadman & Holman 90-100
Christian Focus 90
InterVarsity Press 90
Crossway 85
Christian Ed. Publishers 80
Paulist Press 80
Standard Publishing 75-100
HarperSanFrancisco 75
Multnomah 75
W Publishing Group 75
Love Inspired 72
Liturgical Press 70
WaterBrook Press 70
Moody Publishers 65-70
Tommy Nelson 65
Honor Books 60+
CSS Publishing 60
Fortress Press 60
Kregel 60
Ambassador-Emerald 55
Pilgrim Press 54
Heartsong Presents 52
Harcourt Religion 50-100
Custom Commun. 50-75
Pauline Books 50-60
T & T Clark. 50-60
Warner Faith 50-60
Holy Fire Publishing 50+
Boyds Mills Press 50
Chalice Press 50
Concordia 50
Crossroad Publishing 50
DiskUs Publishing 50
G. P. Putnam's Sons 50
University Press 50

Westminster/John Knox 50
ZonderKidz 50
Capall Bann 46
Howard Publishing 46
Doubleday Religion 45-50
Editores Betania-Caribe 45
RiverOak 45
Selah Publishing 45
Twenty-Third Publications 45
Nelson Books 42
Charisma House 40-50
Faith Kids Books 40-50
Peter Pauper Press 40-50
Jeremy P. Tarcher 40-50
Editorial Portavoz 40+
Group Publishing 40
Health Communications 40
Jossey-Bass 40
Legacy Press 40
Loyola Press 40
P & R Publishing 40
Youth Specialties 40
AMG Publishers 35
Eldridge (plays) 35
Monarch Books 35
Focus on the Family 30-40
Hendrickson 30-40
Morehouse Publishing 30-35
Beacon Hill Press 30
Christian Writer's Ebook 30
Cross Cultural 30
Genesis Communications 30
Good News Publishers (tracts) 30
invert 30
Judson Press 30
Thomas More 30
Pacific Press 30
New Leaf Press 25-30
Sheed & Ward 25-30
Smyth & Helwys 25-30
Bridge-Logos 25
Libros Liguori 25
Liguori Publications 25
Liturgy Training 25
Lutterworth Press 25
Meriwether (plays) 25
WestBow Press 25
New Hope 24-32
Alba House 24
One World 24

St. Augustine's Press 20-40
Chapter Two 20-30
Lighthouse eBooks 20-30
Our Sunday Visitor 20-30
Nelson Ignite 20-25
Univ. of Ottawa Press 20-25
Blue Dolphin 20-24
Carson-Delosa Publishing 20
CharismaKids 20
5th Estate Publishers 20
Jubilant Press 20
Rainbow Pub./Rainbow Books 20
Resource Publications 20
Scepter Publishers 20
Shining Star 20
Third World Press 20
Dimension Books 18
Big Idea 15-20
Catholic Book Publishing 15-20
College Press 15-20
McDougal Publishing 15-20
Branden Publishing 15
Mercer Univ. Press—R 15
Rainbow Pub./Legacy Press 15
Still Waters 15
Wesleyan Publishing House 15
Pathway Press 14-16
Discovery House 12-18
Master Books 12-15
Paragon House 12-15
Siloam Press 12-15
Allegiance Press 12
Forward Movement 12
Lamplighter Publishers 12
Promise Press/Suspense 12
Pflaum Publishing 10-20
Wm. Carey Library 10-15
Gospel Publishing House 10-15
Ragged Edge 10-15
Summit Pub. Group 10-15
Tapestry Press 10-15
Descant Publishing 10-12
E-Digital 10-12
Eerdmans/Young Readers 10-12
Ekklesia Press 10-12
Green Key 10-12
Hiddenspring Books 10-12
Lillenas 10-12
Messianic Jewish Publishers 10-12
St. Anthony Mess. Press 10-12

Starburst Publishers 10-12
Glory Bound Books 10+
ACTA Publications 10
BJU Press/Journey Forth 10
Canon Press 10
Christian Publications 10
FaithWalk Publishing 10
FamilyLife Publishing 10
Georgetown University Press 10
Haworth Press 10
PREP Publishing 10
Silas Publishing 10
Walk Worthy Press 10
Yale Univ. Press 10
Cistercian Publications 8-14
Emmaus Road 8-10
Holy Cross Orthodox 8-10
Lutheran University Press 8-10
Millennium III 8-10
TowleHouse Publishing 8-10
Neibauer Press 8
Oregon Catholic Press 8
Touch Publications 8
Ambassador Books 7
Woodland Gospel 7
Realms 6-10
Kirk House Publishers 6-8
Americana Publishing 6
Church & Synagogue Libraries 6
Filbert Publishing 6
Hope Publishing 6
ICS Publications 6
Inkling Books 6
Langmarc Publishing 6
Northstone Publishing 6
Square One Publishers 6
Trinity Foundation 6
Wilshire Book Co. 6
Greenwood Publishing 5-30
Troitsa Books 5-20
Conciliar Press 5-10
Hensley Publishing 5-10
Rose Publishing 5-10
World Publishing 5-10
Faith One Publishing 5-8
Perigee Books 5-8
Religious Education Press 5-6
ACU Press 5
Baylor Univ. Press 5
Diamond Eyes 5

Four Courts Press 5
Mt. Olive College Press 5
Paradise Research 5
Randall House 5
Friends United Press 4-6
Baker Trittin 4-5
Fair Havens Publications 4-5
Illumination Arts 4-5
Larson Publications 4-5
American Catholic Press 4
Church Growth Institute 4
Iceagle Press 4
Intl. Awakening Press 4
LifeSong Publishers 4
Open Court 4
WindRiver Publishing 4
Cerdic-Publications 3-5
Facts on File 3-5
Northfield Publishing 3-5
Virginia Pines Press 3-5
New Canaan 3-4
Quintessential Books 3-4
Tau-Publishing 3-4
ETC Publications 3
Magnus Press 3
Meriwether 3
Wood Lake Books 3
Baker's Plays 2-8
First Fruits of Zion 2-6
Jireh Publishing 2-5
Obadiah Press 2-5
Canadian Institute for Law 2-4
Frederick Fell 2-4
Regnery Publishing 2-4
UMI Press 2-4
Cladach Publishing 2-3
Daybreak Books/Rodale 2-3
Educational Ministries 2-3
Kindred Productions 2-3
Latimer Press 2-3
Sower's Press 2-3
Canticle Books 2
Devoted to You 2
Earthen Vessel 2
Genesis Press 2
Read 'N Run Books 2
Rising Star Press 2
Barclay Press 1-5
Living Books for All 1-5
Green Pastures Press 1-4

Life Cycle Books 1-3
Hill Street Press 1-2
Players Press 1-2
Write Now 1-2
Aadeon Publishing 1
BelleBooks 1
Gilgal Publications 1
Goetz 1
Good Book 1
Guernica Editions 1
Hay House 1
Noveledit 1
Pelican Publishing 1

SUBSIDY PUBLISHERS

Xulon Press 1,000
Pleasant Word 300+
Brentwood 267
Essence Publishing 100-150+
Black Forest Press 100
Fairway Press 100
Poet's Cove Press 75
American Binding 60
Creation House Press 50-100
WinePress 50+
Insight Publishing Group 50
Guardian Books 40-50
TEACH Services 40-50
ACW Press 40
Southern Baptist Press 25
Impact Christian Books 20+
Elderberry Press 15
Poetry of Today 12
Providence Publishing 12
Catholic Answers 10-20
Hannibal Books 8-10
Longwood Communications 8
Fruit-Bearer Publishing 5-10
Book Publishers 5-8
DCTS Publishing 5
Recovery Communications 4-6
Winer Foundation 4
Lightning Star Press 2-4
Ampelos Press 1-3
Step-by-Step 1-2
Strong Tower Publishing 1-2
Alfred Ali Literary 1
Robbie Dean Press 1

BOOK PUBLISHERS WITH THE MOST BOOKS ON THE BESTSELLER LIST FOR THE LAST YEAR

This tally is based on actual sales in Christian bookstores reported from July 2004 to June 2005 (most recent information available). In the past year, the categories of books tracked has changed, which accounts for some lists being incomplete for the year. However, we have included even the incomplete lists since they show some of the publishers that have done well with those genres. Numbers behind the names indicate the number of titles each publisher had on that particular bestseller list during the year. The combined list indicates the total number a particular publisher had on all the lists added together. If a publisher has more than one imprint listed, they are sometimes combined for these totals. It is interesting to note that in the past the number of publishers on the combined list has varied from a few publishers the first few years (starting at about 26 in 1993), to a much broader number for a couple of years (all time high of 60 in 1996), and then it started to drop again in 1998. By last year it was up to about 56, and this year, although some categories changed, it dropped to 49 different publishers. When we refer to those publishers that appeared on the Top 50 list for the year—that list has only 30 publishers represented. It is interesting to note that although there were very dominant leaders in each category last year, that happened only in Children's Books this year. With a combined total of 89 titles on the list last year, Barbour had shown themselves able not only to produce best-selling books, but to do it in a broad range of categories. This year Zondervan with 67 titles and Nelson with 45 moved ahead of Barbour, whose total dropped to only 41. A close analysis of who is on this list and in what categories will tell you a lot about what publishers to go to with certain projects.

Note: Categories marked with an asterisk (*) were tracked less than one year.

GENERAL INTEREST
1. Barbour 6
2. Howard 3
3. Nelson Books 3
4. Bethany House 2
5. InterVarsity 2
6. Oracle House 1
7. Regal 1
8. Viking 1
9. W Publishing 1

BIBLICAL STUDIES
1. Zondervan 15
2. Nelson 14
3. Baker 2
4. Barbour 2
5. Hendrickson 2
6. InterVarsity 2
7. Moody Publishers 2
8. NavPress 2
9. W Publishing 2
10. Broadman & Holman 1
11. Destiny Image 1
12. Hensley 1
13. Lifeway 1
14. Regal 1
15. Warner Faith 1
16. WaterBrook 1
17. Whitaker House 1
18. Willow Creek (Zondervan) 1

CHARISMATIC BOOKS*
1. Warner Faith 3
2. Harrison House 1
3. Nelson 1

CHRISTIAN LIVING
1. Nelson (Northfield) 15
2. Zondervan 11
3. W Publishing 10
4. Harvest House 7
5. Multnomah 7
6. Warner Faith 6
7. Barbour 5
8. Charisma 5
9. Moody 4
10. Broadman & Holman 3
11. Integrity 3
12. Tyndale 3
13. Crossway 2
14. Howard 2
15. WaterBrook 2
16. Bethany House 1
17. Harrison House 1
18. Penguin 1
19. Revell 1
20. Strang (Siloam) 1
21. Whitaker House 1

CHURCH & MINISTRY
1. Zondervan 8
2. Standard 4

3. Broadman & Holman 3
4. Baker (Academic) 2
5. Gospel Light 1
6. Multnomah 1
7. Nelson Books 1
8. Regal 1

INSPIRATIONAL
1. J Countryman 14
2. Barbour 12
3. Broadman & Holman 5
4. W Publishing 5
5. Zondervan 5
6. Howard 4
7. Nelson Books 3
8. Tyndale 3
9. Warner Faith 3
10. Multnomah 2
11. Penguin 2
12. Regal 2
13. Bethany House 1
14. Charisma 1
15. Harvest House 1
16. Ideal Publications 1
17. WaterBrook 1

MARRIAGE*
1. Harvest House 2
2. Moody 2
3. Multnomah 1

PARENTING*
1. Broadman & Holman 1
2. Harvest House 1
3. Howard 1
4. Revell 1
5. Tyndale 1

PRAYER*
1. Harrison House 2
2. Harvest House 2
3. Multnomah 2
4. Zondervan 2
5. Broadman & Holman 1
6. J Countryman 1
7. InterVarsity 1

RELATIONSHIPS*
1. Multnomah 4
2. Zondervan 1

SPIRITUAL GROWTH*
1. Zondervan 5
2. Broadman & Holman 3
3. Barbour 1
4. Warner Faith 1

THEOLOGY
1. Nelson Books 2
2. Tyndale 2
3. Whitaker House 2
4. Chariot Victor (Cook) 1
5. Crossway 1
6. Multnomah 1
7. Regal 1
8. Victor (Cook) 1

WOMEN'S INTEREST*
1. Harvest House 3
2. Multnomah 2
3. Nelson Books 2
4. WaterBrook 2
5. Moody 1

FICTION
1. Tyndale 19
2. Bethany House 17
3. Zondervan 11
4. Westbow Press (Nelson) 7
5. Multnomah 6
6. Barbour 3
7. Harvest House 3
8. WaterBrook 2
9. Bantam 1
10. Integrity 1
11. Steeple Hill 1
12. Viking 1
13. Warner Faith 1

FICTION: ROMANCE*
1. Multnomah 8
2. Barbour 2

CHILDREN'S BOOKS
1. Zonderkidz 21
2. Tommy Nelson 10
3. Standard 6
4. Barbour 5
5. Tyndale Kids 5
6. Crossway 4
7. Cook/Faith Kidz/Chariot 3
8. Dalmatian Press 3
9. Multnomah 3
10. Integrity 2
11. Legacy Press 2
12. Baker 1
13. Broadman & Holman 1
14. Howard 1
15. Ideals 1
16. Revell 1

YOUNG ADULT BOOKS
1. Tyndale Kids/Thirsty 8
2. Revell 7
3. Howard 4
4. Harvest House 3
5. Multnomah 3
6. Nelson 3
7. Zondervan 3
8. Barbour/Discovery House 2
9. NavPress 2
10. Tyndale 2
11. WaterBrook 2
12. Bethany House 1
13. Charisma 1
14. Integrity 1
15. Moody 1
16. Tommy Nelson 1
17. W Publishing 1

DEVOTIONALS*
1. Zondervan 3
2. Barbour 2
3. J Countryman 2
4. Honor Books (Cook) 1
5. Nelson Books 1
6. W Publishing 1

GIFT BOOKS*
1. J Countryman 9
2. Barbour 3
3. Zondervan 3
4. Broadman & Holman 2
5. Howard 1

6. Tyndale 1
7. W Publishing 1

COMBINED BESTSELLER LISTS
(combination of previous 19 lists)
1. Zondervan 67
2. Nelson Books 45
3. Barbour 41
4. Multnomah 40
5. Tyndale House 31
6. J Countryman 26
7. Bethany House 22
8. Harvest House 22
9. W Publishing 21
10. ZonderKidz 21
11. Broadman & Holman 20
12. Howard 16
13. Warner Books 15
14. Tyndale Kids 13
15. Tommy Nelson 11
16. Moody Press 10
17. Revell 10
18. Standard 10
19. WaterBrook 10
20. Charisma House 7
21. Crossway 7
22. Integrity 7
23. Westbow 7
24. Regal 6
25. Baker 5
26. InterVarsity 5
27. Harrison House 4
28. NavPress 4
29. Whitaker House 4
30. Cook/Faith Kidz/Chariot 3
31. Dalmatian 3
32. Penguin 3
33. Discovery House 2
34. Hendrickson 2
35. Ideals Publications 2
36. Legacy Press 2
37. Viking 2
38. Bantam 1
39. Chariot Victor 1
40. Destiny Image 1
41. Gospel Light 1
42. Hensley 1
43. Honor Books 1
44. Lifeway 1
45. Oracle House 1
46. Steeple Hill 1
47. Strang (Siloam) 1
48. Victor (Cook) 1
49. Willow Creek 1

TOP 50 BOOK PUBLISHERS

This list is based on which publishers had the most books on the list of the Top 50 books each month. It varies from the previous combined list in that it tracks the top 50 sellers regardless of genre. It is interesting to note that there were only 30 publishers with books on this list during the year.

1. Zondervan 24
2. Barbour 17
3. Nelson Books 16
4. W Publishing 14
5. J Countryman 11
6. Multnomah 11
7. Tyndale House 11
8. Harvest House 8
9. Warner Faith 8
10. Howard 6
11. WaterBrook 6
12. Westbow 6
13. Bethany House 5
14. Broadman & Holman 5
15. Charisma 5
16. Moody 4
17. Integrity 3
18. Baker 2
19. Crossway 2
20. InterVarsity 2
21. Penguin 2
22. Revell 2
23. Standard 2
24. Dalmatian Press 1
25. Harrison House 1
26. Ideal 1
27. Tommy Nelson 1
28. Strang/Siloam 1
29. Whitaker House 1
30. Zonderkidz 1

BOOK TOPICS MOST POPULAR WITH PUBLISHERS

Note: The numbers following the topics indicate how many publishers said they were interested in seeing a book on that topic. To find the list of publishers interested in each topic, go to the Topical Listings for books (see Table of Contents).

1. Inspirational 132
2. Prayer 132
3. Spirituality 130
4. Christian Living 129
5. Family Life 126
6. Religion 126
7. Devotional Books 113
8. Women's Issues 111
9. Biography 109
10. Theology 108
11. Bible/Biblical Studies 107
12. Faith 107
13. Parenting 107
14. Marriage 106
15. Discipleship 102
16. Fiction: Adult/Religious 98
17. Church History 91
18. Current/Social Issues 91
19. Evangelism/Witnessing 91
20. Ethics 90
21. Historical 90
22. Christian Education 88
23. Self-help 88
24. Church Life 87
25. Personal Growth 85
26. Leadership 84
27. Church Renewal 83
28. Fiction: Contemporary 81
29. Personal Renewal 78
30. Youth Books (nonfiction) 78
31. Death/Dying 76
32. Healing 76
33. Health 75
34. How-to 75
35. Controversial Issues 73
36. Scholarly 73
37. Doctrinal 72
38. Fiction: Juvenile (ages 8-12) 71
39. Fiction: Adventure 70
40. Men's Books 70
41. Fiction: Historical 69
42. Spiritual Life 69
43. Bible Commentary 67
44. Ethnic/Cultural 67
45. Reference Books 66
46. Pastors' Helps 65
47. Psychology 65
48. Spiritual Gifts 65
49. Forgiveness 64
50. Fiction: Teen/Young Adult 63
51. Gift Books 63
52. Social Justice Issues 63
53. Humor 62
54. Worship 62
55. Autobiography 61
56. Missionary 61
57. Prophecy 61
58. Counseling Aids 60
59. Money Management 60
60. Philosophy 60
61. Personal Experience 59
62. Church Traditions 58
63. Fiction: Biblical 58
64. Fiction: Literary 58
65. Recovery Books 58
66. Singles Issues 58
67. World Issues 58
68. Spiritual Warfare 57
69. Archaeology 56
70. Group Study Books 56
71. Photographs (for covers) 55
72. Divorce 54
73. Stewardship 54
74. Political 53
75. Senior Adult Concerns 53
76. Fiction: Mystery/Suspense 52
77. Worship Resources 52
78. Dating/Sex 51
79. Holy Spirit 50
80. Children's Easy Readers 49
81. Children's Picture Books 49
82. Christian Homeschooling 49
83. Cults/Occult 49
84. Environmental Issues 48
85. Exegesis 48
86. Fiction: Humor 48
87. Miracles 48
88. Christian Business 47
89. Holiday/Seasonal 47
90. Liturgical Studies 47
91. Time Management 47
92. Eschatology 46
93. Fiction: Mystery/Romance 46

94. Memoirs 46
95. Poetry 46
96. Sermons 46
97. Fiction: Romance 45
98. Religious Tolerance 45
99. Retirement 45
100. Science 45
101. Christ 44
102. Economics 43
103. Fiction: Fantasy 43
104. Sociology 43
105. Booklets 41
106. Fiction: Ethnic 41
107. Fiction: Science Fiction 41
108. Fiction: Frontier 40
109. Fiction: Short Story
    Collection 40
110. Homiletics 40
111. Fiction: Historical/Romance 39

112. Curriculum 37
113. Christian School Books 36
114. Drama 36
115. Celebrity Profiles 35
116. Creation Science 35
117. Fiction: Allegory 35
118. Fiction: Frontier/Romance 35
119. Racism 35
120. Sports/Recreation 35
121. Travel 35
122. Apologetics 34
123. Homeschooling Resources 34
124. Cookbooks 32
125. Fiction: Westerns 32
126. Games/Crafts 31
127. Music-Related Books 31
128. Compilations 30
129. Print-on-demand 29
130. Encouragement 28

131. E-books 26
132. Youth Programs 25
133. Charismatic 24
134. Commentaries 24
135. Fiction: Plays 24
136. Fiction: Speculative 24
137. Pamphlets 23
138. Writing How-to 23
139. Church Management 22
140. Fiction: Chick Lit 22
141. Tracts 22
142. Fiction: Novellas 21
143. Canadian/Foreign 20
144. Exposés 19
145. Children's Board Books 14
146. Novelty Books For Kids 13
147. Fiction: Fables/Parables 10
148. Minibooks 8

COMMENTS

If you are a fiction writer, you are more likely to sell adult fiction (98 possible publishers—6 more than last year) than you are juvenile fiction (71 publishers—9 more than last year), or teen fiction (63 publishers—14 more than last year). These figures indicate that the fiction market is greatly improving for children and teen fiction, and even significant improvement in the adult category.

The most popular fiction genres with publishers are (1) Contemporary, 81 markets, (2) Adventure, 70 markets, (3) Historical, 69 markets, (4) Biblical, 58 markets, (5) Literary, 58 markets, (6) Mystery/Suspense, 52 markets, and (7) Humorous, 48 markets. This year, Contemporary stayed at the top, Adventure moved ahead of Historical, and Humorous replaced Mystery/Romance at #7. All the numbers above show an increase in actual markets for each genre, for the sixth year in a row. While last year's numbers ranged from 33 to 69 markets in these categories, this year's range from 48 to 81—a substantial increase.

This year the book market for poetry went up from 37 to 47—a 27% increase in one year. That compares to only 16 in 1994, a 66% increase in the last 12 years. Those numbers should be encouraging to the poets. However, most poets will still want to consider self-publishing (look for subsidy publishers listed in another section of this book). I encourage poets to establish their reputation as a poet by submitting regularly to periodicals before ever considering a book of poetry. Go to the periodical topical listings in this book to find 195 markets for poetry (two less than last year).

Compared to last year, the same 14 topics are at the top, but with most in a different location, and Inspirational at the top.

SUMMARY OF INFORMATION ON CHRISTIAN BOOK PUBLISHERS FOUND IN THE ALPHABETICAL LISTINGS

Note: Following is some general information based on averages of the information supplied by the book publishers in this guide. This information will be valuable in determining if the contract offered by your publisher is in line with other publishers in some of these areas. For further help, check the section on editorial services to find those who offer contract evaluations, which are most valuable.

TOTAL MANUSCRIPTS RECEIVED

About 260 book publishers received combined total of about 250,000 manuscripts during the year. That is an average of over 900 manuscripts per publisher, per year. The actual number of manuscripts received ranges from 5 to 10,000 per publisher.

NUMBER OF BOOKS PUBLISHED

Over 300 publishers reported that they will publish a combined total of almost 12,000 titles during the coming year. That is an average of 40 books per publisher. The actual number per publisher ranges from 1 to 1,000. If each publisher actually publishes his maximum estimate of books for the year, about 5% of the manuscripts submitted will be published.

AVERAGE FIRST PRINT RUN

The average first printing of a book for a new author is just under 4,600 books. Actual print runs ranged from 200 to 20,000 copies. These numbers indicate that publishers are generally publishing about the same number of titles but fewer copies of those titles.

ROYALTIES

Of the almost 300 publishers who indicated that they paid royalties, about 23% pay on the retail price, 53% pay on the wholesale price or net, and the rest did not indicate which. The average royalty based on the retail price of the book was about 9% to 14%. Actual royalties on retail varied from 2% to 50%. The average royalty based on net varied from 10% to 15%. The average royalties in both categories are up this year. Actual royalties on net varied from 2% to 50%. The recommended royalty based on net is 18%, but only 14% of the Christian publishers counted here are paying 18% or higher.

ADVANCES

Not all publishers are willing to disclose whether they pay an advance, and if so, how much. For that reason it is hard to come up with accurate figures. Generally speaking, of those that answered the question about advances, 54% pay an advance, and 46 say they do not. Of those who indicated a specific amount, the average ranged from about $3,000 to $16,000. The actual range is from $250 to $50,000, so ask for the amount that you need or deserve based on past publishing history. (Although one publisher indicated they pay up to a $1 million advance, we didn't include them in order to keep these averages realistic.) Most publishers pay more for established authors or potentially best-selling books. It is not unusual for a first-time author to get no advance or a small one. Once you have one or more books published, feel free to ask for an advance, and raise the amount for each book. Don't be afraid to ask for an advance, even on a first book, if you need the money to support you while you finish the manuscript. Although some publishers say they don't give an advance or are reluctant to name an amount, the truth is, many of those publishers do give advances when warranted.

REPORTING TIME

Waiting for a response from an editor is often the hardest part of the writing business. Of the almost 300 editors who indicated how long you should have to wait for a response from them, the average time was just over 12 weeks. However, since the times they actually gave ranged from 1 to 52 weeks, be sure to check the listing for the publisher you are interested in. Give them a 2- to 4-week grace period; then feel free to write a polite letter asking about the current status of your manuscript. Give them another month to respond, and if you don't hear anything, you can call as a last resort or ask for your manuscript to be returned.

E-MAIL AND WEBSITES

Almost every book publisher has both an e-mail and a Website, but some are reluctant to list their e-mail unless they prefer to be contacted that way.

PREFERRED BIBLE VERSION

Book publishers list their preferred Bible versions as NIV, KJV, NRSV, and NKJV, in that order. Each publisher's preference is indicated in the regular listings.

TOPICAL LISTINGS OF PERIODICALS

As soon as you have an article or story idea, look up that topic in the following topical listings (see table of contents for a full list of topics). Study the appropriate periodicals in the primary/alphabetical listings (as well as their writers' guidelines and sample copies) and select those that are most likely targets for the piece you are writing.

Note that most ideas can be written for more than one periodical if you slant them to the needs of different audiences, for example, current events for teens, or pastors, or women. Have a target periodical and audience in mind before you start writing. Each topic is divided by age group/audience, so you can pick appropriate markets for your particular slant.

If the magazine prefers or requires a query letter, be sure to write that letter first and then follow any guidelines or suggestions they make if they give you a go-ahead.

R—Takes reprints
(*)—Indicates new topic this year
($)—Indicates a paying market

APOLOGETICS

ADULT/GENERAL
Alliance Life
$-Arkansas Catholic—R
$-Bible Advocate—R
Bread of Life—R
$-Catholic Insight
$-Celebrate Life—R
Channels—R
Christian Online
Christian Research
$-Christianity Today—R
Church Herald & Holiness—R
$-City Light News—R
$-Discipleship Journal—R
Eternal Ink—R
Evangelical Advocate—R
$-HonorBound—R
$-Horizons (adult)—R
$-Inside Journal—R
$-Light & Life
$-Lookout
$-Montgomery's Journey
$-National Catholic
$-On Mission
$-Our Sunday Visitor
$-Plain Truth—R
$-Plains Faith—R
Priscilla Papers—R
Randall House Periodicals
Sword and Trumpet—R
Sword of the Lord—R
$-Today's Christian—R
$-Today's Pentecostal Evangel—R

Victory News—R
$-Wesleyan Life—R

PASTORS/LEADERS
$-Catholic Servant
$-Christian Century—R
Theological Digest—R
$-This Rock

BIBLE STUDIES

ADULT/GENERAL
AGAIN—R
$-Alive Now—R
Alliance Life
$-Arlington Catholic
$-Aujourd'hui Credo—R
Bread of Life—R
Breakthrough Intercessor—R
$-Catholic Peace Voice—R
$-Catholic Yearbook—R
Christian Computing—R
Christian Motorsports
Christian Online
Christian Ranchman
Church Herald & Holiness—R
Connecting Point—R
Creation Care—R
$-Culture Wars—R
Desert Call—R
Eternal Ink—R
$-Foursquare World Advance—R
$-Gem—R
$-Generation X—R
Heartlight—R
$-HonorBound—R

HopeKeepers—R
$-Indian Life—R
$-Inside Journal—R
$-Light & Life
$-Lookout
$-Lutheran Journal—R
Mature Times—R
$-Mature Years—R
Men of the Cross
Methodist History
$-My Walk With Jesus
$-New Freeman—R
$-New Wineskins—R
$-Our Sunday Visitor
$-Plain Truth—R
$-Plains Faith—R
$-Positive Thinking—R
PrayerWorks—R
$-Precepts for Living
Priscilla Papers—R
Quaker Life—R
Randall House Periodicals
Singles Scoop—R
$-Sojourners
$-Spiritual Life
$-St. Anthony Messenger
Star of Zion
Sword and Trumpet—R
Sword of the Lord—R
thegoodsteward.com—R
$-Today's Pentecostal Evangel—R
Trumpeter—R
Victory News—R
$-Voice of the Lord

$-War Cry—R
$-Way of St. Francis—R
$-Wesleyan Life—R

CHILDREN
$-Primary Street

CHRISTIAN EDUCATION/ LIBRARY
$-Children's Ministry
Church & Synagogue Lib.—R
$-Church Educator—R
$-Preschool Playhouse
$-RTJ

MISSIONS
Railroad Evangelist—R
Women of the Harvest

PASTORS/LEADERS
$-African American Pulpit
$-Catholic Servant
$-Evangelicals Today—R
$-Let's Worship
$-Ministries Today
$-Pastoral Life—R
$-Pray!—R
Pulpit Helps—R
Quarterly Review
Sewanee Theo. Review
Sharing the Practice—R
$-Small Group Dynamics—R
Strategic Adult Ministries—R
Theological Digest—R
$-This Rock
$-Word & World

TEEN/YOUNG ADULT
GO!
$-Passageway.org—R
$-Student Leadership—R
Teen Light—R
TeensForJC—R
Transcendmag.com—R
$-With—R
$-Young Christian—R
$-Young Salvationist—R

WOMEN
Faithwebbin—R
Precious Times—R
Right to the Heart—R
Women of the Cross

BOOK EXCERPTS

ADULT/GENERAL
AGAIN—R
$-Alive Now—R
$-Animal Trails—R
$-Associated Content—R

Books & Culture
$-Bridal Guides—R
$-Catholic Digest—R
$-Catholic New Times—R
Channels—R
$-Chicken Soup—R
Christian Observer
$-Christian Parenting—R
$-Christian Renewal—R
$-Christian Retailing
$-Christianity Today—R
$-Culture Wars—R
Evangelical Advocate—R
$-Generation X—R
$-HonorBound—R
HopeKeepers—R
$-Ideals—R
$-Indian Life—R
Mature Times—R
Metro Voice—R
New Heart—R
$-New Wineskins—R
Nostalgia—R
Parents & Teens—R
$-Plains Faith—R
$-Portland Magazine
$-Power for Living—R
Priscilla Papers—R
$-Prism—R
Quaker Life—R
Regent Business—R
Sacred Journey—R
Short Stories Bimonthly—R
$-SingleAgain.com
Singles Scoop—R
Spiritual Voice—R
$-Spring Hill Review—R
Steps
thegoodsteward.com—R
$-Today's Christian—R
Tributes—R
Trumpeter—R
$-United Church Observer—R
$-Upscale Magazine
Victory News—R
Walk This Way—R
$-Wesleyan Life—R
$-Wittenburg Door—R

MISSIONS
Intl. Jour./Frontier—R

PASTORS/LEADERS
$-African American Pulpit
$-Christian Century—R
$-Ministries Today
$-Ministry & Liturgy—R
Pastors.com—R

Pulpit Helps—R
Sharing the Practice—R

TEEN/YOUNG ADULT
$-Boundless Webzine—R
$-J.A.M.
$-Passageway.org—R
Teen Light—R
TeensForJC—R
Transcendmag.com—R

WOMEN
Faithwebbin—R
$-Godly Business Woman
Hearts at Home—R
Home-Based Moms—R
$-Link & Visitor—R
$-MOMsense—R
$-SpiritLed Woman

WRITERS
Money the Write Way—R

BOOK REVIEWS

ADULT/GENERAL
$-Abilities
African Voices—R
AGAIN—R
$-America
$-Anglican Journal
$-Arkansas Catholic—R
$-Arlington Catholic
$-Aspiring Retail
$-Associated Content—R
$-Barefoot Path—R
Books & Culture
byFaith
$-Cathedral Age
$-Catholic Insight
$-Catholic Peace Voice—R
Channels—R
$-Charisma
Charlotte World
Christian Computing—R
Christian Current
$-Christian Herald—R
Christian Journal—R
Christian Media—R
Christian Observer
Christian Radio Weekly
$-Christian Renewal—R
Christian Research
$-Christian Retailing
$-Christian Social Action—R
$-Christianity Today—R
Citizen USA—R
$-City Light News—R
$-Cornerstone Christian—R

Creation Care—R
$-Cresset
CrossHome.com
$-Culture Wars—R
Desert Voice
Divine Ascent
$-Dovetail—R
$-Episcopal Life—R
Eternal Ink—R
$-Eureka Street
Evangelical Advocate—R
$-Faith & Family
$-Faith Today
Fire By Nite
$-First Things
Founders Journal
$-Generation X—R
Good News Journal
Good News/S. Florida
Hannah to Hannah—R
Heartland Gatekeeper
$-HonorBound—R
HopeKeepers—R
$-Image/WA
$-Impact—R
$-Indian Life—R
Infuze Magazine
$-Inland NW Christian
$-Interim—R
$-Joy & Praise
LifeLine Journal—R
Light at Home—R
$-Lutheran Journal—R
Maranatha News—R
Mars Hill Review
Mature Times—R
Methodist History
$-Minnesota Christian—R
Mutuality—R
$-New Wineskins—R
$-Parabola—R
Parents & Teens—R
Penwood Review
Perspectives—R
$-Plain Truth—R
$-Plains Faith—R
$-Prairie Messenger—R
Presbyterian Outlook
$-Presbyterians Today—R
Priscilla Papers—R
$-Prism—R
Purpose Magazine
Quaker Life—R
$-Queen of All Hearts
Radix—R
$-Rare Jewel—R
Reformed Quarterly

Regent Business—R
Rock & Sling
Rose & Thorn
Sacred Journey—R
$-Science & Spirit
Short Stories Bimonthly—R
Silver Wings—R
$-SingleAgain.com
Singles Scoop—R
$-Social Justice—R
$-Sojourners
$-Spiritual Life
Spiritual Voice—R
$-Spring Hill Review—R
Star of Zion
Studio—R
$-Testimony—R
thegoodsteward.com—R
$-Tidewater Parent—R
Time of Singing—R
Tributes—R
Trumpeter—R
$-Upscale Magazine
Valparaiso Poetry—R
Victory News—R
Walk This Way—R
$-Way of St. Francis—R
$-Weavings—R
$-Wesleyan Life—R
Winsome Wit—R
$-Wireless Age—R
$-World & I—R
Xavier Review

CHILDREN
$-Barefoot for Kids—R

CHRISTIAN EDUCATION/
LIBRARY
Catholic Library World
Christian Early Education—R
Christian Librarian—R
Christian Library Journal—R
Christian School Education—R
Church & Synagogue Lib.—R
$-Church Libraries—R
Jour. of Christian Education
Jour./Christianity/Foreign Languages
Jour./Ed. & Christian Belief—R
$-Journal/Adventist Educ.—R
Journal/Christian Education
$-Momentum
$-Teachers of Vision—R

MISSIONS
East-West Church
$-Evangelical Missions—R
Missiology

OpRev Equipper—R
Women of the Harvest

MUSIC
$-CCM Magazine
$-Creator—R
Hymn

PASTORS/LEADERS
$-African American Pulpit
$-Barefoot—R
$-Christian Century—R
Christian Education Jour. (CA)—R
Cross Currents
$-Diocesan Dialogue—R
$-Emmanuel
$-Enrichment—R
$-Evangelical Baptist—R
$-Evangelicals Today—R
$-Five Stones—R
$-Horizons (pastor)—R
$-Interpreter
Journal/Pastoral Care—R
$-Leadership—R
$-Let's Worship
Lutheran Forum—R
$-Lutheran Partners—R
$-Ministries Today
$-Ministry
Ministry in Motion—R
$-Pastoral Life—R
Pulpit Helps—R
Quarterly Review
$-Reformed Worship
$-Sermon Notes—R
Sharing the Practice—R
$-Small Group Dynamics—R
Strategic Adult Ministries—R
Theological Digest—R
$-This Rock
$-WCA News—R
$-Word & World
$-Worship Leader
$-Your Church—R

TEEN/YOUNG ADULT
$-Boundless Webzine—R
$-Devo'Zine—R
$-J.A.M.
Teen Light—R
TeensForJC—R
Transcendmag.com—R

WOMEN
Anna's Journal—R
$-Esprit—R
$-Godly Business Woman
Hearts at Home—R
Home-Based Moms—R

$-Horizons (women)—R
$-inSpirit—R
Precious Times—R
Right to the Heart—R

WRITERS
$-Adv. Christian Writer—R
$-Areopagus (UK)
$-Christian Communicator—R
$-Cross & Quill—R
$-Fellowscript—R
Money the Write Way—R
NW Christian Author—R
$-Spirit-Led Writer—R
$-Tickled by Thunder
$-Upper Case
Writer's Lifeline
$-Writers' Journal
Writes of Passage—R

CANADIAN/FOREIGN MARKETS

ADULT/GENERAL
Anglican
$-Abilities
$-Anglican Journal
$-Annals of St. Anne
$-Atlantic Catholic
$-Aujourd'hui Credo—R
$-B.C. Catholic—R
Bread of Life—R
$-Canada Lutheran—R
Canadian Christianity.com
Canadian Lutheran
Canadian Mennonite
$-Catholic Insight
$-Catholic New Times—R
Catholic Register
Challenge Weekly
Challenging Destiny
Channels—R
$-Christian Courier (CAN)—R
$-Christian Herald—R
Christian Herald (UK)
Christian Outlook
$-Christian Renewal—R
Church of England News
$-City Light News—R
Common Ground—R
Crossway/Newsline—R
$-Dreams & Visions—R
$-Eureka Street
Evangelical Times
$-Faith & Friends—R
$-Faith Today
Fellowship Magazine
$-Impact—R

$-Indian Life—R
Insight (for blind)
$-Interim—R
InTouch
Island Catholic News
Lifesite Canada
$-Living Light News—R
Mature Times—R
$-Mennonite Brethren—R
Mennonite Historian—R
$-Messenger/Sacred Heart
$-Messenger/St. Anthony
Mosaic—R
MovieGuide
$-New Freeman—R
Plowman—R
$-Prairie Messenger—R
Singles Scoop—R
Studio—R
Sunday Magazine
$-Testimony—R
Time for Rhyme—R
TJ
$-United Church Observer—R
Walk This Way—R
War Cry (Canada)—R

CHRISTIAN EDUCATION/ LIBRARY
$-Christian Educators Journal—R
Jour. of Christian Education

DAILY DEVOTIONALS
$-Words of Life

MISSIONS
Catholic Missions/Canada
Glad Tidings

PASTORS/LEADERS
$-Evangelical Baptist—R
$-Evangelicals Today—R
$-Horizons (pastor)—R
Ministry Matters
Technologies for Worship—R
Theological Digest—R

WOMEN
Christian Women Today—R
$-Esprit—R
Life Tools for Women
$-Link & Visitor—R
Making Waves
Women Today—R

WRITERS
$-Areopagus (UK)
$-Brady—R
$-Canadian Writer's Journal—R
$-Exchange—R

$-Fellowscript—R
$-Tickled by Thunder
Writer's Lifeline
Writers Manual

CELEBRITY PIECES

ADULT/GENERAL
American Tract Society—R
$-Angels on Earth
$-Arlington Catholic
$-Associated Content—R
Breakthrough Intercessor—R
$-Catholic Digest—R
$-Celebrate Life—R
Challenging Destiny
$-Christian Herald—R
Christian Journal—R
Christian Motorsports
Christian Online
Christian Radio Weekly
Christian Ranchman
$-Christian Social Action—R
Citizen USA—R
$-City Light News—R
$-Cornerstone Christian—R
$-Episcopal Life—R
Eternal Ink—R
Fire By Nite
$-Generation X—R
$-God Allows U-Turns—R
Good News Journal
$-Good News, Etc.—R
$-Grit
$-Guideposts—R
Heartland Gatekeeper
Heartlight—R
$-HonorBound—R
HopeKeepers—R
$-Indian Life—R
$-Inside Journal—R
LifeLine Journal—R
$-Light & Life
$-Live—R
$-Living Light News—R
Maranatha News—R
Metro Voice—R
$-Minnesota Christian—R
$-Montgomery's Journey
Mutuality—R
$-New Wineskins—R
Nostalgia—R
$-Plains Faith—R
$-Positive Thinking—R
$-Power for Living—R
$-Priority!—R
$-Prism—R
Quaker Life—R

Sacred Journey—R
Spiritual Voice—R
$-St. Anthony Messenger
Sunday Magazine
thegoodsteward.com—R
$-Today's Christian—R
Tri-State Voice
Trumpeter—R
$-Vibrant Life—R
Victory News—R
$-War Cry—R
$-Wireless Age—R
$-Wittenburg Door—R

CHILDREN
$-American Girl
$-Cadet Quest—R
$-Guideposts for Kids
$-High Adventure—R
$-SHINEbrightly—R
$-Winner—R

CHRISTIAN EDUCATION/ LIBRARY
$-Children's Ministry

MUSIC
Christian Music Weekly—R

PASTORS/LEADERS
$-Catholic Servant
Ministry in Motion—R
$-Pastoral Life—R

TEEN/YOUNG ADULT
$-Boundless Webzine—R
$-Brio—R
$-Essential Connection
GO!
$-J.A.M.
$-Passageway.org—R
$-Sharing the VICTORY—R
Steelroots
Teen Light—R
TeensForJC—R
Transcendmag.com—R
$-Young Salvationist—R

WOMEN
$-Dabbling Mum.com—R
$-Godly Business Woman
$-Journey
$-MOMsense—R
Precious Times—R

WRITERS
$-Upper Case

CHRISTIAN BUSINESS

ADULT/GENERAL
Alliance Life

$-Angels on Earth
$-Aspiring Retail
Breakthrough Intercessor—R
Business Reform
$-Central Appalachia
$-Christian Courier (CAN)—R
Christian Journal—R
$-Christian Leader—R
Christian Motorsports
Christian News NW—R
Christian Online
Christian Ranchman
$-Christian Retailing
$-ChristianWeek—R
Church Herald & Holiness—R
Citizen USA—R
$-City Light News—R
$-Cornerstone Christian—R
Desert Call—R
Disciple's Journal—R
Discovery—R
$-Faith Today
$-Gem—R
$-Generation X—R
Good News Journal
$-Gospel Today—R
$-Guideposts—R
Heartland Gatekeeper
Heartlight—R
Highway News—R
$-HonorBound—R
$-Indian Life—R
$-Light & Life
$-Living—R
Maranatha News—R
Marketplace
Men of the Cross
Metro Voice—R
$-Minnesota Christian—R
$-Montgomery's Journey
$-New Freeman—R
NRB Magazine—R
$-Our Sunday Visitor
$-Palm Beach—R
$-Plains Faith—R
$-Power for Living—R
$-Prism—R
Purpose Magazine
Randall House Periodicals
Regent Business—R
$-Science & Spirit
$-SingleAgain.com
$-Social Justice—R
$-Sojourners
Spiritual Voice—R
$-St. Anthony Messenger
thegoodsteward.com—R

$-Today's Christian—R
$-Together—R
Trumpeter—R
Victory News—R
$-War Cry—R
$-Wesleyan Life—R
$-Wireless Age—R

CHRISTIAN EDUCATION/ LIBRARY
$-Resource—R
$-Youth & CE Leadership

MISSIONS
$-Evangelical Missions—R

PASTORS/LEADERS
$-African American Pulpit
$-Catholic Servant
$-Christian Century—R
$-Church Administration
$-Clergy Journal—R
$-Evangelicals Today—R
$-InSite—R
$-Interpreter
$-Ministries Today
$-Pastoral Life—R
Pastors.com—R
Sharing the Practice—R
Technologies for Worship—R
$-Today's Parish—R
$-WCA News—R
$-Your Church—R

TEEN/YOUNG ADULT
$-J.A.M.

WOMEN
Christian Women Today—R
$-Dabbling Mum.com—R
$-Esprit—R
$-Godly Business Woman
Home-Based Moms—R
Precious Times—R
Right to the Heart—R

WRITERS
Money the Write Way—R
Writing Corner

CHRISTIAN EDUCATION

ADULT/GENERAL
African Voices—R
$-America
$-Anglican Journal
$-Arlington Catholic
$-B.C. Catholic—R
Breakthrough Intercessor—R
$-Canada Lutheran—R
$-Catholic New Times—R

$-Catholic Peace Voice—R
$-Celebrate Life—R
Channels—R
Christian C. L. RECORD—R
$-Christian Courier (CAN)—R
$-Christian Examiner
$-Christian Home & School
Christian Journal—R
$-Christian Leader—R
Christian News NW—R
Christian Observer
Christian Online
Christian Ranchman
$-Christian Renewal—R
$-Christian Retailing
$-Christianity Today—R
$-ChristianWeek—R
Church Herald & Holiness—R
$-City Light News—R
$-Columbia
$-Company—R
$-Cornerstone Christian—R
$-Covenant Companion—R
$-Culture Wars—R
Desert Call—R
$-Direction
$-Eclectic Homeschool
Evangelical Advocate—R
$-Faith & Family
$-Faith Today
$-Family Digest—R
$-Foursquare World Advance—R
$-Gem—R
$-Generation X—R
Good News Journal
$-Gospel Today—R
Heartlight—R
Highway News—R
$-Homeschooling Today—R
$-HonorBound—R
$-Indian Life—R
$-Inland NW Christian
$-Inside Journal—R
$-Light & Life
$-Living Church
$-Lookout
$-Lutheran Digest—R
Mature Times—R
$-Messenger/Sacred Heart
Methodist History
Metro Voice—R
$-Minnesota Christian—R
$-Montgomery's Journey
Mosaic—R
$-My Walk With Jesus
$-National Catholic
$-New Freeman—R

$-New Wineskins—R
$-ONEvoice!
$-Our Sunday Visitor
$-Palm Beach—R
Penned from the Heart
$-Plains Faith—R
$-Precepts for Living
Presbyterian Outlook
$-Prism—R
Quaker Life—R
Randall House Periodicals
$-SingleAgain.com
Singles Scoop—R
$-Social Justice—R
$-St. Anthony Messenger
Star of Zion
Sword and Trumpet—R
Sword of the Lord—R
$-Testimony—R
thegoodsteward.com—R
$-Today's Pentecostal Evangel—R
$-Together—R
Trumpeter—R
Victory News—R
$-War Cry—R
$-Way of St. Francis—R
$-Wesleyan Life—R

CHILDREN
$-Adventures
$-Guide—R
$-Juniorway
$-My Friend
$-Primary Street

CHRISTIAN EDUCATION/ LIBRARY
$-Catechist
Catholic Library World
$-Children's Ministry
Christian Early Education—R
$-Christian Educators Journal—R
Christian Librarian—R
Christian School Education—R
$-Church Educator—R
$-Ideas Unlimited—R
Jour. of Christian Education
Jour./Christianity/Foreign Languages
Jour./Ed. & Christian Belief—R
$-Journal/Adventist Educ.—R
Journal/Christian Education
$-Kids' Ministry Ideas—R
$-Leader in C. E. Ministries—R
$-Momentum
$-Preschool Playhouse
$-Resource—R
$-RTJ
$-Teach Kids!—R

$-Teachers Interaction
$-Teachers of Vision—R
$-Today's Catholic Teacher—R
$-Youth & CE Leadership

MISSIONS
$-Evangelical Missions—R

PASTORS/LEADERS
$-African American Pulpit
$-Barefoot—R
$-Catholic Servant
$-Christian Century—R
Christian Education Jour. (CA)—R
$-Clergy Journal—R
Cross Currents
$-Enrichment—R
$-Evangelical Baptist—R
$-Evangelicals Today—R
$-Five Stones—R
$-Interpreter
Lutheran Forum—R
$-Lutheran Partners—R
$-Ministries Today
$-Ministry & Liturgy—R
Ministry in Motion—R
$-Parish Life—R
$-Pastoral Life—R
Pastors.com—R
Quarterly Review
Sharing the Practice—R
Technologies for Worship—R
$-This Rock
$-Today's Parish—R
$-Word & World
$-Youthworker

TEEN/YOUNG ADULT
$-J.A.M.
Teen Light—R
TeensForJC—R
Transcendmag.com—R
$-Young Adult Today—R

WOMEN
$-Esprit—R
$-Godly Business Woman
Home-Based Moms—R
$-Horizons (women)—R
$-inSpirit—R
Just Between Us—R
Precious Times—R
Right to the Heart—R
Women of the Cross

CHRISTIAN LIVING

ADULT/GENERAL
AGAIN—R
$-Alive!—R

$-Alive Now—R
Alliance Life
American Tract Society—R
$-Angels on Earth
$-Annals of St. Anne
$-Arlington Catholic
$-B.C. Catholic—R
$-Barefoot Path—R
$-Bible Advocate—R
Bread of Life—R
Breakthrough Intercessor—R
$-Bridal Guides—R
$-Canada Lutheran—R
$-Catholic Digest—R
$-Catholic Forester—R
$-Catholic New York
$-Catholic Yearbook—R
$-Celebrate Life—R
$-CGA World—R
Channels—R
$-Charisma
$-Chicken Soup—R
$-Christian Courier (CAN)—R
Christian Courier (WI)—R
$-Christian Examiner
Christian Journal—R
$-Christian Leader—R
Christian Observer
Christian Online
$-Christian Parenting—R
Christian Radio Weekly
Christian Ranchman
$-Christian Social Action—R
$-Christianity Today—R
$-ChristianWeek—R
Church Herald & Holiness—R
$-Church of God EVANGEL
$-Citizens in America
$-City Light News—R
$-Columbia
Connecting Point—R
$-Cornerstone Christian—R
$-Covenant Companion—R
Crossway/Newsline—R
$-Culture Wars—R
Desert Call—R
$-Discipleship Journal—R
Discovery—R
Divine Ascent
$-Eclectic Homeschool
$-EFCA Today
$-En Confianza
Eternal Ink—R
$-Evangel—R
Evangelical Advocate—R
$-Faith & Family
$-Faith & Friends—R

$-Faith Today
$-Family Digest—R
$-Focus on the Family
$-Foursquare World Advance—R
$-Gem—R
$-Gems of Truth—R
$-Generation X—R
$-God Allows U-Turns—R
$-Good News—R
Good News Journal
$-Gospel Today—R
Gospel Tract—R
$-Guideposts—R
Halo Magazine
Hannah to Hannah—R
Heartlight—R
Highway News—R
$-Homeschooling Today—R
$-HonorBound—R
HopeKeepers—R
$-Horizons (adult)—R
$-Ideals—R
$-Indian Life—R
$-Inland NW Christian
Keys to Living—R
Leaves—R
LifeLine Journal—R
$-Light & Life
Light at Home—R
$-Liguorian
$-Live—R
$-Living—R
$-Living Church
$-Lookout
$-Lutheran Digest—R
$-Lutheran Journal—R
Maranatha News—R
$-Marian Helper—R
$-Mature Living
Mature Times—R
$-Mature Years—R
$-Men of Integrity—R
Men of the Cross
$-Mennonite Brethren—R
MESSAGE/Open Bible—R
$-Messenger/Sacred Heart
Methodist History
Metro Voice—R
$-Minnesota Christian—R
$-Montgomery's Journey
Mosaic—R
Mutuality—R
$-My Walk With Jesus
$-New Freeman—R
New Heart—R
$-New Wineskins—R
Nostalgia—R

$-On Mission
$-ONEvoice!
$-Our Sunday Visitor
$-Over the Back Fence—R
$-Palm Beach—R
Parents & Teens—R
Penned from the Heart
$-Plain Truth—R
$-Plains Faith—R
Plowman—R
$-Positive Thinking—R
$-Power for Living—R
PrayerWorks—R
$-Presbyterians Today—R
$-Psychology for Living—R
$-Purpose—R
Quaker Life—R
Randall House Periodicals
Regent Business—R
$-Science & Spirit
$-Seek—R
$-Senior Living
$-Signs of the Times—R
Silver Wings—R
$-SingleAgain.com
Singles Scoop—R
$-Social Justice—R
$-Sojourners
$-Spiritual Life
Spiritual Voice—R
$-St. Anthony Messenger
$-Standard—R
Storyteller—R
SW Kansas Faith
Sword and Trumpet—R
Sword of the Lord—R
$-Testimony—R
thegoodsteward.com—R
$-Today's Christian—R
$-Today's Pentecostal Evangel—R
$-Together—R
Trumpeter—R
$-U.S. Catholic
$-United Church Observer—R
$-Vibrant Life—R
Victory News—R
$-Vision—R
Voice of the Lord
$-War Cry—R
$-Way of St. Francis—R
$-Wesleyan Life—R
$-Whole Magazine

CHILDREN
$-Adventures
$-Barefoot for Kids—R
$-BREAD/God's Children—R

$-Cadet Quest—R
$-Club Connection
$-Courage—R
$-Focus/Clubhouse Jr.
$-Guide—R
$-High Adventure—R
$-Juniorway
$-My Friend
$-Partners—R
$-Passport—R
$-Pockets—R
$-Primary Street

CHRISTIAN EDUCATION/ LIBRARY
Church & Synagogue Lib.—R
$-Church Educator—R
$-Resource—R
$-Teachers Interaction
$-Teachers of Vision—R
$-Youth & CE Leadership

DAILY DEVOTIONALS
$-Daily Meditation

MISSIONS
$-American Baptists in Mission
$-Evangelical Missions—R
Women of the Harvest

PASTORS/LEADERS
$-African American Pulpit
$-Catholic Servant
$-Christian Century—R
$-Evangelical Baptist—R
$-Evangelicals Today—R
$-Interpreter
$-Ministries Today
Ministry in Motion—R
Net Results
$-Parish Life—R
$-Pastoral Life—R
Pastors.com—R
$-Pray!—R
$-Preaching Well—R
$-Proclaim—R
Pulpit Helps—R
Quarterly Review
$-Review for Religious
$-RevWriter Resource
Sharing the Practice—R
Technologies for Worship—R
$-Today's Christian Preacher—R
$-Word & World

TEEN/YOUNG ADULT
$-Boundless Webzine—R
$-Credo—R
$-Devo'Zine—R

$-Essential Connection
$-J.A.M.
$-Passageway.org—R
$-Real Faith in Life—R
$-Sharing the VICTORY—R
$-Student Leadership—R
Teen Light—R
TeensForJC—R
Transcendmag.com—R
$-With—R
$-Young and Alive—R
$-Young Christian—R
$-Young Salvationist—R

WOMEN
$-At the Center—R
$-Dabbling Mum.com—R
Faithwebbin—R
$-Godly Business Woman
Hearts at Home—R
Home-Based Moms—R
$-Horizons (women)—R
$-inSpirit—R
$-Journey
Just Between Us—R
$-Link & Visitor—R
Lutheran Woman's Quar.
$-MOMsense—R
P31 Woman—R
Precious Times—R
Right to the Heart—R
$-SpiritLed Woman
$-Today's Christian Woman—R
$-Woman's Touch—R
$-Women Alive!—R
Women of the Cross
Women Today—R

CHURCH GROWTH

ADULT/GENERAL
AGAIN—R
Alliance Life
Breakthrough Intercessor—R
$-Bridal Guides—R
$-Catholic Peace Voice—R
Channels—R
$-Christian Examiner
Christian Journal—R
$-Christian Leader—R
Christian News NW—R
Christian Online
$-ChristianWeek—R
Church Herald & Holiness—R
$-City Light News—R
$-Cornerstone Christian—R
$-Covenant Companion—R
$-Culture Wars—R

Desert Call—R
$-Discipleship Journal—R
Evangelical Advocate—R
$-Faith & Family
$-Faith Today
$-Gem—R
$-Generation X—R
$-Good News—R
$-HonorBound—R
$-Indian Life—R
$-Light & Life
$-Living Church
$-Lookout
$-Messenger/Sacred Heart
Mosaic—R
$-My Walk With Jesus
$-National Catholic
$-New Freeman—R
$-New Wineskins—R
$-On Mission
$-Our Sunday Visitor
Penned from the Heart
$-Plains Faith—R
Presbyterian Outlook
$-Presbyterians Today—R
Quaker Life—R
$-Sojourners
$-St. Anthony Messenger
Star of Zion
Sword and Trumpet—R
Sword of the Lord—R
$-Testimony—R
thegoodsteward.com—R
Trumpeter—R
$-U.S. Catholic
Victory News—R
$-Wesleyan Life—R

CHRISTIAN EDUCATION/ LIBRARY
$-Children's Ministry
Church & Synagogue Lib.—R
$-Youth & CE Leadership

MISSIONS
$-Evangelical Missions—R
Missiology
$-PIME World—R

MUSIC
$-Creator—R

PASTORS/LEADERS
$-African American Pulpit
$-Catholic Servant
$-Christian Century—R
$-Clergy Journal—R
$-Enrichment—R
$-Evangelical Baptist—R

$-Evangelicals Today—R
$-Five Stones—R
$-Growth Points—R
$-Horizons (pastor)—R
Interpretation
$-Interpreter
Jour./Amer. Soc./Chur. Growth—R
$-Let's Worship
$-Ministries Today
$-Ministry & Liturgy—R
Ministry in Motion—R
Ministry Matters
Net Results
$-Parish Life—R
$-Pastoral Life—R
Pastors.com—R
Pulpit Helps—R
$-RevWriter Resource
$-Sermon Notes—R
Sharing the Practice—R
Technologies for Worship—R
Theological Digest—R
$-This Rock
$-WCA News—R
$-Worship Leader
$-Your Church—R

TEEN/YOUNG ADULT
$-J.A.M.
$-Passageway.org—R
TeensForJC—R
Transcendmag.com—R
$-Young Christian—R

WOMEN
$-inSpirit—R
Just Between Us—R
Right to the Heart—R

CHURCH HISTORY

ADULT/GENERAL
African Voices—R
$-America
$-Arkansas Catholic—R
$-Bridal Guides—R
$-Catholic Digest—R
$-Catholic Insight
$-Catholic Peace Voice—R
$-Catholic Sentinel
$-Catholic Yearbook—R
Channels—R
$-Christian History—R
Christian Online
$-Christian Renewal—R
Church Herald & Holiness—R
Citizen USA—R
$-Citizens in America
$-City Light News—R

$-Columbia
$-Company—R
$-Covenant Companion—R
Desert Call—R
Divine Ascent
Evangel, The
$-Family Digest—R
Founders Journal
Friends Journal—R
$-Generation X—R
$-HonorBound—R
$-Horizons (adult)—R
$-Indian Life—R
Journal of Church & State
$-Light & Life
$-Lookout
$-Lutheran Journal—R
Maranatha News—R
Mennonite Historian—R
$-Messiah
Methodist History
Mosaic—R
$-National Catholic
$-New Wineskins—R
Nostalgia—R
$-Our Sunday Visitor
$-Plains Faith—R
PrayerWorks—R
Priscilla Papers—R
Randall House Periodicals
$-Science & Spirit
$-Social Justice—R
$-Sojourners
$-St. Anthony Messenger
Star of Zion
Sword and Trumpet—R
Sword of the Lord—R
thegoodsteward.com—R
Trumpeter—R
$-U.S. Catholic
Victory News—R
$-Way of St. Francis—R
$-Wesleyan Life—R

CHILDREN
$-BREAD/God's Children—R
$-Courage—R
$-Guide—R
$-Primary Pal (IL)

CHRISTIAN EDUCATION/ LIBRARY
Catholic Library World
$-Teachers Interaction

MISSIONS
$-Evangelical Missions—R
Missiology
Railroad Evangelist—R

PASTORS/LEADERS
$-African American Pulpit
$-Christian Century—R
$-Clergy Journal—R
Cross Currents
$-Ministries Today
$-Parish Life—R
$-Pastoral Life—R
$-Review for Religious
Theological Digest—R
$-Theology Today
$-This Rock

TEEN/YOUNG ADULT
$-Essential Connection
$-J.A.M.
$-Living My Faith
$-Passageway.org—R
$-Real Faith in Life—R
TeensForJC—R
Transcendmag.com—R
$-Young Christian—R

WOMEN
$-Esprit—R
$-History's Women—R
$-Horizons (women)—R
$-Link & Visitor—R

CHURCH LIFE

ADULT/GENERAL
AGAIN—R
Alliance Life
$-America
$-Arkansas Catholic—R
$-Bible Advocate—R
Breakthrough Intercessor—R
$-Bridal Guides—R
$-Catholic Digest—R
$-Catholic Insight
$-Catholic Sentinel
Catholic World
$-Catholic Yearbook—R
Channels—R
Christian Journal—R
$-Christian Leader—R
Christian Online
$-Christian Standard—R
$-Christianity Today—R
$-ChristianWeek—R
Church Herald & Holiness—R
Citizen USA—R
$-City Light News—R
$-Columbia
$-Company—R
$-Cornerstone Christian—R
$-Covenant Companion—R
Desert Call—R

Eternal Ink—R
Evangelical Advocate—R
$-Faith & Family
$-Faith Today
$-Family Digest—R
$-Gem—R
$-Generation X—R
$-Good News—R
Hannah to Hannah—R
$-HonorBound—R
$-Horizons (adult)—R
$-Impact—R
Leaves—R
$-Light & Life
$-Liguorian
$-Living Church
$-Lookout
$-Lutheran Digest—R
$-Lutheran Journal—R
Maranatha News—R
Mennonite Historian—R
MESSAGE/Open Bible—R
$ Messenger/St. Anthony
$-Minnesota Christian—R
$-Montgomery's Journey
Mosaic—R
Mutuality—R
$-National Catholic
$-New Freeman—R
$-New Wineskins—R
$-On Mission
$-ONEvoice!
$-Our Sunday Visitor
$-Palm Beach—R
Penned from the Heart
$-Plains Faith—R
$-Prairie Messenger—R
PrayerWorks—R
$-Precepts for Living
$-Presbyterians Today—R
Priscilla Papers—R
$-Purpose—R
Quaker Life—R
Randall House Periodicals
Silver Wings—R
$-Sojourners
Spirituality for Today
$-St. Anthony Messenger
Star of Zion
Sword of the Lord—R
$-Testimony—R
thegoodsteward.com—R
$-Today's Christian—R
$-Today's Pentecostal Evangel—R
Trumpeter—R
$-U.S. Catholic
Victory News—R

$-Vision—R
$-Way of St. Francis—R
$-Wesleyan Life—R

CHILDREN
$-Primary Street

CHRISTIAN EDUCATION/ LIBRARY
$-Children's Ministry
$-Church Educator—R
$-Resource—R
$-Youth & CE Leadership

MISSIONS
$-Evangelical Missions—R

PASTORS/LEADERS
$-African American Pulpit
$-Barefoot—R
$-Catholic Servant
$-Christian Century—R
$-Enrichment—R
$-Evangelical Baptist—R
$-Evangelicals Today—R
$-Five Stones—R
$-Horizons (pastor)—R
$-Interpreter
$-Leadership—R
$-Lutheran Partners—R
$-Ministries Today
$-Ministry
$-Ministry & Liturgy—R
Ministry in Motion—R
Ministry Matters
Net Results
$-Parish Life—R
$-Pastoral Life—R
Pastors.com—R
$-Priest
Pulpit Helps—R
Quarterly Review
$-Review for Religious
$-RevWriter Resource
Sharing the Practice—R
Technologies for Worship—R
$-WCA News—R
$-Worship Leader

TEEN/YOUNG ADULT
$-J.A.M.
$-Passageway.org—R
Teen Light—R
$-Young Christian—R

WOMEN
$-Esprit—R
Handmaiden—R
$-Horizons (women)—R

$-inSpirit—R
Right to the Heart—R

CHURCH MANAGEMENT

ADULT/GENERAL
Breakthrough Intercessor—R
$-Bridal Guides—R
Channels—R
Christian Computing—R
$-Christian Leader—R
Christian News NW—R
Christian Online
$-Christian Standard—R
$-ChristianWeek—R
$-Culture Wars—R
Disciple's Journal—R
Evangelical Advocate—R
$-Faith Today
$-Gem—R
$-Generation X—R
$-Good News, Etc.—R
$-Gospel Today—R
$-HonorBound—R
$-Living Church
$-Lookout
$-Lutheran Digest—R
Metro Voice—R
Mosaic—R
$-New Freeman—R
$-ONEvoice!
$-Our Sunday Visitor
$-Presbyterians Today—R
Priscilla Papers—R
Regent Business—R
$-Sojourners
$-St. Anthony Messenger
Star of Zion
Sword of the Lord—R
thegoodsteward.com—R
$-Today's Pentecostal Evangel—R
Trumpeter—R
$-U.S. Catholic
Victory News—R
$-Wesleyan Life—R

CHRISTIAN EDUCATION/ LIBRARY
$-Children's Ministry
$-Church Educator—R
$-Resource—R
$-Youth & CE Leadership

MISSIONS
$-Evangelical Missions—R

PASTORS/LEADERS
$-African American Pulpit
$-Catholic Servant
$-Christian Century—R

Christian Management—R
$-Church Administration
$-Clergy Journal—R
$-Enrichment—R
$-Evangelical Baptist—R
$-Evangelicals Today—R
$-Five Stones—R
$-Growth Points—R
Interpretation
$-Interpreter
Jour./Amer. Soc./Chur. Growth—R
$-Leadership—R
$-Ministries Today
$-Ministry
Ministry in Motion—R
Ministry Matters
Net Results
$-Pastoral Life—R
Pastors.com—R
Pulpit Helps—R
Quarterly Review
$-RevWriter Resource
Sharing the Practice—R
Technologies for Worship—R
$-Word & World
$-Worship Leader
$-Your Church—R

WOMEN
Just Between Us—R
Right to the Heart—R

CHURCH OUTREACH

ADULT/GENERAL
AGAIN—R
$-Alive!—R
$-America
$-Bible Advocate—R
Breakthrough Intercessor—R
$-Bridal Guides—R
$-Cathedral Age
$-Catholic Forester—R
$-Catholic Sentinel
Catholic World
$-Central Appalachia
Channels—R
$-Christian Leader—R
Christian News NW—R
Christian Online
Christian Research
$-Christian Social Action—R
$-Christian Standard—R
$-ChristianWeek—R
Church Herald & Holiness—R
$-Church of God EVANGEL

$-City Light News—R
$-Columbia
$-Company—R
$-Covenant Companion—R
$-Culture Wars—R
Desert Call—R
$-Episcopal Life—R
Eternal Ink—R
$-Evangel—R
Evangelical Advocate—R
$-Faith & Friends—R
$-Faith Today
$-Gem—R
$-Good News—R
Heartland Gatekeeper
$-HonorBound—R
HopeKeepers—R
$-Light & Life
$-Liguorian
$-Living Church
$-Lookout
$-Lutheran Digest—R
Maranatha News—R
Mature Times—R
MESSAGE/Open Bible—R
Metro Voice—R
Mosaic—R
$-My Walk With Jesus
$-National Catholic
Network
$-New Freeman—R
$-New Wineskins—R
$-On Mission
$-ONEvoice!
$-Our Sunday Visitor
$-Precepts for Living
Presbyterian Outlook
$-Presbyterians Today—R
Priscilla Papers—R
$-Prism—R
$-Purpose—R
Quaker Life—R
$-Science & Spirit
Singles Scoop—R
$-Social Justice—R
$-Sojourners
$-St. Anthony Messenger
$-St. Joseph's Messenger—R
Sword of the Lord—R
$-Testimony—R
thegoodsteward.com—R
$-Today's Christian—R
Trumpeter—R
$-U.S. Catholic
Victory News—R

$-Vision—R
$-Way of St. Francis—R
$-Wesleyan Life—R

CHILDREN
$-Primary Street

CHRISTIAN EDUCATION/ LIBRARY
$-Children's Ministry
$-Church Educator—R
$-Journal/Adventist Educ.—R
$-Kids' Ministry Ideas—R
$-Resource—R
$-Youth & CE Leadership

MISSIONS
$-Evangelical Missions—R
Missiology
$-PIME World—R
Railroad Evangelist—R
Wesleyan World—R

PASTORS/LEADERS
$-African American Pulpit
$-Barefoot—R
$-Catholic Servant
$-Christian Century—R
$-Clergy Journal—R
$-Cornerstone Youth—R
$-Enrichment—R
$-Evangelical Baptist—R
$-Evangelicals Today—R
$-Five Stones—R
$-Growth Points—R
$-Interpreter
Jour./Amer. Soc./Chur. Growth—R
$-Leadership—R
$-Let's Worship
$-Lutheran Partners—R
$-Ministries Today
$-Ministry
$-Ministry & Liturgy—R
Ministry in Motion—R
Ministry Matters
Net Results
$-Parish Life—R
$-Pastoral Life—R
Pastors.com—R
Pulpit Helps—R
Quarterly Review
$-Rev.
$-RevWriter Resource
Sharing the Practice—R
Technologies for Worship—R
$-This Rock
$-Today's Parish—R
$-WCA News—R

$-Word & World
$-Worship Leader

TEEN/YOUNG ADULT
$-Credo—R
$-Passageway.org—R
Teen Light—R
TeensForJC—R
Transcendmag.com—R
$-With—R
$-Young Christian—R

WOMEN
$-Esprit—R
Home-Based Moms—R
$-inSpirit—R
Just Between Us—R
Right to the Heart—R
Women Today—R

CHURCH TRADITIONS

ADULT/GENERAL
AGAIN—R
$-America
$-Arkansas Catholic—R
Breakthrough Intercessor—R
$-Bridal Guides—R
$-Canada Lutheran—R
$-Catholic Digest—R
$-Catholic Forester—R
$-Catholic Yearbook—R
$-Celebrate Life—R
Channels—R
$-Christian Examiner
$-Christian History—R
$-Christian Leader—R
Christian Online
Christian Research
$-Citizens in America
$-City Light News—R
$-Columbia
Desert Call—R
$-Faith & Family
$-Faith Today
$-Family Digest—R
$-Gem—R
$-Generation X—R
$-Gospel Today—R
$-HonorBound—R
$-Ideals—R
$-Impact—R
$-Indian Life—R
$-Light & Life
$-Liguorian
$-Living Church
$-Lutheran Journal—R

Maranatha News—R
Mennonite Historian—R
Mosaic—R
$-National Catholic
$-New Freeman—R
$-New Wineskins—R
Nostalgia—R
$-Our Sunday Visitor
$-Palm Beach—R
$-Plains Faith—R
PrayerWorks—R
Priscilla Papers—R
$-Science & Spirit
$-Sojourners
$-St. Anthony Messenger
$-Standard—R
Star of Zion
$-Testimony—R
thegoodsteward.com—R
$-Together—R
Trumpeter—R
$-U.S. Catholic
Victory News—R
$-Way of St. Francis—R
$-Wesleyan Life—R

CHILDREN
$-My Friend

CHRISTIAN EDUCATION/ LIBRARY
$-Children's Ministry
$-RTJ
$-Teachers Interaction
$-Youth & CE Leadership

PASTORS/LEADERS
$-African American Pulpit
$-Clergy Journal—R
$-Evangelicals Today—R
$-Interpreter
$-Ministries Today
$-Parish Life—R
$-Pastoral Life—R
Pastors.com—R
Quarterly Review
$-Review for Religious
Sharing the Practice—R
Theological Digest—R
$-This Rock

TEEN/YOUNG ADULT
$-J.A.M.
$-Passageway.org—R
Teen Light—R
TeensForJC—R
Transcendmag.com—R
$-Young Christian—R

WOMEN
Handmaiden—R
Home-Based Moms—R
$-Horizons (women)—R

CONTROVERSIAL ISSUES

ADULT/GENERAL
AGAIN—R
$-America
American Tract Society—R
$-Associated Content—R
$-Aujourd'hui Credo—R
$-Bible Advocate—R
Biblical Recorder
Canadian Christianity.com
$-Catholic Insight
$-Catholic Peace Voice—R
$-Celebrate Life—R
Challenge Weekly
Channels—R
Christian Citizen USA
$-Christian Courier (CAN)—R
Christian Current
$-Christian Examiner
Christian Herald (UK)
Christian Media—R
$-Christian Networks
Christian Online
Christian Post
Christian Radio Weekly
$-Christian Renewal—R
$-Christian Response—R
$-Christian Social Action—R
$-Christian Standard—R
$-Christianity Today—R
$-ChristianWeek—R
Citizen USA—R
$-Citizens in America
$-City Light News—R
$-Cornerstone Christian—R
Crossway/Newsline—R
$-Culture Wars—R
Desert Christian
Desert Voice
Discovery—R
$-Dovetail—R
DreamSeeker
$-En Confianza
Evangel, The
Evangelical Advocate—R
Evangelical Times
$-Faith Today
$-First Things
$-Generation X—R
$-God Allows U-Turns—R

$-Good News—R
Good News in RI
Good News/S. Florida
Gospel Post
$-Gospel Today—R
Heartland Gatekeeper
$-Homeschooling Today—R
$-HonorBound—R
$-Interim—R
$-Light & Life
$-Living Church
$-Lookout
Mature Times—R
Metro Voice—R
Mid-South Christian
$-Minnesota Christian—R
Mutuality—R
$-National Catholic
$-New Wineskins—R
$-Now What?—R
$-Our Sunday Visitor
$-Palm Beach—R
$-Plain Truth—R
$-Plains Faith—R
$-Prairie Messenger—R
Priscilla Papers—R
$-Prism—R
$-Psychology for Living—R
Quaker Life—R
Rock & Sling
Sacred Journey—R
$-Science & Spirit
$-SingleAgain.com
Singles Scoop—R
$-Social Justice—R
$-Sojourners
Spiritual Voice—R
$-Spring Hill Review—R
$-St. Anthony Messenger
Sunday Magazine
Sword of the Lord—R
thegoodsteward.com—R
$-Today's Christian—R
Tri-State Voice
Trumpeter—R
$-U.S. Catholic
Victory News—R
$-War Cry—R
$-Way of St. Francis—R
$-Whole Magazine
Wichita Chronicle
Winsome Wit—R
$-Wittenburg Door—R
$-World & I—R
World Net Daily
Xavier Review

CHILDREN
$-Passport—R

CHRISTIAN EDUCATION/ LIBRARY
Catholic Library World
$-Children's Ministry
$-Church Educator—R
$-Teachers Interaction
$-Teachers of Vision—R
$-Today's Catholic Teacher—R

MISSIONS
East-West Church
$-Evangelical Missions—R
Intl. Jour./Frontier—R

MUSIC
Hymn

PASTORS/LEADERS
$-African American Pulpit
Alpha News
$-Christian Century—R
$-Clergy Journal—R
Cross Currents
$-InSite—R
$-Interpreter
Journal/Pastoral Care—R
$-Let's Worship
$-Ministry & Liturgy—R
$-Parish Life—R
$-Pastoral Life—R
Pulpit Helps—R
Strategic Adult Ministries—R
$-This Rock
$-Word & World
$-Worship Leader

TEEN/YOUNG ADULT
$-Boundless Webzine—R
$-Brio—R
$-Insight—R
$-J.A.M.
$-Passageway.org—R
$-Student Leadership—R
Teen Light—R
TeensForJC—R
Transcendmag.com—R
$-With—R
$-Young Salvationist—R

WOMEN
$-Esprit—R
$-Godly Business Woman
Home-Based Moms—R
$-inSpirit—R
Precious Times—R
Women Today—R

WRITERS
$-Areopagus (UK)

CRAFTS

ADULT/GENERAL
$-Associated Content—R
$-CGA World—R
Christian Online
$-Citizens in America
$-Eclectic Homeschool
Eternal Ink—R
$-Faith & Family
$-Generation X—R
$-Grit
LifeLine Journal—R
Light at Home—R
$-Living—R
$-Mature Living
Spiritual Voice—R
Sword of the Lord—R
$-World & I—R

CHILDREN
$-Adventures
$-Barefoot for Kids—R
$-BREAD/God's Children—R
$-Cadet Quest—R
$-Celebrate
$-Courage—R
$-Focus/Clubhouse
$-Focus/Clubhouse Jr.
$-Guideposts for Kids
$-High Adventure—R
$-Junior Companion—R
$-Juniorway
$-My Friend
$-On the Line—R
$-Pockets—R
$-Preschool Playhouse (child)
$-Primary Pal (IL)
$-SHINEbrightly—R
Skipping Stones
$-Sparkle
$-Story Friends—R
$-Story Mates—R

CHRISTIAN EDUCATION/ LIBRARY
$-Catechist
$-Children's Ministry
$-RTJ
$-Teach Kids!—R
$-Teachers Interaction

PASTORS/LEADERS
$-Interpreter

TEEN/YOUNG ADULT
$-Brio—R
$-Guideposts Sweet 16—R
$-J.A.M.
Teen Light—R
TeensForJC—R
Transcendmag.com—R

WOMEN
Faithwebbin—R
Home-Based Moms—R
Keeping Hearts & Home
$-MOMsense—R
P31 Woman—R

CREATION SCIENCE

ADULT/GENERAL
$-Catholic New Times—R
$-Christian Courier (CAN)—R
$-Christian Examiner
Christian Observer
$-Christian Renewal—R
Christian Research
Citizen USA—R
$-Citizens in America
$-City Light News—R
$-Creative Nonfiction
Discovery—R
Evangelical Advocate—R
$-Faith Today
$-Homeschooling Today—R
$-HonorBound—R
$-Horizons (adult)—R
$-Live—R
$-Living—R
$-Lookout
Maranatha News—R
Men of the Cross
$-New Freeman—R
$-Palm Beach—R
$-Plains Faith—R
$-Social Justice—R
$-St. Anthony Messenger
Sword and Trumpet—R
Sword of the Lord—R
thegoodsteward.com—R
Trumpeter—R
Victory News—R
$-War Cry—R

CHILDREN
$-Barefoot for Kids—R
$-BREAD/God's Children—R
$-Courage—R
$-Guide—R
$-Nature Friend
$-Primary Pal (IL)

CHRISTIAN EDUCATION/ LIBRARY
$-Journal/Adventist Educ.—R

PASTORS/LEADERS
Cross Currents
$-Pastoral Life—R
Pulpit Helps—R
$-This Rock

TEEN/YOUNG ADULT
$-Boundless Webzine—R
$-J.A.M.
$-Passageway.org—R
$-Real Faith in Life—R

WOMEN
$-Godly Business Woman

CULTS/OCCULT

ADULT/GENERAL
Alliance Life
American Tract Society—R
$-Bible Advocate—R
$-Christian Examiner
$-Christian Renewal—R
Christian Research
Citizen USA—R
$-City Light News—R
$-Culture Wars—R
Discovery—R
$-Faith Today
$-HonorBound—R
$-Lookout
Metro Voice—R
New Heart—R
$-Now What?—R
$-On Mission
$-Plains Faith—R
Randall House Periodicals
$-Social Justice—R
Spiritual Voice—R
Sword of the Lord—R
thegoodsteward.com—R
Trumpeter—R
Victory News—R
$-Voice of the Lord

MISSIONS
Intl. Jour./Frontier—R

PASTORS/LEADERS
$-Word & World

TEEN/YOUNG ADULT
$-Passageway.org—R
$-Real Faith in Life—R
$-Teenage Christian—R

TeensForJC—R
Transcendmag.com—R

WOMEN
$-Journey

CURRENT/SOCIAL ISSUES

ADULT/GENERAL
$-Alive!—R
Alliance Life
American Tract Society—R
$-Anglican Journal
$-Apocalypse Chronicles—R
$-Arlington Catholic
$-Associated Content—R
$-B.C. Catholic—R
$-BGC World—R
$-Bible Advocate—R
Biblical Recorder
Canadian Christianity.com
$-Catholic Insight
$-Catholic New York
$-Catholic Peace Voice—R
Challenge Weekly
Channels—R
Christian Citizen USA
$-Christian Courier (CAN)—R
Christian Courier (WI)—R
Christian Current
$-Christian Examiner
Christian Herald (UK)
$-Christian Leader—R
$-Christian Networks
Christian News NW—R
Christian Observer
Christian Online
Christian Outlook
$-Christian Parenting—R
Christian Post
Christian Ranchman
$-Christian Renewal—R
Christian Research
$-Christian Social Action—R
$-Christian Standard—R
$-Christianity Today—R
$-ChristianWeek—R
$-Church of God EVANGEL
Citizen USA—R
$-Citizens in America
$-City Light News—R
$-Columbia
$-Culture Wars—R
Desert Call—R
Desert Christian
Desert Voice
Discovery—R
$-Dovetail—R

DreamSeeker
$-En Confianza
Eternal Ink—R
$-Eureka Street
Evangelical Advocate—R
Evangelical Times
$-Faith Today
$-First Things
$-Foursquare World Advance—R
Friends Journal—R
$-Gem—R
$-Generation X—R
$-God Allows U-Turns—R
$-Good News—R
Good News Connection
Good News in RI
Good News Journal
Good News/S. Florida
Gospel Post
Hannah to Hannah—R
Heartland Gatekeeper
Heartlight—R
Highway News—R
$-Homeschooling Today—R
$-HonorBound—R
$-Indian Life—R
Indiana Christian News
$-Inland NW Christian
$-Interim—R
Island Catholic News
Journal of Church & State
$-Liberty—R
LifeLine Journal—R
Lifesite Canada
$-Light & Life
Light at Home—R
$-Liguorian
$-Living—R
$-Lookout
$-Marian Helper—R
Mature Times—R
$-Men of Integrity—R
$-Mennonite Brethren—R
$-MESSAGE
MESSAGE/Open Bible—R
$-Messenger/St. Anthony
Metro Voice—R
Mid-South Christian
$-Minnesota Christian—R
$-Montgomery's Journey
Mosaic—R
Mutuality—R
$-National Catholic
$-New Freeman—R
New Heart—R
$-New Wineskins—R

$-Now What?—R
$-On Mission
$-Our Sunday Visitor
$-Palm Beach—R
$-ParentLife
$-Plain Truth—R
$-Plains Faith—R
Plowman—R
$-Prairie Messenger—R
$-Priority!—R
Priscilla Papers—R
$-Prism—R
$-Psychology for Living—R
$-Purpose—R
Quaker Life—R
Sacred Journey—R
$-Senior Living
Silver Wings—R
$-SingleAgain.com
Singles Scoop—R
$-Social Justice—R
$-Sojourners
$-Special Living—R
Spiritual Voice—R
$-Spring Hill Review—R
$-St. Anthony Messenger
$-St. Joseph's Messenger—R
Storyteller—R
Sunday Magazine
Sword of the Lord—R
thegoodsteward.com—R
$-Today's Christian—R
$-Today's Pentecostal Evangel—R
$-Together—R
Tri-State Voice
Trumpeter—R
$-U.S. Catholic
Victory News—R
$-War Cry—R
$-Way of St. Francis—R
West Wind Review
$-Whole Magazine
Wichita Chronicle
Winsome Wit—R
$-Wittenburg Door—R
$-World & I—R
World Net Daily

CHILDREN
$-Barefoot for Kids—R
$-Club Connection
$-Guideposts for Kids
$-Juniorway
$-Passport—R
$-SHINEbrightly—R
Skipping Stones

CHRISTIAN EDUCATION/ LIBRARY
Catholic Library World
$-Children's Ministry
$-Church Educator—R

DAILY DEVOTIONALS
Family Walk

MISSIONS
$-American Baptists in Mission
$-New World Outlook
$-PIME World—R
Women of the Harvest

MUSIC
$-CCM Magazine

PASTORS/LEADERS
$-African American Pulpit
Alpha News
$-Catholic Servant
$-Christian Century—R
$-Evangelicals Today—R
$-Horizons (pastor)—R
$-InSite—R
$-Interpreter
$-Lutheran Partners—R
$-Parish Life—R
$-Pastoral Life—R
Plugged In
Pulpit Helps—R
Quarterly Review
Sharing the Practice—R
Strategic Adult Ministries—R
$-Theology Today
$-This Rock
$-WCA News—R
$-Word & World
Youth Culture

TEEN/YOUNG ADULT
$-Boundless Webzine—R
$-Brio—R
$-Credo—R
$-Devo'Zine—R
GO!
$-J.A.M.
$-Passageway.org—R
Teen Light—R
$-Teenage Christian—R
TeensForJC—R
Transcendmag.com—R
$-With—R
$-Young Adult Today—R
$-Young Salvationist—R

WOMEN
$-Esprit—R

Faithwebbin—R
$-Godly Business Woman
Handmaiden—R
Heart & Soul
Hearts at Home—R
Home-Based Moms—R
$-Horizons (women)—R
$-inSpirit—R
$-Link & Visitor—R
Making Waves
Sisters in the Lord
$-SpiritLed Woman
Women Today—R

WRITERS
$-Areopagus (UK)

DEATH/DYING

ADULT/GENERAL
AGAIN—R
$-Alive!—R
$-America
American Tract Society—R
$-Arlington Catholic
$-Associated Content—R
$-Bible Advocate—R
Breakthrough Intercessor—R
$-Celebrate Life—R
Channels—R
$-Chicken Soup—R
$-Christian Leader—R
Christian Online
$-Christian Parenting—R
Christian Ranchman
$-Christian Social Action—R
$-Christianity Today—R
Citizen USA—R
$-Citizens in America
$-City Light News—R
$-Creative Nonfiction
$-Cup of Comfort—R
Desert Call—R
$-Dovetail—R
Eternal Ink—R
Evangelical Advocate—R
$-Faith Today
$-Gem—R
$-Generation X—R
$-God Allows U-Turns—R
$-Guideposts—R
Heartlight—R
$-Homeschooling Today—R
HopeKeepers—R
$-Horizons (adult)—R
$-Interim—R
Light at Home—R

$-Liguorian
$-Lookout
Mature Times—R
$-Messenger/Sacred Heart
$-National Catholic
$-New Freeman—R
New Heart—R
$-New Wineskins—R
$-Now What?—R
$-Our Sunday Visitor
$-Plain Truth—R
$-Plains Faith—R
$-Positive Thinking—R
$-Prairie Messenger—R
Presbyterian Outlook
$-Presbyterians Today—R
$-Prism—R
$-Psychology for Living—R
Quaker Life—R
Randall House Periodicals
Sacred Journey—R
Silver Wings—R
$-SingleAgain.com
Singles Scoop—R
$-Social Justice—R
Spiritual Voice—R
$-Spring Hill Review—R
$-St. Anthony Messenger
Storyteller—R
Sword of the Lord—R
$-Testimony—R
thegoodsteward.com—R
$-Today's Christian—R
$-Today's Pentecostal Evangel—R
Tributes—R
Trumpeter—R
$-U.S. Catholic
Victory News—R
$-Voice of the Lord
$-War Cry—R
$-Way of St. Francis—R

CHILDREN
$-Guideposts for Kids
Skipping Stones

CHRISTIAN EDUCATION/ LIBRARY
$-Church Educator—R

PASTORS/LEADERS
$-Catholic Servant
$-Christian Century—R
$-Clergy Journal—R
$-Evangelical Baptist—R
$-InSite—R
$-Interpreter

Journal/Pastoral Care—R
$-Parish Life—R
$-Pastoral Life—R
Pulpit Helps—R
Sharing the Practice—R
$-Today's Christian Preacher—R

TEEN/YOUNG ADULT
$-Brio—R
$-J.A.M.
$-Passageway.org—R
Teen Light—R
TeensForJC—R
Transcendmag.com—R
$-With—R
$-Young Salvationist—R

WOMEN
$-Godly Business Woman
$-inSpirit—R
Precious Times—R
Women Today—R

DEVOTIONALS/ MEDITATIONS

ADULT/GENERAL
$-Alive Now—R
$-America
$-Animal Trails—R
$-Annals of St. Anne
$-Arlington Catholic
$-Barefoot Path—R
Bread of Life—R
Breakthrough Intercessor—R
$-Bridal Guides—R
$-Catholic Peace Voice—R
CBN.com—R
$-CGA World—R
$-Chicken Soup—R
Christian Journal—R
Christian Online
Christian Ranchman
Church Herald & Holiness—R
$-Covenant Companion—R
Creation Care—R
CrossHome.com
Desert Call—R
Divine Ascent
Eternal Ink—R
$-Evangel—R
Evangelical Advocate—R
Evangelical Times
$-Faith & Family
$-Faith & Friends—R
Founders Journal
$-Foursquare World Advance—R
$-Gem—R

$-Good News—R
Good News Journal
Gospel Tract—R
Hannah to Hannah—R
Heartlight—R
$-HonorBound—R
HopeKeepers—R
$-Ideals—R
Indiana Christian News
Keys to Living—R
Leaves—R
LifeTimes Catholic
Light at Home—R
$-Liguorian
$-Living Church
Looking Up
Maranatha News—R
$-Mature Living
Mature Times—R
$-Men of Integrity—R
Men of the Cross
$-Mennonite Brethren—R
$-Messenger/Sacred Heart
$-Messenger/St. Anthony
Metro Voice—R
Mosaic—R
Mutuality—R
$-My Walk With Jesus
$-National Catholic
$-New Freeman—R
New Heart—R
$-New Wineskins—R
Penned from the Heart
Perspectives—R
$-Positive Thinking—R
PrayerWorks—R
$-Prism—R
Quaker Life—R
$-Queen of All Hearts
Radix—R
Randall House Periodicals
Silver Wings—R
Singles Scoop—R
Spiritual Voice—R
$-Sports Spectrum
$-St. Anthony Messenger
$-Standard—R
Star of Zion
Sword of the Lord—R
thegoodsteward.com—R
$-Today's Christian—R
$-Today's Pentecostal Evangel—R
Trumpeter—R
$-U.S. Catholic
Victory News—R
$-Vision—R
$-Voice of the Lord

$-War Cry—R
$-Way of St. Francis—R
$-Weavings—R
$-Wesleyan Life—R

CHILDREN
$-Barefoot for Kids—R
$-Club Connection
$-Keys for Kids—R
$-Pockets—R
$-Primary Pal (IL)

CHRISTIAN EDUCATION/ LIBRARY
$-Children's Ministry
Church & Synagogue Lib.—R
$-Church Educator—R

DAILY DEVOTIONALS
Anchor Devotional
Closer Walk
Daily Dev. for Deaf
$-Daily Meditation
$-Devotions
Family Walk
Forward Day by Day
Fruit of the Vine
In His Presence
InDeed
Our Journey
Penned from the Heart
$-Quiet Hour
Quiet Walk
$-Secret Place
$-These Days
$-Upper Room
$-Word in Season
$-Words of Life

MISSIONS
Women of the Harvest

PASTORS/LEADERS
$-Barefoot—R
$-Catholic Servant
$-Church Worship
$-Emmanuel
$-Evangelical Baptist—R
$-Evangelicals Today—R
Jour./Amer. Soc./Chur. Growth—R
Pulpit Helps—R
$-RevWriter Resource
Sharing the Practice—R

TEEN/YOUNG ADULT
$-Brio—R
$-Devo'Zine—R
GO!
$-J.A.M.
$-Passageway.org—R

$-Real Faith in Life—R
Teen Light—R
TeensForJC—R
Transcendmag.com—R
$-With—R
$-Young Adult Today—R
$-Young and Alive—R
$-Young Christian—R
$-Young Salvationist—R

WOMEN
Faithwebbin—R
$-Godly Business Woman
Home-Based Moms—R
$-Horizons (women)—R
Inspired Moms.Com
$-Journey
Keeping Hearts & Home
$-Melody of the Heart
Precious Times—R
$-SpiritLed Woman
$-Woman's Touch—R
$-Women Alive!—R
Women of the Cross

WRITERS
ChristianWriters.com
$-Cross & Quill—R
$-Spirit-Led Writer—R
$-Upper Case

DISCIPLESHIP

ADULT/GENERAL
$-Alive Now—R
Alliance Life
$-Arlington Catholic
$-Barefoot Path—R
$-BGC World—R
$-Bible Advocate—R
Bread of Life—R
Breakthrough Intercessor—R
$-Canada Lutheran—R
$-Catholic New Times—R
Christian Journal—R
$-Christian Leader—R
Christian Motorsports
Christian Online
$-Christian Parenting—R
Christian Ranchman
$-Christian Standard—R
$-ChristianWeek—R
Church Herald & Holiness—R
$-Cornerstone Christian—R
Creation Care—R
Desert Call—R
$-Discipleship Journal—R
Eternal Ink—R

$-Evangel—R
Evangelical Advocate—R
$-Faith & Family
$-Faith & Friends—R
$-Faith Today
$-Family Digest—R
$-Gem—R
$-Good News—R
Heartlight—R
Highway News—R
$-Homeschooling Today—R
$-HonorBound—R
$-Horizons (adult)—R
$-Indian Life—R
$-Inland NW Christian
$-Inside Journal—R
$-Light & Life
$-Liguorian
$-Lookout
$-Men of Integrity—R
Men of the Cross
MESSAGE/Open Bible—R
Metro Voice—R
$-Montgomery's Journey
Mosaic—R
$-My Walk With Jesus
$-National Catholic
$-New Freeman—R
$-New Wineskins—R
NRB Magazine—R
$-On Mission
$-ONEvoice!
Penned from the Heart
$-Plains Faith—R
Plowman—R
PrayerWorks—R
$-Precepts for Living
$-Prism—R
$-Purpose—R
Quaker Life—R
Randall House Periodicals
Regent Business—R
$-Sojourners
$-St. Anthony Messenger
$-St. Joseph's Messenger—R
$-Stewardship—R
Sword of the Lord—R
thegoodsteward.com—R
$-Today's Christian—R
$-Today's Pentecostal Evangel—R
Trumpeter—R
$-U.S. Catholic
Victory News—R
$-Voice of the Lord
Walk This Way—R
$-War Cry—R
$-Way of St. Francis—R

$-Wesleyan Life—R
$-Whole Magazine

CHILDREN
$-Barefoot for Kids—R
$-BREAD/God's Children—R
$-Club Connection
$-Passport—R
$-Primary Street

CHRISTIAN EDUCATION/
LIBRARY
$-Church Educator—R
$-Resource—R
$-Teach Kids!—R

MISSIONS
$-PIME World—R
Wesleyan World—R

PASTORS/LEADERS
$-African American Pulpit
$-Barefoot—R
$-Catholic Servant
Christian Education Jour. (CA)—R
$-Evangelical Baptist—R
$-Evangelicals Today—R
$-Growth Points—R
$-InSite—R
$-Interpreter
Jour./Amer. Soc./Chur. Growth—R
$-Leadership—R
$-Lutheran Partners—R
$-Ministry & Liturgy—R
Ministry in Motion—R
Net Results
$-Parish Life—R
$-Pastoral Life—R
$-Pray!—R
$-Proclaim—R
Quarterly Review
$-Rev.
$-Review for Religious
$-RevWriter Resource
Sharing the Practice—R
$-Small Group Dynamics—R
Theological Digest—R
$-This Rock
$-Word & World

TEEN/YOUNG ADULT
$-Boundless Webzine—R
$-Brio—R
$-Credo—R
$-Devo'Zine—R
$-J.A.M.
$-Passageway.org—R
$-Real Faith in Life—R
$-Student Leadership—R

Teen Light—R
$-Teenage Christian—R
TeensForJC—R
Transcendmag.com—R
$-With—R
$-Young Salvationist—R

WOMEN
Christian Women Today—R
$-Esprit—R
$-Godly Business Woman
$-Horizons (women)—R
$-inSpirit—R
$-Journey
Just Between Us—R
$-Link & Visitor—R
P31 Woman—R
Precious Times—R
Right to the Heart—R
$-Today's Christian Woman—R
$-Woman's Touch—R
$-Women Alive!—R
Women of the Cross

DIVORCE

ADULT/GENERAL
Alliance Life
American Tract Society—R
$-Angels on Earth
$-Arlington Catholic
$-Associated Content—R
$-Bible Advocate—R
Breakthrough Intercessor—R
$-Bridal Guides—R
$-Catholic Digest—R
$-Christian Examiner
Christian Motorsports
Christian Online
$-Christian Parenting—R
Christian Ranchman
$-Christian Social Action—R
Citizen USA—R
$-Cornerstone Christian—R
$-Creative Nonfiction
$-Culture Wars—R
$-Cup of Comfort—R
$-Dovetail—R
Eternal Ink—R
$-Faith Today
$-Focus on the Family
$-Gem—R
$-Generation X—R
$-God Allows U-Turns—R
$-Guideposts—R
Highway News—R
$-Homeschooling Today—R
$-HonorBound—R

HopeKeepers—R
$-Indian Life—R
$-Interim—R
LifeLine Journal—R
Light at Home—R
$-Liguorian
$-Living—R
$-Living Church
$-Lookout
Metro Voice—R
$-Minnesota Christian—R
$-National Catholic
$-New Freeman—R
New Heart—R
$-New Wineskins—R
$-Now What?—R
Parents & Teens—R
$-Plains Faith—R
$-Positive Thinking—R
Priscilla Papers—R
$-Prism—R
$-Psychology for Living—R
Randall House Periodicals
$-SingleAgain.com
$-Smart Families—R
$-Social Justice—R
Spiritual Voice—R
$-Spring Hill Review—R
$-St. Anthony Messenger
Storyteller—R
thegoodsteward.com—R
$-Today's Christian—R
Trumpeter—R
Victory News—R
$-Voice of the Lord
$-War Cry—R
$-World & I—R

CHILDREN
$-Guideposts for Kids
$-SHINEbrightly—R
$-Winner—R

CHRISTIAN EDUCATION/ LIBRARY
$-Children's Ministry

PASTORS/LEADERS
$-Interpreter
$-Pastoral Life—R
Pulpit Helps—R
Sharing the Practice—R
Strategic Adult Ministries—R
$-Word & World

TEEN/YOUNG ADULT
$-Brio—R
$-J.A.M.
$-Listen—R

$-Passageway.org—R
Teen Light—R
$-Teenage Christian—R

WOMEN
$-Godly Business Woman
Home-Based Moms—R
Inspired Moms.Com
$-Journey
$-MOMsense—R
Precious Times—R
Women of the Cross
Women Today—R

DOCTRINAL

ADULT/GENERAL
AGAIN—R
$-Anglican Journal
$-B.C. Catholic—R
$-Bible Advocate—R
Breakthrough Intercessor—R
$-Catholic Insight
Channels—R
Christian Media—R
Christian Online
Christian Research
Church Herald & Holiness—R
$-Culture Wars—R
Evangelical Times
$-Faith & Family
$-Faith Today
$-First Things
Founders Journal
$-Generation X—R
$-Homeschooling Today—R
$-HonorBound—R
$-Horizons (adult)—R
$-Impact—R
$-Inside Journal—R
$-Light & Life
$-Liguorian
$-Lookout
Mature Times—R
MESSAGE/Open Bible—R
Metro Voice—R
$-National Catholic
$-New Freeman—R
$-New Wineskins—R
$-On Mission
$-ONEvoice!
$-Our Sunday Visitor
Perspectives—R
Priscilla Papers—R
$-Queen of All Hearts
Singles Scoop—R
$-Social Justice—R
$-St. Anthony Messenger

Sword and Trumpet—R
Sword of the Lord—R
thegoodsteward.com—R
$-Today's Pentecostal Evangel—R
Trumpeter—R
$-U.S. Catholic
Victory News—R
$-Voice of the Lord
$-Wesleyan Life—R

CHRISTIAN EDUCATION/ LIBRARY
Catholic Library World

MISSIONS
Intl. Jour./Frontier—R
Missiology

PASTORS/LEADERS
$-Catholic Servant
$-Christian Century—R
$-Evangelical Baptist—R
$-Interpreter
$-Lutheran Partners—R
$-Parish Life—R
$-Pastoral Life—R
Pulpit Helps—R
Quarterly Review
Sewanee Theo. Review
Theological Digest—R
$-Theology Today
$-This Rock
$-Word & World
$-Worship Leader

TEEN/YOUNG ADULT
$-Essential Connection
$-J.A.M.
$-Passageway.org—R
$-Real Faith in Life—R
$-Student Leadership—R
$-Teenage Christian—R

WOMEN
$-Esprit—R

ECONOMICS

ADULT/GENERAL
$-America
$-Aspiring Retail
$-Associated Content—R
$-Bridal Guides—R
Business Reform
$-Catholic Peace Voice—R
Christian C. L. RECORD—R
Christian Media—R
Christian Motorsports
Christian Online
Christian Ranchman
$-Christian Renewal—R

$-Christian Retailing
$-Christian Social Action—R
Citizen USA—R
$-Citizens in America
$-City Light News—R
$-Covenant Companion—R
$-Culture Wars—R
$-Faith Today
$-First Things
$-Generation X—R
Good News Journal
$-Homeschooling Today—R
$-HonorBound—R
$-Light & Life
Metro Voice—R
$-National Catholic
$-New Freeman—R
NRB Magazine—R
$-Palm Beach—R
$-Plains Faith—R
$-Positive Thinking—R
$-Prism—R
Regent Business—R
$-Social Justice—R
$-Sojourners
Spiritual Voice—R
$-Spring Hill Review—R
$-St. Anthony Messenger
thegoodsteward.com—R
Trumpeter—R
Victory News—R
$-World & I—R

PASTORS/LEADERS
$-Christian Century—R
$-Pastoral Life—R
$-Today's Parish—R
$-Word & World

TEEN/YOUNG ADULT
$-J.A.M.
Teen Light—R
TeensForJC—R
Transcendmag.com—R

WOMEN
$-Esprit—R
$-Godly Business Woman
Home-Based Moms—R

ENCOURAGEMENT

ADULT/GENERAL
Alliance Life
$-Animal Trails—R
$-Barefoot Path—R
$-Brave Hearts
Bread of Life—R
$-Bridal Guides—R
$-Catholic Digest—R

$-Catholic Forester—R
Channels—R
$-Chicken Soup Magazine
Christian Journal—R
Christian Online
Christian Ranchman
$-Citizens in America
$-Cornerstone Christian—R
$-Cup of Comfort—R
$-Eclectic Homeschool
$-EFCA Today
Eternal Ink—R
$-Evangel—R
Evangelical Advocate—R
$-Faith & Family
$-Faith & Friends—R
$-Faith Today
$-Family Digest—R
$-Gems of Truth—R
$-Generation X—R
$-God Allows U-Turns—R
$-God's Way Books
Halo Magazine
Hannah to Hannah—R
$-Homeschooling Today—R
$-HonorBound—R
HopeKeepers—R
$-Horizons (adult)—R
$-Indian Life—R
InSound
InTouch
$-Joyful Noise!
Keys to Living—R
Leaves—R
$-Lifeglow—R
LifeLine Journal—R
$-Light & Life
Light at Home—R
$-Liguorian
$-Living—R
$-Lookout
$-Lutheran Digest—R
$-Mature Living
$-Men of Integrity—R
Men of the Cross
$-Minnesota Christian—R
Mosaic—R
Mutuality—R
New Heart—R
$-New Wineskins—R
$-Over the Back Fence—R
$-Palm Beach—R
Penned from the Heart
$-Plains Faith—R
PrayerWorks—R
Quaker Life—R
Randall House Periodicals

Regent Business—R
Sacred Journey—R
$-Seek—R
$-Senior Living
Silver Wings—R
Spiritual Voice—R
$-St. Joseph's Messenger—R
$-Standard—R
Storyteller—R
Sword of the Lord—R
$-Today's Christian—R
$-Together—R
Tributes—R
$-UP
Victory News—R
$-Wesleyan Life—R
$-Whole Magazine

CHILDREN
$-Barefoot for Kids—R
$-BREAD/God's Children—R
$-Cadet Quest—R
$-SHINEbrightly—R
$-Sparkle

CHRISTIAN EDUCATION/ LIBRARY
$-Children's Ministry
Christian Early Education—R

MISSIONS
$-American Baptists in Mission

PASTORS/LEADERS
$-Evangelical Baptist—R
Interpretation
$-Pray!—R

TEEN/YOUNG ADULT
$-Brio—R
$-J.A.M.
Teen Light—R
$-Young Christian—R

WOMEN
$-Esprit—R
Faithwebbin—R
Home-Based Moms—R
$-inSpirit—R
$-Journey
$-MOMsense—R
P31 Woman—R
Precious Times—R
$-Today's Christian Woman—R
$-Woman's Touch—R
Women of the Cross

WRITERS
$-Cross & Quill—R
$-Spirit-Led Writer—R

ENVIRONMENTAL ISSUES

ADULT/GENERAL
$-America
$-Anglican Journal
$-Associated Content—R
$-Aujourd'hui Credo—R
$-Bible Advocate—R
$-Catholic Forester—R
$-Catholic Peace Voice—R
$-Christian Courier (CAN)—R
$-Christian Networks
Christian Online
Christian Outlook
$-Christian Social Action—R
Citizen USA—R
$-Citizens in America
Common Ground—R
$-Covenant Companion—R
Creation Care—R
$-Creation Illust.
Desert Call—R
$-Faith Today
$-Generation X—R
Hard Row to Hoe
$-HonorBound—R
HopeKeepers—R
$-Indian Life—R
$-Light & Life
Light at Home—R
$-Liguorian
$-Living Church
Mature Times—R
Metro Voice—R
$-Minnesota Christian—R
$-National Catholic
$-New Freeman—R
$-New Wineskins—R
Pegasus Review—R
Perspectives—R
$-Plains Faith—R
Plowman—R
$-Prairie Messenger—R
Presbyterian Outlook
$-Prism—R
Quaker Life—R
Rock & Sling
Sacred Journey—R
$-Science & Spirit
Singles Scoop—R
$-Sojourners
Spiritual Voice—R
$-Spring Hill Review—R
$-St. Anthony Messenger
$-St. Joseph's Messenger—R
thegoodsteward.com—R
Trumpeter—R

Victory News—R
$-War Cry—R
$-Way of St. Francis—R
$-World & I—R

CHILDREN
$-Barefoot for Kids—R
$-Guideposts for Kids
$-My Friend
$-On the Line—R
$-Pockets—R
$-SHINEbrightly—R
Skipping Stones
$-Sparkle

CHRISTIAN EDUCATION/ LIBRARY
Journal/Christian Education

PASTORS/LEADERS
$-Christian Century—R
$-InSite—R
$-Interpreter
$-Lutheran Partners—R
$-Parish Life—R
$-Pastoral Life—R
$-Word & World

TEEN/YOUNG ADULT
$-Devo'Zine—R
$-J.A.M.
$-Passageway.org—R
$-Student Leadership—R
Teen Light—R
TeensForJC—R
Transcendmag.com—R
$-With—R

WOMEN
$-Esprit—R
$-Godly Business Woman
$-Horizons (women)—R
$-inSpirit—R

ESSAYS

ADULT/GENERAL
African Voices—R
$-America
$-Ancient Paths—R
$-Annals of St. Anne
$-Arlington Catholic
$-Associated Content—R
Books & Culture
$-Brave Hearts
Breakthrough Intercessor—R
$-Catholic Digest—R
$-Catholic Peace Voice—R
$-Celebrations Series—R
$-Chicken Soup—R

Christian Citizen USA
$-Christian Courier (CAN)—R
$-Christian Networks
Christian Online
$-Christian Parenting—R
$-Christian Renewal—R
$-Christianity Today—R
$-Citizens in America
$-Company—R
Creation Care—R
$-Creative Nonfiction
$-Cresset
$-Culture Wars—R
$-Cup of Comfort—R
$-Dovetail—R
Eternal Ink—R
$-Eureka Street
$-Faith Today
$-First Things
$-Flutters of the Heart
$-Gem—R
$-Generation X—R
$-God Allows U-Turns—R
Hannah to Hannah—R
Heartland Gatekeeper
Highway News—R
HopeKeepers—R
$-Ideals—R
$-Impact—R
$-Interim—R
$-Lifeglow—R
Light at Home—R
$-Liguorian
$-Living—R
$-Lookout
Mars Hill Review
Men of the Cross
Metro Voice—R
Mutuality—R
$-My Walk With Jesus
$-National Catholic
$-New Wineskins—R
$-Over the Back Fence—R
$-Parabola—R
Pegasus Review—R
Penwood Review
$-Plain Truth—R
$-Plains Faith—R
$-Portland Magazine
$-Prism—R
Quaker Life—R
Rock & Sling
Rose & Thorn
Sacred Journey—R
$-Senior Living
Short Stories Bimonthly—R

$-Sojourners
$-Spiritual Life
$-Spring Hill Review—R
SR: A Journal—R
$-St. Anthony Messenger
Steps
Storyteller—R
thegoodsteward.com—R
$-Tidewater Parent—R
Tri-State Voice
Tributes—R
Trumpeter—R
$-U.S. Catholic
Valparaiso Poetry—R
Victory News—R
$-War Cry—R
$-Way of St. Francis—R
$-Wittenburg Door—R
$-World & I—R
Xavier Review

CHILDREN
$-Nature Friend

CHRISTIAN EDUCATION/ LIBRARY
Catholic Library World

MISSIONS
$-PFI World Report—R
$-PIME World—R
Railroad Evangelist—R

MUSIC
$-Creator—R

PASTORS/LEADERS
$-African American Pulpit
$-Catholic Servant
$-Christian Century—R
Cross Currents
Journal/Pastoral Care—R
$-Pastoral Life—R
Sharing the Practice—R
Strategic Adult Ministries—R
Theological Digest—R
$-Word & World

TEEN/YOUNG ADULT
$-Boundless Webzine—R
$-Passageway.org—R
Teen Light—R
TeensForJC—R
Transcendmag.com—R
$-Young and Alive—R

WOMEN
Anna's Journal—R
$-Dabbling Mum.com—R
$-Godly Business Woman

$-Horizons (women)—R
$-MOMsense—R
Sisters in the Lord
Women of the Cross

WRITERS
$-Christian Communicator—R
Money the Write Way—R
Once Upon a Time—R
$-Spirit-Led Writer—R
$-Writer
$-Writer's Apprentice
$-Writer's Digest—R

ETHICS

ADULT/GENERAL
AGAIN—R
$-America
$-Angels on Earth
$-Associated Content—R
$-Aujourd'hui Credo—R
Breakthrough Intercessor—R
$-Canada Lutheran—R
$-Catholic Digest—R
$-Catholic Insight
$-Catholic Peace Voice—R
Channels—R
$-Christian Courier (CAN)—R
$-Christian Examiner
Christian Journal—R
Christian Media—R
Christian Observer
Christian Online
$-Christian Renewal—R
Christian Research
$-ChristianWeek—R
$-Citizens in America
$-City Light News—R
$-Culture Wars—R
Desert Call—R
$-Dovetail—R
$-Faith Today
$-First Things
$-Generation X—R
$-God Allows U-Turns—R
Good News Journal
$-Homeschooling Today—R
$-HonorBound—R
$-Horizons (adult)—R
$-Indian Life—R
$-Interim—R
Island Catholic News
Journal of Church & State
$-Light & Life
$-Liguorian
$-Living—R
$-Living Church

$-Lookout
Maranatha News—R
$-Men of Integrity—R
$-Mennonite Brethren—R
Metro Voice—R
$-Minnesota Christian—R
$-National Catholic
$-New Freeman—R
New Heart—R
$-New Wineskins—R
NRB Magazine—R
$-Our Sunday Visitor
Pegasus Review—R
Perspectives—R
$-Plains Faith—R
$-Positive Thinking—R
$-Prairie Messenger—R
Presbyterian Outlook
Priscilla Papers—R
$-Prism—R
Quaker Life—R
Randall House Periodicals
Regent Business—R
Sacred Journey—R
$-Science & Spirit
Silver Wings—R
$-Social Justice—R
$-Sojourners
Spiritual Voice—R
$-Spring Hill Review—R
$-St. Anthony Messenger
thegoodsteward.com—R
Trumpeter—R
$-U.S. Catholic
Victory News—R
$-War Cry—R
$-World & I—R

CHILDREN
$-BREAD/God's Children—R
$-SHINEbrightly—R
Skipping Stones

CHRISTIAN EDUCATION/ LIBRARY
Christian Librarian—R
Journal/Christian Education
$-Teachers Interaction

PASTORS/LEADERS
$-Christian Century—R
$-Clergy Journal—R
Cross Currents
$-Evangelical Baptist—R
$-Interpreter
Journal/Pastoral Care—R
$-Leadership—R
$-Pastoral Life—R

Quarterly Review
Sewanee Theo. Review
Sharing the Practice—R
Theological Digest—R
$-Theology Today
$-This Rock
$-Word & World

TEEN/YOUNG ADULT
$-Devo'Zine—R
GO!
$-Passageway.org—R
$-Real Faith in Life—R
Teen Light—R
$-Teenage Christian—R
TeensForJC—R
Transcendmag.com—R
$-With—R
$-Young Salvationist—R

WOMEN
$-Esprit—R
$-Godly Business Woman
Handmaiden—R
$-inSpirit—R

ETHNIC/CULTURAL PIECES

ADULT/GENERAL
African Voices—R
AGAIN—R
$-America
$-Arlington Catholic
$-Aspiring Retail
$-Associated Content—R
$-Aujourd'hui Credo—R
Breakthrough Intercessor—R
$-Bridal Guides—R
$-Catholic Digest—R
$-Catholic Peace Voice—R
$-Celebrate Life—R
Channels—R
$-Christian Courier (CAN)—R
Christian News NW—R
Christian Online
$-ChristianWeek—R
Citizen USA—R
$-Citizens in America
$-City Light News—R
$-Columbia
$-Commonweal
Creation Care—R
Desert Call—R
$-Dovetail—R
$-En Confianza
$-Episcopal Life—R
Evangelical Advocate—R

$-Faith Today
$-Foursquare World Advance—R
$-Gem—R
$-Generation X—R
$-Good News—R
$-Gospel Today—R
Hannah to Hannah—R
$-Homeschooling Today—R
$-HonorBound—R
$-Impact—R
$-Indian Life—R
Journal of Church & State
$-Light & Life
$-Liguorian
$-Lookout
Maranatha News—R
Mature Times—R
$-Men of Integrity—R
Mennonite Historian—R
$-MESSAGE
MESSAGE/Open Bible—R
$-Minnesota Christian—R
Mutuality—R
$-National Catholic
$-New Freeman—R
$-New Wineskins—R
$-On Mission
Penned from the Heart
$-Plain Truth—R
$-Plains Faith—R
$-Prairie Messenger—R
Priscilla Papers—R
$-Prism—R
Purpose Magazine
Quaker Life—R
Sacred Journey—R
$-Science & Spirit
Singles Scoop—R
$-Sojourners
Spirituality for Today
$-Spring Hill Review—R
$-St. Anthony Messenger
Star of Zion
thegoodsteward.com—R
$-Today's Christian—R
$-Today's Pentecostal Evangel—R
$-Together—R
Trumpeter—R
$-U.S. Catholic
$-Upscale Magazine
Victory News—R
$-War Cry—R
$-Wesleyan Life—R
West Wind Review
$-World & I—R
Xavier Review

CHILDREN
$-Faces
$-Guideposts for Kids
$-On the Line—R
$-SHINEbrightly—R
Skipping Stones
$-Story Friends—R

CHRISTIAN EDUCATION/ LIBRARY
$-Children's Ministry

MISSIONS
$-Evangelical Missions—R
Missiology
OpRev Equipper—R
$-PIME World—R
Wesleyan World—R
Women of the Harvest

PASTORS/LEADERS
$-African American Pulpit
$-Christian Century—R
$-Five Stones—R
$-Interpreter
Jour./Amer. Soc./Chur. Growth—R
Journal/Pastoral Care—R
$-Lutheran Partners—R
Net Results
$-Parish Life—R
$-Pastoral Life—R
Sharing the Practice—R
$-This Rock
$-Worship Leader

TEEN/YOUNG ADULT
$-Boundless Webzine—R
$-Credo—R
$-Devo'Zine—R
$-Essential Connection
$-Passageway.org—R
$-Real Faith in Life—R
$-Student Leadership—R
Teen Light—R
TeensForJC—R
Transcendmag.com—R
$-With—R
$-Young Christian—R
$-Young Salvationist—R

WOMEN
$-Esprit—R
$-Godly Business Woman
Heart & Soul
$-Horizons (women)—R
$-inSpirit—R
$-Link & Visitor—R
$-MOMsense—R

Precious Times—R
$-SpiritLed Woman

EVANGELISM/WITNESSING

ADULT/GENERAL
$-Alive!—R
Alliance Life
$-America
American Tract Society—R
$-Anglican Journal
$-Annals of St. Anne
$-BGC World—R
$-Bible Advocate—R
Bread of Life—R
Breakthrough Intercessor—R
$-Canada Lutheran—R
Channels—R
Christian Courier (WI)—R
$-Christian Leader—R
Christian Online
Christian Ranchman
Christian Research
$-Christianity Today—R
Church Herald & Holiness—R
$-Church of God EVANGEL
$-City Light News—R
$-Cornerstone Christian—R
Creation Care—R
Crossway/Newsline—R
$-Decision
$-Discipleship Journal—R
$-Episcopal Life—R
Eternal Ink—R
$-Evangel—R
Evangelical Advocate—R
$-Faith & Family
$-Faith Today
$-Focus on the Family
$-Gem—R
$-God Allows U-Turns—R
$-Good News—R
Good News in RI
Gospel Tract—R
Halo Magazine
Hannah to Hannah—R
$-HonorBound—R
$-Horizons (adult)—R
$-Indian Life—R
$-Inland NW Christian
$-Inside Journal—R
$-Joyful Noise!
Leaves—R
LifeLine Journal—R
$-Light & Life
$-Liguorian
$-Live—R

$-Living Church
Looking Up
$-Lookout
$-Lutheran Journal—R
Maranatha News—R
Mature Times—R
$-Men of Integrity—R
$-Mennonite Brethren—R
MESSAGE/Open Bible—R
Metro Voice—R
$-Minnesota Christian—R
$-Montgomery's Journey
Mosaic—R
$-New Freeman—R
New Heart—R
$-New Wineskins—R
$-On Mission
$-ONEvoice!
Penned from the Heart
$-Plain Truth—R
$-Plains Faith—R
$-Power for Living—R
PrayerWorks—R
$-Priority!—R
$-Prism—R
$-Purpose—R
Quaker Life—R
Randall House Periodicals
Regent Business—R
$-Seek—R
Sharing—R
$-Signs of the Times—R
Singles Scoop—R
Spiritual Voice—R
$-St. Anthony Messenger
$-Standard—R
Sword of the Lord—R
$-Testimony—R
thegoodsteward.com—R
$-Today's Christian—R
$-Today's Pentecostal Evangel—R
Trumpeter—R
Victory News—R
$-Voice of the Lord
$-War Cry—R
$-Way of St. Francis—R
$-Wesleyan Life—R
$-Whole Magazine

CHILDREN
$-Barefoot for Kids—R
$-BREAD/God's Children—R
$-Club Connection
$-Courage—R
$-Focus/Clubhouse Jr.
$-Guide—R

$-Juniorway
$-Primary Pal (IL)

CHRISTIAN EDUCATION/ LIBRARY
Catholic Library World
$-Children's Ministry
$-Church Educator—R
$-Kids' Ministry Ideas—R
$-Resource—R
$-RTJ
$-Teach Kids!—R
$-Youth & CE Leadership

MISSIONS
$-American Baptists in Mission
$-Evangelical Missions—R
Intl. Jour./Frontier—R
$-Leaders for Today
Missiology
Wesleyan World—R

MUSIC
Christian Music Weekly—R

PASTORS/LEADERS
$-Catholic Servant
$-Christian Century—R
$-Evangelical Baptist—R
$-Evangelicals Today—R
$-Five Stones—R
$-Growth Points—R
$-Horizons (pastor)—R
$-Interpreter
Jour./Amer. Soc./Chur. Growth—R
$-Let's Worship
$-Lutheran Partners—R
$-Ministries Today
Ministry in Motion—R
$-Parish Life—R
$-Pastoral Life—R
Pastors.com—R
Pulpit Helps—R
Quarterly Review
$-Review for Religious
$-RevWriter Resource
$-Sermon Notes—R
Sharing the Practice—R
$-This Rock
$-WCA News—R

TEEN/YOUNG ADULT
$-Credo—R
$-Devo'Zine—R
$-Essential Connection
GO!
$-J.A.M.
$-Passageway.org—R

$-Real Faith in Life—R
$-Student Leadership—R
$-Teenage Christian—R
TeensForJC—R
Transcendmag.com—R
$-With—R
$-Young Christian—R
$-Young Salvationist—R

WOMEN
$-At the Center—R
$-Godly Business Woman
$-inSpirit—R
$-Journey
Just Between Us—R
$-Link & Visitor—R
P31 Woman—R
Precious Times—R
Right to the Heart—R
$-SpiritLed Woman
$-Woman's Touch—R
$-Women Alive!—R

EXEGESIS

ADULT/GENERAL
$-Alive Now—R
$-Catholic Insight
Channels—R
Christian Ranchman
Evangelical Advocate—R
$-HonorBound—R
$-Light & Life
$-Living Church
$-Lookout
$-National Catholic
$-New Freeman—R
Perspectives—R
Pietisten Online
$-Plain Truth—R
PrayerWorks—R
Priscilla Papers—R
Randall House Periodicals
Regent Business—R
$-St. Anthony Messenger
Sword and Trumpet—R
Sword of the Lord—R
Trumpeter—R
Victory News—R
$-Wesleyan Life—R

PASTORS/LEADERS
$-Enrichment—R
$-Pastoral Life—R
Pulpit Helps—R
Sharing the Practice—R
Theological Digest—R
$-Theology Today
$-This Rock

TEEN/YOUNG ADULT
$-Passageway.org—R
$-Young Adult Today—R

FAITH

ADULT/GENERAL
African Voices—R
$-America
$-Animal Trails—R
$-Arkansas Catholic—R
$-Aujourd'hui Credo—R
$-Barefoot Path—R
$-Believer's Bay
$-BGC World—R
$-Bible Advocate—R
$-Brave Hearts
Bread of Life—R
Breakthrough Intercessor—R
$-Bridal Guides—R
byFaith
$-Canada Lutheran—R
$-Catholic Digest—R
$-Catholic Insight
$-Catholic New Times—R
$-Catholic Peace Voice—R
$-Catholic Yearbook—R
$-CGA World—R
Channels—R
$-Christian Courier (CAN)—R
Christian Journal—R
$-Christian Leader—R
$-Christian Networks
Christian Online
Christian Ranchman
Christian Research
$-Christian Retailing
$-Christianity Today—R
$-ChristianWeek—R
$-City Light News—R
$-Columbia
$-Covenant Companion—R
Desert Call—R
Disciple's Journal—R
$-Discipleship Journal—R
$-Dovetail—R
Eternal Ink—R
Evangelical Advocate—R
$-Faith & Family
$-Faith & Friends—R
$-Faith Today
$-Family Digest—R
$-Gem—R
$-Generation X—R
$-God Allows U-Turns—R
Good News Journal
Gospel Tract—R
Hannah to Hannah—R

Highway News—R
$-HonorBound—R
HopeKeepers—R
Island Catholic News
LifeLine Journal—R
LifeTimes Catholic
$-Light & Life
Light at Home—R
$-Liguorian
$-Live—R
$-Living—R
$-Lookout
$-Lutheran Journal—R
Maranatha News—R
$-Mature Living
Mature Times—R
$-Men of Integrity—R
Men of the Cross
$-Minnesota Christian—R
$-Montgomery's Journey
Mosaic—R
$-My Walk With Jesus
$-National Catholic
$-New Freeman—R
New Heart—R
$-New Wineskins—R
$-Now What?—R
$-ONEvoice!
$-Our Sunday Visitor
$-Palm Beach—R
Parents & Teens—R
Pegasus Review—R
Penned from the Heart
$-Plain Truth—R
$-Plains Faith—R
Plowman—R
$-Positive Thinking—R
$-Prairie Messenger—R
PrayerWorks—R
$-Precepts for Living
$-Priority!—R
Priscilla Papers—R
$-Psychology for Living—R
Quaker Life—R
Randall House Periodicals
Reformed Quarterly
Sacred Journey—R
$-Seek—R
$-Signs of the Times—R
Singles Scoop—R
Spiritual Voice—R
$-Spring Hill Review—R
$-St. Anthony Messenger
$-St. Joseph's Messenger—R
$-Standard—R
SW Kansas Faith
Sword and Trumpet—R

Sword of the Lord—R
$-Testimony—R
thegoodsteward.com—R
$-Today's Christian—R
$-Today's Pentecostal Evangel—R
$-Together—R
Trumpeter—R
$-U.S. Catholic
$-United Church Observer—R
Victory News—R
$-Voice of the Lord
$-Way of St. Francis—R
$-Weavings—R
$-Wesleyan Life—R
$-World & I—R

CHILDREN
$-Barefoot for Kids—R
$-BREAD/God's Children—R
$-Courage—R
$-Focus/Clubhouse Jr.
$-Juniorway
$-Our Little Friend—R
$-Partners—R
$-Passport—R
$-Primary Street
$-Primary Treasure—R
$-SHINEbrightly—R
$-Sparkle

CHRISTIAN EDUCATION/ LIBRARY
Catholic Library World
$-Children's Ministry
Christian Librarian—R
$-Teachers of Vision—R
$-Youth & CE Leadership

MISSIONS
$-PIME World—R

MUSIC
Christian Music Weekly—R

PASTORS/LEADERS
$-African American Pulpit
Christian Education Jour. (CA)—R
$-Evangelical Baptist—R
$-Evangelicals Today—R
$-Interpreter
$-Parish Life—R
$-Pastoral Life—R
$-Pray!—R
$-Proclaim—R
Quarterly Review
$-Review for Religious
$-RevWriter Resource
Sharing the Practice—R
$-Worship Leader

TEEN/YOUNG ADULT
$-Boundless Webzine—R
$-Brio—R
$-Credo—R
$-Devo'Zine—R
GO!
$-J.A.M.
$-Passageway.org—R
$-Student Leadership—R
TeensForJC—R
Transcendmag.com—R
$-With—R
$-Young Adult Today—R
$-Young and Alive—R
$-Young Christian—R
$-Young Salvationist—R

WOMEN
$-Dabbling Mum.com—R
$-Esprit—R
Faithwebbin—R
$-Godly Business Woman
Home-Based Moms—R
$-Horizons (women)—R
$-inSpirit—R
$-Journey
Just Between Us—R
Life Tools for Women
P31 Woman—R
$-SpiritLed Woman
$-Today's Christian Woman—R
$-Woman's Touch—R
$-Women Alive!—R
Women of the Cross

WRITERS
$-Areopagus (UK)

FAMILY LIFE

ADULT/GENERAL
$-Abilities
African Voices—R
AGAIN—R
$-Alive!—R
Alliance Life
$-America
$-Angels on Earth
$-Annals of St. Anne
$-Arkansas Catholic—R
$-Arlington Catholic
$-Associated Content—R
$-Aujourd'hui Credo—R
$-B.C. Catholic—R
$-Barefoot Path—R
$-Believer's Bay
$-BGC World—R
$-Bible Advocate—R
$-Brave Hearts

Bread of Life—R
Breakthrough Intercessor—R
$-Bridal Guides—R
byFaith
$-Canada Lutheran—R
$-Catholic Digest—R
$-Catholic Forester—R
$-Catholic Insight
$-Catholic New Times—R
CBN.com—R
$-Celebrations Series—R
$-CGA World—R
Channels—R
$-Chicken Soup—R
$-Chicken Soup Magazine
Christian C. L. RECORD—R
$-Christian Courier (CAN)—R
Christian Courier (WI)—R
$-Christian Home & School
Christian Journal—R
$-Christian Leader—R
Christian Online
$-Christian Parenting—R
Christian Ranchman
$-Christian Renewal—R
$-ChristianWeek—R
Citizen USA—R
$-Citizens in America
$-City Light News—R
$-Columbia
Connecting Point—R
$-Cornerstone Christian—R
$-Covenant Companion—R
$-Culture Wars—R
$-Cup of Comfort—R
$-Decision
Desert Call—R
Disciple's Journal—R
$-Dovetail—R
$-Eclectic Homeschool
$-EFCA Today
Eternal Ink—R
Evangelical Advocate—R
$-Faith & Family
$-Faith & Friends—R
$-Faith Today
$-Family Digest—R
Family Online—R
$-Focus on the Family
$-Foursquare World Advance—R
$-Gem—R
$-God Allows U-Turns—R
Gold Country Families—R
Good News Journal
$-Grand
$-Grit
$-Guideposts—R

Hannah to Hannah—R
Heartlight—R
Highway News—R
$-Homeschooling Today—R
$-HonorBound—R
$-Horizons (adult)—R
$-Ideals—R
$-Indian Life—R
Indiana Christian News
$-Inland NW Christian
$-Interim—R
$-Joy & Praise
Keys to Living—R
LifeLine Journal—R
Lifesite Canada
LifeTimes Catholic
$-Light & Life
Light at Home—R
$-Live—R
$-Living—R
$-Living Church
$-Living Light News—R
$-Lookout
$-Lutheran Digest—R
Maranatha News—R
$-Marriage Partnership—R
Mature Times—R
$-Mature Years—R
$-Men of Integrity—R
Men of the Cross
Mennonite Family History
$-Messenger/St. Anthony
Metro Voice—R
$-Minnesota Christian—R
$-Montgomery's Journey
Mutuality—R
$-New Freeman—R
$-New Wineskins—R
Nostalgia—R
$-On Mission
$-ONEvoice!
$-Our Sunday Visitor
$-Over the Back Fence—R
$-ParentLife
Parents & Teens—R
Pegasus Review—R
Penned from the Heart
$-Plain Truth—R
$-Plains Faith—R
Plowman—R
$-Positive Thinking—R
$-Power for Living—R
$-Prairie Messenger—R
PrayerWorks—R
Priscilla Papers—R
$-Psychology for Living—R
$-Purpose—R

Quaker Life—R
Randall House Periodicals
Sacred Journey—R
$-Science & Spirit
$-Seek—R
$-Signs of the Times—R
$-SingleAgain.com
$-Smart Families—R
$-Social Justice—R
$-Special Living—R
Spiritual Voice—R
$-Spring Hill Review—R
$-St. Anthony Messenger
Steps
Storyteller—R
SW Kansas Faith
Sword and Trumpet—R
Sword of the Lord—R
$-Testimony—R
thegoodsteward.com—R
$-Tidewater Parent—R
$-Today's Christian—R
$-Today's Pentecostal Evangel—R
$-Together—R
Trumpeter—R
$-U.S. Catholic
$-United Church Observer—R
$-Vibrant Life—R
Victory News—R
$-Vision—R
$-War Cry—R
$-Way of St. Francis—R
$-Wesleyan Life—R
West Wind Review
Winsome Wit—R
$-World & I—R

CHILDREN
$-Barefoot for Kids—R
$-BREAD/God's Children—R
$-Club Connection
$-Focus/Clubhouse
$-Focus/Clubhouse Jr.
$-Guide—R
$-Guideposts for Kids
$-Juniorway
$-My Friend
$-Partners—R
$-Pockets—R
$-SHINEbrightly—R
Skipping Stones
$-Sparkle
$-Winner—R
Young Gentleman's Monthly

CHRISTIAN EDUCATION/ LIBRARY
$-Children's Ministry

$-Church Educator—R

MISSIONS
$-American Baptists in Mission
Women of the Harvest

PASTORS/LEADERS
$-African American Pulpit
$-Barefoot—R
$-Catholic Servant
$-Enrichment—R
$-Evangelical Baptist—R
$-Evangelicals Today—R
$-InSite—R
$-Interpreter
Journal/Pastoral Care—R
$-Lutheran Partners—R
$-Pastoral Life—R
$-Preaching Well—R
Pulpit Helps—R
$-Rev.
$-RevWriter Resource
Sharing the Practice—R
$-Today's Christian Preacher—R
$-Today's Parish—R
$-Word & World
Youth Culture

TEEN/YOUNG ADULT
$-Brio—R
$-Credo—R
GO!
$-J.A.M.
$-Listen—R
$-Passageway.org—R
$-Real Faith in Life—R
Teen Light—R
TeensForJC—R
Transcendmag.com—R
$-With—R
$-Young Adult Today—R
$-Young and Alive—R
$-Young Christian—R

WOMEN
Crowned with Silver
$-Dabbling Mum.com—R
$-Esprit—R
Faithwebbin—R
$-Godly Business Woman
Handmaiden—R
Hearts at Home—R
Home-Based Moms—R
$-Horizons (women)—R
Inspired Moms.Com
$-inSpirit—R
$-Journey
Just Between Us—R
Keeping Hearts & Home

Life Tools for Women
$-Link & Visitor—R
Lutheran Woman's Quar.
$-MOMsense—R
P31 Woman—R
Precious Times—R
Shalom Bayit
$-Simple Joy
Sisters in the Lord
$-SpiritLed Woman
$-Today's Christian Woman—R
$-Woman's Touch—R
$-Women Alive!—R
Women of the Cross
Women Today—R

FILLERS: ANECDOTES

ADULT/GENERAL
$-Alive!—R
$-Angels on Earth
$-Animal Trails—R
$-Bridal Guides—R
$-Catholic Digest—R
$-Catholic Yearbook—R
Channels—R
$-Chicken Soup—R
Christian Courier (WI)—R
Christian Journal—R
Christian Motorsports
$-Christian Parenting—R
Christian Ranchman
$-Christian Response—R
Church Herald & Holiness—R
$-Citizens in America
$-City Light News—R
Desert Call—R
Disciple's Journal—R
$-DisciplesWorld
$-Faith & Family
$-Family Digest—R
$-Foursquare World Advance—R
$-Gem—R
$-Generation X—R
$-God Allows U-Turns—R
Good News Journal
Heartlight—R
Highway News—R
$-Impact—R
Light at Home—R
$-Live—R
$-Living—R
$-Lutheran Digest—R
$-Lutheran Journal—R
Maranatha News—R
$-Mature Living
Mature Times—R
MovieGuide

New Heart—R
Nostalgia—R
$-Now What?—R
$-Palm Beach—R
$-Presbyterians Today—R
$-Purpose—R
$-SingleAgain.com
Singles Scoop—R
Spiritual Voice—R
Spirituality for Today
$-St. Anthony Messenger
Star of Zion
Steps
Tributes—R
Victory News—R
$-War Cry—R
$-Way of St. Francis—R

CHILDREN
$-Club Connection
$-Guideposts for Kids
$-High Adventure—R
Skipping Stones

CHRISTIAN EDUCATION/ LIBRARY
Christian Librarian—R
$-RTJ

MISSIONS
Railroad Evangelist—R
Women of the Harvest

MUSIC
$-Creator—R

PASTORS/LEADERS
$-Barefoot—R
$-Leadership—R
Ministry in Motion—R
$-Parish Life—R
$-Pastoral Life—R
$-Preaching Well—R
$-PreachingToday.com
Pulpit Helps—R
$-Sermon Notes—R
Sharing the Practice—R
$-Sunday Sermons—R

TEEN/YOUNG ADULT
$-Credo—R
Teen Light—R
$-Young Christian—R
$-Young Salvationist—R

WOMEN
Anna's Journal—R
Hearts at Home—R
Home-Based Moms—R
Just Between Us—R

Right to the Heart—R
$-Today's Christian Woman—R
$-Woman's Touch—R

WRITERS
$-Areopagus (UK)
$-Cross & Quill—R
$-Fellowscript—R
Money the Write Way—R
NW Christian Author—R
Once Upon a Time—R
$-Tickled by Thunder
Write Touch
$-Writers' Journal
Writes of Passage—R

FILLERS: CARTOONS

ADULT/GENERAL
African Voices—R
$-Alive!—R
$-Alive Now—R
Alliance Life
American Tract Society—R
$-Angels on Earth
$-Animal Trails—R
$-Aspiring Retail
$-Bridal Guides—R
$-Catholic Digest—R
$-Catholic Forester—R
Channels—R
$-Chicken Soup—R
Christian Computing—R
$-Christian Herald—R
Christian Journal—R
Christian Motorsports
Christian Ranchman
Church Herald & Holiness—R
Citizen USA—R
$-Citizens in America
$-City Light News—R
Connecting Point—R
$-Cornerstone Christian—R
$-Culture Wars—R
Disciple's Journal—R
$-DisciplesWorld
Discovery—R
$-Eureka Street
$-Evangel—R
$-Faith & Family
$-Faith & Friends—R
$-Foursquare World Advance—R
$-Gem—R
Good News Journal
$-Gospel Today—R
Heartlight—R
Highway News—R
$-Impact—R

$-Inside Journal—R
$-Interchange
$-Joy & Praise
$-Liguorian
$-Lutheran Digest—R
Maranatha News—R
$-Mature Living
Mature Times—R
$-Mature Years—R
MovieGuide
New Heart—R
Pegasus Review—R
Plowman—R
$-Power for Living—R
$-Presbyterians Today—R
$-Purpose—R
Singles Scoop—R
$-Sojourners
$-Special Living—R
Spiritual Voice—R
$-Spring Hill Review—R
$-St. Anthony Messenger
Star of Zion
Steps
Storyteller—R
thegoodsteward.com—R
Trumpeter—R
$-United Church Observer—R
Victory News—R
$-Way of St. Francis—R
$-Wireless Age—R
$-Wittenburg Door—R

CHILDREN
$-Adventures
$-American Girl
$-Barefoot for Kids—R
$-Club Connection
$-High Adventure—R
$-On the Line—R
$-Passport—R
$-SHINEbrightly—R
Skipping Stones
$-Story Friends—R

CHRISTIAN EDUCATION/ LIBRARY
$-Children's Ministry
Christian Librarian—R
$-Group Magazine
$-Journal/Adventist Educ.—R
$-Teachers of Vision—R
$-Today's Catholic Teacher—R
$-Youth & CE Leadership

MISSIONS
Mission Frontiers
Railroad Evangelist—R

MUSIC
Christian Music Weekly—R
$-Creator—R
$-Senior Musician—R
Tradition

PASTORS/LEADERS
$-Barefoot—R
$-Catholic Servant
$-Christian Century—R
Christian Management—R
$-Diocesan Dialogue—R
$-Enrichment—R
$-Horizons (pastor)—R
$-Leadership—R
$-Lutheran Partners—R
$-Parish Life—R
$-Priest
Pulpit Helps—R
$-Rev.
$-Sabbath School Leadership—R
$-Sermon Notes—R
Sharing the Practice—R
$-Small Group Dynamics—R
$-WCA News—R
$-Your Church—R

TEEN/YOUNG ADULT
$-Credo—R
$-Listen—R
Teen Light—R
TeensForJC—R
Transcendmag.com—R
$-With—R
$-Young Christian—R
$-Young Salvationist—R

WOMEN
Hearts at Home—R
Just Between Us—R
$-Today's Christian Woman—R
$-Women Alive!—R

WRITERS
$-Cross & Quill—R
Heaven—R
Once Upon a Time—R
$-Upper Case
$-Writers' Journal

FILLERS: FACTS

ADULT/GENERAL
$-Alive!—R
Alliance Life
$-Angels on Earth
$-Animal Trails—R
$-Aspiring Retail
$-Bible Advocate—R

Bread of Life—R
$-Bridal Guides—R
$-Catholic Digest—R
$-Catholic Yearbook—R
$-Chicken Soup—R
Christian Courier (WI)—R
$-Christian Herald—R
Christian Motorsports
Christian Ranchman
$-Christian Response—R
$-Citizens in America
$-City Light News—R
$-Cornerstone Christian—R
Desert Call—R
Disciple's Journal—R
Eternal Ink—R
$-Gem—R
$-Generation X—R
$-God Allows U-Turns—R
Good News Journal
Highway News—R
$-Interchange
$-Joy & Praise
Keys to Living—R
Light at Home—R
$-Lutheran Digest—R
$-Lutheran Journal—R
$-Mature Living
Mature Times—R
MESSAGE/Open Bible—R
MovieGuide
Nostalgia—R
$-Now What?—R
PrayerWorks—R
$-SingleAgain.com
Singles Scoop—R
Spiritual Voice—R
$-St. Anthony Messenger
Sword and Trumpet—R
Sword of the Lord—R
$-Vibrant Life—R
Victory News—R
$-Way of St. Francis—R

CHILDREN
$-Adventures
$-Barefoot for Kids—R
$-Club Connection
$-Guideposts for Kids
$-High Adventure—R
$-On the Line—R

CHRISTIAN EDUCATION/ LIBRARY
$-RTJ
$-Teachers of Vision—R
$-Today's Catholic Teacher—R

PASTORS/LEADERS
$-Interpreter
$-Pastoral Life—R
Strategic Adult Ministries—R

TEEN/YOUNG ADULT
$-Real Faith in Life—R
Teen Light—R
TeensForJC—R
Transcendmag.com—R
$-Young Christian—R
$-Young Salvationist—R

WOMEN
Anna's Journal—R
Hearts at Home—R
Home-Based Moms—R

WRITERS
$-Areopagus (UK)
Money the Write Way—R
Write Touch
$-Writers' Journal
Writes of Passage—R

FILLERS: GAMES

ADULT/GENERAL
$-Alive!—R
$-Angels on Earth
$-Catholic Yearbook—R
$-CGA World—R
$-Christian Herald—R
Christian Motorsports
Christian Ranchman
Citizen USA—R
Connecting Point—R
$-Cornerstone Christian—R
$-Creation Illust.
Disciple's Journal—R
$-Faith & Friends—R
$-Gem—R
Good News Journal
Heartlight—R
Light at Home—R
$-Lutheran Journal—R
$-Mature Living
Mature Times—R
MovieGuide
Nostalgia—R
Randall House Periodicals
Singles Scoop—R
$-Smart Families—R
Spiritual Voice—R
$-Spring Hill Review—R
Star of Zion
Victory News—R

CHILDREN
$-Adventures
$-American Girl
$-Barefoot for Kids—R
$-Club Connection
$-Courage—R
$-Guide—R
$-Guideposts for Kids
$-High Adventure—R
$-On the Line—R
$-Pockets—R
$-Primary Pal (IL)
$-SHINEbrightly—R
$-Sparkle

CHRISTIAN EDUCATION/ LIBRARY
Catholic Library World
$-Group Magazine
$-RTJ

PASTORS/LEADERS
$-Barefoot—R

TEEN/YOUNG ADULT
$-Credo—R
$-Listen—R
Teen Light—R
TeensForJC—R
Transcendmag.com—R
$-Young Salvationist—R

WOMEN
Keeping Hearts & Home

WRITERS
$-Areopagus (UK)

FILLERS: IDEAS

ADULT/GENERAL
$-Angels on Earth
$-Animal Trails—R
$-Aspiring Retail
$-Bridal Guides—R
$-CGA World—R
$-Christian Home & School
Christian Motorsports
$-Christian Parenting—R
Christian Ranchman
$-Cornerstone Christian—R
Disciple's Journal—R
Eternal Ink—R
$-Gem—R
$-Generation X—R
$-God Allows U-Turns—R
Good News Journal
Heartlight—R
Highway News—R
Light at Home—R

MovieGuide
$-Seek—R
$-SingleAgain.com
$-Smart Families—R
Spiritual Voice—R
$-St. Joseph's Messenger—R
Victory News—R

CHILDREN
$-Barefoot for Kids—R
$-Club Connection
$-Guideposts for Kids
$-High Adventure—R
$-Pockets—R

CHRISTIAN EDUCATION/ LIBRARY
$-Children's Ministry
Christian Librarian—R
Church & Synagogue Lib.—R
$-Church Educator—R
$-Group Magazine
$-Preschool Playhouse
$-RTJ
$-Teach Kids!—R
$-Teachers Interaction
$-Youth & CE Leadership

MISSIONS
$-Evangelical Missions—R

MUSIC
$-Creator—R
$-Senior Musician—R

PASTORS/LEADERS
$-Barefoot—R
$-Church Worship
$-Enrichment—R
$-Interpreter
$-Lutheran Partners—R
Ministry in Motion—R
$-Pastoral Life—R
$-Pray!—R
$-Preaching Well—R
$-Rev.
$-RevWriter Resource
$-Small Group Dynamics—R
Strategic Adult Ministries—R
$-WCA News—R

TEEN/YOUNG ADULT
$-Campus Life—R
$-Real Faith in Life—R
$-Young Christian—R

WOMEN
Hearts at Home—R
Home-Based Moms—R
Just Between Us—R

P31 Woman—R
Right to the Heart—R
$-Woman's Touch—R

WRITERS
$-Areopagus (UK)
Dedicated Author
Money the Write Way—R
Once Upon a Time—R
$-Tickled by Thunder
Write Touch
Writer's Network
$-Writers' Journal
Writes of Passage—R

FILLERS: JOKES

ADULT/GENERAL
$-Angels on Earth
$-Catholic Digest—R
Christian Journal—R
Christian Motorsports
Christian Ranchman
Citizen USA—R
$-City Light News—R
$-Cornerstone Christian—R
Disciple's Journal—R
Eternal Ink—R
$-Faith & Friends—R
$-Gem—R
$-Generation X—R
Good News Journal
Heartlight—R
$-Impact—R
$-Interchange
Keys to Living—R
Light at Home—R
$-Liguorian
$-Lutheran Digest—R
Maranatha News—R
$-Mature Years—R
MovieGuide
New Heart—R
Nostalgia—R
$-Palm Beach—R
PrayerWorks—R
$-Seek—R
$-SingleAgain.com
Spiritual Voice—R
$-St. Anthony Messenger
Star of Zion
thegoodsteward.com—R
Victory News—R

CHILDREN
$-Barefoot for Kids—R
$-Club Connection
$-Guideposts for Kids

$-High Adventure—R
$-On the Line—R
$-Pockets—R

MUSIC
$-Creator—R

PASTORS/LEADERS
$-Preaching Well—R
Sharing the Practice—R

TEEN/YOUNG ADULT
Teen Light—R
TeensForJC—R
Transcendmag.com—R

WOMEN
Home-Based Moms—R
$-Women Alive!—R

WRITERS
$-Areopagus (UK)
$-Writers' Journal
Writes of Passage—R

FILLERS: KID QUOTES

ADULT/GENERAL
$-Animal Trails—R
$-Bridal Guides—R
$-Chicken Soup—R
Christian Journal—R
Citizen USA—R
$-City Light News—R
$-Cornerstone Christian—R
$-DisciplesWorld
Eternal Ink—R
Highway News—R
$-Indian Life—R
Keys to Living—R
Light at Home—R
MovieGuide
$-SingleAgain.com
Spiritual Voice—R
$-Today's Christian—R
$-Upscale Magazine
Victory News—R

CHILDREN
$-Barefoot for Kids—R

CHRISTIAN EDUCATION/ LIBRARY
$-Children's Ministry

PASTORS/LEADERS
$-Parish Life—R

WOMEN
Home-Based Moms—R

FILLERS: NEWSBREAKS

ADULT/GENERAL
$-Angels on Earth
$-Anglican Journal
$-Arkansas Catholic—R
$-Aspiring Retail
$-B.C. Catholic—R
$-Canada Lutheran—R
$-Catholic New Times—R
$-Catholic Telegraph
$-Celebrate Life—R
Christian Courier (WI)—R
Christian Journal—R
Christian Motorsports
Christian Ranchman
$-Christian Renewal—R
$-City Light News—R
$-Cornerstone Christian—R
Disciple's Journal—R
Friends Journal—R
$-Gem—R
$-God Allows U-Turns—R
Good News Journal
Heartlight—R
Highway News—R
Light at Home—R
Maranatha News—R
MovieGuide
NRB Magazine—R
$-Palm Beach—R
Spiritual Voice—R
Steps
Sword and Trumpet—R
Sword of the Lord—R
Victory News—R

CHILDREN
$-Club Connection

CHRISTIAN EDUCATION/ LIBRARY
Christian Librarian—R

MISSIONS
OpRev Equipper—R

PASTORS/LEADERS
$-Preaching Well—R
Strategic Adult Ministries—R

TEEN/YOUNG ADULT
$-Real Faith in Life—R

WOMEN
Anna's Journal—R

WRITERS
$-Areopagus (UK)

Writer's Network
$-Writers' Journal

FILLERS: PARTY IDEAS

ADULT/GENERAL
$-Animal Trails—R
$-Bridal Guides—R
Christian Ranchman
Citizen USA—R
$-Cornerstone Christian—R
Disciple's Journal—R
Good News Journal
Highway News—R
Light at Home—R
MovieGuide
Spiritual Voice—R
Victory News—R

CHILDREN
$-Adventures
$-Barefoot for Kids—R
$-Club Connection
$-Guideposts for Kids
$-On the Line—R
$-Sparkle

MUSIC
$-Creator—R
$-Senior Musician—R

PASTORS/LEADERS
$-Barefoot—R
$-Pastoral Life—R

TEEN/YOUNG ADULT
$-Credo—R
Teen Light—R
TeensForJC—R
Transcendmag.com—R
$-Young Christian—R

WOMEN
Hearts at Home—R
Home-Based Moms—R
Keeping Hearts & Home
P31 Woman—R
Right to the Heart—R

WRITERS
$-Areopagus (UK)

FILLERS: PRAYERS

ADULT/GENERAL
$-Angels on Earth
$-Animal Trails—R
$-Brave Hearts
$-Bridal Guides—R
$-Catholic Yearbook—R
$-CGA World—R

Channels—R
$-Christian Herald—R
Christian Journal—R
Christian Motorsports
Christian Online
Christian Ranchman
Church Herald & Holiness—R
$-Cornerstone Christian—R
Desert Call—R
Disciple's Journal—R
Eternal Ink—R
$-Family Digest—R
$-Gem—R
$-God Allows U-Turns—R
Good News Journal
Gospel Tract—R
Heartlight—R
Highway News—R
$-Joy & Praise
Keys to Living—R
LifeTimes Catholic
Light at Home—R
$-Mature Years—R
MovieGuide
Plowman—R
PrayerWorks—R
$-SingleAgain.com
Spiritual Voice—R
Spirituality for Today
Star of Zion
Tributes—R
Victory News—R
$-Way of St. Francis—R

CHILDREN
$-Barefoot for Kids—R
$-Pockets—R
$-Primary Pal (IL)
$-SHINEbrightly—R
$-Sparkle

CHRISTIAN EDUCATION/ LIBRARY
$-RTJ
$-Teachers Interaction

DAILY DEVOTIONALS
$-Word in Season

PASTORS/LEADERS
$-Pastoral Life—R

TEEN/YOUNG ADULT
Teen Light—R
TeensForJC—R
Transcendmag.com—R
$-Young Christian—R
$-Young Salvationist—R

WOMEN
Anna's Journal—R
Home-Based Moms—R
Just Between Us—R
Keeping Hearts & Home
Right to the Heart—R

WRITERS
$-Areopagus (UK)
$-Cross & Quill—R
$-Writers' Journal
Writes of Passage—R

FILLERS: PROSE

ADULT/GENERAL
$-Angels on Earth
$-Animal Trails—R
$-Bible Advocate—R
Bread of Life—R
$-Bridal Guides—R
Christian Motorsports
Christian Online
Christian Ranchman
$-Decision
Desert Call—R
Disciple's Journal—R
Discovery—R
Eternal Ink—R
$-Faith & Family
$-Gem—R
$-Generation X—R
$-God Allows U-Turns—R
Good News Journal
Heartlight—R
Highway News—R
Light at Home—R
$-Live—R
MovieGuide
$-Now What?—R
Pegasus Review—R
Plowman—R
$-Presbyterians Today—R
$-SingleAgain.com
Spiritual Voice—R
Sword and Trumpet—R
Sword of the Lord—R
$-Today's Pentecostal Evangel—R
Victory News—R
$-Way of St. Francis—R
$-Wireless Age—R

CHILDREN
$-Guideposts for Kids
$-Partners—R

DAILY DEVOTIONALS
$-Daily Meditation

PASTORS/LEADERS
$-Pastoral Life—R
$-Preaching Well—R
Pulpit Helps—R

TEEN/YOUNG ADULT
$-Brio—R
$-Listen—R
$-Real Faith in Life—R
Teen Light—R
TeensForJC—R
Transcendmag.com—R
$-Young Christian—R

WOMEN
Anna's Journal—R
Home-Based Moms—R
$-Melody of the Heart
$-Today's Christian Woman—R

WRITERS
$-Areopagus (UK)
$-Upper Case
Write Touch
$-Writers' Journal
Writes of Passage—R

FILLERS: QUIZZES

ADULT/GENERAL
$-Alive!—R
$-Angels on Earth
$-Animal Trails—R
$-Bridal Guides—R
$-Catholic Yearbook—R
Christian Motorsports
Christian Online
Christian Ranchman
Church Herald & Holiness—R
Citizen USA—R
Disciple's Journal—R
Eternal Ink—R
$-Faith & Friends—R
$-Gem—R
Good News Journal
$-Impact—R
Light at Home—R
$-Lutheran Journal—R
Mature Times—R
MovieGuide
$-Palm Beach—R
Singles Scoop—R
Spiritual Voice—R
thegoodsteward.com—R
$-Vibrant Life—R
Victory News—R
$-Wittenburg Door—R

CHILDREN
$-Barefoot for Kids—R

$-Cadet Quest—R
$-Club Connection
$-Focus/Clubhouse
$-Guide—R
$-Guideposts for Kids
$-Nature Friend
$-On the Line—R
$-Partners—R
$-SHINEbrightly—R
Skipping Stones
$-Sparkle
$-Story Mates—R

MUSIC
$-Senior Musician—R

TEEN/YOUNG ADULT
$-Credo—R
$-Guideposts Sweet 16—R
$-Listen—R
$-Real Faith in Life—R
Teen Light—R
TeensForJC—R
Transcendmag.com—R
$-Young Christian—R
$-Young Salvationist—R

WOMEN
Anna's Journal—R
Home-Based Moms—R
$-Melody of the Heart

WRITERS
$-Areopagus (UK)
Once Upon a Time—R
$-Writers' Journal

FILLERS: QUOTES

ADULT/GENERAL
Alliance Life
$-Angels on Earth
$-Animal Trails—R
$-Bible Advocate—R
Bread of Life—R
$-Bridal Guides—R
$-Catholic Digest—R
$-Catholic Yearbook—R
$-Chicken Soup—R
$-Christian Herald—R
Christian Journal—R
Christian Motorsports
Christian Ranchman
$-Christian Response—R
Citizen USA—R
$-Culture Wars—R
Desert Call—R
Disciple's Journal—R
$-DisciplesWorld
Eternal Ink—R

$-Faith & Friends—R
$-Gem—R
$-Generation X—R
$-God Allows U-Turns—R
Good News Journal
Heartlight—R
$-Indian Life—R
Keys to Living—R
Light at Home—R
$-Lutheran Journal—R
MESSAGE/Open Bible—R
MovieGuide
$-Now What?—R
$-Palm Beach—R
Pegasus Review—R
PrayerWorks—R
$-Seek—R
$-Smart Families—R
Spiritual Voice—R
Spirituality for Today
$-Spring Hill Review—R
$-St. Anthony Messenger
Storyteller—R
Victory News—R

CHILDREN
$-Adventures
$-Partners—R
Skipping Stones

MISSIONS
Railroad Evangelist—R

PASTORS/LEADERS
$-Pastoral Life—R
Pulpit Helps—R
$-Rev.
Strategic Adult Ministries—R

TEEN/YOUNG ADULT
Teen Light—R
$-Young Christian—R

WOMEN
Anna's Journal—R
Just Between Us—R
Right to the Heart—R

WRITERS
$-Areopagus (UK)
Money the Write Way—R
$-Writers' Journal
Writes of Passage—R

FILLERS: SHORT HUMOR

ADULT/GENERAL
$-Alive!—R
$-Angels on Earth
$-Animal Trails—R

$-Bridal Guides—R
$-Chicken Soup—R
Christian Journal—R
Christian Motorsports
Christian Online
Christian Ranchman
Church Herald & Holiness—R
Citizen USA—R
$-Citizens in America
$-City Light News—R
$-Cornerstone Christian—R
Disciple's Journal—R
$-DisciplesWorld
Eternal Ink—R
$-Family Digest—R
Friends Journal—R
$-Gem—R
$-Generation X—R
$-God Allows U-Turns—R
Good News Journal
Gospel Tract—R
Heartlight—R
Highway News—R
$-Impact—R
$-Indian Life—R
Keys to Living—R
Light at Home—R
$-Living—R
$-Lutheran Digest—R
Maranatha News—R
$-Mature Living
Mature Times—R
MESSAGE/Open Bible—R
MovieGuide
New Heart—R
Nostalgia—R
$-Palm Beach—R
Plowman—R
PrayerWorks—R
$-Presbyterians Today—R
$-Purpose—R
Rose & Thorn
$-Seek—R
$-SingleAgain.com
Singles Scoop—R
Spiritual Voice—R
Steps
Victory News—R
Winsome Wit—R
$-Wittenburg Door—R

CHILDREN
$-Barefoot for Kids—R
$-Club Connection
$-Guideposts for Kids
$-SHINEbrightly—R
$-Sparkle

CHRISTIAN EDUCATION/
LIBRARY
Christian Librarian—R

MISSIONS
Women of the Harvest

MUSIC
Christian Music Weekly—R
$-Creator—R
$-Senior Musician—R

PASTORS/LEADERS
$-Barefoot—R
$-Catholic Servant
$-Enrichment—R
$-Interpreter
$-Leadership—R
$-Parish Life—R
$-Pastoral Life—R
$-Preaching Well—R
Pulpit Helps—R
$-Sermon Notes—R
Sharing the Practice—R
$-WCA News—R

TEEN/YOUNG ADULT
$-Credo—R
$-Real Faith in Life—R
Teen Light—R
TeensForJC—R
Transcendmag.com—R
$-Young Christian—R
$-Young Salvationist—R

WOMEN
Hearts at Home—R
Home-Based Moms—R
Just Between Us—R
Keeping Hearts & Home
$-Melody of the Heart
$-Women Alive!—R

WRITERS
$-Areopagus (UK)
$-Christian Communicator—R
$-Fellowscript—R
Once Upon a Time—R
$-Tickled by Thunder
Write Touch
$-Writers' Journal
Writes of Passage—R

FILLERS: TIPS

ADULT/GENERAL
Alliance Life
$-Animal Trails—R
$-Bridal Guides—R
Eternal Ink—R
Highway News—R

LifeLine Journal—R
Light at Home—R
MovieGuide
Nostalgia—R
$-SingleAgain.com
$-Special Living—R
Storyteller—R
Victory News—R

CHILDREN
$-Adventures
$-Cadet Quest—R

PASTORS/LEADERS
$-Barefoot—R
Ministry in Motion—R
$-Sabbath School Leadership—R
$-Your Church—R

TEEN/YOUNG ADULT
$-Credo—R
Teen Light—R
TeensForJC—R
Transcendmag.com—R
$-Young Christian—R

WOMEN
Home-Based Moms—R

WRITERS
$-Fellowscript—R
Money the Write Way—R
NW Christian Author—R
Once Upon a Time—R
$-Writers' Journal
Writes of Passage—R

FILLERS: WORD PUZZLES

ADULT/GENERAL
$-Alive!—R
$-Animal Trails—R
$-Bridal Guides—R
$-Catholic Yearbook—R
$-CGA World—R
$-Christian Herald—R
Christian Journal—R
Christian Ranchman
Citizen USA—R
Connecting Point—R
$-Cornerstone Christian—R
Disciple's Journal—R
Discovery—R
$-Evangel—R
$-Faith & Friends—R
Friends Journal—R
$-Gem—R
Good News Journal
$-Gospel Today—R
Heartlight—R

$-Horizons (adult)—R
$-Impact—R
$-Joy & Praise
Maranatha News—R
$-Mature Living
$-Mature Years—R
MovieGuide
$-Power for Living—R
Spiritual Voice—R
$-Spring Hill Review—R
$-Standard—R
Star of Zion
Victory News—R

CHILDREN
$-Adventures
$-American Girl
$-Barefoot for Kids—R
$-Cadet Quest—R
$-Club Connection
$-Faces
$-Focus/Clubhouse
$-Guide—R
$-Guideposts for Kids
$-Nature Friend
$-On the Line—R
$-Our Little Friend—R
$-Partners—R
$-Passport—R
$-Pockets—R
$-Primary Pal (IL)
$-SHINEbrightly—R
Skipping Stones
$-Story Friends—R
$-Story Mates—R

CHRISTIAN EDUCATION/ LIBRARY
$-RTJ
$-Youth & CE Leadership

PASTORS/LEADERS
Pulpit Helps—R

TEEN/YOUNG ADULT
$-Credo—R
$-Real Faith in Life—R
Teen Light—R
TeensForJC—R
Transcendmag.com—R
$-Young Christian—R
$-Young Salvationist—R

WOMEN
$-Melody of the Heart

WRITERS
Heaven—R
$-Writers' Journal

FOOD/RECIPES

ADULT/GENERAL
$-Associated Content—R
$-Bridal Guides—R
$-CGA World—R
$-Chicken Soup Magazine
Christian C. L. RECORD—R
Christian Online
Citizen USA—R
$-Citizens in America
$-Cornerstone Christian—R
$-Dovetail—R
$-Faith & Family
$-Faith & Friends—R
$-Grit
HopeKeepers—R
$-Ideals—R
$-Impact—R
LifeLine Journal—R
Light at Home—R
$-Lutheran Digest—R
$-Lutheran Journal—R
$-Mature Living
$-Montgomery's Journey
Nostalgia—R
Parents & Teens—R
Short Stories Bimonthly—R
Spiritual Voice—R
$-St. Anthony Messenger
Victory News—R
$-World & I—R

CHILDREN
$-Adventures
$-American Girl
$-Barefoot for Kids—R
$-Cadet Quest—R
$-Celebrate
$-Club Connection
$-Faces
$-Focus/Clubhouse
$-Focus/Clubhouse Jr.
$-Guideposts for Kids
$-My Friend
$-On the Line—R
$-Pockets—R
Skipping Stones
$-Sparkle

MISSIONS
Women of the Harvest

TEEN/YOUNG ADULT
$-Brio—R
$-J.A.M.
Teen Light—R
TeensForJC—R
Transcendmag.com—R

$-Young Christian—R

WOMEN
Christian Women Today—R
$-Dabbling Mum.com—R
$-Godly Business Woman
Hearts at Home—R
Home-Based Moms—R
Keeping Hearts & Home
$-Melody of the Heart
$-MOMsense—R
Precious Times—R
$-Simple Joy
Sisters in the Lord
$-Woman's Touch—R
Women Today—R

HEALING

ADULT/GENERAL
Alliance Life
$-America
$-Angels on Earth
$-Animal Trails—R
$-Associated Content—R
$-Aujourd'hui Credo—R
$-Bible Advocate—R
$-Brave Hearts
Breakthrough Intercessor—R
$-Bridal Guides—R
$-Canada Lutheran—R
$-Catholic New Times—R
$-Celebrate Life—R
$-CGA World—R
Channels—R
Christian Motorsports
Christian Online
Christian Ranchman
$-City Light News—R
Connecting Point—R
$-Cornerstone Christian—R
$-Cup of Comfort—R
Evangelical Advocate—R
$-Faith Today
$-Foursquare World Advance—R
$-Gem—R
$-God Allows U-Turns—R
$-Good News—R
$-Guideposts—R
Highway News—R
$-HonorBound—R
HopeKeepers—R
Impact Online
LifeLine Journal—R
$-Light & Life
Light at Home—R
$-Liguorian
$-Live—R

Maranatha News—R
Metro Voice—R
$-National Catholic
New Heart—R
$-Now What?—R
$-ONEvoice!
$-Plains Faith—R
$-Positive Thinking—R
Prayer Closet
Quaker Life—R
Sacred Journey—R
Sharing—R
$-SingleAgain.com
$-Sound Body—R
$-Spiritual Life
Spiritual Voice—R
$-St. Anthony Messenger
$-St. Joseph's Messenger—R
Steps
Storyteller—R
$-Testimony—R
thegoodsteward.com—R
$-Today's Christian—R
$-Today's Pentecostal Evangel—R
Tributes—R
Trumpeter—R
$-United Church Observer—R
Victory News—R
$-Vision—R
$-Voice of the Lord
$-World & I—R

CHILDREN
$-BREAD/God's Children—R
Skipping Stones

PASTORS/LEADERS
$-Christian Century—R
Sharing the Practice—R
$-Word & World

TEEN/YOUNG ADULT
$-J.A.M.
$-Young Christian—R

WOMEN
$-Esprit—R
$-Godly Business Woman
$-inSpirit—R
Precious Times—R
$-SpiritLed Woman
$-Woman's Touch—R

WRITERS
$-Areopagus (UK)

HEALTH

ADULT/GENERAL
$-Abilities
$-Alive!—R

$-Angels on Earth
$-Anglican Journal
$-Apocalypse Chronicles—R
$-Associated Content—R
$-B.C. Catholic—R
$-Bible Advocate—R
Breakthrough Intercessor—R
$-Canada Lutheran—R
$-Catholic Forester—R
$-Catholic New Times—R
CBN.com—R
$-Celebrate Life—R
$-CGA World—R
Channels—R
$-Chicken Soup Magazine
$-Christian Courier (CAN)—R
Christian Courier (WI)—R
Christian Journal—R
Christian Online
$-Christian Social Action—R
Citizen USA—R
$-City Light News—R
Common Ground—R
$-Cornerstone Christian—R
Creation Care—R
Disciple's Journal—R
Discovery—R
$-Faith Today
$-Gospel Today—R
$-Guideposts—R
Hannah to Hannah—R
Highway News—R
$-HonorBound—R
HopeKeepers—R
Impact Online
$-Inland NW Christian
Island Catholic News
$-Joy & Praise
$-Lifeglow—R
LifeLine Journal—R
$-Light & Life
Light at Home—R
$-Living—R
$-Lutheran Digest—R
$-Mature Years—R
$-MESSAGE
Metro Voice—R
$-Montgomery's Journey
New Heart—R
$-ONEvoice!
$-Palm Beach—R
Penned from the Heart
$-Plains Faith—R
$-Positive Thinking—R
Purpose Magazine
Quaker Life—R
Sacred Journey—R

$-Senior Living
$-SingleAgain.com
$-Sound Body—R
$-Special Living—R
Spiritual Voice—R
$-Spring Hill Review—R
$-St. Anthony Messenger
$-Testimony—R
thegoodsteward.com—R
$-Today's Christian—R
Tributes—R
Trumpeter—R
$-Upscale Magazine
$-Vibrant Life—R
Victory News—R
$-Voice of the Lord
$-War Cry—R
$-Whole Magazine
$-World & I—R

CHILDREN
$-American Girl
$-Barefoot for Kids—R
$-BREAD/God's Children—R
$-Club Connection
$-Guideposts for Kids
$-Guide—R
$-On the Line—R
Skipping Stones
$-Winner—R

CHRISTIAN EDUCATION/ LIBRARY
$-Children's Ministry
$-Teachers of Vision—R

PASTORS/LEADERS
$-Christian Century—R
$-InSite—R
$-Interpreter
$-Lutheran Partners—R
$-Word & World

TEEN/YOUNG ADULT
$-Brio—R
$-Devo'Zine—R
$-J.A.M.
$-Listen—R
TeensForJC—R
Transcendmag.com—R
$-Young and Alive—R

WOMEN
$-At the Center—R
Christian Women Today—R
$-Esprit—R
Faithwebbin—R
$-Godly Business Woman
Heart & Soul
Hearts at Home—R

$-Horizons (women)—R
Inspired Moms.Com
$-inSpirit—R
$-Journey
Keeping Hearts & Home
Life Tools for Women
Lutheran Woman's Quar.
$-MOMsense—R
Precious Times—R
Sisters in the Lord
$-SpiritLed Woman
$-Today's Christian Woman—R
Women of the Cross
Women Today—R

HISTORICAL

ADULT/GENERAL
AGAIN—R
$-Ancient Paths—R
$-Angels on Earth
$-Animal Trails—R
$-Arlington Catholic
$-Associated Content—R
$-Bridal Guides—R
$-Cappers
$-Cathedral Age
$-Catholic New Times—R
$-Catholic Peace Voice—R
$-Celebrate Life—R
$-CGA World—R
Channels—R
Christian C. L. RECORD—R
$-Christian Courier (CAN)—R
$-Christian History—R
Christian Motorsports
Christian Observer
Christian Online
$-Christian Renewal—R
Citizen USA—R
$-Citizens in America
$-City Light News—R
$-Company—R
$-Dovetail—R
$-Eclectic Homeschool
Evangelical Advocate—R
Evangelical Times
$-Faith Today
$-Generation X—R
$-Grit
$-HonorBound—R
$-Ideals—R
$-Indian Life—R
Journal of Church & State
$-Lifeglow—R
$-Light & Life
$-Liguorian

Looking Up
$-Mature Living
Mennonite Family History
Mennonite Historian—R
$-Messiah
Messianic Times
Methodist History
$-National Catholic
$-New Freeman—R
$-New Wineskins—R
Nostalgia—R
$-Our Sunday Visitor
$-Over the Back Fence—R
$-Plains Faith—R
$-Power for Living—R
PrayerWorks—R
Presbyterian Outlook
Priscilla Papers—R
Quaker Life—R
Rock & Sling
Sharing—R
Short Stories Bimonthly—R
$-Social Justice—R
Spiritual Voice—R
$-Spring Hill Review—R
$-St. Anthony Messenger
Star of Zion
Storyteller—R
Sword of the Lord—R
thegoodsteward.com—R
$-Tidewater Parent—R
Trumpeter—R
$-U.S. Catholic
$-Upscale Magazine
Victory News—R
$-Way of St. Francis—R
$-Wesleyan Life—R
$-Wireless Age—R
$-World & I—R

CHILDREN
$-Barefoot for Kids—R
$-BREAD/God's Children—R
$-Faces
$-Focus/Clubhouse Jr.
$-Guide—R
$-Guideposts for Kids
$-High Adventure—R
$-On the Line—R
$-SHINEbrightly—R
Young Gentleman's Monthly

CHRISTIAN EDUCATION/ LIBRARY
Catholic Library World
$-Teachers of Vision—R

MISSIONS
East-West Church
Women of the Harvest

MUSIC
$-Creator—R
Hymn

PASTORS/LEADERS
Christian Education Jour. (CA)—R
$-Pastoral Life—R
Sewanee Theo. Review
Sharing the Practice—R
Theological Digest—R
$-This Rock
$-Today's Parish—R
$-Word & World

TEEN/YOUNG ADULT
$-J.A.M.
$-Listen—R
$-Passageway.org—R
$-Real Faith in Life—R
$-Student Leadership—R
TeensForJC—R
Transcendmag.com—R
$-Young Adult Today—R
$-Young and Alive—R
$-Young Christian—R

WOMEN
$-History's Women—R
Just Between Us—R
Shalom Bayit
$-SpiritLed Woman

WRITERS
$-Areopagus (UK)
$-Tickled by Thunder

HOLIDAY/SEASONAL

ADULT/GENERAL
$-Alive!—R
$-Alive Now—R
American Tract Society—R
$-Angels on Earth
$-Animal Trails—R
$-Annals of St. Anne
$-Arlington Catholic
$-Barefoot Path—R
$-BGC World—R
$-Brave Hearts
Breakthrough Intercessor—R
$-Bridal Guides—R
$-Canada Lutheran—R
$-Cappers
$-Cathedral Age
$-Catholic Digest—R
$-Catholic Forester—R

$-Catholic New York
$-CGA World—R
Channels—R
$-Chicken Soup—R
Christian C. L. RECORD—R
$-Christian Courier (CAN)—R
Christian Courier (WI)—R
$-Christian Home & School
Christian Online
$-Christian Parenting—R
$-Christian Renewal—R
$-Christian Retailing
Citizen USA—R
$-City Light News—R
Connecting Point—R
$-Covenant Companion—R
Desert Call—R
Discovery—R
$-Dovetail—R
$-Eclectic Homeschool
Eternal Ink—R
$-Evangel—R
Evangelical Advocate—R
$-Faith & Family
$-Faith Today
$-Family Digest—R
$-Foursquare World Advance—R
$-Gem—R
$-Gems of Truth—R
$-Generation X—R
$-God Allows U-Turns—R
Good News Journal
Gospel Tract—R
$-Grit
$-Guideposts—R
Hannah to Hannah—R
Heartlight—R
$-HonorBound—R
HopeKeepers—R
$-Horizons (adult)—R
$-Ideals—R
$-Indian Life—R
$-Inside Journal—R
$-Lifeglow—R
LifeLine Journal—R
$-Light & Life
Light at Home—R
$-Liguorian
$-Live—R
$-Living—R
$-Living Church
$-Living Light News—R
Looking Up
$-Lookout
$-Lutheran Digest—R
$-Marriage Partnership—R

$-Mature Living
Mature Times—R
$-Mature Years—R
$-Men of Integrity—R
MESSAGE/Open Bible—R
$-Minnesota Christian—R
$-Montgomery's Journey
$-National Catholic
$-On Mission
$-Our Sunday Visitor
$-Over the Back Fence—R
Parents & Teens—R
Pegasus Review—R
Penned from the Heart
$-Plain Truth—R
$-Positive Thinking—R
$-Power for Living—R
$-Prairie Messenger—R
PrayerWorks—R
$-Psychology for Living—R
$-Purpose—R
Quaker Life—R
Randall House Periodicals
Sacred Journey—R
$-Seek—R
Sharing—R
Singles Scoop—R
$-Smart Families—R
$-Special Living—R
Spiritual Voice—R
$-Spring Hill Review—R
$-St. Anthony Messenger
$-St. Joseph's Messenger—R
$-Standard—R
Star of Zion
Storyteller—R
Sword of the Lord—R
thegoodsteward.com—R
$-Today's Christian—R
$-Today's Pentecostal Evangel—R
$-Together—R
Tributes—R
Trumpeter—R
$-U.S. Catholic
$-United Church Observer—R
$-Vibrant Life—R
Victory News—R
$-War Cry—R
$-Wesleyan Life—R
$-World & I—R

CHILDREN
$-Barefoot for Kids—R
$-Club Connection
$-Courage—R
$-Focus/Clubhouse
$-Focus/Clubhouse Jr.

$-Guide—R
$-Guideposts for Kids
$-High Adventure—R
$-Junior Companion—R
$-Juniorway
$-My Friend
$-Nature Friend
$-On the Line—R
$-Partners—R
$-Pockets—R
$-Primary Pal (IL)
$-Primary Street
$-SHINEbrightly—R
Skipping Stones
$-Sparkle
$-Winner—R

CHRISTIAN EDUCATION/ LIBRARY
$-Children's Ministry
$-Church Educator—R
$-Ideas Unlimited—R
$-Leader in C. E. Ministries—R
$-Resource—R
$-Teach Kids!—R
$-Teachers of Vision—R
$-Today's Catholic Teacher—R

DAILY DEVOTIONALS
$-These Days

MISSIONS
Railroad Evangelist—R
Women of the Harvest

MUSIC
$-Creator—R

PASTORS/LEADERS
$-Catholic Servant
$-Christian Century—R
$-Church Worship
$-Enrichment—R
$-Five Stones—R
$-Interpreter
$-Ministry & Liturgy—R
Ministry in Motion—R
$-Pastoral Life—R
Pulpit Helps—R
$-Sunday Sermons—R

TEEN/YOUNG ADULT
$-Brio—R
$-Credo—R
$-Essential Connection
$-J.A.M.
$-Listen—R
$-Real Faith in Life—R
Teen Light—R
$-Teenage Christian—R

TeensForJC—R
Transcendmag.com—R
$-Young and Alive—R
$-Young Christian—R
$-Young Salvationist—R

WOMEN
Anna's Journal—R
Christian Women Today—R
$-Dabbling Mum.com—R
$-Esprit—R
Faithwebbin—R
Handmaiden—R
Hearts at Home—R
$-History's Women—R
Home-Based Moms—R
Inspired Moms.Com
$-inSpirit—R
$-Journey
Lutheran Woman's Quar.
$-MOMsense—R
P31 Woman—R
Precious Times—R
$-Today's Christian Woman—R
$-Woman's Touch—R
Women of the Cross
Women Today—R

WRITERS
$-Areopagus (UK)

HOMESCHOOLING

ADULT/GENERAL
$-Anglican Journal
$-Arlington Catholic
$-Aspiring Retail
Breakthrough Intercessor—R
Channels—R
Christian C. L. RECORD—R
Christian Computing—R
$-Christian Examiner
Christian Observer
Christian Online
$-Christian Parenting—R
Citizen USA—R
$-City Light News—R
Creation Care—R
Disciple's Journal—R
Discovery—R
$-Dovetail—R
$-Eclectic Homeschool
$-Faith & Family
$-Faith Today
Good News Journal
Highway News—R
$-Homeschooling Today—R

$-Interim—R
$-Light & Life
Light at Home—R
Metro Voice—R
$-Minnesota Christian—R
Parents & Teens—R
$-Plains Faith—R
$-Psychology for Living—R
$-Smart Families—R
$-Social Justice—R
Spiritual Voice—R
$-Spring Hill Review—R
$-St. Anthony Messenger
Sword of the Lord—R
thegoodsteward.com—R
Trumpeter—R
Victory News—R
$-Voice of the Lord
$-World & I—R

CHILDREN
$-Barefoot for Kids—R
$-BREAD/God's Children—R
$-Guideposts for Kids
$-SHINEbrightly—R
Skipping Stones

CHRISTIAN EDUCATION/ LIBRARY
$-Children's Ministry
Jour./Ed. & Christian Belief—R

MISSIONS
Women of the Harvest

PASTORS/LEADERS
$-Pastoral Life—R

TEEN/YOUNG ADULT
$-J.A.M.
$-Passageway.org—R
Teen Light—R

WOMEN
Crowned with Silver
Hearts at Home—R
Home-Based Moms—R
Inspired Moms.Com
$-Journey
Shalom Bayit
Women of the Cross

HOMILETICS

ADULT/GENERAL
Channels—R
Church Herald & Holiness—R
$-Lookout
Maranatha News—R
$-New Wineskins—R

$-Plains Faith—R
Priscilla Papers—R
Randall House Periodicals
$-St. Anthony Messenger
$-Stewardship—R
$-Testimony—R
Trumpeter—R
Victory News—R
$-Way of St. Francis—R
$-Wesleyan Life—R

PASTORS/LEADERS
$-African American Pulpit
$-Barefoot—R
$-Clergy Journal—R
$-Evangelical Baptist—R
$-Leadership—R
$-Lutheran Partners—R
$-Pastoral Life—R
Preaching—R
$-Preaching Well—R
$-Priest
$-Proclaim—R
Quarterly Review
$-Rev.
$-Sermon Notes—R
Sewanee Theo. Review
Sharing the Practice—R

WOMEN
$-SpiritLed Woman

HOW-TO

ADULT/GENERAL
$-Aspiring Retail
$-Associated Content—R
$-Bridal Guides—R
$-Celebrate Life—R
$-CGA World—R
Channels—R
Christian Journal—R
Christian Motorsports
Christian Observer
Christian Online
$-Christian Parenting—R
$-Christian Retailing
$-Church of God EVANGEL
$-City Light News—R
Connecting Point—R
$-Cornerstone Christian—R
Creation Care—R
$-Direction
Discovery—R
$-Dovetail—R
$-Eclectic Homeschool
$-Faith & Family

$-Faith Today
$-Family Digest—R
$-Generation X—R
Good News Journal
HopeKeepers—R
$-Inland NW Christian
$-Inside Journal—R
$-Joy & Praise
LifeLine Journal—R
$-Light & Life
Light at Home—R
$-Living Church
$-Lutheran Digest—R
Mennonite Historian—R
$-Montgomery's Journey
Mutuality—R
$-On Mission
$-ONEvoice!
$-Plains Faith—R
$-Positive Thinking—R
PrayerWorks—R
Randall House Periodicals
Regent Business—R
$-Smart Families—R
Spiritual Voice—R
$-St. Anthony Messenger
Storyteller—R
$-Testimony—R
thegoodsteward.com—R
$-Tidewater Parent—R
$-Today's Christian—R
Tributes—R
Trumpeter—R
$-U.S. Catholic
$-Vibrant Life—R
Victory News—R
$-World & I—R

CHRISTIAN EDUCATION/ LIBRARY
$-Catechist
Catholic Library World
$-Children's Ministry
$-Christian Educators Journal—R
Christian Librarian—R
Christian Library Journal—R
Church & Synagogue Lib.—R
$-Church Educator—R
$-Church Libraries—R
$-Group Magazine
$-Ideas Unlimited—R
$-Kids' Ministry Ideas—R
$-Leader in C. E. Ministries—R
$-Preschool Playhouse
$-Resource—R
$-RTJ

$-Teachers Interaction
$-Teachers of Vision—R
$-Today's Catholic Teacher—R
$-Youth & CE Leadership

MISSIONS
$-PFI World Report—R

MUSIC
$-Senior Musician—R

PASTORS/LEADERS
$-African American Pulpit
$-Cornerstone Youth—R
$-Evangelical Baptist—R
$-Evangelicals Today—R
$-Leadership—R
$-Ministry
$-Ministry & Liturgy—R
Ministry in Motion—R
Net Results
$-Newsletter Newsletter
$-RevWriter Resource
$-Sabbath School Leadership—R
$-WCA News—R
$-Worship Leader
$-Your Church—R

TEEN/YOUNG ADULT
$-Boundless Webzine—R
$-Brio—R
$-Listen—R
$-Real Faith in Life—R
Teen Light—R
TeensForJC—R
Transcendmag.com—R
$-Young and Alive—R

WOMEN
Christian Women Today—R
$-Dabbling Mum.com—R
$-Esprit—R
Faithwebbin—R
Just Between Us—R
$-Melody of the Heart
$-MOMsense—R
Precious Times—R
Right to the Heart—R
$-Today's Christian Woman—R
Women of the Cross
Women Today—R

WRITERS
$-Adv. Christian Writer—R
$-Cross & Quill—R
$-Exchange—R
Money the Write Way—R
Once Upon a Time—R
$-Spirit-Led Writer—R

$-Writer's Digest—R

HOW-TO ACTIVITIES (JUV.)

ADULT/GENERAL
$-Animal Trails—R
$-Associated Content—R
Channels—R
$-Christian Home & School
Christian Online
$-City Light News—R
$-Cornerstone Christian—R
Creation Care—R
$-Dovetail—R
$-Eclectic Homeschool
Eternal Ink—R
$-Faith & Family
$-Generation X—R
Good News Journal
$-Homeschooling Today—R
$-Indian Life—R
Keys to Living—R
$-Light & Life
Light at Home—R
$-Living—R
$-Lutheran Digest—R
$-Smart Families—R
Spiritual Voice—R
$-St. Anthony Messenger
$-World & I—R

CHILDREN
$-Adventures
$-American Girl
$-Barefoot for Kids—R
$-BREAD/God's Children—R
$-Cadet Quest—R
$-Celebrate
$-Club Connection
$-Courage—R
$-Faces
$-Focus/Clubhouse
$-Focus/Clubhouse Jr.
$-Guide—R
$-Guideposts for Kids
$-High Adventure—R
InspirationStation
$-Junior Companion—R
$-Juniorway
$-My Friend
$-Nature Friend
$-On the Line—R
$-Partners—R
$-Pockets—R
$-Preschool Playhouse
$-Preschool Playhouse (child)

$-Primary Pal (IL)
$-Seeds
$-SHINEbrightly—R
Skipping Stones
$-Sparkle
$-Story Friends—R
$-Winner—R

CHRISTIAN EDUCATION/ LIBRARY
$-Children's Ministry
$-Church Educator—R
$-Kids' Ministry Ideas—R
$-Preschool Playhouse
$-RTJ
$-Teach Kids!—R
$-Teachers Interaction
$-Teachers of Vision—R

PASTORS/LEADERS
$-Evangelical Baptist—R
$-Interpreter

TEEN/YOUNG ADULT
Teen Light—R
$-Young Christian—R
$-Young Salvationist—R

WOMEN
$-Godly Business Woman
Home-Based Moms—R
Just Between Us—R
Women of the Cross

HUMOR

ADULT/GENERAL
$-Alive!—R
Alliance Life
American Tract Society—R
$-Ancient Paths—R
$-Angels on Earth
$-Animal Trails—R
$-Associated Content—R
$-Barefoot Path—R
$-Brave Hearts
Bread of Life—R
$-Bridal Guides—R
$-Catholic Digest—R
$-Catholic Forester—R
$-Catholic Peace Voice—R
$-CGA World—R
Channels—R
$-Chicken Soup—R
Christian C. L. RECORD—R
Christian Computing—R
$-Christian Courier (CAN)—R
Christian Journal—R
Christian Online

$-Christian Parenting—R
Christian Radio Weekly
$-Christianity Today—R
$-Church of God EVANGEL
$-Citizens in America
$-City Light News—R
Connecting Point—R
$-Cornerstone Christian—R
$-Cup of Comfort—R
Disciple's Journal—R
$-Dovetail—R
Eternal Ink—R
$-Evangel—R
Evangelical Advocate—R
$-Faith & Family
$-Faith Today
$-Family Digest—R
$-Gem—R
$-Generation X—R
$-God Allows U-Turns—R
Good News Journal
Gospel Tract—R
Hannah to Hannah—R
Highway News—R
$-Homeschooling Today—R
HopeKeepers—R
$-Horizons (adult)—R
$-Indian Life—R
$-Inland NW Christian
$-Lifeglow—R
$-Light & Life
Light at Home—R
$-Living—R
$-Living Church
$-Living Light News—R
$-Lutheran Digest—R
Maranatha News—R
$-Mature Living
Mature Times—R
$-My Walk With Jesus
$-National Catholic
$-New Freeman—R
New Heart—R
$-New Wineskins—R
Nostalgia—R
$-On Mission
$-Over the Back Fence—R
$-Palm Beach—R
$-ParentLife
Pegasus Review—R
Penned from the Heart
$-Plains Faith—R
Plowman—R
$-Positive Thinking—R
PrayerWorks—R

$-Psychology for Living—R
Quaker Life—R
Randall House Periodicals
Rose & Thorn
Sacred Journey—R
$-Seek—R
$-Senior Living
Silver Wings—R
Singles Scoop—R
$-Smart Families—R
Spiritual Voice—R
$-Spring Hill Review—R
$-St. Anthony Messenger
Storyteller—R
$-Testimony—R
thegoodsteward.com—R
$-Tidewater Parent—R
$-Today's Christian—R
$-Together—R
Trumpeter—R
$-U.S. Catholic
Victory News—R
$-Vision—R
$-War Cry—R
$-Weavings—R
Winsome Wit—R
$-Wittenburg Door—R
$-World & I—R
Xavier Review

CHILDREN
$-Barefoot for Kids—R
$-Cadet Quest—R
$-Club Connection
$-Faces
$-Focus/Clubhouse Jr.
$-High Adventure—R
$-My Friend
$-On the Line—R
$-SHINEbrightly—R
Skipping Stones
$-Sparkle
$-Story Friends—R
$-Winner—R

CHRISTIAN EDUCATION/ LIBRARY
$-Youth & CE Leadership

MISSIONS
Women of the Harvest

MUSIC
Christian Music Weekly—R
$-Creator—R

PASTORS/LEADERS
$-Catholic Servant

$-Enrichment—R
$-Evangelical Baptist—R
$-Evangelicals Today—R
$-Five Stones—R
$-Leadership—R
$-Ministries Today
$-Ministry & Liturgy—R
$-Parish Life—R
$-Pastoral Life—R
$-Preaching Well—R
Pulpit Helps—R
$-Sermon Notes—R
Sharing the Practice—R
$-Small Group Dynamics—R
$-Today's Parish—R
$-WCA News—R

TEEN/YOUNG ADULT
$-Boundless Webzine—R
$-Brio—R
$-Essential Connection
GO!
$-Guideposts Sweet 16—R
$-Listen—R
$-Passageway.org—R
$-Real Faith in Life—R
Teen Light—R
TeensForJC—R
Transcendmag.com—R
$-With—R
$-Young and Alive—R
$-Young Christian—R
$-Young Salvationist—R

WOMEN
$-Esprit—R
Faithwebbin—R
Hearts at Home—R
Home-Based Moms—R
$-Horizons (women)—R
$-inSpirit—R
$-Journey
Just Between Us—R
Keeping Hearts & Home
Lutheran Woman's Quar.
$-Melody of the Heart
$-MOMsense—R
Sisters in the Lord
$-SpiritLed Woman
$-Today's Christian Woman—R
Women Today—R

WRITERS
$-Areopagus (UK)
Beginnings—R
$-Christian Communicator—R
$-Exchange—R

$-Fellowscript—R
Once Upon a Time—R

INNER LIFE

ADULT/GENERAL
$-Barefoot Path—R
$-BGC World—R
$-Bible Advocate—R
$-Bridal Guides—R
$-Catholic Digest—R
Channels—R
Christian Journal—R
$-Discipleship Journal—R
Divine Ascent
$-Faith & Family
$-Faith Today
$-Generation X—R
Halo Magazine
Hannah to Hannah—R
Highway News—R
LifeTimes Catholic
$-Light & Life
Light at Home—R
$-Living—R
$-Lookout
Mature Times—R
$-Mature Years—R
$-Men of Integrity—R
$-Minnesota Christian—R
Mosaic—R
$-National Catholic
$-New Wineskins—R
$-ONEvoice!
$-Palm Beach—R
Penned from the Heart
$-Plains Faith—R
$-Positive Thinking—R
$-Presbyterians Today—R
Quaker Life—R
Reformed Quarterly
Regent Business—R
Sacred Journey—R
Silver Wings—R
Singles Scoop—R
Spiritual Voice—R
$-Spring Hill Review—R
$-Testimony—R
$-Today's Pentecostal Evangel—R
$-Together—R
Victory News—R
$-Weavings—R
$-Whole Magazine
$-World & I—R

CHILDREN
$-BREAD/God's Children—R

CHRISTIAN EDUCATION/ LIBRARY
$-Teachers of Vision—R

PASTORS/LEADERS
$-Evangelical Baptist—R
$-Interpreter
Journal/Pastoral Care—R

TEEN/YOUNG ADULT
TeensForJC—R
Transcendmag.com—R
$-Young Christian—R

WOMEN
$-Esprit—R
$-inSpirit—R
$-Journey
Right to the Heart—R
$-Today's Christian Woman—R
$-Woman's Touch—R

INSPIRATIONAL

ADULT/GENERAL
African Voices—R
$-Alive Now—R
Alliance Life
$-Angels on Earth
$-Annals of St. Anne
$-Arlington Catholic
$-Associated Content—R
$-Barefoot Path—R
$-Brave Hearts
Bread of Life—R
Breakthrough Intercessor—R
$-Bridal Guides—R
$-Canada Lutheran—R
$-Cappers
$-Catholic Forester—R
$-Catholic New Times—R
$-Catholic Peace Voice—R
$-Celebrate Life—R
$-CGA World—R
Channels—R
$-Chicken Soup—R
Christian Herald (UK)
Christian Journal—R
Christian Motorsports
Christian Online
Christian Radio Weekly
Christian Ranchman
Church Herald & Holiness—R
$-Church of God EVANGEL
Connecting Point—R
$-Cornerstone Christian—R
$-Covenant Companion—R
$-Cup of Comfort—R

$-Decision
Divine Ascent
Eternal Ink—R
$-Evangel—R
Evangelical Advocate—R
$-Faith & Family
$-Faith Today
$-Family Digest—R
$-Flutters of the Heart
$-Focus on the Family
$-Foursquare World Advance—R
$-Gem—R
$-God Allows U-Turns—R
$-God's Way Books
$-Good News—R
Good News Journal
$-Gospel Today—R
Gospel Tract—R
$-Grit
$-Guideposts—R
Halo Magazine
Hannah to Hannah—R
Heartlight—R
Highway News—R
HopeKeepers—R
$-Ideals—R
$-Indian Life—R
$-Inland NW Christian
Insight (for blind)
InSound
InTouch
$-Joy & Praise
Keys to Living—R
Leaves—R
$-Lifeglow—R
$-Light & Life
Light at Home—R
$-Live—R
$-Living—R
$-Living Church
$-Lookout
$-Lutheran Digest—R
Maranatha News—R
$-Marian Helper—R
$-Mature Living
Mature Times—R
Men of the Cross
$-Mennonite Brethren—R
MESSAGE/Open Bible—R
$-Messenger/Sacred Heart
$-Minnesota Christian—R
$-Montgomery's Journey
Mosaic—R
Mutuality—R
$-My Walk With Jesus
$-National Catholic

$-New Freeman—R
New Heart—R
$-ONEvoice!
Parents & Teens—R
Pegasus Review—R
Penned from the Heart
$-Plain Truth—R
$-Plains Faith—R
Plowman—R
$-Positive Thinking—R
$-Power for Living—R
$-Prairie Messenger—R
PrayerWorks—R
$-Precepts for Living
$-Psychology for Living—R
Quaker Life—R
$-Queen of All Hearts
Randall House Periodicals
Sacred Journey—R
$-Seek—R
Silver Wings—R
$-SingleAgain.com
Singles Scoop—R
Spiritual Voice—R
$-St. Anthony Messenger
$-St. Joseph's Messenger—R
$-Standard—R
Star of Zion
$-Stewardship—R
Storyteller—R
SW Kansas Faith
Sword and Trumpet—R
Sword of the Lord—R
$-Testimony—R
thegoodsteward.com—R
$-Today's Christian—R
$-Today's Pentecostal Evangel—R
$-Together—R
Trumpeter—R
$-U.S. Catholic
$-United Church Observer—R
$-UP
$-Upscale Magazine
Victory News—R
$-Vision—R
$-War Cry—R
$-Way of St. Francis—R
$-Wesleyan Life—R
$-Whole Magazine
$-World & I—R

CHILDREN
$-Barefoot for Kids—R
$-BREAD/God's Children—R
$-Cadet Quest—R
$-Club Connection

$-Partners—R
$-Primary Street
Skipping Stones

CHRISTIAN EDUCATION/ LIBRARY
$-Children's Ministry
Church & Synagogue Lib.—R
$-Journal/Adventist Educ.—R
$-Resource—R
$-Teachers of Vision—R

MISSIONS
Women of the Harvest

MUSIC
$-Creator—R
$-Senior Musician—R

PASTORS/LEADERS
$-African American Pulpit
$-Catholic Servant
$-Evangelical Baptist—R
$-Evangelicals Today—R
$-Interpreter
$-Leadership—R
$-Let's Worship
$-Pastoral Life—R
Pulpit Helps—R
$-RevWriter Resource
Sharing the Practice—R
Technologies for Worship—R

TEEN/YOUNG ADULT
$-Brio—R
$-Guideposts Sweet 16—R
$-J.A.M.
$-Passageway.org—R
Teen Light—R
$-Teenage Christian—R
TeensForJC—R
Transcendmag.com—R
$-With—R
$-Young Christian—R

WOMEN
Christian Women Today—R
$-Dabbling Mum.com—R
$-Esprit—R
Faithwebbin—R
$-Godly Business Woman
Handmaiden—R
Hearts at Home—R
Home-Based Moms—R
$-Horizons (women)—R
Inspired Moms.Com
$-inSpirit—R
$-Journey
Just Between Us—R

Lutheran Woman's Quar.
P31 Woman—R
Precious Times—R
Right to the Heart—R
$-SpiritLed Woman
$-Today's Christian Woman—R
$-Woman's Touch—R
$-Women Alive!—R
Women of the Cross

WRITERS
$-Areopagus (UK)
NW Christian Author—R
Once Upon a Time—R
$-Writer's Digest—R

INTERVIEWS/PROFILES

ADULT/GENERAL
Anglican
$-Abilities
AGAIN—R
$-Alive!—R
American Tract Society—R
$-Anglican Journal
$-Arlington Catholic
$-Associated Content—R
Baptist Standard
Beacon (AL)
$-BGC World—R
Biblical Recorder
Books & Culture
Breakthrough Intercessor—R
Business Reform
Canadian Christianity.com
$-Catholic New York
$-Catholic Peace Voice—R
CBN.com—R
$-Celebrate Life—R
$-Central Appalachia
Challenge Weekly
Challenging Destiny
Channels—R
Charlotte World
Christian C. L. RECORD—R
Christian Chronicle
Christian Citizen USA
Christian Courier (WI)—R
Christian Current
$-Christian Herald—R
Christian Herald (UK)
Christian Journal—R
Christian Motorsports
Christian News NW—R
Christian Observer
Christian Online
Christian Post

Christian Ranchman
$-Christianity Today—R
$-ChristianWeek—R
Church of England News
$-City Light News—R
$-Columbia
$-Cornerstone Christian—R
Creation Care—R
$-Culture Wars—R
Desert Call—R
Desert Christian
Desert Voice
Divine Ascent
$-Dovetail—R
$-Eclectic Homeschool
$-Episcopal Life—R
Eternal Ink—R
$-Faith Today
Fire By Nite
$-Gem—R
$-Generation X—R
$-God Allows U-Turns—R
$-Good News—R
Good News Connection
Good News in RI
$-Good News, Etc.—R
Good News/S. Florida
$-Gospel Today—R
$-Grit
$-Guideposts—R
Gulf Coast Christian
Heartland Gatekeeper
Heartlight—R
Highway News—R
$-HonorBound—R
HopeKeepers—R
$-Indian Life—R
$-Inside Journal—R
$-Interim—R
$-Joy & Praise
$-Kindred Spirit
$-Lifeglow—R
Lifesite Canada
$-Light & Life
$-Living Church
$-Lookout
Maranatha News—R
Mars Hill Review
Mennonite Historian—R
Metro Voice—R
$-Minnesota Christian—R
$-Montgomery's Journey
Mutuality—R
$-National Catholic
New Heart—R
$-On Mission

$-Plains Faith—R
$-Portland Magazine
$-Positive Thinking—R
$-Power for Living—R
PrayerWorks—R
$-Precepts for Living
Presbyterian Outlook
$-Priority!—R
$-Prism—R
Quaker Life—R
Regent Business—R
Rock & Sling
Rose & Thorn
Sacred Journey—R
$-Science & Spirit
$-Senior Living
Spiritual Voice—R
$-Spring Hill Review—R
$-St. Anthony Messenger
$-Stewardship—R
Sunday Magazine
$-Testimony—R
thegoodsteward.com—R
$-Tidewater Parent—R
$-Today's Christian—R
Tri-State Voice
Tributes—R
Trumpeter—R
$-United Church Observer—R
$-UP
$-Upscale Magazine
Valparaiso Poetry—R
Victory News—R
$-War Cry—R
$-Way of St. Francis—R
$-Weavings—R
Wichita Chronicle
$-Wireless Age—R
$-Wittenburg Door—R
$-World & I—R
World Net Daily

CHILDREN
$-Faces
$-My Friend
$-Pockets—R
$-Primary Street
$-SHINEbrightly—R
$-Sparkle

CHRISTIAN EDUCATION/ LIBRARY
$-Children's Ministry
Christian Early Education—R
Christian Librarian—R
Christian Library Journal—R
$-Church Libraries—R

$-Group Magazine
$-Momentum
$-Teachers of Vision—R

MISSIONS
East-West Church
$-Evangelical Missions—R
$-Leaders for Today
OpRev Equipper—R
$-PFI World Report—R

PASTORS/LEADERS
$-African American Pulpit
Alpha News
$-Catholic Servant
$-Christian Century—R
$-Evangelicals Today—R
$-InSite—R
$-Leadership—R
$-Ministries Today
$-Ministry & Liturgy—R
Ministry in Motion—R
$-Pastoral Life—R
$-Sermon Notes—R
Strategic Adult Ministries—R

TEEN/YOUNG ADULT
$-Boundless Webzine—R
$-Credo—R
$-Essential Connection
$-Guideposts Sweet 16—R
$-Insight—R
$-J.A.M.
$-Listen—R
$-Passageway.org—R
$-Sharing the VICTORY—R
Teen Light—R
$-Teenage Christian—R
TeensForJC—R
Transcendmag.com—R
$-Young and Alive—R
$-Young Salvationist—R

WOMEN
Faithwebbin—R
Hearts at Home—R
Home-Based Moms—R
$-Horizons (women)—R
$-Journey
$-MOMsense—R
Precious Times—R
$-Today's Christian Woman—R

WRITERS
$-Adv. Christian Writer—R
$-Areopagus (UK)
$-Christian Communicator—R
$-Cross & Quill—R
$-Exchange—R

$-Fellowscript—R
Money the Write Way—R
Once Upon a Time—R
$-Upper Case
$-Writer
$-Writer's Digest—R
Writer's Lifeline
Writers Manual
Writes of Passage—R

LEADERSHIP

ADULT/GENERAL
African Voices—R
Alliance Life
$-Angels on Earth
Breakthrough Intercessor—R
Business Reform
Channels—R
$-Christian Courier (CAN)—R
$-Christian Leader—R
Christian Motorsports
Christian Ranchman
$-Christian Retailing
$-Christian Standard—R
$-ChristianWeek—R
$-Church of God EVANGEL
$-Citizens in America
$-City Light News—R
$-Cornerstone Christian—R
$-Culture Wars—R
Disciple's Journal—R
$-EFCA Today
$-Faith Today
$-Foursquare World Advance—R
$-Gem—R
$-Generation X—R
$-Good News—R
Heartlight—R
$-HonorBound—R
HopeKeepers—R
$-Inland NW Christian
$-Light & Life
$-Living Church
$-Lookout
Men of the Cross
$-Minnesota Christian—R
Mosaic—R
Mutuality—R
$-National Catholic
$-New Freeman—R
$-New Wineskins—R
NRB Magazine—R
$-On Mission
$-ONEvoice!
Penned from the Heart
$-Plains Faith—R

Presbyterian Outlook
Priscilla Papers—R
$-Prism—R
Quaker Life—R
Randall House Periodicals
Regent Business—R
Sacred Journey—R
Spiritual Voice—R
$-St. Anthony Messenger
$-Stewardship—R
$-Testimony—R
thegoodsteward.com—R
$-Today's Pentecostal Evangel—R
Trumpeter—R
$-United Church Observer—R
Victory News—R
Walk This Way—R
$-Way of St. Francis—R
$-Wireless Age—R
$-World & I—R

CHILDREN
$-Club Connection
$-SHINEbrightly—R
$-Sparkle

CHRISTIAN EDUCATION/ LIBRARY
Catholic Library World
$-Children's Ministry
Christian Early Education—R
Christian School Education—R
$-Church Educator—R
$-Group Magazine
$-Ideas Unlimited—R
Journal/Christian Education
$-Leader in C. E. Ministries—R
$-Momentum
$-Resource—R
$-Teachers Interaction
$-Today's Catholic Teacher—R
$-Youth & CE Leadership

MISSIONS
$-Leaders for Today
Wesleyan World—R

PASTORS/LEADERS
$-African American Pulpit
$-Barefoot—R
$-Catholic Servant
$-Christian Century—R
Christian Education Jour. (CA)—R
Christian Management—R
$-Church Worship
$-Clergy Journal—R
$-Enrichment—R
$-Evangelical Baptist—R

$-Evangelicals Today—R
$-Five Stones—R
$-Growth Points—R
$-Horizons (pastor)—R
$-InSite—R
$-Interpreter
Jour./Amer. Soc./Chur. Growth—R
$-Leadership—R
$-Lutheran Partners—R
$-Ministries Today
$-Ministry
Ministry in Motion—R
Ministry Matters
Net Results
$-Parish Life—R
$-Pastoral Life—R
Pastors.com—R
Pulpit Helps—R
Quarterly Review
$-RevWriter Resource
$-Sabbath School Leadership—R
$-Sermon Notes—R
Sharing the Practice—R
$-Small Group Dynamics—R
Theological Digest—R
$-WCA News—R
$ Word & World
$-Worship Leader
$-Your Church—R

TEEN/YOUNG ADULT
$-Brio—R
$-Student Leadership—R
Teen Light—R
$-Teenage Christian—R
TeensForJC—R
Transcendmag.com—R

WOMEN
$-Esprit—R
$-Godly Business Woman
$-Horizons (women)—R
$-inSpirit—R
Just Between Us—R
Precious Times—R
Right to the Heart—R
$-SpiritLed Woman
Women Today—R

WRITERS
$-Cross & Quill—R

LITURGICAL

ADULT/GENERAL
AGAIN—R
$-Alive Now—R
$-Arlington Catholic

Breakthrough Intercessor—R
$-Catholic Yearbook—R
Channels—R
$-Culture Wars—R
Divine Ascent
$-Dovetail—R
$-Episcopal Life—R
$-Family Digest—R
$-Living Church
$-Lutheran Journal—R
$-Messenger/Sacred Heart
$-National Catholic
$-New Wineskins—R
$-Our Sunday Visitor
$-Prairie Messenger—R
Silver Wings—R
$-Sojourners
$-St. Anthony Messenger
$-Testimony—R
$-Way of St. Francis—R

CHRISTIAN EDUCATION/
LIBRARY
$-Church Educator—R

PASTORS/LEADERS
$-African American Pulpit
$-Catholic Servant
$-Christian Century—R
$-Church Worship
$-Clergy Journal—R
Cross Currents
$-Diocesan Dialogue—R
$-Leadership—R
$-Lutheran Partners—R
$-Ministries Today
$-Ministry & Liturgy—R
$-Parish Life—R
$-Parish Liturgy—R
$-Pastoral Life—R
Pastors.com—R
$-Preaching Well—R
Quarterly Review
$-Reformed Worship
Sewanee Theo. Review
Sharing the Practice—R
$-This Rock
$-Today's Parish—R
$-Word & World

WOMEN
$-Horizons (women)—R

MARRIAGE

ADULT/GENERAL
$-Alive!—R
Alliance Life

$-Angels on Earth
$-Arlington Catholic
$-Associated Content—R
$-BGC World—R
$-Bible Advocate—R
Bread of Life—R
Breakthrough Intercessor—R
$-Bridal Guides—R
$-Canada Lutheran—R
$-Catholic Digest—R
$-Catholic Forester—R
$-Celebrate Life—R
Channels—R
Christian C. L. RECORD—R
$-Christian Courier (CAN)—R
$-Christian Examiner
$-Christian Home & School
Christian Journal—R
$-Christian Leader—R
Christian Motorsports
Christian Online
$-Christian Parenting—R
Christian Ranchman
$-Christian Social Action—R
Citizen USA—R
$-Citizens in America
$-City Light News—R
$-Columbia
$-Cornerstone Christian—R
$-Culture Wars—R
$-Cup of Comfort—R
$-Decision
Disciple's Journal—R
$-Discipleship Journal—R
$-Dovetail—R
$-EFCA Today
$-Evangel—R
Evangelical Advocate—R
$-Faith & Family
$-Faith Today
$-Family Digest—R
Family Online—R
$-Focus on the Family
$-Foursquare World Advance—R
$-Gem—R
$-Generation X—R
$-God Allows U-Turns—R
Good News Journal
$-Guideposts—R
Hannah to Hannah—R
Heartlight—R
Highway News—R
$-Homeschooling Today—R
$-HonorBound—R
HopeKeepers—R
$-Indian Life—R

$-Interim—R
$-Joy & Praise
$-Lifeglow—R
LifeLine Journal—R
$-Light & Life
Light at Home—R
$-Living—R
$-Living Church
$-Living Light News—R
$-Lookout
$-Lutheran Digest—R
$-Marriage Partnership—R
Mature Times—R
$-Men of Integrity—R
$-Mennonite Brethren—R
Metro Voice—R
$-Minnesota Christian—R
$-Montgomery's Journey
Mosaic—R
Mutuality—R
$-New Freeman—R
$-New Wineskins—R
$-On Mission
$-ONEvoice!
$-Our Sunday Visitor
$-Palm Beach—R
Pegasus Review—R
Penned from the Heart
$-Plain Truth—R
$-Plains Faith—R
$-Positive Thinking—R
$-Prairie Messenger—R
Priscilla Papers—R
$-Prism—R
$-Psychology for Living—R
$-Purpose—R
Quaker Life—R
Randall House Periodicals
$-Signs of the Times—R
$-SingleAgain.com
Singles Scoop—R
$-Smart Families—R
$-Social Justice—R
Spiritual Voice—R
$-Spring Hill Review—R
$-St. Anthony Messenger
$-Standard—R
$-Testimony—R
thegoodsteward.com—R
$-Today's Christian—R
$-Today's Pentecostal Evangel—R
$-Together—R
Trumpeter—R
$-U.S. Catholic
$-Vibrant Life—R
Victory News—R

$-War Cry—R
$-Wesleyan Life—R
$-Whole Magazine
$-World & I—R

MISSIONS
$-American Baptists in Mission

PASTORS/LEADERS
$-African American Pulpit
$-Catholic Servant
$-Christian Century—R
$-Church Administration
$-Evangelical Baptist—R
$-Evangelicals Today—R
$-Interpreter
Journal/Pastoral Care—R
$-Lutheran Partners—R
$-Ministries Today
$-Pastoral Life—R
$-Preaching Well—R
$-Rev.
Sharing the Practice—R
Theological Digest—R
$-Today's Christian Preacher—R
$-Today's Parish—R
$-Word & World

TEEN/YOUNG ADULT
$-Boundless Webzine—R
$-Brio—R
Teen Light—R
TeensForJC—R
Transcendmag.com—R
$-Young Adult Today—R
$-Young and Alive—R

WOMEN
Anna's Journal—R
Crowned with Silver
$-Dabbling Mum.com—R
$-Esprit—R
Faithwebbin—R
$-Godly Business Woman
Heart & Soul
Hearts at Home—R
Home-Based Moms—R
$-Horizons (women)—R
$-inSpirit—R
$-Journey
Just Between Us—R
Lutheran Woman's Quar.
$-MOMsense—R
P31 Woman—R
Precious Times—R
Shalom Bayit
$-Simple Joy
Sisters in the Lord

$-SpiritLed Woman
$-Today's Christian Woman—R
$-Woman's Touch—R
$-Women Alive!—R
Women of the Cross
Women Today—R

MEN'S ISSUES

ADULT/GENERAL
Alliance Life
$-Annals of St. Anne
$-Arlington Catholic
$-Associated Content—R
$-BGC World—R
Bread of Life—R
Breakthrough Intercessor—R
$-Catholic Forester R
$-Catholic New Times—R
Channels—R
$-Chicken Soup—R
$-Christian Examiner
Christian Journal—R
$-Christian Leader—R
Christian Online
$-Christian Parenting—R
Christian Ranchman
$-Christian Social Action—R
$-ChristianWeek—R
Citizen USA—R
$-Citizens in America
$-City Light News—R
$-Columbia
$-Cornerstone Christian—R
Crossway/Newsline—R
Disciple's Journal—R
$-Dovetail—R
$-EFCA Today
$-Evangel—R
$-Faith Today
$-Foursquare World Advance—R
$-Gem—R
$-Generation X—R
$-God Allows U-Turns—R
Good News Journal
Hannah to Hannah—R
Heartlight—R
Highway News—R
$-Homeschooling Today—R
$-HonorBound—R
HopeKeepers—R
$-Indian Life—R
$-Inland NW Christian
$-Inside Journal—R
$-Interim—R
$-Joy & Praise

LifeLine Journal—R
$-Light & Life
Light at Home—R
$-Living—R
Looking Up
$-Lookout
Maranatha News—R
Mature Times—R
$-Men of Integrity—R
Men of the Cross
Metro Voice—R
$-Minnesota Christian—R
$-Montgomery's Journey
Mosaic—R
Mutuality—R
$-New Freeman—R
$-On Mission
$-ONEvoice!
$-Our Sunday Visitor
$-Palm Beach—R
Penned from the Heart
$-Plains Faith—R
$-Positive Thinking—R
Presbyterian Outlook
Priscilla Papers—R
$-Prism—R
$-Psychology for Living—R
$-Purpose—R
Quaker Life—R
Randall House Periodicals
Regent Business—R
$-SingleAgain.com
Singles Scoop—R
$-Smart Families—R
Spiritual Voice—R
$-St. Anthony Messenger
$-Standard—R
Storyteller—R
$-Testimony—R
thegoodsteward.com—R
$-Today's Christian—R
$-Today's Pentecostal Evangel—R
$-Together—R
Trumpeter—R
$-U.S. Catholic
$-United Church Observer—R
$-Vibrant Life—R
Victory News—R
$-Voice of the Lord
$-Wesleyan Life—R
West Wind Review
$-World & I—R

PASTORS/LEADERS
$-African American Pulpit
$-Evangelical Baptist—R

$-Evangelicals Today—R
$-Interpreter
$-Lutheran Partners—R
$-Ministries Today
$-Parish Life—R
$-Pastoral Life—R
Pulpit Helps—R
Sharing the Practice—R
$-Word & World

TEEN/YOUNG ADULT
TeensForJC—R
Transcendmag.com—R

WOMEN
$-At the Center—R
$-Dabbling Mum.com—R
Faithwebbin—R

MIRACLES

ADULT/GENERAL
Alliance Life
$-Angels on Earth
$-Bible Advocate—R
$-Brave Hearts
Bread of Life—R
Breakthrough Intercessor—R
$-Bridal Guides—R
$-CGA World—R
Channels—R
$-Chicken Soup—R
Christian Motorsports
Christian Online
Christian Ranchman
Citizen USA—R
Connecting Point—R
$-Cornerstone Christian—R
$-Culture Wars—R
Divine Ascent
Evangelical Advocate—R
$-Faith Today
$-Gem—R
$-God Allows U-Turns—R
$-Grit
$-Guideposts—R
HopeKeepers—R
$-Lifeglow—R
$-Light & Life
Light at Home—R
$-Live—R
$-Lutheran Digest—R
$-New Freeman—R
New Heart—R
$-Now What?—R
$-ONEvoice!
$-Palm Beach—R
Pegasus Review—R

Penned from the Heart
$-Plains Faith—R
$-Positive Thinking—R
$-Queen of All Hearts
Spiritual Voice—R
$-St. Anthony Messenger
$-Testimony—R
thegoodsteward.com—R
$-Today's Christian—R
$-Today's Pentecostal Evangel—R
Trumpeter—R
Victory News—R
$-Vision—R
$-Voice of the Lord

CHILDREN
$-BREAD/God's Children—R
$-Guide—R
$-Guideposts for Kids

PASTORS/LEADERS
$-Evangelicals Today—R
$-Ministries Today
$-Pastoral Life—R
Sharing the Practice—R
$-Word & World

TEEN/YOUNG ADULT
$-Brio—R
$-Guideposts Sweet 16—R
Teen Light—R
$-With—R
$-Young and Alive—R
$-Young Christian—R

WOMEN
$-Godly Business Woman
Home-Based Moms—R
$-SpiritLed Woman
$-Woman's Touch—R
Women of the Cross

MISSIONS

ADULT/GENERAL
AGAIN—R
$-Alive!—R
Alliance Life
$-Anglican Journal
$-B.C. Catholic—R
Breakthrough Intercessor—R
$-Catholic Yearbook—R
Channels—R
$-Christian Leader—R
Christian Online
$-Christianity Today—R
$-ChristianWeek—R
Church Herald & Holiness—R
Citizen USA—R

$-City Light News—R
Connecting Point—R
$-Culture Wars—R
Disciple's Journal—R
$-Discipleship Journal—R
$-Episcopal Life—R
Eternal Ink—R
Evangelical Advocate—R
$-Faith Today
$-Gem—R
$-Good News—R
Gospel Tract—R
$-Grit
HopeKeepers—R
$-Horizons (adult)—R
LifeLine Journal—R
$-Light & Life
Light at Home—R
$-Live—R
$-Living Church
$-Lookout
$-Lutheran Journal—R
Maranatha News—R
Mature Times—R
$-Men of Integrity—R
Men of the Cross
$-Minnesota Christian—R
$-Montgomery's Journey
Mosaic—R
$-My Walk With Jesus
$-National Catholic
$-New Freeman—R
New Heart—R
$-New Wineskins—R
$-On Mission
$-ONEvoice!
$-Our Sunday Visitor
Penned from the Heart
$-Plains Faith—R
$-Power for Living—R
PrayerWorks—R
Presbyterian Outlook
$-Priority!—R
Priscilla Papers—R
$-Prism—R
$-Purpose—R
Quaker Life—R
Randall House Periodicals
Silver Wings—R
Singles Scoop—R
$-St. Anthony Messenger
$-Standard—R
Sword and Trumpet—R
Sword of the Lord—R
$-Testimony—R
thegoodsteward.com—R

$-Today's Christian—R
Trumpeter—R
Victory News—R
$-Voice of the Lord
Walk This Way—R
$-Way of St. Francis—R
$-Wireless Age—R

CHILDREN
$-BREAD/God's Children—R
$-Guide—R

CHRISTIAN EDUCATION/ LIBRARY
$-Children's Ministry
$-Church Educator—R
$-Teach Kids!—R
$-Youth & CE Leadership

MISSIONS
$-American Baptists in Mission
Catholic Missions/Canada
East-West Church
$-Evangelical Missions—R
Glad Tidings
Intl. Jour./Frontier—R
$-Leaders for Today
Missiology
Mission Frontiers
$-New World Outlook
$-One
OpRev Equipper—R
$-PFI World Report—R
$-PIME World—R
Railroad Evangelist—R
Wesleyan World—R
Women of the Harvest

PASTORS/LEADERS
$-African American Pulpit
$-Clergy Journal—R
$-Enrichment—R
$-Evangelical Baptist—R
$-Evangelicals Today—R
$-Interpreter
$-Lutheran Partners—R
$-Ministries Today
Ministry in Motion—R
$-Pastoral Life—R
Pastors.com—R
Pulpit Helps—R
Sharing the Practice—R
$-This Rock
$-Word & World

TEEN/YOUNG ADULT
$-Brio—R
$-Credo—R
$-Devo'Zine—R

GO!
$-Passageway.org—R
$-Real Faith in Life—R
$-Student Leadership—R
Teen Light—R
$-With—R
$-Young Salvationist—R

WOMEN
$-Godly Business Woman
$-Horizons (women)—R
$-inSpirit—R
$-Journey
Just Between Us—R
$-Link & Visitor—R
$-SpiritLed Woman

MONEY MANAGEMENT

ADULT/GENERAL
$-Anglican Journal
$-Aspiring Retail
$-Associated Content—R
$-Bridal Guides—R
byFaith
$-Catholic Forester—R
CBN.com—R
Channels—R
Christian C. L. RECORD—R
Christian Journal—R
Christian Motorsports
Christian Online
$-Christian Parenting—R
Christian Ranchman
$-ChristianWeek—R
$-Church of God EVANGEL
Citizen USA—R
$-Citizens in America
$-City Light News—R
Connecting Point—R
$-Cornerstone Christian—R
Disciple's Journal—R
$-Faith & Family
$-Faith Today
Family Online—R
$-Gem—R
$-Generation X—R
Gospel Tract—R
Heartlight—R
Highway News—R
$-Homeschooling Today—R
$-HonorBound—R
$-Inland NW Christian
$-Lifeglow—R
LifeLine Journal—R
$-Light & Life

$-Living—R
$-Lookout
$-Mature Years—R
$-Men of Integrity—R
Men of the Cross
$-Montgomery's Journey
NRB Magazine—R
$-Palm Beach—R
Parents & Teens—R
Penned from the Heart
$-Plains Faith—R
Quaker Life—R
Randall House Periodicals
$-SingleAgain.com
$-Smart Families—R
Spiritual Voice—R
$-St. Anthony Messenger
$-Testimony—R
thegoodsteward.com—R
$-Today's Christian—R
$-Today's Pentecostal Evangel—R
$-Together—R
Trumpeter—R
Victory News—R
$-War Cry—R
$-World & I—R

CHILDREN
$-BREAD/God's Children—R

CHRISTIAN EDUCATION/ LIBRARY
$-Church Educator—R
$-Momentum

PASTORS/LEADERS
$-African American Pulpit
$-Clergy Journal—R
$-Enrichment—R
$-Evangelical Baptist—R
$-Evangelicals Today—R
$-Interpreter
$-Ministries Today
Ministry in Motion—R
$-Pastoral Life—R
Pastors.com—R
Sharing the Practice—R
$-Today's Christian Preacher—R
$-Today's Parish—R
$-Your Church—R

TEEN/YOUNG ADULT
$-Boundless Webzine—R
$-Real Faith in Life—R
Teen Light—R
$-Young and Alive—R
$-Young Christian—R

WOMEN
Christian Women Today—R
Faithwebbin—R
$-Godly Business Woman
Heart & Soul
Home-Based Moms—R
$-Horizons (women)—R
Inspired Moms.Com
$-inSpirit—R
$-Journey
Just Between Us—R
Life Tools for Women
Precious Times—R
Sisters in the Lord
$-Today's Christian Woman—R
$-Woman's Touch—R
Women Today—R

WRITERS
Money the Write Way—R

MOVIE REVIEWS

ADULT/GENERAL
$-Abilities
$-Associated Content—R
byFaith
CBN.com—R
Charlotte World
Christian Current
$-Christian Herald—R
Good News/S. Florida
Heartland Gatekeeper
Mars Hill Review
MovieGuide
$-Plains Faith—R
Reformed Quarterly
Rock & Sling
Spiritual Voice—R
$-Spring Hill Review—R

MUSIC
Hymn

MUSIC REVIEWS

ADULT/GENERAL
$-Arlington Catholic
$-Aspiring Retail
$-Associated Content—R
$-Catholic New Times—R
$-Catholic Peace Voice—R
CBN.com—R
Channels—R
$-Charisma
Charlotte World
Christian Current
$-Christian Herald—R
Christian Journal—R

Christian Media—R
Christian Radio Weekly
$-Christian Renewal—R
$-Christian Retailing
Citizen USA—R
$-City Light News—R
$-Cornerstone Christian—R
$-Cresset
$-Faith & Family
$-Faith Today
Good News/S. Florida
Heartland Gatekeeper
Heartlight—R
$-Indian Life—R
Infuze Magazine
$-Interim—R
$-Joy & Praise
LifeLine Journal—R
Light at Home—R
Mars Hill Review
$-Minnesota Christian—R
Parents & Teens—R
$-Plains Faith—R
$-Presbyterians Today—R
$-Prism—R
Quaker Life—R
Reformed Quarterly
Rock & Sling
Rose & Thorn
Spiritual Voice—R
$-Spring Hill Review—R
$-Testimony—R
Trumpeter—R
Victory News—R
Winsome Wit—R
$-Wireless Age—R
$-World & I—R

CHILDREN
$-Club Connection

CHRISTIAN EDUCATION/ LIBRARY
Catholic Library World
$-Church Libraries—R

MISSIONS
Women of the Harvest

MUSIC
$-CCM Magazine
Christian Music Weekly—R
$-Creator—R
$-Senior Musician—R
Tradition

PASTORS/LEADERS
$-Barefoot—R

$-Christian Century—R
$-Interpreter
$-Ministries Today
$-Pastoral Life—R
$-Reformed Worship
Technologies for Worship—R
$-WCA News—R
$-Worship Leader

TEEN/YOUNG ADULT
$-Boundless Webzine—R
$-Credo—R
$-Devo'Zine—R
GO!
Teen Light—R
$-Teenage Christian—R
TeensForJC—R
Transcendmag.com—R
$-With—R
$-Young Salvationist—R

WOMEN
$-Godly Business Woman
Home-Based Moms—R
Precious Times—R

NATURE

ADULT/GENERAL
$-Alive!—R
Angel Face—R
$-Animal Trails—R
$-Associated Content—R
$-Barefoot Path—R
$-Catholic New Times—R
$-Christian Courier (CAN)—R
$-Christian Renewal—R
$-Covenant Companion—R
Creation
Creation Care—R
$-Creation Illust.
$-Cup of Comfort—R
$-Eclectic Homeschool
Eternal Ink—R
$-Gem—R
$-Grit
$-Ideals—R
Keys to Living—R
$-Lifeglow—R
$-Light & Life
Light at Home—R
$-Lutheran Digest—R
Maranatha News—R
$-Over the Back Fence—R
Pegasus Review—R
Penned from the Heart
$-Plains Faith—R

Plowman—R
PrayerWorks—R
Sacred Journey—R
$-Science & Spirit
Spiritual Voice—R
$-Spring Hill Review—R
$-St. Anthony Messenger
Storyteller—R
$-Testimony—R
thegoodsteward.com—R
Trumpeter—R
Victory News—R
$-Vision—R
$-World & I—R

CHILDREN
$-Barefoot for Kids—R
$-BREAD/God's Children—R
$-Cadet Quest—R
$-Club Connection
$-Focus/Clubhouse Jr.
$-Guide—R
$-My Friend
$-Nature Friend
$-Partners—R
$-Passport—R
$-SHINEbrightly—R
Skipping Stones
$-Sparkle
$-Story Friends—R

PASTORS/LEADERS
$-Pastoral Life—R
$-Word & World

TEEN/YOUNG ADULT
$-Devo'Zine—R
Teen Light—R
$-Teenage Christian—R
$-Young and Alive—R

WOMEN
$-inSpirit—R

NEWS FEATURES

ADULT/GENERAL
Anglican
$-Arkansas Catholic—R
$-Associated Content—R
$-Atlantic Catholic
Baptist Standard
Beacon (AL)
$-BGC World—R
Biblical Recorder
Canadian Christianity.com
$-Catholic Insight
$-Catholic New Times—R
$-Catholic New York

$-Catholic Peace Voice—R
$-Catholic Sentinel
Catholic World
CBN.com—R
$-Central Appalachia
Challenge Weekly
$-Charisma
Charlotte World
Christian Chronicle
Christian Citizen USA
Christian Courier (WI)—R
Christian Current
$-Christian Examiner
Christian Herald (UK)
Christian Journal—R
Christian News NW—R
Christian Post
Christian Radio Weekly
$-Christian Renewal—R
Christian Research
$-Christian Response—R
$-Christian Retailing
$-ChristianWeek—R
Church of England News
Citizen USA—R
$-City Light News—R
$-Commonweal
Compass Direct
Desert Christian
Desert Voice
$-Disaster News Network
$-Dovetail—R
Evangel, The
Evangelical Advocate—R
$-Faith Today
Family Online—R
Founders Journal
$-Generation X—R
Good News Connection
Good News in RI
Good News/S. Florida
Gospel Post
Gulf Coast Christian
Heartland Gatekeeper
HopeKeepers—R
$-Impact—R
$-Indian Life—R
Indiana Christian News
$-Interchange
Island Catholic News
$-Liberty—R
Lifesite Canada
$-Light & Life
Metro Voice—R
$-Minnesota Christian—R

$-National Catholic
Network
$-Our Sunday Visitor
$-Palm Beach—R
Pietisten Online
$-Plain Truth—R
$-Plains Faith—R
$-Portland Magazine
PrayerWorks—R
$-Priority!—R
Quaker Life—R
$-Science & Spirit
Spiritual Voice—R
$-St. Anthony Messenger
Sunday Magazine
Sword and Trumpet—R
$-Testimony—R
thegoodsteward.com—R
$-Today's Christian—R
Tri-State Voice
Trumpeter—R
$-Upscale Magazine
Victory News—R
$-War Cry—R
War Cry (Canada)—R
Wichita Chronicle
$-Wireless Age—R
Word News
$-World & I—R
World Net Daily

CHILDREN
$-Partners—R
$-Pockets—R

MISSIONS
OpRev Equipper—R

PASTORS/LEADERS
Alpha News
$-Christian Century—R
Pastors.com—R
Pulpit Helps—R

TEEN/YOUNG ADULT
Teen Light—R

WOMEN
$-Today's Christian Woman—R

WRITERS
$-Fellowscript—R
Money the Write Way—R

NEWSPAPERS/TABLOIDS

Anglican
Alpha News
$-Anglican Journal
$-Arkansas Catholic—R

$-Arlington Catholic
$-Atlantic Catholic
$-B.C. Catholic—R
Baptist Standard
Beacon (AL)
Biblical Recorder
Canadian Christianity.com
$-Catholic New Times—R
$-Catholic New York
Catholic Register
$-Catholic Sentinel
$-Catholic Telegraph
$-Central Appalachia
Challenge Weekly
Charlotte World
Christian Chronicle
Christian Citizen USA
$-Christian Courier (CAN)—R
Christian Courier (WI)—R
Christian Current
$-Christian Examiner
$-Christian Herald—R
Christian Herald (UK)
Christian Journal—R
Christian Media—R
Christian News NW—R
Christian Observer
Christian Ranchman
$-Christian Renewal—R
$-ChristianWeek—R
Church of England News
Citizen USA—R
$-City Light News—R
Common Ground—R
$-Cornerstone Christian—R
Desert Christian
Desert Voice
Disciple's Journal—R
Discovery—R
$-Episcopal Life—R
Evangelical Times
Family Online—R
Faro de Luz
Good News Connection
Good News in RI
Good News Journal
$-Good News, Etc.—R
Good News/S. Florida
Gospel Post
$-Grit
Gulf Coast Christian
Heartland Gatekeeper
$-Indian Life—R
Indiana Christian News
$-Inland NW Christian

$-Inside Journal—R
Insight (for blind)
$-Interim—R
Island Catholic News
$-Layman
Lifesite Canada
$-Living—R
$-Living Light News—R
Maranatha News—R
$-Messenger
Messianic Times
Metro Voice—R
Mid-South Christian
$-Minnesota Christian—R
$-National Catholic
Network
$-New Freeman—R
New Frontier
$-Our Sunday Visitor
$-Palm Beach—R
Pietisten Online
$-Prairie Messenger—R
PrayerWorks—R
Pulpit Helps—R
$-Senior Living
Spiritual Voice—R
Star of Zion
Sunday Magazine
SW Kansas Faith
Sword of the Lord—R
$-Tidewater Parent—R
$-Together—R
Tri-State Voice
Wichita Chronicle
Word News
World Net Daily

NOSTALGIA

ADULT/GENERAL
$-Ancient Paths—R
$-Animal Trails—R
$-Associated Content—R
$-Bridal Guides—R
$-Citizens in America
$-City Light News—R
$-Cup of Comfort—R
Eternal Ink—R
$-God's Way Books
$-Grit
Light at Home—R
$-Lutheran Digest—R
$-Mature Living
Nostalgia—R
$-Over the Back Fence—R
$-Palm Beach—R

PrayerWorks—R
Spiritual Voice—R
$-Spring Hill Review—R
Storyteller—R
$-Testimony—R
$-Tidewater Parent—R
Victory News—R

CHILDREN
$-Faces

DAILY DEVOTIONALS
$-Daily Meditation

WOMEN
Crowned with Silver
$-Journey

ONLINE PUBLICATIONS

ADULT/GENERAL
$-America
$-Anglican Journal
$-Apocalypse Chronicles—R
$-Associated Content—R
$-Barefoot Path—R
$-Believer's Bay
Books & Culture
Canadian Christianity.com
$-Cathedral Age
$-Catholic Digest—R
CBN.com—R
Challenge Weekly
Christian Computing—R
$-Christian Examiner
$-Christian Home & School
Christian Media—R
Christian Online
Christian Outlook
Christian Single Online
$-Christian Standard—R
$-Christianity Today—R
$-Columbia
$-Company—R
Compass Direct
$-Decision
$-Disaster News Network
Disciple's Journal—R
Discovery—R
$-Dragons, Knights & Angels—R
$-Drama Ministry—R
$-Eclectic Homeschool
Eternal Ink—R
$-First Things
$-Flutters of the Heart
Gateway S-F—R
Gold Country Families—R
Heartlight—R

$-Impact—R
Impact Online
$-Interim—R
LifeTimes Catholic
Light at Home—R
$-Lookout
$-Lutheran Digest—R
$-Marian Helper—R
Men of the Cross
$-Messenger/St. Anthony
$-Messianic Sci-Fi
$-Minnesota Christian—R
$-National Catholic
$-New Wineskins—R
$-Now What?—R
NRB Magazine—R
$-On Mission
Parables—R
Parents & Teens—R
Perspectives—R
PrayerWorks—R
$-Priority!—R
Reformed Quarterly
Regent Business—R
$-Relevant
Rose & Thorn
Sacred Journey—R
Salt of the Earth
Short Stories Bimonthly—R
$-Signs of the Times—R
$-SingleAgain.com
$-Smart Families—R
$-Sound Body—R
SR: A Journal—R
$-St. Anthony Messenger
$-Testimony—R
thegoodsteward.com—R
TJ
$-Today's Christian—R
$-Today's Pentecostal Evangel—R
Tributes—R
Trumpeter—R
$-U.S. Catholic
Valparaiso Poetry—R
Walk This Way—R
$-War Cry—R
Wichita Chronicle
Winsome Wit—R
$-World & I—R
World Net Daily

CHILDREN
$-American Girl
$-Barefoot for Kids—R
$-Focus/Clubhouse
$-Focus/Clubhouse Jr.

$-Guideposts for Kids
$-Keys for Kids—R
$-My Friend

CHRISTIAN EDUCATION/ LIBRARY
Christian Library Journal—R
$-Ideas Unlimited—R

DAILY DEVOTIONALS
Forward Day by Day

MISSIONS
Mission Frontiers
OpRev Equipper—R

MUSIC
$-CCM Magazine

PASTORS/LEADERS
$-Barefoot—R
$-InSite—R
$-Interpreter
$-Leadership—R
Ministry in Motion—R
Net Results
$-Newsletter Newsletter
Pastors.com—R
Plugged In
Preaching—R
Pulpit Helps—R
$-Rev.
$-RevWriter Resource
$-Sermon Notes—R
$-Small Group Dynamics—R
Strategic Adult Ministries—R
Technologies for Worship—R
$-WCA News—R
Youth Culture
$-Youthworker

TEEN/YOUNG ADULT
$-Boundless Webzine—R
Journalism Online
$-Passageway.org—R
$-Student Leadership—R
Teen Light—R
TeensForJC—R
Transcendmag.com—R
$-Young Salvationist—R

WOMEN
Anna's Journal—R
$-At the Center—R
Christian Women Today—R
Faithwebbin—R
$-History's Women—R
Inspired Moms.Com
Life Tools for Women

$-Melody of the Heart
Right to the Heart—R
$-Simple Joy
Sisters in the Lord
Women of the Cross
Women Today—R
Women's Ministry

WRITERS
Dedicated Author
Money the Write Way—R
$-Spirit-Led Writer—R
Teachers & Writers
Writing Corner

OPINION PIECES

ADULT/GENERAL
Anglican
$-Annals of St. Anne
$-Arkansas Catholic—R
$-Arlington Catholic
$-Associated Content—R
$-B.C. Catholic—R
$-Bible Advocate—R
$-Bridal Guides—R
$-Catholic New Times—R
$-Catholic New York
$-Catholic Peace Voice—R
$-Christian Courier (CAN)—R
$-Christian Examiner
Christian News NW—R
$-Christian Renewal—R
Christian Research
$-Christian Social Action—R
$-Christianity Today—R
$-ChristianWeek—R
Citizen USA—R
$-City Light News—R
$-Culture Wars—R
$-DisciplesWorld
$-Episcopal Life—R
Eternal Ink—R
$-Faith Today
$-First Things
$-Generation X—R
Good News Journal
HopeKeepers—R
$-Indian Life—R
$-Inland NW Christian
$-Interim—R
Island Catholic News
$-Light & Life
Light at Home—R
$-Living Church
$-Lookout
$-Mennonite Brethren—R

Metro Voice—R
$-Minnesota Christian—R
Mosaic—R
$-National Catholic
$-New Freeman—R
NRB Magazine—R
$-Our Sunday Visitor
Perspectives—R
$-Plain Truth—R
$-Plains Faith—R
$-Portland Magazine
$-Prairie Messenger—R
PrayerWorks—R
Presbyterian Outlook
Regent Business—R
$-Social Justice—R
$-Sojourners
Spiritual Voice—R
$-Spring Hill Review—R
$-St. Anthony Messenger
$-Testimony—R
thegoodsteward.com—R
Trumpeter—R
$-U.S. Catholic
$-United Church Observer—R
Victory News—R
$-Way of St. Francis—R
$-Whole Magazine
Winsome Wit—R
$-Wittenburg Door—R
$-World & I—R

CHILDREN
Skipping Stones

CHRISTIAN EDUCATION/ LIBRARY
Catholic Library World
Jour./Christianity/Foreign Languages

MISSIONS
Glad Tidings
OpRev Equipper—R

PASTORS/LEADERS
$-Catholic Servant
$-Evangelical Baptist—R
$-Pastoral Life—R
Pulpit Helps—R
$-Word & World
$-Worship Leader

TEEN/YOUNG ADULT
$-Boundless Webzine—R
$-Listen—R
Teen Light—R
TeensForJC—R
Transcendmag.com—R
$-Young Christian—R

WOMEN
Anna's Journal—R
Faithwebbin—R

WRITERS
$-Adv. Christian Writer—R
$-Areopagus (UK)
$-Christian Communicator—R
$-Exchange—R
$-Fellowscript—R
Money the Write Way—R

PARENTING

ADULT/GENERAL
American Tract Society—R
$-Ancient Paths—R
$-Angels on Earth
$-Annals of St. Anne
$-Arlington Catholic
$-Associated Content—R
Breakthrough Intercessor—R
$-Bridal Guides—R
$-Canada Lutheran—R
$-Catholic Digest—R
$-Catholic Forester—R
$-Catholic New Times—R
$-Catholic Yearbook—R
$-Celebrate Life—R
$-Chicken Soup—R
$-Christian Courier (CAN)—R
$-Christian Home & School
Christian Journal—R
Christian Motorsports
Christian Observer
$-Christian Parenting—R
Christian Ranchman
$-Christian Renewal—R
$-Christian Social Action—R
Citizen USA—R
$-Citizens in America
$-City Light News—R
$-Columbia
$-Cornerstone Christian—R
Creation Care—R
$-Culture Wars—R
$-Cup of Comfort—R
Disciple's Journal—R
$-Dovetail—R
$-Eclectic Homeschool
Eternal Ink—R
Evangelical Advocate—R
$-Faith & Family
$-Faith Today
$-Family Digest—R
Family Online—R
$-Focus on the Family

$-Foursquare World Advance—R
$-Gem—R
$-Generation X—R
Gold Country Families—R
Good News Journal
$-Grit
Heartlight—R
Highway News—R
$-Homeschooling Today—R
$-HonorBound—R
HopeKeepers—R
$-Indian Life—R
$-Interim—R
LifeLine Journal—R
$-Light & Life
Light at Home—R
$-Living—R
$-Living Light News—R
Looking Up
$-Lookout
$-Lutheran Digest—R
$-Lutheran Journal—R
Maranatha News—R
$-Marriage Partnership—R
$-Men of Integrity—R
$-Mennonite Brethren—R
Metro Voice—R
$-Minnesota Christian—R
$-Montgomery's Journey
Mosaic—R
Mutuality—R
$-New Freeman—R
$-New Wineskins—R
$-ONEvoice!
$-Our Sunday Visitor
$-ParentLife
Parents & Teens—R
Pegasus Review—R
Penned from the Heart
$-Plain Truth—R
$-Plains Faith—R
$-Positive Thinking—R
$-Power for Living—R
$-Prairie Messenger—R
PrayerWorks—R
$-Psychology for Living—R
Quaker Life—R
Randall House Periodicals
$-Signs of the Times—R
$-SingleAgain.com
Singles Scoop—R
$-Smart Families—R
$-Social Justice—R
$-Special Living—R
Spiritual Voice—R
$-Spring Hill Review—R

$-St. Anthony Messenger
$-Standard—R
Storyteller—R
SW Kansas Faith
$-Testimony—R
thegoodsteward.com—R
$-Tidewater Parent—R
$-Today's Christian—R
$-Together—R
Trumpeter—R
$-U.S. Catholic
$-Vibrant Life—R
Victory News—R
$-Vision—R
$-War Cry—R
$-Way of St. Francis—R
$-Wesleyan Life—R
$-Whole Magazine
$-World & I—R

CHILDREN
$-Adventures

CHRISTIAN EDUCATION/ LIBRARY
$-Children's Ministry
Christian Early Education—R

MISSIONS
$-American Baptists in Mission

PASTORS/LEADERS
$-Catholic Servant
$-Evangelical Baptist—R
$-Evangelicals Today—R
$-Interpreter
$-Pastoral Life—R
$-Preaching Well—R
Pulpit Helps—R
Sharing the Practice—R
Strategic Adult Ministries—R
Youth Culture

WOMEN
$-At the Center—R
Crowned with Silver
$-Dabbling Mum.com—R
$-Esprit—R
Faithwebbin—R
$-Godly Business Woman
Handmaiden—R
Heart & Soul
Hearts at Home—R
Home-Based Moms—R
Inspired Moms.Com
$-inSpirit—R
$-Journey
Just Between Us—R

Keeping Hearts & Home
$-Link & Visitor—R
Lutheran Woman's Quar.
$-MOMsense—R
P31 Woman—R
Precious Times—R
Shalom Bayit
$-Simple Joy
$-SpiritLed Woman
$-Today's Christian Woman—R
$-Woman's Touch—R
$-Women Alive!—R
Women of the Cross

PEACE ISSUES

ADULT/GENERAL
$-Associated Content—R
$-Aujourd'hui Credo—R
$-Bridal Guides—R
$-Citizens in America
$-Generation X—R
Light at Home—R
$-Living—R
$-Lookout
Mosaic—R
$-National Catholic
Penned from the Heart
Perspectives—R
$-Plains Faith—R
$-Prairie Messenger—R
$-Purpose—R
Quaker Life—R
Sacred Journey—R
Silver Wings—R
$-Sojourners
Spiritual Voice—R
$-Spring Hill Review—R
$-St. Joseph's Messenger—R
$-Testimony—R
$-Together—R
$-U.S. Catholic
Victory News—R

CHILDREN
$-Pockets—R
Skipping Stones

PASTORS/LEADERS
$-African American Pulpit
$-Clergy Journal—R
$-Interpreter

TEEN/YOUNG ADULT
Teen Light—R

WOMEN
$-Horizons (women)—R
$-inSpirit—R

PERSONAL EXPERIENCE

ADULT/GENERAL
African Voices—R
AGAIN—R
$-Alive Now—R
Alliance Life
$-Angels on Earth
$-Annals of St. Anne
$-Associated Content—R
$-B.C. Catholic—R
$-Barefoot Path—R
$-Bible Advocate—R
Bread of Life—R
Breakthrough Intercessor—R
$-Bridal Guides—R
$-Catholic Digest—R
$-Catholic Forester—R
$-Catholic New Times—R
$-Catholic New York
$-Catholic Peace Voice—R
$-Catholic Yearbook—R
$-Celebrate Life—R
$-CGA World—R
Channels—R
$-Chicken Soup—R
$-Christian Courier (CAN)—R
Christian Journal—R
Christian Motorsports
Christian Observer
Christian Online
Christian Ranchman
$-Christianity Today—R
$-Citizens in America
$-City Light News—R
$-Commonweal
Community Spirit
$-Cornerstone Christian—R
Crossway/Newsline—R
$-Cup of Comfort—R
$-Decision
$-Dovetail—R
$-Eclectic Homeschool
$-EFCA Today
Eternal Ink—R
$-Evangel—R
$-Faith Today
$-Gem—R
$-Generation X—R
$-God Allows U-Turns—R
Good News Journal
$-Grit
$-Guideposts—R
Halo Magazine
Hannah to Hannah—R
Highway News—R

HopeKeepers—R
$-Horizons (adult)—R
$-Ideals—R
$-Indian Life—R
$-Inland NW Christian
$-Inside Journal—R
$-Interim—R
$-Joyful Noise!
Keys to Living—R
Leaves—R
$-Lifeglow—R
$-Light & Life
Light at Home—R
$-Live—R
$-Living—R
$-Living Church
$-Lookout
$-Lutheran Digest—R
$-Lutheran Journal—R
Maranatha News—R
$-Marian Helper—R
$-Marriage Partnership—R
$-Mature Living
Men of the Cross
$-Mennonite Brethren—R
Mutuality—R
$-My Walk With Jesus
$-New Freeman—R
New Heart—R
$-New Wineskins—R
Nostalgia—R
$-Now What?—R
$-On Mission
$-ONEvoice!
$-Palm Beach—R
Parents & Teens—R
Penned from the Heart
$-Plains Faith—R
$-Portland Magazine
$-Positive Thinking—R
PrayerWorks—R
$-Priority!—R
$-Psychology for Living—R
$-Purpose—R
Quaker Life—R
$-Queen of All Hearts
Randall House Periodicals
Sacred Journey—R
$-Seek—R
$-Senior Living
Sharing—R
Silver Wings—R
$-Spiritual Life
Spiritual Voice—R
$-Spring Hill Review—R
$-St. Anthony Messenger

$-Standard—R
Storyteller—R
$-Testimony—R
thegoodsteward.com—R
$-Tidewater Parent—R
$-Today's Christian—R
$-Today's Pentecostal Evangel—R
$-Together—R
Trumpeter—R
$-Upscale Magazine
Victory News—R
$-Vision—R
$-Voice of the Lord
$-War Cry—R
$-Way of St. Francis—R
$-Wesleyan Life—R
$-Whole Magazine
$-Wittenburg Door—R
$-World & I—R

CHILDREN
$-Cadet Quest—R
$-Club Connection
$-Faces
$-Guide—R
$-Partners—R
$-SHINEbrightly—R

CHRISTIAN EDUCATION/ LIBRARY
$-Children's Ministry
$-Journal/Adventist Educ.—R
$-Teachers of Vision—R

MISSIONS
$-PIME World—R
Railroad Evangelist—R
Women of the Harvest

PASTORS/LEADERS
$-Catholic Servant
$-Evangelical Baptist—R
$-Evangelicals Today—R
Journal/Pastoral Care—R
$-Parish Life—R
$-Pastoral Life—R
$-Preaching Well—R
$-Sabbath School Leadership—R
Sharing the Practice—R
Strategic Adult Ministries—R
$-Today's Parish—R
$-Worship Leader

TEEN/YOUNG ADULT
$-Boundless Webzine—R
$-Brio—R
$-Campus Life—R
GO!

$-Listen—R
$-Passageway.org—R
$-Real Faith in Life—R
$-Sharing the VICTORY—R
Teen Light—R
TeensForJC—R
Transcendmag.com—R
$-Young Christian—R

WOMEN

Anna's Journal—R
$-Esprit—R
Faithwebbin—R
$-Godly Business Woman
Handmaiden—R
Hearts at Home—R
Home-Based Moms—R
$-inSpirit—R
$-Journey
Just Between Us—R
$-Melody of the Heart
$-MOMsense—R
Precious Times—R
$-SpiritLed Woman
$-Today's Christian Woman—R
$-Woman's Touch—R
$-Women Alive!—R
Women of the Cross

WRITERS

$-Areopagus (UK)
$-Brady—R
$-Exchange—R
Money the Write Way—R
NW Christian Author—R
Once Upon a Time—R

PERSONAL GROWTH

ADULT/GENERAL

$-Alive Now—R
Alliance Life
$-Annals of St. Anne
$-Associated Content—R
$-Aujourd'hui Credo—R
$-Barefoot Path—R
$-BGC World—R
$-Bible Advocate—R
$-Brave Hearts
Bread of Life—R
Breakthrough Intercessor—R
$-Bridal Guides—R
$-Catholic Digest—R
$-Catholic Forester—R
$-Catholic New Times—R
$-Catholic Peace Voice—R
Channels—R
$-Christian Courier (CAN)—R

Christian Journal—R
Christian Online
Christian Ranchman
$-Church of God EVANGEL
$-Citizens in America
$-City Light News—R
Common Ground—R
$-Cup of Comfort—R
Divine Ascent
$-Dovetail—R
Eternal Ink—R
$-Evangel—R
Evangelical Advocate—R
$-Faith & Family
$-Faith & Friends—R
$-Faith Today
$-Gem—R
$-Generation X—R
$-God Allows U-Turns—R
Good News Journal
Hannah to Hannah—R
HopeKeepers—R
$-Horizons (adult)—R
$-Indian Life—R
$-Joy & Praise
Keys to Living—R
Leaves—R
$-Light & Life
Light at Home—R
$-Living—R
$-Living Church
$-Lookout
Maranatha News—R
Mature Times—R
$-Mature Years—R
Men of the Cross
Mosaic—R
Mutuality—R
$-My Walk With Jesus
New Heart—R
$-New Wineskins—R
$-Now What?—R
$-ONEvoice!
$-Palm Beach—R
Parents & Teens—R
Penned from the Heart
$-Plains Faith—R
$-Positive Thinking—R
PrayerWorks—R
$-Priority!—R
$-Psychology for Living—R
$-Purpose—R
Quaker Life—R
Randall House Periodicals
Regent Business—R
Sacred Journey—R

$-Seek—R
$-SingleAgain.com
Singles Scoop—R
Spiritual Voice—R
$-Spring Hill Review—R
$-St. Anthony Messenger
$-Standard—R
Steps
$-Stewardship—R
Storyteller—R
$-Testimony—R
thegoodsteward.com—R
$-Today's Christian—R
$-Together—R
Tributes—R
Trumpeter—R
Victory News—R
$-Vision—R
Walk This Way—R
$-War Cry—R
$-Way of St. Francis—R
$-World & I—R

CHILDREN

$-BREAD/God's Children—R
$-Cadet Quest—R
$-Guide—R
$-SHINEbrightly—R

CHRISTIAN EDUCATION/LIBRARY

$-Children's Ministry
$-Resource—R
$-Teachers Interaction
$-Youth & CE Leadership

MISSIONS

Women of the Harvest

PASTORS/LEADERS

$-Barefoot—R
Christian Management—R
$-Evangelical Baptist—R
$-Evangelicals Today—R
Ministry in Motion—R
$-Parish Life—R
$-Pastoral Life—R
$-RevWriter Resource
Sharing the Practice—R

TEEN/YOUNG ADULT

$-Brio—R
$-Passageway.org—R
$-Sharing the VICTORY—R
Teen Light—R
TeensForJC—R
Transcendmag.com—R
$-With—R
$-Young Adult Today—R

$-Young Christian—R
$-Young Salvationist—R

WOMEN
Anna's Journal—R
$-Esprit—R
Faithwebbin—R
$-Godly Business Woman
Hearts at Home—R
Home-Based Moms—R
$-Horizons (women)—R
$-inSpirit—R
$-Journey
Just Between Us—R
$-MOMsense—R
P31 Woman—R
Precious Times—R
Right to the Heart—R
$-SpiritLed Woman
$-Today's Christian Woman—R
$-Woman's Touch—R
Women of the Cross

WRITERS
$-Areopagus (UK)

PHOTO ESSAYS

ADULT/GENERAL
$-Animal Trails—R
$-Associated Content—R
$-Bridal Guides—R
Christian Motorsports
Citizen USA—R
$-City Light News—R
$-Cornerstone Christian—R
$-Faith & Family
$-Grit
Maranatha News—R
Men of the Cross
Nostalgia—R
$-Palm Beach—R
$-Plains Faith—R
Rock & Sling
Sacred Journey—R
$-Senior Living
Spiritual Voice—R
$-Spring Hill Review—R
$-St. Anthony Messenger
$-Today's Christian—R
$-Way of St. Francis—R
$-World & I—R

CHILDREN
$-Faces
Skipping Stones

TEEN/YOUNG ADULT
$-Credo—R

$-Passageway.org—R
Teen Light—R
TeensForJC—R
Transcendmag.com—R
$-Young Christian—R

WOMEN
$-Horizons (women)—R
Women of the Cross

PHOTOGRAPHS

Note: "Reprint" indicators (R) have been deleted from this section and "B" for black & white glossy prints or "C" for color transparencies inserted. An asterisk (*) before a listing indicates they buy photos with articles only.

ADULT/GENERAL
African Voices—B
Alive!—B
Alive Now—B/C
American Tract Society
Ancient Paths—B
Angelica—B/C
Anglican Journal—B/C
*Animal Trails—B/C
*Annals of St. Anne—B/C
*Arkansas Catholic—C
Arlington Catholic—B
Aspiring Retail—C
Associated Content—C
Barefoot Path—B/C
BGC World—C
Bible Advocate—C
Brave Hearts
*Bridal Guides—B/C
Canada Lutheran—B
*Cathedral Age—B
*Catholic Digest—B/C
Catholic Forester—B/C
Catholic New Times
Catholic New York—B
Catholic Peace Voice—B/C
Catholic Sentinel—B/C
Catholic Telegraph—B
Catholic Yearbook—C
*Celebrate Life—C
Celebrations Series—B/C
Charisma—C
*Christian Courier (CAN)—B
Christian Drama—B/C
*Christian Examiner—C
*Christian History—B/C
Christian Home & School—C
Christian Journal—B/C

Christian Leader—B/C
*Christian Motorsports—B
*Christian Online
Christian Parenting—B/C
Christian Radio Weekly
Christian Retailing—C
Christian Social Action—B
*Christian Standard—B/C
*Christianity Today—C
ChristianWeek—B/C
Church of God EVANGEL—C
Citizen USA—C
*Citizens in America—B/C
City Light News—B/C
*Commonweal—B/C
Connecting Point—B
Cornerstone Christian
Covenant Companion—B/C
Culture Wars—B/C
*DisciplesWorld
Divine Ascent—B
Dovetail—B
Episcopal Life—B
Eureka Street
*Evangel—B
Evangelical Advocate—B/C
Faith & Family—C
*Faith & Friends—C
*Faith Today—C
Focus on the Family—B/C
Foursquare World Advance
Good News Journal
Gospel Today
Gospel Tract—C
*Grit—B/C
*Guideposts–B/C
Highway News—B
Homeschooling Today—B/C
HonorBound—C
*HopeKeepers—B/C
*Horizons (adult)
Impact—B/C
*Indian Life—C
Inland NW Christian—B
*Inside Journal—B/C
Interchange—B
*Interim—B/C
Island Catholic News
*Layman—B
Leaves—B/C
Liberty—B/C
*Lifeglow—B/C
*LifeLine Journal—C
Light & Life—B/C
*Liguorian—C
Live—B/C

Living—B/C
Living Church—B/C
*Living Light News—B/C
Lookout—B/C
*Lutheran Journal—C
*Maranatha News—B
Marian Helper—B/C
*Mature Living
*Mature Years—C
Mennonite Brethren—B
Messenger—B
*Minnesota Christian—B/C
Montgomery's Journey
*Mosaic—B/C
Mutuality—B/C
*My Walk With Jesus—B
*New Heart—C
New Wineskins—B/C
Nostalgia—B/C
On Mission—B/C
*ONEvoice!—C
Our Sunday Visitor—B/C
Over the Back Fence—C
*Palm Beach—B/C
Parabola—B
*Perspectives—B
*Plains Faith—C
Power for Living—B
Presbyterian Outlook—B/C
Presbyterians Today—B/C
Prism—B/C
*Psychology for Living—C
*Purpose-—B
Quaker Life—B/C
Rhubarb—B
Rock & Sling—B/C
Sacred Journey—B/C
*Seek—C
Signs of the Times—C
Sojourners—C
*Special Living—B/C
Spiritual Life—B
Spiritual Voice—B/C
Sports Spectrum—C
Spring Hill Review—B
*St. Anthony Messenger—B/C
Standard—B
*Star of Zion
*Storyteller—B
*Testimony—B/C
*Today's Christian—B/C
Today's Pentecostal Evangel—B/C
Together—B/C
*Tributes—B/C
*United Church Observer—B/C
Upscale Magazine

*Vibrant Life—C
Vision—B/C
*Voice of the Lord
*Walk This Way—C
War Cry—B/C
War Cry (Canada)
Way of St. Francis—B
West Wind Review—B
White Wing Messenger—C
*World & I—B/C

CHILDREN
American Girl—C
Barefoot for Kids—B/C
Celebrate—C
*Focus/Clubhouse—C
*Focus/Clubhouse Jr.—C
Guideposts for Kids—C
*My Friend—C
Nature Friend—B/C
On the Line—B/C
*Pockets—B/C
Primary Pal (IL)
SHINEbrightly—C
Skipping Stones
Story Friends—B
*Winner—C

CHRISTIAN EDUCATION/ LIBRARY
*Christian Early Education—C
Christian Librarian—B
Church Educator—B
*Church Libraries—B/C
Journal/Adventist Educ.—B
*Leader in C. E. Ministries—B
RTJ—C
Teach Kids!—B/C
*Teachers Interaction—B
*Teachers of Vision—C
*Today's Catholic Teacher—C

DAILY DEVOTIONALS
Our Journey—C
Secret Place—B
Upper Room
Words of Life—B/C

MISSIONS
Evangelical Missions
Intl. Jour./Frontier
*New World Outlook—C
*One—C
OpRev Equipper—B/C
PFI World Report
*PIME World—B/C
*Wesleyan World

MUSIC
Christian Music Weekly—B
*Creator—B/C

PASTORS/LEADERS
Catholic Servant
Christian Century—B/C
Christian Management—C
Environment & Art—B/C
Evangelical Baptist—B/C
*InSite—C
Leadership—B
Lutheran Forum—B
*Lutheran Partners—B
Ministry—B
Parish Life—B/C
Rev.—C
*This Rock—B/C
Today's Parish—B/C
WCA News—C
*Worship Leader—C
Your Church—C

TEEN/YOUNG ADULT
Boundless Webzine
Breakaway—C
Brio—C
Campus Life—C
Credo—B/C
Essential Connection—B/C
Listen—B/C
Passageway.org—B/C
*Real Faith in Life—B
*Sharing the VICTORY—C
Student Leadership—B/C
Teen Light—C
With—B
Young Adult Today—B
*Young and Alive—B
*Young Christian—B/C

WOMEN
Anna's Journal—B
At the Center—C
*Esprit—B
FaithWebbin
Hearts at Home—B/C
*Home-Based Moms
*Link & Visitor—B
MOMsense—B/C
*Precious Times—C
Right to the Heart
Women Alive!—B

WRITERS
*Once Upon a Time
Tickled by Thunder
*Writer's Digest—B

Writes of Passage—B

POETRY

ADULT/GENERAL
African Voices—R
$-Alive Now—R
$-America
$-Ancient Paths—R
Angel Face—R
$-Angelica—R
$-Associated Content—R
$-Barefoot Path—R
$-Bible Advocate—R
$-Brave Hearts
Bread of Life—R
$-Bridal Guides—R
$-Catholic Forester—R
$-Catholic Peace Voice—R
$-Catholic Yearbook—R
Channels—R
$-Christian Courier (CAN)—R
Christian Journal—R
Christian Motorsports
Christian Ranchman
$-Christian Social Action—R
$-Commonweal
Connecting Point—R
$-Cornerstone Christian—R
$-Covenant Companion—R
$-Creation Illust.
$-Cresset
CrossHome.com
$-Culture Wars—R
$-Decision
Desert Call—R
$-DisciplesWorld
$-Dovetail—R
$-Dragons, Knights & Angels—R
Eternal Ink—R
$-Eureka Street
$-Evangel—R
$-First Things
Friends Journal—R
$-Gem—R
Good News Journal
$-Grit
Halo Magazine
Hannah to Hannah—R
Hard Row to Hoe
Highway News—R
$-Ideals—R
$-Image/WA
$-Impact—R
$-Indian Life—R
Infuze Magazine

Island Catholic News
Keys to Living—R
Leaves—R
$-Liberty—R
LifeTimes Catholic
$-Light & Life
Light at Home—R
$-Live—R
Looking Up
$-Lutheran Digest—R
$-Lutheran Journal—R
Mars Hill Review
$-Mature Living
Mature Times—R
$-Mature Years—R
Men of the Cross
$-Mennonite Brethren—R
$-Miraculous Medal
New Heart—R
$-New Wineskins—R
Nostalgia—R
$-Over the Back Fence—R
$-Palm Beach—R
$-Peeks & Valleys—R
Pegasus Review—R
Penned from the Heart
Penwood Review
Perspectives—R
Pietisten Online
Plowman—R
$-Poetry Scout
$-Prairie Messenger—R
Priscilla Papers—R
$-Purpose—R
Quaker Life—R
$-Queen of All Hearts
Radix—R
Rock & Sling
Rose & Thorn
Sacred Journey—R
Sharing—R
Short Stories Bimonthly—R
Silver Wings—R
$-SingleAgain.com
Singles Scoop—R
$-Sojourners
Spiritual Voice—R
$-Spring Hill Review—R
$-St. Anthony Messenger
$-St. Joseph's Messenger—R
St. Linus Review
$-Standard—R
Star of Zion
Storyteller—R
Studio—R

Sword and Trumpet—R
Sword of the Lord—R
$-Testimony—R
Time for Rhyme—R
Time of Singing—R
To God Be the Glory!
Tributes—R
$-U.S. Catholic
Valparaiso Poetry—R
Victory News—R
$-Vision—R
$-War Cry—R
$-Weavings—R
West Wind Review
Winsome Wit—R
$-Wittenburg Door—R
$-World & I—R
Xavier Review

CHILDREN
$-Adventures
$-American Girl
$-Barefoot for Kids—R
$-CharacterS—R
$-Faces
$-Focus/Clubhouse Jr.
$-Guideposts for Kids
$-My Friend
$-On the Line—R
$-Partners—R
$-Pockets—R
$-SHINEbrightly—R
Skipping Stones
$-Story Friends—R
$-Story Mates—R

CHRISTIAN EDUCATION/ LIBRARY
$-Church Educator—R
$-Teachers of Vision—R
$-Today's Catholic Teacher—R

DAILY DEVOTIONALS
$-Daily Meditation
$-Secret Place
$-These Days

MISSIONS
Railroad Evangelist—R
Women of the Harvest

MUSIC
$-Senior Musician—R

PASTORS/LEADERS
$-Catechumenate
$-Christian Century—R
Cross Currents
$-Emmanuel

Journal/Pastoral Care—R
$-Lutheran Partners—R
$-Preaching Well—R
Pulpit Helps—R
$-Review for Religious
Sharing the Practice—R
$-Theology Today

TEEN/YOUNG ADULT
$-Campus Life—R
$-Credo—R
$-Devo'Zine—R
$-Essential Connection
$-Insight—R
$-Student Leadership—R
Teen Light—R
$-Teenage Christian—R
TeensForJC—R
Transcendmag.com—R
$-Young Christian—R
$-Young Salvationist—R

WOMEN
Anna's Journal—R
$-Esprit—R
Handmaiden—R
Hearts at Home—R
Home-Based Moms—R
$-Link & Visitor—R
$-Melody of the Heart
Sisters in the Lord
Women of the Cross

WRITERS
$-Areopagus (UK)
$-Christian Communicator—R
ChristianWriters.com
$-Cross & Quill—R
Heaven—R
NW Christian Author—R
Omnific—R
Once Upon a Time—R
$-Tickled by Thunder
$-Upper Case
Write Touch
$-Writer's Digest—R
Writer's Network
$-Writers' Journal
Writes of Passage—R

POLITICAL

ADULT/GENERAL
African Voices—R
$-Anglican Journal
$-Arlington Catholic
$-Associated Content—R
Business Reform

$-Catholic Insight
$-Catholic New Times—R
$-Catholic Peace Voice—R
Christian C. L. RECORD—R
$-Christian Courier (CAN)—R
Christian Courier (WI)—R
$-Christian Examiner
Christian Media—R
$-Christian Renewal—R
$-Christian Social Action—R
$-Christianity Today—R
Citizen USA—R
$-Citizens in America
$-City Light News—R
$-Commonweal
$-Cornerstone Christian—R
Creation Care—R
Desert Voice
$-Faith Today
$-First Things
$-Generation X—R
Good News/S. Florida
Gospel Post
$-Inland NW Christian
$-Interim—R
Journal of Church & State
$-Light & Life
Metro Voice—R
Mid-South Christian
$-Minnesota Christian—R
$-National Catholic
Network
$-New Wineskins—R
$-Our Sunday Visitor
$-Palm Beach—R
Perspectives—R
$-Plains Faith—R
Presbyterian Outlook
$-Prism—R
$-Social Justice—R
$-Sojourners
Spiritual Voice—R
$-Spring Hill Review—R
$-St. Anthony Messenger
Sunday Magazine
$-Testimony—R
thegoodsteward.com—R
Tri-State Voice
Trumpeter—R
Victory News—R
$-World & I—R

MISSIONS
OpRev Equipper—R

PASTORS/LEADERS
$-Christian Century—R

$-Interpreter
$-Preaching Well—R
$-Word & World

TEEN/YOUNG ADULT
$-Inteen—R
$-With—R

PRAYER

ADULT/GENERAL
African Voices—R
AGAIN—R
$-Alive Now—R
$-Angels on Earth
$-Annals of St. Anne
$-Barefoot Path—R
$-Believer's Bay
$-BGC World—R
$-Bible Advocate—R
Bread of Life—R
Breakthrough Intercessor—R
$-Bridal Guides—R
$-Canada Lutheran—R
$-Catholic Digest—R
$-Catholic New Times—R
$-Catholic Peace Voice—R
$-Catholic Yearbook—R
$-Celebrate Life—R
$-CGA World—R
Christian Journal—R
$-Christian Leader—R
Christian Online
Christian Ranchman
Christian Research
$-Christianity Today—R
$-City Light News—R
$-Columbia
Connecting Point—R
$-Cornerstone Christian—R
$-Covenant Companion—R
Creation Care—R
$-Culture Wars—R
$-Decision
Desert Call—R
$-Discipleship Journal—R
Divine Ascent
$-Dovetail—R
$-Episcopal Life—R
Eternal Ink—R
$-Evangel—R
Evangelical Advocate—R
$-Faith & Family
$-Faith Today
$-Family Digest—R
$-Foursquare World Advance—R
$-Gem—R

$-God Allows U-Turns—R
$-Good News—R
Good News Journal
Gospel Tract—R
Heartlight—R
HopeKeepers—R
$-Horizons (adult)—R
$-Inland NW Christian
Leaves—R
$-Lifeglow—R
$-Light & Life
Light at Home—R
$-Live—R
$-Living Church
$-Lookout
$-Lutheran Digest—R
$-Lutheran Journal—R
Maranatha News—R
$-Marian Helper—R
$-Mature Living
Mature Times—R
$-Mature Years—R
$-Men of Integrity—R
$-Mennonite Brethren—R
Metro Voice—R
$-Montgomery's Journey
Mosaic—R
$-My Walk With Jesus
$-National Catholic
$-New Freeman—R
$-New Wineskins—R
$-Now What?—R
$-On Mission
$-ONEvoice!
$-Palm Beach—R
Pegasus Review—R
Penned from the Heart
$-Plain Truth—R
$-Plains Faith—R
Plowman—R
$-Positive Thinking—R
Prayer Closet
PrayerWorks—R
$-Precepts for Living
Presbyterian Outlook
$-Presbyterians Today—R
$-Priority!—R
Quaker Life—R
$-Queen of All Hearts
Randall House Periodicals
Sacred Journey—R
$-Signs of the Times—R
Silver Wings—R
Singles Scoop—R
$-Social Justice—R
$-Spiritual Life

Spiritual Voice—R
$-Spring Hill Review—R
$-St. Anthony Messenger
$-St. Joseph's Messenger—R
Sword of the Lord—R
$-Testimony—R
thegoodsteward.com—R
$-Today's Christian—R
$-Today's Pentecostal Evangel—R
Trumpeter—R
$-U.S. Catholic
Victory News—R
$-Vision—R
$-Voice of the Lord
$-War Cry—R
$-Way of St. Francis—R
$-Wesleyan Life—R
$-Whole Magazine

CHILDREN
$-Barefoot for Kids—R
$-BREAD/God's Children—R
$-Club Connection
$-Guide—R
$-Passport—R
$-Primary Street

CHRISTIAN EDUCATION/ LIBRARY
Catholic Library World
$-Children's Ministry
$-Church Educator—R
$-Resource—R
$-RTJ
$-Teach Kids!—R
$-Teachers of Vision—R
$-Youth & CE Leadership

DAILY DEVOTIONALS
Quiet Walk

MISSIONS
Intl. Jour./Frontier—R
$-PFI World Report—R
Railroad Evangelist—R
Wesleyan World—R

MUSIC
$-Creator—R

PASTORS/LEADERS
$-Barefoot—R
$-Catholic Servant
$-Church Worship
$-Clergy Journal—R
$-Diocesan Dialogue—R
$-Emmanuel
$-Enrichment—R
$-Evangelical Baptist—R

$-Evangelicals Today—R
$-Interpreter
$-Leadership—R
$-Ministries Today
$-Ministry & Liturgy—R
$-Parish Life—R
$-Pastoral Life—R
Pastors.com—R
$-Pray!—R
$-Preaching Well—R
$-Proclaim—R
Pulpit Helps—R
$-Reformed Worship
$-Review for Religious
Sewanee Theo. Review
Sharing the Practice—R
Theological Digest—R
$-Theology Today
$-Today's Christian Preacher—R
$-Today's Parish—R
$-Word & World
$-Worship Leader

TEEN/YOUNG ADULT
GO!
$-Inteen—R
$-J.A.M.
$-Passageway.org—R
$-Real Faith in Life—R
$-Student Leadership—R
Teen Light—R
$-Teenage Christian—R
TeensForJC—R
Transcendmag.com—R
$-With—R
$-Young and Alive—R
$-Young Christian—R
$-Young Salvationist—R

WOMEN
$-Esprit—R
Faithwebbin—R
Home-Based Moms—R
$-Horizons (women)—R
Inspired Moms.Com
$-inSpirit—R
$-Journey
Just Between Us—R
Lutheran Woman's Quar.
P31 Woman—R
Precious Times—R
Sisters in the Lord
$-SpiritLed Woman
$-Today's Christian Woman—R
$-Woman's Touch—R
$-Women Alive!—R
Women of the Cross

WRITERS
$-Areopagus (UK)

PROPHECY

ADULT/GENERAL
$-Apocalypse Chronicles—R
$-Believer's Bay
$-Bible Advocate—R
Breakthrough Intercessor—R
$-Christian Leader—R
Christian Media—R
Christian Online
Christian Research
Evangelical Advocate—R
$-Foursquare World Advance—R
Gospel Tract—R
Maranatha News—R
Metro Voice—R
Midnight Call
$-My Walk With Jesus
$-New Freeman—R
Penned from the Heart
$-Plains Faith—R
PrayerWorks—R
$-SingleAgain.com
Spiritual Voice—R
$-St. Anthony Messenger
Sword of the Lord—R
$-Testimony—R
thegoodsteward.com—R
Trumpeter—R
Victory News—R
$-Voice of the Lord

CHILDREN
$-BREAD/God's Children—R

PASTORS/LEADERS
$-Ministries Today
$-Pastoral Life—R
Pastors.com—R
Pulpit Helps—R
Sharing the Practice—R
$-Word & World

TEEN/YOUNG ADULT
$-Inteen—R
$-Real Faith in Life—R
TeensForJC—R
Transcendmag.com—R

WOMEN
$-SpiritLed Woman

PSYCHOLOGY

ADULT/GENERAL
$-Associated Content—R
$-Bridal Guides—R

$-Catholic New Times—R
$-Catholic Peace Voice—R
$-Christian Courier (CAN)—R
Christian Online
$-Citizens in America
$-Creative Nonfiction
$-Dovetail—R
Evangelical Advocate—R
$-Gem—R
$-Generation X—R
$-Light & Life
$-Psychology for Living—R
Quaker Life—R
$-Science & Spirit
Short Stories Bimonthly—R
$-Social Justice—R
$-Spiritual Life
Spiritual Voice—R
$-Spring Hill Review—R
$-St. Anthony Messenger
$-Testimony—R
thegoodsteward.com—R
Trumpeter—R
$-Vibrant Life—R
Victory News—R
$-World & I—R

CHRISTIAN EDUCATION/ LIBRARY
$-Church Educator—R

PASTORS/LEADERS
Journal/Pastoral Care—R
$-Ministries Today
$-Pastoral Life—R
Sharing the Practice—R
$-Word & World

PUPPET PLAYS

$-Barefoot for Kids—R
$-Children's Ministry
$-Christian Creative Arts
$-Club Connection
Maranatha News—R
Sharing the Practice—R
$-Sparkle
$-Teach Kids!—R
Teen Light—R

RACISM

ADULT/GENERAL
$-Catholic Peace Voice—R
Christian C. L. RECORD—R
$-Christian Social Action—R
$-Christianity Today—R
$-Creative Nonfiction
$-Dovetail—R

$-Faith Today
$-Generation X—R
$-Light & Life
$-Living—R
$-Lookout
$-Men of Integrity—R
$-Minnesota Christian—R
Mutuality—R
$-New Wineskins—R
$-ONEvoice!
$-Our Sunday Visitor
Perspectives—R
$-Plain Truth—R
$-Plains Faith—R
Priscilla Papers—R
$-Purpose—R
$-Sojourners
$-Spring Hill Review—R
$-St. Anthony Messenger
$-Testimony—R
thegoodsteward.com—R
$-Today's Christian—R
$-Together—R
Trumpeter—R
$-U.S. Catholic
$-Upscale Magazine
Victory News—R
$-World & I—R

CHILDREN
$-Guide—R
$-Our Little Friend—R
$-Primary Treasure—R
Skipping Stones

PASTORS/LEADERS
$-Christian Century—R
$-Clergy Journal—R
Cross Currents
Journal/Pastoral Care—R
$-Lutheran Partners—R
$-Parish Life—R
$-Pastoral Life—R

TEEN/YOUNG ADULT
$-Campus Life—R
$-Passageway.org—R
$-Student Leadership—R
Teen Light—R
TeensForJC—R
Transcendmag.com—R

WOMEN
$-Esprit—R
$-Horizons (women)—R
$-inSpirit—R
Making Waves
$-SpiritLed Woman

WRITERS
Teachers & Writers

RECOVERY*

ADULT/GENERAL
$-Bible Advocate—R
$-City Light News—R
HopeKeepers—R
$-Now What?—R
$-Plains Faith—R
Quaker Life—R
Randall House Periodicals
Spiritual Voice—R
$-Spring Hill Review—R
Steps

PASTORS/LEADERS
Journal/Pastoral Care—R

RELATIONSHIPS

ADULT/GENERAL
Alliance Life
$-Angels on Earth
$-Annals of St. Anne
$-Associated Content—R
$-Barefoot Path—R
$-BGC World—R
Bread of Life—R
Breakthrough Intercessor—R
$-Bridal Guides—R
$-Canada Lutheran—R
Canadian Mennonite
$-Catholic Digest—R
$-Catholic Forester—R
$-Celebrate Life—R
$-Celebrations Series—R
Channels—R
$-Chicken Soup—R
Christian Journal—R
$-Christian Leader—R
Christian Online
Christian Ranchman
$-City Light News—R
$-Cornerstone Christian—R
$-Creative Nonfiction
$-Cup of Comfort—R
Desert Call—R
$-Discipleship Journal—R
$-Dovetail—R
$-Evangel—R
Evangelical Advocate—R
$-Faith Today
$-Foursquare World Advance—R
$-Gem—R
$-Gems of Truth—R
$-Generation X—R

$-God Allows U-Turns—R
Good News Journal
$-Gospel Today—R
$-Guideposts—R
Hannah to Hannah—R
Heartlight—R
Highway News—R
$-Homeschooling Today—R
$-HonorBound—R
HopeKeepers—R
$-Horizons (adult)—R
$-Inside Journal—R
Keys to Living—R
$-Lifeglow—R
LifeLine Journal—R
$-Light & Life
Light at Home—R
$-Live—R
$-Living—R
$-Lutheran Digest—R
$-Marriage Partnership—R
Mature Times—R
$-Mature Years—R
$-Men of Integrity—R
Mennonite Historian—R
Metro Voice—R
$-Minnesota Christian—R
$-Montgomery's Journey
Mutuality—R
New Heart—R
$-New Wineskins—R
$-ONEvoice!
$-Our Sunday Visitor
$-Palm Beach—R
Parents & Teens—R
Pegasus Review—R
Penned from the Heart
$-Plain Truth—R
$-Plains Faith—R
$-Positive Thinking—R
$-Prairie Messenger—R
PrayerWorks—R
Priscilla Papers—R
Quaker Life—R
Sacred Journey—R
$-Science & Spirit
Silver Wings—R
$-SingleAgain.com
Singles Scoop—R
$-Smart Families—R
$-Special Living—R
Spiritual Voice—R
$-Spring Hill Review—R
$-St. Anthony Messenger
$-Standard—R
Steps

Storyteller—R
$-Testimony—R
thegoodsteward.com—R
$-Today's Christian—R
$-Today's Pentecostal Evangel—R
$-Together—R
Trumpeter—R
$-Upscale Magazine
$-Vibrant Life—R
Victory News—R
$-Vision—R
Walk This Way—R
$-War Cry—R
$-Wesleyan Life—R
$-Whole Magazine
$-World & I—R

CHILDREN
$-BREAD/God's Children—R
$-Cadet Quest—R
$-Club Connection
$-Guide—R
$-My Friend
$-Passport—R
$-Sparkle
$-Winner—R

CHRISTIAN EDUCATION/ LIBRARY
$-Resource—R
$-Teachers of Vision—R
$-Youth & CE Leadership

MISSIONS
$-American Baptists in Mission

PASTORS/LEADERS
$-Evangelical Baptist—R
$-Evangelicals Today—R
$-Ministries Today
$-Pastoral Life—R
Sharing the Practice—R
$-Small Group Dynamics—R
Strategic Adult Ministries—R
$-Word & World

TEEN/YOUNG ADULT
$-Boundless Webzine—R
$-Brio—R
$-Credo—R
GO!
$-Guideposts Sweet 16—R
$-Listen—R
$-Passageway.org—R
$-Real Faith in Life—R
$-Student Leadership—R
Teen Light—R
$-Teenage Christian—R
TeensForJC—R

Transcendmag.com—R
$-With—R
$-Young and Alive—R
$-Young Christian—R

WOMEN
$-At the Center—R
$-Dabbling Mum.com—R
$-Esprit—R
Faithwebbin—R
Heart & Soul
Hearts at Home—R
Home-Based Moms—R
Inspired Moms.Com
$-inSpirit—R
$-Journey
Just Between Us—R
Life Tools for Women
$-Link & Visitor—R
Lutheran Woman's Quar.
$-MOMsense—R
P31 Woman—R
Precious Times—R
$-Simple Joy
$-SpiritLed Woman
$-Today's Christian Woman—R
$-Woman's Touch—R
Women of the Cross
Women Today—R

RELIGIOUS FREEDOM

ADULT/GENERAL
$-Arlington Catholic
Breakthrough Intercessor—R
$-Catholic New Times—R
$-Catholic Peace Voice—R
Channels—R
Christian C. L. RECORD—R
Christian Courier (WI)—R
$-Christian Examiner
$-Christian Leader—R
Christian News NW—R
Christian Observer
Christian Online
$-Christian Response—R
$-Christian Social Action—R
$-Christianity Today—R
Citizen USA—R
$-Columbia
$-Commonweal
Compass Direct
Connecting Point—R
$-Cornerstone Christian—R
Desert Voice
$-Dovetail—R
$-Episcopal Life—R
$-Faith Today

$-First Things
$-Gem—R
$-Generation X—R
Good News in RI
Good News/S. Florida
$-Interim—R
Journal of Church & State
$-Liberty—R
$-Lifeglow—R
$-Light & Life
$-Lookout
Maranatha News—R
MESSAGE/Open Bible—R
Metro Voice—R
$-Minnesota Christian—R
$-National Catholic
$-New Freeman—R
$-New Wineskins—R
$-Our Sunday Visitor
$-Palm Beach—R
Pegasus Review—R
$-Plain Truth—R
$-Plains Faith—R
Plowman—R
PrayerWorks—R
Presbyterian Outlook
$-Prism—R
$-Science & Spirit
$-Social Justice—R
$-Spiritual Life
$-Spring Hill Review—R
$-St. Anthony Messenger
$-Standard—R
$-Testimony—R
thegoodsteward.com—R
Trumpeter—R
Victory News—R
Winsome Wit—R
$-World & I—R

CHILDREN
$-Guide—R
Skipping Stones

CHRISTIAN EDUCATION/ LIBRARY
$-Teachers of Vision—R

MISSIONS
East-West Church
$-Evangelical Missions—R
OpRev Equipper—R

PASTORS/LEADERS
$-Catholic Servant
$-Church Worship
Cross Currents
$-Pastoral Life—R

Pulpit Helps—R
Sharing the Practice—R
$-This Rock
$-Word & World

TEEN/YOUNG ADULT
$-Inteen—R
$-Passageway.org—R
Teen Light—R
TeensForJC—R
Transcendmag.com—R

WOMEN
$-Esprit—R
$-SpiritLed Woman

RELIGIOUS TOLERANCE

ADULT/GENERAL
$-Catholic Peace Voice—R
Channels—R
Christian C. L. RECORD—R
$-Christian Examiner
Christian Online
$-Christian Social Action—R
$-Christianity Today—R
$-City Light News—R
$-Columbia
$-Dovetail—R
$-Faith Today
$-Generation X—R
$-Light & Life
$-Minnesota Christian—R
$-National Catholic
$-New Wineskins—R
$-Our Sunday Visitor
$-Palm Beach—R
$-Plains Faith—R
$-Prairie Messenger—R
PrayerWorks—R
$-Science & Spirit
$-Spring Hill Review—R
$-St. Anthony Messenger
Star of Zion
$-Testimony—R
thegoodsteward.com—R
Trumpeter—R
Victory News—R
$-World & I—R

CHILDREN
$-Primary Treasure—R
Skipping Stones

MISSIONS
OpRev Equipper—R

PASTORS/LEADERS
$-Clergy Journal—R
Cross Currents

$-Parish Life—R
$-Pastoral Life—R

TEEN/YOUNG ADULT
$-Campus Life—R
$-Passageway.org—R
$-Student Leadership—R
Teen Light—R
TeensForJC—R
Transcendmag.com—R

WOMEN
$-Esprit—R

WRITERS
Teachers & Writers

REVIVAL*

ADULT/GENERAL
$-Palm Beach—R
Penned from the Heart
$-Plains Faith—R
Spiritual Voice—R

SALVATION TESTIMONIES

ADULT/GENERAL
Alliance Life
American Tract Society—R
$-Believer's Bay
$-BGC World—R
$-Bible Advocate—R
Breakthrough Intercessor—R
Channels—R
Christian Journal—R
Christian Motorsports
Christian Online
Christian Ranchman
Church Herald & Holiness—R
$-Church of God EVANGEL
Connecting Point—R
Crossway/Newsline—R
$-Decision
Eternal Ink—R
Evangelical Advocate—R
$-Faith Today
$-Gem—R
Gospel Tract—R
$-Guideposts—R
Highway News—R
$-Inside Journal—R
$-Joyful Noise!
Leaves—R
$-Lifeglow—R
$-Light & Life
Maranatha News—R
Mature Times—R
$-Men of Integrity—R

$-Mennonite Brethren—R
$-New Freeman—R
New Heart—R
$-Now What?—R
$-Palm Beach—R
Parents & Teens—R
$-Plains Faith—R
$-Power for Living—R
$-Priority!—R
$-Seek—R
$-Signs of the Times—R
Silver Wings—R
Singles Scoop—R
Spiritual Voice—R
$-St. Anthony Messenger
Sword of the Lord—R
$-Testimony—R
thegoodsteward.com—R
$-Today's Christian—R
$-Today's Pentecostal Evangel—R
$-Together—R
Trumpeter—R
Victory News—R
$-War Cry—R
$-Wesleyan Life—R

CHILDREN
$-BREAD/God's Children—R
$-Club Connection
$-Guide—R

CHRISTIAN EDUCATION/ LIBRARY
Catholic Library World
$-Teach Kids!—R

MISSIONS
Railroad Evangelist—R

PASTORS/LEADERS
$-Evangelicals Today—R
$-Pastoral Life—R
Pulpit Helps—R
$-This Rock

TEEN/YOUNG ADULT
GO!
$-Inteen—R
$-Passageway.org—R
TeensForJC—R
Transcendmag.com—R
$-With—R

WOMEN
$-Esprit—R
$-Godly Business Woman
$-History's Women—R
$-Journey
Precious Times—R

$-SpiritLed Woman
Women Today—R

WRITERS
$-Areopagus (UK)

SCIENCE

ADULT/GENERAL
$-Associated Content—R
$-Catholic New Times—R
Christian C. L. RECORD—R
$-Christian Courier (CAN)—R
$-Christian Networks
Christian Post
$-Christian Social Action—R
Citizen USA—R
$-City Light News—R
Creation
$-Creation Illust.
$-Creative Nonfiction
$-Cresset
$-Eclectic Homeschool
$-Faith Today
$-Light & Life
$-Lutheran Digest—R
Men of the Cross
Metro Voice—R
$-National Catholic
$-New Freeman—R
Perspectives—R
$-Plains Faith—R
$-Science & Spirit
$-Spring Hill Review—R
$-St. Anthony Messenger
$-Testimony—R
thegoodsteward.com—R
TJ
Trumpeter—R
$-World & I—R

CHILDREN
$-Barefoot for Kids—R
$-Guideposts for Kids
$-My Friend
$-Nature Friend
$-SHINEbrightly—R
$-Sparkle

MISSIONS
Intl. Jour./Frontier—R

PASTORS/LEADERS
$-Lutheran Partners—R
$-Word & World

TEEN/YOUNG ADULT
$-Inteen—R
$-Passageway.org—R
TeensForJC—R

Transcendmag.com—R
$-Young Christian—R

WOMEN
$-Esprit—R

SELF-HELP

ADULT/GENERAL
$-Associated Content—R
$-Bridal Guides—R
$-Catholic Digest—R
$-CGA World—R
Christian Journal—R
$-City Light News—R
Disciple's Journal—R
$-Dovetail—R
Hannah to Hannah—R
HopeKeepers—R
$-Lifeglow—R
$-Light & Life
Light at Home—R
$-Living—R
$-Marriage Partnership—R
$-Palm Beach—R
$-Plains Faith—R
Randall House Periodicals
$-SingleAgain.com
$-Smart Families—R
$-Social Justice—R
$-Special Living—R
Spiritual Voice—R
$-Spring Hill Review—R
$-St. Anthony Messenger
$-Standard—R
$-Testimony—R
thegoodsteward.com—R
Trumpeter—R
$-Vibrant Life—R
Victory News—R
$-Vision—R
$-World & I—R

CHILDREN
$-Barefoot for Kids—R
Skipping Stones
$-Winner—R

MISSIONS
Women of the Harvest

PASTORS/LEADERS
$-Evangelicals Today—R
$-Interpreter

TEEN/YOUNG ADULT
$-Guideposts Sweet 16—R
Teen Light—R
$-Teenage Christian—R

TeensForJC—R
Transcendmag.com—R
$-Young and Alive—R
$-Young Christian—R

WOMEN
Home-Based Moms—R
$-Journey
$-MOMsense—R
$-Today's Christian Woman—R

WRITERS
Money the Write Way—R

SENIOR ADULT ISSUES

ADULT/GENERAL
$-Alive!—R
$-Angels on Earth
$-Anglican Journal
$-Annals of St. Anne
$-Associated Content—R
$-B.C. Catholic—R
Breakthrough Intercessor—R
byFaith
$-Canada Lutheran—R
$-Catholic Forester—R
$-Catholic New Times—R
$-CGA World—R
Christian Journal—R
Church Herald & Holiness—R
$-Citizens in America
$-City Light News—R
Discovery—R
$-Dovetail—R
$-Evangel—R
Evangelical Advocate—R
$-Gem—R
$-Homeschooling Today—R
HopeKeepers—R
$-Lifeglow—R
LifeLine Journal—R
$-Light & Life
Light at Home—R
$-Live—R
Looking Up
Maranatha News—R
$-Mature Living
$-Mature Years—R
Metro Voice—R
$-New Freeman—R
$-Palm Beach—R
Penned from the Heart
$-Plains Faith—R
$-Power for Living—R
PrayerWorks—R
Quaker Life—R

Randall House Periodicals
$-Senior Living
$-SingleAgain.com
$-Smart Families—R
$-Spring Hill Review—R
$-St. Anthony Messenger
Star of Zion
$-Testimony—R
thegoodsteward.com—R
$-Today's Christian—R
Trumpeter—R
$-U.S. Catholic
Victory News—R
$-Vision—R
$-War Cry—R
$-Wesleyan Life—R

CHRISTIAN EDUCATION/ LIBRARY
$-Church Educator—R
$-Resource—R
$-Youth & CE Leadership

MUSIC
$-Senior Musician—R

PASTORS/LEADERS
Christian Education Jour. (CA)—R
$-Diocesan Dialogue—R
$-Evangelical Baptist—R
$-Evangelicals Today—R
$-Interpreter
$-Parish Life—R
$-Pastoral Life—R
Sharing the Practice—R
$-Word & World

WOMEN
$-Esprit—R
$-Today's Christian Woman—R

SERMONS

ADULT/GENERAL
$-Arlington Catholic
Breakthrough Intercessor—R
$-Cathedral Age
$-Catholic Yearbook—R
Christian Ranchman
Church Herald & Holiness—R
Creation Care—R
$-Lutheran Journal—R
Maranatha News—R
$-My Walk With Jesus
Pegasus Review—R
$-St. Anthony Messenger
Star of Zion
$-Stewardship—R
Sword of the Lord—R

$-Testimony—R
Trumpeter—R
$-Way of St. Francis—R
$-Weavings—R

PASTORS/LEADERS
$-African American Pulpit
$-Church Worship
$-Clergy Journal—R
$-Enrichment—R
$-Evangelicals Today—R
Interpretation
$-Lutheran Partners—R
Preaching—R
$-Preaching Well—R
$-Proclaim—R
Pulpit Helps—R
$-Sermon Notes—R
Sharing the Practice—R
$-Sunday Sermons—R
$-Today's Parish—R

SHORT STORY: ADULT/RELIGIOUS

African Voices—R
$-Alive!—R
$-Alive Now—R
$-Ancient Paths—R
$-Angelica—R
$-Angels on Earth
$-Animal Trails—R
Anna's Journal—R
$-Annals of St. Anne
$-Areopagus (UK)
$-Associated Content—R
$-Aujourd'hui Credo—R
$-Believer's Bay
$-Bridal Guides—R
$-Catholic Forester—R
$-Catholic Yearbook—R
$-CGA World—R
$-Christian Century—R
$-Christian Courier (CAN)—R
$-Christian Educators Journal—R
$-Christian Home & School
Christian Journal—R
Christian Online
Christian Radio Weekly
Christian Ranchman
$-Christian Renewal—R
Church & Synagogue Lib.—R
$-Citizens in America
Connecting Point—R
$-Covenant Companion—R
Cross Currents
$-DisciplesWorld

$-Dragons, Knights & Angels—R
$-Dreams & Visions—R
$-Esprit—R
Eternal Ink—R
$-Eureka Street
$-Evangel—R
$-Faith & Family
Fire By Nite
$-Five Stones—R
$-Gem—R
$-Gems of Truth—R
Good News Journal
Hard Row to Hoe
Heartlight—R
Heaven—R
$-Horizons (adult)—R
$-Horizons (women)—R
$-Ideals—R
$-Image/WA
$-Impact—R
$-Indian Life—R
Infuze Magazine
$-inSpirit—R
$-Joyful Noise!
$-Live—R
$-Living Light News—R
$-Lutheran Journal—R
Lutheran Woman's Quar.
Mars Hill Review
$-Mature Living
Mature Times—R
$-Mature Years—R
$-Melody of the Heart
$-Mennonite Brethren—R
$-Messenger/Sacred Heart
$-Messenger/St. Anthony
$-Miraculous Medal
$-My Legacy—R
$-National Catholic
$-New Wineskins—R
$-Palm Beach—R
Parables—R
Pastors.com—R
$-Peeks & Valleys—R
Pegasus Review—R
$-Plain Truth—R
Plowman—R
PrayerWorks—R
Precious Times—R
$-Proclaim—R
$-Purpose—R
$-Queen of All Hearts
Railroad Evangelist—R
Seeds of Hope
$-Seek—R
$-Shades of Romance—R

Short Stories Bimonthly—R
Singles Scoop—R
Spiritual Voice—R
$-Spring Hill Review—R
$-St. Anthony Messenger
$-St. Joseph's Messenger—R
St. Linus Review
$-Standard—R
Storyteller—R
Studio—R
$-Testimony—R
$-Tickled by Thunder
$-U.S. Catholic
$-Upper Case
$-Vision—R
$-Voice of the Lord
Walk This Way—R
$-War Cry—R
$-Wesleyan Life—R
West Wind Review
$-Whole Magazine
Winsome Wit—R
$-Women Alive!—R
Write Touch

SHORT STORY: ADVENTURE

ADULT
$-Alive!—R
$-Angels on Earth
$-Animal Trails—R
$-Annals of St. Anne
$-Associated Content—R
$-Cappers
$-Christian Century—R
Christian Journal—R
Christian Radio Weekly
$-Citizens in America
$-Cornerstone Christian—R
$-Dreams & Visions—R
Eternal Ink—R
Fire By Nite
$-Gem—R
$-Grit
Heartlight—R
Infuze Magazine
$-Live—R
$-Mature Living
$-My Legacy—R
Parables—R
$-Peeks & Valleys—R
PrayerWorks—R
$-Purpose—R
Rose & Thorn
Spiritual Voice—R

$-Spring Hill Review—R
St. Linus Review
$-Standard—R
Storyteller—R
Studio—R
Victory News—R
$-Vision—R
$-Voice of the Lord
$-Weavings—R

CHILDREN
$-American Girl
$-Barefoot for Kids—R
$-BREAD/God's Children—R
$-Cadet Quest—R
$-Club Connection
Connecting Point—R
$-Cornerstone Christian—R
$-Courage—R
Eternal Ink—R
$-Focus/Clubhouse
$-Focus/Clubhouse Jr.
$-High Adventure—R
$-Junior Companion—R
$-My Friend
$-Partners—R
$-Primary Pal (IL)
$-SHINEbrightly—R
$-Sparkle
Spiritual Voice—R
$-Story Friends—R
Sword of the Lord—R
Victory News—R

TEEN/YOUNG ADULT
$-BREAD/God's Children—R
$-Cadet Quest—R
$-Cornerstone Christian—R
$-Credo—R
$-Inteen—R
$-Partners—R
$-SHINEbrightly—R
Spiritual Voice—R
Sword of the Lord—R
Teen Light—R
$-Teenage Christian—R
TeensForJC—R
Transcendmag.com—R
Victory News—R
$-Young Adult Today—R
$-Young Christian—R
$-Young Salvationist—R

**SHORT STORY:
ALLEGORY**

ADULT
$-Animal Trails—R

$-Associated Content—R
$-Christian Century—R
Christian Journal—R
$-Covenant Companion—R
$-Dragons, Knights & Angels—R
$-Dreams & Visions—R
$-Esprit—R
Fire By Nite
$-Gem—R
Heartlight—R
$-Indian Life—R
Infuze Magazine
$-Mennonite Brethren—R
$-My Legacy—R
$-New Wineskins—R
Parables—R
$-Plain Truth—R
PrayerWorks—R
Railroad Evangelist—R
Spiritual Voice—R
St. Linus Review
Studio—R
$-Vision—R
Walk This Way—R

CHILDREN
$-Barefoot for Kids—R
$-Dragons, Knights & Angels—R
$-Nature Friend
Spiritual Voice—R
Sword of the Lord—R

TEEN/YOUNG ADULT
$-Dragons, Knights & Angels—R
Spiritual Voice—R
$-Student Leadership—R
Sword of the Lord—R
Teen Light—R
$-With—R
$-Young Salvationist—R

**SHORT STORY:
BIBLICAL**

ADULT
$-Animal Trails—R
$-Annals of St. Anne
$-Aujourd'hui Credo—R
Bread of Life—R
$-Catholic Yearbook—R
$-CGA World—R
Christian Journal—R
Christian Online
Christian Ranchman
Church & Synagogue Lib.—R
$-Church Worship
Connecting Point—R
$-Cornerstone Christian—R

$-Dreams & Visions—R
Eternal Ink—R
$-Evangel—R
Fire By Nite
$-Gem—R
Heartlight—R
$-Horizons (women)—R
$-Lutheran Journal—R
Lutheran Woman's Quar.
$-Mennonite Brethren—R
$-My Legacy—R
$-National Catholic
$-New Wineskins—R
Parables—R
PrayerWorks—R
$-Purpose—R
Railroad Evangelist—R
$-Seek—R
Spiritual Voice—R
St. Linus Review
Studio—R
$-Teach Kids!—R
Victory News—R
$-War Cry—R
$-Wesleyan Life—R
$-Whole Magazine

CHILDREN
$-Adventures
$-Barefoot for Kids—R
$-BREAD/God's Children—R
$-Cornerstone Christian—R
Eternal Ink—R
$-Focus/Clubhouse
$-Focus/Clubhouse Jr.
$-Nature Friend
$-Pockets—R
Spiritual Voice—R
Sword of the Lord—R
$-Teach Kids!—R
Victory News—R

TEEN/YOUNG ADULT
$-BREAD/God's Children—R
$-Cornerstone Christian—R
$-Inteen—R
Spiritual Voice—R
$-Student Leadership—R
Sword of the Lord—R
Teen Light—R
$-Teenage Christian—R
TeensForJC—R
Transcendmag.com—R
Victory News—R
$-Young Adult Today—R
$-Young Christian—R

SHORT STORY: CONTEMPORARY

ADULT
African Voices—R
$-Ancient Paths—R
$-Angels on Earth
$-Animal Trails—R
$-Annals of St. Anne
$-Associated Content—R
$-Bridal Guides—R
$-Byline
$-Canada Lutheran—R
$-Christian Century—R
$-Christian Courier (CAN)—R
Christian Radio Weekly
$-Christian Renewal—R
Connecting Point—R
$-Cornerstone Christian—R
$-Covenant Companion—R
$-Dreams & Visions—R
$-Esprit—R
$-Evangel—R
Fire By Nite
$-Gem—R
Hard Row to Hoe
Heartlight—R
&-Horizons (adult)—R
$-Ideals—R
$-Indian Life—R
Infuze Magazine
$-Living Light News—R
$-Mature Living
Mature Times—R
$-My Legacy—R
$-National Catholic
$-New Wineskins—R
Parables—R
$-Peeks & Valleys—R
Precious Times—R
Railroad Evangelist—R
$-Seek—R
Singles Scoop—R
Spiritual Voice—R
$-Spring Hill Review—R
$-St. Anthony Messenger
$-St. Joseph's Messenger—R
St. Linus Review
$-Standard—R
Storyteller—R
Studio—R
$-Teach Kids!—R
$-U.S. Catholic
Victory News—R
$-War Cry—R
West Wind Review

$-Whole Magazine
Xavier Review

CHILDREN
$-Adventures
$-American Girl
$-Barefoot for Kids—R
$-BREAD/God's Children—R
$-Cadet Quest—R
$-Club Connection
$-Cornerstone Christian—R
$-Courage—R
$-Focus/Clubhouse
$-Focus/Clubhouse Jr.
$-Guideposts for Kids
$-My Friend
$-On the Line—R
$-Partners—R
$-Pockets—R
$-Primary Pal (IL)
$-SHINEbrightly—R
Spiritual Voice—R
$-Story Friends—R
$-Story Mates—R
$-Teach Kids!—R
Victory News—R
$-Winner—R

TEEN/YOUNG ADULT
$-BREAD/God's Children—R
$-Cadet Quest—R
$-Campus Life—R
$-Cornerstone Christian—R
$-Essential Connection
$-Living My Faith
$-Partners—R
$-Real Faith in Life—R
Spiritual Voice—R
Teen Light—R
$-Teenage Christian—R
TeensForJC—R
Transcendmag.com—R
Victory News—R
$-Young Christian—R

SHORT STORY: ETHNIC

ADULT
African Voices—R
$-Animal Trails—R
$-Associated Content—R
$-Bridal Guides—R
$-CGA World—R
$-Dreams & Visions—R
$-Esprit—R
Fire By Nite
$-Gem—R
Hard Row to Hoe

$-Indian Life—R
$-Live—R
Parables—R
$-Peeks & Valleys—R
Spiritual Voice—R
St. Linus Review
Studio—R
$-U.S. Catholic
Victory News—R
Xavier Review

CHILDREN
$-BREAD/God's Children—R
$-Club Connection
$-Focus/Clubhouse
$-Focus/Clubhouse Jr.
$-My Friend
Spiritual Voice—R
Victory News—R

TEEN/YOUNG ADULT
$-BREAD/God's Children—R
$-SHINEbrightly—R
Spiritual Voice—R
Teen Light—R
TeensForJC—R
Transcendmag.com—R
Victory News—R
$-Young Christian—R
$-Young Salvationist—R

SHORT STORY: FANTASY

ADULT
$-Associated Content—R
Challenging Destiny
Connecting Point—R
$-Dragons, Knights & Angels—R
$-Dreams & Visions—R
Fire By Nite
Gateway S-F—R
$-Gem—R
$-Impact—R
Infuze Magazine
$-My Legacy—R
Parables—R
$-Peeks & Valleys—R
Rose & Thorn
Spiritual Voice—R
St. Linus Review
Storyteller—R
Studio—R
$-Tickled by Thunder

CHILDREN
$-Barefoot for Kids—R
$-Dragons, Knights & Angels—R
$-Focus/Clubhouse

$-Guideposts for Kids
$-SHINEbrightly—R
$-Sparkle
Spiritual Voice—R
Sword of the Lord—R

TEEN/YOUNG ADULT
$-Credo—R
$-Dragons, Knights & Angels—R
$-Inteen—R
$-SHINEbrightly—R
Spiritual Voice—R
Sword of the Lord—R
Teen Light—R
TeensForJC—R
Transcendmag.com—R
$-With—R
$-Young Adult Today—R
$-Young Salvationist—R

SHORT STORY: FRONTIER

ADULT
$-Animal Trails—R
$-Associated Content—R
$-Cappers
Connecting Point—R
Eternal Ink—R
Fire By Nite
$-Gem—R
$-Grit
$-Indian Life—R
Infuze Magazine
$-My Legacy—R
Parables—R
$-Peeks & Valleys—R
Spiritual Voice—R
St. Linus Review
Storyteller—R
Studio—R
Victory News—R
$-Voice of the Lord

CHILDREN
Beginnings—R
Eternal Ink—R
$-Guideposts for Kids
$-High Adventure—R
$-SHINEbrightly—R
Sword of the Lord—R
Victory News—R

TEEN/YOUNG ADULT
$-Credo—R
Spiritual Voice—R
Sword of the Lord—R
Teen Light—R

Victory News—R
$-Young Christian—R

SHORT STORY: FRONTIER/ROMANCE
$-Associated Content—R
$-Bridal Guides—R
$-Cappers
Connecting Point—R
$-Dreams & Visions—R
Fire By Nite
$-Gem—R
$-Grit
$-My Legacy—R
Parables—R
Spiritual Voice—R
St. Linus Review
Storyteller—R
Studio—R
Teen Light—R
Victory News—R
$-Young Christian—R

SHORT STORY: HISTORICAL

ADULT
$-Alive!—R
$-Ancient Paths—R
$-Animal Trails—R
$-Associated Content—R
$-Aujourd'hui Credo—R
$-Bridal Guides—R
$-Cappers
$-Christian Renewal—R
$-Citizens in America
Connecting Point—R
$-Cornerstone Christian—R
Fire By Nite
$-Gem—R
$-Grit
Heartlight—R
$-Ideals—R
$-Indian Life—R
Infuze Magazine
$-Live—R
Lutheran Woman's Quar.
Mature Times—R
$-My Legacy—R
$-National Catholic
$-Palm Beach—R
Parables—R
$-Peeks & Valleys—R
$-Purpose—R
Railroad Evangelist—R
Rose & Thorn

$-Seek—R
Singles Scoop—R
Spiritual Voice—R
St. Linus Review
Storyteller—R
Studio—R
Victory News—R
$-Voice of the Lord

CHILDREN
$-Barefoot for Kids—R
$-BREAD/God's Children—R
$-Club Connection
$-Cornerstone Christian—R
$-Courage—R
$-Focus/Clubhouse
$-Guideposts for Kids
$-High Adventure—R
$-Nature Friend
$-Palm Beach—R
$-Partners—R
$-SHINEbrightly—R
Spiritual Voice—R
Sword of the Lord—R
Victory News—R
Young Gentleman's Monthly

TEEN/YOUNG ADULT
$-BREAD/God's Children—R
$-Cornerstone Christian—R
$-Credo—R
$-Inteen—R
$-Palm Beach—R
$-Partners—R
$-SHINEbrightly—R
Spiritual Voice—R
Sword of the Lord—R
Teen Light—R
Victory News—R
$-Young Adult Today—R
$-Young Christian—R

SHORT STORY: HISTORICAL/ROMANCE
African Voices—R
$-Areopagus (UK)
$-Associated Content—R
$-Bridal Guides—R
$-Cappers
Connecting Point—R
$-Dreams & Visions—R
Fire By Nite
$-Gem—R
$-Grit
$-My Legacy—R
Parables—R
$-Purpose—R

$-St. Anthony Messenger
St. Linus Review
Storyteller—R
Studio—R
Teen Light—R
Victory News—R
$-Voice of the Lord
$-Young Christian—R

SHORT STORY: HUMOROUS

ADULT
African Voices—R
$-Alive!—R
$-Ancient Paths—R
$-Animal Trails—R
$-Associated Content—R
Beginnings—R
$ Canada Lutheran—R
$-Catholic Forester—R
$-CGA World—R
$-Christian Courier (CAN)—R
Christian Journal—R
Christian Radio Weekly
Church & Synagogue Lib.—R
$-Citizens in America
Connecting Point—R
$-Cornerstone Christian—R
$-Covenant Companion—R
$-Dreams & Visions—R
$-Esprit—R
Eternal Ink—R
Fire By Nite
$-Five Stones—R
$-Gem—R
Gospel Tract—R
Heartlight—R
$-Horizons (adult)—R
Infuze Magazine
Light at Home—R
$-Live—R
$-Living Light News—R
$-Mature Living
Mature Times—R
$-Mature Years—R
$-Miraculous Medal
$-My Legacy—R
$-National Catholic
$-Over the Back Fence—R
$-Palm Beach—R
Parables—R
$-Peeks & Valleys—R
Plowman—R
PrayerWorks—R
$-Seek—R
Singles Scoop—R

Spiritual Voice—R
$-Spring Hill Review—R
St. Linus Review
Storyteller—R
Studio—R
$-Tickled by Thunder
$-U.S. Catholic
Victory News—R
West Wind Review
Winsome Wit—R

CHILDREN
$-Barefoot for Kids—R
$-Cadet Quest—R
$-Club Connection
$-Cornerstone Christian—R
$-Courage—R
Eternal Ink—R
$-Focus/Clubhouse Jr.
$-Guideposts for Kids
$-My Friend
$-Palm Beach—R
$-Sparkle
Spiritual Voice—R
$-Story Friends—R
$-Story Mates—R
Sword of the Lord—R
Victory News—R

TEEN/YOUNG ADULT
$-Brio—R
$-Cadet Quest—R
$-Campus Life—R
$-Cornerstone Christian—R
$-Credo—R
$-Essential Connection
$-Inteen—R
$-Palm Beach—R
Spiritual Voice—R
$-Student Leadership—R
Sword of the Lord—R
Teen Light—R
$-Teenage Christian—R
TeensForJC—R
Transcendmag.com—R
Victory News—R
$-With—R
$-Young Adult Today—R
$-Young Christian—R
$-Young Salvationist—R

SHORT STORY: JUVENILE

$-Adventures
$-American Girl
$-Animal Trails—R
$-Areopagus (UK)

$-Associated Content—R
$-Beginner's Friend—R
$-Bridal Guides—R
$-Cadet Quest—R
$-Catholic Forester—R
$-CharacterS—R
$-Christian Home & School
$-Christian Renewal—R
Church & Synagogue Lib.—R
$-Church Educator—R
$-Club Connection
$-Courage—R
$-Discoveries—R
Eternal Ink—R
$-Faces
$-Faith & Family
$-Focus/Clubhouse
$-Focus/Clubhouse Jr.
$-Guideposts for Kids
$-High Adventure—R
$-Indian Life—R
InspirationStation
$-Junior Companion—R
$-Keys for Kids—R
$-My Friend
$-My Legacy—R
$-Nature Friend
$-On the Line—R
$-Partners—R
$-Pockets—R
$-Primary Pal (IL)
$-Primary Pal (KS)—R
$-SHINEbrightly—R
Skipping Stones
$-Sparkle
Spiritual Voice—R
$-Story Friends—R
$-Story Mates—R
$-Teach Kids!—R
TeensForJC
$-Today's Catholic Teacher—R
Transcendmag.com—R
$-United Church Observer—R
$-Voice of the Lord
$-War Cry—R
$-Winner—R
Write Touch
$-Young Christian—R
Young Gentleman's Monthly
$-Young Salvationist—R

SHORT STORY: LITERARY

ADULT
African Voices—R
$-Ancient Paths—R

$-Associated Content—R
Beginnings—R
$-Byline
$-Christian Century—R
$-Christian Courier (CAN)—R
$-Citizens in America
$-Covenant Companion—R
$-Dreams & Visions—R
Fire By Nite
$-First Things
$-Gem—R
Hard Row to Hoe
$-Horizons (adult)—R
$-Mennonite Brethren—R
$-My Legacy—R
$-National Catholic
$-New Wineskins—R
Parables—R
Rock & Sling
Rose & Thorn
$-Seek—R
Spiritual Voice—R
$-Spring Hill Review—R
$-St. Anthony Messenger
St. Linus Review
$-Standard—R
Storyteller—R
Studio—R
$-Tickled by Thunder
$-U.S. Catholic
Victory News—R
$-War Cry—R
West Wind Review
Xavier Review

CHILDREN
Beginnings—R
$-CharacterS—R
$-My Friend
Spiritual Voice—R
$-Story Friends—R
Victory News—R

TEEN/YOUNG ADULT
Spiritual Voice—R
Teen Light—R
Victory News—R
$-Young Salvationist—R

SHORT STORY: MYSTERY/ROMANCE
$-Associated Content—R
$-Bridal Guides—R
$-Byline
$-Cappers
Connecting Point—R
$-Dreams & Visions—R

Fire By Nite
$-Gem—R
$-Grit
Parables—R
$-Shades of Romance—R
St. Linus Review
Storyteller—R
Studio—R
Teen Light—R
TeensForJC—R
Transcendmag.com—R
Victory News—R
$-Young Christian—R

SHORT STORY: MYSTERY/SUSPENSE

ADULT
$-Angelica—R
$-Animal Trails—R
$-Associated Content—R
$-Bridal Guides—R
$-Byline
$-Cappers
Christian Radio Weekly
Connecting Point—R
$-Dreams & Visions—R
Fire By Nite
$-Gem—R
$-Grit
Heartlight—R
$-Indian Life—R
Infuze Magazine
$-My Legacy—R
Parables—R
$-Peeks & Valleys—R
Spiritual Voice—R
$-Spring Hill Review—R
St. Linus Review
Storyteller—R
Studio—R
$-Tickled by Thunder
Victory News—R
$-Voice of the Lord

CHILDREN
$-American Girl
$-Barefoot for Kids—R
$-Cadet Quest—R
$-Club Connection
$-Courage—R
$-Focus/Clubhouse
$-Guideposts for Kids
$-High Adventure—R
$-My Friend
$-On the Line—R
$-SHINEbrightly—R

Spiritual Voice—R
Sword of the Lord—R
Victory News—R

TEEN/YOUNG ADULT
$-Cadet Quest—R
$-Credo—R
$-Inteen—R
$-SHINEbrightly—R
Spiritual Voice—R
Sword of the Lord—R
Teen Light—R
TeensForJC—R
Transcendmag.com—R
Victory News—R
$-Young Adult Today—R
$-Young Christian—R
$-Young Salvationist—R

SHORT STORY: PARABLES

ADULT
$-Alive Now—R
$-Animal Trails—R
$-Annals of St. Anne
$-Associated Content—R
$-Bridal Guides—R
$-Catholic Yearbook—R
$-Christian Courier (CAN)—R
Christian Journal—R
$-Church Worship
$-Cornerstone Christian—R
$-Covenant Companion—R
$-Dreams & Visions—R
$-Esprit—R
Eternal Ink—R
Fire By Nite
$-Five Stones—R
$-Gem—R
Heartlight—R
$-Impact—R
$-Indian Life—R
$-Lutheran Journal—R
Mature Times—R
$-Mennonite Brethren—R
$-New Wineskins—R
Parables—R
$-Plain Truth—R
PrayerWorks—R
Railroad Evangelist—R
$-Seek—R
Singles Scoop—R
Spiritual Voice—R
$-St. Joseph's Messenger—R
St. Linus Review
Studio—R
$-Testimony—R

CHILDREN
$-Barefoot for Kids—R
$-Church Educator—R
$-Cornerstone Christian—R
Eternal Ink—R
$-Faces
$-Focus/Clubhouse
$-Guideposts for Kids
$-My Friend
$-SHINEbrightly—R
Skipping Stones
$-Sparkle
Spiritual Voice—R

TEEN/YOUNG ADULT
$-Church Educator—R
$-Cornerstone Christian—R
$-Inteen—R
$-SHINEbrightly—R
Spiritual Voice—R
$-Student Leadership—R
Teen Light—R
TeensForJC—R
$-Testimony—R
Transcendmag.com—R
$-With—R
$-Young Adult Today—R
$-Young Christian—R

SHORT STORY: PLAYS

$-Areopagus (UK)
$-Christian Creative Arts
Christian Drama
$-Church Worship
$-Courage—R
$-Drama Ministry—R
$-Faces
$-Guideposts for Kids
$-J.A.M.
$-New Wineskins—R
$-RTJ
$-Sparkle
Studio—R
Teen Light—R
TeensForJC—R
Transcendmag.com—R
$-Voice of the Lord

SHORT STORY: ROMANCE

ADULT
$-Alive!—R
$-Animal Trails—R
$-Associated Content—R
$-Bridal Guides—R
$-Cappers

Connecting Point—R
$-Cornerstone Christian—R
$-Dreams & Visions—R
Fire By Nite
$-Gem—R
$-Grit
Parables—R
$-Peeks & Valleys—R
Precious Times—R
Rose & Thorn
$-Shades of Romance—R
Spiritual Voice—R
St. Linus Review
Storyteller—R
Studio—R

TEEN/YOUNG ADULT
$-Brio—R
Spiritual Voice—R
Teen Light—R
TeensForJC—R
Transcendmag.com—R
$-With—R
$-Young Christian—R
$-Young Salvationist—R

SHORT STORY: SCIENCE FICTION

ADULT
African Voices—R
$-Associated Content—R
Challenging Destiny
Connecting Point—R
$-Dragons, Knights & Angels—R
$-Dreams & Visions—R
Gateway S-F—R
$-Gem—R
Infuze Magazine
$-Messianic Sci-Fi
Parables—R
Rose & Thorn
Spiritual Voice—R
$-Spring Hill Review—R
St. Linus Review
Storyteller—R
Studio—R
$-Tickled by Thunder

CHILDREN
$-Dragons, Knights & Angels—R
$-SHINEbrightly—R
Spiritual Voice—R
Sword of the Lord—R

TEEN/YOUNG ADULT
$-Credo—R
$-Dragons, Knights & Angels—R

$-Inteen—R
$-J.A.M.
$-SHINEbrightly—R
Spiritual Voice—R
Sword of the Lord—R
Teen Light—R
$-With—R
$-Young Adult Today—R
$-Young Salvationist—R

SHORT STORY: SKITS

ADULT
$-Associated Content—R
$-Church Worship
$-Cornerstone Christian—R
$-Drama Ministry—R
$-Five Stones—R
Light at Home—R
Mature Times—R
$-New Wineskins—R
Singles Scoop—R
Studio—R

CHILDREN
$-Barefoot for Kids—R
$-Cornerstone Christian—R
$-SHINEbrightly—R
$-Sparkle
Sword of the Lord—R

TEEN/YOUNG ADULT
$-Cornerstone Christian—R
$-J.A.M.
$-SHINEbrightly—R
$-Student Leadership—R
Sword of the Lord—R
Teen Light—R
TeensForJC—R
Transcendmag.com—R

SHORT STORY: SPECULATIVE

ADULT
$-Associated Content—R
$-Dreams & Visions—R
Fire By Nite
Infuze Magazine
$-National Catholic
Spiritual Voice—R
St. Linus Review
Studio—R
$-Tickled by Thunder

CHILDREN
Spiritual Voice—R

TEEN/YOUNG ADULT
Spiritual Voice—R

Teen Light—R
TeensForJC—R
Transcendmag.com—R

SHORT STORY: TEEN/YOUNG ADULT

$-Animal Trails—R
$-Bridal Guides—R
$-Brio—R
$-Campus Life—R
$-Canada Lutheran—R
$-Catholic Forester—R
$-CharacterS—R
Church & Synagogue Lib.—R
$-Church Educator—R
$-Credo—R
$-Essential Connection
$-Evangel—R
GO!
$-Indian Life—R
$-Inteen—R
$-J.A.M.
$-Living My Faith
Precious Times—R
$-Purpose—R
$-Real Faith in Life—R
Skipping Stones
Spiritual Voice—R
$-St. Anthony Messenger
$-Student Leadership—R
Teen Light—R
$-Teenage Christian—R
TeensForJC—R
$-Testimony—R
Transcendmag.com—R
Victory News—R
$-Voice of the Lord
$-War Cry—R
West Wind Review
$-With—R
Write Touch
$-Young Adult Today—R
$-Young Christian—R
$-Young Salvationist—R
$-Youth Compass (KS)—R

SHORT STORY: WESTERNS

ADULT

$-Associated Content—R
$-Cappers
$-Citizens in America
$-Dreams & Visions—R
Fire By Nite
$-Grit
Infuze Magazine

Parables—R
Spiritual Voice—R
Storyteller—R
Studio—R
$-Tickled by Thunder
Victory News—R

CHILDREN

$-High Adventure—R
Spiritual Voice—R
Sword of the Lord—R
Victory News—R

TEEN/YOUNG ADULT

$-Credo—R
Spiritual Voice—R
Sword of the Lord—R
Victory News—R

SINGLES ISSUES

ADULT/GENERAL

African Voices—R
Alliance Life
$-Annals of St. Anne
$-Associated Content—R
$-BGC World—R
$-Bible Advocate—R
Breakthrough Intercessor—R
$-Bridal Guides—R
Channels—R
$-Christian Examiner
Christian Journal—R
Christian Online
$-Christian Parenting—R
Christian Ranchman
$-Christian Single
$-Christian Social Action—R
$-ChristianWeek—R
$-City Light News—R
$-Cornerstone Christian—R
Crossway/Newsline—R
Disciple's Journal—R
$-Discipleship Journal—R
$-Dovetail—R
$-Evangel—R
Evangelical Advocate—R
$-Faith Today
$-Foursquare World Advance—R
$-Gem—R
$-Generation X—R
Good News Journal
Heartlight—R
$-Homeschooling Today—R
$-HonorBound—R
HopeKeepers—R
$-Indian Life—R
$-Joy & Praise

LifeLine Journal—R
$-Light & Life
$-Living—R
$-Lookout
Mature Times—R
$-Men of Integrity—R
Men of the Cross
Metro Voice—R
$-Minnesota Christian—R
$-Montgomery's Journey
Mutuality—R
$-Our Sunday Visitor
$-Palm Beach—R
Penned from the Heart
$-Plains Faith—R
$-Power for Living—R
Priscilla Papers—R
$-Psychology for Living—R
Quaker Life—R
Randall House Periodicals
$-SingleAgain.com
Singles Scoop—R
$-Smart Families—R
Spiritual Voice—R
$-St. Anthony Messenger
$-Testimony—R
thegoodsteward.com—R
$-Today's Christian—R
$-Today's Pentecostal Evangel—R
$-Together—R
Trumpeter—R
$-U.S. Catholic
$-Vibrant Life—R
Victory News—R
$-Voice of the Lord
$-War Cry—R
$-Wesleyan Life—R
$-World & I—R

CHRISTIAN EDUCATION/ LIBRARY

$-Youth & CE Leadership

MISSIONS

Women of the Harvest

PASTORS/LEADERS

$-Christian Century—R
Christian Education Jour. (CA)—R
$-Evangelical Baptist—R
$-Interpreter
$-Ministries Today
$-Parish Life—R
$-Pastoral Life—R
Sharing the Practice—R
Strategic Adult Ministries—R
$-Word & World

TEEN/YOUNG ADULT
$-Boundless Webzine—R
$-Inteen—R
$-Passageway.org—R
Teen Light—R
TeensForJC—R
Transcendmag.com—R

WOMEN
Anna's Journal—R
$-At the Center—R
Christian Women Today—R
Faithwebbin—R
$-Godly Business Woman
$-inSpirit—R
$-MOMsense—R
Shalom Bayit
Sisters in the Lord
$-SpiritLed Woman
$-Today's Christian Woman—R
$-Woman's Touch—R
Women of the Cross
Women Today—R

SOCIAL JUSTICE

ADULT/GENERAL
$-Arlington Catholic
$-Associated Content—R
$-Aujourd'hui Credo—R
$-Bible Advocate—R
$-Catholic New Times—R
$-Catholic Peace Voice—R
Channels—R
$-Christian Courier (CAN)—R
$-Christian Leader—R
Christian Online
$-Christian Social Action—R
$-Christianity Today—R
$-ChristianWeek—R
Citizen USA—R
$-Citizens in America
$-City Light News—R
$-Commonweal
$-Company—R
$-Covenant Companion—R
$-Culture Wars—R
Desert Call—R
$-Dovetail—R
$-Faith & Family
$-Faith Today
$-Foursquare World Advance—R
$-Gem—R
$-Generation X—R
$-Inland NW Christian
Island Catholic News
$-Light & Life

$-Living—R
$-Lookout
$-Men of Integrity—R
$-Mennonite Brethren—R
$-Minnesota Christian—R
Mosaic—R
Mutuality—R
$-National Catholic
$-New Wineskins—R
$-ONEvoice!
$-Our Sunday Visitor
$-Palm Beach—R
Penned from the Heart
Perspectives—R
$-Plains Faith—R
$-Prairie Messenger—R
$-Priority!—R
Priscilla Papers—R
$-Prism—R
Quaker Life—R
Salt of the Earth
$-Science & Spirit
Silver Wings—R
$-Social Justice—R
$-Spiritual Life
$-Spring Hill Review—R
$-St. Anthony Messenger
$-St. Joseph's Messenger—R
$-Testimony—R
thegoodsteward.com—R
$-Today's Christian—R
$-Together—R
Trumpeter—R
$-U.S. Catholic
$-United Church Observer—R
Victory News—R
$-Way of St. Francis—R
$-World & I—R

CHILDREN
$-Pockets—R
Skipping Stones

CHRISTIAN EDUCATION/ LIBRARY
Catholic Library World
$-Church Educator—R
$-Journal/Adventist Educ.—R
$-RTJ

MISSIONS
Glad Tidings
Missiology

PASTORS/LEADERS
$-African American Pulpit
$-Christian Century—R
$-Clergy Journal—R

$-Interpreter
Journal/Pastoral Care—R
$-Ministries Today
$-Pastoral Life—R
Quarterly Review
Sharing the Practice—R
Theological Digest—R
$-Theology Today

TEEN/YOUNG ADULT
$-Boundless Webzine—R
$-Devo'Zine—R
$-Passageway.org—R
$-Teenage Christian—R
TeensForJC—R
Transcendmag.com—R
$-Young Salvationist—R

WOMEN
$-Esprit—R
$-Horizons (women)—R
$-inSpirit—R
Making Waves

SOCIOLOGY

ADULT/GENERAL
$-Anglican Journal
$-Associated Content—R
$-Catholic New Times—R
$-Catholic Peace Voice—R
$-Christian Courier (CAN)—R
Christian Online
$-Christian Social Action—R
$-Citizens in America
$-City Light News—R
$-Culture Wars—R
$-Dovetail—R
Evangelical Advocate—R
$-Faith Today
$-Gem—R
$-Generation X—R
Journal of Church & State
$-Light & Life
$-Liguorian
$-Montgomery's Journey
$-National Catholic
$-Plains Faith—R
Priscilla Papers—R
$-Science & Spirit
Short Stories Bimonthly—R
$-Social Justice—R
Spiritual Voice—R
$-Spring Hill Review—R
$-St. Anthony Messenger
$-Testimony—R
thegoodsteward.com—R
Trumpeter—R

Victory News—R
$-World & I—R

CHRISTIAN EDUCATION/ LIBRARY
$-Church Educator—R

PASTORS/LEADERS
Jour./Amer. Soc./Chur. Growth—R
$-Parish Life—R
$-Pastoral Life—R
$-Word & World
Youth Culture

TEEN/YOUNG ADULT
$-Inteen—R
TeensForJC—R
Transcendmag.com—R

WOMEN
$-inSpirit—R

SPIRITUAL GIFTS

ADULT/GENERAL
African Voices—R
Alliance Life
$-Arkansas Catholic—R
$-Bible Advocate—R
Bread of Life—R
$-Bridal Guides—R
Channels—R
$-Christian Leader—R
Christian Motorsports
Christian Online
Christian Ranchman
$-Christianity Today—R
$-Cornerstone Christian—R
$-Covenant Companion—R
$-Discipleship Journal—R
$-Dovetail—R
Evangelical Advocate—R
$-Faith & Family
$-Faith & Friends—R
$-Faith Today
Highway News—R
HopeKeepers—R
$-Light & Life
Maranatha News—R
Mature Times—R
$-Mature Years—R
$-Men of Integrity—R
Mosaic—R
Mutuality—R
$-New Freeman—R
$-New Wineskins—R
$-ONEvoice!
Penned from the Heart

$-Plains Faith—R
$-Positive Thinking—R
Priscilla Papers—R
Regent Business—R
Sacred Journey—R
Silver Wings—R
Singles Scoop—R
Spiritual Voice—R
$-St. Anthony Messenger
$-Stewardship—R
Sword and Trumpet—R
$-Testimony—R
thegoodsteward.com—R
$-Today's Christian—R
$-Today's Pentecostal Evangel—R
$-Together—R
Trumpeter—R
Victory News—R
$-Voice of the Lord
$-Way of St. Francis—R

CHILDREN
$-BREAD/God's Children—R
$-Our Little Friend—R
$-Primary Treasure—R
$-SHINEbrightly—R
$-Sparkle

PASTORS/LEADERS
$-Evangelicals Today—R
$-Interpreter
Ministry in Motion—R
$-Pastoral Life—R
$-Pray!—R
Sharing the Practice—R
$-Worship Leader

TEEN/YOUNG ADULT
$-Passageway.org—R
Teen Light—R
TeensForJC—R
Transcendmag.com—R
$-With—R
$-Young Christian—R

WOMEN
$-Esprit—R
$-Godly Business Woman
Home-Based Moms—R
$-inSpirit—R
$-Journey
Just Between Us—R
P31 Woman—R
Precious Times—R
Right to the Heart—R
$-SpiritLed Woman

SPIRITUALITY

ADULT/GENERAL
African Voices—R
AGAIN—R
$-Alive Now—R
Alliance Life
American Tract Society—R
$-Angels on Earth
$-Annals of St. Anne
$-Arkansas Catholic—R
$-Arlington Catholic
$-Associated Content—R
$-Bible Advocate—R
Bread of Life—R
Breakthrough Intercessor—R
$-Bridal Guides—R
$-Cathedral Age
$-Catholic Digest—R
$-Catholic New Times—R
$-Catholic Peace Voice—R
$-CGA World—R
Channels—R
$-Christian Courier (CAN)—R
Christian Journal—R
$-Christian Leader—R
Christian Online
$-Christianity Today—R
$-ChristianWeek—R
Common Ground—R
$-Cornerstone Christian—R
$-Covenant Companion—R
Crossway/Newsline—R
$-Culture Wars—R
Desert Call—R
Divine Ascent
$-Dovetail—R
$-Episcopal Life—R
$-Faith & Family
$-Faith & Friends—R
$-Faith Today
$-Family Digest—R
$-Gem—R
$-Generation X—R
$-God Allows U-Turns—R
$-Good News—R
Good News Journal
$-Guideposts—R
Heartlight—R
Highway News—R
$-Horizons (adult)—R
$-Inland NW Christian
Island Catholic News
Leaves—R
$-Lifeglow—R
LifeTimes Catholic

$-Light & Life
Light at Home—R
$-Living—R
$-Living Church
$-Lookout
Mature Times—R
$-Mature Years—R
$-Men of Integrity—R
Men of the Cross
$-Mennonite Brethren—R
$-Messenger/Sacred Heart
$-Messenger/St. Anthony
$-Minnesota Christian—R
$-My Walk With Jesus
$-National Catholic
$-New Freeman—R
New Heart—R
$-New Wineskins—R
$-Parabola—R
Parents & Teens—R
Pegasus Review—R
Penned from the Heart
Penwood Review
Perspectives—R
$-Plains Faith—R
$-Portland Magazine
$-Positive Thinking—R
$-Prairie Messenger—R
Presbyterian Outlook
$-Presbyterians Today—R
Priscilla Papers—R
$-Prism—R
Quaker Life—R
$-Queen of All Hearts
Randall House Periodicals
Sacred Journey—R
$-Seek—R
$-SingleAgain.com
Singles Scoop—R
$-Social Justice—R
$-Spiritual Life
Spiritual Voice—R
$-Spring Hill Review—R
$-St. Anthony Messenger
$-St. Joseph's Messenger—R
$-Standard—R
Star of Zion
$-Stewardship—R
Sword and Trumpet—R
$-Testimony—R
thegoodsteward.com—R
$-Today's Christian—R
$-Today's Pentecostal Evangel—R
$-Together—R
Trumpeter—R

$-U.S. Catholic
Victory News—R
$-War Cry—R
$-Way of St. Francis—R
$-Weavings—R
$-Whole Magazine
$-Wittenburg Door—R
$-World & I—R

CHILDREN
$-BREAD/God's Children—R
$-Passport—R
Skipping Stones

CHRISTIAN EDUCATION/
LIBRARY
Catholic Library World
$-Church Educator—R
Jour./Ed. & Christian Belief—R
Journal/Christian Education
$-RTJ

MISSIONS
$-Evangelical Missions—R
Missiology

PASTORS/LEADERS
$-Barefoot—R
$-Christian Century—R
Christian Education Jour. (CA)—R
$-Church Worship
$-Diocesan Dialogue—R
$-Emmanuel
$-Evangelical Baptist—R
$-Evangelicals Today—R
$-Interpreter
Journal/Pastoral Care—R
$-Lutheran Partners—R
$-Ministries Today
Ministry in Motion—R
$-Parish Life—R
$-Pastoral Life—R
Pastors.com—R
$-Preaching Well—R
$-Proclaim—R
Quarterly Review
$-Reformed Worship
$-Review for Religious
$-RevWriter Resource
Sharing the Practice—R
Theological Digest—R
$-Theology Today
$-Today's Parish—R
$-Word & World
$-Worship Leader

TEEN/YOUNG ADULT
$-Inteen—R

$-Passageway.org—R
$-Teenage Christian—R
TeensForJC—R
Transcendmag.com—R
$-With—R
$-Young Adult Today—R
$-Young and Alive—R
$-Young Christian—R
$-Young Salvationist—R

WOMEN
$-Esprit—R
$-Godly Business Woman
Handmaiden—R
Heart & Soul
Hearts at Home—R
$-Horizons (women)—R
$-inSpirit—R
$-Journey
Just Between Us—R
Lutheran Woman's Quar.
Precious Times—R
$-SpiritLed Woman
$-Today's Christian Woman—R
Women of the Cross

WRITERS
$-Areopagus (UK)

SPIRITUAL LIFE

ADULT/GENERAL
$-Associated Content—R
$-Aujourd'hui Credo—R
$-Barefoot Path—R
$-BGC World—R
$-Bible Advocate—R
$-Bridal Guides—R
$-Catholic Digest—R
$-Catholic Peace Voice—R
$-Catholic Yearbook—R
CBN.com—R
Channels—R
$-Christian Examiner
Christian Journal—R
Christian Online
Christian Research
$-ChristianWeek—R
$-City Light News—R
$-Discipleship Journal—R
Divine Ascent
$-Eclectic Homeschool
$-En Confianza
Eternal Ink—R
$-Faith & Family
$-Faith & Friends—R
$-Faith Today

$-Family Digest—R
$-God Allows U-Turns—R
$-God's Way Books
Highway News—R
$-Homeschooling Today—R
$-Horizons (adult)—R
$-Indian Life—R
LifeLine Journal—R
$-Light & Life
Light at Home—R
$-Lookout
$-Lutheran Journal—R
$-Men of Integrity—R
$-Minnesota Christian—R
$-Montgomery's Journey
Mosaic—R
$-My Walk With Jesus
$-National Catholic
New Heart—R
$-New Wineskins—R
$-ONEvoice!
Penned from the Heart
$-Plains Faith—R
PrayerWorks—R
$-Presbyterians Today—R
$-Priority!—R
Priscilla Papers—R
$-Purpose—R
Quaker Life—R
Reformed Quarterly
Regent Business—R
Sacred Journey—R
$-Science & Spirit
$-Seek—R
$-Signs of the Times—R
Silver Wings—R
$-SingleAgain.com
Spiritual Voice—R
$-Spring Hill Review—R
$-St. Anthony Messenger
$-Stewardship—R
Sword and Trumpet—R
$-Testimony—R
$-Today's Christian—R
$-Today's Pentecostal Evangel—R
$-Together—R
$-U.S. Catholic
Victory News—R
$-Weavings—R
$-Whole Magazine

CHILDREN
$-Barefoot for Kids—R
$-BREAD/God's Children—R
Skipping Stones

CHRISTIAN EDUCATION/ LIBRARY
$-Children's Ministry
$-Youth & CE Leadership

PASTORS/LEADERS
$-African American Pulpit
Christian Education Jour. (CA)—R
$-Evangelical Baptist—R
$-Interpreter
Journal/Pastoral Care—R
$-Ministry
Ministry in Motion—R
$-Review for Religious
$-RevWriter Resource
$-WCA News—R

TEEN/YOUNG ADULT
$-Young Christian—R

WOMEN
Home-Based Moms—R
$-Horizons (women)—R
$-inSpirit—R
$-Journey
P31 Woman—R
Precious Times—R
Right to the Heart—R

SPIRITUAL RENEWAL

ADULT/GENERAL
Alliance Life
$-Associated Content—R
$-Bible Advocate—R
$-Brave Hearts
$-Bridal Guides—R
Christian Journal—R
Christian Online
Church Herald & Holiness—R
$-Evangel—R
Evangelical Advocate—R
Highway News—R
$-HonorBound—R
$-Indian Life—R
LifeLine Journal—R
$-Lookout
$-Mature Living
$-Men of Integrity—R
Mosaic—R
$-My Walk With Jesus
$-New Wineskins—R
$-ONEvoice!
$-Palm Beach—R
Penned from the Heart
$-Plains Faith—R
PrayerWorks—R
Quaker Life—R

Sacred Journey—R
$-Sojourners
Spiritual Voice—R
Spirituality for Today
Sword and Trumpet—R
$-Testimony—R
$-Today's Christian—R
Victory News—R

PASTORS/LEADERS
$-African American Pulpit
$-Interpreter
$-Lutheran Partners—R
Ministry in Motion—R
$-Pray!—R
$-Review for Religious
Theological Digest—R

TEEN/YOUNG ADULT
Teen Light—R

WOMEN
Home-Based Moms—R
$-Horizons (women)—R
$-inSpirit—R
$-Journey
Precious Times—R
$-Woman's Touch—R

SPIRITUAL WARFARE

ADULT/GENERAL
AGAIN—R
Alliance Life
$-Angels on Earth
$-Associated Content—R
$-Believer's Bay
$-BGC World—R
$-Bible Advocate—R
Breakthrough Intercessor—R
$-Celebrate Life—R
$-CGA World—R
Channels—R
$-Christian Leader—R
Christian Online
Christian Ranchman
Christian Research
$-Christianity Today—R
$-Cornerstone Christian—R
Eternal Ink—R
Evangelical Advocate—R
$-Faith & Friends—R
$-Faith Today
$-Gem—R
$-Good News—R
Gospel Tract—R
Heartlight—R
Highway News—R

Leaves—R
$-Light & Life
$-Lookout
Maranatha News—R
$-Men of Integrity—R
Men of the Cross
Mosaic—R
$-My Walk With Jesus
$-New Freeman—R
New Heart—R
$-New Wineskins—R
$-ONEvoice!
Penned from the Heart
$-Plains Faith—R
Prayer Closet
PrayerWorks—R
$-Purpose—R
Quaker Life—R
Spiritual Voice—R
$-St. Anthony Messenger
Sword and Trumpet—R
Sword of the Lord—R
$-Testimony—R
thegoodsteward.com—R
$-Today's Pentecostal Evangel—R
Trumpeter—R
Victory News—R
$-Voice of the Lord

CHILDREN
$-BREAD/God's Children—R

MISSIONS
Railroad Evangelist—R
Wesleyan World—R

PASTORS/LEADERS
$-Evangelicals Today—R
$-Growth Points—R
Jour./Amer. Soc./Chur. Growth—R
$-Let's Worship
$-Ministries Today
$-Pastoral Life—R
Pastors.com—R
$-Pray!—R
Sharing the Practice—R

TEEN/YOUNG ADULT
$-Brio—R
$-Passageway.org—R
Teen Light—R
TeensForJC—R
Transcendmag.com—R

WOMEN
Faithwebbin—R
$-Godly Business Woman
Handmaiden—R

Home-Based Moms—R
$-inSpirit—R
$-Journey
Just Between Us—R
Precious Times—R
$-Women Alive!—R
Women of the Cross

SPORTS/RECREATION

ADULT/GENERAL
$-Abilities
$-Angels on Earth
$-Arlington Catholic
$-Associated Content—R
$-Bridal Guides—R
Christian Courier (WI)—R
Christian Radio Weekly
Christian Ranchman
$-Christian Renewal—R
$-Citizens in America
$-City Light News—R
Connecting Point—R
$-Cornerstone Christian—R
Discovery—R
Eternal Ink—R
$-Faith Today
$-Gem—R
$-Gospel Today—R
$-Grand
$-Guideposts—R
Heartland Gatekeeper
$-HonorBound—R
$-Lifeglow—R
$-Light & Life
Light at Home—R
$-Living Light News—R
Metro Voice—R
$-Minnesota Christian—R
$-New Freeman—R
$-Palm Beach—R
$-Plains Faith—R
Randall House Periodicals
$-Smart Families—R
Spiritual Voice—R
$-Sports Spectrum
$-St. Anthony Messenger
Storyteller—R
$-Testimony—R
thegoodsteward.com—R
$-Today's Christian—R
Victory News—R
$-World & I—R

CHILDREN
$-Barefoot for Kids—R
$-BREAD/God's Children—R

$-Cadet Quest—R
$-Club Connection
$-Guideposts for Kids
$-SHINEbrightly—R
$-Sparkle

CHRISTIAN EDUCATION/LIBRARY
$-Children's Ministry

PASTORS/LEADERS
$-Cornerstone Youth—R
$-Preaching Well—R

TEEN/YOUNG ADULT
$-Boundless Webzine—R
$-Brio—R
$-Credo—R
$-Inteen—R
$-Listen—R
$-Passageway.org—R
$-Real Faith in Life—R
$-Sharing the VICTORY—R
Steelroots
TeensForJC—R
Transcendmag.com—R
$-Young Christian—R

WOMEN
$-Esprit—R
Home-Based Moms—R

STEWARDSHIP

ADULT/GENERAL
Alliance Life
$-Angels on Earth
$-BGC World—R
$-Bible Advocate—R
Breakthrough Intercessor—R
$-Catholic Yearbook—R
$-Celebrate Life—R
Channels—R
$-Christian Courier (CAN)—R
$-Christian Leader—R
Christian Online
$-Christian Social Action—R
$-ChristianWeek—R
Church Herald & Holiness—R
$-Cornerstone Christian—R
$-Covenant Companion—R
Creation Care—R
$-Discipleship Journal—R
$-Evangel—R
Evangelical Advocate—R
$-Faith Today
$-Family Digest—R
$-Gem—R

Highway News—R
$-Lifeglow—R
$-Light & Life
$-Live—R
$-Living Church
$-Lookout
$-Lutheran Digest—R
$-Lutheran Journal—R
Mature Times—R
$-Men of Integrity—R
NRB Magazine—R
$-ONEvoice!
$-Our Sunday Visitor
Penned from the Heart
Perspectives—R
$-Plains Faith—R
$-Positive Thinking—R
$-Power for Living—R
Presbyterian Outlook
$-Prism—R
Quaker Life—R
Randall House Periodicals
Regent Business—R
Singles Scoop—R
$-St. Anthony Messenger
$-Stewardship—R
$-Testimony—R
thegoodsteward.com—R
$-Today's Christian—R
$-Today's Pentecostal Evangel—R
Trumpeter—R
$-U.S. Catholic
$-United Church Observer—R
Victory News—R
$-Wesleyan Life—R
$-Wireless Age—R

CHILDREN
$-BREAD/God's Children—R
$-Guide—R
$-SHINEbrightly—R
$-Sparkle

CHRISTIAN EDUCATION/
LIBRARY
$-Church Educator—R
$-Momentum

MISSIONS
Wesleyan World—R

PASTORS/LEADERS
Christian Management—R
$-Clergy Journal—R
$-Evangelical Baptist—R
$-Evangelicals Today—R
$-Five Stones—R
$-InSite—R

$-Interpreter
$-Let's Worship
$-Ministries Today
Net Results
$-Pastoral Life—R
Quarterly Review
$-RevWriter Resource
Sharing the Practice—R
$-Your Church—R

TEEN/YOUNG ADULT
$-Passageway.org—R
Teen Light—R
TeensForJC—R
Transcendmag.com—R
$-With—R
$-Young Salvationist—R

WOMEN
$-Esprit—R
$-Godly Business Woman
Home-Based Moms—R
$-Horizons (women)—R
$-inSpirit—R
$-Journey
Just Between Us—R
P31 Woman—R
Precious Times—R
$-Today's Christian Woman—R

TAKE-HOME PAPERS

ADULT/GENERAL
$-Evangel—R
$-Gem—R
$-Gems of Truth—R
$-Horizons (adult)—R
$-Live—R
$-Power for Living—R
$-Purpose—R
$-Seek—R
$-Standard—R
$-Vision—R

CHILDREN
$-Adventures
$-Beginner's Friend—R
$-Celebrate
$-Courage—R
$-Discoveries—R
$-Junior Companion—R
$-Juniorway
$-Our Little Friend—R
$-Partners—R
$-Passport—R
$-Preschool Playhouse (child)
$-Primary Pal (IL)
$-Primary Pal (KS)—R

$-Primary Treasure—R
$-Promise
$-Seeds
$-Story Mates—R

TEEN/YOUNG ADULT
$-Insight—R
$-Youth Compass (KS)—R

THEOLOGICAL

ADULT/GENERAL
AGAIN—R
$-Alive Now—R
$-America
$-Anglican Journal
$-Annals of St. Anne
$-Arkansas Catholic—R
$-Arlington Catholic
$-Aujourd'hui Credo—R
$-B.C. Catholic—R
$-Bible Advocate—R
Breakthrough Intercessor—R
byFaith
$-Catholic New Times—R
$-Catholic Peace Voice—R
$-Catholic Yearbook—R
Channels—R
$-Christian Courier (CAN)—R
$-Christian Leader—R
$-Christian Networks
Christian Online
$-Christian Renewal—R
Christian Research
$-Christian Standard—R
$-Christianity Today—R
$-ChristianWeek—R
Church Herald & Holiness—R
Creation Care—R
$-Culture Wars—R
Divine Ascent
$-Dovetail—R
$-Episcopal Life—R
$-Eureka Street
Evangelical Advocate—R
Evangelical Times
$-Faith Today
$-First Things
Founders Journal
$-Good News—R
$-Horizons (adult)—R
Journal of Church & State
$-Light & Life
$-Living Church
$-Lookout
$-Lutheran Journal—R
Maranatha News—R

Mature Times—R
$-Men of Integrity—R
$-Messenger/Sacred Heart
$-Minnesota Christian—R
$-National Catholic
$-New Freeman—R
$-New Wineskins—R
$-ONEvoice!
$-Our Sunday Visitor
Perspectives—R
Pietisten Online
$-Plain Truth—R
$-Plains Faith—R
$-Prairie Messenger—R
Presbyterian Outlook
Priscilla Papers—R
Purpose Magazine
$-Queen of All Hearts
Randall House Periodicals
Reformed Quarterly
$-Science & Spirit
Singles Scoop—R
$-Social Justice—R
$-Sojourners
$-Spiritual Life
SR: A Journal—R
$-St. Anthony Messenger
Star of Zion
$-Testimony—R
thegoodsteward.com—R
$-Today's Pentecostal Evangel—R
Trumpeter—R
$-U.S. Catholic
$-United Church Observer—R
Victory News—R
$-Way of St. Francis—R

CHRISTIAN EDUCATION/ LIBRARY
$-Church Educator—R
Jour./Christianity/Foreign Languages
$-Teachers Interaction

MISSIONS
$-American Baptists in Mission
East-West Church
Missiology

PASTORS/LEADERS
$-African American Pulpit
$-Catechumenate
$-Christian Century—R
Christian Education Jour. (CA)—R
$-Church Worship
$-Clergy Journal—R
Cross Currents
$-Diocesan Dialogue—R

$-Evangelical Baptist—R
$-Evangelicals Today—R
$-Growth Points—R
$-Horizons (pastor)—R
Interpretation
Jour./Amer. Soc./Chur. Growth—R
Journal/Pastoral Care—R
Lutheran Forum—R
$-Lutheran Partners—R
$-Ministries Today
$-Ministry & Liturgy—R
$-Parish Life—R
$-Pastoral Life—R
Pastors.com—R
$-Preaching Well—R
$-Proclaim—R
Quarterly Review
Sewanee Theo. Review
Sharing the Practice—R
$-Theology Today
$-This Rock
$-Today's Parish—R
$-Word & World
$-Worship Leader

TEEN/YOUNG ADULT
$-Inteen—R
$-Passageway.org—R
TeensForJC—R
Transcendmag.com—R

WOMEN
$-Godly Business Woman
$-Horizons (women)—R
Making Waves

THINK PIECES

ADULT/GENERAL
$-Alive!—R
$-Alive Now—R
$-Annals of St. Anne
$-Associated Content—R
Baptist Standard
$-Catholic Forester—R
$-Catholic New Times—R
$-Catholic Peace Voice—R
$-CGA World—R
Christian C. L. RECORD—R
$-Christian Courier (CAN)—R
Christian Journal—R
$-Christian Leader—R
Christian Online
$-Christian Social Action—R
$-Christian Standard—R
$-Christianity Today—R
$-Citizens in America

$-City Light News—R
$-Cornerstone Christian—R
Creation Care—R
Desert Call—R
$-Dovetail—R
$-Episcopal Life—R
Eternal Ink—R
$-Faith Today
$-First Things
$-Gem—R
$-Generation X—R
Good News Journal
Heartlight—R
$-Lifeglow—R
$-Light & Life
$-Lutheran Digest—R
Metro Voice—R
$-Minnesota Christian—R
$-New Wineskins—R
$-On Mission
$-Palm Beach—R
Pegasus Review—R
Penned from the Heart
Penwood Review
$-Plains Faith—R
$-Positive Thinking—R
PrayerWorks—R
Presbyterian Outlook
Purpose Magazine
$-Science & Spirit
Spiritual Voice—R
$-Spring Hill Review—R
$-St. Anthony Messenger
$-Stewardship—R
$-Testimony—R
thegoodsteward.com—R
$-Today's Christian—R
Trumpeter—R
$-U.S. Catholic
Victory News—R
$-Vision—R
$-Way of St. Francis—R
$-Whole Magazine
Winsome Wit—R
$-Wittenburg Door—R
$-World & I—R

CHILDREN
$-Courage—R

CHRISTIAN EDUCATION/ LIBRARY
$-Children's Ministry

PASTORS/LEADERS
Alpha News
$-Catholic Servant

$-Evangelicals Today—R
$-Ministries Today
Pastors.com—R
Sharing the Practice—R
Strategic Adult Ministries—R
$-Word & World

TEEN/YOUNG ADULT
$-Boundless Webzine—R
$-Passageway.org—R
$-Real Faith in Life—R
TeensForJC—R
Transcendmag.com—R

WOMEN
Anna's Journal—R
$-Godly Business Woman
Home-Based Moms—R
$-inSpirit—R

WRITERS
$-Areopagus (UK)
Money the Write Way—R

TIME MANAGEMENT

ADULT/GENERAL
Alliance Life
$-Aspiring Retail
$-Associated Content—R
Breakthrough Intercessor—R
$-Bridal Guides—R
Business Reform
$-Catholic Forester—R
Christian Journal—R
Christian Online
$-Christian Parenting—R
$-ChristianWeek—R
$-Cornerstone Christian—R
Disciple's Journal—R
Evangelical Advocate—R
$-Gem—R
$-Generation X—R
Good News Journal
$-Homeschooling Today—R
$-HonorBound—R
HopeKeepers—R
$-Lifeglow—R
LifeLine Journal—R
$-Light & Life
Light at Home—R
$-Living—R
$-Living Light News—R
$-Men of Integrity—R
Men of the Cross
NRB Magazine—R
Parents & Teens—R
Penned from the Heart
$-Plains Faith—R

$-Positive Thinking—R
Quaker Life—R
Randall House Periodicals
Regent Business—R
Spiritual Voice—R
$-St. Anthony Messenger
$-Stewardship—R
$-Testimony—R
thegoodsteward.com—R
$-Today's Christian—R
$-Together—R
Trumpeter—R
Victory News—R
$-Wireless Age—R
$-World & I—R

CHILDREN
$-Guideposts for Kids

CHRISTIAN EDUCATION/ LIBRARY
$-Children's Ministry
Christian Librarian—R
$-Resource—R
$-Youth & CE Leadership

PASTORS/LEADERS
$-Barefoot—R
Christian Management—R
$-Enrichment—R
$-Evangelicals Today—R
$-Interpreter
$-Pastoral Life—R
Pastors.com—R
$-RevWriter Resource
Sharing the Practice—R
$-Today's Christian Preacher—R
$-WCA News—R
$-Your Church—R

TEEN/YOUNG ADULT
$-Student Leadership—R
Teen Light—R
TeensForJC—R
Transcendmag.com—R
$-Young and Alive—R
$-Young Christian—R

WOMEN
$-Godly Business Woman
Hearts at Home—R
Home-Based Moms—R
Inspired Moms.Com
$-inSpirit—R
$-Journey
Just Between Us—R
Life Tools for Women
$-MOMsense—R
P31 Woman—R

Precious Times—R
Right to the Heart—R
$-Simple Joy
Sisters in the Lord
$-Today's Christian Woman—R
Women Today—R

WRITERS
$-Adv. Christian Writer—R
$-Christian Communicator—R
$-Fellowscript—R
Money the Write Way—R
$-Writer's Apprentice
$-Writers' Journal
Writes of Passage—R

TRAVEL

ADULT/GENERAL
$-Abilities
$-Alive!—R
$-Angels on Earth
$-Arlington Catholic
$-Associated Content—R
$-Bridal Guides—R
$-Cappers
$-Chicken Soup Magazine
$-Christian Parenting—R
$-Citizens in America
$-City Light News—R
Common Ground—R
$-Cornerstone Christian—R
$-DisciplesWorld
$-Family Digest—R
$-Gem—R
$-Generation X—R
Good News Journal
$-Grand
$-Grit
HopeKeepers—R
$-Joy & Praise
$-Lifeglow—R
LifeLine Journal—R
$-Mature Living
$-Mature Years—R
MovieGuide
Nostalgia—R
$-Over the Back Fence—R
$-Plains Faith—R
Sacred Journey—R
$-Senior Living
$-SingleAgain.com
$-Special Living—R
Spiritual Voice—R
$-Spring Hill Review—R
Storyteller—R
$-Testimony—R
$-Tidewater Parent—R

$-Today's Christian—R
$-Upscale Magazine
Victory News—R
$-World & I—R

CHILDREN
$-Faces
$-SHINEbrightly—R
Skipping Stones
$-Sparkle

MISSIONS
$-PIME World—R

PASTORS/LEADERS
$-Preaching Well—R

TEEN/YOUNG ADULT
Teen Light—R
$-Teenage Christian—R
TeensForJC—R
Transcendmag.com—R
$-Young and Alive—R
$-Young Christian—R

WOMEN
$-Dabbling Mum.com—R
$-Godly Business Woman
Home-Based Moms—R
Inspired Moms.Com
Precious Times—R
Women of the Cross

WRITERS
Money the Write Way—R

TRUE STORIES

ADULT/GENERAL
African Voices—R
$-Alive!—R
$-Ancient Paths—R
$-Angels on Earth
$-Animal Trails—R
Baptist Standard
Beacon (AL)
Biblical Recorder
Breakthrough Intercessor—R
$-Bridal Guides—R
byFaith
$-Catholic Digest—R
$-Catholic New Times—R
Challenge Weekly
Channels—R
Charlotte World
Christian Citizen USA
Christian Herald (UK)
Christian Journal—R
Christian Observer
Christian Online
Christian Post

Christian Ranchman
Church Herald & Holiness—R
$-Citizens in America
$-City Light News—R
Community Spirit
$-Cornerstone Christian—R
Creation Care—R
$-Creative Nonfiction
Crossway/Newsline—R
$-Culture Wars—R
$-Cup of Comfort—R
$-Dovetail—R
$-En Confianza
Eternal Ink—R
Evangelical Times
$-Faith & Family
$-Foursquare World Advance—R
$-Gem—R
$-Gems of Truth—R
$-Generation X—R
$-God Allows U-Turns—R
$-God's Way Books
Good News in RI
Good News Journal
Gospel Post
$-Grit
$-Guideposts—R
Gulf Coast Christian
Hannah to Hannah—R
Heartland Gatekeeper
Heartlight—R
Highway News—R
$-HonorBound—R
HopeKeepers—R
$-Horizons (adult)—R
$-Lifeglow—R
$-Light & Life
Light at Home—R
$-Live—R
$-Lutheran Digest—R
Maranatha News—R
$-Marriage Partnership—R
Men of the Cross
Mennonite Historian—R
MESSAGE/Open Bible—R
Metro Voice—R
$-Minnesota Christian—R
New Heart—R
$-New Wineskins—R
Nostalgia—R
$-Now What?—R
$-On Mission
$-ONEvoice!
$-Over the Back Fence—R
Parents & Teens—R
Penned from the Heart

$-Plain Truth—R
$-Plains Faith—R
$-Power for Living—R
PrayerWorks—R
$-Priority!—R
Sacred Journey—R
$-Science & Spirit
$-Seek—R
$-Signs of the Times—R
Spiritual Voice—R
$-Spring Hill Review—R
$-St. Anthony Messenger
$-St. Joseph's Messenger—R
Storyteller—R
$-Testimony—R
thegoodsteward.com—R
$-Today's Christian—R
Tri-State Voice
Trumpeter—R
$-UP
Victory News—R
$-Vision—R
$-Voice of the Lord
$-War Cry—R
War Cry (Canada)—R
Wichita Chronicle
World Net Daily

CHILDREN
$-Barefoot for Kids—R
$-BREAD/God's Children—R
$-Cadet Quest—R
$-Club Connection
$-Courage—R
$-Focus/Clubhouse Jr.
$-Guide—R
$-High Adventure—R
$-Nature Friend
$-Our Little Friend—R
$-Partners—R
$-Pockets—R
$-Primary Treasure—R
$-SHINEbrightly—R
Skipping Stones
$-Sparkle
$-Story Friends—R
$-Story Mates—R
$-Winner—R

MISSIONS
$-Leaders for Today
OpRev Equipper—R

PASTORS/LEADERS
$-Evangelicals Today—R
$-Pastoral Life—R
$-Preaching Well—R
Sharing the Practice—R

TEEN/YOUNG ADULT
$-Boundless Webzine—R
$-Brio—R
$-Credo—R
$-Essential Connection
$-Guideposts Sweet 16—R
$-Insight—R
$-Listen—R
$-Passageway.org—R
$-Real Faith in Life—R
Teen Light—R
TeensForJC—R
Transcendmag.com—R
$-With—R
$-Young and Alive—R
$-Young Christian—R
$-Young Salvationist—R

WOMEN
$-Godly Business Woman
Hearts at Home—R
$-History's Women—R
Home-Based Moms—R
$-inSpirit—R
$-Journey
Just Between Us—R
Precious Times—R

WRITERS
$-Areopagus (UK)

VIDEO REVIEWS

ADULT/GENERAL
$-Arlington Catholic
$-Aspiring Retail
$-Barefoot Path—R
$-Catholic New Times—R
$-Catholic Peace Voice—R
Channels—R
Charlotte World
Christian Current
Christian Journal—R
Christian Radio Weekly
$-Christian Renewal—R
Citizen USA—R
$-City Light News—R
$-Cornerstone Christian—R
Desert Call—R
$-Dovetail—R
Eternal Ink—R
$-Eureka Street
$-Faith & Family
Good News/S. Florida
Heartland Gatekeeper
$-Interim—R
Light at Home—R
Maranatha News—R

Mature Times—R
$-Minnesota Christian—R
MovieGuide
$-Parabola—R
Parents & Teens—R
$-Plains Faith—R
$-Presbyterians Today—R
$-Prism—R
Quaker Life—R
Reformed Quarterly
Rose & Thorn
$-SingleAgain.com
Singles Scoop—R
Spiritual Voice—R
$-Spring Hill Review—R
$-Testimony—R
Trumpeter—R
Victory News—R
Winsome Wit—R
$-Wireless Age—R

CHILDREN
$-Club Connection

CHRISTIAN EDUCATION/ LIBRARY
Catholic Library World
Christian Library Journal—R
Church & Synagogue Lib.—R
$-Church Libraries—R
Jour./Christianity/Foreign Languages

MISSIONS
East-West Church

PASTORS/LEADERS
$-Christian Century—R
$-Evangelicals Today—R
$-Interpreter
$-Lutheran Partners—R
$-Ministries Today
$-Pastoral Life—R
Sharing the Practice—R
Technologies for Worship—R
$-WCA News—R
$-Worship Leader

TEEN/YOUNG ADULT
$-Credo—R
$-Devo'Zine—R
GO!
TeensForJC—R
Transcendmag.com—R

WOMEN
Home-Based Moms—R
Precious Times—R

WRITERS
$-Fellowscript—R

WEBSITE REVIEWS

ADULT/GENERAL
$-Barefoot Path—R
$-Catholic Peace Voice—R
Charlotte World
Christian Current
$-Christian Home & School
$-Christianity Today—R
Citizen USA—R
$-Dovetail—R
Eternal Ink—R
$-Generation X—R
Good News/S. Florida
Heartland Gatekeeper
HopeKeepers—R
Light at Home—R
$-Minnesota Christian—R
MovieGuide
$-New Wineskins—R
NRB Magazine—R
$-Plains Faith—R
Rose & Thorn
$-SingleAgain.com
Spiritual Voice—R
$-Spring Hill Review—R
Storyteller—R
$-Upscale Magazine
Victory News—R
$-Wireless Age—R
$-World & I—R

CHILDREN
$-Barefoot for Kids—R

CHRISTIAN EDUCATION/ LIBRARY
Christian Librarian—R
Christian Library Journal—R
$-Teachers Interaction

MISSIONS
East-West Church
OpRev Equipper—R

PASTORS/LEADERS
$-Interpreter
Ministry in Motion—R
$-Pastoral Life—R

TEEN/YOUNG ADULT
$-Campus Life—R
GO!
TeensForJC—R
Transcendmag.com—R

WOMEN
Home-Based Moms—R
$-Today's Christian Woman—R

WRITERS
Money the Write Way—R
NW Christian Author—R
$-Writers' Journal

WOMEN'S ISSUES

ADULT/GENERAL
$-Abilities
$-Alive Now—R
$-Anglican Journal
$-Annals of St. Anne
$-Arlington Catholic
$-Aspiring Retail
$-Associated Content—R
$-BGC World—R
Breakthrough Intercessor—R
$-Catholic Forester—R
$-Catholic New Times—R
$-Catholic Peace Voice—R
$-Celebrate Life—R
$-CGA World—R
$-Chicken Soup—R
$-Chicken Soup Magazine
Christian C. L. RECORD—R
$-Christian Courier (CAN)—R
$-Christian Examiner
Christian Journal—R
$-Christian Leader—R
Christian News NW—R
Christian Online
$-Christian Parenting—R
Christian Ranchman
$-Christian Social Action—R
$-ChristianWeek—R
Citizen USA—R
$-City Light News—R
$-Columbia
$-Cornerstone Christian—R
Crossway/Newsline—R
$-Cup of Comfort—R
Disciple's Journal—R
$-Dovetail—R
$-Eclectic Homeschool
$-EFCA Today
$-Episcopal Life—R
$-Evangel—R
Evangelical Advocate—R
$-Faith & Family
$-Faith Today
$-Foursquare World Advance—R
$-Gem—R
$-God Allows U-Turns—R
Good News Journal
$-Gospel Today—R
Hannah to Hannah—R
Heartlight—R

$-Homeschooling Today—R
HopeKeepers—R
$-Indian Life—R
$-Interim—R
$-Joy & Praise
LifeLine Journal—R
$-Light & Life
Light at Home—R
$-Live—R
Looking Up
$-Lookout
Maranatha News—R
$-Mennonite Brethren—R
Metro Voice—R
$-Minnesota Christian—R
$-Montgomery's Journey
Mosaic—R
Mutuality—R
$-National Catholic
$-New Freeman—R
$-New Wineskins—R
$-On Mission
$-Our Sunday Visitor
$-Palm Beach—R
Penned from the Heart
Perspectives—R
$-Plains Faith—R
$-Prairie Messenger—R
Presbyterian Outlook
Priscilla Papers—R
$-Psychology for Living—R
$-Purpose—R
Purpose Magazine
Quaker Life—R
Randall House Periodicals
$-Smart Families—R
$-Sojourners
Spiritual Voice—R
$-Spring Hill Review—R
$-St. Anthony Messenger
$-St. Joseph's Messenger—R
Storyteller—R
$-Testimony—R
thegoodsteward.com—R
$-Today's Christian—R
$-Today's Pentecostal Evangel—R
$-Together—R
Trumpeter—R
$-U.S. Catholic
$-United Church Observer—R
$-Vibrant Life—R
Victory News—R
$-Vision—R
$-Voice of the Lord
$-War Cry—R
$-Wesleyan Life—R

West Wind Review
$-Whole Magazine
$-World & I—R

CHILDREN
Skipping Stones

CHRISTIAN EDUCATION/ LIBRARY
Christian Early Education—R
$-Resource—R
$-Teachers of Vision—R

DAILY DEVOTIONALS
Penned from the Heart

MISSIONS
East-West Church
Women of the Harvest

PASTORS/LEADERS
$-African American Pulpit
$-Enrichment—R
$-Evangelicals Today—R
$-Interpreter
$-Lutheran Partners—R
$-Ministries Today
$-Parish Life—R
$-Pastoral Life—R
Sharing the Practice—R
$-Word & World

TEEN/YOUNG ADULT
$-Boundless Webzine—R
Teen Light—R
TeensForJC—R
Transcendmag.com—R

WOMEN
Anna's Journal—R
$-At the Center—R
Christian Women Today—R
Crowned with Silver
$-Dabbling Mum.com—R
$-Esprit—R
Faithwebbin—R
$-Godly Business Woman
Handmaiden—R
Heart & Soul
Hearts at Home—R
Home-Based Moms—R
$-Horizons (women)—R
$-inSpirit—R
$-Journey
Just Between Us—R
Keeping Hearts & Home
Life Tools for Women
$-Link & Visitor—R
Lutheran Woman's Quar.
Making Waves

$-Melody of the Heart
$-MOMsense—R
P31 Woman—R
Precious Times—R
Right to the Heart—R
Shalom Bayit
$-Simple Joy
Sisters in the Lord
$-SpiritLed Woman
Tapestry (GA)
$-Today's Christian Woman—R
$-Woman's Touch—R
$-Women Alive!—R
Women of the Cross
Women Today—R
$-Women's Faith & Spirit
Women's Ministry

WORKPLACE ISSUES

ADULT/GENERAL
Alliance Life
$-Associated Content—R
$-BGC World—R
Business Reform
byFaith
Channels—R
Christian Citizen USA
Christian Current
$-Christian Examiner
Christian Journal—R
Christian News NW—R
Christian Online
$-Christian Retailing
$-ChristianWeek—R
Citizen USA—R
$-City Light News—R
Desert Voice
$-Evangel—R
Evangelical Advocate—R
$-Faith & Friends—R
$-Faith Today
$-Generation X—R
Good News in RI
Good News/S. Florida
$-Gospel Today—R
Highway News—R
$-HonorBound—R
HopeKeepers—R
LifeLine Journal—R
$-Light & Life
Light at Home—R
$-Liguorian
$-Living—R
$-Lookout
Maranatha News—R
$-Men of Integrity—R
Men of the Cross

$-Minnesota Christian—R
$-Montgomery's Journey
New Heart—R
$-On Mission
$-Our Sunday Visitor
Penned from the Heart
$-Plains Faith—R
$-Positive Thinking—R
$-Prairie Messenger—R
$-Purpose—R
Purpose Magazine
Quaker Life—R
Regent Business—R
Spiritual Voice—R
$-Testimony—R
$-Today's Christian—R
$-Today's Pentecostal Evangel—R
$-Together—R
$-U.S. Catholic
Victory News—R
$-Wireless Age—R
$-World & I—R
World Net Daily

CHRISTIAN EDUCATION/ LIBRARY
Catholic Library World
$-Children's Ministry
Christian Early Education—R
Christian Librarian—R
$-Teachers of Vision—R
$-Today's Catholic Teacher—R

PASTORS/LEADERS
Alpha News
$-Church Administration
$-Interpreter

TEEN/YOUNG ADULT
Teen Light—R

WOMEN
Inspired Moms.Com
$-inSpirit—R
$-Journey
Life Tools for Women
Making Waves
$-MOMsense—R
Sisters in the Lord
$-Today's Christian Woman—R
Women Today—R

WRITERS
$-Adv. Christian Writer—R

WORLD ISSUES

ADULT/GENERAL
AGAIN—R
$-Alive!—R
American Tract Society—R

$-Annals of St. Anne
$-Arlington Catholic
$-Associated Content—R
Baptist Standard
Beacon (AL)
$-Bible Advocate—R
Biblical Recorder
Breakthrough Intercessor—R
Canadian Christianity.com
$-Catholic New Times—R
$-Catholic Peace Voice—R
Catholic Register
$-CGA World—R
Challenge Weekly
Charlotte World
Christian Chronicle
Christian Citizen USA
Christian Current
$-Christian Examiner
Christian Herald (UK)
Christian Journal—R
$-Christian Leader—R
$-Christian Networks
Christian Observer
Christian Online
Christian Post
$-Christian Renewal—R
$-Christian Social Action—R
$-ChristianWeek—R
Church of England News
Citizen USA—R
$-City Light News—R
Compass Direct
$-Cornerstone Christian—R
Creation Care—R
$-Cresset
$-Culture Wars—R
Desert Christian
Desert Voice
$-Dovetail—R
$-Evangel—R
Evangelical Advocate—R
Evangelical Times
$-Faith Today
Friends Journal—R
$-Gem—R
$-Generation X—R
Good News Connection
Good News in RI
Good News Journal
Good News/S. Florida
Gospel Post
Gulf Coast Christian
Heartland Gatekeeper
Heartlight—R
$-Inland NW Christian
$-Interim—R

Journal of Church & State
$-Liberty—R
Lifesite Canada
$-Light & Life
$-Liguorian
$-Living Church
$-Lookout
Maranatha News—R
Metro Voice—R
$-Minnesota Christian—R
$-Montgomery's Journey
Mutuality—R
$-New Freeman—R
$-New Wineskins—R
$-Our Sunday Visitor
$-Palm Beach—R
Penned from the Heart
$-Plain Truth—R
$-Plains Faith—R
$-Prairie Messenger—R
Presbyterian Outlook
$-Purpose—R
Purpose Magazine
$-Rare Jewel—R
Sacred Journey—R
$-Social Justice—R
$-Sojourners
Spiritual Voice—R
$-Spring Hill Review—R
$-St. Anthony Messenger
Sunday Magazine
$-Testimony—R
thegoodsteward.com—R
$-Today's Christian—R
Tri-State Voice
Trumpeter—R
$-United Church Observer—R
Victory News—R
$-War Cry—R
West Wind Review
Wichita Chronicle
$-Wireless Age—R
Word News
$-World & I—R
World Net Daily

CHILDREN
$-Guideposts for Kids
Skipping Stones

CHRISTIAN EDUCATION/ LIBRARY
Catholic Library World

MISSIONS
Intl. Jour./Frontier—R
$-Leaders for Today
Missiology
Mission Frontiers

$-New World Outlook
$-One
OpRev Equipper—R
$-PFI World Report—R
$-PIME World—R
Wesleyan World—R

PASTORS/LEADERS
Alpha News
$-Evangelicals Today—R
$-Ministries Today
$-Pastoral Life—R
$-Preaching Well—R
Quarterly Review
Sharing the Practice—R
$-Theology Today
$-Word & World

TEEN/YOUNG ADULT
$-Boundless Webzine—R
$-Passageway.org—R
Teen Light—R
$-Teenage Christian—R
TeensForJC—R
Transcendmag.com—R
$-Young Christian—R
$-Young Salvationist—R

WOMEN
$-Esprit—R
Home-Based Moms—R
$-Horizons (women)—R
$-inSpirit—R
$-SpiritLed Woman

WRITERS
$-Areopagus (UK)

WORSHIP

ADULT/GENERAL
AGAIN—R
Alliance Life
$-Angels on Earth
$-Annals of St. Anne
$-Arlington Catholic
$-Barefoot Path—R
$-BGC World—R
$-Bible Advocate—R
Breakthrough Intercessor—R
$-Bridal Guides—R
$-Cathedral Age
$-Catholic New Times—R
$-Catholic Yearbook—R
$-CGA World—R
Channels—R
$-Christian Examiner
$-Christian Leader—R
Christian Online
Christian Ranchman
$-Christian Standard—R

$-Christianity Today—R
$-ChristianWeek—R
Church Herald & Holiness—R
$-City Light News—R
$-Columbia
$-Cornerstone Christian—R
Creation Care—R
$-Culture Wars—R
$-Dovetail—R
Eternal Ink—R
$-Evangel—R
Evangelical Advocate—R
$-Faith Today
$-Family Digest—R
$-Foursquare World Advance—R
$-HonorBound—R
HopeKeepers—R
$-Lifeglow—R
$-Light & Life
$-Living Church
Looking Up
$-Lookout
$-Lutheran Journal—R
Mature Times—R
$-Men of Integrity—R
Men of the Cross
$-Minnesota Christian—R
$-Montgomery's Journey
Mosaic—R
$-My Walk With Jesus
$-New Freeman—R
$-New Wineskins—R
$-ONEvoice!
$-Our Sunday Visitor
Penned from the Heart
Perspectives—R
$-Plains Faith—R
$-Power for Living—R
$-Prairie Messenger—R
Presbyterian Outlook
$-Presbyterians Today—R
Priscilla Papers—R
Purpose Magazine
Quaker Life—R
Randall House Periodicals
Silver Wings—R
Singles Scoop—R
$-Spiritual Life
Spiritual Voice—R
$-St. Anthony Messenger
$-Stewardship—R
Sword and Trumpet—R
Sword of the Lord—R
$-Testimony—R
thegoodsteward.com—R
Time of Singing—R
$-Today's Christian—R

$-Today's Pentecostal Evangel—R
Trumpeter—R
$-United Church Observer—R
$-War Cry—R
$-Way of St. Francis—R
$-Wesleyan Life—R
$-World & I—R

CHILDREN
$-Barefoot for Kids—R
$-BREAD/God's Children—R
$-Passport—R
$-Promise

CHRISTIAN EDUCATION/ LIBRARY
$-Children's Ministry
$-Church Educator—R
$-RTJ
$-Teach Kids!—R
$-Youth & CE Leadership

DAILY DEVOTIONALS
Quiet Walk

MUSIC
$-Creator—R

PASTORS/LEADERS
$-African American Pulpit
$-Barefoot—R
$-Church Worship
$-Clergy Journal—R
$-Enrichment—R
$-Environment & Art
$-Evangelical Baptist—R
$-Evangelicals Today—R
$-Growth Points—R
Interpretation
$-Interpreter
$-Leadership—R
$-Let's Worship
$-Lutheran Partners—R
$-Ministries Today
$-Ministry & Liturgy—R
$-Pastoral Life—R
Pastors.com—R
$-Pray!—R
Preaching—R
$-Preaching Well—R
Pulpit Helps—R
$-Reformed Worship
$-Rev.
Sharing the Practice—R
Theological Digest—R
$-Theology Today
$-Today's Parish—R
$-Word & World
$-Worship Leader

TEEN/YOUNG ADULT
$-Brio—R
$-Passageway.org—R
$-Student Leadership—R
Teen Light—R
$-Teenage Christian—R
TeensForJC—R
Transcendmag.com—R
$-With—R
$-Young and Alive—R
$-Young Christian—R

WOMEN
$-Esprit—R
Faithwebbin—R
$-Godly Business Woman
Home-Based Moms—R
$-Horizons (women)—R
$-inSpirit—R
$-Journey
Right to the Heart—R
Women of the Cross

WRITING HOW-TO

ADULT/GENERAL
$-Animal Trails—R
$-Aspiring Retail
$-Associated Content—R
$-Bridal Guides—R
Christian Observer
Christian Online
$-Cornerstone Christian—R
Good News Journal
HopeKeepers—R
Light at Home—R
Men of the Cross
$-On Mission
$-Palm Beach—R
Parents & Teens—R
Penwood Review
Rose & Thorn
Short Stories Bimonthly—R
$-SingleAgain.com
Spiritual Voice—R
$-St. Anthony Messenger
Storyteller—R
$-World & I—R

CHILDREN
$-Guideposts for Kids

CHRISTIAN EDUCATION/ LIBRARY
Christian Librarian—R

PASTORS/LEADERS
$-Evangelicals Today—R
$-Newsletter Newsletter

$-Pastoral Life—R

TEEN/YOUNG ADULT
Teen Light—R
TeensForJC—R
Transcendmag.com—R
$-Young Christian—R

WOMEN
$-Dabbling Mum.com—R
$-Esprit—R
$-Godly Business Woman
Just Between Us—R
Precious Times—R
Women of the Cross

WRITERS
$-Adv. Christian Writer—R
$-Areopagus (UK)
Beginnings—R
$-Brady—R
$-Byline
$-Christian Communicator—R
$-Cross & Quill—R
$-Exchange—R
$-Fellowscript—R
Money the Write Way—R
NW Christian Author—R
Once Upon a Time—R
$-Spirit-Led Writer—R
Teachers & Writers
$-Tickled by Thunder
$-Upper Case
WriteToInspire.com
$-Writer
$-Writer's Apprentice
$-Writer's Digest—R
Writer's Lifeline
Writer's Network
Writers Manual
$-Writers' Journal
Writes of Passage—R
Writing Corner

YOUNG WRITER MARKETS

Note: These publications have indicated they will accept submissions from children or teens (C or T).

ADULT/GENERAL
African Voices
$-Animal Trails
$-Aujourd'hui Credo (C or T)
$-Barefoot Path (T)
$-Bridal Guides (C or T)
$-Catholic Peace Voice (T)
$-Catholic Yearbook (C or T)
$-Celebrate Life (C or T)

$-Celebrations Series (C or T)
Channels (T)
Christian Journal (C or T)
Christian Online (C or T)
$-ChristianWeek (T)
Church Herald & Holiness (C or T)
$-Citizens in America (T)
$-City Light News (T)
$-Creative Nonfiction (T)
$-Drama Ministry (T)
$-Eclectic Homeschool (T)
Eternal Ink (C or T)
$-Generation X (C or T)
$-Gospel Today
Hard Row to Hoe (T)
$-HonorBound (T)
HopeKeepers (T)
$-Interchange (C or T)
LifeLine Journal (T)
LifeTimes Catholic (T)
$-Light & Life (C or T)
Light at Home (C or T)
$-Lutheran Journal (C or T)
Maranatha News (C or T)
Men of the Cross (T)
$-Montgomery's Journey (T)
Mosaic (T)
$-My Walk With Jesus (C or T)
$-ONEvoice! (T)
Parents & Teens (T)
Penned from the Heart (C or T)
$-Plains Faith (C or T)
$-Priority! (C or T)
Quaker Life (C or T)
Short Stories Bimonthly (C or T)
Silver Wings (C or T)
Spiritual Voice (C or T)
$-Spring Hill Review (T)
Storyteller (C or T)
Tributes (T)
Victory News (T)
$-Voice of the Lord (C or T)

CHILDREN
$-Barefoot for Kids (C or T)
$-CharacterS (C or T)
Cliché Finder
$-Pockets
$-American Girl
Skipping Stones

CHRISTIAN EDUCATION/ LIBRARY
Catholic Library World

MISSIONS
$-PIME World (T)

PASTORS/LEADERS
$-Cornerstone Youth
$-Let's Worship
Ministry in Motion

TEEN/YOUNG ADULT
$-Campus Life
$-Credo (T)
$-Essential Connection
$-Insight (T)
$-Listen
Teen Light (T)
TeensForJC
Transcendmag.com
$-Young Christian (C or T)

WOMEN
$-Dabbling Mum.com (C or T)
$-History's Women (T)
Home-Based Moms (C or T)
Precious Times (T)
Women of the Cross (T)
Women Today (T)

WRITERS
Beginnings (C or T)
$-Brady
$-Merlyn's Pen
Money the Write Way
$-Spirit-Led Writer
$-Tickled by Thunder (C or T)
$-Writers' Journal
Writes of Passage (T)

YOUTH ISSUES

ADULT/GENERAL
$-Abilities
Alliance Life
American Tract Society—R
$-Annals of St. Anne
$-Arlington Catholic
$-Associated Content—R
Breakthrough Intercessor—R
$-Catholic Forester—R
$-Catholic New Times—R
$-Catholic Peace Voice—R
Channels—R
$-Chicken Soup—R
$-Christian Examiner
Christian Journal—R
$-Christian Leader—R
Christian Motorsports
Christian News NW—R
Christian Online
$-Christian Parenting—R
Christian Ranchman
$-Christian Renewal—R
$-Christian Social Action—R

$-ChristianWeek—R
Church Herald & Holiness—R
Citizen USA—R
$-Citizens in America
$-City Light News—R
$-Culture Wars—R
$-Dovetail—R
$-EFCA Today
Evangelical Advocate—R
$-Faith & Family
$-Faith Today
Family Online—R
Good News Journal
$-Homeschooling Today—R
$-Indian Life—R
$-Joy & Praise
LifeLine Journal—R
LifeTimes Catholic
$-Light & Life
Light at Home—R
$-Living Church
Looking Up
$-Lookout
$-Lutheran Digest—R
Maranatha News—R
MESSAGE/Open Bible—R
Metro Voice—R
$-Montgomery's Journey
Mosaic—R
$-New Freeman—R
$-ONEvoice!
$-Palm Beach—R
Parents & Teens—R
Penned from the Heart
$-Plains Faith—R
$-Prairie Messenger—R
Presbyterian Outlook
$-Priority!—R
$-Prism—R
Randall House Periodicals
$-SingleAgain.com
$-Smart Families—R
Spiritual Voice—R
$-St. Anthony Messenger
Sword of the Lord—R
$-Testimony—R
thegoodsteward.com—R
$-Today's Christian—R
$-Today's Pentecostal Evangel—R
Trumpeter—R
$-U.S. Catholic
Victory News—R
$-Wesleyan Life—R
$-World & I—R

CHILDREN
$-American Girl

$-BREAD/God's Children—R
$-Cadet Quest—R
$-Club Connection
$-Guideposts for Kids
$-High Adventure—R
$-My Friend
$-SHINEbrightly—R
Skipping Stones

CHRISTIAN EDUCATION/ LIBRARY

$-Church Educator—R
$-Group Magazine
$-Journal/Adventist Educ.—R
$-Leader in C. E. Ministries—R
$-Momentum
$-Resource—R
$-RTJ
$-Teachers of Vision—R

$-Youth & CE Leadership

MISSIONS
East-West Church

PASTORS/LEADERS
$-Barefoot—R
$-Catholic Servant
$-Cornerstone Youth—R
$-Enrichment—R
$-Evangelical Baptist—R
$-Evangelicals Today—R
$-InSite—R
$-Interpreter
$-Lutheran Partners—R
$-Ministries Today
$-Parish Life—R
$-Pastoral Life—R
Plugged In

$-Pray!—R
Sharing the Practice—R
$-Word & World
Youth Culture
$-Youthworker

TEEN/YOUNG ADULT
$-Credo—R
GO!
$-Guideposts Sweet 16—R
Teen Light—R
$-Young Christian—R

WOMEN
$-Godly Business Woman
Home-Based Moms—R
Just Between Us—R
P31 Woman—R
Shalom Bayit

ALPHABETICAL LISTINGS OF PERIODICALS AND E-ZINES

Following are the listings of periodicals. They are arranged alphabetically by type of periodical (see table of contents for a list of types). Nonpaying markets are indicated in bold letters within those listings, e.g. **NO PAYMENT.** Paying markets are indicated with a $ in front of the listing.

If a listing is preceded by an asterisk (*), it indicates that publisher did not send updated information and we were unable to contact them by any means. If it is preceded by a number symbol (#) it was updated from current guidelines, or other available sources. If it is preceded by a (+) it is a new listing. It is important that freelance writers request writer's guidelines and a recent sample copy before submitting to any of these publications.

If you do not find the publication you are looking for, look in the General Index. See the introduction of that index for the codes used to identify the current status of each unlisted publication.

For a detailed explanation of how to understand and get the most out of these listings, as well as solid marketing tips, see the "How to Use This Book" section at the front of this book. Unfamiliar terms are explained in the Glossary at the back of the book.

(*) An asterisk before a listing indicates no or unconfirmed information update.
(#) A number symbol before a listing means it was updated from the current writer's guidelines or other sources.
(+) A plus sign means it is a new listing.
($) A dollar sign before a listing indicates a paying market.
($) A dollar sign in parentheses before a listing indicates they pay in some circumstances.

ADULT/GENERAL MARKETS

$ABILITIES MAGAZINE, 401—340 College St., Toronto ON M5T 3A9, Canada. (416)923-1885, ext. 232. Fax (416)923-9829. E-mail: jaclyn@abilities.ca. Website: www.abilities.ca, or www.enablelink.org. Canadian Abilities Foundation; secular. Jaclyn Law, mng. ed. Canada's foremost cross-disabilities lifestyle magazine. Open to freelance. Query; e-query OK. Pays $50-400 for 1st rts. Articles 500-2,000 wds. No simultaneous submissions. Requires disk. Kill fee 50%. Guidelines & theme list on Website. (Ads)
   Tips: "Ensure your query is strongly Canadian and includes strategies, news, or ideas on living with a disability."

AFRICAN VOICES, 270 W. 96th St., New York NY 10025. (212)865-2982. Fax (212)316-3335. E-mail: africanvoices@aol.com. Website: www.africanvoices.com. African Voices Communications, Inc. Carolyn A. Butts, mng. ed.; Kim Horne, fiction ed.; Debbie Officer, book review ed. Publishes original fiction, nonfiction, and poetry by artists of color. Quarterly mag.; 48 pgs.; circ. 20,000. Subscription $12. 75% unsolicited freelance; 25% assigned. Query/clips; e-query OK. **PAYS IN COPIES** for 1st rts. Articles 500-2,500 wds. (25/yr.); fiction 500-1,500 wds. (20/yr.); book reviews 500-1,200 wds. Responds in 16 wks. Seasonal 4 mos. ahead. Accepts simultaneous submissions & reprints (tell when/where appeared). Requires accepted submissions by e-mail (copied into message). Uses some sidebars. Guidelines; copy $5/9x12 SAE/$1.42 postage (mark "Media Mail"). (Ads)
   Poetry: Layding Kalbia, poetry ed. Accepts 75-80/yr. Free verse, haiku, traditional; to 3 pgs. Submit max. 3 poems.
   Fillers: Accepts 10/yr. Cartoons.

AGAIN MAGAZINE, 10090-A Hwy 9, Ben Lomond CA 95005. (831)336-5118. Fax (831)336-8882. E-mail: tzell@conciliarpress.com. Website: www.conciliarpress.com. Antiochian

Orthodox Archdiocese of North America/Conciliar Press. Father Thomas Zell, mng. ed. Historic Eastern Orthodox Christianity applied to our modern times. Quarterly mag.; 32 pgs.; circ. 5,000. Subscription $16. 1% unsolicited freelance; 99% assigned. Query; e-query OK. **USUALLY PAYS IN COPIES.** Articles 1,500-2,500 wds. (4/yr.); book reviews 800-1,000 wds. Responds in 6-8 wks. Seasonal 4-6 mos. ahead. Serials 2 parts. Accepts reprints (tell when/where appeared). Prefers requested ms on disk or by e-mail (copied into message). Uses some sidebars. Prefers NKJV. Guidelines (also by e-mail); copy for 9x12 SAE/4 stamps. (No ads)

> **Tips:** "We are Orthodox in orientation, and interested in thoughtful, intelligent articles dealing with church history, Protestant/Orthodox dialog, relations between Protestants and Orthodox in foreign countries, also in modern ethical dilemmas—no fluff."

$ALIVE! A Magazine for Vibrant Christians Over 50, PO Box 46464, Cincinnati OH 45246-0464. (513)825-3681. Website: www.missionsalive.org/CSF. Christian Seniors Fellowship. David Lang, ed.; submit to June Lang, office ed. Focuses on activities and opportunities for active Christian senior adults, 55 & older; upbeat rather than nostalgic. Bimonthly mag.; 24 pgs.; circ. 3,000. Subscription/membership $18. 60% unsolicited freelance; 10% assigned. Complete ms/cover letter; no e-query. Pays .04-.06/wd. ($18-75) on publication for one-time or reprint rts. Articles 600-1,200 wds. (25-50/yr.); fiction 600-1,200 wds. (12/yr.). Responds in 9 wks. Seasonal 6 mos. ahead. Accepts reprints (tell when/where appeared). No disk. Uses some sidebars. Guidelines; copy for 9x12 SAE/3 stamps. (Ads)

> **Fillers:** Buys 15/yr. Anecdotes, cartoons, quizzes, short humor, & word puzzles, 50-500 wds.; $2-15.
>
> **Columns/Departments:** Buys 50/yr. Heart Medicine (humor, grandparent/grandchild anecdotes), to 100 wds., $2-25.
>
> **Tips:** "Most open to fresh material of special appeal to Christian adults over 50. Avoid nostalgia. Our market is the over-50 interested in living in the present, not dwelling on the past. We pay little attention to credits/bios; articles stand on their own merit. Stories of seniors in short-term missions or other Christian activities, or active senior groups involved in service—not just social activities."

$ALIVE NOW, PO Box 340004, Nashville TN 37203-0004. (615)340-7218. Fax (615)340-7267. E-mail: alivenow@upperroom.org. Website: www.alivenow.org. United Methodist/ The Upper Room. Melissa Tidwell, ed. Short, theme-based writings in attractive graphic setting for reflection and meditation. Bimonthly mag.; 64 pgs.; circ. 70,000. Subscription $14.95. 25% unsolicited freelance; 75% assigned. Complete ms/cover letter; e-query OK. Pays $50 & up on publication for newspaper, periodical, or electronic rts. Articles 300-500 wds. (25/yr.). Responds 13 wks. before issue date. Seasonal 6-8 mos. ahead. Accepts simultaneous submissions & reprints (tell when/where appeared). Accepts e-mail submissions (copied into message). Uses some sidebars. Prefers NRSV. Guidelines/theme list (also on Website); copy for 6x9 SAE/4 stamps.

> **Poetry:** Avant-garde, free verse, traditional; to 40 lines or one page; $40 & up. Submit max. 5 poems.
>
> **Fillers:** Prayers.
>
> **Tips:** "Write for our theme list and make your submission relevant to the topic. Avoid the obvious and heavy-handed preachiness."

ALLIANCE LIFE, PO Box 35000, Colorado Springs CO 80935-3500. (719)599-5999. Fax (719)599-8234. E-mail: alife@cmalliance.org. Website: www.alliancelife.org. The Christian & Missionary Alliance/denominational. Mark Failing, ed. To teach and inspire readers concerning principles of Christian living. Monthly mag.; circ. 23,000. Subscription free. Open to freelance. Prefers query. **NO PAYMENT.** Articles 900-1,200 wds. Guidelines by e-mail/Website; copy. (Ads)

Tips: "Looking for first-person stories that show God at work and involvement in fulfilling the Great Commission."

****2005, 2004 EPA Award of Merit—Denominational.

\$AMERICA, 106 W. 56th St., New York NY 10019-3893. (212)581-4640. Fax (212)399-3596. E-mail: articles@americamagazine.org. Website: www.americamagazine.org. Catholic. Submit to Editor-in-Chief. For thinking Catholics and those who want to know what Catholics are thinking. Weekly mag. & online version; 32+ pgs.; circ. 46,000. Subscription \$48. 100% unsolicited freelance. Complete ms/cover letter; fax/e-query OK. Pays \$100-200 on acceptance. Articles 1,500-2,000 wds. Responds in 6 wks. Seasonal 3 mos. ahead. No sidebars. Guidelines (also on Website); copy for 9x12 SAE. (Ads) Incomplete topical listings.

Poetry: Buys avant-garde, free verse, light verse, traditional; 20-35 line; \$2-3/line.

AMERICAN TRACT SOCIETY, Box 462008, Garland TX 75046. (972)276-9408. Fax (972)272-9642. E-mail: PBatzing@ATSTracts.org. Website: www.ATSTracts.org. Peter Batzing, tract ed. Majority of tracts written to win unbelievers. Bimonthly new tract releases; 40 new titles produced annually. 5% unsolicited freelance; 2% assigned. Complete ms/cover letter; e-query OK. **PAYS IN COPIES** on publication for exclusive tract rts. Tracts 600-1,200 wds. Responds in 6-8 wks. Seasonal 1 yr. ahead. Accepts simultaneous submissions & reprints (tell when/where appeared). Accepts requested ms on disk or by e-mail (attached or copied into message). Prefers NIV, KJV. Guidelines (also by e-mail)/free samples for #10 SAE/1 stamp. (No ads)

Special Needs: Youth issues, African American, cartoonists, critical issues.

Tips: "Read our current tracts; submit polished writing; relate to people's needs and experiences. Follow guidelines—almost no one does."

\$ANCIENT PATHS, PO Box 7505, Fairfax Station VA 22039. E-mail: ssburris@msn.com. Website: www.editorskylar.com. Christian/nondenominational. Skylar Hamilton Burris, ed. For a literate Christian audience, or non-Christians open to and moved by traditional-themed poetry and fiction. Annual literary mag; 48 pgs.; circ. 175-200. Subscription \$5. 100% unsolicited freelance. Complete ms only; no queries. Pays \$2 for prose & \$3 for artwork on publication for 1st, one-time, reprint, & electronic (optional) rts. Not copyrighted. Fiction (or creative essays/true stories) to 2,500 wds. (5/yr.). Responds in 5 wks. No seasonal. Accepts simultaneous submissions & reprints (tell when/where appeared). Accepts e-mail submissions only from outside U.S. No kill fee. Does not use sidebars. Prefers KJV. Accepts submissions from teens (but must compete with adults). Guidelines (also on Website); copy \$4 (make check to Skylar Burris). (Ads—inserts only)

Poetry: Buys 25-35/yr. Free verse, haiku, traditional; 4-60 lines; pays \$1 & 1 copy. Submit max. 5 poems.

Contest: Occasionally sponsors contest; check Website. Books for prizes.

Tips: "Looking for shorter fiction (under 1,000 wds.). Visit the Website and read sample literature or order a copy. Read the great Christian writers—O'Connor, Lewis, Hopkins, Donne, Herbert, Tennyson, etc. Send your best work, even if it's been previously published (we're open to reprints). Stir your reader's emotions, but don't directly tell him what to think."

ANGEL FACE, PO Box 102, Huffman TX 77336. E-mail: MaryAnkaPress@cs.com. Website: www.maryanka.com. MaryAnka Press/Catholic. Mary Agnes Dalrymple, pub. Religious or secular poetry loosely based on the rosary, birth, rebirth, joy, light, sorrow, epiphany, hope, Jesus, Mary, the seasons of nature and the cycles of life, the search for God in everyday life, etc. (but open to all denominations). Annual literary mag.; 50 pgs.; circ. 100. Subscription \$12. Estab. 2004. 10% unsolicited freelance. Complete ms/cover letter; no phone/fax/e-query. **PAYS 1 COPY** for one-time rts. Poetry only. Responds in 1-6 mos.

Accepts simultaneous submissions & reprints (tell when/where appeared). No submission by e-mail or on disk. Guidelines (also on Website); copy $6.

Poetry: Accepts 35/yr. Free-verse poetry, 60-65 lines. Submit max. 5 poems (typed).

Tips: "Don't be thrown off by the rosary concept. I am open to all viewpoints and have published poems by non-Christians as well as Catholic and protestant writers. Send your best work even if you are not sure it fits the rosary pattern. Info on the rosary pattern can be found on my Website."

$ANGELICA, 207 Grinders Pl., Vicksburg, MS 39180. E-mail: lynettewfuller@yahoo.com. Website: www.angelicamagazine.com. Angelica Publishing. Lynette W. Fuller, ed. Features Contemporary Christian fiction and photography, primarily faith-based suspense/thrillers. Quarterly mag. Estab. 2004. 90% freelance. Pays .20/wd. (.10/wd. for reprints). Short stories 1,700-4,000 wds. (40/yr.). Guidelines by e-mail.

Poetry: Accepts some; see guidelines.

Tips: "We also accept a few stories that are more character/emotion driven, as long as they have a compelling plot."

$ANGELS ON EARTH, 16 E. 34th St., New York NY 10016. (212)251-8100. Fax (212)684-1311. E-mail: angelseditors@guideposts.org. Website: www.angelsonearth.com. Guideposts. Colleen Hughes, ed-in-chief; Meg Belviso, depts. ed. for features and fillers. Presents true stories about God's angels and humans who have played angelic roles on earth. Bimonthly mag.; 75 pgs.; circ. 550,000. Subscription $19.95. 90% unsolicited freelance. Complete ms/cover letter; no phone/fax/e-query. Pays $100-400 on publication for all rts. Articles 100-1,500 wds. (100/yr.); all stories must be true. Responds in 13 wks. Seasonal 6 mos. ahead. No disk or e-mail submissions. Guidelines (also by e-mail/Website); copy for 7x10 SAE/4 stamps.

Fillers: Buys many. Anecdotal shorts of similar nature; 50-250 wds.; $50-100.

Columns/Departments: Buys 20-30/yr. Messages (brief, mysterious happenings), $25. Earning Their Wings (good deeds), 150 wds., $50. Only Human? (human or angel?/mystery), 350 wds.; $100.

Tips: "We are not limited to stories about heavenly angels. We also accept stories about human beings doing heavenly duties."

THE ANGLICAN, 135 Adelaide St. E., Toronto M5C 1L8, Canada. Toll-free (800)668-8932, ext. 247. (416)363-6021. Fax (416)363-7678. E-mail: smann@toronto.anglican.ca. Website: www.toronto.anglican.ca. Anglican Diocese of Toronto. Stuart Mann, ed. Provides timely news, in-depth features, and challenging opinions to Anglicans in this Diocese. Monthly (10X) tabloid; circ. 300. Subscription $8. Open to unsolicited freelance. Not included in topical listings. (Ads)

$ANGLICAN JOURNAL, 80 Hayden St., Toronto ON M4Y 2J6, Canada. (416)924-9199, ext. 306. Fax (416)921-4452. E-mail: editor@national.anglican.ca. Website: www.anglicanjournal.com. Anglican Church of Canada. Leanne Larmondin, ed.; Steve Brickenden, ed. asst. (sbrickenden@national.anglican.ca). National newspaper of the Anglican Church of Canada; informs Canadian Anglicans about the church at home and overseas. Newspaper (10x/yr.) & online; 12-16 pgs.; circ. 215,000. Subscription $10 Cdn., $17 U.S. & foreign. 10% unsolicited freelance. Query only; fax/e-query OK. Pays $50-300 or .23/wd. Cdn., on acceptance for 1st & electronic rts. Articles 600 wds. (12-15/yr.). Responds in 2 wks. Seasonal 2 mos. ahead. No reprints. Guidelines (also by e-mail). (Ads)

$ANIMAL TRAILS, 2660 Peterborough St., Herndon VA 20171. Phone/fax (703)715-1129. E-mail: bridalguides@yahoo.com, or weddingandromancewriters@yahoogroups.com. Tellstar Publishing. Shannon Bridget Murphy, ed. Keeping animal memories alive through writing. Quarterly mag. 85% unsolicited freelance. Complete ms/cover letter; e-query OK. Pays .02-.05/wd. on acceptance for 1st, one-time, reprint, or simultaneous rts. Articles to

2,000 wds.; fiction to 2,000 wds. Responds in 2-8 wks. Seasonal 3 mos. ahead. Accepts simultaneous submissions & reprints (tell when/where appeared). Accepts disk or e-mail submissions (attached or copied into message.). No kill fee. Regularly uses sidebars. Prefers KJV. Guidelines by e-mail. (No ads)

Poetry: Buys variable number. Avant-garde, free verse, haiku, light verse, traditional; any length. Pays variable rates. Submit any number.

Fillers: Buys most types, to 1,000 wds.

Tips: "Send a well-written article that is suitable for this publication."

$THE ANNALS OF SAINT ANNE DE BEAUPRE, PO Box 1000, St. Anne de Beaupre QC G0A 3C0, Canada. (418)827-4538. Fax (418)827-4530. E-mail: mag@revuesteannedebeaupre.ca. Website: www.ssadb.qc.ca. Catholic/Redemptorist Fathers. Fr. Bernard Mercier, C.Ss.R., ed.; submit to Fr. Roch Achard, C.Ss.R., mng. ed. Promotes Catholic family values. Monthly mag.; 32 pgs.; circ. 45,000. Subscription $12.50 U.S., $14.50 Cdn. 80% unsolicited freelance. Complete ms/cover letter; no phone/fax/e-query. Pays .03-.04/wd. on acceptance for 1st N.A. serial rts. only. Articles (350/yr.) & fiction (200/yr.); 500-1,500 wds. Responds in 4-5 wks. Seasonal 6 mos. ahead. No simultaneous submissions or reprints. No disk or e-mail submission. Does not use sidebars. Prefers NRSV. Guidelines; copy for 9x12 SAE/IRC. (No ads)

Tips: "Writing must be uplifting and inspirational, clearly written, not filled with long quotations. We tend to stay away from extreme controversy and focus on the family, good family values, devotion, and Christianity." Rights must be clearly stated. Typed manuscripts only.

$THE APOCALYPSE CHRONICLES, Box 448, Jacksonville OR 97530. Phone/fax (541)899-8888. E-mail: James@ChristianMediaNetwork.com. Websites: www.ChristianMediaDaily.com; www.christianmedianetwork.com; www.christianmediaresearch.com; and www.sound bodycm.com (health articles). Christian Media. James Lloyd, ed./pub. Deals with the apocalypse exclusively. Quarterly & online newsletter; circ. 2,000-3,000. Query; prefers phone query. Payment negotiable for reprint rts. Articles. Responds in 3 wks. Requires KJV. No guidelines; copy for #10 SAE/2 stamps.

Tips: "It's helpful if you understand your own prophetic position and are aware of its name, i.e., Futurist, Historicist, etc."

$ARKANSAS CATHOLIC, PO Box 7417, Little Rock AR 72217. (501)664-0340. Fax (501)664-6572. E-mail: mhargett@dolr.org. Catholic Diocese of Little Rock. Malea Hargett, ed.; Tara Little, assoc. ed. Statewide newspaper for the local diocese. Weekly tabloid; 16 pgs.; circ. 7,000. Subscription $18. 1% unsolicited freelance; 10% assigned. Query/clips; e-query OK. Pays $3/inch on publication for 1st rts. Articles 1,000 wds. Accepts simultaneous submissions & reprints. Accepts requested ms on disk or by e-mail. Uses some sidebars. Prefers Catholic Bible. Guidelines (also by e-mail); copy for 9x12 SAE/2 stamps. (Ads)

Columns/Departments: Tara Little, ed. Buys 2/yr. Seeds of Faith (education). Complete ms. Pays $15.

Tips: "All stories and columns must have an Arkansas connection."

$ARLINGTON CATHOLIC HERALD, 200 N. Glebe Rd., Ste. 600, Arlington VA 22203. (703)841-2590. Fax (703)524-2782. E-mail: editorial@catholicherald.com. Website: http://catholicherald.com/index.htm. Catholic Diocese of Arlington. Michael F. Flach, ed. Regional newspaper for the local diocese. Weekly newspaper; 28 pgs.; circ. 53,000. Subscription $14. 10% unsolicited freelance. Query; phone/fax/e-query OK. Pays $50-150 on publication for one-time rts. Articles 500-1,500 wds. Responds in 2 wks. Seasonal 3 mos. ahead. Accepts simultaneous submissions. Prefers accepted ms on disk. Regular sidebars. Guidelines (also on Website); copy for 11x17 SAE. (Ads)

Columns/Departments: Sports; School News; Local Entertainment; 500 wds.

Tips: "All submissions must be Catholic-related. Avoid controversial issues within the church."

$#ASPIRING RETAIL (formerly *CBA Marketplace*), 9240 Explorer Dr., Colorado Springs CO 80920. Toll-free (800)252-1950. (719)265-9895. Fax (719)272-3510. E-mail: publications@ cbaonline.org. Website: www.cbaonline.org. Christian Booksellers Assn. Submit to The Editor; Carrie Erickson, music/video ed. (cerickson@cbaonline.org). To provide Christian bookstore owners and managers with professional retail skills, product information, and industry news. Monthly trade journal (also in digital edition); 110-260 pgs.; circ. 8,000. Subscription $59.95 (for nonmembers). 0% unsolicited freelance; 30% assigned. Query/clips; fax/e-query OK. Pays .20-.30/wd. on acceptance for all rts. Articles 800-2,000 wds. (30/yr. assigned); book/music/video reviews, 150 wds., $30-35. Responds in 8 wks. Seasonal 4-5 mos. ahead. Prefers requested ms on disk. Regularly uses sidebars. Accepts any modern Bible version. Theme list; copy $5/9x12 SAE/$1.42 postage (mark "Media Mail"). (Ads/Carlton Dunn & Assoc./856-582-0690)

> **Fillers:** Buys 12/yr. Cartoons ($100), retail facts, ideas, trends, newsbreaks.
>
> **Columns/Departments:** Buys 10-20/yr. Industry Watch; Music News; Gift News; Video & Software News; Book News; Kids News; Spanish News; all 100-500 wds. Pays .16-.25/wd. Query.
>
> **Special Needs:** Trends in retail, consumer buying habits, market profiles. By assignment only.
>
> **Tips:** "Looking for writers who have been owners/managers/buyers/sales staff in Christian retail stores. All our articles are by assignment and focus on producing and selling Christian products or conducting retail business. Send cover letter, including related experience and areas of interest, plus samples. We also assign reviews of books, music, videos, Spanish products, kids products, and software. Ask for calendar for product news and market-segment features."

$+ASSOCIATED CONTENT, 222 Milwaukie St., #302, Denver CO 80206. (720)255-9185. E-mail: miguel@associatedcontent.com. Website: www.associatedcontent.com. Associated Content. Miguel Chacon, submissions mngr. Weekly e-zine; 1000+ pgs. Free online. Estab. 2004. 100% unsolicited freelance. Query online. Pays $5-50 on acceptance for nonexclusive, electronic rts. Articles 500-5,000 wds. (1,000+/yr.); fiction 500-5,000 wds. (1,000+/yr.). Responds in 2 wks. Seasonal 1 mo. ahead. Accepts simultaneous submissions & reprints (tell when/where appeared). Accepts submissions online only. Guidelines on Website; copy online.

> **Poetry:** Avant-garde, free verse, haiku, light verse, traditional.
>
> **Tips:** "Look over Website and see what the other writers are doing. Sign up, fill out a profile, and submit your work."

$ATLANTIC CATHOLIC, PO Box 1300, 88 College St., Antigonish NS B2G 2L7, Canada. (902)863-4370. Fax (902)863-1943. E-mail: atlanticcatholic@thecasket.ca. The Casket Printing and Publishing Co. Ken Sims, pub.; Brian Lazzuri, mng. ed. Reports religious news that will inform, educate, and inspire Catholics. Biweekly tabloid; circ. 2,500. Subscription $28. Open to unsolicited freelance. Pays $25/story. Incomplete topical listings. (Ads)

$AUJOURD'HUI CREDO, 1332 Victoria, Longueuil QC J4V 1L8, Canada. (450)466-7733. Fax (450)466-2664. E-mail: davidfines@egliseunie.org. Website: www.united-church.ca. United Church of Canada. David Fines, dir. The only French Reformed magazine in North America. Monthly mag.; 28 pgs.; circ. 250. Subscription $25 Cdn. 20% unsolicited freelance. Complete ms; fax/e-query OK. Pays $50 on publication for nonexclusive rts. Not copyrighted. Articles 1,500 wds. (10/yr.); fiction 800 wds. (6/yr.); reviews 100 wds. Responds in 4 wks. Seasonal 2 mos. ahead. Accepts simultaneous submissions & reprints (tell when/where appeared). Requires e-mail submissions (attached or copied into message). No kill fee. Sometimes uses sidebars. Accepts submissions from children or teens. Prefers TOB. Guidelines/theme list by e-mail; free copy. (Ads)

Poetry: Accepts free verse.

Tips: "Most likely to break in by being inclusive and intelligent. Most preferably written in French."

+THE BAPTIST STANDARD, PO Box 660267, Dallas TX 75266-0267. (214)630-4571. Fax (214)638-8535. E-mail: marvknox@baptiststandard.com. Website: www.baptiststandard.com/postnuke/index.php. Marv Knox, ed. The Texas Baptist news journal. Biweekly newspaper. Subscription $20.50. Incomplete topical listings. No questionnaire returned.

$BAREFOOT PATH, PO Box 3743, Englewood CO 80155. E-mail: jeanne@barefootonholyground.com. Website: www.barefootpath.com. Jeanne Gowen Dennis, ed. Explores childlike wonder and faith for Christian adults who long for a more intimate relationship with their Father/Creator. Quarterly e-zine. Free online. Estab. 2004. 80-90% unsolicited freelance. Complete ms; e-query OK. Pays .01/wd. on publication for 1st, one-time, reprint, simultaneous, electronic, or nonexclusive rts.; right to archive on Website. Not copyrighted. Articles 300-700 wds. (16/yr.); reviews 35-75 wds. Responds in 4-6 wks. Seasonal 2 mos. ahead. Accepts simultaneous submissions & reprints (tell when/where appeared). Requires e-mail submission (copied into message). Does not use sidebars. Accepts submissions from teens. Prefers NIV, NASB, NKJV. Guidelines on Website; copy online. (Ads)

Poetry: Buys 4-8/yr. Free verse, light verse, traditional; 4-25 lines. Prefers unrhymed. Submit max. 5 poems.

Columns/Departments: Accepts 8+/yr. Barefoot on Tiptoe (activity, exercise, or tip to stimulate childlike wonder or faith), 50-100 wds.; Holy Ground (devotional related to childlike wonder or faith), 100-250 wds., plus scripture verse; Roaming the Path (reviews of resources to help readers grow in childlike wonder or faith), 35-75 wds.

Special Needs: "Writing that will inspire wonder at God's great love for us and a childlike spirit of worship in response." Needs illustrators/photographers; features one work of an illustrator/photographer in each issue with a bio and link to their Website.

Tips: "Most open to articles, devotionals, poetry. Understand our focus. To break in, send us quality writing that fits our theme (inspires childlike wonder and faith in readers)."

$B.C. CATHOLIC, 150 Robson St., Vancouver BC V6B 2A7, Canada. (604)683-0281. Fax (604)683-8117. E-mail: bcc@rcav.bc.ca. Website: www.rcav.bc.ca/bcc. Roman Catholic Archdiocese of Vancouver. Paul Schratz, ed. News, education, and inspiration for Canadian Catholics. Weekly (48X) newspaper; 20 pgs.; circ. 20,000. Subscription $32. 20% unsolicited freelance. Query; phone query OK. Pays .15/wd. on publication for 1st rts. Photos $25. Articles 500-1,000 wds. Responds in 6 wks. Seasonal 4 wks. ahead. Accepts simultaneous submissions & reprints. Prefers e-mail submission (copied into message). Guidelines on Website; free copy. (Ads)

Tips: "Items of a Catholic nature are preferred."

+THE BEACON, 980 Hwy 331, Columbiana AL 35051. (205)664-7417. Fax (205)663-0794. E-mail: publisher@newsbeacon.com. Website: www.newsbeacon.com. Teresa Anderson, ed. (editor@newsbeacon.com). Weekly newspaper. Incomplete topical listings. No questionnaire returned.

$BELIEVER'S BAY, PO Box 6362, Clearwater FL 33758. Toll-free (888)564-3534. E-mail: editor@BelieversBay.com. Website: www.BelieversBay.com. Ro Lashua, pub./ed-in-chief. To unite the body of Christ through communication, exhortation, and edification while focusing on ministries in the body of Christ. Monthly online mag. Mostly freelance. Complete ms by e-mail only; e-query OK. Pays $15 for 1st & electronic rts. (keeps posted for 3 mos. & archives with permission). Articles or fiction 900-1,000 wds. Guidelines/monthly topical themes listed on Website submissions page.

Columns/Departments: Columns to 500 wds. One column opening now; however, looking for writers who focus on prophecy. Pays $15.

Special Needs: Focus on prayer every month.

Tips: "We need all submissions via e-mail."

$BGC WORLD, 2002 S. Arlington Heights Rd., Arlington Heights IL 60005-4102. Toll-free (800)323-4215. (847)228-0200. Fax (847)228-5376. E-mail: bputman@baptist general.org. Website: www.bgcworld.org. Baptist General Conference. Bob Putman, ed. Almost exclusively for, about, and by the people and ministries of the Baptist General Conference. Monthly (10X) mag.; 16 pgs.; circ. 44,000. Subscription free. Estab. 2003. 35% unsolicited freelance; 65% assigned. Query; e-query preferred. Pays $30-280 on publication for 1st, reprint, electronic rts. Articles 800-1,300 wds. (12/yr.). Responds in 6-8 wks. Seasonal 8 mos. ahead. Accepts simultaneous submissions & reprints (tell when/where appeared). Prefers accepted mss by e-mail (attached file). Kill fee 50%. Uses some sidebars. Prefers NIV. Guidelines (also by e-mail); free copy. (Ads)

> **Columns/Departments:** Buys 30/yr. New Life (first-person transformation story), 750-1,200 wds.; Profile (third-person story of key leader), 750 wds.; Around the BGC (short news blurb of happenings in churches), 75-200 wds.; Good Ideas (ministries working in BGC churches), 250-400 wds.; $30-115.
>
> **Tips:** "Report on interesting happenings/ministry in BGC churches close to you for our Around the BGC or Good Ideas columns. Or query on a theme-related article."

$BIBLE ADVOCATE, Box 33677, Denver CO 80233. (303)452-7973. Fax (303)452-0657. E-mail: bibleadvocate@cog7.org. Website: www.cog7.org/BA. Church of God (Seventh-day). Calvin Burrell, ed.; Sherri Langton, assoc. ed. Adult readers; 50% not members of the denomination. Monthly (8X) mag.; 32 pgs.; circ. 13,500. Subscription free. 25-35% unsolicited freelance. Complete ms/cover letter; no phone/fax/e-query. Pays $25-55 on publication for 1st, one-time, reprint, electronic, simultaneous rts. Articles 1,000-1,500 wds. (10-20/yr.). Responds in 4-8 wks. Seasonal 9 mos. ahead (no Christmas or Easter pieces). Accepts simultaneous submissions & reprints (tell when/where appeared). Accepts requested ms on disk or by e-mail (copied into message). Regularly uses sidebars. Prefers NIV, NKJV. Guidelines/theme list (also on Website); copy for 9x12 SAE/3 stamps. (No ads)

> **Poetry:** Buys 6-10/yr. Free verse, traditional; 5-20 lines; $20. Submit max. 5 poems.
>
> **Fillers:** Buys 5-10/yr. Facts, prose, quotes; 100-400 wds.; $20.
>
> **Columns/Departments:** Accepts 5/yr. Viewpoint (social or religious issues); 650-675 wds.; pays copies.
>
> **Special Needs:** Articles centering on upcoming themes (ask for theme list).
>
> **Tips:** "If you write well, all areas are open to freelance, especially personal experiences that tie in with the monthly themes. Articles that run 650-700 words are more likely to get in. Also, fresh writing with keen insight is most readily accepted. Writers may submit sidebars that fit our theme for each issue." Magazine was redesigned in 2005.

**This periodical was #28 on the 2003 Top 50 Christian Publishers list (#36 in 2002).

+BIBLICAL RECORDER, PO Box 18808, Raleigh NC 27619. E-mail: biblical@biblical recorder.org. Website: www.biblicalrecorder.org. Baptist. Steve DeVane, mng. ed. Newspaper. Subscription $13.40. Incomplete topical listings. No questionnaire returned.

BOOKS & CULTURE, 465 Gundersen Dr., Carol Stream IL 60188. (630)260-6200. Fax (630)260-8428. E-mail: bceditor@booksandculture.com, or jwilson@christianity today.com. Website: www.booksandculture.com. Christianity Today Intl. John Wilson, ed. To edify, sharpen, and nurture the evangelical intellectual community by engaging the world in all its complexity from a distinctly Christian perspective. Bimonthly & online newsletter.; circ. 12,000. Subscription $24.95. Open to freelance. Query. Incomplete topical listings. (Ads)

**2004 & 2003 EPA Award of Merit—General. 2001 EPA Award of Excellence—General.

$BRAVE HEARTS, 1503 S.W. 42nd St., Topeka KS 66609-1265. Toll-free (800)678-5779, ext.

4345. (785)274-4300. Fax (785)274-4305. Website: www.braveheartsmagazine.com. Ogden Publications/Grit Magazine. Andrea Skallard, ed-in-chief; Jean Teller and Traci Smith, mng. eds. Written by ordinary people who have an inspirational message to share. Quarterly magazine; 48 pgs.; circ. 2,000. Subscription $9.95. 100% unsolicited freelance. Complete ms; no phone/fax/e-query. Pays up to $15 on publication for shared rts. Articles to 900 wds. (100/yr.). Responds in 3-6 mos. Seasonal 6 mos. ahead. Call 800# for guidelines/theme list (also on Website); copy for $4/6x9 SAE.

Poetry: Buys 3-4/yr. Free verse, light verse, traditional, 4-16 lines. Submit max. 5 poems.

Tips: "All departments open to freelancers. Send submissions that correspond with each issue's theme."

THE BREAD OF LIFE, 209 MacNab St. N., Box 395, Hamilton ON L8N 3H8, Canada. (905)529-4496. Fax (905)529-5373. E-mail: steeners@cyberus.ca. Website: www.thebreadoflife.ca. Catholic. Fr. Peter Coughlin, ed. Catholic Charismatic; to encourage spiritual growth in areas of renewal in the Catholic Church today. Bimonthly mag.; 32 pgs.; circ. 2,500. Subscription $30. 5% unsolicited freelance. Complete ms/cover letter; fax query OK. **NO PAYMENT.** Articles 1,100-1,300 wds.; biblical fiction; book reviews 250 wds. Responds in 4-6 wks. Seasonal 6 mos. ahead. Accepts reprints (tell when/where appeared). No disk. Does not use sidebars. Prefers NAB, NJB. Guidelines; copy for 9x12 SAE/$1.42 postage (mark "Media Mail"). (Ads)

Poetry: Accepts little.

Fillers: Accepts 10-12/yr. Facts, prose, quotes; to 250 wds.

Tips: "We do appreciate poetry submissions and shorter articles, 750 words. It is best if a writer includes a 2-3 line biography and photo for publication."

THE BREAKTHROUGH INTERCESSOR, PO Box 121, Lincoln VA 20160. (540)338-5522. Fax (540)338-1934. E-mail: breakthrough@intercessors.org. Website: www.intercessors.org. Nondenominational. Andrea Doudera, ed.; Aledra Hollenbach, mng. ed. Preparing and equipping people who pray; encouraging in prayer and faith. Quarterly mag.; 44 pgs.; circ. 7,000. Subscription $15. 100% unsolicited freelance. Complete ms/cover letter; fax/e-query OK. **NO PAYMENT.** Articles about 1,000 wds. (50/yr.). Accepts simultaneous submissions & reprints (tell when/where appeared). Accepts requested ms on disk or by e-mail. Regularly uses sidebars. Any Bible version. Guidelines; copy for 6x9 SAE/3 stamps. (No ads)

Special Needs: All articles must deal with prayer.

Contest: Pays $25 for article with most reader impact.

Tips: "Break in by submitting true articles/stories about prayer and its miraculous results." Manuscripts acknowledged but not returned.

$BRIDAL GUIDES, 2660 Peterborough St., Herndon VA 20171. Phone/fax (703)715-1129. E-mail: bridalguides@yahoo.com, or weddingandromancewriters@yahoogroups.com. Tellstar Publishing. Shannon Bridget Murphy, ed. Theme-based wedding/reception ideas and planning for Christian wedding planners. Quarterly mag. 85% unsolicited freelance. Complete ms/cover letter; e-query OK. Pays .02-.05/wd. on acceptance for 1st, one-time, reprint, & simultaneous rts. Articles to 2,000 wds.; fiction to 2,000 wds. Responds in 2-8 wks. Seasonal 3 mos. ahead. Accepts simultaneous submissions & reprints (tell when/where appeared). Accepts disk or e-mail submissions (attached or copied into message.). No kill fee. Regularly uses sidebars. Prefers KJV. Guidelines by e-mail. (No ads)

Poetry: Buys variable number. Avant-garde, free verse, haiku, light verse, traditional; any length. Pays variable rates. Submit any number.

Fillers: Buys most types, to 1,000 wds.; .02-.05/wd.

Columns/Departments: Financial Planning (budgeting/planning), 1,000 wds.

Special Needs: All aspects of wedding/reception planning; home-planning articles related to a variety of topics; honeymoon destinations and travel advice. Also romance fiction related to weddings, travel, and home.

+BUSINESS REFORM MAGAZINE, 426 E. 8th St., Ashland OH 44805. (419)207-9977. Fax (419)289-8768. E-mail: managingeditor@businessreform.com. Website: www.business reform.com. Business Reform Foundation. Lyle Becker, mng. ed. Business news from a Christian worldview. Bimonthly mag. Open to freelance. Query. Articles. Guidelines by e-mail. Incomplete topical listings. No questionnaire returned. (Ads)

+BYFAITH (byFaith), 1700 N. Brown Rd., Ste. 105, Lawrenceville GA 30043. (678)825-1000. E-mail: editor@byfaithonline.com. Website: www.byfaithonline.com. Presbyterian Church in America (PCA). Dominic Aquila, ed. Bimonthly mag.; 54 pgs. Subscription $19.95. Open to unsolicited freelance. Complete ms by e-mail ("Editorial Submission" in subject line). **NO MENTION OF PAYMENT.** Articles 500-3,000 wds. Guidelines on Website. Incomplete topical listings.

> **Tips:** "We publish in 5 areas: stories that provoke thinking and creativity; very practical theology; articles that help readers understand the arts and culture; sensible, down-to-earth information; and PCA news."

$CANADA LUTHERAN, 302—393 Portage Ave., Winnipeg MB R3B 3H6, Canada. Toll-free (888)786-6707. (204)984-9170. Fax (204)984-9185. E-mail: editor@elcic.ca, or canaluth@elcic.ca. Website: www.elcic.ca/clweb. Evangelical Lutheran Church in Canada. Ida Reichardt Backman, ed. Denominational. Monthly (8X) mag.; 42 pgs.; circ. 14,000. Subscription $35 U.S. 40% unsolicited freelance; 60% assigned. Query or complete ms/cover letter; fax/e-query OK. Pays $40-110 (.10/wd.) Cdn. on publication for one-time rts. Articles 700-1,200 wds. (15/yr.); fiction 850-1,200 wds. (4/yr.). Responds in 5 wks. Seasonal 10 mos. ahead. Accepts simultaneous submissions & reprints. Prefers e-mail submission (copied into message). Uses some sidebars. Prefers NRSV. Guidelines (also by e-mail). (Ads)

> **Tips:** "Canadians/Lutherans receive priority here; others considered but rarely used. Want material that is clear, concise, and fresh. Articles that talk about real life experiences of faith receive our best reader response."

+CANADIAN CHRISTIANITY.COM, #22-20316—56 Ave., Langley BC V3A 3Y7, Canada. Toll-free (888)899-3777. E-mail: editor@canadianchristianity.com. Website: www.Canadian Christianity.com. A ministry of the Christian Info Society. Flyn Ritchie, ed. Online newspaper. Incomplete topical listings. No questionnaire returned.

THE CANADIAN LUTHERAN, 3074 Portage Ave., Winnipeg MB R3K 0Y2, Canada. Toll-free (800)588-4226. (204)895-3433. Fax (204)897-4319. E-mail: communications@ lutheranchurch.ca. Website: www.lutheranchurch.ca. Lutheran Church-Canada. Ian Adnams, ed. Monthly (9X) mag. Subscription $20. Open to unsolicited freelance. Not in topical listings. (Ads)

CANADIAN MENNONITE, 490 Dutton Dr., Unit C5, Waterloo ON N2L 6H7, Canada. Toll-free (800)378-2524, ext. 225. (519)884-3810. Fax (519)884-3331. E-mail: ed@canadian mennonite.org. Website: www.canadianmennonite.org. Canadian Mennonite Publishing Service/Anabaptist Mennonite. Tim Miller Dyck, ed/pub. Seeks to promote covenantal relationships within the church (Hebrews 10:23-25). Biweekly mag.; circ. 20,000. Subscription $32.50 Cdn.; $52.50 U.S. Open to unsolicited freelance. Pays for assignments only (.10/wd.). Guidelines on Website. Not in topical listings. (Ads)

$CAPPERS, 1503 S.W. 42nd St., Topeka KS 66609. (785)274-4300. Fax (785)274-4305. E-mail: cappers@cappers.com. Website: www.cappers.com. Ogden Publications. Andrea Skalland, ed-in-chief. Timely news-oriented features with positive messages. Biweekly mag.; 40-56 pgs.; circ. 150,000. Subscription $27.98. 40% unsolicited freelance. Complete ms/cover letter by mail only. Pays about $2.50/printed inch for nonfiction on publication, pays $100-400 for fiction on acceptance for one-time rts. Articles to 1,000 wds. (50/yr.); fiction to 2,000 wds., serials to 25,000 wds. (20/yr.). Responds in 2-6 mos. Seasonal 6 mos. ahead. No simultaneous submissions or reprints. Prefers requested ms on CD (Mac). Uses some sidebars. Guidelines (also on Website); copy $4/9x12 SASE/4 stamps. (Ads)

Poetry: Attn: Poetry Editor. Buys 50/yr. Free verse, light verse, traditional; 4-16 lines. Pays $10-15 on acceptance. Submit max. 5 poems.

Fillers: Attn: Fillers Dept. Buys 50/yr. Short humor (humorous or thought-provoking one-liners); 10-50 wds. No payment.

Columns/Departments: Buys 26/yr. Garden Path (gardens/gardening), 500-1,000 wds. Payment varies. This column most open.

Tips: "Our publication is all original material either written by our readers/freelancers or occasionally by our staff. Every department, every article is open. Break in by reading at least 6 months of issues to know our special audience. Most open to nonfiction features and garden stories." Submissions are not acknowledged or status reports given.

$CATHEDRAL AGE, 3101 Wisconsin Ave. N.W., Washington DC 20016. (202)537-5681. Fax (202)364-6600. E-mail: Cathedral_Age@cathedral.org. Website: www.cathedralage.org. Protestant Episcopal Cathedral Foundation. Craig W. Stapert, pub. mngr. News from Washington National Cathedral and stories of interest to friends and supporters of WNC. Quarterly & online mag.; 36 pgs.; circ. 36,000. Subscription $15. 50% assigned freelance. Query; e-query OK. Pays to $600 on publication for all rts. Articles 1,200-1,500 wds. (10/yr.); book reviews 600 wds., ($100). Responds in 6 wks. Seasonal 6 mos. ahead. Requires requested ms on disk or by e-mail (attached file). Kill fee 50%. Uses some sidebars. Prefers NRSV. No guidelines; copy $5/9x12 SAE/5 stamps. (No ads)

Special Needs: Art, architecture, music.

Tips: "We assign all articles, so query with clips first. Always write from the viewpoint of an individual first, then move into a more general discussion of the topic. Human interest angle important."

$CATHOLIC DIGEST, PO Box 180, Mystic CT 06355. (860)536-2611. Fax (860)536-5600. E-mail: catholicdigest@bayard-inc.com. Submissions to: cdsubmissions@bayardpubs .com. Website: www.CatholicDigest.com. Catholic/Bayard Publications. Joop Koopman, ed.; submit to Articles Editor. Readers have a stake in being Catholic and a wide range of interests: religion, family, health, human relationships, good works, nostalgia, and more. Monthly & online mag.; 128 pgs.; circ. 400,000. Subscription $19.95. 15% unsolicited freelance; 20% assigned. Complete ms (for original material)/cover letter, tear sheets for reprints; no e-query. Pays $200-400 ($100 for reprints) on acceptance for one-time rts. Online-only articles receive $100, plus half of any traceable revenue. Articles 1,000-3,500 wds. (60/yr.). Responds in 6-8 wks. Seasonal 5 mos. ahead. Accepts reprints (tell when/where appeared). Accepts requested ms on disk or by e-mail (copied into message). Regularly uses sidebars. Prefers NAB. Guidelines (also on Website: www.catholicdigest.org/ stops/info/writers.html); copy for 7x10 SAE/2 stamps. (Ads)

Fillers: Julie Rattey, asst. ed. Buys 200/yr. Anecdotes, cartoons, facts, jokes, quotes; 1 line to 300 wds.; $2/published line on publication.

Columns/Departments: Buys 75/yr. Open Door (personal stories of conversion to Catholicism); 200-500 wds.; $2/published line. See guidelines for full list.

Special Needs: Family and career concerns of Baby Boomers who have a stake in being Catholic.

Contest: See Website for current contest, or send an SASE.

Tips: "We favor the anecdotal approach. Stories must be strongly focused on a definitive topic that is illustrated for the reader with a well-developed series of true-life, interconnected vignettes."

**This periodical was #48 on the 2005 Top 50 Christian Publishers list (#37 in 2002, #28 in 2001).

\$CATHOLIC FORESTER, Box 3012, Naperville IL 60566-7012. (630)983-3381. Fax (800)811-2140. E-mail: cofpr@aol.com. Website: www.catholicforester.com. Catholic Order of Foresters. Mary Anne File, ed. For mixed audience, primarily parents and grand-parents between the ages of 30 and 80+. Quarterly mag.; 40 pgs.; circ. 100,000. Free/membership. 10% unsolicited freelance. Complete ms/cover letter; no phone/fax/ e-query. Pays .30/wd. on acceptance for 1st, or one-time rts. Articles 1,000-1,500 wds. (5/yr.); fiction for all ages 500-1,200 wds. (5/yr.). Responds in 12-16 wks. Seasonal 4-6 mos. ahead. Accepts simultaneous submissions & reprints (tell when/where appeared). Accepts requested ms by e-mail. Kill fee 5%. Uses some sidebars. Prefers Catholic Bible. Guidelines (also on Website); copy for 9x12 SAE/4 stamps. (No ads)

Poetry: Buys 2/yr. Light verse, traditional. Pay varies. Submit max. 5 poems.

Fillers: Keith Halla, fillers ed. Buys 2/yr. Cartoons. Pay varies.

Tips: "Looking for informational, inspirational articles on finances and parenting. Writing should be energetic with good style and rhythm. Most open to general interest and fiction."
**This periodical was #36 on the 2005 Top 50 Christian Publishers list (#37 in 2004, #15 in 2003, #24 in 2002, #47 in 2001).

\$CATHOLIC INSIGHT, PO Box 625, Adelaide Sta., 31 Adelaide St. E., Toronto ON M5C 2J8, Canada. (416)204-9601. Fax (416)204-1027. E-mail: reach@catholicinsight.com. Website: www.catholicinsight.com. Life Ethics Information Center. Fr. Alphonse de Valk, ed./pub. News, analysis, and commentary on social, ethical, political, and moral issues from a Cath-olic perspective. Monthly (11X) mag.; 40-44 pgs.; circ. 3,500. Subscription $32 Cdn., $42 U.S., International $50. 2% unsolicited freelance; 98% assigned. Query; phone/fax/e-query OK. Pays $200 for 1,500 wds. ($250 for 2,000 wds.) on publication for all rts. Articles 750-1,500 wds. (20-30/yr.); book reviews 750 wds. ($85). Responds in 6-8 wks. Seasonal 2 mos. ahead. Accepts requested ms on disk or by e-mail. Uses some sidebars. Prefers RSV (Catholic). Guidelines (also by e-mail); copy $4 Cdn./9x12 SAE/.90 Cdn. postage or IRC. (Ads)

Tips: "We are interested in intelligent, well-researched, well-presented commentary on a political, religious, social, or cultural matter from the viewpoint of the Catholic Church."

\$CATHOLIC NEW TIMES, 80 Sackville St., Toronto ON M5A 3E5, Canada. (416)361-0761. Fax (416)361-0796. E-mail: editor@catholicnewtimes.org. Website: www.catholicnewtimes .org. New Catholic Times, Inc. Ted Schmidt, ed. An independent journal in the Catholic tra-dition that focuses on faith and social justice. Biweekly newspaper (20X); 20 pgs.; circ. 8,500. Subscription $29. 25% unsolicited freelance; 75% assigned. Query; phone/fax/ e-query OK. Pays $75-300 on publication for one-time rts. Articles 500-1,200+ wds. (40/yr.); book reviews 500-800 wds.; music reviews 500 wds.; video reviews 500-700 wds.; pays $50-100. Guidelines (also by e-mail); copy for 9x12 SAE/3 stamps. (Ads)

Fillers: Newsbreaks.

Columns/Departments: Buys 40/yr. (assigned). Witness (first-person experience) 1,200 wds.; Frontburner (opinion) 500-600 wds.; Faith & Spirituality (experiences of faith) to 1,200 wds.; Canada (Canadian news/features) 300-1,200+ wds.; World (world news) 300-1,200+ wds.; $100. Query.

Tips: "Call me with an idea and we can chat about it. Our office is in Toronto, but we want to reflect all parts of the country, so writers in all provinces and territories are encouraged to get in touch."

\$CATHOLIC NEW YORK, 1011—1st Ave., Rm. 1721, New York NY 10022. (212)688-2399. Fax (212)688-2642. E-mail: cny@cny.org. Website: www.cny.org. Catholic. John Woods, ed-in-chief. To inform New York Catholics. Monthly newspaper; 72 pgs.; circ. 135,000.

Subscription $12. 2% unsolicited freelance. Query or complete ms/cover letter. Pays $15-100 on publication for one-time rts. Articles 500-800 wds. Responds in 5 wks. Copy $3. Columns/Departments: Comment; 325 wds.

$CATHOLIC PEACE VOICE, 532 W. 8th, Erie PA 16502-1343. (814)453-4955. Fax (814)452-4784. E-mail: info@paxchristiusa.org. Website: www.paxchristiusa.org. Pax Christi USA. Dave Robinson, ed. For members of Pax Christi USA, the national Catholic Peace Movement. Bimonthly newsmag.; 16-20 pgs.; circ. 23,000. Subscription $20, free to members. 15-20% unsolicited freelance; 25-30% assigned. Complete ms; phone/fax/e-query OK. Pays $50-75 on publication for all & electronic rts. Articles 500-1,500 wds. (10-15/yr.); reviews 750 wds., $50. Responds in 1-2 wks. Accepts simultaneous submissions & reprints (tell when/where appeared). Accepted ms on disk or by e-mail (attached or copied into message). Uses some sidebars. Accepts submissions from teens. Guidelines (also by e-mail); copy for 9x12 SAE/2 stamps. (Ads)

> **Poetry:** Accepts 1-5/yr. Avant-garde, free verse, haiku, light verse, traditional. Submit max. 2 poems. No payment.

> **Tips:** "Most open to features and news, as well as reviews and resources. E-mailing us and pitching a story is the best way to break into our publication. Emphasis is on nonviolence. No sexist language."

THE CATHOLIC REGISTER, 1155 Yonge St., #401, Toronto ON M4T 1W2, Canada. (416)934-3410. Fax (416)934-3409. E-mail: editor@catholicregister.org. Website: www.catholic register.org. Michey Conlon, mng. ed. To provide reliable information about the world from a Catholic perspective. Weekly (47X) tabloid; circ. 33,000. Subscription $37.20. Open to unsolicited freelance. Not in topical listings. (Ads)

$CATHOLIC SENTINEL, PO Box 18030, Portland OR 97218. (503)281-1191. Fax (503)460-5496. E-mail: sentinel@ocp.org. Website: www.sentinel.org. Oregon Catholic Press. Bob Pfohman, ed. Weekly newspaper; 16-28 pgs.; circ. 16,000. Subscription $28. 2% unsolicited freelance; 0% assigned. Query/clips. Payment negotiable on publication for one-time rts. Articles 600-1,500 wds. Responds in 4 wks. Seasonal 2 mos. ahead. Accepts requested ms on disk or by e-mail (copied into message). Uses some sidebars. Prefers NAS. Incomplete topical listings. Guidelines on Website; copy for 9x12 SAE/3 stamps. (Ads)

> **Tips:** "We're most open to local church news and feature articles."

$CATHOLIC TELEGRAPH, 100 E. 8th St., Cincinnati OH 45202. (513)421-3131. Fax (513)381-2242. E-mail: doconnor@catholiccincinnati.org. Website: www.catholiccincinnati.org. Catholic. Dennis O'Connor, mng. ed. Diocese newspaper for Cincinnati area (all articles must have a Cincinnati or Ohio connection). Weekly newspaper; 24-28 pgs.; circ. 100,000. Limited unsolicited freelance; mostly assigned. Send résumé and writing samples for assignment. Pays varying rates on publication for all rts. Articles. Responds in 2-3 wks. Kill fee. No guidelines; copy $2/#10 SASE.

> **Fillers:** Newsbreaks (local).

> **Special Needs:** Personality features for "Everyday Evangelists" section. These are feature stories that offer a slice of life of a person who is making a difference as a Roman Catholic Christian in their community. Prefer to have a tie within the Archdiocese of Cincinnati; must be an Ohioan. Complete ms.; 800 wds.; pays $40 (extra for photos of individual interviewed).

> **Tips:** "Most likely to accept an article about a person, event, or ministry with an Ohio connection—Cincinnati-Dayton area."

CATHOLIC WORLD REPORT, Domus Enterprises, Inc., Box 1608, South Lancaster MA 01561. (978)365-7208. Fax (978)365-4307. E-mail: editor@cwnews.com. Website: www .cwnews.com. Catholic. Philip Lawler, ed. A news magazine that not only reports on important events in the church but helps to shape them. Monthly mag. Subscription $20. Not in topical listings.

$+THE CATHOLIC YEARBOOK, 7010—6th St. N., Oakdale MN 55128. (651)702-0086. Fax (651)702-0074. E-mail: catholic2@msn.com. Apostolic Publishing Co., Inc./Catholic. Roger Jensen, ed. Family magazine of articles and prayers, promoting the sharing of Christian fellowship among Catholics. Annual mag.; 68-72 pgs.; circ. 400,000. 60% unsolicited freelance; 40% assigned. Complete ms/cover letter. Pays $5-50 on publication for 1st rts. Articles 750-1,500 wds. (20/yr.). Response time varies. No simultaneous submissions; accepts reprints. Accepts articles on disk or by e-mail (attached file). No kill fee. Uses some sidebars. Prefers NIV. Accepts submissions from children/teens. Guidelines. (Ads)

> **Poetry:** Buys 10/yr. Light verse, traditional; 15-50 wds., up to 150 wds. Pays $8-30. Submit max. 3 poems.
>
> **Fillers:** Buys 5-10/yr. Anecdotes, facts, games, prayers, quizzes, quotes, and word puzzles; 50-300 wds. Pays $5-30.

CBN.COM (CHRISTIAN BROADCASTING NETWORK), 977 Centerville Turnpike, Virginia Beach VA 23464. (757)226-3557. Fax (757)226-3575. E-mail: craig.vonbuseck@cbn.org. Website: www.CBN.com. Christian Broadcasting Network. Craig von Buseck, marketing & ministries dir. Online mag.; 1.4 million hits/wk. Free online. Open to unsolicited freelance. E-mail submissions (attached as a Word document). Complete ms. **NO PAYMENT.** Devotions 500-700 wds.; Spiritual Life Teaching, 700-1,500 wds.; Living Features (Family, Entertainment, Health, Finance), 700-1,500 wds.; Movie/TV/Music Reviews, 700-1,000 wds.; Hard News, 300-700 wds.; News Features, 700-1,500 wds.; News Interviews, 1,000-2,000 wds. Accepts reprints (tell when/where appeared). Guidelines by e-mail; copy online.

$CELEBRATE LIFE, PO Box 1350, Stafford VA 22554. (540)659-4171. Fax (540)659-2586. E-mail: clmag@all.org. Website: www.all.org. American Life League. Nicholas Marmalejo, ed.; Melissa Salt, asst. ed. A pro-life, pro-family magazine for Christian audience. Bimonthly mag.; 48 pgs.; circ. 70,000. Subscription $12.95 (donation). 50% unsolicited freelance; 40% assigned. Query/clips or complete ms/cover letter; fax/e-query OK. Pays .30/wd. on publication for one-time or reprint rts. Articles 300-1,500 wds. (40/yr.). Responds in 6 mos. Seasonal 4 mos. ahead. Accepts simultaneous submissions & reprints (tell when/where appeared). Accepts e-mail submissions (attached or copied into message). No kill fee. Uses some sidebars. Accepts submissions from children & teens. Prefers Jerusalem Bible (Catholic). Guidelines/theme list (also by e-mail); copy for 9x12 SAE/4 stamps. (No ads)

> **Fillers:** Buys 5/yr. Newsbreaks (local or special pro-life news); 75-200 wds.; $10.
>
> **Special Needs:** Personal experience about abortion, post-abortion stress/healing, adoption, activism/young people's involvement, death/dying, euthanasia, eugenics, special needs children, personhood, chastity, and large families.
>
> **Tips:** "We are no-exceptions pro-life. The importance of that philosophy should be emphasized. Photos are preferred."

$+THE CELEBRATIONS SERIES OF BOOKS, 1531 Palmer Dr., Fayetteville NC 28303. Phone/fax(910)488-3953. E-mail: PaulAndrewDawkins@yahoo.com. Website: www.the dawkinsproject.net. The Dawkins Project. Paul Andrew Dawkins, pub. & creator. A series of 40 books celebrating loved ones and other special individuals through letters and photos. Paperback books of 300 pgs. 100% freelance. Query, query/clips, or send complete ms; phone/fax/e-query OK. Writers receive 1 copy of the book, plus 2 cents/copy sold for the life of the book, paid annually. Buys 1st, reprint, or electronic rts. Responds in 2-4 wks. Accepts simultaneous submissions & reprints. Accepts ms by e-mail or on disk. Accepts submissions from children/teens. Guidelines (also by e-mail/Website).

> **Photos:** Accepts freelance photos with submissions.
>
> **Tips:** "We accept letters celebrating a loved one or special individuals for our *Celebrations* books, plus essays dealing with a significant day in the lives of individuals for our *A Day in*

the Life books. Especially need letters celebrating grandfathers, brothers, sisters, friends, God, and teachers."

$+CENTRAL APPALACHIA CHRISTIAN NEWS, Rt. 5 Box 435, Grundy VA 24614. (276)935-8520. E-mail: jrthompson@cacnews.com. Website: www.cacnews.com. Regional news. Jim Thompson, ed. Monthly newspaper, 24-28 pgs. Subscription $25. Open to unsolicited freelance. Payment made on individual basis. Articles 800-1,500 wds. Free copy. Incomplete topical listings. No questionnaire returned.

Columns/Departments: Looking for columnists to do business, church, ministry, and individual profiles (from that area).

$CGA WORLD, PO Box 249, Olyphant PA 18447. (570)586-1091. Fax (570)586-7721. E-mail: cgaemail@aol.com. Website: www.catholicgoldenage.org. Catholic Golden Age. Barbara Pegula, mng. ed. For Catholics 50+. Bimonthly mag.; 8 pgs.; circ. 100,000. Subscription/membership $12. Query. Pays .10/wd. on publication for 1st, one-time, or reprint rts. Articles 600-1,000 wds.; fiction 600-1,000 wds. Responds in 6 wks. Seasonal 6 mos. ahead. Accepts reprints (tell when/where appeared). Accepts requested ms on disk. Guidelines; copy for 9x12 SAE/3 stamps. (Ads)

Fillers: Games, ideas, prayers, word puzzles.

Tips: "Most open to stories pertinent to Christians 50 years of age and older."

+CHALLENGE WEEKLY ONLINE, PO Box 168 - 800, Newton, Auckland, New Zealand 1032. Phone (64-9)531 3855. Fax (64-9)531 3855. E-mail: chalpub@internet.co.nz. Website: www.challengeweekly.co.nz. Challenge Publishing Society. Candice Osborne, ed. Proclaiming the good news that Jesus is the Christ. Weekly online newspaper. Subscription $65. Incomplete topical listings. No questionnaire returned.

+CHALLENGING DESTINY, 47 Bridgeport Rd. E., Waterloo ON N2J 2J4, Canada. E-mail: csp@golden.net. Website: http://challengingdestiny.com. Crystalline Sphere Publishing. David M. Switzer, ed. Canadian science fiction and fantasy short story magazine, with reviews and interviews with Canadian authors. Quarterly online mag; circ. 200. 80% unsolicited freelance. Complete ms; e-query OK. Pays .01/wd.(Cdn.) on publication for electronic rts. for 6 mos. Fiction 2,000-10,000 wds./18/yr. (considers shorter or longer stories). Responds in 2-6 wks. Accepts simultaneous submissions & sometimes reprints (tell when/where appeared). Send stories by mail; no e-mail submissions. Guidelines (also on Website); copy $6.50. (No ads)

Tips: "We seek submissions in which violence is not used as a means to solve problems, and in which political, religious, and philosophical themes may be explored. Send a medium-length story, 4,000-6,000 words, with an interesting plot and interesting characters. Read a copy of the magazine to see what we like."

CHANNELS, 3819 Bloor St. W., Toronto ON M9P 1K7, Canada. Phone/fax (519)651-2232. E-mail: cbbrown@rogers.com. Website: www.renewalfellowship.presbyterian.ca. The Renewal Fellowship/Presbyterian (P.C.C.). Calvin Brown, ed. For Presbyterians seeking spiritual renewal and biblical orthodoxy. Quarterly mag.; 20 pgs.; circ. 2,000. Subscription $12. 10% unsolicited freelance; 90% assigned. Query; e-query OK. **PAYS IN COPIES** for one-time rts. Articles 1,000-1,500 wds. (15/yr.); book reviews 300 wds. Responds in 4 wks. Seasonal 4-6 mos. ahead. Accepts reprints (tell when/where appeared). Prefers mss by e-mail (attached file/.RTF). Regularly uses sidebars. Accepts submissions from teens. No guidelines; copy for #10 SAE/3 stamps. (Ads)

Poetry: Accepts 3/yr. Free verse, haiku, light verse, traditional; 3 lines & up. Submit max. 6 poems.

Fillers: Accepts 4/yr. Anecdotes, cartoons, prayers.; 6-100 wds.

$CHARISMA & CHRISTIAN LIFE, 600 Rinehart Rd., Lake Mary FL 32746. (407)333-0600. Fax (407)333-7133. E-mail: charisma@strang.com, or grady@strang.com. Website:

www.charismamag.com. Strang Communications. Lee Grady, exec. ed.; Jimmy Stewart, mng. ed.; Adrienne S. Gaines, book & music review ed. Primarily for the Pentecostal and Charismatic Christian community. Monthly & online mag.; 100+ pgs.; circ. 230,000. Subscription $24.97. 75% assigned freelance. Query only; e-query OK. Pays $100-800 on publication for 1st rts. Articles 1,800-2,500 wds.; book/music reviews, 200 wds., $25-35. Responds in 8-12 wks. Seasonal 4 mos. ahead. Kill fee $50. Prefers accepted ms by e-mail. Regularly uses sidebars. Guidelines; copy $4. (Ads)

> **Tips:** "Most open to news section, reviews, or features. Query (published clips help a lot)." No unsolicited manuscripts.

> **#1 Best-selling Magazine in Christian retail stores.

+THE CHARLOTTE WORLD, 8701 Mallard Creek Rd., Charlotte NC 28262. (704)548-1737. Fax (704)548-1737. E-mail: warren.smith@thecharlotteworld.com. Website: www.the charlotteworld.com. World Newspaper Publishing. Warren Smith, ed. To report unreported, under-reported, or badly reported news, from a Christian perspective. Newspaper; circ. 20,000. Subscription $36. Open to unsolicited freelance. Query preferred. Articles; reviews. Incomplete topical listings. (Ads)

$CHICKEN SOUP FOR THE SOUL, PO Box 30880, Santa Barbara CA 93130. (805)563-2935. Fax (805)563-2945. E-mail: webmaster@chickensoupforthesoul.com. Website: www .chickensoup.com. Barbara LoMonaco, story acquisitions (blomonaco@chickensoup forthesoul.com). Inspirational anthologies to open your heart and rekindle your spirit; audience is open to all ages, races, etc. Quarterly trade paperback books; 385 pgs.; circ. 60 million. $12.95/book. 98% unsolicited freelance. Complete ms/cover letter; fax/e-query OK. Pays a fee on publication for reprint, simultaneous, & electronic rts. Articles 1,200 wds. max. Seasonal anytime. Accepts simultaneous submissions & reprints (tell when/where appeared). Accepts e-mail submissions: stories@chickensoupforthesoul.com (attached file/Word). No kill fee. Guidelines/themes on Website; free sample. (No ads)

> **Fillers:** Anecdotes, cartoons, facts, kid quotes, quotes, short humor; 10-200 wds. Pays.

> **Special Needs:** See Website for a list of upcoming titles.

> **Contest:** See Website for list of current contests.

> **Tips:** "Visit our Website and be familiar with our book series. Send in stories via mail or e-mail, complete with contact information. Submit story typed, double spaced, max. 1,200 words, in a Word document."

$+CHICKEN SOUP FOR THE SOUL MAGAZINE, 5050 Poplar Ave., Ste. 1500, Memphis TN 38157. (901)312-7711. E-mail: staff@chickensoupmagazine.com. Website: www.chicken soupmagazine.com. Modern Media/Chicken Soup for the Soul Enterprises. Jack Canfield & Mark Victor Hansen, exec. eds.; Mignonne Wright, ed-in-chief. Bimonthly mag. Subscription $15. Incomplete topical listings. No questionnaire returned. (Ads)

+THE CHRISTIAN CHRONICLE, Oklahoma Christian University, PO Box 11000, Oklahoma City OK. (405)425-5070. Fax (405)425-5076. E-mail: bailey.mcbride@oc.edu. Website: www.christianchronicle.org. Churches of Christ. Bailey B. McBride, ed. An international newspaper for members of the Church of Christ. Monthly newspaper. Subscription $20 (one-time fee). Incomplete topical listings. No questionnaire returned.

+CHRISTIAN CITIZEN USA, 3651 Wrightway Rd., Dayton OH 45424. (937)233-6227, ext. 16. Fax (937)233-6231. E-mail: psnyder@ccn-usa.net. Website: www.citizenusa.us. Christian Media Group. Pendra Snyder, ed. To report news and information from a Judeo-Christian worldview. Newspaper; circ. 30,000. Subscription free. Open to unsolicited freelance. Query preferred. Articles; reviews. (Ads)

THE CHRISTIAN CIVIC LEAGUE OF MAINE RECORD, Box 5459, Augusta ME 04332. (207)622-7634. Fax (207)621-0035. E-mail: e-mail@cclmaine.org. Website: www .cclmaine.org. Natalie Torgeson, ed. Focuses on public policy, political action, some church and public service. Monthly newsletter; 4 pgs.; circ. 4,600. Free. Some freelance. Query; phone/fax/e-query OK. **NO PAYMENT** for one-time rts. Articles 800-1,200 wds. (10-12/yr.). Responds in 4-8 wks. Accepts simultaneous query & reprints. Guidelines by e-mail/Website; free copy. (No ads)

CHRISTIAN COMPUTING MAGAZINE, PO Box 319, Belton MO 64012. Toll-free phone/fax (800)456-1868. (816)331-8142. Fax (800)456-1868. E-mail: steve@ccmag.com. Website: www.ccmag.com. Steve Hewitt, ed-in-chief. For Christian/church computer users. Monthly (11X) & online mag.; 2 pgs.; circ. 30,000. Subscription $14.95. 40% unsolicited freelance. Query/clips; fax/e-query OK. **NO PAYMENT** for all rts. Articles 1,000-1,800 wds. (12/yr.). Responds in 4 wks. Seasonal 2 mos. ahead. Accepts reprints. Requires requested ms on disk. Regularly uses sidebars. Guidelines; copy for 9x12 SAE.

Fillers: Accepts 6 cartoons/yr.

Columns/Departments: Accepts 12/yr. Telecommunications (computer), 1,500-1,800 wds.

Special Needs: Articles on Internet, DTP, computing.

$CHRISTIAN COURIER (Canada), 1 Hiscott St., St. Catherines ON L2R 1C7, Canada. (U.S. address: Box 110, Lewiston NY 14092-0110). Toll-free (800)969-4838. (905)682-8311. Fax (905)682-8313. E-mail: editor@christiancourier.ca. Website: www.christiancourier.ca. Reformed Faith Witness. Harry DerNederlanden, ed. To present Canadian and international news, both religious and secular, from a Reformed Christian perspective. Biweekly tabloid; 24-28 pgs.; circ. 4,000. 20% unsolicited freelance; 80% assigned. Complete ms/cover letter; fax/e-query OK. Pays $75-120 U.S., up to .10/wd. for assigned ($50-100 for unsolicited); 30 days after publication for one-time, reprint, or simultaneous rts. Not copyrighted. Articles 700-1,500 wds. (40/yr.); fiction to 1,200-2,500 wds. (6/yr.); book discussions 800-1,200 wds. Responds in 1-3 wks. Seasonal 3 mos. ahead. Accepts simultaneous submissions & reprints (tell when/where appeared). Prefers accepted ms by e-mail (attached file). No kill fee. Uses some sidebars. Prefers NIV. No guidelines/theme list/copy. (Ads)

Poetry: Buys 12/yr. Avant-garde, free verse, light verse, traditional; 10-30 lines; $20-30. Submit max. 5 poems.

Tips: "Suggest an aspect of the theme which you believe you could cover well, have insight into, could treat humorously, etc. Show that you think clearly, write clearly, and have something to say that we should want to read. Have a strong biblical world-view and avoid moralism and sentimentality." Responds only if material is accepted.

CHRISTIAN COURIER (WI), 1933 W. Wisconsin Ave., Milwaukee WI 53233. (414)345-3545. Fax (414)345-3544. E-mail: christiancourier@juno.com. ProBuColls Assn. John M. Fisco, Jr., pub.; Don Conklin, ed. To propagate the gospel of Jesus Christ in the Midwest. Monthly newspaper; circ. 10,000. 10% freelance. Query; phone/fax/e-query OK. **PAYS IN COPIES,** for one-time rts. Not copyrighted. Articles 300-1,500 wds. (6/yr.). Responds in 4-8 wks. Seasonal 2 mos. ahead. Accepts reprints. Guidelines; free copy. (Ads)

Fillers: Anecdotes, facts, newsbreaks; 10-100 wds.

Tips: "We are always in need of seasonal feature/filler type of articles: Christmas, Easter, 4th of July, etc."

+CHRISTIAN CURRENT, Box 725, Winnipeg MB R3C 2K3, Canada. (519)829-2525. Fax (204)947-5632. E-mail: managingeditor@christiancurrent.org. Website: www.christiancurrent.org. Fellowship for Print Witness.org. Robert White, ed. To inform, encourage, and inspire the Christian community in Canada. Newspaper; circ. 65,000. Subscription free. Open to unsolicited freelance. Query preferred. Articles; reviews. Incomplete topical listings. (No ads)

CHRISTIAN DRAMA E-MAGAZINE, 1824 Celestia Dr., Walla Walla WA 99362-3619. (509)522-5242. E-mail: hiddennook@hiddennook.com. Phillips Music & Drama. Victor

R. Phillips, ed./pub. Play scripts and articles related to Christian drama. E-magazine. Not currently accepting submissions.

$CHRISTIAN EXAMINER, PO Box 2606, El Cajon CA 92021. Phone/fax (619)668-5100. E-mail: info@christianexaminer.com. Website: www.christianexaminer.com. Keener Communications. Lori Arnold, ed. To report on current events from an evangelical Christian perspective, particularly traditional family values and church trends. Monthly & online newspaper; 24-36 pgs.; circ. 180,000. Subscription $19.95. 0% unsolicited freelance; 5% assigned. Query/clips. Pays .10/wd., on publication for 1st & electronic rts. Articles 600-900 wds. Responds in 4-5 wks. Seasonal 3 mos. ahead. No simultaneous submissions or reprints. Prefers e-mail submissions (copied into message). No kill fee. Uses some sidebars. Guidelines by e-mail; copy $1.50/9x12 SAE. (Ads)

> **Tips:** "We prefer news stories."
> **2005, 2004 EPA Award of Merit—Newspaper.

+CHRISTIAN HERALD, Garcia Estate, Canterbury Rd., Worthing, West Sussex BN13 1EH, United Kingdom. Website: www.christianherald.org.uk. Christian Media Centre, Ltd./interdenominational. Russ Bravo, features ed. Weekly newspaper. Subscription 35 pounds UK. Incomplete topical listings. No questionnaire returned.

$THE CHRISTIAN HERALD, PO Box 68526, Brampton ON L6S 6A1, Canada. (905)874-1731. Fax (905)874-1731. E-mail: info@christianherald.ca. Website: www.christianherald.ca. Covenant Communications. Fazal Karim, Jr., ed-in-chief. A Canadian-Christian tabloid with a focus on Christian arts and entertainment. Monthly tabloid; 24 pgs.; circ. 31,000. Subscription free, or $26.75 mailed. 10% unsolicited freelance; 85% assigned. Query; fax/e-query OK. Pays $20-100 or .10/wd. on publication for 1st rts. Articles 500-1,500 wds.; reviews 150-300 wds. (no payment). Responds in 4 wks. Seasonal 3 mos. ahead. Accepts simultaneous submissions & reprints (tell when/where appeared). Prefers e-mail submissions (attached file). No kill fee. Sometimes uses sidebars. Accepts submissions from teens. Prefers KJV, NKJV, NIV, NLT. Guidelines (also by e-mail); copy for 9x12 SAE/$1.60 Canadian postage. (Ads)

> **Fillers:** Accepts 10/yr. Cartoons, facts, games, jokes, prayers, quotes, and word puzzles; 20-100 wds. No payment.
> **Columns/Departments:** Interviews (Christian newsmakers/personalities), 900 wds., $20-50.
> **Tips:** "Most open to articles/columns with specific reference to Canadians, with Canadian quotes, relevance, etc."

$CHRISTIAN HISTORY & BIOGRAPHY, 465 Gundersen Dr., Carol Stream IL 60188. (630)260-6200. Fax (630)260-0114. E-mail: CHeditor@christianitytoday.com. Website: www.christianhistory.net. Christianity Today Intl. David Neff, exec. ed.; Jennifer Trafton, assoc. ed.; submit to Steve Gertz, asst. ed. To teach Christian history to educated readers in an engaging manner. Quarterly mag. & newsletter; 52 pgs.; circ. 55,000. Subscription $19.95. 5% unsolicited freelance; 95% assigned. E-query only. Pays .10-.20/wd. on acceptance for 1st rts. Articles 1,000-3,000 wds. (1/yr.). Responds in 2 wks. Accepts reprints (tell when/where appeared). Prefers accepted ms by e-mail (attached or copied into message). Kill fee 50%. Regularly uses sidebars. Prefers NIV. Guidelines/theme list (also by e-mail); copy for 9x12 SASE. (Ads)

> **Tips:** "Let us know your particular areas of specialization and any books or papers you have written in the area of Christian history. The Gallery profiles are usually freelanced. We are purely thematic; only submit queries related to upcoming themes. Most open to non-themed departments: Story Behind; People Worth Knowing; Turning Points."
> **2005 EPA Award of Merit—General.

$CHRISTIAN HOME & SCHOOL, 3350 East Paris Ave. S.E., Grand Rapids MI 49512. (616)957-1070, ext. 239. Fax (616)957-5022. E-mail: RogerS@CSIonline.org, or GBordewyk@aol.com. Website: www.CSIonline.org. Christian Schools Intl. Gordon L. Bordewyk, exec. ed.; Roger Schmurr, sr. ed. Focuses on parenting and Christian education; for parents who send their children to Christian schools. Bimonthly & online mag.; 32 pgs.; circ. 66,000. Subscription $13.95. 95% unsolicited; 5% assigned. Complete ms or prefers e-query. Pays $175-250 on publication for 1st rts. Articles 1,000-2,000 wds. (30/yr.); Christmas fiction 1,000-2,000 wds. (5/yr.); book reviews $25 (assigned). Responds in 1 wk. Seasonal 5 mos. ahead. Accepts simultaneous query. Accepts requested ms on disk (clean copy they can scan); prefers e-mail submission (attached file). Regularly uses sidebars. Prefers NIV. Guidelines/theme list (also on Website); copy for 9x12 SAE/4 stamps. (Ads)

Fillers: Parenting ideas; 100-250 wds.; $25-40.

Tips: "Most open to feature articles on parenting and education. Looking for articles on teens, and single parenting. Ask to be assigned to do a book review, or send an article on speculation."

**This periodical was #44 on the 2005 Top 50 Christian Publishers list (#38 on 2004, #33 in 2003). 2001 Award of Excellence—Organizational.

$CHRISTIANITY TODAY, 465 Gundersen Dr., Carol Stream IL 60188-2498. (630)260-6200. Fax (630)260-8428. E-mail: cteditor@christianitytoday.com. Website: www.christianity today.com/ctmag. Christianity Today Inc. David Neff, ed. For evangelical Christian thought leaders who seek to integrate their faith commitment with responsible action. Monthly & online mag.; 65-120 pgs.; circ. 155,000. Subscription $24.95. 80% freelance (mostly assigned). Query only; fax/e-query OK. Pays .20-.30/wd. on publication for 1st rts. Articles 1,000-4,000 wds. (60/yr.); book reviews 800-1,000 wds. (pays per-page rate). Responds in 13 wks. Seasonal 8 mos. ahead. Accepts reprints (tell when/where appeared-payment 25% of regular rate). Kill fee 50%. Does not use sidebars. Prefers NIV. Guidelines; copy for 9x12 SAE/3 stamps. (Ads)

Tips: "Read the magazine."

**The #8 Best-selling Magazine in Christian retail stores. 2005 EPA Award of Excellence— General. 2005, 2004 EPA Award of Merit—Online (for ChristianityToday Online).

THE CHRISTIAN JOURNAL, 1025 Court St., Medford OR 97501. (541)773-4004. Fax (541)773-9917. E-mail: Info@thechristianjournal.org. Website: www.thechristianjournal .org. Chad McComas, ed. Dedicated to sharing encouragement with the body of Christ in Southern Oregon and Northern California. Monthly newspaper; 16-24 pgs.; circ. 15,000. Subscription $20; most copies distributed free. 50% unsolicited freelance; 50% assigned. Complete ms; phone/fax query OK. **NO PAYMENT AT THIS TIME.** Articles & fiction 800-1,000 wds; reviews 300-500 wds.; children's stories 600 wds. Prefer articles on disk or by e-mail (attached file). Accepts submissions from children or teens. Guidelines/theme list; copy $1.20/9x12 SAE/3 stamps. (Ads)

Poetry: Accepts 12-20/yr. Free verse, haiku, light verse, traditional; 4-12 lines. Submit max. 2 poems.

Fillers: Accepts 50/yr. Anecdotes, cartoons, jokes, kid quotes, newsbreaks, prayers, quotes, short humor, or word puzzles; 100-300 wds.

Columns/Departments: Accepts 6/yr. Youth, 800-1,000 wds; Seniors, 800-1,000 wds.; Children's stories, 600 wds.

Tips: "Send articles on themes; each issue has a theme. Theme articles get first choice."

$CHRISTIAN LEADER, PO Box 220, Hillsboro KS 67063-0220. (620)947-5543. E-mail: editor@usmb.org. Website: www.usmb.org. U.S. Conference of Mennonite Brethren.

Connie Faber, ed. Denominational. Monthly mag.; 36 pgs.; circ. 9,800. Subscription $16. 15% unsolicited freelance; 85% assigned. Complete ms; e-query OK. Pays .10/wd. on publication for 1st rts. Articles 1,200 wds. (2/yr.). Responds in 8 wks. Seasonal 4 mos. ahead. Accepts simultaneous submissions & reprints (tell when/where appeared). Prefers requested ms on disk or by e-mail (copied into message). Guidelines/theme list (also by e-mail); no copy. (Ads)

   Tips: "Although we use primarily denominational writers, we are most open to features section. Ask for theme list; query specific topic/article."

CHRISTIAN MEDIA, Box 448, Jacksonville OR 97530. (541)899-8888. E-mail: James@ ChristianMediaNetwork.com. Website: www.ChristianMediaDaily.com, or www.Christian MediaNetwork.com. James Lloyd, ed./pub. Updates on world conditions, politics, economics, in the light of prophecy. Quarterly & online tabloid; 24 pgs.; circ. 25,000. Query; prefers phone query. **NO PAYMENT** for negotiable rts. Articles; book & music reviews, 3 paragraphs. Accepts simultaneous submissions & reprints. Prefers requested ms on disk. Requires KJV. Copy for 9x12 SAE/2 stamps.

   Special Needs: Particularly interested in stories that expose dirty practices in the industry—royalty rip-offs, misleading ads, financial misconduct, etc. No flowery pieces on celebrities; wants well-documented articles on abuse in the media.

CHRISTIAN MOTORSPORTS ILLUSTRATED, PO Box 129, Mansfield PA 16933-0129. E-mail: cpo7@loving-hearts.org. Website: www.christianmotorsports.com. CPO Publishing. Roland Osborne, pub. Covers Christians involved in motorsports. Bimonthly mag.; 64 pgs.; circ. 40,000. Subscription $19.96. 50% unsolicited freelance. Complete ms; no phone/fax/ e-query. **NO PAYMENT.** Articles 500-2,000 wds. (30/yr.). Seasonal 4 mos. ahead. Requires requested ms on disk. Regularly uses sidebars. No guidelines; free copy. (Ads)

   Poetry: Accepts 10/yr. Any type. Submit max. 10 poems.

   Fillers: Accepts 100/yr. Anecdotes, cartoons, facts, games, ideas, jokes, newsbreaks, prayers, prose, quizzes, quotes, short humor.

   Columns/Departments: Accepts 10/yr.

   Tips: "Most open to personal experiences of God's miraculous presence in lives: healing, salvation, deliverance from alcohol, drugs, pornography, etc., with some sort of motorsports as a background. Send a story on a Christian involved in motorsports—cars, tractors, motorcycles, airplanes, go-carts, lawnmowers, etc."

$CHRISTIAN NETWORKS JOURNAL, 228 Robert S. Kerr, Ste. 900, Oklahoma City OK 73102. (405)605-3084. E-mail: gordon@cnj.org. Website: www.cnj.org. ChristianNetworks. Rev. Dr. Gordon McClellan, pres. Examines international and timely issues from many perspectives. Quarterly mag. Pays per article. Articles/essays 1,250-3,000 wds. Gives 10% of net revenue to medical missions. Incomplete topical listings.

CHRISTIAN NEWS NORTHWEST, PO Box 974, Newberg OR 97132. Phone/fax (503)537-9220. E-mail: cnnw@cnnw.com. Website: www.cnnw.com. John Fortmeyer, ed./pub. News of ministry in the evangelical Christian community in western and central Oregon and southwest Washington; distributed primarily through evangelical churches. Monthly newspaper; 28-36 pgs.; circ. 30,000. Subscription $20. 10% unsolicited freelance; 5% assigned. Query; phone/fax/e-query OK. **NO PAYMENT.** Not copyrighted. Articles 300-400 wds. (100/yr.). Responds in 4 wks. Seasonal 3 mos. ahead. Accepts reprints (tell when/where appeared). Accepts e-mail submissions. Regularly uses sidebars. Guidelines (also by e-mail); copy $1.50. (Ads)

   Tips: "Most open to ministry-oriented features. Our space is always tight, but stories on lesser-known, Northwest-based ministries are encouraged. Keep it very concise. Since we focus on the Pacific Northwest, it would probably be difficult for anyone outside the region to break into our publication."

THE CHRISTIAN OBSERVER, 9400 Fairview Ave., Ste. 200, Manassas VA 22110. (703)335-2844. Fax (703)368-4817. E-mail: editor@christianobserver.org. Website: www.Christian Observer.org. Christian Observer Foundation; Presbyterian Reformed. Dr. Edwin P. Elliott, ed. To encourage and edify God's people and families; print version of *Presbyterians-Week.* Monthly newspaper; 32 pgs.; circ. 2,000. Subscription $27. 10% unsolicited freelance; 90% assigned. Query; phone/e-query OK. **NO PAYMENT.** Accepts e-mail submissions. (Ads)

CHRISTIAN ONLINE MAGAZINE. E-mail: darlene@christianmagazine.org. Website: www.ChristianMagazine.org. Darlene Osborne, pub. Strictly founded on the Word of God, this magazine endeavors to bring you the best Christian information on the net. Monthly e-zine. Subscription free. 10% unsolicited freelance; 90% assigned. E-query. Articles 500-1,000 wds. Responds in 1 wk. Seasonal 2 mos. ahead. Prefers accepted ms by e-mail (attached file). **NO PAYMENT.** Regularly uses sidebars. Also accepts submissions from children & teens. Prefers KJV. Guidelines on Website. (Ads)

> **Fillers:** Accepts 50/yr. Prayers, prose, quizzes, short humor; 500 wds.
> **Columns/Departments:** Variety Column, 700-1,000 wds. Query.
> **Contest:** For contest rules and prizes go to Website.
> **Tips:** "Most open to solid Christian articles founded on the Word of God."

+THE CHRISTIAN OUTLOOK, 492 Hob Moor Rd., Yardley, Birmingham B25 8UB, United Kingdom. Phone +44.8701993152. Fax +44.8701376938. Website: www.thechristian outlook.net. Nondenominational. Issues on life and living from a Christian perspective. E-zine. Free online. Open to unsolicited freelance. Submit through Website. Incomplete topical listings. No questionnaire returned.

> **Tips:** "We also maintain forums for online interaction among Christians, and between Christian and non-Christians."

$CHRISTIAN PARENTING TODAY, 465 Gundersen Dr., Carol Stream IL 60188-2498. (630)260-6200. Fax (630)260-0114. E-mail: cpt@christianparenting.net. Website: www .Christianparenting.net. Christianity Today Intl. Caryn Rivadeneira, mng. ed. To encourage and equip parents to nurture the spiritual and moral development of their children as they walk alongside them in a family journey of faith; practical advice for parents (of kids birth to 14). Bimonthly mag.; 76-96 pgs.; circ. 90,000. Subscription $17.95. 50% unsolicited freelance; 50% assigned. Query only; e-query OK. Pays .15-.25/wd. on acceptance for 1st rts. Articles 450-1,500 wds. (50/yr.). Responds in 6-8 wks. Seasonal 6 mos. ahead. Accepts reprints (tell when/where appeared). Accepts requested ms on disk or by e-mail (copied into message). Kill fee 50%. Regularly uses sidebars. Prefers NIV. Guidelines (also on Website); copy $3.95/9x12 SAE. (Ads)

> **Fillers:** Accepts 100/yr. Anecdotes, ideas; 100-400 wds. No payment.
> **Columns/Departments:** Accepts 50/yr. Growing Up, 500 wds.; Ideas That Work (problem-solving ideas), 50 wds.; Life in Our House (funny anecdotes from kids), 50 wds.; Can You Help? (parent-to-parent advice), 50 wds. No payment.
> **Contest:** Sponsors occasional contests.
> **Tips:** "We focus on the spiritual and moral development of children and celebrate the Christian community of parents."
> **The #7 Best-selling Magazine in Christian retail stores. This periodical was #40 on the 2005 Top 50 Christian Publishers list (#14 in 2004, #40 in 2003, #1 in 2002, #4 in 2001).

+THE CHRISTIAN POST, 111 Pine St., Ste. 1725, San Francisco CA 94111. (415)986-3271. E-mail: editor@christianpost.com. Website: www.christianpost.com. Kenneth Chan, ed. Open to freelance. Incomplete topical listings. No questionnaire returned.

CHRISTIAN RADIO WEEKLY: The Information Source for Christian Radio, 5350 N. Academy Blvd., Ste. 200, Colorado Springs CO 80918. (719)536-9000, ext. 123. Fax

(719)598-7461. E-mail: veldo@christianradioweekly.com. Website: www.christianradio weekly.com. Westar Media Group. Jim Veldhuis, mng. ed. For Christian media professionals working in radio and Christian music industry. Weekly mag.; 12 pgs.; circ. 600. Subscription $199/yr. Open to freelance. Query; e-query OK. **NO PAYMENT.** Articles & fiction 800 wds.

THE CHRISTIAN RANCHMAN, 7022-A Lake County Dr., Fort Worth TX 76179. (817)236-0023. Fax (817)236-0024. E-mail: cowboysforchrist@juno.com. Website: www.Cowboys forChrist.net. Interdenominational. Ted Pressley, ed. Monthly tabloid; 20 pgs.; circ. 45,400. No subscription. 85% unsolicited freelance. Complete ms/cover letter. **NO PAYMENT** for all rts. Articles 350-1,000 wds.; book/video reviews (length open). Does not use sidebars.

> **Poetry:** Accepts 40/yr. Free verse. Submit max. 3 poems.
>
> **Fillers:** Accepts all types.
>
> **Tips:** "We're most open to true-life Christian stories, Christian testimonies, and Christian or livestock news."

$CHRISTIAN RENEWAL, Box 770, Lewiston NY 14092-0770, or PO Box 777, Jordan Sta., ON L0R 1S0, Canada. (905)562-5719. Fax (905)562-7828. E-mail: JVANDYK@aol.com, or christianrenewal@hotmail.com. Reformed (Conservative). John Van Dyk, mng. ed. Church-related and world news for members of the Reformed community of churches in North America. Biweekly newspaper; 24 pgs.; circ. 4,000. Subscription $36 U.S./$40 Cdn. (christianrenewal@hotmail.com). 5% unsolicited freelance; 20% assigned. Query/clips; e-query OK. Pays $25-100 for one-time rts. Articles 500-3,000 wds.; fiction 2,000 wds. (6/yr.); book reviews 50-200 wds. Responds in 9 wks. Seasonal 3 mos. ahead. Accepts simultaneous submissions & reprints. Prefers e-mail submission (copied into message). Uses some sidebars. Prefers NIV, NKJV. No guidelines; copy $2. (Ads: christianrenewal@ hotmail.com)

> **Tips:** "Most open to stories written from a reformed, biblical perspective."

CHRISTIAN RESEARCH JOURNAL, PO Box 80250, Rancho Santa Margarita, CA 92688. (949)858-6100. Fax (949)858-6120. E-mail: elliot.miller@equip.org, or response@ equip.org. Website: www.equip.org. Christian Research Institute. Elliot Miller, ed-in-chief. Probing today's religious movements, promoting doctrinal discernment and critical thinking, and providing reasons for Christian faith and ethics. Bimonthly jour.; 64 pgs.; circ. 30,000. Subscription $30. 5% unsolicited freelance. Query or complete ms/cover letter; fax query OK; e-query & submissions OK. Articles to 4,200 wds.; book reviews 1,100-2,500 wds. Responds in up to 16 wks. Accepts simultaneous submissions. Kill fee to 50%. Guidelines (also by e-mail); copy $6. (Ads)

> **Columns/Departments:** Effective Evangelism, 1,700 wds.; Viewpoint, 875 wds.; News Watch, up to 2,500 wds.
>
> **Special Needs:** Viewpoint on Christian faith and ethics, 1,700 wds.; news pieces, 800-1,200 wds.
>
> **Tips:** "Be familiar with the Journal in order to know what we are looking for. We accept freelance articles in all sections (features and departments). E-mail for writer's guidelines."
>
> ****2003 EPA Award of Excellence—Organizational.**

$THE CHRISTIAN RESPONSE, PO Box 125, Staples MN 56479-0125. (218)894-1165. E-mail: hapco2@brainerd.net. Website: www.brainerd.net/~hapco2. HAPCO Industries. Hap Corbett, ed. Exposes anti-Christian bias in America and encourages readers to write letters against such bias. Bimonthly newsletter; 6 pgs. Subscription $13. 10% unsolicited freelance. Complete ms/cover letter; phone/e-query OK. Pays $5-20 on acceptance for one-time rts. Articles 50-700 wds. (4-6/yr.). Responds in 2 wks. Seasonal 6 mos. ahead. Accepts simultaneous submissions & reprints. Does not use sidebars. Guidelines; copy for $1 or 3 stamps. (Ads—classified only)

Fillers: Buys 2-4/yr. Anecdotes, facts, quotes; 150 wds.; $5-20.

Special Needs: Articles on anti-Christian bias; tips on writing effective letters to the editor; pieces on outstanding accomplishments of Christians in the secular media.

Tips: "We are looking for news/articles about anti-Christian bias in the media, and how you, as a writer, responded to such incidents."

$CHRISTIAN RETAILING, 600 Rinehart Rd., Lake Mary FL 32746. (407)333-0600. Fax (407)333-7133. E-mail: andy.butcher@strang.com. Website: www.christianretailing.com. Strang Communications. Andy Butcher, ed. For Christian product industry manufacturers, distributors, retailers. Trade journal published 20X/yr.; circ. 10,000. Subscription $75. 75% assigned. Query/clips; no phone/fax/e-query. Pays .20/wd. on publication. Articles; book reviews. No simultaneous submissions. Accepts requested mss by e-mail (attached file). Kill fee. Uses some sidebars. Prefers NIV. Guidelines on Website. (Ads)

Tips: "Book reviews should focus on what the book contains and how it might help them in their walk with Christ."

$CHRISTIAN SINGLE, One Lifeway Plaza, Nashville TN 37234. (615)251-2230. Fax (615)251-5008. E-mail: christiansingle@lifeway.com, or christiansingle@bssb.com. Website: www .christiansingle.com. Monthly mag. Subscription $20.85. No freelance.

**2003 EPA Award of Merit—General.

CHRISTIAN SINGLE ONLINE, One Lifeway Plaza, Nashville TN 37234-0140. (615)251-2230. Fax (615)251-5008. E-mail: christiansingle@lifeway.com, or christiansingle@bssb.com. Website: www.christiansingle.com. Online version of Christian Single.

$CHRISTIAN SOCIAL ACTION, 100 Maryland Ave. N.E., Washington DC 20002. (202)488-5600. Fax (202)488-1617. E-mail: editor@umc-gbcs.org, or ealsgaard@umc-gbcs.org. Website: www.umc-gbcs.org. United Methodist. Gretchen Hakola, ed. Information and analysis of critical social issues from a theological, denominational perspective. Bimonthly mag.; 32 pgs.; circ. 42,000. Subscription $15. 30% unsolicited freelance; 15% assigned. Query/clips or complete ms/cover letter; e-query OK. Pays $125-175 on publication for 1st rts. Articles 1,500-2,000 wds. (12/yr.); book reviews 500 wds. ($75). Responds in 4-6 wks. Consider simultaneous submissions & reprints (tell when/where appeared). Requires requested ms on disk or by e-mail. Regularly uses sidebars. Prefers RSV. Guidelines (also by e-mail/Website); copy for 9x12 SAE/2 stamps. (Ads)

Poetry: Benediction poetry; $50-75.

Columns/Departments: Buys 10/yr. Talking (readers write), 1,000 wds.; $50-75.

Special Needs: Lectionary items, responsive readings, prayers, litanies on social justice topics.

Tips: "Send a query letter that states your thesis and how you plan to address it. Stories should help readers understand the justice issues but also provide means for hope and for action by readers (what can they do to bring about justice?). Writers need not be United Methodist, but should do their homework and speak to the United Methodist understanding of issues."

$CHRISTIAN STANDARD, 8121 Hamilton Ave., Cincinnati OH 45231. (513)931-4050. Fax (513)931-0950. E-mail: christianstd@standardpub.com, or standardpub@attmail.com. Website: www.christianstandard.com. Standard Publishing/Christian Churches/Churches of Christ. Mark A. Taylor, ed. Devoted to the restoration of New Testament Christianity, its doctrines, its ordinances, and its fruits. Weekly & online mag.; 16 pgs.; circ. 45,000. Subscription $26.99. 40% unsolicited freelance; 60% assigned. Query; no phone/fax/e-query. Pays $20-160 on publication for one-time, reprint, & electronic rts. Articles 800-1,600 wds. (200/yr.). Responds in 9 wks. Seasonal 8-12 mos. ahead. Accepts reprints (tell when/where appeared). Guidelines & copy on Website. (No ads)

**2004 EPA Award of Merit—Most Improved Publication.

$CHRISTIANWEEK, Box 725, Winnipeg MB R3C 2K3, Canada. Toll-free (800)263-6695. Fax (204)947-5632. E-mail: editor@christianweek.org. Website: www.christianweek.org. Fellowship for Print Witness. Kelly Rempel, mng. ed. Canada's leading Christian news source; telling the stories of God and His people in Canada. Biweekly tabloid newspaper (25X/yr.); 12-16 pgs.; circ. 4,000. Subscription $38.45 (Cdn.), $59.95 (U.S.). Query; phone/fax/e-query OK. Pays $30-100 on publication for 1st rts. News articles 300-600 wds. Responds in 1-3 wks. Seasonal 6 mos. ahead. Might accept simultaneous submissions or reprints (tell when/where appeared). Prefers accepted ms by e-mail (attached or copied into message). Uses some sidebars. Prefers NRSV. Accepts submissions from teens. Guidelines/theme list (also by e-mail/Website). (Ads)

    Tips: "Most open to general news, profiles, and features. Writers are encouraged to query first with ideas about people or news events in their own community (Canadian angles, please) or denomination that would be of interest to readers in other denominations or in other areas of the country."

    **2004 EPA Award of Excellence—Newspaper.

CHURCH HERALD AND HOLINESS BANNER, 7407 Metcalf (KS 66212), Box 4060, Overland Park KS 66204. (913)432-0331. Fax (913)722-0351. E-mail: HBeditor@juno.com. Website: www.heraldandbanner.com. Church of God (Holiness)/Herald and Banner Press. Mark D. Avery, ed. Offers the conservative holiness movement a positive outlook on their church, doctrine, future ministry, and movement. Monthly mag.; 24 pgs.; circ. 1,600. Subscription $12.50. 25% unsolicited freelance; 50% assigned. Complete ms/cover letter; e-query OK. **NO PAYMENT** for one-time, reprint, or simultaneous rts. Not copyrighted. Articles 750-1,000 wds. (40/yr.). Responds in 4 wks. Seasonal 3 mos. ahead. Accepts simultaneous submissions & reprints (tell when/where appeared). Accepts requested ms on disk or by e-mail (attached or copied into message). Uses some sidebars. Prefers KJV. Accepts submissions from children or teens. Guidelines (also by e-mail); copy for 6x9 SAE/2 stamps. (No ads)

    Fillers: Anecdotes, quizzes; 150-400 wds.

    Tips: "Most open to short inspirational/devotional articles. Must be concise, well-written, and get one main point across; 200-600 wds."

+CHURCH OF ENGLAND NEWSPAPER, 20-26 Brunswick Pl., London N1 6DZ, England. Phone 020 7417 5800. Fax 020 7216 6410. E-mail: colin.blakely@churchnewspaper.com. Website: www.churchnewspaper.com. Church of England. Colin Blakely, ed. Weekly newspaper; circ. 25,000. Subscription 55 pounds (UK); 85 pounds (U.S.). Incomplete topical listings. No questionnaire returned.

$CHURCH OF GOD EVANGEL, PO Box 2250, Cleveland TN 37320-2250. (423)476-4512. Fax (423)478-7616. E-mail: wilma_amison@pathwaypress.org. Website: www.pathway press.org. Church of God (Cleveland, TN). Bill George, ed. Denominational. Monthly mag.; 40 pgs.; circ. 54,500. Subscription $15. 10-20% unsolicited freelance; 0% assigned. Complete ms/cover letter; e-query OK. Pays $25-50 on acceptance for 1st, one-time, & simultaneous rts. Articles 300-1,200 wds. (50/yr.). Responds in 6-8 wks. Seasonal 4 mos. ahead. Accepts simultaneous submissions. Uses some sidebars. Prefers KJV, NKJV, NIV. Guidelines (also on Website); free copy. (No ads)

    Tips: "We always need short articles (300-500 wds.) with a salvation appeal. Also human interest stories with a spiritual application. Outstanding writing on timely topics will get our attention."

$+CITIZENS IN AMERICA (CIA), 30 Ford St., Glen Cove NY 11542. (516)671-4047. E-mail: ciamc@msn.com. Website: www.CitizensInAmerica.com. Secular publisher that does some inspirational and religious articles; for age 55+, well-educated/informed, and upper income bracket. John J. Maddox, mag. coord. Biweekly mag.; 60-100 pgs. Subscription rate to be determined. 100% unsolicited freelance. Complete ms/cover letter; e-query OK. Pays $40-100 on publication for one-time rts. Articles & fiction to 2,500 wds. Responds in 8 wks. No seasonal. Sometimes accepts simultaneous submissions; no reprints. Accepts requested submissions by e-mail (attached file). No kill fee. Uses some sidebars. Might accept submissions from teens. Guidelines (also on Website); copy $4.95. (Ads)

Poetry: Buys a lot. Avant-garde, free verse, haiku, light verse, traditional; 25+ lines. Pays $10. Submit max. 5 poems.

Fillers: Anecdotes, cartoons, facts. Pays $10.

Columns/Departments: A Choice of Humor (personal humor, made up or heard); to 250 wds. Pays $25.

Tips: "CIA will not accept manuscripts that deliberately promote racial, religious, or gender bigotry. You must request a sample copy before submitting, or visit our Website. Appreciate diversity. The magazine is not celebrity-studded."

+CITIZEN USA, 3651 Wrightway Rd., Dayton OH 45424. (937)233-6227. Fax (937)233-6231. E-mail: editor@CCN-USA.net. Website: www.citizenusa.us. Citizens Media Group, Inc. Submit to Editor-in-Chief. General interest newspaper from a Judeo-Christian editorial perspective. Biweekly newspaper; 20 pgs.; circ. 30,000. Subscription $50/52 issues. 1% unsolicited freelance; 90% assigned. Query/clips; phone/fax/e-query OK. **NO PAYMENT** for all rts. (on assignments). Articles 600-800 wds.; book reviews 500 wds.; music/video reviews 300-400 wds. Accepts requested mss by e-mail (attached file or copied into message). Responds in 4 wks. Seasonal 3 mos. ahead. Accepts reprints (tell when/where appeared). Uses some sidebars. Prefers KJV. Accepts submissions from children/teens. Guidelines/theme list by e-mail; copy. (Ads)

Fillers: Accepts 6/yr. Cartoons, games, jokes, kid quotes, party ideas, quizzes, quotes, short humor, and word puzzles, 300-500 wds.

$+CITY LIGHT NEWS, 9827E Horton Rd. S.W., Calgary AB T2V 2X5, Canada. (403)640-2011. Fax (403)640-2000. E-mail: editor@calgarychristian.com. Website: www.calgarychristian .com. CLN Productions. John Syratt, ed. A Christian newspaper serving the church audience in Central and Southern Alberta. Monthly newspaper; 20-32 pgs.; circ. 12,000. Subscription $24.95. 10% unsolicited freelance; 60% assigned. Query; e-query OK. Pays .10/wd. Cdn., on publication for 1st rts. Articles 600 wds. (12/yr.); reviews 150 wds. ($15). Responds in 2 wks. No simultaneous submissions; accepts reprints (tell when/where appeared). Prefers e-mail submissions (attached file). No kill fee. Uses some sidebars. Accepts submissions from teens. Guidelines/theme list on Website; copy for 10x13 SAE/$2 postage. (Ads)

Fillers: Buys 12/yr. Anecdotes, cartoons, facts, jokes, kid quotes, newsbreaks, short humor. Pays $30-50.

Tips: "Most open to articles of interest to general church audience; news or gripping stories—lighthearted or tragic; and good news stories."

$COLUMBIA, PO Box 1670 (06507-0981), 1 Columbus Plaza, New Haven CT 06510-3326. (203)772-2130. Fax (203)752-4109. E-mail: columbia@kofc.org, or tim.hickey@ kofc-supreme.com. Website: www.kofc.org. Knights of Columbus (Catholic). Tim S. Hickey, ed. Geared to a general Catholic family audience. Monthly & online mag.; 32 pgs.; circ. 1.6 million. Subscription $6; foreign $8. 25% unsolicited freelance; 75% assigned. Query; fax/e-query OK. Pays $250-600 on acceptance for 1st & electronic rts. Articles 500-1,500 wds. (12/yr.). Responds in 2 wks. Seasonal 3 mos. ahead. Occasional reprint (tell when/ where appeared). Prefers e-mail submission (copied into message). Kill fee. Regularly uses sidebars. Free guidelines (also by e-mail)/copy. (No ads)

Special Needs: Essays on spirituality, personal conversion. Catholic preferred. Query first.

Tips: "We welcome contributions from freelancers in all subject areas. An interesting or different approach to a topic will get the writer at least a second look from an editor. Most open to feature writers who can handle church issues, social issues from an orthodox Roman Catholic perspective. Must be aggressive, fact-centered writers for these features." **This periodical was #49 on the 2005 Top 50 Christian Publishers list (#49 in 2002, #30 in 2001).

$COMMON GROUND, Ste. 201, 3091 W. Broadway, Vancouver BC V6K 2G9, Canada. Toll-free (800)365-8897. (604)733-2215. Fax (604)733-4415. E-mail: editor@commonground.ca. Website: www.commonground.ca. Common Ground Publishing. Joseph Roberts, sr. ed. Covers health, environment, spirit, creativity, and wellness. Monthly tabloid; circ. 70,000. 90% unsolicited freelance. Query by e-mail. Pays .10/wd. (Canadian) on publication (although most articles are donated) for one-time or reprint rts. Articles 600-1,500 wds. (to 2,500 wds.), (12/yr.). Responds in 6-13 wks. (returns material only if clearly specified). Seasonal 3 mos. ahead. Accepts simultaneous submissions & reprints. Requires requested ms on disk or by e-mail. Guidelines on Website; copy $5. Incomplete topical listings. (Ads)

> **Tips:** "Donated articles are given priority over paid articles. Once an article has been published, we will contact you with the final word count, after which you may submit an invoice."

$COMMONWEAL, 475 Riverside Dr., Rm. 405, New York NY 10115-0499. (212)662-4200. Fax (212)662-4183. E-mail: editors@commonwealmagazine.org. Website: www.common wealmagazine.org. Commonweal Foundation/Catholic. Paul Baumann, ed. A review of public affairs, religion, literature, and the arts, for an intellectually engaged readership. Biweekly jour.; 32 pgs.; circ. 20,000. Subscription $47. 20% unsolicited freelance. Query/clips; phone query OK. Pays $75-100 on publication for all rts. Articles 2,000-2,500 wds. (30/yr.). Responds in 9 wks. Seasonal 2 mos. ahead. Prefers requested ms on disk or by e-mail. Kill fee 2%. Uses some sidebars. Guidelines on Website; free copy. (Ads)

> **Poetry:** Rosemary Deen and Daria Donnelly, poetry eds. Buys 20/yr. Free verse, traditional; to 75 lines; .75/line. Submit max. 5 poems. Submit October-May.

> **Columns/Departments:** Upfronts (brief, newsy facts and information behind the headlines), 750-1,000 wds.; The Last Word (commentary based on insight from personal experience or reflection), 700 wds.

> **Tips:** "Most open to meaningful articles on social, political, religious, and cultural topics; or columns."

($)COMMUNITY SPIRIT, 8835 S. Memorial, Tulsa OK 74133. (918)307-2323. Fax (918)307-1221. E-mail: Tom@communityspiritmagazine.com. Website: www.communityspirit magazine.com. Independent. Tom McCloud, pub. To glorify God by telling stories of individual Christians whose good works testify to God's active presence in Oklahoma. Monthly mag.; circ. 30,000. Subscription free. Accepts freelance. Prefers query. Pays for assignments only. Incomplete topical listings. No questionnaire returned. (Ads)

$COMPANY: The World of Jesuits and Their Friends, PO Box 60790, Chicago IL 60660. (773)761-9432. Fax (773)761-9443. E-mail: editor@companymagazine.org. Website: www.companymagazine.org. Martin McHugh, ed.; Becky Troha, asst. ed. For people interested in or involved with Jesuit ministries. Quarterly & online mag.; 32 pgs.; circ. 120,000. Free subscription. 40% unsolicited freelance; 60% assigned. Complete ms/cover letter; e-query OK. Pays $250-450 on publication for one-time rts. Articles 1,500 wds. Responds in 6 wks. Seasonal 3 mos. ahead. Accepts simultaneous submissions & reprints (tell when/where appeared). Prefers e-mail submission (attached file). Prefers NRSV, NAB, NJB. Guidelines (also by e-mail); copy for 9x12 SAE/4 stamps. (No ads)

> **Columns/Departments:** Books with a Jesuit connection; Minims and Maxims (short items of interest to Jesuit world), 100-150 wds./photo; Letters to the Editor; Obituaries. No payment (usually).

Tips: "We welcome manuscripts as well as outlines of story ideas and indication of willingness to accept freelance assignments (please include résumé and writing samples with the latter two). Articles must be Jesuit-related, and writers usually have some prior association with and/or knowledge of the Jesuits. Looking for feature articles (Jesuit-related), historical, essays, or ministry-related articles."

COMPASS DIRECT, PO Box 27250, Santa Ana CA 92799. (949)862-0314. Fax (949)752-6536. E-mail: info@compassdirect.org. Website: www.compassdirect.org. David Miller, mng. ed. To raise awareness of and encourage prayer for Christians worldwide who are persecuted for their faith. Monthly e-zine; circ. 700. E-mail subscription $25. Uses little freelance. Articles 800-1,200 wds. Query only. (No ads)

Tips: "An international journalist could submit an article on a current/specific instance of Christian persecution in a country with religious liberty restrictions. We seldom accept freelance work."

CONNECTING POINT, PO Box 6002, Vero Beach FL 32961. (321)773-2691. Fax (321)773-3042. E-mail: lhoward@specialgatherings.com. Linda G. Howard, ed. For and by the mentally challenged (mentally retarded) community; primarily deals with spiritual and self-advocacy issues. Monthly mag.; 12 pgs.; circ. 1,000. Free. 75% unsolicited freelance. Complete ms; phone/fax/e-query OK. **NO PAYMENT** for 1st rts. Articles (24/yr.) & fiction (12/yr.), 250-300 wds. Responds in 3-6 wks. Seasonal 3 mos. ahead. Accepts simultaneous submissions & reprints. Guidelines (also by e-mail); copy for 9x12 SAE/$1.42 postage (mark "Media Mail").

Poetry: Accepts 4/yr. Any type; 4-30 lines. Submit max. 10 poems.

Fillers: Accepts 12/yr. Cartoons, games, word puzzles; 50-250 wds.

Columns/Departments: Accepts 24/yr. Devotion Page, 250 wds.; Bible Study, 250 wds. Query.

Special Needs: Self-advocacy, integration/normalization, justice system.

Tips: "All manuscripts need to be in primary vocabulary."

$CORNERSTONE CHRISTIAN NEWSPAPER, 1111 Sheri Ln., Carlisle OH 45005. (937)743-2371. Fax (937)743-2329. E-mail: NewsCornerstone@aol.com. A Crary Publication. Mark S. Crary, pub./ed.; Vickie Gardner, articles ed. The printed voice for the Tri-State (IN, KY, OH) Christian community. Monthly newspaper; 40 pgs.; circ. 50,000. Subscription $20. 20% unsolicited freelance; 20% assigned. Query; fax/e-query OK. Pays $25-50 on publication for all rts. Articles 1,200 wds. (18/yr.); fiction 1,200 wds.; book/music/video reviews 300 wds. (no payment). Responds in 2 wks. Seasonal 1 mo. ahead. Accepts simultaneous submissions & reprints (tell when/where appeared). Accepts requested ms on disk or by e-mail (copied into message). No kill fee. Some sidebars. Prefers NKJV, NIV. Guidelines (also by e-mail)/theme list; copy for 9x12 SAE/3 stamps. (Ads)

Poetry: Accepts 6-12/yr. Free verse, 50-300 wds. No payment. Submit max. 3 poems.

Fillers: Accepts 24-36/yr. Cartoons, facts, games, ideas, jokes, kid quotes, newsbreaks, party ideas, prayers, short humor, and word puzzles; 50-300 wds. No payment.

Special Needs: Lots of music.

Tips: "We are open and enjoy working with freelancers. The best way a writer can break into our publication is to just get in touch with us and let us see the work they do."

$THE COVENANT COMPANION, 5101 N. Francisco Ave., Chicago IL 60625. (773)784-3000. Fax (773)784-4366. E-mail: communication@covchurch.org. Website: www.covchurch .org. Evangelical Covenant Church. Donald Meyer, ed.; Bob Smietana, features ed. Informs, stimulates thought, and encourages dialog on issues that affect the denomination. Monthly mag.; 40 pgs.; circ. 16,000. Subscription $19.95. 5% unsolicited freelance; 35% assigned. Complete ms/cover letter; fax/e-query OK. Pays $35-100 on publication for one-time or simultaneous rts. Articles 1,200-1,800 wds. (15/yr.). Prefers e-mail submission. Responds in 4 wks. Seasonal 3 mos. ahead. Accepts simultaneous submissions & reprints (tell when/where appeared). Some kill fees. Regularly uses sidebars. Prefers NRSV. Guidelines (also by e-mail/Website); copy for 9x12 SAE/5 stamps or $2.50. (Ads)

*CREATION, PO Box 6302, Acacia Ridge QLD 4110, Australia. Phone 07 3273 7650. Fax 07 3273 7672. E-mail: admin@answersingenesis.com. Website: www.answersingenesis.org. Answers in Genesis. Carl Wieland, ed. A family, nature, science magazine focusing on creation/evolution issues. Quarterly mag.; 56 pgs.; circ. 70,000. Subscription $22. 30% unsolicited freelance. Query; phone/fax/e-query OK. **NO PAYMENT** for all rts. Articles to 1,500 wds. (20/yr.). Responds in 2-3 wks. Prefers requested ms on disk or by e-mail (attached file). Regularly uses sidebars. Guidelines (also by e-mail); copy $6.95. (No ads)

Tips: "Get to know the basic content/style of the magazine and emulate."

CREATION CARE, 275 Edgewood Dr., Americus GA 31709. Toll-free (800)650-6600. (202)554-1955. E-mail: jim@creationcare.org. Website: www.creationcare.org/magazine. Evangelical Environmental Network. Rev. Jim Ball, ed. For Christians who care about reducing pollution and caring for God's creation. Quarterly mag.; 20 pgs.; circ. 5,000. Subscription $25 (free to supporters). 90% unsolicited freelance. Query; fax/e-query OK. **NO PAYMENT.** Articles 500-1,200 wds. (20/yr.); book reviews 200 wds. (no payment). Responds in 6-8 wks. Seasonal 4 mos. ahead. Accepts reprints (tell when/where appeared). Prefers accepted ms by e-mail. Regularly uses sidebars. Prefers NRSV, NIV. Guidelines on Website; copy for 10x13 SAE/4 stamps. (Ads)

Tips: "See past issues on our Website."

$CREATION ILLUSTRATED, PO Box 7955, Auburn CA 95604. (530)269-1424. Fax (530)269-1428. E-mail: creation@foothill.net, or ci@creationillustrated.com. Website: www.creation illustrated.com. Tom Ish, ed./pub. An uplifting, Bible-based Christian nature magazine that glorifies God; for ages 9-99. Quarterly mag.; 68 pgs.; circ. 13,000. Subscription $14.95/19.95. 60% unsolicited freelance; 40% assigned. Query or query/clips; fax/e-query OK. Pays $75-125 within 30 days of publication for 1st rts. (holds rts. for 6 mos.). Articles 1,000-2,000 wds. (25/yr.). Responds in 3 wks. Seasonal 6 mos. ahead. Accepts simultaneous submissions & reprints (tell when/where appeared). Prefers e-mail submission (copied into message). Kill fee 25%. Some sidebars. Prefers NKJV. Guidelines/theme list (also on Website); copy $3/9x12 SAE/$1.42 postage (mark "Media Mail"). (Some ads)

Poetry: Buys 8/yr. Light verse, traditional; 10-20 lines; $15. Submit max. 4 poems.

Fillers: Games, 100-200 wds. Pays variable rates.

Tips: "Most open to an experience with nature/creation that brought you closer to God and will inspire the reader to do the same. Include spiritual lessons and supporting scriptures—at least 3 or 4 of each."

$CREATIVE NONFICTION, 5501 Walnut St., Ste. 202, Pittsburgh PA 15232. (412)688-0304. Fax (412)688-0262. E-mail: information@creativenonfiction.org. Website: www.creative nonfiction.org. Lee Gutkind, ed. Triannual jour.; 140 pgs.; circ. 5,000. Subscription $29.95 for 4 issues. 80% unsolicited freelance; 20% assigned. Complete ms/cover letter; no phone/fax/e-query. Pays $10/published page on publication. Articles to 5,000 wds. (20/yr.). Responds in 3-5 mos. No simultaneous submissions or reprints. E-mail submissions OK. Kill fee sometimes. Does not use sidebars. Accepts submissions from teens. Guidelines (also by e-mail/Website); copy for 7x10 SAE/$1.42 postage (mark "Media Mail").

Contests: Sometimes sponsor contests; see Website for details.

Tips: "We're looking for stories with a strong narrative and an element of research."

$THE CRESSET: A Review of Arts, Literature & Public Affairs, 1409 Chapel Dr., Valparaiso IN 46383-9998. (219)464-6089. E-mail: cresset@valpo.edu. Website: www .valpo.edu/cresset. Valparaiso University/Lutheran. Tom Kennedy, ed. (tom.kennedy@ valpo.edu). For college-educated, professors, pastors, laypeople; serious review essays on religious-cultural affairs. Mag. published 5X/yr.; 60 pgs.; circ. 4,500. Subscription $20. 10% unsolicited freelance; 90% assigned. Query; e-query OK. Pays $100-500 on publication for all rts. Articles 2,000-4,500 wds. (2/yr.); book/music reviews, 1,000 wds. ($150). Responds in 15 wks. No simultaneous submissions or reprints. Prefers requested ms by e-mail (attached or copied into message). Regularly uses sidebars. Prefers NRSV. Guidelines on Website; copy $4.

Poetry: John Ruff, poetry ed. Buys 20/yr. Avant-garde, free verse, light verse, traditional; to 40 lines; $15-25. Submit max. 4 poems.

Columns/Departments: Buys 20/yr. Books; Music; Science & Technology; World Views; all 1,000 wds., $100-250. Query.

+CROSSHOME.COM: Your Christian Home on the Net! E-mail: webmaster@cross home.com. Website: www.crosshome.com. Online mag. Open to solicited freelance. Complete ms by e-mail; e-query OK. **NO PAYMENT** for one-time rts. Articles 300-1,000 wds.; devotionals 300-1,000 wds. (prefers 350-650 wds.); book reviews 300-800 wds. Responds in 1-3 wks. (if accepted). Requires accepted ms by e-mail (attached file in Word). Prefers KJV, NKJV, NIV, NASB. Guidelines on Website (www.crosshome.com/guidelines.shtml); copy online. (Ads)

Poetry: Accepts free verse, traditional; 30-50 wds.

Columns/Departments: Open to submissions for regular columns, or ideas for new ones. (See guidelines.)

Special Needs: See Website/guidelines for list of channels where your writing might fit.

Tips: "We do archive all writing, but any submissions can be deleted by request of the author by e-mail."

*CROSSWAY MAGAZINE/NEWSLINE NEWSLETTER/AVIATION NEWSPAPER, AAACF c/o C.B.C. Officeblock Unit 5, Frimley Road, Camberley, Surrey GU18 5UJ England. Phone/fax 01276 709474. Airline Aviation & Aerospace Christian Fellowship. C. Cowell, gen. sec. For non-Christians working in aviation. Quarterly publications; 16 pgs. Subscription free. 100% unsolicited freelance. Complete ms/cover letter. **NO PAYMENT.** Not copyrighted. Articles on aviation to 2,000 wds. Accepts simultaneous submissions & reprints. Prefers KJV. Not included in topical listings.

$CULTURE WARS, 206 Marquette Ave., South Bend IN 46617-1111. (574)289-9786. Fax (574)289-1461. E-mail: jones@culturewars.com, or letters@culturewars.com. Website: www.culturewars.com. Ultramontagne Associates, Inc. Dr. E. Michael Jones, ed. Issues relating to Catholic families and issues affecting America that affect all people. Monthly (11X) mag.; 48 pgs.; circ. 3,500. Subscription $30. 20% unsolicited freelance. Complete ms/cover letter; fax/e-query OK. Pays $100 & up on publication for all rts. Articles (25/yr.); book reviews $50. Responds in 12-24 wks. Query about reprints. Prefers requested ms on disk. Uses some sidebars. Developing guidelines; copy for 9x12 SAE/5 stamps.

Poetry: Buys 15/yr. Free verse, light verse, traditional; 10-50 lines; $25. Submit max. 2 poems.

Fillers: Buys 15/yr. Cartoons, quotes; 25 wds. & up; variable payment.

Columns/Departments: Buys 25/yr. Commentary, 2,500 wds.; Feature, 5,000 wds.; $100-250.

Tips: "All fairly open except cartoons. Single-spaced preferred; photocopies must be clear."

$A CUP OF COMFORT BOOK SERIES, 57 Littlefield St., 2nd Fl., Avon MA 02322. Toll-free (800)872-5627. (508)427-7100. Fax (508)427-6790. E-mail: cupofcomfort@adams media.com. Website: www.cupofcomfort.com. Adams Media Corp. Colleen Sell, ed. Each anthology is filled with slice-of-life, positive, inspiring, anecdotal stories, written from the heart, about the extraordinary experiences of ordinary people. Publishes 3-4 anthologies/yr.; 360 pgs. 100% freelance. Query/clips; e-query OK. Pays $100 for each story accepted, plus a $500 Grand Prize for best story in each volume, on publication for worldwide book and archival rights for 5 yrs. (with exception of books comprised solely of author's original work); on publication. Stories 1,000-2,000 wds. (no fiction or poetry), 150-200/yr. Responds in 9-12 mos. Accepts simultaneous submissions & reprints (unless published in another anthology). Prefers submissions by disk or e-mail (copied into message). No kill fee. Does not use sidebars. Guidelines (also by e-mail/Website); sample stories posted on Website. (No ads)

Special Needs: Stories of faith, marriage, love, and personal spirituality. See Website for list of possible future themes and deadlines.

Tips: "A Cup of Comfort stories are secular, not religious. We have no Christian-themed anthologies in development at this time, nor planned for the foreseeable future. We publish creative nonfiction (true) stories and essays." Many of the themes listed in the topical files may refer to inclusion only in one of the upcoming anthologies.

$DECISION/DECISION ONLINE, 1 Billy Graham Pkwy., Charlotte NC 28201-0001. (704)401-2432. Fax (704)401-3009. E-mail: submissions@bgea.org. Website: www.decisionmag .org. Billy Graham Evangelistic Assn. Bob Paulson, mng. ed. Evangelism/Christian nurture; all articles must have connection to BGEA. Monthly & online mag.; 44 pgs.; circ. 900,000. Subscription $12. 1% unsolicited freelance; written mostly in-house. Complete ms/cover letter (no queries); no phone/fax/e-query. Pays $55-500 on publication for all, 1st, or electronic rts. Articles 400-1,000 wds. (12-15/yr.). Response time varies. Seasonal 3-5 mos. ahead. Accepts ms by e-mail (attached file). Kill fee. Uses some sidebars. Prefers NIV. Guidelines (also by e-mail/Website); copy for 10x13 SAE/3 stamps. (No ads)

Columns/Departments: Buys 10/yr. Finding Jesus (people who have become Christians through Billy Graham ministries); 400-600 wds.; $85.

Special Needs: Personal experience articles telling how a Billy Graham ministry helped you live out your faith.

Tips: "Nearly all of our articles have some connection with a ministry of the Billy Graham Evangelistic Assn.—through the author's participation in the ministry or through the author's being touched by the ministry."

**2005, 2003 EPA Award of Merit—Organizational. 2001 EPA Award of Merit—Most Improved Publication.

DESERT CALL: Christianity for a Vital Culture, Box 219, Crestone CO 81131. (719)256-4778. Fax (719)256-4719. Website: www.spirituallifeinstitute.org. Spiritual Life Institute/Catholic. Submit to The Editor. Practical spirituality and contemplative prayer; interreligious dialog and culture. Quarterly mag.; 32 pgs.; circ. 2,000. Subscription $16. 15% unsolicited freelance; 10% assigned. Complete ms/cover letter; no phone/fax/e-query. **PAYS 3 COPIES** for 1st rts. Articles 1,000-2,500 wds. (4/yr.). Responds in 15 wks. Seasonal 8 mos. ahead. Accepts reprints (tell when/where appeared). No disk or e-mail submissions. Uses some sidebars. No guidelines; copy $2.50/10x13 SAE. (No ads)

Poetry: Accepts 3/yr. Free verse, haiku, traditional; to 25 lines. Submit max. 2 poems.

Fillers: Accepts 3/yr. Anecdotes, facts, prayers, prose, quotes; 50-250 wds.

Special Needs: Interreligious dialog, arts, and culture.

Tips: "Avoid personal reflection/anecdotal pieces. Prefer articles that are informative, well-researched, accessible to a busy, educated readership of interdenominational background. Avoid moralisms and preachy tone."

+DESERT CHRISTIAN NEWS, PO Box 4196, Palm Desert CA 92261. (760)772-2027. E-mail: desertchristian@aol.com. Susan Miller, ed. To encourage communication and unity amongst Christians in the Coachella Valley by sharing inspiring local news stories, feature articles, and information. Newspaper. Subscription $25. Open to freelance. Query preferred. Articles; reviews. (Ads) Incomplete topical listings. No questionnaire returned.

+THE DESERT VOICE, PO Box 567, Imperial CA 92251. (760)337-9200. Fax (760)355-0197. E-mail: editor@bsafemail.com. Witness Publishing, Inc. Alex Arroyave, ed. To reach the lost, and to provide family-friendly news not found elsewhere. Newspaper; circ. 9,500. Subscription $20. Open to unsolicited freelance. Complete ms. Articles; reviews. Incomplete topical listings. (Ads)

$DIRECTION, PO Box 436987, Chicago IL 60643. Toll-free (800)860-8642. Fax (708)868-6759. E-mail: cywilson@urbanministries.com. Website: www.urbanministries.com. Urban Ministries, Inc. Cheryl Wilson, ed. asst. An adult-level Sunday School quarterly publication consisting of a student book and a teacher's guide. Quarterly mag; 64 pgs.; $16.45 (student) and $24.95 (teacher). 0% unsolicited freelance; 100% assigned. Query or query/clips; phone/fax/e-query OK. Accepts full manuscripts by e-mail. Pays to $250 ($300 for lessons) on acceptance, for all rts. Articles 1,500-3,500 wds. Responds in 4 wks. Seasonal 12 mos. ahead. No simultaneous submissions or reprints. Requires accepted ms on disk or by e-mail (attached or copied into message). Kill fee 50%. Does not use sidebars. Prefers KJV. Guidelines by e-mail; copy for SASE. (No ads)

> **Tips:** "Send query with a writing sample, or attend our annual conference on the first weekend in November each year. Manuscripts are evaluated at the conference."

$DISASTER NEWS NETWORK, 9195C Red Branch Rd., Columbia MD 21045. Toll-free (888)203-384-3028. (410)884-7350. Fax (410)884-7353. E-mail: info@villagelife.org. Website: www.disasternews.net. Village Life Co. Submit to The Editor. Online; an interactive daily news site on the World Wide Web. Query; phone/fax OK; e-query preferred. Pays $85-100 after publication for all rts. Articles 1,000 wds. Requires accepted ms by e-mail. Guidelines on Website. Not in topical listings.

> **Tips:** "Most open to 'people stories' related to faith-based disaster response and/or mitigation. Also, faith-based response to incidents of public violence. Authors are expected to have an e-mail submission address."

$DISCIPLESHIP JOURNAL, Box 35004, Colorado Springs CO 80935. (719)548-9222. Fax (719)598-7128. E-mail: djwriters@navpress.com, or sue.kline@navpress.com. Website: www.discipleshipjournal.com. The Navigators. Sue Kline, ed.; Connie Willems, mng. ed. For motivated, maturing Christians desiring to grow spiritually and to help others grow; biblical and practical. Bimonthly mag.; 82+ pgs.; circ. 130,000. Subscription $23.97. 65% unsolicited freelance; 35% assigned. Query/clips; fax/e-query OK. Pays .25/wd.(.05/wd. for reprints) on acceptance for 1st & electronic rts. Articles 1,500-2,500 wds. (60/yr.). Responds in 6-8 wks. Accepts reprints; simultaneous submissions discouraged. Prefers requested ms by e-mail. Kill fee 50%. Regularly uses sidebars. Prefers NIV. Guidelines (also by e-mail/Website); copy for 9x12 SAE/$1.42 postage (mark "Media Mail"). (Ads)

> **Columns/Departments:** Buys 100+/yr. DJ Plus (ministry how-to on missions, evangelism, serving, discipling, teaching, and small groups), to 500 wds. DJ Plus editor: Connie Willems (connie.willems@navpress.com). Query or complete manuscript. Pays .25/wd.

> **Special Needs:** Biblical exposition of a passage or topic; maturing in Christian character; applying scripture to current topics; character of God; spiritual disciplines.

> **Tips:** "Most open to non-theme articles and DJ Plus. Our articles focus on biblical passages or topics. Articles should derive main principles from a thorough study of Scripture, should illustrate each principle, should show how to put each principle into practice, and should demonstrate with personal illustrations and vulnerability that the author has wrestled with the subject in his or her life."

> **The #4 Best-selling Magazine in Christian retail stores. This periodical was #3 on the 2005 Top 50 Christian Publishers list (#3 in 2004, #3 in 2003, #5 in 2002, #2 in 2001). 2004 EPA Award of Excellence—General; 2005 EPA Award of Merit—General.

DISCIPLE'S JOURNAL, 10 Fiorenza Dr., PO Box 100, Wilmington MA 01887-4421. Toll-free (800)696-2344. (978)657-7373. Fax (978)657-5411. E-mail: dddj@disciples directory.com, or info@disciplesdirectory.com. Website: www.disciplesdirectory.com. Kenneth A. Dorothy, ed. To strengthen, edify, inform, and unite the body of Christ. Monthly & online newspaper; 24-32 pgs.; circ. 8,000. Subscription $14.95. 5% unsolicited freelance. Query; fax/e-query OK. **NO PAYMENT** for one-time rts. Articles 400 wds. (24/yr.); book/music/video reviews 200 wds. Responds in 2 wks. Seasonal 2 mos. ahead. Accepts simultaneous submissions & reprints (tell when/where appeared). Prefers requested ms on disk or by e-mail (attached file). Uses some sidebars. Prefers NIV. Guidelines/theme list (also by e-mail); copy for 9x12 SAE/$1.42 postage (mark "Media Mail"). (Ads)

 Fillers: Accepts 12/yr. All types; 100-400 wds.

 Columns/Departments: Financial; Singles; Men; Women; Business; Parenting; 400 wds.

 Tips: "Most open to men's, women's, or singles' issues; missions; or homeschooling. Send sample of articles for review."

$DISCIPLESWORLD, PO Box 11469, Indianapolis IN 46201-0469. (317)375-8846. Fax (317)375-8849. E-mail: semmons@disciplesworld.com, or editor@disciplesworld.com. Website: www.disciplesworld.com. Christian Church (Disciples of Christ). Sherri Wood Emmons, mng. ed. The journal of news, opinion, and mission for this denomination in North America. Monthly mag.; 48 pgs.; circ. 14,000. Subscription $25. 30% unsolicited freelance; 70% assigned. Complete ms/cover letter; e-query OK. Pays .15/wd. on publication for 1st rts. Articles 600-1,200 wds. (40/yr.); fiction 150-1,500 wds. (8-10/yr.); reviews 600 wds. (no payment). Responds in 2-9 wks. Seasonal 3 mos. ahead. Accepts simultaneous submissions; no reprints. Requires submissions by disk or e-mail (attached file). No kill fee. Uses some sidebars. Prefers NRSV. Guidelines/theme list on Website; copy for #10 SASE. (Ads)

 Poetry: Buys 6-10/yr. Free verse, light verse; 12-30 lines. Pays $10-50. Submit max. 3 poems.

 Fillers: Buys 20/yr. Anecdotes, cartoons, kid quotes, quotes, short humor; 20-200 wds. Pays $10-50.

 Columns/Departments: Buys 12-15/yr. Speak Out (opinion on an issue), 600 wds.; Disciples Go (travel to places relevant to Disciples), 600 wds., plus photos; $100. Quotable Quotes, 200 wds. (no pay).

 Tips: "Looking for humorous short-shorts (200 wds.). Our readers are mostly college-educated, active in their churches, proud of their Disciples heritage, and all over the board politically and theologically. We like things with a Disciples connection."

 **This periodical was #45 on the 2005 Top 50 Christian Publishers list.

DISCOVERY: Central Florida's Online Christian Family Newspaper, 1188 Lake View Dr., Altamonte Springs FL 32714. (407)682-9494. Fax (407)682-7005. E-mail: jadams@wtln.com. Website: www.wtln.com. Radio Stations WTLN & WHIM. John Adams, ed. For the Christian community in Central Florida. Bimonthly print and online newspaper. 20% unsolicited freelance. Complete ms/cover letter; fax/e-query OK. **NO PAYMENT.** Not copyrighted. News-driven articles under 500 wds. Seasonal 1+ mo. ahead. Accepts reprints. Regularly uses sidebars. No disk; e-mail submission OK. No guidelines; free copy. (Ads)

 Fillers: Accepts several/yr. Cartoons, word puzzles.

 Columns/Departments: Local/National News, Local Ministries, Broadcaster's Information, Sports, Christian Living, seasonal-themed features.

 Tips: "We may submit articles to our other publications in Knoxville and Philadelphia."

DIVINE ASCENT: A Journal of Orthodox Faith, PO Box 563, Pt. Reyes Station CA 94956. (415)663-1705. Fax (415)663-0359 or (325)288-6312. E-mail: office@monastery ofstjohn.org. Website: www.monasteryofstjohn.org. Monastery of St. John of Shanghai &

San Francisco/Orthodox Church in America. Fr. Jonah Paffhausen, Abbot & ed-in-chief. Focuses on contemporary Orthodox spirituality as seen in the lives and writings of saints, and holy men and women of our own time. Annual jour.; 150 pgs. Subscription $25/2 yrs. 20% unsolicited freelance; 65% assigned. Query. **NO PAYMENT** for all rts. Articles (6/yr.); book reviews 500 wds. Responds in 4-8 wks. No reprints. Prefers disk or e-mail submissions (attached file). Does not use sidebars. Prefers RSV, KJV, NKJV. Guidelines by e-mail. (Ads, from Orthodox Christian businesses)

Tips: "Nothing Protestant."

$DOVETAIL: A Journal by and for Jewish/Christian Families, 775 Simon Greenwell Ln., Boston KY 40107. (502)549-5499. Fax (549)540-3543. E-mail: di-ifr@bardstown.com. Website: www.dovetailinstitute.org. Dovetail Institute for Interfaith Family Resources. Mary Rosenbaum, ed.(address & e-mail above). Book review ed.: Carol Weiss Rubel, 310 Tulip Cir., Clarks Summit PA 18411-0213; Carol W44@aol.com. Offers balanced, nonjudgmental articles for interfaith families and the professionals who serve them. Bimonthly mag.; 12-16 pgs.; circ. 1,000. Subscription/membership $59.95. 80% unsolicited freelance; 20% assigned. Query or complete ms; phone/fax/e-query OK. Pays $25 on publication for all rts. Articles 800-1,000 wds. (18-20/yr.); book reviews 500 wds., ($15). Responds in 2-6 wks. Seasonal 4 mos. ahead. Accepts simultaneous submissions & reprints (tell when/where appeared). Prefers requested ms on disk or by e-mail (copied into message). Uses some sidebars. Prefers RSV. Guidelines/theme list (also by e-mail); copy for 9x12 SAE/3 stamps. (Ads)

Poetry: Buys 1-2/yr. Traditional; $15. Submit max. 4 poems.

Columns/Departments: Buys 3-6/yr. Food & Family (Jewish & Christian), 500 wds.; Parent's Page, and Reviews; $15. Complete ms.

Special Needs: We are expanding our scope to include other types of interfaith marriages, especially those involving a Muslim partner.

Tips: "Demonstrate real, concrete, practical knowledge of the challenges facing Jewish and Christian partners in a marriage. Do not send pieces of Christian interest only. No proselytizing." Show respect for the religious traditions of their Jewish staff and readers.

$DRAGONS, KNIGHTS, AND ANGELS: The Magazine of Christian Fantasy and Science Fiction, 5461 W. 4605 S., West Valley City UT 84120. E-mail: dkamagazine@quixnet.net. Website: www.dkamagazine.com. Nondenominational. Rebecca Shelley, ed. A family-friendly magazine of Christian fantasy and science fiction. Monthly e-zine; 600 hits/mo. Free online. 80% unsolicited freelance; 0% assigned. Complete ms; e-query OK. Pays $5 on acceptance for one-time electronic rts. Fiction 1,000-4,000 wds. (12/yr.). Responds in 6 wks. Seasonal 3 mos. ahead. Accepts reprints (tell when/where appeared). Accepted mss by e-mail (attached). Does not use sidebars. Accepts submissions from children/teens. Guidelines/copy on Website. (No ads)

Poetry: Accepts 12/yr. Free verse, light verse, traditional; to 50 lines. Pays $1. Submit max. 5 poems.

Tips: "Submissions are only accepted during designated reading periods listed on Website. Submissions sent at other times will be rejected."

$DRAMA MINISTRY, PO Box 681866, Franklin TN 37068-1866. Toll-free (866)859-7622. Fax (615)373-8502. E-mail: service@dramaministry.com. Website: www.dramaministry.com. Belden Street Music Company. Kimberlee Stone, ed. Mag. published 8X/yr. & online; page count varies. 50% unsolicited freelance; 50% assigned. Complete ms/cover letter for scripts; query for articles; e-query OK. Pays $100-150 for scripts on publication for one-time rts. Articles 500-700 wds. (10/yr.); scripts 2-10 minutes (80/yr.). Responds in 6-8 wks. Seasonal 6 mos. ahead. Accepts simultaneous submissions & reprints (tell when/where appeared). Requires submissions by e-mail (attached file). No kill fee. Does not use sidebars. Accepts submissions from teens. Any Bible version. Guidelines/theme list on Website. (No ads)

> **Tips:** "If your script is well-written and you have a true understanding of what works within the church drama ministry, then you will break into our publication easily. Please adhere to and read writer's guidelines thoroughly (see Website). We do not respond unless we choose to publish your script."

$DREAMS & VISIONS: Spiritual Fiction, 35 Peter St. S., Orillia ON L3V 5A8, Canada. Phone/fax (705)329-1770. E-mail: skysong@bconnex.net. Website: www.bconnex.net/ ~skysong. Skysong Press. Steve Stanton, ed. An international showcase for short literary fiction written from a Christian perspective. Semiannual jour.; 56 pgs.; circ. 200. Subscription $12. 100% unsolicited freelance. Complete ms/cover letter; fax/e-query OK. Pays .01/wd. on publication for 1st rts. and one nonexclusive reprint. Fiction 2,000-6,000 wds. (10/yr.). Responds in 4-6 wks. No seasonal. Accepts simultaneous submissions & reprints (tell when/where appeared). Guidelines (also on Website); copy $4.95 (4 back issues to writers $10).

DREAMSEEKER MAGAZINE, 126 Klingerman Rd., Telford PA 18969. (215)723-9125. E-mail: DSM@CascadiaPublishingHouse.com, or editor@CascadiaPublishingHouse.com. Website: www.CascadiaPublishingHouse.com. Cascadia Publishing House. Submit to The Editor. For readers committed to exploring from the heart, with passion, depth, and flair, their own visions and issues of the day. Print & online magazine. Accepts freelance. Guidelines on Website. Not in topical listings. No questionnaire returned.

$#ECLECTIC HOMESCHOOL ONLINE, PO Box 5304, Fallon NV 89407-5304. (775)428-6454. E-mail: articles@eho.org. Website: www.eho.org. Eclectic Homeschool Assn. Beverly S. Krueger, sr. ed. Reaches a diverse homeschool audience interested in new ideas, techniques, or resources that will help them creatively tailor their homeschooling to their children's needs. Biweekly online mag.; circ. 50,000. Subscription $19.95. 25% unsolicited freelance; 25% assigned. Complete ms/cover letter; e-query OK. Pays $35-100 on acceptance for 1st, reprint, electronic, and archival rts. Articles. Responds in 6-8 wks. Seasonal 3 mos. ahead. No simultaneous submissions or reprints. Accepts disk or e-mail submissions (copied into message). No kill fee. Some sidebars. Accepts submissions from teens. Prefers NKJV. Guidelines/copy on Website. (Ads)

> **Columns/Departments:** Buys 25/yr. Homeschooling Methods (for arts, language arts, social sciences, critical thinking, computers, etc.); Making Math Marvelous (math how-to or resources); History (how-to or resources); Science (how-to or resources); all 350 wds. Pays $35.

> **Tips:** "We are looking for short (350 word) pieces for all our departments. Articles must be encouraging, practical, and provide useful content for our readers."

$EFCA TODAY, PO Box 315, Charlottesville VA 22902. (434)961-2500, ext. 508. Fax (434)961-2507. E-mail: Today@EFCA.org, or DianeMc@journeygroup.com. Website: www.efca.org/ today.html. Evangelical Free Church of America/Journey Communications. Diane McDougall, ed. Denominational. Quarterly mag.; 32 pgs.; circ. 60,000. Subscription $12. 5% unsolicited freelance; 95% assigned. Query (preferred) or complete ms/cover letter; fax/e-query OK. Pays .23/wd. on acceptance for 1st and subsidiary (free use on EFCA Website or church bulletins) rts. Articles 200-1,000 wds. (6/yr.). Responds in 6 wks. Seasonal 6 mos. ahead. Accepts simultaneous submissions; rarely uses reprints (tell when/where appeared). Prefers e-mail (attached file) or hard copy. Kill fee 50%. Regularly uses sidebars. Guidelines (also by e-mail); copy $1/10x13 SAE/$1.42 postage (mark "Media Mail"). (Ads)

> **Columns/Departments:** Buys 6/yr. Home Base (topics affecting women's, men's, and youth ministries, as well as families); Cover-Theme Section (variety of topics applicable to church leadership), 550-1,200 wds.; pays .23/wd.

Special Needs: Stories of EFCA churches in action.

Tips: "Have a unique story about a Free Church in action. The vast majority of articles are geared to sharing the Free Church at work."

**2005, 2003 Award of Excellence—Denominational. 2001 EPA Award of Merit—Denominational. This periodical was #44 on the 2004 Top 50 Christian Publishers list.

$EN CONFIANZA, 8675 Explorer Dr., Colorado Springs CO 80920. (719)548-4660. Fax (719)531-3383. E-mail: abeljl@fotf.org. Website: www.enfoqualafamilia.com. Focus on the Family. Graciela Lelli, ed. To provide family-friendly material to our domestic Spanish constituents and inform the Hispanic community of culturally relevant issues that affect their families. Bimonthly mag.; circ. 30,000. Subscription free. Open to unsolicited freelance. Complete ms/cover letter. Articles. Incomplete topical listings. (No ads)

$EPISCOPAL LIFE, 815—2nd Ave., New York NY 10017. Toll-free (800)334-7626, ext. 6009. (212)716-6009. Fax (212)949-8059. E-mail: jhames@episcopalchurch.org. Website: www.episcopal-life.org. Episcopal Church. Jerrold F. Hames, ed. Denominational. Monthly newspaper; 32 pgs.; circ. 280,000. Subscription $16.95. 0% unsolicited freelance; 10% assigned. Query/clips or complete ms/cover letter; phone query on breaking news only; e-query OK. Pays $50-300 on publication for 1st, one-time, or simultaneous rts. Articles 250-1,200 wds. (12/yr.); assigned book reviews 400 wds. ($35). Responds in 5 wks. Seasonal 4 mos. ahead. Accepts simultaneous submissions & reprints. Accepts e-mail submission. Kill fee 50%. Guidelines (by e-mail); free copy. (Ads)

> **Columns/Departments:** Nan Cobbey, column ed. (ncobbey@dfms.org). Buys 36/yr. Commentary on political/religious topics; 300-600 wds.; $35-75. Query.
>
> **Tips:** "All articles must have Episcopal Church slant or specifics. We need topical/issues, not devotional stuff. Most open to feature stories about Episcopalians—clergy, lay, churches, involvement in local efforts, movements, ministries."

+ETERNAL INK, 25 Powers Rd., Lawrenceburg TN 38464. E-mail: fishercaster@yahoo.com. Website: www.eternal-ink.com. Nondenominational. Open to any serious effort or submission. Submit to Administrative Assistant (e-mail above); Carl Phillips, nonfiction ed. (Carl Phil10@aol.com). Biweekly e-zine; circ. 440+. Subscription free. 40% unsolicited freelance; 0% assigned. Complete ms/cover letter; e-query OK. **NO PAYMENT** for 1st or reprint rts. Articles 300-1,500 wds. (26/yr.); some fiction; reviews 400 wds. Responds in 6 wks. Seasonal 3 mos. ahead. Accepts reprints (tell when/where appeared). Accepts e-mail submissions (copied into message). Does not use sidebars. Prefers KJV. Accepts submissions from children and teens. Guidelines/copy on Website. (Ad swaps)

> **Poetry:** Elizabeth Pearson, poetry ed. (roybet630@aol.com). Accepts 26/yr. Free verse, traditional, inspirational; 20-30 lines. Submit max. 3 poems.
>
> **Fillers:** Accepts 26/yr. Facts, ideas, jokes, kid quotes, prayers, prose, quizzes, quotes, short humor, and tips; 100-250 wds.
>
> **Columns/Departments:** Mary Ellen Grisham, columns ed. (meggy88@iwon.com). Accepts many/yr. See information on Website. Query.
>
> **Contest:** See Website.
>
> **Tips:** "Interviews/profiles with Christian athletes are especially needed. Collegiate and professional athletes are requested. Even retired athletes who are involved in ministry are extremely helpful. We want fiction for children, 7-12, and teens. Please send all submissions to appropriate editor."

$EUREKA STREET: A Magazine of Public Affairs, the Arts and Theology, PO Box 553, Richmond VIC 3121, Australia. Phone +613 9427 7311. Fax +613 9428 4450. E-mail: eureka@jespub.jesuit.org.au. Website: www.eurekastreet.com.au/index.html. Jesuit Publications. Marcelle Mogg, ed. Monthly mag. (10X); circ. 13,000. Subscription $70. Accepts freelance. Complete ms by mail or e-mail (attached file). Pays $110 U.S./1,000 wds. for one-time rts. No reprints. Guidelines online (www.eurekastreet.com.au/ab_write.html). Incomplete topical listings.

$EVANGEL, Box 535002, Indianapolis IN 46253-5002. (317)244-3660. E-mail: evangeleditor@ fmcna.org. Free Methodist/Light and Life Communications. Julie Innes, ed. For young to middle-aged adults; encourages spiritual growth. Weekly take-home paper; 8 pgs.; circ. 11,000. Subscription $9. 100% unsolicited freelance. Complete ms/cover letter; no e-query. Pays .04/wd. ($10 min.) on publication for one-time rts. Articles to 1,200 wds. (100/yr.); fiction to 1,200 wds. (100/yr.). Responds in 6-8 wks. Seasonal 12-15 mos. ahead. Accepts simultaneous submissions & reprints (tell when/where appeared). Accepts requested mss by e-mail. Some sidebars. Prefers NIV. Guidelines (also by e-mail); copy for #10 SAE/1 stamp. (No ads)

> **Poetry:** Buys 40+/yr. Free verse, light verse, traditional; 3-16 lines; $10. Submit max. 5 poems. Rhyming poetry not usually taken too seriously.

> **Fillers:** Buys 20/yr. Cartoons, crypto-word puzzles; to 100 wds; $10.

> **Tips:** "Bring fresh insight to a topic like prayer, faith, etc. Be sure to submit material appropriate for the market and audience. Although we will cover a specific issue of concern to men or to women, we prefer that the problem be addressed universally. Don't ramble; stick to one thesis or theme. A returned manuscript isn't always because of poor writing. Don't give up—keep writing and submitting."

THE EVANGEL, PO Box 348, Marlow OK 73055. Toll-free (800)654-3992. (580)658-5631. Fax (817)277-8098. E-mail: umi@umi.org. Website: www.umi.org, or www.watchman.org. Utah Missions, Inc. Dennis A. Wright, dir. A Christian apologetics ministry that exposes major counterfeit religions with a special emphasis upon Mormonism, and explains their doctrine, history, and current events in the light of biblical Christianity. Monthly mag.; 12 pgs.; circ. 3,500. Subscription $15, 6-mo. subscription free to new subscribers. Little freelance. Complete ms; phone/fax/e-query OK. **NO PAYMENT.** Articles 1,000-1,500 wds. Copy. (Ads)

THE EVANGELICAL ADVOCATE, Box 30, 1426 Lancaster Pike, Circleville OH 43113. (740)474-8856. Fax (740)477-7766. E-mail: directordoc@cccuhq.org. Website: www .cccuhq.org. Churches of Christ in Christian Union. Ralph Hux, dir. of communications. Provides news, information, and features which emphasize current events and world-view, appealing to the needs of our constituency, emphasizing fundamental evangelical holiness. Monthly mag.; 24-28 pgs.; circ. 4,000. Subscription $12. 15% unsolicited freelance; 15% assigned. Query (preferred) or complete ms/cover letter; fax/e-query OK. **NO PAYMENT.** Articles 500-1,000 wds. (15-20/yr.). Seasonal 2-3 mos. ahead. Accepts simultaneous submissions & reprints (tell when/where appeared). Prefers e-mail submissions (attached file). Regularly uses sidebars. Prefers KJV, NIV. Theme list (no guidelines); copy for 9x12 SAE. (No ads)

> **Tips:** "Best way to break in is to submit material for review."

+EVANGELICAL TIMES, Faverdale North Industrial Estate, Darlington DL3 0PH, United Kingdom. Phone +44 1325 380232. E-mail: webmaster@evangelical-times.org. Website: www.evangelical-times.org. For churches who hold a biblical, Christ-centered theology and the doctrines of grace; circulated worldwide. Monthly newspaper; 32 pgs.; circ. 40,000. Subscription $25 (surface), $42 (airmail). Incomplete topical listings. No questionnaire returned.

> **Tips:** "Our paper offers UK and world news, Christian comment, and a wide variety of articles (biblical, devotional, practical, topical, doctrinal, and historical), with a strong missionary dimension."

$FAITH & FAMILY: The Magazine of Catholic Living, 432 Washington Ave., North Haven CT 06473. (203)230-3800. Fax (203)230-3838. E-mail: editor@faithandfamilymag.com.

Website: www.faithandfamilymag.com. Catholic/Circle Media, Inc. Tom & April Hoopes, eds.; submit to Robyn Lee, ed. asst. Features writing for Catholics and/or Christian families of all ages. Quarterly mag.; 100 pgs.; circ. 32,000. Subscription $14.95. 10% unsolicited freelance; 90% assigned. Query/clips; e-query OK. Pays .33/wd. on acceptance for 1st rts. Articles 700-3,000 wds. (35/yr.); brief reviews. Responds in 6-8 wks. Seasonal 6-9 mos. ahead. No reprints. Prefers e-mail submission (attached file). Kill fee. Regularly uses sidebars. Accepts illustrations from children. Prefers NAB. Guidelines (also on Website); copy $4.50/10x13 SAE. (Ads)

Fillers: Buys 10/yr. Anecdotes, cartoons, prose (brief).

Columns/Departments: Buys 75/yr. The Home Front (news); The Insider; Flair; The Season; Life Lessons; Faith & Folklore; Celebrations; Entertainment; The Where & How Guide; Spiritual Directions; and Back Porch; 600-1,200 wds. Query.

Tips: "Most open to well-written feature articles employing good quotations, anecdotes, and transitions about an interesting aspect of family life; departments; news items. To break in, submit ideas for The Home Front." Only wants Catholic theme-related material.

**This periodical was #21 on the 2005 Top 50 Christian Publishers list (#5 in 2004).

$FAITH & FRIENDS, 2 Overlea Blvd., Toronto ON M4H 1P4, Canada. (416)422-6226. Fax (416)422-6120. E-mail: faithandfriends@can.salvationarmy.org. Website: www.salvationarmy.ca. The Salvation Army. Geoffrey Moulton, ed. Monthly mag.; 16 pgs.; circ. 60,000. Subscription $16.50 Cdn. 90% assigned. Query/clips; e-query OK. Pays up to $200 Cdn. on publication for one-time rts. Articles 500-1,000 wds. Responds in 2 wks. Seasonal 6 mos. ahead. Accepts simultaneous submissions & reprints (tell when/where appeared). Prefers accepted ms by e-mail (attached file). Uses some sidebars. Prefers NIV. Guidelines (also on Website); free copy. (No ads)

Fillers: Buys 10/yr. Cartoons, games, jokes, quizzes, quotes, word puzzles, recipes; 50 wds.; $25.

Columns/Departments: God in My Life (how Christians in the workplace find faith relevant), 600 wds.; Words to Live By (simple Bible studies/discussions of faith), 600 wds.; Faith Builders; Someone Cares.

$FAITH TODAY: Seeking to Inform, Equip and Inspire Christians Across Canada, M.I.P. Box 3745, Markham ON L3R 0Y4, Canada. (905)479-5885. Fax (905)479-4742. E-mail: ft@efc-canada.com. Website: www.faithtoday.ca. Evangelical Fellowship of Canada. Gail Reid, mng. ed.; Bill Fledderus, sr. ed.; Karen Stiller, assoc. ed. A general-interest publication for Christians in Canada; almost exclusively about Canadians, including Canadians abroad. Bimonthly mag.; 56 pgs.; circ. 18,000. Subscription $25.26 Cdn. 20% unsolicited freelance; 80% assigned. Query only; fax/e-query preferred. Pays $100-500 (.15-.30 Cdn./wd.) within 6 wks. of acceptance for 1st & electronic rts.; reprints .15/wd. Features 800-1,700 wds. (75/yr.); cover stories 2,000 wds.; essays 650-1,200 wds.; profiles 900 wds; reviews 300 wds. Responds in 6 wks. Prefers e-mail submission. Kill fee 30-50%. Regularly uses sidebars. Any Bible version. Guidelines (also by e-mail/Website); copy for 9x12 SAE/$2.05 in Canadian funds. (Ads)

Tips: "Most open to short, colorful items, statistics, stories, profiles for Kingdom Matters department. Must be Canadian." Unsolicited manuscripts will not be returned.

**This periodical was #37 on the 2005 Top 50 Christian Publishers list.

+FAITHWEBBIN, PO Box 8732, Columbia SC 29202. (803)494-6250. E-mail: editor@faithwebbin.net. Website: www.faithwebbin.net. Tywebbin Creations. Mrs. Tyora Moody, ed. For Christian families. Monthly online mag. 100% unsolicited freelance. Complete ms; e-query OK. **NO PAYMENT.** Any Bible version. Articles 800-1,000 wds. (15-20/yr.). Responds in 1-2 wks. Seasonal 2 mos. ahead. Accepts reprints (tell when/where appeared). Requires e-mail submission (attached file). Regularly uses sidebars. Guidelines on Website. (No ads)

Columns/Departments: Accepts 12/yr. Seek (original Bible study lessons and devotions), 1,000-1,200 wds.; Grow (Christian living: family, finance, marriage, etc.), 800-1,000 wds.
Tips: "The two areas exclusively open to freelancers are Seek and Grow. Articles are normally accepted if they meet the length requirement and are not similar to what is already included on the site. Looking for fresh articles; love testimonial type devotions or articles that encourage and motivate the reader."

$THE FAMILY DIGEST, PO Box 40137, Fort Wayne IN 46804. Catholic. Corine B. Erlandson, manuscript ed.; Kelley Renz, issue ed. Dedicated to the joy and fulfillment of Catholic family life and its relationship to the Catholic parish. Bimonthly booklet; 48 pgs.; circ. 150,000. Distributed through parishes. 90% unsolicited freelance. Complete ms/cover letter; no phone/fax/e-query. Pays $40-60, 4-8 wks. after acceptance, for 1st rts. Articles 700-1,200 wds. (60/yr.). Responds in 4-8 wks. Seasonal 7 mos. ahead. Occasionally buys reprints (tell when/where appeared). No disk. Does not use sidebars. Prefers NAB. Guidelines & copy for 6x9 SAE/2 stamps. (No ads)
Fillers: Buys 15/yr. Anecdotes drawn from experience, prayers, short humor; 25-100 wds.; pays $25.
Tips: "Prospective freelance writers should be familiar with the types of articles we accept and publish. We are looking for upbeat articles which affirm the simple ways in which the Catholic faith is expressed in daily life. Articles on family life, parish life, seasonal articles, how-to pieces, inspirational, prayer, spiritual life, and church traditions will be gladly reviewed for possible acceptance and publication."

+FAMILY ONLINE. E-mail: familyonline@trinitynazarene.org. Website: www.trinitynazarene .org/familyonline. Church of the Nazarene. James Tew, ed. Provides solid biblical and practical helps for families in their major areas of concerns. Weekly online newsletter. Open to unsolicited freelance. E-mail complete ms (attached or copied into message); e-query OK. **NO PAYMENT** for one-time & reprint rts. Articles 500-1,000 wds. Accepts reprints (tell when/where appeared). Guidelines/copy on Website. Incomplete topical listings. (no ads)

*FARO DE LUZ, 404 N.W. 14th Ave., Gainesville FL 32601-4215. (352)378-0078. Fax (352)378-0042. Website: www.farodeluz.com. Pastor Rojas, ed. Monthly newspaper; circ. 9,500. For the whole family; promoting the unity of the family, the church, and the body of Christ in general. Subscription $17. Open to freelance. Complete ms. Not in topical listings. (Ads)

FELLOWSHIP MAGAZINE, Box 237, Barrie ON L4M 4T3, Canada. Toll-free (800)678-2607. Fax (705)737-1086. E-mail: jhodgins@sympatico.ca. Website: www.fellowshipmagazine .org. Fellowship Publications/United Church of Canada. Jane Hodgins, ed. To provide a positive voice for orthodoxy and uphold the historic Christian faith of the denomination. Quarterly mag.; circ. 9,000. Subscription free for donation. Open to unsolicited freelance. Not in topical listings. (Ads)

+FIRE BY NITE, 120 East FM544, Ste. 72, PMB 354, Murphy TX 75094. Website: www.fire bynite.com. Submit to The Editor. Showcasing the best in new Christian short fiction, with book reviews and interviews both readers and writers of fiction will enjoy. Quarterly mag. Subscription $9.95. Fiction, interviews, book reviews.
Contest: Fire by Nite Fiction Award. Prizes $50-500. Select entries will be published in magazine. Reading fee $15. Deadline: March 31. Entry form and details on Website.

$FIRST THINGS: A Monthly Journal of Religion and Public Life, 156 Fifth Ave., Ste. 400, New York NY 10010. (212)627-1985. Fax (212)627-2184. E-mail: ft@firstthings.com. Website: www.firstthings.com. Institute on Religion & Public Life. Damon Linker, ed. Shows relation of religion and religious insights to contemporary issues of public life. Monthly (10X) & online mag.; 64-92 pgs.; circ. 32,000. Subscription $34 ($14.97 for students). 70% unsolicited freelance. Complete ms/cover letter; phone/e-query OK. Pays $400-1,000 on publication for all rts. Articles 4,000-6,000 wds.; opinion 1,500 wds. (50-60/yr.); book reviews, 1,500 wds. ($400). Responds in 3 wks. Seasonal 5 mos. ahead. No simultaneous submissions or reprints. Prefers requested ms by e-mail (attached file). Kill fee. Does not use sidebars. Any Bible version. Guidelines/copy for #10 SASE. (Ads)

Poetry: Joseph Bettum, poetry ed. (mailed submissions only). Buys 25-30/yr. Traditional; 4-40 lines; $50.

Columns/Departments: Buys 50-60/yr. Opinion, 1,000-2,000 wds.; $400. Complete ms.

Tips: "Most open to opinion and articles."

$#FLUTTERS OF THE HEART NEWSLETTER, Toll-free (800)854-3143. E-mail: editor@ fluttersoftheheart.com. Website: www.fluttersoftheheart.com. Flutters of the Heart Gift Products. Virginia Villasenor, ed. Online newsletter. Personal essays that warm the heart, touch the soul, or just make you smile; must be tied to one of their products. Monthly newsletter. Accepts freelance. Responds in 1 mo. Complete ms only. Pays $40 on publication. Articles 500-700 wds. No reprints. Prefers e-mail submissions (no attachments). No kill fee. Guidelines on Website. Does not acknowledge receipt of manuscripts; will contact if accepted.

$FOCUS ON THE FAMILY MAGAZINE, 8605 Explorer Dr., Colorado Springs CO 80920. (719)548-4588. Fax (719)531-3499. Website: www.family.org. Focus on the Family. Susan Graham Mathis, mng. ed.; Deb Landers, Single-Parent ed. To help families utilize Christian principles to strengthen their marriages, to improve their child rearing, and to deal with the problems of everyday life. Monthly mag.; 32 pgs., plus an 8-pg. segment for single parents; circ. 2,200,000. Free to donors. 5% unsolicited freelance; 80% assigned. Query/clips; no phone/fax query. Pays $100-300 on publication for one-time & electronic rts. Articles 400-1,100 wds. Responds in 4-6 wks. Seasonal 6 mos. ahead. Kill fee 25%. Regularly uses sidebars. Prefers NIV. Guidelines (also by e-mail/Website); copy for 9x12 SAE/2 stamps. (No ads)

Tips: "This magazine is 90% generated from within our ministry. It's very hard to break in. Must be a unique look at a subject or very interesting topic about marriage, parenting, or family. All topics indicated must have a connection to parenting or marriage."

**2005 EPA Award of Merit—Most Improved Publication.

+THE FOUNDERS JOURNAL, PO Box 150931, Cape Coral FL 33915. (239)772-1400. Fax (239)772-1140. Website: www.founders.org. Founders Ministries/Southern Baptist. Kenneth Puls, ed. Consistent with the doctrines of grace that speak from a historic Southern Baptist perspective. Quarterly mag. Complete ms/cover letter and completed author information form from Website. Articles & book reviews. Responds in 4 mos. or you may contact them. Guidelines on Website. Incomplete topical listings. No questionnaire returned.

$FOURSQUARE WORLD ADVANCE, 1910 W. Sunset Blvd., Ste. 200, Los Angeles CA 90026-0176. (213)989-4230. Fax (213)989-4544. E-mail: comm@foursquare.org, or bshepson@ foursquare.org. Website: www.foursquare.org. International Church of the Foursquare Gospel. Bill Shepson, ed. dir. Quarterly mag. with summer bonus issue; circ. 102,000. Subscription free. Open to unsolicited freelance (query first). Query by letter or e-mail, or complete ms. Responds in 2 wks. Seasonal 6 mos. ahead. Accepts simultaneous submissions & reprints. Accepts e-mail submissions (attached file). Regularly uses sidebars. Free guidelines/theme list on Website; free copy. (No ads)

**2004 EPA Award of Excellence—Most Improved Publication; 2005 Award of Merit—Denominational.

FRIENDS JOURNAL, 1216 Arch St., #2A, Philadelphia PA 19107-2835. (215)563-5629. Fax (215)568-1377. E-mail: info@friendsjournal.org. Website: www.friendsjournal.org. Quaker. Robert Dockhorn, sr. ed. Reflects Quaker life with commentary on social issues, spiritual reflection, Quaker history, and world affairs. Monthly mag.; circ. 8,000. Subscription $29. 70% freelance. Complete ms by e-mail preferred; e-query OK. **NO PAYMENT.** Articles to

2,500 wds.; news items 50-200 wds.; reports of Quaker events 450 wds. Responds in 3-16 wks. Accepts simultaneous submissions or reprints, if notified. Also accepts disk. Guidelines on Website; free copy. Incomplete topical listings.

Poetry: To 25 lines.

Fillers: Games, short humor, newsbreaks, and word puzzles.

GATEWAY S-F MAGAZINE: Stories of Science & Faith, GateWay Publishing House, 12141 Mendocino Pl., Chino CA 91710-2033. (909)591-1481. E-mail (see editors). Website: www.geocities.com/scifieditor/index.html. John A. M. Darnell, ed-in-chief (John.Darnell@ walsworth.com); B. Joseph Fekete Jr., ed./pub. (scifieditor@yahoo.com); Ann Wilkes (azoreannie@sbcglobal.net). Christian science fiction/fantasy for adult sci-fi fans who have a love for Christ and fiction stories. Quarterly e-zine. Free online. 100% unsolicited freelance. Complete ms/cover letter; e-query to editors OK (not to publisher). **NO PAYMENT** for one-time, electronic, or nonexclusive rts. Not copyrighted. Fiction 500-7,500 wds. (80/yr.). Responds in 2-4 wks. No seasonal material. Accepts reprints (tell when/where appeared). Requires accepted ms by e-mail (attached copy). Guidelines by e-mail/Website: www.geocities.com/scifieditor/guidelines.html. (No ads)

   Special Needs: Time-travel stories always welcomed; also stories about the behind-the-scene workings of angels in the sci-fi setting. Also accepts generic sci-fi artwork; payment by agreement with artist.

   Tips: "Submit stories that have solid science-based plot lines, easy reading, straightforward writing without 'creative experimentation,' and religious themes. Also read the online guidelines for specific submission requirements. We are a liberal publication, and disdain dogmatism."

+GATHERING...IN SPIRIT AND IN TRUTH, PO Box 1196, Luling LA 70070. (985)785-2013. E-mail: viviandugas@cox.net. Website: www.gatheringontheweb.com. Nondenominational. Vivian Dugas, ed./pub. Bimonthly mag. Subscription free. (Ads) Not included in topical listings. No questionnaire returned.

$THE GEM, 700 E. Melrose Ave., Box 926, Findlay OH 45839-0926. (419)424-1961. Fax (419)424-3433. E-mail: communications@cggc.org. Website: www.cggc.org. Churches of God, General Conference. Rachel Foreman, ed. Monthly (13X) take-home paper for adults; 8 pgs.; circ. 7,100. Subscription $10. 80% unsolicited freelance; 20% assigned. Complete ms/cover letter; phone/fax/e-query OK. Pays $15 after publication for one-time rts. Articles 300-1,600 wds. (125/yr.); fiction 2,000 wds. (125/yr.); book/music reviews, 750 wds., $10. Responds in 12 wks. Seasonal 3 mos. ahead. Accepts simultaneous submissions & reprints (tell when/where appeared). Accepts requested ms on disk; no e-mail submission. Uses some sidebars. Prefers NIV. Guidelines (also by e-mail)/copy for #10 SAE/2 stamps. (No ads)

   Poetry: Buys 100/yr. Any type, 3-40 lines; $5-15. Submit max. 3 poems.

   Fillers: Buys 100/yr. All types, except party ideas; 25-100 wds; $5-15.

   Special Needs: Missions and true stories. Be sure that fiction has a clearly religious/Christian theme.

   Tips: "Most open to real-life experiences where you have clearly been led by God. Make the story interesting and Christian."

   **This periodical was #24 on the 2005 Top 50 Christian Publishers list (#30 in 2004, #35 in 2003, #25 in 2002).

$GEMS OF TRUTH, PO Box 4060, Overland Park KS 66204. (913)432-0331. Fax (913)722-0351. E-mail: sseditor1@juno.com. Church of God (Holiness)/Herald & Banner Press. Arlene McGehee, Sunday school ed. Denominational. Weekly adult take-home paper; 8 pgs.; circ. 14,000. Subscription $2.25. Complete ms/cover letter; phone/fax/e-query OK (prefers mail or e-mail). Pays .005/wd. on publication for 1st rts. Fiction 1,000-2,000 wds.

Seasonal 6-8 mos. ahead. Accepts simultaneous submissions & reprints (tell when/where appeared). Prefers KJV. Guidelines/theme list; copy. Not in topical listings. (No ads)

$GENERATION X NATIONAL JOURNAL, 411 W. Front, Wayland IA 52654. (319)256-4221. E-mail: genxjournal2004@yahoo.com. Website: www.genxnatljournal.com. Kathy Stoops, mng. ed. For those who came of age during the late 80s and early 90s. Quarterly creative jour.; 60 pgs.; circ. 100. Subscription $12. Estab. 2003. 90% unsolicited freelance; 10% assigned. Query or complete ms.; e-query OK. Pays $5-15 on acceptance for one-time rts. Articles 500-2,000 wds. (100/yr.); fiction 500-2,500 wds. (100/yr.). Responds in 9 wks. Seasonal 6 mos. ahead. Accepts simultaneous submissions & reprints (tell when/where appeared). Requires e-mail submissions (copied into message). No kill fee. Does not use sidebars. Accepts submissions from children & teens. Guidelines/theme list (also by e-mail/Website); copy $3. (Ads)

> **Poetry:** Buys 20-30/yr. Any type; any length; $5. Submit max. 3 poems.
>
> **Fillers:** Buys 20/yr. Anecdotes, facts, ideas, jokes, prose, quotes, short humor; $5.
>
> **Columns/Departments:** Buys 100/yr. Ethnic View (personal perspective); Success Story (personal perspective), Political Views (personal or research); all 500-2,000 wds., $5-10.
>
> **Contest:** Watch Website for future contests.
>
> **Tips:** "Most of our departments are open to freelancers. We believe in being a place for aspiring and established writers."
>
> **This periodical was #5 on the 2005 Top 50 Christian Publishers list.

$GOD ALLOWS U-TURNS BOOK SERIES, The God Allows U-Turns Project, PO Box 717, Faribault, MN 55021-0717. Fax (507)334-6464. E-mail: editor@godallowsuturns.com. Website: www.godallowsuturns.com. Submit to Editor. For a list of current *God Allows U-Turns* books open to submissions, as well as related opportunities, visit Website. Time-lines vary, so send stories any time, as they may fit another volume. Each book in the series will contain up to 100 true short stories written by contributors from all over the world. 98% unsolicited freelance. Includes byline and short bio. Articles 500-1,500 wds. Pays $50 on publication, plus 1 copy of book, for one-time, or reprint rts. (no returns). Accepts simultaneous submissions & reprints (tell when/where appeared). Prefers submissions via e-mail. Submit story typed, double spaced, in an attached Word document. Guidelines and sample story available on Website or by sending #10 SAE/1 stamp. (No ads)

> **Special Needs:** True stories. See Website for current list of titles in development. Open to well-written, personal inspirational pieces showing how faith in God can inspire, encourage, and heal. Hope should prevail. Human-interest stories with a spiritual application, affirming ways in which faith is expressed in daily life. These true stories must touch the emotions. Our contributors are a diverse group with no limits on age or denomination.
>
> **Tips:** "Read prior volumes, or see the sample story on our Website. Keep it real. Ordinary people doing extraordinary things with God's help. We publish the nitty-gritty issues of life—few subjects are taboo. Focus on timeless, universal themes like love, forgiveness, salvation, healing, hope, faith, etc. Be able to tell a good story with drama, description, and dialog. Avoid moralisms and preachy tone. When possible, show how the choice you made, either through a change of heart, attitude, thought, and/or behavior occurred that clearly describes moving closer to God. Using a 'U-turn' lesson/analogy within the story is a plus. Show us how your faith choices have changed your life."
>
> **Deadline:** Deadlines vary; this is an ongoing book series. Check Website for frequent series updates.

$GOD'S WAY BOOK SERIES, 6528 E. 101st St., Ste. 416, Tulsa OK 74133-6754. WhiteStone Publishing. Mark Gilroy, ed. E-mail: stories@godswaybooks.com. Website: www.godsway books.com. For books created to help readers discover and experience God's love and power in their lives through well-crafted, inspirational, and challenging true life stories;

each story enhanced by a compelling quote and Bible verse. True stories 750-2,000 wds./1,200 wds. ideal. (no fiction). Open to freelance. Complete ms sent electronically. Pays $50/story for nonexclusive book rts., plus a copy of the book. Full guidelines and list of current topics available on Website.

GOLD COUNTRY FAMILIES, PO Box 723, Meadow Vista CA 95722. (530)878-8353. E-mail: vgbeninga@yahoo.com, or info@goldcountryfamilies.com. Website: www.goldcountry families.com. Sierra Nevada Gold Country. Victoria Beninga, ed. E-magazine. Subscription free. Open to unsolicited freelance. Complete ms. by e-mail (preferred). **NO PAYMENT.** Articles 300-2,000 wds. (can vary). Accepts reprints. No guidelines; copy online.

$GOOD NEWS, PO Box 150, Wilmore KY 40390. (859)858-4661. Fax (859)858-4972. E-mail: steve@goodnewsmag.org. Website: www.goodnewsmag.org. United Methodist/Forum for Scriptural Christianity, Inc. Steve Beard, ed. Focus is evangelical renewal within the denomination. Bimonthly mag.; 44 pgs.; circ. 100,000. Subscription $20. 20% unsolicited freelance. Query first; no phone/fax/e-query. Pays $100-150 on publication for one-time rts. Articles 1,500-1,850 wds. (25/yr.). Responds in 24 wks. Seasonal 4-6 mos. ahead. Accepts simultaneous submissions & reprints (tell when/where appeared). Accepts requested ms on disk. Kill fee. Regularly uses sidebars. Prefers NIV. Guidelines (also on Website); copy $2.75/9x12 SAE. (Ads)

   Tips: "Most open to features."

+THE GOOD NEWS CONNECTION, 105 Harris Ave., Portland ME 04103. Toll-free (800)357-0203. (207)797-4915. E-mail: goodnewsmaine@aol.com. Website: www.go-gnc.com. Submit to The Editor. Enriching thousands of families, in Maine and New Hampshire, through churches, bookstores, numerous retail outlets, and on the Web. Newspaper; circ. 7,000. Distributed free. Incomplete topical listings. No questionnaire returned.

$GOOD NEWS, ETC., PO Box 2660, Vista CA 92085. (760)724-3075. E-mail: rmonroe@good newsetc.com. Website: www.goodnewsetc.com. Good News Publishers, Inc. of California. Rick Monroe, ed. Feature stories and local news of interest to Christians in San Diego County. Monthly tabloid; 24-32 pgs.; circ. 42,000. Subscription $15. 5% unsolicited freelance; 5% assigned. Query; e-query OK. Pays $20 on publication for all, 1st, one-time, or reprint rts. Articles 500-700 wds. (15/yr.). Responds in 2 wks. Seasonal 2 mos. ahead. Accepts simultaneous submissions & reprints (tell when/where appeared). Prefers accepted ms on disk. Regularly uses sidebars. Prefers NIV. Guidelines; copy for 9x12 SAE/4 stamps. (Ads)

   Tips: "Most open to local (San Diego), personality-type articles. A San Diego connection is needed."

   **2005, 1993 EPA Award of Merit—Newspaper.

+GOOD NEWS IN RI, PMB #141, 300 Quaker Ln., Warwick RI 02886. (401)398-0707. E-mail: larry@goodnewsinri.org. Website: www.goodnewsinri.org. Good News Outreach. Lawrence Lepore, ed. To evangelize the lost and unite the body of Christ. Newspaper; circ. 14,000. Subscription $20. Open to unsolicited freelance. Complete ms. Articles; no reviews. Incomplete topical listings. (Ads)

+GOOD NEWS IN SOUTH FLORIDA, PO Box 101328, Ft. Lauderdale FL 33310. (954)564-5378. Fax (954)453-9291. E-mail: grif@goodnewsfl.org. Website: www.goodnewsfl.org. Calvary Chapel/Ft. Lauderdale. Grif Blackstone, ed. To report news with a biblical perspective, share life-changing stories and encouraging words from people in the community. Newspaper; circ. 60,000. Subscription $19.95. Open to unsolicited freelance. Query preferred. Articles; reviews. Incomplete topical listings. (Ads)

GOOD NEWS JOURNAL, 9701 Copper Creek Dr., Austin TX 78729-3543. (512)249-6535. Fax (512)260-1800. E-mail: goodnews98@aol.com. Evelyn W. Davison, pub. Christian paper for national circulation by subscription, and Central Texas by free distribution. Monthly newspaper; 24 pgs.; circ. 60,000. Subscription $29.95. 40% unsolicited freelance; 60% assigned. Query; fax/e-query OK. **NO PAYMENT** for one-time rts. Articles 200-600 wds. Accepts reprints. Prefers accepted ms by e-mail. Guidelines (also by e-mail/Website); copy for 9x12 SAE/2 stamps. (Ads)

Poetry: Accepts 4-6/yr. Traditional.

Fillers: Accepts many. All types; 10-50 wds.

Tips: "Most open to short helps, funnies, inspirations, and current issues."

+THE GOSPEL POST, 111 Pine St., Ste. 1725, San Francisco CA 94111. (909)576-3297. E-mail: edward@gospelpost.com, or info@gospelpost.com. Website: www.gospelpost.com. Joanna Wong, ed. An evangelical, transdenominational, Christian media company that serves to provide direct, and current news information to the general Christian public. Newspaper. Open to freelance. Submit by e-mail from Website. Incomplete topical listings. No questionnaire returned.

$GOSPEL TODAY MAGAZINE, 286 Highway 314, Ste. C, Fayetteville GA 30214. (770)719-4825. Fax (770)716-2660. E-mail: Gospeltodaymag@aol.com. Website: www.gospel today.com. Horizon Concepts, Inc. Teresa Hairston, pub. Ministry/Christian lifestyle directed toward urban marketplace. Bimonthly (8X) mag.; 64-80 pgs.; circ. 200,000. Subscription $16.97. 5% unsolicited freelance; 90% assigned. Query; e-query OK. Pays $75-250 on publication for all rts. Articles 1,000-3,500 wds. (4/yr.). Responds in 2 wks. Seasonal 3 mos. ahead. Accepts simultaneous submissions & reprints (tell when/where appeared). Prefers accepted ms by e-mail (attached file). Kill fee 15%. Uses some sidebars. Prefers NKJV. Guidelines on Website; copy $3.50. (Ads)

Fillers: Accepts 2-3/yr. Cartoons, word puzzles. No payment.

Columns/Departments: Precious Memories (historic overview of renowned personality), 1,500-2,000 wds.; From the Pulpit (issue-oriented observation from clergy), 2,500-3,000 wds.; Life & Style (travel, health, beauty, fashion tip, etc.), 1,500-2,500 wds.; Broken Chains (deliverance testimony), 1,200 wds. Query. Pays $50-75.

Tips: "Looking for great stories of great people doing great things to inspire others."

GOSPEL TRACT HARVESTER, PO Box 1118, Independence MO 64051. (816)461-6086. Fax (816)461-4305. Gospel Tract Society, Inc. Beth Buttram, ed. For Christians of all ages (few unchurched readers). Monthly mag.; 16 pgs.; circ. 38,000. Subscription free (donations). 20% unsolicited freelance. Query; no phone/fax query. **PAYS UP TO 20 COPIES** for all rts. Not copyrighted. Articles 1,000 wds. (10/yr.). Responds in 4-6 wks. Seasonal 4 mos. ahead. Accepts reprints (tell when/where appeared). Uses some sidebars. Prefers KJV. Guidelines; copy for 9x12 SAE/2 stamps. (No ads)

Fillers: Accepts 8-12/yr. Anecdotes, facts, games, quotes, short humor; 100-500 wds.

Special Needs: Good, fresh, well-written tracts for children and teens.

Tips: "Most open to personal testimonies, if well-written and documented. Have a message to share and a sincere desire to share the message of salvation. Be concise. Be correct in grammar and references."

$+GRAND, 4791 Baywood Point Dr., St. Petersburg FL 33711. E-mail: editor@grand magazine.com. Website: www.grandmagazineonline.com. Secular. Submit to The Editor. Celebrates the vital spirit and active lifestyle of today's grandparents. Bimonthly mag. Subscription $18.95. Open to unsolicited freelance. Query/clips; e-query OK. Pays $250-500, 30 days after acceptance. Articles 800-2,500 wds. Kill fee 25%. Guidelines on Website. Incomplete topical listings. (Ads)

Columns/Departments: Departments, 650 wds., $100-200. Also buys shorter pieces for up-front section, "For Starters."

Special Needs: Topics of interest to grandparents only.

Tips: "Pay close attention to ethnic and socioeconomic balance."

$GRIT, 1503 S.W. 42nd St., Topeka KS 66609. (785)274-4300. Fax (785)274-4305. E-mail: grit@grit.com. Website: www.grit.com. Ogden Publications. Andrea Skalland, ed-in-chief. Features with positive messages. Monthly tabloid; 64 pgs.; min. circ. 100,000. Subscription $27.98. 90% unsolicited freelance. Complete ms/cover letter by mail only. Pays .15/wd. for nonfiction on publication, see guidelines for fiction pay rates; for shared rts. Articles to 2,000 wds. (300/yr.); fiction to 3,500 wds. Responds in 3-6 mos. Seasonal 6 mos. ahead. No simultaneous submissions or reprints. Uses some sidebars. Guidelines; copy $4/9x12 SASE/4 stamps. (Ads)

> **Poetry:** Attn: Poetry Editor. Buys 50/yr. Free verse, light verse, traditional; 4-16 lines. Pays $10-15 on acceptance. Submit max. 5 poems.

> **Columns/Departments:** Buys 100-200/yr. Looking Back (nostalgia with a message), 500 wds.; Cook of the Month (unique people with storyteller recipes), 1,000 wds.; Gardens/Gardening, 500-1,000 wds.; Petting Zoo (pets), 200-1,200 wds. Payment varies.

> **Special Needs:** True inspirational stories, miracles, unique family lifestyles, humor, nature. Always needs seasonal stories and photos (Christmas, Thanksgiving, Easter, Mother's Day, Father's Day, Memorial Day, etc.). Avoid first-person or as-told-to techniques in longer pieces. Also accepts historical, mystery, western, adventure, and romance fiction to 3,500 words. Submit to "Fiction Dept."

> **Tips:** "Our publication is all original material either written by our readers/freelancers or occasionally by our staff. Every department, every article is open. Break in by reading at least 6 months of issues to know our special audience." Submissions are not acknowledged or status reports given.

> **This periodical was #24 on the 2004 Top 50 Christian Publishers list (#18 in 2003, #13 in 2002).

$GUIDEPOSTS, 16 E. 34th St., 21st Fl., New York NY 10016-4397. (212)251-8100. Website: www.guideposts.com. Interfaith. Mary Ann O'Roark, exec. ed. Personal faith stories showing how faith in God helps each person cope with life in some particular way. Monthly mag.; 52 pgs.; circ. 3 million. Subscription $13.94. 30% unsolicited freelance; 20% assigned. Complete ms/cover letter, by mail only; no electronic submissions. Pays $250-500 on acceptance for all rts. Articles 750-1,500 wds. (40-60/yr.), shorter pieces 250-750 wds ($100-250.). Responds only to mss accepted for publication in 2 mos. Seasonal 6 mos. ahead. Accepts simultaneous submissions & reprints. Uses some sidebars. Free guidelines (also by e-mail/Website)/copy. (Ads)

> **Columns/Departments:** Christopher Davis, column ed. Buys 24/yr. His Mysterious Ways (divine intervention), 250 wds.; What Prayer Can Do, 250 wds.; Angels Among Us, 400 wds.; Divine Touch (tangible evidence of God's help), 400 wds. ("This is our most open area. Write in 3rd person."); $100.

> **Contest:** Writers Workshop Contest held on even years with a late June deadline. Winners attend a week-long seminar in New York (all expenses paid) on how to write for Guideposts. Also Young Writers Contest; $36,000 in college scholarships; best stories to 1,200 wds.; deadline November 29, 2006.

> **Tips:** "Be able to tell a good story, with drama, suspense, description, and dialog. The point of the story should be some practical spiritual help that subjects learned through their experience. Use unique spiritual insights, strong and unusual dramatic details." First person only.

> **This periodical was #45 on the 2001 Top 50 Christian Publishers list (#31 in 2001, #22 in 1998).

+GULF COAST CHRISTIAN NEWSPAPER, PO Box 60, Fairhope AL 36533. (334)621-9700. Website: www.siteone.com/religion/gcc1.htm. Interdenominational. Dan Hanson, pub.;

Debbie Hanson, exec. ed. A newspaper by reporters who believe God is real; for Mobile Bay area of Alabama. Monthly newspaper. Subscription $12. Incomplete topical listings. No questionnaire returned.

+HALO MAGAZINE, PO Box 1402, Sterling VA 20167. Phone/fax (703)406-2000. E-mail: halomag@aol.com. Website: www.halomag.com. Marian Newman Braxton, ed. Designed to minister to the unsaved and encourage the Christian; reaches a wide audience, including churches, hospitals, and prison ministries across many states. Magazine. Open to unsolicited freelance. Complete ms by mail or e-mail. **NO PAYMENT FOR NOW.** Incomplete topical listings.

> **Poetry:** Accepts original poems.

HANNAH TO HANNAH, PO Box 5534, Maryville TN 37802-5534. (281)485-8986. E-mail: hannahs@hannah.org. Website: www.hannah.org. Hannah's Prayer Ministries. Jill Amack, ed. Provides encouragement to couples facing infertility or the loss of a child at any time from conception to early infancy. Monthly newsletter.; 15-20 pgs.; circ. 2,300. Subscription free. 40% unsolicited freelance; 60% assigned. Complete ms; e-query OK. Accepts full ms by e-mail. **NO PAYMENT** for all rts. Article length open (15/yr.); book reviews 200 wds. Responds in 2 wks. Seasonal 2 mos. ahead. Accepts simultaneous submissions & reprints (tell when/where appeared). Prefers accepted mss by e-mail (attached file). Does not use sidebars. Prefers NAS/NIV. Guidelines/theme list on Website. (No ads)

> **Poetry:** Accepts 15-20/yr. Free verse, light verse, traditional. Submit max. 10 poems.
> **Tips:** "Articles should be compassionate and practical—all information given should point the reader back to God in difficulties."

HARD ROW TO HOE, PO Box 541-I, Healdsburg CA 95448. (707)433-9786. Secular; Potato Eyes Foundation. Joe E. Armstrong, ed. Focuses on rural literature: poetry, short stories (no blatantly Christian/religious material). Triannual newsletter; 12 pgs.; circ. 200. Subscription $8.00. 90% unsolicited freelance. Complete ms/cover letter; no phone query. **PAYS 2 COPIES** for one-time rts. Rural fiction to 2,000 wds. (3-4/yr.); book reviews 300-400 wds. (no Christian books). Responds in 6-8 wks. No simultaneous submissions or reprints. Sometimes accepts poetry from teens. Guidelines; copy for $3. (no ads)

> **Poetry:** Accepts 20-25/yr. Traditional (rural poems); to 30 lines. Submit max. 6 poems.
> **Special Needs:** Native American.
> **Tips:** "All areas are open—reviews, poetry, and fiction; realistic details of rural life—domestic or foreign. Fiction should be rural, environmental, or Native American (for adults)."

+THE HEARTLAND GATEKEEPER, PO Box 241956, Omaha NE 68124. (402)926-2633. Fax (402)391-8744. E-mail: publisher@heartlandgatekeeper.org. Website: www.heartlandgatekeeper.org. Faith Missions Intl./nondenominational. Irene Jensen, ed./pub. To promote unity in the body of Christ, to encourage spiritual growth, to testify to the goodness of God through reporting from a Christian perspective, to reach those who have yet to know Jesus; for Omaha/Council Bluffs region. Monthly newspaper; circ. 11,500. Subscription $24. Open to freelance. Prefers query; e-query OK. **NO PAYMENT** for one-time or reprint rts. Articles 150-300 wds., 300-700 wds., or feature articles 500-1,000 wds.; reviews. Accepts reprints (tell when/where appeared). E-mail submissions only. Guidelines on Website. Incomplete topical listings. No questionnaire returned. (Ads)

HEARTLIGHT INTERNET MAGAZINE, PO Box 7044, Abilene TX 79608. E-mail: phil@heartlight.org. Website: www.heartlight.org. Westover Hills Church of Christ. Phil Ware & Paul Lee, co-eds. Offers positive Christian resources for living in today's world. Weekly online mag.; 20+ pgs.; circ. 70,000+. Subscription free. 20% unsolicited freelance. E-query. **NO PAYMENT** for electronic rts. Articles 300-450 wds. (25-35/yr.); fiction 500-700 wds. (12-15/yr.). Responds in 3 wks. Seasonal 2 mos. ahead. Accepts simultaneous submissions &

reprints (tell when/where appeared). Prefers e-mail submission. Regularly uses sidebars. Prefers NIV. Copy available on the Internet.

Fillers: Accepts 12/yr. Anecdotes, cartoons, games, ideas, jokes, newsbreaks, prayers, prose, quotes, short humor, word puzzles; to 350 wds.

Tips: "Most open to feature articles, Just for Men or Just for Women, or Heartlight for Children."

HIGHWAY NEWS AND GOOD NEWS, PO Box 303, Denver PA 17517-0303. (717)859-4870. Fax (717)859-4798. E-mail: tfcio@transportforchrist.org. Website: www.transportfor christ.org. Transport for Christ. Jennifer Landis, ed. For truck drivers and their families; evangelistic, with articles for Christian growth. Monthly mag.; 16 pgs.; circ. 35,000. Subscription $30 or donation. 60% unsolicited freelance. Complete ms/cover letter; fax query OK; e-query preferred. **PAYS IN COPIES** for rights offered. Articles 600 or 1,500 wds. Seasonal 4 mos. ahead. Accepts simultaneous submissions & reprints (tell when/where appeared). Prefers requested ms by e-mail (attached or copied into message). Uses some sidebars. Prefers NIV. Guidelines/theme list; free copy for 9x12 SAE. (No ads)

Poetry: Accepts 2/yr.; any type; 3-20 lines. Submit max. 5 poems.

Fillers: Accepts 12/yr. Anecdotes, cartoons, facts, ideas, prayers, prose, short humor, tips; to 100 wds.

Tips: "Looking for items affecting the trucking industry. Need pieces (any length) on health, marriage, and fatherhood. Most open to features and true stories about truckers."

HOLY HOUSE MINISTRIES NEWSLETTER, 9641 Tujunga Canyon Blvd., Tujunga CA 91042. (818)249-3477. Fax (818)249-3432. E-mail: Holy House9@aol.com. Website: http://holy houseministries.tripod.com/. Rev. Kimberlie Zakarian, ed. Bimonthly newsletter. Open to freelance. Prefers accepted ms by e-mail. **PAYS 5 COPIES.** Not included in topical listings. No questionnaire returned.

#HOMECOMING. Contact by e-mail from their Website: www.gaithernet.com/home. Click on Magazine. Bill & Gloria Gaither, pubs.; Joy MacKenzie, ed-at-large; Roberta Croteau, ed-in-chief. Estab. 2003. Open to submissions to several columns.

$HOMESCHOOLING TODAY, PO Box 468, Barker TX 77413. (281)492-6050. Fax (832)201-7620. E-mail: publisher@homeschooltoday.com. Website: www.homeschoolingtoday.com. Family Reformation LLC. Stacy McDonald, ed-in-chief. Practical articles, encouragement, news, and lessons for homeschoolers. Bimonthly mag.; 96 pgs.; circ. 25,000. Subscription $21.99. 40% unsolicited freelance; 60% assigned. Query; query/clips, or complete ms; fax/ e-query OK. Pays .08/wd. on publication for 1st rts. Articles 500-2,500 wds. (30/yr.); book reviews 800 wds. Responds in 5-9 wks. Seasonal 1 yr. ahead. Accepts simultaneous submissions & reprints (tell when/where appeared). Requires requested ms by e-mail (attached file). Kill fee 25%. Uses some sidebars. Any Bible version. Free guidelines/copy. (Ads)

Columns/Departments: Buys 20-24/yr. Parents Speak Out, 500-700 wds. (See guidelines for other departments.) Query. Pays .08/wd.

HOME TIMES FAMILY NEWSPAPER (formerly *Palm Beach Conservative*), 3676 Collins Dr., #16, West Palm Beach FL 33406. (561)439-3509. Fax (561)968-1758. E-mail: publisher@ myconservative.com. Website: www.myconservative.com. Neighbor News, Inc. Dennis Lombard, ed./pub. Conservative, pro-Christian community newspaper. Monthly tabloid; 24-28 pgs.; circ. 5,000. Subscription $16. 20% unsolicited freelance; 30% assigned. Complete ms only/cover letter; no phone/fax/e-query. Pays $5-50 on publication for one-time rts. Articles to 800 wds. (25/yr.); fiction to 800 wds. (6/yr.); book reviews 200 wds. ($5-15). Responds in 2-3 wks. Seasonal 2 mos. ahead. Accepts simultaneous submissions & reprints (tell when/where appeared). Accepts requested ms on disk or by e-mail. No kill fee. Uses some sidebars. Prefers NIV. Guidelines; 3 issues $3. (Ads)

Poetry: Buys several/yr. Light verse, traditional, inspirational; 4-28 lines; $5-10. Submit max. 3 poems.

Fillers: Accepts 30-40/yr. Anecdotes, cartoons, jokes, kid quotes, quotes, short humor; to 100 wds.; pays 3-6 copies.

Columns/Departments: Buys 15/yr. See guidelines for departments, to 600 wds.; $5-15.

Special Needs: Good short stories (creative nonfiction, or fiction). More faith, miracles, and personal experiences.

Tips: "Most open to personal stories or home/family pieces. Very open to new writers, but study guidelines and sample first; we are different. Published by Christians, but not religious. Looking for more positive articles and stories. Open to fiction for all ages."

$+HONORBOUND, 1445 N. Boonville Ave., Springfield MO 65802. (417)862-1447. Fax (417)832-0574. E-mail: honorbound@ag.org. Website: www.honorbound.com. Denominational/Assemblies of God. Andrew Templeton, dir. Targeting men, ages 25-60; Christian/Pentecostal distinctive. Quarterly mag.; 32-40 pgs.; circ. 22,000. 10% unsolicited freelance; 90% assigned. Complete ms; phone/fax/e-query OK. Pays $50-200 for 1st rts. Articles 1,200 wds. (5/yr.); book reviews ($50). Responds in 1 wk. Seasonal 5 mos. ahead. Accepts simultaneous submissions & reprints (tell when/where appeared). Prefers e-mail submissions (attached file). Regularly uses sidebars. Prefers NIV. Accepts submissions from teens. Guidelines/theme list (also by e-mail); copy for 9x12 SAE/3 stamps. (Ads)

Tips: "Most open to topics on family and fathering."

$HOPEKEEPERS MAGAZINE, PO Box 502928, San Diego CA 92150. Toll-free (888)751-7378. (858)486-4685. Toll-free fax (800)933-1078. E-mail: rest@restministries.org. Website: www.restministries.org. Rest Ministries, Inc. Lisa Copen, ed. For people who live with chronic illness or pain; offers encouragement, support, and hope dealing with everyday issues. Quarterly mag.; 64 pgs. Subscription $17.97. Estab. 2004. 40% unsolicited freelance; 60% assigned. Query; fax/e-query OK. **PAYS IN COPIES**; or to be determined for articles with extensive research; on publication. Articles 375-1,500 wds.; book reviews 300 wds. Responds in 6-8 wks. Seasonal 6 mos. ahead. Accepts simultaneous submissions & reprints. Prefers e-mail submissions (attached or copied into message). Regularly uses sidebars. Accepts submissions from teens. Guidelines (also by e-mail/Website); copy $2. (Ads)

Fillers: Accepts 25/yr. Facts, newsbreaks, tips; 40-90 wds.

Columns/Departments: Accepts 4/yr. Refreshments (devotional-style/journal writing), 350 wds.

Tips: "Topics should be 'attention grabbers' about specific emotions (Is it okay to be mad at God?), or experiences (parenting with a chronic illness), or helpful (5 things you should know about illness on the job). Most open to upbeat topical articles that give reader motivation to change/reflect; should be balanced with personal experience, other's experience, facts, and scripture." Fiction is considered, but not used frequently.

$HORIZONS, 1300 N. Meacham Rd., Schaumburg IL 60173-4888. (847)843-1600. Fax (847)843-3757. E-mail: takehomepapers@garbc.org. Website: www.RegularBaptist Press.org. Regular Baptist. Joan E. Alexander, ed. For adults associated with fundamental Baptist Churches. Weekly take-home paper that supports the adult curriculum by assisting adults in being grounded and growing Christians; 4 pgs. weekly. Open to freelance. Complete ms/cover letter including personal testimony; no phone/fax/e-query. Pays .05/wd. and up, on acceptance (usually) for 1st rts. Articles 500-1,200 wds. (if over 600 wds., use subheads); fiction 1,000-1,200 wds. Responds in 8-12 wks. Seasonal 1 yr. ahead. No simultaneous submissions; some reprints. Some sidebars. Prefers KJV. Guidelines/theme list on Website. Incomplete topical listings. (No ads)

Fillers: Buys 10-15/yr. Word puzzles.

Tips: "We look for personal experience stories (both first person and as-told-to), articles with a story element to them, and well-written fiction that helps readers know more of God's character and ways. Check Website quarterly for updates concerning needs, themes, etc."

$IDEALS MAGAZINE, Ideals Publishing, Inc., 535 Metroplex Dr., Ste. 250, Nashville TN 37211. (615)333-0478. Website: www.idealspublications.com. Guideposts, Inc. Marjorie Lloyd, ed. Seasonal, inspirational, nostalgic magazine for mature men and women of traditional values. Bimonthly mag.; 88 pgs.; circ. 180,000. Subscription $15.95. 95% unsolicited freelance. Complete ms/cover letter; no phone/fax/e-query. Pays .10/wd. on publication for one-time rts. Articles 800-900 wds. (20/yr.); fiction 600-800 wds. Responds in 6-8 wks. Seasonal 8 mos. ahead. Accepts simultaneous submissions & reprints (tell when/where appeared). No disk. Does not use sidebars. Prefers KJV. Guidelines; copy $4.

Poetry: Buys 100+/yr. Free verse, light verse, traditional; 12-50 lines; $10. Submit max. 15 poems.

Tips: "Most open to poetry or essays appropriate for current features. Each issue has a particular theme: Easter, Mother's Day, Country, Friendship, Thanksgiving, and Christmas. Check current issue for themes."

$IMAGE, 3307 Third Ave. W., Seattle WA 98119. (206)281-2988. Fax (206)281-2335. E-mail: image@imagejournal.org. Website: www.imagejournal.org. Gregory Wolfe, pub./ed. Publishes the best literary fiction, poetry, nonfiction, and visual arts that engages the Judeo-Christian tradition. Quarterly jour.; 128 pgs.; circ. 4,800. Subscription $36. 50% unsolicited freelance; 50% assigned. Complete ms/cover letter; phone/fax/e-query OK. Payment varies on publication for 1st rts. Articles 5,000-8,000 wds. (8/yr.); fiction 5,000-8,000 wds. (4/yr.); book reviews 2,000 wds. Responds in 10 wks. No seasonal. Accepts simultaneous submissions; no reprints. No kill fees. Does not use sidebars. Any Bible version. Guidelines (also on Website); copy $14. (Ads)

Poetry: Buys 30/yr. Good poetry. Payment varies. Submit max. 8 poems.

Tips: "Read the journal to understand what we publish. We're always thrilled to see high quality literary work in the unsolicited freelance pile, but we really can't typify what we're looking for other than good writing that's honest about faith and the life of faith. No genre fiction."

$IMPACT MAGAZINE, 301 Geylang Rd., #03–04 Geylang Centre, Singapore 389 344. Phone 65 6748 1244. Fax 65 748 3744. Website: www.impact.com.sg. Impact Christian Comm., Ltd. Andrew Goh, ed.; Loy Chin Fen, copy ed. To help young working adults apply Christian principles to contemporary issues. Bimonthly & online mag.; 56 pgs.; circ. 6,000. Subscription $18. 10% unsolicited freelance. Query or complete ms/cover letter; phone/fax/e-query OK. Ranges from no payment up to $20/pg., for all rts. Articles 1,200-1,500 wds. (12/yr.) & fiction (6/yr.); 1,000-2,000 wds. Seasonal 2 mos. ahead. Accepts reprints. Accepts e-mail submission (attached file). Uses some sidebars. Prefers NIV. Guidelines (also by e-mail); copy for $4/$2 postage (surface mail). (Ads)

Poetry: Accepts 2-3 poems/yr. Free verse, 20-40 lines. Submit max. 3 poems.

Fillers: Accepts 6/yr. Anecdotes, cartoons, jokes, quizzes, short humor, and word puzzles.

Columns/Departments: Closing Thoughts (current social issues), 600-800 wds.; Testimony (personal experience), 1,500-2,000 wds.; Parenting (Asian context), 1,000-1,500 wds.; Faith Seeks Understanding (answers to tough questions of faith/Scripture), 80-1,000 wds.

Tips: "We're most open to fillers."

+IMPACT ONLINE, 22 Bond St., Morrilton AR 72110. (501)727-6333. E-mail: only4him@sbcglobal.net. Website: www.onlyforhim.org. Only for Him. Submit to The Editor. For Christian readers looking for quality writing for every member of the family.

Monthly online e-zine. Subscription free. 75% unsolicited freelance. E-query or mail. **NO PAYMENT** for 1st, one-time, or reprint rts. Articles 500-800, up to 1,200 wds. Responds in 4-6 wks. Accepts reprints (tell when/where appeared). Prefers e-mail submissions (copied into message). Guidelines on Website. Not included in topical listings. No questionnaire returned.

> **Columns/Departments:** Survivor's Roost (geared toward cancer survivors).
> **Tips:** "Spend time reading the articles online before submitting."

#INDIANA CHRISTIAN NEWS, 18891 Stockton Dr., Noblesville IN 46060. (317)770-7670. Fax (317)774-8260. E-mail: samgaw@indianachristiannews.com. Website: www.indiana christiannews.com. Flashpoint Ministries. Sam Gaw, ed.; Kelly Gaw, assoc. ed. (kellygaw@ indianachristiannews.com). A Christian company dedicated to building up the church, which is the body of Christ, unifying churches in the community, and giving Christian men, women, and children a voice in our community. Monthly newspaper. Subscription $25. Query on Website. Incomplete topical listings. No questionnaire returned.

$INDIAN LIFE, PO Box 3765, Redwood Post Office, Winnipeg MB R2W 3R6, Canada. U.S. address: Box 32, Pembina ND 58271. (204)661-9333. Fax (204)661-3982. E-mail: viola .editor@indianlife.org. Website: www.indianlife.org. Indian Life Ministries/nondenominational. Viola Jones, ed. An evangelistic publication for English-speaking aboriginal people in North America. Bimonthly tabloid newspaper; 16 pgs.; circ. 22,000. Subscription $12. 3% unsolicited freelance; 5% assigned. Query (query or complete ms for fiction); fax/ e-query OK. Pays .10/wd (to $150) on publication for 1st rts.; Internet rts. negotiable. Articles 200-500 wds. (20/yr.); reviews, 100 wds. Responds in 8 wks. Seasonal 4 mos. ahead. Accepts simultaneous submissions & reprints (tell when/where appeared). Accepts requested ms by e-mail (attached or copied into message). No kill fee. Uses some sidebars. Prefers New Life Version, NIV. Guidelines (also by e-mail); copy for 9x12 SAE/$1 postage (check or money order). (Ads)

> **Poetry:** Buys 2 poems/yr.; free verse, light verse, traditional, to 100 wds.; pays $20. Submit max. 3 poems.
> **Fillers:** Kid quotes, quotes, short humor, 50-200 wds.; $10-25.
> **Special Needs:** Celebrity pieces must be aboriginal only. Looking for legends.
> **Tips:** "Most open to testimonies from Native Americans/Canadians—either first person or third person—news features, or historical fiction with strong and accurate portrayal of Native American life from the Indian perspective. A writer should have understanding of some Native American history and culture. We suggest reading some Native American authors. Native authors preferred, but some others are published. Aim at a 10th-grade reading level; short paragraphs; avoid multisyllable words and long sentences."
> **2003, 2001 EPA Award of Excellence—Newspaper.

INFUZE MAGAZINE: Art, Entertainment and Faith (formerly *Fuse Magazine*), 1902 N. Centennial St., High Point NC 27262. (336)687-0157. E-mail: creative@infuzemagazine.com. Website: www.infuzemag.com. Mr. Robin Parrish, ed./pub. Online mag. Open to unsolicited freelance. **NO PAYMENT FOR NOW.** Fiction 3,000 wds. and up. Guidelines on Website.

> **Poetry:** Accepts poetry. "We prefer poetry about people and what they feel, think, or experience." No length requirements.
> **Special Needs:** Original artwork short films, and comic books. See guidelines.
> **Tips:** "No preachy fiction—a thought-provoking moral to the story is enough for us. This publication is unique. Be sure to send for guidelines before submitting."

$INLAND NORTHWEST CHRISTIAN NEWS, 222 W. Mission, #132, Spokane WA 99201. (509)328-0820. Fax (509)326-4921. E-mail: inldnwchrist@spocom.com. John McKelvey, ed. To inform, motivate, and encourage evangelical Christians in Spokane and the Inland Northwest. Monthly newspaper; 12 pgs.; circ. 8,000. Subscription $14.95. 30% freelance.

Query; phone query OK. Pays $1/column-inch on publication for 1st rts. Articles 350 wds. Responds in 9 wks. (Ads)

$INSIDE JOURNAL, PO Box 2206, Ashburn VA 20146. (703)478-0100, ext. 3553. Fax (703)554-8570. E-mail: Jeff_Peck@pfm.org. Website: www.pfm.org. Prison Fellowship. Jeff Peck, mng. ed. To proclaim the gospel to non-Christian prisoners within the context of a prison newspaper. Bimonthly (8X) tabloid; 8 pgs.; circ. 395,000. Subscription $10. 5% unsolicited freelance; 10% assigned. Query; phone/fax/e-query OK. Modest payment (depending on situation) on acceptance for one-time rts. Articles to 1,200 wds. (25/yr.). Responds in 4 wks. Seasonal 4 mos. ahead. Accepts requested ms on disk or by e-mail. Regularly uses sidebars. Guidelines (also by e-mail); free copy. (No ads)

> **Columns/Departments:** Buys 15-20/yr. Shortimer (those preparing for release within 6 wks.), 500 wds.; Especially for Women (issues for incarcerated women), 600-800 wds. Variable payment.
>
> **Tips:** "Always need seasonal material for Christmas, Easter, and Thanksgiving. Also celebrity stories that demonstrate triumph over adversity. Address our prison audience with authenticity. Preachy church talk doesn't work. Be practical. Inspire or equip prisoner to serve his/her sentence or live a new life when released."
>
> **2003 EPA Award of Merit—Newspaper.

INSIGHT, 40 St. Clair Ave. E., #202, Toronto ON M4T 1M9, Canada. (416)960-3953. Fax (416)960-3570. E-mail: admin@jmsblind.ca. Website: www.jmsblind.ca. John Milton Society for the Blind in Canada. Rebekah Chevalier, ed. To provide Christian inspiration and information to blind and visually impaired Canadians in an accessible format. Bimonthly large-print newspaper; circ. 2,000. Open to unsolicited freelance. Not in topical listings. (No ads)

INSOUND, 40 St. Clair Ave. E., #202, Toronto ON M4T 1M9, Canada. (416)960-3953. Fax (416)960-3570. E-mail: admin@jmsblind.ca. Website: www.jmsblind.ca. John Milton Society for the Blind in Canada. Graham Down, ed. To provide Christian inspiration and information to blind and visually impaired Canadians in an accessible format. Bimonthly audio cassettes; circ. 200. Open to unsolicited freelance. Not in topical listings. (No ads)

$INTERCHANGE, 412 Sycamore St., Cincinnati OH 45202-4179. (513)421-0311. Fax (513)421-0315. E-mail: richelle_thompson@episcopal-dso.org. Website: www.episcopal-dso .org. Episcopal Diocese of Southern Ohio. Richelle Thompson, dir. of communications. Regional paper for the Episcopal and Anglican Church in southern Ohio. Monthly tabloid; 16 pgs.; circ. 12,000. Free. 20% unsolicited freelance. Query or complete ms/cover letter. Pays $50-150 on acceptance for all rts. Articles 500-2,000 wds. (8-10/yr.). Responds in 4 wks. Accepts simultaneous submissions. Prefers requested ms on disk/CD. Regularly uses sidebars. Accepts submissions from children or teens. Copy for 9x12 SASE.

> **Fillers:** Cartoons, facts, jokes.
>
> **Tips:** "Most open to features, especially with a local angle."

$THE INTERIM, 104 Bond St., Toronto ON M5B 1X9, Canada. (416)204-1687. Fax (416)204-1027. E-mail: interim@lifesite.net. Website: www.lifesite.net. The Interim Publishing Co. Paul Tuns, ed. Abortion, euthanasia, pornography, feminism, and religion from a pro-life perspective; Catholic and evangelical Protestant audience. Monthly & online newspaper; 24 pgs.; circ. 20,000. Subscription $35 Cdn. or U.S. 60% unsolicited freelance. Query; phone/fax/e-query OK. Pays $50-150 Cdn., on publication. Articles 400-750 wds.; book, music, video reviews, 500 wds. ($50-75 Cdn.). Responds in 2 wks. Seasonal 2 mos. ahead. Accepts simultaneous submissions & reprints (tell when/where appeared). Prefers e-mail submission (copied into message). Kill fee. Uses some sidebars. Prefers RSV & others. No guidelines; catalog. (Ads)

> **Tips:** "We are most interested in articles relating to issues of human life and the family."

INTOUCH, 40 St. Clair Ave. E., #202, Toronto ON M4T 1M9, Canada. (416)960-3953. Fax (416)960-3570. E-mail: admin@jmsblind.ca. Website: www.jmsblind.ca. John Milton Society for the Blind in Canada. Rebekah Chevalier, ed. To provide Christian inspiration and information to blind and visually impaired Canadians in an accessible format. Quarterly Braille mag. Open to unsolicited freelance. Not in topical listings. (No ads)

+IPHC EXPERIENCE, PO Box 9, Franklin Springs GA 30639-0009. Toll-free (800)541-1376. (706)245-7272. Fax (706)245-5488. Website: www.lifesprings.net. International Pentecostal Holiness Church. Not included in topical listings. No questionnaire returned.

ISLAND CATHOLIC NEWS, PO Box 5721, Victoria BC V8R 6S8, Canada. (250)727-9429. E-mail: icn@islandnet.com. Website: www.islandnet.com/~icn. Island Catholic News Society. Patrick Jamieson, mng. ed.; Larry Rumsby, chairman of board. News and features about spirituality, social justice, health, ethical and poverty issues from a faith perspective. Monthly tabloid; circ. 3,000. Subscription $30 Cdn.; $40 U.S./foreign. Open to unsolicited freelance. E-submissions OK (copied into message). (Ads: e-mail sample for cost.)

JOURNAL OF CHURCH AND STATE, Baylor University, One Bear Pl., #97308, Waco TX 76798-7308. (254)710-1510. Fax (254)710-1571. E-mail: Derek_Davis@Baylor.edu. Website: www.baylor.edu/~church_state. J. M. Dawson Institute of Church-State Studies/Baylor University. Dr. Derek H. Davis, dir. Provides a forum for the critical examination of the interaction of religion and government worldwide. Quarterly jour.; 225 pgs.; circ. 1,700. Subscription $25 (indiv.); $39 (institution). 75% unsolicited freelance; 25% assigned. Complete ms (3 copies)/cover letter (also by e-mail); phone/fax query OK; no e-query. **NO PAYMENT** for all rights. Articles 25-30 pgs./footnotes (24/yr.). Responds in 9-18 wks. Prefers requested ms on disk, e-mail submission OK. Does not use sidebars. Prefers KJV. Guidelines (also by e-mail); copy $8/$1.42 postage (mark "Media Mail"). (Ads)

　　Special Needs: Church-state issues.

　　Tips: "Open to feature articles only. Send three copies of manuscript and cover letter. Follow writers' guidelines."

$JOY AND PRAISE, PO Box 284, Swarthmore PA 19081-0284. Toll-free (866)800-5JOY. (610)565-5526. Fax (610)565-4553. E-mail: sonya@joyandpraise.org. Website: www.joyandpraise.org. Blessed Communications and Entertainment, Inc. Sonya Crew, pub.; Crystal Morgan, mng. ed. (submissions to: submissions@joyandpraise.org). Youth Ministry Supplement; biblically based articles. Biannual mag.; 60 pgs. Subscription $4.50. Estab. 2003. 40% unsolicited freelance; 60% assigned. Query/clips; e-query OK. Pays $50-250 on acceptance for 1st & electronic rts. Articles; reviews $10-50. Responds in 8 wks. Guidelines on Website. Incomplete topical listings. (Ads).

　　Fillers: Cartoons, facts, prayers, and word puzzles; $2-25.

　　Columns/Departments: Pays $50-75.

　　Tips: "Articles must relay insightful, personal accounts of your Christian experience. Be certain these accounts are original, enlightening, and encouraging to others in their Christian walk." Log onto Website and click on writer's section.

$+JOYFUL NOISE! MAGAZINE, PO Box 41224, North Charleston SC 29423. (843)557-6849. E-mail: joyfulnoisemag@yahoo.com. Website: www.joyfulnoisemagazine.com. UPLIFT Publishing Co. LaVondilyn J. Watson, ed. Praise and worship magazine. Open to unsolicited freelance. Prefers e-query. Payment is negotiable. Articles & fiction 1,000-1,500 wds. Incomplete topical listings.

KEYS TO LIVING, 105 Steffens Rd., Danville PA 17821. (570)437-2891. E-mail: owcam@chilitech.net. Connie Mertz, ed./pub. Educates, encourages, and challenges readers through devotional and inspirational writings; also nature articles, focusing primarily on wildlife in eastern U.S. Quarterly newsletter; 12 pgs.; circ. 200. Subscription $10. 20% unsolicited freelance (needs freelance). Complete ms/cover letter; no phone query. **PAYS**

2 COPIES for one-time or reprint rts. Articles 350-500 wds. Responds in 4 wks. Accepts reprints. No disk; e-mail submission OK (copied into message). Prefers NIV. Guidelines/theme list; copy for 7x10 SAE/2 stamps. (No ads)

Poetry: Accepts if geared to family, personal living, and current theme. Traditional with an obvious message.

Fillers: Facts, jokes, kid quotes, prayers, quotes, short humor; one paragraph. Must pertain to current theme.

Special Needs: More freelance submissions on themes only.

Tips: "We are a Christ-centered family publication. It's best to request a sample copy. Submissions must focus on our current theme, which is included with Writers' Guidelines. No holiday material. Stay within word count. We are a ministry."

$+KINDRED SPIRIT, 3909 Swiss Ave., Dallas TX 75204. (214)841-3556. Fax (972)222-1544. E-mail: sglahn@dts.edu. Website: www.dts.edu/ks. Dallas Theological Seminary. Sandra Glahn, ed-in-chief. Publication of Dallas Theological Seminary. Quarterly mag.; 16-20 pgs.; circ. 30,000. Subscription free. 75% unsolicited freelance. Query/clips; fax/e-query OK. Pays $350 flat fee on publication. Articles.

Tips: "Most open to profiles of DTS graduates and faculty."

$THE LAYMAN, 136 Tremont Park Dr., PO Box 2210, Lenoir NC 28645. (828)758-8716. Fax (828)758-0920. E-mail: laymanletters@layman.org, or art@abts.net. Website: www.layman .org. Presbyterian Lay Committee. Parker T. Williamson, CEO; Craig M. Kibler, dir. of publications. For members of the Presbyterian Church (USA). Bimonthly & online newspaper; 24 pgs.; circ. 485,000. No subscriptions. 10% unsolicited freelance. Query. Pays negotiable rates on publication for 1st rts. Articles 800-1,200 wds. (12/yr.). Responds in 2 wks. Seasonal 2 mos. ahead. Prefers requested ms on disk. Regularly uses sidebars. Copy for 9x12 SAE/3 stamps. (No ads)

LEAVES, PO Box 87, Dearborn MI 48121-0087. (313)561-2330. Fax (313)561-9486. E-mail: leaves-mag@juno.com. Website: www.rc.net/detroit/mariannhill/leaves.htm. Catholic/Mariannhill Mission Society. Jacquelyn M. Lindsey, ed. For all Catholics; promotes devotion to God and His saints and publishes readers' spiritual experiences, petitions, and thanksgivings. Bimonthly mag.; 24 pgs.; circ. 50,000. Subscription free. 50% unsolicited freelance. Complete ms/cover letter; phone/fax/e-query OK. **NO PAYMENT** for 1st or reprint rts. Not copyrighted. Articles 500 wds. (6-12/yr.). Responds in 4 wks. Seasonal 4 mos. ahead. Accepts reprints. Accepts e-mail submissions (copied into message). Does not use sidebars. Prefers NAB, RSV (Catholic edition). No guidelines or copy. (No ads)

Poetry: Accepts 6-12/yr. Traditional; 8-20 lines. Submit max. 4 poems.

Special Needs: Testimonies of conversion or reversion to Catholicism.

Tips: "Besides being interestingly and attractively written, an article should be confidently and reverently grounded in traditional Catholic doctrine and spirituality. The purpose of our magazine is to edify our readers."

$LIBERTY, Dept. of Public Affairs and Religious Liberty, 12501 Old Columbia Pike, Silver Springs MD 20904-1608. (301)680-6690. Fax (301)680-6695. E-mail: steeli@nad.adventist.org. Website: www.libertymagazine.org. Seventh-day Adventist. Lincoln Steed, ed. Deals with religious liberty issues for government officials, civic leaders, and laymen. Bimonthly mag.; 32 pgs.; circ. 200,000. Subscription $6.95. 95% unsolicited freelance. Query/clips; phone/fax/ e-query OK. Pays $250 & up on acceptance for 1st rts. Articles & essays 1,000-2,500 wds. Responds in 5-13 wks. Requires requested ms on disk or by e-mail. Guidelines; copy.

$#LIFEGLOW, Box 6097, Lincoln NE 68506. (402)448-0981. Fax (402)488-7582. Website: www.christianrecord.org. Christian Record Services, Inc. Gaylena Gibson, ed. For sight-impaired adults over 25; interdenominational Christian audience; inspirational/devotional articles. Quarterly mag.; 65-70 pgs. (lg. print); circ. 30,000. Free to sight-impaired. 95%

unsolicited freelance. Complete ms; no phone/e-query. Pays .04-.05/wd. on acceptance for one-time rts. Articles & true stories 750-1,400 wds. Responds in 52 wks. Seasonal anytime. Accepts simultaneous submissions & reprints. Accepts requested ms on disk. Does not use sidebars. Guidelines; copy for 7x10 SAE/5 stamps. (No ads) Note: Due to an overabundance of manuscripts, this publication will not be accepting manuscripts until 2009.

$+LIFELINE JOURNAL, PO Box 487, Destin FL 32540. (850)837-6630. Fax (850)837-9299. E-mail: Diana@LifeLineJournal.com. Website: www.LifeLineJournal.com. Diana Jernigan, sr. ed. Encourages the family to put biblical precepts into practical everyday living. Bimonthly mag.; 48 pgs.; circ. 25,000. Subscription $19.99. 30% unsolicited freelance; 30% assigned. Query; e-query OK. Pays .10-.20/wd. (or free advertisement) on publication for 1st or reprint rts. How-to articles 400-500 wds.; teaching and features 800-1,200 wds. Responds in 6 wks. Seasonal 6 mos. ahead. Accepts simultaneous submissions & reprints (tell when/where appeared). Accepted mss by e-mail (attached file). No kill fee. Uses some sidebars. Prefers NIV. Accepts submissions from teens. Guidelines by e-mail/Website; copy for 9x12 SAE/$1.50 postage. (Ads)

> **Fillers:** Prayers, prose, short domestic tips for busy families, 250 wds. No payment.

> **Tips:** "Most open to short, catchy how-tos for the busy reader; up to 500 wds."

+LIFESITE CANADA, 301—104 Bond St. E., Toronto ON M5B 1X9, Canada. (866)787-9947. E-mail: lsn@lifesite.net. Website: www.lifesite.net. Interim Publishing/Campaign Life Coalition. Dedicated to the issues of culture, life, and family. Daily newspaper. Incomplete topical listings. No questionnaire returned.

LIFETIMES CATHOLIC eZINE. E-mail: bjubar@parishwebmaster.com. Website: www.Parish Webmaster.com. Catholic. Brandon Jubar, ed. Designed to spread the Good News and minister to people online. Online publication. Open to submissions. Query first. **NO PAYMENT.** Articles 300-600 wds. (300/yr.). Accepts submissions from teens. Guidelines on Website.

> **Columns:** Weekly Reflection; Catholic Catechism; Faith & Spirituality; Family; Self-Improvement; Teen Issues; Teen 2 Teen.

$LIGHT & LIFE, Box 535002, Indianapolis IN 46253-5002. (317)244-3660. Fax (317)248-9055. E-mail: LLMAuthors@fmcna.org. Website: www.freemethodistchurch.org/Magazine. Free Methodist Church of North America. Doug Newton, ed.; Cynthia Schnereger, mng. ed.; submit to Margie Newton, ms manager. Interactive magazine for maturing Christians; contemporary-issues oriented, thought-provoking; emphasizes spiritual growth, discipline, holiness as a lifestyle. Bimonthly mag.; 32 pgs. (plus pull-outs); circ. 50,000. Subscription $16. 95% unsolicited freelance. Query first; e-query OK. Pays .10-.15/wd. on acceptance for 1st rts. Articles 600-1,500 wds. (24/yr.). Responds in 8-12 wks. Seasonal 12 mos. ahead. No simultaneous submissions. Prefers e-mail submission (attached file) after acceptance. No kill fee. Uses some sidebars. Prefers NIV. Accepts submissions from children or teens. Guidelines (also on Website); copy $5. (Ads)

> **Tips:** "Best to write a query letter. We are emphasizing contemporary issues articles, well researched. Ask the question, 'What topics are not receiving adequate coverage in the church and Christian periodicals?' Seeking unique angles on everyday topics."

> **2001 EPA Award of Excellence—Denominational.

+LIGHT AT HOME, 10117 S.E. Sunnyside Rd., Ste. F#518, Clackamas OR 97015. Toll-free (888)889-3665. E-mail: lightathome@comcast.net. Website: www.lightathome.com. Batdorf & Associates. Lindy Batdorf, ed./pub. Dedicated to enhancing life at home by offering encouraging words, household hints, organizational tips, inspiring funny stories, and more. Weekly e-zine; 2-3 pgs.; circ. 29,000. Subscription free. Open to unsolicited freelance. Complete ms/cover letter if under 300 wds. (query if over 300 wds.); e-query OK. **NO PAYMENT** for one-time rts. Not copyrighted. Articles 25-400 wds. (150/yr.); humorous fiction to 400 wds. (40/yr.); reviews 100 wds. Responds in 4 wks. Seasonal 1-2 mos. ahead. Accepts simultaneous submissions & reprints (tell when/where appeared). Prefers e-mail submissions. Regularly uses sidebars. Any Bible version. Accepts submissions from children/teens. Guidelines by e-mail/Website; copy online. (Ads & trades links)

Poetry: Accepts poetry to 30 lines, prefers short. Submit max. 1 poem by e-mail or 10 by snail mail.

Fillers: Accepts 150/yr. All except cartoons or word puzzles; to 400 wds.

Columns/Departments: Household Secrets (tips & hints); Encouraging Words (quotes, thoughts); Sweet Memories; Everyday Heroes; Just Fun (clean jokes, funny or embarrassing moments); Recycling Tips; Recipes; Crafts; Money Savers; Gardening Tips. Looking for columnists (contact editor).

Special Needs: Original household hints; sweet stories/memories of people making a difference; innovative money-saving tips; tips for pet owners; building faith through trying circumstances. Short holiday skits for kids.

Contest: Occasionally sponsors contests. Sign up for newsletter to receive details.

Tips: "We have a constant need for fresh, interesting, or helpful material on just about any topic associated with home life and family. Make it brief and meaningful. Facts must be accurate, and household hints must be tested and safe."

$LIGUORIAN, One Liguori Dr., Liguori MO 63057-9999. Toll-free (800)464-2555. (636)464-2500. Toll-free fax (800)325-9526. (636)464-8449. E-mail: liguorianeditor@liguori.org. Website: www.liguorian.org. Catholic/Liguori Publications. William Parker, C.Ss.R., ed-in-chief; Cheryl Plass, mng. ed. To help Catholics of all ages better understand the gospel and church teachings and to show how these teachings apply to life and the problems confronting them as members of families, the church, and society. Monthly (10X) mag.; 40 pgs.; circ. 200,000. Subscription $20. 30-40% unsolicited freelance; 60% assigned. Query, query/clips, or complete ms; phone/fax/e-query OK. Pays .12-.15/wd. on acceptance for 1st rts. Articles 1,500-1,800 wds. (30-50/yr.); fiction 2,000 wds. (10/yr.); book reviews 250 wds. No simultaneous submissions or reprints. Responds in 8-12 wks. Seasonal 6-8 mos. ahead. Prefers requested ms by e-mail (attached file). Uses some sidebars. Prefers NRSV. Guidelines (also by e-mail/Website); copy for 9x12 SAE/3 stamps. (Ads)

Fillers: Buys 10/yr. Cartoons, jokes.

Tips: "Most open to 1,000 word meditations; 1,800 word fiction; or 1,500 word personal testimonies. Send complete manuscript for fiction. Polish your own manuscript."

**This periodical was #6 on the 2005 Top 50 Christian Publishers list (#42 in 2004, #39 in 2003).

$LIVE, 1445 N. Boonville Ave., Springfield MO 65802-1894. (417)862-2781. Fax (417)862-6059. E-mail: rl-live@gph.org. Website: www.radiantlife.org. Assemblies of God/Gospel Publishing House. Paul W. Smith, adult ed. Inspiration and encouragement for adults. Weekly take-home paper; 8 pgs.; circ. 62,000. Subscription $14.50. 100% unsolicited freelance. Complete ms/cover letter; no phone/fax query. Pays .10/wd. (.07/wd. for reprints) on acceptance for 1st, one-time, simultaneous, or reprint rts. Articles 500-1,200 wds. (80-90/yr.); fiction 800-1,200 wds. (20/yr.). Responds in 4-6 wks. Seasonal 12-18 mos. ahead. Accepts simultaneous submissions & reprints (tell when/where appeared). Accepts e-mail submissions (copied into message). Few sidebars. Prefers NIV, KJV. Guidelines (also by e-mail/Website); copy for #10 SAE/1 stamp. (No ads)

Poetry: Buys 15/yr. Any type; 12-20 lines; $60 ($35 for reprints) when scheduled. Submit max. 3 poems.

Fillers: Buys 6-8/yr. Anecdotes, prose; 200-700 wds.; .10/wd. (.07/wd. for reprints).

Tips: "All areas open to freelance—human interest, inspirational, and difficulties overcome with God's help. Fiction must be especially good with biblical application. Follow our guidelines. Most open to well-written personal experience with biblical application. Send no more than two articles in the same envelope and send a SASE. We always need holiday articles."

**This periodical was #9 on the 2005 Top 50 Christian Publishers list (#6 in 2004, #5 in 2003, #4 in 2002, #12 in 2001).

$LIVING, 1251 Virginia Ave., Harrisonburg VA 22802. Toll-free (888)833-3333. (540)433-5351. Fax (540)434-0247. E-mail: Tgether@aol.com. Website: www.churchoutreach.com. Shalom Foundation, Inc. Melodie M. Davis, ed. A positive, practical, and uplifting publication for the whole family; mass distribution. Quarterly tabloid; 32 pgs.; circ. 50,000. Subscription free. 95% unsolicited freelance. Query or complete ms/cover letter; e-query OK. Pays $35-60 on publication for one-time rts. Articles 500-1,200 wds. (40-50/yr.). Responds in 13-18 wks. Seasonal 4 mos. ahead. Accepts simultaneous submissions & reprints (tell when/where appeared). Accepts requested ms on disk or by e-mail (copied into message; include e-mail address in message). Uses some sidebars. Prefers NIV. Guidelines/theme list (also by e-mail); copy for 9x12 SAE/4 stamps. (Ads)

Fillers: Buys 4-8/yr. Anecdotes, short humor; 100-200 wds.; $20-25.

Tips: "We are directed toward the general public, many of whom have no Christian interests, and we're trying to publish high-quality writing on family issues/concerns from a Christian perspective. That means religious language must be low key. Too much of what we receive is directed toward a Christian reader. We get far more than we can use, so something really has to stand out. Please carefully consider before sending. Need more articles of interest to men. Our articles need to have a family slant or fit the descriptor 'encouragement for families.'" When submitting by e-mail, put title of magazine and title of your piece in subject line. Also include your e-mail address in body of message.

$THE LIVING CHURCH, PO Box 514036, Milwaukee WI 53203-3436. (414)276-5420, ext. 11. Fax (414)276-7483. E-mail: tlc@livingchurch.org. Website: www.livingchurch.org. Episcopal/The Living Church Foundation, Inc. John Schuessler, mng. ed. Independent news coverage of the Episcopal Church for clergy and lay leaders. Weekly mag.; 24+ pgs.; circ. 9,000. Subscription $39.50. Open to freelance. Query; phone/fax/e-query OK. Pays $25-100 (for solicited articles, nothing for unsolicited) for one-time rts. Articles 1,000 wds. (10/yr.). Responds in 2-4 wks. Seasonal 2 mos. ahead. Prefers requested ms on disk or by e-mail (attached or copied into message). Uses some sidebars. Guidelines (by e-mail); free copy. (Ads)

Columns/Departments: Accepts 5/yr. Benediction (devotional/inspirational), 200 wds. Complete ms. No payment.

Tips: "Most open to features, as long as they have something to do with the Episcopal Church."

$LIVING LIGHT NEWS, #200, 5306—89th St., Edmonton AB T6E 5P9, Canada. (780)468-6397. Fax (780)468-6872. E-mail: shine@livinglightnews.org. Website: www.livinglight news.org. Living Light Ministries. Jeff Caporale, ed. To motivate and encourage Christians; witnessing tool to the lost. Bimonthly (7X) tabloid; 36 pgs.; circ. 34,000. Subscription $19.95 U.S. 40% unsolicited freelance; 60% assigned. Query; fax/e-query OK. Pays $20-125 (.05-.10/wd. Cdn. or .08/wd. U.S.) on publication for all, 1st, one-time, simultaneous, or reprint rts. Articles 350-700 wds. (75/yr.); fiction 500-1,200 wds. (3/yr. for Christmas only). Responds in 4 wks. Seasonal 3-4 mos. ahead. Accepts simultaneous submissions & reprints (tell when/where appeared). Accepts requested ms on disk or by e-mail (attached file in rich text format or copied into message). Regularly uses sidebars. Prefers NIV. Guidelines (also by e-mail/Website); copy for 9x12 SAE/$2.50 Cdn. postage or IRCs (no U.S. postage). (Ads)

Columns/Departments: Buys 20/yr., 450-600 wds., $10-30. Parenting; relationships. Query.

Special Needs: Celebrity interviews/testimonials of well-known personalities; humorous fiction and interesting nonfiction stories related to Christmas (Christmas fiction only). Fun or informative articles (250-700 wds.) for Christian education supplement.

Tips: "Most open to a timely article about someone who is well known in North America, in sports or entertainment, and has a strong Christian walk."

**2002, 2001 EPA Award of Merit—Newspaper. This publication was #34 on the 2005 Top 50 Christian Publishers list (#25 in 2004, #14 in 2003, #10 in 2002).

LOOKING UP MAGAZINE, PO Box 24, Southington OH 44470. (330)647-4849. Fax (330)898-0687. E-mail: LookingUpMag@aol.com or LookingUpMag@yahoo.com. Website: www.lookingupmagazine.com. Jeannie Schmucker, ed-in-chief. Monthly mag. Subscription $19. **PAYS ONE COPY.** Articles and devotions to 700 wds.; poetry. Guidelines/theme list on Website. Incomplete topical listings.

$THE LOOKOUT, 8121 Hamilton Ave., Cincinnati OH 45231-9981. (513)931-4050. Fax (513)931-0950. E-mail: lookout@standardpub.com. Website: www.lookoutmag.com. Standard Publishing. Shawn McMullen, ed. For adults who are interested in learning more about applying the gospel to their lives. Weekly & online mag.; 16 pgs.; circ. 100,000. Subscription $26.99, plus $5 postage. 30% unsolicited freelance; 70% assigned. Query for theme articles; complete ms for others; e-query OK. Pays .09-.12/wd. on acceptance. Articles 500-1,600 wds.(200/yr.). Responds in 10 wks. Seasonal 6 mos. ahead. Accepts simultaneous submissions; no reprints. No disks or e-mail submissions. Kill fee 50%. Regularly uses sidebars. Prefers NIV. Guidelines/theme list (also by e-mail/Website); copy for #10 SAE/$1 postage. (No ads)

Columns/Departments: Buys 24/yr. The Outlook (personal opinion); Salt & Light (innovative ways to reach out into the community); Faith Around the World; all 500-800 wds.; .09/wd. Query.

Tips: "Most open to feature articles according to our theme list. Get a copy of our theme list and query about a theme-related article at least six months in advance. Request sample copies of our magazine to familiarize yourself with our publishing needs. Send samples of published material."

**This periodical was #4 on the 2005 Top 50 Christian Publishers list (#2 in 2004, #24 in 2003, #11 in 2002, #49 in 2001).

$THE LUTHERAN DIGEST, Box 4250, Hopkins MN 55343. (952)933-2820. Fax (952)933-5708. E-mail: tldi@lutherandigest.com. Website: www.lutherandigest.com. Lutheran. David L. Tank, ed. Blend of secular and light theological material used to win nonbelievers to the Lutheran faith. Quarterly & online mag.; 64 pgs.; circ. 105,000. Subscription $14. 100% unsolicited freelance. Query/clips or complete ms/cover letter; no phone/fax query. Pays $25-50 on acceptance for one-time rts. Articles to 1,000 wds. (25-30/yr.). Responds in 4-9 wks. Seasonal 6-9 mos. ahead. Accepts reprints (70% is reprints). No disk. Uses some sidebars. Guidelines (also on Website); copy $3.50/6x9 SAE/3 stamps. (Ads)

Poetry: Accepts 45-50/yr. Light verse, traditional; any length; no payment. Submit max. 3 poems.

Fillers: Anecdotes, cartoons, facts, jokes, short humor; to 100 wds.; no payment.

Tips: "We need well-thought-out, well-written, professional articles. More nature pieces. Compose well-written, short pieces that would be of interest to middle-aged and senior Christians—and also acceptable to Lutheran church pastors. (The word *hope* is frequently associated with our publication.) So much of the material we receive is poorly written and we spend too much time trying to clean it up. Research your market first. To catch our attention, the topic has to be catchy or stand out from the usual and must be well-written."

$THE LUTHERAN JOURNAL, 7010—6th St. N., PO Box 28158, Oakdale MN 55128. (651)702-0086. Fax (651)702-0074. E-mail: christianad2@msn.com. Submit to Editor.

Family magazine for, by, and about Lutherans, and God at work in the Lutheran world. Semi-annual mag.; 24-32 pgs.; circ. 100,000. Subscription $6. 60% unsolicited freelance; 40% assigned. Complete ms/cover letter; fax query OK. Pays $5-50 on publication for 1st rts. Articles 750-1,500 wds. (20/yr.). Response time varies. Seasonal 4-5 mos. ahead. Accepts reprints. Uses some sidebars. Prefers NIV, NAS, KJV. Accepts requested ms on disk. Accepts submissions from children or teens. Guidelines; copy for 9x12 SAE/3 stamps. (Ads)

Poetry: Buys 10/yr. Light verse, traditional; 50-150 wds.; $5-30. Submit max. 3 poems.

Fillers: Buys 5-10/yr. Anecdotes, facts, games, prayers, quizzes, quotes; 50-300 wds.; $5-30.

Columns/Departments: Buys 40/yr. Apron Strings (short recipes); About Books (reviews), 50-150 wds.; $5-25.

Tips: "Most open to Lutheran lifestyles or Lutherans in action."

MARANATHA NEWS, PO Box 328, Jupiter FL 33468. (561)744-9336. Fax (561)744-8897. E-mail: maranews@aol.com. Assemblies of God. Waldir DeOliveira, ed. Quarterly tabloid; 16 pgs.; circ. 4,000. Subscription free. Open to freelance. Complete ms; e-query OK. **NO PAYMENT** for 1st rts. Not copyrighted. Articles (2/yr.). Responds in 2 wks. Seasonal 2 mos. ahead. Accepts reprints (tell when/where appeared). No kill fee. Uses some sidebars. Accepts submissions from children or teens. No guidelines; copy for 7x10 SAE. (Ads)

Fillers: Anecdotes, cartoons, jokes, newsbreaks, short humor, and word puzzles.

$MARIAN HELPER, Marian Helpers Center, Eden Hill, Stockbridge MA 01263. (413)298-3691. Fax (413)298-3583. E-mail: came@marian.org. Website: www.marian.org. Catholic/Marians of the Immaculate Conception. Dave Came, exec. ed.; Steve LaChance, review ed. Quarterly & online mag.; circ. 500,000. Rarely uses unsolicited; 25% assigned freelance. Query/clips or complete ms/cover letter. Pays $250 for 1,000-1,200 wds. (2-page feature), for 1st rts. Articles 500-900 wds. Responds in 6 wks. Seasonal 6 mos. ahead. Kill fee 30%. Guidelines/copy for #10 SAE. (No ads)

Tips: "Write about God's mercy touching people's everyday lives, or about devotion to the Blessed Virgin Mary in a practical, inspirational, or fresh way."

MARKETPLACE, 12900 Preston Rd., Ste. 1215, Dallas TX 75230-1328. Toll-free (800)775-7657. (972)385-7657. Fax (972)385-7307. E-mail: art.stricklin@marketplace ministries.com. Website: www.marketplaceministries.com. Marketplace Ministries. Art Stricklin, ed. Focus is on working in the corporate workplace. Triannual mag.; 12 pgs.; circ. 16,000. Subscription free. 10% assigned. Query or complete ms; e-query OK. **NO PAYMENT** for all rts. Articles. Prefers e-mail submission. No copy. Incomplete topical listings. (No ads)

Tips: "We are attempting to cut back on freelance and use only assigned stories."

$MARRIAGE PARTNERSHIP, 465 Gundersen Dr., Carol Stream IL 60188. (630)260-6200. Fax (630)260-0114. E-mail: mp@marriagepartnership.com. Website: www.marriagepartnership .com, or www.christianitytoday.com/marriage. Christianity Today Intl. Ginger Kolbaba, mng. ed. To promote and strengthen Christian marriages. Quarterly mag.; 74 pgs.; circ. 53,000. Subscription $19.95. 5% unsolicited freelance; 95% assigned. Query only; fax/e-query OK. Pays .15-.25/wd. on acceptance for 1st rts. Articles 500-2,000 wds. Responds in 8-10 wks. Seasonal 9 mos. ahead. Accepts reprints (tell when/where appeared). Prefers accepted ms by e-mail (copied into message). Kill fee 50%. Regularly uses sidebars. Prefers NIV. Guidelines (also on Website); copy $5/9x12 SAE. (Ads)

Columns/Departments: Buys 4/year/department. Work It Out (working out a marriage problem); Back from the Brink (real-life story of a marriage in recovery), 1,800 wds.; Starting Out (views from the early years, married 5 years or less), 900 wds., pays $150; That Thing We Do (unique hobby you share as a couple), 400 wds. Query with ideas.

Tips: "Please, only articles on marriage—if it's a parenting piece, it needs to be how that topic affects marriage. Know the magazine. Read a few issues to get the correct tone and feel. Most open to the departments listed above. Be fresh, creative, and have a thorough, well-crafted query."

MARS HILL REVIEW, PO Box 10506, Bainbridge Island WA 98110-0506. Toll-free (800)990-MARS. Fax (877-349-7880. E-mail from Website. Website: www.marshillreview.com. Sarah Koops Vanderveen, ed. Revealing Christ in the various texts of our contemporary culture. Triannual literary jour.; 200 pgs. Subscription $36. Open to unsolicited freelance. For longer submissions query first. Pays for solicited submissions only; **NO PAYMENT** for unsolicited. Essays/studies up to 3,000-5,000 wds.; fiction up to 3,000-5,000 wds. Responds in 10-12 wks. Requires disk. Guidelines on Website.

Poetry: Marlene Muller, poetry ed.

Special Needs: Deadlines for issues are Spring/Winter, October 1; Summer, February 1; and Fall, June 1.

$MATURE LIVING, One Lifeway Plaza, MSN 175, Nashville TN 37234-0175. (615)251-5677. E-mail: rene.holt@lifeway.com. LifeWay Christian Resources/Southern Baptist. David T. Seay, ed-in-chief; submit to Rene Holt, ed. Christian leisure reading for senior adults (50+) characterized by human interest and Christian warmth. Monthly mag.; 52 pgs.; circ. 318,000. Subscription $20.25. 90% unsolicited freelance; 10% assigned. Complete ms/cover letter; no phone/fax/e-query. Pays $75-105 on acceptance for all rts. Articles 600-1,200 wds. (85/yr.); senior adult fiction 600-1,200 wds. (12/yr.). Responds in 13 wks. Seasonal 8 mos. ahead. No simultaneous submissions or reprints. Accepts disk or e-mail submissions. No kill fee. Uses some sidebars. Prefers KJV, HCSB. Accepts submissions from children or teens. Guidelines (also by e-mail); copy for 9x12 SAE/4 stamps. (Ads)

Poetry: Buys 24/yr. Light verse, traditional; 12-16 lines; $25. Submit max. 3 poems.

Fillers: Buys 120/yr. Anecdotes, cartoons, word puzzles; to 50 wds.; $15-40.

Columns/Departments: Buys 300+/yr. Cracker Barrel (brief humor), 25-30 wds., $15; Grandparent's Brag Board, 50-100 wds., $15. Columns pay $15-40. See guidelines for full list.

Tips: "Almost all areas open to freelancers, except medical and financial matters."

**This periodical was #47 on the 2004 Top 50 Christian Publishers list (#46 in 2003, #44 in 2001, #43 in 1999).

*MATURE TIMES, 374 Sheppard Ave. E., Toronto ON M2N 3B6, Canada. (416)222-3341, ext. 142. Fax (416)222-3344. The Peoples Church/Toronto Canada. Dr. T. Starr, mng. ed. For readers aged 55 and older. Quarterly mag.; 24 pgs. Subscription free/donation. 15% unsolicited freelance; 85% assigned. Complete ms/cover letter. **NO PAYMENT.** Articles 500 wds. (20/yr.); fiction 350-500 wds.; book/video reviews 150 wds. Responds in 2 wks. Seasonal 3 mos. ahead. Accepts simultaneous submissions & reprints (tell when/where appeared). Accepts requested ms on disk. Regular sidebars. Prefers NIV. Guidelines/theme list; copy for 9x12 SAE/$1.20 Cdn. postage. (Ads)

Poetry: Accepts 1-2/yr.

Fillers: Accepts 1-5/yr.; 50 wds. Anecdotes, cartoons, facts, games, quizzes, short humor; 25-40 wds.

Columns/Departments: Accepts 20/yr. Complete ms.

Note: This Website is for sale, so publication may be going out of business.

$MATURE YEARS, Box 801, Nashville TN 37202. (615)749-6292. Fax (615)749-6512. E-mail: matureyears@umpublishing.org. United Methodist. Marvin W. Cropsey, ed. Inspiration, information, and leisure reading for persons of retirement age. Quarterly mag.; 112 pgs.; circ. 70,000. Subscription $19. 60% unsolicited freelance; 40% assigned. Complete ms/cover letter; fax/e-query OK. Pays .05/wd. on acceptance for one-time rts. Articles 900-2,000 wds. (60/yr.); fiction 1,200-2,000 wds. (4/yr.). Responds in 9 wks. Seasonal 14 mos. ahead. Accepts reprints. Prefers accepted ms by e-mail (copied into message). Regularly uses sidebars. Prefers NRSV, NIV. Guidelines (also by e-mail); copy $5. (No ads)

Poetry: Buys 24/yr. Free verse, haiku, light verse, traditional; 4-16 lines; pays $.50-1.00/line. Submit max. 6 poems.

Fillers: Buys 20/yr. Anecdotes (to 300 wds.), cartoons, jokes, prayers, word puzzles (religious only); to 30 wds.; $5-25.

Columns/Departments: Buys 20/yr. Health Hints, 900-1,200 wds.; Modern Revelations (inspirational), 900-1,100 wds.; Fragments of Life (true-life inspirational), 250-600 wds.; Going Places (travel), 1,000-1,500 wds.; Money Matters, 1,200-1,800 wds.

Special Needs: Articles on crafts and pets. Fiction on older adult situations. All areas open except Bible studies.

**This periodical was #31 on the 2005 Top 50 Christian Publishers list (#35 in 2004, #43 in 2003, #33 in 2002, #34 in 2001).

$MENNONITE BRETHREN HERALD, 3-169 Riverton Ave., Winnipeg MB R2L 2E5, Canada. (204)654-5760. Fax (204)654-1865. E-mail: mbherald@mbconf.ca. Website: www.mbherald.com. Canadian Conference of Mennonite Brethren Churches. Susan Brandt, acting ed.; Dora Dueck, assoc. ed. Denominational; for information, communication, and spiritual enrichment. Biweekly mag.; 32 pgs.; circ. 17,000. Subscription $30. 75% unsolicited freelance; 25% assigned. Query or complete ms/cover letter; phone/e-query OK. Pays $30-40 (.07/wd.) on publication for 1st or one-time rts. Not copyrighted. Articles 250-1,500 wds. (40/yr.); fiction 1,000-2,000 wds. (10/yr.). Responds in 26 wks. Seasonal 5 mos. ahead. Accepts reprints (tell when/where appeared). Prefers requested ms on disk or by e-mail. Regularly uses sidebars. Prefers NIV. Guidelines/theme list; copy for 9x12 SAE/$1 Canadian postage. (Ads)

Poetry: Buys 6-12/yr. Avant-garde, free verse, traditional; to 25 lines; pays to $10.

Tips: "Most open to feature articles on relevant topics, but not with an American bias."

***MENNONITE FAMILY HISTORY,** 219 Mill Rd., Morgantown PA 19543-9516. Lois Ann Mast, ed. Incomplete topical listings. No questionnaire returned. (No ads)

($)MENNONITE HISTORIAN, 600 Shaftesbury Blvd., Winnipeg MB R3P 0M4, Canada. (204)888-6781. Fax (204)831-5675. E-mail: aredekopp@mennonitechurch.ca. Website: www.mennonitechurch.ca. Mennonite Church Canada. Alf Redekopp, ed. dir. Gathers and shares historical material related to Mennonites; focus on North America, but also beyond. Quarterly newsletter; 8 pgs.; circ. 2,600. Subscription $11. 40% unsolicited freelance; 20% assigned. Complete ms/cover letter; phone/e-query OK. **NO PAYMENT EXCEPT BY SPECIAL ARRANGEMENT** for 1st rts. Articles 250-1,000 wds. (6/yr.). Responds in 3 wks. Seasonal 3 mos. ahead. Accepts simultaneous submissions & reprints (tell when/where appeared). Prefers e-mail submission (attached file). Does not use sidebars. Guidelines (also by e-mail); copy $1/9x12 SAE. (Ads)

Tips: "Must be Mennonite related (i.e., related to the life and history of the denomination, its people, organizations, and activities). Most open to lead articles. Write us with your ideas. Also genealogical articles."

$MEN OF INTEGRITY, 465 Gundersen Dr., Carol Stream IL 60188. (630)260-6200. Fax (630)260-0114. E-mail: mail@menofintegrity.net. Website: www.MenofIntegrity.net. Christianity Today, Inc. Harry Genet, mng. ed. Uses narrative to apply biblical truth to specific gritty issues men face. Bimonthly pocket-sized mag.; 64 pgs.; circ. 102,000. Subscription $19.95. 10% unsolicited freelance. Complete ms. Pays $50 on acceptance for one-time and electronic rts. Articles 225 wds. (15/yr.). Responds in 5 wks. Accepts simultaneous submissions & reprints (tell when/where appeared). Accepts requested ms on disk or by e-mail (attached file or copied into message). Does not use sidebars. Prefers NLT. Guidelines/theme list (also by e-mail); copy $4/#10 SAE. (Ads)

MEN OF THE CROSS, 920 Sweetgum Creek, Plano TX 75023. (972)517-8553. E-mail: info@menofthecross.com. Website: www.menofthecross.com. Mission Ware.com. Greg Paskal, content mngr. (greg@gregpaskal.com). Encouraging men in their walk with the Lord; strong emphasis on discipleship and relationship. Online community. 50% unsolicited freelance. Query by e-mail. **NO PAYMENT.** Not copyrighted. Articles 500-1,000 wds. (10/yr.). Responds in 2-4 wks. Seasonal 3 mos. ahead. Accepts simultaneous submissions; no reprints. Prefers e-mail submissions (attached or copied into message). Uses some sidebars. Prefers NIV, NKJV, NASB. Accepts submissions from teens. Guidelines by e-mail; copy online. (No ads)

> **Poetry:** Accepts 1/yr. Avant-garde, free verse; 50-250 lines. Submit max. 1 poem.
> **Special Needs:** Christian living in the workplace.
> **Tips:** "Appropriate topic could be a real, first-hand account of how God worked in the author's life. We are looking for humble honesty in hopes it will minister to those in similar circumstances. View online forums for specific topics."

$MESSAGE, Review and Herald Pub. Assn., 55 W. Oak Ridge Dr., Hagerstown MD 21740. (301)393-4099. Fax (301)393-4103. E-mail: message@RHPA.org, or ronsmith@rhpa.org. Website: www.messagemagazine.org. Review & Herald/Seventh-day Adventist. Dr. Ron Smith, ed. For African Americans and all people seeking practical Christian guidance on current events and a better lifestyle. Bimonthly mag.; 32 pgs.; circ. 80,000. Subscription $14.95. Most articles assigned. Query or complete ms/cover letter; fax/e-query OK. Pays $50-250 on acceptance for 1st rts. Articles 700-1,200 wds.; fiction for children (ages 5-8), 500 wds. Responds in 6-10 wks. Seasonal 6 mos. ahead. Prefers requested ms by e-mail. Regularly uses sidebars. Prefers KJV. Guidelines (also on Website); copy for 9x12 SAE/2 stamps. (No ads)

> **Columns/Departments:** Buys for each issue. Healthspan (health issues), 700 wds.; MESSAGE Jr. (biblical stories or stories with clear-cut moral for ages 5-8), 500 wds.; $75-150.
> **Tips:** "As with any publication, writers should have a working knowledge of *Message.* They should have some knowledge of our style and our readers."

MESSAGE OF THE OPEN BIBLE, 2020 Bell Ave., Des Moines IA 50315-1096. (515)288-6761. Fax (515)288-2510. E-mail: message@openbible.org. Website: www.openbible.org. Open Bible Standard Churches. Andrea Johnson, ed. To inspire, inform, and educate the Open Bible family. Bimonthly mag.; 16 pgs.; circ. 3,000. Subscription $9.95. 3% unsolicited freelance; 3% assigned. Query or complete ms/cover letter; e-query OK. **PAYS 5 COPIES.** Not copyrighted. Articles 750 wds. (2/yr.). Responds in 4 wks. Seasonal 4 mos. ahead. Accepts simultaneous submissions & reprints (tell when/where appeared). Accepts requested ms on disk or by e-mail. Regularly uses sidebars. Prefers NIV. Guidelines/theme list (also by e-mail); copy for 9x12 SAE/2 stamps. (No ads)

> **Fillers:** Accepts 6/yr. Facts, quotes, short humor; 50 wds.
> **Tips:** "A writer can best break in by giving us material for an upcoming theme, or something inspiring, specifically as it would relate to an Open Bible lay person."

$*MESSENGER, Box 18068, Covington KY 41018-0068. Fax (859)283-6226. Catholic. Diane Reder, news ed. Diocese paper of Covington KY. Weekly (45X) newspaper; 24 pgs.; circ. 16,000. Subscription $18. 40% unsolicited freelance. Query/clips. Pays $1.25/column inch on publication for 1st rts. Articles 500-800 wds. Responds in 1 wk. Seasonal 1 mo. ahead. Accepts simultaneous submissions. Guidelines; free copy. (Ads)

$THE MESSENGER OF SAINT ANTHONY, Via Orto Botanico 11, 35123 Padova, Italy (U.S. address: Anthonian Assn., 101 Saint Anthony Dr., Mt. Saint Francis IN 47146). (812)923-6356 or 049 8229924. Fax (812)923-3200 or 049 8225651. E-mail: m.conte@mess-s-antonio.it (editor); messenger@mess-s-antonio.it (ed. sec.), or info@saintanthonyofpadua.net. Website: www.saintanthonyofpadua.net. Catholic/Provincia Padovana F.M.C. Fr. Mario Conte

OFM, ed.; Corrado Roeper, ed. sec. For middle-aged and older Catholics in English-speaking world; articles that address current issues. Monthly & online mag.; 50 pgs.; circ. 35,000. Subscription $25 U.S. 10% unsolicited freelance; 90% assigned. Query (complete ms for fiction); phone/fax/e-query OK. Pays $40/pg. (600 wds./pg.) for one-time rts. Articles 600-2,400 wds. (40/yr.); fiction 900-1,200 wds. (11/yr.). Responds in 8-10 wks. Seasonal 3 mos. ahead. Prefers e-mail submission (attached file or copied into message). Regularly uses sidebars. Prefers NEB (Oxford Study Edition). Guidelines (also by e-mail); free copy. (No ads)

> **Columns/Departments:** Buys 50-60/yr. Documentary (issues), 600-2,000 wds.; Spirituality, 600-2,000 wds.; Church Life, 600-2,000 wds.; Saint Anthony (devotional), 600-1,400 wds.; Living Today (family life), 600-1,400 wds.; $55-200. Complete ms.
>
> **Special Needs:** Short story of a moral or religious nature; St. Anthony.
>
> **Tips:** "Most open to short stories; Saint Anthony, and devotional articles on parishes named after Saint Anthony, local feasts/shrines in Saint Anthony's honour."

$MESSENGER OF THE SACRED HEART, 661 Greenwood Ave., Toronto ON M4J 4B3, Canada. (416)466-1195. Catholic/Apostleship of Prayer. Rev. F. J. Power, S.J., ed. Help for daily living on a spiritual level. Monthly mag.; 32 pgs.; circ. 13,000. Subscription $14. 20% freelance. Complete ms; no phone query. Pays .06/wd. on acceptance for 1st rts. Articles 800-1,500 wds. (30/yr.); fiction 800-1,500 wds. (12/yr.). Responds in 5 wks. Seasonal 5 mos. ahead. No disk. Does not use sidebars. Guidelines; copy $1/9x12 SAE. (No ads)

> **Tips:** "Most open to inspirational stories and articles."

$MESSIAH MAGAZINE, PO Box 620099, Littleton CO 80162-0099. Fax (303)933-0997. Website: www.ffoz.org. First Fruits of Zion. Hope Egan, ed. Dedicated to the study, exploration, and celebration of our righteous and sinless Torah-observant King—Yeshua of Nazareth. Mag. published 5X/yr.; 34 pgs.; circ. 10,000. Subscription for donation. Open to freelance. Query; fax query OK. Pays on acceptance for all rts. Articles (15-20/yr.). Responds in 3 wks. Seasonal 6 mos. ahead. Accepts simultaneous submissions; no reprints. Requires e-mail submissions (attached file). Does not use sidebars. Prefers NASB. Copy for $4/9x12 SAE/5 stamps. Incomplete topical listings. (No ads)

> **Tips:** "F.F.O.Z. is a nonprofit ministry devoted to strengthening the love and appreciation of the Body of the Messiah for the land, people, and scriptures of Israel. Since our focus is unique, please be very familiar with our magazine before submitting your query. Our Torah Testimony column is always open, as are some of the others. Looking for something on Hebrew roots."

$*MESSIANIC SCI-FI ONLINE. E-mail: msf-submit@heartofisrael.org, or info@heartofisrael.org. Website: www.heartofisrael.org/msf. Pia Cruz, Stephanie Lutz, Joe Applegate, eds. Quarterly e-zine. 100% freelance. Heavily Bible-based science fiction that glorifies God. Welcomes new writers. Authors paid per download through offsite service. All legal issues/rights/finances are between that service and the author. Publishes (a) author's testimony (b) introduction (like a book jacket cover) and (c) "Teaser": first 200 words of ms. Will maintain archives so new visitors/readers can buy older stories from authors and will allow (and may help) authors create their own individual Website to promote their work to increase sales of their story. Pays 1/8 cent/wd., for original stories only, for one-time rts. Articles to 2,000 words (also accepts serials). Responds within 1-3 mos. No simultaneous submissions. Requires submissions by e-mail (copied into message). See Website for guidelines, topics, and deadlines, and suggested biblical Scripture references (for inspiration) for 2006.

> **Tips:** "For classic topics (e.g., apocalyptic fiction), we seek a very fresh approach in an area that has been done to death! Primary motivation for writing: glorify God with your talent."

THE MESSIANIC TIMES, PO Box 2190, Niagara Falls NY 14302. (905)685-4072. Fax (905)685-7371. E-mail: editor@messianictimes.com. Website: www.messianictimes.com.

Donita Painter, ed. To unify the Messianic Jewish community around the world, to serve as an evangelistic tool to the Jewish community, and to educate Christians about the Jewish roots of their faith. Bimonthly newspaper; circ. 35,000. Subscription free to donors. Accepts freelance. Not in topical listings. No questionnaire returned. (Ads)

METHODIST HISTORY, PO Box 127, Madison NJ 07940. (973)408-3189. Fax (973)408-3909. E-mail: cyrigoyen@gcah.org. Website: www.gcah.org. United Methodist. Charles Yrigoyen Jr., ed. History of the United Methodism and Methodist/Wesleyan churches. Quarterly jour.; 64 pgs.; circ. 800. Subscription $20. 100% unsolicited freelance. Query; phone/fax/e-query OK. **PAYS IN COPIES** for all rts. Historical articles to 5,000 wds. (15/yr.); book reviews 500 wds. Responds in 8 wks. Requires requested ms on disk. Does not use sidebars. Guidelines (also on Website); no copy. (Ads)

> **Special Needs:** United Methodist church history.

METRO VOICE, 305 S.W. Market, Ste. 4, Lee's Summit MO 64063. (816)524-4522. Fax (816)282-0010. E-mail: metrovoice@kcweb.net. Website: www.metrovoicenews.com. Nondenominational. Dwight & Anita Widaman, pubs. To promote Christian business, ministries, and organizations and provide thought-provoking commentary for edification of the body of Christ. Monthly newspaper; circ. 35,000. Subscription $19.95. 50% unsolicited freelance. Complete ms/cover letter or e-mail query; short phone query OK. **PAYS IN COPIES** or limited amount for well-researched pieces, for one-time or reprint rts. Not copyrighted. Articles to 1,200 wds. (100/yr.). Responds in 6 wks. Seasonal 6 mos. ahead. Accepts reprints. Guidelines.

> **Tips:** "We look for up-to-date information. Willing to work with new writers who want to learn. Interested in investigative features and current events."

MIDNIGHT CALL MAGAZINE, PO Box 280008, Columbia SC 29228. Toll-free (800)845-2420. (803)755-0733. Fax (803)755-6002. E-mail: info@midnightcall.com. Website: www.midnightcall.com. Arno Froese, ed. The world's only international voice of prophecy regarding end-time events. Subscription $24.50.

MID-SOUTH CHRISTIAN BANNER, PO Box 40086, Memphis TN 38174-0086. (662)280-1304. Fax (662)280-1301. E-mail: abholmes@bellsouth.net; publisher@christianbanner.com. Website: www.christianbanner.com. Independent. Mary Ann Marchbanks, pub.; Warren Smith, ed. Holding forth truth and traditional Judeo-Christian values as found in God's Word, and seeking to increase awareness and activism among its readers related to moral, ethical, political, and biblical issues that affect the Christian community. Monthly newspaper. Subscription $24 (free to churches). Open to freelance articles, press releases, and news of interest to readers. Guidelines on Website. Not in topical listings. No questionnaire returned. (Ads)

$MINNESOTA CHRISTIAN CHRONICLE, 623 N. Lilac Dr., Ste. A, Golden Valley MN 55422. (763)746-2468. Fax (763)746-2469. E-mail: editor@mcchronicle.com. Website: www.mcchronicle.com. World Newspaper Publishing. Bryan Malley, ed. Local news and features of interest to the Christian community. Biweekly & online newspaper; 20-24 pgs.; circ. 25,000. Subscription $29.95. 20% unsolicited freelance; 80% assigned. Query; phone/fax/e-query OK. Prefers e-mail submissions (attached file). Pays $20-200 one month after publication for all rts. Articles 250-1,000 wds. (50-100/yr.); reviews 400 wds. Responds in 5 wks. Seasonal 2 mos. ahead. Rarely accepts simultaneous submissions or reprints (tell when/where appeared). No kill fee. Regularly uses sidebars. Guidelines by e-mail; copy $2. (Ads)

> **Tips:** "Looking for church trend stories. We most often use freelancers in our local news and feature article sections. Stories with a strong Minnesota hook will be accepted. Unique ministries, events, and/or people interest our readers the most. We also encourage participation in communities."
> **2005 EPA Award of Merit—Newspaper.

$THE MIRACULOUS MEDAL, 475 E. Chelten Ave., Philadelphia PA 19144-5785. (215)848-1010. Fax (215)848-1014. Website: www.cammonline.org. Catholic. Rev. James O. Kiernan, C.M., ed. Fiction and poetry for Catholic adults, mostly women. Quarterly mag.; 36 pgs.; circ. 200,000. Subscription free to members. 25% unsolicited freelance. Query by mail only. Pays .02/wd. and up, on acceptance, for 1st rts. Religious fiction 1,000-2,400 wds.; some 1,000-1,200 wds. (6/yr.). Responds in 26 wks. Seasonal anytime. Accepts simultaneous submissions. Guidelines (also by e-mail); copy for 6x9 SAE/2 stamps. (No ads)
> **Poetry:** Buys 6/yr. Free verse, traditional; to 20 lines; .50 & up/line. Send any number. "Must have religious theme, preferably about the Blessed Virgin Mary."
> **Tips:** "Most open to good short stories, 1,500-2,500 wds., or poetry, with light religious theme."

$MONTGOMERY'S JOURNEY, 555 Farmington Rd, Montgomery AL 36109-4609. (334)213-7940. Fax (334)213-7990. E-mail: Journey@watsonmedia.com. Website: www.watson media.com. Keep Sharing, LLC. DeAnne Watson, pub. (submit to: Deanne@montgomerys journey.com). For protestant Christians and Christian families. Monthly mag.; 60-72 pgs.; circ. 8,000. Subscription $20. Open to freelance. Complete ms by e-mail. Pays $25 on publication for one-time or reprint rts. Articles 1,800-2,000 wds. Seasonal 3 mos. ahead. Accepts requested ms on disk or by e-mail (attached file). No kill fee. Regularly uses sidebars. Accepts submissions from teens. No guidelines or copy. (Ads)
> **Tips:** "Mainly open to feature stories."

MOSAIC, 4315 Village Centre Ct., Mississauga ON L4Z 1S2, Canada. (905)848-2600. Fax (905)848-2603. E-mail: howdenl@fmc-canada.org. Website: www.fmc-canada.org. Free Methodist Church in Canada. Lisa Howden, mng. ed. Reflecting the diversity of ministry expression within the Free Methodist family. Bimonthly tabloid; 8 pgs.; circ. 4,000. Open to unsolicited freelance. Query; phone/e-query OK. **NO PAYMENT.** Articles 800-1,200 wds. Responds in 2 wks. Seasonal 4 mos. ahead. Accepts reprints (tell when/where appeared). Accepts e-mail submissions (attached file). Guidelines/theme list by e-mail/ Website; no sample copy. (Ads)
> **Tips:** "Most open to inspirational pieces."

MOVIEGUIDE, 2510-G Los Posas Rd., #502, Camarillo CA 93010. (805)383-2000. Fax (805)383-4089. E-mail: office@movieguide.org. Website: www.movieguide.org. Good News Communications/Christian Film & TV Commission. Dr. Theodore Baehr, pub. Family guide to media entertainment from a biblical perspective. Biweekly mag.; 23+ pgs.; circ. 3,000. Subscription $40. 40% unsolicited freelance. Query/clips. **NO PAYMENT** for all rts. Articles 1,200 wds. (100/yr.); book/music/video/movie reviews, 1,200 wds. Responds in 6 wks. Seasonal 6 mos. ahead. Accepts requested ms on disk. Regularly uses sidebars. Guidelines/theme list; copy for SAE/4 stamps. (Ads)
> **Fillers:** Accepts 1,000/yr.; all types; 20-50 wds.
> **Columns/Departments:** MovieGuide; TravelGuide; VideoGuide; CDGuide, etc.; 1,200 wds.

($)MUTUALITY, 122 W. Franklin Ave., Ste. 218, Minneapolis MN 55404-2451. (612)872-6898. Fax (612)872-6891. E-mail: mutuality@cbeinternational.org. Website: www.cbeinter national.org. Christians for Biblical Equality. Jaime Hunt, ed. Seeks to provide inspiration, encouragement, and information about equality within the Christian church around the world. Quarterly mag.; 32 pgs.; circ. 2,200. Subscription $30/free to members & donors. 80% assigned freelance. Query/clips; fax/e-query OK. **PAYS A GIFT CERTIFICATE TO THEIR BOOKSTORE** on publication for 1st or electronic rts. Articles 500-2,500 wds. (12/yr.); book reviews 600 wds. Responds in 6 wks. Accepts reprints (tell when/where appeared). Accepts requested ms on disk or by e-mail (attached file). Regularly uses sidebars. Prefers NRSV, NIV, TNIV. Guidelines (also on Website); copy for 9x12 SAE/3 stamps. (Ads)

$+MY WALK WITH JESUS, PO Box 1483, Travelers Rest SC 29690. Phone/fax (864)834-4404. E-mail: james4436@charter.net. Website: www.christianlink.com/publish/mwwj. Nondenominational. James Ianbragulia, pub. Monthly newsletter; 16 pgs. Subscription $18. Estab. 2006. 30% unsolicited freelance; 70% assigned. Query; phone/fax/e-query OK. Pays $20 for one-time rts. Articles 1-2 pgs. (single-spaced). Responds in 1 wk. Seasonal 2 mos. ahead. Accepts simultaneous submissions & reprints. Accepts e-mail submissions (attached or copied into message). Prefers KJV. Accepts submissions from children/teens. Guidelines on Website; no copy.

$NATIONAL CATHOLIC REPORTER, 115 E. Armour Blvd., Kansas City MO 64111. (816)531-0538. Fax (816)968-2280. E-mail from Website: www.natcath.org. Catholic. Thomas Fox, pub.; Tom Roberts, ed-in-chief. Independent. Weekly (44X) & online newspaper; 44-48 pgs.; circ. 120,000. Query/clips. Pays .20/wd. on publication, or varying rates by agreement. Articles & short stories, varying lengths. Responds in up to 6 wks. Accepts simultaneous submissions. Guidelines (also by e-mail/Website); copy on Website.

Columns/Departments: Query with ideas for columns.

NETWORK, PO Box 131165, Birmingham AL 35213-6165. (205)328-7112. Website: www.networknewspaper.org. Interdenominational. Dolores Milazzo Hicks, ed./pub. (dolores@networknewspaper.org). To encourage and nurture dialog, understanding, and unity in Christian communities. Monthly tabloid; 12-16 pgs.; circ. 10,000. Subscription $18. 50% unsolicited freelance. Phone/fax/e-query OK. **NO PAYMENT.** Not copyrighted. Articles to 500 wds. Accepts simultaneous submissions. Articles and news.

Tips: "Most open to feature stories that express the unity of the body of Christ and articles that encourage and uplift our readers. We also cover state, local, national, and international news."

$THE NEW FREEMAN, One Bayard Dr., Saint John NB E2L 3L5, Canada. (506)653-6806. Fax (506)653-6818. E-mail: tnf@nbnet.nb.ca. Roman Catholic Diocese of St. John. Margie Trafton, ed. Weekly tabloid; 12 pgs.; circ. 7,300. Subscription $18.69 Cdn., $30 U.S. 70% unsolicited freelance; 30% assigned. Query/clips; phone/fax/e-query OK. Pays variable rates on publication. Not copyrighted. Articles about 200 wds. Seasonal 2 mos. ahead. Accepts simultaneous submissions & reprints (tell when/where appeared). Accepts requested ms on disk or by e-mail (attached/.txt format or copied into message). Kill fee. Uses some sidebars. No guidelines/copy. (Ads)

Tips: "We are very open to all sorts of freelance possibilities."

NEW FRONTIER, 180 E. Ocean Blvd., 4th Fl., Long Beach CA 90802. (562)491-8343. Fax (562)491-8791. E-mail from Website: www.salvationarmy.usawest.org/newfrontier. Salvation Army—Western Territory. Robert L. Docter, ed. To share the good news of the gospel and the work of The Salvation Army in the western territory with salvationists and friends. Biweekly newspaper; circ. 25,500. Subscription $10. Open to freelance. Prefers query. Not in topical listings. (Ads)

A NEW HEART, Box 4004, San Clemente CA 92674-4004. (949)496-7655. Fax (949)496-8465. E-mail: HCFUSA@juno.com. Website: www.HCFUSA.com. Aubrey Beauchamp, ed. For Christian healthcare givers; information regarding medical/Christian issues. Quarterly mag.; 16 pgs.; circ. 5,000. Subscription $25. 20% unsolicited freelance; 10% assigned. Complete ms/cover letter; phone/fax/e-query OK. **PAYS 2 COPIES** for one-time rts. Not copyrighted. Articles 600-1,800 wds. (20-25/yr.). Responds in 2-3 wks. Accepts simultaneous submissions & reprints. Accepts e-mail submission. Does not use sidebars. Guidelines (also by fax); copy for 9x12 SAE/3 stamps. (Ads)

Poetry: Accepts 1-2/yr. Submit max. 1-3 poems.

Fillers: Accepts 3-4/yr. Anecdotes, cartoons, facts, jokes, short humor; 100-120 wds.

Columns/Departments: Accepts 20-25/yr. Chaplain's Corner, 200-250 wds.; Physician's Corner, 200-250 wds.

Tips: "Most open to real-life situations which may benefit and encourage healthcare givers and patients. True stories with medical and evangelical emphasis."

$NEW WINESKINS, PO Box 41028, Nashville TN 37204-1028. (615)292-2940. Fax (615)292-2931. E-mail: gtaylor@woodmont.org. Website: www.wineskins.org. The ZOE Group, Inc. Greg Taylor, mng. ed. Combines biblical and cultural scholarly focus with popular-level articles and art for a powerful journal/magazine hybrid. Bimonthly e-zine; 15-20 articles/mo. Subscription $19.95 (online). 40% unsolicited freelance; 60% assigned. Query; e-query preferred. Pays $50-100 for online 2-3 mos. after publication for one-time and electronic rts. Articles 800-2,500 wds. (100/yr.); fiction 1,000-2,500 wds. (10/yr.); book reviews 800-1,200 wds. ($50-100). Responds in 6-8 wks. Seasonal 6 mos. ahead. Accepts simultaneous submissions & reprints (tell when/where appeared). Prefers e-mail submissions (attached or copied into message). No kill fee. Sometimes uses sidebars. Accept submissions from children or teens. Prefers NIV or NRSV. Guidelines by e-mail/Website; copy on Website. (Ads)

Poetry: Buys 4-5/yr. Avant-garde, free verse, light verse; 100-2,000 wds. Pays $50. Submit max. 1 poem.

Tips: "Best way to break in is by reviewing books, specifically ones we request. Also by writing well-shaped and well-researched pieces that are more than just opinions."

**This periodical was #47 on the 2005 Top 50 Christian Publishers list.

NOSTALGIA, 1703 N. Normandie St., Spokane WA 99205. (509)323-2086. Fax (509)323-2096. E-mail: mcarter@NostalgiaMagazine.us. Website: www.nostalgiamagazine.net. King's Publishing Group, Inc. Mark Carter, ed. We provide a forum for baby boomers and before to share photos and stories of yesterday that enrich life today; we use exclusively dated images/photos. Monthly mag.; 48 pgs. Subscription $24.95. Estab. 2004. 90% unsolicited freelance; 10% assigned. Complete ms/cover letter; e-query OK. **PAYS COPIES** on publication for 1st, one-time, reprint, simultaneous, or electronic rts. Articles 400-1,500 wds. (150/yr.). Responds in 8 wks. Seasonal 4 mos. ahead. Accepts simultaneous submissions & reprints (tell when/where appeared). Prefers e-mail submissions (attached or copied into message). No kill fee. Regularly uses sidebars. Guidelines (also by e-mail); query for themes/topics; copy $2/9x12 SAE. (Ads)

Poetry: Accepts 6-12/yr. Free verse, light verse, traditional; variable length. Pays in copies. Submit max. 1 poem. Send photo with poem.

Fillers: Accepts 25+/yr. Anecdotes, facts, games, jokes, short humor, tips, historic photos; 50-400 wds. Pays copies.

Columns/Departments: Buys 50+/yr. Old Recipes; Hitch-Hiking; Games We Used to Play; Historic Household Hints; Old Movie Reviews; Yesterday's Kitchen (old favorite recipes or household hints); all 400 wds.

Special Needs: Photos and family memories from 1940s and 1950s.

Tips: "Looking for personal family memories with interesting photos: traveling, camping, working together. Specific episodes are better than generalities (400-2,000 wds., 1 photo/400 wds.). No genealogies."

$NOW WHAT?, Box 33677, Denver CO 80233. (303)452-7973. Fax (303)452-0657. E-mail: bibleadvocate@cog7.org. Website: http://nowwhat.cog7.org. Church of God (Seventh-day). Calvin Burrell, ed.; Sherri Langton, assoc. ed. Articles on salvation, Jesus, social issues, life problems that are seeker sensitive. Monthly online mag.; available only online. 100% unsolicited freelance. Complete ms/cover letter; no query. Pays $25-55 on publication for first, one-time, electronic, simultaneous, and reprint rts. Articles 1,000-1,500 wds. (20/yr.).

Responds in 4-8 wks. Accepts simultaneous submissions & reprints (tell when/where appeared). Accepts requested ms on disk or by e-mail (copied into message). Regularly uses sidebars. Prefers NIV. Guidelines (also on Website); copy of online article for #10 SAE/1 stamp. (No ads)

Fillers: Buys 5-10/yr. Anecdotes, facts, prose, quotes; 50-100 wds.; $20.

Special Needs: "Personal experiences must still show a person's struggle that either brought him/her to Christ or deepened faith in God. The entire *Now What?* site is built around a personal experience each month."

Tips: "The whole e-zine is open to freelance. Think how you can explain your faith, or how you overcame a problem, to a non-Christian. It's a real plus for writers submitting a personal experience to also submit an objective article related to their story. Or they can contact Sherri Langton for upcoming personal experiences that need related articles."

NRB MAGAZINE, 9510 Technology Dr., Manassas VA 20110-4167. (703)330-7000. Fax (703)330-7100. E-mail: vfraedrich@nrb.org. Website: www.nrb.org. National Religious Broadcasters. V. Fraedrich, ed. Topics relate to Christian radio, television, satellite, church media, Internet, and all forms of communication; promoting access and excellence in Christian communications. Monthly (9X) & online mag.; 52 pgs.; circ. 9,300. Subscription $24; Canadians add $6 U.S.; foreign add $24 U.S. 70% unsolicited freelance. Complete ms/cover letter; fax/e-query OK. **PAYS 6 COPIES** ($100-200 for assigned) on publication for 1st or reprint rts. Articles 1,000-2,000 wds. (30/yr.). Responds in 6 wks. Seasonal 6 mos. ahead. Accepts simultaneous submissions & reprints (tell when/where appeared). Prefers accepted ms by e-mail. Regularly uses sidebars. Prefers NAS. Guidelines/theme list (also by e-mail); free copy. (Ads)

Columns/Departments: Valerie Fraedrich, asst. ed. Accepts 9/yr. Trade Talk (summary paragraphs of news items/events in Christian broadcasting), 50 wds.; Opinion (social issues), 750 wds. Columns coordinated in-house, 500 wds.

Special Needs: Electronic media; education. All articles must relate in some way to broadcasting: radio, TV, programs on radio/TV, or Internet.

Tips: "Most open to feature articles relevant to Christian communicators. Become acquainted with broadcasters in your area and note their struggles, concerns, and victories. Find out what they would like to know, research the topic, then write about it." Contact assistant editor for guidelines, reprint permission, classified ads, additional copies, etc.

$+ONEVOICE! (ONEvoice!), 1201 E. 5th St., Anderson IN 46012. (765)648-2202. E-mail: onevoice@chog.org. Website: www.onevoicemag.org. Church of God Ministries/Denominational. Steven Beverly, ed. Tells the stories of Church of God people, congregations, and ministries as they live out the love of Christ. Bimonthly mag.; 36 pgs. 80% unsolicited freelance; 20% assigned. Query or complete ms/cover letter; phone/e-query OK. Pays .20/printed wd. on publication for 1st rts. Articles 1,000-1,500 wds. (60/yr.). Responds in 9 wks. No simultaneous submissions or reprints. Prefers e-mail submissions (attached file). Kill fee $50 (sometimes). Uses some sidebars. Prefers NIV. Guidelines by e-mail/Website; copy for 9x12 SAE/$1.25 postage. (Ads)

Columns/Departments: Buys 60/yr. ONEstory (COG ministry organizations at work), 1,500-2,000 wds.; ONElife (COG individuals living out the love of Christ), 1,500-2,000 wds.; ONEbody (stories of unity in COG), 1,500-2,000 wds.; SPIRIT & Truth (worship stories in the COG), 1,000-1,500 wds.; OUTreach (Evangelism stories in the COG), 1,000-1,500 wds.; MASTERclass (discipleship stories in the COG), 1,000-1,500 wds.; WORKSHOP (equipping people for ministry in the COG), 1,000-1,500 wds.

Tips: "The features (ONEstory, ONElife, and ONEbody) and the departments (SPIRIT & truth, OUTreach, WORKSHOP, and MASTERclass) are all open to freelancers."

$ON MISSION, 4200 North Point Pkwy., Alpharetta GA 30022-4176. (770)410-6382. Fax (770)410-6105. E-mail: onmission@namb.net. Website: www.onmission.com. North American Mission Board, Southern Baptist. Carol Pipes, ed. Helping readers share Christ in the real world. Quarterly & online mag.; 64 pgs.; circ. 100,000. Subscription $14.95. 1-5% unsolicited freelance; 50-60% assigned. Query/clips; no phone/fax query; e-query OK. Pays .25/wd. on acceptance for 1st rts. Articles 600-1,800 wds. (20/yr.). Responds in 8 wks. Seasonal 8 mos. ahead. Accepts simultaneous submissions; no reprints. Accepts e-mail submission (attached and copied into message). Kill fee. Regularly uses sidebars. Prefers NIV. Guidelines (also on Website); copy for 9x12 SAE/$1.95 postage. (Ads)

> **Special Needs:** Needs articles on these topics: sharing Christ, starting churches, volunteering in missions, sending missionaries, impacting the culture, and equipping leaders.
>
> **Tips:** "We are primarily a Southern Baptist publication reaching out to Southern Baptist pastors and lay people, equipping them to share Christ, start churches, volunteer in missions, and impact the culture. Write a solid, 750-word, how-to article geared to 20- to 40-year-old men and women who want fresh ideas and insight into sharing Christ in the real world in which they live, work, and play. Send a résumé, along with your best writing samples. We are an on-assignment magazine, but occasionally a well-written manuscript gets published."
>
> **2005 EPA Award of Merit—Most Improved Publication.

$OUR SUNDAY VISITOR, 200 Noll Plaza, Huntington IN 46750. (260)356-8400. Fax (260)359-9117. E-mail: oursunvis@osv.com. Website: www.osv.com. Catholic. Gerald Korson, ed. Vital news analysis, perspective, spirituality for today's Catholic. Weekly newspaper; 24 pgs.; circ. 68,000. 10% unsolicited freelance; 90% assigned. Query or complete ms; fax/e-query OK. Pays $100-300 on acceptance for 1st & electronic rts. Articles to 1,100 wds. (25/yr.). Responds in 6 wks. Seasonal 2 mos. ahead. No simultaneous submissions; rarely accepts reprints (tell when/where appeared). Kill fee. Regularly uses sidebars. Prefers RSV. Guidelines (also by e-mail/Website); copy for 10x13 SASE. (Ads)

> **Columns/Departments:** Faith; Family; Trends; Profile; Heritage; Media; Q & A. See guidelines for details.
>
> **Tips:** "Our mission is to examine the news, culture, and trends of the day from a faithful and sound Catholic perspective—to see the world through the eyes of faith."
>
> **This periodical was #14 on the 2005 Top 50 Christian Publishers list.

$OVER THE BACK FENCE, PO Box 756, Chillicothe OH 45601. (740)772-2165. Fax (740)773-7626. E-mail: backfenc@bright.net. Website: www.pantherpublishing.com. Panther Publishing, Inc. Sarah Williamson, mng. ed. Positive news about Southern Ohio. Quarterly mag.; 64 pgs.; circ. 15,000. Subscription $9.97. 60% unsolicited freelance. Query/clips; fax/e-query OK. Pays .10-.20/wd. on publication for one-time rts. Articles 750-1,000 wds. (9-12/yr.); fiction 300-850 wds. (4/yr.). Responds in 13 wks. Seasonal 1 yr. ahead. Accepts simultaneous submissions & reprints (tell when/where appeared). Requires requested ms on disk or by e-mail (copied into message). Regularly uses sidebars. Guidelines (also on Website); copy $4/9x12 SAE, or on Website. (Ads)

> **Poetry:** Buys 4/yr. Free verse, light verse, traditional; 1 pg.; $25 min. Submit max. 5 poems.
>
> **Columns/Departments:** Buys 10-20/yr. Profiles From the Past (interesting history that never made the headlines), 800-1,000 wds.; Heartstrings (touching essays), 800 wds.; Shorts (humorous essays), 800 wds. Complete ms. Pays $80-120.
>
> **Special Needs:** Think upbeat and positive. Articles on nature, history, travel, nostalgia, and family.
>
> **Tips:** "We need material for our columns most often—Humor, Profiles from the Past, and Heartstrings. It is best for writers to send things with appeal for Midwest readers and be generally positive. We do not publish articles that criticize or create a negative feeling about a geographical area or people."

$PALM BEACH CONSERVATIVE—See *Home Times Family Newspaper.*

+PARABLES, 1400 E. 35th St., #61, Texarkana AR 71854. (870)772-4983. Fax (870)216-2687. E-mail: editors@parablesmag.com. Website: www.parablesmag.com. Nondenominational. Rosalind Morris, ed./pres. Dedicated to showcasing stellar works of Christian fiction. Bimonthly online mag.; 80-90 pgs. Subscription $18. Estab. 2004. 100% unsolicited free-lance. Complete ms by e-mail (attached file); put genre in subject line. **PAYS ONE COPY** for rights for 1 publication yr. Fiction 1,500-5,000 wds. (36/yr.) Responds in 3-5 wks. Accepts reprints (tell when/where appeared). Guidelines on Website; copy $3.50. (Ads)

$#PARABOLA: Myth, Tradition, and the Search for Meaning, 135 E. 15th St., New York NY 10003-3557. (212)505-9037. Fax (212)979-7325. E-mail: editors@parabola.org, or parabola@panix.com. Website: www.parabola.org. The Society for the Study of Myth and Tradition. Natalie Baan, mng. ed. Devoted to the exploration of the search for meaning as expressed in the myths, symbols, rituals, and art of the world's religious traditions. Quar-terly jour.; 144 pgs.; circ. 40,000. Subscription $24. 60% unsolicited freelance; 40% assigned. Query; fax/e-query OK. Pays $150-400 on publication for 1st, one-time, or reprint rts. Articles 1,000-3,000 wds. (40/yr.); book/video reviews 500-700 wds., $75. Responds in 12 wks. Accepts simultaneous submissions & reprints (tell when/where appeared). Accepts e-mail submissions after query (attached file or copied into message). Kill fee varies. Uses some sidebars. Prefers KJV. Guidelines/theme list (also by e-mail/Web-site); copy $7.50. (Ads)

> **Columns/Departments:** Buys 40/yr. Reviews (books, audios, videos, software), to 700 wds.; Epicycles (retellings of traditional stories), to 1,500 wds.; $75-150.
>
> **Tips:** "All submissions must relate to themes. We look for well-researched, well-written, and authentic material that strikes a balance between the personal and the objective. No journalistic or self-improvement articles, evangelism, or profiles of specific persons or organizations. No witnessing, no pieces solely focused on Christianity as the only religious truth. We are a multifaith journal and seek reflections on the truths that underlie all forms of religious and spiritual search. Visit our hints page at www.parabola.org/hints.html, for suggestions."

$PARENTLIFE, One Lifeway Plaza, Nashville TN 37234-0172. (615)251-2021. Fax (615)277-8142. E-mail: parentlife@lifeway.com. Website: www.lifeway.com. LifeWay Christian Resources. William Summey, ed-in-chief. A child-centered magazine for parents of children 12 and under. Monthly mag.; 52 pgs.; circ. 100,000. Subscription $22.65. 5% unsolicited freelance; 95% assigned. Query; e-query OK. Pays on publication for nonexclusive rts. Arti-cles 1,000 wds. Responds in 8 wks. Seasonal 1 yr. ahead. Accepts simultaneous submis-sions; no reprints. Accepts e-mail submissions (attached file). No kill fee. Regularly uses sidebars. Accepts submissions from children. Prefers HCSB. Guidelines (also by e-mail); copy for 10x13 SASE. (No ads)

> **Columns/Departments:** Buys 60/yr. The Funny Life (funny family stories), 100 wds.; $20. Complete ms.
>
> **Tips:** "Most open to a feature article with cutting edge approach to current issues affecting parents/children."

#PARENTS & TEENS. E-mail: submissions@parentsandteens.com. Website: www.parentsand teens.com. Lyn Gregory, ed./pub. (lyngregory@ntlworld.com). To help parents connect with their teens. Biweekly e-zine; 20 pgs.; circ. 10,000. Subscription free. 10% unsolicited freelance. E-mail submissions only. Accepts full ms by e-mail. **PAYS IN COPIES AND LINK TO YOUR WEBSITE/BIO OR E-BOOKS** for 1st, one-time, reprint, or electronic rts. Articles 400-1,200 wds. (12/yr.); reviews 500 wds. ($5). Responds in 1-2 wks. Sea-sonal 3 mos. ahead. Accepts simultaneous submissions & reprints (tell when/where appeared). Prefers e-mail submission (copied into message). Does not use sidebars.

Accepts submissions from teens. Guidelines on Website; copy on site archive. (Ads)
Special Needs: Parenting teens and frugal living. Also articles from dads of teens.
Tips: "Query by e-mail."

$PEEKS & VALLEYS: A Fiction Journal, 702 S. Twyckenham Dr., South Bend IN 46615.
E-mail: editor@peeksandvalleys.com. Website: www.peeksandvalleys.com. Brink Publications. Meagan Church, ed. Literary magazine of short stories. Quarterly mag. 100% freelance.
Complete ms by e-mail only. Pays $5 on publication for one-time rts. Fiction to 2,600 wds.
Responds in 3 mos. Accepts simultaneous submissions & reprints, if indicated. Copy $5.75.
   Poetry: Buys 8/yr. Light verse, traditional; to 30 lines. Submit max. 2 poems.
   Special Needs: "We seek writing that leaves an impression and has a purpose—however tangible that may be."
   Tips: "Review a sample copy before submitting. No sci-fi, fantasy, recipes, interview/profiles, sex, or profanity."

THE PEGASUS REVIEW, PO Box 88, Henderson MD 21640-0088. (410)482-6736. E-mail: bounds1@comcast.net. Art Bounds, ed. Theme-oriented poetry, short fiction, and essays; not necessarily religious; in calligraphy format. Bimonthly mag.; 10-12 pgs.; circ. 125.
Subscription $12. 100% unsolicited freelance. Query or complete ms/cover letter; e-query OK. **PAYS 2 COPIES** for one-time rts. Fiction 2.5 pgs. is ideal, single-spaced (6-10/yr.); also one-page essays. Responds in 4-5 wks. Seasonal 2 mos. ahead. Accepts simultaneous submissions & reprints (tell when/where appeared). No disk or e-mail submissions. Does not use sidebars. Prefers KJV. Accepts submissions from teens. Guidelines/theme list (also by e-mail); copy $2.50. (No ads)
   Poetry: Accepts 100/yr. Any type; 4-25 lines (shorter the better—pay attention to line length). Theme oriented. Submit max. 3 poems.
   Fillers: Accepts 10-20/yr. Cartoons, prose, essays; 100-150 wds.
   Special Needs: 2006 themes: Jan/Feb—Discovery; Mar/Apr—Books; May/Jun—Family; Jul/Aug—Age/Youth; Sep/Oct—Earth; and Nov/Dec—Perseverance.
   Tips: "Don't talk about that book, poem, or play you are planning to write. Do it! And once written, keep that submission circulating. Perseverance will eventually be worth the effort."

PENTECOSTAL MESSENGER, PO Box 850, Joplin MO 64802. Toll-free (800)444-4674.
(417)624-7050. Fax (417)624-7102 or (800)982-5687. E-mail: johnm@pcg.org. Website: www.pcg.org. Denominational/Pentecostal Church of God. John Mallinak, ed. Monthly (11X) mag.; circ. 5,000. Subscription $12. Accepts freelance. Prefers query. Complete ms. Articles and reviews. Copy $1.50. Not in topical listings. No questionnaire returned. (Ads)

THE PENWOOD REVIEW, PO Box 862, Los Alamitos CA 90720-0862. E-mail: penwood review@charter.net. Website: http://webpages.charter.net/penwoodreview/penwood .htm. Lori Cameron, ed. Poetry, plus thought-provoking essays on poetry, literature, and the role of spirituality and religion in the literary arts. Biannual jour.; 40+ pgs.; circ. 50-100.
Subscription $12. 99% unsolicited freelance; 1% assigned. Complete ms (February 25 & August 25 deadlines); no e-query. **NO PAYMENT** ($2 off subscription & 1 free copy), for one-time and electronic rts. Articles 2 pgs. Responds in 9-12 wks. Accepts requested ms on disk or by e-mail (copied into message). Guidelines (also by e-mail/Website); copy $6.
   Poetry: Accepts 100-120/yr. Avant-garde, free verse, traditional; to 2 pgs. Submit max. 5 poems.
   Special Needs: Faith and the literary arts; religion and literature. Needs essays (up to 2 pages, single spaced).
   Tips: "We publish poetry almost exclusively and are looking for well-crafted, disciplined poetry, not doggerel or greeting-card-style poetry. Poets should study poetry, read it extensively, and send us their best, most original work. Visit our Website or buy a copy for an idea of what we publish."

PERSPECTIVES: A Journal of Reformed Thought, PO Box 1196, Holland MI 49422-1196. (616)392-8555. Fax (616)392-7717. E-mail: perspectives@rca.org. Website: www .perspectivesjournal.org. Reformed Church Press. Dr. Scott Hoezee, Dr. David Timmer, and Dr. James Bratt, eds. To express the Reformed faith theologically; to engage issues that Reformed Christians meet in personal, ecclesiastical, and societal life; and thus to contribute to the mission of the church of Jesus Christ. Monthly & online mag.; 24 pgs.; circ. 3,000. Subscription $30. 75% unsolicited freelance; 25% assigned. Complete ms/cover letter or query; fax/e-query OK. **PAYS 6 COPIES** for 1st rts. Articles (10/yr.) and fiction (3/yr.), 2,500-3,000 wds.; reviews 1,000 wds. Responds in 20 wks. Seasonal 10 mos. ahead. Accepts reprints (tell when/where appeared). Prefers requested ms by e-mail (attached file). Uses some sidebars. Prefers NRSV. Guidelines on Website; no copy. (Ads)

> **Poetry:** Accepts 2-3/yr. Traditional. Submit max. 3 poems.
>
> **Columns/Departments:** Accepts 12/yr. As We See It (editorial/opinion), 750-1,500 wds.; Inside Out (biblical exegesis), 750 wds. Complete ms.
>
> **Tips:** "I would say that a reading of past issues and a desire to join in a contemporary conversation on the Christian faith would help you break in here."

+PIETISTEN ONLINE, 3232—47th Ave. S., Minneapolis MN 55406. E-mail: pietist@mtn.org. Website: www.pietisten.org. Pietisten, Inc. Phil Johnson, mng. ed. Takes its inspiration and design from the newspaper of the same name that was published is Sweden during the 19th and early 20th centuries. Print and online newspaper. Subscription $10/3 issues. Incomplete topical listings. No questionnaire returned.

> **Poetry:** Bruce Carlson, poetry ed.
>
> **Tips:** "We base our format on what were regular and frequent elements of the original Pietisten: commentaries on the lectionary texts by Luther, Rosenius, Waldenstrom, and others; ecclesiastical concerns; theological discussions; hymns; poetry; and selected news items. We welcome your participation and responses to any and all articles."

$+PLAINS FAITH MAGAZINE, PO Box 52407, Amarillo TX 79159. (806)857-2350. Fax (806)857-2350. E-mail: plainsfaith@amaonline.com. Website: www.plainsfaith.com. Wellsaid Publications. Debra Wells, pub. Features the people, places, and events of the High Plains region, from Southwestern Kansas to the South Texas Panhandle, from eastern New Mexico to Oklahoma. Quarterly mag. Estab. 2003. 10% unsolicited freelance; 90% assigned. Query; e-query OK. Pays .05/wd. on publication for 1st rts. Not copyrighted. Articles 2,000 wds. (5/yr.); reviews 50 wds.($20). Responds in 4 wks. Seasonal 5 mos. ahead. Accepts reprints (tell when/where appeared). Accepts submissions by e-mail (copied into message). No kill fee. Regularly uses sidebars. Any Bible version. Guidelines by e-mail or Website; copy for 9x12 SAE/$2 postage. (Ads)

> **Columns/Departments:** Buys 5/yr. Last, Best Lesson (Sunday school teachers—preferable from the High Plains region—talk about their favorite lessons), 1,000 wds. Pays .05/wd. Query.
>
> **Special Needs:** Stories and articles from the region.
>
> **Tips:** "We're looking for writers who will take the initiative to get out and interview people for high-interest feature articles."

$THE PLAIN TRUTH, 300 W. Green St., Pasadena CA 91129. (626)304-6181. Fax (626)304-8172. E-mail: laura.urista@ptm.org. Website: www.ptm.org. Plain Truth Ministries. Greg Albrecht, ed.; submit to Laura Urista, asst. ed. Proclaims Christianity without the religion, emphasizing the central, main and plain, core teachings of historic Christianity. Bimonthly mag.; 32 pgs.; circ. 95,000. Subscription free (1 yr.) in U.S. & Canada; Intl. $29.95. 10% unsolicited freelance; 90% assigned. Query only; fax/e-query OK. Pays .25/wd.(.15/wd. for reprints) on publication for 1st, one-time, reprint, or world (all languages) rts. Articles 750-2,500 wds., prefers 800-1,200 wds. (48-50/yr.); fiction. Responds in 4-6 wks. Seasonal 6 mos. ahead. Accepts simultaneous submissions & reprints (tell when/where appeared). Requires requested ms on disk or by e-mail (attached or copied into message). Kill fee $50. Regularly uses sidebars. Prefers NIV. Guidelines (also by e-mail/Website); copy for 9x12 SAE/5 stamps. (Ads)

Columns/Departments: Buys 18/yr. Family (family issues), 1,500 wds.; Commentary (hot topic editorials), 550-650 wds.

Tips: "Most open to articles. Best to send tear sheets of previously published articles, and submit detailed query for standard articles."

**This periodical was #29 on the 2005 Top 50 Christian Publishers list (#39 in 2004, #26 in 2003, #12 in 2002, #22 in 2001).

THE PLOWMAN, Box 414, Whitby ON L1N 5S4, Canada. (905)668-7803. The Plowman Ministries/Christian. Tony Scavetta, ed./pub. Poetry and prose of social commentary; any topics. Annual newsletter; 20 pgs.; circ. 5,000. Subscription $10 U.S. 100% unsolicited freelance. Query; phone query OK. **NO PAYMENT.** Articles (10/yr.) & fiction (50/yr.), 1,000 wds. Responds in 2-4 wks. Accepts simultaneous submissions & reprints. No disk. Does not use sidebars. Free guidelines/copy for 9x12 SAE. (Ads)

Poetry: Accepts 100/yr. All types; to 38 lines (55 characters across max.). Submit max. 4 poems.

Fillers: Accepts 25/yr. Cartoons, prayers, short humor; 25-30 wds.

Special Needs: Also publishes chapbooks; 20% royalties.

Contest: Sponsors monthly poetry contests; $2/poem entry fee.

Tips: "All sections open, especially poetry and short stories. Send in submissions for review."

$+POETRY SCOUT, PO Box 325, Cedar Park TX 78613. (512)528-8170. Fax (603)309-0782. E-mail: director@poetryscout-centreministry.com. Website: www.poetryscout-centreministry .com. Poetry Scout–Centre Ministry. Tommy Lee Means, ministry dir. Seeking Christian inspirational poetry writers to share in a partnership book publishing contract. Poetry only. (Ads only as Website links)

Poetry: Accepts 10 pages per poet per publishing contract; ten pages of theme-oriented poetry, quotes, and elaborating thoughts. Free verse or traditional (theme oriented); up to 32 lines/poem. Payment is based on contractual agreement with affiliated publisher, and within a partnership cost-share plan.

$*PORTLAND MAGAZINE: The University of Portland Quarterly, 5000 N. Willamette Blvd., Portland OR 97203. Catholic. Brian Doyle, ed. University of Portland news, issues, and concerns; spirituality issues (especially Catholic). Quarterly mag.; circ. 28,000. 70% unsolicited freelance. Query/clips or complete ms. Pays $100-500 on publication for 1st rts. Articles 1,000-3,000 wds. (6/yr.). Responds in 5 wks. Seasonal 8 mos. ahead. Free guidelines/copy. Incomplete topical listings.

$POSITIVE THINKING: Finding Joy & Fulfillment Every Day, 66 E. Main St., Pauling NY 12564. (845)855-5000. Fax (845)855-1036. E-mail: PPlaneta@guideposts.org. Website: www.guideposts.org. Guideposts. Patricia Planeta, ed. Spiritually oriented, based on positive thinking and faith. Monthly (10X) mag.; 36 pgs.; circ. 400,000. Subscription $10. 30% unsolicited freelance. Query preferred; phone/fax/e-query OK. Pays $75/pg. on publication for one-time rts. Articles 500-2,300 wds. (8/yr.). Responds in 3-4 wks. Seasonal 6 mos. ahead. Accepts reprints. Accepts submissions by e-mail. Does not use sidebars. Guidelines; copy for #10 SAE/1 stamp.

Special Needs: Contemporary heroes; overcoming (addiction, etc.) through faith. (1) Life-changing experiences that bring about faith in Jesus Christ. (2) Ways to improve prayer and spiritual life. (3) How positive thinking and faith provide answers to life's problems.

Tips: "Most open to true stories of finding faith through difficult circumstances. Avoid preachiness. How-tos (if applicable), stories (nonfiction only) that touch the heart and soul. Have a deep, living knowledge of Christianity. Our audience is 65-70% female, average age is 55."

$POWER FOR LIVING, 4050 Lee Vance View, Colorado Springs CO 809118. Toll-free (800)708-5550. (719)536-0100. Fax (719)535-2928. Website: www.cookministries.org. Cook Communications/Scripture Press Publications. Don Alban Jr., ed. To expressly demonstrate the relevance of specific biblical teachings to everyday life via reader-captivating profiles of exceptional Christians. Weekly take-home paper; 8 pgs.; circ. 250,000. Subscription $12. 15% unsolicited freelance; 85% assigned. Complete ms; no phone/fax/e-query. Pays up to .175/wd. (reprints up to .10/wd.) on acceptance for 1st rts. Profiles 700-1,500 wds. (20/yr.). Responds in 10 wks. Seasonal 1 yr. ahead. Accepts simultaneous submissions & reprints (tell when/where appeared). Accepts requested ms on disk. Kill fee. Requires KJV. Guidelines/copy for #10 SAE/1 stamp. (No ads)

   Special Needs: Third-person profiles of truly out-of-the-ordinary Christians who express their faith uniquely. We use very little of anything else.

   Tips: "Most open to vignettes, 450-1,500 wds., of prominent Christians with solid testimonies or profiles from church history. Focus on the unusual. Signed releases required."

$PRAIRIE MESSENGER: Catholic Journal, PO Box 190, Muenster SK S0K 2Y0, Canada. (306)682-1772. Fax (306)682-5285. E-mail: pm.editor@stpeters.sk.ca. Website: www.stpeters.sk.ca/prairie_messenger. Catholic/Benedictine Monks of St. Peter's Abbey. Peter Novecosky, OSB, ed.; Maureen Weber, assoc. ed. For Catholics in Saskatchewan and Manitoba, and Christians in other faith communities. Weekly tabloid (46X); 20 pgs.; circ. 7,300. Subscription $29.50 Cdn. 10% unsolicited freelance; 90% assigned. Complete ms/cover letter; phone/fax/e-query OK. Pays $50-60 ($2.75/column inch for news items) on publication for 1st, one-time, simultaneous, and reprint rts. Not copyrighted. Articles 800-900 or 2,500 wds. (15/yr.). Responds in 9 wks. Seasonal 3 mos. ahead. Accepts simultaneous submissions & reprints. Regularly uses sidebars. Guidelines (also by e-mail/Website); copy for 9x12 SAE/$1 Cdn./$1.29 U.S. (Ads)

   Poetry: Accepts 30/yr. Avant-garde, free verse, haiku, light verse; 4-30 lines. Pays $20 Cdn.

   Columns/Departments: Accepts 5/yr. Pays $50.

   Special Needs: Ecumenism; social justice; native concerns.

   Tips: "Comment/feature section is most open; send good reflection column of about 800 words; topic of concern or interest to *Prairie* readership. It's difficult to break into our publication."

   **This periodical was selected #1 for general excellence by the Canadian Church Press (10 times during the last 16 years).

THE PRAYER CLOSET, 595 Stratton Rd., Decatur, MS 39327. (601)635-2180. Fax (601)635-4025. E-mail: prayer@prayerclosetministries.org. Website: www.prayerclosetministries .org. Dr. Kevin Meador, ed. Challenges and equips believers in the area of prayer, fasting, spiritual warfare, journaling, and healing. Monthly newsletter; circ. 3,000. Free subscription. **PAYS IN COPIES.** Prefers NKJV. Guidelines.

   Tips: "We are looking for sound, biblically based articles concerning the above-listed topics."

PRAYERWORKS, PO Box 301363, Portland OR 97294. (503)761-2072. E-mail: VannM1@aol.com. Website: www.prayerworksnw.org. The Masters Work. V. Ann Mandeville, ed. For prayer warriors in retirement centers; focuses on prayer. Weekly newspaper and online (soon); 4 pgs.; circ. 1,000. Subscription free. 100% unsolicited freelance. Complete ms. **PAYS IN COPIES/SUBSCRIPTION** for one-time rts. Not copyrighted. Articles (30-40/yr.) & fiction (30/yr.); 300-500 wds. Responds in 3 wks. Seasonal 2 mos. ahead. Accepts simultaneous submissions & reprints. Does not use sidebars. Guidelines; copy for #10 SAE/1 stamp. (No ads)

Poetry: Accepts 20-30/yr. Free verse, haiku, light verse, traditional. Submit max. 10 poems.
Fillers: Accepts up to 50/yr. Facts, jokes, prayers, quotes, short humor; to 50 wds.
Tips: "Write tight and well. Half our audience is over 70, but 30% is young families. Subject matter isn't important as long as it is scriptural and designed to help people pray. Have a strong, catchy take-away."

$PRECEPTS FOR LIVING UMI, Annual Sunday School Commentary, PO Box 436987, Chicago IL 60643. Toll-free (800)860-8642. Fax (708)868-7105. Website: www.urbanministries .com. Urban Ministries, Inc. K. Hall, mng. ed. *Precepts for Living* is a verse-by-verse Sunday School commentary geared toward an African American adult audience. Word studies are presented in the original Greek and Hebrew languages to further illuminate understanding of the text. KJV Scriptures. 500 pgs. $16.95 complete with an enhanced CD-ROM Bible study tool for interactive learning. The CD-ROM contains electronic versions of the New Living Translation Bible, *Strong's Concordance, Strong's Greek and Hebrew Dictionary,* and other helpful resources including a video tutorial feature. Strict adherence to guidelines. Query/clips; fax/e-query OK. Pays $200 per Bible Study lesson and $250 per verse-by-verse commentary which includes Greek and Hebrew word studies, 120 days after acceptance, for all rts. Requires accepted ms on disk.

THE PRESBYTERIAN OUTLOOK, Box 85623, Richmond VA 23285-5623. Toll-free (800)446-6008. (804)359-8442. Fax (804)353-6369. E-mail: editor@pres-outlook.com. Website: www.pres-outlook.com. Presbyterian Church (USA)/Independent. O. Benjamin Sparks, interim ed.; Randy Harris, book review ed. For ministers, members, and staff of the denomination. Weekly (43X) mag.; 16-40 pgs.; circ. 10,000. Subscription $39.95. 5% unsolicited freelance; 95% assigned. Query; phone/fax/e-query OK. **NO PAYMENT** for all rts. Not copyrighted. Articles to 1,000 wds.; book reviews 1 pg. Responds in 1-2 wks. Seasonal 2 mos. ahead. Requires requested ms on disk; accepts e-mail submissions. Uses some sidebars. Prefers NRSV. Guidelines (also by e-mail); free copy. (Ads)
  Tips: "Correspond (mail or e-mail) with editor regarding current needs; most open to features. Most material is commissioned; anything submitted should be of interest to Presbyterian church leaders."

$PRESBYTERIANS TODAY, 100 Witherspoon St., Louisville KY 40202-1396. Toll-free (888)728-7228, ext. 5637. (502)569-5637. Fax (502)569-8632. E-mail: today@pcusa .org. Website: www.pcusa.org/today. Presbyterian Church (U.S.A.). Eva Stimson, ed.; John Sniffen, assoc. ed. Denominational; not as conservative or evangelical as some. Monthly (10X) mag.; 48 pgs.; circ. 58,000. Subscription $19.95. 65% unsolicited freelance. Query or complete ms/cover letter; phone/fax/e-query OK. Pays $75-300 on acceptance for 1st rts. Articles 800-2,000 wds. (prefers 1,000-1,500). (20/yr.). Also uses short features 250-600 wds. Responds in 5 wks. Seasonal 3 mos. ahead. Few reprints. Accepts requested ms on disk or by e-mail. Prefers NRSV. Guidelines (also by e-mail/Website: www.pcusa.org/ today/guidelines/guidelines.htm); free copy. (Ads)
  Fillers: Cartoons, $25; and short humor to 150 wds., no payment.
  Tips: "Most open to feature articles about Presbyterians—individuals, churches with special outreach, creative programs, or mission work. Do not often use inspirational or testimony-type articles."
  ****This periodical was #32 on the 2005 Top 50 Christian Publishers list (#32 in 2004, #27 in 2003).

$PRIORITY!, 440 W. Nyack Rd., West Nyack NY 10994. (845)620-7450. Fax (845)620-7223. E-mail: linda_johnson@use.salvationarmy.org. Website: www.prioritypeople.org. The Salvation Army. Linda D. Johnson, ed.; Robert Mitchell, assoc. ed. Quarterly & online mag.; 48-56 pgs.; circ. 27,000. Subscription $6.95. 50% assigned. Query/clips; e-query OK. Pays $200-800 on acceptance for 1st rts. Articles 400-1,700 wds. (8-10/yr.). All articles assigned. Responds in 2 wks. Occasionally buys reprints (tell when/where appeared). Prefers accepted ms by e-mail (in Word or copied into message). Kill fee 50%. Regularly uses sidebars. Prefers NIV. Occasionally buys submissions from children/teens. Guidelines/theme list by e-mail; copy $1/9x12 SAE. (Ads from nonprofits only)

> **Columns/Departments:** Buys 5-10/yr. Prayer Power (stories about answered prayer, or harnessing prayer power); Who's News (calling attention to specific accomplishments or missions); Q & A (answers to current questions); all 400-700 wds.; $200-400. Query.
>
> **Special Needs:** All articles must have a connection to The Salvation Army. Can be from any part of the U.S. Looking especially for freelancers with Salvation Army connections. Christmas recollections.
>
> **Tips:** "Most open to features on people. Every articles, whether about people or programs, tells a story. Stories focus on evangelism, holiness, prayer. The more a writer knows about The Salvation Army, the better. We are interested in finding a group of freelancers we can assign to specific features."

PRISCILLA PAPERS, 122 W. Franklin Ave., Ste. 218, Minneapolis MN 55404-2451. (612)872-6898. Fax (612)872-6891. E-mail: mdinkler@stanfordalumni.org. Website: www.cbeinternational.org. Christians for Biblical Equality. William D. Spencer, ed. Addresses biblical interpretation and its relationship to gender, race/ethnicity, economic class, and age issues in the society, the Christian community, and the family. Quarterly jour.; 32 pgs.; circ. 2,000. Subscription $30. 85% unsolicited freelance; 15% assigned. Query preferred; fax/e-query OK. **PAYS 3 COPIES, PLUS A FREE BOOK** for 1st & electronic rts. Articles 600-5,000 wds.; book review 600 wds (free book). Responds in 4 wks. Seasonal 3 mos. ahead. Accepts simultaneous submissions & reprints (tell when/where appeared). Prefers accepted ms on disk or by e-mail (attached file). No kill fee. Uses some sidebars. Prefers NIV, TNIV, NRSV. Guidelines on Website; copy for 9x12 SAE/$1.06 postage. (Ads)

> **Poetry:** Accepts 1/yr. Avant-garde, free verse, traditional; pays a free book.
>
> **Tips:** "All sections are open to freelancers. Any article presenting a solid exegetical and hermeneutical approach to biblical equality will be considered for publication."

$PRISM: America's Alternative Evangelical Voice, 10 E. Lancaster Ave., Wynnewood PA 19096-3495. (610)645-9390. Fax (610)649-8090. E-mail: prism@esa-online.org, or kristyn@esa-online.org. Website: www.esa-online.org. Evangelicals for Social Action. Kristyn Komarnicki, ed. For Christians who are interested in the social and political dimensions of the gospel. Bimonthly mag.; 40 pgs.; circ. 9,000. Subscription $35. 25% unsolicited freelance. Query/clips; fax/e-query OK. Pays to $200, 6 wks. after publication for 1st or reprint rts. Articles 500-2,800 wds. (10-12/yr.); no fiction; book/video reviews, 500 wds., $0-100. Responds in 2-9 wks. Seasonal 6 mos. ahead. Accepts reprints (tell when/where appeared). Prefers requested ms on disk. Regularly uses sidebars. Prefers NRSV. Guidelines; copy $3. (Ads)

> **Tips:** "Looking for analysis on religious right; social justice fiction. Understand progressive evangelicals and E.S.A. Read Tony Campolo, Ron Sider, and Richard Foster. Most open to features."

$PSYCHOLOGY FOR LIVING, 250 W. Colorado Blvd., Ste. 200, Arcadia CA 91007. (626)821-8400. Fax (626)821-8409. E-mail: rwi@ncfliving.org. Website: www.ncfliving.org. Narramore Christian Foundation. Dick Innes, ed. Addresses issues of everyday life from a Christian and psychological viewpoint. Quarterly mag.; 8 pgs. (one issue 24 pgs.); circ. 7,000. Subscription for $20 donation. Open to freelance. Complete ms/cover letter; fax OK, e-query preferred. Pays $75-200, plus a subscription, on publication for 1st, one-time, or reprint rts. Articles 1,000-1,700 wds. Responds in 2-4 wks. Seasonal 4 mos. ahead. Accepts reprints (tell when/where appeared). Prefers accepted ms by e-mail (attached file). Uses some sidebars. Prefers NIV. Guidelines (also by e-mail); free copy. (No ads)

Tips: "Tell a story or illustration that tells how a psychological/emotional problem was dealt with in a biblical and psychologically sound manner. Not preachy."

$PURPOSE, 616 Walnut Ave., Scottdale PA 15683-1999. (574)537-0891. Fax (724)887-3111. E-mail: Horsch@mph.org. Website: www.mph.org. Mennonite Publishing Network. James E. Horsch, ed. Denominational, for older youth and adults. Weekly take-home paper; 8 pgs.; circ. 9,000. Subscription $21.20. 95% unsolicited freelance; 5% assigned. Complete ms (only)/cover letter; e-mail submissions preferred. Pays up to .06/wd. on acceptance for one-time rts. Articles & fiction, to 700 wds. (70/yr.). Responds in 13 wks. Seasonal 6 mos. ahead. Accepts simultaneous submissions & reprints (tell when/where appeared). Regularly uses sidebars. Guidelines (also by e-mail); copy $2/6x9 SAE/2 stamps. (No ads)

Poetry: Buys 130/yr. Free verse, light verse, traditional; 3-12 lines; up to $2/line ($7.50-20). Submit max. 10 poems.

Fillers: Buys 80/yr. Anecdotes, cartoons, short humor; 300-600 wds.; up to .05/wd.

Tips: "All areas are open. Articles must carry a strong story line. First person is preferred. Don't exceed maximum word length, send no more than 3 works at a time."

**This periodical was #50 on the 2005 Top 50 Christian Publishers list (#28 in 2004, #48 in 2003, #40 in 2002, #9 in 2001).

+PURPOSE MAGAZINE, 2720 Airport Dr., Columbus OH 43219. (614)418-1785. Fax (614)253-2283. E-mail: purpose@iwaynet.net; ella@iwaynet.net. Website: www.purpose magazine.com. Ellavation Enterprises, Inc. Ella Coleman, pub./ed-in-chief. Christian magazine for a predominately African American audience; personal and family empowerment to inspire, motivate, and educate readers to live their God-given purpose. Biweekly mag.; 32-40 pgs.; circ. 5,000. Subscription $25. 25% unsolicited freelance; 75% assigned. Query/clips; e-query OK. **PAYS A SUBSCRIPTION & PROMOTION.** Accepts reprints (tell when/where appeared). Prefers e-mail submissions (attached file in Word). Regularly uses sidebars. Accepts submissions from children & teens. Prefers NKJV. Guidelines on Website; copy for 9x12 SASE. (Ads)

Poetry: Accepts very few; 30-40 lines. Submit max. 20 poems.

Fillers: Most types; 200-500 wds.

Columns/Departments: Financial wisdom. Complete ms.

Contests: Occasionally sponsors a contest.

QUAKER LIFE, 101 Quaker Hill Dr., Richmond IN 47374. (765)962-7573. Fax (765)962-1293. E-mail: quakerlife@fum.org. Website: www.fum.org/ql. Friends United Meeting. Trish Edwards-Konic, ed. For Christian Quakers, focusing on news around the world, peace and justice, simplicity, and inspiration. Monthly (10X) mag.; 36 pgs.; circ. 7,000. Subscription $24. 50% unsolicited freelance; 50% assigned. Query; fax/e-query OK. Accepts full ms by e-mail. **PAYS 3 COPIES** on publication for 1st rts. Articles to 1,500 wds. (40/yr.); book reviews 300 wds.; music/video reviews, 200 wds. Responds in 4 wks. Seasonal 4 mos. ahead. Accepts some reprints (tell when/where appeared). Accepts e-mail submissions (attached in Word or copied into message). No kill fee. Uses some sidebars. Prefers RSV. Accepts submissions from children or teens. Guidelines/theme list (also by e-mail); copy for 9x12 SAE. (Ads)

Poetry: Accepts 4/yr.

Columns/Departments: Turning Point (first-person spiritual experiences); Ideas That Work (ideas from churches); Peace Notes (peace and justice news and ideas); each 750 wds. Query or complete ms.

Special Needs: Leadership, church growth, personal experience.

Tips: "Write on current issues or a personal spiritual experience from a Christian perspective. Be more practical than academic. For general readers who are Christian Quakers."

$QUEEN OF ALL HEARTS, 26 S. Saxon Ave., Bay Shore NY 11706-8993. (631)665-0726. Fax (631)665-4349. E-mail: montfort@optonline.net. Website: www.montfortmissionaries .com. Catholic/Montfort Missionaries. Rev. Roger M. Charest, SMM, mng. ed. Focus is Mary, the Mother of Jesus. Bimonthly mag.; 48 pgs.; circ. 1,500. Subscription $22. 60% unsolicited freelance; 40% assigned. Not copyrighted. Query or complete ms/cover letter; phone/fax query OK. Pays $40-60 on publication for one-time rts. Not copyrighted. Articles 1,000-2,000 wds. (40/yr.) and fiction 1,500-2,000 wds. (6/yr.); book reviews 100 wds. Responds in 1 mo. Seasonal 4 mos. ahead. No simultaneous submissions or reprints. No disk. Uses some sidebars. Prefers NRSV. Guidelines (also by e-mail); copy for $3.50/9x12 SAE. (No ads)

> **Poetry:** Joseph Tusiani, poetry ed. Buys 12/yr. Free verse; to 25 lines; Marian themes only. No payment. Submit max. 2 poems.

RADIX MAGAZINE, PO Box 4307, Berkeley CA 94704. (510)548-5329. E-mail: RadixMag@aol.com. Website: www.RadixMagazine.com. Sharon Gallagher, ed.; Luci Shaw, poetry ed. Features in-depth articles for thoughtful Christians who are interested in engaging the culture. Quarterly mag.; 32 pgs. Subscription $15. 10% unsolicited freelance; 90% assigned. E-queries only. **PAYS IN COPIES** for 1st rts. Meditations, 300-500 wds. (2/yr.); book reviews 700 wds. Responds in 6 wks. to e-mail only. Seasonal 6 mos. ahead. No simultaneous submissions; accepts reprints (tell when/where appeared). Accepted submissions by e-mail (attached file). Uses some sidebars. Prefers NRSV. Guidelines by e-mail; copy $5. (Ads)

> **Poetry:** Accepts 12/yr. Avant-garde, free verse, haiku, traditional; 4-30 lines. Submit max. 3 poems.
>
> **Tips:** "Most open to poetry, book reviews, meditations. Familiarity with the magazine is key."

+RANDALL HOUSE PERIODICALS—See "Special Needs" in their book publishers' listing for details.

$+RARE JEWEL MAGAZINE, PO Box 7, Fairfield MT 59436. (406)467-2340. E-mail: tim@rarejewelmag.com. Website: www.rarejewelmag.com. Rare Jewel Ministries. Tim Ewing, pub.; Rick Marschall, mng. ed. Empowering Christians to exercise a biblical worldview (Proverbs 20:15). Bimonthly mag.; 48 pgs.; circ. 1,000. Subscription $23.97. Estab. 2004. 20% unsolicited freelance; 80% assigned. Query/clips; e-query OK. Pays up to .10./wd. on publication for 1st rts. Articles 1,500-2,500 wds. (50/yr.); book reviews, 1,000-1,500 wds. Responds in 2 wks. Seasonal 4 mos. ahead. Accepts reprints (tell when/where appeared). Requires e-mail submissions (attached file). Kill fee 20%. Regularly uses sidebars. Prefers NIV. Accepts submissions from teens. Guidelines by e-mail; copy for 9x12 SAE/$1.95 postage. (Ads)

> **Columns/Departments:** Buys 12/yr.

THE REFORMED QUARTERLY, 1231 Reformation Dr., Oviedo FL 32765. Toll-free (800)543-2703. (407)366-9425. Fax (407)366-9425. E-mail: lperez@rts.edu. Website: www.rts.edu. Reformed Theological Seminary. Lyn Perez, ed.; Ken McMullen, Website ed. To provide theological and biblical articles and other information helpful to the church. Quarterly mag.; circ. 40,000. Subscription free. Open to unsolicited freelance. Prefers query. Articles/reviews. Incomplete topical listings. (No ads)

REGENT BUSINESS REVIEW, 1000 Regent University Dr., Virginia Beach VA 23464. E-mail: michzig@regent.edu. Website: www.regent.edu/review. Regent University School of Business. Michael A Zigarelli, ed. For Christian leaders and managers who take their faith seriously and who give genuine thought to how to live out that faith in the workplace and everywhere else. Bimonthly e-zine; 30 pgs.; circ. 10,000. Free online. 25% unsolicited freelance; 75% assigned. Query/clips by e-mail only. **NO PAYMENT** for electronic rts. Articles 1,500-3,500 wds. (10/yr.); book reviews 300-500 wds. Responds in 2 wks. Seasonal 6 mos. ahead. No simultaneous submissions; accepts reprints. Requires accepted mss by e-mail (attached file). Regularly uses sidebars. Prefers NIV. Guidelines on Website.

Columns/Departments: Tool Kit (tips and resources) 1,000-2,000 wds.; Research Translations, 1,000-1,500 wds.

Tips: "Anyone can offer an idea for Christian leadership. We're looking to publish only those ideas that have a proven track record for success."

$RELEVANT & RELEVANTMAGAZINE.COM. Toll-free (866)512-1108. (407)3433-7152. E-mail: editorial@relevantmagazine.com. Website: www.RelevantMediaGroup.com. Cara Davis, ed. dir. (cara@relevantmediagroup.com); Erika Larson, asst. ed. (erika@relevant mediagroup.com); submit to Won Kim (won@relevantmediagroup.com). Targets culture-savvy twentysomethings who are looking for purpose, depth, and spiritual truth. Bimonthly & online mag.; 100 pgs. Subscription $10. Send a one-paragraph query; prefers e-mail; no phone/fax query. Pays .10/wd. within 45 days of publication for 1st rts. and all electronic rts. for 6 mos.; nonexclusive rts. thereafter. Features 1,000 wds.; reviews 400-600 wds. Prefers submissions as Word attachments. Guidelines on Website; copy $2.98. No questionnaire returned.

RHUBARB, 606-100 Arthur St., Winnipeg MB R3B 1H3, Canada. E-mail: rhubarb@mts.net. Website: www.mennolit.com. Mennonite Literary Society. Submit to The Editor. Designed to provide an outlet for the (loosely defined) Mennonite voice, reflecting the changing face of the Mennonite community, promoting dialog, and encouraging the Anabaptist tradition of reformation and protest. Quarterly mag. Subscription $25 Cdn., $20 U.S. Open to unsolicited freelance. Query for nonfiction; e-query OK. **NO REFERENCE TO PAYMENT.** Articles & fiction to 2,500 wds. Guidelines/theme list on Website.

ROCK & SLING: A Journal of Literature, Art and Faith, PO Box 30865, Spokane WA 99223. Fax (509)276-2971. E-mail: editors@rockandsling.org. Website: www.rockandsling.org. Kris Christensen, Susan Cowger, Laurie Klein, eds. A literary journal created to give forum to the spiritual journey, while exploring the Christian point of view. Biannual jour. Subscription $18. 70% unsolicited freelance; 30% assigned. Complete ms/cover letter; no phone/fax/e-query. **PAYS 2 COPIES** for 1st rts. Articles & fiction to 5,000 wds. (10,000 max.). Responds in 6 wks. Accepts simultaneous submissions (if indicated), no reprints. Any Bible version. Guidelines on Website; copy $10. Incomplete topical listings.

Poetry: Accepts poetry to 60 lines (longer if exceptional). Submit max. 5 poems.

Contest: Virginia Brendemuehl Prize for Poetry. Prize: $1,000, plus publication. Deadline July 30. Entry fee $10/3 poems. Send SASE for guidelines.

Tips: "Writers should be familiar with literary prose and poetry. We do not accept genre writing or didacticism. No devotions or testimonies. We publish writing with broad or explicit associations to Christian faith or its history, including fiction, nonfiction, memoir, poetry, translations, interviews, critical reviews of books, music, and film, and scholarly articles by qualified authors. We want complexity of thought and emotion, but not esotericism to the point of inaccessibility. We also publish art and photography. Submissions accepted year round."

THE ROSE & THORN: A Literary E-zine. E-mail: BAQuinn@aol.com. Website: www.therose andthornezine.com. Secular. B. A. Quinn, ed. Showcases short fiction, poetry, essays, and anything of a literary nature; no children's or juvenile stories. Quarterly online literary mag. Open to freelance. Complete ms. **NO PAYMENT** but will provide a link to your Website. One-time nonexclusive rts. Articles, fiction, reviews; all to 2,000 wds. Requires accepted ms by e-mail (copied into message). Guidelines on Website.

Poetry: Now accepting poetry. Submit max. 3 poems; prefers shorter poems. E-mail to poetryeditor@hotmail.com.

Special Needs: Fiction, vignettes, and flash fiction; creative essays, perspective, humor, reviews, and interviews. Author interviews and writing how-to articles.

Tips: "We have eclectic tastes, so go ahead and give us a shot."

SACRED JOURNEY: The Journal of Fellowship in Prayer, 291 Witherspoon St., Princeton NJ 08542. (609)924-6863. Fax (609)924-6910. E-mail: editorial@sacredjourney.org. Website: www.sacredjourney.org. Fellowship in Prayer, Inc. Louise Hutner, ed. Multifaith spirituality. Bimonthly jour. & e-zine; 48 pgs.; circ. 4,500. Subscription $18. 75% unsolicited freelance; 30% assigned. Complete ms/cover letter; phone/fax/e-query OK. **PAYS 5 COPIES & SUBSCRIPTION** for 1st & electronic rts. Articles to 1,500 wds. (30/yr.); reviews 500 wds. Responds in 9 wks. Seasonal 4 mos. ahead. Accepts simultaneous submissions & reprints (tell when/where appeared). Requires requested ms on disk or by e-mail. Does not use sidebars. Guidelines (also by e-mail/Website); copy $1.70/6x9 SAE. (No ads)

> **Poetry:** Accepts 6-8/yr. Free verse, haiku, light verse, traditional; 10-35 lines. Submit max. 3 poems.

> **Columns/Departments:** Accepts 30/yr. A Transforming Experience (personal experience of spiritual significance); Pilgrimage (journey taken for spiritual growth or service); Spirituality and the Family; Spirituality and Aging; to 1,500 wds.

> **Special Needs:** Meditation and service to others.

> **Tips:** "Write well about your own spiritual experience and we'll consider it. Most open to a transforming experience feature."

SALT OF THE EARTH: Your Online Resource for Social Justice, 205 W. Monroe St., Chicago IL 60606. (312)236-7782. Fax (312)236-8201. E-mail: clarkek@claretianpubs .org. Website: http://salt.claretianpubs.org. The Claretians/Catholic. Kevin Clarke, mng. ed. Monthly online mag.

$#SCIENCE & SPIRIT MAGAZINE, 300 Conshohocken State Rd., #500, West Conshohocken PA 19428-3801. (617)769-2904. Fax (617)745-3932. E-mail: editorial@science-spirit .org. Website: www.science-spirit.org. Science & Spirit Resources, Inc./Heldref Publications. Karl Giberson, ed. Well-researched and reported articles on the intersection of science and religion in health, environment, human relationships, technology, and ethics. Bimonthly mag; circ. 10,000. Subscription $23.95. 20% freelance. Query by mail first. Pays $700 for feature articles on publication for all rts. No reprints. Feature articles 1,500-1,800 wds. Responds in 6 mos. Guidelines; copy $4.95.

> **Columns/Departments:** Interlude (social/science environmental topic), 1,200 wds.; Critical Mass (news briefs covering all areas of science—physics, gender, space, psychology, etc.); pays $200-300. See Website for samples of departments.

> **Tips:** "Common mistakes include shallow reporting, lack of in-depth writing, lack of diversity in religious perspectives. We're looking for well-researched articles that include interviews with scientists, theologians, and everyday people. The best articles include citations for recent research and current books. Thoughtful leads, transitions, and conclusions based on the writer's research and insight are a must."

SEEDS OF HOPE, 602 James Ave., Waco TX 76706-1476. (254)755-7745. Fax (254)753-1909. E-mail: SeedsHope@aol.com. Website: www.seedspublishers.org. Seeds of Hope Publishers. Katie Cook, ed. Committed to the healing of hunger and poverty in our world. Quarterly worship packet; 20 pgs. of camera-ready resources. Subscription $120. Individual packet $50. Back issues less expensive. Also quarterly newsletter, *Hunger News & Hope,* published through denominational offices of national churches. E-query OK. **NO PAYMENT.**

$SEEK, 8121 Hamilton Ave., Cincinnati OH 45231. (513)521-1789. Fax (513)931-0950. E-mail: seek@standardpub.com. Website: www.Standardpub.com. Standard Publishing. Margaret K. Williams, ed. Light, inspirational, take-home reading for young and middle-aged adults. Weekly take-home paper; 8 pgs.; circ. 29,000. Subscriptions $14.69 (sold only in sets of 5). 75% unsolicited freelance; 25% assigned. Complete ms; no phone/fax/ e-query. Pays .07/wd. on acceptance for 1st rts., .05/wd. for reprints. Articles 400-1,200 wds. (150-200/yr.); fiction 400-1,200 wds. Responds in 18 wks. Seasonal 1 yr. ahead. Accepts reprints (tell when/where appeared). Prefers submissions by e-mail (attached file). Kill fee. Uses some sidebars. Guidelines/theme list (also on Website); copy for 6x9 SAE/2 stamps. (No ads)

Fillers: Buys 50/yr. Ideas, jokes, short humor; $15.

Tips: "We now work with a theme list. Only articles tied to these themes will be considered for publication. Check Website for theme list and revised guidelines."

**This periodical was #27 on the 2005 Top 50 Christian Publishers list (#20 in 2004, #49 in 2003, #29 in 2002, #45 in 2001).

$SENIOR LIVING NEWSPAPERS, 2010 S. Stewart, Springfield MO 65804. (417)862-0852. Fax (417)862-9079. E-mail: elefantwalk@msn.com. Website: www.seniorlivingnews papers.com. Metropolitan Radio Group, Inc. Joyce Yonker O'Neal, mng. ed. Positive, upbeat paper for people 55+; includes religious articles. Monthly newspaper; 40 pgs.; circ. 40,000. 25-50% unsolicited freelance. Query or complete ms/cover letter; no phone/fax/ e-query. Pays $20-35 for assigned, $5-35 for unsolicited, 30 days after publication for 1st, reprint, and electronic rts. Articles 600-700 wds. (65/yr.). Responds in 2-5 wks. Seasonal 4 mos. ahead. Guidelines; copy for 9x12 SAE/5 stamps.

SHARING: A Journal of Christian Healing, 6807 Forest Haven, San Antonio TX 78240. (210)681-5146. Fax (210)681-5146. E-mail: Marjorie.George@dwtx.org. Website: www.orderofstluke.org. Order of St. Luke the Physician. Marjorie George, ed. For Christians interested in spiritual and physical healing. Monthly (10X) jour.; 16 pgs.; circ. 9,000. Subscription $20. 100% unsolicited freelance. Complete ms/cover letter. **NO PAYMENT** for one-time or reprint rts. Articles 750-900 wds. (50/yr.). Responds in 3 wks. Seasonal 2 mos. ahead. Accepts simultaneous submissions & reprints (tell when/where appeared). Prefers ms by e-mail. Some sidebars. Prefers RSV. Guidelines; copy for 8x10 SAE/2 stamps.

Poetry: Accepts 10-12/yr. Free verse, traditional; 6-14 lines.

Tips: "We're looking for crisp, clear, well-written articles on the theology of healing and personal witness of healing. We do not return manuscripts or poems, nor do we reply to inquiries regarding manuscript status."

+SHORT STORIES BIMONTHLY, 5713 Larchmont Dr., Erie PA 16509. Phone/fax (814)866-2543. E-mail: 75562.670@compuserve.com. Website: www.thepoetryforum.com. Poetry Forum. Gunvor Skogsholm, ed. Poetry and prose that takes an honest look at the human condition. Converting from a print publication to an e-zine; 16 pgs. 90% unsolicited freelance; 10% assigned. Complete ms; fax/e-query OK. **NO PAYMENT** for one-time or electronic rts. Not copyrighted. Articles 200 wds.; fiction 1,500 wds.; book reviews 100 wds. Responds in 4 wks. Seasonal 3 mos. ahead. Accepts reprints. Prefers requested ms by e-mail (copied into message). Uses some sidebars. Accepts submissions from children/teens. Guidelines (also by e-mail/Website); copy online. (Ads)

Poetry: All types.

$SIGNS OF THE TIMES, Box 5398, Nampa ID 83653-5398. (208)465-2579. Fax (208)465-2531. E-mail: signs@pacificpress.com, or mmoore@pacificpress.com. Website: www.signs times.com. Seventh-day Adventist. Marvin Moore, ed. Biblical principles relevant to all of life; for general public. Monthly mag. & partial online version; 32 pgs.; circ. 200,000. Subscription $18.95. 40% unsolicited freelance; 60% assigned. Complete ms/cover letter. Pays $100-300 (.10-.20/wd.) on acceptance for all, 1st, reprint rts. Articles 500-1,500 wds. (75/yr.). Responds in 4-9 wks. Seasonal 1 yr. ahead. Accepts simultaneous submissions & reprints (tell when/where appeared). Prefers requested ms by e-mail (copied into message).

Kill fee 50%. Uses some sidebars. Guidelines (also by e-mail/Website); copy for 9x12 SAE/3 stamps. (No ads)

> **Tips:** "Most open to gospel, Christian lifestyle, or Amazing Grace column (conversion, answers to prayer, victory over temptation, or God's leading)."

SILVER WINGS, PO Box 2340, Clovis CA 93613-2340. (559)347-0194. E-mail: cloviswings@ aol.com. Poetry on Wings/Evangelical. Jackson Wilcox, ed. Christian understanding and uplift through poetry. Bimonthly mag.; 16 pgs.; circ. 300. Subscription free with donation. 100% unsolicited freelance. Query or complete ms; phone query OK. **PAYS ONE COPY** for articles for 1st rts.; book reviews 200 wds. Not copyrighted. Poetry only. Responds in 3 wks. Seasonal 3-12 mos. ahead. Sometimes accepts simultaneous submissions & reprints (tell when/where appeared). No disk or e-mail submissions. Does not use sidebars. Prefers KJV. Accepts submissions from children/teens. Guidelines; copy for 6x9 SAE/2 stamps. (No ads)

> **Poetry:** Accepts 175/yr. Free verse, haiku, light verse, traditional; 3-20 lines. Submit max. 3 poems. No payment. "Any poetry that conforms to Christian conduct, teaching, and morality."
>
> **Fillers:** Original sayings. No payment.
>
> **Contest:** Annual poetry contest on a theme(December 31 deadline); send SASE for details. Winners published in March. $200 in prizes. $3 entry fee. Theme for 2006: Seasons of Change.
>
> **Tips:** "We like poems with clear Christian message, observation, or description. Poetry should be easy to read and understand. Short poems get best attention. We are open to topics and material making a point that agrees with Christian teaching. We will even consider views that vary within the Christian community."

$SINGLE AGAIN.COM WEBZINE & NEWSLETTER, 1237 Crescendo Dr., Roseville CA 95678-5165. (916)773-7337. E-mail: publisher@singleagain.com. Website: www.singleagain.com. Christian. Rev. Paul Scholl, pub. Caters to people trying to put their lives back together after divorce, separation, or death of a significant other. Quarterly & online newsletter; 8-10 pgs. Subscription $12. Open to freelance. Complete ms/cover letter by mail or e-mail (preferred). **NO PAYMENT** for simultaneous rts. Articles 500 wds. (50-75/yr.). Responds in 6 wks. Accepts simultaneous submissions & reprints (tell when/where appeared). Accepts requested mss by e-mail (attached file in Word only). Does not use sidebars. Guidelines on Website. Incomplete topical listings. (Ads)

> **Poetry:** Accepts 6-12/yr. Any type to 24 lines. Submit max. 6 poems.
>
> **Fillers:** Accepts 15-12/yr. Anecdotes, facts, ideas, jokes, kid quotes, prayers, prose, short humor, tips.
>
> **Tips:** "Write from your heart first. Don't worry about your article being perfect. We will help you with any final editing."

*SINGLES SCOOP, 374 Sheppard Ave. E., Toronto ON M2N 3B6, Canada. (416)222-3341, ext. 142. Fax (416)222-3344. The Peoples Church/Toronto Canada. Dr. T. Starr, mng. ed. For singles, ages 35-65. Quarterly mag.; 24 pgs. Subscription free/donation. 15% unsolicited freelance; 85% assigned. Complete ms/cover letter. **NO PAYMENT.** Articles 500 wds. (20/yr.); fiction 350-500 wds.; book/video reviews 150 wds. Responds in 2 wks. Seasonal 3 mos. ahead. Accepts simultaneous submissions & reprints (tell when/where appeared). Accepts requested ms on disk. Regularly uses sidebars. Prefers NIV. Guidelines/theme list; copy for 9x12 SAE/$1.20 Cdn. postage. (Ads) Website up for sale; may be defunct.

> **Poetry:** Accepts 1-2/yr.
>
> **Fillers:** Accepts 1-5/yr.; 50 wds. Anecdotes, cartoons, facts, games, quizzes, short humor; 25-40 wds.
>
> **Columns/Departments:** Accepts 20/yr. Complete ms. No payment.

$SMART FAMILIES, PO Box 1125, Murrieta CA 92564-1125. (858)513-7150. Fax (951)461-3526. E-mail: plewis@smartfamilies.com. Website: www.smartfamilies.com. Smart Families, Inc. Paul Lewis, ed./pub. Christian parenting, with strong crossover to secular families. Bimonthly online newsletter & 16 pg. print mag.; circ. 140,000. 20% unsolicited freelance. Complete ms preferred; fax/e-query OK. Pays $50-250 on publication for 1st rts. Articles 200-1,000 wds. Responds in 1-3 wks. Seasonal 4 mos. ahead. Accepts simultaneous submissions & reprints. Prefers e-mail submission (attached file). Uses some sidebars. Prefers NIV. No guidelines or copy. (No ads)

> **Fillers:** Games, ideas, quotes.
>
> **Tips:** "We are not a typical 'magazine' and have tight length requirements. Because of crossover audience, we do not regularly print Scripture references or use traditional God-word language."

$SOCIAL JUSTICE REVIEW, 3835 Westminster Pl., St. Louis MO 63108-3472. (314)371-1653. E-mail: centbur@juno.com. Website: www.socialjusticereview.org. Catholic Central Union of America. Rev. John H. Miller, C.S.C., ed. For those interested in the social teaching of the Catholic Church. Bimonthly jour.; 32 pgs.; circ. 4,950. Subscription $20. 90% unsolicited freelance. Query or complete ms/cover letter. Pays .02/wd. on publication for one-time rts. Not copyrighted. Articles to 3,000 wds. (80/yr.); book reviews 500 wds. (no pay). Responds in 1 wk. Seasonal 3 mos. ahead. Accepts reprints (tell when/where appeared). Does not use sidebars. Guidelines; copy for 9x12 SAE/3 stamps. (No ads)

> **Columns/Departments:** Virtue; Economic Justice; variable length. Query.
>
> **Tips:** "Fidelity to papal teaching and clarity and simplicity of style; thoughtful and thought-provoking writing."

$SOJOURNERS/SOJO.NET, 3333—14th St. N.W., Washington DC 20009. Toll-free (800)714-7474. (202)328-8842. Fax (202)328-8757. E-mail: sojourners@sojo.net. Website: www.sojo.net. Submit to Manuscript Editor. For those who seek to turn their lives toward the biblical vision for justice and peace and the union of faith and politics. Monthly & online mag.; 54 pgs.; circ. 35,000. Subscription $39.95. 1% unsolicited freelance; 85% assigned. Complete ms/cover letter; fax/e-query OK. Accepts full ms by e-mail. Pays $50-400 on publication for all rts. Articles 600-3,000 wds. (12/yr.); reviews 650 wds., $50-100. Responds in 8 wks. Seasonal 6 mos. ahead. No simultaneous submissions or reprints. Accepts submissions by e-mail (attached file). Kill fee. Uses some sidebars. Prefers NRSV. Guidelines (also by e-mail/Website); no copy. (Ads)

> **Poetry:** Rose Marie Berger, poetry ed. Buys 6-10/yr. Free verse, haiku; $25. Submit max. 3 poems.
>
> **Fillers:** Accepts 6 cartoons/yr.; also other unsolicited artwork and photographs.
>
> **Tips:** "Most open to features, Culture Watch reviews, and short pieces on individuals and groups working successfully in their communities to empower the poor, create jobs, and promote peace and reconciliation."
>
> ****2004 ACP Award: Best in Class.**

+SOUL SOURCE MAGAZINE, (248)249-2320. E-mail: pamperry@ministrymarketing solutions.com. Website: www.ministrymarketingsolutions.com. Ministry Marketing Solutions. Pam Perry, pub. Inserted in *The Michigan Chronicle* and distributed at major Christian events and select churches throughout metro Detroit. Monthly tabloid. Subscription free. Not included in topical listings. No questionnaire returned.

$SOUND BODY, Box 448, Jacksonville OR 97530. Phone/fax (541)899-8888. E-mail: James@ChristianMediaNetwork.com. Websites: www.SoundBodycm.com. Christian Media. James Lloyd, ed./pub. A health newsletter with an alternative slant. Quarterly & online newsletter. Query; prefers phone query. Payment negotiable for reprint rts. Articles. Responds in 3 wks. Requires KJV. No guidelines; copy for #10 SAE/2 stamps.

*SOUTHERN RENAISSANCE, PO Box 1199, Boutte LA 70039. E-mail: Boris3128@aol.com. Catholic. Allen Lottinger, ed. Articles & columns to 1,200 wds. Include your e-mail address. Looking mainly for Catholic writers.

SOUTHWEST KANSAS FAITH AND FAMILY, PO Box 1454, Dodge City KS 67801. (620)225-4677. Fax (620)225-4625. E-mail: stan@swkfaithandfamily.org. Website: www.swkfaith andfamily.org. Independent. Stan Wilson, pub. Dedicated to sharing the Word of God and news and information that honors Christian beliefs, family traditions, and values that are the cornerstone of our nation. Monthly newspaper; circ. 5,000. Subscription $18. Accepts freelance. Prefers e-query. Complete ms. Incomplete topical listings. (Ads)

$SPECIAL LIVING, PO Box 1000, Bloomington IL 61702. E-mail: gareeb@aol.com. Website: www.specialiving.com. Betty Garee, pub./ed. For and about physically disabled adults, mobility impaired individuals. Quarterly mag.; 88 pgs.; circ. 12,000. Subscription $12. 90% unsolicited freelance; 5% assigned. Query; phone/fax/e-query OK. Pays .10/wd. on publication for 1st rts. Articles 300-800 wds. (50/yr.). Responds in 3 wks. Seasonal 6 mos. ahead. Accepts simultaneous submissions & reprints (tell when/where appeared). Prefers requested ms on disk. No kill fee. Uses some sidebars. No guidelines; copy $2. (Ads)

    Fillers: Buys 20/yr. Cartoons, tips.

    Tips: "Query with a specific idea. Have good photos to accompany your article."

SPIRITUALITY FOR TODAY, PO Box 7466, Greenwich CT 06836. (203)316-9394. Fax (203)316-9396. E-mail: Clemons10@aol.com. Website: www.spirituality.org. Clemons Productions, Inc. Dorothy Riera, asst. ed. Adults' spiritual renewal with articles that challenge reflection. Monthly mag.; 13-15 pgs.; circ. 495,000. Subscription free. Open to freelance. E-query OK. **NO PAYMENT.** Articles 1.5 pgs. Incomplete topical listings. (Ads)

    Fillers: Accepts anecdotes, prayers, quotes.

    Tips: "Most open to human interest pertaining to the church (2 pages); and human values." Spanish page included.

$SPIRITUAL LIFE, 2131 Lincoln Rd. N.E., Washington DC 20002-1199. Toll-free (888)616-1713. (202)832-8489. Fax (202)832-8967. E-mail: editor@spiritual-life.org. Website: www.Spiritual-Life.org. Catholic. Edward O'Donnell, O.C.D., ed. Essays on Christian spirituality with a pastoral application to everyday life. Quarterly jour.; 64 pgs.; circ. 11,000. Subscription $18. 90% unsolicited freelance. Complete ms/cover letter; phone/fax/e-query OK. Pays $50-250 ($50/pg.) on acceptance for 1st rts. Articles/essays 5,000-8,000 wds. (20/yr.); book reviews 1,500 wds. ($15). Responds in 8-10 wks. Seasonal 9 mos. ahead. Accepts simultaneous submissions. Requires requested ms on disk. Does not use sidebars. Prefers NAB. Guidelines; copy for 7x10 SAE/5 stamps.

    Tips: "No stories of personal healing, conversion, miracles, etc."

SPIRITUAL VOICE NEWS, PO Box 45, Kennett Square PA 19348. (610)347-6766. Fax (610)347-6765. E-mail: Linda@Kennett.net. Website: www.spiritualvoyages.cc. Regional news. Linda T. Eckman, ed./pub. For backslid Christians or the unsaved; available free at convenience stores, restaurants, etc. Quarterly newspaper; 16 pgs.; circ. 10,000. Subscription free. 100% unsolicited freelance. Complete ms/cover letter (by e-mail); phone/fax/e-query OK. **PAYS IN COPIES** for one-time, reprint, or simultaneous rts. Not copyrighted. Articles (500 wds.); all genres of fiction (500 wds.); book/music/movie reviews. Responds in 1 wk. Seasonal 2 wks. to 1 mo. ahead. Accepts simultaneous submissions & reprints. Requires e-mail submissions (attached file or copied into message—preferred); no hard copies. Uses some sidebars. Accepts submissions from children or teens. Guidelines/theme list (also by e-mail); copy for 6x9 SAE/3 stamps. (Ads)

    Poetry: Accepts 30/yr. Any type. Send any number. No payment. Needs more.

    Fillers: Accepts many. Any type. No payment. Needs more.

Special Needs: Column writers; more puzzles. Editor looking for a column linking physical and spiritual health.

Tips: "This paper is very open to new writers. If you have a heart for those who have been far from God or hurt by the 'religious authority,' your work *will* get published."

$SPORTS SPECTRUM, 105 Corporate Blvd., Ste. 2, Indian Trail NC 28105. (704)821-2971. Fax (704)821-2669. E-mail: dbranon@rbc.org. Website: www.sportsspectrum.com. Sports Spectrum Publishing. Dave Branon, mng. ed. Designed to feature sports people and issues as a way of introducing the gospel to non-Christian sports fans and encouraging Christian sports fans. Bimonthly daily-devotional mag.; 56 pgs.; circ. 30,000. Subscription $27.52. 0% unsolicited freelance; 80% assigned. Query/clips; e-query OK. Pays .21/wd. on acceptance for all rts. Not copyrighted. Articles 1,200-2,000 wds. (40/yr.). Responds in 3-4 wks. Requires accepted ms by e-mail (attached file). Kill fee 30-50%. Regularly uses sidebars. Prefers NIV. Guidelines (also by e-mail/Website); no sample copy. (Ads)

   Tips: "The best thing a writer can do is to be aware of the special niche *Sports Spectrum* has developed in sports ministry. Then find athletes who fit that niche and who haven't been covered in the magazine."

   ****2005, 2004, 2003 EPA Award of Merit—General.

$SPRING HILL REVIEW, PO Box 621, Brush Prairie WA 98606. (360)892-1178. E-mail: Springhillreview@aol.com. Carolyn Schultz-Rathbun, pub./mng. ed. A general market publication that examines and challenges Pacific Northwest U.S. culture, seeking to encourage its audience to re-view contemporary culture through the lens of biblical truth. Monthly jour.; 16 pgs.; circ. 6,200. Subscription $20. 80% unsolicited freelance; 20% assigned. Complete ms/cover letter; e-query preferred. Pays $10-15 on publication for 1st, reprint, or simultaneous rts. Articles 500-800 wds. (30/yr.); fiction to 2,000 wds. (13/yr.); reviews 500-700 wds. (20/yr.) Responds in 4-6 wks. Seasonal 2 mos. ahead. Accepts simultaneous submissions & reprints (tell when/where appeared). Prefers submitted ms on disk or by e-mail (attached file); accepts disk in MS Word only. No kill fee. Uses some sidebars. Accepts submissions from teens. Guidelines (also by e-mail); copy $2. (Ads)

   Poetry: Lucy S. R. Austen, poetry ed. Buys 30/yr. Avant-garde, free verse, haiku, traditional; to 35 lines; $5-10. Submit max. 6 poems.

   Fillers: Buys 12/yr. Cartoons (single-frame, B & W cartoons; would consider a regular monthly multiframe cartoon), games, word puzzles, poetry, and essays; 500 wds./20 lines; $5-10.

   Columns/Departments: Buys 50/yr. Book of the Hour (new book reviews); The Reel Deal (movie reviews); The Play's the Thing (Northwest Theater reviews); Northwest Book Nook (books with a N.W. connection); Video Corner (old and new video reviews); The Poetry Corner; all 600-800 wds.; $10-15.

   Special Needs: Frequently uses an in-depth examination of multiple books/CDs/movies on the same theme or by the same author/artist/director, up to 1,000 wds. Needs seasonal material. Information and opinion pieces on politics, arts, history, social and spiritual issues, especially those with a N.W. U.S. angle.

   Tips: "We are always looking for good reviews of books (especially Northwest authors), movies, CDs, and videos. And we never have enough good fiction. No overtly evangelistic material, please, and no material written for a specifically Christian audience. Write to connect with a secular, post-modern audience, but don't check your faith at the door. Our tone and approach are quite different from those of most Christian publications. We receive a large number of submissions written for a Christian audience, but we can't use them because our audience is primarily non-Christian. You can write a wonderful story or article dealing with spiritual issues from a Christian perspective, but if your reader stops reading after the first paragraph, you haven't communicated. Read a sample copy before submitting." Deadline is the 15th of each month.

**This periodical was #30 on the 2003 Top 50 Christian Publishers list (#48 in 2002).

SR: A JOURNAL FOR LUTHERAN REFORMATION. E-mail: jglange@allwest.net. Website: http://members.aol.com/SemperRef. Semper Reformada. Rev. Jonathan G. Lange, ed. Publishes reformation theses only. Query from Website. Open to original articles & reprints of essays from old theological journals. No mention of payment. Submissions must be sent to full editorial board from the Website. Guidelines on Website.

$STANDARD, 6401 The Paseo, Kansas City MO 64131. (816)333-7000. Fax (816)333-4439. E-mail: evlead@nazarene.org. Website: www.nazarene.org. Nazarene. Dr. Everett Leadingham, ed. Examples of Christianity in everyday life for adults, college-age through retirement. Weekly take-home paper; 8 pgs.; circ. 150,000. Subscription $11.95. 100% unsolicited freelance. Complete ms. Pays .035/wd.(.02/wd. for reprints) on acceptance for one-time rts. Articles (20/yr.) or fiction (200/yr.) 700-1,500 wds. Responds in 12 wks. Seasonal 6-9 mos. ahead. Accepts simultaneous submissions & reprints (tell when/where appeared). No disk; accepts e-mail submissions (attached). Kill fee. Does not use sidebars. Prefers NIV. Guidelines (also by e-mail); copy for #10 SAE/2 stamps. (No ads)

> **Poetry:** Buys 50/yr. Free verse, haiku, traditional; to 50 lines; .25/line. Submit max. 5 poems.
> **Fillers:** Buys 50/yr. Word puzzles; $20.
> **Tips:** "Fiction or true-experience stories must demonstrate Christianity in action. Show us, don't tell us. Action in stories must conform to Wesleyan-Arminian theology and practices." Themes follow the Christian year, not celebrating national holidays.
> **This periodical was #38 on the 2003 Top 50 Christian Publishers list (#30 in 2002, #23 in 2001).

$ST. ANTHONY MESSENGER, 28 W. Liberty St., Cincinnati OH 45210-1298. (513)241-5615. Fax (513)241-0399. E-mail: SamAdmin@AmericanCatholic.org. Website: www.American Catholic.org. Pat McCloskey, O.F.M., ed. For Catholic adults & families. Monthly & online mag.; 60 pgs.; circ. 310,000. Subscription $25. 40% unsolicited freelance. Query; fax/e-query OK. Pays .15/wd. on acceptance for 1st, reprint (right to reprint), and electronic rts. Articles 1,500-3,000 wds., prefers 2,000-2,500 (45-50/yr.); fiction 1,500-2,500 wds. (12/yr.); book reviews 500 wds., $40. Responds in 8 wks. Seasonal 6+ mos. ahead. Kill fee. Uses some sidebars. Prefers NAB. Guidelines (also on Website); copy for 9x12 SAE. (Ads)

> **Poetry:** Christopher Heffron, poetry ed. Buys 20/yr. Free verse, haiku, traditional; 3-25 lines; $2/line ($20 min.) Submit max. 2 poems.
> **Fillers:** Cartoons.
> **Tips:** "Most open to articles, fiction, profiles, interviews of Catholic personalities, personal experiences, and prayer. Writing must be professional; use Catholic terminology and vocabulary. Writing must be faithful to Catholic belief and teaching, life, and experience. Our online writers' guidelines indicate the seven categories of articles. Texts of articles reflecting each category are linked to the online writers' guidelines for nonfiction articles."
> **This periodical was #40 on the 2005 Top 50 Christian Publishers list (#40 in 2004, #45 in 2003, #36 in 2001).

STAR OF ZION, PO Box 26770, Charlotte NC 28221-6770. (704)599-4630, ext. 318. Fax (704)688-2546. E-mail: editor@starofzion.org. Submissions to jasnead@amezhqtr.org. Website: www.starofzion.org. African Methodist Episcopal Zion Church. Mike Lisby, ed. Religious denominational newspaper for A.M.E. Zion church members, pastors, and national officers. Bimonthly newspaper; 16 pgs.; circ. 9,200. Subscription $38. 10% unsolicited freelance; 75% assigned. Query/clips; fax/e-query OK. **NO PAYMENT; SUBSCRIP-**

TION FOR ESTABLISHED COLUMNS for 1st rts. Articles to 750 wds.; book reviews 500-750 wds. Responds in 4 wks. Seasonal 2 mos. ahead. Accepts simultaneous submissions. Prefers e-mail submissions (attached file or copied into message). No kill fee. Uses some sidebars. Copy of 9x12 SAE/$1.42 postage (mark "Media Mail"). (Ads)

Poetry: Accepts 12-24/yr. African American themes; traditional. Submit max. 12 poems.

Fillers: Accepts 24/yr. Anecdotes, cartoons, games, jokes, prayers, and word puzzles; 25-175 wds.

Columns/Departments: Accepts 24/yr. Motivational Message (sermon text), 500-1,000 wds.; 5-Minute Sermon (brief lesson), 500-750 wds.; From the Pulpit (pastor recollections and anecdotes). Query.

Contest: Annual essay contest: What Zion Means to Me.

Tips: "Most open to columns, Black history articles, religious poems, humor, church (A.M.E. Zion) histories, and pastor biographies."

STEPS: A Magazine of Hope and Healing for Christians in Recovery, PO Box 215, Brea CA 92822-0215. (714)529-6227. Fax (714)529-1120. E-mail: barbaram@christian recovery.com. Website: www.nacronline.com. National Assn. for Christian Recovery. Barbara Milligan, assoc. ed. Serves a broad audience of individuals, families, couples, church leaders, pastors, support-group leaders, and mental-health professionals. Quarterly mag. Subscription with $30 membership. Open to freelance. E-query only (see guidelines first on Website); no complete mss. **PAYS ONE YEAR HONORARY MEMBERSHIP/SUB-SCRIPTION.** Articles to 1,000 wds. Uses some sidebars.

Fillers: Anecdotes, cartoons, newsbreaks, short humor; to 350 wds. All on a recovery theme.

Special Needs: Healing, restoration, reconciliation, depression, substance abuse, co-dependency, domestic violence, loss, sexual abuse, spiritual abuse, eating disorders, shame, bitterness, guilt, distorted images of self, distorted images of God, distorted images of others, sexual addiction, broken relationships, anger/rage, grief, family dysfunction, woundedness, fear, workaholism, the Twelve Steps, self-disclosure, support groups, boundaries, forgiveness, trust, God's grace, God's love, God's help.

Tips: "Freelance articles usually appear in a feature titled 'Illumination: Observations, Opinions and an Occasional Rant.' Emphasize the *process* of being changed by God, not just the results. We look for honesty and a solid grounding in reality. If your article is a personal story, what specifically did you struggle with? What image describes how that struggle felt to you? And what did you eventually learn about God or about yourself as a result of that struggle? Be sure to visit our Website and read sample articles from back issues."

$STEWARDSHIP, PO Box 1561, New Canaan CT 06840. (203)966-6470. Fax (203)966-4654. E-mail: guy@parishpublishing.org. Website: www.parishpublishing.org. Parish Publishing, LLC. Guy Brossy, principal. Inspires parishioners to give to their church—abilities, time, and monies. Monthly newsletter; 4 pgs.; circ. 1 million. 50% unsolicited freelance; 50% assigned. Fax/e-query with cover letter. Pays $50 on acceptance for all & reprint rts. Articles 160, 200, or 250 wds. (50/yr.) Responds in 2 wks. Seasonal 3 mos. ahead. Accepts simultaneous submissions & reprints. Accepts e-mail submissions (attached or copied into message). Regularly uses sidebars. Free guidelines/copy. (No ads)

Tips: "Write articles that zero in on stewardship—general, time, talent, or treasure—as it relates to the local church."

$ST. JOSEPH'S MESSENGER AND ADVOCATE OF THE BLIND, PO Box 288, Jersey City NJ 07303-0288. (201)798-4141. Catholic/Sisters of St. Joseph of Peace. Sister Mary Kuiken, CSJP, ed. For older Catholics interested in supporting ministry to the aged, young, blind, and needy. Biannual mag.; 12-16 pgs.; circ. 14,000. Subscription $5. 30% unsolicited freelance. Complete ms. Pays $20-30 on acceptance for 1st rts. Articles 800-1,000 wds. (24/yr.); fiction 800-1,000 wds. (30/yr.). Responds in 5 wks. Seasonal 3 mos. ahead. Accepts simultaneous submissions & reprints (tell when/where appeared). Does not use sidebars. Guidelines; copy for 9x12 SAE/2 stamps. (No ads)

Poetry: Buys 25/yr. Light verse, traditional; 4-16 lines; $5-15 on publication. Submit max. 4 poems.

Fillers: Buys 20/yr. Ideas, 50-100 wds.; $5-10.

Tips: "Most open to contemporary fiction. No Christmas issue."

ST. LINUS REVIEW, 5239 S. Sandusky, Tulsa OK 74135. (918)906-7059. E-mail: editor@ stlinusreview.com. Website: www.stlinusreview.com. Catholic. William Ferguson, ed./pub. Poetry and short prose by and for orthodox Catholics. Semiannual mag.; circ. 50. Subscription $12. Estab. 2003. 95% unsolicited freelance; 5% assigned. Complete ms.; e-query OK. **PAYS 1 COPY,** plus $1 for 1st rts. Fiction 2,500 wds. (8/yr.). Responds when selections are made. Seasonal poetry or fiction. No simultaneous submissions or reprints. Accepts e-mail submissions (MS Word attachment). Does not use sidebars. Accepts submissions from teens. Prefers RSV for Catholics. Guidelines on Website; copy for $6/9x12 SAE. (Ads)

Poetry: Accepts 30-50/yr. All types; prefers rhyming. Pays 1 copy. Submit max. 3 poems.

Contest: Offers small cash prize for "Best of Review."

Tips: "Send us poetry or fiction."

THE STORYTELLER, 2441 Washington Rd., Maynard AR 72444. (870)647-2137. Fax (870)847-2454. E-mail: storyteller1@cox-internet.com. Website: http://freewebz.com/fossilcreek. Fossil Creek Publishing. Regina Cook Williams, ed./pub.; Ruthan Riney, review ed. Family audience; geared to (but not limited to) new writers. Quarterly mag.; 72 pgs.; circ. 600. Subscription $20. 100% unsolicited freelance. Complete ms/cover letter; phone/e-query OK. **NO PAYMENT** for 1st rts. Articles 1,500 wds. (60/yr.); fiction 1,500 wds. (100-125/yr.). Responds in 3-4 wks. Seasonal 3 mos. ahead. Accepts simultaneous submissions & reprints (tell when/where appeared). No disk or e-mail submissions. Does not use sidebars. Accepts submissions from children or teens. Guidelines (also on Website); copy $6/#10 SAE/5 stamps. (Ads)

Poetry: Accepts 100/yr. Free verse, haiku, light verse, traditional; 3-40 lines. Submit max. 3 poems.

Fillers: Accepts 10-20/yr. Cartoons, quotes, tips; 25-50 wds. Writing-related only.

Special Needs: Original artwork. Funny or serious stories about growing up as a pastor's child or being a pastor's wife. Also westerns and mysteries.

Contest: Offers 1 or 2 paying contests per year, along with People's Choice Awards, and Pushcart Prize nominations. Go to www.freewebs.com/Fossilcreekpub, for announcements of all forthcoming contests for the year (contest site only).

Tips: "All sections of the magazine are open to freelancers. To break in, write a good story, of course, but send as clean a copy as possible, learn how to set up the manuscript, and include a cover letter. We like to know who wrote the story. Show us you are a serious writer."

STUDIO: A Journal of Christians Writing, 727 Peel St., Albury NSW 2640, Australia. Phone/fax +61 2 6021 1135. E-mail: studio00@bigpond.net.au. Submit to Studio Editor. Quarterly journal; 36 pgs.; circ. 300. Subscription $60 AUS. 90% unsolicited freelance; 10% assigned. Query. **PAYS IN COPIES** for one-time rts. Articles 3,000 wds. (15/yr.); fiction 3,000 wds. (50/yr.); book reviews 300 wds. Responds in 3 wks. Accepts simultaneous submissions & reprints (tell when/where appeared). No disks; e-mail submissions OK. Does not use sidebars. Guidelines (send IRC); copy for $10 AUS. (Ads)

Poetry: Accepts 200/yr. Any type; 4-100 lines. Submit max. 3 poems.

Contest: See copy of journal for details.

Tips: "We accept all types of fiction and literary article themes."

+SUNDAY MAGAZINE, PO Box 53529, Victoria BC V8X 5KS, Canada. (250)592-6071. Fax (250)592-8217. E-mail: info@sundaymagazine.org. Website: www.sundaymagazine.org. Vancouver Island Christian Communications Society. Adele Wickett, ed. To build up, inform, and promote unity within the body of Christ on Vancouver Island and beyond, through communication media. Newspaper; circ. 11,000. Subscription $30 Cdn./$42 U.S. Open to unsolicited freelance. Prefers query. Articles. Incomplete topical listings. No questionnaire returned. (Ads—Mavis Reynolds)

THE SWORD AND TRUMPET, PO Box 575, Harrisonburg VA 22803-0575. Phone/fax (540)867-9419. Mennonite. Paul Emerson, ed. Primarily for conservative Bible believers. Monthly mag.; 37 pgs.; circ. 3,300. Subscription $12. **NO PAYMENT.** Articles. Prefers KJV. (No ads)

SWORD OF THE LORD NEWSPAPER, PO Box 1099, Murfreesboro TN 37133. (615)893-6700. Fax (615)895-7447. E-mail through Website. Website: www.swordofthelord.com. Independent Baptists and other fundamentalists. Dr. Terry Frala, editorial dept. supervisor. Revival and soul-winning. Biweekly newspaper; 24 pgs.; circ. 70,000. Subscription $15. Open to freelance. Query; phone/fax/e-query OK. **NO PAYMENT.** Articles 500-1,000 wds.; fiction for 4-7 & 8-12 yrs. and teenagers. Responds in 13 wks. Seasonal 3 mos. ahead. Accepts simultaneous submissions & reprints (tell when/where appeared). Accepts disk or e-mail submissions (attached file). No kill fee. Does not use sidebars. Requires KJV. Guidelines (also by e-mail); no copy. (Ads)

> **Poetry:** Accepts variable number. Free verse, light verse, traditional; any length.
>
> **Fillers:** Accepts variable number. Facts, newsbreaks, prose.
>
> **Columns/Departments:** Accepts variable number. Kid's Korner (children's stories); Teen Talk (teen issues); both 500-700 wds.
>
> **Tips:** "Most open to Bible study, soul-winning material, Christian growth and youth character building that does not stress graphic portrayals of 'what's really going on out there'. Only works from a fundamentalist viewpoint and using the KJV are considered."

$TESTIMONY, 2450 Milltower Ct., Mississauga ON L5N 5Z6, Canada. (905)542-7400. Fax (905)542-7313. E-mail: testimony@paoc.org. Website: www.paoc.org/testimony. The Pentecostal Assemblies of Canada. Submit to The Editor. Focus is inspirational and Christian living; Pentecostal holiness slant. Monthly & online mag.; 24 pgs.; circ. 15,000. Subscription $24 U.S./$19.05 Cdn. (includes GST). 10% unsolicited freelance; 90% assigned. Query; fax/e-query OK. Pays $20-75 on publication for 1st rts. (no pay for reprint rts.). Articles 800-1,000 wds. Responds in 6-8 wks. Seasonal 4 mos. ahead. Accepts reprints (tell when/where appeared). Prefers e-mail submission (copied into message). Regularly uses sidebars. Prefers NIV. Guidelines/theme list (also by e-mail/Website); copy $2/9x12 SAE. (Ads)

> **Special Needs:** See Website.
>
> **Tips:** "View our theme list on our Website and query us about a potential article regarding one of our themes. Our readership is 98% Canadian. We prefer Canadian writers or at least writers who understand that Canadians are not Americans in long underwear. We also give preference to members of this denomination, since this is related to issues concerning our fellowship."

($)THEGOODSTEWARD.COM, 2514 Plantation Dr., Ste. B, Matthews NC 28105. Toll-free (866)324-7097. (828)396-7966. Fax (828)396-9490. E-mail: editor@thegoodsteward.com. Website: www.thegoodsteward.com. Wall Watchers. Michael Barrick, ed. (michaelb@thegoodsteward.com). To increase the level of giving to Christian ministries and provide a central source of information on those ministries. Weekly e-zine. 2% unsolicited freelance; 10% assigned. Query; e-query OK. **USUALLY NO PAYMENT,** except for providing a link to your e-mail or Website on publication. Articles 500-750 wds.; book reviews 500-750 wds. Responds in 2 wks. Seasonal 2 mos. ahead. Accepts simultaneous submissions & reprints.

Requires e-mail submissions (attached file). Does not use sidebars. Guidelines on Website. (No ads)

Special Needs: Looking for information/articles that match well with the site's themes—biblical stewardship, life stewardship, environmental stewardship, and responsible giving. Books reviewed must have been published within last 90 days.

Tips: "Subject areas include: Biblical Principles (general precepts of biblical stewardship); Life Stewardship (physical health, fitness and well being, spiritual gifts, talents, use of time, and relationships); Financial Matters (saving, budgeting, investing, tax strategy, insurance, and estate planning); Giving Wisely (tithing and responsible giving); and Environment (ecology, recycling, environmental management, and conservation)." Is working on design/content changes; check Website for updated guidelines.

$*TIDEWATER PARENT, 1300 Diamond Springs Rd., Ste. 102, Virginia Beach VA 23455. (757)222-3100. Fax (757)363-1767. E-mail: jodonnel@pilotonline.com. Portfolio Publishing. Jennifer O'Donnell, ed. For parents of children 0-11 years; help for facing the everyday challenges of parenting. Monthly tabloid; circ. 40,000. 85% unsolicited freelance. Complete ms. or query; fax/e-query OK. Pays $35-200 on publication for 1st rts. Articles 500-3,000 wds. (60/yr.); reviews 600-800 wds. ($35-50). Responds in 1-4 mos. Seasonal 3 mos. ahead. Accepts simultaneous submissions & reprints. Kill fee 10%. Free guidelines & copy. (Ads)

Tips: "Write in an informal, familiar tone." A secular publication that accepts religious articles.

TIME FOR RHYME, PO Box 1055, Battleford SK S0M 0E0, Canada. (306)445-5172. Family Books. Richard W. Unger, ed. Poetry only; not strictly Christian (but editor is). Quarterly mag.; 32 pgs.; circ. about 100. Subscription $12 U.S./Cdn.; $17 foreign. 80% unsolicited freelance; 0% assigned. Complete ms/cover letter; phone query OK. **PAYS IN COPIES** for 1st rts. Responds as soon as possible. Seasonal 1 yr. ahead. Accepts reprints (tell when/where appeared). Prefers KJV. Guidelines; copy $3.25 U.S./Cdn.; $5.50 foreign. (Classified ads)

Poetry: Accepts 70/yr.; light verse or traditional; 2-32 lines. Rhyming only; light or serious. Submit max. 5 poems.

Tips: "Write poetry honest to the heart. Truly see, smell, etc., the experience first—focus. Then write. Don't hold readers at arm's length; let them experience it with you (show, don't tell)." U.S. authors can send a $1 U.S. bill to cover return postage—no U.S. stamps.

TIME OF SINGING: A Magazine of Christian Poetry, PO Box 149, Conneaut Lake PA 16316. (814)382-8667. E-mail: timesing@zoominternet.net. Website: www.timeofsinging .bizland.com. Lora Zill, ed. We try to appeal to all poets and lovers of poetry. Quarterly booklet; 44 pgs.; circ. 250. Subscription $17. 95% unsolicited freelance; 5% assigned. Complete ms; e-query OK. **PAYS IN COPIES** for 1st, one-time, or reprint rts. Poetry only (some book reviews by assignment). Responds in 12 wks. Seasonal 6 mos. ahead. Accepts simultaneous submissions & reprints (tell when/where appeared). Accepts e-mail submission (attached file). Guidelines (also by e-mail/Website); copy $4 ea. or 2/$6.

Poetry: Accepts 150-200/yr. Free verse, haiku, light verse, traditional; 3-60 lines. Submit max. 5 poems. Always need form poems (sonnets, villanelles, triolets, etc.) with Christian themes. Fresh rhyme. "Cover letter not needed—your work speaks for itself."

Contest: Sponsors 1-2 annual poetry contests on specific themes or forms ($2 entry fee/poem) with cash prizes (send SASE for rules).

Tips: "Study poetry, read widely—both Christian and non-Christian. Work at the craft. Be open to suggestions and critique. If I have taken time to comment on your work, it is close to publication. If you don't agree, submit elsewhere. I appreciate poets who take chances, who write outside the box. *Time of Singing* is a literary poetry magazine, so I'm not looking for greeting card verse or sermons that rhyme."

*TJ: The In-depth Journal of Creation, PO Box 6302, Acacia Ridge D. C., QLD 4110, Australia. Phone 07 3273 7650. Fax 07 3273 7672. E-mail: admin@answersingenesis.com. Website: www.answersingenesis.org. Answers in Genesis. Pierre Jerlstrom, chief editorial coord. An international journal devoted to the presentation and discussion of the technical aspects of the sciences as they relate to biblical creation and Noah's flood. Triannual & online journal; 128 pgs.; circ. 5,000. Subscription $37. 90% unsolicited freelance; 10% assigned. Complete ms/cover letter; phone/fax/e-query OK. **NO PAYMENT** for all rts. Articles to 5,000 wds.; include an abstract of 200 wds. Responds in 2-3 wks. Prefers requested ms on disk or by e-mail (attached file). Guidelines on Website (www.answersingenesis .org/Home/Area/Magazines/TJ/Tjguidelines.asp). Not included in topical listings. (No ads)

$TODAY'S CHRISTIAN, 465 Gundersen Dr., Carol Stream IL 60188-2498. (630)260-6200. Fax (630)260-0114. E-mail: tceditor@christianitytoday.com. Website: www.todays-christian .com. Christianity Today Intl. Ed Gilbreath, mng. ed. A Christian *Reader's Digest* that uses both reprints and original material. Bimonthly & online mag.; 64 pgs.; circ. 125,000. Subscription $17.95. 35% unsolicited freelance; 20% assigned. Complete ms/cover letter; phone/fax/e-query OK. Pays .10/wd. on acceptance for 1st, reprint & electronic rts. Articles 500-1,500 wds. (50/yr.). Responds in 6-8 wks. Seasonal 9 mos. ahead. Accepts reprints ($50-100, tell when/where appeared). Accepts e-mail submissions (copied into message). Kill fee. Sidebars, 150-300 wds. Prefers NIV. Guidelines/theme list (also on Website); copy for 6x9 SAE/4 stamps. (Ads)

> **Columns/Departments:** Cynthia Thomas, columns ed. Buys 150/yr. Lite Fare (adult church humor); Kids of the Kingdom (kids say and do funny things); all to 250 wds.; $35.
> ****This periodical was #18 on the 2005 Top 50 Christian Publishers list (#16 in 2004, #6 in 2003, #14 in 2002, #7 in 2001). 2001 EPA Award of Merit—General.

$TODAY'S PENTECOSTAL EVANGEL, 1445 N. Boonville, Springfield MO 65802-1894. (417)862-2781. Fax (417)862-0416. E-mail: pe@ag.org. Website: www.pe.ag.org. Assemblies of God. Hal Donaldson, ed-in-chief; Ken Horn, mng. ed.; submit to Ashli O'Connell, asst. ed. Denominational; Pentecostal. Weekly & online mag.; 32-48 pgs.; circ. 215,000. Subscription $24.99. 5% unsolicited freelance; 95% assigned. Complete ms/cover letter; no phone/fax/e-query. Pays .08/wd. (.04/wd. for reprints) on acceptance for 1st and electronic rts. Articles 500-1,200 wds.; testimonies 200-300 wds. Responds in 6-8 wks. Seasonal 6-8 mos. ahead. Kill fee 100%. Prefers e-mail submission (attached file). Regularly uses sidebars. Prefers NIV, KJV. Guidelines (also on Website); no copy. (Ads)

> **Fillers:** Practical, how-to pieces on family life, devotions, evangelism, seasonal, current issues, Christian living; 50-200 wds.; $20.
> **Tips:** "Most of the material published from unsolicited submissions centers on the personal experience of the writer. Bible exposition and most teaching articles, as well as controversial issues, are assigned to tested writers. Send samples of previous things published and indicate you are open for assignments. Special themes done mostly by assignment, but holiday themes are used if submitted well in advance (preferably 6 months). Our news editor is open to news leads and gives small stories on assignment occasionally. Best opportunity for first-time feature writer is an article about a compelling personal experience written in a down-to-earth manner. Avoid a melodramatic or preachy tone."
> ****2003, 2001 EPA Award of Merit—Denominational.

$TOGETHER, 1251 Virginia Ave., Harrisonburg VA 22802. Toll-free (888)833-3333. (540)433-5351. Fax (540)434-0247. E-mail: Tgether@aol.com. Website: www.church outreach.com. Shalom Foundation, Inc. Melodie Davis, ed. An outreach magazine distributed by churches to attract the general public to Christian faith and life. Quarterly tabloid; 8 pgs.; circ. 2,000. Free. 95% unsolicited freelance. Complete ms/cover letter; e-query OK. Pays up to $50 after publication for one-time rts. Articles 500-1,200 wds. (16/yr.).

Responds in 12-16 wks. Seasonal 4 mos. ahead. Accepts simultaneous submissions & reprints. Accepts requested ms on disk or by e-mail (copied into message). Uses some sidebars. Prefers NIV. Guidelines/theme list (also by e-mail/Website); copy for 9x12 SAE/4 stamps. (No ads)

> **Tips:** "Deal with contemporary themes with fresh style. We need a variety of salvation testimonies from all racial/ethnic groups, with excellent photos available (don't submit photos until requested)." When submitting by e-mail, put title of magazine and title of your piece in subject line. Also include your e-mail address in body of message.

+TO GOD BE THE GLORY! POETRY MAGAZINE, 525 N. Arlington, #D-2, Kalamazoo MI 49006. (269)547-5212. E-mail: Reynolds_Ink@yahoo.com. Website: www.geocities.com/reynolds_ink/my_page.html. Reynolds INK. M. J. Reynolds, owner/CEO. Devoted to lifting up the name of our precious Lord and Savior Jesus Christ. Bimonthly mag.; 18-20 pgs. Subscription $21. Estab. 2005. 100% unsolicited freelance. Query; no phone/fax/e-query. **NO PAYMENT** for one-time rts. Not copyrighted. Poetry only. Prefers KJV. Guidelines; copy $4. (Ads)

> **Poetry:** Accepts a large number/yr. Traditional (mainly about Jesus Christ); to 20 lines. Submit max. 3 poems.
>
> **Contest:** Holds a poetry contest in each issue. Cash prize for winner, consolation prize for 2nd & 3rd places, and certificates for 4th-7th places.
>
> **Tips:** "We're open to all freelancers. There is a $2 reading fee for nonsubscribers, and $1 fee for subscribers. (Fees go to pay contest winner.)"

TRIBUTES, 5008 Rolling Meadows Dr., Durham NC 27703. (919)596-7663. E-mail: wisler@mindspring.com. Website: www.geocities.com/griefhope/index.html. Daniel's House Publications. Alice Wisler, ed. To reach those who have had a child or sibling die, and for those who care and want to help the bereaved. Monthly online mag; circ. 500+. Free (send blank e-mail to wisler@mindspring.com). 95% unsolicited freelance; 5% assigned. Complete ms. by e-mail only. **NO PAYMENT,** but gives generous bio and Website links. Articles 800-900 wds.; reviews 600-700 wds. Responds in 1 wk. Seasonal 2 mos. ahead. Accepts reprints. Accepts mss by e-mail (copied into message). Accepts submissions from teens. Guidelines by e-mail. (Ads)

> **Poetry:** Accepts 35/yr. Free verse, haiku, light verse, traditional; to 60 lines. Submit max. 2 poems.
>
> **Fillers:** Accepts 15/yr. Anecdotes and prayers to 100 wds.
>
> **Tips:** "*Tributes* is geared to helping those in grief, specifically bereaved parents and bereaved siblings. Make sure articles and poetry are within the range of this theme."

+TRI-STATE VOICE, PO Box 110282, Nutley NJ 07110. (973)235-0776. Fax (973)235-1688. E-mail: tristatevoice@aol.com; editor@tristatevoice.com; staff@tristatevoice.com. Website: www.tristatevoice.com. Tom Campisi, ed. To be a voice to the Christian community in Greater NYC. Newspaper; circ. 22,000. Subscription $24. Open to freelance. Articles. Incomplete topical listings. No questionnaire returned. (Ads)

#THE TRUMPETER, 7757 S.W. 86th St., Ste. C-109, Miami FL 33143. (305)274-4880. Fax (302)370-1485. E-mail: martiele@thetrumpeter.com. Website: www.thetrumpeter.com. Swanko Communications. Martiele Swanko, ed-in-chief. Unites all South Florida Christian denominations, ethnic groups, and cultures. Bimonthly & online mag.; 80+ pgs.; circ. 20,000. Subscription $19.95. 90% unsolicited freelance. Query; fax/e-query OK. **NO PAYMENT** for one-time rts. Features & sports, 900-1,000 wds.; articles 500-1,200 wds.; book/music/video reviews, 100 wds. Responds in 4 wks. Accepts reprints (tell when/where appeared). Requires requested ms on disk or by e-mail. Regularly uses sidebars. Prefers KJV. Guidelines/theme list (also by e-mail/Website). (Ads)

> **Fillers:** Cartoons.

Columns/Departments: Accepts 100/yr. Around Town (local talk), 100-125 wds.; Arts & Entertainment, 400 wds.; Legal, 450 wds.; Political/Viewpoint, 100-125 wds.

Tips: "Call us for a special feature assignment. Be a good writer. Know how to effectively write a paragraph by the rules and use active verbs instead of adjectives."

$THE UNITED CHURCH OBSERVER, 478 Huron St., Toronto ON M5R 2R3, Canada. (416)960-8500. Fax (416)960-8477. E-mail: mduncan@ucobserver.org. Website: www .ucobserver.org. United Church of Canada. Muriel Duncan, ed. To voice hope for individual Christians, for the United Church, for God's World. Monthly mag.; circ. 70,000. Subscription $20. Uses a limited amount of material from non-United Church freelancers. (Ads)

$#UP: The Magazine of Hope & Encouragement, 102 S. 2nd St., Ste. 204, Stillwater MN 55082. (715)294-4580. Fax (651)439-4668. E-mail: julie@upmagazine.us. Website: www.upmagazine.us. Julie Holmquist, pub. Regional stories about how God is working in lives and through ministries. Bimonthly mag.; 36 pgs.; circ. 10,000. Subscription $18. Estab. 2003. 0% unsolicited freelance; 10% assigned. Query/clips; e-query OK. Pays $40, copies & subscription, on publication for all rts. Articles 1,500-2,000 wds. (4/yr.) Responds in 2 wks. No simultaneous submissions or reprints. Accepts submissions by e-mail (attached file). Regularly uses sidebars. No guidelines; copy for $1.50/9x12 SAE. (Ads)

$UPSCALE MAGAZINE: Exposure to the World's Finest, 600 Bronner Brothers Way S.W., Atlanta GA 30310. (404)758-7467. Fax (404)755-9892. E-mail: features@upscale mag.com. Website: www.upscalemagazine.com. Upscale Communications, Inc. Joyce E. Davis, sr. ed. To inspire, inform, and entertain African Americans. Monthly mag.; circ. 250,000. Subscription $12. 75-80% unsolicited freelance. Query; fax/e-query OK. Pays $100 & up on publication for 1st rts. Articles (135/yr.); novel excerpts. Seasonal 6 mos. ahead. Accepts simultaneous submissions. Responds in 5-9 wks. Kill fee 25%. Guidelines on Website; copy online.

Columns/Departments: Buys 6-10/yr. News & Business (factual, current); Lifestyle (travel, home, wellness, etc.); Beauty & Fashion (tips, trends, upscale fashion, hair); Arts & Entertainment. Query. Payment varies. These columns most open to freelance.

Tips: "We are open to queries for exciting and informative nonfiction." Uses inspirational and religious articles.

$U.S. CATHOLIC, 205 W. Monroe St., Chicago IL 60606. (312)236-7782. Fax (312)236-8207. E-mail: editors@uscatholic.org. Website: www.uscatholic.org. The Claretians. Meinrad Schrer Emunds, ed. dir.; Heidi Schlumpf, mng. ed.; Rev. John Molyneau C.M.F., ed. Devoted to starting and continuing a dialog with Catholics of diverse lifestyles and opinions about the way they live their faith. Monthly & online mag.; 52 pgs.; circ. 40,000. Subscription $22. 95% unsolicited freelance. Complete ms/cover letter; phone/fax/e-query OK. Pays $250-600 (fiction $300-400) on acceptance for all rts. Articles 2,500-4,000 wds.; fiction 2,500-3,500 wds. Responds in 5 wks. Seasonal 6 mos. ahead. Accepts requested ms on disk or by e-mail. Regularly uses sidebars. Guidelines; copy for 10x13 SASE. (Ads: Tom Toussaint, 312-236-7782, ext. 854)

Poetry: Submit poetry (and fiction) to literaryeditor@uscatholic.org. All types but light verse, to 50 lines; $75.

Columns/Departments: (See guidelines first.) Sounding Board, 1,100-1,300 wds., $250; Practicing Catholic, 750 wds., $150.

Tips: "Most open to features and essays. All manuscripts (except for fiction or poetry) should have an explicit religious dimension that enables readers to see the interaction between their faith and the issue at hand. Fiction should be well written, creative, with solid character development."

**This periodical was #22 on the 2004 Top 50 Christian Publishers list (#33 in 2004).

VALPARAISO POETRY REVIEW, Dept. of English, Valparaiso University, Valparaiso IN 46383-6493. E-mail: VPR@Valpo.edu. Website: www.valpo.edu. Academic. Edward Byrne, ed. Presents new, emerging, and well-known voices in contemporary poetry. Online literary jour. Reads unsolicited submissions year round. Complete ms/cover letter; e-submissions OK (copied into message). **NO PAYMENT** for one-time rts. Essays, book reviews, author interviews. Accepts simultaneous submissions & reprints (tell when/where appeared). Guidelines on Website; copy online.

> **Poetry:** Accepts unpublished and previously published poems. Submit max. 5 poems, once per month.
>
> **Tips:** "Unsolicited book reviews are welcome. Small press publishers and poets are encouraged to send books for review to address above."

$VIBRANT LIFE, 55 W. Oak Ridge Dr., Hagerstown MD 21740-7390. (301)393-4019. Fax (301)393-4055. Website: www.vibrantlife.com. Seventh-day Adventist/Review & Herald. Charles Mills, ed. Total health publication (physical, mental, and spiritual); plus articles on family and marriage improvement; ages 30-50. Bimonthly mag.; 32 pgs.; circ. 28,000. Subscription $19.95. 50% unsolicited freelance; 30% assigned. Query/clips; fax/e-query OK. Pays $75-300 on acceptance for 1st, one-time, reprint, or electronic rts. Articles 600-1,500 wds. (50-60/yr.). Responds in 9 wks. Seasonal 9 mos. ahead. Accepts simultaneous submissions & reprints (tell when/where appeared). Accepts e-mail submissions (attached file). Kill fee 50%. Regularly uses sidebars. Prefers NIV. Guidelines (also by e-mail/Website); copy $1/9x12 SAE. (Ads)

> **Fillers:** Buys 6-12/yr. Facts, quizzes; 50-500 wds.; $25-100.
>
> **Columns/Departments:** Buys 12-18/yr. Fit People (people whose lives are changed for the better when applying timeless health principles/before and after photos), 500-650 wds.; Times of Your Life (family-oriented, everyday tips), 500-600 wds.; $75-200. Query.
>
> **Tips:** "Articles need to be very helpful, practical, and well documented. Don't be preachy. Sidebars are a real plus." Not accepting submissions until end of year; see Website.
>
> **This periodical was #7 on the 2005 Top 50 Christian Publishers List (#7 in 2004, #4 in 2003, #22 in 2002, #26 in 2001, #16 in 2000).

VICTORY NEWS, 2723 Steamboat Cir., Arlington TX 76006. (817)548-1124. E-mail: luotto@comcast.net. Website: wwwfranklinpublishing.net. Franklin Publishing Company. Dr. Ludwig Otto, pub. Positive news about the Christian experience. Quarterly jour.; 200 pgs.; circ. 1,000. Subscription $185. 100% unsolicited freelance. Complete ms.; phone/e-query OK. **NO PAYMENT** for nonexclusive rts. Articles (100/yr.) & fiction (75/yr.) to 7,000 wds.; reviews to 1,000 wds. Responds in 3 wks. Seasonal 1 mo. ahead. Accepts simultaneous submissions & reprints. Requires requested ms by e-mail (attached file in Word format). Does not use sidebars. Accepts submissions from teens. Any Bible version. Guidelines/theme list on Website; no copy. (Ads)

> **Poetry:** Accepts 1,000/yr.; all types. Submit max. 10 poems.
>
> **Fillers:** Accepts 200/yr.; all types except games and word puzzles.
>
> **Columns/Departments:** Accepts 20/yr.
>
> **Special Needs:** Communications; public relations; marketing, management; fund-raising; grant development; TV, newspaper, and radio projects; music; building or construction; government relations; public and private education; and special event planning.
>
> **Tips:** "Articles and stories may advocate any Christian position for all issues concerning our mission."

$THE VISION, 8855 Dunn Rd., Hazelwood MO 63042-2299. (314)837-7300. Fax (314)837-4503. E-mail: WAP@upci.org. Website: www.upci.org. United Pentecostal Church. Richard M. Davis, ed.; submit to Lisa Henson, ed. designer. Denominational. Weekly take-home paper; 4 pgs.; circ. 10,000. Subscription $1.85/quarter. 95% unsolicited freelance. Complete ms/cover letter; no e-query. Pays $18-25 on publication for 1st rts. Articles 1,200-1,600 wds. (to 120/yr.); fiction 1,200-1,600 wds. (to 120/yr.). Seasonal 9 months ahead. Accepts simultaneous submissions & reprints. Guidelines (also by e-mail); free copy. (No ads)

Poetry: Buys 30/yr.; $3-12.

Tips: "Most open to fiction short stories, real-life experiences, and short poems. Stay within word count. Be sure manuscript has a pertinent, spiritual application."

$VOICE OF THE LORD, 3675 S. Westshore Blvd., PMB 156, Tampa FL 33639-8235. (412)232-6801. E-mail: SwordofTruthmin@hotmail.com. Website: www.SwordofTruth.org. International Charismatic Bible Ministries (ICBM)/Sword of Truth Ministries. Rev. Jay Baldwin, gen. overseer. Healing, spiritual warfare, and prayer from a Charismatic/Pentecostal perspective. Quarterly mag.; up to 40 pgs.; circ. 1,850-2,150. Free subscription. 25-35% unsolicited freelance; 65-75% assigned. Query only; e-query OK. Pays negotiable rates on publication for 1st North American & international rts., and all electronic rts. Articles 150-700 wds. Responds in 8-10 wks. Seasonal 3 mos. ahead. Accepts simultaneous submissions; no reprints. No disk or e-mail submissions. Uses some sidebars. Prefers KJV. Accepts submissions from children or teens. Guidelines; copy for #10 SAE/3 stamps. (Ads)

Special Needs: Charismatic deliverance, prophetic intercession, and declarations beyond 2006.

Tips: "Issues are topic oriented—the same each year. Most open to fiction or monthly topic. We are looking for bold Charismatic pieces. Spiritual warfare, healing, deliverance topics are the best to write about. Must be Pentecostal/Charismatic in doctrine, and writer will have to agree to adhere to our Statement of Beliefs (charismatic) before publication will be done. Articles dealing with first person and/or reports of physical healing have a much better chance of publication if confirmed documentation from a physician is included. Be truthful—we check."

WALK THIS WAY: Extreme Discipleship Web-zine, Prolongacion de Paraiso #153-A, Colonia Rincon de San Juan, Tepic, Nayarit 63138 Mexico. (311)214-6200. E-mail: editor@walk-this-way.com. Website: www.walk-this-way.com. Walk This Way Ministries. Submit to R. Cody Smith, ed. (submissionseditor@walk-this-way.com). Monthly e-zine; 20 pgs. Subscription free. 50% unsolicited freelance; 50% assigned. Complete ms/cover letter; e-query OK. **NO PAYMENT** for 1st, one-time, reprint, simultaneous, or electronic rts. Articles 800-1,600 wds. (25/yr.); fiction 800-1,600 wds. (2/yr.); book reviews 300-500 wds. Responds in 4 wks. Seasonal 3 mos. ahead. Accepts simultaneous submissions & reprints (tell when/where appeared). Requires submissions by e-mail (attached or copied into message). Does not use sidebars. Prefers NIV. Guidelines on Website; copy online. (No ads)

Special Needs: New Testament Reformation; house church.

$WAR CRY, 615 Slaters Ln., Alexandria VA 22313. (703)684-5500. Fax (703)684-5539. E-mail: War_cry@USN.salvationarmy.org. Website: www.salvationarmyusa.org. The Salvation Army. Lt. Col. Marlene Chase, ed-in-chief; Jeff McDonald, mng. ed. Pluralistic readership reaching all socioeconomic strata and including distribution in institutions. Biweekly & online mag.; 24 pgs.; circ. 500,000. Subscription $10. 10% unsolicited freelance. Complete ms/brief cover letter; no phone/fax query; e-query OK. Pays .18-.25/wd.(.15/wd. for reprints) on acceptance for 1st or reprint rts. Articles (40/yr.) & fiction (5-10/yr.) 800-1,500 wds. Responds in 4-6 wks. Seasonal 1 yr. ahead. Accepts simultaneous submissions & reprints (tell when/where appeared). Prefers accepted ms by e-mail. Regularly uses sidebars. Prefers NIV. Guidelines/theme list (also on Website); copy free or online. (No ads)

Poetry: Buys 10-20/yr. Free verse, traditional; to 16 lines. Inspirational only. Pays $25 and up. Submit max. 5 poems.

Fillers: Buys 10-20/yr. Anecdotes (inspirational), 200-500 wds.; .15-.20/wd.

Tips: "We are soliciting more short fiction, inspirational articles, and poetry; interviews with Christian athletes, evangelical leaders, and celebrities; and theme-focused articles. Always looking for theologically sound coverage of essential Christian doctrine and how it applies to daily living. Also short, contemporary articles (400 wds.) with an evangelical message."

**This periodical was #33 on the 2005 Top 50 Christian Publishers list (#21 in 2004, #23 in 2003, #43 in 2002, #17 in 2001).

THE WAR CRY (Canada), 2 Overlea Blvd., Toronto ON M4H 1P4, Canada. (416)422-6114. Fax (416)422-6120. E-mail: warcry@can.salvationarmy.org, or Kenneth_Smith@can.salvation army.org. Website: www.salvationarmy.ca/magazines/thewarcry. The Salvation Army/Canada. Kenneth Smith, ed. To provide news and information about the people, programs, and potential of The Salvation Army at work. Monthly mag.; 24 pgs.; circ. 25,000. Subscription $26.50. Open to unsolicited freelance. Complete ms/with cover letter; e-submissions OK (attached or copied into message). **PAYS 3 COPIES.** Feature articles; news 100-150 wds.; departments 650-750 wds. Accepts reprints (tell when/where appeared). Guidelines on Website. Incomplete topical listings. (Ads)

$THE WAY OF ST. FRANCIS, 1112—26th St., Sacramento CA 95816-5610. (916)443-5717, ext. 16. Fax (916)443-2019. E-mail: ofmcaway@att.net. Website: www.sbfranciscans.org. Franciscan Friars of California/Catholic. David Elliott, mng. ed. For those interested in the message of St. Francis of Assisi as lived out by contemporary people. Bimonthly mag.; 48 pgs.; circ. 5,000. Subscription $12. 10% unsolicited freelance; 65% assigned. Complete ms/cover letter; no phone/fax query; e-query OK. Pays $25-100 (or copy & subscription) on publication for 1st rts. Articles 500-1,500 wds. (4-6/yr.). Responds in 8 wks. (manuscripts are not returned). Seasonal 6 mos. ahead. Accepts simultaneous submissions & reprints (tell when/where appeared). Prefers requested ms on disk or by e-mail (attached file). Regularly uses sidebars. Any Bible version. Guidelines/theme list (also by e-mail); copy for 6x9 SAE/$1.42 postage (mark "Media Mail"). (No ads)

Fillers: Anecdotes, cartoons, facts, prayers, prose; to 100 wds.; $25-50.

Columns/Departments: Buys 12/yr. First Person (opinion/issue), to 900 wds.; Portrait (interview or personality), to 1,200 wds.; Inspirations (spiritual), to 1,200 wds.; $25-50.

Contest: Annual Simon Scanlon Writing Awards. Articles 1,500-2,000 wds. Prizes: $250-1,000. Deadline October 4. Details on Website.

Tips: "Make direct connection to St. Francis, St. Clare, or a recognizable aspect of their life and vision."

$WEAVINGS, 1908 Grand Ave., PO Box 340004, Nashville TN 37203-0004. (615)340-7200. E-mail: weavings@upperroom.org. Website: www.upperroom.org. The UpperRoom. Submit to The Editor. For clergy, lay leaders, and all thoughtful seekers who want to deepen their understanding of, and response to, how God's life and human lives are being woven together. Bimonthly mag. Open to freelance. Complete ms. Pays .12/wd. & up on acceptance. Articles 1,250-2,500 wds.; sermons & meditations 500-2,500 wds.; stories (short vignettes or longer narratives) to 2,500 wds.; book reviews 750 wds. Responds within 13 wks. Accepts reprints. Accepts requested ms on disk or by e-mail. Guidelines (also on Website: www.upperroom.org/weavings/guidelines.asp)/theme list; copy for 7.5 x 10.5 SAE/5 stamps. Incomplete topical listings.

Poetry: Pays $75 & up.

Tips: "All contributions should reflect simplicity, authenticity, and inclusiveness."

$WESLEYAN LIFE, Box 50434, Indianapolis IN 46250-0434. (317)774-7909. Fax (317)774-7913. E-mail: communications@wesleyan.org. Website: www.wesleyan.org. The Wesleyan Church Corp. Dr. Norman G. Wilson, gen. ed.; Jerry Brecheisen, mng. ed. Denominational. Quarterly mag.; 34 pgs.; circ. 50,000. Subscription controlled. 10% freelance. E-mail submissions only. Pays $50-80 for unsolicited on publication for 1st or simultaneous rts. Articles 400-500 wds. (50/yr.). Responds in 2 wks. Seasonal 6 mos. ahead. Accepts simultaneous submissions & reprints (tell when/where appeared). Guidelines (also by e-mail/Website); copy $2. (Ads-limited)

Tips: "Most open to ministry pieces, personal testimonies, and general articles. No poetry."

WEST WIND REVIEW, 1250 Siskiyou Blvd., Ashland OR 97520. (541)552-6518. E-mail: West Wind@students.sou.edu. Website: www.sou.edu/English/westwind. Southern Oregon University. Student editor changes each year. Strives to bring well-written, insightful stories and poems to the public. Annual anthology; 100-200 pgs.; circ. 250-500. 100% unsolicited freelance. Complete ms/cover letter & bio; no phone/e-mail query. **PAYS 1 COPY OF ANTHOLOGY** for 1st rts. Not copyrighted. Fiction (8-15/yr.). Accepts mss from May 15 through November 20. Responds in 5-10 wks. No simultaneous submissions or reprints. Does not use sidebars. No e-mail submissions. Guidelines on Website; copy $3. (No ads)

Poetry: Any type; any length. Submit max. 5 poems. Pays one copy of the anthology.

Special Needs: Poetry or short stories that reflect moving, human interest—in a tasteful manner. Fiction should be thoughtful, literary, and contemporary.

Tips: "We accept all submissions for consideration, and observe no borders in order to encourage original creativity. We accept all forms of poetry, prose, short story, and black & white photos. No erotica, sci-fi/fantasy, or racial bias."

WHITE WING MESSENGER, PO Box 2970, Cleveland TN 37320-2970. (423)559-5128. Fax (423)559-5444. E-mail: jenny@cogop.org. Website: www.cogop.org. Church of God of Prophecy. Virginia Chatham, mng. ed. Official voice of the denomination. Monthly mag.; 36 pgs.; circ. 7,000. Subscription $18. Open to freelance. Query; phone/fax/e-query OK. **NO PAYMENT.** Articles 500-1,000 wds. Responds in 3-4 wks. Not in topical listings. (No ads)

$+WHOLE MAGAZINE, 127 Audubon Dr., #162-C, North Little Rock AR 72113. E-mail: publisher@wholemagazine.com. Website: www.wholemagazine.com. L. Marie Trotter, pub. A Christian living publication focusing on "wholeness" for the body of Christ: witness, health, opinion, lifestyle, and evangelism topics for the entire family of God. Quarterly mag; 32 pgs.; circ. 5,000. Subscription $16. 50% unsolicited freelance; 50% assigned. Complete ms/cover letter; e-query OK. Pays $50-150 on publication for one-time rts. Articles 1,000-3,000 wds.; fiction 1,200-2,000 wds. Responds in 4 wks. Seasonal 4 mos. ahead. Uses some sidebars. Guidelines; copy for 9x12 SAE/3 stamps.

Tips: "Looking for in-depth and feature-length articles on a multitude of topics. Do your Bible and current-events homework. Christian short stories must be very well written and polished. Don't be afraid to address controversial issues, but be ready to 'wrap it up' or 'round it off,' as it were, with a clear, uncompromised Christian perspective."

+THE WICHITA CHRONICLE, PO Box 781079, Wichita KS 67278. (316)733-6539. E-mail: editor@wichitachronicle.com. Website: www.wichitachronicle.com. Kansas' largest Christian newspaper. Monthly newspaper; weekly online version; circ. 16,500. Subscription $13. Incomplete topical listings. No questionnaire returned.

WINSOME WIT, 12971 Fieldstone Rd., Milaca MN 56353. (320)983-5910. E-mail: jbeuoy@winsomewit.com. Website: www.winsomewit.com. Nondenominational. Jay Beuoy, ed. We write to persuade the unbeliever through the use of satire, from a Christian worldview. Online e-zine. 75% unsolicited freelance. Complete ms; e-query OK. **NO PAYMENT FOR NOW** for one-time and electronic rts. Not copyrighted. Articles & short stories 500-2,000 wds.; reviews 500-700 wds. Responds in 1 wk. No seasonal. Accepts simultaneous submissions & reprints (tell when/where appeared). Prefers accepted ms by e-mail (attached as Word.doc or copied into message). Guidelines & copy on Website. (Ads)

Poetry: Open to poetry if it fits their style; any type; to 100 lines. Submit max. 10 poems.

Fillers: Short humor.

Special Needs: "Writers with a good sense of humor. We want satire, but keep it friendly."

Contest: Details on Website.

Tips: "Check our Website. We encourage you to submit if you can write from a Christian perspective; use satire, parody, and the like; and be creative. We do not lampoon the church. Please don't send religious satire; we satirize secular culture."

$WIRELESS AGE: The Information Source for Christian Media, 1305 B Clearview Dr., Latrobe PA 15650. (724)532-3300. Fax (724)532-3399. E-mail: wmg@wpa.net. Website: www.westarmediagroup.com. Westar Media Group, Inc. Dave Koch, pub./ed. For Christian media professionals working in the industry—especially those in radio. Quarterly mag.; 48 pgs.; circ. 4,000. 15% unsolicited freelance; 85% assigned. Query; fax/e-query OK. Pays variable rates for 1st rts. Articles 300-2,500 wds.; book reviews 150-250 wds. Responds in 2 wks. Accepts simultaneous submissions & reprints (tell when/where appeared). Prefers accepted ms by e-mail (attached or copied into message). Regularly uses sidebars. Prefers NIV. Guidelines (also by e-mail); copy for 10x13 SAE/$1.42 postage (mark "Media Mail"). (Ads)

Fillers: Buys 3/yr. Cartoons, prose, 50-300 wds.; pay varies.

Columns/Departments: Buys 48-55/yr. TV/Film (Christian TV/film issues/concerns); Radio (Christian broadcasting issues/concerns); Internet (using the Internet effectively); Programming/Production (radio program and production development); Music (profiles, reviews, news); Publishing (publishing concerns/issues); Technology (reviews, technology issues); Ministry (highlights, development of); plus others; all 800 wds., payment varies.

Special Needs: Technology pieces, affecting the way Christians communicate the gospel.

$THE WITTENBURG DOOR (formerly *The Door*), 5634 Columbia Ave., Dallas TX 75214. (214)827-2625. Fax (254)752-4915. E-mail (submissions): dooreditor@earthlink.net. Website: www.wittenburgdoor.com. Trinity Foundation. Robert Darden, sr. ed. Satire of evangelical church, plus issue-oriented interviews. Bimonthly mag.; 50 pgs.; circ. 14,000. Subscription $29.95. 90% unsolicited freelance; 10% assigned. Complete ms; e-query OK. Pays $60-200 on publication for 1st rts. Articles to 1,500 wds., prefers 750-1,000 wds. (30/yr.). Responds in 8 wks. Accepts simultaneous submissions & reprints (if from non-competing markets). Guidelines (also by e-mail); copy $7. (Ads)

Tips: "We look for biting satire/humor—*National Lampoon* not *Reader's Digest*. You must understand our satirical slant. Read more than one issue to understand our 'wavelength.' We desperately need genuinely funny articles with a smart, satiric bent. Write funny stuff about religion. Interview interesting people with something to say about faith and/or religion."

+WORD & WAY, 3236 Emerald Ln., Ste. 400, Jefferson City MO 65109. (573)635-5939, ext. 202. Fax (573)635-1774. E-mail: jconley@wordandway.org. Website: www.wordand way.org. Jan Conley, communications asst.

+THE WORD NEWS, 1420 Main St., Buffalo NY 14209. Toll-free (866)469-9673. Fax (877)225-0423. E-mail: submissions@wordmagazine.net, or editor@wordmagazine.net. Website: www.wordmagazine.net. David R. McCleary, exec. ed. (davemc@wordmagazine .net). To publish the news from a godly perspective. Newspaper. Open to unsolicited free-lance. Query or complete ms by e-mail. Articles. Incomplete topical listings. No question-naire returned.

Tips: "It is our purpose to share information and educate the general public on community and civic issues, and to promote dialogue and stimulate individuals to critical thinking on such matters."

$#THE WORLD & I: The Magazine for Lifelong Learners, 3600 New York Ave. N.E., Washington DC 20002-1947. (202)635-4000. Fax (202)269-9353. Website: www.world andi.com. Washington Times Corp. Morton A. Kaplan, ed./pub.; Michael Marshall, exec. ed.; submit to Gary Rowe, editorial office mngr. Scholarly and encyclopedic. Monthly & online journal.; 350 pgs.; print circ. 30,000. Subscription rates on Website. 5-8% unsolicited freelance; 85% assigned. Query/clips; e-query OK. Pays $400-800 on publication for all rts. Articles 2,500 wds. (1,200/yr.); book reviews 2,000-2,500 wds. ($400-500). Responds in 6-10 wks. Seasonal 5 mos. ahead. Accepts reprints. Prefers requested ms on disk. Kill fee 20%. Uses some sidebars. Guidelines (also by e-mail); copy $7.95/9x12 SAE/$1.42 postage (mark "Media Mail"). (Ads)

Poetry: Buys few. Haiku (Asian translation); $30-75. Submit max. 5 poems.

Columns/Departments: Buys 60/yr., plus 12 photo essays. Seven different columns, various lengths. See sample copy.

Tips: "Life and Culture areas most open to freelancers. Offer a great/original idea (with established background as a writer), and writing samples. We especially appreciate scholarly contributions."

**This periodical was #49 on the 2004 Top 50 Christian Publishers list (#31 in 2003).

+WORLD NET DAILY, PO Box 1087, Grants Pass OR 97528. (541)474-1776. Fax (541)474-1770. Website: www.worldnetdaily.com. WorldNetDaily.Com, Inc. A fiercely independent news site committed to hard-hitting investigative reporting of government waste, fraud, and abuse. Daily news-zine. Incomplete topical listings. No questionnaire returned.

XAVIER REVIEW, 1 Drexel Dr., Box 110C, Xavier University of Louisiana, New Orleans LA 70125. (504)520-7549. E-mail: rcollins@xula.edu. Richard Collins, ed. Publishes non-dogmatic, thought-provoking, and sometimes humorous and even irreverent work on religious subject matters. Semiannual literary jour; 75 pgs.; circ. 300. Subscription $10 (individuals), $15(institutions). 90% unsolicited freelance; 10% assigned. Complete ms/cover letter; e-query OK. **PAYS IN COPIES** for 1st rts. Articles 250-5,000 wds. (3/yr.); fiction 250-5,000 wds.(6/yr.); book reviews 250-750 wds. Responds in 4 wks. Accepts simultaneous submissions; no reprints. Prefers accepted mss by e-mail (attached). No kill fee. Does not use sidebars. Guidelines by e-mail; copy for $2/7x10 SAE/3 stamps. (No ads)

Poetry: Accepts 20/yr. Avant-garde, free verse, traditional; 5-60 lines. Submit max. 5 poems.

CHILDREN'S MARKETS

$ADVENTURES, 6401 The Paseo, Kansas City MO 64131-1213. (816)333-7000, ext. 2247. Fax (816)333-4439. E-mail: jjsmith@nazarene.org. Website: www.wordaction.com. Julie Smith, ed.; submit to Denise Willemen, ed. asst. For 6- to 8-yr.-olds (1st & 2nd graders); emphasis on principles, character building. Weekly take-home paper; 4 pgs.; circ. 40,000. Subscription $11.96 ($2.99/child/quarter). Estab. 2003. 45% unsolicited freelance. Query; e-query OK. Pays $15-25 on publication for all rts. Biblical or contemporary fiction 100 wds. Responds in 4-6 wks. Accepts simultaneous submissions; no reprints. Accepts requested ms by e-mail (attached file). Prefers NIV. Guidelines/theme list (also by e-mail); copy for #10 SAE/1 stamps. (No ads)

Poetry: Buys free verse, light verse, traditional; 4-8 lines; .25/line, with $2 min. Submit any number.

Fillers: Buys cartoons, facts, games, party ideas, quotes, tips, word puzzles. Pays $15 for cartoons; $25 for 4-panel strip.

Special Needs: Rebus stories; interesting facts/trivia; trivia puzzles; recipes and crafts; activities. Also needs material for Parent Connections: activities for parent/child; upbeat advice for parents or caretakers.

Tips: "We accept a limited amount of material." Not accepting submissions until September 2006.

$AMERICAN GIRL, 8400 Fairway Pl., Middleton WI 53562. (608)836-4848. Fax (608)831-7089. E-mail: im_agmag_editor@pleasantco.com. Website: www.americangirl.com. Pleasant

Company Publications. Kristi Thom, ed.; Barbara E. Stretchberry, mng. ed. Secular; for girls ages 8-12 to recognize and celebrate girls' achievements yesterday and today, inspire their creativity, and nurture their hopes and dreams. Bimonthly & online mag.; 50 pgs.; circ. 700,000. Subscription $19.95. 5% unsolicited freelance; 10% assigned. Query (complete ms for fiction); no e-query. Pays $1/wd. ($300 minimum) on acceptance for 1st or all rts. Articles 150-1,000 wds. (10/yr.); fiction to 2,500 wds. (6/yr.- $500 min.). Responds in 13 wks. Seasonal 6 mos. ahead. Accepts simultaneous submissions & reprints. Kill fee 50%. Uses some sidebars. Guidelines (also on Website); copy $3.95 (check)/9x12 SAE/$1.42 postage (mark "Media Mail"). (No ads)

Poetry: All poetry is by children.

Fillers: Cartoons, puzzles, word games; $50.

Columns/Departments: Buys 10/yr. Girls Express (short profiles on girls), to 150 wds. (query); Giggle Gang (visual puzzles, mazes, word games, math puzzles, seasonal games/puzzles), send complete ms. Pays $50-200.

Contest: Contests vary from issue to issue.

Tips: "Girls Express offers the most opportunities for freelancers. We're looking for short profiles of girls who are doing great and interesting things. Key: a girl must be the 'star' and the story written from her point of view. Be sure to include the ages of the girls you are pitching to us. Write for 8- to 12-year-olds—not teenagers."

$BAREFOOT FOR KIDS, PO Box 3743, Englewood CO 80155. E-mail: jeanne@barefooton holyground.com. Website: www.barefootforkids.com. Jeanne Gowen Dennis, ed. Encourages children, ages 6-12, to live their lives fully in a loving relationship with God. Quarterly e-zine. Free online. Estab. 2004. 80% unsolicited freelance. Complete ms; e-query OK. Pays .005/wd. on publication for 1st, reprint, simultaneous, electronic, or nonexclusive rts.; right to archive on Website. Not copyrighted. Articles 300-500 wds. (8/yr.); fiction 300-800 wds. (4-8/yr.); book reviews 25-250 wds. Responds in 4-6 wks. Seasonal 2 mos. ahead. Accepts simultaneous submissions & reprints (tell when/where appeared). Requires e-mail submission (copied into message). Encourages submissions from children. Uses some sidebars. Prefers NIV or Children's NIV. Guidelines/copy online. (Ads)

Poetry: Buys several/yr. Free verse, haiku, light verse, traditional; 4-12 lines. Submit max. 5 poems.

Fillers: Buys several/yr. Cartoons, facts, games, ideas, jokes, kid quotes, party ideas, prayers, quizzes, short humor, word puzzles; devotionals, recipes; 25-100 wds.

Columns/Departments: Buys 4-8/yr. Treasure Hunt (fun activities and puzzles that require children to use their Bibles to find answers), up to 600 wds.

Special Needs: Looking for book reviews of great children's classics; fun, hands-on activities; short stories; recipes; and treasure hunt submissions.

Tips: "We're looking for high quality writing that will entice children away from TV and video games into enriching and fun activities. Our main goal is to guide them toward greater intimacy with God through an active life and faith."

$BEGINNER'S FRIEND, PO Box 4060, Overland Park KS 66204. (913)432-0331. Fax (913)722-0351. E-mail: sseditor1@juno.com. Church of God (Holiness)/Herald and Banner Press. Arlene McGehee, Sunday school ed. Denominational; for young children. Weekly take-home paper; 4 pgs.; circ. 2,700. Subscription $1.50. Complete ms/cover letter; phone/fax/e-query OK (prefers mail or e-mail). Pays .005/wd. on publication for 1st rts. Fiction 500-800 wds. Seasonal 6-8 mos. ahead. Accepts simultaneous submissions & reprints (tell when/where appeared). Prefers KJV. Guidelines/theme list; copy. Not in topical listings.

$BREAD FOR GOD'S CHILDREN, Box 1017, Arcadia FL 34265-1017. (863)494-6214. Fax (863)993-0154. E-mail: BREAD@sunline.net. Website: www.breadministries.org. Bread

Ministries, Inc. Judith M. Gibbs, ed. A family magazine for serious Christians who are concerned about their children or grandchildren. Bimonthly mag.; 32 pgs.; circ. 10,000. Subscription free. 20-25% unsolicited freelance. Complete ms; no e-query. Pays $25 ($40-50 for fiction) on publication for 1st rts. Not copyrighted. Articles 600-800 wds. (6/yr.); fiction & true stories 600-900 wds. for 4-10 yrs., 900-1,500 wds. for teens aged 14 and up (6/yr.). Responds in 8-12 wks. (may hold longer). Uses some simultaneous submissions & reprints (tell when/where appeared). Some sidebars. Prefers KJV. Guidelines (also by e-mail); 3 magazine copies for 9x12 SAE/5 stamps; 1 copy 3 stamps. (No ads)

> **Columns/Departments:** Buys 5-8/yr. Let's Chat (discussion issues facing children), 500-800 wds.; Teen Page (teen issues), 600-900 wds.; and Idea Page (object lessons or crafts for children), 300-800 wds.; $10-30.

> **Tips:** "We need good stories for the younger children-ages 4-10 years. Most open to fiction or real-life stories of overcoming through faith in Jesus Christ and/or guidance from godly principles. No tag endings or adult solutions coming from children. Create realistic characters and situations. No 'sudden inspiration' solutions. Open to any areas of family life related from a godly perspective."

$CADET QUEST, PO Box 7259, Grand Rapids MI 49510. (616)241-5616. E-mail: submissions @CalvinistCadets.org. Website: www.CalvinistCadets.org. Calvinist Cadet Corps. G. Richard Broene, ed. To show boys ages 9-14 how God is at work in their lives and in the world around them. Mag. published 7X/yr.; 24 pgs.; circ. 9,500. 35% unsolicited freelance. Complete ms/cover letter. Pays .04-.06/wd. on acceptance for 1st, one-time, or reprint rts. Articles 500-1,000 wds. (7/yr.); fiction 900-1,500 wds. (14/yr.). Responds in 4 wks. Accepts simultaneous submissions & reprints (tell when/where appeared). Accepts ms by e-mail (copied into message). Uses some sidebars. Prefers NIV. Guidelines, theme list (also on Website); copy for 9x12 SAE/4 stamps. (Ads-limited)

> **Fillers:** Buys several/yr. Quizzes, tips, word puzzles; 20-200 wds.; $5 & up.

> **Tips:** "Most open to fiction or fillers tied to themes; request new theme list in January of each year (best to submit between January and April each year). Also looking for simple projects/crafts, and puzzles (word, logic)."

$CELEBRATE, 6401 The Paseo, Kansas City MO 64131. (816)333-7000, ext. 2358. Fax (816)333-4439. E-mail: acallison@nazarene.org. Website: www.wordaction.com. Word-Action Publishing Co., Church of the Nazarene. Andrea Callison, ed. asst. Weekly activity/ story paper connects Sunday school learning to life for preschoolers (3 & 4), kindergartners (5 & 6), and their families. Weekly take-home paper; 4 pgs.; circ. 40,000. Subscription $10. 50% unsolicited freelance. Query or complete ms/cover letter; e-query OK. Pays $15 or .25/line on acceptance for multiple-use rts. Responds in 4-6 wks. No seasonal. Accepts simultaneous submissions; no reprints. Accepts e-mail submissions (attached file). Prefers NIV. Guidelines (also by e-mail)/theme list/copy for #10 SAE/1 stamp. (No ads)

> **Special Needs:** Activities, recipes, poems, piggyback songs, and crafts for 3- to 6-year-olds.

> **Tips:** "We accept a limited amount of material."

$+CHARACTERS, PO Box 708, Newport NH 03773-0708. (603)863-5896. Fax (603)863-8198. E-mail: hotdog@nhvt.net. Website: www.cdavisnh.com. Davis Publications. Cindy Davis, ed. Literary magazine of short stories. Quarterly mag. 100% unsolicited freelance. Complete ms; e-submissions OK. Pays $5 on publication for one-time or reprint rts. Not copyrighted. Fiction to 1,500 wds. (30/yr.). Responds in 4-9 wks. Seasonal 6 mos. ahead. Accepts simultaneous submissions & reprints. Accepts submissions from children/teens. Guidelines; copy $5. Incomplete topical listings.

> **Poetry:** Buys 5/yr. Light verse, traditional; to 14 lines. Submit max. 2 poems.

> **Special Needs:** Short stories and art submissions by children.

Contest: Annual Short Story Contest with August 31 deadline. Six prizes in 2 categories: adult authors and children authors (to age 16). All genres to 1,000 words. $3 entry fee per story. Details in Website.

Tips: "No talking animals, sex, or obscenity."

$CLUB CONNECTION, 1445 N. Boonville Ave., Springfield MO 65802-1894. (417)862-2781. Fax (417)862-0503. E-mail: clubconnection@ag.org. Website: www.clubconnection .ag.org, or www.ag.org/missionettes. Gospel Publishing House. Submit to The Editor. For girls, ages 6-12 (with leader edition for Missionettes leaders). Quarterly mag.; 32 pgs.; circ. 12,000. Subscription $6.50 (leader's $7.50). 25% freelance. Complete ms/cover letter; fax/e-query OK. Pays $25-50 on publication for 1st or one-time rts. Articles 250-800 wds. (8/yr.); fiction 250-800 wds. (8/yr.). Responds in 5-10 wks. Seasonal 9-12 mos. ahead. Accepts requested ms on disk. Regular sidebars. Prefers NIV. Guidelines/theme list on Website; free copy.

  Fillers: Buys 6-8/yr. Anecdotes, cartoons, facts, games, ideas, jokes, newsbreaks, party ideas, quizzes, short humor, word puzzles; 20-50 or 100 wds.; $5-20.

  Columns/Departments: Buys 4-6/yr.; $10-50.

  Special Needs: Send for theme list each year.

$COURAGE, 1300 N. Meacham Rd., Schaumburg IL 60173-4806. Toll-free (888)588-1600. (847)843-1600. Fax (847)843-3757. E-mail: takehomepapers@garbc.org. Website: www .garbc.org/rbp. Regular Baptist Press. Joan Alexander, ed. For children, 9-11, in Sunday school. Weekly take-home paper; 4 pgs. Subscription $2.49/quarter. Complete ms/cover letter including personal testimony; no phone/fax/e-query. Pays .05/wd. and up, on acceptance for first and reprint rts. (needs multiple reprint rights so they can reprint 2-3 times until next revision). Lead stories 800-1,200 wds. (40/yr.). Fiction & true stories (40-50/yr.); some serials. Responds in 8-12 wks. Seasonal 1 yr. ahead. No simultaneous submissions; occasionally accepts reprints (tell when/where appeared). No mss by e-mail. Uses some sidebars. Accepts submissions from children. Requires KJV. Guidelines/theme list on Website (go to RBP site map/site index/About Us/Write for RBP); copy for 9x12 SAE/3 stamps. (No ads)

  Fillers: Accepts 15-25/yr. Puzzles and projects. "Not word puzzles; we're looking for logic puzzles, visual puzzles, and other innovative approaches to solving problems." Pays for fillers.

  Special Needs: Looking for well-written stories that show the truth about God (related to the weekly Sunday school lesson) as it comes to bear in the lives of children today. Need stories for boys, or that have both boy and girl characters.

  Tips: "Writer can best break into our market by being well acquainted with our audience and writing well in a way that supports the RBP mission. Check Website quarterly for updates concerning needs, themes, etc.: www.RegularBapristPress.org."

$DISCOVERIES, 6401 The Paseo, Kansas City MO 64131. (816)333-7000. Fax (816)333-4439. E-mail: vfolsom@nazarene.org. Website: www.nazarene.org. Nazarene/Word Action Publishing. Virginia Folsom, ed.; submit to Sarah Weatherwax, ed. asst. (sweatherwax@ nazarene.org). For 8- to 10-yr.-olds, emphasizing Christian values and holy living; follows theme of Sunday school curriculum. Weekly take-home paper; 4 pgs.; circ. 30,000. 80% unsolicited freelance; 20% assigned. This publication has announced that it will be accepting no more freelance submissions until 2007.

  **This periodical was #41 on the 2004 Top 50 Christian Publishers list (#44 in 2003).

$FACES, 30 Grove St., Ste. C, Peterborough NH 03458. (603)924-7209. Fax (603)924-7380. E-mail: facesmag@yahoo.com. Website: www.cobblestonepub.com. Cobblestone Publishing/secular. Elizabeth Crooker, ed. Introduces young readers (ages 9-14) to different world cultures, religion, geography, government, and art. Monthly mag.; circ. 15,000. Subscription $29.95. 90-100% freelance. Query only; e-query OK. Pays .20-.25/wd. on publication for all rts. Articles 300-800 wds. (45-50/yr.); fiction to 800 wds. (retold folktales, legends, plays; related to theme). Responds in 4 wks. to 4 mos. Accepts simultaneous submissions. Prefers disk or hard copy. Kill fee 50%. Guidelines/themes (also on Website); copy $4.95/9x12 SAE/$2 postage; also online.

Poetry: Any type to 100 wds.

Fillers: Activities, 100-600 wds.; .20-.25/wd.

$FOCUS ON THE FAMILY CLUBHOUSE, 8605 Explorer Dr., Colorado Springs CO 80920. (719)531-3400. Website: www.clubhousemagazine.com. Focus on the Family. Jesse Florea, ed.; Suzanne Hadley, assoc. ed. For children 8-12 years who desire to know more about God and the Bible. Monthly & online mag.; 24 pgs.; circ. 101,100. Subscription $15. 15% unsolicited freelance; 25% assigned. Complete ms/cover letter; no phone/fax/e-query. Pays .15-.25/wd. for articles, up to $200 for fiction on acceptance for 1st, one-time, electronic rts. Articles to 800 wds. (5/yr.); fiction 500-1,800 wds. (30/yr.). Responds in 8 wks. Seasonal 6 mos. ahead. Accepts simultaneous submissions; no reprints. No disk or e-mail submissions. Kill fee. Uses some sidebars. Prefers NIV. Accepts submissions from children. Guidelines; copy (call 1-800-232-6459). (No ads)

Fillers: Buys 6-8/yr. Quizzes, word puzzles, recipes; 200-800 wds.; .15-.25/wd.

Tips: "Most open to fiction, biblical fiction, and how-to pieces with a theme. Avoid stories dealing with boy-girl relationships, poetry, and contemporary, middle-class family settings (current authors meet this need). Biggest need is for biblical fiction stories (less than 1,000 wds.) that stay true to the Bible, but bring text to life; also historical or other cultures; or how-to with a theme (doing stuff for dad, making neighborhood beautiful, Christmas crafts, etc.). Send mss with list of credentials. Read past issues."

**2005, 2004 EPA Award of Merit—Youth.

$FOCUS ON THE FAMILY CLUBHOUSE JR., 8605 Explorer Dr., Colorado Springs CO 80920. (719)531-3400. Website: www.clubhousemagazine.org. Focus on the Family. Annette Bourland, ed.; Suzanne Hadley, assoc. ed. For 4- to 8-year-olds growing in a Christian family. Monthly & online mag.; 24 pgs.; circ. 78,000. Subscription $18. 25% unsolicited freelance; 50% assigned. Complete ms/cover letter; no phone/fax/e-query. Pays $25-200 ($50-100 for fiction) on acceptance for 1st, one-time, electronic rts. Articles 100-500 wds. (1-2/yr.); fiction 250-1,000 wds. (10/yr.); Bible stories 250-800 wds.; one-page rebus stories to 200 wds. Responds in 4-6 wks. Seasonal 5-6 mos. ahead. Kill fee 25%. Uses some sidebars. Guidelines; copy (call 1-800-232-6459). (No ads)

Poetry: Buys 4-8/yr. Traditional; 10-25 lines (to 250 wds.); $50-100.

Fillers: Buys 4-8/yr. Recipes/crafts; 100-500 wds.; $50-100.

Special Needs: Bible stories, rebus, fiction, and crafts.

Tips: "Most open to short, nonpreachy fiction, beginning reader stories, and read-to-me. Be knowledgeable of our style and try it out on kids first. Looking for stories set in exotic places; nonwhite, middle-class characters; historical pieces; humorous quizzes; and craft and recipe features are most readily accepted."

**2004 EPA Award of Excellence—Youth.

$GOD'S WORLD NEWS, PO Box 2330, Asheville NC 28802. (828)253-8063. Fax (828)253-1556. E-mail: nbomer@gwpub.com. God's World Publications. Norman W. Bomer, sr. ed. No longer accepting freelance.

$GUIDE, 55 W. Oak Ridge Dr., Hagerstown MD 21740. (301)393-4037. Fax (301)393-4055. E-mail: Guide@rhpa.org. Website: www.guidemagazine.org. Seventh-day Adventist/Review and Herald Publishing. Randy Fishell, ed.; Rachel Whitaker, asst. ed. A Christian journal for 10- to 14-yr.-olds, presenting true stories relevant to their needs. Weekly mag.; 32 pgs.; circ. 30,000. Subscription $46.95/yr. 65% unsolicited freelance; 20% assigned. Complete ms/cover letter; fax/e-query OK. Pays .06-.12/wd. on acceptance for 1st or reprint rts. True stories 500-1,200 wds. (150/yr.). Responds in 6-8 wks. Seasonal 7 mos. ahead. Accepts reprints (tell when/where appeared; pays 50% of standard rate). Prefers requested ms by e-mail (attached file). Uses some sidebars. Prefers NIV. Guidelines on Website; copy for 6x9 SAE/2 stamps. (No ads)

Fillers: Buys 50/yr. Games, quizzes, word puzzles on a spiritual theme; 20-50 wds.; $20-50. Accepting very few games, only the most unusual concepts.

Special Needs: "Most open to true action/adventure, Christian humor, and true stories showing God at work in a 10- to 14-year-old's life. Stories must have energy and a high level of intrinsic interest to kids. Put it together with dialog and a spiritual slant, and you're on the 'write' track for our readers. School life."

Tips: "We use only true stories, including school situations, humorous circumstances, adventure, short historical and biographical stories, and almost any situation relevant to 10- to 14-year-olds. Stories must have a spiritual point or implication."

**This periodical was #25 on the 2005 Top 50 Christian Publishers list (#34 in 2004, #19 in 2003, #8 in 2002, #11 in 2001).

$GUIDEPOSTS FOR KIDS ON THE WEB, 1050 Broadway, Ste. 6, Chesterton IN 46304. (219)929-4429. Fax (219)926-3839. E-mail: rtolin@guideposts.org. Website: www.gp4k.com. Guideposts, Inc. Mary Lou Carney, ed.; submit to Rosanne Tolin, mng. ed. For kids 6-11 yrs. (emphasis at upper level). Online mag. Free online. 40% unsolicited freelance; 60% assigned. Query/clips (complete ms for fiction); no phone/fax/e-query. Pays $50-350 (.50-.70/wd.); $100-350 for fiction; on acceptance for all electronic rts. & nonexclusive print rts. Articles 300-1,200 wds. (24/yr.); fiction to 900 wds. (6/yr.). Responds in 4-6 wks. Seasonal 6 mos. ahead. No disk or e-mail submissions. Kill fee. Regularly uses sidebars. Prefers NIV. Guidelines (also on Website); copy online. (No ads)

Poetry: Buys 4-6/yr. Any type; 3-20 lines; $15-50. Submit max. 5 poems.

Fillers: Buys 15-20/yr. Anecdotes, cartoons, facts, games, ideas, jokes, party ideas, prose, quizzes, short humor, word puzzles; to 300 wds.; $20-75.

Columns/Departments: Buys 20/yr. Cool Kids (amazing kids doing great things to help their communities, or excelling in a sport, etc.), 300-600 wds.; Tips from the Top (Christian celebrities/sports figures), 500-700 wds.; $100-200.

Contest: Has giveaways, art and writing contests in Home School Zone (section of the e-zine).

Tips: "Keep online links in mind that might be of interest on your topic. Polaroid snapshots are helpful as well. Cool Kids column is a good place to break in. Also stories on school and sports; craft and recipe ideas; animals; and celebrity profiles."

**This periodical was #41 on the 2005 Top 50 Christian Publishers list (#32 in 2001).

$HIGH ADVENTURE, 1445 N. Boonville Ave., Springfield MO 65802-1894. (417)862-2781, ext. 4177. Fax (417)831-8230. E-mail: RoyalRangers@ag.org. Website: www.rangers .ag.org. Assemblies of God. Submit to High Adventure Editor. For the Royal Rangers (boys), from kindergarten through high school; emphasis toward elementary through high school. Quarterly mag.; 16 pgs.; circ. 86,000. 25% unsolicited freelance; 60% assigned. Complete ms/cover letter; e-query OK. Pays .06/wd. on publication for 1st, one-time, simultaneous, or reprint rts. Articles 500-900 wds. (30/yr.); fiction 500-900 wds. (15/yr.). Responds in 4-5 wks. Seasonal 7 mos. ahead. Accepts simultaneous submissions & reprints (tell when/where appeared). Regularly uses sidebars. Prefers NIV. Guidelines (also by e-mail); copy for 9x12 SAE/3 stamps. (No ads)

Fillers: Buys 30/yr. Cartoons, jokes, short humor; 50 wds., $25-30; quizzes, word puzzles, $12-15.

Tips: "Both fiction and nonfiction are open to freelancers. Space is a major issue. We look for writers who are precise in their descriptions of events , but who can still meet the word count."

**This periodical was #46 on the 2002 Top 50 Christian Publishers list.

+INSPIRATIONSTATION MAGAZINE, 1119 S. Despelder, #6, Grand Haven MI 49417. (616)846-7283. E-mail: kevinscottcollier@hotmail.com. Website: www.inspirationstation .faithweb.com. Kevin Scott Collier, pub. Online Christian children's mag.

$JUNIOR COMPANION, PO Box 4060, Overland Park KS 66204. (913)432-0331. Fax (913)722-0351. E-mail: sseditor1@juno.com. Church of God (holiness)/Herald and Banner Press. Arlene McGehee, Sunday school ed. Denominational; for 4th-6th graders. Weekly take-home paper; 4 pgs.; circ. 3,500. Subscription $1.50. Complete ms/cover letter; phone/fax/e-query OK (prefers mail or e-mail). Pays .005/wd. on publication for 1st rts. Fiction 500-1,200 wds. Seasonal 6-8 mos. ahead. Accepts simultaneous submissions & reprints (tell when/where appeared). Prefers KJV. Guidelines/theme list; copy. Not in topical listings.

$JUNIORWAY, PO Box 436987, Chicago IL 60643. Toll-free (800)860-8642. Fax (708)868-6759. Website: www.urbanministries.com. Urban Ministries, Inc. Submit to The Editor. Sunday school take-home paper for 4th-6th graders. Open to freelance. Query/clips; fax/e-query OK. Pays $150, 120 days after acceptance, for all rts. Articles. Responds in 4 wks. Seasonal 6 mos. ahead. Accepts simultaneous submissions. Requires accepted ms on disk. Prefers NIV. Guidelines; copy for #10 SASE. (No ads) Incomplete topical listings.

> **Tips:** "Send query with a writing sample. Looking for those with educational or Sunday school teaching experience."

$KEYS FOR KIDS, PO Box 1001, Grand Rapids MI 49501-1001. (616)647-4500. Fax (616)647-4950. E-mail: Hazel@cbhministries.org, or geri@cbhministries.org. Website: www.cbhministries.org. CBH Ministries. Hazel Marett, ed.; Geri Walcott, ed. A daily devotional booklet for children (8-14) or for family devotions. Bimonthly booklet and online version; 80 pgs.; circ. 100,000. Subscription free. 100% unsolicited freelance. Complete ms. Pays $20-25 on acceptance for 1st, reprint, or simultaneous rts. Not copyrighted. Devotionals (includes short fiction story) 375-425 wds. (60-70/yr.). Responds in 2-4 wks. Seasonal 4-5 mos. ahead. Accepts simultaneous submissions & reprints. Prefers NKJV. Guidelines (also by e-mail); copy for 6x9 SAE. (No ads)

> **Tips:** "We want children's devotions. If you are rejected, go back to the sample and study it some more."

$LIVE WIRE, 8121 Hamilton Ave., Cincinnati OH 45231. (513)931-4050. Fax (513)931-0950. E-mail: cgirton@standardpub.com. Website: www.StandardPub.com. No freelance.

$MY FRIEND: The Catholic Magazine for Kids, 50 Saint Pauls Ave., Boston MA 02130-3491. (617)522-8911. Fax (617)541-9805. E-mail: mgdateno@paulinemedia.com. Website: www.myfriendmagazine.org. Pauline Books & Media. Sr. Maria Grace Dateno, ed. Christian formation, inspiration, and entertainment for Catholic children, ages 7-12. Monthly (10X) & online mag.; 32 pgs.; circ. 9,000. Subscription $24.95. 30% unsolicited freelance; 30% assigned. Complete ms/cover letter; e-query OK for nonfiction. Pays $70-150 for articles & fiction on acceptance for 1st, electronic, & worldwide rts. Articles 200-1,000 wds. (5/yr.); fiction 500-1,200 wds. (25/yr.). Responds in 8 wks. Seasonal 11 mos. ahead. Kill fee. Uses some sidebars. Prefers CEV. Guidelines/theme list (also on Website); copy $2/9x12 SAE/5 stamps. (No ads)

> **Poetry:** Buys 5-6/yr. Light verse, traditional; theme-related or seasonal; $20-50. Submit any number.

> **Fillers:** Buys 5-6/yr. Math puzzles. Pays $5-20.

> **Special Needs:** Needs more nonfiction and fiction for Christmas issue. Also profiles of kids making a difference in the world. Theme-related fiction.

Tips: "We publish freelance fiction in every issue. We are looking for engaging stories with realistic dialog, good character development, and current lingo. Watch out for being too predictable or too preachy. Please check out our guidelines, theme list, and a sample copy. Go to Website and click on 'For Contributors.'"

$NATURE FRIEND, 2673 Township Rd. 421, Sugarcreek OH 44681-9486. (330)852-1900. Fax (330)852-3285 or (800)852-4482. Carlisle Press. Marvin Wengerd, ed. For children (ages 6-14); about God's wonderful world of nature and wildlife. Monthly mag.; 24 pgs.; circ. 13,000. Subscription $22. 10% unsolicited freelance; 40% assigned. Complete ms/cover letter; no phone/fax query. Pays .05/wd. on publication for 1st or one-time rts. Articles 250-750 wds. (50/yr.); or fiction 500-750 wds. (40/yr.). Responds in 12-13 wks. Seasonal 4 mos. ahead. Accepts simultaneous submissions; no reprints. No disk. Uses some sidebars. Any version except KJV. Guidelines $4; copy $2.50/9x12 SAE/3 stamps. (No ads)

Fillers: Buys 12/yr. Quizzes, word puzzles; 100-500 wds.; $10-25.

Tips: "We're looking for detailed science experiments for our 'Learning by Doing' feature. Choose a nature/wildlife-related topic, do it yourself, take good photos, and you're almost guaranteed a yes. Don't bother submitting to us unless you have seen our guidelines and a sample copy. We are very conservative in our approach. Everything must be nature-related. Write on a children's level—stories, facts, puzzles about animals, and nature subjects. No evolution."

$ON THE LINE, 616 Walnut Ave., Scottdale PA 15683-1999. (724)887-8500. Fax (724)887-3111. E-mail: otl@mph.org. Website: www.mph.org/otl. Mennonite Publishing House/Herald Press. Mary Clemens Meyer, ed. Reinforces Christian values in 9- to 14-yr.-olds. Monthly mag.; 24 pgs.; circ. 5,500. Subscription $27.95. 90% unsolicited freelance; 10% assigned. Complete ms; fax/e-query OK. Pays .03-.05/wd. on acceptance for one-time or reprint rts. Articles 300-500 wds. (25-30/yr.); fiction 1,000-1,800 wds. (45-50/yr.). Responds in 5 wks. Seasonal 6 mos. ahead. Accepts simultaneous submissions & reprints (tell when/where appeared). No e-mail submission. Regularly uses sidebars. Prefers NIV, NRSV. Guidelines (also by e-mail or Website); copy for 7x10 SAE/2 stamps. (No ads)

Poetry: Buys 10-15/yr. Free verse, haiku, light verse, traditional; 3-24 lines; $10-25.

Fillers: Buys 25-30/yr. Cartoons, facts, games, jokes, party ideas, quizzes, word puzzles; to 350 wds.; $10-25.

Tips: "Watch kids 9-14. Listen to them talk. Write stories that sound natural—not moralizing, preachy, with adults quoting Scripture. We look for stories of ordinary kids solving everyday problems; humor helps. Our readers like puzzles, especially theme crosswords and word-finds. Most sections of our magazine rely on freelancers for material; especially need fiction, puzzles, how-tos, and recipes for each issue."

**This periodical was #39 on the 2005 Top 50 Christian Publishers list. (#27 in 2004, #36 in 2003, #28 in 2002, #19 in 2001).

$OUR LITTLE FRIEND, Box 5353, Nampa ID 83653-5353. (208)465-2580. Fax (208)465-2531. E-mail: ailsox@pacificpress.com. Website: www.pacificpress.com. Seventh-day Adventist. Aileen Andres Sox, ed. To teach children Christian belief, values, and practice; God loving us and our loving Him makes a difference in every facet of life, from how we think and act to how we feel. Weekly take-home paper for 0- to 5-yr.-olds; 8 pgs. 25% unsolicited freelance (or reprints); 50% assigned. Complete ms by e-mail. Pays $25-40 on acceptance for one-time or reprint rts. True stories 450-550 wds. (52/yr.); no articles. Responds in 26 wks. Seasonal 7 mos. ahead. Accepts simultaneous submissions & reprints; no serials. Prefers e-mail submissions (attached file). Guidelines (also on Website); copy for 9x12 SAE/2 stamps. (No ads)

$PARTNERS, Christian Light Publications, Inc., Box 1212, Harrisonburg VA 22803-1212. (540)434-0768. Fax (540)433-8896. E-mail: partners@clp.org. Mennonite. Etta Martin, ed. Helping 9- to 14-yr.-olds to build strong Christian character. Weekly take-home paper; 4 pgs.; circ. 6,389. Subscription $9.80. 99% unsolicited freelance; 1% assigned. Complete ms; e-query OK. Pays up to .03-.05/wd. on acceptance for 1st, multiuse, or reprint rts. Articles 200-1,000 wds. (50/yr.); fiction & true stories 1,000-1,600 wds. (70/yr.); serial stories up to 1,600 wds./installment; short-short stories to 400 wds. Responds in 6 wks. Seasonal 6 mos. ahead. Accepts reprints (tell when/where appeared); serials 2-4 parts. Prefers e-mail submissions (attached or copied into message). No kill fee. Requires KJV. Guidelines/theme list (also by e-mail); copy for 9x12 SAE/3 stamps. (No ads)

Poetry: Buys 100/yr. Traditional, story poems; 4-24 lines; .50-.70/line. Submit max. 6 poems.

Fillers: Buys 100/yr. Prose, quizzes, quotes, word puzzles (Bible-related); 200-800 wds.; .03-.05/wd. Must be theme-related.

Columns/Departments: Character Corner; Cultures & Customs; Historical Highlights; Maker's Masterpiece; Missionary Mail; Torches of Truth; or Nature Nook; all 200-800 or 1,000 wds.

Tips: "Most open to character-building articles and stories that teach a spiritual lesson. Many new writers will submit their manuscript without asking for or reading our guidelines. That is folly and a waste of everyone's time. Someone who has experienced a genuine spiritual 'rebirth' has a much better chance of receiving an acceptance. Write in a lively way (showing, not telling) and on a child's level of understanding (ages 9-14). We do not require that you be Mennonite, but we do send a questionnaire for you to fill out if you desire to write for us."

**This periodical was #15 on the 2005 Top 50 Christian Publishers list (#12 in 2004, #21 in 2003, #21 in 2002, #25 in 2001).

$#PASSPORT, 6401 The Paseo, Kansas City MO 64131. (816)333-7000, ext. 2243. Fax (816)333-4439. Church of the Nazarene. Submit to The Editor. For preteens, 10- to 12-year-olds; supports the Sunday school lesson and provides an exciting way to learn about God and life. Weekly take-home paper; 4 pgs.; circ. 18,000. 30% unsolicited freelance. No freelance until 2007.

$POCKETS, PO Box 340004, Nashville TN 37203-0004. (615)340-7333. Fax (615)340-7267. E-mail: pockets@upperroom.org. Website: www.pockets.org. United Methodist. Submit to Lynn W. Gilliam, ed. Devotional magazine for children (6-11 yrs.). Monthly (11X) mag.; 48 pgs.; circ. 93,000. Subscription $19.95. 75% unsolicited freelance. Complete ms/brief cover letter. Pays .14/wd. on acceptance for 1st rts. Articles 400-800 wds. (20/yr.) & fiction 500-1,500 wds. (40/yr.). Responds in 4 wks. Seasonal 1 yr. ahead. Accepts reprints (tell when/where appeared). No mss by e-mail. Uses some sidebars. Prefers NRSV. Accepts submissions from children through age 12. Guidelines/theme list (also by e-mail/Website); copy for 9x12 SAE/4 stamps. (No ads)

Poetry: Buys 25/yr. Free verse, haiku, light verse, traditional; 4-24 lines; $2/line. Submit max. 7 poems.

Fillers: Buys 44/yr. Games, ideas, jokes, prayers, riddles, word puzzles; $25.

Columns/Departments: Buys 40/yr. Kids Cook; Pocketsful of Love (ways to show love), 200-300 wds.; Peacemakers at Work (children involved in environmental, community, and peace/justice issues; include action photos and name of photographer), to 600 wds.; Pocketsful of Prayer, 400-600 wds.; Someone You'd Like to Know (preferably a child whose lifestyle demonstrates a strong faith perspective).

Special Needs: Two-page stories for ages 5-7, 600 words max. Need role model stories, retold Biblical stories, Someone You'd Like to Know, and Peacemakers at Work.

Contest: Fiction-writing contest; submit between 3/1 & 8/15 every yr. Prize $1,000 and publication in *Pockets*. Length 1,000-1,500 wds. Must be unpublished and not historical fiction. Previous winners not eligible. Send to Pockets Fiction Contest at above address, and include an SASE for return of manuscript and response.

Tips: "Well-written fiction that fits our themes is always needed. Make stories relevant to the lives of today's children and show faith as a natural part of everyday life. All areas open to freelance. Nonfiction probably easiest to sell for columns (we get fewer submissions for those). Read, read, read and study—be attentive to guidelines, themes, and study past issues."

**This periodical was #10 on the 2005 Top 50 Christian Publishers list (#4 in 2004, #1 in 2003, #9 in 2002, #5 in 2001).

$PRAYKIDS! PO Box 35004, Colorado Springs CO 80935. (719)531-3555. Fax (719)598-7128. Website: www.praykids.com. *Pray!* magazine/NavPress. Submit to The Editor. Focus is on prayer for 8- to 12-year-olds. They will not be publishing any new issues in this series, so will not be needing new material. Re-running originals.

$PRESCHOOL PLAYHOUSE, PO Box 436987, Chicago IL 60643. (708)868-7100. Fax (708)868-6759. Website: www.urbanministries.com. Urban Ministries. Submit to The Editor. Sunday school magazine with activities for 2- to 5-year-olds with accompanying teacher's manual. Quarterly magazine for teachers; take-home paper for students; 96 pgs. Subscription $4.85 (teacher) and $2.85 (student). 80% assigned. Query/clips; fax/e-query OK. Pays $150, 120 days after acceptance, for all rts. Articles 6,000 characters for teacher, 2,900 characters for student (4/yr.). Responds in 4 wks. Seasonal 6 mos. ahead. Accepts simultaneous submissions. Requires accepted ms on disk. Prefers NIV. Guidelines; copy $2.25/#10 SASE. (No ads)

Tips: "Send a query with writing samples."

$PRIMARY PAL (IL), 1300 N. Meacham Rd., Schaumburg IL 60173-4806. (847)843-1600. Fax (847)843-3757. E-mail: takehomepapers@garbc.org. Website: www.garbc.org/rbp. Regular Baptist Press. Joan Alexander, ed. For ages 6-8; fundamental, conservative. Weekly take-home paper. Complete ms/cover letter including personal testimony; no e-query. Pays .04/wd. & up, on acceptance for all rts. Lead stories 450-525 wds. Requires KJV. Currently in a reprint cycle. (No ads)

Fillers: Buys 40+/yr. Word Puzzles; one page (include copy of solution). Payment. "We need items with a bit of visual puzzling. Writers also need to set the puzzle in a 'frame,' writing something to help child anticipate the challenge in solving the puzzle and receiving a take-away in finding the solution."

Tips: "We also use crafts and service projects. In fiction, we want mainstream stories of daily life for children of this age. May have elements of suspense, adventure, or humor—but pointed toward an understanding of God's character and ways as they apply today. Check Website quarterly for updates concerning needs, themes, etc."

$PRIMARY PAL (KS), PO Box 4060, Overland Park KS 66204. (913)432-0331. Fax (913)722-0351. E-mail: sseditor1@juno.com. Church of God (holiness)/Herald and Banner Press. Arlene McGehee, Sunday school ed. Denominational; for 1st-3rd graders. Weekly take-home paper; 4 pgs.; circ. 2,900. Subscription $1.50. Complete ms/cover letter; phone/fax/e-query OK (prefers mail or e-mail). Pays .005/wd. on publication for 1st rts. Fiction 500-1,000 wds. Seasonal 6-8 mos. ahead. Accepts simultaneous submissions & reprints (tell when/where appeared). Prefers KJV. Guidelines/theme list; copy. Not in topical listings.

$PRIMARY STREET, 1551 Regency Ct., Calumet City IL 60409. (708)832-3304. Fax (708)868-6759. E-mail: Jhull@urbanmisnistries.com. Website: www.urbanministries .com. Urban Ministries, Inc. Dr. Judith Hull, sr. ed. Sunday school curriculum for African American children, ages 6-8. Quarterly lesson folder for students & teacher's guide; 96 pgs. for teacher, 4 pages weekly for students. 100% assigned. Query/clips; phone/e-query OK.

Pays $150/lesson on acceptance for all rts. Requires submissions on disk or by e-mail (attached file). Prefers NIV. Guidelines by e-mail; copy for 9x12 SAE/3 stamps.

> **Tips:** "Writer may submit a résumé, testimony, and writing sample to be considered for an assignment."

$PRIMARY TREASURE, Box 5353, Nampa ID 83653-5353. (208)465-2500. Fax (208)465-2531. E-mail: ailsox@pacificpress.com. Website: www.pacificpress.com. Seventh-day Adventist. Aileen Andres Sox, ed. To teach children Christian belief, values, and practice; God's loving us and our loving him makes a difference in every facet of life, from how we think and act to how we feel. Weekly take-home paper for 6- to 9-yr.-olds (1st-4th grades); 16 pgs. 50% freelance (assigned), 25% reprints or unsolicited. Complete ms by e-mail preferred. Pays $25-50 on acceptance for one-time or reprint rts. True stories 900-1,000 wds. (52/yr.); articles used rarely (query). Responds in 13 wks. Seasonal 7 mos. ahead. For simultaneous submissions & reprints see guidelines; serials to 10 parts (query). E-mail submission preferred (attached file). Guidelines (also on Website); copy for 9x12 SAE/2 stamps. (No ads)

> **Tips:** "We need true adventure stories with a spiritual slant; positive, lively stories about children facing modern problems and making good choices. We always need strong stories about boys and stories featuring dads. We need a spiritual element that frequently is missing from submissions."

$PROMISE, 2621 Dryden Rd., Moraine OH 45439. (937)293-1415. Fax (937)293-1310. E-mail: service@pflaum.com. Website: www.pflaum.com. Catholic. Joan Mitchell CSJ, ed. For kindergarten and grade 1; encourages them to participate in parish worship. Weekly (32X) take-home paper. Not in topical listings.

$SEEDS, 2621 Dryden Rd., Moraine OH 45439. (937)293-1415. Fax (937)293-1310. E-mail: service@pflaum.com. Website: www.pflaum.com. Catholic. Joan Mitchell CSJ, ed. Prepares children to learn about God; for preschoolers. Weekly (32X) take-home paper; 4 pgs. Not in topical listings.

$SHINE BRIGHTLY, Box 7259, Grand Rapids MI 49510. (616)241-5616, ext. 3034. Fax (616)241-5558. E-mail: christina@gemsgc.org, or servicecenter@gemsgc.org. Website: www.gemsgc.org. GEMS Girls Clubs. Christina Malone, mng. ed. To show girls ages 9-14 that God is at work in their lives and in the world around them. Monthly (9X) mag.; 24 pgs.; circ. 13,000. Subscription $12.50. 80% unsolicited freelance; 20% assigned. Complete ms; no e-query. Pays .03-.05/wd. on publication for 1st or reprint rts. Articles 100-400 wds. (10/yr.); fiction 400-900 wds. (30/yr.). Responds in 4-6 wks. Seasonal 10 mos. ahead. Accepts simultaneous submissions & reprints. Accepts requested ms on disk. Regularly uses sidebars. Prefers NIV. Guidelines/theme list (also by e-mail/Website); copy $1/9x12 SAE/3 stamps. (No ads)

> **Fillers:** Buys 10/yr. Cartoons, games, party ideas, prayers, quizzes, short humor, word puzzles; 50-200 wds.; $5-10.

> **Special Needs:** Craft ideas that can be used to help others. Articles on how words can help build others up or tear people down.

> **Tips:** "Be realistic—we get a lot of fluffy stories with Pollyanna endings. We are looking for real-life-type stories that girls relate to. We mostly publish short stories but are open to short reflective articles. Know what girls face today and how they cope in their daily lives. We need angles from home life and friendships, peer pressure, and the normal growing-up challenges girls deal with."

SKIPPING STONES: A Multicultural Magazine, PO Box 3939, Eugene OR 97403. Phone/fax (541)342-4956. E-mail: editor@skippingstones.org. Website: www.skippingstones.org. Interfaith/multicultural. Arun N. Toké, exec. ed.; Mary Drew, asst. ed. A multicultural awareness and nature appreciation magazine for young people 7-17, worldwide. Bimonthly

(5X) mag.; 36 pgs.; circ. 2,500. Subscription $25. 85% unsolicited freelance; 15% assigned. Query or complete ms/cover letter; no phone query; e-query/submissions OK. **PAYS IN COPIES** for 1st, electronic, and nonexclusive reprint rts. Articles (15-25/yr.) 500-750 wds.; fiction for teens, 750-1,000 wds. Responds in 9-13 wks. Seasonal 2-4 mos. ahead. Accepts simultaneous submissions. Accepts requested ms on disk. Regularly uses sidebars. Guidelines/theme list (also by e-mail/Website); copy $5/4 stamps. (No ads)

Poetry: Only from kids under 18. Accepts 100/yr. Any type; 3-30 lines. Submit max. 4-5 poems.

Fillers: Accepts 10-20/yr. Anecdotes, cartoons, games, quizzes, short humor, word puzzles; to 250 wds.

Columns/Departments: Accepts 10/yr. Noteworthy News (multicultural/nature/international/social, appropriate for youth), 200 wds.

Special Needs: Stories and articles on your community and country, peace, nonviolent communication, compassion, kindness, spirituality, tolerance, and giving.

Contest: Annual Book Awards for published books and authors (deadline February 1); Annual Youth Honor Awards for students 7-17. Send SASE for guidelines. June 20 deadline.

Tips: "Most of the magazine is open to freelance. We're seeking submissions by minority, multicultural, international, and/or youth writers. Do not be judgmental or preachy; be open or receptive to diverse opinions."

$SPARKLE, Box 7259, Grand Rapids MI 49510. (616)241-5616. Fax (616)241-5558. E-mail: sara@gemsgc.org, or servicecenter@gemsgc.org. Website: www.gemsgc.org. GEMS Girls Clubs (nondenominational). Christina Malone, mng. ed. To show girls, grades 1-3, that God is at work in their lives and the world around them. Triannual mag. Subscription $5. 80% unsolicited freelance; 20% assigned. Complete ms; no e-query. Pays .03/wd. on publication for 1st, reprint, or simultaneous rts. Articles 200-400 wds. (10/yr.); fiction 400-1,000 wds. (30/yr.). Responds in 6 wks. Seasonal 10 mos. ahead. Accepts simultaneous submissions & reprints. Accepts requested ms on disk. Regularly uses sidebars. Prefers NIV. Guidelines/theme list (also by e-mail/Website); copy $1/9x12 SAE/3 stamps. (No ads)

Fillers: Buys 10/yr. Games, party ideas, prayers, quizzes, short humor; 50-200 wds.; $5-15.

$STORY FRIENDS, 616 Walnut St., Scottdale PA 15683. (724)887-8500. Fax (724)887-3111. E-mail: rstutz@mph.org, or bmiller@mph.org. Website: www.mph.org. Faith and Life Press/Mennonite Publishing House. Rose Mary Stutzman, ed. For children 4-9 yrs.; reinforces Christian values in a nonmoralistic manner. Monthly mag.; 20 pgs.; circ. 6,000. Subscription $18. 70% freelance. Complete ms/cover letter; no e-query. Pays .03-.05/wd. on acceptance for 1st or one-time rts. Articles (5-10/yr.) 100-300 wds.; fiction (30/yr.), 300-800 wds. Responds in 8 wks. Seasonal 6 mos. ahead. Accepts simultaneous submissions & reprints (tell when/where appeared). Prefers NIV. Guidelines; copy for 9x12 SAE/2 stamps.

Poetry: Buys 12/yr. Traditional; 6-12 lines; $10. Submit max. 3 poems.

Fillers: Buys 2-3/yr. Cartoons, word puzzles.

Ethnic: Targets all ethnic groups involved in the Mennonite church.

Tips: "Send stories that show rather than tell. Realistic fiction (no fantasy). Send good literary quality with a touch of humor that will appeal to children. Cover letter should give your experience with children."

$STORY MATES, Box 1212, Harrisonburg VA 22803-1212. (540)434-0768. Fax (540)433-8896. E-mail: StoryMates@clp.org. Website: www.clp.org. Mennonite/Christian Light Publications, Inc. Crystal Shank, ed. For 4- to 8-yr.-olds. Weekly take-home paper; 4 pgs.; circ. 6,275. Subscription $9.80. 90% unsolicited freelance. Complete ms. Pays up to .04/wd. on acceptance for 1st rts. (.05/wd. for 1st rts., plus reprint rts.). Realistic or true stories to 800-900 wds. (50-75/yr.); picture stories 120-150 wds. Responds in 6 wks. Seasonal 6 mos. ahead. Accepts simultaneous submissions & reprints (tell when/where appeared). No disk. Requires KJV. Guidelines/theme list (also by e-mail); copy for 9x12 SAE/3 stamps. Will send questionnaire to fill out. (No ads)

Poetry: Buys 25/yr. Traditional, any length. Few story poems. Pays up to .50/line.

Fillers: Quizzes, word puzzles, craft ideas. "Need fillers that correlate with theme list; Bible related." Pays about $7.

Special Needs: True or true-to-life stories the children can relate to.

Tips: "Carefully read our guidelines and understand our conservative Mennonite applications of Bible principles." Very conservative.

$WINNER MAGAZINE, 55 W. Oak Ridge Dr., Hagerstown MD 21740. Phone/fax (301)393-3294. E-mail: winner@healthconnection.org. Website: www.winnermagazine.org. The Health Connection. Jan Schleifer, ed. For elementary school children, grades 4-6; Saying No to Drugs, and Yes to Life. Monthly (during school year) mag.; 16 pgs.; circ. 12,000. Subscription $18.25. 30% unsolicited freelance; 70% assigned. Query by e-mail. Pays $50-80 on acceptance for 1st rts. Articles 600-650 wds. (25-30/yr.); fiction 600-650 wds. (18/yr.) Responds in 4-13 wks. Seasonal 6-8 mos. ahead. Accepts simultaneous submissions & reprints (tell when/where appeared). Prefers e-mail submission (attached file). Kill fee 50%. Uses some sidebars. Guidelines (also on Website); copy $2/9x12 SAE/2 stamps.

Tips: "*Winner* is a positive lifestyle magazine. Most open to self-help stories, factuals on tobacco, alcohol, and other drugs—in story format (include sources), with a catchy ending. Each article needs at least three questions relating to the story and a puzzle/activity."

*YOUNG GENTLEMAN'S MONTHLY, PO Box 23, West Charleston VT 05872-0023. Stepping Out of the Darkness. Sharon White, ed. For Christian boys, ages 7-11. Monthly (8X). Subscription $12, includes club membership. Open to freelance. Complete ms. **NO PAYMENT.** Articles 200-600 wds.; fiction 200-800 wds. No guidelines; copy $2/SASE. Incomplete topical listings. (Ads)

Fillers: Accepts 8/yr. Historical fillers, 200 wds. (What did boys learn and do 200-300 years ago?)

Columns/Departments: Diligence; Work Ideas; Manners; Sabbath Keeping; How to Care for and Protect the Family; 200-600 wds.

Special Needs: Short stories need to be old-fashioned—moral, character building. No contemporary problems or situations. Articles should be devout Christian/Messianic Jewish based.

Tips: "Please request a sample issue before submitting. We're always willing to work with new writers. Be sensitive to the growing need of leading our children away from modernism and back to the old paths of moralism, courage, and men being men."

CHRISTIAN EDUCATION/LIBRARY MARKETS

$CATECHIST, 2621 Dryden Rd., 3rd Fl., Dayton OH 45439. (937)847-5900. Fax (937)293-1410. E-mail: kdotterweich@peterli.com. Website: www.catechist.com. Catholic; Peter Li Education Group. Kass Dotterweich, ed. For Catholic school teachers and parish volunteer catechists. Mag. published 7X/yr.; 52 pgs.; circ. 50,000. Subscription $19.95. 30% unsolicited freelance; 70% assigned. Query (preferred) or complete ms. Pays $25-150 on publication. Articles 1,200-1,500 wds. Responds in 9-18 wks. Guidelines (also on Website); copy $3.

Tips: "Most open to short features and how-to lesson plans and crafts."

CATHOLIC LIBRARY WORLD, 100 North St., Ste. 224, Pittsfield MA 01201-5109. (413)443-2252. Fax (413)442-2252. E-mail: cla@cathla.org. Website: www.cathla.org. Catholic Library Assn. Sr. Mary E. Gallagher, gen. ed. For libraries at all levels—preschool to post-secondary to academic, parish, public, and private. Quarterly jour.; 80 pgs.; circ. 1,000. Subscription $60/$70 foreign. 90% unsolicited freelance; 10% assigned. Query or complete ms; phone/fax/e-query OK. **PAYS 1 COPY.** Articles; book/video reviews, 300-500 wds. Accepts requested ms on disk. Uses some sidebars. No guidelines; copy for 9x12 SAE. (Ads)

Special Needs: Topics of interest to academic libraries, high school and children's libraries, parish and community libraries, archives, and library education. Reviewers cover areas such as theology, spirituality, pastoral, professional, juvenile books and material, and media.

Tips: "Review section considers taking on new reviewers who are experts in field of librarianship, theology, and professional studies. No payment except a free copy of the book or materials reviewed. Query us by mail or e-mail."

$CHILDREN'S MINISTRY MAGAZINE, 1515 Cascade Ave., Loveland CO 80539. Toll-free (800)447-1070. Fax (970)292-4360. E-mail: cyount@cmmag.com. Website: www.cmmag.com. Group Publishing/nondenominational. Christine Yount, exec. ed.; submit to Jennifer Hooks, assoc. ed. (jhooks@cmmag.com). The leading resource for adults who work with children (ages 0-12) in the church. Bimonthly mag.; 140 pgs.; circ. 90,000. Subscription $24.95. 80% unsolicited freelance; 20% assigned. Complete ms/cover letter; e-query OK. Pays $25-400 on acceptance for all & electronic rts. Articles 50-1,800 wds. (250-300/yr.). Responds in 8-10 wks. Seasonal 6-9 mos. ahead. No simultaneous submissions or reprints. Accepts requested ms by e-mail (attached or copied into message). Kill fee 100%. Regularly uses sidebars. Accepts submissions from children & teens. Prefers NIV. Guidelines (also by e-mail/Website); copy $2/9x12 SAE/.80 postage. (Ads)

Fillers: Buys 25-50/yr. Cartoons, kid quotes; 25-50 wds.; $25-60.

Columns/Departments: Buys 200+/yr. Age-level insights (age-appropriate ideas); Family Ministry (family ideas); Reaching Out (outreach ideas); 150-250 wds. Teacher Telegram (ideas for teachers); For Parents Only (parenting ideas); 150-300 wds.; $40-150. Complete ms.

Special Needs: Seasonal ideas, outreach ideas, volunteer management, and family ministry.

Tips: "All areas open to freelancers. We're looking for stand-out ideas. Big need for cartoons depicting kids and faith. Break in with ideas unless you are a published writer. We seek features from 'experts'—through practice or theory."

**This periodical was #1 on the 2005 Top 50 Christian Publishers list (#14 in 2004).

#CHRISTIAN EARLY EDUCATION, PO Box 65130, Colorado Springs CO 80962-5130. (719)528-6906. Fax (719)531-0631. E-mail: earlyeducation@acsi.org. Website: www.acsi.org. Assn. of Christian Schools Intl. D'Arcy Maher, sr. ed. Equips individuals serving children ages birth to five from a biblical perspective. Quarterly mag.; 40 pgs.; circ. 5,500. Subscription $14. 10% unsolicited freelance; 90% assigned. Query; phone/fax/e-query OK. **PAYS IN COPIES.** Not copyrighted. Articles 600-1,800 wds. (12-15/yr.). Responds in 4 wks. Seasonal 10 mos. ahead. Accepts reprints (tell when/where appeared). Prefers e-mail submissions (attached file). Does not use sidebars. Prefers NIV. Guidelines/theme list (also by e-mail); copy $1.50/9x12 SAE. (Ads)

Columns/Departments: Accepts up to 10/yr. Staff Training (training for teachers of young children, to use in staff meeting), 400 wds.; Parents Place (material suitable for parents of young children), 400 wds. Complete ms.

$CHRISTIAN EDUCATORS JOURNAL, 73 Highland Ave., St. Catherines ON L2R 4H9, Canada. Phone/fax (905)684-3991. E-mail: bert.witvoet@sympatico.ca. Christian Educators Journal Assn. Bert Witvoet, mng. ed. For educators in Christian day schools at the elementary, secondary, and college levels. Quarterly jour.; 36 pgs.; circ. 4,200. Subscription $7.50 (c/o James Rauwerda, 2045 Boston St. S.E., Grand Rapids MI 49506, 616-243-2112). 50% unsolicited freelance; 50% assigned. Query; phone/e-query OK. Pays $30 on publication for one-time rts. Articles 750-1,500 wds. (20/yr.); fiction 750-1,500 wds. Responds in 5 wks. Seasonal 4 mos. ahead. Accepts simultaneous submissions & reprints. Guidelines/ theme list; copy $1.50 or 9x12 SAE/4 stamps. (Limited ads)

Poetry: Buys 6/yr. On teaching day school; 4-30 lines; $10. Submit max. 5 poems.

Tips: "No articles on Sunday school, only Christian day school. Most open to theme topics and features."

THE CHRISTIAN LIBRARIAN, Ryan Library, PLNU, 3600 Lomaland Dr., San Diego CA 92106. (619)849-2208. Fax (619)849-7024. E-mail: anne-elizabethpowell@ptloma.edu. Website: www.acl.org. Assn. of Christian Librarians. Anne-Elizabeth Powell, ed-in-chief. Geared toward academic librarians of the Christian faith. Quarterly (3X) jour.; 40 pgs.; circ. 800. Subscription $30. 50% unsolicited freelance; 50% assigned. E-mail; fax/e-query OK. **NO PAYMENT** for one-time rts. Not copyrighted. Articles 1,000-3,500 wds.; research articles to 5,000 wds. (6/yr.); reviews 150-300 wds. Responds in 5 wks. Accepts simultaneous submissions & reprints (tell when/where appeared). Prefers accepted ms by e-mail (attached file). Uses some sidebars. Guidelines (also by e-mail/Website); copy $5. (No ads)

Fillers: Anecdotes, ideas, short humor; 25-300 wds.

Special Needs: Articles dealing with the intersection of faith and professional duties in libraries. Interviews with library leaders, profiles of Christian academic libraries, international librarianship.

Tips: "Reviews are a good way to gain publication. Write a tight, well-researched article about a current 'hot topic' in librarianship as it is defined in a Christian setting; or ethics of librarianship. Articles on 'how we did it right' are good entry publications."

CHRISTIAN LIBRARY JOURNAL, 1225 Johnson St., Wenatchee WA 98801-3109. (509)662-7455. Fax (509)267-8109. E-mail: nlhesch@ChristianLibraryJ.org. Website: www.christian libraryj.org. Christian Library Services. Nancy Hesch, ed./pub. Provides reviews of library materials and articles about books, authors, and libraries for the Christian librarian. Irregular online mag. (about 4/yr.); 70+ pgs.; circ. 20,000. Subscription $20. 10% unsolicited freelance; 90% assigned. Query by e-mail only. **PAYS 1 COPY OR SUBSCRIPTION** for 1st or reprint rts. Articles 1,000-1,500 wds. (20/yr.); book/video reviews, 200-300 wds. (see the Website if you want to be a reviewer), book or other item, plus subscription, in payment. Responds in 10-12 wks. Accepts reprints (tell when/where appeared). Requires accepted ms by e-mail (attached file or copied into message). Copy online.

Special Needs: Library how-tos, Websites, author profiles, and annotated bibliographies.

Tips: "Most open to articles, book reviews, especially written by librarians and teachers."

CHRISTIAN SCHOOL EDUCATION, PO Box 65130, Colorado Springs CO 80962-5130. (719-528-6906. Fax (719)531-0631. E-mail: cse@acsi.org. Website: www.acsi.org. Association of Christian Schools, Intl. Steven C. Babbitt, ed. To provide accurate information as well as provoke thought and reflection about the ministry of Christian school education worldwide. 5X/yr. mag.; 56 pgs.; circ. 70,000. Subscription $16. 2% unsolicited freelance; 98% assigned. Query preferred; phone query OK. **NO PAYMENT.** Asks for photocopy permission for member schools. Articles 600-2,400 wds.; book reviews 600 wds. Responds in 12 wks. No seasonal material. Accepts simultaneous submissions & reprints (tell when/where appeared). Requires submissions by disk or e-mail (attached file). Regularly uses sidebars. Prefers NIV, NKJV. Guidelines by e-mail/Website. Incomplete topical listings. (Ads)

CHURCH & SYNAGOGUE LIBRARIES, PO Box 19357, Portland OR 97280-0357. (503)244-6919. Fax (503)977-3734. E-mail: csla@worldaccessnet.com. Website: www.worldaccess net.com/~csla. Church and Synagogue Library Assn. Judith Janzen, exec. dir. To help librarians run congregational libraries. Bimonthly; 24 pgs.; circ. 3,000. Subscription $25, $35 Cdn., $45 foreign. Query; no e-query. **NO PAYMENT.** Requires accepted ms on disk. Articles. Book & video reviews 1-2 paragraphs. Guidelines; copy available. (Ads)

Fillers: Ideas.

$CHURCH EDUCATOR, 165 Plaza Dr., Prescott AZ 86303. Toll-free (800)221-0910. (928)771-8601. Fax (928)771-8621. E-mail: edmin2@aol.com. Website: www.educational ministries.com. Educational Ministries, Inc. Robert G. Davidson, ed. For mainline Protestant Christian educators. Monthly jour.; 32 pgs.; circ. 4,500. Subscription $28, Cdn. $34, foreign $36. 95% unsolicited freelance. Complete ms/cover letter; phone/fax/e-query OK. Pays .03/wd. 60 days after publication for 1st rts. Articles 500-2,000 wds. (200/yr.); fiction 500-1,500 wds. (10/yr.). Responds in 2-17 wks. Seasonal 7 mos. ahead. Accepts simultaneous submissions & reprints (tell when/where appeared). Regularly uses sidebars. Guidelines/theme list; copy for 9x12 SAE/4 stamps.

> **Fillers:** Bible games and Bible puzzles.

> **Tips:** "Talk to the educators at your church. What would they find useful? Most open to seasonal articles dealing with the liturgical year. Write up church programs with specific how-tos of putting the program together."

> ****This periodical was #17 on the 2005 Top 50 Christian Publishers list (#17 in 2004, #16 in 2003, #38 in 2002, #39 in 2001).

$CHURCH LIBRARIES, 9731 N. Fox Glen Dr., #6F, Niles IL 60714-4222. (847)296-3964. Fax (847)296-0754. E-mail: lin@ECLAlibraries.org. Website: www.ECLAlibraries.org. Evangelical Church Library Assn. Lin Johnson, mng ed. To assist church librarians in setting up, maintaining, and promoting church libraries and media centers. Quarterly mag.; 40 pgs.; circ. 500. Subscription $30. 25% unsolicited freelance. Complete ms or queries by e-mail only. Pays .04/wd. on acceptance for 1st or reprint rts. Articles 500-1,000 wds. (24-30/yr.); book/music/video/cassette reviews by assignment, 75-150 wds., free product. Responds in 4-6 wks. Seasonal 6 mos. ahead. Accepts reprints (tell when/where appeared). Requires e-mail submission. Regularly uses sidebars. Prefers NIV. Guidelines (also by e-mail/Website); copy for 9x12 SAE/$1.42 postage (mark "Media Mail"). (Ads)

> **Tips:** "Talk to church librarians or get involved in library or reading programs. Most open to articles and promotional ideas; profiles of church libraries; roundups on best books in a category (query on topic first). Need for reviewers fluctuates; if interested e-mail for availability."

> ****This periodical was #48 on the 2002 Top 50 Christian Publishers list.

$GROUP MAGAZINE, Box 481, Loveland CO 80538. (970)669-3836. Fax (970)679-4360. E-mail: rlawrence@grouppublishing.com, or kdieterich@grouppublishing.com. Website: www.grouppublishing.com, or www.groupmag.com. Rick Lawrence, ed.; Kathleen Dieterich, asst. ed. For leaders of Christian youth groups; to supply ideas, practical help, inspiration, and training for youth leaders. Bimonthly mag.; 85 pgs.; circ. 55,000. Subscription $29.95. 50% unsolicited freelance; 50% assigned. Query; fax/e-query OK. Pays $125-350 on acceptance for all rts. Articles 175-2,000 wds. (100/yr.). Responds in 6-9 wks. Seasonal 5 mos. ahead. No simultaneous submissions or reprints. Accepts e-mail submissions (copied into message). No kill fee. Uses some sidebars. Any Bible version. Guidelines on Website; copy $2/9x12 SAE/3 stamps. (Ads)

> **Fillers:** Buys 5-10/yr. Cartoons, games, ideas; $40.

> **Columns/Departments:** Buys 30-40/yr. Try This One (youth group activities), to 300 wds.; Hands-on-Help (tips for leaders), to 175 wds.; Strange But True (profiles remarkable youth ministry experience), 500 wds. Pays $40. Complete ms.

> **Special Needs:** Articles geared toward working with teens; programming ideas; youth ministry issues.

> **Tips:** "We're always looking for effective youth ministry ideas—especially those tested by youth leaders in the field. Most open to Hands-On-Help column (use real-life examples, personal experiences, practical tips, scripture, and self-quizzes or checklists)."

$IDEAS UNLIMITED FOR EFFECTIVE CHILDREN'S MINISTRY, PO Box 12624, Roanoke VA 24027. (540)342-7511. E-mail: ccmbbr@juno.com. Website: www.CreativeChristian Ministries.com. Betty Robertson, ed. For anyone ministering to children. Monthly e-zine; circ. 4,200. Subscription free. 25% unsolicited freelance; 75% assigned. Query; no phone/fax query; e-query OK. Pays $5-10 on acceptance for 1st, one-time, or simultaneous rts. Not copyrighted. Articles 100-600 wds. Responds in 3 wks. Seasonal 6 mos. ahead. Accepts simultaneous submissions & reprints. Guidelines by e-mail.

$THE JOURNAL OF ADVENTIST EDUCATION, 12501 Old Columbia Pike, Silver Springs MD 20904-6600. (301)680-5075. Fax (301)622-9627. E-mail: rumbleb@gc.adventist.org. Website: www.education.gc.adventist.org/jae. General Conference of Seventh-day Adventists. Beverly J. Robinson-Rumble, ed. For Seventh-day teachers teaching in the church's school system, kindergarten to university. Bimonthly (5X) jour.; 48 pgs.; circ. 7,500. Subscription $17.25 (add $1 outside U.S.). Percentage of freelance varies. Query or complete ms; phone/fax/e-query OK. Pays $25-300 on publication for 1st North American and translation rts. Articles 1,000-1,500 wds. (2-20/yr.). Responds in 6-18 wks. Seasonal 6 mos. ahead. Accepts reprints (tell when/where appeared). Accepts requested ms on disk. Kill fee to 25%. Regularly uses sidebars. Guidelines (also by e-mail); copy for 10x12 SAE/5 stamps.

  Fillers: Cartoons only, no pay.

  Special Needs: "All articles in the context of parochial schools (*not* Sunday school tips); professional enrichment and teaching tips for Christian teachers. Need feature articles."

JOURNAL OF CHRISTIAN EDUCATION, PO Box 602, Epping NSW 1710, Australia. Phone/fax 61 2 9868 6644. E-mail: ahukins@bigpond.com, submit to editor@acfe.org.au. Website: http://jce.acfe.org.au. Australian Christian Forum on Education, Inc. Dr. Allan G. Harkness, ed. To consider the implications of the Christian faith for the entire field of education. Triannual jour.; 64 pgs.; circ. 500. Subscription $40 AUS, $35 U.S. for individuals; $50 AUS, $45 U.S. for institutions. 40% unsolicited freelance; 60% assigned. Complete ms/cover letter; phone/fax/e-query OK. **NO PAYMENT** for one-time rts. Articles 3,000-5,000 wds. (6/yr.); book reviews 400-600 wds. Responds in 4 wks. Seasonal 6 mos. ahead. Accepts requested ms on disk or by e-mail (attached file). Does not use sidebars. Accepts submissions from children & teens. Free guidelines (also on Website) & copy. (No ads)

  Tips: "Send for a sample copy, study guidelines, and submit manuscript. Most open to articles or book reviews. Open to any educational issue from a Christian perspective."

JOURNAL OF CHRISTIANITY AND FOREIGN LANGUAGES, Dept. of Germanic and Asian Languages, Calvin College, 3201 Burton St. S.E., Grand Rapids MI 49546. (616)957-8609. Fax (616)526-8583. E-mail: dsmith@calvin.edu. Website: www.spu.edu/orgs/NACFLA. North American Christian Foreign Language Assn. Dr. David Smith, ed. Scholarly articles dealing with the relationship between Christian belief and the teaching of foreign languages and literatures; mainly for college faculty. Annual jour.; 100 pgs.; circ. 100. Subscription $16 (indiv.), $27 (library). Open to freelance. Complete ms/cover letter; phone/fax/e-query OK. **PAYS IN COPIES/OFFPRINTS.** Articles 2,000-4,000 wds. (6/yr.); book/video reviews, 750 wds. Responds in 12-16 wks. Rarely accepts reprints (tell when/where appeared). Requires requested ms on disk or by e-mail (attached file). Does not use sidebars. Guidelines (also on Website); no copy. (Ads)

  Columns/Departments: Accepts 1-3/yr. Forum (position papers, pedagogical suggestions), 1,000-1,500 wds.

  Tips: "Most open to Forum column; see www.spu.edu/orgs/nacfla/for guidelines. Also see Website for abstracts and samples. Book reviews and opinion pieces must be related to Christianity and education in foreign languages and literature."

JOURNAL OF EDUCATION & CHRISTIAN BELIEF, Dept. of Germanic Languages, Calvin College, 3201 Burton St. S.E., Grand Rapids MI 49546. (616)957-8609. Fax (616)526-8583. E-mail: jecb@stapleford-centre.org. Website: www.stapleford-centre.org. Association of Christian Teachers. Editors: Dr. David Smith (use above address) & Dr. John Shortt, 1 Kiteleys Green, Leighton Buzzard, Beds LU7 3LD, United Kingdom. Phone +44 0 1525 379709. Semiannual jour.; 80 pgs.; circ. 400. Subscription 20-80 pounds. 80% unsolicited freelance; 20% assigned. Complete ms/cover letter; e-query OK. **NO PAYMENT** for 1st rts. Articles 5,000 wds. (12/yr.). Responds in 4-8 wks. Accepts reprints (tell when/where appeared). Prefers requested ms on disk or by e-mail (attached file). Does not use sidebars. Guidelines by e-mail; no copy. (No ads)

> **Tips:** "Most open to reviews of books related to education and Christian belief; should be expert reviews addressed to an academic audience."

JOURNAL OF RESEARCH ON CHRISTIAN EDUCATION, Andrews University, Information Services Bldg., Ste. 101, Berrien Springs MI 49104. (269)471-6080. Fax (269)471-6224. E-mail: jrce@andrews.edu. Website: www.andrews.edu/jrce. Andrews University. Larry D. Burton, ed.; Janet Mallory, book rev. ed. Research related to Christian schooling (all levels) within the Protestant tradition. Biannual jour.; 150+ pgs.; circ. 400. Subscription $60.100% unsolicited freelance. Complete ms/cover letter; phone/fax/e-query OK. **NO PAYMENT.** Articles 13-26, double-spaced pgs. (12-18/yr.); book reviews, 2-5 pgs. Responds in 1 wk.; decision within 6 mos. (goes through review board). No simultaneous submissions. Requires requested ms on disk. Does not use sidebars. Guidelines (also by e-mail). (No ads)

> **Tips:** "This is a research journal. All manuscripts should conform to standards of scholarly inquiry. Manuscripts are submitted to a panel of 3 experts for their review. Publication decision is based on recommendation of reviewers. Authors should submit manuscripts written in scholarly style and focused on Christian schooling. Submit 5 copies along with a 100-word abstract and 30-word bio-sketch indicating institutional affiliation."

$KIDS' MINISTRY IDEAS, 55 W. Oak Ridge Dr., Hagerstown MD 21740. (301)393-4082. Fax (301)393-3209. E-mail: KidsMin@rhpa.org. Seventh-day Adventist. Ginger Church, ed. For adults leading children (birth-8th grade) to Christ. Quarterly mag.; 32 pgs.; circ. 1,700. Guidelines on request.

$LEADER IN CHRISTIAN EDUCATION MINISTRIES, PO Box 801, Nashville TN 37202-0801. (615)749-6791. Fax (615)749-6512. E-mail: jshoup@umpublishing.org. Website: www.cokesburynewsstand.com. United Methodist. Marvin Cropsey, ed.; Joan M. Shoup, assoc. ed. Estab. 2003. Focuses on issues of concern to leaders in the field of Christian education. Quarterly mag.; 40 pgs.; circ. 3,500. Subscription $20. 5% unsolicited freelance. 95% assigned. Query or complete ms/cover letter; e-query OK. Pays $50-150 on acceptance for all rts. Articles 600-4,000 wds. (4/yr.). Responds in 8 wks. Seasonal 1 yr. ahead. Accepts simultaneous submissions & reprints (tell when/where appeared). Prefers e-mail submission (attached or copied into message). No kill fee. Regularly uses sidebars. Prefers NRSV (never The Living Bible). Guidelines/theme list (also by e-mail); copy for 9x12 SAE. (No ads)

> **Columns/Departments:** Features on Christian education, 600-5,000 wds.; $50-100. Holidays (reflection that may suggest a program), 600-1,200 wds.

> **Tips:** "We occasionally accept articles in our features section or for the Holiday column. Most of our articles are assigned, however. We rarely accept freelance submissions." Online version is available through the Teaching & Learning Portal.

$MOMENTUM, 1077—30th St. N.W., Ste. 100, Washington DC 20007-3852. (202)337-6232. Fax (202)333-6706. E-mail: momentum@ncea.org. Website: www.ncea.org. National Catholic Educational Assn. Brian Gray, ed. Features outstanding programs, issues, and research in education. Quarterly jour.; 88 pgs.; circ. 25,000. Subscription $20 (free to members). 50% unsolicited freelance; 30% assigned. Query or complete ms; phone/e-query OK. Pays $50-100 on publication for 1st rts. Articles 500-1,500 wds. (25-30/yr.); book reviews 400 wds. ($50). No simultaneous submissions. Accepts full mss by e-mail. Regularly uses sidebars. Guidelines (also by e-mail/Website); copy $5/9x12 SAE/$1.42 postage (mark "Media Mail"). (Ads)

Columns/Departments: From the Field (success ideas that can be used by other Catholic schools); DRE Directions (guidance for directors of religious education programs); both 700 wds.

Special Needs: Religious education; teaching methods; Catholic school administration.

Tips: "We recommend that writers call or send e-mail before submitting. Conversation often leads to additional ideas. Articles should have applicability to Catholic elementary and high schools. Especially need brief articles about successful youth religious education programs in Catholic parishes. Also, how are weekend religious education programs absorbing students in areas where Catholic schools are closing?"

$PRESCHOOL PLAYHOUSE, PO Box 436987, Chicago IL 60643. Toll-free (800)860-8642. (708)868-7100. Fax (708)868-7105. Website: www.urbanministries.com. Urban Ministries, Inc. K. Steward, ed. Sunday school magazine with activities for 2- to 5-year-olds with accompanying teacher's manual. Quarterly mag. for teachers; take-home paper for students; 96 pgs. Subscription $4.99 (teacher/64 pgs.) and $2.85 (student). 80% assigned. Query/clips; fax/e-query OK. Pays $150, 120 days after acceptance, for all rts. Articles 6,000 characters for teacher, 2,900 characters for student (4/yr.). Responds in 4 wks. Seasonal 6 mos. ahead. Accepts simultaneous submissions. Requires requested ms on disk. Prefers NIV. Guidelines; copy $2.25/#10 SASE. (No ads)

$RESOURCE, 6401 The Paseo, Kansas City MO 64131. (816)333-7000, ext. 2343. Fax (816)363-7092. E-mail: ssmith@nazarene.org. Website: www.nazarene.org. Church of the Nazarene. David Graves, dir.; submit to Shirley Smith, ed. asst. To provide information, training, and inspiration to those who are involved in ministering within the Christian Life and Sunday school departments of the local church. Quarterly mag.; 32 pgs.; circ. 25,000. Subscription $6.25. 95% unsolicited freelance; 5% assigned. Complete ms; phone/fax/e-query OK. Pays .05/wd. on publication for all, one-time, reprint, or simultaneous rts. Articles 1,000-2,000 wds. (150/yr.). Seasonal 9-12 mos. ahead. Accepts simultaneous submissions & reprints. Accepts requested ms on disk or by e-mail (attached or copied into message). Uses some sidebars. Prefers NIV, NRSV. Guidelines/theme list (also by e-mail); copy for 9x12 SAE/2 stamps. (No ads)

Tips: "Focus on issues, skills, concerns central to a particular age group; how-tos, examples, illustrations; skill development; roles of teachers/leaders; organizational tips."

**This periodical was #41 on the 2002 Top 50 Christian Publishers list (#46 in 2000).

$RTJ: The Magazine for Catechist Formation, (formerly *Religion Teacher's Journal*), Box 180, Mystic CT 06355. (860)536-2611. Fax (860)572-0788. E-mail: aberger@twentythirdpublications.com. Website: www.twentythirdpublications.com. Catholic Publishers/Bayard. Alison Berger, ed. For volunteer religion teachers who need practical, hands-on information as well as spiritual and theological background for teaching religion to kindergarten through high school. 7X/yr. mag.; 40 pgs.; circ. 32,000. Subscription $22.95. 40% unsolicited freelance; 60% assigned. Complete ms/cover letter; fax/e-query OK. Pays $50-125 on acceptance for 1st rts. Articles to 1,300 wds. (40/yr.); plays. Responds in 2-4 wks. Seasonal 6 mos. ahead. Accepts simultaneous submissions and rarely accepts reprints (tell when/where appeared). Prefers requested ms on disk or by e-mail (attached file). No kill fee. Regularly uses sidebars. Prefers NRSV (Catholic edition). Guidelines/theme list (also by e-mail); copy for 9x12 SAE/3 first class stamps. (Ads)

Fillers: Buys 20-30/yr. Anecdotes (about teaching), games, ideas, quizzes, crafts, successful class activities (especially seasonal); 50-300 wds.; $20-50.

Special Needs: Partnering with families; teaching the sacraments; prayer and prayer services; celebrating the seasons; spiritual formation for religion teachers/catechists; successful faith formation programs.

Tips: "Most open to articles on teaching skills; successful activity ideas/lessons; involving parents in religious education, especially in sacrament preparation; celebrating Advent and Lent; spiritual formation. Looking for clear, concise articles written from experience, for catechists and religion teachers (K-12). Articles should help readers move from theory/doctrine to concrete application." Unsolicited manuscripts not returned without an SASE.

**This periodical was #43 on the 2005 Top 50 Christian Publishers list (#43 in 2004, #22 in 2003, #47 in 2002).

$TEACHERS INTERACTION, 3558 S. Jefferson Ave., St. Louis MO 63118-3968. (314)268-1083. Fax (314)268-1329. E-mail: tom.nummela@cph.org. Website: www.cph.org. Concordia Publishing House/Lutheran Church—Missouri Synod. Tom Nummela, ed. Supports volunteer Sunday school teachers and those who serve with teaching ideas, resources, and articles about education and theology. Quarterly mag.; 32 pgs.; circ. 11,000. Subscription $16.60. 5% unsolicited freelance; 95% assigned. Query; fax/e-query OK. Pays $55-110 on acceptance for all rts. One-page articles, 450 wds., feature articles 1,200 wds. (4/yr.). Responds in 4-8 wks. Seasonal 1 yr. ahead. Prefers requested ms on disk or by e-mail. Uses some sidebars. Prefers NIV or ESV. Guidelines/theme list (also by e-mail); copy $4.99. (No ads)

Songs: Buys occasionally. First rts.; $50.

Fillers: Buys 48/yr. Teacher tips/ideas, 50-150 wds.; $20-40 on publication.

Columns/Departments: Departments for early childhood teachers, lower elementary grade teachers, middle school teachers, The Adaptive Teacher, Parents As Teachers, Law and Gospel, Outreach/Evangelism, and Support Staff (pastors, directors of CE, and superintendents); 450 wds., $55.

Special Needs: Practical, how-to articles that will help the volunteer church worker.

Tips: "Most freelance material is used in our 'Teacher's Toolbox' section; practical teaching ideas for the Sunday school classroom. We also need feature articles in four areas—inspiration, theology, practical application, and information—in the area of volunteer Christian education. Theology must be compatible with Lutheranism."

$TEACHERS OF VISION MAGAZINE, Box 41300, Pasadena CA 91114. (626)798-1124. Fax (626)798-2346. E-mail: judy@ceai.org. Website: www.ceai.org. Christian Educators Assn., Intl. Judy Turpen, contributing ed.; F. L. Turpen, editorial dir.; Denise Trippett, mng. ed. To encourage, equip, and empower Christian educators serving in public and private schools. Biannual mag.; circ. 10,000. Subscription $20. 50-60% unsolicited freelance; 40-50% assigned. Query; phone/fax/e-query OK. Pays $40 ($30 for reprints) on publication for 1st or reprint rts. Articles 1,000-2,500 wds. (12-15/yr.); mini-features 400-750 wds., $25; very few book reviews 50 wds., (pays copies). Responds in 4-6 wks. Seasonal 4 mos. ahead. Accepts simultaneous submissions & reprints (tell when/where appeared). Accepts requested ms on disk or by e-mail (attached or copied into message). Regularly uses sidebars. Any Bible version. Guidelines/theme list (also by e-mail/Website); copy for 9x12 SAE/5 stamps. (Ads)

Poetry: Accepts 2-3/yr. Free verse, haiku, light verse, traditional; 4-16 lines; no payment. Submit max. 3 poems.

Fillers: Accepts 6/yr. Cartoons, facts; 20-100 wds.; no payment. Educational only.

Special Needs: Legal and other issues in public education. Interviews; classroom resource reviews; living out your faith in your work.

Tips: "Know public education; write from a positive perspective as our readers are involved in public education by calling and choice. Most open to tips for teachers for living out their faith in the classroom in legally appropriate ways. All topics covered must be public-education related."

$TEACH KIDS!, (formerly *Evangelizing Today's Child*), PO Box 348, Warrenton MO 63383-0348. (636)456-4321. Fax (636)456-9935. E-mail: Editor@TeachKidsMag.com. Website: www.TeachKidsMag.com. Child Evangelism Fellowship. Elsie C. Lippy, ed. To equip Christians to lead the world's children (ages 4-11) to Christ and disciple them in the Word of God. Bimonthly mag.; 64 pgs.; circ. 12,000. Subscription $24. 25% unsolicited freelance; 75% assigned. Complete ms; no phone/fax query; e-query OK. Payment rate varies; pays within 60 days of acceptance for one-time rts. Articles 800-900 wds. (24/yr.); fiction 800-850 wds. (12/yr.). Responds in 4-6 wks. Seasonal 1 yr. ahead. Accepts few reprints (tell when/where appeared). Disk or e-mail submission OK. Kill fee 30%. Regularly uses sidebars. Prefers NIV. Guidelines (also by e-mail/Website); copy $3/9x12 SAE. (Ads)

Easy Ideas: Complete ms, 250-300 wds.; $35-150 for teaching tips, object lessons, missions incentives, seasonal ideas, crafts with spiritual focus, attendance boosters, verse drills, and lesson reviews that teachers can use with children ages 4-11.

Special Needs: Hands-on creative preschool teaching ideas that are theme related.

Tips: "Fictional read-aloud stories and Easy Ideas are good areas to break into. A writer should be actively working with children in order to gain fresh anecdotes and insight to share with the readers. Fiction should be written at the third- to fourth-grade level. Feature contemporary settings with scriptural solutions to problems faced by children."

**This periodical was #46 on the 2005 Top 50 Christian Publishers list (#45 in 2004).

$TODAY'S CATHOLIC TEACHER, 2621 Dryden Rd., Dayton OH 45439. (937)293-1415. Fax (937)293-1310. E-mail: mnoschang@peterli.com. Website: www.catholicteacher.com. Catholic; Peter Li Education Group. Mary C. Noschang, ed. Directed to personal and professional concerns of teachers and administrators in K-12 Catholic schools. Monthly mag. (6X during school yr.); 60 pgs.; circ. 45,000. Subscription $14.95. 30% unsolicited freelance; 30% assigned. Query; phone/fax/e-query OK. Pays $100-250 on publication for 1st rts. Articles 600-800, 1,000-1,200, or 1,200-1,500 wds. (40-50/yr.). Responds in 18 wks. Seasonal 3 mos. ahead. Accepts simultaneous submissions & reprints (tell when/where appeared). Prefers requested ms by e-mail (attached file). Regularly uses sidebars. Guidelines/theme list (also on Website); copy $3/9x12 SAE. (Ads)

Special Needs: Activity pages teachers can copy and pass out to students to work on. Try to provide classroom-ready material teachers can use to supplement curriculum.

Tips: "Looking for material teachers in grades 3-9 can use to supplement curriculum material. Most open to articles or lesson plans."

$YOUTH AND CHRISTIAN EDUCATION LEADERSHIP, 1080 Montgomery Ave., Cleveland TN 37311. (423)478-7597. Fax (423)478-7616. E-mail: wanda_griffith@pathwaypress.org. Website: www.pathwaypress.org. Church of God/Pathway Press. Wanda Griffith, ed. To inform, equip, and inspire Christian education teachers and leaders. Quarterly mag.; 32 pgs.; circ. 11,000. Subscription $8. 10% unsolicited freelance; 90% assigned. Query; phone/fax/e-query OK. Pays $25-50 on publication for 1st rts. Articles 500-1,200 wds. (4/yr.). Responds in 4 wks. Seasonal 6 mos. ahead. Accepts requested ms on disk or by e-mail (attached file). No kill fee. Uses some sidebars. Accepts submissions from teens. Prefers NIV. Guidelines by e-mail/Website; copy for 9x12 SAE/4 stamps. (No ads)

Fillers: Cartoons, ideas, word puzzles.

Special Needs: Most open to how-to articles relating to Christian education. Local church ministry stories; articles on youth ministry, children's ministry, Christian education, and Sunday school.

**2004 EPA Award of Excellence—Denominational.

DAILY DEVOTIONAL MARKETS

Due to the nature of the daily devotional market, the following market listings give a limited amount of information. Because most of these markets assign all material, they do not wish to be listed in the usual way.

If you are interested in writing daily devotionals, send to the following markets for guidelines and sample copies, write up sample devotionals to fit each one's particular format, and send to the editor with a request for an assignment. **DO NOT** submit any other type of material to these markets unless indicated.

ANCHOR DEVOTIONAL, PO Box 5100, Costa Mesa CA 92628. Toll-free (800)65HAVEN. Fax (951)710-1115. E-mail: ministry@havenministries.com. Website: www.havenministries .com. Haven Ministries. Joyce Gibson, ed. Quarterly devotional mag. Devotions 200 wds. Assigns one month of devotions on a theme (author picks theme). Query first for theme.

CLOSER WALK, 4201 N. Peachtree Rd., Atlanta GA 30341. (770)458-9300. Fax (770)454-9313. E-mail: pubsinfo@walkthru.org. Website: www.walkthru.org. Walk Thru the Bible. Read through the New Testament in a year. Monthly mag. Requires NKJV.

DAILY DEVOTIONS FOR THE DEAF, 21199 Greenview Rd., Council Bluffs IA 51503-4190. (712)322-5493. Fax (712)322-7792. E-mail: DeafMissions@deafmissions.com. Website: www.deafmissions.com. Jo Krueger, ed. Quarterly. Circ. 26,000. Prefers to see completed devotionals; 225-250 wds. **NO PAYMENT.** E-mail submissions OK.

$*DAILY MEDITATION, PO Box 2710, San Antonio TX 78299. (210)735-5247. Emilia Devno, ed. Inspirational religious articles. Semiannual booklet; circ. 775. Subscription $16. Complete ms; no e-query. Pays .015-.02/wd. on acceptance for 1st rts. Articles 300-1,650 wds. Responds in 3-8 wks.

  Poetry: Buys poetry; 4-12 lines; pays .14/line.

  Fillers: Buys prose fillers, to 350 wds.

$DEVOTIONS, 8121 Hamilton Ave., Cincinnati OH 45231. (513)931-4050. Fax (513)931-0904. E-mail: gwilde1@cfl.rr.com. Website: www.standardpub.com. Gary Allen, ed. Assigned by work-for-hire contract to previously published writers only. Query by e-mail only. Pays $20/devotion. Send list of credits rather than a sample.

FAMILY WALK, 4201 N. Peachtree Rd., Atlanta GA 30341. (770)458-9300. Fax (770)454-9313. E-mail: pubsinfo@walkthru.org. Website: www.walkthru.org. Walk Thru the Bible. Topical devotional guide for families with children 6 years and older. Explores a different issue each week (rather than daily Bible readings). Monthly mag. Subscription $18. Requires NIV.

FORWARD DAY BY DAY, 300 W. Fourth St., Cincinnati OH 45202-2665. Toll-free (800)543-1813. (513)721-6659. Fax (513)721-0729. E-mail: esgleason@forwarddaybyday.com, or orders@forwarddaybyday.com. Website: www.forwardmovement.org. Edward S. Gleason, ed./dir. Also online version. Send complete devotions, or send samples and request an assignment. Also likes author to complete an entire month's worth of devotions. E-mail submissions OK. Length: 2 paragraphs. **NO PAYMENT.** (No ads)

FRUIT OF THE VINE, Barclay Press, 211 N. Meridian St., #101, Newberg OR 97132. (503)538-9775. Fax (503)554-8597. E-mail: info@barclaypress.com. E-mail submissions accepted at phampton@barclaypress.com. Website: www.barclaypress.com. Editorial team: Susan Fawver, Sherry Macy, Paula Hampton. Send samples and request assignment. Prefers 250-290 wds. **PAYS FREE SUBSCRIPTION & 6 COPIES.** Guidelines.

INDEED, PO Box 562, Mt. Morris IL 61054-8197. (770)458-9300. Fax (770)454-9313. Website: www.walkthru.org. Walk Thru the Bible. Chris Tiegreen, ed. Bimonthly mag.; circ. 13,000. By assignment only.

  **2005, 2004 EPA Award of Excellence—Devotional.

+IN HIS PRESENCE, PO Box 9609, Kansas City MO 64134-0609. Toll-free (800)525-8627. (816)763-7800. Fax (816)765-2522. Website: http://stonecroft.gospelcom.net. Stonecroft Ministries. Devotions for women. Assigns a whole month to one writer. Query.

OUR JOURNEY (formerly *Soul Journey*), 3000 Kraft Ave. S.E., Grand Rapids MI 49512. (616)974-2663. E-mail: articles@ourjourneyonline.org. Website: www.ourjourney online.org. RBC Ministries. Tom Felton, ed. Devotionals for today's young adults and older. Monthly devotional; 64 pgs. Subscription for a gift of any amount. Open to unsolicited freelance. Complete ms.(as a Word attachment). **PAYS 10 COPIES.** Articles/devotions 325-350 wds. Guidelines on Website.

    Special Needs: Art and photographs. See guidelines.

    Tips: "Submit one article at a time, once a month."

($)+PENNED FROM THE HEART, 26 Everbreeze Dr., Hadley PA 16130. (724)253-2635. E-mail: gloworm@certainty.net. Website: www.gloriaclover.com. Son-Rise Publications. Gloria Clover, ed. Annual daily devotional book; about 240 pgs.; 5,000 copies/yr. 100% unsolicited freelance. Complete ms/cover letter; phone/e-query OK. **PAYS ONE COPY OF THE BOOK + A DISCOUNT TO RESELL BOOKS.** One-time rts. Devotions up to 250 wds. (365/yr.). Responds in 8 wks. No simultaneous submissions; accepts reprints (tell when/where appeared). Accepts mss by e-mail (copied into message). Prefers NIV. Accepts submissions from children/teens. Guidelines & copy on Website. (No ads)

    Poetry: Accepts any type; to 24 lines. Pays one copy. Submit max. 10 poems.

    Fillers: Accepts anecdotes, prayers, and quotes; to 250 wds.

    Tips: "Devotions should include instruction and encouragement and should be biblically based. Follow guidelines, specifically 250 words or less. I am open to all well-written topics that either instruct or encourage."

$THE QUIET HOUR, 4050 Lee Vance View, Colorado Springs CO 80919. (719)536-0100. Fax (407)359-2850. E-mail: gwilde1@cfl.rr.com. Website: www.cookministries.com. Cook Communications Ministries. Gary Wilde, ed. 100% unsolicited freelance. Pays $15-35/devotional on acceptance. Send list of credits only, rather than a sample. Accepts e-mailed sample devotional. Responds in 3 mos.

QUIET WALK, 4201 N. Peachtree Rd., Atlanta GA 30341. (770)458-9300. Fax (770)454-9313. E-mail: pubsinfo@walkthru.org. Website: www.walkthru.org. Walk Thru the Bible. Emphasis on personal worship and prayer. Monthly mag. Subscription $18. Requires NKJV.

$THE SECRET PLACE, Box 851, Valley Forge PA 19482-0851. (610)768-2000. Fax (610)768-2441. E-mail: thesecretplace@abc-usa.org. Website: www.judsonpress.com. Kathleen Hayes, sr. ed. Prefers to see completed devotionals, 200 wds. (use unfamiliar Scripture passages). 64 pgs. Circ. 150,000. 100% freelance. Pays $15 for 1st rts. Accepts poetry and buys photos (B & W). Accepts e-mail submissions. Guidelines.

$THESE DAYS, 100 Witherspoon St., Louisville KY 40202-1396. (502)569-5052. Fax (502)569-8308. E-mail: vpatton@presbypub.com. Website: www.ppcpub.com. Presbyterian Publishing Corp. Vince Patton, ed. Subscription $6.95. Query/samples. 95% unsolicited freelance. Pays $14.25/devotion for 1st and nonexclusive reprint rts. (makes work-for-hire assignments); 200 wds. (including key verse and short prayer). Uses poetry (2-6/yr.), pays $15. Wants short, contemporary poetry on church holidays and seasons of the year—overtly religious (15 lines, 33-character/line maximum). Query for their two feature segments (short articles): "These Moments" and "These Times."

$THE UPPER ROOM, PO Box 340004, Nashville TN 37203-0004. (615)340-7252. Fax (615)340-7267. E-mail: TheUpperRoomMagazine@upperroom.org. Website: www.upper room.org. Mary Lou Redding, mng. ed. 95% unsolicited freelance. Pays $25/devotional on publication. 72 pgs. This publication wants freelance submissions and does not make assignments. Phone/fax/e-query OK. Send devotionals up to 250 wds. Buys explicitly religious art, in various media, for use on covers only (transparencies/slides requested); buys one-time, worldwide publishing rts. Accepts e-mail submissions (copied into message). Guidelines (also on Website); copy for 5x7 SAE/2 stamps.(No ads)

Tips: "We do not return submissions. Accepted submissions will be notified in 6-9 wks. Follow guidelines. Need meditations from men." Always include postal address with e-mail submissions.

$THE WORD IN SEASON, PO Box 1209, Minneapolis MN 55440-1209. Fax (612)330-3215. E-mail: rochelle@liferhymecoaching.com. Website: www.augsburgfortress.org. Augsburg Fortress. Rev. Rochelle Y. Melander, ed./mngr. 96 pgs. Devotions to 200 wds. Pays $18/devotion; $50 for prayers. Accepts e-mail submissions (copied into message) after reading guidelines. Guidelines for #10 SAE/2 stamps; copy for 9x12 SAE/4 stamps.

Tips: "We prefer that you write for guidelines. We will send instructions for preparing sample devotions. We accept new writers based on the sample devotions we request and make assignments after acceptance. Do not send samples or request guidelines by e-mail."

$WORDS OF LIFE: Daily Reflections for Your Spirit, St. Paul University, 249 Main St., Ottawa ON K1S 1C5, Canada. (613)236-1393, ext. 3036. Fax (613)782-3004. E-mail: words-of-life@ustpaul.ca. Website: www.ustpaul.ca. Caryl Green, ed. Send samples and request an assignment. Prefers 135 wds. Pays $45 Cdn. Buys photos.

MISSIONS MARKETS

$AMERICAN BAPTISTS IN MISSION, PO Box 851, Valley Forge PA 19482-0851. (610)768-2000. Fax (610)768-2320. E-mail: richard.schramm@abc-usa.org. Website: www.abc-usa.org. Richard W. Schramm, ed. Denominational. Bimonthly mag.; 24-32 pgs.; circ. 39,000. Subscription free. 10% unsolicited freelance; 90% assigned. Query; fax/e-query OK. Pays negotiable rates on publication. Articles 750-1,000 wds. (few/yr.). Prefers e-mail submission (attached file). Uses some sidebars. Prefers NRSV. Guidelines (also by e-mail); copy. Incomplete topical listings but will accept any article of substantial interest to American Baptists. (Ads)

CATHOLIC MISSIONS IN CANADA, 1155 Yonge St., #201, Toronto ON M4T 1W2, Canada. Toll-free (866)937-2642. (416)934-3424. Fax (416)934-3425. E-mail: magazine@cmic.info. Website: www.cmic.info. Catholic Missions in Canada. Patria C. Rivera, ed. To share the faith journeys of missionaries as they share the love of Jesus in needy Catholic missions across Canada. Quarterly digest-sized mag.; circ. 25,000. Subscription free to donors. Open to unsolicited freelance. Incomplete topical listings. (No ads)

EAST-WEST CHURCH & MINISTRY REPORT, Southern Wesleyan University, Box 1020, Central SC 29630. (864)644-5221. Fax (864)644-5902. E-mail: melliott@swu.edu. Website: www.swu.edu/~melliott. Dr. Mark Elliott, ed. Encourages Western Christian ministry in Central and Eastern Europe and the former Soviet Union that is effective, culturally sensitive, and cooperative. Quarterly newsletter; 16 pgs.; circ. 430. Print subscription $44.95; online subscription $19.95. 25% unsolicited freelance; 75% assigned. Query; phone/fax/e-query OK. **NO PAYMENT** for all rts. Articles 1,500 wds. (4/yr.); book reviews, 100 wds. Responds in 4 wks. Prefers requested ms on disk or by e-mail. Regularly uses sidebars. Any Bible version. Guidelines (also by e-mail/Website); copy $11.95. (No ads)

Tips: "All submissions must relate to Central and Eastern Europe or the former Soviet Union."

**2001 EPA Award of Merit—Newsletter.

$EVANGELICAL MISSIONS QUARTERLY, PO Box 794, Wheaton IL 60189. (630)752-7158. Fax (630)752-7155. E-mail: emqjournal@aol.com, or emis@wheaton.edu. Website: www .BillyGrahamCenter.org/emis. Evangelism and Missions Information Service (EMIS). Gary

Corwin, ed.; Minnette Northcutt, mng. ed. For missionaries and others interested in missions trends, strategies, issues, problems, and resources. Quarterly jour.; 136 pgs.; circ. 7,000. Subscription $24.95. 65% unsolicited; 35% assigned. Query; fax/e-query OK. Pays $100 on publication for all rts. Articles 2,500 wds. (30/yr.); book reviews 400 wds. (query/pays $25). Responds in 4 wks. Accepts few reprints (tell when/where appeared). Prefers requested ms on disk or by e-mail (copied into message). Uses some sidebars. Prefers NIV. Free guidelines (also by e-mail)/copy. (Ads)

> **Columns/Departments:** Buys 4/yr. In the Workshop (tips to increase missionary effectiveness), 1,500-2,000 wds.; $100.

> **Tips:** "We consider all submissions. It is best to check our Website for examples and guidelines. Present an article idea and why you are qualified to write it. All articles must target evangelical, cross-cultural missionaries. 'In the Workshop' is most open to freelancers. Most authors have a credible connection to and experience in missions."

GLAD TIDINGS, 50 Wynford Dr., Toronto ON M3C 1J7, Canada. Toll-free (800)619-7301.(416)441-1111. Fax (416)441-2825. E-mail: hwilson@presbyterian.ca. Website: www.presbyterian.ca/wms/index.html. Women's Missionary Society/Presbyterian. Holly Wilson, ed. To challenge concerned Christians to reflect on their faith through articles and reports related to mission and social justice issues; encourages readers to become informed, inspired, and motivated to action. Bimonthly mag.; circ. 5,000. Subscription $12 Cdn. Open to unsolicited freelance. Not in topical listings. (Ads)

INTERNATIONAL JOURNAL OF FRONTIER MISSIONS, 1539 E. Howard St., Pasadena CA 91104. (626)398-2108. Fax (626)398-2185. E-mail: ijfm@wciu.edu. Website: www.ijfm.org. Rory Clark, mng. ed. Dedicated to frontiers in missions. Quarterly jour.; 48 pgs.; circ. 500. Subscription $15. 75% unsolicited freelance. Complete ms/cover letter; phone/fax/e-query OK. **NO PAYMENT** for one-time rts. Articles 2,000-8,500 wds. Seasonal 3 mos. ahead. Accepts simultaneous submissions & reprints. Accepts e-mail submissions. Does not use sidebars. Guidelines/theme list (also by e-mail/Website); copy $2/10x13 SAE. (Ads)

> **Special Needs:** Contextualization, church in missions, training for missions, mission trends and paradigms, de-westernization of the gospel and missions from the Western world, biblical world-view development, mission theology, Animism, Islam, Buddhism, Hinduism, nonliterate peoples, tent making, mission member care, reaching nomadic peoples, mission history, new religious movements and missions, science and missions, etc.

> **Tips:** "Writers on specific issues we cover are always welcome. Although the circulation is small, the print run is 2,000 and used for promotional purposes. Highly recommended for mission schools, libraries, and mission executives."

$LEADERS FOR TODAY, Box 13, Atlanta GA 30370. (770)449-8869. Fax (770)449-8457. E-mail: hiatlanta@haggai-institute.com. Website: www.haggai-institute.com. Haggai Institute. Roland Moody, exec. production. Primarily for donors to ministry; focus is alumni success stories. Quarterly mag.; 16 pgs.; circ. 7,500. Subscription free. 100% assigned to date. Query; fax query OK. Pays .10-.25/wd. on acceptance for all rts. Articles 1,000-2,000 wds. Responds in 2-3 wks. Requires requested ms on disk or by e-mail (attached file). Kill fee 100%. Regularly uses sidebars. Prefers NIV. Guidelines/theme list; copy for 9x12 SAE/4 stamps. (No ads)

> **Tips:** "If traveling to a developing country, check well in advance regarding the possibility of doing an alumni story. All articles are preassigned; query first."

> **2005 EPA Award of Merit—Missionary.

MISSIOLOGY: An International Review, 204 N. Lexington Ave., Wilmore KY 40390. (859)858-2216. Fax (859)858-2375. E-mail: missiology@asburyseminary.edu. Website: www.asmweb.org. American Society of Missiology/Asbury Theological Seminary. Terry C.

Muck, ed. A scholarly journal for those who study and practice missions worldwide. Quarterly jour.; 128-136 pgs.; circ. 1,500. Subscription $24. 60% unsolicited freelance; 40% assigned. Complete ms/cover letter. **PAYS 20 COPIES** for 1st rts. Articles 3,000-4,000 wds. (20/yr.); book reviews 400 wds. Responds in 12 wks. No seasonal. No simultaneous submissions or reprints. Prefers requested ms by e-mail (attached file) or on disk. No kill fee. Uses some sidebars. Any Bible version. Guidelines (also by e-mail); copy for 6x9 SAE/$2 postage ($5 foreign). (Ads)

MISSION FRONTIERS, 1605 Elizabeth St., Pasadena CA 91104. (626)797-1111. Fax (626) 398-2263. E-mail: mission.frontiers@uscwm.org. Website: www.missionfrontiers.org. U.S. Center for World Mission. Darrell Dorr, mng. ed. To stimulate a movement to establish indigenous churches where still needed around the world. Bimonthly & online mag.; 24 pgs.; circ. 81,000. Subscription by donation. No unsolicited freelance; 100% assigned. Query. **NO PAYMENT.** Articles. Rarely responds. Accepts requested ms on disk or by e-mail (copied into message). Regularly uses sidebars. No guidelines; free copy. Incomplete topical listings. (Ads)

> **Fillers:** Cartoons.

> **Tips:** "Be a published missionary or former missionary. Be on the cutting edge of strategic breakthrough or methods of reaching an unreached ethnic group." Looking for true-life, short sidebars of Muslims accepting Jesus, or impact of prayer in missions.

$NEW WORLD OUTLOOK, 475 Riverside Dr., Rm. 1476, New York NY 10115-0122. (212)870-3765. Fax (212)870-3940. E-mail: nwo@gbgm-umc.org. Website: http://gbgm-umc.org/nwo. United Methodist. Christie R. House, ed. Denominational missions. Bimonthly mag.; 48 pgs.; circ. 24,000. Subscription $15. 20% unsolicited freelance. Query; fax/e-query OK. Pays $50-300 on publication for all & electronic rts. Articles 500-2,000 wds. (24/yr.); book reviews 200-500 wds. (assigned). No guaranteed response time. Seasonal 4 mos. ahead. Kill fee 50% or $100. Prefers e-mail submission (Word Perfect 6.1 or 8.1 in attached file). Regularly uses sidebars. Prefers NRSV. Guidelines; copy $3. (Ads)

> **Tips:** "Ask for a list of United Methodist mission workers and projects in your area. Investigate them, propose a story, and consult with the editors before writing. Most open to articles and/or color photos of U.S. or foreign mission sites visited as a stringer, after consultation with the editor."

$ONE, 1011 First Ave., New York NY 10022-4195. Toll-free (877)228-8239. (212)826-1480. Fax (212)826-8979. E-mail: mjl@cnewa.org. Website: www.cnewa.org. Catholic Near East Welfare Assn. Michael La Civita, exec. ed. Interest in cultural, religious, and human rights development in Middle East, N.E. Africa, India, and Eastern Europe. Bimonthly mag.; 40 pgs.; circ. 100,000. Subscription $12. 20% unsolicited freelance; 50% assigned. Query/clips; fax query OK. Pays .20/edited wd.($200) on publication for all rts. Articles 2,000-3,000 wds. (15/yr.). Responds in 9 wks. Accepts requested ms on disk. Kill fee $200. Prefers NAS. Guidelines (also by e-mail); copy for 7x10 SAE/2 stamps.

> **Tips:** "We strive to educate our readers about the culture, faith, history, issues, and people who form the Eastern Christian churches. Anything on people in Palestine/Israel, Eastern Europe, or India. Material should not be academic. Include detailed photographs with story or article."

OPREV EQUIPPER, PO Box 3488, Monument CO 80132-3488. (719)572-5908. Fax (775)248-8147. E-mail: bside@oprev.org. Website: www.oprev.org. Mission To Unreached Peoples. Bruce T. Sidebotham, dir. Provides information to equip U.S. military Christians for cross-cultural ministry. Quarterly & online newsletter; 8 pgs.; circ. 1,500. Subscription free. 40% unsolicited freelance; 60% assigned. Query; phone/e-query OK. **PAYS IN COPIES** for one-time rts. Not copyrighted. Articles 250-1,000 wds. (4/yr.). Responds in 4 wks. Seasonal 4 mos. ahead. Accepts simultaneous submissions & reprints (tell when/

where appeared). Accepts requested ms on disk. No kill fee. Regularly uses sidebars. Prefers NIV. No guidelines; copy .50/9x12 SAE/4 stamps. (No ads)

Fillers: Accepts 4/yr. Newsbreaks, to 150 wds.

Columns/Departments: Accepts 4/yr. Agency Profile (describes a mission agency's history and work), 200-300 wds.; Area Profile (describes spiritual landscape of a military theater of operations), 300-750 wds., Resource Review (describes a cross-cultural ministry tool), 100-200 wds. Query.

Special Needs: Ministry in Afghanistan and Iraq. World news and analysis; cross-cultural communication; area profiles and people profiles on military theaters of operation.

Tips: "We need insights and case studies on U.S. service personnel being used in cross-cultural Christian ministry."

$PFI WORLD REPORT, Box 17434, Washington DC 20041. (703)481-0000. Fax (703)481-0003. E-mail: info@pfi.org, or chris@pfi.org. Website: www.pfi.org. Prison Fellowship, Intl. Christopher P. Nicholson, ed. Targets issues and needs of prisoners, ex-prisoners, justice officials, victims, families, PFI staff, and volunteers in 75 countries. Bimonthly newsletter; 4-8 pgs.; circ. 4,750. Subscription free. 10% unsolicited freelance. Query; fax/e-query OK. Pays $100-350 on acceptance for all rts. Articles 500-750 wds. (4/yr.). Responds in 2 wks. Seasonal 4 mos. ahead. Accepts simultaneous submissions & reprints (tell when/where appeared). Accepts requested ms on disk. Kill fee. Regularly uses sidebars. Guidelines (also on Website); copy for #10 SAE/1 stamp. (No ads)

Special Needs: Prison issues, justice issues, anything that relates to international prison ministry.

Tips: "Looking for personal profiles of people active in prison ministry (preferably PFI officials); ex-prisoner success stories; how-to articles about various aspects of prison ministry. Avoid American slant."

$PIME WORLD, 17330 Quincy St., Detroit MI 48221-2765. (313)342-4066. Fax (313)342-6816. E-mail: pimeworld@pimeusa.org. Website: www.pimeusa.org. Pontifical Inst. for Foreign Missions/Catholic. Cari Hartman, publications mngr. For those interested in and supportive of foreign missions. Published 5X/yr., plus newsletter supplement; 24 pgs.; circ. 16,000. Subscription $15. 10% unsolicited freelance. Complete ms; e-query OK. Pays $15-25 on publication for one-time rts. Photos $10. Articles 500-1,000 wds. Responds in 2 wks. Seasonal 4 mos. ahead. Accepts reprints (tell when/where appeared). Prefers e-mail submission (attached file). Uses some sidebars. Prefers NAB. Accepts submissions from teens. Guidelines/theme list; copy for 6x9 SAE/2 stamps. (No ads)

Tips: "Features are open to freelancers. Needs missionary profiles; articles on PIME missionaries; interfaith dialog/experiences; and missions in Africa, especially Ivory Coast, Guinea Bissau, and Cameroon. Also issues like hunger, human rights, women's rights, peace, and justice as they are dealt with in developing countries by missionaries and locals alike."

THE RAILROAD EVANGELIST, PO Box 5026, Vancouver WA 98668-5026. (360)699-7208. E-mail: rrjoe@comcast.net. Railroad Evangelistic Assn. Joe Spooner, ed. For railroad and transportation employees and their families. Triannual mag.; 16 pgs.; circ. 2,500. Subscription $8. 100% unsolicited freelance. Complete ms/no cover letter; phone query OK. **NO PAYMENT.** Articles 100-700 wds. (10-15/yr.); railroad-related fiction only, for children or teens. Seasonal 4 mos. ahead. Accepts simultaneous submissions & reprints. Accepts e-mail submissions. Does not use sidebars. Guidelines (also by e-mail); copy for 9x12 SAE/2 stamps. (No ads)

Poetry: Accepts 4-8/yr. Traditional, any length. Send any number.

Fillers: Accepts many. Anecdotes, cartoons, quotes; to 100 wds.

Tips: "We need 400- to 700-word railroad-related salvation testimonies; or railroad-related human-interest stories; or model railroads. Since we publish only three times a year, we are focusing on railroad-related articles only. Just write and tell us or send us what you have. We'll let you know if we can use it or not."

WESLEYAN WORLD, 13300 Olio Rd., Noblesville IN 46060. (317)774-7943. Fax (317)774-7958. E-mail: djbray42@msn.com. Website: www.PrayGiveGo.com. The Wesleyan Church. Joy Bray, ed. For members and those who attend a Wesleyan church and are world-missions minded. Quarterly mag.; 34 pgs.; circ. 38,700. Subscription free or $15 (suggested donation). 10% unsolicited freelance; 90% assigned. Complete ms/cover letter. **NO PAYMENT.** Articles 1,200 wds. Accepts simultaneous submissions & reprints (tell when/where appeared). Regularly uses sidebars. (Ads—denominational only)

Special Needs: Leadership in missions; children's ministries; biblical teaching on spiritual warfare. Describe a personal missions experience.

WOMEN OF THE HARVEST, PO Box 151297, Lakewood CO 80215-9297. (303)985-2148. Fax (303)989-4239. E-mail: snelson@womenoftheharvest.com. Website: www.womenoftheharvest.com. Women of the Harvest Ministries Intl., Inc. Stephanie Nelson, ed.; Blair Sellke, submissions ed. To support and encourage women serving in cross-cultural missions. Bimonthly mag.; 16 pgs.; circ. 2,500. Subscription $24. 90% unsolicited freelance; 10% assigned. Complete ms; e-query OK. **NO PAYMENT** for one-time rts. Articles 350-650 wds. Seasonal 3 mos. ahead. Prefers requested ms on disk or by e-mail. Guidelines (also by e-mail); copy for SASE. (No ads)

Poetry: Free verse, traditional, haiku; variable length. Submit max. 5 poems.

Fillers: Anecdotes, short humor; 100 wds.

Tips: "This is a magazine designed especially for women serving cross-culturally. We need articles, humor, and anecdotes related to this topic. Best way to break in is by having a cross-cultural missions experience or to be heading to the mission field."

**2004 EPA Award of Merit—Christian Ministries.

MUSIC MARKETS

$CCM MAGAZINE, 104 Woodmont Blvd., 3rd Fl., Nashville TN 37205-2245. (615)386-3011. Fax (615)385-4112. E-mail: CCMWebEditors@ccmcom.com, or feedback@ccmmagazine.com. Website: www.ccmmagazine.com. Salem Communications, Inc. Jay Schwartzendruber, ed. Encourages spiritual growth through contemporary music; provides news and information about the Christian music market. Monthly & online mag.; 80 pgs.; circ. 70,000. Subscription $19.95. 75% unsolicited freelance. Query/clips; phone/fax query OK. Pays .20/wd. for short pieces, or $100/published pg. for features, on publication for all rts. Articles 500-2,500 wds.; music reviews 250-350 wds. Responds slowly. Seasonal 3 mos. ahead. Kill fee 50%. Prefers requested ms on disk or by e-mail (copied into message). Regularly uses sidebars. Guidelines; copy for 9x12 SAE/$4. (Ads)

**The #2 Best-selling Magazine in Christian retail stores.

CHRISTIAN MUSIC WEEKLY, 7057 Bluffwood Ct., Brownsburg IN 46112-8650. (317)892-5031. Fax (317)892-5034. E-mail through Website. Website: www.ChristianMusicWeekly.com. Joyful Sounds. Rob Green, ed. Trade paper for Worship, Inspirational, Adult Contemporary, and Southern Gospel Music radio formats. Weekly trade paper; 12 pgs.; circ. 300-1,200. Subscription $104 (paper) or $52 (PDF via e-mail). 25% unsolicited freelance; 75% assigned. Query by e-mail only. **PAYS IN COPIES** (will publish photo of writer and tiny bio). Articles 600-2,000 wds.; music reviews, 100-300 wds. Responds in 2 wks. Seasonal 2 mos. ahead. Accepts reprints. Requires requested ms on disk (DOS-ASCII), prefers e-mail submission. Guidelines by e-mail; copy for 9x12 SAE/2 stamps. (Ads)

Fillers: Cartoons, short humor (particularly radio or music related).

Columns/Departments: Insider (artist interview); Programming 101 (radio technique); retail, inspirational, especially for musicians and radio people; 600-2,000 wds.

Special Needs: Songwriting and performance.

Tips: "Most open to artist interviews. Must be familiar with appropriate music formats."

$CREATOR MAGAZINE, PO Box 480, Healdsburg CA 95448. Toll-free (800)777-6713. (707)837-9071. E-mail: creator@creatormagazine.com. Website: www.creatormagazine .com. Rod Ellis, ed. For interdenominational music ministry; promoting quality, diverse music programs in the church. Bimonthly mag.; 48-56 pgs.; circ. 6,000. Subscription $32.95. 35% unsolicited freelance. Query or complete ms/cover letter; fax/e-query OK. Pays $30-75 for assigned, $30-60 for unsolicited, on publication for 1st, one-time, or reprint rts. Articles 1,000-10,000 wds. (20/yr.); book reviews ($20). Responds in 4-12 wks. Seasonal 4 mos. ahead. Accepts simultaneous submissions & reprints (tell when/where appeared). Prefers requested ms on disk. Regularly uses sidebars. Prefers NRSV. Guidelines/theme list; copy for 9x12 SAE/5 stamps. (Ads)

   Fillers: Buys 20/yr. Anecdotes, cartoons, ideas, jokes, party ideas, short humor; 10-75 wds.; $5-25.

   Special Needs: Articles on worship; staff relationships.

THE HYMN: A Journal of Congregational Song, School of Theology, Boston University, 745 Commonwealth Ave., Boston MA 02215-1401. Toll-free (800)THE-HYMN. Fax (617)353-7322. E-mail: hymneditor@aol.com. Website: www.bu.edu/sth/hymn, or www.hymnsociety .org. Hymn Society in the U.S. & Canada. Beverly A. Howard, ed. (5423 Via Alberca, River-side CA 92507-6477). For church musicians, hymnologists, scholars; articles related to the congregational song. Quarterly jour.; 60 pgs.; circ. 3,000. Subscription $65. 85% unso-licited freelance; 15% assigned. Query; phone/e-query OK. **NO PAYMENT** for all rts. Arti-cles any length (12/yr.); book and music reviews any length. Responds in 4 wks. Seasonal 4 mos. ahead. Prefers requested ms on disk, no e-mail submission. Regularly uses side-bars. Any Bible version. Guidelines (also on Website); free copy. (Ads)

   Special Needs: Articles on history of hymns or practical ways to teach or use hymns. Con-troversial issues as related to hymns and songs. Contact editor.

   Contest: Hymn text and tune contests for special occasions or themes.

   Tips: "Controversial Issues in congregational song; focus all articles on congregational song."

   Note: Also see "Resources: Songwriting" in the Resources section in the front of this book.

$THE SENIOR MUSICIAN, One Lifeway Plaza., Nashville TN 37234-0170. (615)251-2913. Fax (615)251-2614. E-mail: jere.adams@lifeway.com. Website: www.lifeway.com. Southern Baptist. Jere V. Adams, ed. Easy choir music for senior adult choirs to use in worship, min-istry, and recreation; for music directors, pastors, organists, pianists, and choir coordina-tors. Quarterly mag.; 32 pgs.; circ. 32,000. 90% unsolicited freelance; 10% assigned. Com-plete ms. Pays .07/wd. on publication for 1st rts. Articles 500-900 wds. (6-7/yr.). Responds in 2-4 wks. Seasonal 1 yr. ahead. Some simultaneous submissions; reprints. Guidelines; free copy. (No ads for now)

   Poetry: Buys 2-3/yr. Traditional.

   Fillers: Buys 3-4/yr. Cartoons, ideas, party ideas, musical quizzes, short humor.

   Special Needs: Leisure reading, music training, fellowship suggestions, and choir projects for personal growth.

   Tips: "All topics must relate to senior adult musicians and senior choirs—anything else will be returned. Our publication includes 8 pages of literary and 24 pages of music."

TRADITION MAGAZINE, PO Box 492, Anita IA 50020. Phone/fax (712)762-4363. E-mail: bobeverhart@yahoo.com. Website: www.oldtimemusic.bigstep.com. National Traditional Country Music Assn., Inc. Bob Everhart, pres./ed. Bimonthly mag.; 56 pgs.; circ. 3,500.

Subscription $25. 30% unsolicited freelance; 70% assigned. Query. **PAYS IN COPIES** for one-time rts. Articles 1,000-2,000 wds. (4/yr.). Responds in 6-8 wks. Uses some sidebars. Prefers KJV. Guidelines; copy for 9x12 SAE/2 stamps. (Ads)

Fillers: Cartoons.

Columns/Departments: Accepts 4-6/yr. Query.

Tips: "Most articles need to deal with traditional or old-time music."

PASTOR/LEADERSHIP MARKETS

$THE AFRICAN AMERICAN PULPIT, PO Box 15347, Pittsburgh PA 15237. Toll-free (800)509-8227. Phone/fax (412)364-1688. E-mail: Info@theafricanamericanpulpit.com. Website: www.TheAfricanAmericanPulpit.com. Hope for Life Intl., Inc. Victoria McGoey, project mngr.; Martha Simmons, pub. The only journal focused exclusively on the art of black preaching. Quarterly jour.; 96 pgs.; circ. 4,000. Subscription $35 ($54 to libraries). 50% unsolicited freelance; 50% assigned. Complete ms/cover letter; phone/e-query OK. Pays $50 (flat fee) on publication for all rts. Articles 1,500 wds., sermons 2,500 wds. Responds in 13-26 wks. Seasonal 6-9 mos. ahead. Requires requested ms on disk or by e-mail. Does not use sidebars. Any Bible version. Guidelines (also by e-mail/Website); copy. (Ads)

Special Needs: Any type of sermon by African American preachers, and related articles or essays.

Contest: Sponsors contest occasionally; advertised in the magazine.

Tips: "The entire journal is open to freelancers. We strongly encourage freelancers to submit to us (as many pieces as you can), and freelancers can call anytime with questions. We are always looking for how-to articles, sermon helps, homiletic-method essays, seminarian pieces, and practical pieces."

+ALPHA NEWS, 74 Trinity Pl., 9th Fl., New York NY 10006-2001. (212)406-8687. Fax (212)406-7521. E-mail: info@alphausa.org. Website: www.Alphausa.org. Alpha North America. Claudia Roux, ed. To keep church leaders informed about the Alpha course. Newspaper; circ. 195,000. Subscription free. Open to unsolicited freelance. Query preferred. Not in topical listings. (Ads)

$BAREFOOT, PO Box 419527, Kansas City MO 64141. Toll-free (866)355-9933. (816)931-1900. Fax (816)753-4071. E-mail: bfeditor@barefootministries.com. Website: www.bare footministries.com. Bo Cassell, ed. Dedicated to resourcing and equipping youth workers and youth. Weekly e-zine. Subscription free online. 10% unsolicited freelance; 90% assigned. E-query preferred; fax query OK. Pays $50-100 on publication for all rts. Articles for youth workers 1,000 wds. (15-20/yr.); articles for youth, 500-1,000 wds. (15-20/yr.); fiction 500-1,000 wds.; reviews 500 wds. ($25). Responds in 8 wks. Seasonal 6 mos. ahead. Accepts reprints (tell when/where appeared). Accepts e-mail submissions (attached or copied into message). Some kill fees. Does not use sidebars. Prefers NIV. Accepts submissions from teens. Guidelines by e-mail; copy online. (No ads)

Fillers: Buys 20-40/yr. Anecdotes, cartoons, games, ideas, party ideas, short humor, and tips, 100-200 wds.; $20-40.

Special Needs: Youthworker and youth issues.

Tips: "We are most open to freelancers in the areas of product, music, and entertainment reviews. Also for fillers and any materials written for teens. Where youth ministry articles and curricular pieces are concerned, we usually assign those to established youth ministry professionals."

$CATECHUMENATE: A Journal of Christian Initiation, 1800 N. Hermitage Ave., Chicago IL 60622-1101. Toll-free (800)933-1800. (773)486-8970. Fax (800)933-7094. E-mail:

editors@ltp.org. Website: www.LTP.org. Catholic. Victoria M. Tufano, ed. For clergy and laity who work with those who are planning to become Catholic. Bimonthly jour.; 48 pgs.; circ. 5,600. Subscription $20. Complete ms/cover letter; phone/fax/e-query OK. Pays $100-250 on publication for all rts. Articles 1,500-3,000 wds. (10/yr.). Responds in 2-6 wks. Accepts simultaneous submissions. Prefers requested ms on disk. Kill fee. Does not use sidebars. Guidelines; copy for 6x9 SAE/4 stamps.

Poetry: Buys 6/yr. Free verse, traditional; 5-20 lines; $75. Submit max. 5 poems. One-time rts.

Columns/Departments: Buys 12/yr. Sunday Word (Scripture reflection on Sunday readings, aimed at catechumen); 450 wds.; $200-250. Query for assignment.

Special Needs: Christian initiation; reconciliation.

Tips: "It helps if the writer has experience working with Christian initiation. Approach is that this is something we are all learning together through experience and scholarship."

$THE CATHOLIC SERVANT, 3204 E. 43rd St., Minneapolis MN 55406. (612)729-7321. Fax (612)724-8695. E-mail: jcsondag@mninter.net. Catholic. John Sondag, ed./pub. For Catholic evangelization, catechesis, and apologetics. Monthly tabloid; 12 pgs.; circ. 41,000 (during school yr.; 33,000 summer). Query/clips; fax query OK. Pays $60 on publication. Articles 750-1,000 wds. (12/yr.). Responds in 4 wks. Seasonal 3 mos. ahead. Requested mss by e-mail only. Uses some sidebars. (Ads)

Fillers: Cartoons & short humor.

Columns/Departments: Opinion column, 500-750 wds.

Tips: "We buy features or column only."

$THE CHRISTIAN CENTURY, 104 S. Michigan Ave., Ste. 700, Chicago IL 60603. (312)263-7510. Fax (312)263-7540. E-mail: main@christiancentury.org. Website: www.christian century.org. Christian Century Foundation. Submit to: Attention Manuscripts. For ministers, educators, and church leaders interested in events and theological issues of concern to the ecumenical church. Biweekly mag.; 48 pgs.; circ. 30,000. Subscription $49. 20% unsolicited freelance; 80% assigned. Query (complete ms for fiction); phone/fax query OK. Pays $75-200 ($75-150 for unsolicited) on publication for all or one-time rts. Articles 1,500-3,000 wds. (150/yr.); fiction 1,000-3,000 wds. (3/yr.); book reviews, 800-1,500 wds.; music or video reviews 1,000 wds.; pays $0-75. Responds in 1-9 wks. Seasonal 4 mos. ahead. No simultaneous submissions. Accepts reprints (tell when/where appeared). No kill fee. Regularly uses sidebars. Prefers NRSV. Guidelines/theme list (also by e-mail); copy $5. (Ads)

Poetry: Buys 50/yr. Any type (religious but not sentimental); to 20 lines; $50. Submit max. 10 poems.

Special Needs: Film, popular culture commentary; news topics and analysis.

Tips: "Keep in mind our audience of sophisticated readers, eager for analysis and critical perspective that goes beyond the obvious. We are open to all topics if written with appropriate style for our readers."

$CHRISTIAN CREATIVE ARTS ASSN., PO Box 1128, Franklin TN 37065. (877)CH-DRAMA. E-mail: info@ccaaonline.org. Website: www.ccaaonline.org. Christy Haines, exec. dir. Conservative, evangelical dramas for stage, street, and sanctuary. Open to freelance. Scripts must adhere to guidelines for submissions; e-mail for guidelines first. Looking for any-length scripts for drama, puppetry, clowning, mime, interpretive movement, and comedy.

CHRISTIAN EDUCATION JOURNAL (CA), 13800 Biola Ave., LaMirada CA 90639. (562)903-6000, ext. 5528. Fax (562)906-4502. E-mail: editor.cej@biola.edu. Website: www.biola.edu/cej. Talbot School of Theology, Biola University. Kevin E. Lawson, ed. Academic journal on the practice of Christian education; for students, professors, and thoughtful ministry leaders in Christian education. Semiannual jour.; 200-250 pgs.; circ. 750. Subscription $25. Open to freelance. Query; e-query OK. Accepts full mss by e-mail. **NO**

PAYMENT for 1st rts. Articles 3,000-6,000 wds. (20/yr.); book reviews 2-5 pgs. Responds in 4-6 wks. No seasonal. Might accept simultaneous submissions & reprints (tell when/where appeared). Requires e-mail submissions (attached file in Word format). Does not use sidebars. Any Bible version. Guidelines on Website; no copy. (Ads)

Special Needs: Children's spiritual life.

Tips: "Focus on foundations and/or research with implications for the conception and practice of Christian education." Book reviews must be preassigned and approved by the editor; guidelines on Website.

CHRISTIAN MANAGEMENT REPORT, PO Box 4090, San Clemente CA 92674-4090. (949)487-0900. Fax (949)487-0927. E-mail: DeWayne@CMAonline.org, or cma@cmaon line.org. Website: www.CMAonline.org. Christian Management Assn. DeWayne Herbrandson, exec. ed. Management resources and leadership training for Christian nonprofit organizations and growing churches. Bimonthly jour.; 48 pgs.; circ. 3,500+. Subscription $39.95. 100% assigned. Complete ms; e-query encouraged. **PAYS 10 COPIES** for all, 1st, one-time, reprint, or electronic rts. Articles 770-1,500 wds./bio; book reviews 100-200 wds. Responds in 4 wks. Seasonal 6 mos. ahead. No simultaneous submissions; limited reprints. CMA members first choice. Prefers accepted ms by e-mail (attached file). No kill fee. Regularly uses sidebars. Prefers NIV, NLT. Guidelines (also by e-mail); free copy. (Ads)

Fillers: Cartoons.

Columns/Departments: Accepts 6/yr. Living with Integrity (leadership integrity issues), 750-1,500 wds.; Ministry Profile (management issues with various ministries), 1,500 wds.; Coaching as Ministry (how to mentor and coach one's staff), 750-1,500 wds.

Special Needs: Evangelical Calendar of Events, Ministry Profiles/Case Studies; hot ministry news, and trends.

Tips: "All areas open. Submit a synopsis of article idea dealing with leadership and management issues relevant to megachurches or parachurch organizations. Send by e-mail (attached file)."

$*CHURCH ADMINISTRATION, One Lifeway Plaza, Nashville TN 37234. (615)251-2297. Fax (615)251-3866. Website: www.lifeway.com. Southern Baptist. Chris Johnson, ed. Practical pastoral ministry/church administration ideas for pastors and staff. Quarterly mag.; 50 pgs.; circ. 12,000. 15% unsolicited freelance. Query. Pays .065/wd. on acceptance for all rts. Articles 1,600-2,000 wds. (60/yr.). Responds in 8 wks. Guidelines/copy for #10 SAE/2 stamps.

Columns/Departments: Buys 60/yr. Weekday Dialogue; Minister's Mate; Secretary's File; all 2,000 wds.

Tips: "Manuscripts must be typed and have return postage."

$CHURCH WORSHIP, 165 Plaza Dr., Prescott AZ 86303. (928)771-8601. Fax (928)771-8621. E-mail: edmin2@aol.com. Website: www.educationalministries.com. Educational Ministries. Robert Davidson, ed. Supplementary resources for church worship leaders. Monthly jour.; 24 pgs.; circ. 1,500. Subscription $24. 100% unsolicited freelance. Complete ms/cover letter; phone/fax/e-query OK. Pays .03/wd., 60 days after publication, for 1st rts. Articles 500-1,500 wds.; fiction 100-1,500 wds. Responds in 3-18 wks. Seasonal 6 mos. ahead. Guidelines/theme list; copy for 9x12 SAE/4 stamps. (No ads)

Special Needs: Complete worship services; seasonal sermons.

Tips: "Most open to creative worship services using music, drama, or art."

$THE CLERGY JOURNAL, 6160 Carmen Ave. E., Inver Grove Heights MN 55076-4422. (651)451-9945. Fax (651)457-4617. E-mail: sfirle@logosstaff.com. Website: www.logos productions.com. Logos Productions, Inc. Sharon Firle, mng. ed. Directed mainly to clergy—a practical guide to church leadership and personal growth. Monthly (9X) mag.; 56 pgs.; circ. 6,000. Subscription $39.20. 5% unsolicited freelance; 95% assigned. Complete ms/cover letter; fax/e-query OK. Pays $75-150 on publication for 1st rts. Articles 1,000-1,500 wds. (25/yr.) Responds in 4 wks. Seasonal 8 mos. ahead. Accepts simultaneous submissions & reprints (tell when/where appeared). Prefers requested ms by e-mail (attached file). No kill fee. Uses some sidebars. Prefers NRSV. Guidelines/theme list (also by e-mail/Website); copy for 9x12 SAE/4 stamps. (Ads—struran@logosstaff.com)

> **Columns/Departments:** Ministry Issues; Preaching & Worship; Personal Issues. Pays $75-150.
>
> **Special Needs:** Church technology issues.
>
> **Tips:** "Our greatest need is sermon writers who can write on assigned texts. Instructions sent on request. Our readers are mainline Protestant. We are interested in meeting the personal and professional needs of clergy in areas like worship planning, church and personal finances, and self-care—spiritual, physical, and emotional."

$CORNERSTONE YOUTH RESOURCES, 55 W. Oak Ridge Dr., Hagerstown MD 21740. Fax (817)926-5845. E-mail: plhumphrey@earthlink.net. Seventh-day Adventist. Patricia Humphrey, ed. For Christian youth leaders; a practical resource filled with ideas for creative youth ministry and programming. Quarterly mag.; 48 pgs.; circ. 2,200. 5% unsolicited freelance; 95% assigned. Query/clips; fax query OK; best to e-mail as editor lives in Texas. Pays $25-350 on acceptance for 1st rts. Articles 700-900 wds. (16/yr.). Responds in 8-12 wks. Seasonal 12 mos. ahead. Accepts reprints (tell when/where appeared). Accepts e-mail submissions (attached file). No kill fee. Regularly uses sidebars. Prefers KJV, NKJV, NIV. Accepts submissions from teens. Guidelines (also by e-mail); copy for 9x12 SAE/$1.42 postage (mark "Media Mail"). (Ads)

> **Columns/Departments:** Outreach Ideas (service activity ideas for teens), 800-1,000 wds.; Super Social Suggestions (social activities and games for teen groups), 800-1,000 wds.; Program Ideas (creative youth programming ideas), variable lengths.
>
> **Special Needs:** Articles dealing with understanding and teaching youth. Innovative concepts in youth ministry.
>
> **Tips:** "Areas most open to freelancers are the Super Social and Outreach Ideas. We are always looking for creative activity ideas that teen leaders can do with youth, ages 14-18. The activities should be fun to do and well-written with clear, easy-to-follow instructions. Ideas that are tested and have worked well with your own youth group are preferred."

CROSS CURRENTS, 475 Riverside Dr., Ste. 1945, New York NY 10015. (212)870-2544. Fax (212)870-2539. E-mail: careym@mindspring.com. Website: www.crosscurrents.org. Association for Religion and Intellectual Life. Carey Monserrate, mng. ed. For thoughtful activists for social justice and church reform. Quarterly mag.; 144 pgs.; circ. 5,000. Subscription $30. 25% unsolicited freelance; 75% assigned. Mostly written by academics. Complete ms/cover letter; e-query OK. **PAYS IN COPIES** for all rts. Articles 3,000-5,000 wds.; fiction 3,000 wds.; book reviews 1,000 wds. Responds in 6-8 wks. Seasonal 6 mos. ahead. No simultaneous submissions or reprints. Prefers requested ms on disk or by e-mail (attached file). No kill fee. Does not use sidebars. Guidelines (also on Website); no copy. (Ads)

> **Poetry:** Beverly Coyle, poetry ed. Accepts 12/yr. Any type or length; no payment. Submit max. 5 poems.
>
> **Tips:** "Looking for focused, well-researched articles; creative fiction and poetry. Send two double-spaced copies; SASE; use *Chicago Manual of Style* and nonsexist language."

$DIOCESAN DIALOGUE, 16565 S. State St., South Holland IL 60473. (708)331-5485. Fax (708)331-5484. E-mail: acp@acpress.org. Website: www.americancatholicpress.org. A Mexican Catholic Press. Fr. Michael Gilligan, editorial dir. Targets Latin-Rite dioceses in the U.S. that sponsor a mass broadcast on TV or radio. Annual newsletter; 8 pgs.; circ. 750. Free. 20% unsolicited freelance. Complete ms/cover letter; no phone/fax/e-query. Pays on publication for all rts. Responds in 10 wks. Accepts simultaneous submissions & reprints. Uses some sidebars. Prefers NAB (Confraternity). No guidelines; copy $3/9x12 SAE/2 stamps. (No ads)

Fillers: Cartoons, 2/yr.

Tips: "Writers should be familiar with TV production of the Mass and/or the needs of senior citizens, especially shut-ins."

$EMMANUEL, 5384 Wilson Mills Rd., Cleveland OH 44143. (440)449-2103. Fax (440)449-3862. E-mail: emmanuelpublishing@sbcglobal.net. Website: www.blessedsacrament.com. Catholic. Paul Bernier SSS, ed. (pbernier@earthlink.net). Eucharistic spirituality for priests and others in church ministry. Bimonthly mag.; 96 pgs.; circ. 3,000. Subscription $26; $31 foreign. 30% unsolicited freelance. Query or complete ms/cover letter; e-query OK. Pays $75-150 for articles, $50 for meditations, on publication for all rts. Articles 2,000-2,750 wds.; meditations 1,000-1,250 wds.; book reviews 500-750 wds. Responds in 2 wks. Seasonal 4 mos. ahead. Accepts manuscripts on disk or as e-mail attachments. Guidelines (also by e-mail)/theme list. (Ads)

Poetry: Buys 15/yr. Free verse, light verse, traditional; 8 lines & up; $35. Submit max. 3 poems.

Tips: "Most open to articles, meditations, poetry oriented toward Eucharistic spirituality, prayer, and ministry."

$ENRICHMENT: A Journal for Pentecostal Ministry, 1445 N. Boonville Ave., Springfield MO 65802. (417)862-2781, ext. 4095. Fax (417)862-0416. E-mail: enrichmentjournal@ ag.org. Website: www.enrichmentjournal.ag.org. Assemblies of God. Gary R. Allen, exec. ed.; Rick Knoth, mng. ed. (rknoth@ag.org). Directed to part- or full-time ministers and church leaders. Quarterly jour.; 128-144 pgs.; circ. 33,000. Subscription $24, $42/2 yrs.; foreign add $10. 5-10% unsolicited freelance. Complete ms/cover letter. Pays .10/wd. ($75-175) on acceptance for one-time rts. Articles 1,200-1,500 wds. (25/yr.); book reviews, 250 wds. ($25). Responds in 8-12 wks. Seasonal 1 yr. ahead. Accepts simultaneous submissions & reprints (tell when/where appeared). Requires requested ms on disk or by e-mail (copied into message). Kill fee 50%. Regularly uses sidebars. Prefers NIV. Guidelines/theme list; copy for $3/10x13 SAE. (Ads)

Fillers: Cartoon; $50-75.

Columns/Departments: Buys many/yr. For Women in Ministry (leadership ideas), Associate Ministers (related issues), Managing Your Ministry (how-to), Financial Concepts (church stewardship issues), Family Life (minister's family), When Pews Are Few (ministry in smaller congregation); Worship in the Church; Leader's Edge; Preaching That Connects; all 1,200-1,500 wds.; $125-150.

Tips: "Open to sermon outlines."

$*ENVIRONMENT & ART LETTER, 1800 N. Hermitage Ave., Chicago IL 60622-1101. Toll-free (800)933-1800. (773)486-8970, ext. 267. Fax (773)486-7094. E-mail: mbrennan@ LTP.org. Website: www.LTP.org. Catholic. Margaret Brennan, ed. For artists, architects, building professionals, pastors, parish committees interested in church architecture, art, and decoration. Monthly newsletter; 12 pgs.; circ. 2,500. Subscription $20. 80% unsolicited freelance. Query/clips; phone/fax query OK. Pays $25/ms page on publication for all rts. Responds in 18 wks. Seasonal 2 mos. ahead. Accepts simultaneous submissions. Theme list; copy for 9x12 SAE/3 stamps.

Tips: "Need a thorough knowledge of the liturgical documents pertaining to architecture and art, especially environment and art for Catholic worship."

$THE EVANGELICAL BAPTIST, 679 Southgate Dr., Guelph ON N1G 4S2, Canada. (519)821-4830. Fax (519)821-9829. E-mail: eb@fellowship.ca. Website: www.fellowship.ca. Fellowship of Evangelical Baptist Churches in Canada. Ginette Cotnoir, mng. ed., (18 Louvigny,

Lorraine QC J6Z 1T7 Canada). To enhance the life and ministry of pastors and leaders in local churches. Bimonthly (5X) mag.; 32 pgs.; circ. 3,000. Subscription $12. 5-10% unsolicited freelance; 20% assigned. Complete ms/cover letter; e-query preferred. Pays $30-150 on publication for one-time rts. Articles 500-2,400 wds.(12-15/yr.) Responds in 6-8 wks. Accepts simultaneous submissions & reprints. Guidelines (also by e-mail); copy for 9x12 SAE/$1.50 Cdn. postage. (Ads)

>   **Columns/Departments:** Buys 10/yr. Joy in the Journey (inspiration in everyday life), 600-800 wds.; Point of View (respectful and well-argued opinion pieces about a subject relevant to believers or the church), 800-900 wds; $25-50. Complete ms.

>   **Special Needs:** Church Life department looking for practical church ministry ideas; how to enhance Sunday school, small groups, worship, youth ministry, women's ministries, etc.; 600-800 wds.

>   **Tips:** "This magazine is for church leaders—pastors, elders, deacons, and anyone involved in a church ministry. Most articles are assigned. Most open to columns. Preference given to writers from Fellowship Baptist Churches in Canada."

$*EVANGELICALS TODAY, 62 Molave St., Project 3, Quezon City 1102, Philippines. (632)433-1546 to 1549. Fax (632)913-1675. Philippine Council of Evangelical Churches. Bishop Efraim M. Tendero, exec. ed. To equip pastors, Christian leaders/workers, and the rest of Christ's Body in the various areas of Christian life and ministry by providing inspiring and enriching articles and relevant news reports. Bimonthly mag.; 36 pgs.; circ. 3,000. Subscription $6.25 (local) or $50 (foreign). 5% unsolicited freelance; 95% assigned. Complete ms by e-mail. Pays $12.50/article on publication. Articles 1,000-1,500 wds. Responds in 2 wks. Seasonal 2 mos. ahead. Accepts simultaneous submissions & reprints (tell when/where appeared). Prefers requested ms on disk or by e-mail (attached file or copied into message). Prefers NIV. No guidelines. (Ads)

$THE FIVE STONES, 155 Brown St., Providence RI 02906. Phone/fax (401)861-9405. E-mail: pappas@tabcom.org. Website: www.tabcom.org. American Baptist. Anthony G. Pappas, ed. Primarily to small church pastors and laity, denominational staff, and seminaries; to equip for service. Quarterly jour.; 16 pgs.; circ. 1,000. Subscription $8-12. 100% unsolicited freelance. Complete ms/cover letter. Pays $5 on publication for one-time rights. Not copyrighted. Articles (20/yr.) & fiction (4/yr.), 500-2,000 wds.; book reviews 500 wds. ($5). Responds in 10-12 wks. Seasonal 10 mos. ahead. Accepts simultaneous submissions & reprints. Prefers requested ms on disk or by e-mail. Uses some sidebars. Any Bible version. Guidelines/theme list; copy for 9x12 SAE/4 stamps. (Ads)

>   **Tips:** "Always looking for everything related to small church life (nature and dynamics of small churches); fresh programming. Good place for unpublished to break in. Use first person. Best to call and talk."

$GROWTH POINTS, (formerly *Church Growth Network*), PO Box 892589, Temecula CA 92589-2589. Phone/fax (909)506-3086. E-mail: cgnet@earthlink.net. Website: www.mcintoshcgn.com. Dr. Gary L. McIntosh, ed. For pastors and church leaders interested in church growth. Monthly newsletter; 2 pgs.; circ. 8,000. Subscription $16. 10% unsolicited freelance; 90% assigned. Query; fax/e-query OK. Pays $25 for one-time rts. Not copyrighted. Articles 1,000-2,000 wds. (2/yr.). Responds in 4 wks. Accepts simultaneous submissions & reprints. Accepts requested ms on disk. Does not use sidebars. Guidelines; copy for #10 SAE/1 stamp. (No ads)

>   **Tips:** "Write articles that are short (1,200 words), crisp, clear, with very practical ideas that church leaders can put to use immediately. All articles must have a pro church-growth slant, be very practical, have how-to material, and be very tightly written with bullets, etc."

$HORIZONS, 2 Overlea Blvd., Toronto ON M4H 1P4, Canada. (416)422-6226. Fax (416)422-6120. E-mail: horizons@can.salvationarmy.org. Website: www.horizons.salvationarmy.ca.

The Salvation Army. Geoff Moulton, sr. ed. For officers and lay leaders of The Salvation Army; focusing on leadership, discipleship, theology, social issues, and Christian ministry. Bimonthly mag.; 24 pgs.; circ. 4,600. Subscription $14 Cdn. 100% assigned. Query/clips; fax/e-query OK. Pay negotiated for 1st rts. Articles 1,500 wds. (30/yr.); reviews 250 wds. Responds in 2 wks. Accepts simultaneous submissions & reprints (tell when/where appeared). Prefers e-mail submission (attached file). Uses some sidebars. Prefers NIV. Guidelines (also on Website); free copy. Incomplete topical listings. (No ads)

Fillers: Cartoons.

Columns/Departments: Accepts 20/yr. Future Frontiers (what's new in church ministry), 850 wds.; Practical Ministry (practical helps), 850 wds.; Strategic Advance (church leadership/growth issues), 1,500 wds.; Reaching Out (evangelism), 1,500 wds.; Bookmarks (reviews), 250-300 wds.; Creed & Deed (theology), 850 wds. No payment.

$INSITE (formerly *Christian Camp & Conference Journal*), PO Box 62189, Colorado Springs CO 80962-2189. (719)260-9400. Fax (719)260-6398. E-mail: editor@cciusa.org. Website: www.christiancamping.org. Christian Camping Intl./USA. Alison Hayhoe, ed.; Justin Boles, mng. ed. To inform, inspire, and motivate all who serve in Christian camps and conferences. Bimonthly & online mag.; 40 pgs.; circ. 8,700. Subscription $26.95. 15% unsolicited freelance; 85% assigned. Query; e-query OK. Pays .16/wd. on publication for 1st and electronic rts. Articles 1,500-2,000 wds. (12/yr.); features 1,000-1,200 wds. (30/yr.); sidebars 500 wds. (15-20/yr.) Responds in 4 wks. Seasonal 6 mos. ahead. Accepts simultaneous submissions & reprints (tell when/where appeared). Prefers e-mail submission (attached file) with fax backup. Kill fee. Regularly uses sidebars. Prefers NIV. Guidelines (also by e-mail); copy $4.95/10x13 SAE/$1.60 postage. (Ads)

Special Needs: Outdoor setting; purpose and objectives; administration and organization; personnel development; camper/guest needs; programming; health and safety; food service; site/facilities maintenance; business/operations; marketing and PR; relevant spiritual issues; and fund-raising.

Tips: "Most open to nonfiction; get guidelines, then query first. Don't send general camping-related articles. We print stories specifically related to Christian camp and conference facilities; changed lives or innovative programs; how a Christian camp or conference experience affected a present-day leader. Review several issues so you know what we're looking for."

**2004 & 2005 EPA Award of Merit—Christian Ministries.

INTERPRETATION, 3401 Brook Rd., Richmond VA 23227. Toll-free (877)522-7799. Website: www.interpretation.org. James A. Brashler, ed.; Jenna A. Bowen, mng. ed. Enhances lifelong theological education and recharges ministers in their work with individuals, study groups, and congregations. Quarterly & online mag. Subscription $23. Incomplete topical listings. No questionnaire returned.

$INTERPRETER and INTERPRETER ONLINE (formerly *Interpreter Magazine*), PO Box 320, Nashville TN 37202-0320. (615)742-5407. Fax (615)742-5460. E-mail: knoble@umcom.org. Website: www.InterpreterMagazine.org. United Methodist Church. Kathy Noble, ed. For lay leaders and pastors of the United Methodist Church; focus on ministry ideas and resources, spiritual growth issues, with a practical slant. Bimonthly & online mag.; 44+ pgs.; circ. 225,000. Subscription $12. 5% unsolicited freelance; some assigned. Query/clips; fax/e-query OK (form online). Pays $150-500 on acceptance for all rts. Articles 500-1,000 wds. (10/yr.); book/music/video reviews, $100. Responds in 8 wks. Seasonal 6 mos. ahead. No simultaneous submissions or reprints. Prefers requested ms on disk or by e-mail (attached file). No kill fee. Uses some sidebars. Prefers NRSV. No guidelines; copy for 9x12 SAE/4 stamps. (Ads)

Fillers: Buys several/yr. Facts, ideas, short humor; 50-75 wds.

Columns/Departments: Buys 10/yr. Youth (how parents/church can reach and serve);

Worship (new ideas/special days); Evangelism (new ideas for); Relationships (strengthening); Jumpstart Your Ministry (ideas for ministry/missions); Living Your Faith in the Real World (practical discipleship); all to 200 wds.; payment varies.

Tips: "All articles must have a specific and prominent United Methodist connection. Very difficult for unsolicited freelancers to break in, as we have an excellent pool and depend on them for referrals."

**This periodical was #19 on the 2005 Top 50 Christian Publishers list (#31 in 2004, #42 in 2003, #32 in 2002).

THE JOURNAL OF PASTORAL CARE & COUNSELING, 1068 Harbor Dr. S.W., Calabash NC 28467. Phone/fax (910)579-5084. E-mail: OrloS@aol.com. Website: www.jpcp.org. Dr. Orlo Strunk Jr., mng. ed. For chaplains/pastors/professionals involved with pastoral care and counseling in other than a church setting. Quarterly jour.; 116 pgs.; circ. 10,000. Subscription $35. 95% unsolicited freelance; 5% assigned. Query; phone/fax/e-query OK. **PAYS 10 COPIES** for 1st rts. Articles 5,000 wds. or 20 pgs. (30/yr.); book reviews 5 pgs. Responds in 8 wks. Accepts requested ms on disk. Does not use sidebars. Guidelines (also on Website); no copy. (Ads)

Poetry: Accepts 16/yr. Free verse; 5-16 lines. Submit max. 3 poems.

Special Needs: "We publish brief (500-600 wds.) 'Personal Reflections'—but they need to deal with clinical experiences that have led the writer to reflect on the religious and/or theological meaning generated."

Tips: "Most open to poems and personal reflections. Readers are highly trained clinically, holding professional degrees in religion/theology. Writers need to be professionals on topics covered."

JOURNAL OF THE AMERICAN SOCIETY FOR CHURCH GROWTH, c/o Dr. Gary L. McIntosh, ed., Talbot School of Theology, 13800 Biola Ave., LaMirada CA 90639. (562)944-0351. Fax (562)906-4502. E-mail: gary.mcintosh@biola.edu. Website: www.ascg.org. American Society for Church Growth. Dr. Gary L. McIntosh, ed. Targets professors, pastors, denominational executives, and seminary students interested in church growth and evangelism. Quarterly jour. (3X-fall, winter, spring); 100 pgs.; circ. 400. Subscription $24. 66% unsolicited freelance; 33% assigned. Complete ms/cover letter; phone/fax/e-query OK. **PAYS IN COPIES** for one-time rts. Not copyrighted. Articles 15 pgs. or 4,000-5,000 wds. (10/yr.); book reviews 750-2,000 wds. Responds in 8-12 wks. Accepts simultaneous submissions & reprints (tell when/where appeared). Prefers requested ms on disk or by e-mail. Does not use sidebars. Any Bible version. Guidelines (also in journal)/theme list; copy $10. (Ads)

Tips: "Provide well-researched and tightly written articles related to some aspect of church growth. Articles should be academic in nature, rather than popular in style. We're open to new writers at this time."

$#LEADERSHIP, 465 Gundersen Dr., Carol Stream IL 60188. (630)260-6200. Fax (630)260-0114. E-mail: LJEditor@LeadershipJournal.net. Website: www.leadershipjournal.net. Christianity Today Intl. Marshall Shelley, ed.; Eric Reed, mng. ed. Practical help for pastors/church leaders. Quarterly & online jour.; 130 pgs.; circ. 65,000. Subscription $24.95. 20% unsolicited freelance; 80% assigned. Query or complete ms; fax/e-query OK. Pays $75-375 (.15/wd) on acceptance for 1st rts., right to reprint, and electronic rts. Articles 500-3,000 wds. (50/yr.). Responds in 3-5 wks. Seasonal 6 mos. ahead. Accepts reprints (tell when/where appeared). Accepts requested ms on disk or by e-mail (copied into message). Kill fee 50%. Regularly uses sidebars. Prefers NIV, NLT. Guidelines/theme list (also on Website); copy $3. (Ads)

Fillers: Buys 80/yr. Cartoons, short humor; to 150 wds.; $25-50.

Columns/Departments: Buys 80/yr. Ideas That Work, 150 wds.; To Illustrate (sermon illustrations), 150 wds.; $25-50. Complete ms.

Tips: "*Leadership* is a practical journal for pastors. We look for articles that provide practical help for problems church leaders face, not essays expounding on a topic, editorials arguing a position, or homilies explaining biblical principles. We want 'how-to' articles based on first-person accounts of real-life experiences in ministry."
**2005, 2004, 2003, 2001 EPA Award of Merit—Christian Ministries. This periodical was #8 on the 2005 Top 50 Christian Publishers list (#8 in 2004, #12 in 2003, #16 in 2002, #14 in 2001).

$LET'S WORSHIP, One Lifeway Plaza, MSN 175, Nashville TN 37234-0170. (615)251-2769. Fax (615)251-2795. E-mail: mtullos@lifeway.com. Website: www.lifeway.com. Southern Baptist/LifeWay Christian Resources. Matt Tullos, ed-in-chief. Resources for pastors and worship leaders; countering the norm with contagious ideas. Quarterly mag.; 96 pgs.; circ. 5,500. Subscription $14.95. 10% unsolicited freelance; 90% assigned. Complete ms by e-mail only. Pays .105/wd. on acceptance for all, 1st, or one-time rts. Articles 1,500 wds. (50/yr.); book reviews 300 wds. ($50). Responds in 10 wks. Seasonal 10 mos. ahead. Accepts simultaneous submissions. Requires ms by e-mail (attached file or copied into message). Regularly uses sidebars. Prefers HCSB. No guidelines/copy. (No ads)

> **Columns/Departments:** Wednesday Words (4-week Bible study with listening sheets); Bible study, 625 wds.; listening sheet, 200 wds.; Drama (original scripts), 900 wds.
>
> **Special Needs:** Offer testimonials: How we do drama, start a drama ministry, use mime, transition worship, etc. in our church. Offer original scripts for short drama or reader's theater.
>
> **Tips:** "Most open to short dramas, dramatic readings, dramatic monologues/dialogs."

LUTHERAN FORUM, PO Box 327, Delhi NY 13753-0327. (607)746-7511. E-mail: dkralpb@ aol.com. Website: www.alpb.org. American Lutheran Publicity Bureau. Ronald Bagnall, ed. For church leadership—clerical and laity. Quarterly jour.; 64 pgs.; circ. 3,200. Subscription $24.95. 80% unsolicited freelance. Complete ms/cover letter. **NO PAYMENT.** Articles 1,000-3,000 wds. Responds in 26-32 wks. Accepts simultaneous submissions & reprints. Requires requested ms on disk. Guidelines; copy for 9x12 SAE/$1.42 postage (mark "Media Mail"). (Ads)

$LUTHERAN PARTNERS, 8765 W. Higgins Rd., Chicago IL 60631-4101. Toll-free (800)638-3522, ext. 2884. (773)380-2884. Fax (773)380-2829. E-mail: lpartmag@elca.org or LUTHERAN_PARTNERS@ecunet.org. Website: www.elca.org/lp. Evangelical Lutheran Church in America. William A. Decker, ed. To encourage and challenge rostered leaders in the ELCA, including pastors and lay ministers. Bimonthly mag.; 40+ pgs.; circ. 20,000. Subscription $12.50 (free to leaders), $18.75 outside North America. 10-15% unsolicited freelance; 85-90% assigned. Query; phone/fax/e-query OK. Pays $120-170 on publication for one-time rts. Articles 500-1,500 wds. (12-15/yr.). Responds in 16 wks. Seasonal 9 mos. ahead. Accepts simultaneous submissions & reprints (tell when/where appeared). Kill fee (rare). Prefers requested ms on disk or by e-mail (attached file). Regularly uses sidebars. Prefers NRSV. Guidelines/theme list (also by e-mail/Website); copy $2/9x12 SAE/5 stamps. (Ads)

> **Poetry:** Buys 6-10/yr. Free verse, traditional; $50-75. Keep concise. Submit max. 6 poems.
>
> **Fillers:** Buys 4-5/yr. Cartoons; ideas for parish ministry (called Jottings); to 500 wds.; $25.
>
> **Special Needs:** Book reviews. Query the editor. Uses books predominately from mainline denominational and some evangelical publishers. Payment is copy of book. Youth and family issues, rural and urban ministry issues, men's issues. More articles from women and ethnic authors (especially if ordained or are in official lay-ministry leadership roles).
>
> **Tips:** "Query us with solid ideas. First, we are a leadership publication. Our audience includes pastors and lay church staff. Your articles must answer concerns that leadership has. Secondly, understand Lutheran Church theology and ELCA congregational life. Perti-

nent topics include preaching, Christian education, youth and family issues, Lutheran identity, worship, Scripture and theology, and social issues."

$MINISTRIES TODAY, 600 Rinehart Rd., Lake Mary FL 32746. (407)333-0600. Fax (407)333-7133. E-mail: ministries@strang.com, or shepson@strang.com. Website: www.ministries today.com. Strang Communications. Bill Shepson, ed.; Adrienne Gaines, review ed. Helps for pastors and church leaders, primarily in Pentecostal/charismatic churches. Bimonthly mag.; 90 pgs.; circ. 30,000. Subscription $24.95. 60-80% freelance. Query; fax/e-query preferred. Pays $50 or $500-800 on publication for all rts. Articles 1,800-2,500 wds. (25/yr.); book/music/video reviews, 300 wds., $25. Responds in 4 wks. Prefers accepted ms by e-mail. Kill fee. Regularly uses sidebars. Prefers NIV. Guidelines; copy $6/9x12 SAE. (Ads)

Columns/Departments: Buys 36/yr.

Tips: "Most open to columns. Write for guidelines and study the magazine."

$MINISTRY & LITURGY, 160 E. Virginia St., #290, San Jose CA 95112. (408)286-8505. Fax (408)287-8748. E-mail: mleditor@rpinet.com. Website: www.rpinet.com/ml. Resource Publications, Inc. Donna M. Cole, ed. dir. To help liturgists and ministers make the imaginative connection between liturgy and life. Monthly (10X) mag.; 50 pgs.; circ. 20,000. Subscription $50. Query only; fax/e-query OK. Pays a stipend on publication for 1st rts. Articles 1,500 wds. (30/yr.). Responds in 4 wks. Seasonal 6 mos. ahead. Accepts reprints (tell when/where appeared). Requires requested ms on disk. Regularly uses sidebars. Guidelines/theme list; copy $4/11x14 SAE/2 stamps. (Ads)

Contest: Visual Arts Awards.

MINISTRY IN MOTION E-ZINE, 451 Hawthorne Ln., Benicia CA 94510. (707)751-3707. E-mail: customerservice@ministryinmotion.net. Website: www.ministryinmotion.net. Non-denominational. Teena Stewart, ed. Dedicated to helping individuals uncover and use their gifts and abilities for ministry, and to providing ministry resources and tips for volunteers and church leaders. Biweekly e-zine; circulation 200+. Subscription free. 50% unsolicited freelance; 50% assigned. Complete ms/cover letter; e-query OK. **NO PAYMENT** (for now) for 1st, reprint, electronic, nonexclusive rts., but provides a blurb on the author or the author's Website, ministry, or book. Not copyrighted. Articles 500-1,000 wds. (20/yr.); book reviews 250 wds. Responds in 1-2 wks. Seasonal 3 mos. ahead. Accepts simultaneous submissions & reprints (tell when/where appeared). Prefers submissions by e-mail (copied into message). Does not use sidebars. Prefers NIV or MSG (no KJV). Guidelines and theme list by e-mail/Website; copy online. (Ads)

Fillers: Accepts anecdotes and tips, to 2 paragraphs.

Columns/Departments: Evangelism/outreach (from a church perspective), 500-1,000 wds.; Christian Living, Small Groups, Lay Counseling, Single's Ministry, Worship Arts Ministry, Teaching, Small Groups, Men's Ministry, Discipleship, etc.; 800-1,000 wds. We are looking for columnists. If you have a column you think will fit, query us.

Special Needs: Practical how-tos. We want to hear about what churches are doing as they minister. Let us see how you do what you do.

Tips: "Share leadership tips and insights. The more practical and how-to, the better. No theology or heavily scholastic articles; we are for the everyday church worker. We are always looking for good interviews with those who are actively involved in ministry. This is a great way to promote your ministry. A writer will do best if they are in ministry—whether volunteer or vocational—and are a good writer. If no experience, break in with book reviews or short ministry tips. We look for church ministry that is on the cutting edge—very contemporary—non-denominational. Avoid church culture terms and lingo related to your own denomination."

$MINISTRY MAGAZINE: International Journal for Pastors, 12501 Old Columbia Pike, Silver Spring MD 20904. (301)680-6510. Fax (301)680-6502. E-mail: norcottj@ gc.adventist.org. Website: www.ministrymagazine.org. Seventh-day Adventist. Willmore D.

Eva, ed.; Julia W. Norcott, asst. ed. For pastors. Monthly jour.; 32 pgs.; circ. 19,000. Subscription $29.95. 90% unsolicited freelance. Query; fax/e-query OK. Pays $50-300 on acceptance for all rts. Articles 1,000-1,500 wds.; book reviews 100-150 wds. ($25). Responds within 13 wks. Prefers requested ms on disk. Uses some sidebars. Guidelines (also on Website)/theme list; copy for 9x12 SAE/5 stamps. (Ads)

*MINISTRY MATTERS, 80 Hayden St., Toronto ON M4Y 3G2, Canada. (905)833-6200. Fax (905)833-2116. E-mail: ministry.matters@national.anglican.ca, or cmccormick@canadads.com. Website: www.national.anglican.ca/mm. Anglican Church of Canada. Vianney (Sam) Carriere, ed. To produce articles, resources, and information to inspire you and support your ministry. Mag. published 3X/yr. Open to unsolicited freelance. Not in topical listings. (Ads)

NET RESULTS, 5001 Ave. N, Lubbock TX 79412-2993. (806)726-8094, ext. 198. Fax (806)762-8873. E-mail: netresults@netresults.org. Website: www.netresults.org. Net Results, Inc. Karen Medlin, mng. ed. (kmedlin@netresults.org). Offers Christian church leaders practical, ministry vitalization ideas and methods. Monthly (10X) & online mag.; 32 pgs.; circ. 12,000. Subscription $29.95. 20% unsolicited freelance; 80% assigned. Query; fax/e-query OK. Accepts full ms through e-mail. **PAYS IN COPIES/SUBSCRIPTION** on publication for one-time rts. Articles 1,000-2,000 wds. (20/yr.). Response time varies. Seasonal 6 mos. ahead. No simultaneous submissions or reprints. Requires accepted ms by e-mail (attached file). No kill fee. Regularly uses sidebars. Prefers NRSV. Copy for 9x12 SAE. (Limited ads)

Tips: "We prefer practical, how-to articles on ideas that have worked in a local church setting."

$THE NEWSLETTER NEWSLETTER, PO Box 36269, Canton OH 44735. Toll-free (800)992-2144. E-mail: jburns@comresources.com. Website: www.newsletternewsletter.com. Communication Resources. John Burns, ed. To help church secretaries and church newsletter editors prepare their newsletter. Monthly & online newsletter; 14 pgs. Subscription $44.95. 0% unsolicited freelance; 70% assigned. Complete ms; e-query OK. Pays $50-150 on acceptance for all rts. Articles 800-1,000 wds. (12/yr.). Responds in 4 wks. Seasonal 8 mos. ahead. Accepts simultaneous submissions. Requires requested ms on disk; accepts e-mail submissions. Kill fee. Regular sidebars. Guidelines (also by e-mail); copy for 9x12 SAE/3 stamps.

Tips: "Most open to how-to articles on various aspects of newsletter production—writing, graphics, layout and design, postal, printing, etc."

$PARISH LIFE (formerly *Eucharistic Ministries*), 115 E. Armour Blvd., Box 419493, Kansas City MO 64111. (816)531-0538. Fax (816)968-2291. E-mail: nwagner@natcath.org. Website: www.ncrpub.com. Celebration Publications. Nick Wagner, ed. For Eucharistic ministers; One Bread, One Body, One Spirit, One Mission. Monthly newsletter; 8 pgs.; circ. 50,000. Subscription $48. 20% unsolicited freelance; 80% assigned. Complete ms/cover letter; phone/fax/e-query OK. Pays $50-125 on publication for one-time rts. Articles 500-1,250 wds. (12/yr.). Responds in 1-2 wks. Seasonal 6 mos. ahead. Accepts reprints (tell when/where appeared). Prefers accepted ms by e-mail (attached or copied into message). Does not use sidebars. Guidelines (also by e-mail); copy for 10x13 SAE/2 stamps. (Ads—e-mail for specifications).

Fillers: Buys 10-12/yr. Anecdotes, cartoons, short humor.

Columns/Departments: Buys 12/yr. Living My Ministry (reflections on minister's experiences, anecdotes, inspirational personal experiences), 500 wds., $50. Complete ms.

Tips: "Feature articles need to be eucharistically, theologically, and/or ministerially based; practical, inspirational, or motivational. They need to be simple and direct enough for the average person to read easily—no heavy theology, pious inspiration, or excess verbiage. General focus—rather than personal accounts—a must."

$PARISH LITURGY, 16565 S. State St., South Holland IL 60473. (708)331-5485. Fax (708)331-5484. E-mail: acp@acpress.org. Website: www.americancatholicpress.org. Catholic. Father Michael Gilligan, ed. dir. A planning tool for Sunday and holy day liturgy. Quarterly mag.; 40 pgs.; circ. 1,200. Subscription $24. 5% unsolicited freelance. Query; no phone/e-query. Pays variable rates for all rts. Articles 400 wds. Responds in 4 wks. Seasonal 4 mos. ahead. Accepts simultaneous submissions & reprints (tell when/where appeared). Uses some sidebars. Prefers NAB. No guidelines; copy available. (No ads)

   Tips: "We only use articles on the liturgy—period."

$PASTORAL LIFE, PO Box 595, Canfield OH 44406-0595. (330)533-5503. Fax (330)533-1076. E-mail: plmagazine@hotmail.com. Website: www.albahouse.org. This publication has been temporarily suspended, probably until spring 2006.

PASTORS.COM, 20 Empire Dr., Lake Forest CA 92630-2244. Toll-free (866)829-0300. (929)829-0300. Fax (949)829-0400. E-mail: editor@pastors.com. Website: www.pastors.com. Jon Walker ed. dir. To mentor pastors worldwide. Weekly e-zine; circ. 140,000. Free e-mail newsletter. 30% unsolicited freelance; 30% assigned. Query; fax/e-query OK. **NO PAYMENT** for one-time, reprint, simultaneous, and electronic rts. Articles 500-1,000 wds. (250/yr.); fiction 500-1,000 wds. (25/yr.). Responds in 6-8 wks. Seasonal 4 mos. ahead. Accepts simultaneous submissions & reprints (tell when/where appeared). Prefers accepted ms by e-mail (attached file). Uses some sidebars. Guidelines by e-mail; copy by e-mail. (No ads)

   Special Needs: Time management, conflict resolution, facilitating change, communication and preaching, stewardship, worship, lay ministry, temptation, spiritual vitality, family matters, finances, creative ideas for ministry, vision, power, and authority.

   Tips: "We're very open to freelance contributions. Although we are unable to pay, this is a worldwide ministry to pastors."

PLUGGED IN, 8605 Explorer Dr., Colorado Springs CO 80920. Toll-free (800)232-6459. (719)531-3400. Fax (719)531-3347. E-mail: waliszrs@fotf.org, or pluggedin@family.org. Website: www.pluggedinmag.com. Focus on the Family. Bob Smithouser, print ed.; Steven Isaac, online ed. Helping parents and youth leaders guide teens through the world of popular youth culture. Monthly & online newsletter; 12 pgs.; circ. 50,000. Subscription $20. Freelance OK. Query. **NO PAYMENT.** No guidelines. Not in topical listings. (No ads)

   **2005, 2003 EPA Award of Excellence—Newsletter; 2004, 2001 EPA Award of Merit—Newsletter.

$PRAY!, PO Box 35004, Colorado Springs CO 80935-3504. (719)531-3585. Fax (719)598-7128. E-mail: pray@navpress.com. Website: www.praymag.com. The Navigators. Jonathan L. Graf, ed.; submit to Cynthia Bezek, asst. ed. A magazine entirely about prayer for believers who want to grow in their relationship with Christ through prayer and intercession—whether new to prayer, seasoned prayer warriors, or prayer leaders. Bimonthly mag.; 56-64 pgs.; circ. 39,000. Subscription $19.97. 70% unsolicited freelance; 30% assigned. Complete ms/cover letter or query; e-query OK. Pays .10/wd. (.05/wd. for reprints), plus a subscription, on acceptance for 1st, reprint, & electronic rts. Articles 800-1,500 wds., or 500 wds. or less. (30/yr.). Responds in 8-12 wks. Accepts simultaneous submissions & reprints (tell when/where appeared). Prefers e-mail submission. Kill fee 50%. Regularly uses sidebars. Prefers NIV. Guidelines/theme list (also by e-mail/Website); copy for 9x12 SAE/$2.56 postage. (Ads)

   Fillers: Ideas on prayer (no prayers); 150-500 wds.; .10/wd.

   Columns/Departments: Buys 28/yr. Prayer Journeys (tells a personal story of a breakthrough, milestone, epiphany, or even setback you experienced in your prayer journey, which can teach others and draw them closer to Jesus through prayer); 800 wds. Prayer Ideas (short, practical articles that offer fresh and helpful ideas for readers to try in either personal or corporate prayer), 150-500 wds. Prayer News (using journalistic style, tells of a prayer event, preferably interdenominational and city- or region-wide, to encourage or inspire others), 200-400 wds. Complete ms. Pays .10/wd.

Special Needs: Especially needs articles that move readers beyond praying for personal needs and toward praying for neighborhoods, churches, cities, and the nation.

Tips: "Please note that any topics indicated in the topical listings must be closely related to prayer (no general articles on those topics). Most open to prayer journeys, prayer ideas, non-theme features. Make sure you move people toward prayer as a relationship with Jesus and not just into more religious forms and structures. Be personal, vulnerable, biblical, and passionate."

**#9 Best-selling Magazine in Christian retail stores. This periodical was #42 on the 2005 Top 50 Christian Publishers list (#36 in 2004, #37 in 2003, #34 in 2002, #18 in 2001).

PREACHING, PREACHING ON-LINE & PREACHING NOW, PO Box 681868, Franklin TN 37068. (615)599-9889. Fax (615)599-8985. E-mail: mail@preaching.com. Website: www.preaching.com. American Ministry Resources. Dr. Michael Duduit, ed. Subscription $39.95. 50% unsolicited freelance; 50% assigned. Query; fax/e-query OK. **PAYS A SUBSCRIPTION** for one-time & electronic rts. Responds in 4-8 wks. Seasonal 10-12 mos. ahead. Reprints from books only. Prefers requested ms on disk or by e-mail (attached file). Uses some sidebars. Guidelines on Website; copy online. (ads). *Preaching Online* is a professional resource for pastors that supplements *Preaching Magazine.* Includes all content from magazine, plus additional articles and sermons. **NO PAYMENT** for material used only online. *Preaching Now* is a weekly e-mail/online e-zine; circ. 12,500. No freelance submissions; accepts books for review.

$PREACHINGTODAY.COM, 465 Gundersen Dr., Carol Stream IL 60188-2498. (630)260-6200. Fax (630)260-8428. E-mail: editor@preachingtoday.com. Website: www.preaching today.com. Christianity Today Intl. Open to fresh sermon illustrations from various sources for preachers (no recycled illustrations from other illustration sources). E-mail submissions only. Guidelines on Website. Sermon illustrations only.

$PREACHING WELL, (formerly *Spiritual Spinach*), PO Box 3102, Margate NJ 08402. Toll-free (800)827-9401. (609)822-9401. Fax (609)822-1638. E-mail: sermons@voicings.com. Website: www.voicings.com. Voicings Publications. James Colaianni Jr., pub. Sermon illustration resource for professional clergy. Monthly newsletter, 12 pgs. Subscription $37.50. 5% unsolicited freelance; 0% assigned. Complete ms; e-query OK. Pays .10/wd. on publication for any rts. Illustrations/anecdotes 50-250 wds. Responds in 6 wks. Seasonal 4 mos. ahead. Accepts reprints. Prefers requested ms on disk or by e-mail. Guidelines/topical index (also by e-mail); copy for 9x12 SAE. (Ads)

Poetry: Light verse, traditional; 50-250 lines; .10/wd. Submit max. 3 poems.

Fillers: Various; sermon illustrations; 50-250 wds.; .10/wd.

Tips: "All sections open."

$THE PRIEST, 200 Noll Plaza, Huntington IN 46750-4304. (260)356-8400. Fax (260)356-8472. E-mail: tpriest@osv.com. Website: www.osv.com. Catholic/Our Sunday Visitor, Inc. Msgr. Owen F. Campion, ed.; submit to Murray Hubley, assoc. ed. For Catholic priests, deacons, and seminarians; to help in all aspects of ministry. Monthly jour.; 48 pgs.; circ. 6,500. Subscription $39.95. 40% unsolicited freelance. Query (preferred) or complete ms/cover letter; phone/fax/e-query OK. Pays $50-250 on acceptance for 1st rts. Articles 1,500-5,000 wds. (96/yr.); some 2-parts. Responds in 5-13 wks. Seasonal 4 mos. ahead. Uses some sidebars. Prefers disk or e-mail submissions (attached file). Prefers NAB. Free guidelines/copy. (Ads)

Fillers: Murray Hubley, fillers ed. Cartoons; $35.

Columns/Departments: Buys 36/yr. Viewpoint, to 1,000 wds.; $75.

Tips: "Write to the point, with interest. Most open to nuts-and-bolts issues for priests, or features. Keep the audience in mind; need articles or topics important to priests and parish life. Include Social Security number."

**This periodical was #41 on the 2001 Top 50 Christian Publishers list.

$PROCLAIM, PO Box 1561, New Canaan CT 06840. Toll-free (888)320-5576. Fax (203)966-4654. E-mail: meg@parishpublishing.org, or info@parishpublishing.org. Website: www.parishpublishing.org. Parish Publishing, LLC. Guy Brossy, principal. The leading inspirational preaching resource for church leaders. Weekly newsletter; 4 pgs. Subscription $59.95. 20% unsolicited freelance; 80% assigned. Query/clips. Pays to $100 on publication or acceptance for reprint rts. Articles or fiction. Responds in 2 wks. Seasonal 3 mos. ahead. Prefers accepted mss by e-mail (attached file). (No ads)

Tips: "*Proclaim* follows the Catholic Lectionary and the Revised Common Lectionary (RCL). Writers are usually priests and ministers, or in seminary."

PULPIT HELPS, 6815 Shallowford Rd., Chattanooga TN 37421. Toll-free (800)251-7206. (423)894-6060. Fax (423)510-8074. E-mail: publisher@pulpithelps.com. Website: www.pulpithelps.com. AMG International. Bob Dasal, ed-in-chief. To help evangelical preachers and serious students of the Bible. Monthly & online tabloid; 36 pgs.; circ. 75,000. Subscription $22.99. 25% unsolicited freelance; 75% assigned. Query; e-query OK. **NO PAYMENT.** Articles 700-900 wds. (60-80/yr.); book reviews 400 wds. Responds in 4 wks. Seasonal 4 mos. ahead. Accepts simultaneous submissions & reprints (tell when/where appeared). Accepts e-mail submission (attached or copied into message). Uses some sidebars. Prefers KJV. Guidelines/theme list (also by e-mail); copy for 9x12 SAE/2 stamps. (Ads)

Poetry: Accepts 10-12/yr. Traditional; short. Submit max. 3 poems.

Fillers: Ted Kyle, fillers ed. Accepts 10-20/yr. Anecdotes, cartoons, prose, quotes, short humor, word puzzles; 300-500 wds.

Columns/Departments: Ted Kyle, mng. ed. Family Helps, 100-1,000 wds.; Illustrations (for sermons), 50-100 wds.; Sermon Starters (brief).

Tips: "Most open to Illustrations and Sermon Starters—short, pointed anecdotes/articles preachers can use as illustrations. Follow submission guidelines."

QUARTERLY REVIEW: A Journal of Theological Resources for Ministry, 1001—19th Ave. S., PO Box 340007, Nashville TN 37203-0007. (615)340-7334. Fax (615)340-7048. E-mail: hpieterse@gbhem.org. Website: www.quarterlyreview.org. United Methodist. Dr. Hendrik R. Pieterse, ed. A theological approach to subjects of interest to clergy—Scripture study, ethics, and practice of ministry in Wesleyan tradition. Quarterly jour.; 112 pgs.; circ. 1,100. Subscription $24. 20% unsolicited; 80% assigned. Complete ms/cover letter; phone/fax/e-query OK. **PAYS IN COPIES** for 1st rts. Articles to 5,000 wds. (20/yr.); book reviews to 1,000 wds. Responds in 6-8 wks. Seasonal 8 mos. ahead. Prefers requested ms on disk, no e-mail submission. Does not use sidebars. Prefers NRSV. Guidelines/theme list (also by e-mail); copy for 9x12 SAE/$1.42 postage (mark "Media Mail"). (No ads)

Tips: "A section called 'Outside the Theme' is reserved for articles of high quality unrelated to the theme of the issue. I often consider unsolicited manuscripts for this section. We look for writers who have strong academic/theological training and whose work addresses concerns and interests of those in ministry. Awareness of current scholarly literature, a well-developed argument, and clear expository prose are essential."

$REFORMED WORSHIP, 2850 Kalamazoo S.E., Grand Rapids MI 49560-0001. Toll-free (800)777-7270. Fax (616)224-0834. E-mail: info@reformedworship.org. Website: www.reformedworship.org. Christian Reformed Church in North America. Dr. Emily R. Brink, ed. To provide liturgical and musical resources for pastors, church musicians, and other worship leaders. Quarterly mag.; 48 pgs.; circ. 5,000. Subscription $25.95. 10%

unsolicited freelance; 70% assigned. Query or complete ms/cover letter; e-query OK. Pays .05/wd. on publication for 1st rts. Articles 2,000 wds.; book reviews 250 wds. Responds in 4 wks. Seasonal 6 mos. ahead. Rarely accepts reprints (tell when/where appeared). Prefers e-mail submission (copied into message). Regularly uses sidebars. Prefers NRSV. Guidelines/theme list (also by e-mail); copy for 9x12 SAE/$1.42 postage (mark "Media Mail"). (No ads)

Columns/Departments: Songs for the Season (music and background notes, usually 3 songs), 2,000 wds.; Worship Technology (intersection of worship and technology), 900 wds. Query.

Tips: "You need to understand the Reformed tradition of worship."

**2004 EPA Award of Merit—General.

$REVIEW FOR RELIGIOUS, 3601 Lindell Blvd., Rm. 428, St. Louis MO 63108-3393. (314)977-7363. Fax (314)977-7362. E-mail: review@slu.edu. Website: www.reviewfor religious.org. Catholic/Jesuits of Missouri Province. Rev. David L. Fleming, S.J., ed. A forum for shared reflection on the lives and experience of all who find that the church's rich heritages of spirituality support their personal and apostolic Christian lives. Quarterly mag.; 112 pgs.; circ. 7,000. Subscription $24. 100% unsolicited freelance. Complete ms/cover letter; no phone/fax/e-query. Pays $6/pg. on publication for 1st rts. Articles 1,500-5,000 wds. (50/yr.). Responds in 9 wks. Seasonal 8 mos. ahead. Accepts requested ms on disk. Does not use sidebars. Prefers RSV, NAB. Guidelines (also by e-mail); copy for 10x13 SAE/5 stamps. (No ads)

Poetry: Buys 10/yr. Light verse, traditional; 3-12 lines; $6. Submit max. 4 poems.

Tips: "Be familiar with at least three past issues. Submit an article based on our guidelines."

$REV. MAGAZINE, PO Box 481, Loveland CO 80539-0481. (970)669-3836. Fax (970)679-4392. E-mail: therev@onlinerev.com. Website: www.revmagazine.com. Group Publishing, Inc. Paul Allen, ed. For pastors; partnering with pastors. Bimonthly & online mag.; 104 pgs.; circ. 45,000. Subscription $24.86. 25% unsolicited freelance; 75% assigned. Complete ms/cover letter; e-query OK. Pays $300-400 on acceptance for all rts. Articles 1,800-2,000 wds. (18-24/yr.) Responds in 9 wks. Seasonal 8 mos. ahead. Prefers requested ms on disk or by e-mail (attached file). Regularly uses sidebars. Guidelines on Website; copy $2/9x12 SAE/5 stamps. (Ads)

Fillers: Buys 3/yr. Cartoons, ideas, sermon illustrations; $30-50.

Columns/Departments: Ministry (preaching, worship, discipleship, outreach, family); Life (personal growth, health beat, home front); Leadership (church business, team work, leadership); Insight (today's trends, current culture, in the know); all 150-300 wds; $35-50.

Tips: "We are most open to short (250 word) practical articles for our departments. Write articles that deal with personal and professional topics for pastors."

$THE REVWRITER RESOURCE, PO Box 81, Perkasie PA 18944. (215)453-5066. Fax (215)453-8128. E-mail: editor@revwriter.com. Website: www.revwriter.com. Nondenominational. Rev. Susan M. Lang, ed. An electronic newsletter for busy lay and clergy congregational leaders. Monthly e-zine.; circ. 400. Subscription free. 50% unsolicited freelance; 50% assigned. Query; e-query preferred. Pays $20 on publication for 1st electronic rts. and one-year archival rts. Articles 800-1,000 wds.; questions or exercises for group use, 250-500 wds. No simultaneous submissions or reprints. Guidelines on Website; copy online. Incomplete topical listings. (No ads)

Fillers: Buys 10/yr. Ideas; Ministry Resources List to accompany article; 250-400 wds. These are usually written by the feature-article writer.

Tips: "Articles should be practical how-tos for busy church leaders—materials they can use in their ministry settings. Be sure to read archived issues for previous formats and ministry resources already covered. Looking for a new approach to stewardship. Most open to devotion writing in Lent and Advent, and the monthly articles and discussion questions. Send me an e-query detailing the article you'd like to write and include your expertise in this area. The material must be practical and applicable to life as a busy congregational leader. They want information they can use."

$SABBATH SCHOOL LEADERSHIP, 55 W. Oak Ridge Dr., Hagerstown MD 21740. (301)393-4090. Fax (301)393-4055. E-mail: fcrumbly@rhpa.org, or SabbathSchoolLeadership@rhpa.org. Website: www.Sabbathschool.com. Seventh-day Adventist/Review & Herald. Faith Crumbly, ed. Nurtures, educates, and supports adult Bible study and program leaders by providing training in leadership and interpersonal skills, plus programs. Monthly mag.; 32 pgs.; circ. 8,100. Subscription $29.95 (add $6 for addresses outside U.S., Canada, and Bermuda). 10% unsolicited freelance; 90% assigned. Complete ms. Pays $25-100 on acceptance for 1st rts. Articles 600-1,200 wds. (120-150/yr.). Responds in 1-2 wks. Seasonal 6-8 mos. ahead. Accepts reprints (tell when/where appeared). Prefers accepted ms by e-mail (attached file). Uses some sidebars. Guidelines/theme list; copy. (For ads, contact: Margie Tooley at margie.tooley@rhpa.org.)

  Fillers: Cartoons; $70-100.

  Columns/Departments: Buys 5/yr. Leadership Tips (interpersonal skills, organization, mentoring, training), 600-800 wds. Query. Pays $70-100.

$SERMON NOTES, 465 Gundersen Dr., Carol Stream IL 60188. Website: www.sermon notes.com. Christianity Today. Kevin Miller, ed. Sermon helps for ministers. Quarterly & online mag.; 96 pgs.; circ. 5,000. Subscription $39. 25% unsolicited freelance. Complete ms/cover letter; fax/e-query OK. Pays $35-50 for articles & sermons ($5 for illustrations) on publication for one-time rts. Sermons & articles (8/yr.) 1,500 wds.; illustrations 80-100 wds.; book reviews 500 wds., $20. Responds in 5 wks. Seasonal 4 mos. ahead. Accepts reprints (tell when/where appeared). Prefers requested ms on disk. Regularly uses sidebars. Prefers NIV. Guidelines/theme list; copy $2/6x9 SAE. (Ads)

  Fillers: Buys 12/yr. Cartoons, short humor, or church newsletter ideas; $15.

  Columns/Departments: Buys 6/yr. Q&A (interview with Christian leader), 1,000-1,500 wds.; Pastor's Library (book or product review), 500 wds.; $35-50.

  Tips: "We are always interested in sermons. Right now we have an even greater interest in articles about church growth, preaching, or about a particular minister who is pastoring a growing church of any size." Also publishes on diskette.

SEWANEE THEOLOGICAL REVIEW, University of the South, 335 Tennessee Ave., Sewanee TN 37383-0001. (931)598-1475. E-mail: STR@sewanee.edu. Website: www.sewanee.edu/theology/str/strhome. Anglican/Episcopal. Jim D. Jones, mng. ed. For Anglican/Episcopal clergy and interested laity. Quarterly jour.; 120 pgs. Subscription $21. Open to freelance. Complete ms/cover letter; no e-query. **NO PAYMENT** for all rts. Articles (24/yr.). Responds in 9-26 wks. Seasonal 24 mos. ahead. No simultaneous submissions or reprints. Prefers requested ms on disk or by e-mail (attached file). Prefers NRSV. No guidelines; copy $7. Incomplete topical listings.

  Special Needs: Anglican and Episcopal theology, religion, history, doctrine, ethics, homiletics, liturgies, hermeneutics, biography, prayer, practice.

SHARING THE PRACTICE, 100 S. Chestnut St., Kent OH 44240-3402. (330)678-0187. E-mail: journal@apclergy.org. Website: www.apclergy.org. Academy of Parish Clergy/Ecumenical/Interfaith. Dr. Donald W. Shilling, ed-in-chief; Dr. Forrest V. Fitzhugh, book rev. ed. (bond007@texas.net). Growth toward excellence through sharing the practice of parish ministry. Quarterly international jour.; 40 pgs.; circ. 250 (includes 80 seminary libraries and publishers). Subscription $25/yr. (send to APC, 2249 Florinda St., Sarasota FL 34231-1414). 100% unsolicited freelance. Complete ms/cover letter; e-query OK. **PAYS IN**

COPIES for 1st, reprint, simultaneous, or electronic rts. Articles 500-2,500 wds. (25/yr.); reviews 200 wds. Responds in 2 wks. Seasonal 6 mos. ahead. Accepts simultaneous submissions & reprints (tell when/where appeared). Prefers e-mail submissions (copied into message). Uses some sidebars. Prefers NRSV. Guidelines/theme list (also by e-mail); free copy. (No ads)

Poetry: Accepts 12/yr. Any type; 25-35 lines. Submit max. 2 poems.

Fillers: Accepts 6/yr. Anecdotes, cartoons, jokes, short humor; 50-100 wds.

Contest: Book of the Year Award ($100+), Top Ten Books of the Year list, Parish Pastor of the Year Award ($200+). Inquire by e-mail to DIELPADRE@aol.com.

Tips: "We desire articles and poetry by practicing clergy of all kinds who wish to share their practice of ministry."

$SMALL GROUP DYNAMICS, PO Box 621, Zionville IN 46077. (317)769-0945. E-mail: office@smallgroups.com. Website: http://smallgroups.com. Small Group Network. Dan Lentz, owner. How-to for small groups. Online e-zine/newsletter. Query; e-query OK. Pays $40-60 for all rts. Articles 500-1,000 wds. Seasonal 2-3 mos. ahead. Prefers requested ms by e-mail (attached file). Accepts reprints. Prefers NIV. Guidelines/theme list: http://small groups.com/themes.htm.

Fillers: Small group cartoons.

Special Needs: Brief testimonies of how God has worked in your group; humor in groups; icebreaker ideas, etc.

Tips: "Follow our themes. We use mostly practical, how-to oriented articles."

STRATEGIC ADULT MINISTRIES ONLINE JOURNAL (SAM Journal), 4050 Lee Vance View, Colorado Springs CO 80918. (719)536-0100, ext. 3438. Fax (719)536-3202. E-mail: samresources@cookministries.org. Website: www.samresources.com. Cook Communications Ministries. Susan Tjaden, mng. ed. For pastors and lay leaders involved in ministry with single or young adults. Online jour. 10% unsolicited freelance. Query; fax/e-query OK. **USUALLY NO PAYMENT** for 1st rts. Articles 200-2,500 wds. (2/yr.); book reviews 50-300 wds. ($15-75). Responds in 4 wks. Seasonal 1 yr. ahead. Accepts simultaneous submissions & reprints (tell when/where appeared). Prefers e-mail submission (copied into message). Prefers NIV. Theme list; copy online.

Fillers: Buys 0-5/yr. Facts, newsbreaks, quotes; 25-200 wds.; $10-50.

Tips: "Write to the pastor or leader, not to the singles or young adults themselves. Interview young adults or the leaders who work with them. Want very practical, how-to or 600-word essay on a controversial topic of interest to young adult leaders."

*STRATEGIES FOR TODAY'S LEADER, 1230 U.S. Hwy. 6, Corunna IN 46730. Accepts freelance. Not in topical listings. No questionnaire returned.

$SUNDAY SERMONS, PO Box 3102, Margate NJ 08402. Toll-free (800)827-9401. (609)822-9401. Fax (609)822-1638. E-mail: sermons@voicings.com. Website: www.voicings.com. Voicings Publications. James Colaianni Jr., pub. Full-text sermon resource serving professional clergy since 1970. Bimonthly booklet; 60 pgs. Subscription $59. 5% unsolicited freelance; 0% assigned. Complete ms; e-query OK. Pays .10/wd. on publication for any rts. Complete sermon manuscripts 1,200-1,500 wds.; illustrations/anecdotes 50-250 wds. Responds in 6 wks. Seasonal 4 mos. ahead. Accepts reprints. Prefers requested ms on disk or by e-mail. Guidelines/topical index (also by e-mail); copy for 9x12 SAE. Incomplete topical listings.

Fillers: Various; sermon illustrations; 50-250 wds.; .10/wd.

Tips: "Submit complete sermon, 1,200-1,500 words."

TECHNOLOGIES FOR WORSHIP, 3891 Holborn Rd., Queensville ON L0G 1R0, Canada. (905)473-9822. Fax (905)473-9928. E-mail: krc@tfwm.com, or info@tfwm.com. Website: www.tfwm.com. ITC Inc. Kevin Rogers Cobus, ed. Bimonthly & online mag.; 92+ pgs.; circ.

35,000. Subscription $14.95/29.95. 100% unsolicited freelance. Query; phone/fax/e-query OK. **NO PAYMENT** for one-time rts. Articles 700-1,200 wds. Responds in 2 wks. Seasonal 2 mos. ahead. Accepts simultaneous submissions & reprints (tell when/where appeared). Prefers accepted ms by e-mail (attached or copied into message). Uses some sidebars. Free guidelines/theme list (also on Website)/copy. (Ads)

> **Special Needs:** Website streaming resources for churches and ministries; technologies: audio, video, music, computers, broadcast, lighting, and drama; 750-2,500 wds.
>
> **Tips:** "Call/fax/e-mail the editor to discuss idea for article or column. The publication is open to technical, educational articles that can benefit the church, providing hints, tips, guidelines, examples, studies, tutorials, etc. on new technology and new uses for it in the church."

THEOLOGICAL DIGEST & OUTLOOK, 415 Linwell Rd., St. Catherines ON L2M 2P3, Canada. (905)935-5369. Fax (905)935-7134. E-mail: p-d@magara.com. Website: www.church alivecanada.org. United Church of Canada. Paul Miller, ed. For clergy and informed laity; evangelical/orthodox slant within denomination. Semiannual mag.; 32 pgs.; circ. 400. Subscription $15 Cdn., $19 U.S. 100% unsolicited freelance. Complete ms; phone/fax/e-query OK. **NO PAYMENT.** Articles 1,500-5,000 wds. (6-8/yr.). Responds in 2 wks. Accepts reprints (tell when/where appeared). Prefers disk or e-mail submissions. Does not use sidebars. Any Bible version. No guidelines. (No ads)

> **Tips:** "Just submit."

$THEOLOGY TODAY, PO Box 821, Princeton NJ 08542-0803. (609)497-7714. Fax (609)497-7870. E-mail: theology.today@ptsem.edu. Website: http://theologytoday.ptsem.edu. Princeton Theological Seminar. Patrick D. Miller (patrick.miller@ptsem.edu) & Ellen T. Charry (ellen.charry@ptsem.edu), eds. Explores key issues, current thoughts and trends in the fields of religion and theology. Quarterly jour.; 144-160 pgs.; circ. 14,000. Subscription $29. 50% unsolicited freelance; 50% assigned. Complete ms/cover letter and disk; phone query OK. Pays to $250 on publication for all rts. Articles 13-17 manuscript pgs. Responds in several wks. Seasonal 1 yr. ahead. Regularly uses sidebars. Guidelines (also by e-mail/Website); free copy. (Display ads)

> **Poetry:** Buys 12/yr. Free verse, traditional; $50. Submit max. 5 poems.
>
> **Tips:** "We rarely accept unsolicited material, but do look for new talent. The best route to acceptance is strong familiarity with the journal and types of articles we publish. We expect inclusive language."

$THIS ROCK, 2020 Gillespie Way, El Cajon CA 92020. (619)387-7200. Fax (619)387-0042. E-mail: editor@catholic.com. Website: www.catholic.com. Catholic Answers. Cherie Peacock, ed. Deals with doctrine, evangelization, and apologetics. Monthly (10X) mag.; 48 pgs.; circ. 15,870. Subscription $39.95. 10% unsolicited freelance; 90% assigned. Complete ms/cover letter; e-query OK. Pays $80-500 on acceptance for 1st & electronic rts. Articles 1,500-3,000 wds. (80/yr.); book reviews 800 wds. ($80). Responds in 4 wks. Seasonal 9 mos. ahead. Prefers RSV (Catholic version). No simultaneous submissions or reprints. Prefers e-mail submissions (attached file). Kill fee sometimes. Regularly uses sidebars. Guidelines (also by e-mail/Website); copy for 9x12 SAE/$1.42 postage (mark "Media Mail"). (No ads)

> **Columns/Departments:** Buys 10/yr. Damascus Road (personal conversion story), 1,800-3,000 wds. Complete ms. Pays $200.
>
> **Tips:** "Most open to Damascus Road stories."

$TODAY'S CHRISTIAN PREACHER, 7 Chinkapin Dr., Fleetwood PA 19522. (610)944-9445. Fax (610)944-1555. E-mail: publications@rightideas.us. Website: www.rightideas.us. Right Ideas, Inc. Jerry Thacker, ed. To provide material on current topics to help preachers in their personal lives. Quarterly mag.; 20 pgs.; circ. 30,000. Subscription free. 20% unsolicited freelance; 80% assigned. Query preferred; fax/e-query OK. Pays $150 on publication for one-time or simultaneous rts. Articles 800-1,000 wds. (16/yr., 2-3 freelance). Responds in 6-8 wks. Seasonal 1 yr. ahead. Accepts simultaneous submissions & reprints (tell when/where appeared). Prefers requested ms by e-mail. Requires KJV. Guidelines (also by e-mail); copy for 9x12 SAE/3 stamps. (No ads)

Tips: "Most open to very practical articles on everyday life—not sermons or how to run a church."

$TODAY'S PARISH, Box 180, Mystic CT 06355. (860)536-2611. Fax (860)536-5674. Websites: www.todaysparish.com, or www.twentythirdpublications.com. Catholic/Twenty-Third Publications. Submit to The Editor. Practical ideas and issues relating to parish life, management, and ministry. Mag. published 7X/yr.; 40 pgs.; circ. 14,800. Subscription $24.95. Very little unsolicited freelance. Query or complete ms. Pays $75-100 on publication for 1st rts. Articles 800-1,800 wds. (15/yr.). Responds 13 wks. Seasonal 6 mos. ahead. Guidelines; copy for 9x12 SASE.

$WCA NEWS, PO Box 3188, Barrington IL 60011-5046. (847)765-0070. Fax (847)765-5046. E-mail: Paulb@willowcreek.com. Website: www.willowcreek.com. Willow Creek Assn. Paul Braoudakis, mng. ed. For church leaders who are willing to take risks for the sake of the gospel. Quarterly & online newsletter; 28 pgs.; circ. 10,000. Subscription $39. 10% unsolicited; 25-30% assigned. Query/clips or complete ms; phone/fax/e-query OK. Pays .20/wd. on publication for all rts. Articles 500-1,000 wds.; book/music reviews 500 wds., video reviews 300 wds. Responds in 2 wks. Seasonal 2 mos. ahead. Accepts simultaneous submissions & reprints (tell when/where appeared). Requires requested ms on disk or by e-mail (attached file). Some sidebars. Prefers NIV. Free copy. (No ads)

Fillers: Buys cartoons, ideas, short humor; 50-75 wds.; $10.

Columns/Departments: News From the Frontlines (creative ministries within the church), 50-100 wds.; Strategic Trends (trends from growing churches), 200-250 wds.; $10-25. Complete ms.

Tips: "Submit articles that will help other churches do what they do better. Any articles that pertain to doing a seeker-sensitive type of ministry will be considered. Also leadership issues in the church, outreach ideas, and effective evangelism."

$WORD & WORLD: Theology for Christian Ministry, 2481 Como Ave., St. Paul MN 55108. (651)641-3210. Fax (651)641-3354. Website: www.luthersem.edu/word&world. E.L.C.A./Luther Theological Seminary. Frederick J. Gaiser, ed. (fgaiser@luthersem.edu); Mark Thronveit, book rev. ed. (mthrontv@luthersem.edu). Addresses ecclesiastical and secular issues from a theological perspective and addresses pastors and church leaders with the best fruits of theological research. Quarterly jour.; 104 pgs.; circ. 2,500. Subscription $24. 10% unsolicited freelance. Complete ms/cover letter; phone query OK. Pays $50 on publication for all rts. Articles 3,500 wds. Responds in 2-8 wks. Guidelines/theme list; copy $7.

Tips: "Most open to general articles. We look for serious theology addressed clearly and interestingly to people in the practice of ministry. Creativity and usefulness in ministry are highly valued."

$WORSHIP LEADER, 26311 Junipero Serra, Ste. 130, San Juan Capistrano CA 92675. (949)240-9339. Fax (949)240-0038. E-mail: editor@wlmag.com. Website: www.worshipleader.com. Worship Leader Partnership. Julie Reid, exec. ed. A resource for current trends, theological insights, and planning programs for all those involved in church worship. Bimonthly mag.; 64-72 pgs.; circ. 45,000. Subscription $19.95. 20% unsolicited freelance; 80% assigned. Complete ms. by fax/e-mail OK. Pays $200-800 for assigned, $200-500 for unsolicited, on publication for all or 1st rts. Articles 1,200-2,000 wds. (15-30/yr.);

reviews 300 wds. Responds in 6-13 wks. Seasonal 6 mos. ahead. Accepts e-mail submissions (attached file—MS Word). Kill fee 50%. Uses some sidebars. Prefers NIV. Guidelines/theme list (also by e-mail); copy $5. (Ads)

> **Tips:** "Read our magazine. Become familiar with our themes. Submit a detailed and well-thought-out idea that fits our vision."
>
> **2003 EPA Award of Merit—Christian Ministries.

$YOUR CHURCH, 465 Gundersen Dr., Carol Stream IL 60188. (630)260-6200. Fax (630)260-0114. E-mail: YCEditor@yourchuch.net. Website: www.yourchurch.net. Christianity Today Intl. Harold Smith, exec. ed.; submit to Mike Schreiter, mng. ed. We give pastors and church leaders practical information to help them in managing the business side of the church. Bimonthly trade journal; 80+ pgs.; circ. 150,000. Subscription free to church administrators. 10% unsolicited freelance; 90% assigned. Query; phone/fax/e-query OK. Query for electronic submissions. Pays .15/wd. on acceptance for 1st & electronic rts. Articles 1,000-2,000 wds. (60/yr.). Responds in 2-4 wks. Seasonal 6 mos. ahead. Accepts reprints (tell when/where appeared). Prefers e-mail submission (attached file). Accepts full manuscripts by e-mail. Kill fee 50%. Uses some sidebars. Prefers NIV. Guidelines/theme list; copy for $1 postage. (Ads: 630-260-6202)

> **Fillers:** Cartoons, $125.
>
> **Columns/Departments:** Leadership Notes (tips on leadership from high-profile writer—often an article or book excerpt, but also original material).
>
> **Special Needs:** Church management articles; audio/visual equipment; books/curriculum resources; music equipment; church products; furnishings; office equipment; computers/software; transportation (bus, van); video projectors; church architecture/construction.
>
> **Tips:** "Write and ask to be considered for an assignment; tell of your background, experience, strengths, and writing history. Most assigned articles include a list of companies that must be interviewed. Unsolicited manuscripts should be informative, how-to articles without referring to any companies. Direct information to nontechnical readership (pastors and church administrators)."
>
> **This periodical was #16 on the 2005 Top 50 Christian Publishers list (#46 in 2004, #50 in 2003, #44 in 2002, #46 in 2001).

YOUTHCULTURE@TODAY, PO Box 414, Elizabethtown PA 17022-0414. (717)361-8429. Fax (717)361-8964. E-mail: cpyu@cpyu.org, or media@cpyu.org. Website: www.cpyu.org. Center for Parent/Youth Understanding. Walt Mueller, pres. To equip parents, teens, and youth workers with analysis and commentary on youth culture and cross-generational ministry. Quarterly & online mag.; 24 pgs.; circ. 10,000. Subscription $15 donation. 100% assigned. (No ads)

> **2003 EPA Award of Merit—Newsletter.

$YOUTHWORKER: The Contemporary Journal for Youth Ministry, 104 Woodmont Blvd., Ste. 300, Nashville TN 37205. (615)312-4250. Fax (615)385-4112. E-mail: Will@Youth Specialties.com. Website: www.Youthworker.com. Salem Communications. Will Penner, ed. For youth workers/church and parachurch. Bimonthly & online jour.; 72 pgs.; circ. 20,000. Subscription $39.95. 80% unsolicited freelance. Query or complete ms (only if already written); e-query preferred. Pays $200-300 on acceptance for all rts. Articles 1,500-3,000 wds. (30/yr.); length may vary. Responds in 8 wks. Seasonal 10 mos. ahead. No reprints. Kill fee $50. Guidelines/theme list (also on Website: www.youthworker.com/editorial_guidelines.php); copy $3/10x13 SAE. (Ads)

> **Columns/Departments:** Buys 10/yr. International Youth Ministry, and Technology in Youth Ministry.
>
> **Tips:** "Read *Youthworker;* imbibe its tone (professional, though not academic; conversational, though not chatty). Query me with specific, focused ideas that conform to our

editorial style. It helps if the writer is a youth minister, but it's not required. Check Website for additional info, upcoming themes, etc."
**2003 Award of Merit—Most Improved Publication & 2003 Award of Excellence—Christian Ministries.

TEEN/YOUNG ADULT MARKETS

$BOUNDLESS WEBZINE, 8605 Explorer Dr., Colorado Springs CO 80920. (714)548-5928. Fax (719)548-4666. E-mail: roeberdb@boundless.org. Website: www.boundless.org. Focus on the Family. Blake Roeber, ed. For college students exploring love, faith, and cultural issues in the context of a Christian world-view. Online Web mag. 20,000 visitors/wk. 15% unsolicited freelance; 85% assigned. Complete ms; e-query OK. Pays .35-.40/wd. on publication for one-time rts. Articles 700-1,200 wds. (5/yr.); reviews 700-1,200 wds. Responds in 3 wks. Seasonal 1-2 mos. ahead. Accepts simultaneous submissions & reprints (tell when/where appeared). Requires e-mail submission (attached or copied into message). Prefers NIV. Guidelines (by e-mail/Website); copy online. (No ads)
    Columns/Departments: Pages (book reviews/excerpt); @Play (entertainment/culture); Beyond Buddies (relationships); Campus Culture (college life/issues); Head and Heart (spirituality); Finding Your Place (career/future planning); Isms & Ologies (world-view); The Podium (speeches); all 1,000-2,000 wds., .20-.40/wd.
    Tips: "Develop an understanding of Web journalism and a voice that will compel college students."
    **2004 EPA Award of Merit—Online. This periodical was #23 on the 2005 Top 50 Christian Publishers list (#22 in 2004, #32 in 2003, #23 in 2002, #27 in 2001).

$BREAKAWAY, 8605 Explorer Dr., Colorado Springs CO 80921. (719)531-3400. Fax (719)531-3499. E-mail: breakaway@family.org. Website: www.breakawaymag.com. Focus on the Family. Michael Ross, ed. The 15-year-old unchurched teen (boy) in the public school is our target; boys 12-17 yrs. Monthly mag.; 32 pgs.; circ. 96,000. Subscription $18. 25% unsolicited freelance; 75% assigned. Query preferred, or complete ms/cover letter; no phone/fax/e-query. Pays .12-.15/wd. on acceptance for 1st, one-time, or electronic rts. Articles 400-1,000 wds. (6/yr.); fiction to 2,000 wds. (3-4/yr.). Responds in 9-13 wks. Seasonal 6 mos. ahead. No simultaneous submissions or reprints. Kill fee $25. Uses some sidebars. Accepts submissions from teens. Prefers NIV. Guidelines; copy for $1.50/9x12 SAE/3 stamps. (No ads)
    Columns/Departments: Buys 2-3/yr. Truth Encounter (devotional); 700-900 wds.
    Tips: "Most open to nontypical, historical, and biblical fiction. Need strong lead. Brevity and levity a must. Have a teen guy or two read it. Make sure the language is up to date, but not overly hip." Needs drama-in-life stories involving boys.
    **2005, 2004, 2003 EPA Award of Merit—Youth. This periodical was #7 on the 2003 Top 50 Christian Publishers list (#2 in 2002, #10 in 2001).

$BRIO, 8605 Explorer Dr., Colorado Springs CO 80920. (719)548-4577. Fax (719)531-3499. E-mail: brio@macmail.fotf.org. Website: www.briomag.com. Focus on the Family. Susie Shellenberger, ed.; submit to Mrs. Marty Kasza, assoc. ed. For teen girls, 12-15 yrs. Monthly mag.; 38-48 pgs.; circ. 142,500. Subscription $18. 25-50% unsolicited freelance; 50-75% assigned. Complete ms/cover letter; e-query OK. Pays .08-.15/wd. on acceptance for 1st rts. Articles 800-1,000 wds. (10/yr.); fiction 1,200-2,000 wds. (10/yr.). Accepts requested ms by e-mail or disk. Responds in 2-4 wks. Seasonal 8 mos. ahead. Rare kill fee $100. Uses some sidebars. Guidelines (also by e-mail); copy $1.50. (No ads)
    Special Needs: All topics of interest to female teens are welcome: boys, makeup, dating, weight, ordinary girls who have extraordinary experiences, female adjustments to puberty, etc. Also teen-related female fiction.

Tips: "Study at least 3 issues of *Brio* before submitting. We're looking for a certain fresh, hip-hop, conversational style. Most open to fiction, articles, and quizzes."

**The #5 Best-selling Magazine in Christian retail stores. Also 2001 EPA Award of Merit—Youth. This periodical was #50 on the 2004 Top 50 Christian Publishers list.

$CAMPUS LIFE, 465 Gundersen Dr., Carol Stream IL 60188. (630)260-6200. Fax (630)260-0114. E-mail: clmag@campuslife.net. Website: www.campuslife.net. Christianity Today Inc. Christopher Lutes, ed. Seeks to help teenagers navigate adolescence with their Christian faith intact. Bimonthly (plus 4 special Christian-college issues) mag.; 68-94 pgs.; circ. 100,000. Subscription $19.95. 20% assigned. Query or query/clips; fax/e-query OK. Pays .20-.25/wd. on acceptance for 1st rts. Articles 1,200-2,000 wds. (5-10/yr.); fiction 1,000-2,000 wds. (1-5/yr.). Responds in 6 wks. Seasonal 6 mos. ahead. Accepts reprints (tell when/where appeared). Accepts requested ms by e-mail (attached file). Kill fee 50%. Uses some sidebars. Accepts queries from teens. Guidelines (also on Website); copy $3/9x12 SAE. (Ads)

Poetry: Buys 1-5/yr. Free verse; 5-20 lines; $25-50. Submit max. 2 poems. Rarely purchase.

Tips: "Most open to as-told-to stories. Interview students and get their stories."

**This periodical was #42 on the 2001 Top 50 Christian Publishers list. 2003, 2002, 2001 EPA Award of Merit—Youth.

$+CREDO MAGAZINE, PO Box 419527, Kansas City MO 64141. (816)931-1900. Fax (816)412-8312. E-mail: credomag@barefootministries.com. Website: www.credo magazine.com. Barefoot Ministries. Stephanie McNelly, ed. A cutting-edge devotional magazine that also challenges teens in their spiritual walk with relevant articles dealing with the issues they are facing. Monthly mag.; 48 pgs.; circ. 15,000. Subscription $23.40. Estab. 2005. 20-30% unsolicited freelance; 70-80% assigned. Complete ms; query OK. Pays $40-60 for articles; $60 for fiction; on acceptance for all rts. Articles 500-800 wds. (20-30/yr.); fiction 700-800 wds. (10-15/yr.); reviews 500 wds. ($25). Responds in 4-6 wks. Seasonal 4-6 mos. ahead. No simultaneous submissions; accepts reprints (tell when/where appeared). Requires e-mail submission (attached or copied into message). Kill fee. Some sidebars. Prefers NIV. Encourages submissions from teens. Guidelines/theme list (also by e-mail/Website); copy for 6x9 SAE/$1 postage (additional copies $1.95 ea.). (No ads)

Poetry: Accepts 10-15/yr. Any type. Will be used in the magazine or on the Web. No payment. Submit any number.

Fillers: Buys 20-40/yr. Anecdotes, cartoons, games, party ideas, quizzes, short humor, and tips; 100-500 wds. Pays $20-40.

Columns/Departments: Buys 30-40/yr. Real Deal (life issues/relationships), 700-850 wds.; Kung Pao (features student's creative work—poetry, lyrics, short stories, essays, art, photos. etc.), 100-500 wds.; Unreal (fiction piece—looking for 4-6 part series with each part able to stand on its own), 800 wds.; Tune-Up (interviews/profiles/news on Christian artists and bands—e-mail for a suggested question list), 800-850 wds.; Life Zone (articles about youth God is using in cool ways), 800 wds. Pays $40-60.

Special Needs: All topics must be geared to teens.

Tips: "We are most open to freelancers in the areas of Kung Pao, Tune-Up, Life Zone, Unreal (fiction), and seasonal/fun articles written for teens. Also to fillers, and music and entertainment reviews."

$DEVO'ZINE, PO Box 340004, Nashville TN 37203-0004. (615)340-7247. Fax (615)340-1783. E-mail: devozine@upperroom.org, or smiller@upperroom.org. Website: www .devozine.org. Upper Room Ministries. Sandy Miller, ed. Devotional; to help teens (12-18) develop and maintain their connection with God and other Christians. Bimonthly mag.; 64 pgs.; circ. 100,000. Subscription $20. 85% unsolicited freelance; 15% assigned. Query; phone/fax/e-query OK. Pays $25 for meditations, $100 for feature articles (assigned) on acceptance for these one-time rts.: newspaper, periodical, electronic, and software-driven rts., and the right to use in future anthologies. Meditations 150-250 wds. (350/yr.), articles 350-500 wds.; book/music/video reviews, 350-500 wds., $100. Responds in 16 wks. Seasonal 6-8 mos. ahead. Accepts occasional reprints (tell when/where appeared). Accepts requested ms by e-mail or online submission. Regular sidebars. Prefers NRSV, NIV, CEV. Guidelines/theme list (also by e-mail/Website); copy/7x10 SASE. (No ads)

> **Poetry:** Buys 25-30/yr. Free verse, light verse, haiku, traditional; to 150 wds. or 10-20 lines; $25. Submit max. 1 poem/theme, 9 themes/issue.

> **Tips:** "E-mail with ideas for weekend features related to specific themes."

> **This periodical was #2 on the 2005 Top 50 Christian Publishers list (#1 in 2004, #2 in 2003, #3 in 2002, #3 in 2001).

$ESSENTIAL CONNECTION, One Lifeway Plaza, Nashville TN 37234-0174. (615)251-2008. Fax (615)277-8271. E-mail: ec@lifeway.com. LifeWay Christian Resources of the Southern Baptist Convention. Bob Bunn, ed-in-chief. Christian leisure reading and devotional guide for 7th-12th graders. Monthly mag.; 60 pgs.; circ. 120,000. Subscription $1.32/issue. 10% unsolicited freelance; 90% assigned. Query; e-query OK. Pays $80-120 on acceptance for all rts. Articles 800-1,200 wds. (12/yr.); fiction 1,200 wds. (12/yr.). Responds in 10 wks. Seasonal 9 mos. ahead. No simultaneous submissions or reprints. Prefers e-mail submission (attached file or copied into message). No kill fee. Uses some sidebars. Prefers NIV. Guidelines (also by e-mail); free copy. (No ads)

> **Poetry:** Accepts 36/yr. All types. From teens only.

> **Special Needs:** Always in search of Christian humor; sports profiles. Most open to fiction (send complete ms).

GO! MAGAZINE, 4200 North Point Pkwy, Alpharetta GA 30022. (770)410-6100. Fax (770)410-6033. E-mail: go@namb.net. Website: www.GOstudents.net. North American Mission Board/Southern Baptist Convention. Jana Jones & Brent Moxey, eds. To encourage Christian teens to make an impact on their world for Christ. Annual & online mag.; 64 pgs.; circ. 85,000. Subscription $1.95/copy (bulk). Open to freelance. Prefers e-query. Articles; music/video/Website reviews. (Ads)

> **2004, 2003, 2001 EPA Award of Excellence—Youth.

> **Tips:** "Most open to stories about youth sharing Christ in the real world. Mostly accept freelance for our new Website."

$GUIDEPOSTS SWEET 16, 1050 Broadway, Ste. 6, Chesterton IN 46304. (219)929-4429. Fax (219)926-3839. E-mail: writers@guidepostssweet16mag.com. Website: www.guideposts sweet16.com. Guideposts, Inc. Mary Lou Carney, ed-in-chief; Betsy Kohn, mng. ed.; Allison Ruffing, assoc. ed. For teen girls 11-17; features true, first-person stories about real teens. Our watchwords are "wholesome," "current," "fun," and "inspiring." Bimonthly mag.; 48 pages.; circ. 200,000. Subscription $19.95. 50% unsolicited freelance; 50% assigned. Query/clips; fax/e-query OK. Pays $300-500 for true stories, $100-300 for shorter pieces on acceptance for all rts. Articles 500-1,500 wds. Responds in 4 wks. Seasonal 6 mos. ahead. Accepts simultaneous submissions & reprints (tell when/where appeared). Accepts disk or e-mail submission (copied into message). Kill fee 25%. Some sidebars. Guidelines (also by e-mail); copy $4.50.

> **Columns/Departments:** Allison Ruffing, assoc. ed. Buys 40/yr. Query. Positive Thinker (single-page feature on teen girl who has overcome something remarkable and kept a positive outlook), 300 wds; Too Good to Be True (profile of teen guy who is cute, wholesome, and doing something very, very cool), 250 wds; DIY (trendy crafts, DIY fashion/beauty, bedroom accessories, anything a teen girl would find cool, fun, easy to create); Fashion/Beauty/Self-Help (fun, trendy, seasonal pieces about a single topic in beauty or fashion); 500-1,000 wds; Quizzes (teen issues, approached with humor), 500-900 wds. Pays $175-400.

Special Needs: Need 1st-person (ghostwritten) true stories of teen girls (5/issue); see guidelines. Also need Mysterious Moments ("strange-but-true" stories of miracles, unexplained coincidences, by teen girl or boy narrators), 250 words.

Tips: "We'll publish the occasional action/adventure true story, but our ongoing focus will be on relationships and real-life teen issues: friendship, romance, peer pressure, etc. We need 'light' true stories about finding a date and learning to drive, as well as 'catch-in-the-throat' stories. Language and subject matter must be current, uplifting, and teen-friendly. No preaching or lecturing, please! We do not publish fiction or poetry."

**This periodical was #38 on the 2005 Top 50 Christian Publishers list.

$INSIGHT, 55 W. Oak Ridge Dr., Hagerstown MD 21740-7301. (301)393-4038. Fax (301)393-4055. E-mail: insight@rhpa.org. Website: www.insightmagazine.org. Review and Herald/Seventh-day Adventist. Dwain Esmond, ed. A magazine of positive Christian living for Seventh-day Adventist high school students. Weekly take-home mag.; 16 pgs.; circ. 13,600. Subscription $49.95. 60% unsolicited freelance. Complete ms/cover letter; e-query OK. Pays $10-125 on acceptance for one-time rts. Not copyrighted. Articles 500-1,500 wds. (100/yr.). Responds in 4 wks. Seasonal 6 mos. ahead. Accepts reprints (tell when/where appeared). Prefers e-mail submission (attached file). Kill fee. Regularly uses sidebars. Prefers NIV. Accepts submissions from teens. Guidelines (also by e-mail/Website); copy $2/9x12 SAE/2 stamps. (No ads)

Poetry: Buys to 36/yr. All types; to 1 pg.; $10. By high school and college students only.

Columns/Departments: Buys 50/yr. On the Edge (drama in real life), 800-1,500 wds., $50-100; It Happened To Me (personal experience in first person), 600-900 wds., $50-75; Big Deal (big topics, such as prayer, premarital sex, knowing God's will, etc.) with sidebar, 1,200-1,700 wds., $75 + $25 for sidebar; So I Said (first-person opinion), 300-500 wds., $25-100.

Contest: Sponsors a nonfiction and poetry contest; includes a category for students under 21. Prizes to $250. June deadline (varies). Send SASE for rules.

Tips: "We are desperately in need of true, dramatic stories involving Christian young people. Also need stories by male authors, particularly some humor. Also profiles of Seventh-day Adventist teenagers who are making a notable difference."

**This periodical was #28 on the 2005 Top 50 Christian Publishers list (#19 in 2004, #20 in 2003, #26 in 2002, #24 in 2001).

$INTEEN, PO Box 87618, Chicago IL 60680-0168. Toll-free (800)860-8642. (708)868-7100, ext. 239. Fax (708)868-7105. Website: www.urbanministries.com. Urban Ministries, Inc. Submit to The Editor. Teen curriculum for ages 15-17 (student and teacher manuals). Quarterly booklet; 32 pgs.; circ. 20,000. Subscription $11.25. 1% unsolicited freelance; 99% assigned. Query/clips; phone query OK; no e-query. Pays $75-150 on acceptance for all rts. Articles & fiction 1,200 wds. Responds in 4 wks. Seasonal 9 mos. ahead. Accepts some reprints (tell when/where appeared). Accepts requested ms on disk or by e-mail (copied into message). Prefers NIV. Free guidelines/theme list/copy for 10x13 SAE. (No ads)

Poetry: Buys 4/yr. Free verse; variable length; $25-60.

Tips: "Write in with sample writings and be willing and ready to complete an assignment. We prefer to make assignments. Most open to Bible study guides applicable and interesting for teens. Writers who can accurately explain scriptures to teens are always welcome."

$J.A.M.: JESUS AND ME, PO Box 436987, Chicago IL 60643. (708)868-7100, ext. 290. Fax (708)868-6759. E-mail: ctaylor@urbanministries.com. Website: www.urbanministries.com. Urban Ministries, Inc. C. Taylor, ed. Magazine for 12- to 14-year-olds. Open to freelance. Query/clips; fax/e-query OK. Pays up to $150, 120 days after acceptance, for all rts. Articles 200-400 wds. Responds in 4 wks. Seasonal 6 mos. ahead. Accepts simultaneous submissions. Requires accepted ms on disk. Prefers NIV. Guidelines; copy for #10 SASE. (No ads)

Tips: "Send query with a writing sample, or attend our annual conference on the first weekend in November each year. Manuscripts are evaluated at the conference."

$LISTEN, 55 W. Oak Ridge Dr., Hagerstown MD 21740. (301)393-4019. Fax (301)393-3294. E-mail: editor@listenmagazine.org. Website: www.listenmagazine.org. The Health Connection. Celeste Perrino-Walker, ed. Positive lifestyle magazine for teens/young adults; emphasizes values in a secular tone. Monthly mag. (September-May); 32 pgs.; circ. 20,000/exposure 100,000. Subscription $26.95. 50% unsolicited freelance; 50% assigned. Query or complete ms; phone/fax/e-query OK. Pays .06-.10/wd.($50-150) on acceptance for 1st or reprint rts. Articles 800-1,200 wds. (30-50/yr.); true stories 800 wds. (15/yr.). Responds in 2 wks.-3 mos. Seasonal 1 yr. ahead. Accepts simultaneous submissions & reprints (tell when/where appeared). Accepts requested ms on disk or by e-mail (attached file). Regularly uses sidebars. Guidelines/theme list (also by e-mail/Website); copy $2/9x12 SAE/2 stamps. (No ads)

Poetry: From high school students only. Pays comps.

Fillers: Uses 500-word quizzes and shorts based on topic in our theme list.

Special Needs: Anti-drug, tobacco, alcohol; positive role models. For true stories, needs stories dealing with everyday problems: peer pressure, decision making, friendship, family conflict, self-discipline, divorce, abuse, anorexia/bulimia, and making positive choices.

Tips: "Need good true stories. We've recently stopped using fiction. While it isn't always possible, we like to feature stories about individuals who overcome the temptation to experiment with drugs and alcohol, and/or who find a creative way to deal with a bad situation."
**This periodical was #13 on the 2005 Top 50 Christian Publishers List (#11 in 2004, #9 in 2003).

$LIVING MY FAITH, 1300 N. Meacham Rd., Schaumburg IL 60173-4888. (847)843-1600. Fax (847)843-3757. E-mail: livingmyfaith@garbc.org. Website: www.rbpstudentministries.org. Regular Baptist Press. Mel Walker, dir. of student ministries. For junior high youth (12-14); conservative/fundamental. Weekly devotional booklet; 12 pgs. Complete ms; no e-query. Pays .04/wd. and up, on acceptance. Lead stories 450-550 wds; articles 300-800 wds.; true & fiction stories to 1,000 wds. Requires KJV. Check Website for guidelines before submitting at www.rbpstudentministries.org/contribute.

Tips: "Check Website quarterly for updates concerning needs, themes, etc."

$PASSAGEWAY.ORG, 1 Billy Graham Pkwy., Charlotte NC 28201. (704)401-2432. E-mail: ed@passageway.org. Website: www.passageway.org. Billy Graham Evangelistic Assn. Steve Knight, sr. ed.; Blaine Howard, asst. ed. Online publication for teens, 15-17 yrs. Biweekly e-zine. 10% unsolicited freelance; 90% assigned. Complete ms/cover letter; no phone query/e-query OK. Pays $100-250 on publication for all, electronic, or reprint rts. Articles 500-1,000 wds. (52/yr.); no fiction. Responds in 6-8 wks. Seasonal 2 mos. ahead. Accepts simultaneous submissions & reprints (tell when/where appeared). Prefers e-mail submission (attached or copied into message). Some kill fees 50%. Uses some sidebars. Prefers NIV. Guidelines on Website (www.passageway.org/guidelines); copy online. (No ads)

Columns/Departments: Grow and Pop Culture sections.

Tips: "Most open to a well-written article for the Grow section; it is the best way to break in. Also open to unique Pop Culture features that are relevant to teens. This is a youth Website, and writing that does not work for youth or the Web will not be considered."
**2004 EPA Award of Merit—Online.

$REAL FAITH IN LIFE, 1300 N. Meacham Rd., Schaumburg IL 60173-4888. (847)843-1600. Fax (847)843-3757. E-mail: realfaith@garbc.org. Website: www.rbpstudentministries.org. Regular Baptist Press. Mel Walker, dir. of student ministries. For senior high youth (15-18); conservative/fundamental. Quarterly devotional planner; 96 pgs. Complete ms; no e-query. Pays .04/wd. and up, on acceptance for first (preferred) or one-time rts. Articles

400-1,200 wds. (if more than 600 wds., include subheads). Using mostly assignment writers who are using the RBP student ministries materials or are familiar with churches who do. Some reprints. Guidelines (also on Website: www.rbpstudentministries.org/contribute); copy.

Tips: "Check Website quarterly for updates concerning needs, themes, etc."

$SHARING THE VICTORY, 8701 Leeds Rd., Kansas City MO 64129-1680. Toll-free (800)289-0909. (816)921-0909. Fax (816)921-8755. E-mail: stv@fca.org. Website: www.Fca.org. Fellowship of Christian Athletes (Protestant and Catholic). Jill Ewert, ed. Equipping and encouraging athletes and coaches to take their faith seriously, in and out of competition. Monthly (9X-double issues in Jan., Jun. & Aug.) mag.; 40 pgs.; circ. 80,000. Subscription $18. 10% unsolicited freelance; 40% assigned. Query only/clips; e-query OK. Pays $150-400 on publication for 1st rts. Articles 500-1,000 wds. (5-20/yr.). Responds in 13 wks. Seasonal 6 mos. ahead. Accepts reprints, pays 50% (tell when/where appeared). Accepts requested ms on disk or by e-mail (attached or copied into message). Kill fee .05%. Uses some sidebars. Prefers NIV. Guidelines on Website; copy $1/9x12 SAE/3 stamps. (Ads)

Special Needs: Articles on FCA camp experiences. All articles must have an athletic angle. Need stories featuring Christian female professional athletes with a FCA connection.

Tips: "FCA angle important; pro and college athletes and coaches giving solid Christian testimony; we run stories according to athletic season. Need articles on Christian pro athletes—all sports. It is suggested that writer actually look at the magazine for general style and presentation."

+STEELROOTS MAGAZINE, PO Box 410800, Charlotte NC 28241-0800. (704)561-7602. E-mail: info@steelroots.com. Website: www.steelroots.com, or http://steelrootsproshop .com. Steelroots, Inc. Submit to The Editor. Provides a look into the lives of professional skaters, snowboarders, and surfers through articles written about and by athletes; intended for Christian and secular audience. Mag.; circ. 30,000. Distributed through Christian bookstores, specialty shops, and at youth events. Articles. Copy $5. Incomplete topical listings. (Ads)

$STUDENT LEADERSHIP JOURNAL, Box 7895, Madison WI 53707-7895. (608)274-9001, ext. 3694. Fax (608)274-7882. E-mail: slj@intervarsity.org. Website: www.intervarsity .org/slj. InterVarsity Christian Fellowship. Jeff Yourison, ed. Undergraduate college student Christian leaders, single, ages 18-26. Triannual & online jour.; 32 pgs.; circ. 9,500. Subscription $12. 2% unsolicited; 20% assigned. Query/clips; no e-query. Pays $35-125 on acceptance for 1st or one-time rts. Articles to 2,000 wds. (3/yr.). Responds in 16 wks. Seasonal 8 mos. ahead. Accepts reprints. No e-mail submissions. Regularly uses sidebars. Guidelines/theme list; copy $4/9x12 SAE/4 stamps. (No ads)

Poetry: Buys 4-6/yr. Avant-garde, free verse; to 15 lines; $25-50. Submit max. 5 poems.

Columns/Departments: Buys 6-10/yr. Collegiate Trends, 20-100 wds.; Student Leadership Network, 500-800 wds.; Chapter Strategy (how-to planning strategy for campus groups), 500-800 wds.; $10-75. Query.

Special Needs: Campus issues/trends/ministry/spiritual growth/leadership; Kingdom values; multiethnic reconciliation.

Tips: "Most open to main features targeted to college-age students. Be upbeat, interesting, and fresh. Writers who were involved in campus fellowship as students have the 'write' perspective and experience."

$TEENAGE CHRISTIAN, PO Box 2227, Brentwood TN 37024-2227. Toll-free (800)637-2613. E-mail: teenagechristian@bellsouth.net. Website: www.teenagechristian.net. Church of Christ/Christian Publishing Inc. Ben Forrest, ed. Spiritual answers to tough questions for Christian teens (13-19 yrs.). Quarterly mag.; 32 pgs.; circ. 10,500. Subscription $14.95. 50% unsolicited freelance. Prefers submissions through e-mail or Website. Pays $35 on publication for one-time & reprint rts. Articles 600-1,200 wds. (20/yr.); fiction 600-1,500 wds. (9/yr.). Responds in 2-3 mos. Accepts requested ms on disk. Seasonal 6 mos. ahead. Accepts simultaneous submissions & reprints (tell when/where appeared). Rarely uses sidebars. Prefers NIV. Copy $2.50/9x12 SAE. (Ads)

Poetry: Buys 3-4/yr. Free verse; 10-25 lines; $15-25. Submit max. 5 poems.

Fillers: Buys 5-10/yr. Cartoons, quizzes, prayers, word puzzles; 150-350 wds.; $15-25.

Tips: "Most open to practical nonfiction. Fiction should be excellent, realistic, and up to date."

TEEN LIGHT: The Teen 2 Teen Christian Magazine, 6118 Bend of River, Dunn NC 28334. (910)980-1126. E-mail: publisher@teenlight.org. Website: www.teenlight.org. Writers' Ministries, Inc. Annette Dammer, pub.; submit to Rebekah Hamrick. Totally teen authored; uses professional Christian writers to mentor their teen journalists so they may reach the world for Christ. Bimonthly & online mag.; circ. 3,000. Subscription $11.95. 20% unsolicited freelance; 80% assigned. Complete ms/cover letter; e-query OK. **PAYS IN COPIES & FREE CLASSES** for nonexclusive rts. Articles 500-1,000 wds. (25/yr.); short fiction (12/yr.). Responds in 2 mos. Seasonal 4-6 mos. ahead. Accepts simultaneous submissions & reprints (tell when/where appeared). Prefers accepted mss by e-mail (copied into message). Uses some sidebars. Accepts submissions from children & teens. Guidelines (also by e-mail/Website); copy for 9x12 SAE/3 stamps. (Ads)

Poetry: Accepts 26/yr. All types; pays in copies. Submit max. 5 poems.

Fillers: Accepts 26/yr. Anecdotes, cartoons, facts, games, jokes, party ideas, prayers, prose, quizzes, quotes, short humor, tips, and word puzzles; pays in copies.

Special Needs: Fashion, art, photo journalism; true-life teen triumphs and testimonies.

Contest: Emaleigh's Writer's Contest held every year.

Tips: "Write from your heart and your life. Be honest, open, and fallible. Most of all, our writers must be 22 years old or younger. Even our publisher doesn't write for us. By teens, for teens—that is our appointed mission."

TEENS FOR JC.COM, 2855 Lawrenceville-Suwanee Rd., Ste. 760-355, Suwanee GA 30024. Phone/fax (770)831-8622. E-mail: uvaldes@aol.com. Website: www.teensforjc.com. PLGK Communications, Inc. Quentin Plair, pres./CEO. Salutes the fun and exhilaration of being a Christian teen. Monthly e-zine. 90% unsolicited freelance; 10% assigned. Complete ms/cover letter; no phone/fax/e-query. Accepts requested ms on disk or by e-mail (attached file). **NO PAYMENT** for one-time rts. Not copyrighted. Articles 100-5,000 wds. (15/yr.) & fiction 100-5,000 wds. (12/yr.); reviews 200 wds. Responds in 12 weeks. Seasonal 4 mos. ahead. Accepts simultaneous submissions & reprints (tell when/where appeared). No kill fee. Uses some sidebars. Accepts submissions from teens. Guidelines (also on Website). (Ads)

Poetry: Accepts many; any type; 1-200 lines.

Fillers: Accepts many; cartoons, facts, games, jokes, party ideas, prayers, prose, quizzes, short humor, tips, word puzzles; 10-750 wds.

Columns/Departments: Accepts 36/yr. School tips (teen tips for scholarly excellence); Scoop (current info); Music (music reviews/stories); Speak Out (opinion articles by teens); all 100-500 wds.

Tips: "Provide information teens need to lay a foundation for a successful life. Looking for great stories."

TRANSCENDMAG.COM, 2855 Lawrenceville-Suwanee Rd., Ste. 760-355, Suwanee GA 30024. Phone/fax (770)831-8622. E-mail: uvaldes@aol.com. Website: www.transcendmag.com. PLGK Communications, Inc. Quentin Plair, mng. ed. Salutes the fun and exhilaration of being an African American teen. Monthly e-zine. 100% assigned. Complete ms/cover letter (for fiction query/clips); no phone/fax/e-query. **NO PAYMENT** for one-time rts. Not copyrighted. Articles 100-5,000 wds. (15/yr.); fiction 100-5,000 wds. (12/yr.); reviews 200 wds. Responds in 12 weeks. Seasonal 4 mos. ahead. Accepts simultaneous submissions & reprints (tell when/where appeared). Prefers requested ms on disk or by e-mail (attached file). No kill fee. Uses some sidebars. Accepts submissions from children & teens. Guidelines (also on Website); copy on Website. (Ads)

Poetry: Accepts many; 1-200 lines. Submit any number.

Fillers: Accepts many; cartoons, facts, games, jokes, party ideas, prayers, prose, quizzes, short humor, tips, word puzzles; 10-750 wds.

Columns/Departments: Accepts 36/yr. School Tips (tips for scholarly excellence); Speak Out (opinion articles by teens); Scoop (current info); Music (music reviews/stories); all 100-500 wds.

Tips: "Looking for great stories. Provide information teens need to lay a foundation for a successful life. Great publication for freelancers."

$WITH: The Magazine for Radical Christian Youth, Box 347, Newton KS 67114-0347. (316)283-5100. Fax (316)283-0454. E-mail: carold@mennoniteusa.org. Website: www.withonline.org. Faith & Life Press/Mennonite, Brethren & Mennonite Brethren. Carol Duerksen, ed. For high-school teens (15-18 yrs.), Christian and non-Christian. Bimonthly mag.; 32 pgs.; circ. 4,000. Subscription $23.50. 20% unsolicited freelance; 80% assigned. Query (on first-person and how-to articles); complete ms on others/cover letter; no phone/fax/e-query. Pays .06/wd. (.03/wd. for reprints) on acceptance for 1st, one-time, simultaneous, or reprint rts. Articles 500-1,800 wds. (15/yr.); fiction 1,000-2,000 wds. (15/yr.); music reviews 500 wds., .05/wd. (query for assignment). Responds in 4 wks. Seasonal 6 mos. ahead. Accepts simultaneous submissions & reprints (tell when/where appeared). No disk. Kill fee 25-50%. Regularly uses sidebars. Prefers NRSV. Guidelines/theme list (also by e-mail); copy for 9x12 SAE/4 stamps. Separate guidelines for 1st-person and how-to articles sent only when requested. (No ads)

Fillers: Buys 20 cartoons/yr.; $35-40.

Tips: "We need good Christmas stories; true, powerful stories or fiction that reads as well as truth. Send for theme list and write for the theme. Write a story from a teen's perspective that grabs the reader and leaves the reader thinking and going away with a new insight. Humor—both cartoons and short articles—are hard to find. Our readers expect high-quality humor."

**This periodical was #35 on the 2002 Top 50 Christian Publishers list.

$YOUNG ADULT TODAY, PO Box 436987, Chicago IL 60643. Toll-free (800)860-8642. (708)868-7100, ext. 239. Fax (708)868-7107. E-mail from Website. Website: www.urbanministries.com. Urban Ministries, Inc. Submit to The Editor. Young-adult curriculum for ages 18-24 (student and teacher manuals). Quarterly booklet; 80 pgs.; circ. 10,000. Subscription $14.75. 99% assigned. Query/clips; phone query OK; no e-query. Pays $75-150 on acceptance for all rts. Articles (24/yr.) & fiction (12/yr.); under 1,000 wds. Responds in 4 wks. Seasonal 9 mos. ahead. Accepts some reprints (tell when/where appeared). Accepts requested ms on disk or by e-mail (copied into message). Prefers KJV. Free guidelines/theme list/copy for 10x13 SAE. (No ads)

Poetry: Buys 4/yr. Free verse; variable length; $25-60.

Tips: "We assign articles based on the Uniform Lesson Series for Sunday schools. Writers should send samples of their writing to be considered for an assignment. We very rarely publish unassigned submissions. Assignments are made to writers who demonstrate knowledge of the audience and the publication as well as biblical text and life application."

$#YOUNG AND ALIVE, Box 6097, Lincoln NE 68506. (402)488-0981. E-mail: info@christianrecord.org. Website: www.christianrecord.org. Christian Record Services, Inc. Gaylena Gibson, ed. For sight-impaired young adults, 12-25 yrs.; for interdenominational Christian audience. Quarterly mag.; 65-70 pgs.; circ. 25,000. Free to sight-impaired. 90% unsolicited freelance. Complete ms by mail. Pays .04-.05/wd. on acceptance for one-time rts. Articles & true stories 800-1,400 wds. (40/yr.). Responds in 52 wks. Seasonal anytime. Accepts simultaneous submissions & reprints (tell when/where appeared, no tear sheets). Accepts requested ms on disk. Does not use sidebars. Guidelines; copy for 7x10 SAE/5 stamps. (No ads) Note: due to an overabundance of manuscripts, this publication will not be accepting submissions until 2009.

$YOUNG CHRISTIAN, 2660 Petersborough St., Herndon VA 20171. Phone/fax (703)715-1129. E-mail: youngchristianmagazine@yahoo.com. Website: http://groups.yahoo.com/group/youngchristianmagazine. Tellstar Publishing. Shannon Bridget Murphy, ed. Christian writing with the Lord's message for children and teens. Quarterly mag. 85% unsolicited freelance. Complete ms/cover letter; e-query OK. Pays .02-.05/wd. on acceptance for 1st or one-time rts. Articles 500-2,000 wds.; fiction 500-2,000 wds.; book/tape reviews. Responds in 2-8 wks. Seasonal 3-6 mos. ahead. Accepts simultaneous submissions & reprints (tell when/where appeared). Accepts disk; prefers e-mail submissions (attached or copied into message). No kill fee. Regularly uses sidebars. Prefers KJV. Guidelines by e-mail. (No ads)

> **Poetry:** Buys variable number. Avant-garde, free verse, haiku, light verse, traditional; any length; variable rates. Submit any number.

> **Fillers:** Buys anecdotes, cartoons, facts, ideas, kid quotes, party ideas, prayers, prose, quizzes, quotes, short humor, tips, and word puzzles; to 1,000 wds.

> **Tips:** "Freelancers have the best chance of breaking in if they send a manuscript that is well-written and suitable for our audience."

$YOUNG SALVATIONIST, PO Box 269, Alexandria VA 22313-0269. (703)684-5500. Fax (703)684-5539. E-mail: ys@usn.salvationarmy.org. Website: http://publications.salvationarmyusa.org. The Salvation Army. Curtiss A. Hartley, ed. (Curtiss_Hartley@USN.Salvationarmy.org). For teens and young adults in the Salvation Army. Monthly (10X) & online mag.; 24 pgs.; circ. 48,000. Subscription $4. 80% unsolicited freelance; 20% assigned. Complete ms preferred; e-query OK. Pays .15/wd.(.10/wd. for reprints) on acceptance for 1st, one-time, or reprint rts. Articles (60/yr.) & fiction (10/yr.), 600-1,200 wds.; short evangelistic pieces, 350-600 wds. Responds in 9 wks. Seasonal 6 mos. ahead. Accepts reprints (tell when/where appeared). Accepts requested ms on disk or by e-mail. Uses some sidebars. Prefers NIV. Guidelines/theme list (also on Website); copy for 9x12 SAE/3 stamps. (No ads)

> **Contest:** Sponsors a contest for fiction, nonfiction, poetry, original art, and photography. Send SASE for details.

> **Tips:** "Our greatest need is for nonfiction pieces that are relevant to the readers and offer clear application to daily life. We are most interested in topical pieces on contemporary issues that affect a teen's daily life, and pieces that work with the day-to-day challenges of faith. Although we use fiction and poetry, they are a small percentage of the total content of each issue."

> **This periodical was #12 on the 2005 Top 50 Christian Publishers list (#9 in 2004, #10 in 2003, #6 in 2002, #6 in 2001).

$YOUTH COMPASS, PO Box 4060, Overland Park KS 66204. (913)432-0331. Fax (913)722-0351. E-mail: sseditor1@juno.com. Church of God (holiness)/Herald and Banner Press. Arlene McGehee, Sunday school ed. Denominational; for teens. Weekly take-home paper; 4 pgs.; circ. 4,800. Subscription $1.50. Complete ms/cover letter; phone/fax/e-query OK (prefers mail or e-mail). Pays .005/wd. on publication for 1st rts. Fiction 800-1,500 wds. Seasonal 6-8 mos. ahead. Accepts simultaneous submissions & reprints (tell when/where appeared). Prefers KJV. Guidelines/theme list; copy. Not in topical listings.

YOUTHWALK (GA), 4201 N. Peachtree Rd., Atlanta GA 30341. (770)451-9300. Fax (770)454-

9313. E-mail: twalker@walkthru.org. Website: www.youthwalk.org. Walk Thru the Bible Ministries. Tim Walker, ed.; Laurin Makohon, asst. ed. To encourage teens to have a real faith by reading their Bible daily and to have a real relationship with a real God who cares about every aspect of their lives. Monthly mag.; circ. 55,000. Subscription $18. Open to freelance. Query or complete ms. Requires NIV. (No ads)

Tips: "We accept freelance for feature articles and profiles only; no devotionals."
**2001 Award of Merit—Youth.

WOMEN'S MARKETS

*ANNA'S JOURNAL, PO Box 341, Ellijay GA 30540. Phone/fax (706)276-2309. E-mail: annas@ellijay.com. Catherine Ward-Long, ed. Spiritual support for childless couples who for the most part have decided to stay that way. Print publication being converted to an e-zine. 80% unsolicited freelance; 20% assigned. Complete ms/cover letter; fax/e-query OK. 1st, simultaneous, or reprint rts. Not copyrighted. Articles 500-2,000 wds. (8-12/yr.); fiction 1,000-2,000 wds. (1-3/yr.). Seasonal 3 months ahead. Accepts simultaneous submissions & reprints (tell when/where appeared). No disk; e-mail OK (copied into message). Does not use sidebars. Prefers KJV. No guidelines or copy. (No ads) Note from publisher: "*Anna's Journal* has recently gone out of business."

Poetry: Accepts 4-10/yr. Any type. Submit max. 3 poems.

Fillers: Accepts 3-4/yr. Anecdotes, facts, newsbreaks, prose, prayers, quizzes, quotes, letters; 50-250 wds.

Special Needs: Articles from married, childless men; articles discussing the meaning of childless, childfree, and childless by choice.

Tips: "Looking for innovative ways to improve the child-free lifestyle and self-esteem. It helps if writer is childless."

$AT THE CENTER, PO Box 100, Morgantown PA 19543. Toll-free (800)588-7744. (610)856-6830. Fax (610)856-6831. E-mail: publications@rightideas.us, or elaine@rightideas.us. Website: www.atcmag.com. Right Ideas, Inc. Jerry Thacker, ed.; submit to Elaine Williams, asst. ed. Designed to help staff, volunteers, and board members of Crisis Pregnancy Centers/Pregnancy Care Centers with relevant information and encouragement. Triannual & online mag.; 24 pgs.; circ. 30,000. Subscription free. 20% unsolicited freelance; 80% assigned. Complete ms; phone/fax query OK; e-query preferred. Pays $150 on publication for 1st, reprint, or simultaneous rts. Articles 800-1,000 wds. (15/yr.). Responds in 8-10 wks. Seasonal 6-8 mos. ahead. Accepts simultaneous submissions & reprints. Accepts e-mail submissions (attached or copied into message). No kill fee. Uses some sidebars. Prefers KJV, ESV, or NASB. Guidelines/idea list (also by e-mail); copy for 9x12 SAE/3 stamps. (Ads—elaine@rightideas.us)

Special Needs: Articles that give ideas for other centers in the areas of recruiting and retaining volunteers, ways to reach abortion-minded clients, and creative fund-raising ideas.

Tips: "Looking for practical articles of help and encouragement for those involved in the work of CPC/PCC ministry. If someone has been involved in crisis pregnancy work, their insight into many areas of the ministry can be helpful to staff and board. Need good techniques for counseling abortion-minded clients."

**2001 EPA Award of Merit—Organizational.

CHRISTIAN WOMEN TODAY, Box 300, Sta. A, Vancouver BC V6C 2X3, Canada. (604)514-2000. Fax (604)514-2124. E-mail: editor@christianwomentoday.com. Website: www.christianwomentoday.com. French Website: www.chretiennes.com. Campus Crusade for Christ, Canada. Karen Schenk, pub.; Stacy Wiebe, ed. For Christian women, 20-60 yrs.

Monthly online mag.; 2 million hits/mo. 30% unsolicited freelance. Query first; e-query preferred. **NO PAYMENT.** Lifestyle articles 200-500 wds.; features 500-1,000 wds.; life stories 500 wds. Seasonal 4 mos. ahead. Accepts simultaneous submissions & reprints (tell when/where appeared). Prefers e-mail submission (attached file). Guidelines/theme list on Website (www.christianwomentoday.com/volunteer/submissions.html). (Ads)

> **Tips:** "The writer needs to have a global perspective, have a heart to build women in their faith, and help develop them to win others to Christ. Text should be written for online viewing with subheads and bullets in the body of the article."

CHURCHWOMAN, 475 Riverside Dr., Ste. 1626, New York NY 10115. Toll-free (800)298-5551. (212)870-2347. Fax (212)870-2338. E-mail: cwu@churchwomen.org. Website: www.churchwomen.org. Church Women United. Annie Llamoso-Songco, ed. Shares stories of women acting on their faith and engaging in the work for peace and justice around the world. Quarterly mag.; 28 pgs.; circ. 3,000. Subscription $10. 1% unsolicited freelance. Query. **PAYS IN COPIES.** Articles to 3 pgs. Prefers accepted ms by e-mail (copied into message). Guidelines; copy $1.

CROWNED WITH SILVER, PO Box 10, Masonville CO 80541. E-mail: crownedwithsilver@yahoo.com. Website: www.crownedwithsilver.com. Submit to The Editor. Return to biblical femininity; Christian homemaking encouragement regarding home schooling, etiquette, marriage, womanhood, and nostalgic wisdom from the past. Quarterly mag. Subscription $14. Incomplete topical listings. No questionnaire returned.

$+THE DABBLING MUM.COM, 9919 Marilyn Collins Way, Knoxville TN 37931. (865)691-7739. E-mail: dm@thedabblingmum.com. Website: www.thedabblingmum.com. Nondenominational. Alyice Edrich, ed. Balance your life while you glean from successful entrepreneurs, parents, and Christians—just like you. Weekly online mag.; circ. 40,000. Subscription free online. 90% unsolicited freelance; 10% assigned. Complete ms submitted online. Pays $20-30 (reprints $5) on publication for 1st & nonexclusive archival rts. Articles 500-1,500 wds. (98/yr.). Accepts submissions from children & teens, if it fits the topic. Responds in 8 wks. Seasonal 1 mo. ahead. No simultaneous submissions; accepts reprints (tell when/where appeared). Accepts disk or via online form. No kill fee or sidebars. Prefers KJV. Guidelines/editorial calendar/copy on Website. (Ads)

> **Contest:** Every 2-3 months they have an essay contest (http://thedabblingmum.com/contests/index.htm).
>
> **Tips:** "Writers really need to study our publication. We receive far too many articles on writing and not enough on parenting or home business area. See editorial calendar."

$ESPRIT, Evangelical Lutheran Women, 302-393 Portage Ave., Winnipeg MB R3B 3H6, Canada. (204)984-9160. Fax (204)984-9162. E-mail: esprit@elcic.ca. Website: www.elw.ca. Evangelical Lutheran Church in Canada. Catherine Pate, ed. For Christian women. Quarterly mag.; 36 pgs.; circ. 5,400. Subscription $17 Cdn., $26 U.S. 50% unsolicited freelance; 50% assigned. Complete ms/cover letter; phone/fax/e-query OK. Pays $16.50/pg. Cdn. on publication for 1st or one-time rts. Articles (34/yr.) & fiction (4/yr.) 350-1,300 wds. Responds in 2-4 wks. Seasonal 4 mos. ahead. Accepts simultaneous submissions & reprints (tell when/where appeared). Prefers accepted mss by e-mail (attached). Uses some sidebars. Requires NRSV. Guidelines (also on Website); copy for #10 SAE/.90 Cdn. postage or $1 U.S. (Limited ads)

> **Poetry:** Light verse, traditional; 8-100 lines; $16.50. Submit max. 3 poems.
>
> **Columns/Departments:** Buys 4/yr., 325 wds.
>
> **Tips:** "Articles must be in accordance with Lutheran theology. Preference is given to Canadian Lutheran women writers. Use inclusive language (no male pronoun references to God), focus on women and spiritual/faith, and topical issues. Looking for humorous articles that see the joy and play in life; well-researched topical issues that stretch our reader's understanding of faith."

**This periodical was #30 on the 2005 Top 50 Christian Publishers list (#18 in 2004, #34 in 2003, #19 in 2002).

$THE GODLY BUSINESS WOMAN, PO Box 181004, Casselberry FL 32718-1004. Toll-free (800)560-1090. (407)696-2805. Fax (407)695-8033. E-mail: info@godlybusiness woman.com, or tracey@godlybusinesswoman.com. Website: www.godlybusinesswoman .com. Kathleen B. Jackson, pub; Tracey Davison, mng. ed. Our goal is to educate, inspire, and encourage women to be all they can be through Jesus Christ; to be a resource that will shed light on God's view of the responsibilities we have been given. Mag.; 48 pgs.; circ. 25,000. Subscription $15.99. 30% unsolicited freelance; 70% assigned. Query; prefers e-queries. Pays $20. Articles 750-1,500 wds. Regularly uses sidebars. Guidelines. (Ads)

Columns/Departments: Women on the Move; Missions Hall of Fame; Mind; 250-650 wds. Query. No payment.

Tips: "Our goal is to encourage educated decision-making and harmony in women's lives, whether they are in or out of the workplace."

THE HANDMAIDEN, PO Box 76, Ben Lomond CA 95005. Toll-free (800)967-7377. (831)336-5118. Fax (831)336-8882. E-mail: czell@conciliarpress.com, or vhnieuwsma@prodigy .com. Website: www.conciliarpress.com. Antiochian Orthodox Archdiocese of North America. Virginia Nieuwsma & Carla Zell, co-eds. For women serving God within the Eastern Orthodox tradition. Quarterly jour.; 64 pgs.; circ. 3,000. Subscription $16.50. 5% unsolicited freelance; 95% assigned. Query; e-query OK. **PAYS IN COPIES/SUBSCRIPTION.** Articles 1,000-2,000 wds. (8/yr.). Responds in 6-8 wks. Seasonal 6 mos. ahead. Accepts reprints (tell when/where appeared). Prefers hard copy or e-mail submissions (copied into message). Uses some sidebars. Prefers NKJV. Guidelines (also by e-mail)/theme list; copy for 7x10 SAE/4 stamps. (No ads)

Poetry: Donna Farley, poetry ed. Accepts 4-8/yr. Free verse, light verse, traditional. Submit max. 3 poems.

Columns/Departments: Heroines of the Faith (lives of women saints within Orthodox tradition), 1,000-2,000 wds.

Tips: "Most open to theme features, sidebars, and poetry."

+HEART & SOUL, One N. Charles St., 25th Fl., Baltimore MD 21202. (410)576-9199. Fax (410)-576-8298. E-mail: heartandsoul@vanguarde.com. Website: www.heartandsoul.com. Secular. Corynne Corbett, ed-in-chief. The African American woman's ultimate guide to total well-being (body, mind, and spirit). Bimonthly mag.; circ. 300,000. Subscription $16.97. Open to unsolicited freelance. Query preferred. Pays on acceptance. Articles 800-1,500 wds. (Ads) Incomplete topical listings.

HEARTS AT HOME, 900 W. College Ave., Normal IL 61761. (309)888-6667. Fax (309)888-4525. E-mail: hearts@hearts-at-home.org. Website: www.hearts-at-home.org. Connected to annual conferences by the same name (held in Normal IL, Lansing MI, and Rochester MN). Rachel Kitson, ed-in-chief. To encourage and educate mothers at home. Bimonthly mag.; 24 pgs.; circ. 1,500. Subscription $10. 30-40% unsolicited freelance; 60-70% assigned. Complete ms by mail or e-mail; e-query OK. **PAYS 5 COPIES** for one-time rts. Articles 350-900 wds. (40-50/yr.); devotionals to 750 wds.; book reviews 500 wds. Responds in 2 wks. Seasonal 3 mos. ahead. Accepts reprints (tell when/where appeared). Prefers e-mail submissions (attached Word file to mag@hearts-at-home.org). No kill fee. Some sidebars. Any Bible version. Guidelines/theme list (also by e-mail/Website); copy $2/6x9 SAE/2 stamps. (No ads)

Poetry: Accepts 5-8/yr. Light verse, traditional; 10-25 lines (to 250 wds.). Submit max. 3 poems.

Fillers: Accepts 100/yr. Anecdotes, cartoons, facts, ideas, party ideas, short humor; 25-100 wds.

Columns/Departments: Accepts 15-20/yr.; Motherhood; Parenting; Marriage; Personal Growth; Spiritual Growth; Family Management; to 750 wds.

Special Needs: Articles that challenge mothers in their growth as a parent; uplift spouses in relationship with each other and children; encourage spiritual growth; educate mothers on networking, finding time for themselves, or overcoming personal challenges; tips on saving time and money; and using personal experiences to better parent kids. Looking for more articles by, for, and about moms at home with older children (preteen and older).

Tips: "Submit a well-written, balanced, positive article which will encourage, educate, and/or entertain our audience. Personal stories of the triumphs and trials of being an at-home mom are preferred. This publication is designed to be by moms and for moms. Please include a short biography to go with your article."

($)HISTORY'S WOMEN, 22 Williams St., Batavia NY 14020. (585)343-2810. Fax (585)343-3245. E-mail: patti@historyswomen.com. Website: www.historyswomen.com. PC Publications. Patti Chadwick, ed. Online magazine highlighting the extraordinary achievements of women throughout history. Weekly e-zine; 20 pgs.; circ. 17,000. Subscription free. 20% unsolicited freelance. E-query/e-submissions only. **PAYS IN COPIES & FREE E-BOOKS** (occasionally pays $10, if budget permits) for 1st, one-time, reprint, or electronic rts. Articles 500-1,000 wds. (20/yr.). Responds in 1-2 wks. Seasonal 3 mos. ahead. Accepts simultaneous submissions & reprints (tell when/where appeared). Prefers e-mail submission (copied into message). Does not use sidebars. Accepts submissions from teens. Guidelines on Website; copy on site archive. (Ads)

Columns/Departments: Buys 10-20/yr. Women to Admire, in these columns: Women of Faith; First Women (pioneers in their field); Social Reformers; Amazing Moms; Women Who Ruled (women rulers); Early America; all 500-1,000 wds., $10. Query or complete ms.

+HOME-BASED MOMS: AUDIOZINE, PO Box 570, Theodore AL 36590-0570. (866)324-2893, ext. 8117. E-mail: melissahowell@mchsi.com. Website: www.homebasedmom.org. Melissa Howell Ministries/Nondenominational. Melissa Howell, founder/ed. Christian audio magazine for stay-at-home moms on the run. Bimonthly audio mag. on CD. Estab. 2005. 50% unsolicited freelance; 50% assigned. Query; phone/e-query OK. **PAYS IN COPIES** for one-time rts. Audio articles. Responds in 3 wks. Seasonal 3 mos. ahead. Accepts simultaneous submissions & reprints (tell when/where appeared). Accepts e-mail submissions (attached as a MP3 audio file). Any Bible version. Accepts submissions from children & teens. Guidelines (also by e-mail/Website); copy for 7x10 SAE/$1.42 postage. (No ads)

Poetry: Accepts 1-2/yr. Avant-garde, free verse, haiku, traditional, 6-12 lines. Submit max. 6 poems.

Fillers: Accepts 20-30/yr. Anecdotes, facts, ideas, jokes, kid quotes, party ideas, prayers, prose, quizzes, short humor, tips. Query for length.

Columns/Departments: Accepts 6/yr. Getting to Know Your Fellow Home-based Moms (short story about your life as a stay-at-home mom); In the Kitchen with_____ (easy, affordable recipes). Query.

Tips: "Everything needs to be slanted toward busy, stay-at-home moms. At this time all areas of HBM are open to freelancers. Especially open to stay-at-home moms who are also writers. The best way to break in is to query by e-mail and be patient with replies. Also must be open to learning how to submit audio files."

$HORIZONS, 100 Witherspoon St., Louisville KY 40202-1396. (502)569-5897. Fax (502)569-8085. E-mail: yhileman@ctr.pcusa.org. Website: www.pcusa.org/horizons. Presbyterian Church (USA). Presbyterian Women. Yvonne Hileman, asst. ed. Justice issues and spiritual life for Presbyterian women. Bimonthly mag. & annual Bible study; 40 pgs.; circ. 20,000. Subscription $18. 10% unsolicited freelance; 90% assigned. Query; fax/e-query OK. Pays

$50-125/printed pg. on acceptance for 1st rts. Articles 600-1,800 wds. (10/yr.) & fiction 1,200-1,800 wds. (5/yr.); book reviews 100 wds. ($25). Seasonal 6 mos. ahead. Accepts simultaneous submissions & reprints (tell when/where appeared). Accepts requested ms on disk or by e-mail (attached file or copied into message). Kill fee. Regularly uses sidebars. Prefers NRSV. Guidelines/theme list (also by e-mail/Website); copy $4. (No ads)

Poetry: Buys 5/yr. All types; $50-100. Submit max. 5 poems.

Fillers: Cartoons, church-related graphics; $50.

Tips: "Most open to devotionals, mission stories, justice and peace issues. Writer should be familiar with constituency of Presbyterian women and life in the Presbyterian Church (USA)."

**This periodical was #11 on the 2005 Top 50 Christian Publishers list (#10 in 2004, #8 in 2003, #15 in 2002).

+INSPIRED MOMS.COM, PO Box 293477, Lewisville TX 75077. (972)979-7438. E-mail: editor@ inspiredmoms.com. Website: www.inspiredmoms.com. Inspired Life Ministries, Inc. Wendy Stewart-Hamilton, site ed. Monthly e-zine. Open to unsolicited freelance. Complete ms/bio; e-query OK. **PAYS WITH BIOGRAPHY, BYLINE, AND PROMOTION RESOURCES FOR MOMS.** Articles to 1,200 wds.; devotionals to 500 wds. Responds in 2-3 wks. Guidelines/theme list on Website.

Tips: "Devotionals must be written to themes, and feature articles are theme-based."

$INSPIRIT MAGAZINE, 5101 N. Francisco Ave., Chicago IL 60625. (773)907-3332. Fax (773)784-1128. E-mail: wmc@covchurch.org. Website: www.covchurch.org./cov/cwm. Dept. of Women's Ministries. Ruth Hill, ed-in-chief. To inform and inspire women across the Covenant denomination. Quarterly mag.; 50 pgs.; circ. 2,500. Subscription $10. 40% unsolicited freelance; 60% assigned. Complete ms/cover letter; phone/fax/e-query OK. Pays $20-35 on publication. Articles about 800 wds. (36/yr.); fiction 750-800 wds. (4/yr.). Seasonal 2.5 mos. ahead. Accepts simultaneous submissions & reprints (tell when/where appeared). Accepts e-mail submissions (attached file). Uses some sidebars. Prefers TNIV or NIV. Guidelines/theme list (also by e-mail); copy for 6x9 SAE & $1. (Ads)

Tips: "Follow themes printed in issues and guidelines posted on our Website."

$JOURNEY: A Woman's Guide to Intimacy with God, One Lifeway Plaza, Nashville TN 37234-0175. (615)251-5659. Fax (615)277-8272. E-mail: journey@lifeway.com. Website: www.lifeway.com. LifeWay Christian Resources. Pamela Nixon, lead ed.; Tammy Drolsum, ed. Devotional magazine for women 30-50 years old. Monthly mag.; 44 pgs.; circ. 215,000. 15% unsolicited freelance; 85% staff or assigned. Subscription $22.05. Query/clips or complete ms/cover letter; no phone/fax/e-query or e-submissions. Pays $50-100 on acceptance for all rts. Articles 350-1,000 wds. (10-12/yr.). Responds in 8 wks. Seasonal 6-7 mos. ahead. Regularly uses sidebars. Prefers HCSB. Accepts requested ms on disk. Guidelines; copy for 6x9 SAE/2 stamps.

Special Needs: Strong feature articles, 750-1,000 words (including sidebars) on topics of interest to women 30-50 years old ranging from practical applications of faith to spiritual growth, as well as profiles of Christian women in leadership positions.

Tips: "Most open to feature articles that are well-written with a thorough understanding of our magazine and target audience. Strong sample devotionals written in *Journey* style may be considered for assignment of a devotional."

JUST BETWEEN US, 777 S. Barker Rd., Brookfield WI 53045. Toll-free (800)260-3342. (262)786-6478. Fax (262)796-5752. E-mail: jbu@elmbrook.org. Website: www.just betweenus.org. Elmbrook Church, Inc. Shelly Esser, ed. Ideas, encouragement, and resources for wives of evangelical ministers and women in leadership. Quarterly mag.; 32 pgs.; circ. 8,000. Subscription $19.95. 85% unsolicited freelance; 15% assigned. Query; phone/fax/ e-query OK. **NO PAYMENT** for one-time rts. Articles 250-500 wds. or 1,200-1,500 wds.

(50/yr.). Responds in 8 wks. Accepts simultaneous submissions & reprints. Regularly uses sidebars. Prefers NIV. Guidelines/theme list (also by e-mail/Website); copy $4/9x12 SAE. (Ads)

Fillers: Accepts 15/yr. Anecdotes, cartoons, ideas, prayers, quotes, short humor; 50-250 wds.

Columns/Departments: Accepts 12/yr. Hospitality; Keeping Your Kids Christian; Women's Ministry (program ideas); all 700-900 wds.

Tips: "Most open to feature articles addressing the unique needs of women in leadership (Bible-study leaders, women's ministry directors, pastor's wives, missionary wives, etc.). Some of these needs would include relationship with God, staff, leadership skills, ministry how-tos, balancing ministry and family, and marriage. The best way to break in is to contact the editor directly. Follow themes."

KEEPING HEARTS & HOME, W9109 Holmes Junction Rd., Beecher WI 54156. E-mail: articles@keepinghearts.org. Website: www.keepinghearts.org. Jocelyn Zichterman, ed/pub.; Sarah Burton, asst. ed. Uplifting and heart-warming; to encourage and inspire women in every stage of life. Quarterly mag.; 30 pgs. Subscription $14. Estab. 2003. Open to freelance. Complete ms by e-mail. **NO PAYMENT.** Articles 1,000-1,200 wds. Prefers e-mail submissions. Guidelines on Website. Incomplete topical listings. (Ads)

Fillers: Accepts games, household tips, party plans, prayers, short humor.

Columns/Departments: Has several columns.

Tips: "We prefer testimony-type articles—not necessarily instructional."

LIFE TOOLS FOR WOMEN: Online Women's Lifestyle Magazine, 40 Macewan Park Rise, N.W., Calgary AB T3K 3Z9, Canada. (403)295-1932. Fax (403)291-2515. E-mail: editor@life toolsforwomen.com. Website: www.lifetoolsforwomen.com. Judy Rushfeldt, ed. Equipping women to reach their potential. Monthly online mag. Monthly page views: 45,000. Articles 500-1,200 wds. **NO PAYMENT.** Provides a byline and up to 50-word bio, including e-mail & Website link. Prefers e-query & e-submission (attached file). Guidelines on Website.

$THE LINK & VISITOR, 1-315 Lonsdale Rd., Toronto ON M4V 1X3, Canada. (416)544-8550. E-mail: linkvis@baptistwomen.com. Website: www.baptistwomen.com. Baptist Women of Ontario and Quebec. Esther Barnes, ed. A positive, practical Baptist magazine for Canadian women who want to reach others for Christ. Bimonthly mag.; 24 pgs.; circ. 4,000. Subscription $16 Cdn., $16 U.S. 15% unsolicited freelance; 85% assigned. Complete ms; e-query OK. Pays .06-.10/wd. Cdn., on publication for one-time or simultaneous rts.; some work-for-hire. Articles 750-1,500 wds. (30/yr.). Responds in 16 wks. Seasonal 3 mos. ahead. Accepts simultaneous submissions & reprints (tell when/where appeared). Requires e-mail submission (copied into message). No kill fee. Uses some sidebars. Prefers NIV (inclusive language), NRSV, NLT. Guidelines/theme list on Website; copy for 9x12 SAE/.90 Cdn. postage. (Ads—limited/Canadian)

Poetry: Buys 3/yr. Free verse; 12-32 lines; $10-20. Submit max. 3 poems.

Tips: "Feature writers who know our magazine and our readers will know what topics and types of stories we are looking for. Canadian writers only, please."

LUTHERAN WOMAN'S QUARTERLY, 3121 Chelsea Ct., South Bend IN 46614-2207. Phone/fax (574)291-8297. E-mail: djs3121@yahoo.com, or lwml@lwml.org. Website: www.lwml .org. Lutheran Women's Missionary League. Donna Streufert, ed-in-chief. For women of the Lutheran Church—Missouri Synod. Quarterly mag.; 44 pgs.; circ. 200,000. Subscription $4.50. 25% unsolicited freelance; 75% assigned. Complete ms/cover letter. **NO PAYMENT.** Not copyrighted. Articles 750-1,200 wds. (4/yr.); fiction 750-1,200 wds. (4/yr.). Responds in 2 wks. Seasonal 5 mos. ahead. Regularly uses sidebars. Prefers NIV. Guidelines/theme list (also by e-mail); no copy.

Tips: "Most open to articles. Must reflect the Missouri Synod teachings. Most of our writers are from the denomination. We set themes two years ahead. Contact us for themes and guidelines."

MAKING WAVES, 47 Queen's Park Cr. E., Toronto ON M5S 2C3, Canada. (416)929-5184. Fax (416)929-4064. E-mail: barfoot@wicc.org. Website: www.wicc.org. Women's Inter-Church Council of Canada. Karen Hincke, pub. A Christian feminist journal committed to addressing issues related to women, justice, and theology from an ecumenical faith perspective. Bimonthly mag.; circ. 4,000. Subscription $16. Open to unsolicited freelance. Incomplete topical listings. (Ads)

> **Tips:** "We are connected to a wider network of women and men working to free church and society from racism, ageism, and sexism, and from the teachings and practices that discriminate against women."

$MELODY OF THE HEART E-ZINE: Reconciling Hearts; Offering Hope, 8409 S. Elder Glenwood St., Broken Arrow OK 74011-8286. (918)451-4017. Cell (918)695-4528. E-mail: editor1@epistleworks.com (do not e-mail directly; use submission form at site). Website: http://epistleworks.com/HeartMelody. Please: No fax or postal submissions. Published by EpistleWorks Creations. JoAnn Reno Wray, owner, ed./pub. For women, 30-60+ yrs. Vivid writing with scriptural accuracy to bring a practical and joyful approach to life. Quarterly e-zine; 130,000 hits a month. Open to freelance. Query only (using only the online form provided on Website). Pays $15-20 for articles, $20-25 for fiction, on publication for 1st or reprint electronic rts. Contracts issued for work used (archived for one issue only/3 mos.; exclusive for 1 month then may market elsewhere). Articles 500-900 wds.; short fiction 600-900 wds. Tries to respond but normally can't unless the queries meet editorial needs. Seasonal 6 mos. ahead. Guidelines/theme list/submission form on Website. PDF guidelines available online to download.

> **Poetry:** Music of the Poet Department—poems on theme of targeted issue. Buys 8+/yr.; 4-24 lines. Submit max. 2 poems; theme-related. Wait for response before submitting more. Complete ms. Pays $6.00-8.50. First or one-time electronic rts. "Avoid overused rhymes; try forms other than iambic pentameter; use words to paint vivid images and scenes to help readers see scriptural truths. More poetry is rejected than any other type of writing due to telegraphed end rhymes, or overused, tired ideas or inappropriate content. Use online form for poetry submissions."

> **Fillers:** Buys 15-30 fillers/year. Short humor, news, kids sayings, anecdotes, husband/wife shorts, animal antics, interesting facts, health info, household tips, devotions. Needs more of these. Send complete ms via online form. Under 200 wds.; prefers under 150. Pays $3-10.

> **Columns/Departments:** Life Steps (illustrates the work of God in your life in some way), 500-900 wds.; How Do I? (how-to), 500-750 wds.; Just Do It! (what you do that ministers God's love to others), 500-900 wds.; It's the Little Things (lessons learned or insights gained from the seemingly insignificant), 500-750 wds.; Teen Quest (teen interest), 500-750 wds.; Crafting Love (instructions for craft projects), 900 wds.; Cooking with Taste (recipes), 900 wds. Book Reviews (new and about to be released books), 350-800 wds. New and needed: Quiet Heart Profiles (true stories of those in community who are quietly doing work of the Lord). Query only via online form. Pays $15-25. Open to new column proposals from writers. If accepted, they become staff columnists. Must include 2 sample columns and commit to 4/year. Use online form. Pays $30 per column.

> **Tips:** "Biggest lack in quality submissions is in Fiction Fountain (short fiction), Cook's Corner (recipes and their stories),Crafting Love (crafts), and the new Quiet Heart Profiles. Being previously unpublished is no hindrance to being published here. However, over 65% of submissions miss the mark due to failure to study guidelines and read content online. Follow guidelines to the best of your ability. If you have questions, then send them by e-mail using the form on the Connections Page (http://epistleworks.com/HeartMelody/INFO/connections.html). Must include a short bio with your query or submission. Target your submission or queries to a specific issue's theme (choose from form) and to a specific

department. Be patient; I work alone here. Never submit by postal mail; always use the form."

$MOMSENSE, 2370 S. Trenton Way, Denver CO 80231. (303)733-5353. Fax (303)733-5770. E-mail: MOMsense@mops.org. Website: www.mops.org. MOPS Intl., Inc. (Mothers of Preschoolers). Elizabeth Jusino, ed. Nurtures mothers of preschoolers from a Christian perspective with articles that both inform and inspire on issues relating to womanhood and motherhood. Bimonthly mag.; 24 pgs.; circ. 100,000. Subscription $19.95. 20% unsolicited freelance; 30% assigned. Query; fax/e-query OK. Pays .15/wd. on publication for 1st rts. Articles 600-1,000 wds. (15/yr.). Responds in 6-8 wks. Seasonal 6 mos. ahead. Accepts simultaneous submissions & reprints (tell when/where appeared). Prefers requested ms by e-mail (attached file or copied into message). Kill fee 10%. Uses some sidebars. Prefers NIV. Guidelines/theme list (also by e-mail); copy for 9x12 SAE. (No ads)

  Contest: Sponsors several contests per year for writing and photography. Check Website for details on current contests.

  Tips: "Most open to theme-specific features. Writers are more seriously considered if they are a mother with some connection to MOPS (but not required). Looking for original content ideas that appeal to Christian and non-Christian readers."

  **2001 EPA Award of Merit—Most Improved Publication.

#PRAISE MAGAZINE (PRA!SE), PO Box 66434, Baltimore MD 21239-6434. E-mail: submissions@praisemagazine.com. Website: www.praisemagazine.com. Geared toward African American women. Submit to The Editor. Bimonthly mag. Open to freelance. Complete ms; e-query OK. **NO PAYMENT** for one-time rts. (Articles may be held for use in future issues.) Articles 500-1,500 wds.; book reviews (fiction & nonfiction). Accepts e-mail submissions (copied into message). Guidelines by e-mail; themes on Website.

  Poetry: Accepts poetry.

  Special Needs: Skin, hair, fashion design/trends/tips, health advice, home decorating, recipes. Movie & music reviews.

  Tips: "Relax. Be warm and personal. Think about what information the readers can take away with them. How can this help create balance in their life?"

+PRECIOUS TIMES, 3857 Birch St., Newport Beach CA 92660-2660. Toll-free (800)299-0696. (714)564-3949. E-mail: editor@precioustimesmag.com. Website: www.precious timesmag.com. Independent. Pamela Caldwell, sr. ed. To help Black women (ages 20-60) grow in their relationship with God, self, and others; biblical, but not preachy. Quarterly mag.; 76 pgs.; circ. 350,000. Subscription $18. 90% unsolicited freelance; 10% assigned. Complete ms; e-query OK. **PAYS 5 COPIES** for 1st rts. Personal testimonies, 1,800-2,000 wds.; everyday-life information, 1,200-2,400 wds.; health/fitness/beauty, 1,200 wds.; celebrity/personality interviews 1,800-2,400 wds.; book reviews 250-300 wds.; music reviews, 200-500 wds; fiction, 2,400-3,200. (20 articles/yr.; 4 fiction). Responds in 12 wks. Seasonal 10 mos. ahead. Accepts simultaneous submissions & reprints (tell when/where appeared). Requires e-mail submissions (attached or copied into message in Word only). Uses some sidebars. Prefers NIV. Accepts submissions from teens. Guidelines (also by e-mail/Website); copy $5/9x12 SAE. (Ads)

  Columns/Departments: Business, Health, Beauty, Finance; 600 wds.

  Tips: "Provide practical theology for contemporary issues. All articles should have a personal perspective, be relevant, and use real life anecdotes. We prefer a Black woman's perspective on life issues."

P31 WOMAN, 616-G Matthews-Mint Hill Rd., Matthews NC 28105. (704)849-2270. Fax (704)849-7267. E-mail: editor@proverbs31.org. Website: www.proverbs31.org. Proverbs 31 Ministries. Glynnis Whitwer, ed. Seeks to offer a godly woman's perspective on life. Monthly mag.; 16 pgs.; circ. 10,000. Subscription for donation. 50% unsolicited freelance;

50% assigned. Complete ms; e-query OK. **PAYS IN COPIES** for one-time rts. Not copyrighted. Articles 200-1,000 wds. (40/yr.). Responds in 4-6 wks. Seasonal 3 mos. ahead. Accepts simultaneous submissions & reprints (tell when/where appeared). Prefers accepted ms by e-mail (attached file or copied into message). Uses some sidebars. Prefers NIV. Guidelines/theme list (also on Website); copy on Website. (No ads)

   Fillers: Accepts 12/yr. Ideas, party ideas, prose; to 100 wds.

   Tips: "Looking for articles that encourage women and offer practical advice as well."

REFLECTIONS, 5351 N.W. 11th St., Lauderhill FL 33313-6406. (954)587-0129. E-mail: thesilentwoman2@aol.com. Ellen Waldron, pub. Good news and inspiration for all ages. Quarterly newsletter; 20+ pgs. Subscription $15. 90% unsolicited freelance; 10% assigned. Complete ms/cover letter. **PAYS 4 COPIES.** Not copyrighted. Articles 400 wds. (6/yr.); fiction 1,000 wds. (6/yr.). Responds in 6-8 wks. Seasonal 2 mos. ahead. Accepts e-mail submissions. Uses some sidebars. Guidelines/theme list; copy for $2/10x13 SAE/$1.42 postage (mark "Media Mail"). (Ads)

   Poetry: Accepts 10/yr. Free verse, haiku, light verse, traditional; 5-30 lines. Submit max. 5 poems. Poetry to reach those who have suffered abuse and found the Lord.

   Columns/Departments: Accepts 6/yr. Pen Pals Corner (write service families in armed forces); Helpful Hints (ideas to help others), 400 wds.; Joy, Joy, Joy (good news), 400 wds.; Chicklette Gazette (children ages 4-12), 200 wds.; Teen Corner (sharing ideas for 13- to 19-year-olds), 400 wds.; On the Road (travel).

   Tips: "Have an interest in writing; write from the heart. No foul language or anything offensive. Writers must send a notarized release before we can print their work (under 18 years, parent must sign). Fiction is for children or teens."

RIGHT TO THE HEART OF WOMEN E-ZINE, PO Box 6421, Longmont CO 80501. (303)772-2035. Fax (303)678-0260. E-mail: Rebekah@rebekahmontgomery.com. Website: www.righttotheheartofwomen.com. Rebekah Montgomery, ed. Encouragement and helps for women in ministry. Bimonthly online e-zine; 20 pgs.; circ. 4,000. Subscription free. 10% unsolicited freelance; 90% assigned. Query; e-query OK. **NO PAYMENT** for nonexclusive rts. Articles 100-300 wds. (20/yr.); book reviews 100 wds. Responds in 2 wks. Seasonal 4 mos. ahead. Accepts simultaneous submissions & reprints (tell when/where appeared). Requires accepted mss by e-mail (copied into message). Does not use sidebars. No guidelines; copy on Website. (Ads)

   Fillers: Accepts 12/yr. Anecdotes, ideas, party ideas, prayers, quotes; 50-200 wds.

   Columns/Departments: Accepts 10/yr. Women Bible Teachers; Profiles of Women in Ministry; Women's Ministry Tips; Author's and Speaker's Tips; 100 wds. Query.

   Special Needs: Book reviews must be in first person, by the author. Looking for women's ministry event ideas.

   Tips: "For free subscription, subscribe at Website above; also view e-zine. We want to hear from those involved in women's ministry or leadership. Also accepts manuscripts from AWSAs (see www.awsawomen.com). Query with your ideas."

($)SHALOM BAYIT: Peace in the Home, PO Box 23, West Charleston VT 05872. E-mail: puritanstore@aol.com. Website: www.thepuritanlight.com. The Puritan Light Ministry. Sharon White, ed. For old-fashioned keepers at home. Quarterly mag.; 32 pgs. Subscription $12. 40% unsolicited freelance; 30% assigned. Complete ms/cover letter; e-query OK (no attachments). Pays $10 for assigned articles only; copy only for unsolicited. Articles 400-1,500 wds. (16/yr.). Responds in 2 mos. Seasonal 6 mos. ahead. No simultaneous submissions or reprints. Accepts e-mail submissions (copied into message). Does not use sidebars. Accepts submissions from children & teens. Guidelines on Website; copy $3. (Ads)

   Columns/Departments: Memories of Grandmother (nostalgic stories of grandmother), 500-1,000 wds.; Dear Daughter (letter to a future keeper at home), 800 wds.; Etiquette (share how ladies behaved long ago), 400 wds.; Education at Home (helpful and thrifty tips for homeschooling your children), 500 wds.; Fashion and Home (stories and ideas for homemaking and modest apparel), 300-600 wds. Complete ms.

Tips: "The magazine is geared to very old-fashioned homemakers who strive to be devoutly religious, gentle-spirited mothers, and loving wives. The editor owns and operates a country store in rural Vermont. We focus on home business, home schooling, tender mothering, peaceful/lifelong marriage, and old-fashioned living. Order a sample issue, study it, consider if this is a good fit for your style of writing, then submit your work. You must be willing to make changes quickly and professionally and alter your work to meet our publishing goals. Be patient waiting for responses. If you are looking for assignments, submit constantly and regularly. If we continue to print your work, we will eventually begin to trust you and assign paid work."

SHARE, 10 W. 71st St., New York NY 10023-4201. (212)877-3041. Fax (212)724-5923. E-mail: CDofANatl@aol.com. Website: www.catholicdaughters.org. Catholic Daughters of the Americas. Peggy O'Brien, exec. dir.; submit to Peggy Eastman, ed. For Catholic women. Quarterly mag.; circ. 100,000. Free with membership. Most articles come from membership, but is open. **NO PAYMENT.** Buys color photos & covers. Guidelines/copy. Not in topical listings. (Ads)

Tips: "We use very little freelance material unless it is written by Catholic Daughters."

$SIMPLE JOY. E-mail: JeanAnn@simplejoy.org. Website: www.simplejoy.org. Jean Ann Duckworth, pub.; submit to The Editor. For women (target age 30-55) interested in a simpler way of life; secular. Monthly online mag. Open to freelance. Query first; e-query OK (queries@simplejoy.org). Pays $10 honorarium on publication for articles to 1,000 wds. (72-120/yr.); within 60 days of publication; for one-time rts. Seasonal 4 mos. ahead. Prefers e-mail (attached file in Word format). Guidelines by e-mail (guidelines@simple joy.org). Upcoming needs listed on Website. Incomplete topical listings.

Columns/Departments: Simple Home; Simple Celebrations; Simple Traditions; Joy for Couples; Joy with Children; Simple Garden; Simple Cooking; all to 1,000 wds. Recipes; no payment.

Special Needs: Focuses on 4 specific areas: reducing stress, enhancing joy, simplifying life, and building/strengthening relationships.

Tips: "Keep in mind our Three Rules of Simple Joy as you write your articles. (See Website.)"

+SISTERS IN THE LORD MAGAZINE. E-mail: submissions@sistersinthelord.org. Website: www.sistersinthelord.org/magazine/submit_step2.html. Dian Moore, ed-in-chief (dian@ sistersinthelord.org). Women helping women come to Christ. Monthly mag. Estab. 2003. Open to unsolicited freelance. Complete ms by e-mail (attached file). **NO PAYMENT** for one-time rts. Articles 200-2,000 wds. Responds in 1 wk. Guidelines on Website. Incomplete topical listings.

Poetry: Accepts avant-garde, haiku, free verse, light verse, traditional; to 1,000 wds. Submit max. 3 poems.

Columns/Departments: A Man's Viewpoint (humorous, informative, encouraging, enlightening), 500-2,000 wds.; And Then, God Laughed (humor), 500-2,000 wds.; Answered Prayers (true), 500-1,500 wds.; Deliver Us from Darkness (overcoming various types of abuse), 500-2,000 wds.; Food for the Soul (food & occasions to enjoy food), 200-1,000 wds., recipes to 300 wds.; Heavenly Hindsight (lessons learned from past events), 500-1,500 wds.; Single Parents 500-2,000 wds.; Spitfire (controversial issues) 500-2,000 wds. See Website for additional departments and details.

$SPIRITLED WOMAN, 600 Rinehart Rd., Lake Mary FL 32746. (407)333-0600. Fax (407)333-7133. E-mail: spiritledwoman@strang.com. Website: www.spiritledwoman.com. Strang Communications. Brenda J. Davis, ed. To call women, ages 20-60, into intimate fellowship with God so He can empower them to fulfill His purpose for their lives. Bimonthly mag.; 100 pgs.; circ. 100,000. Subscription $17.95. 1% unsolicited freelance; 99% assigned. Query (limit to 500 wds.); e-query OK. Pays to $300 ($50 for humor, $75 for testimonies) on publication for 1st and all electronic rts. Articles 1,200-2,000 wds. Responds in 18-26 wks. No simultaneous submissions. Guidelines (also by e-mail); copy. (Ads)

Columns/Departments: Testimonies; Final Fun (funny stories or embarrassing moments, to 200 wds.); cartoons; $25-50.

Tips: "Most of our articles are commissioned. Mainly we want high-impact feature articles that depict a practical and spiritual application of scriptural teachings. Need brief testimonies of 300 words or less (open to all); profiles of women in ministry. Articles need to deal with the heart issues that hold a woman back. Also humorous anecdotes and book excerpts."

*TAPESTRY: A Woman's Guide to Intimacy with God, 4201 N. Peachtree Rd., Atlanta GA 30341. (770)458-9300. Fax (770)454-9313. E-mail: pubsinfo@walkthru.org. Website: www.walkthru.org. Walk Thru the Bible. Monthly mag. Requires NIV.

**2005 Award of Merit—Devotional; 2004 EPA Award of Excellence—Christian Ministries.

$TODAY'S CHRISTIAN WOMAN, 465 Gundersen Dr., Carol Stream IL 60188-2498. (630)260-6200. Fax (630)260-0114. E-mail: TCWedit@christianitytoday.com. Website: www.Todays ChristianWoman.com. Christianity Today Intl. Jane Johnson Struck, ed.; submit to Lisa Cockrel, assoc. ed. To help Christian women (20-49 yrs.) grow in their relationship to God by providing practical, biblical perspectives on marriage, sex, parenting, work, health, friendship, single life, and self. Bimonthly mag.; 80-150 pgs.; circ. 250,000. Subscription $17.95. 25% unsolicited freelance; 75% assigned. Query only; fax/e-query OK. Pays .20/published wd. on publication (on acceptance for assignments) for 1st rts. Articles 1,000-1,800 wds. (6-12/yr.); no fiction. Responds in 8 wks. Seasonal 6 mos. ahead. Accepts reprints (tell when/where appeared); no simultaneous submissions. Accepts e-mail submission (copied into message). Regularly uses sidebars. Prefers NIV. Guidelines; copy $5. (Ads)

Columns/Departments: Camerin Courtney, ed. of My Story. Buys 6/yr. My Story (dramatic story of overcoming a difficult situation), 1,500 wds., $300. Faith@Work (how you shared faith in the marketplace), 300 wds., $25. Reader's Picks (personal book or CD review), 200 wds.

Special Needs: Articles slanted for mature Christians that deal with spiritual life topics; short humor pieces.

Tips: "Break in by submitting to our reader-solicited questions or My Story. Make sure your writing has a fresh approach to a relational topic and that it has a personal tone and anecdotal approach. Please query first."

**The #3 Best-selling Magazine in Christian retail stores.

+A VIRTUOUS WOMAN, 594 Ivy Hill, Harlan KY 40831. E-mail: melissaringstaff@avirtuous woman.org. Website: www.avirtuouswoman.org. Melissa Ringstaff, dir. Online newsletter for women based on Proverbs 31. Monthly e-newsletter; circ. 12,000 online. Looking for practical articles of interest to women—homemaking, mothering, financial, working moms, health (vegetarian), faith, devotionals. Open to freelance. Not included in topical listings.

$WOMAN'S TOUCH, 1445 N. Boonville Ave., Springfield MO 65802-1894. (417)862-2781. Fax (417)862-0503. E-mail: womanstouch@ag.org. Website: www.ag.org/womanstouch. Assemblies of God Women's Ministries Dept. Darla J. Knoth, mng. ed. Inspirational magazine for women. Bimonthly mag.; 36 pgs.; circ. 16,000. Subscription $9.95. 20% unsolicited freelance; 80% assigned. Query only; fax/e-query OK. Pays $20-35 (.06/wd) on publication for one-time and electronic rts. Articles 500-800 wds. (20/yr.). Responds in 13 wks. Seasonal 10 mos. ahead. Accepts simultaneous submissions & reprints (tell when/where appeared). Accepts e-mail submission. Kill fee. Regularly uses sidebars. Prefers NIV. Guidelines/theme list (also by e-mail); copy for 9x12 SAE/3 stamps. (No ads)

Columns/Departments: Buys 30/yr. The Single Woman (never married, widowed, divorced), 400 wds.; Family Matters (single or married moms); I Still Do! (marriage), 400 wds.; $10-40.

Tips: "Request guidelines and theme list for guidance on types of articles needed." **2005 EPA Award of Merit—General; 2003 EPA Award of Excellence—Most Improved Publication.

$WOMEN ALIVE!, PO Box 480052, Kansas City MO 64148. Phone/fax (913)402-1369. E-mail: ahinthorn@kc.rr.com. Website: www.womenalivemagazine.org. Aletha Hinthorn, ed. To encourage women to live holy lives by applying Scripture to their daily lives. Bimonthly mag.; 20 pgs.; circ. 5,000-6,000. Subscription $13.95. 50% unsolicited freelance; 0% assigned. Complete ms/no cover letter; no phone/fax query. Pays $25-50 on publication for 1st or reprint rts. Articles 300-1,800 wds. (7/yr.). Responds in 4-6 wks. Seasonal 4 mos. ahead. Accepts reprints. Uses some sidebars. No disk. Prefers KJV, NIV. Guidelines/theme list (also by e-mail); copy for 9x12 SAE/4 stamps. (No ads)

Fillers: Buys 0-1/yr. Cartoons, jokes, short humor.

Tips: "We look for articles that draw women into a deeper spiritual life—articles on surrender, prayer, Bible study—yet written with personal illustrations."

WOMEN OF THE CROSS, 920 Sweetgum Creek, Plano TX 75023. (972)517-8553. E-mail: info@womenofthecross.com. Website: www.womenofthecross.com. Mission Wares.com. Greg Paskal, content mngr. (greg@gregpaskal.com). Encouraging women in their walk with the Lord; strong emphasis on discipleship and relationship. Online community. 50% unsolicited freelance. Complete ms by e-mail; e-query OK. **NO PAYMENT.** Articles 500-1,500 wds. (10/yr.). Responds in 2-4 wks. Seasonal 3 mos. ahead. Accepts simultaneous submissions; no reprints. Prefers e-mail submissions (attached or copied into message). Uses some sidebars. Prefers NIV, NKJV, NASB. Accepts submissions from teens. Guidelines by e-mail. (No ads)

Poetry: Accepts 2/yr. Avant-garde, free verse, haiku, or light verse; 50-250 lines. Submit max. 1 poem.

Columns/Departments: Accepts 10/yr. Features (Christian living, encouragement); Article (to other women); all 500-1,500 wds.

Special Needs: Personal stories of growing in the Lord; faith-stretching stories about international adoption.

Tips: "Appropriate topics could be first-hand accounts of how God worked in the author's life through a personal or family experience. View online forum for specific topics."

$*WOMEN'S FAITH & SPIRIT, 125 Park Ave., New York NY 10017. Meredith Corp. Pamela Guthrie O'Brien, ed. Explores what faith means to the reader and how it affects daily life and the way women view the world. Monthly mag.; 112 pgs.; circ. 350,000. No information on openness to freelance. Not included in topical listings. No questionnaire returned.

WOMEN'S MINISTRY MAGAZINE, 4319 S. National Ave., #303, Springfield MO 65810-2607. (417)888-2067. Fax (417)888-2095. E-mail: publisher@womensministry.net. Website: www.womensministry.net. Jennifer and Philip Rothschild, pubs. Where more than 9,000 women's ministry leaders find news, events, and tips for women's ministry in the local church. Online newsletter. Subscription free. Open to freelance. Guidelines by e-mail.

Special Needs: Punchy, practical tips and ideas related to leading effective women's ministry.

WOMEN TODAY MAGAZINE, Box 300, Sta. A, Vancouver BC V6C 2X3, Canada. Toll-free (800)563-1106, ext. 252. (604)514-2000 (no phone calls). Fax (604)514-2002. E-mail: editor@womentodaymagazine.com. Website: www.womentodaymagazine.com. Campus Crusade for Christ, Canada. Karen Schenk, pub.; Claire Colvin, ed. For the professional, pre-seeking woman, 20-60 years; provides quality information that leads into a discussion of spiritual things and a presentation of the gospel. Monthly e-zine; 1.5 million hits/mo.; 60,000 unique visitors/mo. 60% unsolicited freelance; up to 10% assigned. Query; fax/e-query OK. Accepts full ms by e-mail. **NO PAYMENT** for one-time or reprint rts. Articles 300-1,000 wds. (12-24/yr.). Responds in 8-12 wks. Seasonal 2 mos. ahead. Accepts simultaneous submissions & reprints (tell when/where appeared). Prefers e-mail submission (attached). Does not use sidebars. Accepts submissions from teens. Guidelines on Website. (Ads)

> **Columns/Departments:** Columns tend toward how-to; 600-1,000 wds. Beauty & Fashion; Health & Fitness; Food & Cooking; Advice.

> **Tips:** "Beauty/fashion, relationships, and self-esteem are big draws on our site, and we can always use more great content. To break in, make your article approachable to an unchurched audience, avoid Christian jargon, and speak the truth plainly."

WRITERS' MARKETS

$ADVANCED CHRISTIAN WRITER, 9731 N. Fox Glen Dr., #6F, Niles IL 60714-4222. (847)296-3964. Fax (847)296-0754. E-mail: lin@wordprocommunications.com. Website: www.ACWriters.com. American Christian Writers/Reg Forder, Box 110390, Nashville TN 37222. Toll-free (800)21-WRITE. E-mail: ACWriters@aol.com (for samples, advertising, and subscriptions). Lin Johnson, mng. ed. A professional newsletter for published writers. Bimonthly newsletter; 8 pgs.; circ. 500. Subscription $19.95. 60% unsolicited freelance; 0% assigned. Query, correspondence, & mss by e-mail only. Pays $20 on publication for 1st or reprint rts. Articles 500-1,000 wds. (18/yr.). Responds in 4-6 wks. Seasonal 6 mos. ahead. Accepts reprints (tell when/where appeared). Regularly uses sidebars. Requires e-mail submission. Prefers NIV. Guidelines (also by e-mail); copy for #10 SAE/1 stamp. (Ads)

> **Special Needs:** Behind the scenes look at a publishing house (how it started, how editorial operates, current needs, submission procedures); how-to profiles; opinion pieces; time management; workplace issues.

> **Tips:** "We accept articles only from professional, well-published writers and from editors. We need manuscripts about all aspects of being a published freelance writer and how to increase sales and professionalism; on the advanced level; looking for depth beyond the basics."

$AREOPAGUS MAGAZINE (UK). Fax 0870 1346384. E-mail for UK: areopagus@church net.org.uk. Website: www.churchnet.org.uk/areopagus/index.html. Areopagus Publications. Julian Barritt, ed. For amateur and semiprofessional Christian writers, producing both secular and Christian writing. Quarterly mag.; 32 pgs.; circ. 150. Subscription $17 (now on sale in U.S.). 80% unsolicited freelance; 20% assigned. Complete ms/cover letter (if subscriber); e-query OK. Pays 3-7 pounds (or equivalent in dollars) on publication for 1st & electronic rts. Articles 1,800 wds. (40/yr.); fiction 1,800 wds. (15/yr.); book reviews 300 wds. Responds in 2 wks. Seasonal 4 mos. ahead. Accepts e-mail submissions (attached or copied into message). Does not use sidebars. Any Bible version. Guidelines; copy (also on Website) for 9x12 SAE/equivalent of 31 pence for postage. (Ads)

> **Poetry:** Buys 40/yr. Any type; to 60 lines. Pays 3 pounds. Submit max. 5 poems.

> **Fillers:** Accepts 12/yr. Facts, ideas, newsbreaks, prayers, prose, short humor, to 200 wds. No payment.

> **Contest:** Sponsors a quarterly, subscribers-only, writing competition (fiction, nonfiction, or poetry theme) with prizes of 25 pounds.

> **Tips:** "Send an idea with short sample in the first instance. Items are selected by merit from subscribers only. If not accepted, a recommendation for re-submission is given if there is potential." Purchases manuscripts from subscribers only.

AUTHOR-ME.COM. E-mail: ccfictioneditor@aol.com. Website: www.Author-Me.com. Independent. Bruce L. Cook, pub. Endeavors to encourage and nurture new writers in their craft. Accepts freelance. Complete ms. **NO PAYMENT.** No submissions from writers under age 14. Edit manuscripts before submitting. Requires e-mail submissions (attached or copied into message). Guidelines on Website.

> **Poetry:** Submit max. 4 poems.

BEGINNINGS: A Magazine for Novice Writers, PO Box 214, Bayport NY 11705. E-mail: jenineb@optonline.net. Website: www.scbeginnings.com. The only magazine that caters exclusively to the new writer. Jenine Killoran, ed/pub. Triannual mag.; 48 pgs.; circ. 1,500. Subscription $14. 95% unsolicited freelance; 5% assigned. Charges a reading fee of $10 if you send more than one ms or 5 poems at a time. Complete ms/cover letter. **PAYS IN COPIES** for one-time rts. Articles any length (10/yr.) & short stories to 3,000 wds. (27-30/yr.). Responds in 14-16 wks. Accepts simultaneous submissions & reprints (tell when/where appeared). Requested ms by mail only. Uses some sidebars. Guidelines (also by e-mail/Website—www.scbeginnings.com/guidelines.htm); copy for 10x13 SAE/$1.42 postage. (Ads)

> **Poetry:** Freada Dillon, poetry ed. Accepts 60/yr. Any type; reasonable length. Submit only by mail. Submit max. 2 poems.
>
> **Fillers:** Cartoons.
>
> **Special Needs:** Short stories, poetry, or artwork by children. Written work: ages 5-12. Or same material from young adults: 13-19 yrs. Artwork must be on plain, unruled white paper.
>
> **Contest:** Sponsors poetry and short story contests, 4 contests for each season. See Website for current contests and details.
>
> **Tips:** "Read a sample copy! See Website!" Fiction for 5-12 year olds.

$BRADY MAGAZINE, 165 Old Muskoka Rd., Ste. 306, Gravenurst ON P1P 1N3, Canada. (705)687-3963. Fax (705)687-8736. E-mail: submissions@bradymagazine.com. Website: www.bradymagazine.com. Krissy Brady, ed-in-chief; Jennifer Hollowell, submissions ed. Help for writers; set apart from the competition because we back up our advice with action to personally help writers succeed. Monthly e-zine; 60 hits/day. Subscription free. Estab. 2003. 100% unsolicited freelance. Complete ms by e-mail only (use submissions form on Website); no attached files. Pays $10-15 Cdn. on acceptance for 1st, reprint, electronic rts. Articles 1,000-2,500 wds. (24/yr.). Responds in 2 wks. Accepts simultaneous submissions & reprints (tell when/where appeared). Does not use sidebars. Accepts submissions from children & teens if writing related. Guidelines by e-mail/Website. (Ads)

> **Special Needs:** Writing success stories, 200-500 wds.; pays $10.
>
> **Contests:** Plans to sponsor contests in the future.
>
> **Tips:** "We only accept articles for our section The Written Word. Don't just show us your talent in your articles, show us your personality as well."

$BYLINE, Box 5240, Edmond OK 73083-5240. Phone/fax (405)348-5591. E-mail: Mpreston@bylinemag.com. Website: www.BylineMag.com. Secular. Marcia Preston, ed.; Carolyn Wall, fiction ed. Offers practical tips, motivation, and encouragement to freelance writers and poets. Monthly (11X) mag.; 32 pgs.; circ. 3,000+. Subscription $22. 80% unsolicited freelance. Query or complete ms; no phone/fax/e-query. Pays $75 for features; $100 for fiction; less for shorts, on acceptance for 1st rts. Articles 1,500-1,800 wds. (75/yr.); personal essays 700 wds.; fiction 2,000-4,000 wds. (11/yr.). Responds in 6 wks. Seasonal 6 mos. ahead. Accepts simultaneous submissions. No e-mail submissions. Encourages sidebars. Guidelines on Website; copy $5. (Ads)

> **Poetry:** Sandra Soli, poetry ed. Buys 50-100/yr. Any type; to 30 lines; $10. Writing themes only. Submit max. 3 poems.

Fillers: Anecdotes, prose, short humor for humor page; 50-400 wds.; $15-25. Must pertain to writing.

Columns/Departments: Buys 50-60/yr. End Piece (personal essay on writing theme), 700 wds., $35; First Sale accounts, 300 wds., $20; Only When I Laugh (writing humor), short, $15-25. Complete ms.

Contests: Sponsors many year round; details included in magazine, on Website, or send SASE for flier.

Special Needs: Accepts articles only about writing and selling; likes mainstream fiction.

Tips: "All areas except our regular columns are open to freelancers. We get much more fiction than nonfiction. Always looking for instructive, well-written articles."

**This periodical was #48 on the 2004 Top 50 Christian Publishers list.

$CANADIAN WRITER'S JOURNAL, White Mountain Publications, Box 1178, New Liskeard ON P0J 1P0, Canada. Canada-wide toll-free (800)258-5451. (705)647-5424. Fax (705)647-8366. E-mail: cwj@cwj.ca. For submissions: submissions@cwj.ca. Website: www.cwj.ca. Deborah Ranchuk, ed./pub. How-to articles for writers. Bimonthly mag.; 64 pgs.; circ. 350. Subscription $37.45. 75% unsolicited freelance; 15% assigned. Complete ms/cover letter or query; phone/fax/e-query OK. Pays $7.50 Cdn./published pg.(about 450 wds.) on publication (2-9 mos. after acceptance) for one-time rts. Articles 400-2,000 wds. (200/yr.); fiction to 1,200 wds (see contest below); book/music/video reviews 250-500 wds., $7.50. Responds in 9 wks. Seasonal 3 mos. ahead. Accepts simultaneous submissions & reprints (tell when/where appeared). Prefers e-mail submission (copied into message only). Some sidebars. Prefers KJV. Accepts submissions from teens. Guidelines (also by e-mail/Website); copy $8. (Ads)

Poetry: Buys 40-60/yr. All types; to 40 lines; $2-5. Submit max. 10 poems.

Fillers: Buys 15-20/yr. Anecdotes, cartoons, ideas, quotes; 20-200 wds.; $3-5.

Contest: Sponsors semiannual short fiction contest (March 31 and September 30 deadlines); to 1,200 wds. Entry fee $5. Prizes $100, $50, $25. All fiction needs are filled by this contest. E-mail: cwc-calendar@cwj.ca.

Tips: "Send clear, complete, concise how-to-write articles with a sense of humor and usefulness. Read the guidelines and follow them, please."

$CHRISTIAN COMMUNICATOR, 9731 N. Fox Glen Dr., #6F, Niles, IL 60714-4222. (847)296-3964. Fax (847)296-0754. E-mail: lin@wordprocommunications.com. Website: www.ACWriters.com. American Christian Writers/Reg Forder, Box 110390, Nashville TN 37222. Toll-free (800)21-WRITE , fax (615)834-0450; ACWriters@aol.com (for samples, advertising or subscriptions). Lin Johnson, mng. ed. For Christian writers/speakers who want to improve their writing craft and speaking ability, stay informed about writing markets, and be encouraged in their ministries. Monthly (11X) mag.; 20 pgs.; circ. 3,000. Subscription $29.95. 70% unsolicited freelance. Complete ms/queries by e-mail only. Pays $5-10 on publication for 1st or reprint rts. Articles 650-1,000 wds. (22/yr.). Responds in 4-6 wks. Seasonal 6 mos. ahead. Accepts reprints (tell when/where appeared). Requires e-mail submission. Guidelines by e-mail; copy for 9x12 SAE/3 stamps to Nashville address. (Ads)

Poetry: Buys 11/yr. Poems on writing or speaking; $5. Send to Gretchen Sousa, gretloriat@earthlink.net.

Columns/Departments: Buys 80/yr. A Funny Thing Happened on the Way to Becoming a Communicator (humor), 75-300 wds.; Interviews (published authors or editors), 650-1,000 wds.; Speaker's Corner (techniques for speakers), 600-1,000 wds.

Tips: "I need editor profiles and articles for speaker's column."

CHRISTIANWRITERS.COM. Website: www.christianwriters.com. A free online writers' resource community to provide a supportive, family atmosphere where writers may easily access the tools and resources to create, market, and publish their work. Accepts articles, short fiction, poetry, and devotionals. Submit through Website. Guidelines on Website.

$CROSS & QUILL, 1624 Jefferson Davis Rd., Clinton SC 29325-6401. (864)697-6035. E-mail: cwfi@cwfi-online.org. Website: www.cwfi-online.org. Christian Writers Fellowship Intl. Sandy Brooks, ed./pub. For Christian writers, editors, agents, conference directors. Bimonthly newsletter; 16 pgs.; circ. 1,000+. Subscription $25; CWFI membership $40. 75% unsolicited freelance; 25% assigned. Complete ms; query for electronic submissions. Pays honorarium for feature articles on publication for 1st or reprint rts. Articles 800-1,000 wds. (24/yr.); book reviews 100 wds. (pays copies). Responds in 2 mos. Seasonal 6 mos. ahead. Accepts reprints (tell when/where appeared). Regularly uses sidebars. Accepts e-mail submission to CQArticles@cwfi-online.org. Guidelines; copy $2/9x12 SAE/2 stamps. (Ads)

Poetry: Accepts 12/yr. Any type; to 12 lines. Submit max. 3 poems. Must pertain to writing/publishing.

Fillers: Accepts 12/yr. Anecdotes, cartoons, prayers; 25-100 wds. Pays in copies.

Columns/Departments: Accepts 36/yr. Writing Rainbows! (devotional), 500-600 wds.; Writers Helping Writers (how-to), 200-800 wds.; Editor's Roundtable (interview with editor), 200-800 wds.; Tots, Teens & In-Betweens (juvenile market), 200-800 wds.; Business-Wise (business side of writing), 200-800 wds.; Connecting Points (how-to on critique group), 200-800 wds.

Special Needs: Good "meaty" informational articles on children's writing; writing for teens; how-tos on organizing and operating writers' groups; program ideas for groups; and how to organize and run a writer's workshop, conference, or seminar.

Tips: "Most open to informational articles that explain how to improve writing skills, how to keep records, how to organize and run a writers' group. Keep in mind our audience is primarily writers and others associated with Christian publishing. Stick to informational, nuts and bolts type articles, and follow our guidelines."

$EXCHANGE, 1275 Markham Rd., #305, Toronto ON M1H 3A2, Canada. (416)439-4320. Fax (416)439-5089. E-mail: audrey@dorschedit.ca. Website: www.dorschedit.ca. Audrey Dorsch, ed. A forum for Christian writers to share information and ideas. Quarterly newsletter; 8 pgs.; circ. 300. Subscription $19.26 Cdn., $15 U.S. 65% unsolicited freelance; 30% assigned. Complete ms OK (as e-mail attachment; no hard copy); e-query OK. Pays .12 Cdn. & .08 U.S./wd. on publication for one-time rts. Not copyrighted. Articles 400-600 wds. (20/yr.). Responds in 4-6 wks. Accepts reprints (tell when/where appeared). Accepts requested ms on disk, prefers e-mail submission (attached file). Does not use sidebars. Prefers NIV. Guidelines/copy at www.dorschedit.ca/publications.html. (Ads—classified)

Special Needs: Material geared to experienced, professional writers.

Tips: "Take a very deliberate approach to the 'how' of good writing. I get too much for the novice writer. If you submit something an experienced writer will learn from, you face much less competition."

$FELLOWSCRIPT, 333 Hunter's Run, Edmonton AB T6R 2N9, Canada. (780)988-5622. Fax (780)430-0139. E-mail: submissions@inscribe.org. Website: www.inscribe.org. Inscribe Christian Writers' Fellowship. Elsie Montgomery & Janet Sketchley, eds. To provide encouragement, instruction, news, and helpful information to Christians who write. Quarterly newsletter; 32-44 pgs.; circ. 175-250. Subscription $40 (includes membership, if desired). 55% unsolicited freelance; 45% assigned. Complete ms/cover letter; no e-query. Accepts full mss by e-mail. Pays .025/wd. Cdn. for 1st rts., .015 Cdn. for reprint rts., on publication. Articles 400-1,200 wds. (30-50/yr.); book reviews, 400 wds. Responds in 1-4 wks. Seasonal 6 mos. ahead. Accepts simultaneous submissions & reprints (nothing from Internet; tell when/where appeared; pays .015/wd. Cdn.). Prefers requested ms by e-mail (copied into message). No kill fee. Uses some sidebars. Prefers NIV. Guidelines (also by e-mail/Website); copy $3.50 Cdn., $3.50 U.S., plus $1.60 in Canadian stamps or IRCs. (Ads if writing related)

Fillers: Accepts 5-10/yr. Anecdotes, short humor, tips; 100-200 wds. Pays one tear sheet.

Columns/Departments: Accepts 20-25/yr. Opportunities (market news, publishing opportunities, contests, etc.), 25-100 wds., no payment.

Special Needs: Articles of practical help to writers, from beginners to advanced.

Contest: Fall contest in conjunction with Inscribe's Fall Conference. Details on Website, or write and ask to be on mailing list. Spring contest for members only.

Tips: "Most open to 600-1,200 words with strong take-away value for writers (at all levels, in most genres)."

$FICTION FIX NEWSLETTER: The Nuts and Bolts of Crafting Better Fiction. Articles@ coffeehouseforwriters.com. Website: www.coffeehouseforwriters.com/news.html. Carol Lindsay, ed. For writers and aspiring writers of short stories and novels. Monthly; circ. 5,000. To subscribe, send blank e-mail to FictionFix-subscribe@topica.com. E-query only. Responds in 2-3 wks. Pays to $20 ($30-50 for assigned) within 10 days of publication for 1st electronic rts. How-to articles 300-500 wds. Prefers submission by e-mail (copied into message/see guidelines for specifics). Guidelines on Website.

Columns/Departments: This Writer's Opinion (reviews of writing books), 300-500 wds.; The Writing Life (personal writing stories). No payment.

HEAVEN, 207 Willow Wind Dr., Artemas PA 17211. (814)458-3102. E-mail: willowwind@here intown.net. Kay Weems, ed. Published every even year. $7/copy. 100% unsolicited freelance. Phone/e-query OK. **NO PAYMENT.** Short stories to 2,500 wds. Responds before typing begins. Accepts simultaneous submissions & reprints.

Poetry: All types of poetry on heaven, to 36 lines (or slightly longer). Submit max. 10 poems. Helpful hints: Subject could be "finding the right road to heaven," "suppose through a mistake you go to the wrong place," "would you have a memory of earth?" "can you still see earth or visit?" or "are animals there?" Use your imagination. This is an endless subject.

Tips: "In addition to this collection, I also publish 2-3 different themes throughout the year, along with my regular publications."

$#MERLYN'S PEN: Fiction, Essays, and Poems by America's Teens, PO Box 2550, Providence RI 02906-0550. Toll-free (800)247-2027. (401)885-5192. Fax (401)885-5199. E-mail: merlyn@merlynspen.org. Website: www.merlynspen.com. Secular. Jim Stahl, ed. Magazine; circ. 5,000. Subscription $29.95. Query; no e-query. Pays $20-200 on publication for all rts. Articles 500-5,000 wds.; fiction to 8,500 wds. Responds in 10-12 wks.

Poetry: Free verse, metric verse; $20-50.

($)MONEY THE WRITE WAY, PO Box 488, Dobbins CA 95935. (916)205-4763. E-mail: carmel@moneythewriteway.com. Website: www.moneythewriteway.com. Write Spirit Publishing. Carmel Mooney, pub. Educates, inspires, and supports Christian writers, travel writers, authors, and e-publishing enthusiasts in making money as a writer of integrity. Monthly e-zine; 8-15 pgs.; circ. 4,000. Subscription free. 80% unsolicited freelance; 10% assigned. Query; e-query OK. **PAYS IN COPIES,** free advertising for writer, and occasionally up to $10; for one-time rts. Articles 300-800 wds. (36/yr.); book reviews 300-500 wds. Responds in 2-4 wks. Seasonal 2 mos. ahead. Accepts simultaneous submissions & reprints (tell when/where appeared). Accepts mss by e-mail (attached file). Does not use sidebars. Prefers NIV. Guidelines; copy for #10 SAE or by e-mail. (Ads)

Fillers: Accepts 6-12/yr. Anecdotes, facts, ideas, quotes, tips; 50-100 wds. No payment (usually), or up to $5.

Columns/Departments: Accepts 36+/yr. Marketing for Writers—Marketing with Integrity, 300-800 wds.; monthly guest article (how-to or personal experience essay), 300-800 wds.; Boast Post (short pieces on personal writing accomplishments), 50-100 wds.

Special Needs: Christian writing: tips, resources, how-to, reviewing, travel writing, success stories, and marketing. Propose a column for us.

Contest: Occasionally sponsors writing contests.

Tips: "Most open to Boast Post (column), or how-to-write/marketing/breaking-in articles. Send a concise, focused query that is an example of writer's tone and expertise."

$MY LEGACY, 207 Willow Wind Dr., Artemas PA 17211. (814)458-3102. E-mail: willowwind@ hereintown.net. Kay Weems, ed. For young adults & up. Quarterly booklet; 70-80 pgs.; circ. 200+. Subscription $16. 100% unsolicited freelance. Pays $5 for editor's favorite stories. No articles; fiction to 2,500 wds. Responds in 16-20 wks. Accepts simultaneous submissions & reprints. Guidelines; copy $4.50/6x9 SAE/4 stamps. This publication currently being published irregularly.

NORTHWEST CHRISTIAN AUTHOR, PO Box 428, Enumclaw WA 98022. Toll-free (800)731-6292. E-mail: acquisitions@nwchristianwriters.org. Website: www.nwchristianwriters.org. Northwest Christian Writers Assn. Bob Haslam, acq. ed. To encourage Christian authors to share the gospel through the written word and to promote excellence in writing. Bimonthly newsletter; 8 pgs.; circ. 150. Subscription $10. 40% unsolicited freelance; 60% assigned. Complete ms/cover letter; e-query OK. **PAYS 3 COPIES** for one-time or reprint rts. Not copyrighted. Articles 300-800 wds. (16/yr.); book reviews 100 wds. Responds in 2 wks. Accepts simultaneous submissions & reprints (tell when/where appeared). Prefers e-mail submission (attached file). Uses some sidebars. Accepts submissions from teens. Guidelines on Website; no copy. (No ads)

Poetry: Accepts 3/yr. Free verse, light verse. Submit max. 3 poems.

Fillers: Anecdotes, tips; 50-250 wds.

Special Needs: How-tos on nonfiction and fiction writing. Focus on genre techniques.

Tips: "Most open to articles on writing techniques, particularly for specific genres. We've had too many how-to-submit articles. Stay within word count. E-queries should have 'NW Christian Author' in subject line. Include 1-2 sentence author bio with article."

OMNIFIC, 207 Willow Wind Dr., Artemas PA 17211. (814)458-3102. E-mail: willowwind@ hereintown.net. Kay Weems, ed. Family-type publication for writers/adults. Semiannual booklet; approx. 100 pgs.; circ. 300+. Subscription $10 ($5/issue). 100% unsolicited freelance. **NO PAYMENT.** Accepts simultaneous submissions & reprints. No articles; poetry only. Guidelines; copy for 6x9 SAE/4 stamps & $5 (payable to Weems Concepts).

Poetry: Any type; to 36 lines. Submit max. 4-8 poems.

ONCE UPON A TIME, 553 Winston Ct., St. Paul MN 55118. (651)457-6223. E-mail: audreyouat@ comcast.net. Website: http://onceuponatimemag.com. Audrey B. Baird, ed./pub. Highly specialized magazine for children's writers and illustrators, offering help, instruction, encouragement in an over-the-fence-type friendly way. Quarterly mag.; 32 pgs.; circ. 1,000. Subscription $26. 50% unsolicited freelance. Complete ms/cover letter; no phone/fax/ e-query. **PAYS IN COPIES** for one-time rts. Articles 100-900 wds. (80-100/yr.). Responds in 6 wks. Seasonal anytime. Accepts simultaneous submissions & reprints (tell when/where appeared—must be 1 yr. from last publication). Uses some sidebars. Guidelines (also on Website); copy $5. (Ads)

Poetry: Accepts 80-100/yr. Free verse, haiku, light verse, traditional; to 30 lines. Writing/illustrating related. Submit max. 6 poems. "About rhyming poetry: pay attention to rhythm—it's not enough to rhyme—rhyming poetry must have rhythm (and near rhyme is not enough). I'm willing to help and to edit and to suggest, but do your part first with revision until the piece is as good as you can get it."

Fillers: Accepts 20-30/yr. Anecdotes, cartoons, ideas, short humor, tips (all writing/illustrating related); to 100 wds.

Special Needs: How-to articles on writing and illustrating (by those qualified to write them) up to 800 wds.; short pieces on writing & illustrating, 100-400 wds.

Tips: "Send a good, tight article on the writing life—any aspect—that is either educational, informative, entertaining, humorous, or inspiring. We like a friendly, upbeat tone. Humor is always looked for. We get too many articles on rejection. I am open to them if you state what you learned from them or how you persevered in spite of them. Articles on good advice you've received that resulted in publication for you are always good. We like success stories and particularly look for how-to pieces. Perseverance is a strong theme for us. Read the writing books. Read the market guides. Attend conferences. Learn how to write before you attempt it."

$SHADES OF ROMANCE MAGAZINE. E-mail: sormag@mail.com. Website: www.sormag.com. LaShaunda Hoffman, ed. A guide for readers and writers of multicultural romance and fiction. Bimonthly magazine. Subscription $12. E-query only. Pays $20 for articles, $25 for fiction within 30 days of publication (through PayPal). Articles 500-800 wds.; short stories 500-1,500 wds.; devotions 200-500 wds. Responds in 2-4 wks. Accepts reprints (pays $10). Guidelines/themes online; no copy.

Poetry: Buys romantic poetry to 1 pg.; $5.

Fillers: Buys fillers; $10. Tips on freelancing time management, writing exercises, and romance. Humorous anecdotes.

Columns/Departments: The Writer's Path (articles on writing multicultural romance and fiction); Shades of Motivation (inspiring thoughts on writing); The Marketing Path (how to market); The Publishing Path (business of writing and promoting).

$SPIRIT-LED WRITER. E-mail: spiritwriter@att.net. Website: www.SpiritLedWriter.com. Lisa A. Crayton, pub./ed. Internet magazine for Christian beginning, intermediate, and advanced writers. Monthly e-zine. Query by e-mail (put "Query: [subject]" in subject line). Pays $10-20 on publication for one-time, reprint, and electronic rts. Articles to 1,200 wds. (70+/yr.); reviews to 500 wds. Responds in 8 wks. Accepts reprints. Submit accepted mss by e-mail (no attachments). Regularly uses sidebars. Accepts submissions from teens. Guidelines by e-mail/Website; copy online. (Ads)

Columns/Departments: Buys several/yr. Musing Dept. (writing-related personal reflections), 700-900 wds.; God's Glory Dept. (writing success stories), 500-700 wds.; Business (articles on the business of writing), to 1,200 wds.; Children's Column (how-to on writing for youth), to 1,200 wds.; $10-20.

Special Needs: Writing-related devotionals; conference coverage (700-900 wds.); and book reviews of writing books, 250-500 wds. ($5-10, depending on whether they supply the book). Also articles on writing for youth or on advanced writing topics.

Tips: "Easiest to break in with a success story (God's glory), musing article, or devotional. We seek how-to and feature articles with a writing theme. We are not a general, Christian-living publication. We reject many manuscripts because they are general, not writing-related. Make it relevant to writing and writers."

TEACHERS & WRITERS, 5 Union Square W., New York NY 10003-3306. (212)691-6590. Fax (212)675-0171. E-mail: info@twc.org. Website: www.twc.org. Christopher Edgar, pub. dir. (cedgar@twc.org) & Christina Davis, ed. (cdavis@twc.org). On teaching creative and imaginative writing for children. Mag. published 5X/yr. & online; circ. 3,000. Query; phone/fax/e-query OK. **PAYS IN COPIES.** Articles 3,000-6,000 wds. Guidelines by e-mail; copy $2.50.

$TICKLED BY THUNDER, 14076—86A Ave., Surrey BC V3W 0V9, Canada. (604)591-6095. E-mail: info@tickledbythunder.com. Website: www.tickledbythunder.com. Larry Lindner, ed. For writers wanting to better themselves. Quarterly chapbook (3-4X); 24 pgs.; circ.

1,000. Subscription $12 Cdn. (or $10 U.S.). 90% unsolicited freelance; 10% assigned. Complete ms/cover letter; e-query OK from subscribers only. Pays $2-5 (in Cdn. or U.S. stamps) on publication for one-time rts. Articles 1,500 wds. (5/yr.); fiction 2,000 wds. (20/yr.); book/music/video reviews 1,000 wds. Responds in 16 wks. Seasonal 6 mos. ahead. Accepts simultaneous submissions. Prefers requested ms on disk, no e-mail submission. Uses some sidebars. Accepts submissions from children & teens. Guidelines (also by e-mail/Website); copy $2.50/6x9 SAE. (Ads)

Poetry: Accepts 20-40/yr. Any type; to 40 lines. Submit max. 5-7 poems. "Try sending seasonal poetry well in advance."

Contest: For fiction (February 15 annual deadline) and poetry (February 15, May 15, August 15, and October 15 annual deadlines). Article contests for subscribers only (February 15, May 15, August 15, and October 15 deadlines). Send SASE for guidelines.

Tips: "Write a 300-word article describing how you feel about your successes/failures as a writer. Be specific, and focus—don't be at all general or vague, tell what works for you. Be original; say something classic in a new way. Use imagery. I also like fiction that surprises me. Need book reviews of writing books."

$THE UPPER CASE, PO Box 2505, Cranberry PA 16066. Fax (724)776-7228. Website: www.StDavidsWriters.com. St. Davids Christian Writers' Assn. Nancy E. James, ed. Triannual newsletter. Subscription $10 to nonmembers. Open to freelance. Complete ms. or query. Pays $10/half page for one-time rts. Articles 300-900 wds.; short-short stories 150-300 wds.; devotionals 150-200 wds.; book reviews 200-300 wds. Guidelines in newsletter/on Website; copy for 9x12 SAE/3 stamps. (No ads)

Poetry: Any form; to 20 lines.

Fillers: Short fillers and cartoons.

Special Needs: Articles on writing, book reviews, devotions, interviews with published writers (query first for interviews).

$WIN-INFORMER, PO Box 11337, Bainbridge Island WA 98110. (206)842-9103. Fax (206)842-0536. E-mail: writersinfonetwork@juno.com. Website: www.christianwriters info.net. Writers Information Network. Elaine Wright Colvin, ed. Send books to be announced or reviewed to 5359 Ruby Pl. N.E., Bainbridge Island WA 98110. CBA industry news and trends to keep professional writers, editors, agents, and speakers in touch with the changing marketplace. Bimonthly (6X) mag.; 24-32 pgs.; circ. 1,000. Subscription $49.95 ($60 Canada/foreign in U.S. funds). 33% unsolicited; 20% assigned. Complete ms submitted in body of e-mail only. Pays $5-50 (or subscription) on acceptance for 1st rts. Articles 100-800 wds. (30/yr.); book reviews, 100-300 wds. Accepts e-mail submissions only. Uses some sidebars. Guidelines on Website; copy $10. (No ads, but likes to announce news of members' successes)

Poetry: Any type; writing related.

Fillers: Anecdotes, facts, ideas, newsbreaks, quizzes, quotes, prayers, short humor; 50-300 wds.; $10-20.

Columns/Departments: Columns are continuously changing to meet the needs of an evolving industry. Check a recent copy for current column needs.

Special Needs: "Hot news of our growing, changing market whenever and wherever you hear it—at a writers conference, in a magazine news announcement, from your editor or agent, at your writers group—pass it on. If you make it into a round-up article of what many industry insiders are saying, we'll even pay you. Our readers want to be kept on the cutting-edge of what is happening in the CBA industry."

Tips: "If it works for you, we want to hear about it. If you learn a hot tip, we'd love to share it. We are in a crowded marketplace and a tight book-publishing industry. We really do need each other! This industry is built on networking and relationships. We want tried and proven ideas—what's working for you and other professional writers and speakers. Give us great hints on book promotion, preparing for radio and TV appearances, promoting book signings, and other speaking engagements. 'Without good direction, people lose their way; the more wise counsel you follow, the better your chances' (Prov. 11:14, MSG)."

$THE WRITER, 21027 Crossroads Cir., Waukesha WI 53187. (262)796-8776. Fax (262)798-6468. E-mail: editor@writermag.com. Website: www.writermag.com. Secular. Elfrieda Abbe, ed.; Jeff Reich, mng. ed. How-to for writers; lists religious markets periodically. Monthly mag.; 68 pgs.; circ. 38,000. Subscription $29 (single issue $5.50). 80% unsolicited freelance. Query; no phone/fax query (prefers hard copy, but will accept e-query at queries@writermag.com). Pays $75-500 for feature articles; book reviews ($50-varies); on acceptance for 1st rts. Features 575-3,000 wds. (60/yr.). Responds in 4 wks. Uses some sidebars. Guidelines (also on Website), copy $5.50. (Ads)

> **Fillers:** Prose; cartoons $50.
>
> **Columns/Departments:** Buys 24+/yr. Get Published (shorter pieces on the business of writing); Off the Cuff (personal essays about writing; avoid writer's block stories); Poet to Poet (a poet writes on writing poetry—should show a technique); Syntax (on language; please, no articles on basic grammar or punctuation). All 800-1,200 wds. Pays $150-400 for columns; $50-75 for reviews. Query 4 months ahead.
>
> **Special Needs:** How-to on the craft of writing only.
>
> **Contests:** Occasionally sponsors a contest.
>
> **Tips:** "General features are most open to freelancers. It's important to have a sense of what we've covered in the past year or two, as well as the general tone and approach of our articles. Personal essays must provide take-away advice and benefits for writers ; we shun the 'navel-gazing' type of essay. Include plenty of how-to, advice, and tips on techniques. Be specific. Query for features six months ahead."

$WRITER'S APPRENTICE, 607 N. Cleveland St., Merrill WI 54452. Phone/fax (715)536-3167. E-mail: tina@writersapprentice.com. Website: www.writersapprentice.com. Prairie River Publishing. Tina Miller, ed./pub. For aspiring, beginning, and intermediate writers. Monthly mag.; circ. 10,000. Subscription free. 90% freelance. Prefers e-mail query or complete ms.; fax query OK. Articles 300-900 wds. ($15-50), essays 300-600 wds. ($10-25). First rts.; no reprints. Not copyrighted. Pays on publication for 1st rts. Responds in 1-6 mos. Seasonal 6-9 mos. ahead. Guidelines on Website; copy for 9x12 SAE/4 stamps. (Ads)

> **Tips:** "Your best chance of breaking in is with a very niche-specific, fair, and objective article that presents both sides of an issue relevant to aspiring, beginning, or intermediate writers, and include at least two quotes from experts or others with actual experience on each side of the issue."

$#WRITER'S CHRONICLE: The Magazine for Serious Writers, The Association of Writers & Writing Programs, George Mason University, MSN 1E3, Fairfax VA 22030-4444. (703)993-4301. Fax (703)993-4302. E-mail: services@awpwriter.org. Website: www.awp writer.org. D. W. Fenza, ed-in-chief. Bimonthly mag. Subscription $20. Pays $8/100 wds. on publication for 1st rts. No kill fee. Guidelines on Website.

> **Special Needs:** Author interviews, essays, trends, and literary controversies. No poetry or fiction.

$WRITER'S DIGEST, 4700 E. Galbraith Rd., Cincinnati OH 45236. (513)531-2690, ext. 1483. E-mail: wdsubmissions@fwpubs.com. Website: www.writersdigest.com. Secular/F & W Publications. Submit to Submissions Editor. To inform, instruct, or inspire the freelancer. Monthly mag.; 76 pgs.; circ. 150,000. Subscription $27. 20% unsolicited; 60% assigned. Strongly prefers e-query (responds in 2 wks.). Pays .30-.50/wd. on acceptance for 1st and electronic (sometimes) rts. Articles 1,000-2,000 wds. (60/yr.). Responds to mail query in 3 mos. Seasonal 8 mos. ahead. Requires requested ms on disk or by e-mail (attached file or copied into message). Kill fee 25%. Regularly uses sidebars. Guidelines/editorial calendar on Website; copy $5.25 (attn: Lyn Menke). (Ads)

Contests: Sponsors annual contest for articles, short stories, poetry, and scripts. Also The National Self-Publishing Book Awards. Send SASE for rules.

Tips: "We're looking for fiction technique pieces by published authors."

$WRITERS' JOURNAL, PO Box 394, Perham MN 56573-0394. (218)346-7921. Fax (218)346-7924. E-mail: writersjournal@lakesplus.com. Website: www.writersjournal.com. Val-Tech Media/Secular. Leon Ogroske, ed. Advice, tools, and markets for writers, communicators, and poets. Bimonthly mag.; 68 pgs.; circ. 26,000. Subscription $19.97. 90% unsolicited freelance; 10% assigned. Complete ms/cover letter; e-query OK. Pays $10-30, plus subscription, on publication for one-time rts. Articles 800-2,500 wds. (45/yr.); fiction 2,000 wds. Responds in 6-28 wks. Accepts simultaneous submissions; no reprints. Accepts requested ms by e-mail (copied into message). No kill fee. Uses some sidebars. Guidelines (also by e-mail); copy $5. (Ads)

Poetry: Esther M. Leiper, poetry ed. Buys 25/yr. All types; to 10 lines; $5/poem. Submit max. 4 poems.

Fillers: Buys 20/yr. Any type, 10-200 wds. Pays $1-10.

Contest: Runs several contests each year. Prizes up to $300. Categories are short story, horror/ghost, romance, travel writing, and fiction; 3 poetry; 2 photo. Send an SASE requesting guidelines.

Tips: "We are looking for a well-written article on freelance income; articles on how to write better and how to sell what authors write. Also looking for articles on obscure income markets for writers. General story construction and grammar tips."

*WRITER'S LIFELINE, Box 1641, Cornwall ON K6H 5V6, Canada. (613)932-2135. Fax (613)932-7735. E-mail: stefgill@hotmail.com. Stephen Gill, mng. ed. For professional freelancers and beginning writers. Bimonthly mag.; 16-35 pgs.; circ. 1,500. Needs articles of interest to writers, news items of national and international interest, letters to the editor, poetry, interviews. Needs book reviewers; **PAYS IN BOOK REVIEWED & COPIES.**

WRITERS MANUAL, 7231—120th St., Ste. 105, Delta BC V4C 6P5, Canada. E-mail: writers manual@yahoo.com. Website: www.writersmanual.com (click on "Get Interviewed!"). Krista Barrett, ed-in-chief. Looking for author and/or freelance interviews. One-time rts.

+WRITER'S NETWORK NEWS, 106 Fletcher Dr., Logansport LA 71049. (318)697-5649. E-mail: mamarcy5@cs.com. Marcy Simmons, ed/pub. For poets and writers of all genres. Monthly tabloid. Open to unsolicited freelance. Complete ms by mail. **PAYS 5 COPIES** for 1st or one-time rts. Articles to 1,500 wds. Seasonal several mos. ahead. Guidelines; copy. Incomplete topical listings.

Poetry: Accepts poetry on any aspect of writing, up to 20 lines. Submit max. 5 poems.

Special Needs: Market news up to 1,500 wds.; contest news up to 1,500 wds.

WRITES OF PASSAGE, 3706 N.E. Shady Lane Dr., Gladstone MO 64119. Phone/fax (816)459-8016. E-mail: JeanetteDL@earthlink.net. Website: www.hacwn.org. Heart of America Christian Writers' Network. Jeanette Littleton, ed. Monthly newsletter; 4 pgs.; circ. 150. Subscription $25. 50% unsolicited freelance; 50% assigned. Complete ms/cover letter; phone/e-query OK. **NO PAYMENT** for 1st rts. Not copyrighted. Articles 400 wds. (15/yr.); book reviews 200 wds. Responds in 8 wks. Accepts simultaneous submissions; no reprints. Accepts requested mss by e-mail. Uses some sidebars. Accepts submissions from teens. Guidelines by e-mail. (Ads)

Poetry: Accepts 5/yr. Free verse, light verse, traditional; to 12 lines. Submit max. 3 poems.

Fillers: Accepts 25/yr. Anecdotes, facts, ideas, jokes, prayers, prose, quotes, short humor, tips.

Columns/Departments: Query for columns.

WRITETOINSPIRE.COM. E-mail: editor@writetoinspire.com?subject=Submission. Website: www.writetoinspire.com. Online publication. Provides good how-to information for Christian writers. **NO PAYMENT** for 1st or one-time rts. Articles 500-700 wds., written in an online style. Send submissions in body of e-mail (no attachments). Guidelines on Website.

***THE WRITE TOUCH,** 1714 Soland Dr. N.E., Albuquerque NM 87110-4930. Tim Anderson, ed. For writers trying to get published. Monthly newsletter; 12 pgs.; circ. 40. Subscription $15/yr. 100% unsolicited freelance. Complete ms/cover letter. **PAYS 3 COPIES,** for one-time rts. Essays on various subjects (120/yr.) & fiction for all ages (120/yr.), 100-500 wds. Responds in 2-4 wks. Seasonal 2 mos. ahead. Discourages simultaneous submissions & reprints. Accepts requested ms on disk. Guidelines; copy $1.

> **Poetry:** Any type; 4-30 lines. Submit max. 3 poems.
>
> **Fillers:** Anecdotes, facts, ideas, prose, short humor; 15-50 wds.

+**WRITING CORNER.** E-mail: edit-wc@writingcorner.com. Website: www.writingcorner.com. Shirley Kawa-Jump, ed. Online publication. Open to unsolicited freelance. Query or complete ms. by e-mail (no attachments). **NO PAYMENT** for nonexclusive rts. Articles 600-900 wds.; fiction 600-900 wds. Responds in 2 wks. Accepts reprints. Guidelines on Website: www.writingcorner.com/admin/sub-guidelines.htm.

MARKET ANALYSIS

PERIODICALS IN ORDER BY CIRCULATION

ADULT/GENERAL

Guideposts 3,000,000
Focus on the Family 2,200,000
Columbia 1,600,000
Decision 900,000
Angels on Earth 550,000
Marion Helpers 500,000
War Cry 500,000
Spirituality for Today 495,000
Catholic Digest 400,000
Catholic Yearbook 400,000
Positive Thinking 400,000
Mature Living 318,000
St. Anthony Messenger 310,000
Anglican Journal 272,000
Power for Living 250,000
Upscale Magazine 250,000
Charisma 230,000
Today's Pentecostal Evangel 215,000
Gospel Today 200,000
Liberty 200,000
Liguorian 200,000
Miraculous Medal 200,000
Signs of the Times 200,000
Ideals 180,000
Christianity Today 155,000
Cappers 150,000
Family Digest 150,000
Standard 150,000
Tomorrow's Christian Graduate
   150,000
Smart Families 140,000
Discipleship Journal 130,000
Today's Christian 125,000
Company 120,000
Lutheran Digest 105,000
Presbyterian Survey 105,000
Foursquare World Advance 102,000
Men of Integrity 102,000
Catholic Forester 100,000
CGA World 100,000
Good News (KY) 100,000
Lookout 100,000
Lutheran Journal 100,000
On Mission 100,000
ParentLife 100,000
Message 80,000
Plain Truth 80,000
Christian Parenting Today 78,000

Alive Now 70,000
Celebrate Life 70,000
Common Ground 70,000
Creation 70,000
Heartlight Internet 70,000
Live 70,000
Mature Years 70,000
Sword of the Lord 70,000
United Church Observer 70,000
Our Sunday Visitor 68,000
Christian Home & School 66,000
Presbyterians Today 62,000
Christian Standard 60,000
EFCA Today 60,000
Christian History 55,000
Church of God Evangel 54,500
Marriage Partnership 53,000
Bridal Guides 50,000
Faith & Friends 50,000
Leaves 50,000
Light & Life 50,000
Wesleyan Life 50,000
Christian Social Action 48,000
Annals of St. Anne 45,000
BGC World 44,000
America 41,000
Christian Motorsports 40,000
Parabola 40,000
Reformed Quarterly 40,000
Senior Living 40,000
U.S. Catholic 40,000
Gospel Tract 38,000
Cathedral Age 36,000
Highway News 35,000
Messenger of St. Anthony 35,000
Messianic Times 35,000
Faith & Family 32,000
First Things 32,000
Christian Computing 30,000
Christian News Northwest 30,000
Christian Research Journal 30,000
Community Spirit 30,000
en confianza 30,000
Kindred Spirit 30,000
Lifeglow 30,000
Sojourners 30,000
Sports Spectrum 30,000
World & I 30,000
Light at Home 29,000
Seek 29,000

Portland Magazine 28,000
Vibrant Life 28,000
Priority! 27,000
Canadian Lutheran 26,000
Homeschooling Today 25,000
LifeLine Journal 25,000
War Cry (Canada) 25,000
Alliance Life 23,000
Catholic Peace Voice 23,000
HonorBound 22,000
African Voices 20,000
Canadian Mennonite 20,000
Commonweal 20,000
Interim 20,000
Trumpeter 20,000
Faith Today 18,000
Mennonite Brethren Herald 17,000
Covenant Companion 16,000
Marketplace 16,000
Wittenburg Door 16,000
Over the Back Fence/SW 15,000
Testimony 15,000
Canada Lutheran 14,000
DisciplesWorld 14,000
Gems of Truth 14,000
St. Joseph's Messenger 14,000
Bible Advocate 13,500
Creation Illustrated 13,000
Messenger/Sacred Heart 13,000
Books & Culture 12,000
Special Living 12,000
Evangel 11,000
Spiritual Life 11,000
Christian Retailing 10,000
Disciple's Journal 10,000
Messiah Magazine 10,000
Parents & Teens 10,000
Presbyterian Outlook 10,000
Regent Business Review 10,000
Spiritual Voice News 10,000
Vision 10,000
Christian Leader 9,800
Breakthrough Intercessor 9,300
NRB Magazine 9,300
Fellowship Magazine 9,000
Living Church 9,000
Prism 9,000
Purpose 9,000
Sharing 9,000
Catholic New Times 8,500

CBA Marketplace 8,000
The Gem 7,100
MN Christian Chronicle 7,000
Montgomery's Journey 7,000
Psychology for Living 7,000
Quaker Life 7,000
Review for Religious 7,000
White Wing Messenger 7,000
Impact 6,000
Spring Hill Review 5,400
AGAIN 5,000
Creation Care 5,000
Creative Nonfiction 5,000
New Heart 5,000
Pentecostal Messenger 5,000
Plowman 5,000
Purpose Magazine 5,000
TJ 5,000
Way of St. Francis 5,000
WHOLE Magazine 5,000
Social Justice Review 4,950
Christian Civic League/ME 4,600
Cresset 4,500
Resource 4,500
Sacred Journey 4,500
Christian Courier (CAN) 4,000
Christian Renewal 4,000
Evangelical Advocate 4,000
Image 4,000
Maranatha News 4,000
Mosaic (Free Methodist) 4,000
Wireless Age 4,000
Catholic Insight 3,700
Cross Currents 3,500
Culture Wars 3,500
Evangel 3,500
Sword and Trumpet 3,300
Alive! 3,000
Evangelical Baptist 3,000
Message/Open Bible 3,000
MovieGuide 3,000
Perspectives 3,000
Prayer Closet 3,000
Mennonite Historian 2,600
Bread of Life 2,500
Railroad Evangelist 2,500
Hannah to Hannah 2,300
Mutuality 2,200
Apocalypse Chronicles 2,000-3,000
Brave Hearts 2,000
Channels 2,000
Desert Call 2,000
Priscilla Papers 2,000
Voice of the Lord 1,850-2,150
Jour./Church & State 1,700
Church Herald/Holiness Banner 1,600
Connecting Point 1,500

Queen of All Hearts 1,500
Dovetail 1,000
Rare Jewel 1,000
Victory News 1,000
Methodist History 800
Compass Direct 700
Christian Radio Weekly 600
The Storyteller 600
Tributes 500+
Eternal Ink 440+
Silver Wings 300
Studio 300
Xavier Review 300
West Wind Review 250-500
Aujourd'hui Credo 250
Time of Singing 250
Challenging Destiny 200
Dreams & Visions 200
Hard Row to Hoe 200
Insound 200
Keys to Living 200
Ancient Paths 175-200
Pegasus Review 125
Angel Face 100
Time for Rhyme 100
Penwood Review 50-100
St. Linus Review 50

CHILDREN

American Girl 700,000
Guideposts for Kids Online 200,000+
FOF Clubhouse 101,100
Keys for Kids 100,000
Pockets 93,000
High Adventure 86,000
FOF Clubhouse Jr. 78,000
Our Little Friend 45,000-50,000
Adventure 40,000
Celebrate 40,000
Courage 40,000
Primary Treasure 35,000
GUIDE 30,000
Passport 18,000
Faces 15,000
Nature Friend 13,000
SHINE brightly 13,000
Club Connection 12,000
The Winner 12,000
BREAD for God's Children 10,000
Cadet Quest 9,500
My Friend 9,000
Partners 6,389
Story Mates 6,275
Story Friends 6,000
On the Line 5,500
Junior Companion 3,500
Primary Pal (KS) 2,900

Beginner's Friend 2,700
Skipping Stones 2,500

CHRISTIAN EDUCATION/LIBRARY

Christian School Education 70,000
Children's Ministry 60,000
Group 55,000
Catechist 50,000
Today's Catholic Teacher 45,000
RTJ 32,000
Momentum 25,000
Resource 25,000
Christian Library Journal 20,000
Teach Kids! 12,000
Teachers Interaction 11,000
Youth & CE Leadership 11,000
Teachers of Vision 10,000
Jour./Adventist Ed. 7,500
Christian Early Education 5,500
Church Educator 4,500
Christian Educator's Journal 4,200
Ideas Unlimited 4,200
Leader/Chr. Ed. Ministries 3,500
Church & Synagogue Libraries 3,000
Kids' Ministry Ideas 1,700
Catholic Library World 1,000
Christian Librarian 800
Christian Education Journal (CA) 750
Church Libraries 500
Jour./Christian Education 500
Jour./Ed. & Christian Belief 400
Jour./Research on C. E. 400
Jour./Christianity/Foreign Languages 100

DAILY DEVOTIONALS

Secret Place 150,000
Our Journey 80,000
Daily Devotions for the Deaf 26,000
InDeed 13,000
Daily Meditation 775

MISSIONS

CNEWA World 100,000
Mission Frontiers 81,000
American Baptists in Mission 39,000
Wesleyan World 38,700
Catholic Missions in Canada 25,000
New World Outlook 24,000
PIME World 16,000
Leaders for Today 7,500
Evangelical Missions 7,000
Glad Tidings 5,000
PFI World Report 4,750
Women of the Harvest 2,500
Cornerstone Youth Resource 2,200

Missiology 1,500
OpRev Equipper 1,500
Intl. Jour./Frontier 600
East-West Church 430

MUSIC

CCM Magazine 70,000
Senior Musician 32,000
Creator 6,000
Tradition 3,500
The Hymn 3,000
Christian Music Weekly 300-1,200

NEWSPAPERS

Layman 485,000
Inside Journal 395,000
Episcopal Life 280,000
Anglican Journal 215,000
Alpha News 195,000
Christian Examiner 180,000
Catholic New York 135,000
National Catholic Reporter 120,000
Catholic Telegraph 100,000
Grit 100,000
Living 90,000
Pulpit Helps 75,000
Common Ground 70,000
Sword of the Lord 70,000
Our Sunday Visitor 68,000
Christian Current 65,000
Good News Journal 60,000
Good News/S. Florida 60,000
Arlington Catholic Herald 53,000
Cornerstone Christian 50,000
Living 50,000
Christian Ranchman 45,400
Good News, Etc. 42,000
Evangelical Times 40,000
Senior Living 40,000
Tidewater Parent 40,000
Messianic Times 35,000
Metro Voice 35,000
Living Light News 34,000
Catholic Register 33,000
Christian Herald 31,000
Christian Citizen USA 30,000
Christian News NW 30,000
Citizen USA 30,000
Interim 30,000
New Frontier 25,500
Christian Media 25,000
Minnesota Chr. Chronicle 25,000
Life Gate 23,000
Indian Life 22,000
B.C. Catholic 20,000
Charlotte World 20,000
Wichita Chronicle 16,500

Catholic Sentinel 16,000
Messenger 16,000
Christian Journal 15,000
Christian Voice 15,000
Good News in RI 14,000
City Light News 12,000
Interchange 12,000
Christian Courier (WI) 10,000
Network 10,000
Spiritual Voice News 10,000
Desert Voice 9,500
Faro de Luz 9,500
Star of Zion 9,200
Catholic New Times 8,500
Disciple's Journal 8,000
Inland NW Christian 8,000
New Freeman 7,300
Prairie Messenger 7,300
Arkansas Catholic 7,000
Palm Beach Conservative 5,000
SW KS Faith & Family 5,000
Christian Courier (Canada) 4,000
Christian Renewal 4,000
Christianweek 4,000
Maranatha News 4,000
Island Catholic News 3,000
Atlantic Catholic 2,500
Christian Observer 2,000
Insight (for the blind) 2,000
Together 2,000
B.C. Christian News 1,000
Hunted News 1,000
Prayerworks 1,000
Anglican 300

PASTORS/LEADERS

Interpreter 225,000
Your Church 150,000
Pastors.com 140,000
Growing Churches 85,000
Pulpit Helps 75,000
Leadership 65,000
Parish Life 50,000
Plugged In 50,000
Rev. 45,000
Worship Leader 43,000
Pray! 39,000
Technologies/Worship 35,000
Catholic Servant 33,000
Enrichment 33,000
Christian Century 30,000
Ministries Today 30,000
Today's Christian Preacher 30,000
Lutheran Partners 20,000
Ministry & Liturgy 20,000
Youthworker 20,000
Ministry 19,000

This Rock 15,870
Today's Parish 14,800
Theology Today 14,000
Church Administration 12,000
Net Results 12,000
Jour./Pastoral Care 10,000
Watchman Expositor 10,000
WCA News 10,000
YouthCulture 10,000
Student Leadership Journal 9,500
Preaching 9,000
Christian Camp & Conference 8,700
Sabbath School Leadership 8,100
Growth Points 8,000
The Priest 8,000
Review for Religious 7,000
Christian Ministry 6,500
Clergy Journal 6,000
Jour./Christian Camping 6,000
Catechumenate 5,600
Let's Worship 5,600
Cross Currents 5,000
Reformed Worship 5,000
Ministry Matters 4,500
African American Pulpit 4,000
Christian Management Report 3,500+
Lutheran Forum 3,200
Emmanuel 3,000
Evangelicals Today 3,000
Sermon Notes 3,000
Single Adult Min. Jour. 3,000
Environment & Art 2,500
Word & World 2,500
Pastoral Life 2,000
Reaching Children at Risk 2,000
Preaching On-Line 1,500
Church Worship 1,200
Parish Liturgy 1,200
Quarterly Review 1,100
Five Stones 1,000
Hunted News 1,000
Jour./Amer. Soc./Chur. Growth 400
RevWriter Resource 400
Theological Digest 400
Ministry in Motion 200+

TEEN/YOUNG ADULT

Guideposts Sweet 16 200,000
Brio 142,500
Essential Connection 120,000
Campus Life 100,000
Devo'Zine 100,000
Breakaway 96,000
Sharing the Victory 80,000
YouthWalk/GA 55,000
Young Salvationist 48,000
Young & Alive 25,000

Inteen 20,000
Listen 20,000
Real Faith in Life 18,000
Living My Faith 16,000
Credo 15,000
Insight 13,600
Teenage Christian 10,500
Young Adult Today 10,000
Student Leadership 8,500
The Conqueror 6,000
Beautiful Christian Teen 5,000
Youth Compass 4,800
With 4,000
Teen Light 3,000

WOMEN

Precious Times 350,000
Today's Christian Woman 250,000
Journey 215,000
Lutheran Woman's Quarterly 200,000
MOMSense 100,000
Share 100,000
SpiritLed Woman 100,000
Dabbling Mum.com, 40,000
At the Center 30,000

Godly Business Women 25,000
Horizons 20,000
History's Women 17,000
Woman's Touch 16,000
Women of Spirit 15,000
P31 Woman 10,000
Women's Ministry 8,000
Just Between Us 7,000
Esprit 5,400
Women Alive! 5,000-6,000
Link & Visitor 4,000
Making Waves 4,000
Right to the Heart 4,000
Tapestry 3,700
ChurchWoman 3,000
Handmaiden 3,000
inSpirit 2,500
Women of God's Word 1,700
Hearts at Home 1,500
Melody of the Heart 500+

WRITERS

Writer's Digest 150,000
The Writer 38,000
Writers' Journal 26,000

Writer's Apprentice 10,000
Fiction Fix Newsletter 5,000
Money the Write Way 4,000
Byline 3,000+
Christian Communicator 3,000
Teachers & Writers 3,000
Beginnings 1,500
Writer's Lifeline 1,500
Cross & Quill 1,000+
New Writing 1,000
Once Upon a Time 1,000
Tickled by Thunder 1,000
WIN-Informer 1,000
Advanced Christian Writer 500
Canadian Writer's Journal 385
Omnific 300+
Exchange 300
Gotta Write Network 300
My Legacy 200+
FellowScript 175-250
Areopagus (UK) 150
Northwest Christian Author 150
Writes of Passage 150
The Write Touch 40

PERIODICAL TOPICS IN ORDER OF POPULARITY

NOTE: Following is a list of topics in order by popularity. To find the list of publishers interested in each of these topics, go to the Topical Listings for periodicals and find the topic you are interested in. The numbers indicate how many periodical editors said they were interested in seeing something of that type or on that topic. (*—new topic this year)

1. Christian Living 253
2. Family Life 251
3. Photographs 247
4. Current/Social Issues 217
5. Book Reviews 209
6. Interviews/Profiles 204
7. Inspirational 202
8. Prayer 202
9. Holiday/Seasonal 200
10. Poetry 195
11. Faith 188
12. Personal Experience 188
13. Spirituality 179
14. Humor 178
15. Evangelism/Witnessing 171
16. Marriage 170
17. Women's Issues 166
18. Relationships 165
19. Christian Education 163
20. Devotionals/Meditations 161

21. Parenting 158
22. True Stories 155
23. Controversial Issues 149
24. Discipleship 148
25. Online Publications 147
26. Worship 144
27. Personal Growth 142
28. World Issues 141
29. Church Outreach 139
30. Leadership 138
31. Missions 132
32. Church Life 131
33. Ethnic/Cultural Pieces 131
34. Fillers: Cartoons 131
35. Theological 125
36. Essays 124
37. How-to 123
38. Youth Issues 123
39. Health 121
40. Historical 119

41. Men's Issues 114
42. Ethics 112
43. Short Story: Adult/Religious 112
44. Encouragement 108
45. News Features 108
46. Singles Issues 106
47. Death/Dying 105
48. Money Management 101
49. Church Growth 100
50. Spiritual Life 99
51. Fillers: Anecdotes 98
52. Social Justice 98
53. Bible Studies 97
54. Fillers: Short Humor 97
55. Stewardship 96
56. Newspapers/Tabloids 95
57. Celebrity Pieces 94
58. Christian Business 93
59. Opinion Pieces 93

60. Time Management 93
61. Divorce 92
62. Short Story: Contemporary 92
63. Church History 90
64. Short Story: Humorous 90
65. Canadian/Foreign Markets 85
66. Church Traditions 85
67. Environmental Issues 85
68. Religious Freedom 85
69. Think Pieces 85
70. Young Writer Markets 84
71. Healing 83
72. Spiritual Gifts 81
73. Spiritual Warfare 81
74. Music Reviews 80
75. Workplace Issues 80
76. Salvation Testimonies 79
77. Fillers: Ideas 77
78. Short Story: Adventure 77
79. Fillers: Facts 76
80. Book Excerpts 75
81. Church Management 75
82. Doctrinal 75
83. How-to Activities (juv.) 74
84. Senior Adult Issues 71
85. Video Reviews 69
86. Miracles 68
87. Fillers: Word Puzzles 67
88. Short Story: Historical 67
89. Short Story: Biblical 66
90. Sports/Recreation 66
91. Food/Recipes 64
92. Nature 63

93. Writing How-to 63
94. Fillers: Prayers 62
95. Homeschooling 62
96. Inner Life 62
97. Political 62
98. Travel 62
99. Fillers: Quotes 61
100. Short Story: Parables 60
101. Fillers: Prose 57
102. Crafts 56
103. Fillers: Quizzes 56
104. Fillers: Games 55
105. Racism 55
106. Short Story: Juvenile 55
107. Short Story: Mystery/Suspense 55
108. Economics 54
109. Fillers: Jokes 53
110. Self-help 51
111. Creation Science 47
112. Liturgical 47
113. Science 47
114. Spiritual Renewal 47
115. Short Story: Literary 46
116. Website Reviews 46
117. Religious Tolerance 45
118. Fillers: Newsbreaks 43
119. Sociology 43
120. Prophecy 40
121. Short Story: Fantasy 40
122. Short Story: Teen/Young Adult 39
123. Apologetics 38

124. Short Story: Allegory 37
125. Short Story: Ethnic 36
126. Cults/Occult 34
127. Photo Essays 34
128. Psychology 34
129. Sermons 34
130. Short Story: Science Fiction 34
131. Exegesis 33
132. Fillers: Party Ideas 33
133. Peace Issues 33
134. Short Story: Frontier 33
135. Fillers: Tips 32
136. Homiletics 32
137. Short Story: Romance 29
138. Take-home Papers 29
139. Nostalgia 27
140. Fillers: Kid Quotes 24
141. Short Story: Skits 23
142. Short Story: Historical/Romance 22
143. Short Story: Westerns 21
144. Short Story: Mystery/Romance 20
145. Short Story: Frontier/Romance 18
146. Movie Reviews 17
147. Short Story: Plays 17
148. Short Story: Speculative 14
149. Recovery 11*
150. Puppet Plays 9
151. Revival 4*

COMMENTS

If you are a short story writer, the biggest market is for adult fiction (112 markets), next is children's with 55, followed by teen with 39. These numbers all show significant drops from last year, but that appears to be a difference in how the database counted them this year—rather than indicating such a large drop in the market (this will be corrected for next year). The most popular genres (in order) are Contemporary, Humorous, Adventure, Historical, Biblical, Parables, Mystery/Suspense, and Literary. This represents several changes in order from last year—although the topics are the same. Biblical dropped from third to fifth; Adventure rose from fifth to third; and Historical rose from sixth to fourth. The least popular are still the genre romances. Publishers continue to show more interest in Fantasy and Science Fiction.

This year poetry rose to 195 markets, up from 191 last year, 197 the year before, 200 the year before, and 210 the year before that. There is good news for poets as far as poetry books goes—with the number of publishers for book publishers rising from 37 to 47. I still recommend that the serious poet pursue the periodical markets and establish a good reputation as a poet before ever attempting to sell a book of poetry.

This year the same topics are in the top 15, although every topic has changed places, except Christian Living, which remains number one.

SUMMARY OF INFORMATION ON CHRISTIAN PERIODICAL PUBLISHERS FOUND IN THE ALPHABETICAL LISTINGS

NOTE: Following is some general information based on averages of the information supplied by the periodical publishers in this guide. This information will be valuable in determining what numbers are typical in the various categories.

WANTS QUERY OR COMPLETE MANUSCRIPT

Of the more that 600 periodicals that indicated a preference, 47% ask for or will accept a complete manuscript, and 37% want or will accept a query. Only 3% require a query. Thirteen percent of all reporting will accept either.

ACCEPTS PHONE QUERY

This year, even fewer periodical publishers are accepting phone queries. Many seem now to prefer e-mail or even faxes to phone queries. It is suggested that you reserve phone queries for timely material that won't wait for the regular mailed query. If you phone in a query, be sure you have your idea well thought out and can present it succinctly and articulately.

ACCEPTS FAX QUERY

Most publishers have faxes, but many are asking for their fax number to be dropped from their listing—mostly because they prefer an e-mail query or are trying to avoid having complete manuscripts come by fax. Last year, 30% of all the periodical publishers accepted fax queries. This year, less than 28% will accept them. Since a fax query will not have an SASE, it is suggested that you make fax queries only if you have your own fax machine to accept their response.

ACCEPTS E-MAIL QUERY

As expected, the number of publishers with e-mail addresses continues to grow. Last year over 400 publishers were open to receiving messages or submissions by e-mail. This year it is up to about 450. Because most publishers now have both e-mail and Websites, we are no longer tracking the actual numbers who have them.

SUBMISSIONS ON DISK

Of the almost 250 periodicals that responded to the question about whether or not they accepted, preferred, or required accepted submissions on disk, 41% said they accepted disks, 25% preferred disks, only 14% required disks, and 20% no longer want disks—preferring e-mail submissions.

SUBMISSIONS BY E-MAIL

This area continues to show some significant changes in editors' perceptions of e-mail submissions. When asked if they would accept submissions by e-mail, about a third said yes. Of those, 38% wanted them copied into the message, 40% wanted them sent as an attached file, and the last 22% would accept them either way. These percentages are almost the same as last year. Generally speaking, those who prefer it copied into the message fear viruses, while those who prefer an attached copy don't like losing the coding when you copy it into the message.

PAYS ON ACCEPTANCE OR PUBLICATION

Of the publishers that indicated, 40% of the publishers pay on acceptance, while 60% pay on publication. Not encouraging.

PERCENTAGE OF FREELANCE

Many of the publishers responded to the question about how much freelance material they use. We now make the question more definitive by asking them to specify the percentage unsolicited and the percentage assigned, and each year a greater number of them give us both figures. Based on the figures we have, for the average publisher, 46% of the material purchased is unsolicited freelance and 54% is assigned.

CIRCULATION

In dividing the list of periodicals into three groups, according to size of circulation, the list comes out as follows: Publications with a circulation of 100,000 or more (up to 3,000,000), 14.8%; publications with a circulation between 50,000 and 100,000, 9.4%; the remaining 75.8%, a circulation of 50,000 or less. These percentages are slightly higher for the highest category and slightly lower for the other two, compared to last year. If we break that last group into three more groups by circulation, we come out with 10% of those from 33,000-50,000; 17% from 17,000-32,000; and the remaining 73% with less than 17,000. That means that 52% of all the periodicals that reported their circulation are at a circulation of 17,000 or less—four percentage points lower than last year. Circulations seem to be dropping overall.

RESPONSE TIME

According to the publishers who indicated response time, the average response time moved up to just over 8 weeks, one week longer than reported two years ago. Those who are writing and submitting regularly will have no problem confirming that most publishers are taking longer to respond to submissions.

REPRINTS

Nearly 50% of the periodicals included in the market guide accept reprints. Although until the last few years it was not necessary to tell a publisher where a piece had been published previously, that has changed. Most Christian publishers are now wanting a tear sheet of the original publication and a cover letter telling when and where it appeared originally. Be sure to check the individual listings to see if a publisher wants to know when and where a piece has appeared previously. Most are also paying less for reprints than for original material.

PREFERRED BIBLE VERSION

Although we are not running the percentages anymore, it is obvious that the most preferred Bible version is the New International Version, the preference of more than half the publishers. Other preferred versions are the King James Version, the New Revised Standard Version, the New American Bible, New American Standard, Revised Standard Version, and New King James. The NIV seems a good choice for those who didn't indicate a preference, although the more conservative groups seem to favor the KJV.

GREETING CARD/GIFT/SPECIALTY MARKETS

PLEASE NOTE: This listing contains both Christian/religious card publishers and secular publishers who have religious lines or produce some religious or inspirational cards. Keep in mind that the secular companies may produce other lines of cards that are not consistent with your beliefs, and that for a secular company, inspirational cards usually do not include religious imagery. The dollar sign ($) has been deleted from these listings, since they are all assumed to be paying markets.

(*) Indicates that publisher did not return questionnaire
(#) Indicates that listing was updated from guidelines or other sources
(+) Indicates new listing

NOTE: See the end of this listing for specialty product lists.

CARD PUBLISHERS

AFRICAN AMERICAN EXPRESSIONS, 3127 Fite Circle, Ste. I, Sacramento CA 95827. (916)424-5000. Fax (916)424-5053. E-mail: gperkins@black-gifts.com. Website: www.black-gifts.com. Greg Perkins, pres. Christian card publishers and specialty products. Open to freelance; buys 5-10 ideas/yr. Prefers outright submissions. Pays $35 on acceptance. No royalty. Responds in 2 wks. Uses rhymed, unrhymed, traditional, and light verse. Produces invitations and conventional, humorous, informal, inspirational, juvenile, novelty, and religious cards. Needs anniversary, birthday, Christmas, friendship, get well, graduation, keep in touch, love, miss you, Mother's Day, new baby, relatives (all occasions), sympathy, valentines, wedding, and pastor appreciation. Holiday/seasonal 9 mos. ahead. Open to ideas for new card lines, calendars/journals, novelty/gift items, magnets, and stationery. No guidelines; free catalog.

ALEGRIA COLLECTION, PO Box 835008, Miami FL 33283-5008. (305)271-6183. Fax (786)551-7985. E-mail: ventas@alegriacollection.com. Website: www.alegriacollection.com. Spanish greeting cards.

AMERICAN GREETINGS, 1 American Rd., Cleveland OH 44144-2398. (216)252-7300. Website: www.americangreetings.com. Kathleen McKay, ed. No unsolicited material.

ARTFUL GREETINGS, PO Box 52428, Durham NC 27717. (919)598-7599. Fax (919)598-8909. Website: www.artfulgreetings.com. Black art greeting cards and gifts.

BLESS HIS NAME GREETINGS, 127 Audubon Dr., #162-C, North Little Rock AR 72113. E-mail: Marie@blesshisnamegreetings.com. Website: www.blesshisnamegreetings.com. L. Marie Trotter, pub. A Christian/religious card publisher. Open to freelance. Prefers e-mail contact. Pays $50 on acceptance for all rts. No royalties. Responds in 4 wks. Uses rhymed, unrhymed; variable lengths. Produces inspirational and religious cards. Needs anniversary, birthday, Christmas, congratulations, Easter, Father's Day, friendship, get well, graduation, keep in touch, love, miss you, Mother's Day, new baby, relative (all occasion), sympathy, Thanksgiving, thank you, valentine, and wedding; cards with Names of God from the Old and New Testaments of the Bible. Holiday seasonal 3 mos. ahead. Open to ideas for new card lines. Submit max. 5-10 ideas. Open to ideas for bookmarks, gift books, greeting books, prints, and T-shirts. Guidelines for SAE/$1 postage; catalog for 9x12 SAE/$1.50 postage.

> **Tips:** "Our author division is the Names of God. Please study each name thoroughly before you attempt to write a card. Card verse should minister a specific Name of God to a specific life situation."

BLUE MOUNTAIN ARTS, INC., PO Box 1007, Boulder CO 80306-1007. (303)449-0536. Fax (303)447-0939. E-mail: editorial@spsstudios.com. Website: www.sps.com. Submit to Editorial Department. General card publisher that does a few inspirational cards. Open to freelance; buys 50-100 ideas/yr. Prefers outright submissions. Pays $300 for all rts. for use on a greeting card, or $50 for one-time use in a book, on publication. No royalties. Responds in 12-16 wks. Uses unrhymed or traditional poetry; short or long, but no one-liners. Produces inspirational and sensitivity. Needs anniversary, birthday, Christmas, congratulations, Easter, Father's Day, friendship, get well, graduation, keep in touch, love, miss you, Mother's Day, new baby, please write, relatives, sympathy, thank you, valentines, wedding, reaching for dreams. Holiday/seasonal 3 mos. ahead. Open to ideas for new card lines. Send any number of ideas (1 per pg.). Open to ideas for gift books. Guidelines; no catalog.

> **Contest:** Sponsors a poetry card contest online. Details on Website.

> **Tips:** "We are interested in reviewing poetry and writings for greeting cards, and expanding our field of freelance poetry writers."

+WILLIAM CARROLL DESIGNS, 2742—14th St. N., Naples FL 34103-4538. (239)434-8722. Fax (239)434-2510. E-mail: carobi5@aol.com. Website: www.williamcarrolldesigns.com. Carol Fitzgerald, pres. A general card publisher with one or more inspirational lines. Open to freelance. Buys about 12 verses/yr. Submit by e-mail. Unrhymed verse; conventional, humorous, inspirational. Submit max. 10-15 ideas/batch. Pays $20-40/idea on acceptance for North American rts.; more if accompanied by artwork or photograph. No royalties. Responds in 3-4 wks. Uses unrhymed, traditional, light verse; short. Produces conventional, humorous, inspirational. Needs birthday, Christmas, get well, sympathy, thank you. Holiday/seasonal 9 mos. ahead. Open to ideas for new card lines and gift books. Specializes in photo cards (children and nature). Cute thought or humor for children's cards; inspirational for nature cards. No guidelines; catalog for 9x12 SAE/96 cents postage.

CELEBRATION GREETINGS, (a div. of Leanin' Tree), Box 9500, Boulder CO 80301. (303)530-1442. Website: www.celebrationgreetings.com. Nancy Trumble Fox, VP Product. Christian/religious card publisher and specialty products. No freelance for now.

CHRISTIAN INSPIRATIONS, 30 E. 33rd St., New York NY 10016. (212)685-0751. Fax (212)889-6868. Suzanne Kruck, VP. Christian card publisher. No unsolicited submissions; request permission in writing to send submissions. Pays on acceptance; no royalty. Responds in 4-6 wks. All types of verse, 4-6 lines. All kinds of cards and greetings, except Halloween and St. Patrick's. Seasonal 12 mos. ahead. Not open to new card lines or specialty products. No guidelines; catalog.

CREATIVE CHRISTIAN GIFTS, PO Box 915441, Longwood FL 32791-5441. Toll-free (866)325-1857. (407)924-9186. E-mail: sales@creativechristiangifts.com. Website: www.creativechristiangifts.com. Renee Purner. Greeting cards & note cards.

CURRENT, INC., PO Box 2559, Colorado Springs CO 80901. (719)594-4100. Fax (719)534-6259. Mar Porter, freelance coordinator. No freelance.

DAYSPRING CARDS, INC., Box 1010, 20984 Oak Ridge Rd., Siloam Springs AR 72761. (479)549-6303. Fax (479)524-8959. E-mail: info@dayspring.com (type "write" in message or subject line). Website: www.dayspring.com. Christian/religious card publisher. Please read guidelines before submitting. Prefers outright submission. Pays $60/idea on acceptance for all rts. No royalty. Responds in 4-8 wks. Uses unrhymed, traditional, light verse, conversational, contemporary; various lengths. Looking for inspirational cards for all occasions, including anniversary, birthday, relative birthday, congratulations, encouragement, friendship, get well, new baby, sympathy, thank you, wedding. Also needs seasonal cards for friends and family members for Christmas, Valentine, Easter, Mother's Day,

Father's Day, Thanksgiving, graduation, and Clergy Appreciation Day. Include scripture verse with each submission. Send 10 ideas or less. Guidelines by phone or e-mail; no catalog.

Tips: Prefers submissions on 8 x 11 inch sheets, not 3x5 cards (one idea per sheet).

DESIGNER GREETINGS, PO Box 140729, Staten Island NY 10314. Toll-free (800)654-6960. (718)981-7700. Fax (718)981-0151. E-mail: info@designergreetings.com. Website: www.designergreetings.com. Fern Gimbelman, art dir. 50% freelance. Holiday/seasonal 6 mos. ahead. Responds in 2 mos. Pays on acceptance for greeting card rts. Guidelines on Website. Uses rhymed or unrhymed verse. Produces announcements, conventional, humorous, informal, inspirational, invitations, juvenile, sensitivity, soft line, studio. Up to 50% freelance.

GIBSON GREETINGS, PO Box 371804, Cincinnati OH 45222-1804. E-mail: wcallah@gibson greetings.com. Website: www.gibsongreetings.com. No freelance.

GIFTS OF FAITH, (formerly TON Communications), 2295 Towne Lake Pkwy, #116-127, Woodstock GA 30189-5520. Toll-free (800)572-8866. Fax (800)722-0778. E-mail: info@jpatton catalog.com. Websites: www.giftsoffaith.com. Bought out by Dicksons. Christian humor cards. Willing to look at ideas from freelancers.

+#HEAVENLY DESIGNS, 118 Burnell Pl. S.E., Leesburg VA 20175. Toll-free (866)707-0113. Fax (703)737-0113. E-mails: cindyjames@birthverse.com, or bjames@birthverse.com. Bob & Cindy James, owners. Inspirational greeting cards.

*THE HERITAGE COLLECTION, 2 Forest Ln., Monroe NJ 08831-3256. Submit to Creative Director. General card publisher with a religious line. 20% freelance; buys 50-60 ideas/yr. Outright submission. Pays $35 on publication for domestic rts. No royalties. Responds in 4 wks. Prefers unrhymed; to 3 paragraphs. Produces announcements, inspirational, religious, and sensitivity. Needs anniversary, birthday, congratulations, friendship, get well, keep in touch, love, miss you, new baby, sympathy, thank you, and wedding. Also open to ideas for mugs. Guidelines/needs list; free catalog.

INSPIRATIONART & SCRIPTURE, INC., PO Box 5550, Cedar Rapids IA 52406-5550. Toll-free (800)728-5550. (319)365-4350. Fax (319)861-2103. E-mail: Charles@inspiration art.com. Website: www.inspirationart.com. Publishes Christian posters. Charles Edwards, creative dir. Open to freelance. Buys 20-30 ideas/yr. Prefers e-mail contact. Pays $150-250, 30 days after publication, for right to publish as a poster; or royalties 5% of net. Responds in 4 wks. Seasonal 6 mos. ahead. Open to new ideas for posters, bookmarks, or puzzles. Submit up to 3 ideas. Guidelines (also on Website); catalog on Website.

INSPIRATIONS UNLIMITED, PO Box 5097, Crestline CA 92325. Toll-free (800)337-6758. (909)338-6758. Fax (909)338-2907. Website: www.InspirationsUnlimited.org. General card publisher that does a few inspirational/religious cards. Open to freelance. Buys 50 ideas/yr. Prefers outright submission. Pays $25 on acceptance. No royalties. Responds in 4 wks. Prefers unrhymed verse (something that tugs at the heart). Produces conventional, informal, inspirational, religious, sensitivity. All types. Holiday/seasonal 1 yr. ahead. Open to ideas for new card lines, plaques, stationery, note cards, and gift tags. Send up to 10 ideas. No guidelines or catalog.

LAWSON FALLE PUBLISHING, 290 Pinebush Rd., Cambridge ON N1R 5X9, Canada. (821)623-7200. Fax (812)623-7201. E-mail: lsandman@nalu.net. Website: www.lawsonfalle.com. Larry Sandman, chief ed. General card publisher with an inspirational line. Open to freelance; buys 20 ideas/yr. Prefer outright submission or e-mail contact. Buys rights to publish in CBA. Pays variable amounts. Royalties 3-5% of wholesale on publication. Responds in 3 wks. Prefers rhymed, unrhymed, traditional, and light verse, under 40 wds. Produces announcements, conventional, humorous, informal, inspirational, invitations, juvenile, novelty. Needs all types except Halloween, especially humorous birthday cards. Seasonal 18 mos. ahead. Not open to new card lines. Send 10 ideas. Open to ideas for calendars/journals, gift/novelty items, greeting books, and stationery. No guidelines or catalog.

Tips: "We need good but clean humor."

LAURA LEIDEN CALLIGRAPHY, INC., PO Box 141, Watkinsville GA 30677. (706)769-6989. Fax (706)769-0628. E-mail: llc@lauraleiden.com. Website: www.lauraleidencalligraphy.com. Submit to: Freelance submissions. General card publisher with one or more inspirational (not religious) lines, and producer of specialty products. Open to freelance. Buys 10-20 ideas/yr. Outright submission. Responds in 12 wks. Buys all rts. on acceptance. No royalties. Prefers rhymed verse; sentimental/nostalgic; 4 stanzas, 4 lines ea. stanza. Produces conventional, inspirational. Needs Christmas, friendship, get well, mother, father, son, daughter, baby, animal lover, sympathy. Prefers 4-10 ideas/submission. Holiday/seasonal 8 mos. ahead. Not open to ideas for new card lines or specialty items. Also produces plaques. Send SASE for guidelines first; no catalog.

LIFE GREETINGS, Box 468, Little Compton RI 02837. Website: www.LifeGreetings.com. (401)635-8535. Fax (401)635-4918. Kathy Brennan, ed. Christian/religious card publisher. Not currently accepting freelance submissions.

+MASTERPIECE STUDIOS/EXPRESSIONS OF FAITH, PO Box 8660, Mankato MN 56002. Toll-free (800)447-0219. Fax (800)541-6309. Website: www.masterpiecestudios.com. Cards.

NORTHERN CARDS, Creative Department, 5694 Ambler Dr., Mississauga ON L4W 2K9, Canada. Toll-free (877)627-7444. (905)625-4944. Fax (905)625-5995. E-mail: artists@northern cards.com. Website: www.northerncards.com/docs/artists.shtml. Open to writers and artists. Greeting cards.

NOVO CARD PUBLISHERS, INC., 3630 W. Pratt Ave., Lincolnwood IL 60712. Toll-free (800)624-2426. (847)763-0077. Fax (847)763-0020. E-mail: art@novocard.net. Website: www.novocard.net. Submit to Art Production. General card publisher that does a few inspirational and religious cards. Open to freelance; buys 10 ideas/yr. Prefers outright submissions. Pays $2/line on acceptance for all rts. No royalties. Responds in 5 wks. Uses traditional and light verse; 5-20 lines (nothing too brief). Produces baby announcements, conventional, humorous, inspirational, invitations, juvenile, religious, studio. Needs anniversary, birthday, Christmas, congratulations, Easter, Father's Day, friendship, get well, miss you, Mother's Day, new baby, relatives (all occasions), sympathy, Thanksgiving, thank you, valentines, wedding. Seasonal 6-8 mos. ahead. Open to ideas for new card lines. Submit enough ideas to show style. Guidelines/needs list; no catalog.

Tips: "We don't want anything too brief or too lengthy. We like verse that holds everyone's hearts, especially the male gender."

+PLESH CREATIVE GROUP, INC., 38 A Park St., Medfield MA 02052. (508)359-6400. Fax (508)359-6448. E-mail: PleshCreativeGroup@verizon.net. Website: www.PleshCreative.com. Submit to: Suzanne Comeru. General card publisher with a religious line. Open to freelance. Prefers outright submissions. Buys all rts. Pays $25-35 on acceptance. No royalties. Responds in several wks. Uses rhymed, unrhymed, traditional, and light verse; 8-10 lines. Produces conventional, humorous, inspirational, juvenile, religious. Needs birthday, Easter, friendship, get well, and sympathy.

PRINTESSDI, 2058 N. Mills Ave., #520, Claremont CA 91711. (909)437-0808. E-mail: cards@printessdi.com. Website: www.printessdi.com. Diane Cooley, design ed. A general card publisher with one or more inspirational lines. Open to freelance. Buys 10-20 ideas/yr. Prefers outright submissions (read guidelines first). Buys all rts. Pays $20 on acceptance. Royalties 10%. Responds in 2-3 wks. Uses unrhymed, traditional, light verse; brief and to the point. Produces conventional, humorous, informal, inspirational, novelty. Needs birthday, Christmas, friendship, get well, love, Mother's Day, new baby, sympathy, thank you, valentines. Holiday/seasonal 6 mos. ahead. Open to new card lines. Prefers 3-10 ideas/submission tied together by theme and/or style. Guidelines/needs list (also on Website); no catalog.

Tips: "Need artwork: fresh, simple images (any media) with plain or no background. We do not use 'all over' card designs. Think 'clean, simple, classy.'"

P. S. GREETINGS, 5730 N. Tripp Ave., Chicago IL 60646-6723. Toll-free (800)621-8823. (773)267-6150. Fax (773)267-6055. E-mail: artdirector@psgreetings.com. Website: www.psgreetings.com. Fantus Paper Products. Jennifer Dodson, art dir. 100% freelance; 200-300 ideas/yr. Holiday/seasonal 6 mos. ahead. Responds in 1 mo. Pays flat fee on acceptance; no royalty. Rhymed or unrhymed verse. Produces conventional, humorous, inspirational, invitations, juvenile, sensitivity, soft line, and studio. Send 10 ideas. Submit on disk or by e-mail (copied into message). Guidelines/market list for #10 SASE (also on Website).

+PUMPERNICKEL PRESS, 508 Jack Enders Blvd., PO Box 603, Berryville VA 22611. (540)955-5770. Fax (540)955-5771. Website: www.pumpernickelpress.com. Angela Schwarzkopf, art dir. A general card publisher with one or more inspirational lines. Open to freelance. Buys 50-75 pieces of art/yr. Query. Buys greeting cards with artwork. Pays 5% royalty on publication. Uses light verse, 4-8 sentences. Inspirational cards.

RED FARM STUDIO, 1135 Roosevelt Ave., Pawtucket RI 02861-0347. (401)728-9300. Fax (401)728-0350. E-mail: sscott@redfarmstudio.com. Website: www.redfarmstudio.com. Thomas Scott, pres.; Steven Scott, VP; submit to Production Coordinator. General card publisher with a religious line. 100% freelance; buys 100 ideas/yr. Outright submission. Pays variable rates (about $4/line) within 1 mo. of acceptance for exclusive rts. No royalties. Responds in 2 mos. Use traditional and light verse; 1-4 lines. Produces announcements, invitations, religious. Needs anniversary, birthday, Christmas, friendship, get well, new baby, sympathy, wedding. Holiday 6 mos. ahead. Not open to ideas for new card lines. Submit any number of ideas. Guidelines/needs list for SASE.

*RIVER M, 29742—400th St., Le Sueur MN 56058. Toll-free (866)474-8376. Inspirational display cards.

BOB SIEMON DESIGNS INC., 3501 W. Segerstrom Ave., Santa Ana CA 92704-6497. (714)549-0678. Fax (714)979-2627. Website: www.bobsiemon.com. No freelance.

+SMILING MOON STUDIOS, 12930 Ventura Blvd., #907, Studio City CA 91604. Toll-free (877)752-6777. E-mail: info@smilingmoon.com. Website: www.smilingmoon.com. Christmas "Knockouts!" card line.

+SOLE SOURCE GREETINGS, Attn: Art Submissions or Attn: Copy Submissions, PO Box 5487, Bend OR 97708. Toll-free (800)346-5860. E-mail: submissions@solesourcegreetings .com. Website: www.solesourcegreetings.com. Send artwork via e-mail as a JPG or PDF file (see Website for size details). Check Website for samples of greetings. Open to: thinking of you, birthday, thank you, sympathy, new baby, congratulations, anniversary, wedding, etc. Also business-specific cards. Pays up to $500 for artwork; pays $25/message. Royalties 5% on retail sales; 2.5% on wholesale catalog sales.

WARNER PRESS INC., 1200 E. 5th St., PO Box 2499, Anderson IN 46018-9988. (765)644-7721. Fax (765)640-8005. E-mail: krhodes@warnerpress.org. Website: www.warner press.com. Karen Rhodes, sr. ed. Produces greeting cards. 30% freelance; buys 15-25 ideas/yr. Pays on acceptance. No royalties. Responds in 3-4 mos. Uses unrhymed prose, traditional & free verse for cards. Devotionals for bulletins—reflective, 110-150 wds, with scripture. Accepts 10 ideas/submission. Prefers e-mail submissions; be sure name and address are on each page. Guidelines on Website; no catalog.

Tips: "Most of our present purchases are for church bulletins; send bulletin submissions August-October only. Send greeting card submissions August-September. Those received at other times will be returned or held for possible use later, IF requested by the sender." Manuscripts/requests sent by regular mail without an SASE will not be returned.

ADDITIONAL CARD PUBLISHERS

NOTE: Following is a list of card publishers who did not respond to our questionnaire. You may want to contact them on your own to see if they are open to freelance submissions.

APPALACHIAN BIBLE CO. INC., 506 Princeton Rd., Johnson City TN 37601.

JOAN BAKER DESIGNS, 1130 Via Callejon, San Clemente, CA 92673.

BERG CHRISTIAN ENTERPRISES, 4525 S.E. 63rd Ave., Portland OR 97206.

BLACK FAMILY GREETING CARDS, 20 Cortlandt Ave., New Rochelle NY 10801. Bill Harte, pres.

BLACKSMITH CARDS & PRINTS, 37535 Festival Dr., Palm Desert CA 92211. Bob Smith, pres.

CD GREETING CARDS, PO Box 5084, Brentwood TN 37024-5084.

CRT CUSTOM PRODUCTS, INC., 7532 Hickory Hills Ct., Whites Creek TN 37189.

DESIGNS FOR BETTER LIVING, 1716 N. Vista St., Los Angeles CA 90046.

#KRISTIN ELLIOTT, INC., 10 Industrial Way, Amesbury MA 01913-3223.

EXPRESSIONS OF FAITH, PO Box 35777, Colorado Springs CO 80935-3577.

GOOD NEWS IN SIGHT, 2610 Mirror Lake Dr., Fayetteville NC 28303-5212.

GRACE PUBLICATIONS, 2125 Martindale S.W., Grand Rapids MI 49509.

GREENLEAF, INC., 951 S. Pine St., #250, Spartanburg SC 29302-3370. Greenleaf Foundation, Inc.

HERMITAGE ART CO., INC., 5151 N. Ravenswood Ave., Chicago IL 60640.

HIGHER HORIZONS, PO Box 78399, Los Angeles CA 90016-0399.

JODY HOUGHTON DESIGNS, INC., 2253 Lois Ln., West Linn OR 97068.

LORENZ CO., 1208 Cimmaron Dr., Waco TX 76712-8174.

LUCY & ME GALLERY, 13232 Riviera Pl. N.E., Seattle WA 98125-4645. Diane Roger, card ed.

ALFRED MAINZER, INC., 27-08—40th Ave., Long Island City NY 11101. Toll-free (800)22-cards. (718)392-4200. Fax (718)392-2681.

MCBETH CORP, PO Box 400, Chambersburg PA 17201.

MORE THAN A CARD, 5010 Baltimore Ave., Bethesda MD 20816.

OAKSPRINGS IMPRESSIONS, PO Box 572, Woodacre CA 94973-0572.

FREDERICK SINGER & SONS, INC., 2–15 Borden Ave., Long Island City NY 11101.

THESE THREE, INC., 314 Washington Rd., #1001, South Hills PA 15216-1638. Jean P. Bridgers, card ed.

RANDALL WILCOX PUBLISHING, 826 Orange Ave., #544, Coronado CA 92118.

CAROL WILSON FINE ARTS, PO Box 17394, Portland OR 97217. Gary Spector, ed.

GAME MARKETS

BIBLE GAMES CO., 14389 Cassell Rd., PO Box 237, Fredericktown OH 43019. Toll-free (800)824-2637. (740)694-8042. Fax (740)694-8072. E-mail: info@biblegamescompany.com. Website: www.biblegamescompany.com. JoAnn Vozar, operations mngr. Produces Bible games. 10% freelance. Buys 1-2 ideas/yr. Query. Pays on publication for all rts. (negotiable). Royalties 8%. Responds in 6-8 wks. Open to new ideas. One game per submission. Guidelines & catalog online.

> **Tips:** "Send developed and tested game play, target market, and audience. Must be totally nonsectarian and fully biblical—no fictionalized scenarios." Board games, CD-ROMs, computer games, and video games.

CACTUS GAME DESIGN, INC., 751 Tusquittee St., Hayesville NC 28904. (828)389-1536. Fax (828)389-1534. E-mail: rob@cactusgamedesign.com. Website: www.cactusgamedesign

.com. Rob Anderson, pres. Produces card games, board games, and computer games. Open to freelance submissions. Buys 2-4 ideas/yr. Query by e-mail. Pays variable amounts on acceptance for game rts. Pays 5-15% royalty for complete games only. Responds in 4 wks. Open to new ideas for games. Guidelines; catalog for .60 postage.

GOODE GAMES INTERNATIONAL, 211 Stirrup Cir., Nicholasville KY 40356. Toll-free (800)257-7767. (859)881-4513. Fax (859)881-0765. E-mail: info@goodegames.com. Website: www.goodegames.com. Contact: Mike Goode.

*GOOD STEWARD GAME CO., 6412 Sunnyfield Way, Sacramento CA 95823-5781. William Parker, ed.

#PRISMATECH PUBLISHING, 5680 Oakbrook Pkwy., Ste. 135, Norcross GA 30093. Toll-free (888)316-3206. (770)242-1898. Fax (770)242-6123. E-mail: WFWilliams@prismatech-inc .com. Website: www.prismatech-inc.com. Contact: Bill Williams. Board games.

#TALICOR, 22853 Rio Lobos Rd., Diamond Bar CA 91765-4196. (909)517-0076. Fax (909)517-1962. E-mail: webmaster@Talicor.com. Website: www.Talicor.com. Lew Herndon, pres. Produces board games and puzzles. 100% freelance; buys 10 ideas/yr. Outright submissions. Pays variable rates on publication for all rts. Royalty 4-6%. Responds in 4 wks. Seasonal 6 mos. ahead. Open to new ideas for puzzles or toys. Submit 1-4 ideas. No guidelines; catalog for 9x12 SAE/$1.42 postage (mark "Media Mail").

WISDOM TREE, PO Box 8682, Tucson AZ 85738-8682. Toll-free (800)772-4253. (520)825-5702. Fax (520)825-5710. E-mail: wisdom@christianlink.com. Website: www.wisdomtree games.com. Brenda Huff, owner. Produces Bible-based computer games. 30% freelance (Beta versions). Query. Negotiable rts. Pays variable rates on publication. Variable royalties. Responds in 1-6 wks. Seasonal 8 mos. ahead. Open to review beta versions of computer games, computer software, or video games. No guidelines; catalog on request.

   Special Needs: "Storybook/puzzle game engine."

GIFT/SPECIALTY ITEM MARKETS

ACTIVE DISCIPLE, PO Box 2045, Redmond WA 98073-2045. (425)260-6936. Fax (425)644-1777. E-mail: steveo@activedisciple.com. Website: www.activedisciple.com. Apparel.

ANCHOR WALLACE PUBLISHERS, 1000 Hwy 4 S., PO Box 7000, Sleepy Eye MN 56085-0007. Toll-free (800)533-3570. Fax (800)582-2352. E-mail: contactus@anchorwallace.com. Website: www.anchorwallace.com. Calendars and bulletins.

ARTBEATS, 129 Glover Ave., Norwalk CT 06850-1311. (203)847-2000. Fax (203)846-2105. E-mail: Richard@nygs.com. Website: www.NYGS.com. New York Graphic Society. Richard Fleischmann, pub. Produces prints and posters. Open to freelancers; purchases 100 ideas/yr. Outright submissions. Pays on publication. Royalties 10%. Responds in 3 wks. Does conventional, inspirational, juvenile, religious, and sensitivity prints and posters. Open to new ideas. Guidelines; no catalog.

ART 2 INSPIRE, INC., (formerly Contemporary Christian Art Posters), 140 E. 52nd St., Ste. 2C, New York NY 10022. Toll-free (888)999-4188. (212)486-7700. Fax (212)486-7077. E-mail: kingdavid18@aol.com. Website: www.Art-2-inspire.com. Catholic art posters.

*BE ONE CHRISTIAN SPORTSWEAR, 3208 Merrywood Dr., Sacramento CA 95825. (916)483-7630. Christian clothing.

CARPENTREE, INC., Carpentree Design, 2724 N. Sheridan, Tulsa OK 74115. Toll-free (800)736-2787. (918)582-3600. Fax (918)587-4329. Website: www.carpentree.com. Submit to Design Dept. Produces framed art and verse. Buys several ideas/yr. Prefers outright submission. Rights purchased are negotiable. Pays on publication; negotiable royalty. Responds in 12-15 wks. Uses rhymed, unrhymed, and traditional verse for framed art; 4-16 lines. Open to ideas for new specialty items. Submit max 3-10 ideas. Open to ideas for framed art, tabletop items, and gift/novelty items. Guidelines; catalog $5/10x13 SAE.

#CHRISTIAN ART GIFTS, 1025 N. Lombard Rd., PO Box 1443, Lombard IL 60148. Toll-free (800)521-7807. (630)599-0240. Fax (630)599-0245. Website: www.christianart gifts.com. Friendship cards, greeting books, bookmarks, mugs.

DEPENDING ON THE SON CHRISTIAN PATCHWORKS, 639 S. Everett Ave., Columbus OH 43213-2778. Toll-free (866)204-6011. E-mail from Website. Website: www.jcpatch.com. Iron-on patches.

DESTINY IMAGE GIFTS, PO Box 310, Shippensburg PA 17257. Toll-free (800)722-6774. (717)532-3040. Fax (717)532-9291. E-mail: dlm@destinyimage.com. Website: www .destinyimage.com. Don Milam, ed. mngr. No e-mail submissions. Gift books.

DEXSA: The Giving Company, PO Box 109, Hudson WI 54016. Toll-free (800)933-3972. (715)386-8701. Fax (888)559-1603. Website: www.dexsa.com. John Larson, owner.

+EAGLES WINGS, 2343 Clay St., Kissimmee FL 34741. (407)870-8800. Fax (407)932-0828. Website: www.eagleswings.com. Apparel.

+EXODUS WEAR, Exodus Enterprises, LLC, 9766—19th St., #401, Alta Loma CA 91737. Toll-free (888)3-EXODUS. Fax (909)899-7024. Website: www.exoduswear.com. Christian apparel.

FAMILYLIFE, PO Box 23840, Little Rock AR 72221-3840, or PO Box 7111, Little Rock AR 72223. Toll-free (800)358-6329. Website: www.familylife.com. Mark Whitlock, acq. ed. Producer of specialty products. Open to freelance. Prefers a query/SASE; e-query OK. Buys all rts. Payment negotiable. Pays 1/4 on acceptance and 3/4 on publication. Royalty 2-18% of gross. Responds within 24 mos. Holiday/seasonal 24 mos. ahead. Open to ideas for specialty items. Does activity/coloring books, audiotapes, bookmarks, calendars/journals, gift books, gift/novelty items, magnets, videos, and interactive multipiece resources. Guidelines; catalog for 9x12 SAE/4 stamps.

Tips: "We do content product. Please do not send us trinkets or cheap specialties. Study our resources and read our guidelines on our Website."

+GREENACRE WORKSHOP. Toll-free (800)851-7715. Fax (401)728-0350. E-mail: info@greenacreworkshop.com. Website: www.greenacreworkshop.com. Coloring/activity books; Paintables.

#GREGG GIFT COMPANY, 15281 Barranca Pkwy, Ste. H, Irvine CA 92618-2202. Toll-free (800)447-3440. (949)955-5900. Fax (949)955-1198. E-mail: sales@gregggiftcompany .com. Website: www.gregggiftcompany.com. Makes a variety of gift items. Open to freelance art. Prefers e-mail submissions.

HERITAGE PUZZLE, INC., 340 Witt St., Winston-Salem NC 27103. Toll-free (888)348-3717. Fax (336)760-3041. E-mail: heritagepuzzle@triad.rr.com. Website: www.heritage puzzle.com. Religious jigsaw puzzles.

+HIS TEN, INC., 2090 Idaho Dr., Pella IA 50219. (641)620-1020. E-mail: histen@iowatelcom .net. Website: www.histen.com. Christian apparel.

INSPIRIO GIFTS/ZONDERVAN PUBLISHING HOUSE, 5300 Patterson S.E., Grand Rapids MI 49530-0002. Toll-free (800)727-1309. Website: www.inspiriogifts.com. Gift company offering Bible and book covers, gift books, devotionals, boutique products, and home decor lines.

KNOW HIM CHRISTIAN GEAR, 6200 S. Troy Cir., #240, Englewood CO 80111. Toll-free (888)256-6944. (303)662-9512. Fax (303)662-9942. E-mail: Doug.Mckenna@knowhim .com. Website: www.knowhimcom. Doug McKenna, pres. Christian apparel.

JAMES LAWRENCE COMPANY, 1501 Livingstone Rd., PO Box 188, Hudson WI 54016. Toll-free (800)546-3699. (715)386-3082. Fax (800) 875-7578. (715)386-3699. E-mail:

admin@jameslawrencecompany.com. Website: www.jameslawrencecompany.com. Chuck Hetland, product development. Produces wall decor. Open to freelance. Buys 12-20 ideas/yr. Prefers outright submissions. Prefers exclusive rts. Pays $50-100/verse on acceptance. No royalties. Responds in 3 wks. Inspirational verse no shorter than 4 lines and no longer than 5 stanzas of 4 lines ea. Holiday 9-12 mos. ahead. Open to new ideas for mugs, plaques, pictures. Send any number of ideas. Guidelines; no catalog.

LIVING EPISTLES, 3401 Greensboro Ave., Tuscaloosa AL 35401. Toll-free (800)294-8637. Website: www.livingepistles.com. Apparel.

MULTNOMAH GIFTS, a Division of Multnomah Publishers, Inc., 601 N. Larch St., Sisters OR 97759. (541)549-1144. Fax (541)549-8048. E-mail: comments@multnomahbooks.com. Website: www.multnomahgifts.com. Produces 4-color gift books. Not open to freelance submissions. Guidelines; no catalog.

*PEELE ENTERPRISES SHIRT PRINTS, 3401 Hwy. 25N, Hodges SC 29653. Shirts.

POWERMARK: Comics Worth Reading, 380 E. Hwy. CC, Ste. B104, Nixa MO 65714. Toll-free (877)769-2669. Fax (417)724-0119. E-mail: webmaster@powermarkcomics.com. Website: www.powermarkcomics.com. Contact: Steve Benintendi. Christian comic books.

*PRINTS OF PEACE, PO Box 717, Camino CA 95709. (530)644-7044.

*RED LETTER 9, 2910 Kerry Forest Pkwy, D4, Tallahassee FL 32309. (866)804-4833. Fax (866)804-4832. Apparel and gift items.

+SIGNS OF THE SAVIOR, Oceanside CA. (619)991-7713 or (760)224-6258. E-mail: info@signsofthesavior.com. Website: www.signsofthesavior.com. Decals, apparel, hats, T-shirts, sweatshirts, flags, banners, magnets, etc.

SOLID LIGHT CO., PO Box 330, Lewis Center OH 43035-0330. Toll-free (800)726-9606. Fax (740)548-1223. E-mail: info@solidlightco.com. Website: www.solidlightco.com. Apparel.

SONTEEZ CHRISTIAN T-SHIRTS, PO Box 44106, Phoenix AZ 85064. Toll-free (800)874-4485. E-mail: info@sonteez.com. Website: www.sonteez.com. T-shirts.

SWANSON INC., 1200 Park Ave., Murfreesboro TN 37129. (615)896-4114. Fax (866)431-1313. E-mail: adam@swansoninc.com. Website: www.swansoninc.com. Adam Swanson, marketing. Produces specialty products. Just opening up to freelancers. Query. Pays on publication. No royalties. Responds in 8-10 wks. Uses rhymed, unrhymed, traditional, and light verse; short. Inspirational/Christian. Open to new ideas. Send any number. Open to ideas for coloring books, gift/novelty items, magnets, mugs, postcards, puzzles, T-shirts. No guidelines or catalog.

*WARFARE STORE, PO Box 681, Ocoee FL 34761. Toll-free (888)769-9931. Fax (208)972-1164. Website: www.warfarestore.com. Produces and distributes specialty products and cards. Open to freelance. Buys 3-4 ideas/yr. Prefers outright submissions. Pays on publication. Royalties 5-8%. Responds in 8-10 wks. Produces conventional cards; keep in touch, wedding, and humor. Open to ideas for new card lines or specialty items. Prefers more than one idea per submission. Guidelines; no catalog.

    Special Needs: Apparel for teen audience (skater, goth, punk, rave, etc.).

    Tips: "Visit our Website to see if your idea fits our audience. We resell products as well as manufacture our own products. Please send us your 'out of the box' ideas."

WARNER PRESS INC., 1200 E. 5th St., PO Box 2499, Anderson IN 46018-9988. (765)644-7721. Fax (765)640-8005. E-mail: krhodes@warnerpress.org. Website: www.warner press.com. Karen Rhodes, product mktg. ed. Producer of church resources (greeting cards, bulletins, coloring books, puzzle books). 30% freelance; buys 30-50 ideas/yr. Query for guidelines. Pays $30-35 on acceptance (for bulletins); material for bulletins cannot be sold elsewhere for bulletin use, but may be sold in any other medium. No royalties. Responds in 6-8 wks. Uses rhymed, unrhymed, traditional verse, and devotionals for bulletins; 16-24 lines. Accepts 10 ideas/submission. Also open to ideas for coloring books, church resource items. Guidelines for bulletins; no catalog.

SOFTWARE DEVELOPERS

AMG SOFTWARE, 6815 Shallowford Rd. (37421), PO Box 22000, Chattanooga TN 37422. Toll-free (800)266-4977. (423)894-6060, ext. 275. Fax (800)265-6690 or (423)894-9511. E-mail: danp@amginternational.org. Website: www.amgpublishers.org. AMG International. Dan Penwell, dir. of prod. dev./acq. Bible software.

BAKER BOOKS, Box 6287, Grand Rapids MI 49516-6287. (616)676-9185. Fax (616)676-9573. Website: www.BakerBooks.com. Baker Publishing Group.

BIBLESOFT, 22014—7th Ave. S., Seattle WA 98198-6235. (206)824-0547. Fax (206)824-1828. Website: www.biblesoft.com.

BROADMAN & HOLMAN SOFTWARE, 127 Ninth Ave. N., Nashville TN 37234. (615)251-3638. Website: www.broadmanholman.com.

DISCOVERY HOUSE SOFTWARE, PO Box 3566, Grand Rapids MI 49501. Toll-free (800)653-8333. Website: www.dhp.org. Does Bible study software.

ELLIS ENTERPRISES, INC., 5100 N. Brookline, #465, Oklahoma City OK 73112. (405)948-1766. E-mail: mail@ellisenterprises.com. Website: www.ellisenterprises.com, or www.BibleLibrary.com. Contact person: John Ellis. Produces the Micro Bible, Ultra Bible, Mega Bible, and Maxima Bible. Check out additional products on their Website.

LARIDIAN, 1733 Lake Terrace Rd. S.E., Cedar Rapids IA 52403. (319)378-4940. Fax (413)208-8477. E-mail: craigr@laridian.com, or support@laridian.com. Website: www.laridian.com. Craig Rairdin, pres. Send ideas by e-mail. Bible software for hand-held and palmtop computers.

LOGOS RESEARCH SYSTEMS, 1313 Commercial St., Bellingham WA 98225-4307. Phone/fax (360)527-1700. E-mail: info@logos.com. Website: www.logos.com. Contact: Dan Pritchett (DAN@logos.com), mkt. mngr. Publishes the Logos Bible Software Series X—Scholar's Library, Pastor's Library, and Bible Study Library. Over 3,800 titles from more than 100 publishers now compatible with the system.

*NAVPRESS SOFTWARE, 16002 Pool Canyon Rd., Austin TX 78734.

+OLIVE TREE BIBLE SOFTWARE, PO Box 48271, Spokane WA 99228-1271. Website: www.OliveTree.com. Bible software.

+RIVER DEEP, 100 Pine St., Ste. 1900, San Francisco CA 94111. (415)659-2000. E-mail: infor@riverdeep.com. Website: www.riverdeep.com. Software developer.

SILAS PUBLISHING SOFTWARE, 1154 Westchester Dr., Lilburn GA 30047. (404)625-9217. E-mail: scott@silasinteractive.com. Website: www.silasinteractive.com. Dr. Scott Philip Stewart, ed. Christian self-help books with software; develops companion software for printed books and computer-based training.

ZONDERVAN NEW MEDIA, 5300 Patterson St. S.E., Grand Rapids MI 49530. Toll-free (800)226-1122. (616)698-6900. Fax (616)698-3483. Website: www.zondervan.com. Contact: Britt Dennison. Software.

VIDEO/CD MARKETS

+ALPHA OMEGA PUBLICATIONS, 300 N. McKemy Ave., Chandler AZ 85226. Toll-free (866)444-4498. (602)438-2717. Website: www.AOP.com. Videos & DVDs.

AMG PUBLISHERS, 6815 Shallowford Rd. (37421), PO Box 22000, Chattanooga TN 37422. Toll-free (800)266-4977. (423)894-6060, ext. 275. Fax (800)265-6690 or (423)894-9511. E-mail: danp@amginternational.org. Website: www.amgpublishers.org. AMG International. Dan Penwell, dir. of prod. dev./acq. Bible CD-ROMs.

BIG IDEA PRODUCTIONS, INC., 230 Franklin Rd., #2A, Franklin TN 37064. (615)224-2200. Website: www.bigidea.com. Query; no unsolicited ideas. Movies, videos, music, books, and games.

CANDLELIGHT MEDIA GROUP, 566 Watson Branch Rd., Franklin TN 37064. Toll-free (800)747-2696. E-mail: info@candlelightmedia.com. Website: www.candlelightmedia .com. Videos, DVDs.

CHRISTIAN DUPLICATIONS INTL., INC., 1710 Lee Rd., Orlando FL 32810. Toll-free (800)327-9332.(407)299-7363. Fax (407)299-6004. E-mail: info@CDIMediasolutions .com. Website: www.CDIMediaSolutions.com. Videos.

CLOUD TEN PICTURES, PO Box 1440, Niagara Falls NY 14302. Or, One St. Paul St., Ste. 401, The Penthouse, St. Catherines ON L2R 7L2, Canada. (905)684-5561. Fax (905)684-7946. E-mail: movies@cloudtenpictures.com. Website: www.cloudtenpictures.com. Mario Falvo, corp. controller. Film production, theatrical release, video distribution, and marketing. Cloud Ten Pictures (maker of the Left Behind movies) is committed to maintaining its position as the industry leader in the production, distribution, and acquisition of quality faith-based family entertainment. For all media inquiries, contact Jessica Parker, Publicist. (905)684-5561, ext. 47, or e-mail: jessicap@cloudtenpictures.com.

CROWN VIDEO/CROWN COMEDY, 15397—117 Ave., Edmonton AB T5M 3X4, Canada. Toll-free (800)661-9467. (780)471-1417. Fax (780)474-0418. E-mail: info@crownvideo.com. Website: www.crownvideo.com. Precision Media Group. Videos, DVDs.

*DALLAS CHRISTIAN VIDEO, PO Box 450474, Garland TX 75045-0474. Toll-free (800)350-9458. Fax (972)644-5926. E-mail: DCV6681@aol.com. Contact: Bob Hill. Videos.

RUSS DOUGHTEN FILMS, INC., 5907 Meredith Dr., Des Moines IA 50322. Toll-free (800)247-3456. (515)278-4737. Fax (515)278-4738. E-mail: jmurphy@rdfilms.com. Website: www.rdfilms.com. Submit to Production Dept. Produces and distributes feature-length Christian movies. Open to ideas. Guidelines; free catalog.

GOODTIMES ENTERTAINMENT, 16 E. 40th St., New York NY 10016. Toll-free (800)285-6920. (212)951-3000. Fax (212)951-9319. E-mail: information@goodtimes.com. Website: www.goodtimesentertainmsnt.com. Videos.

GOSPEL COMMUNICATIONS, PO Box 455, Muskegon MI 49443-0455. Toll-free (800)467-7353. (231)774-3361. Fax (231)777-1847. Website: www.ChristianMediaSource.com. Videos, DVDs, books, Bibles, and music.

TOMMY NELSON VIDEOS, PO Box 141000, Nashville TN 37214. E-mail: breeves@tommynelson .com. Website: www.tommynelson.com. Contact: Bill Reeves, entertainment dir. Video producer.

PROPHECY PUBLICATIONS, PO Box 7000, Oklahoma City OK 73153. Toll-free (800)475-1111. Fax (405)636-1054. E-mail: JRChurch@swbell.net. Website: prophecyinthe news.com. Contact: J. R. Church. Religious education videos; fiction videos.

RANDOLF PRODUCTIONS, INC., 18005 Sky Park Cir., Ste. K, Irvine CA 92614-6514. Toll-free (800)266-7741. (949)794-9109. Fax (949)794-9117. E-mail: randy@randolfproductions .com. Website: www.randolfproductions.com. Distributor of music and video from Campus Crusade for Christ. Contact: Randy Ray. Videos, CD-ROMs, and DVDs.

SILAS PUBLISHING/VIDEO/CDs, 1154 Westchester Dr., Lilburn GA 30047. (404)625-9217. E-mail: info@silasinteractive.com. Website: www.silasinteractive.com. Dr. Scott Philip Stewart, ed. Interactive multimedia; book/CD sets.

ST. ANTHONY MESSENGER PRESS. See book listing for contact information.

TYNDALE FAMILY VIDEO, 351 Executive Dr., Carol Stream IL 60188. (630)668-8300. Website: www.tyndale.com. Videos.

VISION VIDEO/GATEWAY FILMS, PO Box 540, Worcester PA 19490-0540. (610)584-3500. Fax (610)584-6643. E-mail: info@VisionVideo.com. Website: www.VisionVideo.com. Contact: Karen Rutt.

VIVA ENTERTAINMENT, LLC, (formerly Soldiers of Light Productions), 10852 Plainview Ave., Tujunga CA 91042-1649. (818)951-6703. Contact: Jeff Varga. Specializes in supernatural horror movies from a Christian perspective.

WACKY WORLD STUDIOS, 148 E. Douglas Rd., Oldsmar FL 34677. (813)818-8277. Fax (813)818-8396. E-mail: info@wackyworld.tv. Website: www.wackyworld.tv. Full service custom art and design studio. Videos, DVDs.

+WHITAKER AUDIO, 30 Hunt Valley Cir., New Kensington PA 15068. Toll-free (877)793-9800. (724)334-2920. Toll-free fax (866)773-7001. Fax (724)334-2932. Website: www.whitakerhouse.com. Audio Bibles and books.

+WHITAKER ENTERTAINMENT, 30 Hunt Valley Cir., New Kensington PA 15068. Toll-free (877)793-9800. (724)334-2920. Toll-free fax (866)773-7001. Fax (724)334-2932. Website: www.whitakerhouse.com. Videos/CDs/DVDs.

WORLD WIDE PICTURES, INC., PO Box 668029, Charlotte NC 28266-8029. Toll-free (800)745-4318. Fax: (704)401-3013. E-mail: info@wwp.org. Website: www.wwp.org. Billy Graham Assn. DVDs.

ZONDERVAN NEW MEDIA, 5300 Patterson St. S.E., Grand Rapids MI 49530. Toll-free (800)226-1122. (616)698-6900. Fax (616)698-3483. Website: www.zondervan.com. Contact: T. J. Rathbun. Videos.

SPECIALTY PRODUCTS TOPICAL LISTINGS

NOTE: Most of the following publishers are greeting card/specialty market publishers, but some will be found in the book publisher listings.

ACTIVITY/COLORING BOOKS

Broadman & Holman
Cook Communications
Greenacre Workshop
Rainbow Publishers
Warfare Store
Warner Press Cards

AUDIOTAPES

AMG Software
Bible Games
Eldridge Plays
Fair Havens
McRuffy Press
Success Publishers
Tyndale House
W Publishing
Warfare Store
World Publishing
Zondervan New Media

BANNERS

Signs of the Savior

BOARD GAMES/GAMES

Bethel Publishing
Bible Games
Big Idea
Cactus Game
Carson-Dellosa

Cook Communications
Goode Games
Good Steward Game
Joshua Morris
Master Books
Prismatech
Review and Herald
Standard Publishing
Tyndale House
Warfare Store

BOOKMARKS

Bless His Name
Christian Art Gifts
Christian Inspirations

BULLETINS

Anchor Wallace
Broadman & Holman
Warner Press Cards

CALENDARS/DAILY JOURNALS

Abingdon Press
African American Expressions
American Tract Society
Anchor Wallace
Barbour Publishing
Christian Inspirations
Group Publishing
Lawson Falle

Neibauer Press
Tyndale House
Women of the Promise

CD-ROMs

AMG Software
Bible Games
Cactus Game
Cook Communications
Fair Havens
Georgetown Univ. Press
Group Publishing
Our Sunday Visitor
St. Anthony Mess.
Twenty-Third Public.
World Publishing

CHARTS

Rose Publishing

COMIC BOOKS

Cactus Game
InFuze Magazine
Kaleidoscope Press
Lighthouse Ebooks
Nelson Books
Powermark

COMPUTER GAMES

Bible Games
Big Idea

Cactus Game
Caribe-Betania Editores
Cook Communications
Dean Press, Robbie
Wisdom Tree
Wood Lake Books

COMPUTER SOFTWARE

AMG Software
Logos Research
Regal Books
Resource Public.
Wisdom Tree
Zondervan New Media

DVDs

Big Idea
Candlelight Media
Crown Video
Gospel Communications
Latimer Press
Wacky World
World Wide Pictures

GIFT BOOKS

Bless His Name
Blue Mountain Arts
Carroll Designs, William
Christian Inspirations
Destiny Image
Inspirio Gifts
Multnomah Gifts
Review and Herald

GIFT/NOVELTY ITEMS

Abingdon Press
African American Expressions
Carson-Dellosa
Christian Art Gifts
Christian Inspirations
Cook Communications
Depending on the Son
Houghton Designs, Jody
Lawson Falle
River M
Signs of the Savior
Zondervan New Media

GREETING BOOKS

Bless His Name
Blue Mountain Arts
Christian Art Gifts
Christian Inspirations
Houghton Designs, Jody
Lawson Falle

MAGNETS

African American Expressions
Christian Inspirations
Houghton Designs, Jody
Signs of the Savior

MUGS

Christian Art Gifts
Christian Inspirations
Heritage Collection
Lawrence Co., James
Warfare Store

NOTE CARDS

Creative Christian Gifts

PLAQUES

Christian Inspirations
Houghton Designs, Jody
Inspirations Unlimited
Lawrence Co., James
Leiden, Laura

POSTCARDS

Abingdon Press
Broadman & Holman Software
Houghton Designs, Jody
Warner Press Cards
Zondervan New Media

POSTERS

Art 2 Inspire
Bless His Name
Life Cycle Books
Warfare Store

PUZZLES

Bible Games
Christian Inspirations
Heritage Puzzle
Warfare Store

STATIONERY

African American Expressions
Christian Inspirations
Inspirations Unlimited
Lawson Falle

SUNDAY BULLETINS

Broadman & Holman Software
Christian Inspirations
Warner Press Cards

TOYS

Standard Publishing
Warfare Store

T-SHIRTS/APPAREL

Active Disciple
Be One Christian
Bless His Name
Christian Inspirations
Eagles Wings
Exodus Wear
His Ten
Know Him
Living Epistles
Peele Enterprises
Red Letter 9
Signs of the Savior
Solid Light

VIDEOS/VIDEO GAMES

Abingdon Press
AMG Video/CD
Bible Games
Big Idea
Big Idea Productions
Cactus Game
Candlelight Media
Christian Duplications
Cook Communications
Crown Video
Destiny Image
Doughten Films, Russ
Editorial Unilit
Fair Havens
Focus on the Family
GoodTimes
Gospel Communications
Group Publishing
Howard Publishing
Latimer Press
Master Books
Moody Press
Nelson Videos, Tommy
Pauline Books
Prophecy Publications
Regal Books
St. Anthony Mess.
Tyndale House
Victor Books
Viva Entertainment
W Publishing
Wacky World
Warfare Store
Wisdom Tree

CHRISTIAN WRITERS' CONFERENCES AND WORKSHOPS

(*) Indicates information was not verified or updated by the conference director
(+) Indicates a new listing

Note: Visit the following Websites for information on these and other conferences available across the country: www.freelancewriting.com/conferences, or www.screenwriter.com/insider/WritersCalendar.html. Link to the following conference sites at www.stuartmarket.com. Also visit the site below for help in preparing for your next conference:

WRITERS CONFERENCE GUIDELINES. Website: www.WritersConferenceGuidelines.com. A Website dedicated to helping writers master the conference submissions process. Learn what goes into writing your submission package, and how to do it right. Information on cover letters, queries, book proposals, article and manuscript formats, genre tips, meeting with faculty, making the most of your conference, and much more. Contributions from editors, publishers, agents, and experienced writers.

ALABAMA

SOUTHERN CHRISTIAN WRITERS CONFERENCE. Tuscaloosa/First Baptist Church; June 2006. Contact: Joanne Sloan, SCWC, PO Box 1106, Northport AL 35473. (205)333-8603. Fax (205)339-4528. E-mail: SCWCworkshop@aol.com. Website www.magazinewriting.com/scwc. Attendance: 220.

ARIZONA

AMERICAN CHRISTIAN WRITERS PHOENIX CONFERENCE. October 20-21, 2006; October 19-20, 2007. Contact: Reg A. Forder, Box 110390, Nashville TN 37222. 1-800-21-WRITE. E-mail: ACWriters@aol.com. Website: www.ACWriters.com. Attendance: 40-80.

CATHOLIC WRITERS CONFERENCE AND RETREAT. Redemptorist Renewal Center at Picture Rocks/near Tucson; February 2006. Contact: Thomas M. Santa, CSSR, 7101 W. Picture Rocks Rd., Tucson AZ 85743. (520)744-3400. Fax (520)744-8021. E-mail: office@desertrenewal.org. Website: www.desertrenewal.org. Speakers: Working professionals and select editors from Catholic publishers. Attendance: 40-50. Awards an annual $500 scholarship to attend this conference. Applicants must send a 250-word statement, explaining why they should receive the scholarship, by e-mail only to: CBPA3@aol.com. Also Sessions One and Two for Beginning Writers on January 13-17, 2006, and March 22-26, 2006. Editors in attendance.

SOUTH-EASTERN ARIZONA CHRISTIAN WRITERS WORKSHOP. Benson; November 4, 2006 (always the 1st Saturday of November). Contact: Floyd Pierce, 6565 Jeffords Trail, Willcox AZ 85643. (520)384-3064.

ARKANSAS

ANNUAL ARKANSAS WRITERS CONFERENCE. Little Rock; June 2-3, 2006 (always 1st Friday & Saturday of June). Contact: Barbara Mulkey, 9317 Claremore, Little Rock AR 72227. (501)312-1747. E-mail: blm@aristotle.net. Attendance: 200. Sponsors 32 contests; one $6 entry free covers all contests.

OZARK CREATIVE WRITERS CONFERENCE. Eureka Springs; October 12-14, 2006 (always

2nd weekend, Thursday-Saturday, of October). Contact: Clarissa Willis, 2603 W. Walnut, Johnson City TN 37604. (423)929-1049. E-mail: ozarkcreativewriters@earthlink.net. Website: www.ozarkcreativewriters.org. Editors and agents in attendance. Sponsors 25-30 contests each year. Attendance: 200.

CALIFORNIA

#ACT ONE: WRITING FOR HOLLYWOOD. Hollywood; July/August 2006. Contact: Barbara R. Nicolosi, 1763 N. Gower St., Hollywood CA 90028. (323)464-0815. Fax (323)462-2550. E-mail: Actone@fpch.org or info@actoneprogram.com. Website: www.ActOneProgram.com. These are month-long intensive training session for screenwriters. No editors or agents in attendance. Limited to 30 students (by application).

ALL DAY FICTION. Tehachapi; not being held in 2006. Contact: Lauraine Snelling (instructor), 19872 Highline Rd., Tehachapi CA 93561. (661)823-0669. Fax (661)823-9427. E-mail: TLSnelling@yahoo.com. Website: www.LauraineSnelling.net. Attendance: limited to 15.

AMERICAN CHRISTIAN WRITERS ANAHEIM CONFERENCE. October 13-14, 2006; October 12-13, 2007. Contact: Reg A. Forder, Box 110390, Nashville TN 37222. 1-800-21-WRITE. E-mail: ACWriters@aol.com. Website: www.ACWriters.com. Attendance: 40-80.

+AUTHORIZEME. Contact: Sharon Norris Elliott, PO Box 1519, Inglewood CA 90308. (323)357-9497. E-mail: AuthorizeMe@sbcglobal.net. Website: www.AuthorizeMe.net. Offers 12-hr. seminars to assist writers in fully visualizing, organizing, outlining, and jump-starting their book projects. Authors leave the seminar equipped with full chapter synopsis, proposal, and beginning marketing ideas. Seminars offered nationwide. For a list of scheduled seminars or to sponsor a seminar in your area, e-mail or mail your request to Sharon Elliott (see above).

BIOLA MEDIA CONFERENCE. La Mirada; April 2006. Contact: Craig Detweiler, Biola University, 13800 Biola Ave., La Mirada CA 90639. Toll-free (866)334-2266. Website: www.biola.edu/media.

CASTRO VALLEY CHRISTIAN WRITERS SEMINAR. Castro Valley; February 17-18, 2006; February 2007. Contact: Pastor Jon Drury, 19300 Redwood Rd., Castro Valley CA 94546-3465. (510)886-6300. Fax (510)581-5022. E-mail: jond@redwoodchapel.org. Website: www.christianwriter.org. Speaker 2006: Lee Roddy. On occasion has editors/agents in attendance. Attendance: 200.

FICTION INTENSIVE, for fiction writers who want to go deeper. Tehachapi; June 2006. Contact: Lauraine Snelling (instructor), 19872 Highline Rd., Tehachapi CA 93561. (661)823-0669. Fax (661)823-9427. E-mail: TLSnelling@yahoo.com. Website: www.LauraineSnelling.net. Attendance: limited to 10-12.

HANDS-ON WRITER'S WEEKEND. Lake Elsinore; April & October 2006. Contact: Beverly Caruso, PO Box 1388, Lake Elsinore CA 92530. (951)245-4082. E-mail: rancho@across2u.com. Website: www.cross2u.com/writersweekend.html. This is a small (no more than 10) interactive workshop/instruction & personal time with Beverly Caruso. Editors in attendance; no agents.

+HIGH DESERT CHRISTIAN WRITER'S CONFERENCE. Quartz Hill; May 5-6, 2006. Sponsored by the High Desert Christian Writer's Guild and Quartz Hill School of Theology. Theme: Streams in the Desert. Contact: Don Patterson, 6223 Almond Valley Way, Quartz Hill CA 93536. (661)722-5695. E-mail: streams@theology.edu. Website: www.theology.edu/writers.

LODI ALL-DAY WRITERS SEMINAR. Stockton; not scheduled at this time. General writing conference; not just Christian writers. Contact: Dee Porter, PO Box 1863, 103 Koni Ct. (95240), Lodi CA 95241. Phone/fax (209)334-0603. E-mail: crcomm@lodinet.com. Write or e-mail for conference information.

MOUNT HERMON CHRISTIAN WRITERS CONFERENCE. Mount Hermon (near Santa Cruz); April 7-11, 2006; March 30-April 3, 2007; also Mentoring Clinic November 2006. Offers a Career Track for professional writers. Also offers a teen track. Contact: David R. Talbott, Box 413, Mount Hermon CA 95041-0413. (831)335-4466. Fax (831)335-9413. E-mail: dtalbott@mhcamps.org. Website: www.mounthermon.org/writers. Many editors and agents in attendance. Attendance: 450.

#ORANGE COUNTY CHRISTIAN WRITERS FELLOWSHIP WRITERS DAYS. Location to be announced; April 2006, and possibly fall 2006. Contact: Beverly Bush Smith or Bonnie Compton Hanson, PO Box 982, Lake Forest CA 92630. (714)639-6546. Fax (949)458-1807. E-mail: bonnieh1@worldnet.att.net, or b2smith@pacbell.net, or editor@occwf.org. Website: www.occwf.org. Attendance: 100.

THE PUBLISHING GAME WORKSHOP. San Francisco; check Website for date. Contact: Alyza Harris, Peanut Butter and Jelly Press, PO Box 590239, Newton MA 02459. Phone/fax (617)630-0945. E-mail: workshop@PublishingGame.com. Website: www.PublishingGame .com (registration form on Website). Speaker: Fern Reiss. Attendance: limited to 18.

SAN DIEGO CHRISTIAN WRITERS GUILD FALL CONFERENCE. San Diego; September 22-23, 2006. Contact: Jennie Gillespie, PO Box 270403, San Diego CA 92198. (619)221-8183. Fax (619)255-1131. E-mail: info@sandiegocwg.org. Website: www.sandiegocwg.org. Editors and agents in attendance. Attendance: 180.

SANTA BARBARA CHRISTIAN WRITERS CONFERENCE. Westmont College; October 7, 2006. Contact: Rev. Opal Mae Dailey, PO Box 42429, Santa Barbara CA 93140. Phone/fax (805)682-0316. E-mail: cwgsb@sbcglogal.net. Attendance: 50.

SCBWI WRITERS & ILLUSTRATORS CONFERENCE IN CHILDREN'S LITERATURE. New York City, early February 2006; Los Angeles; early August 2006. Society of Children's Book Writers & Illustrators. Contact: Lin Oliver, 8271 Beverly Blvd., Los Angeles CA 90048. (323)782-1010. Fax (323)782-1892. E-mail: scbwi@scbwi.org. Website: www.scbwi.org. Includes a track for professionals. Editors and agents in attendance. Attendance: 900.

WRITERS SYMPOSIUM BY THE SEA. San Diego/Point Loma Nazarene University; February 8-11, 2006. Contact: Dean Nelson, Professor, Journalism Dept., PLNU, 3900 Lomaland Dr., San Diego CA 92106. (619)849-2592. Fax (619)849-2566. E-mail: deannelson@ptloma .edu. Website: www.ptloma.edu/writers. Sometimes has editors in attendance. Speakers include Barbara Taylor Brown and Donald Miller. Attendance: 300-1,000.

COLORADO

AD LIB CHRISTIAN ARTS RETREAT. St. Malo Retreat and Conference Center/Allenspark; September/October 2006. Contact: Judith Deem Dupree, PO Box 365, Pine Valley CA 91962-0365. Phone/fax (619)473-8683, or (303)823-9938. E-mail: adlib@ixpres.com, or joan nekirwin@yahoo.com. Website: www.adlibchristianarts.org. Retreat and forum for literary, visual, and performing arts. Designed as a forum and format for renewal. Solitude, fellowship, issues and ideas, critiquing. Notable speakers. No "working" editors or agents. Attendance: 35-40.

AMERICAN CHRISTIAN WRITERS COLORADO SPRINGS CONFERENCE. September 8-9, 2006; September 7-8, 2007. Contact: Reg A. Forder, Box 110390, Nashville TN 37222. 1-800-21-WRITE. E-mail: ACWriters@aol.com. Website: www.ACWriters.com. Attendance: 40-80.

CLASS REUNION. Denver; July 2006 (limited to first 80 CLASS graduates). Marketing conference for writers. Includes appointments with editors. Contact: Marita Littauer, PO Box 66810, Albuquerque, NM 87193-6810. (505)899-4283. Fax (505)899-9282. E-mail: info@classervices.com. Website: www.classervices.com.

COLORADO CHRISTIAN WRITERS CONFERENCE. Estes Park; May 17-20, 2006 at the YMCA of the Rockies. Director: Marlene Bagnull, LittD, 316 Blanchard Rd., Drexel Hill, PA 19026-3507. Phone/fax (610)626-6833. E-mail: mbagnull@aol.com. Website: www.write hisanswer.com/Colorado. Conferees choose six hour-long workshops from 42 offered or a Fiction Clinic (by application) plus one 6.5 hour continuing session from seven offered. One-on-one appointments, paid critiques, editors panels, and general sessions. Wednesday or Thursday evening concert by Marty Goetz. Teens Write Saturday afternoon, plus teens are welcome to attend the entire conference at half price. Contest (registered conferees only) awards four $75 discounts off May 16-19, 2007, conference. Faculty of 40-45 authors, editors, and agents. Attendance: 250.

GLEN EYRIE FICTION WRITER'S CONFERENCE. Colorado Springs; January 23-26, 2006. Contact: Craig Dunham, 3820 N. 30th, Colorado Springs CO 80904. Toll-free (800)944-GLEN. (719)272-7749. E-mail: craig_dunham@navigators.org. Website: www.gleneyrie group.org. Speaker: Ted Dekker. Some editors/agents in attendance. Attendance: 100.

+GMA MUSIC IN THE ROCKIES CONFERENCE. Estes Park; July 31-August 6, 2006; July 30-August 5, 2007. Contact: John W. Styll, dir., 1205 Division St., Nashville TN 37203. (615)242-0303. Fax (615)254-9755. Website: www.gospelmusic.org. Offers advanced track and teens track; critiques, talent, competition, and seminars. A & R and industry reps on site; teaching and judging. Attendance: 1,200.

INTERNATIONAL CHRISTIAN RETAIL SHOW (formerly CBA International Convention). (Held in a different location each year.) July 9-13, 2006, Denver CO. Contact: CBA, Box 62000, Colorado Springs CO 80962-2000. Toll-free (800)252-1950. (719)265-9895. Website: www.christianretailshow.com. Entrance badges available through book publishers or Christian bookstores. Attendance: 14,000.

JERRY B. JENKINS CHRISTIAN WRITERS GUILD WRITING FOR THE SOUL CONFERENCE. Colorado Springs; February 16-19, 2006; February 15-18, 2007. Sponsored by the Jerry B. Jenkins Christian Writers Guild. Held at the luxurious 5-star, 5-diamond Broadmoor Hotel. Host: Jerry B. Jenkins. Speakers include: Frank Peretti, Sue Buchanan, Dennis Hensley, and McNair Wilson. Gourmet meals during keynote sessions and in-depth workshops on 9 tracks, including a track exclusively for teens. Over 30 editors and agents in attendance. Payment plans are available. Special meal rates offered for nonparticipating spouses or parents of teens. Offers multiple general sessions with national keynote speakers and in-depth workshops on 6 tracks; plus appointments with publisher's reps. Contact: Wayne Atcheson, PO Box 88196, Black Forest CO 80908. Toll-free (866)495-5177, ext. 37. Fax (719)495-5181. E-mail: ContactUs@christianwritersguild.com. Website: www .christianwritersguild.com. Attendance: 350. See contest listings for Operation First Book Contests.

+WRITE AWAY WEEKEND. Frisco; check Website for dates. Christian writing retreat for women. Contact: Linda Evans Shepherd through Website only. Website: www.WriteAway Weekend.com. Speaker: Linda Evans Shepherd. No editors or agents in attendance. Attendance: limited to 6-8.

CONNECTICUT

WESLEYAN WRITERS CONFERENCE. Wesleyan University/Middletown; June 18-23, 2006 (always 3rd week). Contact: Anne Greene, 279 Court St., Middletown CT 06457. (860)685-3604. Fax (860)685-2441. E-mail: agreene@wesleyan.edu. Website: www.wesleyan.edu/ writers. Includes an advanced track. Editors and agents in attendance. Offers fellowship and scholarship awards. Attendance: 100.

DELAWARE

+**DELAWARE CHRISTIAN WRITERS CONFERENCE,** on the campus of University of Delaware; Newark; April 20-22, 2006. (302)834-4910. E-mail: dechristianwritersconference@ yahoo.com. Website: www.Ilovetowriteday.org. Director: John Riddle. Editors, publishers, agents, and professional writers will offer over 22 workshops. Scholarships available.

DISTRICT OF COLUMBIA

ACT ONE: WRITING FOR HOLLYWOOD. Washington DC; May 1-31, 2006. Contact: Barbara R. Nicolosi, 2690 Beachwood Dr., Lower Fl., Hollywood CA 90068. (323)464-0815. Fax (323)464-0851. E-mail: info@actoneprogram.com. Website: www.ActOneprogram.com. Limited to 30 students. These are month-long intensive training session for screenwriters.

FLORIDA

AMERICAN CHRISTIAN WRITERS ORLANDO CONFERENCE. November 18, 2006; November 17, 2007. Contact: Reg A. Forder, Box 110390, Nashville TN 37222. 1-800-21-WRITE. E-mail: ACWriters@aol.com. Website: www.ACWriters.com. Attendance: 40-80.

EVANGELICAL PRESS ASSOCIATION CONVENTION. Orlando (held in different location each year); May 7-10, 2006. Contact: Doug Trouten, dir., PO Box 28129, Crystal MN 55428. (763)535-4793. Fax (763)535-4794. E-mail: mailto:director@epassoc.org. Website: www.epassoc.org. Attendance: 300-400. Annual convention for editors of evangelical periodicals; freelance communicators welcome.

FLORIDA CHRISTIAN WRITERS CONFERENCE. Bradenton; March 2-5, 2006. Contact: Billie Wilson, 2344 Armour Ct., Titusville FL 32780. (321)269-5831. Fax (321)264-0037. E-mail: billiewilson@cfl.rr.com. Website: www.flwriters.org. Offers advanced track. Editors and agents in attendance. Offers awards in 10 categories. Attendance: 225.

+**2006: A ROMANCE ODYSSEY.** Cocoa Beach; February 3-5, 2006. Contact: Marilyn Ivison, PO Box 410787, Melbourne FL 32941-0787. (321)757-9506. E-mail: msivison@bell south.net. Website: www.authorsofromance.com. Sponsors a contest called "Launching a Star" (see details on Website). Speakers: Rachel Gibson and Madeline Hunter, plus 20 published authors. Editors and agents in attendance (4 each). Attendance: 250.

WORD WEAVERS CHRISTIAN WRITERS RETREAT. Vero Beach; January 2006 (unconfirmed). Contact: Eva Marie Everson, 122 Fairway Ten Dr., Casselberry FL 32707-4823. Phone/fax (407)695-9366. E-mail: EvaMarieEverson@aol.com.

WRITING STRATEGIES FOR THE CHRISTIAN MARKET. Not offered in seminar; only as independent studies, with manual and assignments. Contact instructor: Rosemary J. Upton, 2712 S. Peninsula Dr., Daytona Beach FL 32118-5706. Phone/fax (386)322-1111. E-mail: rupton@cfl.rr.com. E-mail name and address to request a brochure on Writing Strategies for the Christian Market course.

GEORGIA

AMERICAN CHRISTIAN WRITERS ATLANTA CONFERENCE. May 19-20, 2006; July 6-7, 2007. Contact: Reg Forder, Box 110390, Nashville TN 37222. 1-800-21-WRITE. E-mail: ACWriters@aol.com. Website: www.ACWriters.com. Attendance: 40-80.

SOUTHEASTERN WRITERS CONFERENCE. Epworth-by-the-Sea, St. Simons Island; mid-June 2006. Contact: Holly McClure, Dir., 210 Harrington Rd., St. Simons Island GA 31522 (holly.mcc@mindspring.com), or Donna Bond, 265 Lake Valley Rd., Hendersonville TN

37075 (Donna.mari@comcast.net). E-mail: info@southeasternwriters.com. Website: www.southeasternwriters.com. Attendance: limited to 100. Awards cash prizes to attendees in every genre, and free manuscript critiques.

HAWAII

MAUI WRITERS RETREAT AND CONFERENCE. Wailea. Retreat, August 25-30, 2006; Conference, Labor Day weekend, September 1-4, 2006. Contact: Shannon and John Tullius, Maui Writers Foundation, PO Box 1118, Kihei HI 96753. (808)879-0061. Fax (808)879-6233. E-mail: writers@mauiwriters.com. Website: www.mauiwriters.com. Download forms or sign up from Website. Secular. Editors and agents in attendance. Sponsors the Rupert Hughes Writing Contest.

ILLINOIS

KARITOS CHRISTIAN ARTS CONFERENCE. Elgin; July 2006. Contact: Bob Hay, 24 N. Belmont Ave., #B, Arlington Heights IL 60004. (847)749-1284. E-mail: bob@karitos.com. Website: www.karitos.com. Karitos is a festival conducting classes and showcases in all areas of the arts, including writing. Attendance: 300-400.

WRITE-TO-PUBLISH CONFERENCE. Wheaton (Chicago area); June 7-10, 2006. Contact: Lin Johnson, 9731 N. Fox Glen Dr., #6F, Niles IL 60714-4222. (847)296-3964. Fax (847)296-0754. E-mail: lin@WriteToPublish.com. Website: www.WriteToPublish.com. Offers advanced track (prerequisite 2 published books). Keynote speaker: Lynn Austin. Majority of faculty are editors; also has agents. Attendance: 275.

INDIANA

AMERICAN CHRISTIAN WRITERS FORT WAYNE CONFERENCE. Holiday Inn; April 7-8, 2006; March 30-31, 2007. Contact: Reg A. Forder, Box 110390, Nashville TN 37222. 1-800-21-WRITE. E-mail: ACWriters@aol.com. Website: www.ACWriters.com. Attendance: 40-80.

AMERICAN CHRISTIAN WRITERS INDIANAPOLIS CONFERENCE. July 29, 2006; August 4, 2007. Contact: Reg A. Forder, Box 110390, Nashville TN 37222. 1-800-21-WRITE. E-mail: ACWriters@aol.com. Website: www.ACWriters.com. Attendance: 40-80.

+AMERICAN CHRISTIAN WRITERS SOUTH BEND CONFERENCE. March 31-April 1, 2006; March 23-24, 2007. Contact: Reg A. Forder, Box 110390, Nashville TN 37222. 1-800-21-WRITE. E-mail: ACWriters@aol.com. Website: www.ACWriters.com. Attendance: 40-80.

BETHEL COLLEGE CHRISTIAN WRITERS' WORKSHOP. Bethel College/Mishawaka; planning a conference with American Christian Writers, March 31-April 1. Contact: Kim Peterson, 1001 W. McKinley Ave., Mishawaka IN 46545-5509. (574)257-3375. E-mail: petersk@bethelcollege.edu. Offers tracks for beginning & advanced writers. Attendance: 110.

EARLHAM SCHOOL OF RELIGION ANNUAL COLLOQUIUM: THE MINISTRY OF WRITING. Richmond; October 20-21, 2006 (always 3rd weekend). Editors in attendance. Contact: '06 Writing Colloquium, Director, Earlham School of Religion, 228 College Ave., Richmond IN 47374. Toll-free (800)432-1377. (765)983-1423. Fax (765)983-1688. E-mail: esr@earlham.edu. Website: www.esr.earlham.edu. Attendance: 150.

MIDWEST WRITERS WORKSHOP. Muncie/Ball State University Alumni Center; July 27-29, 2006 (always the last Thursday, Friday, and Saturday of July). Contact: Dept. of Journalism, Ball State University, Muncie IN 47306-0484. Director: Jama Kehoe Bigger. (765)282-1055. Fax (765)285-7997. E-mail: info@midwestwriters.org. Website: www.midwestwriters.org. Editors and sometimes agents in attendance. Attendance: 125. Also sponsors a 2-day writers' retreat in May.

IOWA

IOWA SUMMER WRITING FESTIVAL. University of Iowa/Iowa City; June & July 2006. This is a secular writer's conference that comes highly recommended for good, solid instruction. Contact: Iowa Summer Writing Festival, C215 Seashore Hall, University of Iowa, Iowa City IA 52242-5000. (319)335-4160. Fax (319)335-4039. E-mail: iswfestival@uiowa.edu. Website: www.uiowa.edu/~iswfest. For two months, June and July, you can sign up for either one-week workshops or weekend workshops on a wide variety of topics. Write for a catalog of offerings (available in February).

+QUAD-CITIES CHRISTIAN WRITERS' CONFERENCE. Bettendorf; March 31-April 1, 2006. Contact: Twila Belk, 4350 Tanglewood Rd., Bettendorf IA 52722. (563)332-1622. E-mail: iamstraightway@aol.com. Website: www.gottatellsomebody.com. Speakers: Wayne Holmes, Chris White, Myrna Strasser, Twila Belk, Dr. Dennis Hensley, and others. No editors or agents in attendance. Attendance 100+.

KANSAS

CALLED TO WRITE. Girard; March 31-April 1, 2006. Contact: Deborah Vogts, 17300 Ness Rd., Erie KS 66733. (620)244-5619. E-mail: debvogts@terraworld.net. Website: www.christian writersgirard.org. Sponsors a contest for attendees only. Attendance: 45-50.

***LITERARY ARTS FESTIVAL.** The Milton Center/Wichita; February 2006. Cosponsored with Newman University English Department. Contact: Dr. Bryan Dietrich, Newman University, 3100 McCormick, Wichita KS 67213-2097. (316)942-4291. Fax (316)942-4483. Website: www.newmanu.edu/miltoncenter. Offers advanced track. Sometimes has editors in attendance; usually not agents. Sponsors a contest.

KENTUCKY

AMERICAN CHRISTIAN WRITERS LOUISVILLE CONFERENCE. July 22, 2006; June 2, 2007. Contact: Reg A. Forder, Box 110390, Nashville TN 37222. 1-800-21-WRITE. E-mail: ACWriters@aol.com. Website: www.ACWriters.com. Attendance: 40-80.

#ANNUAL KENTUCKY CHRISTIAN WRITERS' CONFERENCE. Memorial United Methodist Church, Elizabethtown; June 2006. Contact: Crystal Murray, 1440 Shingo Ave., Louisville KY 40215-1132. (502)361-7078. E-mail: crystalamurray@insightbb.com. Speaker: Dr. Dennis Hensley. Editors in attendance. Attendance: 60-100.

LOUISIANA

+BAYOU WRITERS' GROUP WORKSHOP. Lake Charles. November 2006. Contact: Randy Dupre, PO Box 602, Iota LA 70543. One-day seminar.

MAINE

#STATE OF MAINE WRITERS' CONFERENCE. Ocean Park; August 2006. Contact: Jim Brosnan. E-mail: Jim.Brosnan@jwu.edu. Attendance: 30. Sponsors several contests. Editors in attendance.

MARYLAND

SANDY COVE CHRISTIAN WRITERS CONFERENCE. Sandy Cove/North East; October 1-4, 2006. Offers Advanced and Teen Tracks. Contact: Jim Watkins, Writers' Conference Director, Sandy Cove Ministries, 60 Sandy Cove Rd., North East MD 21901. Toll-free (800)234-2683. E-mail: info@sandycove.com. Website: www.jameswatkins.com/sandycove.htm. Editors and agents in attendance. Attendance: 150.

WISE PEN CHRISTIAN WRITERS GUILD SEMINAR. Bel Air; October 2006. Contact: Anne Perry, 5714 Denwood Ave., Baltimore MD 21017. (410)488-3761. Attendance: 50.

MASSACHUSETTS

CAPE COD ANNUAL SUMMER WRITERS' CONFERENCE AND YOUNG WRITERS' WORKSHOP (ages 12-16). Craigville Conference Center; August 2006. Contact: Jacqueline M. Loring, dir., PO Box 408, Osterville MA 02665. (508)420-0200. Fax (508)420-0212. E-mail: ccwc@capecod.net. Website: www.capecodwriterscenter.org. Editors and agents in attendance. Attendance: 150.

THE PUBLISHING GAME WORKSHOP. Boston; September 26, 2006. Contact: Alyza Harris, Peanut Butter and Jelly Press, PO Box 590239, Newton MA 02459. Phone/fax (617)630-0945. E-mail: workshop@PublishingGame.com. Website: www.PublishingGame.com (registration form on Website). Speaker: Fern Reiss. Attendance: limited to 18.

MICHIGAN

+ACW DETROIT CONFERENCE. Detroit; fall 2006. Contact: Pam Perry, 21442 Hamilton, Farmington Hills MI 48336. (248)426-2300. Fax (248)471-2422. E-mail: PamPerry@ministrymarketing.com. Website: www.ministrymarketing.com. Speakers: Dr. Gail Hayes and Denise Stinson. Offers class/track for advanced writers. Attendance: 300. Editors/agents in attendance.

"ADVANCED SPEAK UP WITH CONFIDENCE" SEMINAR. Hillsdale; check Website for 2006 dates. Contact: Carol Kent, 1614 Edison Shores Pl., Port Huron MI 48060. Toll-free (888)870-7719. (810)982-0898. Fax (810)987-4163. E-mail: Speakupinc@aol.com. Website: www.SpeakUpSpeakerServices.com. Speakers: Carol Kent and Jennie Afman Dimkoff. Speaking seminar. Offers advanced training. Also offers a seminar on writing for speakers who write. Attendance: 100. Also offers several Basic Speak Up Seminars.

AMERICAN CHRISTIAN WRITERS GRAND RAPIDS CONFERENCE. June 23-24, 2006; June 22-23, 2007. Contact: Reg Forder, Box 110390, Nashville TN 37222. 1-800-21-WRITE. E-mail: ACWriters@aol.com. Website: www.ACWriters.com. Attendance: 40-80.

MARANATHA CHRISTIAN WRITERS SEMINAR. Maranatha Bible & Missionary Conference/Muskegon; August 2006. Contact: Maranatha, 4759 Lake Harbor Rd., Muskegon MI 49441-5299. (231)798-2161. E-mail: info@maranatha-bmc.org. Website: www.maranatha-bmc.org. Editors in attendance. Attendance: 50.

MINNESOTA

AMERICAN CHRISTIAN WRITERS MINNEAPOLIS CONFERENCE. August 4-5, 2006; August 10-11, 2007. Contact: Reg Forder, Box 110390, Nashville TN 37222. 1-800-21-WRITE. Website: www.ACWriters.com. Attendance: 40-80.

MINNESOTA CHRISTIAN WRITERS SPRING & FALL SEMINARS. Minneapolis; spring seminar, early April 2006; fall seminar, early November 2006. Contact: Barbara Majchrzak, 18469 Jaeger Path, Lakeville MN 55044. (952)892-0438. E-mail: barbara.majchrzak@charter.net. Website: www.mnchristianwriters.org. No editors or agents in attendance. Attendance: 50.

THE WRITING ACADEMY SEMINAR. Mount Olivet Retreat Center outside Minneapolis; July 2006. Sponsors year-round correspondence writing program and annual seminar in various locations. Contact: Mar Korman, 1128 Mule Lake Dr. N.E., Outing MN 56662. (218)792-5144. E-mail: pattyk@wams.org. Website: www.wams.org. Attendance: 30-40. Sponsors a contest open to nonattendees (rules are posted on Website).

WRITING SEMINARS/NORTH HENNEPIN COMMUNITY COLLEGE. Brooklyn Park/Minneapolis; new classes every quarter. Instructor: Louise B. Wyly. Topics include Fiction I, II, III; children and teen writing; personal experiences; Beginning & Advanced; The Artist's Way; and memoirs. Now offers a Creative Writing Certificate. Attendance: 24 (2 classes each quarter). Contact: Louise Wyly, 7411—85th Ave. N., Brooklyn Park MN 55445-2299. (763)533-6207. E-mail: Lsnowbunny@aol.com. Website: www.nhcc.edu (click on Training and Development); watch NHCC Bulletin for details, or call (612)424-0880 to inquire. Offers "Creative Writing Certificate" and "Advanced Creative Writing Certificate" for required classes in creative writing.

MISSOURI

AMERICAN CHRISTIAN WRITERS SPRINGFIELD CONFERENCE. Springfield; August 12, 2006; August 18, 2007. Contact: Reg A. Forder, Box 110390, Nashville TN 37222. 1-800-21-WRITE. E-mail: ACWriters@aol.com. Website: www.ACWriters.com. Attendance: 40-80.

HEART OF AMERICA CHRISTIAN WRITERS' NETWORK CONFERENCE. Kansas City MO; November 2006. Contact: Mark and Jeanette Littleton, 3706 N.E. Shady Lane Dr., Gladstone MO 64119. Phone/fax (816)459-8016. E-mail: mlittleton@earthlink.net. Website: www.HACWN.org. Offers classes for new and advanced writers. Has editors and agents in attendance. Attendance: 100.

NEBRASKA

MY THOUGHTS EXACTLY WRITERS RETREAT. St. Benedict Retreat Center/Schuyler; November 17-19, 2006. Contact: Cheryl Paden, PO Box 1073, Fremont NE 68026-1073. (402)727-6508. Geared toward the beginning writer. Attendance: 10.

NEW HAMPSHIRE

WRITERS WORKSHOPS BY MARY EMMA ALLEN. Taught as requested by writer's groups, conferences, schools, and libraries. Topics include: Workshops for Young Writers (for schools and home parenting groups); Workshops for Teachers and Home-parenting Parents; Writing for Children Workshop; Travel Writing Workshop; Writing for Regional Markets; Poetry Writing Workshop; Writing Family History Workshop; Self-Publishing Workshop; Writer & the Internet Workshop; Writing for the Weekly Newspaper Workshop; Writing Columns for Newspaper, Magazine, and Online Publications; and Writing for Publication Workshop. Contact: Mary Emma Allen (instructor), 55 Binks Hill Rd., Plymouth NH 03264. (603)536-2641. Fax (603)536-4851. E-mail: me.allen@juno.com. Website: http://homepage.fcgnetworks.net/jetent/mea.

NEW JERSEY

+NORTH JERSEY A REASON TO WRITE CONFERENCE. Ringwood; May 13, 2006 (usually in May). Contact: Louise Bergman DuMont, PO Box 36, Ringwood NJ 07456. (973)962-9267.E-mail: word.worker@verizon.net. Blog site: www.njcwg.blogspot.com. Attendance: 50. Teaching conference. No editors or agents in attendance.

NEW MEXICO

THE GLEN WORKSHOP. St. John's College/Santa Fe; July 30-August 6, 2006. Includes fiction, poetry, nonfiction, memoir, on-site landscape painting, figure drawing, collage and mixed media, and several master classes. Contact: Gregory Wolfe, Image, 3307 Third Ave. W., Seattle WA 98119. (206)281-2988. Fax (206)281-2335. E-mail: glenworkshop@image journal.org. Website: www.imagejournal.org/glen. No editors/agents in attendance. Attendance: 200.

GLORIETA CHRISTIAN WRITERS' CONFERENCE. Glorieta (18 mile N. of Santa Fe); October 11-15, 2006. Offers 7 continuing classes (including beginning, advanced, fiction, nonfiction, magazines, children, and at least one specialty topic); 80+ workshops, paid critiques, and much more. Editors and agents in attendance. Speakers include James Scott Bell and Becky Tirabassi. Contact: CLASServices, 3311 Candelaria N.E., Ste. I, Albuquerque, NM 87107-1952. Toll-free (800)433-6633. (505)899-4283. Fax (505)899-9282. E-mail: linda@classervices.com. Website: www.glorietaCWC.com. Attendance: 350-400.

SOUTHWEST WRITERS MINI CONFERENCES. Albuquerque; February, May, August, and November 2006. Contact: Southwest Writers, 3721 Morris St. N.E., Ste. A, Albuquerque NM 87111-3611. (505)265-9485. Fax (505)265-9483. E-mail: swriters@aol.com. Website: www.southwestwriters.org. Send SASE/2 stamps for brochure. Secular. Sponsors the Southwest Writers Contest (send SASE for details and entry form).

NEW YORK

ANNUAL INTERNATIONAL CONFERENCE ON HUMOR, HOPE AND HEALING. Saratoga Springs; April 2006. Secular. Contact: The HUMOR Project, Inc., 480 Broadway, Ste. 210, Saratoga Springs NY 12866. (518)587-8770. Fax (800)600-4242. E-mail: info@humor project.com. Website: www.humorproject.com.

THE PUBLISHING GAME WORKSHOP. New York; September 19, 2006. Contact: Alyza Harris, Peanut Butter and Jelly Press, PO Box 590239, Newton MA 02459. Phone/fax (617)630-0945. E-mail: workshop@PublishingGame.com. Website: www.PublishingGame.com (registration form on Website). Speaker: Fern Reiss. Attendance: limited to 18.

NORTH CAROLINA

AMERICAN CHRISTIAN WRITERS CHARLOTTE CONFERENCE. Marriott Hotel; March 17-18, 2006; Greensboro in 2007. Contact: Reg A. Forder, Box 110390, Nashville TN 37222. 1-800-21-WRITE. E-mail: ACWriters@aol.com. Website: www.ACWriters.com. Attendance: 40-80.

+AMERICAN CHRISTIAN WRITERS GREENSBORO CONFERENCE. March 9-10, 2007. Contact: Reg A. Forder, Box 110390, Nashville TN 37222. 1-800-21-WRITE. E-mail: ACWriters@ aol.com. Website: www.ACWriters.com. Attendance: 40-80.

*BLUE RIDGE MOUNTAIN CHRISTIAN WRITERS CONFERENCE. Lifeway Ridgecrest Conference Center; April 2006. Contact: Ron Pratt, LifeWay Christian Resources, One Lifeway Plaza, Nashville TN 37234-0106. Fax (615)277-8232. E-mail: ron.pratt@lifeway.com, or Yvonne Lehman, PO Box 188, Black Mountain NC 28770. Editors and agents in attendance. Sponsors a contest. Attendance: 200.

JERRY B. JENKINS CHRISTIAN WRITERS GUILD WRITING FOR THE SOUL CONFERENCE. Ashville/The Cove; no August conference offered in 2006. Hosted by Left Behind author Jerry B. Jenkins. Held at the Billy Graham Training Center. Offers morning and evening general sessions with national keynote speakers, 6 continuing classes, and 6 workshop tracks, plus appointments with publisher's reps and agents. Contact: Wayne Atcheson, PO Box 88196, Black Forest CO 80908. (866)495-5177, ext. 37. Fax (719)495-5181. E-mail: ContactUs@christianwritersguild.com. Website: www.christianwritersguild.com. Editors and agents in attendance. Attendance: 200-250.

OHIO

AMERICAN CHRISTIAN WRITERS COLUMBUS CONFERENCE. June 9-10, 2006; June 8-9, 2007. Hosted by Columbus Christian Writers Assn./Pat Zell, (937)593-9207. Contact: Reg Forder, Box 110390, Nashville TN 37222. 1-800-21-WRITE. E-mail: ACWriters@aol.com. Website: www.ACWriters.com. Attendance: 40-80.

+AMERICAN CHRISTIAN WRITERS DAYTON CONFERENCE. August 19, 2006; July 28, 2007. Contact: Reg A. Forder, Box 110390, Nashville TN 37222. 1-800-21-WRITE. E-mail: ACWriters@aol.com. Website: www.ACWriters.com. Attendance: 40-80.

DAYTON CHRISTIAN WRITERS GUILD, INC. Contact: Tina V. Toles, PO Box 251, Englewood OH 45322-2227. Phone/fax (937)836-6600. E-mail: Poet11@ureach.com. Sponsoring a seminar August 5-6, 2006 (always first week-end).

NORTHWEST OHIO CHRISTIAN WRITERS SEMINAR. Toledo; September 2006. Contact: Judy Gyde, 3072 Muirfield, Toledo OH 43614-3766. (419)382-7582. E-mail: begyde@glasscity.net. Usually no editors or agents in attendance. Attendance: 50.

OKLAHOMA

AMERICAN CHRISTIAN WRITERS OKLAHOMA CITY CONFERENCE. La Quinta Hotel; February 24-25, 2006; February 23-24, 2007. Contact: Reg Forder, Box 110390, Nashville TN 37222. 1-800-21-WRITE. E-mail: ACWriters@aol.com. Website: www.ACWriters.com. Attendance: 40-80.

WRITING WORKSHOPS. Various locations and dates. Contact: Kathryn Fanning, PO Box 18472, Oklahoma City OK 73154-0472. (405)524-9619. E-mail: oklahomawriter@earthlink.net. Attendance varies: 25-200.

OREGON

HEART TALK. A workshop for women beginning to speak or write for publication. Portland/Western Seminary; March 8-11, 2006 (speaking); March 2007 (writing). Beverly Hislop, dir. Contact: Women's Center for Ministry, Western Seminary, 5511 S.E. Hawthorne Blvd., Portland OR 97215. (503)517-1881. Fax (503)517-1889. E-mail: bhislop@westernseminary.edu. Website: www.westernseminary.edu/women. Attendance: 125. This conference alternates with a writing conference one year and a speaking conference the next. The 2006 conference is on speaking with Carol Kent as featured speaker. Check Website for details.

OREGON CHRISTIAN WRITERS COACHING CONFERENCE. Canby Grove Christian Conference Center/Portland area; July 31-August 3, 2006. Contact: Pat Rushford. E-mail: prushford@comcast.net. Website: www.OregonChristianWriters.com. Includes about 7 hours of training under a specific coach/topic. Offers advanced track. Editors and agents in attendance. Attendance: 250.

PENNSYLVANIA

+AMERICAN CHRISTIAN WRITERS PITTSBURGH CONFERENCE. March 25, 2006. Contact: Reg A. Forder, Box 110390, Nashville TN 37222. 1-800-21-WRITE. E-mail: ACWriters@aol.com. Website: www.ACWriters.com. Attendance: 40-80.

GREATER PHILADELPHIA CHRISTIAN WRITERS' CONFERENCE. Philadelphia Biblical University, Langhorne; mid-August 2006. Founder and director: Marlene Bagnull, LittD, 316 Blanchard Rd., Drexel Hill, PA 19026-3507. Toll-free (888)760-9041. Phone/fax (610)626-6833. E-mail: mbagnull@aol.com. Website: www.writehisanswer.com/Philadelphia. Conferees choose six hour-long workshops from 42 offered or a Fiction Clinic (by application) plus one 6.5 hour continuing session from 7 offered. One-on-one appointments, paid critiques, editors panels, and general sessions. Contest (registered conferees only) awards four $75 discounts off 2007 conference. Especially encourages African American writers. Faculty of 40-50 authors, editors, and agents. Attendance: 225.

MERCER ANNUAL ONE-DAY WRITERS' WORKSHOP (sponsored by St. David's Writers' Conference); April 2006. Contact: Gloria C. Peterman. (724)253-2635. E-mail: gloworm@certainty.net. Website: www.stdavidswriters.com. Attendance: 135.

MONTROSE CHRISTIAN WRITERS CONFERENCE. Montrose; July 23-28, 2006; July 2007. Contact: Patti Souder, c/o Montrose Bible Conference, 5 Locust St., Montrose PA 18801-1112. Toll-free (800)598-5030. (570)278-1001. Fax (570)278-3061. E-mail: mbc@montrosebible.org. Website: www.montrosebible.org. Features wide range of classes for beginning and advanced writers in many different areas. Attendance: 120. Editors in attendance.

REVWRITER WRITERS CONFERENCE. Sellersville; October 14, 2006. Contact: RevWriter, Rev. Susan M. Lang, PO Box 81, Perkasie PA 18944. (215)453-5066. Fax (215)453-8128. E-mail: conference@revwriter.com. Website: www.revwriter.com. Editors in attendance. Focuses on supporting those writing for the local congregation and for the larger Christian market. Attendance: 50.

#ST. DAVIDS CHRISTIAN WRITERS' CONFERENCE. Geneva College/Beaver Falls, near Pittsburgh; June 2006. Offers writer's retreat and a special pastor's day. Contest in 10 categories for attendees only. Lora Zill, director. Contact: Audrey Stallsmith, registrar, 87 Pines Rd. E., Hadley PA 16130-1019. (724)253-2738. Fax (724)946-3689. E-mail: audstall@stdavids writers.com. Website: www.stdavidswriters.com. Attendance: 70.

WEST BRANCH CHRISTIAN WRITERS MINI-CONFERENCE. Montoursville. Contact: Roberta Updegraff, 332 S. Pine Run Rd., Linden PA 17744. (570)584-2280. E-mail: bobbiup@suscom.net. Sponsors an annual one-day mini-conference, October 2006. Also sponsors a contest. Attendance: 100.

TENNESSEE

+AMERICAN CHRISTIAN WRITERS MEMPHIS CONFERENCE. April 29, 2006; April 14, 2007. Contact: Reg A. Forder, Box 110390, Nashville TN 37222. 1-800-21-WRITE. E-mail: ACWriters@aol.com. Website: www.ACWriters.com. Attendance: 40-80.

AMERICAN CHRISTIAN WRITERS MENTORING RETREAT. Nashville; June 2-3, 2006. Contact: Reg Forder, Box 110390, Nashville TN 37222. 1-800-21-WRITE. E-mail: ACWriters@aol.com. Website: www.ACWriters.com. Attendance: 40-80.

CBA ADVANCE. Nashville (held in a different location each year). January 23-27, 2006; January 29-February 3, 2007 (Indiana Convention Center, Indianapolis). Contact: CBA, Box 62000, Colorado Springs CO 80962-2000. Toll-free (800)252-1950. (719)265-9895. Website: www.cbaonline.org. Entrance badges available through book publishers or Christian bookstores.

CLASS CAREER COACHING CONFERENCE. February 2006 in Nashville (limited to first 80 CLASS graduates). Marketing conference for writers, includes training and appointments with editors. CLASS, PO Box 66810, Albuquerque, NM 87193-6810. Toll-free (800)433-6633. (505)899-4283. Fax (505)899-9282. E-mail info@classervices.com. Website www.classervices.com.

TEXAS

AMERICAN CHRISTIAN WRITERS DALLAS CONFERENCE. Dallas Plaza Hotel; February 17-18, 2006; February 16-17, 2007. Contact: Reg Forder, Box 110390, Nashville TN 37222. 1-800-21-WRITE. E-mail: ACWriters@aol.com. Website: www.ACWriters.com. Attendance: 40-80.

ART & SOUL INTL. FESTIVAL OF RELIGIOUS FAITH AND LITERARY ART AT BAYLOR UNIVERSITY. Baylor University, Waco; Spring 2007 (held biennially in odd years). Contact: Doug Henry, Institute for Faith & Learning, One Bear Pl., #97270, Waco TX 76798-7270. Toll-free (800)BAYLOR-U. (254)710-4805. Fax (254)710-4713. E-mail: Vickie_Dunnam@baylor.edu. Website: www.baylor.edu/Rel_Lit. Editors in attendance.

AUSTIN CHRISTIAN WRITERS' SEMINAR. February 10-12, 2006. Contact: Lin Harris, 129 Fox Hollow Cove, Cedar Creek TX 78612-4844. (512)601-2216. Fax (240)208-3201. E-mail: linharris@austin.rr.com. Attendance: 100.

EAST TEXAS CHRISTIAN WRITERS CONFERENCE. Marshall; June 3, 2006 (1st Saturday of June annually). Contact: Dr. Jerry Hopkins, East Texas Baptist University, 1209 N. Grove St., Marshall TX 75670. (903)923-2269. E-mail: Jhopkins@ETBU.edu. Website: www.ETBU.edu/news/CWC/default.htm.

INSPIRATIONAL WRITERS ALIVE!/AMARILLO SEMINAR. April 22, 2006 (always first Saturday after Easter). Contact: Jerry McClenagan, 6808 Cloud Crest, Amarillo TX 79124. (806)355-7117. E-mail: jerrydalemc@sbcglobal.net. Attendance: 50. Sponsors an annual contest.

NORTH TEXAS CHRISTIAN WRITERS' CONFERENCE. Keller; September 8-9, 2006; September 7-8, 2007. Contact: Frank Ball, NTCW Conference, Anchor Church, PO Box 2200, Keller TX 76244. (817)431-9500. E-mail: frank.ball@ntchristianwriters.com. Website: www.ntchristianwriters.com. Track for teens. Speaker: Dr. Dennis Hensley. No editors or agents in attendance. Attendance: 200.

TEXAS CHRISTIAN WRITERS CONFERENCE. Houston; August 5, 2006; August 4, 2007. Contact: Martha Rogers, 6038 Greenmont, Houston TX 77092-2332. (713)686-7209. E-mail: marthalrogers@sbcglobal.net. Speakers 2006: Wayne Holmes, Dr. Dennis Hensley. Editors in attendance; agents when available. Sponsors a contest: Inspirational Writers Alive! Open Competition. Attendance: 65.

YWAM HANDS-ON SCHOOL OF WRITING AND WRITERS TRAINING WORKSHOPS. Lindale; March-June 2006. Contact: Carol Scott, PO Box 1380, Lindale TX 75771-1380. (903)882-9663. Fax (903)882-1161. E-mail: writing@ywamwoodcrest.com. Website: www.ywamwoodcrest.com. Send SASE for list of workshops. Attendance: 10-20.

VIRGINIA

AMERICAN CHRISTIAN WRITERS RICHMOND CONFERENCE. Wyndam Airport Hotel; March 10-11, 2006; March 16-17, 2007. Contact: Reg A. Forder, Box 110390, Nashville TN 37222. 1-800-21-WRITE. E-mail: ACWriters@aol.com. Website: www.ACWriters.com. Attendance: 45-80.

+PENINSULA CHRISTIAN WRITERS INTENSIVE MENTORING CLINIC. Yorktown, March 15-18, 2006. Yvonne Ortega, leader; contact: Nancy Stevens (757)499-0461; or Donna Himes (757)989-6681. E-mail: yvonne@whro.net. Speaker: Cecil Murphey. ACW Chapter.

RICHMOND CHRISTIANS WHO WRITE SEMINAR. Richmond; Fall 2006. Contact: Rev. Thomas C. Lacy, 12114 Walnut Hill Dr., Rockville VA 23146-1854. (804)749-4050. Fax (804)749-4939. E-mail: RichmondCWW@aol.com.

WASHINGTON

AMERICAN CHRISTIAN WRITERS SPOKANE CONFERENCE. September 15-16, 2006; September 14-15, 2007. Contact: Reg Forder, Box 110390, Nashville TN 37222. 1-800-21-WRITE. E-mail: ACWriters@aol.com. Website: www.ACWriters.com. Attendance: 40-80.

IMAGE FESTIVAL OF LITERATURE AND THE ARTS. Fall 2006. Contact: Gregory Wolfe, Image, 3307 Third Ave. W., Seattle WA 98119. (206)281-2988. Fax (206)281-2335. E-mail: conference@imagejournal.org. Website: www.imagejournal.org.

+NCWA CHRISTIAN WRITERS ALASKAN CRUISE. From Seattle; September 2006; August 2007. Contact: Carla Williams, PO Box 856, Enumclaw WA 98022-4856. (360)802-2547. Fax (360)802-2551. E-mail: events@nwchristianwriters.org. Website: www.nwchristian writers.org. Editors in attendance. Attendance: 30.

SEATTLE PACIFIC CHRISTIAN WRITERS RENEWAL. Seattle; May 5-6, 2006. Contact: Clint Kelly, Seattle Pacific University, 3307 Third Ave. W., Ste. 116, Seattle WA 98119. (425)488-2900. E-mail: jabodmere@hotmail.com. Website: www.spu.edu/fellows. Speaker: Calvin Miller.

WRITE ON THE BEACH. Ocean Shores; January 27-29, 2006. Contact: Don Clark, Write on the Beach, PO Box 2284, Ocean Shores WA 98569. Toll-free (800)76-BEACH. (360)289-2451. Website: www.wotbeach.com. Editors and agents in attendance. Sponsors a contest. Secular. Attendance: 100.

WRITER'S WEEKEND AT THE BEACH. Ocean Park; February 24-26, 2006. Contact: Birdie Etchison/Pat Rushford, PO Box 877, Ocean Park WA 98640-0877. (360)665-6576. E-mail: etchison@pacifier.com. Website: www.patriciarushford.com. (Registration form on Website.) Offers an advanced track. Sponsors a limerick contest. Editors and sometimes agents in attendance. Attendance: 50-60.

WISCONSIN

CHRISTIANS IN THEATRE ARTS (CITA) NATIONAL NETWORKING CONFERENCE. New York City; June 15-18, 2006. Contact: Dr. Dale Savidge, dir., PO Box 26471, Greenville SC 29616. (864)679-1898. Fax (864)679-1899. E-mail: admin@cita.org. Website: www.conference.cita.org. Advanced track. Sponsors a play contest (rules on Website). Sometimes editors in attendance; no agents. Attendance: 200.

GREEN LAKE CHRISTIAN WRITER'S CONFERENCE. Green Lake; July 29-August 4, 2006. Contact: Russann Hadding, Green Lake Conference Center, W2511 State Hwy. 23, Green Lake WI 54941-9300. Toll-free (800)558-8898. (920)294-7364. Fax (920)294-3848. E-mail for information: RussannHadding@glcc.org, or program@glcc.org. Website: www.glcc.org. Sometimes has editors or agents. Attendance: 100. Also provides Christian Writer's Weeks when you can stay at the conference center for writing time; January, March, November (may vary).

OBADIAH PRESS CHRISTIAN WRITER'S CONFERENCE. Merrill; April 28-29, 2006. Contact: Tina L. Miller, 607 N. Cleveland St., Merrill WI 54452. (715)536-3167. E-mail: tina@obadiahpress.com. Website: www.obadiahpress.com/conference.htm. No editors or agents in attendance.

WFCA WRITERS CONFERENCE (formerly Wisconsin PAW Conference). Milwaukee area; April 8, 2006. Contact: Patti Wolf, 2215 Hall Rd., Hartford WI 53027. (262)673-2775. E-mail: wolfrosebud@purescreen.net. Website: www.wisconsinchristianauthors.com. Register on Website. No editors or agents in attendance. Attendance: 50-100.

CANADA/FOREIGN

AMERICAN CHRISTIAN WRITERS CARIBBEAN CRUISE. November 26-December 3, 2006; November 25-December 2, 2007. Contact: Reg A. Forder, Box 110390, Nashville TN 37222. 1-800-21-WRITE. E-mail: ACWriters@aol.com. Website: www.ACWriters.com. Attendance: 15-30.

CARIBBEAN CHRISTIAN WRITER'S CONFERENCES. Various Caribbean locations; schedule unknown for 2006. Contact: Patricia Varlack, PO Box 645, St. Maarten, Netherlands Antilles. (599)524-5405. Fax (599)547-5393. E-mail: pvarlack@sintmaarten.net. Website: www.greaterthings.an. Attendance: 20. This conference may be on hold for now.

COMIX35 CHRISTIAN COMICS TRAINING. Various international locations; Sidney, Australia, May 2006; other dates for 2006 not set yet. Contact: Nathan Butler, PO Box 27470, Albuquerque NM 87125-7470. (505)232-3500. Fax (775)307-8202. E-mail: comix35@comix35.org. Website: www.comix35.org. Often has editors in attendance; no agents.

INSCRIBE CHRISTIAN WRITERS' FELLOWSHIP FALL CONFERENCE. Edmonton AB, Canada; September 30-October 1, 2006. Contact: Eunice Matchett, 5304—45 St., Drayton Valley AB T7A 1G7, Canada. (780)542-7950. E-mail: info@inscribe.org. Website: www.inscribe.org (click on Events). Some editors in attendance, no agents. Runs two tracks: beginners and intermediate/advanced. Sponsors a fall contest open to nonmembers; details on Website. Attendance: 115. May also hold a spring conference in April (check Website).

LITT-WORLD CONFERENCE. Sao Paulo, Brazil; November 12-17, 2006 (held every two years on even years). Contact: John D. Maust, director, 130 N. Bloomingdale Rd., Ste. 101, Bloomingdale IL 60108-1035. (630)893-1977. Fax (630)893-1141. E-mail: MaiLittWorld@sbcglobal.net. Website: www.littworld.org. Editors in attendance. Attendance: 140.

+MENTORING CLINIC WITH CECIL MURPHEY. Bognor Regis, West Sussex, England, November 1-4, 2006. Contact: Cecil Murphey. (770)270-9883. Fax (770)270-1756. E-mail: cec_haraka@msn.com. Participants must have a manuscript in process and a laptop computer. Limited to 12-14 students.

WRITE! CANADA. Guelph, Ontario; June 15-17, 2006 (tentative). Contact: Nancy J. Lindquist or Wendy Nelles, Box 487, Markham ON L3P 3R1, Canada. (905)294-6482. Fax (905)471-6912. E-mail: info@thewordguild.com. Website: www.thewordguild.com. Hosted by The Word Guild, an association of Canadian writers and editors who are Christian. Editors and agents in attendance. Contests for attendees. Attendance: 240. Also sponsors one-day conferences in various Canadian cities.

WRITING SERVICES INSTITUTE (WSI)/MARSHA L. DRAKE, #109, 4351 Rumble St., Burnaby BC V5J 2A2, Canada. Phone/fax (604)321-3555. E-mail: write@shaw.ca. Offers several correspondence and online courses: Write for Fun and Profit; Write for Success; Write Fiction from Plot to Print; Write with Power; Write for You; Magazine Article Writing; Write Yes!; Write Now; Young Author's Tutorial; Write Write—with Computers; and Write On! Write or e-mail for details and information on correspondence courses. Also writes company histories, biographies, résumés, and offers online tutorial. Charges negotiable fees for consultation, editing, and critique. See www.vsb-adult-ed.com for further information on courses and author biography.

CONFERENCES THAT CHANGE LOCATIONS

#AMERICAN CHRISTIAN FICTION WRITERS CONFERENCE/WRITE FROM THE HEART. September 2006. Contact: Tammy Alexander, PO Box 101066, Palm Bay FL 32910-1066. E-mail: alexandertammy@yahoo.com. Website: www.acrw.net. Editors and agents in attendance. Sponsors a contest (details on Website). Formerly American Christian Romance Writers.

AMERICAN CHRISTIAN WRITERS CONFERENCES. Various dates and locations (see individual states where held). Also sponsors an annual Caribbean cruise, November 26-December 3, 2006; November 25-December 2, 2007. Contact: Reg A. Forder, Box 110390, Nashville TN 37222. 1-800-21-WRITE. E-mail: ACWriters@aol.com. Website: www.AC Writers.com. Attendance 40-80.

ASSOCIATED CHURCH PRESS ANNUAL CONVENTION. Chicago; March/April 2006. Contact: Mary Glenn Hendrickson, The Associated Church Press, PO Box 30379, Chicago IL 60630-0379. (608)877-0011. Website: www.associatedchurchpress.org.

BEFORE ACT ONE WEEKEND SEMINARS. See Website for dates and locations. Contact: Act One, 2690 Beachwood Dr., Lower Fl., Hollywood CA 90068. (323)464-0815. Fax (323)464-0851. E-mail: info@ActOneProgram.com. Website: www.ActOneprogram.com. Open to anyone who is interested in learning more about the craft of screenwriting.

CATHOLIC PRESS ASSOCIATION ANNUAL CONVENTION. Location unannounced; late May or early June 2006. Contact: Owen McGovern, exec. dir., 3555 Veterans Memorial Hwy., Unit O, Ronkonkoma NY 11779-7636. (631)471-4730. Fax (631)471-4804. E-mail: CathJourn@aol.com. Website: www.catholicpress.org. For media professionals. Annual book awards. Attendance: 400.

CHILDREN'S AUTHORS' BOOTCAMPS. Held in several locations each year; various dates. Secular. Contact: Bootcamp c/o Linda Arms White, PO Box 231, Allenspark CO 80510. Phone/fax (303)747-1014. E-mail: CABootcamp@aol.com. Website: www.WeMake Writers.com. Upcoming dates and details on Website.

CHRISTIAN LEADERS AND SPEAKERS SEMINARS (The CLASSeminar). Sponsors several seminars across the country each year. Check Website for CLASSeminar dates and locations. For anyone who wants to improve their communication skills for either the spoken or written word, for professional or personal reasons. Speakers: Florence Littauer and Marita Littauer. Contact: CLASS, 3311 Candelaria N.E., Ste. I, Albuquerque, NM 87107-1952. Toll-free (800) 433-6633. (505) 899-4283. Fax (505) 899-9282. E-mail: linda@classervices.com. Website: www.classervices.com. Attendance: 75-120.

EVANGELICAL PRESS ASSOCIATION CONVENTION. Orlando FL; May 7-10, 2006 (held in a different location each year). Contact: Doug Trouten, dir., PO Box 28129, Crystal MN 55428. (763)535-4793. Fax (763)535-4794. E-mail: director@epassoc.org. Website: www.epassoc.org. Attendance: 300-400. Annual convention for editors of evangelical periodicals; freelance communicators welcome.

INTERNATIONAL CHRISTIAN RETAIL SHOW/(formerly CBA CONVENTION). Held in a different location each year. July 8-13, 2006, Denver CO. Contact: CBA, Box 62000, Colorado Springs CO 80962-2000. Toll-free (800)252-1950. (719)265-9895. Website: www.cbaonline.org. Entrance badges available through book publishers or Christian bookstores. Attendance: 14,000. Future dates: July 7-12, 2007, Atlanta GA; July 12-17, 2008, Orlando FL; July 11-16, 2009, Denver CO.

JERRY B. JENKINS CHRISTIAN WRITERS GUILD. PO Box 88196, Black Forest CO 80908. Toll-free (866)495-5177. Fax (719)495-5181. E-mail: contactus@christianwriters guild.com. Website: www.christianwritersguild.com. Contact: Wayne Atcheson. Owned by Jerry B. Jenkins, author of the Left Behind series. Students enrolled in correspondence courses are personally mentored by seasoned professional writers or editors. The Guild also offers annual memberships, a critique service, associated benefits (advocacy, supplemental insurance, etc.), conferences, and contests. Call for a Free Starter Kit.

+MENTORING CLINICS WITH CECIL MURPHEY. Various dates & locations. Contact: Cecil Murphey. (770)270-9883. Fax (770)270-1756. E-mail: cec_haraka@msn.com. Participants must have a manuscript in process and a laptop computer. Limited to 12-14 students. Clinics for 2006 are: Yorktown VA, March 15-18; Atlanta, August; Kingman AZ September; and Bognor Regis, West Sussex, England, November 1-4.

ORTHODOX AUTHOR'S ASSN. ANNUAL CONVENTION. National organization. Contact: Donna Jones, 1563 Three Sisters Way, Kodiak AK 99615. (907)486-2529. E-mail: seraphima@ak.net. Membership (70) open. This group is currently reorganizing, but not defunct.

THE PUBLISHING GAME WORKSHOP. Various cities throughout the year (see individual states or check Website for dates and locations). Contact: Alyza Harris, Peanut Butter and Jelly Press, PO Box 590239, Newton MA 02459. Phone/fax (617)630-0945. E-mail: work shop@PublishingGame.com. Website: www.PublishingGame.com (dates, locations, and registration forms on Website). Speaker: Fern Reiss. Most workshops held at the Four Seasons Hotel. Attendance: limited to 18.

SPAN's SMALL PUBLISHERS MARKETING CONFERENCE. Location unannounced; October 2006. Sponsored by the Small Publishers Assn. of North America. A marketing-specific, information-packed conference for authors, self-publishers, and independent presses. Contact: Scott Flora, PO Box 1306, Buena Vista CO 81211-1306. (719)395-4790. Fax (719)395-8374. E-mail: scott@SPANnet.org, or span@spannet.org. Website: www.SPANnet .org/2006. No editors or agents in attendance. Attendance: 100.

WINSUN COMMUNICATIONS WRITING SEMINARS/MARK LITTLETON. Various dates and locations. Available for your conference at your location. Contact: Mark Littleton, WINSUN Communications, 3706 N.E. Shady Lane Dr., Gladstone MO 64119. Phone/fax: (816)459-8016. E-mail: Mark Litt@aol.com.

"WRITE HIS ANSWER" SEMINARS & RETREATS. Various locations around U.S.; dates throughout the year; a choice of focus on periodicals or books (includes self-publishing or mastering the craft). Contact: Marlene Bagnull, LittD, 316 Blanchard Rd., Drexel Hill PA 19026-3507. Phone/fax (610)626-6833. E-mail: mbagnull@aol.com. Website: www.write hisanswer.com. Attendance: 20-50. One- and two-day seminars by the author of *Write His Answer: A Bible Study for Christian Writers.*

AREA CHRISTIAN WRITERS' CLUBS, FELLOWSHIP GROUPS, AND CRITIQUE GROUPS

(*) An asterisk before a listing means the information was not verified or updated by the group leader.
(+) A plus sign before a listing indicates a new listing.

ALABAMA

CHRISTIAN FREELANCERS. Tuscaloosa. Contact: Joanne Sloan, 4195 Waldort Dr., Northport AL 35473. (205)333-8603. Fax (205)339-4528. E-mail: cjosloan@aol.com. Membership (25) open.
OAKWOOD COLLEGE LITERARY GUILD. Huntsville. Contact: Dr. Cicely Daly, 3903 Nelson Dr. N.W., Huntsville AL 35810-3919. (256)852-8656. Fax (256)726-7042. E-mail: cdaly@ oakwood.edu. Membership (15) open. ACW Chapter. Sponsors occasional writers' event.

ARIZONA

EAST VALLEY CHRISTIAN WRITERS. Mesa. Contact: B. K. Jackson, 519 E. 8th Ave., Mesa AZ 85204. (480)827-1545. E-mail: BrendaAtTheRanch@yahoo.com. Membership (10) open.
FOUNTAIN HILLS CHRISTIAN WRITERS GROUP. Contact: Jewell Johnson, 14223 N. Westminster Pl., Fountain Hills AZ 85268. (480)836-8968. E-mail: TykeJ@juno.com. Membership (10-20) open. ACW Chapter.

ARKANSAS

ACW FAMILYLIFE CHAPTER. Little Rock. Contact: Sabrina Beasley, 5800 Ranch Rd., Little Rock AR 72223. (501)228-1756. Fax (501)224-2529. E-mail: sbeasley@familylife.com. Membership (15) open. ACW Chapter. Sponsors a contest for members only.
ARK-LA-TEX PEN-SHELL ACW CHAPTER. Texarkana. Contact: Rosalind Morris, 1400 E. 35th St., Apt. 61, Texarkana AR 71854. (870)772-4983.
ROGERS AREA CHRISTIAN WRITERS GUILD. Rogers. Contact: Karin Croft, 729 N. Wharton Rd., Lowell AR 72745-9366. (479)936-7945. Membership (6) open.
SILOAM SPRINGS WRITERS. Contact: Margaret Weathers, 716 W. University, Siloam Springs AR 72761-2658. (479)524-6598. Website: http://sswc.flash57.com. Membership (20) open. Periodically sponsors a contest open to nonmembers and a seminar.

CALIFORNIA

+BAKERSFIELD CRITIQUE GROUP. Contact: Kathy Summers, 4307 Horseshoe Ct., Bakersfield CA 93311. (661)654-0584. Membership open.
BAY AREA WRITERS CRITIQUE GROUP. Fremont. Contact: Dianne Smith, 55 Montalban Dr., Fremont CA 94536. (510)791-7804. Fax (510)791-7804. E-mail: dmsfremont55@ sbcglobal.net. Membership (5) open to experienced writers only.
CASTRO VALLEY CHRISTIAN WRITERS GROUP. Contact: Pastor Jon Drury, 19300 Redwood Rd., Castro Valley CA 94546-3465. (510)886-6300. Fax (510)581-5022. E-mail: jond@redwoodchapel.org. Website: www.christianwriter.org. Membership (15-20) open. Sponsoring a Christian Writers Seminar, February 17-18, 2006; February 2007. Keynote speaker 2006: Lee Roddy.

CHINO VALLEY CHRISTIAN WRITERS CRITIQUE GROUP. Chino Hills. Contact: Nancy I. Sanders, 6361 Prescott Ct., Chino CA 91710-7105. (909)590-0226. E-mail: jeffandnancys@ peoplepc.com. Membership (15) open. This group wrote a book called *Writing to Give God the Glory: A Potpourri of Devotions, Encouragement, & Tips for the Christian Who Writes.* Available on Amazon.com.

+CHRISTIAN WRITERS GROUP. Vacaville area. Contact: Phyllis Seminoff, PO Box 6148, Vacaville CA 95696. (707)451-2211. E-mail: PSeminoff@aol.com. Membership open.

CHRISTIAN WRITERS' GROUP INTERNATIONAL. Fountain Valley. Contact: Penelope Alexander, PO Box 1122, Huntington Beach CA 92647-1122. (714)979-3098. Membership (1) open.

DIABLO VALLEY CHRISTIAN WRITERS GROUP. Danville. Marcy Weydemuller, leader. Contact: Sue Massie, 2674 Derby Dr., San Ramon CA 94583. (925)828-8667. Fax (925)556-1590. E-mail: redfox@ix.netcom.com. Membership (10-14) open.

HIGH DESERT CHRISTIAN WRITERS GUILD. Quartz Hill. Contact: Don Patterson, 6223 Almond Valley Way, Quartz Hill CA 93536. (661)722-5695. E-mail: don@theology.edu. Website: www.theology.edu/writers. Membership (30) open. Presents the Sable Quill-Pacesetter Award each year to the writer in the group who has shown the most progress or professional achievement. Planning a 2-day conference for May 5-6, 2006.

+IRVINE CRITIQUE GROUP. Contact: Diana Kightlinger, PO Box 10875, Santa Ana CA 92711. (949)559-1895. E-mail: ticklemice@earthlink.net. Membership limited to 6. Contact to see if they are open.

LODI WRITERS ASSOCIATION. (General membership, not just Christian.) Contact: Dee Porter, PO Box 1863, Lodi CA 95241. Phone/fax (209)334-0603. E-mail: crcomm@lodinet .com. Membership (70) open. Sponsors one-day workshop, usually in July.

MARIPOSA CHRISTIAN WRITERS. Contact: Steve Radanovich, 4194 Sebastopol Rd., Mariposa CA 95338-9775. Phone/fax (209)742-5463 or (209)966-3047. E-mail: oz333@ sierratel.com. Membership (8) open. ACW Chapter.

NOVEL IDEA, CHRISTIAN WRITERS SWARM. Norwalk. Contact: Derrell B. Thomas, 11239 1/2 Ferina St., Norwalk CA 90650-5507, (562)863-3132. E-mail: luv2writ@yahoo.com. Membership (6) open.

ORANGE COUNTY CHRISTIAN WRITERS FELLOWSHIP. Various groups meeting throughout the county. Contact: Peggy Matthews Rose (editor@occwf.org) or write OCCWF, PO Box 982, Lake Forest CA 92630. Membership (200+) open. Annual membership includes a bimonthly newsletter, information on local critique groups, advance notice of writing opportunities through an e-mail list, and reduced fees for annual Spring Writer's Day (usually the last Saturday in April; see Website for details). Conference includes keynote speakers, workshops, and consultations. See Website for details: www.occwf.org.

+PEGGY LESLIE'S CRITIQUE GROUP. El Cajon. Contact: Peggy Leslie, 329 Quail Run, El Cajon CA 92019. (619)447-6258. E-mail: ghpleslie@cox.net. Membership (6-10) not currently open.

SACRAMENTO CHRISTIAN WRITERS. Citrus Heights/North Sacramento. Contact: Beth Miller Self, 2012 Rushing River Ct., Elverta CA 95626-9756. (916)992-8709. E-mail: cwbself@ msn.com. Website: www.scwgroup.org. Membership (36) open. Sponsors a contest open to members only. Sponsors a seminar every 5 years; the next one, in 2010, will be their 30th anniversary as a group.

SAN DIEGO COUNTY CHRISTIAN WRITERS' GUILD. Contact: Jennie & Robert Gillespie, PO Box 270403, San Diego CA 92198. (619)221-8183. Fax (619)255-1131. E-mail: info@sandiegocwg.org. Website: www.sandiegocwg.org. Membership (150) open. To join their Internet newsgroup, e-mail your name and address to: info@sandiegocwg.com. Sponsors critique groups, fall seminar (September 2006), and spring awards banquet.

SANTA CLARA VALLEY CHRISTIAN WRITER'S GROUP. Los Gatos. Contact: Richard M. Hinz, 550 S. 4th St., Apt. E, San Jose CA 95112. (408)297-3336. E-mail: Rickhinz@yahoo.com. Membership (14) open.

S.C.U.M. San Leandro. Contact: John B. Olson, 1261 Estrudillo Ave., San Leandro CA 94577. (510)357-4441. E-mail: john@litany.com. Membership (15) open, by invitation.

SONRISE CHRISTIAN WRITERS. East of Sacramento. Contact: Marlys Norris, PO Box 5144, Fair Oaks CA 95628. (916)961-0575. Membership (10) open.

SOUTHERN CALIFORNIA WRITERS ASSN. Fountain Valley. Contact: Roy King, 15772 Heatherdale Rd., Victorville CA 92394-1317. (760)955-5027. Website: www.ocwriter.com. Membership (100) open. Secular group/many Christians.

SOUTH VALLEY CHRISTIAN WRITERS. Group connects by e-mail only. Contact: Mary Elizabeth Kirk, 247 E. Cortner St., Hanford CA 93230-1845. (559)582-8442. E-mail: mkirk@sti.net. ACW Chapter.

TEMECULA CHRISTIAN WRITERS CRITIQUE GROUP. Contact: Rebecca Farnbach, 41403 Bitter Creek Ct., Temecula CA 92591-1545. (951)699-5148. Fax (951)699-4208. E-mail: sunbrook@hotmail.com. Website: www.sandiegocwg.org. Membership (12) open.

VALLEY BIBLE CHURCH CHRISTIAN WRITERS GROUP. Hercules. Contact: Sandy Ormeo, 1477 Willow Ave., Hercules CA 94547. (510)779-3171. Fax (510)799-3174. E-mail: writersgroup@valleybible.org. Website: www.valleybible.org. Membership (10-15) open.

COLORADO

*CHRISTIAN WRITERS GROUP. Colorado Springs area. Contact: Julie Schroeder, PO Box 202, Simla CO 80835-0202. E-mail: WriteHeart@aol.com. Membership open in this new group.

DELAWARE

DELMARVA CHRISTIAN WRITERS' FELLOWSHIP. Georgetown. Contact: Candy Abbott, PO Box 777, Georgetown DE 19947-0777. (302)856-6649. Fax (302)856-7742. E-mail: candy.abbott@verizon.net. Website: www.delmarvawriters.com. Membership (36) open.

FLORIDA

+ADVENTURES IN CHRISTIAN WRITING. Orlando. Contact: Joanna Adicks Wallace, 1107 E. Amelia St., Orlando FL 32803-5327. (407)841-2157. E-mail: joannaw@quixnet.net. Membership (15) open.

BRANDON CHRISTIAN WRITERS. Contact: Ruth C. Ellinger, 1405 S. Lithia Pinecrest Rd., Brandon FL 33511-6719. (813)685-7387. E-mail: WrightandRuth@verizon.net. Membership (10) open.

BROWARD COUNTY ACW CHAPTER. Coral Springs. Contact: Lynne Cooper Sitton, 105 N.W. 104th Ter., Coral Springs FL 33071-7364. (954)341-2627. E-mail: LynneCSitton@cs.com. Membership (10) open.

CHRISTIAN WRITERS GROUP. Contact: Roy Proctor, 1715 Dalby Ct., Middleburg FL 32068. E-mail: royp2000@bellsouth.net. Membership (5) open.

+MARTIN COUNTY ACW; Stuart. Contact: Ave Pennington, 8122 S.W. Yachtsmans Dr., Stuart FL 34997. (772)781-8599. E-mail: rusavapen@yahoo.com. Open to new members.

MIAMI-DADE AMERICAN CHRISTIAN WRITERS CHAPTER. Miami. Contact: Jeanette Windle, 10886 S.W. 151st Pl., Miami FL 33196. (305)383-3366. Fax (305)388-1013. E-mail: windle5@bellsouth.net. Membership (20+) open.

MID-FLORIDA CHRISTIAN WRITERS. Winter Garden. Contact: Joy Shelton, 1040 Glensprings Ave., Winter Garden FL 34787. (407)654-9076. Fax (407)654-9079. E-mail: JoySprinkles@aol.com. Membership (10) open.

SUNCOAST CHRISTIAN WRITERS. Clearwater. Contact: Elaine Creasman, 13014—106th Ave. N., Largo FL 33774-5602. Phone/fax (727)595-8963. E-mail: emcreasman@aol.com. Membership (10) open.

WORD WEAVERS. Longwood. Contact: Eva Marie Everson, 122 Fairway Ten Dr., Casselberry FL 32707-4823. Phone/fax (407)695-9366. E-mail: EvaMarieEverson@aol.com. Membership (50) open. Yearly contest for members. Planning a conference for January 2006 (date unconfirmed) in Vero Beach, Florida.

WRITING STRATEGIES CRITIQUESHOP. Daytona Beach. Meets monthly (10X). Sponsors workshops the 2nd Friday of each month for working authors who have completed one course of Writing Strategies (see conference listing). Send SASE for brochure. Contact: Rosemary J. Upton, 2712 S. Peninsula Dr., Daytona Beach FL 32118-5706. Phone/fax (386)322-1111. E-mail: rupton@cfl.rr.com. Website: www.ruptonbooks.com. Membership (10+) open.

GEORGIA

AMERICAN CHRISTIAN WRITERS IN ATLANTA. Contact: Kay Shostak, 2242 Blenheim Ct., Marietta GA 30066. (770)591-9057. E-mail: kshostak@comcast.net. Membership (20) open.

+CENTRAL GEORGIA CHRISTIAN WRITERS. Warner Robins. Contact: Judy Davis, 100 Wesleyan Dr., Warner Robins GA 31093. (478)922-5599. E-mail: judys12@juno.com. Website: www.flwriters.org/judydavis.htm. Membership (6) open.

CHRISTIAN AUTHORS GUILD. Woodstock. Contact: Diana Baker, 6413 Bells Ferry Rd., Woodstock GA 30189.E-mail: info@christianauthorsguild.org, or DianaJBaker@cs.com. Website: www.christianauthorsguild.org. Membership (40) open.

EAST METRO ATLANTA CHRISTIAN WRITERS. Covington. Contact: Colleen Jackson, 215 High Point Forest Dr., Covington GA 30016. (404)444-7514. E-mail: cjac401992@aol.com. Membership (15) open. Sponsoring a seminar in April or September 2006.

GEORGIA WRITERS ASSN./CHRISTIAN WRITERS POD. Woodstock. Contact: Lloyd Blackwell, 3049 Scott Rd. N.E., Marietta GA 30066. (770)421-1203. E-mail: lloydblackwell@worldnet.att.net. Membership (45) open. Sponsors a contest. Sponsors a seminar in September.

LAMBLIGHTERS CRITIQUE GROUP. Roswell area. Contact: Cisi Morrow-Smith, 4626 Pond House Rd., Flowery Branch GA 30542. (770)518-6101. Membership (4-6) open.

NORTHEAST GEORGIA WRITERS. Gainesville. Contact: Elouise Whitten, 660 Crestview Ter., Gainesville GA 30501-3110. (770)532-3007. Membership (32) open. Sponsors contest open to members.

SOUTHEASTERN WRITERS ASSN. Contact: Amy Munnell (amunnell@earthlink.net), 125 University Ave., Athens GA 30605. E-mail: info@southeasternwriters.com. Website: www.southeasternwriters.com. Sponsors an annual conference; June 2006. Membership open.

IDAHO

CHRISTIAN WRITERS OF IDAHO. Boise. Contact: Debbie Castaneda, 8830 San Anita Dr., Boise ID 83704. (208)375-7297. E-mail: christianwritersofid@yahoo.com. Membership (25+) open. ACW Chapter. Occasionally holds contests for members. Usually sponsors a conference every other year.

INDIANA

BLOOMINGTON AREA CHRISTIAN WRITERS. Bloomington/Nashville. Contact: Debbie Hill, PO Box 1952, Nashville IN 47448. Phone/fax (812)988-8992. E-mail: debb@simplegifts .org. Membership (14) open.

FORT WAYNE CHRISTIAN WRITERS CLUB. Fort Wayne. Contact: Linda R. Wade, 739 W. Fourth St., Fort Wayne IN 46808-2613. (260)422-2772. E-mail: linda_wade@juno.com. Membership (20) open. Co-sponsors conference with ACW; April 6-7, 2006.

OPEN DOOR CHRISTIAN WRITERS. Westport. Contact: Janet Teitsort, PO Box 129, Westport IN 47283-0129. Phone/fax (812)591-2210. E-mail: Janetteitsort@comcast.net. Membership (12) open.

+SHORT STORY CRITIQUE GROUP. Jasonville area. Contact: Janie Orman, RR 1 Box 143, Jasonville IN 47438. E-mail: ShortStoryCrits-subscribe@yahoogroups.com. Website: http://groups.yahoo.com/group/ShortStoryCrits. Membership (9) open.

STEUBEN CHRISTIAN WRITERS GROUP (ACW CHAPTER). Angola. Contact: Tatiana Claudy, 6160 S. 800 W., Pleasant Lake IN 46779-9763. (260)475-5908. E-mail: akclaudy@ netscape.net. Membership (10) open.

IOWA

CEDAR RAPIDS CHRISTIAN WRITER'S GROUP. Contact: Susan Fletcher, 513 Knollwood Dr. S.E., Cedar Rapids IA 52403. (319)365-9844. Membership (5) open.

KANSAS

CHRISTIAN WRITERS FELLOWSHIP. Girard. Contact: Deborah Vogts, 17300 Ness Rd., Erie KS 66733. (620)244-5619. E-mail: debvogts@terraworld.net. Membership (29) open. Sponsors a contest and a seminar in April.

HEART OF AMERICA CHRISTIAN WRITERS' NETWORK. Kansas City MO. Contact: Mark and Jeanette Littleton, 3706 N.E. Shady Lane Dr., Gladstone MO 64119. Phone/fax (816)459-8016. E-mail: MLittleton@earthlink.net. Membership (150) open. Sponsors monthly meetings, a contest (open to nonmembers), and two conferences: a major one in November and a mentoring conference in April.

KENTUCKY

INFINITE INK CHRISTIAN WRITERS. Paris. Contact: Annita Bruening, 348 Northland Dr., Paris KY 40361. (859)987-6543. Membership (10-14) open.

LOUISVILLE CHRISTIAN WRITERS. Contact: Lana Jackson, pres., 8516 Missionary Ct., Louisville KY 40291-4436. (502)968-3602. E-mail: LanaHJackson@aol.com. Website: www.LCWriters.com. Membership (25) open. ACW Chapter.

LOUISIANA

+BAYOU WRITERS' GROUP. Lake Charles area. Contact: Randy Dupre, PO Box 602, Iota LA 70543. Membership open. Sponsors an annual conference in November.

SOUTHERN CHRISTIAN WRITERS GUILD. Slidell. Contact: Grace Booth or Marlaine Peachey, 160 Lake David Dr., Picayune MS 39466-9119. (601)799-3248. Fax (985)624-3108. E-mail: ruwriting@datastar.net. Website under construction. Membership (35) open. Presents quarterly workshops. Dues are $25/yr.

MAINE

#MAINE FELLOWSHIP OF CHRISTIAN WRITERS. China. Contact: Beth Rogers, 720 Essex St., Bangor ME 04401. (207)942-1616. E-mail: BethR58@aol.com. Membership (20) open.

MARYLAND

ANNAPOLIS FELLOWSHIP OF CHRISTIAN WRITERS. Annapolis. Contact: Jeri Sweany, 3107 Ervin Ct., Annapolis MD 21403-4620. (410)267-0924. Membership (7-11) open.

+BALTIMORE AREA ACW. Contact: Theresa Wilson, PO Box 47182, Windsor Mill MD 21244-3571. E-mail: acwritersgroup@aol.com. Website: www.writersinthemarketplace.org. Membership (25) open. Sponsoring a spring one-day seminar.

NATIONAL TELECONFERENCE FOR CHRISTIAN WRITERS. Bimonthly teleconference. Contact: Sharon Ricks, 12912 Belle Meade Trace, Bowie MD 20720-4676. (301)262-1816. E-mail: rickssharon@comcast.net. Membership (25) open.

THIRD SATURDAY CHRISTIAN WRITERS GROUP. Howard County. Contact: Claire K. DeBakey. (410)545-0407. E-mail: c.debakey@att.net. Membership (6-8) open.

WISE PEN CHRISTIAN WRITERS GUILD. Belcamp. Contact: Anne Perry, 5714 Denwood Ave., Baltimore MD 21206. (410)488-3761. Nonfiction group. Membership (7) open. Sponsors a seminar in October in Bel Air MD.

MASSACHUSETTS

CENTRAL MASSACHUSETTS CHRISTIAN WRITERS FELLOWSHIP. Sturbridge. Contact: Barbara Shaffer, 168 Warren Rd., Brimfield MA 01010. (413)245-9620. Membership (10) open.

WESTERN MASSACHUSETTS CHRISTIAN WRITERS FELLOWSHIP. Springfield. Contact: Barbara A. Robidoux, 127 Gelinas Dr., Chicopee MA 01020-4813. (413)594-4741. Fax (413)594-8375. E-mail: ebwordpro@aol.com. Website: www.scribesnscribblers.com. Membership (54) open.

MICHIGAN

ACW DETROIT. Contact: Pamela Perry, 21442 Hamilton Ave., Farmington Hills MI 48336-5840. (248)426-2300. Fax (248)471-2422. E-mail: PamPerry@ministrymarketingsolutions.com. Website: www.ministrymarketingsolutions.com. Membership (100) open. Sponsors a fall seminar in Detroit and book signing parties.

THE CALLED AND READY WRITERS. Detroit. Contact: Mary Edwards, 20700 Civic Center Dr., Ste. 170, Southfield MI 48076. (248)663-2363. Fax (313)861-7578. E-mail: mwwginc@aol.com. Website: www.thecalledandreadywriters.org. Sponsoring a spring conference, May or June 2006. Fall retreat, workshops, seminars, and special book signing events. Poetry critique available. Membership (70) open (over 25 published book authors).

CAPSTONE COMPOSERS. Bancroft. Contact: Rebecca L. Durling, 6986 Cole Rd., Bancroft MI 48414. (989)634-9237. Fax (989)634-5984. E-mail: durfar@michonline.net. Membership (14) open.

CHRISTIAN WRITERS GROUP. Vassar. Contact: Arlene Knickerbocker, 810-793-0316. E-mail: writer@thewritespot.org. Membership (6+) open.

EAT, MEET AND CRITIQUE. Grandville. Contact: Flavia Crowner, 211 S. Maple St., Fennville

MI 49408. (616)561-5296. E-mail: flacro@datawise.net. Membership (10) open. ACW Chapter.

SOUTHEASTERN MICHIGAN ACW CHAPTER. Ypsilanti. Contact: Debbie Mitchell, 1191 Stamford Rd, Yypsilanti MI 48198. (734)483-5444. Fax (734)769-5134. E-mail: all things@ameritech.net. Membership (10) open.

MINNESOTA

MINNESOTA CHRISTIAN WRITERS GUILD. Edina (Minneapolis area). Contact: Sharon Knudson, pres., 1596 Beechwood Ave., St. Paul MN 55116-2408. (651)695-0609. Fax: same/call first. E-mail: sharonknudson@hotmail.com. Website: www.mnchristianwriters.org. Sponsors a spring contest for members only and annual spring (early April) and fall (early November) seminars in Minneapolis/St. Paul. Monthly meetings (Sept.-May); monthly newsletter. Sponsors critique circles throughout Minnesota. Membership (110) open.

MISSISSIPPI

BYHALIA CHRISTIAN WRITERS/ACW CHAPTER. Byhalia. Contact: Marylane Wade Koch, 2573 W. Church St., Byhalia MS 38611-9576. (662)838-2451. E-mail: rwkoch@att.net. Membership (15) open.

MISSOURI

CHRISTIAN WRITERS WORKSHOP OF ST. LOUIS. Day group contact: Ruth Houser, 3148 Arnold-Tenbrook Rd., Arnold MO 63010-4732. (636)464-1187. E-mail: HouserRA@juno.com. Also contact Ruth McDaniel (636)464-1187. Membership (15-20) open. ACW Chapter.

MONTANA

WRITERS IN THE BIG SKY. Helena. Contact: Lenore Puhek, 1215 Hudson, Helena MT 59601-1848. (406)443-2552. Membership (9) currently closed. There is a waiting list.

NEBRASKA

CENTRAL NEBRASKA FELLOWSHIP OF CHRISTIAN WRITERS, ARTISTS, AND MUSICIANS. Kearney. Contact: Carolyn Scheidies, 415 E. 15th, Kearney NE 68847-6959. (308)234-3849. E-mail: crscheidies@hotmail.com (put C-WAM in subject line). Membership (20) open.

MY THOUGHTS EXACTLY WRITERS GROUP. Fremont. Contact: Cheryl A. Paden, PO Box 1073, Fremont NE 68025. (402)727-6508. Membership (6) open. Periodically sponsors a writers' retreat; November 17-19, 2006 in Schuyler.

WORDSOWER'S CHRISTIAN WRITER'S GROUP. Omaha. Contact: Kelly Haack, 5712 S. 91st St., Omaha NE 68127. (402)593-7936. E-mail: haackkj@cox.net. Membership (15) open. ACW Chapter.

NEW HAMPSHIRE

#WORDSMITHS' CHRISTIAN WRITERS' FELLOWSHIP. Nashua. Contact: Susan Peel, 497 Hooksett Rd., #2-344, Manchester NH 03102-7112. (603)669-0264. E-mail: speel@icwriters.com. Website: www.icwriters.com/Wordsmiths/index.htm. Membership (40) open.

NEW JERSEY

CENTRAL JERSEY CHRISTIAN WRITERS' FELLOWSHIP. Zarephath. Contact: Catherine J. Barrier, 13 Oliver St., Somerset NJ 08873-2142. (732)545-5168. Fax (732)545-0640. E-mail: CJBnotice@juno.com. Membership (5) open.

NEW JERSEY SOCIETY OF CHRISTIAN WRITERS. Three chapters: Vineland, Voorhees, and Delanco. Liz Fabiani, dir. Contact: Lillian Baker, membership dir., 1370 S. Main Rd., PMB #7, Vineland NJ 08360. (856)690-0186. Fax (856)327-0291. E-mail: Newriter57@aol .com. Website: www.njscw.com. Membership in all 3 groups (49) open.

NORTH JERSEY CHRISTIAN WRITER'S GROUP. Ringwood. Contact: Louise Bergmann DuMont, PO Box 36, Ringwood NJ 07456. (973)962-9267. E-mail: word.worker@verizon .net. Website: www.louisedumont.com. Writers blog: www.njcwg.blogspot.com. Membership (32) open. E-mail for information. Sponsoring a conference May 13, 2006.

NEW MEXICO

SOUTHWEST CHRISTIAN WRITERS ASSOCIATION. Farmington. Contact: Barbara Kugle, SCWA, 240 S. Ash, Cortez CO 81321. (970)564-9449. E-mail: barbarakugle@earthlink.net. Website: www.swchristianwriter.org. Membership (12) open. Sponsors annual one-day seminar the third Saturday in April (April 15, 2006) in Farmington NM.

SOUTHWEST WRITERS. Albuquerque. Contact: Robert Spiegel, pres., SWW, 3721 Morris St. N.E., Ste. A, Albuquerque NM 87111-3611. (505)265-9485. Fax (505)265-9483. E-mail: swriters@aol.com. Website: www.southwestwriters.com. Membership (700) open. Sponsors a contest (open to nonmembers) and a series of mini-conferences in Albuquerque, in February, May, August, and November 2006. Secular.

NEW YORK

BROOKLYN WRITER'S CLUB. Contact: Ann Dellarocco, PO Box 184, Bath Beach Sta., Brooklyn NY 11214-0184. (718)680-4084. Membership (10-20) open.

NEW YORK CHRISTIAN WRITERS GROUP. New York City (Manhattan). Contact: Marilyn Driscoll, 350 First Ave., New York NY 10010-4911, (212)529-6087. Membership (10) open.

THE SCRIBBLERS. Riverhead. Contact: Bill Batcher, pres., c/o First Congregational Church, 103 First St., Riverhead NY 11901. E-mail: bbatcher@optonline.net. Membership (12) open. ACW Chapter #3049.

SOUTHERN TIER CHRISTIAN WRITERS' FELLOWSHIP. Binghamton. Contact: Kenneth Cetton, 20 Pine St., Port Crane NY 13833-1512. (607)648-7249. E-mail: KC1933@juno.com. Membership (5) open.

NORTH CAROLINA

COVENANT WRITERS. Cherryville. Contact: Robert Redding, 3392 Hwy. 274, Cherryville NC 28021-9634. (704)445-4962. E-mail: minwriter@yahoo.com. Membership (10) open.

+KERNERSVILLE ACW CHAPTER. Contact: Barbie Gourley, 5204 Folgers Mill Rd., Julian NC 27283. (336)685-0704. E-mail: barbiepaul@bellsouth.net. Membership open.

SEVEN SERIOUS SCRIBES. Cary. Contact: Katherine W. Parrish, 103 Chimney Rise Dr., Cary NC 27511-7214. (919)467-1924. E-mail: servantsong@aol.com. Critique group. Membership (7) not currently open, but encourages others to start similar groups in the area. ACW chapter.

OHIO

ASHLAND AREA CHRISTIAN WRITERS GUILD. Contact: April Boyer, 1552 County Rd. 995, Ashland OH 44805. (419)281-1766. E-mail: oboy@bright.net. Website: http://april boyer.com (includes pertinent information). Membership (8) open. Meets twice a month. Holds a variety of events, activities, and speakers.

COLUMBUS CHRISTIAN WRITERS ASSN. Contact: Barbara Taylor Sanders, 9220 Shawnee Trl., Powell OH 43065. (614)764-9220. E-mail: BTSanders@columbus.rr.com. Membership (25) open. Cosponsoring a writers' workshop with the American Christian Writers, June 9-10, 2006.

DAYTON CHRISTIAN SCRIBES. Kettering. Contact: Lois Pecce, Box 41613, Dayton OH 45441-0613. (937)433-6470. E-mail: epecce@compuserve.com. Membership (30) open.

GREATER CINCINNATI CHRISTIAN WRITERS' FELLOWSHIP. Contact: John Turney, 12042 Marwood Ln., Cincinnati OH 45246-1909. (513)671-2833. E-mail: turn2him@earth link.net. Website: http://gccwf.com. Membership (20-30) open.

+NORTHGATE ACW. Contact: Lark Lamontagne, 450 Township Rd. 208, Marengo OH 43334. (740)625-6032.

NORTHWEST OHIO CHRISTIAN WRITERS. Toledo. Contact: Judy Gyde, 3072 Muirfield Ave., Toledo OH 43614-3766. (419)382-7582. E-mail: judygyde@sbcglobal.net. Membership (45) open. Sponsors a Saturday seminar in September.

OKLAHOMA

FELLOWSHIP OF CHRISTIAN WRITERS (FCW), PO Box 700635, Tulsa OK 74170-0635. Membership 90+; 1 satellite group; at-large membership 80+. Ready Writer Online, FCW's Website at http://fcwreadywriter.com. JoAnn R. Wray, Web master, e-mail newsletter director (epistle1@fcwreadywriter.com). Linda Cravens, secretary/treasurer (lcravens@fcw readywriter.com). James Tate, poetry director/greeter (jetate@fcwreadywriter.com). Trudy Graham, print newsletter editor/publicist (gfgram@fcwreadywriter.com); Betty Pharris, devotion director (bpharris@fcwreadywriter.com). Lavon Lewis & Jan Warren, prayer directors. Satellite group: Vinita OK, Lavon Lewis, director (lavonl@fcwreadywriter.com). Local groups meet monthly or more often; open to new groups. Info on Website. FCW also has a Free List Serve at Yahoo Groups—http://groups.yahoo.com/group/FCW—or send an e-mail to FCW-subscribe@yahoogroups.com. Apply online at Yahoo groups and fill out questionnaire. 600+ members. Has daily interaction, markets, encouragement, tips, definitions, prayer, contests, and more. Online critique groups in various genres for members. See Website for details on joining. Free e-mail newsletter: (over 750 subscribers), *Ready Writer Light,* with different content than the print newsletter which goes to paid members only. Subscribe at the Website through provided form. Paid local memberships: yearly fee $35 offers many benefits including our 10-page monthly print newsletter, membership card, resources, bookmarks, magnets, eligibility to members' only contests with cash prizes, product discounts, critique groups, special speakers, and workshops, free listing at the Members Online bookstore, and much more. Tapes of speakers and workshops available for sale online. At-large memberships for those not near a local group $25/year. See Website for details/form. Special rates for teens and for more than one person per household. Contact: JoAnn R. Wray, 8409 S. Elder, Broken Arrow, OK 74011; Phone (918)451-4017; cell (918)695-4528; e-mail: epistle1@fcwreadywriter.com. Brochure on request.

WORDWRIGHTS OKLAHOMA CITY CHRISTIAN WRITERS. Contact: Milton Smith, 6457 Sterling Dr., Oklahoma City OK 73132. (405)721-5026. E-mail: jerri-milton@juno.com. Membership (20) open. Cosponsors an annual writers' conference with American Christian Writers, February 24-25, 2006, in Oklahoma City; send an SASE for information. Sponsors 2 or 3 contests through the year for members only.

OREGON

GOD'S WORDSMITHS—ADVANCED. King City. Contact: Crystal Ortmann, 11625 S.W. King George Dr., King City OR 97224-2624. (503)372-0529. Fax (503)372-0529. E-mail: cjortmann@earthlink.net. Membership (3) not currently open.

OREGON CHRISTIAN WRITERS. Contact: Jennifer Anne Messing. 6214 S.E. Sherman St., Portland OR 97215-4064. Phone/fax (503)775-6039. E-mail: JenniferAnneMessing@comcast.net. Website: www.oregonchristianwriters.org. Meets for 4 all-day Saturday conferences annually: February 18, 2006, in Salem; May 6, 2006, in Eugene; September in Medford area; and October 21, 2006, in Portland. Newsletter published one month before each one-day conference. Annual 4-day Coaching Conference July 31-August 3, 2006, in Canby Grove. Occasionally sponsors a contest. Membership (360+) open.

PORTLAND CHRISTIAN WRITERS GROUP. Contact: Stan Baldwin, (503)659-2974. Serious group; must write regularly. Waiting list available.

SALEM I CHRISTIAN WRITERS GROUP. Contact: Marcia Mitchell, 4144 Sunnyview Rd. N.E., #115, Salem OR 97305-1893. (503)588-0372. Membership (10) not currently open.

WORDSMITHS. Gresham/sometimes E. Portland or Vancouver WA. Contact: Susan Thogerson Maas, 27526 S.E. Carl St., Gresham OR 97080-8215. (503)663-7834. E-mail: susan.maas@verizon.net. Membership (6-8) open. Christian and secular writers.

WRITER'S DOZEN CRITIQUE GROUP. Eugene/Springfield. Contact: Geni J. White, 1455 Larkspur Ave., Eugene OR 97401-1924. E-mail: samcivy@comcast.net. Membership (9) occasionally open.

PENNSYLVANIA

THE FIRST WORD. Sewickley. Contact: Shirley S. Stevens, 326 B Glaser Ave., Pittsburgh PA 15202-2910.(412)761-2618. E-mail: poetcat@earthlink.net. Membership (12) open. Affiliated with the St. Davids Conference.

GREATER PHILADELPHIA CHRISTIAN WRITERS' FELLOWSHIP. Newtown Square. Contact: Marlene Bagnull, 316 Blanchard Rd., Drexel Hill, PA 19026. Phone/fax (610)626-6833. E-mail: Mbagnull@aol.com. Website: www.writehisanswer.com. Membership (20) open. Meets one Thursday morning a month, October-June. Sponsors annual writers' conference (mid-August 2006) and contest (open to registered conferees only).

INDIANA CHRISTIAN WRITERS FELLOWSHIP. Indiana PA. Contact: Jan Woodard, 270 Sunset Dr., Indiana PA 15701. (724)465-5886. E-mail: bcroce@localnet.com (Barb Croce). Membership (10) open. Annual fall and winter writers' retreats.

INDIAN VALLEY CHRISTIAN WRITERS FELLOWSHIP. Telford. Contact: Cheryl Wallace, 952 Route 113, Sellersville PA 18960-2962. (215)453-0415. E-mail: wallacewriter@earth link.net. Membership (25+) open. ACW Chapter. Sponsors a seminar every other year; next one in 2007.

INSPIRATIONAL WRITERS' FELLOWSHIP. Brookville. Contact: Jan R. Sady, 2026 Langville Rd., Mayport PA 16240. (814)856-2560. E-mail: janfran@alltel.net. Membership (15) open. Sponsors a contest in February open to nonmembers. Sponsors a conference in October in Ringgold.

JOHNSTOWN CHRISTIAN WRITERS' GUILD. Johnstown area. Contact: Betty Rosian, 108 Deerfield Ln., Johnstown PA 15905-5703. (814)255-4351. E-mail: wordsforall@atlanticbb .net. Membership (15) open.
LANCASTER AREA CHRISTIAN WRITERS FELLOWSHIP. Contact: A. Martha Stahl, 1001 E. Oregon Rd., Lititz PA 17543. (717)509-5829. E-mail: omstahl@juno.com. Membership open.
WEST BRANCH CHRISTIAN WRITERS. Williamsport. Contact: Eileen Berger, 866 Penn Dr., Hughesville PA 17737. (570)584-2280. E-mail: emberger@sunlink.net. Membership (20) open. Sponsors an annual one-day mini-conference each fall, usually in October.

SOUTH CAROLINA

COLUMBIA CHRISTIAN WRITERS. Irmo. Contact: Kim Andrysczyk, 201 Sutton Way, Irmo SC 29063. (803)781-3510. E-mail: kimbocraig@juno.com. Meets monthly. Membership (8) open.
+GREATER ANDERSON ACW. Contact: Marla Fuller, 3514B Hopewell Rd., Anderson SC 29621. (864)375-9125.
GREENVILLE CHRISTIAN WRITERS GROUP. Contact: Nancy Parker, 3 Ben St., Greenville SC 29601. (864)232-1705. E-mail: Nancy@jjparker.com. Membership (15) open.
+SPARTANBURG WRITERS GROUP. Contact: Linda Gilden, 105 Pheasant Dr., Spartanburg SC 29302. E-mail: rosewriter@aol.com. Membership open.
STEVENS CREEK WRITERS GROUP. Augusta. Contact: Gene Jennings, pres., 1203 Crestview Dr., North Augusta SC 29841. (706)863-7002. E-mail: genepjennings@aol.com. Membership (10) open. ACW Chapter.
WRITING 4 HIM. Spartanburg. Contact: Linda Gilden, PO Box 2928, Spartanburg SC 29304. E-mail: Rosewriter@aol.com. Membership (12+) open.

TENNESSEE

CHATTANOOGA ACW CHAPTER. Contact: Keith Troop, 3207 Mount View Dr., Chattanooga TN 37411. (423)629-6990.
+GERMANTOWN ACW. Contact: Earl Adams, 7465 Germantown Square S., Germantown TN 38138. (901)751-3311. E-mail: erladms@wmconnect.com.
WEST TENNESSEE WORD WEAVERS. Henderson. Contact: Sue Hite, pres., PO Box 12, Henderson TN 38340. (731)989-0265. E-mail: fright@earthlink.net. Membership (16) open. ACW Chapter.

TEXAS

AUSTIN CHRISTIAN WRITERS' GUILD. Contact: Lin Harris, 129 Fox Hollow Cv., Cedar Creek TX 78612-4844. (512)601-2216. Fax (240)208-3201. E-mail: linharris@austin.rr.com. Website: http://pw1.netcom.com/~linjer/acwg.html. Membership (60) open. Meetings, workshops, and conferences announced on Website. February conference.
CHRISTIAN WRITERS GROUP OF GREATER SAN ANTONIO. Universal City/San Antonio area. Contact: Brenda Blanchard, 2827 Olive Ave., Schertz TX 78154-3719. (210)945-4163. Fax (210)945-6613. E-mail: ZBGP1@aol.com. Has 4-8 speakers/yr. Membership (25) open.
DALLAS CHRISTIAN WRITERS GUILD. Plano. Contact: Sue Palencia, 2800 Valley Ridge Dr., Richardson TX 75080. E-mail: suepalencia@dallaschristianwriters.com. Website: www .dallaschristianwriters.com. Membership (50) open.

INSPIRATIONAL WRITERS ALIVE! Groups meet in Houston, Pasadena, Jacksonville, Amarillo, and Humble. Contact: Martha Rogers, 6038 Greenmont, Houston TX 77092-2332. (713)686-7209. E-mail: marthalrogers@sbcglogal.net. Membership (130 statewide) open. Sponsors summer seminar, August 2006, monthly newsletter, and annual contest (November 1-April 1) open to nonmembers.

INSPIRATIONAL WRITERS ALIVE!/AMARILLO CHAPTER. Contact: Helen Luecke, 2921 S. Dallas, Amarillo TX 79103. (806)376-9671. E-mail: hcoluecke@arn.net. Sponsors a seminar, first weekend in April 2006.

INSPIRATIONAL WRITERS ALIVE!/EAST TEXAS CHAPTER. Jacksonville. Contact: Maxine Holder, director & founding member, Rt. 4, Box 81-H, Rusk TX 75785-9410. (903)795-3986. E-mail: mholder787@aol.com. President of chapter: Judith Robinson, 15777 Meadow Cr., Bullard TX 75757. (903)825-2416. Membership (16) open. Connects with chapters in Houston and Amarillo for spring (Amarillo) and summer (Houston) conferences. When possible, East Texas chapter holds a fall, one-day seminar in Tyler. New: A new chapter has formed in Marshall, at East Texas Baptist University. Contact: Jerry Hopkins, Asst. Professor/History. E-mail: jhopkins@etbu.edu.

INSPIRATIONAL WRITERS ALIVE!/FIRST BAPTIST HOUSTON CHAPTER. Contact: Carl Grjalba. (281)531-9034. E-mail: csgrjalba@yahoo.com.

INSPIRATIONAL WRITERS ALIVE!/HUMBLE CHAPTER. Contact: Dalphna Barnes, 20319 Belleau Wood Dr., Humble TX 77338. (281)852-3521. Membership (20) open.

#NORTH DALLAS CHAPTER OF ACW. Dallas. Contact: Earma Brown, Carrollton TX. (469)892-1574. E-mail: earma@acwchapter.com. Website: www.acwchapter.com.

READY WRITERS. Lewisville. Contact: Frank Ball, PO Box 820802, Fort Worth TX 76182-0802. (817)915-1688. E-mail: frank.ball@ntchristianwriters.com. Membership (10) open. ACW Chapter.

ROCKWALL CHRISTIAN WRITERS' GROUP. Contact: Leslie Wilson, 535 Cullins Rd., Rockwall TX 75032-6017. (972)772-3442. Cell (214)505-5336. E-mail: les5points@aol.com. Membership (10-15) open. Assists with the Greenville Christian Writers' Conference.

SEED SOWERS. Arlington. Contact: Frank Ball, PO Box 820802, Fort Worth TX 76182-0802. (817)915-1688. E-mail: frank.ball@ntchristianwriters.com. Membership (9) open. ACW Chapter.

SUPER SCRIBES. Keller (North Ft. Worth). Contact: Frank Ball, PO Box 820802, Fort Worth TX 76182-0802. (817)915-1688. E-mail: frank.ball@ntchristianwriters.com. Membership (18) open. ACW Chapter.

+WORDS FOR THE JOURNEY CHRISTIAN WRITERS GUILD. The Woodlands. Contact: Sharen Watson or Linda Kozar, 1703 Indigo Park Dr., Spring TX 77386. (281)298-6791 or (281)362-1791. E-mail: IRite4Him@aol.com. Website: www.wordsforthejourney.org. Membership (40) open.

UTAH

UTAH CHRISTIAN WRITERS FELLOWSHIP. Salt Lake City area. Contact: Julie Scott, PO Box 3, Bountiful UT 84011-0003. (801)294-5485. E-mail: compelled2tell@mac.com, or ucwf@cyber-servant.com. Membership (9) open.

VIRGINIA

CAPITAL CHRISTIAN WRITERS. Fairfax. Leader: Betsy Dill, PO Box 873, Centreville VA 20122-0873. Phone/fax (703)803-9447. E-mail: ccwriters@juno.com. Website: www.ccwriters

.org. Meets the second Monday of each month except August and December. Speakers one month, critiquing the next. Sponsors a contest for members only. Membership (70) open.

CHRISTIAN WRITER'S CIRCLE. Fredericksburg. Contact: Sarah Sumpolec, dir., 6210 Forest Grove Dr., Fredericksburg VA 22407. (540)548-1460. E-mail: Sarah@sarahannesumpolec .com. Membership open. Group may be on hiatus, but is collecting names of interested writers so they can resume meeting.

NEW COVENANT WRITER'S GROUP. Newport News. Contact: Mary Tatem, 451 Summer Dr., Newport News VA 23606-2515. Phone/fax (757)930-1700. E-mail: rwtatem@juno.com. Membership (6) open.

PENINSULA CHRISTIAN WRITERS. Yorktown. Yvonne Ortega, leader; contact: Nancy Stevens (757)499-0461; or Donna Himes (757)989-6681. E-mail: yvonne@whro.net. ACW Chapter. Membership (20) open. Sponsors an Intensive Mentoring Clinic, March 15-18, 2006.

RICHMOND CHRISTIANS WHO WRITE. Contact: Rev. Thomas C. Lacy, 12114 Walnut Hill Dr., Rockville VA 23146-1854. (804)749-4050. Fax (804)749-4939. E-mail: Richmond CWW@aol.com.Membership (40) open. Sponsors a seminar, Fall 2006. ACW Chapter.

TIDEWATER CHRISTIAN WRITERS FORUM. Norfolk. Contact: Peter D. Mallett, 1270 Pall Mall St., #A, Norfolk VA 23513. (757)889-9917. E-mail: F18Pete@aol.com. Website: www.yahoogroups.com/tidewaterchristianwf. ACW Chapter. Membership (8) open.

WASHINGTON

ADVENTIST WRITERS ASSOCIATION OF WESTERN WASHINGTON. Auburn. Contact: Marian Forschler, PO Box 58785, Renton WA 98058-1785. (425)235-1435. Fax (425)204-2070. E-mail: msf1944@cs.com. Membership (40) open. Newsletter $10/yr. Sponsors annual writers' conference in late June.

CHRISTIAN WRITERS FELLOWSHIP OF MOSES LAKE. Contact: Judith Gonzales, 1108 W. Rose Ave., Moses Lake WA 98837-2062. (509)765-4829. Fax: (509)766-4284. E-mail: gonzalesjm92@genext.net. This group is currently not meeting, but open to restarting if there is interest.

MEMOIR WRITERS. Federal Way. Contact: Bernice Large, 1013 S. 325th St., Federal Way WA 98003-5933. (253)946-2782. Membership (12-13) open.

NORTHWEST CHRISTIAN WRITERS ASSN. Bellevue WA. Contact: Diana Savage Kruger, PO Box 428, Enumclaw WA 98022-4428. Toll-free (800)731-6292. E-mail: president@ nwchristianwriters.org. Website: www.nwchristianwriters.org. Membership (125+) open. Sponsoring an Alaskan Cruise (leaving from Seattle) in August/September 2006 (events@nwchristianwriters.org).

SPOKANE NOVELISTS. Contact: Betsy Tan, 211 S. Whipple Rd., #3, Spokane WA 99206. (509)926-4121. E-mail: MOCHEL@aol.com. Membership (18) open. Secular group with mostly Christian members. Membership (7-10) open.

WALLA WALLA VALLEY CHRISTIAN SCRIBES. College Place. Contact: Helen Heavirland, PO Box 146, College Place WA 99324-0146. Phone/fax (541)938-3838. E-mail: hlh@bmi.net. Membership (15) open.

WENATCHEE CHRISTIAN WRITERS' FELLOWSHIP. Contact: David Peckham, PO Box 236, Chelan WA 98816. (509)682-5591. E-mail: david@onhisshoulders.com. Membership (25) open.

+WRITERS IN THE ROUGH. Arlington. Contact: Darlene Paterson, 19105—11th Ave. N.E., Arlington WA 98223-9663. (360)652-9279.E-mail: dpat777@verizon.com. Website: www.geocities.com/writersintherough. Membership (15) open.

WISCONSIN

+**LIGHTHOUSE CHRISTIAN WRITERS.** Oconto. Contact: Lois Wiederhoeft, 901 Aubin, Peshtigo WI 54157. (715)582-1024. E-mail: 2-loisw115@centurytel.net. Website: www.mychristiansite.com/ministries/lhchristianwriters. Membership (10) open.

WORD AND PEN CHRISTIAN WRITERS CLUB. Menasha. Contact: Chris Stratton, 107 E. McArthur St., Appleton WI 54911-2109. (920)739-0752. E-mail: wordandpen@mychristiansite.com. Website: http://mychristiansite.com/ministries/wordandpen. Membership (9) open. ACW Chapter.

WORDSMITHS (W.R.W.A.). Marinette/Menominee. Wisconsin Regional Writers Assn. (secular group that includes Christians). Contact: Mildred Utke, 2709 Northland Cir. Dr., Marinette WI 54143-4277. (715)735-0127. Membership (6) open.

+**WRITER'S CRITIQUE GROUP.** Fort Atkinson. Contact: James B. Robar, N2963 Buena Vista Rd., Fort Atkinson WI 53538. (920)568-1677. E-mail: jimcin@compufort.com. Membership (5) open.

CANADA/FOREIGN

*****ASSOCIATION OF CHRISTIAN WRITERS.** London + network of area groups in England. Contact: Jenny Kyriacou, Administrator, All Saints Vicarage, 43 All Saints Close, Edmonton, London N9 9AT, United Kingdom. Phone/fax 020 8884 4348. E-mail: admin@christian writers.org.uk. Membership (900) open. Sponsors a biennial writers' weekend for members only. Next one first weekend in July 2006 in Hertfordshire.

FRASER VALLEY CHRISTIAN WRITERS GROUP. Abbotsford BC. Contact: Helmut Fandrich, 2461 Sunnyside Pl., Abbotsford BC V2T 4C4, Canada. Phone/fax (604)850-0666. E-mail: helmut@coneharvesters.com. Membership (20) open.

INSCRIBE CHRISTIAN WRITERS' FELLOWSHIP. Calgary & Edmonton (various locations across Canada). Contact: Eunice Matchett, 5304—45 St., Drayton Valley AB T7A 1G7 Canada. (780)542-7950. E-mail: scrappi@telusplanet.net. Website: www.inscribe.org. Membership (250) open. Sponsors a newsletter and 2 contests, details on Website (one open to nonmembers). Also sponsors annual conferences in April and September.

MANITOBA CHRISTIAN WRITERS ASSN. Winnipeg. Contact: Alma Barkman, 583 Municipal Rd., Winnipeg MB R3R 1J2, Canada. (204)895-2353. E-mail: alb@mts.net. Membership (25-30) open.

PLC ONTARIO WRITES! Sudsbury area. Contact: Emily Betty, 374 Bressie St., Unit 3, Sudsbury ON P3C, Canada. (705)673-0544. ACW Chapter.

NATIONAL/INTERNATIONAL GROUPS (no state location)

AMERICAN CHRISTIAN FICTION WRITERS. Website: www.americanchristianfiction writers.com. E-mail loop, online courses, critique groups, and newsletter for members. Send membership inquiries to address above. Membership (470) open. Sponsors a contest open to nonmembers. Sponsoring a seminar in Houston, September 2006.

AMERICAN CHRISTIAN WRITERS SEMINARS. Sponsors conferences in various locations around the country (see individual states for dates and places). Call or write to be placed on mailing list for any conference. Events are Friday and Saturday unless otherwise noted. Brochures usually mailed three months prior to event. Contact: Reg Forder, Box 110390, Nashville TN 37222. 1-800-21-WRITE. Website: www.ACWriters.com.

CHRISTIAN WRITERS FELLOWSHIP INTL. (CWFI). Contact: Sandy Brooks, 1624 Jefferson Davis Rd., Clinton SC 29325-6401. (864)697-6035. E-mail: cwfi@cwfi-online.org. Website:

www.cwfi-online.org. To contact Sandy Brooks personally: sandybrooks@cwfi-online.org. No meetings, but offers market consultations, critique service, writers books, and conference workshop tapes. Connects writers living in the same area, and helps start writers' groups. Membership (1,000+) open.

FAITH, HOPE & LOVE is the inspirational chapter of Romance Writers of America. Dues for the chapter are $24/yr., but you must also be a member of RWA to join (dues $75/yr.). Chapter offers these services: online list service for members, a Web page, 20-pg. bimonthly newsletter, annual contest, monthly online guest chats with multipublished authors and industry professionals, connects critique partners by mail or e-mail, and latest romance-market information. To join, contact RWA National Office, 16000 Stuebner Airline Rd., Ste. 140, Spring TX 77379. (832)717-5200. Fax (832)717-5201. Website: www.rwanational.org. Or go to FHL Website: www.faithhopelove-rwa.org. Inspirational Readers Choice Contest by subgenre categories for published works; deadline April 1; cash prizes. Send SASE for guidelines. Membership (150+) open.

+JERRY B. JENKINS CHRISTIAN WRITERS GUILD. Contact: Wayne Atcheson, PO Box 88196, Black Forest, CO 80908. Toll-free (866) 495-5177. E-mail: ContactUs@ChristianWriters Guild.com. Website: www.ChristianWritersGuild.com. This international organization of more than 1,500 members offers annual memberships, mentor-guided correspondence courses for adults (two-year "Apprentice" and advanced one-year "Journeyman") and youth ("Pages": ages 9-12 and "Squires": 13 and up), writing contests, conferences, critique service, writers resource books, monthly newsletter, and more. Critique service accepts prose samples of 1-15 pages. Professional writing assessment covers proper language usage, pacing, presentation, purpose, and persuasiveness. Call for pricing structure. Members receive 10% off.

NATIONAL ASSN. OF WOMEN WRITERS. Secular. Contact: Sheri McConnell, PO Box 700696, San Antonio TX 78270. Toll-free (866)821-5829. Toll-free fax (866)821-5829. E-mail: naww@onebox.com. Website: www.naww.org. Over 40 chapters across the U.S. (see Website for list of locations, under Chapters link). Membership (2,500+) open. Sponsors regional events across the U.S.

PEN-SOULS (prayer and support group, not a critique group). Conducted entirely by e-mail. Contact: Janet Ann Collins, (510)522-7681. E-mail: jan@janetanncollins.com. Membership (12) open.

THE PRESBYTERIAN WRITERS GUILD. No regular meetings. National writers' organization with a quarterly newsletter. Dues $15/year. Contact: Nancy Regensburger, 3111 Greenridge Dr., Lancaster PA 17601-1369. Membership (220) open. Sponsors contests for members each year. Sponsors annual conference.

THE WRITING ACADEMY. Contact: Inez Schneider, 4010 Singleton Rd., Rockford IL 61114. (815)877-9675. E-mail: Inezmarie@aol.com. Website: www.wams.org. Membership (75) open. Sponsors year-round correspondence writing program and annual seminar in August (held in various locations); currently in Minneapolis.

Note: If your group is not listed here, please send information to Sally Stuart, 1647 S.W. Pheasant Dr., Aloha OR 97006. June 5 is the deadline for next year's edition.

EDITORIAL SERVICES

The following listing is included because so many writers contact me looking for experienced/qualified editors who can critique or evaluate their manuscripts. These people from all over the country offer this kind of service. I cannot personally guarantee the work of any of those listed, so you may want to ask for references or samples of their work.

The following abbreviations indicate what kinds of work they are qualified to do:

GE—general editing/
   manuscript evaluation
LC—line editing or
   copyediting

GH—ghostwriting
CA—coauthoring
B—brochures

NL—newsletters
SP—special projects
BCE—book contract evaluation

The following abbreviations indicate the types of material they evaluate:

A—articles
SS—short stories
P—poetry
F—fillers
N—novels
NB—nonfiction books

BP—book proposals
JN—juvenile novels
PB—picture books
QL—query letter
BS—Bible studies

GB—gift books
TM—technical material
E—essays
D—devotionals
S—scripts

Always send a copy they can write on and an SASE for return of your material.

(*) Indicates that editorial service did not return questionnaire
(#) Indicates updated from Website, brochure, or other sources
(+) Indicates new listing

ARIZONA

CARLA'S MANUSCRIPT SERVICE/CARLA BRUCE, 10229 W. Andover Ave., Sun City AZ 85351-4509. Phone/fax (623)876-4648. E-mail: CarlaBrc@aol.com. Call/e-mail/write with deposit of $100. GE/LC/GH/typesetting/PDF files for publishers. Does A/SS/P/F/N/NB/BP/QL/BS/GB/TM/E/D. Charges $25/hr. or gives a project estimate after evaluation. Does ghostwriting for pastors and teachers; professional typesetting. Twenty-three years ghostwriting/editing; 12 years typesetting.

PROFESSIONAL PROOFREADING/JODI DECKER, 5642 W. Carol Ave., Glendale AZ 85302. (623)521-3064. E-mail: jodidecker@msn.com. Call/e-mail. GE/LC. Does A/SS/N/NB/JN/GB/TM/E/D. Charges by the page. Has MEd; BA in communication; college writing teacher; editor of 5 published books; award-winning freelance writer. References available.

CALIFORNIA

CHRISTIAN COMMUNICATOR MANUSCRIPT CRITIQUE SERVICE/SUSAN TITUS OSBORN, 3133 Puente St., Fullerton CA 92835-1952. (714)990-1532. Toll-free (877)428-7992. (714)990-1532. Fax (714)990-0310. E-mail: Susanosb@aol.com. Website: www.christiancommunicator.com. Call/e-mail/write. For book, send material with $115 deposit. Staff of 14 editors. GE/LC/GH/CA/SP/BCE. Does A/SS/P/F/N/NB/BP/JN/PB/QL/BS/GB/TM/E/D/S. $72 for short pieces/picture books. Three-chapter book proposal $115. Additional editing $25/hr. Twenty-eight years' experience.

+EDITORIAL SERVICE/ARLENE PLANT, 9237 Greenback Ln., #139, Orangevale CA 95662-4855. (916)838-3729. E-mail: aplant@pngusa.net. E-mail/write. GE. Does A/SS/N/NB/BS/D. Charges $10/hr. Has 3+ years' experience editing for a Christian organization. Also does transcription and typing from cassette tapes. Uses Microsoft Word.

+EDITORIAL SERVICE/KATHY IDE, 203 Panorama Ct., Brea CA 92821. (714)529-1212. Fax (714)529-5267. E-mail: Kathy@kathyide.com. Website: www.KathyIde.com. Contact by e-mail. GE/LC/GH/CA/B/NL/WS, proofreading, mentoring. Does A/SS/F/N/NB/BP/QL/JN/BS/GB/D/S. Charges by the hour (mention this listing and get a $5/hr. discount). Freelance author, editor (full-time since 1998), and speaker. Has done proofreading and editing for Moody, Thomas Nelson, Barbour/Heartsong, and WinePress.

*VICKI HESTERMAN, PhD/WRITING, EDITING, PHOTOGRAPHY, PO Box 6788, San Diego CA 92166. E-mail: vhvh@earthlink.net. E-mail/write; will follow with phone call. GE/LC/CA/SP. Does A/NB/BP/QL/BS/GB/E/D/photo books, memoirs. Quotes/rates based on project. Edits/develops nonfiction material, including editorials; works with book and article writers and publishers as coauthor, line editor, or in editorial development.

DARLENE HOFFA, 512 Juniper St., Brea CA 92821. (714)990-5980. E-mail: jack.darlene .hoffa@adelphia.net. E-mail contact. GE. Does A/F/NB/BP/D. Eighteen years' experience; author of 11 books. Charges $20/hr. or $1.50/ms pg.

LIGHTHOUSE EDITING/DR. LON ACKELSON, 13326 Community Rd., #11, Poway CA 92064-4754. (858)748-9258. Fax (858)748-7431. E-mail: Isaiah68LA@aol.com. Website: www .lighthouseedit.com. E-mail/write. GE/LC/GH/CA/B/NL/BCE. Does A/SS/N/NB/BP/QL/BS/E/D. Charges $30 for article/short story critique; $50 for 3-chapter book proposal. Send SASE for full list of fees. Editor since 1981; senior editor 1984-2002.

KAREN O'CONNOR COMMUNICATIONS/KAREN O'CONNOR, 2050 Pacific Beach Dr., #205, San Diego CA 92109-6269. (858)483-3184. Fax (858)483-0427. E-mail: karen@karen oconnor.com. Website: www.karenoconnor.com. E-mail; send material/deposit. GE/LC/BCE. Does A/F/NB/BP/QL/PB/BS/GB/E/D. One-hour free consultation; $75-90/hr. or flat fee depending on project. Has 30 years of writing/editing; 20 years teaching writing.

SHIRL'S EDITING SERVICE/SHIRL THOMAS, 9379 Tanager Ave., Fountain Valley CA 92708-6557. (714)968-5726. E-mail: Shirlth@aol.com. E-mail (preferred)/write, and send material with $100 deposit. GE/LC/GH/SP/rewriting/analysis. Does A/SS/P/F/N/NB/BP/QL/GB/D/greeting cards/synopses. Consultation/evaluation, $60/hr.; evaluation/critique, $60/hr.; copyediting $55/hr.; content editing/rewriting $65/hr.

LAURAINE SNELLING/KMB COMMUNICATIONS, INC., 19872 Highline Rd., Tehachapi CA 93561-7796. (661)823-0669. Fax (661)823-9427. E-mail: TLsnelling@yahoo.com. Website: www.LauraineSnelling.net. Call/write/e-mail. GE. Does N/BP/QL/JN. Charges $50/hr. with $100 deposit, or by the project after discussion with client. Author of 45 books (YA and adult fiction, 2 nonfiction).

+THE STRONG WORD COMMUNICATION SERVICES/ANITA PALMER, 5800 Lake Murray Blvd., Unit 14, La Mesa CA 91942. (619) 697-1823. E-mail: edit@strongword.com. Website: www.strongword.com. Call/write/e-mail. GE/LC/B/SP. Does A/SS/F/NB/JN/QL/E/D. Competitive rates; happy to negotiate. Published author. Former newspaper and magazine editor with 25 years' experience; experienced in media relations and marketing. Have freelanced for most of the major Christian publishing houses and some secular houses. Quick, trustworthy, and reliable.

+#THE WORD WORKS/SONJA L. STRUTHERS, 40960 California Oaks Rd., Ste. 136, Murrieta CA 92562. Phone/fax (951-696-5631). Website: www.mywriter.net. Writing/editing services, Web content, ghostwriting.

COLORADO

ALPHA TRANSCRIPTION/CHERYL A. JONES, 1832 S. Lee St., Unit G, Lakewood CO 80232-6255. (303)978-9596. E-mail: alphatranscription@juno.com. E-mail/write. Typing for authors, preferably from cassette tapes, but will consider legible longhand material. Rate determined after discussion with client. Has worked with Dr. Larry Crabb, David Wilkerson, and literary agents since 1988.

*ARIEL COMMUNICATIONS & DESIGN, INC./DEBBIE BARKER, 18445 Shady Knoll Ct., Peyton CO 80831. (719)749-0166. Fax (719)749-0188. E-mail: dbarker@cnonline.net. Editing and proofreading. No poetry. Call for rates and turn-around times.

EDIT RESOURCE/ERIC & ELISA STANFORD, 7645 N. Union Blvd., PMB 235, Colorado Springs CO 80920. (719)599-7808. E-mail: info@editresource.com. Website: www.edit resource.com. E-mail contact. GE/LC/GH/CA/B/NL/SP. Does A/F/N/NB/BP/BS/GB/TM/E/D/book doctoring. Rates determined after discussion with client. Combined 25 years of professional editing experience.

MARKETING CONSULTANT/CECILE COOPER HIGGINS, 11126 W. 69th Pl., Arvada CO 80004. (303)456-1511. E-mail: cecilehiggins@yahoo.com. A marketing consultant for the publishing world. Regularly leads workshops and gives talks on self-publishing marketing. Consults on an individual basis with people seeking marketing advice on self-publishing.

OMEGA EDITING/MICHAEL P. COLCHIN, 1832 S. Lee St., Unit G, Lakewood CO 80232-6255. (303)978-0880. E-mail: omegaediting@juno.com. E-mail. GE/LC/GH/CA/B/NL/SP. Does A/SS/NB/BP/QL/BS/TM/D. Charges $45/hr. and up, or by the project after discussion with client. Works in partnership with authors and publishers as ghostwriter, coauthor, editor, or in editorial development. Published book and article author, 10 years' experience as freelance editor.

+THE PERFECT PAPER/PATRICIA UNGER, 16695 Von Neuman Dr., Monument CO 80132. E-mail: dpunger@adelphia.net. Call/e-mail/send with $100 deposit. GE/LC/B/NL/SP/WS. Does A/SS/P/F/N/NB/BP/QL/JN/PB/BS/GB/TM/E/D/S. Charges $2.50-3.50/page for smaller projects (up to 30 pgs.); $60/hr. for projects over 30 pgs. Ten years' experience proofreading and copyediting; 25 years' experience with word processing of all kinds.

SCRIBBLE COMMUNICATIONS/BRAD LEWIS, 6762 Lange Cir., Colorado Springs CO 80918. Phone/fax (719)260-8651. E-mail: scribblecom@adelphia.net. Website: www.scribble communications.com. E-mail contact. GE/GH/SP/developmental/substantive editing. Does A/NB/BP/BS/Website content. Edited 60 books; former senior book and magazine editor; 5+ years as a freelancer. Charges by project, mutually agreed upon with publisher, and stated in editor's/author's agreement.

STANFORD CREATIVE SERVICES. See Edit Resource.

A WAY WITH WORDS/RENEE GRAY-WILBURN, 1820 Smoke Ridge Dr., Colorado Springs CO 80919-3458. (719)265-6626. Fax (719)266-8040. E-mail: waywords@earthlink.net. Call/e-mail. LC/CA/B/NL/SP. Does A/SS/F/N/NB/JN/PB/BS/GB/TM/E/D. Line editing/copyediting: $20/hr. Project prices negotiable. Has had a writing company for over 10 years. Works with authors, Christian publishers, ministries, and small businesses.

THE WELL-WRITTEN WORD/NICKIE DUMKE, 1877 Polk Ave., Louisville CO 80027-1117. Phone/fax (303)666-8253. E-mail: dumke@earthlink.net. Website: www.food-allergy.org. Call or e-mail. GE/LC/GH/CA/NL/SP/health and medical editing and writing. Does A/SS/F/N/NB/JN/PB/BS/GB/TM/E/D/cookbooks. Fifteen years' experience in writing, editing, and publishing; author of 4 books and several booklets. Charges $25/hr.; flat rate for project after evaluating material.

FLORIDA

EDITORIAL SERVICES/LESLIE SANTAMARIA, 1024 Walnut Creek Cv., Winter Springs FL 32708-4735. E-mail: santamaria@mpinet.net. Write or e-mail. GE/LC. Does A/SS/N/NB/BP/ QL/JN/BS/TM/E/D. Critiques: $65 for short pieces/picture books; $100 for 3-chapter book proposals. Editing services: $25/hr. Published author and book reviewer with extensive book and magazine editing experience and a BA in English.

LIGHTPOST COMMUNICATIONS/SEAN FOWLDS, 305 Pinecrest Rd., Mount Dora FL 32757-5929. (352)383-2485. Fax (775)249-5732. E-mail: sfowlds@earthlink.net. Website: www .home.earthlink.net/~sfowlds. E-mail. GE/LC/B/NL/SP/copy for Websites. Does A/SS/P/F/ NB/BP/QL/PB/BS/GB/TM/E/D/S. Offers speaking, writing, and editing services. Negotiated sliding scale starting at $30/hr. Former editor of a national publication.

REACH OUT EXPRESSIONS, INC./CAROL C. TONGUE, PO Box 1861, Mt. Dora FL 32756. (352)669-6789. E-mail: Reach_Out@yahoo.com. Website: www.ReachOutExpressions .com. E-mail/write/send with $15 deposit. GE/LC/GH/CA/B/NL/SP. Does A/SS/P/F/N/NB/BP/ QL/JN/BS. Fees start at $20/hr.; negotiable for special projects. Works in partnership with authors, political leaders, and ministries as a ghostwriter, co-author, and editor. Twelve years editorial experience; published author.

WILDE CREATIVE SERVICES/GARY A. WILDE, 183 Lawn St., Oviedo FL 32765-8089. (407)977-3869. GE/GH/CA/SP. A publishing support company providing book doctoring, editorial project management, collaborative writing, and copywriting services. Negotiated flat fee based on $50/hr. Former staff editor for major publisher.

GEORGIA

JILL COX'S WRITE MIND, 1986 Morning Walk, Acworth GA 30102. Phone/fax (770)917-1539. E-mail: jcoxwritemind@aol.com. E-mail/write. GE/LC/SP/BCE/media-related résumés and book proposals. Does A/N/NB/BP/QL/BS/GB/E/D/S. Thirteen years in television; 3 years as a professor; currently a magazine editor. Charges $15-25/hr or $5-9/pg., depending on service provided.

BONNIE C. HARVEY, PhD, 5579B Chamblee Dunwoody Rd., Ste. 357, Atlanta GA 30038. (404)299-6149. Fax (404)297-6651. E-mail: BoncaH@aol.com. Call/e-mail/write to discuss terms & payment. GE/LC/GH/CA/SP/theology. Does A/SS/P/N/NB/QL/JN/BS/GB/ E/D/S/theological and academic articles. Does critiquing, editing, book consulting, book proposals, and rewriting. Charges $20/hr. for reading/critiquing; $20/hr. for proofreading; $25/hr. for editing, $45-75/hr. for rewriting. Has PhD in English; 14 years teaching college-level English; 25 years' experience as editor; has ghostwritten books and authored 22 books. Also does some agenting.

#LAMBLIGHTERS LITERARY SERVICE/CISI MORROW-SMITH, 4626 Pond House Rd., Flowery Branch GA 30542-3742. (770)518-6101. Call/write/send with $25-35 deposit. GE/LC/ GH/CA/SP/BCE/tutors writing (child or adult). Does A/SS/P/F/N/NB/BP/QL/JN/PB/ TM/E/D/S. Phone consultation $25 (initial hour free). Charges $35-75/hr., $30 min.; long-term projects negotiable. Has BA in journalism/creative writing; 28 years' experience.

+ON-TIME EDITORIAL SERVICES/LEIGH DELOZIER, 1009 Crown River Pkwy., McDonough GA 30252. (770)914-3812. Fax (866)321-9914. E-mail: leighdelozier@bellsouth .net. Website: www.leighdelozier.net. Call/e-mail/write. GE/LC/B/NL/SP/WS. Does A/SS/ QL/GB/E/D/brochures & other marketing materials. Fees by the hour, page, or project, depending on the work. Proofreading $25/hr.; editing/rewriting $35-75/hr. BS in journalism; 17 years' experience in publishing and public relations; published writer.

POSITIVE DIFFERENCE COMMUNICATIONS/ROSS WEST, 100 Martha Dr., Rome GA 30165-4138. (706)232-9325. Fax (706)235-2716. E-mail: drrwest@comcast.net. Website: www.positivedifference.com. Call/write/e-mail. GE/LC/GH. Does A/NB/BS. Charges by the page or provides a project cost estimate. Published professional; author of two books and several articles; more than 20 years editing experience.

IDAHO

MAX JAMES, 393 W. Willowbrook Dr., Meridian ID 83642. (208)288-0983. E-mail: Max Diana@aol.com.

ILLINOIS

ALICE 'N INK/ALICE PEPPLER, 6007 N. Sheridan Rd., Apt. 6D, Chicago IL 60660-3061. (773)878-5943. Fax (773)878-6264. E-mail: apeppler@aol.com. Website: www.apeppler .com. Call/e-mail/write. GE/LC. Does A/SS/P/F/N/NB/BP/QL/JN/PB/BS/GB/E/D. Three-chapter book proposal, including market analysis $103; additional editing $30/hr. Publishing experience of 25 years. Quality work; quick turnaround.

AMACK EDITING SERVICES/JILL S. AMACK, 808 Corday Dr., #202, Naperville IL 60540. (630)848-1948. E-mail: amackediting@earthlink.net. Website: www.pensite.org (listed under Membership). E-mail. GE/LC. Does A/N/NB/BP/QL/PB/BS/GB/TM/D/back-cover copy. Full-time copy editor; freelance editing for over 6 years; newsletter editor; graduate of Denver Publishing Institute. Charges $25/hr. or flat rate.

INNOVATIVE MEDIA SOLUTIONS/BILL SPILMAN, 1134 N. Henderson St., Ste. D, Galesburg IL 61401. (309)342-3211. Fax (309)342-3212. E-mail: Bill@innovativemedia solutions.com. Website: www.innovativemediasolutions.com. Contact by e-mail. GE/LC/B/NL/SP/WS. Does A/SS/NB. Provides PR and editorial services, business cards, press-release writing, and distribution. Rates available on request. Professional journalist since 1987.

THE WRITER'S EDGE, PO Box 1266, Wheaton IL 60189. E-mail: info@writersedgeservice .com. Website: www.WritersEdgeService.com. No phone calls. A manuscript screening service for 75 cooperating Christian publishers. Charges $79 to evaluate a book proposal and if publishable, they will send a synopsis of it to 75 publishers who might be interested. If not publishable they will tell how to improve it. If interested, send an SASE for guidelines and a Book Information Form; request a form via e-mail or copy from Website. The Writer's Edge now handles previously published books that are out of print and available for reprint. Requires a different form, but cost is the same. Reviews novels, nonfiction books, juvenile novels, Bible studies, devotionals, biography, and theology. See Website for details.

INDIANA

DENEHEN, INC./DR. DENNIS E. HENSLEY, 6824 Kanata Ct., Fort Wayne IN 46815-6388. (260)485-9891. Fax (260)485-9891. E-mail: dnhensley@H51mail.com. E-mail; send ms. GE/LC/GH/CA. Does A/SS/F/N/NB/BP/QL/JN/BS/E/D/comedy/academic articles/editorials/Op-Ed pieces/columns/speeches/interviews. Rate sheet for SASE. Author of 44 books; PhD in English; college English professor.

EDITORIAL SERVICES/APRIL STIER, 7768 N. 100 E., Ossian IN 46777-9360. (260)622-4756. E-mail: april_lynn03@hotmail.com. E-mail/Write. GE/LC/CA. Does A/SS/F/N/NB/BP/QL/BS/GB/E/D. Charges $15/hr. for proofreading/copyediting; $18/hr. for line editing, and $250 and up for manuscript evaluation. Send SASE for rate sheet. BA in English, AA in writing, BA in biblical studies; published writer.

EPIPHANY LANE PRODUCTIONS/STEPHEN R. CLARK, PO Box 868, Fishers IN 46038-0868. (317)435-9673. E-mail: stephen@stephenrclark.com. Website: www.StephenRClark .com. E-mail. LC/GH/CA/SP/Websites/speechwriting/consulting. Does A/NB/BS/GB/TM/E/D. Charges $95/hour (negotiable). Projects negotiable. Ghostwriting $5,000 and up. Details on Website. Writer/editor for 20+ years.

XARIS COM/JAMES WATKINS, PO Box 117, Laotto IN 46763-0117. (260)897-2575. E-mail: jim@jameswatkins.com. Website: www.jameswatkins.com. E-mail; send $50 deposit. GE. Does A/NB/BP/D. Award-winning author & editor; 20+ years' experience. Charge $50 for 2,000 words of critique, editing, market suggestions.

KENTUCKY

EDITORIAL SERVICE/MARILYN A. ANDERSON, 127 Sycamore Dr., Louisville KY 40223-2956. (502)244-0751. Fax (502)452-9260. E-mail: shelle12@aol.com. Call/e-mail. GE/LC. Does A/F/NB/BS/TM/E/D. Charges $15-20/hr. for proofreading; $25/hr. for extensive editing; or negotiable by the job or project. Holds an MA and BA in English; former high school English teacher; freelance consultant since 1993. References available. Contributing member of The Christian PEN.

+EDITORIAL SERVICES/MISHAEL AUSTIN, 844 Keystone Way, Louisville KY 40223-3530. Phone/fax (502)489-5485. E-mail: Mishael1830@aol.com. Call/e-mail. GE/LC/GH/B/NL/SP/transcription/typing. Does A/SS/F/N/NB/BP/QL/JN/BS/GB/E/D. Light editing/proofreading: $2.50/pg.; extensive editing (including formatting): $4/pg.; typing: $2/pg.; transcription: $15-20/hr. Special projects and writing fees negotiable. BA and MA in psychology; 3.5 years proofreading/editing experience for academic and news media corporations; familiarity with APA, MLA, and *Chicago Manual of Style* writing formats.

BETTY L. WHITWORTH, 11740 S. Hwy 259, Leitchfield KY 42754. (270)257-2461. E-mail: Blwhit@bbtel.com. Call/e-mail/write. GE/GH/SP. Does A/SS/N/NB/D. Typing fees based on project (reasonable). Editing for novels and nonfiction books: $50 deposit with first 100 pgs., fee based on amount of work. Retired English teacher, newspaper columnist for 18 yrs., published over 1,000 stories/articles; have worked with 50 writers.

MARYLAND

OPINE PUBLISHING INTERACTIVE SERVICE FOR FIRST BOOK AUTHORS. This service gives writers a direct, interactive publisher's contact. Gain a unique view of key elements most likely to influence a publisher. Obtain publisher's view of frequently overlooked items, a unique query packet, personal guidance and critique of documents, plus thorough critique of three manuscript chapters. Contact: publisher@opinebooks.com. Participation does not insure consideration for publication by Opine.

OWEN-SMITH & ASSOCIATES, INC./RHONDA OWEN-SMITH, 2916 Old Court Rd., Pikesville MD 21208. (410)659-2247. Fax (410)659-9758. E-mail: mapreos@aol.com. Does GH/CA/B/NL/SP/BP/biographies/market analysis/marketing and PR plans/potential publisher identification/press kits/interview scheduling/book signings. Will consider other requests. Charges a flat fee or hourly rate based upon the project.

MASSACHUSETTS

WORD PRO/BARBARA A. ROBIDOUX, 127 Gelinas Dr., Chicopee MA 01020-4813. (413)592-4386. Fax (413)594-8375. E-mail: Ebwordpro@aol.com. Call/e-mail. GE/LC/GH/CA. Does A/SS/F/N/NB/BP/QL/BS/GB/TM/E/D. Charges $25/hr.; $115 for book proposal/3 chapters.

BA in English; 18 years as freelancer; book reviewer; on staff of TCC Manuscript Critique Service.

MICHIGAN

CALLED AND READY WRITERS CONSULTATION SERVICE/MARY EDWARDS, 20700 Civic Center Dr., Ste. 170, Southfield MI 48076. (248)663-2363. Fax (313)861-7578. E-mail: medwards4487@comcast.net. Website: www.thecalledandreadywriters.org. Contact by e-mail. LC. Does A/SS/N/NB/BS/GB/E/D. Charges $45/hr. (negotiable). Twenty plus years editing books and writing; copyeditor for secular newspaper; author of 6 books. Also leads workshops on "How to Write a Book."

WALLIS EDITORIAL SERVICES/DIANA WALLIS, 547 Cherry St. S.E., #6C, Grand Rapids MI 49503-4755. Phone/fax (616)459-8836. E-mail: WallisEdit@sirus.com. Call/e-mail. GE/LC/GH/CA/B/NL/SP/research/fact and reference checking/rewriting/proofreading/ markup for typesetting/coding for electronic publications. Does A/SS/F/N/NB/BS/ TM/E/D/advertising and promotional material, Website content, technical material for non-technical readers. Charges $25/hr. Will negotiate on larger projects (20+ hours). Deposit of 50% required for first-time clients. Commercial advertising and technical writing experience; published book author and editor.

MINNESOTA

NORTH COUNTRY TRANSCRIPTION (Psalm 96:13): Writing, Editing and Secretarial Services/CONNIE PETTERSEN. (218)927-6176. E-mail: PSALM9613@mlecwb.net. Call or write. Manuscript typing; edit for punctuation/spelling/grammar, etc. Nationally published freelance writer: fiction, nonfiction; local newspaper feature and news writer; 28 years secretarial/transcription experience. Windows XP, Corel 8. Transcription: voice file digital, standard or micro-cassette tapes. Fees: by the 65-character line or hourly rate; free estimates. Confidential.

MISSOURI

BLUE MOUNTAIN EDITORIAL SERVICE/BARBARA WARREN, Rte. 3 Box 3200, Exeter MO 65647. (417)835-3235. E-mail: barbarawarren@mo-net.com. E-mail. GE. Does A/SS/N/ BP/QL/JN/BS/GB/E/D. Rate sheet send on request. Eighteen years' experience.

PRO WORD WRITING & EDITORIAL SERVICES/MARY R. RUTH, PO Box 155, Labadie MO 63055-0155. (636)742-3663. E-mail: prowordusa@juno.com. Call/e-mail. GE/LC/ SP/manuscript or script typing, scan hard copy to disk, proofreading, indexing. Does A/SS/N/NB/BP/JN/BS/TM/E/D/S/biographies/textbooks. Call to discuss your project. Reasonable rates/professional results. MC/Visa available.

+THERE'S AN ANGEL IN YOUR INKWELL/CAROL NEWMAN, PO Box 480835, Kansas City MO 64148-0835. (913)681-1168. Fax (913)681-1173. E-mail: carol@angelinyour inkwell.com. Website: www.angelinyourinkwell.com. Contact by e-mail. GE/GH. Does A/SS/P/F/NB/BP/QL/E/D. Variable rates according to project; average $40/hr.; 1/2 hr. free consultation. Twenty years national inspirational writer, teacher, and writing coach.

MONTANA

NOVELEDIT AND ALONG COUNTRY ROADS/JIM COTTON, (2 business names) 652 Treece Gulch Rd., Stevensville MT 59870. (406)777-5191. E-mail: noveledit2003@yahoo.com.

Websites: www.noveledit.com and www.alongcountryroads.com. E-mail/write. GE. Does N/JN/memoirs only; specializes in tutorial critique for novels. Also online editing using MS Word 2000. Charges $30 for 30 pgs. for critique; electronic rates available. Has 25 years' experience in journalism and magazine editing; novel coach and tutor since 1995.

NEW HAMPSHIRE

AMDG ENTERPRISES/SALLY WILKINS, Box 273, Amherst NH 03031-0393. (603)673-9331. E-mail: SEDWilkins@aol.com. Write. GE/LC. Does A/F/JN/PB/BS/TM. Rate sheet for SASE.

NEW JERSEY

*D'EDRA Y. ARMSTRONG. New Jersey. E-mail: MLHUB21@aol.com or thesoulssolace@aol.com. E-mail. LC/GH/CA/B/NL/SP. Does SS/N/NB/QL/E/D. Charges $20/hr.; technical $40/hr. Over 15 years copywriting/editing experience.

WRITER'S RELIEF, INC./RONNIE L. SMITH, 245 Teaneck Rd., #3, Ridgefield Park NJ 07660-2003. (201)641-3003. Fax (201)641-1253. E-mail: Ronnie@wrelief.com. Website: www.wrelief.com. Call (8:30 a.m.–2:30 p.m. ET) or e-mail. GE/LC. Does A/SS/P/N/NB/BP/QL/E/S. An author's submission service, handling your manuscript submissions for an hourly rate of $45-60 (plus postage and copying), or a flat fee after completing review. Prepares manuscripts, proofreads, writes query and cover letters, tracks submissions, keeps records, etc.

NEW YORK

ELIZABETH CRISPIN, Box 134 Schulyer Rd., Oswegatchie NY 13670-3126. (315)848-7401. Fax (315)848-9860. E-mail: JMYPoet@aol.com. Write/call/e-mail, or send with $25 deposit and SASE. GE/LC/GH/CA/B/SP. Does A/SS/P/BP/JN/PB/BS/GB/E/D. Charges $25 basic charge; others on contractual basis. Published book and magazine author.

#I AM THE VINE PUBLISHING SERVICES/SUSAN RESCIGNO, 2927 Lexington Ave., Mohegan Lake NY 10547. (914)526-4947. E-mail: srescigno@aol.com. Website: www.iamthevine.net. Call/e-mail. GE/LC/NL. Does A/SS/N/NB/JN. Fifteen years' experience in publishing industry. Hourly or page rates available for copyediting or proofreading.

LAST WORD OFFICE WORKS/MARY A. LACLAIR, PO Box 435, Vernon NY 13476-0435. (315)829-3356. Fax (315)829-3356 (auto switch). E-mail: mlaclair1@juno.com. Write; send material with $25 deposit. GE/LC. Does A/SS/N/JN/BS/D. Estimates for projects, about $2-5/pg. or $10-20/hr. (depending on amount of editing needed). Published writer; Op-Ed guest column in NY and FL newspapers, weekly columnist in VA newspaper, published articles in 5 different national magazines.

NORTH CAROLINA

ANNA W. FISHEL, 3416 Hunting Creek Dr., Pfafftown NC 27040. (336)924-5880. E-mail: awfishel@triad.rr.com. Call/write/e-mail. GE/CA/SP. Does A/SS/P/N/NB/JN/E/D. Charges by the hour. Estimates offered. Professional editor for over 17 years; editor with major Christian publishing house for over 10 years; published author.

PREP PUBLISHING/PATTY SLEEM, 1110½ Hay St., Fayetteville NC 28305. (910)483-6611. Fax (910)483-2439. E-mail: preppub@aol.com. Website: www.prep-pub.com. Write. GE/LC/SP. Does N/NB. Project price based on written query and initial free telephone consultation. BA in English, MBA from Harvard, author of more than 25 books.

LESLIE H. STOBBE, 300 Doubleday Rd., Tryon NC 28782. (828)859-5964. Fax (978)945-0517. E-mail: lstobbe@alltel.net. E-mail. GE/GH/CA/BCE. Does A/NB/BP/D. Considers writing assignments of all kinds, including promotional and fund-raising, coauthoring with pastors and professionals, biographies, research-based Bible studies, adult curriculum, small group Bible studies, major rewriting of manuscripts, specialized editing. Fifty years as writer/editor/agent; including 14 books and well over 700 articles, newsletter writer, and fund-raising writer. Able to meet client needs despite tight deadlines. Charges $50-75/hr.; rate sheet on request.

OHIO

+CRYSTAL CLEAR EDITING SERVICES/KATHLEEN FULLER, 4374 Austin Rd., Geneva OH 44041. (440)363-5671. E-mail: Kathy@kathleenfuller.com. Website: www.kathleen fuller.com. Contact by e-mail. GE/LC/GH/B/NL. Does A/SS/F/N/BP/QL/BS/E/D. Charges $10/hr. Multipublished fiction and nonfiction author; 5 years' experience critiquing/editing. References available on request.

OKLAHOMA

EDITORIAL SERVICES/CHRISTY PHILLIPPE, 5736 S. Quincy Pl., Tulsa OK 74105. (918)749-0098. E-mail: christy6871@aol.com. E-mail. GE/LC/GH/SP/research/indexing. Does A/SS/NB/BP/QL/BS/GB/D. Critiques: $3/pg.; line editing: $15-17/hr.; other projects negotiable. Deposit usually required. Ten year's experience in Christian publishing; former editor; ghostwritten books on bestseller list; former college English instructor.

EPISTLEWORKS CREATIONS/JOANN RENO WRAY, 8409 S. Elder Ave., Broken Arrow OK 74011-8286. (918)451-4017. Cell: (918)695-4528. E-mail: epistle1@epistleworks.com. Website: http://epistleworks.com. Call/write/e-mail (prefers). GE/LC/GH/CA/B/NL/SP/research. Does A/SS/P/F/N/NB/BP/D. Charges start at $25/hr. Accepts checks, money orders, or payment by PayPal. See site for details on services. Most editing requires min. $25 deposit. Binding estimates given. Designs and creates Websites. Offers e-mail classes on writing. Available as speaker/teacher. Experienced artist, writer, and editor since 1974.

+TWEEN WATERS EDITORIAL SERVICES/TERRI KALFAS, PO Box 1233, Broken Arrow OK 74013-1233. (918)346-7960. Fax (918)451-3595. E-mail: tkalfas@valornet.com. E-mail/call/write. GE/LC/GH/CA/B/SP/BCE. Does A/N/NB/BP/QL/BS/TM/project management/book doctoring. Multiple editorial and freelance writing services. Project fees negotiable. Twenty years' experience as reporter, writer, editor, editorial development director, and director of publishing. Equally skilled in copywriting for catalogs, direct marketing, and fund-raising. Former tech school writing instructor. Award-winning fiction writer. Available as conference speaker and workshop teacher.

WINGS UNLIMITED/CRISTINE BOLLEY, PO Box 691532, Tulsa OK 74169-1532. (918)250-9239. Fax (918)250-9597. E-mail: WingsUnlimited@aol.com. Website: www.wingsun limited.com. E-mail. GE/GH/CA/SP. Does NB/D. Charges by the page; negotiated in advance. Former editorial acquisition editor with 25 yrs. experience in book development of bestselling titles and author/coauthor/ghostwriter of 30+ titles. Also available to teach workshops at writer's conferences.

THE WRITE WORD/IRENE MARTIN, PO Box 300332, Midwest City OK 73140-5641. E-mail: write1word@aol.com. Write/e-mail (detailing project). GE/LC. Does A/SS/F/N/BP/QL/JN. Charges $3/pg., min. $15 for 5 pgs. Workshops and editorial consulting done on a project-by-project basis. Has MA in English Creative Writing; published novelist; instructor/editor for Writer's Digest School; former college writing instructor.

OREGON

BALDWIN WRITERS SERVICES/STANLEY C. BALDWIN, 12900 S.E. Nixon, Portland OR 97222. (503)659-2974. E-mail: scbaldwin@juno.com. Evaluation of your organizational publication; Writers Workshops; manuscript critiquing by mail, contract evaluation. Send an SASE for rate sheet.

+THE EDITING GALLERY/CAROL L. CRAIG, 2622 Willona Dr., Eugene OR 97408. (541)342-7300. E-mail: carollcraig@cs.com. Website: www.editinggallery.com. Call/e-mail. GE/LC. Does SS/N/QL/JN/synopses. English major. Fee scale available on Website.

EDITORIAL SERVICES/ANNA LLOYD STONE, PO Box 2251, Lake Oswego OR 97035. (503)691-8349. E-mail: astone@att.net. Contact by e-mail. LC. Does A/SS/F/N/NB/BP/QL/JN/BS/TM/E/D/S/advertising/copywriting. Charges $50/hr. Send ms/SASE or can edit by e-mail. BA in humanities/writing, 3 years copywriting experience.

I'LL READ IT! EDITORIAL SERVICES/DONNA FLEISHER, PO Box 871, Lincoln City OR 97367. (541)994-2630. E-mail: donna@illreadit.com. Website: www.illreadit.com. Call/e-mail/write. GE/LC. Does SS/N/JN. Charges $500 flat fee for entire manuscript, which includes a complete edit and free future consultations.

BONNIE LEON, PO Box 774, Glide OR 97443. (541)496-3787. E-mail: leon@rosenet.net. Call/write/e-mail. GE/LC/GH/NL/SP. Does A/SS/F/N/BP/QL/D. Charges $25/hr. ($50 min.); larger projects negotiated. Author of 10 books; editorial services, writing instructor, speaker.

MARCIA A. MITCHELL, 4144 Sunnyview Rd. N.E., #115, Salem OR 97305-1893. (503)588-0372. E-mail: bzrytr@msn.com. E-mail/write; send $25 deposit with ms. GE/LC/GH/CA/NL. Does A/SS/F/N/NB/JN/D. Charges $25/hr for long projects; $25 for up to 5,000 wds.; $50 for 5,000-10,000 wds. Published writer.

PICKY, PICKY INK/SUE MIHOLER, 1075 Willow Lake Road N., Salem OR 97303-5790. (503)393-3356. E-mail: miholer@viser.net. E-mail. GE/LC. Does A/F/N/NB/BS/D. Manuscript preparation available. $25 an hour or negotiable by job. Freelance writer and copyeditor for several publishers for 7 years. "Helping you write it right," whether it's a postcard or a doctoral dissertation.

PRINT PREVIEW, INC./PAT JOHNSON, 10214 S.W. 36th Ct., Portland OR 97219-6100. (503)244-4460. Fax (503)244-4153. E-mail: pjdj01@aol.com. Call/e-mail/write. LC/NL/SP. Does A/SS/F/N/NB/BP/QL/JN/PB/BS/TM/D/S/typing. Charges $18/hr.; $35 min. Editing, proofreading experience.

SALLY STUART, 1647 S.W. Pheasant Dr., Aloha OR 97006. (503)642-9844. Fax (503)848-3658. E-mail: stuartcwmg@aol.com. Website: www.stuartmarket.com. Call/write/e-mail. GE/BCE/agent contracts. Does A/SS/N/NB/BP/GB/JN/E. No poetry or picture books. Charges $35/hr. for critique; $40/hr. for consultations. Contact for availability. For books, send a copy of your book proposal: cover letter, chapter-by-chapter synopsis, and the first three chapters. Comprehensive publishing contract evaluation $75-125. Author of 32 books and over 37 years' experience as a writer, teacher, marketing expert.

PENNSYLVANIA

AUTHORCOACHING.COM: A Coaching Service for Inspirational Authors (formerly Manuscript Placement Service), PO Box 428, Newburg PA 17240. (717)423-6621. Fax (717)423-6944. E-mail: keith@authorcoaching.com. Website: www.AuthorCoaching.com. Coach: Keith Carroll. Estab. 2000. Deals with all inspirational material. Contact by letter, fax, phone, e-mail. Visit Website for detailed description of fees.

VAL CINDRIC EDITING & WRITING SERVICES, 662 N. Main St., Greensburg PA 15601-1695. (724)838-9011. Fax (724)838-9336. E-mail: pcindric@earthlink.net. Call/e-mail/write. GE/LC/GH/CA. Does A/SS/F/N/NB/BP/GB/D. Fee based on complexity and subject matter of the material (call for rate); generally $1-2/pg. Reduced rate for nonprofits. Over twenty years' experience in professional editing and coauthoring for Christian publishers, authors, pastors, and mission organizations.

SPREAD THE WORD/MAURCIA DELEAN HOUCK, 106 Danny Rd., Sanatoga PA 19464-7215. (610)970-6931. E-mail: m-houck@verizon.net. E-mail/write. GE/LC. Does A/SS/N/NB/BP/JN/BS. Charges $1.75/pg. (double-spaced), or as quoted; 50% deposit required. E-mail for possible discount for over 300 pgs. Author of 2 books and over 1,500 articles and former newspaper editor.

STRONG TOWER PUBLISHING/HEIDI NIGRO, PO Box 973, Milesburg PA 16853-0973. E-mail: strongtowerpubs@aol.com. Website: www.strongtowerpublishing.com. E-mail contact. GE/LC/GH/B/NL/SP/WS. Does A/SS/P/F/N/NB/QL/BS/GB/TM/E/D. Manuscript evaluation, $59-109; proofing, $2 per 250-word-page; copyediting, $4/250-word-page. Other projects negotiable. Provides free 5-page sample edit. Theological manuscripts must be consistent with basic statement of faith. Twenty years' experience in editing/publishing.

WRITE HIS ANSWER MINISTRIES/MARLENE BAGNULL, LittD, 316 Blanchard Rd., Drexel Hill PA 19026-3507. Phone/fax: (610)626-6833. E-mail: mbagnull@aol.com. Website: www.writehisanswer.com. Call/write. GE/LC/typesetting. Does A/SS/N/NB/BP/JN/BS/D. Charges $30/hr.; estimates given. Call or write for information on At-Home Writing Workshops, a correspondence study program. Author of 5 books; compiler/editor of 3 books; over 1,000 sales to Christian periodicals.

SOUTH CAROLINA

+EDITORIAL SERVICE/LINDA J. LEE, A-11, 1208 Bush River Rd., Columbia SC 29210-7563. (803)798-0943. E-mail: ljlee@bellsouth.net. E-mail/write. GE/LC/B/NL/SP/academically oriented research. Does A/SS/F/NB/PB/QL/BS/GB/TM/E/D/S. Charges $20/hr. MEd; BA in English; 4 years as college writing tutor; published writer and contributing editor. Experienced in both technical and creative writing. References available.

TENNESSEE

CHRISTIAN WRITERS INSTITUTE MANUSCRIPT CRITIQUE SERVICE, PO Box 110390, Nashville TN 37222. Toll-free (800)21-WRITE. E-mail: ACWriters@aol.com. Website: www.ACWriters.com. Call/write. GE/LC/GH/CA/SP/BCE. Does A/SS/P/F/N/NB/BP/JN/PB/BS/TM/E/D/S. Send SASE for rate sheet and submission slip.

EDIT PLUS/CHARLES STROHMER, PO Box 4325, Sevierville TN 37876. (865)453-7120. Fax (865)428-0029. E-mail: wiselife@esper.com. Call/e-mail. GE/LC/CA/NL/SP. Does A/NB/BP/QL/BS/TM/E/D. Twenty years of experience as author and editor for major Christian publishers. Call/e-mail to discuss project and rates. Rates vary according to the type of work, e.g., ms evaluation, line editing, rewriting, or book proposal.

#THE YEOMAN'S SERVICE/VIRGINIA S. YOUMANS, 3227 Ella West Cir., Lynnville TN 38472-5228. (931)527-0101. E-mail: sergevirge@bellsouth.net. Website: www.bellsouth pwp.net/s/v/svyoumans. E-mail (preferred), write, or see Website; send ms/full payment. GE. Does N/NB/JN/BS/D. Charges $20/hour. BA in English, plus over 20 years' experience as an editor.

TEXAS

SYLVIA BRISKEY, Dallas TX. (214)521-7507. Call. GE/LC. Does P/JN/PB/BS/GB/children's stories/secular articles. Poetry, charges $5.60 plus $1/line; fiction $30 to 2,000 wds., $2.50/page thereafter. Writing teacher; writes children's books and poetry.

PWC EDITING/PAUL W. CONANT, 527 Bayshore Pl., Dallas TX 75217-7755. (972)913-9123. Fax (972)557-7558. E-mail: editor@pwc-editing.com. Website: www.pwc-editing.com. Contact by e-mail. LC/NL/SP/Websites/magazine editing. Does A/SS/F/N/NB/BS/TM/E/D/S/dissertations/textbooks/Web pages. Writer, editor; proofreader for book publishers and magazines. Dissertations, $18/hr.; short works, $25/hr.; negotiable terms for long works.

WORDS IN PROGRESS/CARRIE M. WOOD, 310 Lakewood Dr., Buda TX 78610-2575. (512)295-2592. E-mail: pclwood@netzero.net. Website: www.carriewood.com. E-mail or send synopsis and first three chapters with $30 deposit. GE. Does A/SS/N/NB/BP/QL/JN/PB/BS/GB/D/S/audio dramas. Charges $30/hr. (negotiable), discount for ACW and CWFI members. Introductory offer for new clients: $30 flat fee for 3 chapters. Quick turnaround. Project estimates after evaluation of services needed. Four years editing experience. References available.

UTAH

RIVERWRITERS.COM/KATHLEEN DAMP WRIGHT. Phone/fax (801)572-5227. E-mail: kathleen@riverwriters.com. Website: www.riverwriters.com. E-mail contact. GE/fiction coaching. Does N/QL/fiction synopsis. Also a writing coach. Charges by the hour; e-mail for current rate. BA in journalism, 20+ years editing/writing experience.

VIRGINIA

EDITOR FOR YOU/MELANIE RIGNEY, 4201 Wilson Blvd., #110328, Arlington VA 22203-1859. (571)235-1743. E-mail: info@editorforyou.com. Website: www.editorforyou.com. Contact by e-mail. GE/LC. Does SS/N/NB/BP/QL. Charges .01/wd. for copyediting; $50/hr. for content editing; $150-300 for ms evaluation. Editor of Writer's Digest Magazine for 5 years; book editor/manager of Writer's Digest Books for 3 years; 27 years of editing experience.

+EDITORIAL SERVICES/SKYLAR HAMILTON BURRIS, PO Box 7505, Fairfax Station VA 22039. (775)206-3883 (voice mail). E-mail: SSburris@msn.com. Website: www.editor skylar.com. E-mail contact. LC/B/NL/SP. Does A/SS/P/F/N/NB/BP/QL/JN/BS/GB/TM/E/D/S. Charges authors $1.75/double-spaced pg. for editing. Charges businesses $35/hr. (for newsletter editing, writing, design). Specializes in working with self-publishing and POD authors. BA and MA in English. Current editor. Free sample edit of 2 pages.

+EDITORIAL SERVICES/WHITNEY HOPLER, 13112 Pelfrey Ln., Fairfax VA 22033. E-mail: WhitneyVLH@cox.net. Experience in editing on staff at Christian publications.

SCRIVEN COMMUNICATIONS/KATHIE NEE SCRIVEN, 1902 Stevens Rd., #1406, Woodbridge VA 22191-2748. Phone/fax (703)492-6442. Call/write; send material for a free estimate. GE/LC/B/SP. Does A/SS/P/F/N/NB/BP/QL/JN/PB/BS/GB/TM/E/D/S/tracts/pamphlets/résumés/job application letters/biographical sketches/grant proposals. Charges $20/hr (negotiable); 1/2 deposit up front. Discount for ministries. Brochure available for SASE. Has a BS in mass communication/journalism; 18 years' experience in print media; has edited 32 books. Specializes in spiritual growth books for adults.

SOLUTIONS UNLIMITED/SHARLENE PRITCHETT WADE, PO Box 1, Fisherville VA 22939. (540)241-1599. E-mail: solutions@rockbridge.net. Call/e-mail. GE/LC/GH/CA/B/NL/SP. Does A/P/F/NB/GB/E/D. Competitive pricing by page or project. Creator of several works, newsletter designer, author, editor.

WASHINGTON

BOOKHOUSE COMMUNICATIONS/TRICIA LAWRENCE, Box 24687, Federal Way WA 98093-1687. Phone/fax (253)661-0371. E-mail: sensibility@proaxis.com. Website: www.real brilliant.com. Call. GE/LC/GH/CA/B/NL/SP. Does A/SS/N/NB/BP/QL/JN/PB/GB. Nine years as a published author and freelance editor. Charges $5/pg. and up, or $250 for a book proposal evaluation. Call or e-mail for details.

BRISTOL EDITING SERVICES/SANDRA E. HAVEN, PO Box 1000, Carlsborg WA 98324-1000. (360)582-9478. E-mail: mailto:services@bristolservicesintl.com. Website: www.bristol servicesintl.com. E-mail contact. GE/SP. Does A/SS/N/NB/BP/QL/JN/E. Critique (comprehensive edit) is .01/wd. Edits complete manuscripts as well as offering a "Write as We Go" service for writers working on book-length manuscripts. Fees and services fully explained on Website, or send SASE for services and rate sheet. Editor of *Writers' Intl. Forum,* 1990-1999 (award-winning publication); contributing editor to *1995 Novel & Short Story Writer's Market;* profiled as a leading editor for young writers in latest *Market Guide for Young Writers;* 15 years' experience in general editing.

MARION DUCKWORTH, 15917 N.E. 41st St., Vancouver WA 98682-7473. (360)896-8599. E-mail: mjduck@comcast.net. Call/e-mail/write. GE. Does A/N/NB/PB/BS; also does consultations. Charges $25/hr. for critique or consultation. Negotiates on longer projects. Author (for over 25 years) of 16 books and 300 articles; writing teacher for over 25 years.

EDITORIAL SERVICES/NANCY SWANSON, 10234—38th Ave. S.W., Seattle WA 98146-1118. (206)932-2161. E-mail: sannanvan@yahoo.com. Write/e-mail. GE/LC/GH/CA/B/NL/SP. Does A/SS/P/F/N/NB/JN/BS/E/D/S. Rates currently under revision; projects priced as mutually agreed. Former English teacher; editing course; 30+ years' experience editing.

KALEIDOSCOPE PRESS/PENNY LENT, 2507—94th Ave. E., Edgewood WA 98371-2203. (253)848-1116. E-mail: K.press@earthlink.net. Call/e-mail/write; send negotiated deposit. GE/LC/GH/CA/B/NL/SP/BCE. Does A/SS/P/F/N/NB/BP/QL/JN/PB/BS/GB/TM/E/D/S. Also market analysis, newsletters, brochures (graphic design & layout). All editing contracted by negotiated agreement. Discount given on larger projects. Thirty years as published author on radio, in magazines, newspapers, and 9 books. Editor for book publishers.

LOGOS WORD DESIGNS, INC./LINDA L. NATHAN, PO Box 735, Maple Falls WA 98266-0735. (360)599-3429. Fax (360)392-0216. E-mail: linda@logosword.com. Website: www.logos word.com. Call/e-mail. GE/LC/GH/CA/B/NL/SP/résumés, consultations, writing assistance, manuscript submission services. Does A/SS/F/N/NB/BP/QL/JN/PB/BS/TM/E/D/S/academic, legal, apologetics, conservative political. Over 30 years' experience in wide variety of areas, including publicity, postdoctoral; BA Psychology; some MA work. See Website or e-mail/call for rates.

PATRICIA RUSHFORD, Vancouver WA. E-mail: prushford@comcast.net. Website: www.patricia rushford.com. Prefers e-mail contact. GE. Does A/SS/N/NB/BP/JN. Fee schedule varies. Author of over 40 fiction and nonfiction books; author for 25 years.

WORD SOURCE, INC./MONICA COGLAS, PO Box 331, Mountlake Terrace WA 98043-0331. (425)481-4847. E-mail: info@monicacoglas.com. Website: www.monicacoglas.com. E-mail/write/$20 deposit. GE/LC/B. Does A/SS/N/NB/BP/QL/JN/PB/BS/GB/E/D. National award-winning author, business editor, newsletter editor, critique service, contest judge, and legal secretary. Charges $25/hr. or $5/pg. (4-page min.). Payment agreement must be signed in advance.

WISCONSIN

BRIAR PEN EDITORIAL SERVICES/SALLIE BACHAR, N1261 Briarwood Ln., Merrill WI 54452. (715)536-2450. E-mail: briarpen@msn.com. Call/e-mail/write. GE/LC. Does A/SS/F/NB/E/D. Charges $25/hr. Associate editor of a national Christian magazine, published author, columnist, and journalist.

MARGARET HOUK, West 2355 Valleywood Ln., Appleton WI 54915-8712. (920)687-0559. Fax (920)687-0259. E-mail: marghouk@juno.com. Call/write. GE/LC. Does A/F/NB/BP/QL/E/D (all for teens or adults). Charges *Writer's Market* suggested rates. Author of 5 books and 700 articles; has taught writing and manuscript marking for many years.

WYOMING

#MOODY LITERARY AGENCY/VIRGINIA A. MOODY, PO Box 35, Ranchester WY 82839-0035. E-mail: vamoody638@hotmail.com. Call/e-mail/write. LC/GH/CA/NL/SP/BCE. Does A/SS/N/NB/BP/QL/JN/PB/BS/GB/D/S. Charges $3.50/pg. or as agreed. Initially, send three pages and $9 for evaluation. Has edited spiritual romance and Bible study books.

CANADIAN/FOREIGN

+AOTEAROA EDITORIAL SERVICES/VENNESSA NG, PO Box 228, Oamaru 8901, New Zealand. Phone 0064273033738. E-mail: aotearao.editorial@xtra.co.nz. E-mail or write. GE. Does N. Full edit/critique $1.50/pg. Proofread only: $50/100 pgs. (Rates are in U.S. dollars and can be paid by PayPal.) Five years critiquing experience.

+CORRECT EDITING/MERILYN WALLACE, PO Box 19, Bonville NSW 2441, Australia. Phone: (02) 6653 5000. Fax (02) 6653 5200. E-mail: correctediting@bigpond.com. Call/e-mail/write. GE/LC/GH/CA/B/NL/SP/WS. Does A/SS/F/N/NB/BP/QL/JN/PB/BS/GB/TM/E/D. Ask for a quote. Over 20 year's experience in editing and writing.

DORSCH EDITORIAL/AUDREY DORSCH, 1275 Markham Rd., #305, Toronto ON M1H 3A2, Canada. (416)439-4320. Fax (416)439-5089. E-mail: audrey@dorschedit.ca. Website: www.dorschedit.ca. Audrey Dorsch, ed. Editorial services: substantive editing, copyediting, indexing, proofreading, layout.

+EDITORIAL SERVICE/KEVIN MILLER, 2779 Victoria St., Abbotsford BC V2T 2T7, Canada. (604)853-4920. E-mail: author@kevinwrites.com. Website: www.kevinwrites.com. Contact by e-mail. GE/LC/GH/CA/B/NL/SP/BCE. Does A/SS/P/N/MB/BP/QL/JN/PB/BS/GB/E/D/S. Charges per word, per page, or per project. Send e-mail for free estimate and free samples. Has written, co-written, or contributed to more than 24 books, fiction and nonfiction; helped dozens of writers prepare their work for publication.

BERYL HENNE, 711—60 Bridge St. W., Belleville ON K8P 1J3, Canada. (613)961-1791. Fax (613)961-1792. E-mail: b.henne@sympatico.ca. Write or e-mail. GE/LC/B/NL/SP. Does A/SS/NB/BS/TM/E/D. Charges $25/hr., will negotiate on larger projects. Has 5 years book and magazine editing, plus 18 years freelancing. Has worked with many self-publishing authors.

WENDY SARGEANT, PO Box 5617, Alexandra Hills QLD 4161, Australia. Phone 0427 870 330. Fax 07 3822 3054. E-mail: WendySargeant@bigpond.com. Website: www.editorsqld.com/

freelance/Wendy_Sargeant.htm. Editing, newsletters, proofreading, research, writing. Special interests: Annual/business reports, children's books, educational books (primary, secondary, tertiary, and above), fiction, history, legal, technical material (business humour). Manuscript assessor and instructional designer with The Writing School. Award-winning author published in major newspapers and magazines. Editing educational manuals. Project officer and instructional designer for Global Education Project, United Nationals Assoc. Information specialist for Australian National University.

VINEMARC LITERARY SERVICES/MARCIA LEE LAYCOCK, 5007—42A St., Ponoka AB T4J 1M3, Canada. (403)783-3044. Fax (403)783-6500. Contact by E-mail: Marcia@vinemarc.com. Website: www.vinemarc.com. GE. Does A/SS/P/N/NB/JN/D; others by arrangement. Rated listed on Website. Editing courses; speaks at conferences and teaches writing workshops and online courses through Inscribe Christian Writers' Fellowship. Blog for writers: www.writer-lee.blogspot.com.

CHRISTIAN LITERARY AGENTS

The references in these listings to "published authors" refer to those who have had one or more books published by royalty publishers, or who have been published regularly in periodicals. If a listing indicates that the agent is "recognized in the industry," it means they have worked with the Christian publishers long enough to be recognized (by the editors) as credible agents.

Note: Visit this Website to find information on agents or agents other writers have found less than desirable: www.agentresearch.com, or contact Professor Jim Fisher, Criminal Justice Dept., Edinboro University of Pennsylvania, Edinboro PA 16444, (814)732-2409, e-mail: Jfisher@edinboro.edu. Another such site, www.sfwa.org/beware/agents.html, is sponsored by the Science Fiction and Fantasy Writers of America. At the site for the Association of Authors' Representatives, www.aar-online.org, you will find a list of agents who don't charge fees, except for office expenses. You may also send for their list of approved agents (send $7 with a #10 SAE/1 stamp) to: PO Box 237201, Ansonia Station, New York NY 10003. I also suggest that you check out any potential agents at their local Better Business Bureau or local attorney general's office. Additional agent sites: http://fictionaddiction.net/agents.html; www.anotherealm.com/prededitors; www.agentquery.com; www.literaryagents.com; www.authorlink.com; and www.AuthorsTeam.com/agents.

As the information is available, listings will indicate which agents belong to the Association of Authors' Representatives, Inc. (address above). Those members have subscribed to a set code of ethics. However, lack of such a designation does not indicate the agent is unethical; most Christian agents are not members. If they do happen to be members, it should give an extra measure of confidence.

We do not intentionally list agents who charge fees beyond ordinary office expenses. If you run across one on this list, please let us know. Some of these are Christian agents; some are secular agents who handle Christian books.

(*) Indicates that agent did not return questionnaire
(#) Indicates that listing was updated from Website, brochure, or other sources
(+) Indicates new listing

AGENT RESEARCH & EVALUATION, INC., 25 Barrow St., New York NY 10014. (212)924-9942. Fax (212)924-1864. E-mail: info@agentresearch.com. Website: www.agentresearch.com. This is not an agency but a service that tracks the public record of literary agents and helps authors use the data to obtain effective literary representation. Charges fees for this service. Offers a free "agent verification" service at the site. (Answers the question of whether or not the agent has created a public record of sales.) Also offers a newsletter, *Talking Agents,* that is $35/yr. U.S., slightly higher elsewhere. See Jerry Jenkins's comments on this service on their Website, in the "Story So Far" section.

ALIVE COMMUNICATIONS, 7680 Goddard St., Ste. 200, Colorado Springs CO 80920. (719)260-7080. Fax (719)260-8223. E-mail: submissions@alivecom.com. Website: www.alivecom.com. Agents: Rick Christian, president; Lee Hough, Don Pape, and Beth Jusino. Well known in the industry. Estab. 1989. Represents 100+ clients. New clients on referral only. Handles adult and teen novels and nonfiction, gift books, children's books, crossover and general market books. Deals in both Christian (70%) and general market (30%). Member Author's Guild.

    Contact: E-mail to: submissions@alivecom.com.
    Commission: 15%
    Fees: Only extraordinary costs with client's preapproval; no review/reading fee.

Tips: If you have a referral, send material by mail and be sure to mark envelope "Requested Material." Unable to return unsolicited materials.

ALLRED AND ALLRED LITERARY AGENTS, 7834 Alabama Ave., Canoga Park CA 91304-4905. Fax (818)346-4313. Agents: Robert Allred & Kim Allred. Estab. 1991. Not yet recognized in industry. Represents 5 clients. Open to unpublished authors and new clients. Handles religious/inspirational fiction and nonfiction for all ages, screenplays, TV/movie scripts, and secular/crossover books.

> **Contact:** Query. Responds in 3 wks. to 2 mos.
>
> **Commission:** 10%; foreign 10%.
>
> **Fees:** None.
>
> **Tips:** "Be professional. If a project has a certain doctrinal slant that makes it of interest to a limited audience, let us know that."

AMBASSADOR AGENCY, PO Box 50358, Nashville TN 37205. (615)370-4700. Fax (615)661-4344. E-mail: Wes@AmbassadorAgency.com. Website: www.AmbassadorAgency.com. Agent: Wes Yoder. Estab. 1973. Recognized in the industry. Represents 15 clients. Open to unpublished authors and new clients. Handles adult novels and nonfiction, crossover books. Also has a Speakers Bureau.

> **Contact:** E-mail.

MEREDITH BERNSTEIN LITERARY AGENCY, 2112 Broadway, Ste. 503A, New York NY 10023. (212)799-1007. Fax (212)799-1145. Agents: Meredith Bernstein and Elizabeth Cavanaugh. Estab. 1981. Represents 85 clients. Open to unpublished authors and new clients. Handles nonfiction on spirituality. Member AAR.

> **Contact:** Query with SASE.
>
> **Commission:** 15%; foreign 20%.
>
> **Fees:** Charges $75/yr. disbursement fee.
>
> **Tips:** "We obtain most of our new clients through conferences and referrals from others."

BIGSCORE PRODUCTIONS, INC., PO Box 4575, Lancaster PA 17604. (717)293-0247. Fax (717)293-1945. E-mail: bigscore@bigscoreproductions.com. Website: www.bigscoreproductions.com. Agents: David A. Robie, Sharon Hanby Robie. Recognized in industry. Estab. 1995. Represents 40-50 clients. Open to unpublished and new clients. Handles all types of fiction and nonfiction, gift books, secular, crossover books, self-help, health, history, business, teen/children, and general nonfiction.

> **Contact:** Query by e-mail only. No longer accepts queries or proposals by mail.
>
> **Commission:** 15%, foreign and film 20%.
>
> **Fees:** Photocopying, overnight, etc. No reading fees.
>
> **Tips:** "Very open to taking on new clients. Bigscore deals extensively with the general market, as well as the Christian market. Submit a well-prepared proposal that will take minimal fine tuning for presentation to publishers. Fiction: Your work must be extremely well written. Nonfiction: You must be highly marketable and media savvy. The more established in speaking or your profession, the better."

BOOKS & SUCH/JANET KOBOBEL GRANT, 52 Mission Circle, Ste. 122, PMB 170, Santa Rosa CA 95409-5370. (707)538-4184. E-mail: janet@janetgrant.com. Website: www.booksandsuch.biz. Agents: Janet Kobobel Grant, Wendy Lawton. Recognized in industry. Estab. 1997. Represents 50 clients. Open to new or unpublished authors (with recommendation only). Handles fiction and nonfiction for all ages, picture books, gift books, crossover, and secular books.

> **Contact:** Letter or e-mail (no attachments).
>
> **Commission:** 15%.
>
> **Fees:** Photocopying and phone calls.
>
> **Tips:** "Especially looking for women's nonfiction. Also fiction that depicts everyday life and everyday faith struggles. Always interested in a strong nonfiction manuscript."

CURTIS BROWN, LTD., 10 Astor Pl., New York NY 10003-6935. (212)473-5400. West coast office: 1750 Montgomery St., San Francisco CA 94111. (415)954-8566. Agent: Perry Knowlton, chairman; Ellen C. Geiger. Member AAR. Secular agent; handles adult religious/ inspirational novels & nonfiction.

> **Contact:** Query with SASE; no fax/e-query. Responds in 3 wks. to query; 5 wks. to ms.

PEMA BROWNE LTD., 11 Tena Pl., Valley Cottage NY 10989-2215. (845)268-0029. Website: www.pemabrowneltd.com. Agents: Perry Browne & Pema Browne. Recognized in industry. Estab. 1966. Represents 20 clients (1 religious). Open to unpublished authors; no new clients at this time. Handles novels for adults and teens, nonfiction for all ages; picture books/novelty books, gift books, crossover books. Only accepts mss not previously sent to publishers.

> **Contact:** Letter query with credentials; no phone, fax or e-mail. Must include SASE.
> **Commission:** 15%; 20% foreign.
> **Fees:** None.
> **Tips:** "Check at the library in reference section, in *Books in Print,* for books similar to yours. Have good literary skills, neat presentation. Know what has been published and research the genre that interests you."

BROWNE & MILLER LITERARY ASSOCIATES, 410 S. Michigan Ave., Ste. 460, Chicago IL 60605. (312)922-3063. Fax (312)922-1905. E-mail: mail@browneandmiller.com. Website: www.browneandmiller.com. Agent: Danielle Egan-Miller. Recognized in the industry. Estab. 1971. Represents 15 clients. Open to unpublished authors and new clients if talented and professional. Handles teen and adult fiction, adult nonfiction, gift books, crossover and secular books. Member AAR.

> **Contact:** Query letter/SASE only; no fax/e-query.
> **Commission:** 15%, foreign 20%.
> **Fees:** No fees.

SHEREE BYKOFSKY ASSOCIATES, INC., 16 W. 36th St., 13th Fl., New York NY 10018. E-mail: ShereeBee@aol.com. Website: www.shereebee.com. Agent: Sheree Bykofsky. Estab. 1984. Agent is a former editor and an author. Represents a limited number of clients. Open to unpublished authors and new clients. Handles adult religious/inspirational fiction and nonfiction. Member AAR.

> **Contact:** Query with SASE.
> **Commission:** 15%; foreign 15%.
> **Fees:** Charges for postage, photocopying, and fax.
> **Tips:** "I get new clients through the recommendations of others. No poetry, children's material, or screenplays."

CAMBRIDGE LITERARY ASSOCIATES, 135 Beach Rd., Unit C3, Salisbury MA 01952-2255. (978)499-0374. Fax (978)499-9774. Website: www.cambridgeliterary.com. Agent: Michael R. Valentino. Represents 20 clients. Open to unpublished authors and new clients. Open to adult and teen fiction and nonfiction, screenplays, TV/movie scripts, and secular/ crossover books. Member AAR.

> **Contact:** Query letter.
> **Commission:** 15%; 20% foreign.
> **Fees:** None.
> **Tips:** "Christian fiction has become increasingly popular, especially works dealing with contemporary issues. Touch the readers where they live."

CASTIGLIA LITERARY AGENCY, 1155 Camino del Mar, Ste. 510, Del Mar CA 92014. (858)755-8761. Fax (858)755-7063. E-mail: JacLAgency@aol.com. Agents: Julie Castiglia and Sally Van Haitsma. Estab. 1993. Recognized in the industry. Represents 50 clients. Open to unpublished authors (with credentials) and selected new clients. Handles adult religious/inspirational nonfiction, Christian fiction, and secular crossover books. Member AAR.

Contact: Letter/SASE. No e-query.

Commission: 15%; 25% foreign.

Fees: For excessive postage and copying.

Tips: "I do not look at unsolicited manuscripts."

THE CREATIVE CULTURE, 72 Spring St., Ste. 304, New York NY 10012. E-mail: ndaustin@the creativeculture.com. Website: www.thecreativeculture.com. Agent: Nicole Diamond Austin. Open to unpublished authors and new clients. Handles adult religious/spiritual nonfiction.

Contact: Query with SASE; no e-query.

CS INTERNATIONAL, 43 W. 39th St., New York NY 10018. (212)921-1610. E-mail: csliterary@ aol.com. Website under construction. Agent: Cynthia Neeseman. Handles adult fiction and nonfiction; screenplays; and seeks foreign sales for translations of books published in the U.S.

Contact: Query.

DEFIORE & CO., 72 Spring St., Ste. 304, New York NY 10012. (212)925-7744. Fax (212)925-9803. E-mail: submissions@defioreandco.com. Website: www.defioreandco.com. Agents: Brian Defiore, Laurie Abkemeier, and Kate Garrick. Estab. 1999. Represents 35 clients. Open to new and unpublished authors. Secular agent; handles religious/inspirational nonfiction. Member of AAR.

Contact: Query with SASE, or e-query (no attachments).

Commission: 15%; foreign 20%.

Fees: Charges office expenses after book has sold.

JAN DENNIS LITERARY AGENCY, 19350 Glen Hollow Cir., Monument CO 80132. (719)481-0118. E-mail: jpdennislit@msn.com. Agent: Jan Dennis.

SANDRA DIJKSTRA LITERARY AGENCY, PMB 515, 1155 Camino del Mar, Del Mar CA 92014. (858)755-3115. E-mail: sdla@dijkstraagency.com. Website: www.dijkstraagency.com. Agent: Sandra Dijkstra. Open to unpublished authors and new clients. Secular agent. Handles adult religious nonfiction.

Contact: Query with outline, bio, SASE, plus 50-page synopsis for fiction and formal proposal for nonfiction. Simultaneous queries OK; no e-queries.

Commission: 15%; foreign 20%.

DYSTEL & GODERICH LITERARY MANAGEMENT, INC., 1 Union Square W., Ste. 904, New York NY 10003. (212)627-9100. Fax (212)627-9313. E-mail: Miriam@dystel.com. Website: www.dystel.com. Agents: Jane Dystel, Miriam Goderich, Stacey Glick, Michael Bourret, Jim McCarthy, and Lauren Abramo. Estab. 1994. Recognized in the industry. Represents 5-10 religious book clients. Open to unpublished authors and new clients. Handles fiction and nonfiction for adults, gift books, secular/crossover books. Member AAR.

Contact: Query letter with bio. Brief e-query; no simultaneous query.

Commission: 15%; foreign 19%.

Fees: Photocopying is author's responsibility.

Tips: "Send a professional, well-written query to a specific agent."

+EAMES LITERARY AGENCY. Website: www.eamesliterary.com. Agents: John Eames (John@ eamesliterary.com) and Dan Mann (Dan@eamesliterary.com). Open to unpublished authors and new clients. Handles adult religious/inspirational novels & nonfiction.

+EPIC LITERARY AGENCY, 7107 S. Yale Ave., #327, Tulsa OK 74136. (918)267-3248. Fax (918)267-3244. E-mail: KevinD@EpicLiterary.com, or info@EpicLiterary.com. Website: www.EpicLiterary.com. Agent: Kevin D. Decker. Estab. 1996. Represents up to 12 clients. Not currently open to unpublished authors; possibly open to new clients. Handles adult & children's novels & nonfiction, picture books, screenplays, TV/movie scripts, gift books, crossover books.

Commission: 15%; foreign 20%.

Fees: Charges only for special travel or out-of-ordinary expenses.

Tips: "Please query first; we do not accept unsolicited manuscripts."

FARRIS LITERARY AGENCY, INC., PO Box 570069, Dallas TX 75357-0069. (972)203-8804. Fax (972)226-1799. E-mail: farris1@airmail.net, or agent@farrisliterary.com. Website: www.farrisliterary.com. Agents: Mike Farris and Susan Morgan Farris. Open to unpublished authors and new clients. Handles Christian adult and teen fiction, spiritual or inspirational nonfiction, screenplays, secular/crossover books.

Contact: Mail or e-mail query (no attachments).

Commission: 15%; foreign 20%.

Fees: Expense for copies and postage only.

Tips: Please keep your query to one page and allow 2 weeks for a response to queries and 4-6 weeks for response to submissions.

THE FOGELMAN LITERARY AGENCY, 7515 Greenville Ave., Ste. 712, Dallas TX 75231, (214)361-9956. Fax (214)361-9553. And 445 Park Ave., New York NY 10022. (212)836-4803. E-mail: foglit@aol.com, or info@fogelman.com. Website: www.fogelman.com. Agent: Evan M. Fogelman. Estab. 1990. Recognized in the industry. Represents 100 clients. Open to few unpublished authors and new clients. Handles adult novels and nonfiction, women's fiction and nonfiction, gift books, secular/crossover books. Member AAR.

Contact: Query by e-mail, phone, or letter; no unsolicited manuscripts.

Commission: 15%; foreign 10%.

Fees: None.

SARA A. FORTENBERRY LITERARY AGENCY, 1001 Halcyon Ave., Nashville TN 37204. (615)385-9074. Recognized in the industry. Estab. 1995. Represents 30 clients. Open to unpublished authors or new clients only by referral. Handles adult nonfiction and novels, picture books, gift books, and secular crossover books.

Contact: Unpublished authors query by mail; published authors by phone or mail. Query letters should be accompanied by referral, book proposal, and SASE.

Commission: 15%; foreign 10%, plus subagent commission.

Fees: Standard expenses directly related to specific projects (copies, messenger, overnight shipping, and postage).

Tips: "For my purposes, a published author is one who has had a book published by a commercial (royalty) publisher."

SAMUEL FRENCH, INC., 45 W. 25th St., New York NY 10010-2751. (212)206-8990. Fax (212)206-1429.E-mail: samuelfrench@earthlink.net, or info@samuelfrench.com. Website: www.samuelfrench.com. Editor: Lawrence Harbison. Estab. 1830. Handles rights to some religious/inspirational stage plays.

Contact: Query or send complete manuscript.

Commission: Varies.

Fees: None.

GENESIS CREATIVE GROUP, 28126 Peacock Ridge, Ste. 104, Rancho Palos Verdes CA 90275. (310)541-9232. Fax (310)541-9532. E-mail: KenRUnger@aol.com. Agent: Ken Unger. Estab. 1998; developing recognition in industry. Represents 10 clients. Open to new clients. Handles completed screenplays only; no books.

Contact: Send one-page query with personal information, project description, and target market, by mail or e-mail only. No phone calls; no unsolicited manuscripts.

Commission: 15%; may vary by type of project.

Fees: Office fees for long distance calls and postage only.

Tips: "We formed this company to represent material to film and television community. We want material that presents values based on Judeo-Christian tradition."

MARK GILROY COMMUNICATIONS, INC., 6528 E. 101st St., Ste. 416, Tulsa OK 74133. Phone/fax (918)298-0041. E-mail: mark@markgilroy.com. Website: www.markgilroy .com. Agent: Mark K. Gilroy. Recognized in the industry. Represents 10 clients. Open to a limited number of new or unpublished clients. Handles adult nonfiction, gift books, crossover books, and secular books.

GOLDEN LITERARY AGENCY, 210 S. Holman Way, Golden CO 80401. (303)947-3524. Fax (303)384-9055. E-mail: goldenliterary@msn.com. Agent: Mary Ann Jeffreys. Estab. 2004. Gaining a reputation in the industry. Open to unpublished authors and new clients. Handles adult Christian novels & nonfiction, especially related to health and aging; teen/young adult novels; Bible studies; or how-to-minister books. No children's books, poetry, romance novels, or drama.

    Contact: Proposal by mail or e-mail (preferred).

    Commission: 15%; foreign 20%.

    Fees: Office expenses only.

    Tips: "Looking for authors who are passionate about their writing."

SANFORD J. GREENBURGER ASSOCIATES, INC., 55 Fifth Ave., New York NY 10003. (212)206-5600. Fax (212)463-8718. Website: www.greenburger.com. Agents: Heide Lange, Faith Hamlin, Dan Mandel, Matthew Bialer. Estab. 1945. Represents 500 clients. Open to unpublished authors and new clients. Secular agent; handles adult religious/inspirational nonfiction. Member of AAR.

    Contact: Query Heide Lange by mail with SASE, or by fax. Responds in 3 wks. to query; 2 mos. to ms.

    Commission: 15%; foreign 20%.

    Fees: Charges for photocopying and foreign submissions.

GROSVENOR LITERARY AGENCY, 5510 Grosvenor Ln., Bethesda MD 20814. Phone/fax (301)564-6231. E-mail: dcgrosveno@aol.com. Agent: Deborah Grosvenor. Estab. 1995. Represents 30 clients. Open to few unpublished authors and new clients. Secular agent; handles adult religious/inspirational nonfiction.

    Contact: Letter. Responds in 1-2 mos.

    Commission: 15%; foreign 20%.

    Fees: None.

JOY HARRIS LITERARY AGENCY, 156 Fifth Ave., Ste. 617, New York NY 10010. (212)924-6269. Fax (212)924-6609. E-mail: gen.office@jhlitagent.com. Agent: Joy Harris. Represents 100 clients. Handles religious/inspirational fiction. Member of AAR.

    Contact: Proposal/outline. Responds in 2 mos.

    Commission: 15%; foreign 20%.

    Fees: Charges some office expenses.

HARTLINE LITERARY AGENCY, 123 Queenston Dr., Pittsburgh PA 15235. (412)829-2483. Fax (412)829-2450. E-mail: joyce@hartlineliterary.com. Website: www.hartlineliterary .com. Agents: Joyce A. Hart, adult novels (romance, mystery/suspense, women's fiction) and nonfiction; Janet Benrey, adult fiction (romance, mystery/suspense, women's) and nonfiction, Janet@hartlineliterary.com; Tamela Hancock Murray, children's and young adult fiction, adult fiction (romance, mystery/suspense, women's) and nonfiction, tamela@ hartlineliterary.com; Andrea Boeshaar, women's fiction and romance, andrea@hartline literary.com. Recognized in industry. Estab. 1992. Represents 150 clients. Open to published authors (or selected unpublished). Handles novels and nonfiction for all ages, gift books, secular/crossover books. No poetry.

    Contact: Phone, letter, fax, or e-mail.

    Commission: 15%; foreign negotiable.

    Fees: Office expenses; no reading fee.

Tips: "Be sure to include your biography and publishing history with your proposal. Please ask for our literary guidelines if you have questions about preparing proposals. Working together we can make sure your manuscript gets the exposure and attention it deserves."

+HELMERS LITERARY AGENCY, PO Box 50737, Colorado Springs CO 80949-0737.E-mail: helmersliterary@msn.com. Agent: Kathryn A. Helmers.

JEFF HERMAN AGENCY, PO Box 1522, Stockbridge MA 01262. (413)298-0077. Fax (413)298-8188. E-mail: Jeff@jeffherman.com. Website: www.jeffherman.com. Agents: Jeff Herman and Deborah Herman. Estab. 1987. Recognized in the industry. Represents 20+ clients with religious books. Open to unpublished authors and new clients. Handles adult nonfiction (recovery/healing, spirituality), gift books, and secular/crossover; fiction.

    Contact: Query by mail/SASE; or by e-mail or fax. Accepts simultaneous submissions & e-query.: 15%; foreign 10%.

    Fees: No reading or management fees; just copying and shipping.

    Tips: "I love a good book from the heart. Have faith that you will accomplish what has been appointed to you."

SUSAN HERNER RIGHTS AGENCY, PO Box 57, Pound Ridge, NY 10576. (914)234-2864. Fax (914)234-2866. E-mail: sherneragency@optonline.net. Agent: Susan Herner. Estab. 1987. Represents 100 clients. Handles adult religious/inspirational nonfiction.

    Contact: Proposal/2-3 sample chapters. Responds in one month.

    Commission: 15%; foreign 20%.

    Fees: Charges only for extraordinary copying costs.

    Tips: "Particularly interested in revisionist biblical history, women's religious/spiritual experience, and comparative religious thought rather than traditional religious viewpoints."

HIDDEN VALUE GROUP, 1499 Iris Grove Dr., Corona CA 92881. Phone/fax (951)549-8891. E-mail: njernigan@HiddenValueGroup.com. Website: www.HiddenValueGroup.com. Agent: Nancy Jernigan. Estab. 2001. Recognized in the industry. Represents 7 clients with religious books. Open to previously published authors only. Handles adult & children's novels, adult & teen nonfiction, picture books, gift books, and crossover books.

    Contact: Prefers letter; e-mail OK.

    Commission: 15%; foreign 15%.

    Fees: None.

    Tips: "No poetry, articles, or short stories."

HORNFISCHER LITERARY MANAGEMENT, PO Box 50544, Austin TX 78763. E-mail: queries@hornfischerlit.com, or jim@hornfischerliterarymanagement.com. Website: www.hornfischerliterarymanagement.com. Agent: James D. Hornfischer. Estab. 2001. Represents 45 clients. Open to unpublished authors and new clients. Considers simultaneous submissions. Responds in 1 mo. Secular agent; handles adult religious/inspirational nonfiction.

    Contact: E-query only for fiction; query or proposal for nonfiction.

    Commission: 15%; foreign 20%.

JELLINEK & MURRAY LITERARY AGENCY, 2024 Mauna Pl., Honolulu HI 96822. (808)521-4057. Fax (808)521-4058. E-mail: r.jellinek@verizon.net. Agent: Roger Jellinek. Estab. 1995. Represents 5 clients/religious bks. New to this market. Open to unpublished authors and new clients. Handles adult religious/inspirational novels for teens and adults, adult nonfiction, screenplays by book clients, gift books, crossover books, and secular books.

    Contact: Prefers e-mail.

    Commission: 15%, foreign 20-25%.

    Fees: No fees.

LAWRENCE JORDAN AGENCY, 345 W. 121st St., New York NY 10027. (212)662-7871. Fax

(212)662-8138. E-mail: LJLAgency@aol.com. Agent: Lawrence Jordan. Estab. 1978. Represents 40 clients. Open to unpublished authors and new clients. Recognized in the industry. Responds in 3-6 wks. Handles adult novels and adult nonfiction (including religious/inspirational), gift books, short stories, crossover, and secular books.

Contact: Letter or e-mail only.

Commission: 15%; foreign 20%.

Fees: Office expenses only.

Tips: "Actively seeking spiritual and religious books."

NATASHA KERN LITERARY AGENCY INC., PO Box 1069, White Salmon WA 98672. (509)493-3803. Fax (509)493-3826. E-mail: nkern@natashakern.com. Website: www.natashakern .com. Agent: Natasha Kern. Recognized in the industry. Estab. 1987. Represents 40 clients, 12 religious. Open to unpublished authors and new clients. Secular agent; handles adult religious/inspirational fiction, crossover, and secular books.

Contact: Accepts queries by letter; 3 pg. synopsis & 3 sample pgs.; SASE if mailed.

Commission: 15%; 20% foreign (includes foreign-agent commission).

Fees: No reading fee.

Tips: "We represent a wide range of inspirational fiction and nonfiction; adult only." Responds in 3-8 wks. See submission guidelines on Website.

THE STEVE LAUBE AGENCY, 5501 N. 7th Ave., #502, Phoenix AZ 85013. (602)336-8910. E-mail: krichards@stevelaube.com. Website: www.stevelaube.com. Agent: Steve Laube. Estab. 2004. Recognized in the industry. Represents 50+ clients. Open to new and unpublished authors. Handles adult Christian fiction and nonfiction, history, theology, how-to, health, Christian living. No YA, children's books, or poetry.

Contact: Letter with proposal and sample chapters by mail is preferred. Open to e-queries.

Commission: 15%; foreign 20%.

Fees: No fees.

Tips: "Looking for fresh and innovative ideas. Make sure your proposal contains an excellent presentation."

THE LESCHER AGENCY, 47 E. 19th St., New York NY 10003. (212)529-1790. E-mail: susan lescher@aol.com. Website: www.lescherltd.com. Agent: Susan Lescher.

LEVINE GREENBERG LITERARY AGENCY, INC., 307—7th Ave., Ste. 1906, New York NY 10001. (212)337-0934. Fax (212)337-0948. Website: www.jameslevine.com. Agent: James Levine. West Coast Office: 112 Auburn St., San Refael CA 94901. (415)785-1582. Fax (415)785-1583. Agent: Arielle Eckstut. Estab. 1989. Represents 250 clients. Open to unpublished authors and new clients. Secular agent; handles adult religious/inspirational nonfiction. Member AAR.

Contact: See guidelines/submission form on Website; prefers e-query.

Commission: 15%; foreign 20%.

Fees: Office expenses.

Tips: "Our specialties include spirituality and religion."

PAUL S. LEVINE LITERARY AGENCY, 1054 Superba Ave., Venice CA 90291-3940 (310)450-6711. Fax (310)450-0181. E-mail: pslevine@ix.netcom.com. Agent: Paul S. Levine. Estab. 1996. Represents 100 clients. Open to unpublished authors and new clients. Considers simultaneous submissions. Responds in one day to 2 mos. Secular agent; handles adult religious/inspirational novels, nonfiction, and scripts.

Contact: Query with SASE by mail, e-mail, or fax. Accepts simultaneous submissions. Responds in 1 day to query; 2 mos. to ms.

Commission: 15%; foreign 20%.

Fees: Actual office expenses; no up-front payment.

+LINDSEY'S LITERARY SERVICES, 7502 Greenville Ave., Ste. 500, Dallas TX 75231. (214)890-9262. Fax (214)890-9265. E-mail: bonedges001@aol.com. Agents: Bonnie James and Emily Armenta. Estab. 2002. Represents 10 clients. Open to unpublished authors and new clients. Considers simultaneous submissions. Responds in 6 wks. to 3 mos. Secular agency; handles adult religious/inspirational novels.

> **Contact:** Query with SASE.
> **Commission:** 15%; foreign 20%.

THE LITERARY GROUP INTL, 270 Lafayette St., #1505, New York NY 10012. (212)274-1616. Fax (212)274-9876. E-mail: Fweimann@theliterarygroup.com, or js@theliterarygroup .com. Website: www.theliterarygroup.com. Agent: Frank Weimann, Ian Kleinert. Recognized in the industry. Estab. 1986. Represents 300 clients (120 for religious books). Open to new and unpublished authors. Handles adult fiction and nonfiction, history, secular, crossover, gift books, how-to, health, spiritual guidance.

> **Contact:** Letter.
> **Commission:** 15%; foreign 20%.
> **Fees:** No fees.
> **Tips:** "Looking for fresh, original spiritual fiction and nonfiction. We offer a written contract which may be canceled after 30 days."

LITERARY MANAGEMENT GROUP, INC., offices in Nashville TN & Gainesville FL. Mailing address: 407 N.W. 122nd St., Gainesville FL 32607. (615)812-4445 (Bruce Barbour); (615) 812-1884 (Margaret Langstaff). Fax (352)332-0081. E-mail: brucebarbour@literary managementgroup.com. Website: www.literarymanagementgroup.com. Agents: Bruce R. Barbour & Margaret Langstaff. Estab. 1995. Well recognized in the industry. Represents 100+ clients. Open to unpublished authors and new clients who have a platform and a compelling story or idea. Handles nonfiction only. Other services offered: editorial and rewrites, book packaging, and consulting

> **Contact:** E-mail preferred.
> **Commission:** 15%; foreign 20%.
> **Fees:** No fees or expenses on agented books.
> **Tips:** Follow guidelines, proposal outline, and submissions format on Website. Use Microsoft Word. Study the market and know where your book will fit in. Include return postage for unsolicited materials.

+LITWEST GROUP, LLC. E-mail: kboyle1@mindspring.com. Website: www.litwest.com. Agents: Katie Boyle or Nancy Ellis. Represents 160 clients. Open to unpublished authors and new clients. Considers simultaneous submissions. Responds in 1 mo. or more. Secular agency; handles adult religious/inspirational novels & nonfiction.

> **Contact:** Query with SASE.
> **Commission:** 15%; foreign 20%.

LUKEMAN LITERARY MANAGEMENT, INC., 157 Bedford Ave., Brooklyn NY 11211-2037. E-mail: Agency@lukeman.com. Website: www.lukeman.com. Agent: Noah Lukeman. Estab. 1996. Recognized in the industry. Represents 10 clients. Rarely open to unpublished authors or new clients (most are already publishing). Handles adult religious/inspirational novels and nonfiction.

> **Contact:** Not accepting submissions at this time. Check Website for availability.
> **Commission:** 15%; foreign 20%.
> **Fees:** None.

RICIA MAINHARDT AGENCY, 612 Argyle Rd., #L5, Brooklyn NY 11230. (718)434-1893. Fax (718)434-2157. E-mail: ricia@ricia.com. Website: www.ricia.com. Handles adult and young adult fiction, nonfiction, picture books, and early readers.

Contact: For fiction send a 3-5 page synopsis with first 20-30 pages (ending at a chapter break); for nonfiction, a chapter-by-chapters synopsis and 2 chapters; for children's send complete ms. Call for e-mail submissions instructions.

Fees: No reading fees.

MARCH MEDIA, INC., 1114 Oman Dr., Brentwood TN 37027. (615)377-1146. Fax (615)373-1705. E-mail: etta.wilson@comcast.net. Agents: Etta Wilson & Cathey Clark. Estab. 1989. Recognized in the industry. Represents 27 clients. Handles teen/YA and children's novels and nonfiction, some adult novels, picture books, and gift books for adults.

Contact: E-mail contact; no phone calls.

Commission: 15%.

Fees: Only if agreed on in contract. Offers consultation services on a fee basis for authors regarding contract negotiation.

Tips: "I prefer strong Christian values."

MCHUGH LITERARY AGENCY, 1033 Lyon Rd., Moscow ID 83843. (208)882-0107. Fax (603)688-6437. E-mail: elisabetmch@turbonet.com. Agent: Elisabet McHugh. Estab. 1995. Represents 49 clients. Recognized in the industry. Open to unpublished authors and new clients. Secular agent; handles adult and teen religious/inspirational nonfiction, crossover, and secular books.

Contact: E-mail.

Commission: 15%; foreign 20%.

Fees: None, but clients provide copies of manuscripts.

Comments: Be professional!

WILLIAM MORRIS LITERARY AGENCY, 1600 Division, Ste. 300, Nashville TN 37203. (615)963-3376. Fax (615)963-3094. E-mail: vs@wma.com. Website: www.wma.com. Agent: Valerie Summers. Recognized in the industry. Estab. 1898. Hundreds of clients with religious books. Not open to unpublished authors or new clients. Handles all types of material. Member AAR.

Contact: By e-mail.

Commission: 15%.

Fees: None.

DEE MURA ENTERPRISES, INC., 269 W. Shore Dr., Massapequa NY 11758-8225. (516)795-1616. Fax (516)795-8797. E-mail: samurai5@ix.netcom.com. Agents: Dee Mura, Karen Roberts, Frank Nakamura. Estab. 1987. Open to unpublished authors and new clients. Secular agency; handles religious/inspirational scripts.

Contact: Query with SASE; e-query OK (without attachment); no fax query. Responds in 2 weeks. Responds more quickly to mailed queries.

Commission: 15%; foreign 20%.

Fees: Charges for photocopying, long distance phone calls and faxes, and postage.

Tips: Offers written contract.

KATHI J. PATON LITERARY AGENCY, 19 W. 55th St., New York NY 10019-4907. (212)265-6586. (908)647-2117. E-mail: KJPLitBiz@optonline.net. Agent: Kathi Paton. Estab. 1987. Handles adult religious/inspirational nonfiction.

Contact: Prefers e-mail query.

Commission: 15%; foreign 20%.

Fees: For photocopying.

PATRICK-MEDBERRY ASSOCIATES, 11684 Ventura Blvd., #215, Studio City CA 91604. (818)422-1649. Fax (818)980-5820. E-mail: patrickmedberry@sbcglobal.net. Agent: Peggy Patrick. Estab. 2005. Newly established management company specializing in Christian writers, directors, and producers, as well as religious and inspirational novels, screenplays, TV/movie scripts, crossover books, secular books and screenplays. Open to unpublished authors and new clients.

Contact: Query by letter, fax, or e-mail; no calls.
Commission: 10%.
Fees: None.

PELHAM LITERARY AGENCY, 2451 Royal St. James Dr., El Cajon CA 92019-4408. (619)447-4468. E-mail: jmeals@pelhamliterary.com. Website: www.pelhamliterary.com. Agent: Jim Meals. Not yet known in the Christian industry. Estab. 1993. Open to unpublished authors and new clients. Handles adult and teen novels, adult nonfiction, secular/crossover books.
> **Contact:** Brief query letter preferred; e-query OK. Provides a list of published clients and titles.
> **Commission:** 15%; foreign 20%.
> **Fees:** Charges for postage and copying only.
> **Tips:** "We are actively seeking writers for the Christian fiction market although also open to Christian nonfiction. We specialize in genre fiction and enjoy working with new writers."

STEPHEN PEVNER, INC., 382 Lafayette St., 8th Fl., New York NY 10003. (212)674-8403. Fax (212)529-3692. E-mail: spevner@aol.com. Agent: Stephen Pevner. Estab. 1991. Represents under 50 clients. Open to unpublished authors and new clients. Responds in 2-5 wks. Secular agent; handles religious/inspirational nonfiction.
> **Contact:** Query/outline/proposal.
> **Commission:** 15%; foreign 20%.
> **Fees:** Commission only.

A PICTURE OF YOU AGENCY, 2372 W. Minster Dr., Fairfield OH 45014-3744. Phone/fax (513)863-1108. E-mail: apoy1@aol.com. Agent: Lenny Minelli. Estab. 1995. Branching out into Christian market. Represents 15 clients. Open to unpublished authors and new clients. Handles only screenplays, TV/movie scripts.
> **Contact:** Query with proposal.
> **Commission:** 10%; 15% foreign.
> **Fees:** Charges $125/yr. for office expenses.
> **Tips:** "Make sure your material is the best it can be before seeking an agent. Always enclose an SASE."

+QUICKSILVER BOOKS ONLINE. E-mail: QBOnline@artsnet.net. Website: www.quicksilver books.com. Agent: Bob Silverstein. Estab. 1987. Represents 50 clients. Open to unpublished authors and new clients. Secular agent; handles adult religious/inspirational nonfiction.
> **Contact:** Query by e-mail. Considers simultaneous submissions. Responds in 2-5 wks.
> **Commission:** 15%; foreign 20%.
> **Fees:** No fees.

RLR ASSOCIATES, LTD., Literary Dept., 7 W. 51st St., New York NY 10019. (212)541-8641. Fax (212)541-6052. Website: www.rlrassociates.net, or www.rlrliterary.net. Agent: Tara Mark (TMark@rlrassociates.net). Represents 50 clients. Open to unpublished authors and new clients. Secular agency; handles adult religious/inspirational nonfiction.
> **Contact:** Query with SASE. Considers simultaneous submissions. Responds in 5 wks.
> **Commission:** 15%; foreign 20%.

RITA ROSENKRANZ LITERARY AGENCY, 440 West End Ave., Ste. 15D, New York NY 10024-5358. (212)873-6333. Agent: Rita Rosenkranz. Estab. 1990. Represents 30 clients. Open to unpublished authors and new clients. Secular agent; handles adult religious/inspirational nonfiction. Member AAR.
> **Contact:** Proposal package (outline and sample chapter); no fax/e-query. Accepts simultaneous submissions. Responds in 2 wks. to query.
> **Commission:** 15%; foreign 20%.
> **Tips:** "A strong cover letter is very important. Be sure to identify competition to your book, and be sure it's a valid project."

GAIL ROSS LITERARY AGENCY, 1666 Connecticut Ave. N.W., #500, Washington DC 20009. (202)328-3282. Fax (202)328-9162. E-mail: jennifer@gailross.com. Website: www.gail ross.com. Contact: Jennifer Manguera. Estab. 1988. Represents 200 clients. Open to unpublished authors and new clients. Secular agent; handles adult religious/inspirational nonfiction, history, health, and business books.

> **Contact:** Query letter/SASE; no e-query.
> **Commission:** 15%; foreign 25%.
> **Fees:** Office expenses.

DAMARIS ROWLAND AGENCY, 5 Peter Cooper Rd., #13H, New York NY 10010. (212)475-8942. Fax (212)358-9411. Agent: Damaris Rowland. Estab. 1994. Represents 40 clients. Open to unpublished authors and new clients. No New Age material. Very selective.

> **Contact:** Query letter.
> **Commission:** 15%; foreign 20%.
> **Fees:** Some office expenses.

SCHIAVONE LITERARY AGENCY, INC., 236 Trails End, West Palm Beach FL 33413-2135. Phone/fax (561)966-9294. E-mail: profschia@aol.com. Website: www.publishersmarket place.com/members/profschia. Agent: James Schiavone, EdD. Recognized in the industry. Estab. 1997. Represents 6 clients. Open to unpublished and new clients. Handles adult, teen and children's fiction and nonfiction; picture books; celebrity biography; secular/ crossover books.

> **Contact:** Query letter/SASE; one-page e-mail query (no attachments).
> **Commission:** 15%, foreign 20%.
> **Fees:** No reading fees; authors pay postage only.
> **Tips:** Works primarily with published authors; will consider first-time authors with excellent material. Actively seeking books on spirituality, major religions, and alternative health. Very selective on first novels.

SUSAN SCHULMAN, A LITERARY AGENCY, 454 W. 44th St., New York NY 10036. (212)713-1633. Fax (212)581-8830. E-mail: schulman@aol.com. Website: www.susanschulman agency.com. Agent: Linda Migalti. Estab. 1980. Building recognition in the industry. Represents 3 clients with religious books. Open to unpublished authors and new clients. Handles religious/spiritual nonfiction and fiction for all ages, picture books, and secular books. Member AAR.

> **Contact:** Query/SASE.
> **Commission:** 15%; foreign 20% (shared 50/50 with foreign co-agent).
> **Fees:** No fees.
> **Tips:** "We are interested in sophisticated religious and spiritual material, especially nonfiction or historically based or appropriate for a well-educated audience."

+SCRIBBLERS HOUSE, LLC, PO Box 1007, Cooper Station, New York NY 10276-1007. Agent: Stedman Mays.

SEDGEBAND LITERARY ASSOCIATES, 7312 Martha Ln., Fort Worth TX 76112-5336. (817)496-3652. E-mail: queries@sedgeband.com. Website: www.sedgeband.com. Agents: Ginger Norton and David Duperre. Estab. 1997. Recognized in the industry. Represents 5 clients with religious books. Open to new clients. Handles religious fiction and nonfiction for teens and adults, secular & crossover books. Manuscripts must be at least 70,000 wds., and complete.

> **Contact:** No unsolicited complete mss. Submit using online form from Website, or e-mail.
> **Commission:** 15%; foreign 20%.
> **Fees:** Office expenses only.
> **Tips:** "Write your query with as much care as you wrote your manuscript. Watch spelling and grammar. Never be rude or egotistical; impress the agent with your style and ability."

SE LITERARY PROPERTIES, PO Box 67385, St. Pete Beach FL 33706. E-mail: stephen@ excellentnovels.com. Website: www.seliterary.homestead.com. Agent: Stephen Everett.
>**Contact:** Mail or e-mail (no attachments).
>**Commission:** 15%.
>**Fees:** Office expenses only.

SERENDIPITY LITERARY AGENCY, LLC, 732 Fulton St., Ste. 3, Brooklyn NY 11238. Phone/fax (718)230-7689. E-mail: rbrooks@serendipitylit.com. Website: www.serendipitylit.com. Agent: Regina Brooks. Estab. 2000. Represents 30 clients. Open to unpublished authors and new clients. Secular agent; handles adult religious/inspirational nonfiction.
>**Contact:** Outline/1 chapter. No simultaneous submissions. Responds in 2-3 mos.
>**Commission:** 15%; foreign 20%.
>**Fees:** $200 for office expenses.

THE SEYMOUR AGENCY, 475 Miner St. Rd., Canton NY 13617. (315)386-1831. Fax (315)386-1037. E-mail: marysue@slic.com. Website: www.theseymouragency.com. Agent: Mary Sue Seymour. Estab. 1992. Recognized in the industry. Represents 25 religious clients. Open to unpublished authors and new clients. Handles romance novels, and nonfiction for all ages, gift books, secular/crossover books.
>**Contact:** Query letter or e-mail with first 50 pages of ms; no fax query. For nonfiction, send proposal with chapter one. Simultaneous query OK. Responds in 2 wks. for queries and 2-3 mos. for mss.
>**Commission:** 15% for unpublished authors; 12% for published authors; foreign 20%.
>**Fees:** None.
>**Tips:** Mary Sue is a New York State certified (but retired) teacher. Former Sunday school teacher and superintendent. "Looking for Christian chick lit."

THE SHEPARD AGENCY, 73 Kingswood Dr., Bethel CT 06801. (203)790-4230. Fax (203)798-2924. E-mail: shepardagcy@mindspring.com. Website: http://home.mindspring.com/ ~shepardagcy. Agent: Jean Shepard. Recognized in the industry. Estab. 1987. Represents 11 clients. Open to unpublished authors; no new clients at this time. Handles fiction and nonfiction for all ages; no picture books; especially business, reference, professional, self-help, cooking, and crafts. Books only.
>**Contact:** By e-mail.
>**Commission:** 15%; foreign variable.
>**Fees:** None except long-distance calls and copying.

KEN SHERMAN & ASSOCIATES, 9507 Santa Monica Blvd., Beverly Hills CA 90210. (310)273-3840. Fax (310)271-2875. Agent: Ken Sherman. Estab. 1989. Represents 50 clients. Open to unpublished authors and new clients. Handles adult religious/inspirational novels, nonfiction, and scripts.
>**Contact:** By referral only. Responds in 1 mo.
>**Commission:** 15%; foreign 15%; dramatic rts. 15%.
>**Fees:** Charges office expenses and other negotiable expenses.

JACQUELINE SIMENAUER LITERARY AGENCY, PO Box AG, Mantoloking NJ 08738-0390. (732)262-0783. Open to unpublished authors. Handles spiritual fiction & nonfiction.
>**Contact:** For fiction, query with first 3 chapters, synopsis, bio, and SASE. For nonfiction, send query with SASE. Simultaneous & e-query OK.
>**Commission:** 15%; foreign 20%.

MICHAEL SNELL LITERARY AGENCY, PO Box 1206, Truro MA 02666-1206. (508)349-3718. Agent: Michael Snell. Estab. 1978. Represents 200 clients. Open to unpublished authors and new clients. Secular agent: handles adult religious/inspirational nonfiction.
>**Contact:** Query with SASE. No simultaneous submissions. Responds in 1-2 wks.
>**Commission:** 15%; foreign 15%.

SPENCERHILL ASSOCIATES, LTD./KAREN SOLEM, 24 Park Row, PO Box 374, Chatham NY 12037. (518)392-9293. Fax (518)392-9554. E-mail: ksolem@klsbooks.com. Agent: Karen Solem. Recognized in the industry. Estab. 2001 (previously with Writers House). Represents 20 clients. Open to unpublished authors and new clients. Handles adult novels and nonfiction, secular, and crossover books.

> **Contact:** A brief e-mail query is OK. If sending a proposal with chapters, send by mail.
> **Commission:** 15%; foreign 20%.
> **Fees:** Photocopying and Express Mail charges only.

LESLIE H. STOBBE, 300 Doubleday Rd., Tryon NC 28782. (828)859-5964. Fax (978)945-0517. E-mail: lstobbe@alltel.net. Well recognized in the industry. Estab. 1993. Represents 72 clients. Open to unpublished authors and new clients. Handles adult fiction and nonfiction.

> **Contact:** By e-mail or letter.
> **Commission:** 15%
> **Fees:** Only when engaged as a consultant/mentor.
> **Tips:** "I will not accept clients whose theological positions in their book differ significantly from mine."

STONE MANNERS AGENCY, 6500 Wilshire Blvd., Ste. 550, Los Angeles CA 90048. (323)655-1313. Fax (323)655-7676. Agent: Michael Sheehy. Handles religious/inspirational scripts and well as all others.

> **Contact:** Queries only.

SUITE A MANAGEMENT TALENT AGENCY, 120 El Camino Dr., Ste. 202, Beverly Hills CA 90212. (310)278-0801. Fax (310)278-0807. E-mail: suite-A@juno.com. Agent: Lloyd D. Robinson. Recognized in the industry. Estab. 2001. Several clients. Open to new and unpublished clients (if published in other media). Specializes in screenplays and novels for adaptation to TV movies.

> **Commission:** 10%
> **Comments:** Representation limited to adaptation of novels and true-life stories for film and television development. Work must have been published for consideration.

+MARK SWEENEY & ASSOCIATES, 28540 Altessa Way, Bonita Springs FL 34135. (239)594-1957. Fax (239)594-1935. E-mail: sweeney2@comcast.net. Agent: Mark Sweeney. Recognized in the industry. Estab. 2003. Open to unpublished authors and new clients on a restricted basis. Handles adult religious/inspirational novels & nonfiction for all ages, picture books, gift books, crossover, and secular books.

> **Contact:** E-mail.
> **Commission:** 15%; foreign 20%.
> **Fees:** None.

MARY M. TAHAN LITERARY AGENCY, PO Box 1060, Gracie Station, New York NY 10028-1060. Agent: Mary M. Tahan. Estab. 2004.

TALCOTT NOTCH LITERARY SERVICES, 276 Forest Rd., Milford CT 06460. (203)877-1146. Fax (203)876-9517. E-mail: editorial@talcottnotch.net. Website: www.talcottnotch.net. Agent: Gina Panettieri. Not yet recognized in the industry; building a Christian presence. Estab. 2003. Represents 3 clients. Open to unpublished authors and new clients. Handles nonfiction for all ages.

> **Contact:** By e-mail.
> **Commission:** 15%; foreign 20%.
> **Fees:** None.
> **Tips:** "We specifically seek nonfiction in areas of parenting, self-help, and current events. We are open to academic/scholarly work as well as commercial projects."

3 SEAS LITERARY AGENCY, PO Box 8571, Madison WI 53708. (608)221-4306. E-mail: three seaslit@aol.com. Website: www.threeseaslit.com. Agent: Michelle Grajkowski. Estab. 2000. Represents 40 clients. Open to unpublished authors and new clients. Secular agent; handles adult religious/inspirational novels & nonfiction.

> **Contact:** Query with proposal/first 3 chapters. Considers simultaneous submissions. Responds in 2-3 mos.
> **Commission:** 15%; foreign 20%.

TOAD HALL, INC., RR 2 Box 2090, Laceyville PA 18623. (570)869-2942. Fax (570)869-1031. E-mail: toadhallco@aol.com. Website: www.laceyville.com/toad-hall. Agent: Sharon Jarvis. Not yet known in the industry. Estab. 1983. Represents 1 religious client. Not open to unpublished authors and new clients. Handles adult religious/inspirational nonfiction; fiction only from published authors.

> **Contact:** Letter or e-mail. Do not send any text unless requested.
> **Commission:** 15%; foreign 10%.
> **Fees:** Office expenses (photocopying, bank fees, special postage). $50 fee to read the first 50 pages plus synopsis/table of contents and provide a detailed written analysis.
> **Tips:** "All queries should include (1) the category, (2) the word count, (3) brief summary, (4) bio, (5) SASE." Has their own small press, plus a partnership with an independent e-book company for authors considering self-publishing or a co-op arrangement.

+VAN DIEST LITERARY AGENCY, PO Box 1482, Sisters OR 97759. Website: www.working mom.com/david-van-diest.htm. Agent: David Van Diest. Open to unpublished authors and new clients. Handles adult religious/inspirational novels & nonfiction.

> **Contact:** Query with a 50-word summary of book idea, outline of the chapters, author bio, and contact information.

VINES AGENCY, INC., 648 Broadway, Ste. 901, New York NY 10012. (212)777-5522. Fax (212)777-5978. E-mail: jv@vinesagency.com. Website: www.vinesagency.com. Agents: James C. Vines, Paul Surdi, Ali Ryan, and Alexis Caldwell. Estab. 1995. Represents 52 clients. Open to unpublished authors and new clients. Secular agency; handles adult religious/inspirational nonfiction.

> **Contact:** Send outlines/3 sample chapters/SASE; fax/e-mail query OK. Simultaneous & e-queries OK.
> **Commission:** 15%; foreign 25%.
> **Fees:** For foreign postage, photocopying, and messenger service.
> **Tips:** "We get most of our clients through query letters, conferences, recommendations from others."

+WATERSIDE PRODUCTIONS, INC., 2187 New Castle Ave., #204, Cardiff-by-the-Sea CA 92007. (760)632-9190. Fax (760)632-9295. E-mail: webrown@waterside.com. Website: www.waterside.com. Agent: William E. Brown, 12234 Crestwood Dr., Carmel IN 46033-4323. (317)844-8786. Christian agent at a secular agency. Interested in handling Christian books.

WESTPHAL LITERARY AGENCY, PO Box 148, Shelby IN 46377. (219)552-9027. E-mail: Pennie West@aol.com. Agents: Richard & Pennie Westphal. Not yet recognized in the industry. Represents 3 clients with religious books. Open to unpublished authors and new clients. Handles adult & teen novels & nonfiction, short stories, stage plays, and secular books.

> **Contact:** Query with SASE or by e-mail.
> **Commission:** 15%; foreign 15%.
> **Fees:** Charges $85 annually for office expenses.
> **Tips:** "Best to query first and follow our submission guidelines. In secular books, we want nothing overtly sexual."

+KATHERINE WHITLOW LITERARY AGENT, 6700 Providence Rd., Charlotte NC 28226. E-mail: agent@KWhitLit.com. Website: www.KWhitLit.com. Agent: Katherine Whitlow. Open to unpublished authors and new clients. Handles adult religious/inspirational novels & non-fiction.

WILLIAMS AGENCY, 909 Knox Rd., Kosciusko MS 39090. (662)290-0617. Fax (315)893-5138. E-mail: submissions@williamsliteraryagency.com (no attachments). Website: www.williamsliteraryagency.com. Agents: Sheri Homan Williams (book rts.); Maxx Williams (film & TV rts.). Estab. 1997. Recognized in the industry. Represents 25 clients. Not open to unpublished authors; open to new clients (1-page query first). Handles adult and teen fiction and nonfiction, TV/movie scripts, gift books, crossover books, and secular books (secular books must be family-friendly). Foreign commission 20%.

> **Contact:** Query by mail or e-mail; 1-page letter with synopsis only. No complete mss unless requested (unsolicited returned or discarded). No phone calls. Adhere to guidelines on Website. Allow up to 3 months for reply.
> **Commission:** 15%; 25% foreign.
> **Fees:** No reading or signing fees.
> **Tips:** "No unsolicited manuscripts. SASE for reply. No calls. Always follow guidelines as posted on our Website. Multiple e-mails or calls inquiring as to the status of your manuscript does not increase your chances; in fact, it hurts them."

WINSUN LITERARY AGENCY, 3706 N.E. Shady Ln. Dr., Gladstone MO 64119. Phone/fax (816)459-8016. E-mail: mlittleton@earthlink.net. Agents: Mark and Jeanette Littleton. Recognized in the industry. Represents 20 clients. Somewhat open to unpublished authors and open to new clients. Handles fiction and nonfiction for all ages, picture books, gift books.

> **Contact:** E-mail.
> **Commission:** 15%; foreign 20%.
> **Fees:** Postage and copying for new clients only.
> **Tips:** "Send only your absolutely best work, i.e., work that has been rewritten to perfection, put through critique groups, and so on."

WOLGEMUTH & ASSOCIATES, INC., 8600 Crestgate Cir., Orlando FL 32819. (407)909-9445. Fax (407)909-9446. E-mail: rwolgemuth@cfl.rr.com. Agent: Robert D. Wolgemuth. Well recognized in the industry. Estab. 1992. Represents 18 clients. No new clients or unpublished authors. Handles mostly adult nonfiction; most other types of books handled only for current clients.

> **Contact:** By letter.
> **Commission:** 15%.
> **Fees:** None.
> **Tips:** "We work with authors who are either best-selling authors or potentially best-selling authors. Consequently, we want to represent clients with broad-market appeal."

WOMACK PUBLISHING AGENCY, PO Box 2341, Merced CA 95344-2341. (928)785-6140. E-mail: WomackAgency@aol.com. Agent: David A. Womack. E-mail queries only.

+WORDSERVE LITERARY GROUP, 10152 S. Knoll Cir., Highlands Ranch CO 80130. (303)471-6675. Fax (303)471-1297. E-mail: greg@wordserveliterary.com. Website: www.wordserveliterary.com. Agent: Greg Johnson. Estab. 2003. Represents 20+ clients. Recognized in the industry. Open to unpublished authors (fiction primarily) and new clients. Handles novels & nonfiction for all ages, gift books, crossover books, and secular books.

> **Contact:** Short e-mail initially; then letter with samples by mail, with SASE.
> **Commission:** 15%; foreign 10-15%.
> **Fees:** None.
> **Tips:** "Nonfiction: First impressions count. Make sure your proposal answers all the ques-

tions on competition, outline, audience, felt need, etc. Fiction: Make sure your novel is completed before you submit a proposal (synopsis, plus 5 chapters)."

THE WRITER'S EDGE. See listing under Editorial Services—Illinois.

WRITERS HOUSE, 21 W. 26th St., New York NY 10010. (212)685-2400. Fax (212)685-1781. Website: www.writershouse.com. Agent: Albert Zuckerman. Estab. 1974. Represents 600 clients. Secular agency; handles adult religious/inspirational fiction. Member of AAR.

> **Contact:** One-page query by mail/SASE. Responds in 1 mo. to query.
> **Commission:** 15%; foreign 20%.
> **Fees:** No fees.
> **Tips:** "See Website for details. Write a compelling query so we'll ask to see your manuscript."

WYLIE-MERRICK LITERARY AGENCY, 1138 S. Webster St., Kokomo IN 46902-6357. (765)459-8258, or (765)457-3783. E-mail for submissions: wmliterary@yahoo.com. Website: www.wylie-merrick.com. Agents: S. A. Martin (smartin@wylie-merrick.com) and Robert Brown (rbrown@wylie-merrick.com). Estab. 1999. Secular agent; handles juvenile and adult religious/inspirational novels.

> **Contact:** Query with SASE/first 10 pgs. for fiction. Proposal package for nonfiction. Considers simultaneous submissions. Responds in 1-3 mos.
> **Commission:** 15%; foreign 20%.
> **Fees:** Office expenses.

YATES & YATES, LLP, 1100 W. Town and Country Rd., Ste. 1300, Orange CA 92868-4654. (714)480-4000. Fax (714)480-4001. E-mail: email@yates-yates.com. Website: www.yates-yates.com. Estab. 1989. Recognized in the industry. Represents 50+ clients. Not currently open to unpublished authors or new clients. Handles adult novels, nonfiction for adults and teens, TV/Movie scripts, secular/crossover books.

> **Contact:** Letter or fax.
> **Commission:** Negotiable
> **Fees:** Negotiable.
> **Tips:** "The law firm of Yates & Yates, LLP, in addition to providing traditional literary agenting services, also serves the legal needs of its author clients, having extensive experience in intellectual property law (including copyright and trademark), entertainment law, tax law, estate planning, and business law."

ALAN YOUNGREN, LITERARY AGENT, 1243 Hawthorne, Downers Grove IL 60515. Fax (630)964-2109. E-mail: Ayoungren@sbcglobal.net. Estab. 1998. Recognized in the industry. Represents 15 clients. Open to unpublished authors and new clients. Handles adult fiction and nonfiction, crossover books.

> **Contact:** Letter, fax, or e-mail (no phone calls).
> **Commission:** 15%; 20% foreign.
> **Fees:** No reading fees.

ADDITIONAL AGENTS

NOTE: The following agents did not return a questionnaire, but have been identified as secular agents who handle religious/inspirational manuscripts. Be sure to send queries first if you wish to submit to them. Always check out an agent thoroughly before committing to work with him or her. Ask for references and a list of books represented, check with the Better Business Bureau, and ask your writing friends.

+A+B WORKS, 615 Fort Washington Ave., #2E, New York NY 1040. E-mail: amy@aplusb works.com. Website: www.aplusbworks.com. Agent: Amy Jameson. Open to unpublished authors and new clients. Secular agent. Handles adult religious nonfiction.

+THE ANDERSON LITERARY AGENCY, INC., 435 Convent Ave., Ste. 5, New York NY 10031. E-mail: gilesa@rcn.com. Agent: Giles Anderson. Open to unpublished authors and new clients. Secular agent. Handles adult religious nonfiction.

*AVATAR LITERARY AGENCY, 3389 Sheridan St., Ste. 308, Hollywood FL 33021. Agent: Karen Weiss.

+DAVID BLACK LITERARY AGENCY, 156 Fifth Ave., Ste. 608, New York NY 10010. Agent: David Black. Handles religious nonfiction.

    Contact: Query by mail. No e-query. Not currently accepting unsolicited queries.

+THE BLUMER LITERARY AGENCY, PO Box 20754, Park West Station, New York NY 10025. Agent: Olivia Blumer. Open to unpublished authors and new clients. Secular agent. Handles adult religious nonfiction.

    Contact: Query with SASE.

*LIZA DAWSON ASSOCIATES, 240 W. 35th St., Ste. 500, New York NY 10001. Agent: Liza Dawson.

+JOELLE DELBOURGO ASSOCIATES, 516 Bloomfield Ave., Ste. 5, Montclair NJ 07042. E-mail: joelle@delbourgo.com. Website: www.delbourgo.com. Agent: Joelle Delbourgo. Open to unpublished authors and new clients. Handles adult religious nonfiction.

    Contact: Query with SASE; no e-query.

+DUNOW, CARLSON & LERNER, 27 W. 20th St., Ste. 1003, New York NY 10011. Agent: Betsy Lerner. Open to unpublished authors and new clients. Secular agent. Handles adult religious nonfiction.

+CANDICE FUHRMAN LITERARY AGENCY, 60 Greenwood Way, Mill Valley CA 94941. Agent: Candice Fuhrman. Open to unpublished authors and new clients. Secular agent. Handles adult religion/spirituality nonfiction.

    Contact: Query with SASE.

+FULL CIRCLE LITERARY, LLC., 7676 Hazard Center Dr., Ste. 500, San Diego CA 92108. E-mail: lilly@fullcircleliterary.com. Website: www.fullcircleliterary.com. Agents: Lilly Ghahremani & Stefanie Von Borstel. Open to unpublished authors and new clients. Secular agent. Handles adult religious/spirituality nonfiction.

+THE GARAMOND AGENCY, 12 Horton St., Newburyport MA 01950. E-mail: lisa .adams@garamondagency.com. Website: www.garamondagency.com. Agent: Lisa Adams. Open to unpublished authors and new clients. Secular agent. Handles adult religious nonfiction.

    Contact: Query with SASE; no e-query.

+THE THOMAS GRADY AGENCY, 209 Bassett St., Petaluma CA 94952. Agent: Thomas Grady. Open to unpublished authors and new clients. Secular agent. Handles adult religious nonfiction.

+LINDA KONNER LITERARY AGENCY, 10 W. 15th St., Ste. 1918, New York NY 10011. E-mail: ldkonner@cs.com. Agent: Linda Konner. Open to unpublished authors and new clients. Secular agent. Handles adult religious/spirituality nonfiction.

    Contact: Query with SASE.

+LITERARY AND CREATIVE ARTISTS, INC., 3543 Albemarle St. N.W., Washington DC 20008. E-mail: muriel@lcadc.com. Website: www.lcadc.com. Agent: Muriel Nellis. Open to unpublished authors and new clients. Secular agent. Handles adult religious nonfiction.

+STERLING LORD LITERISTIC, INC., 65 Bleecker St., 12th Fl., New York NY 10012. E-mail: claudia@sll.com. Agent: Claudia Cross. Open to new clients. Handles adult Christian fiction & spiritual nonfiction.

    Contact: Query with SASE; no e-query.

+DENISE MARCIL LITERARY AGENCY, 685 West End Ave., New York NY 10025, or 156— 5th Ave, Ste. 625, New York NY 10011. Agent: Denise Marcil. Secular agent. Handles religious nonfiction. Member of AAR.

+NEW BRAND AGENCY GROUP. E-mail: queries@literaryagent.net. Website: www.literary agent.net. Handles inspirational, spirituality/religious fiction and nonfiction. Member AAR.

+ALICKA PISTEK LITERARY AGENCY, 302A W. 12th St., #124, New York NY 10014. E-mail: info@alickapistek.com. Website: www.alickapistek.com. Agent: Alicka Pistek. Open to unpublished authors and new clients. Secular agent. Handles adult religious nonfiction.

　　Contact: Query with SASE; no e-query.

+THE AMY RENNERT AGENCY, 98 Main St., #302, Tiburon CA 94920. E-mail: arennert@ pcabell.net. Agent: Amy Rennert. Open to unpublished authors and new clients. Secular agent. Handles adult religious nonfiction.

　　Contact: Query with SASE; no e-query.

+PETER RUBIE LITERARY AGENCY, LTD., 240 W. 35th St., Ste. 500, New York NY 10001. E-mail: peterrubie@prlit.com. Website: www.prlit.com. Agent: Peter Rubie. Open to unpublished authors and new clients. Secular agent. Handles adult religion/spirituality nonfiction.

+SCOVIL, CHICHAK, GALEN LITERARY AGENCY, 381 Park Ave. S., Ste. 1020, New York NY 10016. E-mail: annaghosh@scglit.com. Website: www.scglit.com. Agent: Anna Ghosh. Open to unpublished authors and new clients. Secular agent. Handles adult religious/ spirituality nonfiction.

+WENDY SHERMAN ASSOCIATES, 450 Seventh Ave., Ste. 3004, New York NY 10123. E-mail: tracy@wsherman.com. Website: www.wsherman.com. Agent: Tracy Brown. Open to unpublished authors and new clients. Secular agent. Handles adult religious nonfiction.

+SOBEL WEBER ASSOCIATES, 146 E. 19th St., New York NY 10003. Agent: Nat Sobel. Open to unpublished authors and new clients. secular agent. Handles adult religious nonfiction.

+TRIDENT MEDIA GROUP, LLC., 41 Madison Ave., 36th Fl., New York NY 10010. E-mail: pfedorko@tridentmediagroup.com. Website: www.tridentmediagroup.com. Agent: Paul Fedorko. Open to unpublished authors and new clients. Secular agent. Handles adult religious nonfiction.

*STEPHANIE VON HIRSCHBERG LITERARY AGENCY, 1385 Baptist Church Rd., Yorktown Heights NY 10598. (914)243-9250.

+VRATTOS LITERARY AGENCY, 708 Gravenstein Hwy. N., #185, Sebasapol CA 95472. E-mail: VrattosLitAgency@aol.com. Agent: John Vrattos & Francesca Vrattos. Open to unpublished authors and new clients. Secular agent. Handles adult religious nonfiction.

+TED WEINSTEIN LITERARY MANAGEMENT, 35 Stillman St., Ste. 203, San Francisco CA 94107. Agent: Ted Weinstein. Open to unpublished authors and new clients. Secular agent. Handles adult religious nonfiction.

+WILSON MEDIA, PO Box 613, Hastings-on-Hudson NY 10706. E-mail: wilsonmedia@ verizon.net. Agent: Robert Wilson. Open to unpublished authors and new clients. Secular agent. Handles adult religious nonfiction.

CONTESTS

Note: Below is a listing of all the contests mentioned throughout this guide, plus additional contests that will be of interest. Some are sponsored by book publishers or magazines, some by conferences or writers' groups included in this guide. The contests are arranged by genre or type of material they are looking for such as poetry, fiction, nonfiction, etc. Send an SASE to each one you are interested in to obtain a copy of their complete contest rules and guidelines, or copy from their Website. A listing here does not guarantee the legitimacy of a contest. For guidelines on evaluating contests and to determine if a contest is legitimate or just a scam, go to: www.sfwa.org/beware/contests.html. Also note that because many contests had not set deadlines and final details for the next year's contests when this guide was written, details as given may change, so always get a copy of their current guidelines before entering.

CHILDREN/YOUNG ADULT CONTESTS, WRITING FOR

+ANNUAL CONTEST FOR A FIRST MIDDLE-GRADE NOVEL, Delacorte Dell Yearling Contest, Random House, Inc., 1745 Broadway, 9th Fl., New York NY 10019. Website: www.randomhouse.com/kids/writingcontests. For writers of their first middle-grade novel, 96-160 pgs. June 30 deadline. Contemporary or historical fiction set in North America, for readers 9-12. Prize: $1,500 cash, $7,500 advance against royalties, plus a book contract.

+CHILDREN'S WRITERS FICTION CONTEST, Stepping Stones, PO Box 8863, Springfield MO 65801-8863. (417)863-7369. E-mail: verwil@alumni.pace.edu. V. R. Williams, dir. Annual contest for unpublished fiction. Entry fee $10. Prize is $260, and/or publication in *Hodge Podge*. Send SASE for guidelines.

MARGUERITE DE ANGELI PRIZE, Delacorte Press/Random House, Inc. Open to U.S. and Canadian authors who have not previously published a book for middle-grade readers. Submissions must be contemporary or historical fiction for ages 8-12 (80-144 ms pages) that examines the diversity of the American experience. Deadline: April 1–June 30th. Winner receives a $1,500 cash prize and book contract with a $7,500 advance against royalties. For rules, send SASE to: Marguerite de Angeli Contest, Bantam Doubleday Dell BFYR, 1745 Broadway, New York NY 10019. (212)782-9000. Website: www.randomhouse.com/kids.

DEVOTED TO YOU BOOKS, PO Box 300, Sartell MN 56377. Toll-free (800)704-7250. E-mail: info@devotedtoyoubooks.com. Website: www.devotedtoyoubooks.com. Nondenominational. Tracy Ryks, pub. Seeks to teach children that God is present in their lives today; children's picture books for ages 1-8. Publishes 2 titles/yr. Sponsors a book contest. See Website.

+GUIDEPOSTS YOUNG WRITERS CONTEST, Guideposts, 16 E. 34th St., New York NY 10016. (212)251-8100. E-mail: ywcontest@guideposts.org. Website: www.gp4teens.com. Annual contest for unpublished high school juniors and seniors. Deadline November 24. Prizes $250 gift certificate to $10,000.

HIGHLIGHTS FOR CHILDREN, 803 Church St., Honesdale PA 18431. (570)253-1080. Website: www.highlights.com. Marileta Robinson, sr. ed. *Highlights for Children* Fiction Contest. Offers 3 prizes of $1,000 each for stories up to 800 words for children. Stories for beginning readers to 500 words. Send SASE for guidelines and current topic. No crime, violence, or derogatory humor. No entry fee or form required. Entries must be postmarked between January 1 and February 28.

+CORETTA SCOTT KING BOOK AWARD, Coretta Scott King Task Force, American Library Assn., 50 E. Huron St., Chicago IL 60611. (800)545-2433. E-mail: feedback@ala.org.

Website: www.ala.org. Annual award for children's books by African American authors and/or illustrators, published the previous year. Books must fit one of these categories: preschool-grade 4; grades 5-8; grades 9-12. Deadline December 1. Send SASE for guidelines. Winner receives an honorarium, framed citation, and a set of encyclopedias.

MILKWEED PRIZE FOR CHILDREN'S LITERATURE, Milkweed Editions, Open Book Bldg., Ste. 300, 1011 Washington Ave. S., Minneapolis MN 55415-1246. Toll-free (800)520-6455. (612)332-3192. Fax (612)215-2550. E-mail: webmaster@milkweed.org. Website: www.milkweed.org/2_1_2.html. Children's novels for ages 8-13 years; 90-200 pgs. Ongoing competition. Prize: $5,000 advance against royalties with publication of the book. Follow guidelines for their children's books on Website. All book submissions are automatically entered in this contest.

POCKETS, PO Box 340004, Nashville TN 37203-0004. (615)340-7333. Fax (615)340-7267. E-mail: pockets@upperroom.org. Website: www.pockets.org. United Methodist. Lynn W. Gilliam, ed. Devotional magazine for children (6-11 yrs.). Fiction-writing contest; submit between 3/1 and 8/15 every yr. Prize $1,000 and publication in Pockets. Length 1,000-1,600 wds. Must be unpublished and not historical fiction. Previous winners not eligible. Send to Pockets Fiction Contest at above address, designating "Fiction Contest" on outside of envelope. Send an SASE for return and response.

SKIPPING STONES: A Multicultural Magazine, PO Box 3939, Eugene OR 97403. Phone/fax (541)342-4956. E-mail: editor@skippingstones.org. Website: www.skippingstones.org. Not specifically Christian. Arun N. Toké, ed.; Mary Drew, asst. ed. A multicultural awareness and nature appreciation magazine for young people 8-17, worldwide. Annual Book Awards for published books and authors (deadline February 1); Annual Youth Honor Awards for students 7-17. Send SASE for guidelines. June 20 deadline.

FICTION CONTESTS

+AIM MAGAZINE SHORT STORY CONTEST, PO Box 1174, Maywood IL 60153-8174. (708)344-4414. E-mail: apiladoone@aol.com. Website: www.aimmagazine.org. Myron Apilado, ed. Awards a $100 prize to best unpublished short story, to 4,000 words. "Promoting brotherhood among people and cultures." August 15 deadline.

AMERICAN CHRISTIAN FICTION WRITERS CONTEST. Rachel Hauck, pres.; PO Box 101066, Palm Bay FL 32910-1066. Website: www.acrw.net. E-mail loop, online courses, critique groups, and newsletter for members. Sponsors a contest open to nonmembers. See Website for current contest.

ANCIENT PATHS, PO Box 7505, Fairfax Station VA 22039. E-mail: ssburris@msn.com. Website: www.editorskylar.com. Christian/nondenominational. Skylar Hamilton Burris, ed. For a literate Christian audience, or non-Christians open to and moved by traditional-themed literature. Occasionally sponsors contest; check Website.

+BOSTON REVIEW SHORT STORY CONTEST, Boston Review, E53-407 MIT, Cambridge MA 02139. Website: www.bostonreview.mit.edu. Offers a $1,000 prize (plus publication) for an unpublished short story to 4,000 words. Entry fee $20. Deadline October 1.

BOULEVARD SHORT FICTION CONTEST FOR EMERGING WRITERS, PMB 325, 6614 Clayton Rd., Richmond Heights MO 63117. (314)862-2643. Website: www.boulevard magazine.com/contest.htm. Prize of $1,500, plus publication in *Boulevard Magazine*. For writers who have not had a book published with a nationally distributed publisher. Story to 8,000 wds. Entry fee $15. December 15 deadline. Not held every year; check Website for current contest.

BULWER-LYTTON FICTION CONTEST. For the worst opening line to a novel. Deadline: April 15. Website: www.bulwer-lytton.com. Rules on Website.

CANADIAN WRITER'S JOURNAL SHORT FICTION CONTEST, White Mountain Publications, Box 1178, New Liskeard ON P0J 1P0, Canada. (705)647-5424. Canada-wide toll-free (800)258-5451. Fax (705)647-5424. E-mail: cwj@cwj.ca. Website: www.cwj.ca. Deborah Ranchuk, ed./pub. Sponsors semiannual short fiction contest (March 31 and September 30 deadlines); to 1,200 wds. Entry fee $5. Prizes $100, $50, $25. All fiction needs are filled by this contest. E-mail: cwc-calendar@cwj.ca.

+CHARACTERS ANNUAL SHORT STORY CONTEST, PO Box 708, Newport NH 03773-0708. (603)863-5896. Fax (603)863-8198. E-mail: hotdog@nhvt.net. Website: www.cdavisnh .com. Davis Publications. Cindy Davis, ed. Literary magazine of short stories. Annual Short Story Contest with August 31 deadline. Six prizes in 2 categories: adult authors and children authors (to age 16). All genres to 1,000 words. $3 entry fee per story. Details in Website.

THE CHRISTY AWARDS. Donna Kehoe, Administrator, 1571 Glastonbury Rd., Ann Arbor MI 48103. Phone/fax (734)663-7931. E-mail: CA2000DK@aol.com. Website: www.christy awards.com/home.htm. Awards in 9 fiction genres for excellence in Christian fiction: allegory, contemporary/general, futuristic, historical (international and North American), romance, suspense/mystery, western, plus first novel. For submission guidelines and other information, see Website: www.christyawards.com. Awards are presented at an Annual Christy Awards Banquet held Friday prior to the annual CBA international convention in June or July.

+FIRE BY NITE FICTION AWARD, 120 East FM544, Ste. 72, PMB 354, Murphy TX 75094. Website: www.firebynite.com. Submit to The Editor. Showcasing the best in new Christian short fiction, with book reviews and interviews both readers and writers of fiction will enjoy. Quarterly mag. Fire by Nite Fiction Award. Prizes $50-500. Select entries will be published in magazine. Reading fee $15. Deadline March 31. Entry form and details on Website.

GLIMMER TRAIN PRESS FICTION OPEN. Secular. Must be postmarked by June 30. Entry fee: $15. Prizes: $2,000 and publication, $1,000, and $600. Open to all writers, all themes, any length. Submit original, unpublished stories. Send SASE for results. Glimmer Train Press, 1211 N.W. Glisan St., #207, Portland OR 97209. (503)221-0836. Fax (503)221-0837. Website: www.glimmertrain.com.

GLIMMER TRAIN PRESS SHORT STORY AWARD FOR NEW WRITERS. Secular. Must be postmarked between February 1 and March 31. Also sponsors a fall contest with deadline between August 1 and September 30. Open to any writer who hasn't been published in a national magazine with a circulation over 5,000; unpublished stories 1,200-7,500 wds.; no children's stories; prizes $1,200, $500, and $300; staple pages together with name, address, and phone on first page, no SASE (will not be returned); $12 entry fee/story. Send to: Short-Story Award, Glimmer Train Press, 1211 N.W. Glisan St., #207, Portland OR 97209. (503)221-0836. Fax (503)221-0837. E-mail: info@glimmertrain.com. Website: www.glimmertrain.com. Results announced on July 1.

GLORY BOUND BOOKS/ONCE UPON A TWISTED TALE, PO Box 278, Cass City MI 48726. (989)635-7520. E-mail: info@gloryboundenterprises.com. Website: www.theglorybound bookcompany.com. Leah Berry, pub. Annual contest for previously unpublished Christian authors for this series. Winner(s) will first be published on the Web and then in a paperback volume of "Tales," receiving 25% of the profit from all sales. Simultaneous submissions acceptable. Preview the current stories for "Once Upon a Twisted Tale" on the Website in the Collect-A-Book category to understand what they are looking for. Submit a 12-chapter manuscript of similar length to those on the site by December 31. Entry fee $20. Guidelines on Website.

LORIAN HEMINGWAY SHORT STORY COMPETITION, PO Box 993, Key West FL 33041. E-mail: info@shortstorycompetition.com. Website: www.shortstorycompetition.com. First prize $1,000; 2nd and 3rd $500 apiece. Up to 3,000 wds. May deadline. Entry fee $10-15. Details on Website.

HIDDEN TALENTS ANNUAL SHORT STORY CONTEST. Sponsored by Tall Tales Press (a small Canadian publisher), 20 Tuscany Valley Park N.W., Calgary BC T3L 2B6, Canada. (403)874-4293. E-mail: talltalespress@shaw.ca. Website: www.talltalespress.com. May 31 deadline. Prizes of $25-500. Entry fee $10 U.S. or Cdn. Details on Website: www.tall talespress.com/pages/882188/index.htm.

IOWA SHORT FICTION AWARD and JOHN SIMMONS SHORT FICTION AWARD are open to any writer who has not published a volume of prose fiction. Award-winning manuscripts will be published by the University of Iowa Press under their standard contract. The manuscript must be a collection of short stories of at least 150 pages. Submit between August 1 and September 30. No submission fee. Also sponsors a poetry contest. (319)335-2000. E-mail: uipress@uiowa.edu. Details: www.uiowa.edu/uiowa press/prize-rules.htm. Submit to: Iowa Short Fiction Award, Iowa Writers Workshop, 102 Dey House, Iowa City IA 52242-1000.

JAMES JONES FIRST NOVEL FELLOWSHIP for an American author with a first novel in progress. Offers a $6,000 fellowship/award. Deadline is March 1. Winners notified by September 1. Entry fee $20. Details: www.wilkes.edu/humanities/jones.asp. E-mail: english@wilkes.edu. James Jones First Novel Fellowship, c/o Dept. of English, Wilkes University, Wilkes-Barre PA 18766.

C. S. LEWIS CONTESTS. Check Website for current contests: www.cslewisclassics.com.

THE LONG FICTION CONTEST. Website: http://members.aol.com/wecspress/page4.htm. Stories 8,000-14,000 wds. December 15 postmark.

THE MARY MCCARTHY PRIZE IN SHORT FICTION, PO Box 4456, Louisville KY 40204. Website: www.sarabandebooks.org. Prize: $2,000 and publication of a collection of short stories, novellas, or a short novel. Postmark between January 1 and February 15. Entry fee: $20.

MEMPHIS MAGAZINE FICTION CONTEST with $1,000 grand prize, plus two $500 honorable mentions. August 1 deadline. Entrants must live within 150 miles of Memphis. Reading fee $10. Stories 3,000-4,500 wds. Details on Website: www.memphismagazine.com/fictioncontest rules.asp. Fiction Contest, c/o *Memphis Magazine,* PO Box 1738, Memphis TN 38101.

MID-LIST PRESS FIRST SERIES AWARD FOR SHORT FICTION, 4324—12th Ave. S., Minneapolis MN 55407-3218. (612)822-3733. Fax (612)823-8387. E-mail: guide@midlist.org. Website: www.midlist.org. Annual contest of short fiction for previously unpublished writers. Deadline July 1. Entry fee $30. Awards include publication and advance against royalties. Send #10 SASE for guidelines and entry form; also on Website.

MID-LIST PRESS FIRST SERIES AWARD FOR THE NOVEL, 4324—12th Ave. S., Minneapolis MN 55407-3218. (612)822-3733. Fax (612)823-8387. E-mail: guide@midlist.org. Website: www.midlist.org. Annual contest of novels for previously unpublished writers. Mss 50,000 words and up. Send #10 SASE for guidelines and entry form; also on Website.

+NATIONAL WRITERS ASSOCIATION NOVEL WRITING CONTEST, The National Writers Assn., 3140 S. Peoria, #295, Aurora CO 80014. (303)841-0246. Fax (303)841-2607. E-mail: sandywrter@aol.com. Website: www.nationalwriters.com. Sandy Whelchel, dir. Annual novel contest. April 1 deadline. Entry fee $35. Prizes $200, $300, $500. Send SASE for guidelines.

+NATIONAL WRITERS ASSOCIATION SHORT STORY CONTEST, The National Writers Assn., 3140 S. Peoria, #295, Aurora CO 80014. (303)841-0246. Fax (303)841-2607. E-mail: sandywrter@aol.com. Website: www.nationalwriters.com. Sandy Whelchel, dir. Annual nonfiction contest. July 1 deadline. Entry fee $15. Prizes $50, $100, $200. Send SASE for guidelines.

NELLIGAN PRIZE FOR SHORT FICTION, *Colorado Review*, Dept. of English, Colorado State University, Fort Collins CO 80523. Website: www.coloradoreview.com. Best short story. First prize $1,000, plus publication in the fall issue of *Colorado Review.* Entry fee $10. Deadline March 1 (may vary).

THE FLANNERY O'CONNOR AWARD FOR SHORT FICTION, University of Georgia Press, 330 Research Dr., Athens GA 30602. For submission guidelines, go to Website: www.ugapress .uga.edu. Cash award of $1,000, plus publication under royalty book contract. Submission fee: $20. Submit between April 1 and May 31 (postmark).

OPERATION FIRST NOVEL. Sponsored by the Jerry B. Jenkins Christian Writers Guild, PO Box 88196, Black Forest, CO 80908. For unpublished authors who are students or annual members of the Christian Writers Guild. Winner receives publication by Tyndale House Publishers, plus $15,000 advance against royalties. Length 75,000–100,000 wds. Entry deadline October 18, 2006. Winner announced at the *Writing for the Soul* conference, February 2007. For contest rules, go to www.ChristianWritersGuild.com.

+THE PARABLE AWARD, 420 N. Meridian St., #5798, Newberg OR 97132. E-mail: write_the_word@yahoo.com. Website: www.parableaward.tripod.com. Christine Hahn-Steichen, ed. To promote excellence in Christian fiction. December 1 deadline. Entry fee $1. Prize $25.

TAMARAK AWARD, 600 U.S. Trust Bldg., 730 S. 2nd Ave., Minneapolis MN 55402. Website: www.minnesotamonthly.com. Short fiction to 4,000 wds. $10,000 prize. Winning story to be published in the fall issue of *Minnesota Monthly.* For residents of Minnesota, North Dakota, South Dakota, Iowa, Wisconsin, and Michigan only. Spring deadline (March 1–May 16; varies).

TOBIAS WOLFF AWARD IN FICTION. Send manuscripts to: The Tobias Wolff Award for Fiction, Mail Stop 9053, Western Washington University, Bellingham WA 98225. (360)650-4863. E-mail: bhreview@cc.wwu.edu. Website: www.wwu.edu/~bhreview. Short story or novel excerpt to 8,000 wds. Entries must be postmarked between December 1 and March 15. Entry fee $15/story or chapter. First prize of $1,000. Unpublished works only.

+WORD SMITTEN'S TENTEN FICTION COMPETITION, Word Smitten, LLP, PO Box 5067, St. Petersburg FL 33737. E-mail: story@wordsmitten.com. Website: www.word smitten.com. Annual contest for a short story of exactly 1,010 words. Deadline July 1. Entry fee $15. Prize is $1,010.

+WRITER'S JOURNAL FICTION CONTEST, Val-Tech Media, PO Box 394, Perham MN 56573. E-mail: writersjournal@writersjournal.com. Website: www.writersjournal.com. January 30 deadline. $15 reading fee. Maximum 5,000 wds. Prizes $15-50.

NONFICTION CONTESTS

THE AFRICAN AMERICAN PULPIT, PO Box 15347, Pittsburgh PA 15237. Toll-free (800)509-8227. Phone/fax (412)364-1688. E-mail: Info@theafricanamericanpulpit.com. Website: www.TheAfricanAmericanPulpit.com. Hope for Life Intl., Inc. Victoria McGoey, project mngr.; Martha Simmons, pub. The only journal focused exclusively on the art of black preaching. Sponsors contest occasionally; advertised in the magazine.

THE AMY FOUNDATION sponsors the Amy Writing Awards, which is a call to present spiritual truth reinforced with biblical references in secular, nonreligious publications. First prize is $10,000 with a total of $34,000 given annually. The Amy Writing Awards is designed to recognize creative, skillful writing that presents in a sensitive, thought-provoking manner a biblical position on issues affecting the world today. To be eligible, submitted articles must be published in a secular, nonreligious publication, and must be reinforced with at least one passage of Scripture. For details on The Amy Writing Awards and a copy of last year's winning entries, contact: The Amy Foundation, PO Box 16091, Lansing MI 48901-6091. (517)323-6233. E-mail: amyfoundtn@aol.com. Website: www.amyfound.org. Deadline is January 31 of following year.

AMY PASTOR AWARDS, PO Box 16091, Lansing MI 48901. Toll-free (877)727-4260. E-mail: amyfoundtn@aol.com. Website: www.amyfound.org. $10,000 first prize, plus 14 additional prizes from $200-$5,000, for 10 sermon outlines. Only open to pastors or associate pastors actually serving an organized congregation. Details on Website. Deadline is June 30.

+ANNUAL FAMILY HISTORY WRITING CONTEST, 417 Irving Dr., Burbank CA 91504-2408. E-mail: scgs@scgsgenealogy.com. Website: www.scgsgenealogy.com. Southern California Genealogy Society. Three categories, 1,000-2,000 wds. Unpublished family or local history articles, character sketches, or memoirs. Prizes $50-250. No e-mail entries. Details on Website.

+ANNUAL SIMON SCANLON WRITING AWARDS, The Way, 1112—26th St., Sacramento CA 95816-5610. E-mail: ofmcaway@att.net. Website: www.sbfranciscans.org. Sponsored by *The Way of St. Francis.* Articles 1,500-2,000 wds. Prizes: $250-1,000. Deadline October 4. Details on Website.

ERMA BOMBECK WRITING COMPETITION. Website: www.wcpl.lib.oh.us/adults/erma.html. No entry fee. Offers cash prizes. Personal essay, 450 wds. Submit between January 6 and February 20 (may vary). Use online entry form.

THE BROSE PRIZE, The Brose Foundation, Lake Forest College, 555 N. Sheridan, Lake Forest IL 60045. (847)735-5175. Fax (847)735-6192. E-mail: rmiller@lfc.edu. Professor Ron Miller, contact person. Offered only every 10 years for unpublished work; next contest 2010. September 1 deadline in contest year. Prizes from $4,000-$15,000; entries become the property of the college. Open to a book or treatise on the relationship between any discipline or topic and the Christian religion. Send SASE for guidelines.

+THE DABBLING MUM.COM CONTESTS, 9919 Marilyn Collins Way, Knoxville TN 37931. (865)691-7739. E-mail: dm@thedabblingmum.com. Website: www.thedabblingmum.com. Nondenominational. Alyice Edrich, ed. Balance your life while you glean from successful entrepreneurs, parents, and Christians—just like you. Weekly online mag.

   Contest: Every 2-3 months they have an essay contest (http://thedabblingmum.com/contests/index.htm).

ANNIE DILLARD AWARD IN CREATIVE NONFICTION. Contact: Brenda Miller. Essays on any subject to 9,000 wds. Entries must be postmarked between December 1 and March 15. Entry fee $15. First prize: $1,000. Unpublished works only, to 8,000 wds. Send manuscripts to contest at: Bellingham Review, Mail Stop 9053, Western Washington University, Bellingham WA 98225. (360)650-4863. E-mail: bhreview@cc.wwu.edu. Website: www.wwu.edu/~bhreview.

+RALPH WALDO EMERSON AWARD, The Phi Beta Kappa Society, 1606 New Hampshire Ave. N.W., Washington DC 20009. (202)265-3808. Fax (202)986-1601. E-mail: sbeasley@pbk.org. Website: www.pbk.org/scholarships/books. Contact: Sandra Beasley. May recognize work in the fields of history, philosophy, or religion. Work must have appeared in print and be submitted by the publisher. Prize: $2,500. Details on Website.

GUIDEPOSTS CONTEST, 16 E. 34th St., New York NY 10016. (212)251-8100. Website: www.guideposts.org. Interfaith. Submit to The Editor. Writers Workshop Contest held on even years with a late June deadline. True, first-person stories (yours or someone else's), 1,500 wds. Needs one spiritual message, with scenes, drama, and characters. Winners attend a week-long seminar (all expenses paid) on how to write for *Guideposts.* Also Young Writers Contest (see separate listing).

+CORETTA SCOTT KING AWARDS, American Library Assn., 50 E. Huron St., Chicago IL 60611. (800)545-2433, ext. 4294. E-mail: olos@ala.org. Website: www.ala.org/srrt/csking.

Offered annually to an African American author and illustrator to promote understanding and appreciation of culture and the contributions of all people. Send SASE for guidelines. Prize $1,000, plus a set of encyclopedias.

MID-LIST PRESS FIRST SERIES AWARD FOR CREATIVE NONFICTION, 4324—12th Ave S., Minneapolis MN 55407-3218. (612)822-3733. Fax (612)823-8387. E-mail: guide@midlist.org. Website: www.midlist.org. Annual contest of creative nonfiction for previously unpublished writers. Mss 50,000 wds. & up. Submit entire manuscript between April 1 and July 1. Prize is $1,000 advance against royalties, plus publication. Entry fee: $30.

MONEY THE WRITE WAY, PO Box 488, Dobbins CA 95935-0488. (916)205-4763. E-mail: carmel@moneythewriteway.com. Website: www.moneythewriteway.com. Write Spirit Publishing. Carmel Mooney, pub. Educates, inspires, and supports Christian writers, travel writers, authors, and e-publishing enthusiasts in making money as a writer of integrity. Occasionally sponsors writing contests.

+NATIONAL WRITERS ASSOCIATION NONFICTION CONTEST, The National Writers Assn., 3140 S. Peoria, #295, Aurora CO 80014. (303)841-0246. Fax (303)841-2607. E-mail: sandywrter@aol.com. Website: www.nationalwriters.com. Sandy Whelchel, dir. Annual nonfiction contest. December 31 deadline. Entry fee: $18. Prizes $50, $100, $200. Send SASE for guidelines.

THE NEUBY AWARD, PO Box 1785, Georgetown TX 78628. Sponsored by WordWright.Biz, Inc. and the Writer's League of Texas. Website: www.wordwright.biz/neubyaward.shtml. For authors of nonfiction books, previously unpublished by royalty houses. First place, royalty contract; 2nd place, $250; 3rd place, $150. Entry form on Website.

THE POWER OF PURPOSE AWARDS, 5105 Peachtree Industrial Blvd., Ste. 250, Atlanta GA 30341. (770)457-5800. Fax (770)234-9338. A Worldwide Essay Competition. Website: www.powerofpurpose.org. John Templeton Foundation. Essays to 3,500 wds. No entry fee. Nineteen prizes totaling $500,000 (Grand prize $100,000). Deadline May 31. Intended to encourage people to think about the benefits of purpose. Entries may be published or unpublished. Word length: up to 3,500 wds.

WINSOME WIT, 12971 Fieldstone Rd., Milaca MN 56353. (320)983-5910. E-mail: jbeuoy@ winsomewit.com. Website: www.winsomewit.com. Nondenominational. Jay Beuoy, ed. We write to persuade the unbeliever through the use of satire, from a Christian world-view. Online e-zine. Deadline January 7. Contest details on Website.

LAMAR YORK PRIZE FOR NONFICTION, The Chatahoochee Review, Georgia Perimeter College, 2101 Womack Rd., Dunwoody GA 30338-4497. (770)551-3091. Website: www.gpc .edu/~gpccr/lamaryork.html. Reading fee $10. Prize $1,000. Unpublished essays to 5,000 wds. Must be postmarked between October 1 and January 31.

PLAY/SCRIPTWRITING/SCREENWRITING CONTESTS

THE AMERICAN ACCOLADES SCREENWRITING COMPETITION. Website: http://american accolades.com/contest_rules.htm. February deadline.

BAKER'S PLAYS HIGH SCHOOL PLAYWRITING CONTEST, PO Box 699222, Quincy MA 02269. (617)745-0805. Fax (617)745-9891. E-mail: 411@bakersplays.com. Website: www.bakersplays.com. Deidre Shaw, mng. ed. High School Play Writing Contest. Deadline: January 31. No entry fee. Prizes: $500 (with publication), $250, $100. Plays about the high-school experience or appropriate for high-school productions. Requires a signature from a sponsoring drama or English teacher.

CHESTERFIELD FILM COMPANY WRITER'S FILM PROJECT. Website: www.chesterfield-co .com. Any genre. Awards up to five winners $20,000 stipends for a one-year fellowship based in Los Angeles to learn more about the craft of screenwriting. Currently on hiatus.

CITA PLAY DEVELOPMENT COMPETITION, PO Box 26471, Greenville SC 29616. E-mail: information@cita.org. Website: www.CITA.org. (click on "Playwriting"). To encourage Christian playwrights, the writing of new plays and musicals that are informed by a biblical world-view in influencing our culture and furthering the Kingdom of God. Entries may be a full-length play, approximately 60+ pages, or a one-act play to 60 pages. Entry fee: $20. Deadline for entries: March 15 (may vary). Entry form on Website.

CITA THEATRICAL SKETCH WRITING CONTEST, Lin Sexton, 501 Coronado Way, Modesto CA 95350. E-mail: information@cita.org. Dramatic or comedy sketch not to exceed 8 minutes in length. Deadline for entries: March 1 annually. Writers must be members of CITA (go to www.CITA.org for info on membership). Contest categories are Comedy and Drama. Entry fee: $10. Download entry form and rules on Website.

WALT DISNEY STUDIOS/ABC TV FELLOWSHIP PROGRAM. Website: www.abcnewtalent .disney.com. Spring competition. Awards a residency program in Los Angeles for 8 lucky winners, with round-trip airfare and one month's accommodations.

THE FIREHOUSE THEATRE PROJECT, 1609 W. Broad St., Richmond VA 23220. Website: www.firehousetheatre.org/contest.htm. Annual Festival of New American Plays. First prize is $1,000 with staged reading and possible full production, and second prize is $500 and a stage reading. Deadline August 31 (may vary).

NICHOLL FELLOWSHIPS IN SCREENWRITING. E-mail: nicholl@oscars.org. Website: www.oscars.org/nicholl/index.html. An international contest held annually is open to any writer who has not optioned or sold a treatment, teleplay, or screenplay for more than $5,000. Up to five $30,000 fellowships are offered each year to promising authors.

OPEN DOOR SCREENPLAY COMPETITION. Website: www.scriptmag.com/contests/index .htm. Winner receives $3,000 cash.

SCREENPLAY FESTIVAL. Annual festival where you can submit your screenplay. $1,000 grand prize in each category. Website: www.screenplayfestival.com. Early deadline: July 1. Final deadline: September 1.

THE WRITERS NETWORK ANNUAL SCREENPLAY & FICTION COMPETITION. E-mail: writersnet@aol.com. May 31 deadline (may vary). Over $10,000 in prizes. Website: www .fadeinonline.com.

POETRY CONTESTS

ANHINGA PRIZE FOR POETRY, PO Box 10595, Tallahassee FL 32302. (850)521-9920. Fax: (850)442-6363. E-mail: info@anhinga.org. A $2,000 prize for original poetry book in English. Winning manuscript published by Anhinga Press. For poets trying to publish a first or second book of poetry. Self-published books and chapbooks do not make you ineligible. Submissions must be 48-80 pages, excluding front matter (do not staple or bind manuscript). Number pages and include $20 reading fee. Submissions must be received between February 15 and May 1 each year. For details, go to: www.anhinga.org/contest.html.

ANNUAL CAVE CANEM POETRY PRIZE. Supports the work of African American poets with excellent manuscripts who have not found a publisher for their first book. May 14 deadline. Winner receives $500, publication of their book by a national press, and 50 copies of the book. Details on Website: www.cavecanempoets.org/pages/prize.html#guidelines. Mailing address: 2006 Cave Canem Poetry Prize, Cave Canem Foundation, Inc., 584 Broadway, Ste. 508, New York NY 10012.

ANNUAL KENYON REVIEW PRIZE FOR POETRY, c/o Zoo Press, PO Box 3528, Omaha NE 68103. E-mail: editors@zoopress.org. Website: http://zoopress.org. For previously unpublished book of poems in English, 48-100 pages, by an author who has not yet published a full-length book of verse. First prize $3,500 advance against royalties, publication by Zoo

Press. Entry fee: $25. Deadline in mid-March (see Website to verify date). Mail or e-mail for rules.

ATLANTA REVIEW INTERNATIONAL POETRY COMPETITION, PO Box 8248, Atlanta GA 31106. E-mail: contest@atlantareview.com. Website: www.atlantareview.com. Dan Veach, ed. Prize of $1,000 and publication in the *Atlanta Review* given for an unpublished poem; five prizes of $100 each. Twenty International Publication Awards appear in over 120 countries in *Atlanta Review.* May 16 (postmark) deadline. Submit poems of any length with a $5 entry fee for the first poem, and $3 each for any additional poems. Discount on subscriptions and contest issue to all entrants. Send SASE, e-mail, or visit Website for details.

MURIEL CRAFT BAILEY MEMORIAL POETRY AWARD. Awarded annually. July 1 deadline. Prizes of $100 to $1,000. Finalists published in the Comstock Review. Unpublished poems up to 40 lines. Entry fee $3 for each poem. Details on Website: www.comstockreview.org.

BOSTON REVIEW ANNUAL POETRY CONTEST. Deadline is June 1. First prize is $1,000, plus publication. Submit up to 5 unpublished poems; $15 entry fee (includes a subscription to *Boston Review*). Submit manuscripts in duplicate with cover note. Send manuscript and fee to: Poetry Contest, *Boston Review,* E53-407 MIT, Cambridge MA 02139. Website: www.bostonreview.net

+BOULEVARD POETRY CONTEST FOR EMERGING WRITERS, PMB 325, 6614 Clayton Rd., Richmond Heights MO 63117. (314)862-2643. Website: www.boulevardmagazine.com/ contest.htm. Prize money, plus publication in *Boulevard Magazine.* For writers who have not had a book published with a nationally distributed publisher. Entry fee $15 for 3 poems. May 15 deadline. Not held every year; check Website for current contest.

+VIRGINIA BRENDEMUEHL PRIZE FOR POETRY, *ROCK & SLING: A Journal of Literature, Art and Faith,* PO Box 30865, Spokane WA 99223. Fax (509)276-2971. E-mail: editors@ rockandsling.org. Website: www.rockandsling.org. Kris Christensen, Susan Cowger, Laurie Klein, eds. A literary journal created to give forum to the spiritual journey, while exploring the Christian point of view. Prize: $1,000, plus publication. Deadline July 30. Entry fee $10/3 poems. Send SASE for guidelines.

CAMPBELL CORNER POETRY PRIZE. Once a year, on October 15, a prize of $2,500 for best entry is awarded by an outside panel of distinguished poets and writers. Entry fee $25. Winner and two finalists invited to give a reading at Sarah Lawrence College, plus publication. Submit 1-3 poems. See Website for theme: http://pages.slc.edu/~eraymond/corner. Twelve pgs. max. Send three sets in hard copy and one disk in ASCII text format only. Submit to: Dean of Graduate Studies, c/o Office of Graduate Studies, Sarah Lawrence College, 1 Mead Way, Bronxville NY 10708-5999. Deadline: March 15.

CHRISTIAN ONLINE CONTESTS, E-mail: darlene@christianmagazine.org. Website: www.ChristianMagazine.org. Darlene Osborne, pub. Strictly founded in the Word of God, this magazine endeavors to bring you the best Christian information on the net. Monthly e-zine. Guidelines on Website. Sponsors a monthly contest. For details go to Website.

DREAM HORSE PRESS ORPHIC PRIZE FOR POETRY, PO Box 640746, San Jose CA 95164. E-mail: dreamhorsepress@yahoo.com. Send 16-24 pages of poetry (paginated), plus two title pages (one with title, name, address, phone number, and e-mail address, and one with title only), table of contents, acknowledgment page, bio, and SASE. Entry fee: $12. Deadline May 1 (may vary). Prize: $300 and 25 copies of the book. Previously published OK, if not in book form. Manuscripts will be recycled. See Website for details: www.dreamhorse press.com. Electronic submissions OK, with electronic fee payment.

49TH PARALLEL POETRY CONTEST. Contact: Brenda Miller. Poems in any style or on any subject. Entries must be postmarked between December 1 and March 15. Entry fee $15 for first entry (up to 3 poems), $10 for each additional entry. First prize of $1,000. Unpublished works only. Send manuscripts to: 49th Parallel Poetry Award, Mail Stop 9053, West-

ern Washington University, Bellingham WA 98225. (360)650-4863. E-mail: bhreview@cc
.wwu.edu. Website: www.wwu.edu/~bhreview.

GRIFFIN POETRY PRIZE. Contact: Ruth Smith, mngr., The Griffin Trust for Excellence in
Poetry, 6610 Edwards Blvd., Mississauga ON L5T 2V6, Canada. (905)565-5993. E-mail:
info@griffinpoetryprize.com. Website: www.griffinpoetryprize.com. Makes two $50,000
awards (one to a Canadian and one to a poet from anywhere in the world) for a collection
of poetry published in English during the preceding year. Details on Website.

+KATHRYN HANDLEY PROSE-POEM PRIZE, National League of American Pen Women, Nob
Hill, San Francisco Branch, 1544 Sweetwood Dr., Colma CA 94015-2029. E-mail: pen
nobhill@aol.com. Website: www.soulmakingcontest.us. Contact: Eileen Malone. One-page
poems only (single- or double-spaced). Up to 3 poems/entry. Deadline November 30. Entry
fee $5. Prizes $25, $50, $100.

SARA HENDERSON HAY PRIZE, The Pittsburgh Quarterly, 36 Haberman Ave., Pittsburgh PA
15211-2144. Enter up to 3 poems of no more than 100 lines each. Prize is $500. Entry fee
$10. Unpublished poems only. Details: www.city-net.com/~tpq.

HONICKMAN FIRST BOOK PRIZE IN POETRY is sponsored by The American Poetry Review.
Open to any U.S. citizen who has not published a book of poetry. Prize is $3,000, publica-
tion, distribution, and a $1,000 grant for a book tour. Entry fee $20. Deadline October 31.
Details: www.aprweb.org.

BARBARA MANDIGO KELLY PEACE POETRY AWARDS, Nuclear Age Peace Foundation, PMB
121, 1187 Coast Village Rd., Ste. 1, Santa Barbara CA 93108-2794. (805)965-3443. Fax
(805)568-0466. E-mail: development@napf.org. Website: www.wagingpeace.org. An annual
series of awards to encourage poets to explore and illuminate positive visions of peace and the
human spirit. Deadline July 1. Prizes: $1,000 for Adult; $200 for Youth 13-18 years; and $200
for Youth ages 12 and under. Adult entry fee: $15 for up to 3 poems (no youth fee).

THOMAS MERTON POETRY OF THE SACRED CONTEST. Poetry that expresses, directly or
indirectly, a sense of the holy or that, by mode of expression, evokes the sacred. The tone
may be religious, prophetic, or contemplative. Deadline: December 31. First prize: $500;
three Honorable Mentions, $50 each. Submit 1 poem. No entry fee. No poems returned.
Submit poems to: The Thomas Merton Prize, The Thomas Merton Foundation, 2117 Payne
St., Louisville KY 40206-2011, or e-mail to: hgraffy@mertonfoundation.org. For additional
information, call (502)899-1991 or visit Website: www.mertonfoundation.org.

MID-LIST PRESS FIRST SERIES AWARD FOR POETRY, 4324—12th Ave S., Minneapolis MN
55407-3218. (612)822-3733. Fax (612)823-8387. E-mail: guide@midlist.org. Website:
www.midlist.org. Annual contest of poetry for writers who have never published a book of
poetry. Manuscript must be at least 60 pages. Guidelines and entry form on Website, or
send #10 SASE.

+MISSISSIPPI VALLEY NON-PROFIT POETRY CONTEST, Midwest Writing Center, PO Box
3188, Rock Island IL 61204-3188. (563)359-1057. Max Molleston, chairman. Annual
contest with the following categories: adult general, student, Mississippi Valley, senior citizen, religious, rhyming, jazz, humorous, haiku, history, and ethnic. Submit 5 poems max.
Deadline is April 1. Entry fee $8 for adults, $5 for students. Cash prizes totaling $1,200.

KATHRYN A. MORTON PRIZE IN POETRY, Sarabande Books, PO Box 4456, Louisville KY
40204. (502)458-4028. E-mail: sarabanden@aol.com. Website: www.sarabande
books.org. Kirby Gann, mng. ed. Prize: $2,000, plus publication of a book of poetry. Sub-
mit a minimum of 48 pages of poetry. Entry fee: $20. Deadline is January 1–February 15.

+NATIONAL WRITERS ASSOCIATION POETRY CONTEST, The National Writers Assn., 3140
S. Peoria, #295, Aurora CO 80014. (303)841-0246. Fax (303)841-2607. E-mail: sandy
wrter@aol.com. Website: www.nationalwriters.com. Sandy Whelchel, dir. Annual poetry
contest. Entry fee: $10. Prizes $25, $50, $100. Send SASE for guidelines.

HOWARD NEMEROV SONNET AWARD, The Formalist, 320 Hunter Dr., Evansville IN 47711. Entry fee: $3/sonnet. Original, unpublished sonnets. Winning entries will be published in *The Formalist.* June 15 deadline. Prize: $1,000, plus publication. Put name, address, and phone number on back of entry. Send SASE for complete list of rules or for contest results.

+THE OPEN WINDOW IV, Hidden Brook Press, 412—701 King St. W., Toronto ON M5V 2W7, Canada. (416)504-3966. Fax (801)751-1837. E-mail: writers@hiddenbrookpress.com. Website: www.hiddenbrookpress.com/an-ow.htm. Annual poetry anthology contest. Deadline July 15. Entry fee $15 for 3 poems. Prizes from $10-100.

THE PLOWMAN, Box 414, Whitby ON L1N 5S4, Canada. (905)668-7803. The Plowman Ministries/Christian. Tony Scavetta, ed./pub. Poetry and prose of social commentary; any topics. Sponsors monthly poetry contests; $2/poem entry fee.

POETRY OF TODAY PUBLISHING, 2073 Stanford Village Dr., Antioch TN 37013-4450. (615)337-2725. Fax (347)823-9608. E-mail: info@poetryoftoday.com. Website: www .poetryoftoday.com. Patrice M. Clark, pub. Specializes in Christian poetry. Sponsors a monthly poetry contest.

POETRY SOCIETY OF VIRGINIA POETRY CONTEST, PO Box 35160, Richmond VA 23235. Website: www.poetrysocietyofvirginia.org. Categories for adults and students. Prizes from $10-100. Entry fee per poem for nonmembers: $3.

+NICHOLAS ROERICH POETRY PRIZE, Story Line Press, Three Oaks Farm, PO Box 1240, Ashland OR 97520-0055. (541)512-8792. Fax (541)512-8793. E-mail: mail@storyline press.com. Website: www.storylinepress.com. Roerich Prize Coordinator. Annual contest for full-length book of poetry from a writer who has not had a full-length book of poetry published (48 pages or more). Postmarked between May 1 and October 31. Entry fee $20. Prize is $1,000, plus publication. Guidelines on Website or for SASE.

SHORT STORIES BIMONTHLY CHAPBOOK CONTEST, 5713 Larchmont Dr., Erie PA 16509. Phone/fax (814)866-2543. E-mail: 75562.670@compuserve.com. Website: www.thepoetry forum.com. Poetry Forum. Gunvor Skogsholm, ed. Poetry and prose that takes an honest look at the human condition. Chapbook contest, $12 entry fee. Prize: publication and 20 copies. Send SASE for information. December 15 deadline (may vary).

SILVER WINGS CONTEST, PO Box 2340, Clovis CA 93613-2340. (559)347-0194. E-mail: cloviswings@aol.com. Poetry on Wings/Baptist Evangelical. Jackson Wilcox, ed. Christian understanding and uplift through poetry, plus a sermon. Contest: Annual poetry contest on a theme(December 31 deadline); send SASE for details. Winners published in March. $200 in prizes. $3 entry fee. Theme for 2006: Seasons of Change.

SLIPSTREAM ANNUAL POETRY CHAPBOOK COMPETITION, Box 2071, Niagara Falls NY 14301. Website: www.slipstreampress.org/contest.html. Prize: $1,000, plus 50 copies of chapbook. December 1 deadline annually. Send up to 40 pages of poetry. Reading fee: $15.

SPS STUDIOS POETRY CARD CONTEST, SPS Studios, Inc., publisher of Blue Mountain Arts, PO Box 1007, Dept. E, Boulder CO 80306-1007. (303)449-0536. Fax (303)447-0939. E-mail: editorial@spsstudios.com. Website: www.sps.com. Sponsors a biannual poetry card contest. Prizes for this contest range from $50-300. Deadlines: December 31 and June 30. Details on Website.

STORY LINE PRESS'S ANNUAL FREDERICK MORGAN POETRY PRIZE. Roerich Competition, Three Oaks Farm, PO Box 1240, Ashland OR 97520-0055. E-mail: contest@story linepress.com. Website: www.storylinepress.com/projects/roerich.htm. Manuscripts of original poetry must be in English, and at least 48 pages in length. Poems may have previously appeared in magazines (including online), anthologies, or chapbooks, or in printed press runs of less than 500 copies. Prize: $1,000. Entry fee: $20. Deadline: October 31.

HOLLIS SUMMERS POETRY PRIZE COMPETITION, Ohio University Press, The Ridges, Bldg. 19, Athens OH 45701. E-mail: oupress@ohio.edu. Details on Website: www.ohiou.edu/

oupress/poetryprize.htm. For unpublished collection of original poems, 60-95 pgs. Entry fee $20. Deadline October 31. Prize: $500, plus publication.

THE MAY SWENSON POETRY AWARD, Utah State University Press, 7800 Old Main Hill, Logan UT 84322-7800. (435)797-1362. E-mail: michael.spooner@usu.edu. Website: www.usu .edu/usupress. Michael Spooner. Annual. Collections of original poetry, 50-100 pgs. September 30 deadline. Prize: $1,000 award, publication the following spring, and royalties. Reading fee $25. Details on Website.

TIME OF SINGING: A Magazine of Christian Poetry, PO Box 149, Conneaut Lake PA 16316. (814)382-8667. E-mail: timesing@toolcity.net. Website: www.timeofsinging.bizland.com. Lora Zill, ed. Sponsors 1-2 annual poetry contests on specific themes or forms ($2 entry fee/poem) with cash prizes (send SASE for rules).

+TO GOD BE THE GLORY! POETRY CONTESTS, 525 N. Arlington, #D-2, Kalamazoo MI 49006. (269)547-5212. E-mail: Reynolds_Ink@yahoo.com. Website: www.geocities.com/ reynolds_ink/my_page.html. Reynolds INK. M. J. Reynolds, owner/CEO. Devoted to lifting up the name of our precious Lord and Savior Jesus Christ. Bimonthly mag.

> **Contest:** Holds a poetry contest in each issue. Cash prize for winner, consolation prize for 2nd & 3rd places, and certificates for 4th-7th places.

KATE TUFTS DISCOVERY AWARD is presented annually for a first or very early work by a poet of genuine promise. Award is $10,000. Work submitted must be a book published between September 15, 2005, and September 15, 2006. Deadline is September 15. Details and entry form on Website: www.cgu.edu/tufts.

UTMOST CHRISTIAN POETRY CONTEST, New Leaf Works, 121 Morin Maze, Edmonton AB T6K 1V1, Canada. E-mail: nathan@snowfaux.com. Website: www.utmostchristian writers.com/poetry-contest/poetrycontest.htm. Nathan Harms. Prizes of $25-1,000. Deadline is February 28 (may vary). Contest details on Website.

WAR POETRY CONTEST. Website: www.winningwriters.com/annualcontest.htm. Sponsored by Winning Writers. Submit 1-3 unpublished poems on the theme of war, up to 500 lines total. $1,500 first prize; $3,000 in total prizes. Submit between November 15 and May 31. Entry fee $12.

THE WRITER MAGAZINE/EMILY DICKINSON AWARD, Poetry Society of America, 15 Gramercy Park S., New York NY 10003. (212)254-9628. Fax (212)673-2352. E-mail: brett@poetrysociety.org. Website: www.poetrysociety.org. Brett Lauer, program associate. Annual contest for poem inspired by Emily Dickinson (not necessarily in her style). Deadline is December 22. Prize $250. Guidelines on Website and for SASE. Open to members of PSA only.

*YALE UNIVERSITY PRESS, 302 Temple St. (06511), PO Box 209040, New Haven CT 06520. (203)432-0960. Fax (203)432-0948. E-mail: robert.flynn@yale.edu. Website: www.yale .edu/yup. Robert Flynn, ed./religion. Yale Series of Younger Poets competition. Open to poets under 40 who have not had a book of poetry published. Submit manuscripts of 48-64 pgs. in February only. Entry fee $15. Send SASE for guidelines (also on Website).

MULTIPLE-GENRE CONTESTS

ALEXANDRA WRITERS' CENTRE SOCIETY FREEFALL FICTION & POETRY CONTEST. Website: www.alexandrawriters.org/ctest.html. October 1 deadline. Fiction to 3,000 wds.; 5 poems. Prizes of $200 & $100 in both categories. Entry fee: $20.

THE AMERICAN DREAM GROUP WRITING CONTESTS. Various contests on Website: http://achieve-the-dream.net.

AMERICAN LITERARY REVIEW CONTEST, PO Box 311307, University of North Texas, Denton TX 76203. Category is different each year. Winner receives $1,000 and publication in fall issue of the magazine. Reading fee $10. Check Website for current category and details: www.engl.unt.edu/alr/contest.htm.

AUTHOR LINK CONTESTS. Website: www.authorlink.com. Sponsors a variety of contests each year; check Website for current listings. Scroll down to "Authorlink News/Info" and click on "Contests."

BAKELESS LITERARY PUBLICATION PRIZES. Website: www.bakelessprize.org. Book series competition for new authors of literary works of poetry, fiction, and nonfiction. Processing fee: $10. Submit between October 1 and November 15.

BEGINNINGS: A Magazine for Novice Writers, PO Box 214, Bayport NY 11705. (631)205-5542. E-mail: jenineb@optonline.net. Website: www.scbeginnings.com. Jenine Boisits, ed-in-chief. Sponsors poetry and short story contests, 4 contests for each season. See Website for current contests and details.

BRISTOL SERVICES WRITING COMPETITIONS, PO Box 1000, Carlsborg WA 98324-1000. E-mail: services@bristolservicesintl.com. Website: www.bristolservicesintl.com. Recent contests for short stories and stories for children. Check Website for current contests.

BYLINE, Box 5240, Edmond OK 73083-5240. Phone/fax (405)348-5591. E-mail: Mpreston@bylinemag.com. Website: www.BylineMag.com. Secular. Marcia Preston, ed.; Carolyn Wall, fiction ed. Sponsors many contests year-round; details included in magazine, on Website, or send SASE for flier.

CATHOLIC DIGEST, PO Box 180, Mystic CT 06355. (860)536-2611. Fax (860)536-5600. E-mail: catholicdigest@bayard-inc.com. Submissions to: cdsubmissions@bayardpubs.com. Website: www.CatholicDigest.com. Catholic/Bayard Publications. Joop Koopman, ed.; submit to Articles Editor. Readers have a stake in being Catholic and a wide range of interests: religion, family, health, human relationships, good works, nostalgia, and more. See Website for current contest, or send an SASE.

CHICKEN SOUP BOOKS. Website: www.chickensoup.com. See Website for list of current contests.

COLUMBIA FICTION/POETRY/NONFICTION CONTEST. Website: www.columbia.edu/cu/arts/journal. Length: 20 double-spaced pages or up to 5 poems. Entry fee: $10. Prize: $500, plus publication. Deadline: February 1 (varies).

*ESSENCE PUBLISHING CO., INC., 20 Hanna Ct., Belleville ON K8P 5J2, Canada. (613)962-2360. Toll-free (800)238-6376. Fax (613)962-3055. E-mail: publishing@essence group.com. Website: www.essencegroup.com. Essence Communications Group. Cathy Jol, submissions ed. Sponsors The Essence Treasury Writing Competition.

+ETERNAL INK CONTEST, 25 Powers Rd., Lawrenceburg TN 38464. E-mail: fisher caster@yahoo.com. Website: www.eternal-ink.com. Nondenominational. Open to any serious effort or submission. Submit to Administrative Assistant (e-mail above); Carl Phillips, nonfiction ed. (CarlPhil10@aol.com). See Website for contest details.

GENERATION X NATIONAL JOURNAL CONTESTS, 411 W. Front, Wayland IA 52654. (319)256-4221. E-mail: genxjournal2004@yahoo.com. Website: www.genxnatljournal .com. Kathy Stoops, mng. ed. For those who came of age during the late 80s and early 90s. Quarterly creative jour. Watch Website for future contests.

INSIGHT WRITING CONTEST, 55 W. Oak Ridge Dr., Hagerstown MD 21740-7301. (301)393-4038. Fax (301)393-4055. E-mail: insight@rhpa.org. Website: www.insightmagazine.org. Review and Herald/Seventh-day Adventist. Dwain N. Esmond, ed. A magazine of positive Christian living for Seventh-day Adventist high school. Sponsors a nonfiction and poetry contest; includes a category for students under 21. Prizes to $250. June deadline (varies). Send SASE for rules.

INTERNATIONAL LIBRARY OF PHOTOGRAPHY FREE PHOTO CONTEST, 3600 Crondall Ln., Ste. 101, Owings Mills MD 21117. Website: www.picture.com. Ongoing contest.

$10,000 first prize; $60,000 in prizes to amateur photographers. Send one photo in one of these categories: Action, Children, Humor, Nature, People, Animals/Pets, Portraiture, Sports, Travel, or Other. Color or black & white, up to 8x10. Photos will not be returned, but photographer retains all rights to the photo. Entry form on Website.

"IN THE BEGINNING WAS THE WORD..." LITERARY ARTS CONTEST. Sponsored by the Lake Oswego, Oregon, United Church of Christ. Categories include short fiction, creative nonfiction, or poetry; previously unpublished; to 4,000 words. One submission per person. Deadline: September 1 each year. Prizes of $500, $250, and $100 for first three places. Also sponsors a Young Writers' Contest for those 18 years and younger (write or call for details). Send SASE for official entry form to: Lake Oswego United Church of Christ, 1111 S.W. Country Club Rd., Lake Oswego OR 97034, (503)635-4348, or e-mail: loucc@pacifier.com.

+LIGHT AT HOME CONTESTS, 10117 S.E. Sunnyside Rd., Ste. F#518, Clackamas OR 97015. Toll-free (888)889-3665. E-mail: lightathome@comcast.net. Website: www.lightathome .com. Batdorf & Associates. Lindy Batdorf, ed./pub. Dedicated to enhancing life at home by offering encouraging words, household hints, organizational tips, inspiring funny stories, and more. Weekly e-zine. Occasionally sponsors contests. Sign up for newsletter to receive details.

JOHN T. LUPTON NEW VOICES IN LITERATURE AWARDS. Website: www.booksforlife foundation.com/php/luptonawards.php#guidelines. Professional query letters and proposals to submit to agents or publishers. Prizes are $10,000 for each category. Entry fee: $35. Deadline November 15 (varies).

MINISTRY & LITURGY VISUAL ARTS AWARDS, 160 E. Virginia St., #290, San Jose CA 95112. (408)286-8505. Fax (408)287-8748. E-mail: mleditor@rpinet.com. Website: www.rpinet .com/ml, or www.rpinet.com/vaaentry.pdf. Resource Publications, Inc. Nick Wagner, ed. dir. To help liturgists and ministers make the imaginative connection between liturgy and life. Visual Arts Awards. $100 cash prize. Entry fee $30. Different deadline for each category (see Website).

MISSISSIPPI REVIEW PRIZE. Website: www.mississippireview.com/contest.html. Fiction & Poetry. $1,000 prize in each category. April 1 to October 1 (may vary). Entry fee: $15 per entry.

MOMSENSE, 2370 S. Trenton Way, Denver CO 80231. (303)733-5353. Fax (303)733-5770. E-mail: info@mops.org, or MOMsense@mops.org. Website: www.mops.org. MOPS Intl., Inc. (Mothers of Preschoolers). Elizabeth Jusino, mng. ed. Nurtures mothers of preschoolers from a Christian perspective with articles that both inform and inspire on issues relating to womanhood and motherhood. Sponsors several contests per year for writing and photography. Check Website for details on current contests.

NEW MILLENNIUM AWARDS. Website: www.newmillenniumwritings.com/awards.html. Fiction, poetry, and nonfiction; $1,000 award for each. Fiction and nonfiction to 6,000 wds.; 3 poems to 5 pgs. total. Entry fee: $17. June deadline.

MONA SCHREIBER PRIZE FOR HUMOROUS FICTION AND NONFICTION, 11362 Homedale St., Los Angeles CA 90049. Website: http://home.pcmagic.net/brashcyber/mona.htm. Humorous fiction and nonfiction to 750 wds. Prizes: $500, $250, and $100. Entry fee: $5. Deadline: December 1.

SHARING THE PRACTICE, 100 S. Chestnut St., Kent OH 44240-3402. (330)678-0187. E-mail: dunmovin720@aol.com. Website: www.apclergy.org. Academy of Parish Clergy/Ecumenical/Interfaith. Dr. Darryl Zoller, ed-in-chief (journal@apclergy.org); Dr. Forrest V. Fitzhugh, book rev. ed. (bond007@texas.net). Growth toward excellence through sharing the practice of parish ministry. Book of the Year Award ($100+), Top Ten Books of the Year list, Parish Pastor of the Year award ($200+). Inquire by e-mail to: DIELPADRE@ aol.com.

SOUL-MAKING LITERARY COMPETITION. November 30 deadline. Prose and poetry. Submit up to 3 poems, one per page. First prize $100; $5 entry fee. For complete guidelines, send SASE to: Soul-Making Literary Competition, Webhallow House, 1544 Sweetwood Dr., Colma CA 94015-2029; or e-mail: PenNobHill@aol.com. Website: www.SoulMakingContest.us.

SOWING SEEDS ANNUAL WRITING CONTEST. E-mail: LarryDavies@sowingseeds offaith.com. Soliciting entries in four categories: Devotions (600-750 wds.); Sermons (to 2,000 wds.); Prayer; and Poetry. Winner in each category gets $100, plus publication on their Web page. Winners will also be submitted to other publications. Entries must be post-marked by June 30. Entry fee is $25 for first submission, $18 each additional. For details and sample entries, go to their Website at www.sowingseedsoffaith.com/writing.htm. Send submissions to: Sowing Seeds Ministry, 21649 Timberlake Rd., Lynchburg VA 24502.

THE STORYTELLER, 2441 Washington Rd., Maynard AR 72444. (870)647-2137. Fax (870)647-2454. E-mail: storyteller1@cox-internet.com. Contest Website: www.freewebs .com/fossilcreekpub. Fossil Creek Publishing. Regina Cook Williams, ed./pub.; Ruthan Riney, review ed. Family audience; geared to (but not limited to) new writers. Offers 1 or 2 paying contests per year, along with People's Choice Awards, and Pushcart Prize nominations.

STUDIO: A Journal of Christians Writing, 727 Peel St., Albury NSW 2640, Australia. Phone/fax +61 2 6021 1135. E-mail: studio00@bigpond.net.au. Submit to Studio Editor. See copy of journal for contest details.

+TEEN LIGHT ANNUAL WRITING CONTEST, 6118 Bend of River, Dunn NC 28334. (910)980-1126. E-mail: publisher@teenlight.org. Website: www.teenlight.org. Writers' Ministries, Inc. Annette Dammer, pub.; submit to Rebekah Hamrick. Totally teen authored; uses professional Christian writers to mentor their teen journalists so they may reach the world for Christ. Emaleigh's Writer's Contest held every year. See Website.

TICKLED BY THUNDER, 14076—86A Ave., Surrey BC V3W 0V9, Canada. (604)591-6095. E-mail: info@tickledbythunder.com. Website: www.tickledbythunder.com. Larry Lindner, ed. Contest for fiction (February 15 annual deadline) and poetry (February 15, May 15, August 15, and October 15 annual deadlines). Article contests for subscribers only (February 15, May 15, August 15, and October 15 deadlines). Prizes range from $5-150 & up. Send SASE for guidelines.

THE WHITBREAD BOOK AWARDS. Go to: www.whitbread-bookawards.co.uk. The site lists a number of writing contests in the UK.

WOMEN'S EMPOWERMENT AWARDS WRITING COMPETITION/RELIGIOUS FICTION WRITING CONTEST, E.F.S. Enterprises, Inc., 2844 Eighth Ave., Ste. 6E, New York NY 10039. (212)283-8899. E-mail: info@efs-enterprises.com. Website: www.efs-enterprises .com. Rita Baxter, contest director. Fiction, nonfiction, poetry, and scripts. Deadline: May 31. Entry fee $25. Prizes: Online publishing contract for 1st and 2nd place winners. For fiction, plays, and essays. See Website for entry form and additional information.

+THE WRITER CONTESTS, 21027 Crossroads Cir., Waukesha WI 53189. (262)796-8776. E-mail: editor@writermag.com. Website: www.writermag.com. Secular. Elfreida Abbe, ed. How-to for writers; lists religious markets periodically. Occasionally sponsors a contest. Check Website.

WRITER'S DIGEST, 4700 E. Galbraith Rd., Cincinnati OH 45207. (513)531-2690, ext. 1483. Fax (513)531-1843. E-mail: wdsubmissions@fwpubs.com. Website: www.writersdigest .com. Secular/F & W Publications. Jane Friedman, mng. ed. To inform, instruct, or inspire the freelancer. Sponsors annual contest for articles, short stories, poetry, children's fiction and scripts (categories vary); May deadline (varies). More than $25,000 in prizes. Also The National Self-Publishing Book Awards with $6,000+ in prizes, including $1,500 grand prize. Send SASE for rules, or visit Website: www.writersdigest.com/novalearn.asp. Plus National Zine Publishing Awards. Official rules and entry forms are available online at:

www.writersdigest.com/catalog/contest_frame.html. And International Screenplay Competition; $5,000, plus trip to a screenwriting conference; deadline October 31.

WRITERS' JOURNAL CONTESTS, PO Box 394, Perham MN 56573-0394. (218)346-7921. Fax (218)346-7924. E-mail: writersjournal@lakesplus.com. Website: www.writersjournal .com. Val-Tech Media/Secular. Leon Ogroske, ed. Runs several contests each year. Prizes up to $300. Categories are short story, horror/ghost, romance, travel writing, and fiction; 3 poetry; 2 photo. Different starter lines and deadlines for each category (see Website). Guidelines on Website, or send SASE.

WRITERS' UNION OF CANADA AWARDS & COMPETITIONS, 90 Richmond St. E., Ste. 200, Toronto ON M5C 1P1, Canada. (416)703-8982. Fax (416)504-9090. E-mail: info@writers union.ca. Website: www.writersunion.ca/compete.htm. Various competitions. See Website for details.

YOUNG SALVATIONIST, PO Box 269, Alexandria VA 22313-0269. (703)684-5500. Fax (703)684-5539. E-mail: ys@usn.salvationarmy.org. Website: http://publications.salvation armyusa.org. The Salvation Army. Laura Ezzell, mng. ed. For teens & young adults in the Salvation Army. Sponsors a contest for fiction, nonfiction, poetry, original art, and photography. Send SASE for details.

SPONSORED BY WRITERS' CONFERENCES/GROUPS

(This list includes only those contests that are open to nonmembers of the groups or nonattendees at the conferences.)

AMERICAN CHRISTIAN FICTION WRITERS CONTESTS. Complete guidelines for contest on Website: www.acrw.net. Various contests listed.

ARKANSAS WRITERS CONTEST. Conference in Little Rock, AR; June 2-3, 2006 (always 1st Friday & Saturday of June). Contact: Barbara Mulkey, 9317 Claremore, Little Rock AR 72227. (501)312-1747. E-mail: blm@aristotle.net. Attendance: 200. Sponsors 32 contests; one $6 entry free covers all contests.

*BETHEL CHRISTIAN WRITERS' CONTEST. Bethel College. Contact: Kim Peterson, 1001 W. McKinley Ave., Mishawaka IN 46545-5509. (574)257-3375. E-mail: petersk@bethel college.edu. May sponsor a contest.

BLUE RIDGE MOUNTAIN CHRISTIAN WRITERS CONFERENCE. Lifeway Ridgecrest Conference Center; April 2006. Contact: Ron Pratt, LifeWay Christian Resources, One Lifeway Plaza, Nashville TN 37234-0106. (615)241-2065. Fax (615)277-8232. E-mail: ron.pratt@ lifeway.com, or Yvonne Lehman, PO Box 188, Black Mountain NC 28770. Sponsors a contest.

EVANGELICAL PRESS ASSOCIATION, PO Box 28129, Crystal MN 55428. (763)535-4793. Fax (763)535-4794. E-mail: mailto:director@epassoc.org. Website: www.epassoc.org. Sponsors annual contest for member publications. New "Best Freelance Article" category open to articles in EPA publications authored by freelancers who are members of EPA.

FAITH, HOPE & LOVE is the inspirational chapter of Romance Writers of America. Dues for the chapter are $24/yr., but you must also be a member of RWA to join (dues $75/yr.). Chapter offers these services: online list service for members, a Web page, 20-pg. bimonthly newsletter, annual contest, monthly online guest chats with multipublished authors and industry professionals, connections to critique partners by mail or e-mail, and latest romance-market information. To join, contact RWA National Office, 16000 Stuebner Airline Rd., Ste. 140, Spring TX 77379. (832)717-5200. Fax (832)717-5201. Website: www.rwanational.org. Or go to FHL Website: www.faithhopelove-rwa.org. Inspirational Readers Choice Contest by subgenre categories for published works; deadline April 1; cash prizes. See Website or send SASE for guidelines.

FELLOWSCRIPT CONTEST. Marcia Laycock, 5007—42A St., Ponoka AB T4J 1M3, Canada. (403)783-3044. E-mail: info@inscribe.org. Website: www.inscribe.org. Inscribe Christian Writers' Fellowship. Spring contest; members only; March 1 deadline. Fall contest in conjunction with Inscribe's Fall Conference; deadline August 6 (varies). Details on Website, or write and ask to be on mailing list. Sponsors two conferences each year, one open and one for members only.

FELLOWSHIP OF CHRISTIAN POETS ANNUAL CONTESTS, PO Box 831413, Ocala FL 34483. E-mail: john@christianpoets.com. Website: www.christianpoets.com. Sponsors 6 contests a year. Check Website for current contests and details. Open to members only.

HEART OF AMERICA CHRISTIAN WRITERS' NETWORK. Overland Park KS. Contact: Mark and Jeanette Littleton, 3706 N.E. Shady Lane Dr., Gladstone MO 64119. Phone/fax (816)459-8016. E-mail: MLittleton@earthlink.net. Sponsors a contest (open to nonmembers).

+RUPERT HUGHES WRITING CONTEST. Contest held in conjunction with the Maui Writers' Conference. Contact: Shannon and John Tullius, Maui Writers Foundation, PO Box 1118, Kihei HI 96753. (808)879-0061. Fax (808)879-6233. E-mail: writers@mauiwriters.com. Website: www.mauiwriters.com. Sponsors the Rupert Hughes Writing Contest.

INSCRIBE CHRISTIAN WRITERS' FELLOWSHIP. Contact: Eunice Matchett, 5304—45 St., Drayton Valley AB T7A 1G7, Canada. (780)542-7950. E-mail: scrappi@telusplanet.net. Website: www.inscribe.org. Sponsors 2 contests: one in conjunction with their spring workshop (April), and one in conjunction with their fall conference (September). See Website for details.

INSPIRATIONAL WRITERS ALIVE! AMARILLO CONTEST. Contact: Helen Luecke, 2921 S. Dallas, Amarillo TX 79103. (806)376-9671. E-mail: hcoluecke@arn.net. Sponsors a contest; one category opened to nonmembers.

INSPIRATIONAL WRITERS ALIVE! OPEN COMPETITION. Groups meet in Houston, Pasadena, Jacksonville, Amarillo, and Humble TX. Contact: Martha Rogers, 6038 Greenmont, Houston TX 77092-2332. (713)686-7209. E-mail: marthalrogers@sbcglobal.net. Sponsors annual contest. Annual deadline: May 15. Seven categories. Include 10x13 SAE for return. E-mail for official rules and entry form.

INSPIRATIONAL WRITERS FELLOWSHIP CONTEST. Contact: Jan R. Sady, 2026 Langville Rd., Mayport PA 16240. (814)856-2560. E-mail: janfran@alltel.net. Sponsors a contest in February (February 14 deadline) open to nonmembers.

OZARK CREATIVE WRITERS CONTESTS. Contact: Clarissa Willis, 2603 W. Walnut, Johnson City TN 37604. (423)929-1049. E-mail: ozarkcreativewriters@earthlink.net. Website: www.ozarkcreativewriters.org. Sponsors 25-30 contests each year.

SOUTHWEST WRITERS ANNUAL CONTEST. Contact: Southwest Writers, 3721 Morris St. N.E., Ste. A, Albuquerque NM 87111-3611. (505)265-9485. Fax (505)265-9483. E-mail: swriters@aol.com. Website: www.southwestwriters.com. Sponsors the Southwest Writers Contest (send SASE for details and entry form). Deadline: May 1. Prizes: $150, $100, $50. Guidelines on Website.

STATE OF MAINE WRITERS' CONFERENCE. Contact: Jim Brosnan. E-mail: Jim.Brosnan@ jwu.edu. Sponsors several contests.

+WEST BRANCH CHRISTIAN WRITERS CONTEST. Contact: Roberta Updegraff, 332 S. Pine Run Rd., Linden PA 17744. (570)584-2280. E-mail: bobbiup@suscom.net. Sponsors an annual one-day miniconference, October 2006. Also sponsors a contest.

THE WORD GUILD CANADIAN WRITING AWARDS, an association of Canadian writers and editors who are Christians. Exec. Director: N. J. Lindquist, Box 487, Markham ON L3P 3R1, Canada. (905)294-6482. Fax (905)471-6912. E-mail: info@thewordguild.com. Website: www.thewordguild.com. Sponsors the Write! Canada Conference, plus additional one-day conferences in various locations, and several contests open to nonmembers.

THE WRITING ACADEMY CONTEST. Sponsors year-round correspondence writing program and annual seminar in various locations. Contact: Mar Korman, 1128 Mule Lake Dr. N.E., Outing MN 56662. (218)792-5144. E-mail: pattyk@wams.org. Website: www.wams.org. Sponsors a contest open to non attendees (rules are posted on Website). Prizes $25-100. $5 entry fee for nonmembers.

RESOURCES FOR CONTESTS

BYLINE MAGAZINE CONTEST LISTINGS. www.bylinemag.com.

CONTESTS LINK PAGE. www.wordsmithshoppe.com. Good information on entering contests and avoiding scams.

FREELANCE WRITING: WEBSITE FOR TODAY'S WORKING WRITER. www.freelance writing.com/contests.html.

KIMN SWENSON GOLLNICK'S WEBSITE. Contest listings. Website: www.KIMN.net.

+LITERARY SCAMS. For help in determining if a contest is legitimate or not, go to: www.wind pub.com/literary.scams.

DENOMINATIONAL LISTING OF BOOK PUBLISHERS AND PERIODICALS

An attempt has been made to divide publishers into appropriate denominational groups. However, due to the extensive number of denominations included, and sometimes incomplete denominational information, some publishers inadvertently may have been included in the wrong list. Additions and corrections are welcome.

ANTIOCHIAN ORTHODOX

Book Publishers:
Conciliar Press
Periodicals:
Again
The Handmaiden

ASSEMBLIES OF GOD

Book Publishers:
Gospel Publishing House
Logion Press
Periodicals:
Club Connection
Discovery Trails
Enrichment
High Adventure
HonorBound
Live
Maranatha News
Poetry Scout
Testimony (Canada)
Today's Pentecostal Evangel
Woman's Touch

BAPTIST, FREE WILL

Book Publishers:
Randall House
Periodicals:
CoLaborer
Heartbeat
Randall House Publications

BAPTIST, SOUTHERN

Book Publishers:
Baylor Univ. Press
Broadman & Holman
Founders Press
New Hope Publishers
Southern Baptist Press
Periodicals:
Church Administration
Crusader
Founders Journal
Glory Songs
HomeLife

Journey
Let's Worship
Light
Living with Teenagers
Mature Living
Music Makers
Music Time
On Mission
ParentLife
Senior Musician
Stand Firm

BAPTIST (other)

Book Publishers:
Baptist Publishing House
Earthen Vessel (Reformed)
R.H. Boyd (Missionary)
Judson Press (American)
Mercer Univ. Press
Periodicals:
African American Pulpit (American)
American Baptist in Missions
BGC World
CoLaborer (Free Will)
Courage (Regular)
Friends Journal
Heartbeat (Free Will)
Link & Visitor
Living My Faith (Regular)
Primary Pal (Regular)
Real Faith in Life (Regular)
Secret Place (American)
Sword of the Lord (Independent)
Writer's Forum

CATHOLIC

Book Publishers:
ACTA Publications
Alba House
American Catholic Press
Canticle Books
Catholic Book Publishing
Catholic Univ. of America Press
Cistercian Publications
Cross Cultural Publications
Dimension Books

HarperSanFrancisco (Cath. bks.)
ICS Publications
Libros Liguori
Liguori Publications
Liturgical Press
Loyola Press
Thomas More
Novalis
Oregon Catholic Press
OSL Publications
Our Sunday Visitor
Pauline Books
Paulist Press
Pflaum Publishing
Regnery Publishing
Small Helm Press
St. Anthony Messenger
Tau-Publishing
Twenty-Third Publications
Periodicals:
America
Angel Face
Annals of St. Anne
Arkansas Catholic
Arlington Catholic Herald
Atlantic Catholic
Bread of Life
Canticle
Catechist
Catechumenate
Catholic Answer
Catholic Courier
Catholic Digest
Catholic Faith & Family
Catholic Forester
Catholic Insight
Catholic Library World
Catholic Missions in Canada
Catholic New Times
Catholic New York
Catholic Parent
Catholic Peace Voice
Catholic Register
Catholic Rural Life
Catholic Sentinel
Catholic Servant

Catholic Telegraph
Catholic Yearbook
Celebration
CGA World
CNEWA WORLD
Columbia
Commonweal
Culture Wars
Desert Call
Diocesan Dialogue
Emmanuel
Environment & Art
Eucharistic Ministries
Faith & Family
Family Digest
Good News for Children
Immaculate Heart Messenger
Interim
Island Catholic News
Leaves
Liguorian
Marian Helper
Messenger (KY)
Messenger/Sacred Heart
Messenger/St. Anthony
Miraculous Medal
Montana Catholic
My Friend
National Catholic Reporter
New Covenant
New Freeman
Notre Dame
Oblates
Oblate World
Our Sunday Visitor
Parish Liturgy
Pastoral Life
Portland Magazine
Prairie Messenger
Priest
Queen of All Hearts
Review for Religious
RTJ
Seeds
Share
Social Justice Review
Southern Renaissance
Spiritual Life
St. Anthony Messenger
St. Joseph's Messenger
St. Linus Review
St. Willibrord Journal
Sursum Corda!
This Rock
Today's Catholic Teacher
Today's Parish
U.S. Catholic

Visions
Way of St. Francis

CHRISTIAN CHURCH/ CHURCH OF CHRIST

Book Publishers:
ACU Press
Chalice Press (Disciples of Christ)
College Press (Church of Christ)
Periodicals:
Christian Standard
DisciplesWorld (Disciples of Christ)
Encounter
Kidz Chat
Lookout
Teenage Christian (Church of Christ)

CHURCH OF GOD (Anderson, IN)

Book Publisher:
Warner Press
Periodical:
ONEvoice!
Pathways to God

CHURCH OF GOD (Cleveland, TN)

Book Publishers:
Editorial Evangelica
Pathway Press
Periodicals:
Church of God EVANGEL
Save Our World
Youth and CE Leadership

CHURCH OF GOD (holiness)

Periodicals:
Beginner's Friend
Church Herald and Holiness Banner
Gems of Truth
Junior Companion
Primary Pal (KS)
Youth Compass

CHURCH OF GOD (other)

Periodicals:
Bible Advocate (Seventh-day)
Church Advocate
Gem
Now What? (Seventh-day)
Spirit (Pentecostal Church of God)
2 Soar (Church of God in Christ)
White Wing Messenger (Church of
    God of Prophecy)

CHURCH OF THE NAZARENE

Book Publishers:
Beacon Hill Press
Lillenas (music)
Periodicals:
Adventures
Celebrate
Children's Church Exch.
Discoveries
Holiness Today
Passport
Preacher's Magazine
Resource
Standard
Team NYI

EPISCOPAL/ANGLICAN

Book Publishers:
Alban Institute
Forward Movement
Latimer Press
Morehouse Publishing
Periodicals:
Cathedral Age
Episcopal Life
Interchange
Living Church
Sewanee Theological Review

LUTHERAN

Book Publishers:
Concordia
Langmarc Publishing
Lutheran University Press
Northwestern Publishing
Openbook Publishers
Periodicals:
Canada Lutheran (ELCC)
Canadian Lutheran
Cresset
Esprit (ELCC)
Forward in Christ
Lutheran (ELCA)
Lutheran Digest
Lutheran Educ. (MO Synod)
Lutheran Forum
Lutheran Journal
Lutheran Parent
Lutheran Parent's Wellspring
Lutheran Partners (ELCA)
Lutheran Witness (MO Synod)
Lutheran Woman's Quarterly
    (MO Synod)
Lutheran Woman Today (ELCA)
Northwestern Lutheran

Teachers Inter. (MO Synod)
Word & World (ELCA)

MENNONITE

Book Publishers:
Green Pastures Press
Kindred Productions
Periodicals:
Canadian Mennonite
Christian Leader
Companions
Mennonite Brethren Herald
Mennonite Historian
Mennonite Weekly Review
On the Line
Partners
Purpose
Story Friends
Story Mates
With

METHODIST, FREE

Book Publisher:
Light and Life Communications
Periodicals:
Evangel
Light and Life
World Mission People

METHODIST, UNITED

Book Publishers:
Abingdon Press
Cokesbury
Dimensions for Living
United Methodist Publishing House
Upper Room Books
Periodicals:
Alive Now
Christian Social Action
Good News
Interpreter
Leader/Christian Education
    Ministries
Mature Years
Methodist History
Michigan Christian Advocate
New World Outlook
Pockets
Quarterly Review
Upper Room

MISSIONARY CHURCH

Periodical:
Emphasis/Faith & Living

PENTECOSTAL, UNITED

Periodicals:
Conqueror
Vision (adult)

PRESBYTERIAN

Book Publishers:
Canon Press
P & R Publishing
Westminster John Knox
Periodicals:
Channels (PCC)
Glad Tidings
Horizons (USA)
PCA Messenger
Presbyterian Layman (USA)
Presbyterian Outlook (USA)
Presbyterian Record
Presbyterians Today
Reflections (EPC)

QUAKER/FRIENDS

Book Publishers:
Barclay Press
Friends United Press
Periodicals:
Fruit of the Vine
Quaker Life

REFORMED CHURCHES

Periodicals:
Perspectives
Reformed Worship
Vision (MI)

SEVENTH-DAY ADVENTIST

Book Publishers:
Pacific Press
Review and Herald
Periodicals:
Cornerstone Youth Resources
GUIDE Magazine
Insight (MD)
Journal/Adventist Ed
Kids' Ministry Ideas
Liberty

Message
Ministry
Our Little Friend
Primary Treasure
Sabbath School Leadership
Signs of the Times
Vibrant Life
Young and Alive

WESLEYAN CHURCH

Book Publisher:
Wesleyan Publishing House
Periodicals:
Friend
Wesleyan Life
Wesleyan World

MISCELLANEOUS DENOMINATIONS

Armenian Holy Apostolic
Pourastan
Christian & Missionary Alliance
Christian Publications
Covenant Church
inSpirit
Evangelical Covenant Church
Cornerstone
Covenant Companion
Evangelical Free Church
EFCA Today
Evangelical Beacon
Pursuit
Foursquare Gospel Church
Foursquare World Advance
Greek Orthodox
Holy Cross Orthodox Press
Open Bible Standard Churches
MESSAGE of the Open Bible
Orthodox Church in America
Divine Ascent
Plymouth Brethren
Chapter Two (books)
United Church of Canada
Aujourd'hui Credo
Fellowship Magazine
Theological Digest & Outlook
United Church Observer
United Church Publishing House
United Church of Christ
Pilgrim Press
United Church Press

LIST OF BOOK PUBLISHERS AND PERIODICALS
BY CORPORATE GROUP

Following is a listing of book publishers first and then periodicals that belong to the same group or family of publications.

CCM COMMUNICATIONS

CCM
Worship Leader
Youthworker
The CCM Update

CHRISTIANITY TODAY, INTL.

Books & Culture
Campus Life
Christian Bible Studies.com
Christian History & Biography
Christianity Today
Christianity Today.com
Christian Parenting Today
Leadership Journal
Marriage Partnership
Men of Integrity
PreachingToday.com
Sermon Notes
Today's Christian
Today's Christian Woman
Your Church

CHRISTIAN MEDIA

Christian Media (books)
The Apocalypse Chronicles
Christian Media
Sound Body

COOK COMMUNICATIONS MINISTRIES

Chariot Books
Chariot Victor Books
Honor Books
Lion Publishing (books)
RiverOak Publishing
Counselor
I.D.
Power for Living
Primary Days
Quiet Hour
Real Time
The Rock
Strategic Adult Ministries Online

FOCUS ON THE FAMILY

Focus on the Family (books)
Boundless Webzine

Breakaway
Brio
Brio and Beyond
Citizen
Clubhouse
Clubhouse Jr.
Focus on the Family
Plugged-In

BILLY GRAHAM EVANG. ASSN.

Decision
Passageway.org

GROUP PUBLICATIONS, INC.

Group Publishing, Inc. (books)
Group's Faithweaver Bible Curriculum
Children's Ministry
Group Magazine

GUIDEPOSTS

Guideposts Books
Angels on Earth
Clarity
Guideposts
Guideposts for Kids on the Web
Guideposts Sweet 16
Ideals Magazine
Ideals Publications
Positive Thinking

HARPERCOLLINS

HarperSanFrancisco
ZonderKidz
Zondervan

THE NAVIGATORS

NavPress
Pray!
PrayKids!

THOMAS NELSON PUBLISHERS

J. Countryman
Thomas Nelson Publishers (books)
Tommy Nelson (books)
W Publishing Group (books)

PLGK COMMUNICATIONS

Setmag.com
TeensforJC.com
Transcendmag.com

THE SALVATION ARMY

Faith & Friends
Horizons
War Cry
Young Salvationist

STANDARD PUBLISHING

Standard Publishing (books)
Christian Standard
Encounter
Kidz Chat
The Lookout
Seek

STRANG COMMUNICATIONS

Charisma House (books)
Creation House Press (co-publishing)
Charisma & Christian Life
Christian Retailing
Ministries Today
New Man
Vida Cristiana

THE UPPER ROOM

Upper Room Books
alive now!
Devo'Zine
The Upper Room
Weavings

URBAN MINISTRIES

Direction
InTeen
J.A.M.: Jesus and Me
Juniorway
Precepts for Living
Preschool Playhouse
Primary Street
Young Adult Today

GLOSSARY OF TERMS

NOTE: This is not intended to be an exhaustive glossary of terms. It includes primarily those terms you will find within the context of this market guide.

Advance. Amount of money a publisher pays to an author up front, against future royalties. The amount varies greatly from publisher to publisher, and is often paid in two or three installments (on signing contract, on delivery of manuscript, and on publication).

All rights. An outright sale of your material. Author has no further control over it.

Anecdote. A short, poignant, real-life story, usually used to illustrate a single thought.

Assignment. When an editor asks a writer to write a specific piece for an agreed-upon price.

Avant-garde. Experimental; ahead of the times.

Backlist. A publisher's previously published books that are still in print a year after publication.

Bar code. Identification code and price on the back of a book read by a scanner at checkout counters.

Bible versions. CEV—Contemporary English Version; ESV—English Standard Version; GNB—Good News Bible; HCSB—Holman Christian Standard Bible; ICB—International Children's Bible; KJV—King James Version; MSG—The Message; NAB—New American Bible; NAS—New American Standard; NEB—New English Bible; NIrV—New International Reader's Version; NIV—New International Version; NJB—New Jerusalem Bible; NKJV—New King James Version; NLT—New Living Translation; NRSV—New Revised Standard Version; RSV—Revised Standard Version; TNIV—Today's New International Version.

Bimonthly. Every two months.

Biweekly. Every two weeks.

Bluelines. Printer's proofs used to catch errors before a book is printed.

Book proposal. Submission of a book idea to an editor; usually includes a cover letter, thesis statement, chapter-by-chapter synopsis, market survey, and 1-3 sample chapters.

Byline. Author's name printed just below the title of a story, article, etc.

Camera-ready copy. The text and artwork for a book that are ready for the press.

Chapbook. A small book or pamphlet containing poetry, religious readings, etc.

Circulation. The number of copies sold or distributed of each issue of a publication.

Clips. See "Published Clips."

Column. A regularly appearing feature, section, or department in a periodical using the same heading; written by the same person or a different freelancer each time.

Contributor's copy. Copy of an issue of a periodical sent to the author whose work appears in it.

Copyright. Legal protection of an author's work.

Cover letter. A letter that accompanies some manuscript submissions. Usually needed only if you have to tell the editor something specific or to give your credentials for writing a piece of a technical nature. Also used to remind the editor that a manuscript was requested or expected.

Critique. An evaluation of a piece of writing.

Devotional. A short piece that shares a personal spiritual discovery, inspires to worship, challenges to commitment or action, or encourages.

Editorial guidelines. See "Writer's guidelines."

Electronic submission. The submission of a proposal or article to an editor by electronic means, such as by e-mail or on disk.

Endorsements. Flattering comments about a book; usually carried on the back cover or in promotional material.

EPA/Evangelical Press Assn. A professional trade organization for periodical publishers and associate members.

E-proposals. Proposals sent via e-mail.

E-queries. Queries sent via e-mail.

Eschatology. The branch of theology that is concerned with the last things, such as death, judgment, heaven, and hell.

Essay. A short composition usually expressing the author's opinion on a specific subject.

Evangelical. A person who believes that one receives God's forgiveness for sins through Jesus Christ, and believes the Bible is an authoritative guide for daily living.

Exegesis. Interpretation of the Scripture.

Feature article. In-depth coverage of a subject, usually focusing on a person, an event, a process, an organization, a movement, a trend or issue; written to explain, encourage, help, analyze, challenge, motivate, warn, or entertain as well as to inform.

Filler. A short item used to "fill" out the page of a periodical. It could be a timeless news item, joke, anecdote, light verse or short humor, puzzle, game, etc.

First rights. Editor buys the right to publish your piece for the first time.

Foreign rights. Selling or giving permission to translate or reprint published material in a foreign country.

Foreword. Opening remarks in a book introducing the book and its author.

Freelance. As in 50% freelance: means that 50% of the material printed in the publication is supplied by freelance writers.

Freelancer or freelance writer. A writer who is not on salary but sells his material to a number of different publishers.

Free verse. Poetry that flows without any set pattern.

Galley proof. A typeset copy of a book manuscript used to detect and correct errors before the final print run.

Genre. Refers to type or classification, as in fiction or poetry. Such types as westerns, romances, mysteries, etc., are referred to as genre fiction.

Glossy. A black-and-white photo with a shiny, rather than matte, finish.

Go-ahead. When a publisher tells you to go ahead and write up or send your article idea.

Haiku. A Japanese lyric poem of a fixed 17-syllable form.

Hard copy. A typed manuscript, as opposed to one on disk or in an e-mail.

Holiday/seasonal. A story, article, filler, etc., that has to do with a specific holiday or season. This material must reach the publisher the stated number of months prior to the holiday/season.

Homiletics. The art of preaching.

Honorarium. If a publisher indicates they pay an honorarium, it means they pay a small flat fee, as opposed to a set amount per word.

Humor. The amusing or comical aspects of life that add warmth and color to an article or story.

Interdenominational. Distributed to a number of different denominations.

International Postal Reply Coupon. See "IRC."

Interview article. An article based on an interview with a person of interest to a specific readership.

IRC or IPRC. International Postal Reply Coupon: can be purchased at your local post office and should be enclosed with a manuscript sent to a foreign publisher.

ISBN number. International Standard Book Number; an identification code needed for every book.

Journal. A periodical presenting news in a particular area.

Kill fee. A fee paid for a completed article done on assignment that is subsequently not published. Amount is usually 25-50% of original payment.

Libel. To defame someone by an opinion or a misquote and put his or her reputation in jeopardy.

Light verse. Simple, lighthearted poetry.

Little/Literary. Small circulation publications whose focus is providing a forum for the literary writer, rather than on making money. Often do not pay, or pay in copies.

Mainstream fiction. Other than genre fiction, such as romance, mystery, or science fiction. Stories of people and their conflicts handled on a deeper level.

Mass market. Books intended for a wide, general market, rather than a specialized market. These books are produced in a smaller format, usually with smaller type, and are sold at a lower price. The expectation is that their sales will be higher.

Ms. Abbreviation for manuscript.

Mss. Abbreviation for more than one manuscript.

Multiple submissions. Submitting more than one piece at a time to the same publisher, usually reserved for poetry, greeting cards, or fillers, not articles. Also see "Simultaneous submissions."

NASR. Abbreviation for North American serial rights.

Newsbreak. A newsworthy event or item sent to a publisher who might be interested in publishing it because it would be of interest to his particular readership.

Nondenominational. Not associated with a particular denomination.

Not copyrighted. Publication of your piece in such a publication will put it into public domain and it is not then protected. Ask that the publisher carry your copyright notice on your piece when it is printed.

On acceptance. Periodical or publisher pays a writer at the time manuscript is accepted for publication.

On assignment. Writing something at the specific request of an editor.

One-time rights. Selling the right to publish a story one time to any number of publications (usually refers to publishing for a nonoverlapping readership).

On publication. Publisher pays a writer when his/her manuscript is published.

On speculation/On spec. Writing something for an editor with the agreement that he will buy it only if he likes it.

Overrun. The extra copies of a book printed during the initial print run.

Over the transom. Unsolicited articles that arrive at a publisher's office.

Payment on acceptance. See "On acceptance."

Payment on publication. See "On publication."

Pen name/Pseudonym. Using a name other than your legal name on an article or book in order to protect your identity or the identity of people included, or when the author wishes to remain anonymous. Put the pen name in the byline under the title, and your real name in the upper, left-hand corner.

Permissions. Asking permission to use the text or art from a copyrighted source.

Personal experience story. A story based on a real-life experience.

Personality profile. A feature article that highlights a specific person's life or accomplishments.

Photocopied submission. Sending an editor a photocopy of your manuscript, rather than an original. Some editors prefer an original.

Piracy. To take the writings of others just as they were written and put your name on them as the author.

Plagiarism. To steal and use the ideas or writings of another as your own, rewriting them to make them sound like your own.

Press kit. A compilation of promotional materials on a particular book or author, usually organized in a folder, used to publicize a book.

Public domain. Work that has never been copyrighted, or on which the copyright has expired. Subtract 75 from the current year, and anything copyrighted prior to that is in public domain.

Published clips. Copies of actual articles you have had published, from newspapers or magazines.

Quarterly. Every three months.

Query letter. A letter sent to an editor telling about an article you propose to write and asking if he or she is interested in seeing it.

Reporting time. The number of weeks or months it takes an editor to get back to you about a query or manuscript you have sent in.

Reprint rights. Selling the right to reprint an article that has already been published elsewhere. You must have sold only first or one-time rights originally, and wait until it has been published the first time.

Review copies. Books given to book reviewers or buyers for chains.

Royalty. The percentage an author is paid by a publisher on the sale of each copy of a book.

SAE. Self-addressed envelope (without stamps).

SAN. Standard Account Number, used to identify libraries, book dealers, or schools.

SASE. Self-addressed, stamped envelope. Should always be sent with a manuscript or query letter.

SASP. Self-addressed, stamped postcard. May be sent with a manuscript submission to be returned by publisher indicating it arrived safely.

Satire. Ridicule that aims at reform.

Second serial rights. See "Reprint rights."

Semiannual. Issued twice a year.

Serial. Refers to publication in a periodical (such as first serial rights).

Sidebar. A short feature that accompanies an article and either elaborates on the human interest side of the story or gives additional information on the topic. It is often set apart by appearing within a box or border.

Simultaneous rights. Selling the rights to the same piece to several publishers simultaneously. Be sure everyone is aware that you are doing so.

Simultaneous submissions. Sending the same manuscript to more than one publisher at the same time. Usually done with nonoverlapping markets (such as denominational or newspapers) or when you are writing on a timely subject. Be sure to state in a cover letter that it is a simultaneous submission and why.

Slanting. Writing an article so that it meets the needs of a particular market.

Slush pile. The stack of unsolicited manuscripts that have arrived at a publisher's office.

Speculation. See "On speculation."

Staff-written material. Material written by the members of a magazine staff.

Subsidiary rights. All those rights, other than book rights, included in a book contract such as paperback, book club, movie, etc.

Subsidy publisher. A book publisher who charges the author to publish his book, as opposed to a royalty publisher who pays the author.

Synopsis. A brief summary of work from one paragraph to several pages long.

Tabloid. A newspaper-format publication about half the size of a regular newspaper.

Take-home paper. A periodical sent home from Sunday school each week (usually) with Sunday school students, children through adults.

Think piece. A magazine article that has an intellectual, philosophical, or provocative approach to a subject.

Third World. Reference to underdeveloped countries of Asia and Africa.

Trade magazine. A magazine whose audience is in a particular trade or business.

Traditional verse. One or more verses with an established pattern that is repeated throughout the poem.

Transparencies. Positive color slides, not color prints.

Unsolicited manuscript. A manuscript an editor didn't specifically ask to see.

Vanity publisher. See "Subsidy publisher."

Vignette. A short, descriptive literary sketch or a brief scene or incident.

Vitae/Vita. An outline of one's personal history and experience.

Work-for-hire. Signing a contract with a publisher stating that a particular piece of writing you are doing for him is "work-for-hire." In the agreement you give the publisher full ownership and control of the material.

Writers' guidelines. An information sheet provided by a publisher that gives specific guidelines for writing for the publication. Always send an SASE with your request for guidelines.

GENERAL INDEX

This index includes periodicals, books, and greeting cards/specialty markets, as well as some of the various organizations/resources and specialty lists or areas you may need to find quickly. Conferences, groups, and editorial services are listed alphabetically by state; agents are listed alphabetically by the name of the agency. Check the table of contents for the location of supplementary listings.

Note: Due to the many changes in the market, and to help you determine the current status of any publisher you might be looking for, all markets will be listed in this index. If they are not viable markets, their current status will be indicated here, rather than in separate listings as they were in earlier years. The following codes will be used: (ABD) asked to be deleted, (BA) bad address, phone number, e-mail/Website, (ED) editorial decision, (NF) no freelance, (NR) no recent response, (OB) out of business. These changes will be noted in this listing for five years before being dropped altogether.

2/06 - 4/06 2